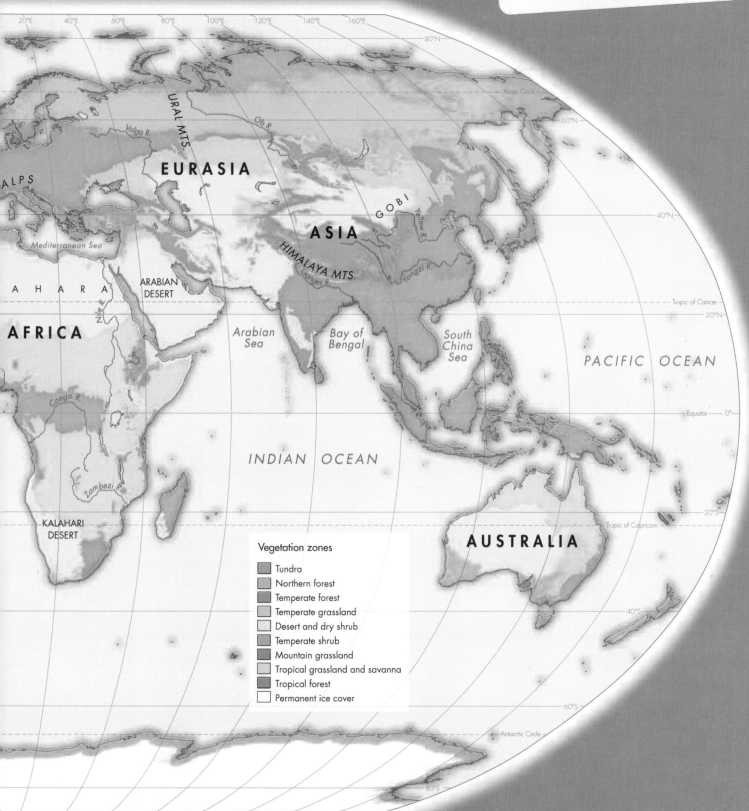

EURASIA

ALPS

URAL MTS.

Volga R.

Ob R.

Arctic Circle

80°N

60°N

40°N

ASIA

GOBI

Yellow R.

HIMALAYA MTS.

Ganges R.

Yangzi R.

Mediterranean Sea

S A H A R A

ARABIAN DESERT

Nile R.

AFRICA

Arabian Sea

Bay of Bengal

South China Sea

PACIFIC OCEAN

Tropic of Cancer

20°N

Congo R.

INDIAN OCEAN

Equator 0°

Zambezi R.

KALAHARI DESERT

AUSTRALIA

20°S

Tropic of Capricorn

40°S

Vegetation zones

Tundra
Northern forest
Temperate forest
Temperate grassland
Desert and dry shrub
Temperate shrub
Mountain grassland
Tropical grassland and savanna
Tropical forest
Permanent ice cover

60°S

Antarctic Circle

80°S

20°E   40°E   60°E   80°E   100°E   120°E   140°E   160°E

Learn how this book can improve your performance on tests and exams.

SEE PAGES xii–xix.

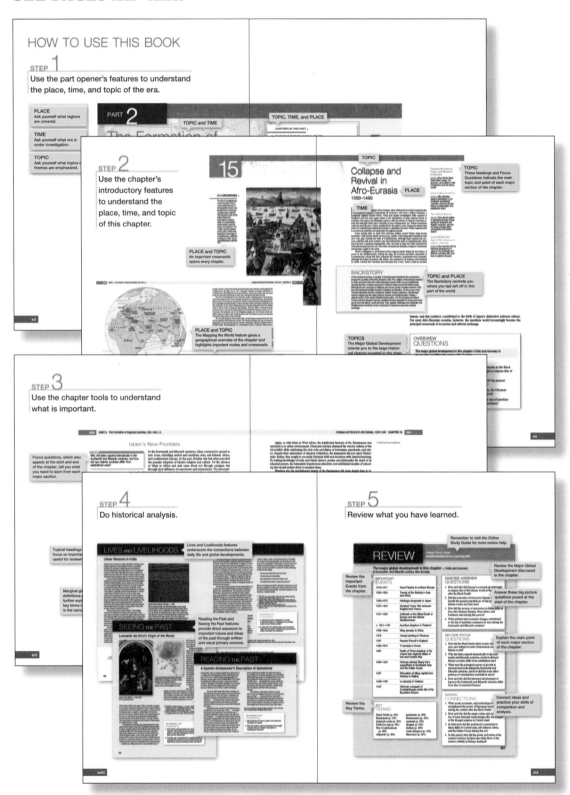

For more resources, visit the Web site for

Crossroads and Cultures
A HISTORY OF THE WORLD'S PEOPLES

bedfordstmartins.com/smith

FREE ONLINE STUDY GUIDE
Get instant feedback on your progress with

- Chapter self-tests
- Key terms review
- Map quizzes
- Timeline activities
- Note-taking outlines

FREE HISTORY RESEARCH AND WRITING HELP
Refine your research skills and find plenty of good sources with

- A database of useful images, maps, documents, and more at *Make History*
- A guide to online sources for history
- Help with writing history papers
- A tool for building a bibliography
- Tips on avoiding plagiarism

Crossroads and Cultures

A History of the World's Peoples

Crossroads and Cultures

A History of the World's Peoples

Bonnie G. Smith
Rutgers University

Marc Van De Mieroop
Columbia University

Richard von Glahn
University of California, Los Angeles

Kris Lane
Tulane University

Bedford/St. Martin's

Boston ■ New York

FOR BEDFORD/ST. MARTIN'S

Publisher for History: Mary Dougherty
Executive Editor for History: Elizabeth M. Welch
Director of Development for History: Jane Knetzger
Senior Developmental Editor: Heidi Hood
Senior Production Editor: Anne Noonan
Senior Production Supervisor: Andrew Ensor
Executive Marketing Manager: Jenna Bookin Barry
Associate Editor: Jennifer Jovin
Assistant Production Editor: Laura Deily
Editorial Assistant: Emily DiPietro
Production Assistant: Elise Keller
Copy Editor: Dan Otis
Map Editor: Charlotte Miller
Indexer: Leoni Z. McVey
Cartography: Mapping Specialists, Ltd.
Photo Researcher: Rose Corbett Gordon
Permissions Manager: Kalina K. Ingham
Senior Art Director: Anna Palchik
Text Designer: Jerilyn Bockorick
Cover Designer: Billy Boardman
Cover Art: Turkey, Istanbul, mosques and Bosporus.
© Richard Nowitz/Getty Images
Composition: Cenveo Publisher Services
Printing and Binding: RR Donnelley and Sons

President: Joan E. Feinberg
Editorial Director: Denise B. Wydra
Director of Marketing: Karen R. Soeltz
Director of Production: Susan W. Brown
Associate Director, Editorial Production: Elise S. Kaiser
Managing Editor: Elizabeth M. Schaaf

Library of Congress Control Number: 2011943843

Manufactured in the United States of America.

7 6 5 4 3 2
f e d c b a

For information, write: Bedford/St. Martin's, 75 Arlington Street, Boston, MA 02116   (617-399-4000)

ISBN: 978-0-312-41017-9   (Combined edition)
ISBN: 978-0-312-57158-0   (Loose leaf)
ISBN: 978-0-312-44213-2   (Volume 1)
ISBN: 978-0-312-57159-7   (Loose leaf)
ISBN: 978-0-312-44214-9   (Volume 2)
ISBN: 978-0-312-57160-3   (Loose leaf)
ISBN: 978-0-312-57161-0   (Volume A)
ISBN: 978-0-312-57167-2   (Volume B)
ISBN: 978-0-312-57168-9   (Volume C)

A CONVERSATION WITH THE AUTHORS

The Story Behind *Crossroads and Cultures*

Bonnie G. Smith
Rutgers University

Marc Van De Mieroop
Columbia University

Richard von Glahn
University of California,
Los Angeles

Kris Lane
Tulane University

Bedford/St. Martin's is proud to publish *Crossroads and Cultures: A History of the World's Peoples,* which incorporates the best current cultural history into a fresh and original narrative that connects global patterns of development with life on the ground. This new synthesis highlights the places and times where people interacted and exchanged goods and ideas and in doing so joined their lives to the broad sweep of global history. Below the authors discuss their goals and approach.

Q. How does the title *Crossroads and Cultures: A History of the World's Peoples* tell the story of your book?

Crossroads

Bonnie: From the beginning we knew that we would be stressing interactions and engagements among the world's peoples. We looked for the places where they would meet—the **crossroads**— whether those were actual places or the intersections reflected in the practices of everyday life. We

want students to see how crossroads, interactions, and connections among the world's peoples have changed over time and continue to shape their own lives.

Richard: This focus is a result of our recognition that world history is not simply a matter of covering more areas of the world; it requires rethinking what matters in world history. World history must center on cross-cultural interactions and the ways in which peoples and cultures are influenced and are sometimes transformed by political engagement, cultural contact, economic exchange, and social encounters with other societies.

Cultures

Bonnie: The second half of our title reflects our heartfelt judgment that the past is shaped by **cultures**. Beliefs, ways of living, artistic forms, technology, and intellectual accomplishments are fundamental to historical development and are a part of the foundation of politics and economies. Cultures also produce structures such as caste, class, ethnicity, race, religion, gender, and sexuality—all of which are important themes in our book.

> **"We looked for the places where the world's peoples would meet —the crossroads—whether those were actual places or the intersections reflected in the practices of everyday life."**

A History of the World's Peoples

Marc: The book's subtitle, *A History of the World's Peoples*, is crucial. History often focuses on kings and states, but in the end the peoples of the past are the most interesting to study, however difficult that may be considering the nature of the sources for world history. People interact with their immediate and more distant neighbors, and these interactions are, indeed, often a cause of historical change.

Bonnie: *Crossroads and Cultures* focuses on people—individual and collective historical actors—who have lived the history of the world and produced global events. We want to capture their thoughts and deeds, their everyday experiences, their work lives, and their courageous actions—all of which have helped to create the crossroads we travel today.

Q. To follow up on the idea of "crossroads," what are some of the places and interactions that you emphasize in the book, and why?

Marc: In the ancient world, the period that I cover in the book (Part 1, from human origins to 500 C.E.), two regions figured prominently by virtue of their location—the Middle East and Central Asia. From earliest times, the Middle East formed a nexus of interactions among the African, European, and Asian continents, which I try to convey when I discuss the first human migrations out of Africa and when I show how the Roman and Persian empires met—and yes, battled! But I emphasize as well that vast open areas also served as crossroads in antiquity. Indeed, Central Asia, an enormous region, acted as a highway for contacts between the cultures at its fringes: China, South Asia, the Middle East, and Europe. Seas also can play this role, and I include the gigantic Pacific Ocean, which, although a formidable barrier, functioned as a road for migration for centuries.

> **"The crossroads that we describe are often the obvious ones of war, empire building, and old and new forms of trade, but we also enthusiastically feature the more ordinary paths that people traveled."**

Richard: Since I also deal with a period remote from the present (Part 2, 500–1450 C.E.), I try to balance my coverage between familiar and recognizable places that remain crossroads today—Rome and Jerusalem, Baghdad and Istanbul, Beijing and Delhi, the Nile Delta and the Valley of Mexico—and places that have faded from view, such as the trading cities of the West African savanna; Melaka, the greatest port of Asia in the fifteenth century; Samarkand, which had a long history as the linchpin of the Central Asian Silk Road; and the Champagne fairs in France, which operated as a "free trade" zone and became the incubator of new business practices that enabled Europeans to surpass the older economic centers of the Mediterranean world.

Kris: Since my section of the book (Part 3, 1450–1750) treats the early modern period, when the entire globe was interconnected for the first time in recorded history, I have almost too many crossroads to choose from. In this period, Seville and Lisbon emerged as hugely rich and important ports and sites of redistribution, but so also did Manila, Nagasaki, and Macao. Most of the obvious crossroads of this seafaring era were ports, but great mining centers like Potosí, deep in the highlands of present-day Bolivia, also became world-class cosmopolitan centers. In other books many of these sites have been treated simply as nodes in an expanding European world, but I try to show how local people and other non-European residents made Manila and Potosí quite different from what the king of Spain might have had in mind. Indeed, I emphasize crossroads as places of personal opportunity rather than imperial hegemony.

Bonnie: The crossroads that we describe are often the obvious ones of war, empire building, and old and new forms of trade, but we also enthusiastically feature the more ordinary paths that people traveled. For example, in my own section of the book (Part 4, 1750 to the present), I trace the route of the young Simon Bolivar, whose travels in Spain, France, and the new United States helped to inspire his own liberation struggles. I also follow the rough road from factory to factory along which a seven-year-old English orphan, Robert Blincoe, traveled. His life occurred at the crossroads of industrial development, where he suffered deliberate torture as the world began industrializing. For me, these personal journeys—filled with interactions—are at the heart of our endeavor to make history vivid and meaningful for students.

Q. Author teams of world history textbooks typically divide the work based on geographic specialty. Why did you decide to take responsibility for eras instead of regions?

Bonnie: Our goal is to show the interactions of the world's peoples over time and space. Had we divided history by region, our purpose would have been confounded from the start. Many books still take a "civilizational" approach, shifting from one region or nation to another and dividing each author's coverage according to national specialization. We aimed for a more interconnected result by each taking responsibility for narrating developments across the globe during a particular period of time.

Marc: When we look at any period globally, we can see certain parallels between the various parts of the world. There is a huge benefit to weighing what happened in different places at the same time.

Richard: Right. World history fundamentally is about making comparisons and connections. Defining our subject matter by time period rather than by geographic region enabled us to see the connections or parallel developments that make societies part of world history—as well as the distinctive features that make them unique. Our format has the virtue of bringing a coherent perspective to the many stories that each part of the book tells.

Kris: In my chapters, certain themes, such as slavery and the spread of silver money, took on new meaning as I traced them across cultures in ways that regional specialists had not considered. Writing the book this way entailed a huge amount of reading, writing, and reconsideration, but I feel it was a great decision. It allowed each of us to explore a bit before coming back together to hash out differences.

Q. The table of contents for *Crossroads and Cultures* blends both thematic and regional chapters. Why did you organize the book this way?

Bonnie: There is no orthodoxy in today's teaching of world history. Although textbooks often follow either a

> **"Defining our subject matter by time period rather than by geographic region enabled us to see the connections or parallel developments that make societies part of world history—as well as the distinctive features that make them unique."**

regional or a thematic structure, we felt that neither of these told the story that a blended approach could tell.

Richard: I particularly relished the opportunity to develop thematic chapters—for example, on cross-cultural trade and business practices, or on educational institutions and the transmission of knowledge—that illustrate both convergence and diversity in history. The thematic chapters were especially suitable for introducing individuals from diverse levels of society, to help students appreciate personal experiences as well as overarching historical trends.

Kris: In my period, the rapid integration of the world due to expanding maritime networks had to be balanced against the persistence of land-based cultures that both borrowed from new technologies and ideas and maintained a regional coherence. The Aztecs, the Incas, the Mughals, and the Ming were all land-based, tributary empires headed by divine kings, but whereas the first two collapsed as a result of European invasion, the latter two were reinforced by contact with Europeans, who introduced powerful new weapons. I felt it was necessary to treat these empires in macroregional terms before grappling with more sweeping themes. I found that in the classroom my students made better connections themselves after having time to get a firm handle on some of these broad regional developments.

Q. Each chapter includes a Counterpoint section as substantial as the main sections of the narrative itself. What purposes do the Counterpoints serve?

Kris: The **Counterpoint** feature helps students and teachers remember that alternative histories—or paths—are not only possible but that they exist alongside "master narratives." In each chapter we have selected a people, a place, or a movement that functions as a Counterpoint to the major global development traced in that chapter. Some Counterpoints highlight different responses to similar circumstances—the successful resistance of the Mapuche of Chile against the European conquistadors, for example, in a chapter that tells the story of the collapse of the Aztec and Incan empires. Other Counterpoints show cultures adapting to a particular environment that either enables persistence or requires adaptation—such as the Aborigines of Australia, gatherer-hunters by choice, in a chapter that treats the rise of agriculture and spread of settled farming. Counterpoint is about human difference and ingenuity.

Richard: The Counterpoint feature is fundamental to our approach. It reminds us that there is much diversity in world history and helps us to think about the causes underlying divergence as well as convergence.

Marc: Right. It helps counter the idea that everyone goes through the same stages of evolution and makes the same choices. There is no uniform history of the world, as nineteenth-century scholars used to think.

Bonnie: One of my favorite Counterpoints centers on the importance of nonindustrialized African women farmers to the world economy during the Industrial Revolution. From a pedagogical standpoint, Counterpoints not only expose basic questions that historians grapple with but also offer material within a single chapter for compare-and-contrast exercises.

Q. Each chapter also offers a special feature devoted to the way that people made their living at different times and at different crossroads in the past. Would you explain how this Lives and Livelihoods feature works?

Richard: The **Lives and Livelihoods** feature helps us provide more in-depth study of one of our key themes, namely how people's lives intersect with larger cross-cultural interactions and global change.

Bonnie: We often spotlight new means of making a living that arose as the result of cross-cultural exchange or that contributed to major global developments. For example, the Lives and Livelihoods feature in Chapter 6 shows students how papermaking originated as a carefully guarded invention in classical China and became a worldwide technology that spawned numerous livelihoods. Similarly, the feature in Chapter 24 on workers on the trans-Siberian railroad exemplifies influence in both directions: the workers built a transportation network that advanced interconnections and fostered global change—change that they and their families experienced in turn.

> "The Lives and Livelihoods feature supports one of our key themes: how people's lives intersect with larger cross-cultural interactions and global change."

Q. *Crossroads and Cultures* has a rich art and map program, and it also includes plentiful primary-source excerpts and clear reading aids. Can you talk about how you had students in mind as you developed these features of the book?

Kris: Throughout the book we chose **images** to match as closely as we could the themes we wanted to stress. We did not conceive of the images as mere illustrations but rather as documents worthy of close historical analysis in their own right, products of the same places and times we try to evoke in the text.

Richard: And our carefully developed **map program** provides sure-footed guidance to where our historical journey is taking us—a crucial necessity, since we travel to so many places not on the usual Grand Tour! Our **Seeing the Past** and **Reading the Past** features, which provide excerpts from visual and written primary sources, give students direct exposure to the ideas and voices of the people we are studying. These features also help students build their analytical skills by modeling how historians interpret visual and written evidence.

Bonnie: Among the many reading aids, one of my favorites is the chapter-opening **Backstory**, which provides a concise overview of previously presented material to situate the current chapter for the student. It is at once a review and an immediate preparation for the chapter to come.

Richard: And we use every opportunity—at the start of chapters and sections, in the features, and at the end of each chapter—to pose **study questions** to help students think about what they are reading and make connections across time and space.

Kris: We wanted to hit as many bases as possible in order to make our book accessible for different kinds of learners. I imagine I'm like most teachers in that I never teach a course in exactly the same way each year. I like to use or emphasize different aspects of a textbook each time I assign it, sometimes hammering on chronology or working through study questions and sometimes paying closer attention to maps, works of art, or material culture. It all needs to be there; I like a complete toolbox.

Q. You have written many well-received and influential works. What response to *Crossroads and Cultures: A History of the World's Peoples* would please you most?

Bonnie: Our hope is that our approach to world history will engage students and help them master material that can otherwise seem so remote, wide-ranging, and seemingly disconnected from people's lives.

Richard: I would like from students who read this book what I want from my own students: a recognition and appreciation of the diversity of human experience that fosters understanding not only of the past and where we have come from but also of our fellow world citizens and the future that we are making together.

Kris: The practical side of me wants simply to hear, "At last, a world history textbook that works." The idealistic side wants to hear, "Wow, a world history textbook that makes both me and my students think differently about the world and about history."

Marc: And I hope that students start to realize not only that the pursuit of answers to such questions is absorbing and satisfying but also that the study of history is fun!

Crossroads and Cultures: A History of the World's Peoples **makes its new synthesis accessible and memorable for students through a strong pedagogical design, abundant maps and images, and special features that heighten the narrative's attention to the lives and voices of the world's peoples. To learn more about how the book's features keep the essentials of world history in focus for students, see the "How to Use This Book" introduction on the following pages.**

HOW TO USE THIS BOOK

STEP 1

Use the part opener's features to understand the place, time, and topic of the era.

PLACE
Ask yourself what regions are covered.

TIME
Ask yourself what era is under investigation.

TOPIC
Ask yourself what topics or themes are emphasized.

PART 2

TOPIC and TIME

The Formation of Regional Societies
500–1450 C.E.

CH 9

ALTHOUGH NO SINGLE LABEL adequately reflects the history of the world in the period 500–1450, its most distinctive feature was the formation of regional societies based on common forms of livelihoods, cultural values, and social and political institutions. The new age in world history that began in around 500 C.E. marked a decisive break from the "classical" era of antiquity. The passing of classical civilizations in the Mediterranean, China, and India shared a number of causes, but the most notable were invasions by nomads from the Central Asian steppes. Beset by internal unrest and foreign pressures, the empires of Rome, Han China, and Gupta India crumbled. As these once-mighty empires fragmented into a multitude of competing states, cultural revolutions followed. Confidence in the values and institutions of the classical era was shattered, opening the way for fresh ideas. Christianity, Buddhism, Hinduism, and the new creed of Islam spread far beyond their original circles of believers. By 1450 these four religious traditions had supplanted or transformed local religions in virtually all of Eurasia and much of Africa.

The spread of foreign religions and the lifestyles and livelihoods they promoted produced distinctive regional societies. By 1000, Europe had taken shape as a coherent society and culture even as it came to be divided between the Roman and Byzantine Christian churches. The shared cultural values of modern East Asia—rooted in the literary and philosophical traditions of China but also assuming distinctive national forms—also emerged during the first millennium C.E. During this era, too, Indian civilization expanded into Southeast Asia and acquired a new unity expressed through the common language of Sanskrit. The rapid expansion of Islam across Asia, Africa, and

266

CH 10 →

TOPIC
Read the part overview to learn how the chapters that follow fit into the larger story.

TOPIC, TIME, and PLACE

CH 11

even parts of Europe demonstrated the power of a shared reli-

500–1450 C.E.

CH 13

faiths grew ever wider. The rise of steppe empires—above all, the explosive expansion of the Mongol empires—likewise transformed the political and cultural landscape of Asia. Historians today recognize the ways in which the Mongol conquests facilitated the movement of people, goods, and ideas across Eurasia. But contemporaries could see no farther than the ruin sowed by the Mongols wherever they went, toppling cities and laying waste to once-fertile farmlands.

After 1300 the momentum of world history changed. Economic growth slowed, strained by the pressure of rising populations on productive resources and the effects of a cooling climate, and then it stopped altogether. In the late 1340s the Black Death pandemic devastated the central Islamic lands and Europe. It would take centuries before the populations in these parts of the world returned to their pre-1340 levels.

By 1400, however, other signs of recovery were evident. Powerful national states emerged in Europe and China, restoring some measure of stability. Strong Islamic states held sway in Egypt, Anatolia (modern Turkey), Iran, and India. The European Renaissance—the intense outburst of intellectual and artistic creativity envisioned as a "rebirth" of the classical civilization of Greece and Rome—flickered to life, sparked by the economic vigor of the Italian city-states. Similarly, Neo-Confucianism—a "renaissance" of China's classical learning—whetted the intellectual and cultural aspirations of ed...

Eurasia's major land-based economies struggled to regain their earlier prosperity.

In 1453 Muslim Ottoman armies seized Constantinople and deposed the Byzantine Christian emperor, cutting the last thread of connection to the ancient world. The fall of Constantinople symbolized the end of the era discussed in Part 2. Denied direct access to the rich trade with Asia, European monarchs and merchants began to shift their attention to the Atlantic world. Yet just as Columbus's discovery of the "New World" (in fact, a very ancient one) came as a surprise, the idea of a new world order centered on Europe—the modern world order—was still unimaginable.

CH 15

TIME and PLACE
Scan the timeline to see how events and developments in different regions of the world fit together.

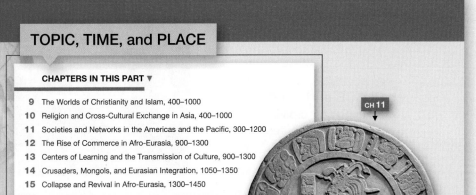

	500	750	1000	1250	1500
Americas	• 500 First permanent settlements in Chaco Canyon / 500–1000 Andean state of Tiwanaku / 550–650 Collapse of Teotihuacán	800–900 Collapse of the Maya city-states / Rise of Chimu state 900 / 700–900 Heyday of Andean state of Wari	950–1150 Height of Toltec culture / 1050 Consolidation of Cahokia's dominance	• 1200 Incas move into Cuzco region / 1150 Abandonment of pueblos in Chaco Canyon / 1250–1300 Collapse of Cahokia	Columbus reaches the Americas 1492 • / • 1325 Aztecs found Tenochtitlán / 1430–1532 Inca Empire
Europe	• 507 Clovis defeats Visigoths and converts to Christianity / Charles Martel halts Muslim advance into Europe 732 • / 590–604 Papacy of Gregory I / Charlemagne crowned emperor 800 •	• 793 Earliest record of Viking raids on Britain	• 988 Rus prince Vladimir converts to Christianity / • 1066 Norman conquest of England	• 1150 Founding of first university at Paris / 1347–1350 Outbreak of Black Death / 1150–1300 Heyday of the Champagne fairs / 1270–1300 Introduction of overseas navigational aids / Mongol conquest of Kiev 1240 •	1400–1550 Italian Renaissance / 1337–1453 Hundred Years' War / Reconquista
Middle East	527–565 Reign of Byzantine emperor Justinian I / 570–632 Life of Muhammad / • 680 Permanent split between Shi'a and Sunni Islam / 661–743 Umayyad caliphate / 750–850 Abbasid caliphate at its height		First Crusade ends with Christian capture of Jerusalem 1099 • / • 1120 Founding of order of Knights of the Temple / Saladin recaptures Jerusalem 1187 •	• 1291 Mamluks recapture Acre, last Christian stronghold in Palestine / • 1258 Mongols sack Baghdad / 1347–1350 Outbreak of Black Death	• 1453 Fall of Constantinople to the Ottomans
Africa	• 500 Spread of camel use; emergence of trans-Saharan trade routes	• 750 Islam starts to spread via trans-Saharan trade routes	969 Fatimids capture Egypt / Fall of kingdom of Ghana 1076 •	Reign of Sunjata, founder of Mali Empire 1230–1255 / 1250–1517 Mamluk dynasty / 1250 Kingdom of Benin founded / 1100–1500 Extended dry period in West Africa prompts migrations	
Asia and Oceania	581–618 Sui Empire / 618–907 Tang Empire / 600–1000 Polynesian settlement of Pacific islands	• 668 Unification of Korea under Silla rule / 755–763 An Lushan rebellion	850–1267 Chola kingdom / 939 Vietnam achieves independence from China / 960–1279 Song Empire	1100–1500 Easter Island's stone monuments / Formation of first Hawaiian chiefdoms 1200–1400 / 1206–1526 Delhi Sultanate / 1271–1368 Yuan Empire	1336–1573 Ashikaga Shogunate / 1368–1644 Ming Empire / 1392–1910 Korean Yi dynasty

STEP 2

Use the chapter's introductory features to understand the place, time, and topic of this chapter.

15

AT A CROSSROADS ▶

The fall of Constantinople to the Ottoman Turks in 1453 marked the end of the Byzantine Empire and heralded the coming age of gunpowder weapons. The Ottoman forces under Sultan Mehmed II breached the massive walls of Constantinople using massive cannons known as *bombards*. The Turkish cannons appear in the center of this book illustration of the siege of Constantinople, published in France in 1455. (The Art Archive/Bibliothèque Nationale Paris.)

PLACE and TOPIC
An important crossroads opens every chapter.

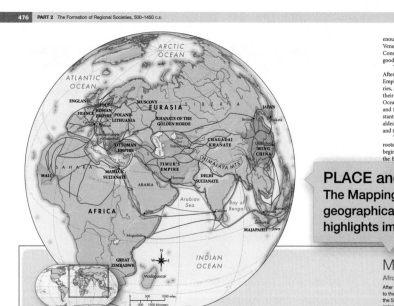

enough cannons to match the heavily armed Ottoman army and navy, which expelled the Venetians from the Black Sea in 1475. Although Venetian merchants still flocked to Constantinople, which Mehmed renamed Istanbul, to obtain spices, silks, and other Asian goods, the Ottomans held the upper hand and could dictate the terms of trade.

The fall of Constantinople to the Ottomans marks a turning point in world history. After perpetuating ancient Rome's heritage and glory for a thousand years, the Byzantine Empire came to an end. Islam continued to advance; in the fourteenth and fifteenth centuries, it expanded most dramatically in Africa and Asia. Italian merchants and bankers lost their dominance in the eastern Mediterranean and turned westward toward the Atlantic Ocean in search of new commercial opportunities. And this shift in commercial power and focus was not the only profound change that followed the Ottoman capture of Constantinople. The bombards cast by the Hungarian engineer for the Ottoman sultan heralded a military revolution that would decisively alter the balance of power among states and transform the nature of the state itself.

The new global patterns that emerged after Constantinople changed hands had their roots in calamities of the fourteenth century. The Ottoman triumph came just as Europe was beginning to recover from the previous century's catastrophic outbreak of plague known as the Black Death. The demographic and psychological shocks of epidemic disease had se-

PLACE and TOPIC
The Mapping the World feature gives a geographical overview of the chapter and highlights important routes and crossroads.

MAPPING THE WORLD
Afro-Eurasia in the Early Fifteenth Century

After the Mongol Empire disintegrated, trans-Eurasian trade shifted from the overland Silk Road to the maritime routes stretching from China to the Mediterranean. Muslim merchants crossed the Sahara Desert and the Indian Ocean in pursuit of African gold, Chinese porcelain, and Asian spices. Although Chinese fleets led by Admiral Zheng He journeyed as far as the coasts of Arabia and Africa, the Ming rulers prohibited private overseas trade.

ROUTES ▼
— Major trade route
— Silk Road
— Voyages of Zheng He

Timeline:

- 1315–1317 Great Famine in northern Europe
- 1325–1354 Travels of Ibn Battuta in Asia and Africa
- 1336–1573 Ashikaga shogunate in Japan
- 1337–1453 Hundred Years' War between England and France
- • 1378 Ciompi uprising in Florence
- • 1381 Peasant Revolt in England
- 1392–1910 Yi dynasty in Korea
- • 1405 Death of Timur; breakup of his empire into regional states in Iran and Central Asia
- • 1453 Ottoman conquest of Constantinople marks fall of the Byzantine Empire

| 1300 | 1325 | 1350 | 1375 | 1400 | 1425 | 1450 |

- 1347–1350 Outbreak of the Black Death in Europe and the Islamic Mediterranean
- c. 1351–1782 Ayudhya kingdom in Thailand
- 1368–1644 Ming dynasty in China
- 1405–1433 Chinese admiral Zheng He's expeditions in Southeast Asia and the Indian Ocean
- • 1421 Relocation of Ming capital from Nanjing to Beijing
- 1428–1788 Le dynasty in Vietnam

TIME and TOPIC
The timeline previews key events and developments discussed in the chapter.

Collapse and Revival in Afro-Eurasia

1300–1450

armies of the Ottoman sultan Mehmed II encircled Constantinople, the Byzantine emperor Constantine XI received a visit from a fellow Christian, a Hungarian engineer named Urban. Urban had applied metallurgical skills acquired at Hungary's rich iron and copper mines to the manufacture of large cannons known as *bombards*. He came to the Byzantine capital to offer his services to repel the Ottoman assault. But although Urban was a Christian, he was a businessman, too. When Constantine could not meet his price, Urban quickly left for the sultan's camp. Facing the famed triple walls of Constantinople, Mehmed promised to quadruple the salary Urban requested and to provide any materials and manpower the engineer needed.

Seven months later, in April 1453, Ottoman soldiers moved Urban's huge bronze bombards—with barrels twenty-six feet long, capable of throwing eight-hundred-pound shot—into place beneath the walls of Constantinople. Although these cumbersome cannons could fire only seven rounds a day, they battered the walls of Constantinople, which had long been considered impenetrable. After six weeks of siege the Turks breached the walls and swarmed into the city. The vastly outnumbered defenders, Emperor Constantine among them, fought to the death.

Urban's willingness to put business before religious loyalty helped tip the balance of power in the Mediterranean. During the siege, the Genoese merchant community at Constantinople—along with their archrivals, the Venetians—maintained strict neutrality. Although the Italian merchants, like Urban, were prepared to do business with Mehmed II, within a decade the Venetians and Ottomans were at war. Venice could not produce

BACKSTORY

In the fourteenth century, a number of developments threatened the connections among the societies of the Afro-Eurasian world. The collapse of the Mongol empires in China and Iran in the mid-1300s disrupted caravan traffic across Central Asia, diverting the flow of trade and travel to maritime routes across the Indian Ocean. Although the two centuries of religious wars known as the Crusades ended in 1291, they had hardened hostility between Christians and Muslims. As the power of the Christian Byzantine Empire contracted, Muslim Turkish sultanates—the Mamluk regime in Egypt and the rising Ottoman dynasty in Anatolia (modern Turkey)—gained control of the eastern Mediterranean region. Yet the Crusades and direct contact with the Mongols had also whetted European appetites for luxury and exotic goods from the Islamic world and Asia. Thus, despite challenges and obstacles, the Mediterranean remained a lively crossroads of commerce and cross-cultural exchange.

Fourteenth-Century Crisis and Renewal in Eurasia

FOCUS How did the Black Death affect society, the economy, and culture in Latin Christendom and the Islamic world?

Islam's New Frontiers

FOCUS Why did Islam expand dramatically in the fourteenth and fifteenth centuries, and how did new Islamic societies differ from established ones?

The Global Bazaar

FOCUS How did the pattern of international trade change during the fourteenth and fifteenth centuries, and how did these changes affect consumption and fashion tastes?

COUNTERPOINT
Age of the Samurai in Japan, 1185–1450

FOCUS How and why did the historical development of Japan in the fourteenth and fifteenth centuries differ from that of mainland Eurasia?

---

bazaar, and this isolation contributed to the birth of Japan's distinctive national culture. For most Afro-Eurasian societies, however, the maritime world increasingly became the principal crossroads of economic and cultural exchange.

OVERVIEW QUESTIONS

The major global development in this chapter: Crisis and recovery in fourteenth- and fifteenth-century Afro-Eurasia.

As you read, consider:

1. In the century after the devastating outbreak of plague known as the Black Death, how and why did Europe's economic growth begin to surpass that of the Islamic world?

2. Did the economic revival across Eurasia after 1350 benefit the peasant populations of Europe, the Islamic world, and East Asia?

3. How did the process of conversion to Islam differ in Iran, the Ottoman Empire, West Africa, and Southeast Asia during this period?

4. What political and economic changes contributed to the rise of maritime commerce in Asia during the fourteenth and fifteenth centuries?

STEP 3

Use the chapter tools to understand what is important.

Islam's New Frontiers

Focus questions, which also appear at the start and end of the chapter, tell you what you need to learn from each major section.

> **FOCUS**
> Why did Islam expand dramatically in the fourteenth and fifteenth centuries, and how did new Islamic societies differ from established ones?

In the fourteenth and fifteenth centuries, Islam continued to spread to new areas, including central and maritime Asia, sub-Saharan Africa, and southeastern Europe. In the past, Muslim rule had often preceded the popular adoption of Islamic religion and culture. Yet the advance of Islam in Africa and Asia came about not through conquest, but through slow diffusion via merchants and missionaries. The universalism and egalitarianism of Islam appealed to rising merchant classes in both West Africa and maritime Asia.

During this period, Islam expanded by adapting to older ruling cultures rather than seeking to eradicate them. Timur, the last of the great nomad conquerors, and his descendants ruled not as Mongol khans but as Islamic sultans. The culture of the Central Asian states, however, remained an eclectic mix of Mongol, Turkish, and Persian traditions, in contrast to the strict adherence to Muslim law and doctrine practiced under the Arab regimes of the Middle East and North Africa. This pattern of cultural adaptation and assimilation was even more evident in West Africa and Southeast Asia.

Islamic Spiritual Ferment in Central Asia 1350–1500

The spread of Sufism in Central Asia between 1350 and 1500 played a significant role in the process of cultural assimilation. **Sufism**—a mystical tradition that stressed self-mastery, practical virtues, and spiritual growth through personal experience of the divine—had already emerged by 1200 as a major expression of Islamic values and social identity. Sufism appeared in many variations and readily assimilated local cultures to its beliefs and practices. Sufi mystics acquired institutional strength through the communal solidarity of their brotherhoods spread across the whole realm of Islam. In contrast to the orthodox scholars and teachers known as *ulama*, who made little effort to convert nonbelievers, Sufi preachers were inspired by missionary zeal and welcomed non-Muslims to their lodges and sermons. This made them ideal instruments for the spread of Islam to new territories.

Topical headings in the margin focus on important topics and are useful for reviewing the chapter.

Timur

One of Sufism's most important royal patrons was Timur (1336–1405), the last of the Mongol emperors. Born near the city of Samarkand (SAM-ar-kand) when the Mongol Ilkhanate in Iran was on the verge of collapse, Timur—himself a Turk—grew up among Mongols who practiced Islam. He rose to power in the 1370s by reuniting quarreling Mongol tribes in common pursuit of conquest. Although Timur lacked the dynastic pedigree enjoyed by Chinggis Khan's descendants, like Chinggis he held his empire together by the force of his personal charisma.

From the early 1380s, Timur's armies relentlessly pursued campaigns of conquest, sweeping westward across Iran into Mesopotamia and Russia and eastward into India. In 1400–1401 Timur seized and razed Aleppo and Damascus, the principal Mamluk cities in Syria. In 1402 he captured the Ottoman sultan in battle. Rather than trying to consolidate his rule in Syria and Anatolia (modern Turkey), however, Timur turned his attention eastward. He was preparing to march on China when he fell ill and died early in 1405. Although Timur's empire quickly fragmented, his triumphs would serve as an inspiration to later empire builders, such as the Mughals in India and the Manchus in China. Moreover, his support of Sufism would have a lasting impact, helping lay the foundation for a number of important Islamic religious movements in Central Asia.

The institutions of Timur's empire were largely modeled on the Ilkhan synthesis of Persian civil administration and Turkish-Mongol military organization. Like the Ilkhans and the Ottomans, Timur's policies favored settled farmers and urban populations over pastoral nomads, who were often displaced from their homelands. While Timur allowed local princes a degree of autonomy, he was determined to make Samarkand a grand imperial capital.

Marginal glossary definitions provide further explanation of key terms boldfaced in the narrative.

Sufism A tradition within Islam that emphasizes mystical knowledge and personal experience of the divine.

Cultural Innovations

Again, as with Islam in West Africa, the intellectual ferment of the Renaissance was nurtured in an urban environment. Humanist scholars shunned the warrior culture of the old nobility while celebrating the civic roles and duties of townsmen, merchants, and clerics. Despite their admiration of classical civilization, the humanists did not reject Christianity. Rather, they sought to reconcile Christian faith and doctrines with classical learning. By making knowledge of Latin and Greek, history, poetry, and philosophy the mark of an educated person, the humanists transformed education and established models of schooling that would endure down to modern times.

Nowhere was the revolutionary impact of the Renaissance felt more deeply than in visual arts such as painting, sculpture, and architecture. Artists of the Renaissance exuded supreme confidence in the ability of human ingenuity to equal or even surpass the works of nature. The new outlook was exemplified by the development of the techniques of perspective, which artists used to convey a realistic, three-dimensional quality to physical forms, most notably the human body. Human invention also was capable of improving on nature by creating order and harmony through architecture and urban planning. Alberti advocated replacing the winding narrow streets and haphazard construction of medieval towns with planned cities organized around straight boulevards, open squares, and monumental buildings whose balanced proportions corresponded to a geometrically unified design.

Above all, the Renaissance transformed the idea of the artist. No longer mere manual tradesmen, artists now were seen as possessing a special kind of genius that enabled them to express a higher understanding of beauty. In the eyes of contemporaries, no one exemplified this quality of genius more than Leonardo da Vinci (1452–1519), who won renown as a painter, architect, sculptor, engineer, mathematician, and inventor. Leonardo's father, a Florentine lawyer, apprenticed him to a local painter at age eighteen. Leonardo spent much of his career as a civil and military engineer in the employ of the Duke of Milan, and developed ideas for flying machines, tanks, robots, and solar power that far exceeded the engineering capabilities of his time. Leonardo sought to apply his knowledge of natural science to painting, which he regarded as the most sublime art (see Seeing the Past: Leonardo da Vinci's *Virgin of the Rocks*).

> The final Counterpoint section offers an important exception to the Major Global Development discussed in the chapter.

The flowering of artistic creativity in the Renaissance was rooted in the rich soil of Italy's commercial [...] from the Islamic world and Asia. International [...] production across maritime Asia and gave [...] nd consumption. In Japan, however, grow [...] fostered the emergence of a national cultu [...] ted the rest of East Asia.

COUNTERPOINT
Age of the Samurai in Japan 1185–1450

In Japan as in Europe, the term *Middle Ages* brings to mind an age of warriors, a stratified society governed by bonds of loyalty between lords and vassals. In Japan, however, the militarization of the ruling class intensified during the fourteenth and fifteenth centuries, a time when the warrior nobility of Europe was crumbling. Paradoxically, the rise of the **samurai** (sah-moo-rye) ("those who serve") warriors as masters of their own estates was accompanied by [...] e increasing independence of peasant communities.

FOCUS

How and why did the historical development of Japan in the fourteenth and fifteenth centuries differ from that of mainland Eurasia?

> Phonetic spellings follow many potentially unfamiliar terms.

[...] pter, Japan became more isolated from [...] ural exchanges with China reached a pea [...] invasion of Japan in 1281, ties with conti [...] panese see this era as the period in which Japan's unique national identity—expressed most distinctly in the ethic of *bushidō* (boo-shee-doe), the "Way of the Warrior"—took its definitive form. Samurai warriors became the

samurai Literally, "those who serve"; the hereditary warriors who dominated Japanese society and culture from the twelfth to the nineteenth centuries.

STEP 4

Do historical analysis.

LIVES AND LIVELIHOODS

Lives and Livelihoods features underscore the connections between daily life and global developments.

Urban Weavers in India

Industry and commerce in India, especially in textiles, grew rapidly beginning in the fourteenth century. Specialized craftsmen in towns and regional groups of merchants formed guilds that became the nuclei of new occupational castes, *jati* (JAH-tee). Ultimately these new occupational castes would join with other forces in Indian society to challenge the social inequality rooted in orthodox Hindu religion.

It was growth in market demand and technological innovations such as block printing that drove the rapid expansion of India's textile industries. Luxury fabrics such as fine silks and velvet remained largely the province of royal workshops or private patronage. Mass production of textiles, on the other hand, was oriented toward the manufacture of cheaper cotton fabrics, especially colorful chintz garments. A weaver could make a woman's cotton *sari* in six or seven days, whereas a luxury garment took a month or more. Domestic demand for ordinary cloth grew steadily, and production for export accelerated even more briskly. At the beginning of the sixteenth century, the Portuguese traveler Tomé Pires, impressed by the craftsmanship of Indian muslins and calicoes (named after the port of Calicut), observed that "they make enough of these to furnish the world."[1]

Weaving became an urban industry. It was village women who cleaned most of the cotton and spun it into yarn; they could easily combine this simple if laborious work with other domestic chores. But peasants did not weave the yarn into cloth, except for their own use. Instead, weaving, bleaching, a...
professional...
living in sepa...

Like oth...
pation that c...
Families of w...
guilds with b...
within their g...
not have exc...
could include...
could become...

South...
and Rai...

Indian Block-Printed Textile, c. 1500
Block-printed textiles with elaborate designs were in great demand both in India and throughout Southeast Asia, Africa, and the Islamic world. Craftsmen carved intricate designs on wooden blocks (a separate block for each color), which were then dipped in dye and repeatedly stamped on bleached fabric until the entire cloth was covered. This cotton fabric with geese, lotus flower, and rosette designs was manufactured in Gujarat in western India. (Ashmolean Museum, University of Oxford/...)

The rising prosperity of weavers whetted their aspirations for social recognition. Amid the whirl and congestion of city life, it was far more difficult than in villages to enforce the laws governing caste purity and segregation. As a fourteenth-century poet wrote about the crowded streets of his hometown of Jaunpur in the Ganges Valley, in the city "one person's caste-mark gets stamped on another's forehead, and a brahman's holy thread will be found hanging around an untouchable's neck."[2] Brahmans objected to this erosion of caste boundaries, to little avail. Weaver guilds became influential patrons of temples and often served as trustees and accountants in charge of managing temple endowments and revenues.

In a few cases the growing economic independence of weavers and like-minded artisans prompted complete rejection of the caste hierarchy. Sufi preachers and *bhakti* (BAHK-tee)—devotional movements devoted to patron gods and goddesses—encouraged the disregard of caste distinctions in favor of a universal brotherhood of devout believers. The fifteenth-century bhakti preacher Kabir, who was strongly influenced by Sufi teachings, epitomized the new social radicalism coursing through the urban artisan classes. A weaver himself, Kabir joined the dignity of manual labor to the purity of spiritual devotion, spurning the social pretension and superficial piety of the brahmans ("pandits") and Muslim clerics ("mullahs"):

a trinity of labor, charity, and spiritual devotion. The Sikhs, who gained a following principally among traders and artisans in the northwestern Punjab region, drew an even more explicit connection between commerce and piety. In the words of a hymn included in a sixteenth-century anthology of Sikh sacred writings:

> The true Guru [teacher] is the merchant;
> The devotees are his peddlers.
> The capital stock is the Lord's Name, and
> To enshrine the truth is to keep His account.[4]

Sikh communities spurned the distinction between pure and impure occupations. In their eyes, holiness was to be found in honest toil and personal piety, not ascetic practices, book learning, or religious rituals.

---

1. Tomé Pires, *The Suma Oriental of Tomé Pires*, ed. and trans. Armando Cortes (London: Hakluyt Society, 1944), 1:53.
2. Vidyapati Thakur, *Kirtilata*, quoted in Eugenia Vanina, *Urban Crafts and Craftsmen in Medieval India (Thirteenth–Eighteenth Centuries)* (New Delhi: Munshiram Manoharlal, 2004), 443.
3. Quoted in Vanina, *Urban Crafts and Craftsmen*, 149.
4. *Sri Guru Granth Sahib*, trans. Gophal Singh (Delhi: Gur Das Kapur & Sons, 1960), 2:427.

at ease
... mullahs,
...come
... toil,
...asure.
...sieced
...ered on

... *India*. Delhi: Oxford University Press, 1985.
... *India (Thirteenth–Eighteenth Centuries)*. New Delhi: Munshiram Manoharlal, 2004.

QUESTIONS TO CONSIDER

1. In what ways did the organization of textile production reinforce or challenge the prevailing social norms of Hindu society?

2. In what ways did religious ideas and movements reflect the new sense of dignity among prosperous Indian merchants and craftsmen?

SEEING THE PAST

Reading the Past and Seeing the Past features provide direct exposure to important voices and ideas of the past through written and visual primary sources.

Leonardo da Vinci's *Virgin of the Rocks*

Virgin of the Rocks, c. 1483–1486
(Erich Lessing/Art Resource.)

Leonardo's Botanical Studies with Star-of-Bethlehem, Grasses, Crowfoot, Wood Anemone, and Another Genus,
c. 1500–1506 (The Royal Collection © 2011 Her Majesty Queen Elizabeth II/Bridgeman Art Library.)

the menacing...
the cavern; de...
there was any...
thing within."[1]

Fantastic as the sce...
might seem, Leonardo's
meticulous rendering of
rocks and p...
based on cl...
of nature. Th...
lehem flowe...
left of the pa...
izing purity a...
also appear...
contempora...
cal drawing...
Geologists h...
Leonardo's I...
sandstone n...
and his prec...
of plants wh...
most likely t...

Master...
the *Virgin o...*
display Leonardo's careful study of human an...
landscapes, and botany. Although he admire...
tion of nature, Leonardo also celebrated the h...
rational and aesthetic capacities, declaring th...
arts may be called the grandsons of God."[2]

While living in Milan in the early 1480s, Leonardo accepted a commission to paint an altarpiece for the chapel of Milan's Confraternity of the Immaculate Conception, a branch of the Franciscan order. Leonardo's relationship with the friars proved to be stormy. Leonardo's first version of the painting (now in the Louvre), reproduced here, apparently displeased his patrons and was sold to another party. Only after a fifteen-year-long dispute over the price did Leonardo finally deliver a modified version in 1508.

In portraying the legendary encounter between the child Jesus and the equally young John the Baptist during the flight to Egypt, Leonardo replaced the traditional desert setting with a landscape filled with rocks, plants, and water. Leonardo's dark grotto creates an aura of mystery and foreboding, from which the figures of Mary, Jesus, John, and the angel Uriel emerge as if in a vision. A few years before, Leonardo had written about "coming to the entrance of a great cavern, in front of which I stood for some time, stupefied and uncomprehending. . . . Suddenly two things arose in me, fear and desire: fear of

1. Arundel ms. (British Library), p. 115 recto, cited i...
   Leonardo da Vinci: The Marvelous Works of Nat...
   (Oxford: Oxford University Press, 2006), 78.
2. John Paul Richter, ed., *The Notebooks of Leona...*
   of 1883 ed.; New York: Dover, 1970), Book IX, 32...

EXAMINING THE EVIDENCE

1. How does Leonardo express the conne... between John (at left) and Jesus throug... gesture, and their relationships with the... Mary and the angel Uriel?

2. The friars who commissioned the painting sought to celebrate the sanctity and purity of their patron, the Virgin Mary. Does this painting achieve that effect?

Thus, China influenced patterns of international trade not only as a producer, as with

READING THE PAST

A Spanish Ambassador's Description of Samarkand

In September 1403, an embassy dispatched by King Henry III of Castile arrived at Samarkand in hopes of enlisting the support of Timur for a combined military campaign against the Ottomans. Seventy years old and in failing health, Timur lavishly entertained his visitors, but made no response to Henry's overtures. The leader of the Spanish delegation, Ruy Gonzalez de Clavijo, left Samarkand disappointed, but his report preserves our fullest account of Timur's capital in its heyday.

> The city is rather larger than Seville, but lying outside Samarkand are great numbers of houses that form extensive suburbs. These lay spread on all hands, for indeed the township is surrounded by orchards and vineyards. . . . In between these orchards pass streets with open squares; these are all densely populated, and here all kinds of goods are on sale with breadstuffs and meat. . . .
>
> Samarkand is rich not only in foodstuffs but also in manufactures, such as factories of silk. . . . Thus trade has always been fostered by Timur with the view of making his capital the noblest of cities; and during all his conquests . . . he carried off the best men to people Samarkand, bringing thither the master-craftsmen of all nations. Thus from Damascus he carried away with him all the weavers of that city, those who worked at the silk looms; further the bow-makers who produce those cross-bows which are so famous; likewise armorers; also the craftsmen in glass and porcelain, who are known to be the best in all the world. From Turkey he

had brought their gunsmiths who make the arquebus. . . . So great therefore was the population now of all nationalities gathered together in Samarkand that of men with their families the number they said must amount to 150,000 souls . . . [including] Turks, Arabs, and Moors of diverse sects, with Greek, Armenian, Roman, Jacobite [Syrian], and Nestorian Christians, besides those folk who baptize with fire in the forehead [i.e., Hindus]. . . .

> The markets of Samarkand further are amply stored with merchandise imported from distant and foreign countries. . . . The goods that are imported to Samarkand from Cathay indeed are of the richest and most precious of all those brought thither from foreign parts, for the craftsmen of Cathay are reputed to be the most skillful by far beyond those of any other nation.

Source: Ruy Gonzalez de Clavijo, *Embassy to Tamerlane, 1403–1406*, trans. Guy Le Strange (London: Routledge, 1928), 285–289.

EXAMINING THE EVIDENCE

1. What features of Timur's capital most impressed Gonzalez de Clavijo?

2. How does this account of Samarkand at its height compare with the chapter's description of Renaissance Florence?

STEP 5

Review what you have learned.

> Remember to visit the Online Study Guide for more review help.

REVIEW

Online Study Guide
bedfordstmartins.com/smith

The major global development in this chapter ▶ Crisis and recovery in fourteenth- and fifteenth-century Afro-Eurasia.

> Review the Major Global Development discussed in the chapter.

> Review the Important Events from the chapter.

IMPORTANT EVENTS

1315–1317	Great Famine in northern Europe
1325–1354	Travels of Ibn Battuta in Asia and Africa
1336–1573	Ashikaga shogunate in Japan
1337–1453	Hundred Years' War between England and France
1347–1350	Outbreak of the Black Death in Europe and the Islamic Mediterranean
c. 1351–1782	Ayudhya kingdom in Thailand
1368–1644	Ming dynasty in China
1378	Ciompi uprising in Florence
1381	Peasant Revolt in England
1392–1910	Yi dynasty in Korea
1405	Death of Timur; breakup of his empire into regional states in Iran and Central Asia
1405–1433	Chinese admiral Zheng He's expeditions in Southeast Asia and the Indian Ocean
1421	Relocation of Ming capital from Nanjing to Beijing
1428–1788	Le dynasty in Vietnam
1453	Ottoman conquest of Constantinople marks fall of the Byzantine Empire

CHAPTER OVERVIEW QUESTIONS

1. How and why did Europe's economic growth begin to surpass that of the Islamic world in the after the Black Death?

2. Did the economic revival across Eurasia a benefit the peasant populations of Europe Islamic world, and East Asia?

3. How did the process of conversion to Islam differ in Iran, the Ottoman Empire, West Africa, and Southeast Asia during this period?

4. What political and economic changes contributed to the rise of maritime commerce in Asia during the fourteenth and fifteenth centuries?

> Answer these big-picture questions posed at the start of the chapter.

SECTION FOCUS QUESTIONS

1. How did the Black Death affect society, the omy, and culture in Latin Christendom and Islamic world?

2. Why did Islam expand dramatically in the fourteenth and fifteenth centuries, and how did new Islamic societies differ from established ones?

3. What were the principal sources of growth in international trade during the fourteenth and fifteenth centuries, and how did this trade affect patterns of consumption and fashion tastes?

4. How and why did the historical development of Japan in the fourteenth and fifteenth centuries differ from that of mainland Eurasia?

> Explain the main point of each major section of the chapter.

> Review the Key Terms.

KEY TERMS

Black Death (p. 478)
humanism (p. 498)
janissary corps (p. 489)
Little Ice Age (p. 479)
Neo-Confucianism (p. 486)
oligarchy (p. 483)

pandemic (p. 478)
Renaissance (p. 498)
samurai (p. 501)
shogun (p. 503)
Sufism (p. 488)
theocracy (p. 489)
trade diaspora (p. 492)

MAKING CONNECTIONS

1. What social, economic, and technological c strengthened the power of European mona during the century after the Black Death?

2. How and why did the major routes and con ties of trans-Eurasian trade change after the collapse of the Mongol empires in Central Asia?

3. In what ways did the motives for conversion to Islam differ in Central Asia, sub-Saharan Africa, and the Indian Ocean during this era?

4. In this period, why did the power and status of the samurai warriors in Japan rise while those of the warrior nobility in Europe declined?

> Connect ideas and practice your skills of comparison and analysis.

507

VERSIONS AND SUPPLEMENTS

Adopters of *Crossroads and Cultures: A History of the World's Peoples* and their students have access to abundant extra resources, including documents, presentation and testing materials, the acclaimed Bedford Series in History and Culture volumes, and much, much more. See below for more information, visit the book's catalog site at bedfordstmartins .com/smith/catalog, or contact your local Bedford/St. Martin's sales representative.

Get the Right Version for Your Class

To accommodate different course lengths and course budgets, *Crossroads and Cultures: A History of the World's Peoples* is available in several different formats, including three-hole punched loose-leaf Budget Books versions and e-books, which are available at a substantial discount.

- Combined edition (Chapters 1–31)—available in hardcover, loose-leaf, and e-book formats
- Volume 1: To 1450 (Chapters 1–16)—available in paperback, loose-leaf, and e-book formats
- Volume 2: Since 1300 (Chapters 15–31)—available in paperback, loose-leaf, and e-book formats
- Volume A: To 1300 (Chapters 1–14)—available in paperback
- Volume B: 500–1750 (Chapters 9–22)—available in paperback
- Volume C: Since 1750 (Chapters 23–31)—available in paperback

Your students can purchase *Crossroads and Cultures: A History of the World's Peoples* in popular e-book formats for computers, tablets, and e-readers by visiting bedfordstmartins .com/ebooks. The e-book is available at a discount.

Online Extras for Students

The book's companion site at bedfordstmartins.com/smith gives students a way to read, write, and study by providing plentiful quizzes and activities, study aids, and history research and writing help.

FREE **Online Study Guide.** Available at the companion site, this popular resource provides students with quizzes and activities for each chapter, including multiple-choice self-tests that focus on important concepts; flashcards that test students' knowledge of key terms; timeline activities that emphasize causal relationships; and map quizzes intended to strengthen students' geography skills. Instructors can monitor students' progress through an online Quiz Gradebook or receive e-mail updates.

FREE **Research, Writing, and Anti-plagiarism Advice.** Available at the companion site, Bedford's **History Research and Writing Help** includes **History Research and Reference Sources**, with links to history-related databases, indexes, and journals; **More Sources and How to Format a History Paper**, with clear advice on how to integrate primary and secondary sources into research papers and how to cite and format sources correctly; **Build a Bibliography**, a simple Web-based tool known as the Bedford Bibliographer that generates bibliographies in four commonly used documentation styles; and **Tips on Avoiding Plagiarism**, an online tutorial that reviews the consequences of plagiarism and features exercises to help students practice integrating sources and recognize acceptable summaries.

Resources for Instructors

Bedford/St. Martin's has developed a rich array of teaching resources for this book and for this course. They range from lecture and presentation materials and assessment tools to course management options. Most can be downloaded or ordered at bedfordstmartins.com/smith/catalog.

HistoryClass for Crossroads and Cultures. *HistoryClass*, a Bedford/St. Martin's Online Course Space, puts the online resources available with this textbook in one convenient and completely customizable course space. There you and your students can access an interactive e-book and primary source reader; maps, images, documents, and links; chapter review quizzes; interactive multimedia exercises; and research and writing help. In *HistoryClass* you can get all our premium content and tools and assign, rearrange, and mix them with your own resources. For more information, visit yourhistoryclass.com.

Bedford Coursepack for Blackboard, WebCT, Desire2Learn, Angel, Sakai, or Moodle. We have free content to help you integrate our rich materials into your course management system. Registered instructors can download coursepacks easily and with no strings attached. The coursepack for *Crossroads and Cultures: A History of the World's Peoples* includes book-specific content as well as our most popular free resources. Visit bedfordstmartins.com/ coursepacks to see a demo, find your version, or download your coursepack.

Instructor's Resource Manual. Written by Rick Warner, an experienced teacher of the world-history survey course, the instructor's manual offers both experienced and first-time instructors tools for preparing lectures and running discussions. It includes chapter review material, teaching strategies, and a guide to chapter-specific supplements available for the text.

Computerized Test Bank. The test bank includes a mix of fresh, carefully crafted multiple-choice, matching, short-answer, and essay questions for each chapter. It also contains the Overview, Focus, Making Connections, Lives and Livelihoods, Reading the Past, and Seeing the Past questions from the textbook and model answers for each. The questions appear in Microsoft Word format and in easy-to-use test bank software that allows instructors to easily add, edit, resequence, and print questions and answers. Instructors can also export questions into a variety of formats, including WebCT and Blackboard.

The Bedford Lecture Kit: Maps, Images, Lecture Outlines, and i>clicker Content. Look good and save time with *The Bedford Lecture Kit*. These presentation materials are downloadable individually from the Instructor Resources tab at bedfordstmartins.com/smith/catalog and are available on *The Bedford Lecture Kit* Instructor's Resource CD-ROM. They provide ready-made and fully customizable PowerPoint multimedia presentations that include lecture outlines with embedded maps, figures, and selected images from the textbook and extra background for instructors. Also available are maps and selected images in JPEG and PowerPoint formats; content for i>clicker, a classroom response system, in Microsoft Word and PowerPoint formats; the Instructor's Resource Manual in Microsoft Word format; and outline maps in PDF format for quizzing or handing out. All files are suitable for copying onto transparency acetates.

Make History—Free Documents, Maps, Images, and Web Sites. *Make History* combines the best Web resources with hundreds of maps and images, to make it simple to find the source material you need. Browse the collection of thousands of resources by course or by topic, date, and type. Each item has been carefully chosen and helpfully annotated to make it easy to find exactly what you need. Available at bedfordstmartins.com/makehistory.

Videos and Multimedia. A wide assortment of videos and multimedia CD-ROMs on various topics in world history is available to qualified adopters through your Bedford/St. Martin's sales representative.

Package and Save Your Students Money

For information on free packages and discounts up to 50%, visit bedfordstmartins.com/smith/catalog, or contact your local Bedford/St. Martin's sales representative.

Sources of Crossroads and Cultures. The authors of *Crossroads and Cultures* have carefully developed this two-volume primary source reader themselves to reflect the textbook's geographic and thematic breadth and the key social, cultural, and political developments discussed in each chapter. *Sources of Crossroads and Cultures* extends the textbook's emphasis on the human dimension of global history through the voices of both notable figures and everyday individuals. With a blend of major works and fresh perspectives, each chapter contains approximately six sources, an introduction, document headnotes, and questions for discussion. Available free when packaged with the print text.

Sources of Crossroads and Cultures e-Book. The reader is also available as an e-book for purchase at a discount.

The Bedford Series in History and Culture. More than one hundred titles in this highly praised series combine first-rate scholarship, historical narrative, and important primary documents for undergraduate courses. Each book is brief, inexpensive, and focused on a specific topic or period. For a complete list of titles, visit bedfordstmartins.com/history/series. Package discounts are available.

Rand McNally Historical Atlas of the World. This collection of almost seventy full-color maps illustrates the eras and civilizations in world history from the emergence of human societies to the present. Available for $3.00 when packaged with the print text.

The Bedford Glossary for World History. This handy supplement for the survey course gives students historically contextualized definitions for hundreds of terms—from *abolitionism* to *Zoroastrianism*—that they will encounter in lectures, reading, and exams. Available free when packaged with the print text.

World History Matters: A Student Guide to World History Online. Based on the popular "World History Matters" Web site produced by the Center for History and New Media, this unique resource, edited by Kristin Lehner (The Johns Hopkins University), Kelly Schrum (George Mason University), and T. Mills Kelly (George Mason University), combines reviews of 150 of the most useful and reliable world history Web sites with an introduction that guides students in locating, evaluating, and correctly citing online sources. Available free when packaged with the print text.

Trade Books. Titles published by sister companies Hill and Wang; Farrar, Straus and Giroux; Henry Holt and Company; St. Martin's Press; Picador; and Palgrave Macmillan are available at a 50% discount when packaged with

Bedford/St. Martin's textbooks. For more information, visit bedfordstmartins.com/tradeup.

A Pocket Guide to Writing in History. This portable and affordable reference tool by Mary Lynn Rampolla provides reading, writing, and research advice useful to students in all history courses. Concise yet comprehensive advice on approaching typical history assignments, developing critical reading skills, writing effective history papers, conducting research, using and documenting sources, and avoiding plagiarism—enhanced with practical tips and examples throughout—have made this slim reference a best-seller. Package discounts are available.

A Student's Guide to History. This complete guide to success in any history course provides the practical help students need to be effective. In addition to introducing students to the nature of the discipline, author Jules Benjamin teaches a wide range of skills from preparing for exams to approaching common writing assignments, and he explains the research and documentation process with plentiful examples. Package discounts are available.

Worlds of History: A Comparative Reader. Compiled by Kevin Reilly, a widely respected world historian and community college teacher, *Worlds of History* fosters historical thinking through thematic comparisons of primary and secondary sources from around the world. Each chapter takes up a major theme—such as patriarchy, love and marriage, or globalization—as experienced by two or more cultures. "Thinking Historically" exercises build students' capacity to analyze and interpret sources one skill at a time. This flexible framework accommodates a variety of approaches to teaching world history. Package discounts are available.

NOTE ON DATES AND USAGE

Where necessary for clarity, we qualify dates as B.C.E. ("Before the Common Era") or C.E. ("Common Era"). The abbreviation B.C.E. refers to the same era as B.C. ("Before Christ"), just as C.E is equivalent to A.D. (*anno Domini,* Latin for "in the year of the Lord"). In keeping with our aim to approach world history from a global, multicultural perspective, we chose these neutral abbreviations as appropriate to our enterprise. Because most readers will be more familiar with English than with metric measures, however, units of measure are given in the English system in the narrative, with metric and English measures provided on the maps.

We translate Chinese names and terms into English according to the *pinyin* system, while noting in parentheses proper names well established in English (e.g., Canton, Chiang Kai-shek). Transliteration of names and terms from the many other languages traced in our book follow the same contemporary scholarly conventions.

BRIEF CONTENTS

CONTENTS

PART 1   The Ancient World, from Human Origins to 500 C.E.

5

The Greeks and the
Wider World,
1200–30 B.C.E.   *138*

Major Global Development ▶ The cultural and political innovations of the ancient Greeks and the expansion of Greek ideals and institutions.

6

Peoples and World
Empires: Classical
India, the Kushan
Empire, and China,
500 B.C.E.–500 C.E.   *170*

Major Global Development ▶ The revolutionary religious and cultural developments in India and China that took place between 500 B.C.E. and 500 C.E. and remained fundamental to the history of Asia.

9

The Worlds of Christianity and Islam, 400–1000 *270*

Major Global Development ▶The spread of Christianity and Islam and the profound impact of these world religions on the societies of western Eurasia and North Africa.

10

Religion and Cross-Cultural Exchange in Asia, 400–1000 *304*

Major Global Development ▶The cultural and commercial exchanges during the heyday of the Silk Road that transformed Asian peoples, cultures, and states.

13

Centers of Learning and the Transmission of Culture, 900–1300 *406*

Major Global Development ▶ The expansion of learning and education across Eurasia in the period from 900 to 1300 and its relationship with the rise of regional and national identities.

14

Crusaders, Mongols, and Eurasian Integration, 1050–1350 *440*

Major Global Development ▶ The Eurasian integration fostered by the clashes of culture known as the Crusades and the Mongol conquests.

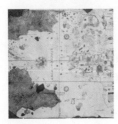

19

Trade and Empire in the Indian Ocean and South Asia, 1450–1750 *612*

20

Consolidation and Conflict in Europe and the Greater Mediterranean, 1450–1750 *646*

21

Expansion and Isolation in Asia, 1450–1750 *682*

> **Major Global Development** ▶ The general trend toward political and cultural consolidation in early modern Asia.

22

Transforming New Worlds: The American Colonies Mature, 1600–1750 *718*

> **Major Global Development** ▶ The profound social, cultural, and environmental changes in the Americas under colonial rule.

23

Atlantic Revolutions and the World,
1750–1830 *758*

Major Global Development ▶ The Atlantic revolutions and their short- and long-term significance.

24

Industry and Everyday Life, 1750–1900 *790*

Major Global Development ▶ The Industrial Revolution and its impact on societies and cultures throughout the world.

25

The Rise of Modern Nation-States, 1850–1900 *824*

Major Global Development ▶The causes and consequences of nation building in the nineteenth century.

26

Imperial Order and Disorder, 1850–1914 *856*

Major Global Development ▶The accelerated competition among nineteenth-century nation-states for empire.

29

The Emergence of New Nations in a Cold War World, 1945–1970 *958*

Major Global Development ►The political transformations of the postwar world and their social and cultural consequences.

30

Technological Transformation and the End of Cold War, 1960–1992 *988*

Major Global Development ►The technological revolution of the late twentieth century and its impact on societies and political developments around the world.

31

A New Global Age, 1989 to the Present *1022*

Major Global Development ▸ The causes and consequences of intensified globalization.

MAPS

SPECIAL FEATURES

Seeing the Past

ACKNOWLEDGMENTS

Writing *Crossroads and Cultures* has made real to us the theme of this book, which is connections among many far-flung people of diverse livelihoods and talents. From the first draft to the last, the authors have benefited from repeated critical readings by many talented scholars and teachers who represent an array of schools and historical interests. Our sincere thanks go to the following instructors, who helped us keep true to our vision of showing connections among the world's people and whose comments often challenged us to rethink or justify our interpretations. Crucial to the integrity of the book, they always provided a check on accuracy down to the smallest detail.

Alemseged Abbay, *Frostburg State University*
Heather J. Abdelnur, *Augusta State University*
Wayne Ackerson, *Salisbury University*
Kathleen Addison, *California State University, Northridge*
Jeffrey W. Alexander, *University of Wisconsin–Parkside*
Omar H. Ali, *The University of North Carolina at Greensboro*
Monty Armstrong, *Cerritos High School*
Pierre Asselin, *Hawai'i Pacific University*
Eva Baham, *Southern University at Baton Rouge*
William Bakken, *Rochester Community and Technical College*
Thomas William Barker, *The University of Kansas*
Thomas William Barton, *University of San Diego*
Robert Blackey, *California State University, San Bernardino*
Chuck Bolton, *The University of North Carolina at Greensboro*
Robert Bond, *San Diego Mesa College*
James W. Brodman, *University of Central Arkansas*
Gayle K. Brunelle, *California State University, Fullerton*
Samuel Brunk, *The University of Texas at El Paso*
Jurgen Buchenau, *The University of North Carolina at Charlotte*
Clea Bunch, *University of Arkansas at Little Rock*
Kathy Callahan, *Murray State University*
John M. Carroll, *The University of Hong Kong*
Giancarlo Casale, *University of Minnesota*
Mark Chavalas, *University of Wisconsin–La Crosse*
Yinghong Cheng, *Delaware State University*
Mark Choate, *Brigham Young University*
Sharon Cohen, *Springbrook High School*
Christine Colin, *Mercyhurst College*
Eleanor Congdon, *Youngstown State University*
Dale Crandall-Bear, *Solano Community College*
John Curry, *University of Nevada, Las Vegas*
Michelle Danberg-Marshman, *Green River Community College*
Francis Danquah, *Southern University at Baton Rouge*
Sherrie Dux-Ideus, *Central Community College*

Peter Dykema, *Arkansas Tech University*
Tom Ewing, *Virginia Polytechnic Institute and State University*
Angela Feres, *Grossmont College*
Michael Fischbach, *Randolph-Macon College*
Nancy Fitch, *California State University, Fullerton*
Terence Anthony Fleming, *Northern Kentucky University*
Richard Fogarty, *University at Albany, The State University of New York*
Nicola Foote, *Florida Gulf Coast University*
Deanna Forsman, *North Hennepin Community College*
John D. Garrigus, *The University of Texas at Arlington*
Trevor Getz, *San Francisco State University*
David Goldfrank, *Georgetown University*
Charles Didier Gondola, *Indiana University–Purdue University Indianapolis*
Sue Gronewold, *Kean University*
Christopher Guthrie, *Tarleton State University*
Anne Hardgrove, *The University of Texas at San Antonio*
Donald J. Harreld, *Brigham Young University*
Todd Hartch, *Eastern Kentucky University*
Janine Hartman, *University of Cincinnati*
Daniel Heimmermann, *The University of Texas at Brownsville*
Cecily M. Heisser, *University of San Diego*
Timothy Henderson, *Auburn University at Montgomery*
Ted Henken, *Baruch College, The State University of New York*
Marilynn J. Hitchens, *University of Colorado Denver*
Roy W. Hopper, *University of Memphis*
Timothy Howe, *St. Olaf College*
Delridge Hunter, *Medgar Evers College, The City University of New York*
Bruce Ingram, *Itawamba Community College*
Erik N. Jensen, *Miami University*
Steven Sandor John, *Hunter College, The City University of New York*
Deborah Johnston, *Lakeside School*
David M. Kalivas, *Middlesex Community College*
Carol Keller, *San Antonio College*
Ian Stuart Kelly, *Palomar College*
Linda Kerr, *University of Alberta*
Charles King, *University of Nebraska at Omaha*
Melinda Cole Klein, *Saddleback College*
Ane Lintvedt-Dulac, *McDonogh School*
Ann Livschiz, *Indiana University–Purdue University Fort Wayne*
George E. Longenecker, *Vermont Technical College*
Edward Lykens, *Middle Tennessee State University*
Susan Maneck, *Jackson State University*
Chandra Manning, *Georgetown University*
Michael Marino, *The College of New Jersey*

Thomas Massey, *Cape Fear Community College*

Mary Jane Maxwell, *Green Mountain College*

Christine McCann, *Norwich University*

Patrick McDevitt, *University at Buffalo, The State University of New York*

Ian F. McNeely, *University of Oregon*

M. E. Menninger, *Texas State University–San Marcos*

Kathryn E. Meyer, *Washington State University*

Elizabeth Mizrahi, *Santa Barbara City College*

Max Okenfuss, *Washington University in St. Louis*

Kenneth Orosz, *Buffalo State College, The State University of New York*

Annette Palmer, *Morgan State University*

David Perry, *Dominican University*

Jared Poley, *Georgia State University*

Elizabeth Ann Pollard, *San Diego State University*

Dana Rabin, *University of Illinois at Urbana-Champaign*

Norman G. Raiford, *Greenville Technical College*

Stephen Rapp, *Universität Bern*

Michele Reid, *Georgia State University*

Chad Ross, *East Carolina University*

Morris Rossabi, *Queens College, The City University of New York*

Steven C. Rubert, *Oregon State University*

Eli Rubin, *Western Michigan University*

Anthony Santoro, *Christopher Newport University*

Linda B. Scherr, *Mercer County Community College*

Hollie Schillig, *California State University, Long Beach*

Michael Seth, *James Madison University*

Jessica Sheetz-Nguyen, *University of Central Oklahoma*

Rose Mary Sheldon, *Virginia Military Institute*

David R. Smith, *California State Polytechnic University, Pomona*

Ramya Sreenivasan, *University at Buffalo, The State University of New York*

John Stavens, *Bristol Eastern High School*

Catherine Howey Stearn, *Eastern Kentucky University*

Richard Steigmann-Gall, *Kent State University*

Anthony J. Steinhoff, *The University of Tennessee at Chattanooga*

Stephen J. Stillwell, *The University of Arizona*

Heather Streets, *Washington State University*

Jean Stuntz, *West Texas A&M University*

Guy Thompson, *University of Alberta*

Hunt Tooley, *Austin College*

Wendy Turner, *Augusta State University*

Rick Warner, *Wabash College*

Michael Weber, *Gettysburg College*

Theodore Weeks, *Southern Illinois University*

Guy Wells, *Lorain County Community College*

Sherri West, *Brookdale Community College*

Kenneth Wilburn, *East Carolina University*

Pingchao Zhu, *University of Idaho*

Alexander Zukas, *National University*

Many colleagues, friends, and family members have helped us develop this work as well. Bonnie Smith wishes to thank in particular Michal Shapira and Molly Giblin for their research assistance and Patrick Smith, who gave helpful information on contemporary world religions. Her colleagues at Rutgers, many of them pioneers in world history, were especially helpful. Among these, expert historian Donald R. Kelley shaped certain features of the last section of the book and always cheered the author on. Marc Van De Mieroop thanks the friends and colleagues who often unknowingly provided insights and information used in this book, especially Irene Bloom, William Harris, Feng Li, Indira Peterson, Michael Sommer, and Romila Thapar. Richard von Glahn thanks his many colleagues at UCLA who have shaped his thinking about world history, especially Ghislaine Lydon, Jose Moya, Ron Mellor, Sanjay Subrahmanyam, and Bin Wong. He is also grateful for the exposure to pathbreaking scholarship on world history afforded by the University of California's Multi-Campus Research Unit in World History. Kris Lane thanks the many wonderful William & Mary students of History 192, "The World Since 1450," as well as colleagues Abdul-Karim Rafeq, Scott Nelson, Chitralekha Zutshi, Hiroshi Kitamura, Philip Daileader, Chandos Brown, and Ron Schechter. All offered valuable advice on framing the early modern period. He also owes a huge debt to the University of Minnesota for graduate training and teaching assistant experience in this field.

We also wish to acknowledge and thank the publishing team at Bedford/St. Martin's, who are among the most talented people in publishing that we as a group have ever worked with and who did so much to bring this book into being. Among them, our special thanks go to former publisher for history Patricia A. Rossi, who inspired the conceptual design of the book and helped bring us together. The current publisher for history, Mary Dougherty, then picked up the reins from Tisha and advanced the project, using her special combination of professional expertise and personal warmth. It is hard to convey sufficiently our heartfelt appreciation to president Joan E. Feinberg and editorial director Denise Wydra. They always kept us alert to Bedford's special legacy of high-quality textbooks, a legacy based on the benefits a book must have for students and teachers alike. We aimed to be part of that legacy while writing *Crossroads and Cultures*.

President emeritus and founder Charles Christensen was also present at the beginning of this project, and he always cheerfully lent his extraordinary knowledge of publishing to the making and actual production of this book. We know that it would have been less than it is without his wisdom. Alongside all these others, director of development for history Jane Knetzger patiently and skillfully guided the development process, during which each chapter (and sentence) was poked and prodded. We thank Jane for being such a quiet force behind the progress of *Crossroads and*

Cultures. Special thanks go to senior editor and expert facilitator Heidi Hood and the editorial assistants who joined Heidi in providing invaluable help on many essential tasks: Lynn Sternberger, Jennifer Jovin, and Emily DiPietro. All of them moved the project along in myriad ways that we hardly know. We also appreciate the countless schedules, tasks, and layouts juggled so efficiently and well by senior production editor Anne Noonan. On the editorial team were John Reisbord and Daniel Otis, who helped edit and polish our final draft. All along the way Rose Corbett Gordon and Charlotte Miller, our superb photo researcher and talented map editor, respectively, provided us with striking and thought-provoking images and up-to-date, richly informative, and gorgeous maps. No author team could ask for more than to have the book's content laid out in such a clear and attractive design as that provided by Jerilyn Bockorick, with assistance from senior art director Anna Palchik. Jerilyn's special attention to the overall look of our work makes us feel that we and our readers are especially lucky. Senior designer Billy Boardman created our six beautiful covers with help from senior art director Donna Dennison. We are grateful for their craft in building the book's appeal.

Crossroads and Cultures has a wealth of materials for students and teachers to help support the text. Editor Annette Fantasia has guided our creation of the sourcebook that accompanies the main book, and we could hardly have achieved this task without her help; she also edited the instructor's resource manual. The work of associate editor Jack Cashman, who supervised the development of the other elements in our impressive array of supplements, will be appreciated by all teachers and students who use these materials. Jenna Bookin Barry, senior executive marketing manager; Sally Constable, senior market development manager; and Katherine Bates, market development manager, have worked tirelessly at our side to ensure that the book is in the best shape to meet the needs of students and teachers. We are deeply grateful for all the work they have done in the past and all that they will do in so sincerely advocating for the success of *Crossroads and Cultures* in today's classrooms.

Among the authors' greatest *Crossroads* experiences has been our relationship with brilliant executive editor Elizabeth M. Welch and her support team of ace development editors Sylvia Mallory, Margaret Manos, and Jim Strandberg. Beth has guided many a successful book from inception to completion—all to the benefit of tens of thousands of students and their instructors. We thank her for bringing us her historical, conceptual, visual, and publishing talent, all of which she has offered with such generosity of spirit, good humor, and grace. It has been a privilege for all of us to work with Beth and to have spent these *Crossroads* years with the entire Bedford team.

Finally, our students' questions and concerns have shaped much of this work, and we welcome all our readers' suggestions, queries, and criticisms. We know that readers, like our own students, excel in spotting unintended glitches and also in providing much excellent food for thought. Please contact us with your comments at our respective institutions.

Bonnie G. Smith
Marc Van De Mieroop
Richard von Glahn
Kris Lane

Crossroads and Cultures

A History of the World's Peoples

PART 1

The Ancient World

from Human Origins to 500 C.E.

CH 1

THE STORY WE TELL in this book begins around 4 million years ago, when the lines of human ancestors diverged from those of the great African apes, and our exploration of the ancient period of world history ends at about the year 500 C.E. If one wrote a four-hundred-page book that gave equal space to every century in all of world history, the period from 500 C.E. to today would take up only one-sixth of the final page. All previous pages would treat what we call the ancient world.

It would be hard for a historian to fill many of the four hundred pages of this book, however. The first 399 would describe foraging peoples who moved around during most of the year and consequently left little evidence for us to study. All the evidence is archaeological—that is, the material objects humans left behind. Only late in the period, some five thousand years ago, did people invent writing. That skill had a limited geographical spread, however, and even in societies that had developed writing, it was restricted by social class and to a small number of people. Archaeological remains provide much information, but they have limitations; they do not reveal what languages people spoke, their names, and many other things we know about those people to whom we have access through their writings.

This was the era of origins, the period in which human populations invented all the major elements we associate with culture. The modern human species itself originated over millions of years, and our ancestor species invented basic tools, some of which—such as the needle—we still use today. Humans migrated across the globe, sometimes helped by natural events; the last ice age, for instance, lowered sea level to create a land bridge that allowed people to move into the Americas. About ten thousand years ago, modern humans in various parts of the world invented agriculture, which remains an important livelihood for some of the world's peoples into the twenty-first century C.E. The development of agriculture allowed villages and, later, cities to arise, where people with special skills had an opportunity to invent and refine new technologies. As cities and states grew larger and people interacted more closely, they needed means of regulating their societies. This gave rise to such developments as laws, diplomacy, and tools for managing financial transactions, among many others.

CH 2

2

CH 3

All of the writing systems we use today had their roots in these early times. Some ancient scripts died out before 500 C.E., including Babylonian cuneiform, Egyptian hieroglyphs, and Greek Linear B. Others, such as Chinese script, have remained in use from the second millennium B.C.E. until today. The alphabet invented in western Asia in the second millennium B.C.E. had particularly widespread success, with Greeks, Romans, Indians, and many others adopting and then modifying it to serve their specific needs. In later history, it sometimes replaced long existing writing systems, such as those of the Americas.

Peoples of the ancient world also developed a wide variety of political structures. The overall trend was toward larger and more complex organizations, from small bands of up to forty gatherer-hunters to enormous empires incorporating millions of people. Eurasia's classical empires—so called because the revolutionary ideas that shaped these empires long outlived them and gave rise to the fundamental, or "classical," cultural traditions of Eurasia—flourished from about 500 B.C.E. to 500 C.E. Among them were the Qin Empire, which gave its name to the country of China, and the Old Persian Empire of Iran, whose Parthian and Sasanid successors inspired the people of the region until very recently. In western Eurasia, the Roman Empire gave us the term *empire* itself, which is derived from *imperium* (meaning "rule"), and its history inspired ideas of political domination up to modern times. We consider the classical period of antiquity to have ended at the time when many empires disappeared: the Roman in the Mediterranean, Sasanid in the Middle East, Gupta in India, and Han in China. Political organization was far from uniform

CH 4

CH 5

CH 6 →

in this era, however, and states we give the same label—empire—took varied approaches to rule. Some states gave power to one individual, others to a group of bureaucrats. Still others professed ideals of popular participation in government, but even in these only a select group of people was involved in governing.

Although many people lived in relative isolation, ancient societies were often in contact over great distances. Trade routes ran across Eurasia, for example, and women in China made silk cloth that people in Rome would wear. Those contacts waxed and waned over time, but they ignored political boundaries, and often continued even between societies at war. Migrant peoples sometimes carried technologies over vast expanses; Bantu speakers, for instance, spread agriculture and ironworking over much of sub-Saharan Africa. Not all historical developments and innovations resulted from contact and migration, however. Often people living far apart separately created similar technologies and tools. Pottery, for example, was invented independently in Japan, the Middle East, Mesoamerica, and the Andes.

The ancient world produced the classical eras of the literate cultures of Eurasia. Many religions and philosophies begun in this period remain influential to this day, including Indian Buddhism and Hinduism, Chinese Confucianism, Daoism, and Legalism, and in the Mediterranean region Judaism, Christianity, and Greek philosophies. Major genres of literature stem from this period, and authors from a variety of cultures wrote works still read today, including Greek and Sanskrit epics and tragedies, the Five Classics of

CH 7 →

	4000 B.C.E.		3000 B.C.E.	2000 B.C.E.
Americas	• 4000 Spread of agriculture		3000–1800 Norte Chico culture	
Europe	• 4000 Spread of agriculture and Indo-European languages		3000–1650 Minoan culture	
Middle East	• 4000 Spread of agriculture	Uruk, the first city; Mesopotamian cuneiform script 3200 •	3000–2350 Competing city-states in Mesopotamia 2350–2200 Akkadian dynasty	
Africa	• 4000 Spread of agriculture		• 3000 Unification of Egypt; Egyptian hieroglyphic script; start of southward migration of the Bantu • 2550 Khufu's pyramid at Giza	
Asia and Oceania	• 4000 Spread of agriculture		2600–1900 Mature Indus Valley culture Oxus culture 2100–1700 3000–750 First wave of Austronesian migrations	

Chinese literature, and historical accounts, among many others. Some were short poems, others volumes of vast length.

World history was not a uniform process, however, as people everywhere chose the lifestyles and livelihoods best suited to their environments. Sometimes this led them to abandon techniques that most others saw as advances. People in Polynesia stopped making pottery, for example; people in Australia opted not to farm. In certain regions, structures that elsewhere provided the foundation for later developments suddenly ceased to exist. The urban cultures of the Oxus River Valley disappeared, for instance. Perhaps the primary characteristic of early world history is the sheer variety of the cultures that flourished in this period.

CH 8

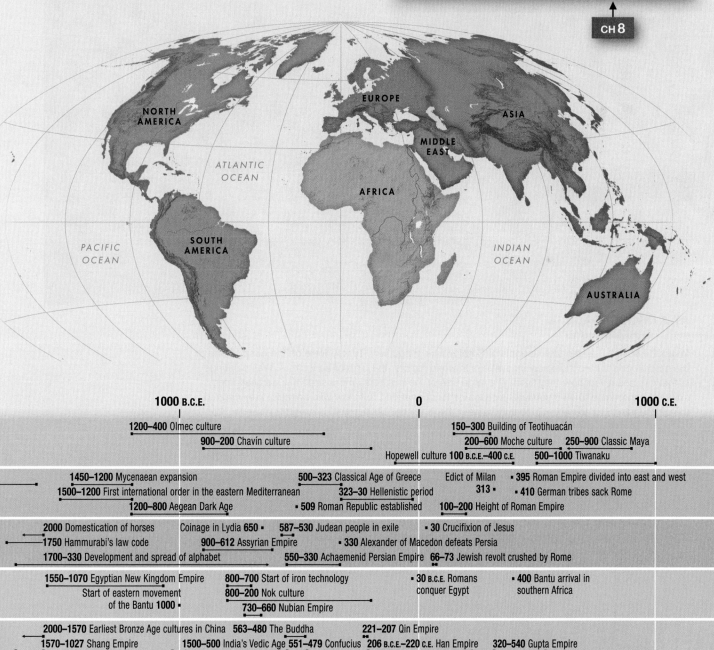

| 1000 B.C.E. | 0 | 1000 C.E. |

1200–400 Olmec culture
150–300 Building of Teotihuacán
900–200 Chavín culture
200–600 Moche culture   250–900 Classic Maya
Hopewell culture 100 B.C.E.–400 C.E.   500–1000 Tiwanaku

1450–1200 Mycenaean expansion   500–323 Classical Age of Greece   Edict of Milan   395 Roman Empire divided into east and west
1500–1200 First international order in the eastern Mediterranean   323–30 Hellenistic period   313   410 German tribes sack Rome
1200–800 Aegean Dark Age   509 Roman Republic established   100–200 Height of Roman Empire

2000 Domestication of horses   Coinage in Lydia 650   587–530 Judean people in exile   30 Crucifixion of Jesus
1750 Hammurabi's law code   900–612 Assyrian Empire   330 Alexander of Macedon defeats Persia
1700–330 Development and spread of alphabet   550–330 Achaemenid Persian Empire   66–73 Jewish revolt crushed by Rome

1550–1070 Egyptian New Kingdom Empire   800–700 Start of iron technology   30 B.C.E. Romans   400 Bantu arrival in
Start of eastern movement   800–200 Nok culture   conquer Egypt   southern Africa
of the Bantu 1000   730–660 Nubian Empire

2000–1570 Earliest Bronze Age cultures in China   563–480 The Buddha   221–207 Qin Empire
1570–1027 Shang Empire   1500–500 India's Vedic Age 551–479 Confucius   206 B.C.E.–220 C.E. Han Empire   320–540 Gupta Empire
1400–200 Lapita culture   321–185 Mauryan Empire   50–233 Kushan Empire   Polynesian settlement 600–1000

AT A CROSSROADS ▲

In around 6000 B.C.E., the townspeople of Çatal Höyük in southern Turkey were on the cusp of one of the most important technological innovations in world history: the birth of agriculture. Wall paintings in their houses reveal how they lived. The large size of the bull here emphasizes this domesticated animal's importance to their survival. Humans no longer needed to follow wild animals; they created the surroundings for the animals to survive near them. (ullstein bild-Archiv Gerstenberg/The Image Works.)

Peopling the World

to 4000 B.C.E.

In August 1856 quarry workers opening up a cave in the Neander Valley of northwest Germany discovered a skull and bones. The skull was curious: it was long, with a bulge in the back, and the large brow ridges arched prominently over the eye sockets. Johann Fuhlrott, a local teacher and amateur student of natural history, identified them as the remains of an early species of human, thus challenging the ideas about creation that prevailed among the nineteenth-century Christians who lived in the area. Finds of other fossils and stone tools near lakes and riverbeds had convinced Fuhlrott and others, however, that modern humans had developed through a process of evolution rather than creation.

Three years later, in 1859, the British natural historian Charles Darwin published a detailed explanation of evolution in his famous book, *On the Origin of Species*. Darwin argued that the species of all living beings had evolved over millions of years through adaptation to their environment. He wrote in his *Autobiography* that, "Natural Selection . . . tends only to render each species as successful as possible in the battle for life with other species, in wonderfully complex and changing circumstances."[1] But many opposed the idea that earlier species of humans had existed and explained the strange fossil finds in the Neander Valley (*Neanderthal* in German) in other ways. One professor of anatomy claimed that the skeleton belonged to a man with severe vitamin deficiency and arthritis. Another said he was a Cossack horseman who had been wounded in battle and crawled into the

BACKSTORY

Some five billion years ago the earth came into being. For 99.9 percent of the time since then, the planet only gradually developed the conditions in which humans evolved. Humans with all the physical characteristics we have today have lived on the planet only for the last fifty thousand years, a short blip in the immense period that earth has existed. The era we can study through our ancestors' own written records is much shorter still. Less than five thousand years ago people in a few places invented writing, a skill that very gradually spread over the globe. Writing is the source that tells historians people's names and gives us access to their actions and thoughts.

We start this book by examining the period before people invented writing, however, at the moment when a separate species of uniquely human ancestors originated. With its appearance began world history—not the history of the world, but of humans in the world. Over time, people's interactions with one another and their environment caused fundamental changes not only in their physical features and behavior but in the natural world. We are one of the most recent species on earth, but we are also the one whose impact on the planet has been the greatest.

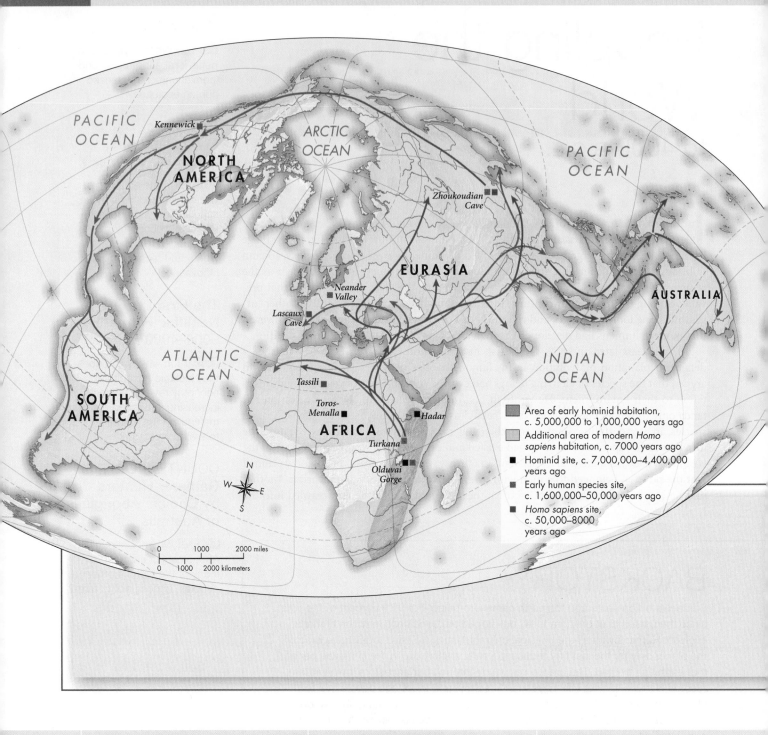

PACIFIC OCEAN

Kennewick ■

NORTH AMERICA

ARCTIC OCEAN

PACIFIC OCEAN

Zhoukoudian Cave ■■

EURASIA

AUSTRALIA

Neander Valley ■

Lascaux Cave ■

ATLANTIC OCEAN

INDIAN OCEAN

SOUTH AMERICA

Tassili ■

Toros-Menalla ■

Hadar ■

AFRICA

Turkana ■

Olduvai Gorge ■■

N W E S

0   1000   2000 miles
0   1000   2000 kilometers

■ Area of early hominid habitation, c. 5,000,000 to 1,000,000 years ago

Additional area of modern *Homo sapiens* habitation, c. 7000 years ago

■ Hominid site, c. 7,000,000–4,400,000 years ago

■ Early human species site, c. 1,600,000–50,000 years ago

■ *Homo sapiens* site, c. 50,000–8000 years ago

▪ **c. 7 million years ago (mya)** Oldest hominid on record, *Sahelanthropus tchadensis*, lives in central Africa

▪ **c. 3.2 mya** *Australopithecus afarensis* (Lucy) lives in the region of modern Ethiopia

▪ **c. 1 mya** Ancestors of *Homo erectus* enter Asia

7 million years ago (mya) | **3 mya** | **1 mya**

▪ **c. 2 mya** First hominin and first stone tools

▪ **4.4 mya** *Ardipithecus ramidus* lives in the region of modern Ethiopia

cave; the agonizing pain he suffered had deformed his skull. Only in the early twentieth century, after numerous finds of similar fossils, were most scholars convinced that the Neanderthal represented an early human species, as Johann Fuhlrott had concluded.

Disagreements such as those over the Neanderthal skeleton characterize the study of early humans and their ancestors to the present day. Specialists often come to conflicting conclusions in their interpretation of such finds, and consequently they develop different narratives about the course of human evolution. This is understandable, given the challenges involved. Scholars have a limited number of archaeological remains, which come from all over the globe and cover a span of millions of years, and they must place them into a sequence that is logically consistent with the observable differences.

A major difficulty in interpretation is uncertainty in dating finds related to human evolution. Archaeologists assign widely differing dates to the skeleton remains they discover, which leads to divergent reconstructions of when certain human ancestors existed and how they relate to one another. Moreover, new finds often upset existing theories. In late 2009, for example, archaeologists announced the discovery in northern Ethiopia of remains that demonstrate the existence of an entirely new species of human ancestors, *Ardipithecus ramidus* (ahr-dih-PITH-eh-kihs rahm-IH-dihs), which lived 4.4 million years ago and had attributes scholars had thought developed more than a million years later. It will take years of further research to integrate these finds into the general reconstruction of human evolution.

Despite their varying viewpoints, scholars agree that humans developed over millions of years, and that a number of species preceded the modern human. The wide range of material evidence we explore in this chapter reveals that each species had distinctive characteristics that resulted from adaptations to different environments. Gradually our ancestors acquired the skills to manipulate the natural surroundings for their own purposes. After millions of years of gathering foodstuffs available in the wild, they began to control the growth of plants and animals through farming and herding. The implications of this development were numerous and profound. Farming made settled communities

MAPPING THE WORLD

Out of Africa

Several species of human ancestors migrated out of Africa at different times, ultimately settling in almost every part of the globe by 5000 B.C.E., about seven thousand years ago. Their ability to spread depended in part on ecological conditions such as the expansion of the Arctic ice cap and low sea levels, but it also involved such technological achievements as the construction of boats to reach islands. The first species to migrate were the ancestors of *Homo erectus* some one million years ago; the last was *Homo sapiens*, about one hundred thousand years ago.

ROUTES ▼

→ Migration of early *Homo* species, c. 1,000,000–500,000 years ago

→ Migration of *Homo sapiens*, c. 100,000–5000 years ago

- **c. 500,000 B.C.E.** Ancestors of Neanderthal enter western Eurasia

- **c. 400,000 B.C.E.** First evidence of *Homo sapiens* in Africa

- **c. 100,000 B.C.E.** Some *Homo sapiens* leave Africa

- **c. 30,000 B.C.E.** *Homo sapiens* becomes the only human species

| 500,000 B.C.E. | 100,000 B.C.E. | 50,000 B.C.E. | 10,000 B.C.E. |

c. 400,000–30,000 B.C.E. Neanderthal lives in western Eurasia

- **c. 15,000 B.C.E.** *Homo sapiens* enters the Americas

c. 35,000–10,000 B.C.E. Paleolithic cave paintings

c. 10,000–8,000 B.C.E. Development of agriculture in Southwest Asia

possible, which in turn led to the development of increasingly complex societies, cultures, and governments.

Not all humans decided to practice agriculture, however. In some parts of the world, such as Australia, they continued to forage even after they knew farming was possible. Examples like this show that natural conditions always influenced people's choices: they had to work with the resources available. To a great extent, the world's diverse geography explains the various forms of livelihood we observe in human history.

OVERVIEW QUESTIONS

The major global development in this chapter: The adaptation of early humans to their environment and their eventual domestication of plants and animals.

As you read, consider:

1. What caused humans to introduce technological and other innovations?

2. How did these innovations increase their ability to determine their own destinies?

3. How did the relationship between humans and nature change?

4. How have historians and other scholars reconstructed life in the earliest periods of human existence despite the lack of written records?

Human Origins

FOCUS

What physical and behavioral adaptations and innovations characterized human evolution?

Over the past two centuries archaeologists have uncovered fossils all over the world that show a startling range of human ancestors. The oldest finds come from Africa, which is also the source of the largest variety of fossils, especially the eastern part of the continent (see Map 1.1). Consequently, most scholars agree that Africa was the birthplace of the human species. Only after their origins in Africa did human ancestors start to spread out of the continent, which took place in several waves (see again Mapping the World, pages 8 and 9).

Students of human evolution have benefited immensely from recent advances in DNA analysis—in particular, the analysis of mitochondrial DNA, which passes on from the mother to her children. Similarities and differences in the mitochondrial DNA of populations across the world have enabled researchers to establish genetic connections among various population groups, as well as their ancestry. This information provides crucial support to the idea that Africa was the home of the modern human species.

Human evolution was not a process of constant, steady development. It unfolded unevenly, as bursts of change interrupted long periods of overall stability. Scholars understand human evolution in the context of changes in the natural environment, which often triggered and shaped physical and behavioral changes in human ancestors. Although today all humans belong to the same species, in the past different species of our ancestors coexisted. The sole surviving species, *Homo sapiens*, was the one best adapted to new conditions. Thus, from the very beginning, environmental adaptation and its consequences have been at the heart of the story of human history.

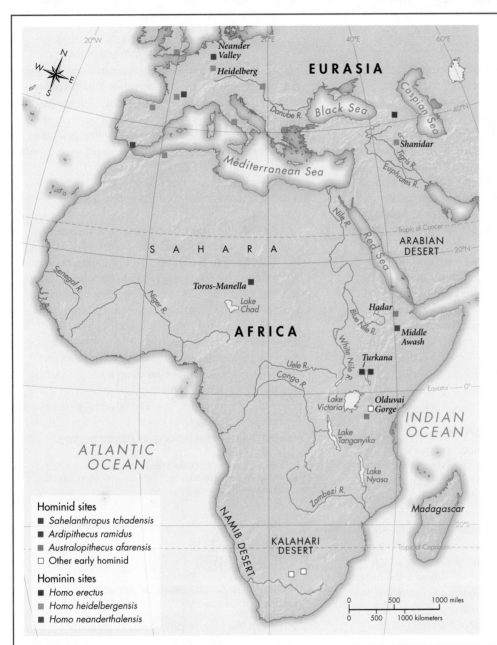

Human Fossil Finds in Africa and Western Eurasia

Archaeologists continue to find the remains of skeletons of human ancestors, so they can determine where and when different species lived. Certain regions are especially rich in skeletons. Many of the earliest hominid remains have been found in northeast Africa; the earliest are from 4.4 million years ago. Southwestern Eurasia has also produced many hominid finds, from one million to thirty thousand years ago. But isolated finds complicate our reconstruction of the history of human evolution, such as the single find of *Sahelanthropus tchadensis* in West Central Africa, dating to seven million years ago.

Evolution of the Human Species

The great African apes are the closest relatives of the human species. Indeed, we share 98 percent of our genetic makeup with them. Although recent finds suggest that human ancestors may have separated from those of the great apes beginning 7 million years ago (see Reading the Past: Fossil Hunting), secure evidence dates to only 5 to 4 million years ago. At that time, human ancestors, or **hominids**, moved out of dense forests into the more open woodlands and grasslands of eastern Africa; the ancestors of the great apes remained in the forest. A sustained drought that diminished the size of the African forest may have inspired the move. Adapting to the new environment led to several changes in the physical appearance and behavior of hominids. Three main physical traits came to distinguish humans from apes and other primates: upright walking, flexible hands, and the ability to communicate through speech.

hominid The biological family that includes modern humans and their human ancestors.

Fossil Hunting

New fossil finds occur regularly, and they often force scholars to reconsider existing theories of human evolution. Indeed, ideas about the evolutionary process have fundamentally changed in recent decades. Whereas scholars previously saw human evolution as linear, with each early species showing a single stage of evolution, today they see the various human species as coexisting during the same period, each having adapted to regional circumstances. Further, they now view evolutionary milestones as taking place not just in eastern Africa, where most early fossils were discovered, but in other parts of the world where they have found evidence of important developments. Moreover, scholars now think the divergence between the ancestors of humans and great African apes began earlier than they thought formerly. Until recently they thought this happened four or five million years ago. The discovery announced in 2002 of an almost complete skull that mixes ape and hominid features may force a reinterpretation. The find is surprising because of its very early date, 6–7 million years ago, and its location, Chad in central Africa.

The following is one of the earliest English-language reports on the remarkable find.

After more than a decade of digging, researchers working in Chad have made the fossil discovery of a lifetime: a nearly complete skull of the oldest and most primitive member of the human family yet known. Nicknamed Toumaï—or "hope of life" in the local Goran language—it belongs to an entirely new genus and species of hominid, *Sahelanthropus tchadensis*. And at almost 7 million years old, it has taken scientists several crucial steps closer to the point in time at which humans and chimpanzees diverged. Yet as is the case for most spectacular finds, this one raises as many questions, if not more, than it answers.

For one, until now almost all of the next earliest hominid fossils unearthed so far have come from East Africa, leading some scholars to posit that the origin of humans was essentially an "East Side story." Toumaï, however, comes from central Africa. And then there's his (the skull is thought to be that of a male) surprising

combination of primitive and advanced features. Characteristics of the face and teeth clearly align Toumaï with hominids, say team leader Michel Brunet of the University of Poitiers in France and his colleagues. But the braincase is comparable in size to that of a small ape. (Whether or not Toumaï and his kind were bipedal remains a matter of uncertainty. No skeletal elements have been found, but features on the base of the skull and the face resemble those of known bipedal hominids.)

As the oldest hominid on record, *S. tchadensis* could be the ancestor of all later hominids—including us—according to Brunet and his collaborators, who announced their discovery today in the journal *Nature*. But that will be difficult to prove, cautions Bernard Wood of George Washington University in an accompanying commentary. "My prediction is that *S. tchadensis* is just the tip of an iceberg of taxonomic diversity during hominid evolution 5–7 million years ago," he writes. Whatever the case, it seems certain that this find will have a tremendous impact on the study of human origins. "It's a lot of emotion to have in my hand the beginning of the human lineage," Brunet muses. "I have been looking for this for so long."

Source: Kate Wong, "Meet the Oldest Member of the Human Family," *Scientific American*, July 11, 2002, http://www.scientificamerican.com/article.cfm?id=meet-the-oldest-member-of.

EXAMINING THE EVIDENCE

1. What makes *S. tchadensis* an especially significant discovery?

2. What are the fossil's physical characteristics? Why does it upset the accepted theories about human evolution?

3. Why does a find such as this raise more questions than answers?

Upright Walking   Initially, the three developments that revealed an evolutionary split between humans and the great apes were all a matter of degree. Apes walk on two legs only in unusual circumstances, but people do so easily. This characteristic was the first of the three to develop, and the earliest signs of upright walking now seem to come from northern Ethiopia. The skeleton of the *Ardipithecus ramidus* from that region shows that the species could walk upright but did not yet have the arched foot that makes walking easy. The first evidence of smooth upright walking is fossilized footprints in what is today northern

Tanzania in a river canyon called Olduvai (ohl-DOO-vy) Gorge. These footprints show that 3.6 million years ago an adult and a child walked fully upright, using the same stride as modern humans.

Upright walking changed the skeleton and musculature and shifted the body's weight to a vertical axis. It reduced the space available for digestive organs, which led to a need for food that was easier to digest and more nutritious. Instead of hard plant materials, such as leaves, human ancestors now ate fruits and nuts. Moreover, the upright posture freed the hands for uses other than walking, such as carrying food, stones, and offspring—uses that offered potential survival advantages. Thus, upright walking created conditions favorable to the further evolution of human hands, because individuals with more flexible hands had improved chances of surviving and passing on their genetic inheritance.

Human hands and those of apes have thumbs that can face the four other fingers, but human hands have a much more powerful and precise grasp. Greater dexterity allowed humans to make tools to aid them in their daily tasks. The use of tools itself is not a distinguishing characteristic of humans—chimpanzees, for example, use peeled branches to catch ants. What is unique is the human capacity to use tools to create other tools. Many scholars agree that this skill may have developed late in human evolution, around 2 million years ago. The earliest preserved tools are made of stone, which because of their durability offer the archaeologist a rich set of evidence. With toolmaking, humans' ability to manipulate the environment to meet their needs took an enormous step forward.

Fossilized Footprints

In 1978, the archaeological team led by Mary Leakey discovered these revealing sets of footprints at Laetoli in northern Tanzania. Made by a child and an adult who walked through volcanic ash some 3.6 million years ago, they were preserved after the ash solidified. They are the earliest evidence of human ancestors walking upright using the same stride we use today. This change in walking resulted in important new skeletal and behavioral developments. (Tom Reader/PhotoResearchers, Inc.)

Flexible Hands

Humans took another step forward with speech, which gave them the capacity to work more effectively in groups and to pass on the benefits of experience to their offspring. Humans have a much greater ability to communicate than other primates. With their migration into the flat grasslands, human ancestors needed to live in larger groups for their safety. They were relatively small, weak, and slow—easy targets for predators—and cooperation offered their only defense. For example, they coordinated the throwing of rocks (a uniquely human and highly efficient skill), which gave them substantial protection. The heightened need for cooperation led to greater social interaction and organization, and over time, humans developed speech—the capacity to speak and to understand what others say.

Speech

The human attributes of walking upright, manual versatility, and speech both depended on and contributed to an increase in brain size. The brain became larger not only in absolute terms, but relative to the entire body. To accommodate the larger organ, the skull's shape had to change, and the new grasslands diet helped make that possible. The fruits and nuts human ancestors ate were easier to chew than the bark and leaves of the forest. Consequently, teeth and jawbones gradually grew smaller, which changed the shape of the skull. The very structure of the brain changed, too, as new areas developed, such as the one that controls speech and language. Thus, changes in human brains, like other key human characteristics, evolved out of a complex set of environmental pressures and corresponding adaptations. This pattern of adaptation to environmental pressures continued as humans evolved from the earliest human species to *Homo sapiens,* modern human beings.

The Changing Brain

As we have seen, recently published research on skeletal material from northern modern-day Ethiopia indicates that 4–5 million years ago a human ancestor lived who had

Human Ancestors

very apelike characteristics but also new abilities. This species, *Ardipithecus ramidus*, had a brain the size of a modern chimpanzee's and arms that permitted swift movement in trees, but it also had legs that enabled upright walking, albeit rather awkwardly. The species ate nuts and plants rather than the fruits that apes consume.

Around 4 million years ago, human ancestors of the *Australopithecus* (aw-strah-loh-PITH-uh-kihs) species developed. The term *Australopithecus* literally means "southern ape," and branches of the species inhabited eastern and southern Africa up to 1.5 million years ago. The most famous individual from this lengthy period is Lucy, a woman who lived 3.2 million years ago in what is now northern Ethiopia, near where the *Ardipithecus ramidus* remains were found. In 1974, archaeologists discovered her relatively well-preserved skeleton, and concluded from it that she was twenty-five to thirty years old, about 3.5 feet tall, and weighed no more than sixty pounds. She was much smaller and lighter than *Ardipithecus ramidus*, and she could walk much better because her foot had the archlike structure of the modern human. Her long arms indicated that Lucy still climbed trees, probably to escape from predators. Her teeth resembled those of hominids, and the wear on them suggested that she ate mostly fruits, berries, and roots. It is possible that all later hominids derived from Lucy's species, which we call *Australopithecus afarensis*.

Starting around 2 million years ago, the last members of the *Australopithecus* species started to coexist with the human ancestors we identify with the term **hominin**. They are distinguished from previous hominids by their much larger brains, which may have developed as a result of eating more nutritious foods, especially meat. Indeed, the eating habits of early hominins may have been their most important characteristic. They originated in a period when the climate fluctuated between wet and dry periods, forcing hominids to explore new sources of food. Among the foods most sought after, meat became preeminent.

One of the earliest representatives of hominins in the fossil record is Turkana boy, whose almost complete skeleton archaeologists found in the mid-1980s in the north of modern-day Kenya. He was no more than twelve years old when he died some 1.6 million years ago. Compared with Lucy, he stood more upright and his arms were shorter relative to the rest of his body. But his brain was larger and he was much taller. He already measured 5.3 feet at his young age, and biologists estimate he would have reached 6 feet when fully grown. Although his brain size was still very limited and he probably could not speak, Turkana boy resembled modern humans in many ways.

Around 1 million years ago, the first human ancestors moved from Africa into Asia,

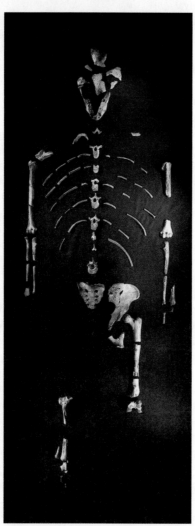

Comparing Skeletons

When paleontologists compare ancient skeletons to determine how human ancestors changed physically over time, they have to piece together evidence from many fragments. Compare the remains of an *Ardipithecus ramidus* more than 4 million years old (left) with those of the famous *Australopithecus afarensis*, Lucy, estimated to be 3.2 million years old (right). It is easy to see that the *Ardipithecus* had much longer arms and shorter legs, whereas Lucy's bones were lighter. Detailed analysis also shows that her skull had space for stronger teeth and a larger brain. (Tim White (left) and Dave Einsel/Getty Images (right).)

where they reached the areas of modern China and Indonesia. These groups developed into the species scholars call *Homo erectus* ("upright person"). Remains of their campsites show that they collaborated to kill large animals and they made fires. In fact, the use of fire made emigration out of Africa possible, because it allowed human ancestors to survive in the cold northern climates. Excavated hearths indicate that the fires, though small, allowed *Homo erectus* to shelter in caves. Fire also enabled them to cook, so they could soften otherwise inedible plants and more easily separate meat from bones. In this way, the invention of cooking meant that the frontal teeth could grow even smaller. *Homo erectus* existed in Asia until perhaps fifty thousand years ago, while in Africa and Europe new hominins developed.

At the same time that *Homo erectus* evolved in Asia, other human ancestors who remained in Africa developed substantially larger brains. One new African species, *Homo heidelbergensis*, was the first to migrate to Europe, establishing self-sustaining populations in Europe around five hundred thousand years ago. The hominids residing in Europe very slowly developed into a separate branch, *Homo neanderthalensis*, or **Neanderthals**, whose fossils led to the nineteenth-century debates over human origins discussed earlier. Flourishing in Europe and western Asia from four hundred thousand to thirty thousand years ago, Neanderthals had long, large faces that projected sharply forward, and they had larger front teeth than modern humans, which may have allowed them to consume the large amounts of meat they hunted. Their brains were slightly larger than those of modern humans, and their bones show that they were stockier. These physical characteristics may have helped them to survive in colder climates.

Simultaneous with the development of the Neanderthal in Europe, the earliest forms of the modern human species, **Homo sapiens** ("consciously thinking person"), arose in Africa around four hundred thousand years ago. This species continued to evolve slowly until it attained the physical characteristics humans have today, perhaps as recently as fifty thousand years ago. *Homo sapiens* is especially distinct from other hominids in the size and structure of the brain. Larger and more sophisticated brains allow them to improve skills such as tool-making and communication, giving the species a marked advantage over other hominids.

Homo sapiens may have used these abilities to monopolize available resources. For millions of years, various hominid species coexisted, but around thirty thousand years ago *Homo sapiens* became the sole human species on earth. It is possible that *Homo sapiens'* extraordinarily successful adaptation caused the extinction of all other human species. Then, as now, the development and adaptation of one human population had consequences for all human populations.

Homo Sapiens

Out of Africa

Various human ancestors migrated out of Africa at different times—the ancestors of *Homo erectus* some 1 million years ago, the ancestors of the Neanderthal some five hundred thousand years ago, and finally *Homo sapiens* about one hundred thousand years ago. Climate change, a desire to follow a particular type of prey, and social pressures probably triggered these movements. When the climate became wetter, for example, African animals grazing on grasslands spread into zones that were previously too dry to feed them, and the hominins who ate them probably followed. Moreover, when human groups became too large to survive on the natural resources of their territory, some members moved away and explored new areas.

The final migration—that of *Homo sapiens*—was a remarkable success. Scholars now think that the species survived times when its numbers dwindled to several thousand individuals, or even fewer. This did not prevent *Homo sapiens* from spreading to all corners of the earth, even into the most inhospitable environments, such as polar regions and desert fringes. The movement of early peoples from Africa into Eurasia was relatively easy, because these continents are connected by land. But to colonize the distant regions of the Americas, Australia, and other islands, humans had to take advantage of changes in the physical environment—as they did with the advent of the ice ages.

Hominin Migrations

hominin The biological subsection of the hominid family that includes species identified with the term *Homo*.

Neanderthal A hominid species that inhabited Europe and western Asia from four hundred thousand to thirty thousand years ago.

Homo sapiens The species of hominids to which modern humans belong; "sapiens" refers to the ability to think.

Ice Ages

In climatic terms, the earth's last seven hundred thousand years saw a series of dramatic fluctuations between warm and cold conditions. In cold periods, the so-called ice ages, the absorption of water into massive glaciers at the polar caps led to a drastic drop in the sea level, to more than 330 feet lower than today. As ocean waters receded into the ice sheets, islands grew larger and landmasses previously separated by water became connected.

The last ice age started 110,000 years ago and lasted almost 100,000 years. By 40,000 years ago, *Homo sapiens* had settled most of mainland Eurasia, and were migrating into Australia and its surrounding islands from southeast Asia. This required that they cross the sea by boat, often to places they could not see from the opposite shore.

Human Adaptation to the New Environment

There is much debate about when humans first entered the Americas, but no convincing evidence exists that any hominid species other than fully developed *Homo sapiens* made this journey. The earliest Americans had fire, stone tools, and the means to obtain clothing, food, and shelter. They most likely arrived fifteen thousand years ago when the last ice age lowered sea levels to produce a land bridge between northeast Asia and North America (see Map 1.2). Possibly others migrated by boat to the Americas from other parts of Asia. Kennewick Man, so-called from the site in the state of Washington where he was discovered in 1996, anatomically seems unlike other early humans of the continent, although he appears to have lived some eight thousand years ago. His physical characteristics resemble those of inhabitants of southeast Asia rather than of northeast Asia. Was he a descendant of another migration or not? The question remains unanswered.

The remarkable adaptability of *Homo sapiens* allowed the species to deal with differences in heat, sunlight, and other climatic and geographical conditions. Communities in various parts of the world developed diverse physical traits. One adaptation was a change in skin color. The pigment melanin, present in relatively high concentration in dark skin, protects against the ultraviolet in sunlight. This protection is essential in sun-drenched Africa or Australia, but not in the north, where it can even be counterproductive because it prevents absorption of vitamin D. Thus, through adaptation, inhabitants of most northern regions developed lighter skin to avoid vitamin deficiency.

Similarly, the size of human limbs varied from climate to climate. Long limbs allow for cooling of the body and short limbs retain heat. These and other distinctions are minor, however, when compared with the biological similarities that humans all over the globe share. The human genetic makeup is much more uniform than that of other species: two chimpanzees living in close proximity to one another have ten times as much variability in their DNA as two humans living on different continents.

A second vehicle for humans' adaptation to new environments is change in the languages they speak, change that can be substantial over short periods. The work of linguists—specialists in the study of language—suggests that on average, people who originally spoke the same language would preserve only 85 percent of the common features after living in separate communities for a thousand years. This relatively rapid change explains linguistic diversity. For example, many scholars assume that most inhabitants of the Americas before the arrival of the Italian explorer Christopher Columbus in

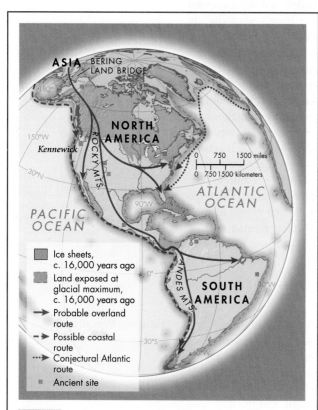

MAP 1.2

Settling the Americas

The last ice age created a land bridge across the Bering Sea, allowing humans to migrate from Eurasia into North America. The first humans probably entered fifteen thousand years ago, and their descendants continued expanding southward over land and by boat along the coasts. By seven thousand years ago, humans lived in the entire continent from the modern state of Alaska to the southern tip of South America, except for some regions in the dense Amazonian forest.

1492 C.E. descended from the people who had migrated there some fifteen thousand years earlier, and who had spoken a common language. Yet by Columbus's arrival, America had enormous linguistic variety, several thousand mutually unintelligible languages. This variety developed in part because populations lived in different environments and focused on different activities for their livelihoods. Some hunted, others fished, and later, farmers and herders developed vocabularies to suit their circumstances. Other processes also caused the languages of separate communities to diverge.

Any aspect of a language can change, including pronunciation, grammar, and vocabulary. Grammatical forms are abandoned or newly created; words change their meanings, disappear, or are invented. Word meanings can differ even among speakers of the same language. For example, *corn* in the United States refers to maize, whereas in England the word *corn* refers to wheat. Languages may drop the names of animals and plants if these species do not appear where the speakers live. They borrow terms from other languages to indicate new tools or foods. People all over the world today write "e-mails," using a newly invented English word in very different languages. The diversity of languages is one of the main features that distinguish human populations, and it shows how people adjust habits to their local situations. It also demonstrates that evolution is an ongoing process. Just as human language continues to develop in response to changing circumstances, humans themselves continue to evolve in response to new environmental conditions, whether those new conditions are the result of natural processes or of the impact of humans on their environment.

Paleolithic Food Gatherers   2,000,000–9000 B.C.E.

Having traced the biological evolution of *Homo sapiens*, we turn now to the development of human communities. To study the distant human past, scholars rely on archaeological remains, primarily tools made of hard stones such as flint and obsidian that leave a sharp edge when chipped. Items made of other materials, such as bone and wood, survive much less often. The record is thus biased toward stone tools, but they are undeniably important. Scholars commonly divide the period that used stone as the main material for tools into the **Paleolithic** ("Old Stone Age") and the **Neolithic** ("New Stone Age"). Based on the type of tools people used, these terms indicate critical differences in people's livelihoods as well: in the early period they hunted and gathered their food; in the later period they farmed. The transition from one livelihood to the other was not simultaneous worldwide. On the contrary, it took many millennia for agriculture to spread from the regions where it was first invented, and in some parts of the world people did not farm until the modern period.

> **FOCUS**
>
> In the absence of written sources, what have scholars learned about the Paleolithic economy, adaptations to the natural world, and technological innovations?

The Paleolithic is by far the longest period of hominin existence. For close to 2 million years, our predecessors collected food from their environments using stone tools. Seasonal cycles determined what was available and when. Only in the recent past, starting eleven thousand years ago, did people in some parts of the world take a next step in manipulating the environment by controlling food supplies through farming.

The Gatherer-Hunter Economy

All living things need food to survive, and they use resources in their natural surroundings to secure it. Humans are the most versatile of all living primates in this respect. If necessary, they are willing to consume anything with nutritional value. This flexibility allowed humans to adapt to new environments as they migrated all over the globe.

A major breakthrough in the quest for food occurred around 2 million years ago with the use of stone tools, which gave human ancestors enormous advantages. They could

Paleolithic Literally "Old Stone Age," the period when modern humans and their ancestors used stone tools and lived as foragers.

Neolithic Literally "New Stone Age," the period when humans developed a special set of stone tools to harvest cultivated plants.

quickly cut off parts of dead prey and run to a safe place. With tools they could pierce animal skins, cut meat from bones, and crush bones for marrow, increasing the availability of highly nutritious food. As we have seen, eating such foods allowed greater brain expansion, which in turn facilitated toolmaking abilities.

Paleolithic Toolmakers
At first, Paleolithic people did little to modify the stones they employed as tools. They chipped off flakes that had very sharp edges, allowing them to cut, and they used the cores as hammers to crush bones. Starting around 1.65 million years ago, however, they began to shape cores much more extensively, flaking off pieces symmetrically on both sides to create sharp hand axes that resembled large teardrops. This development reveals their ability to imagine in advance what the tool should look like. Hand axes were extremely popular and were an important part of the human tool arsenal until around 250,000 years ago. Human ancestors who migrated from Africa into Eurasia took the technology with them. Only when they reached distant regions such as China and southeast Asia did they stop making such hand axes, possibly because suitable stone was unavailable.

With the emergence of *Homo sapiens* toolmaking expanded dramatically. These physically modern humans created a wide variety of stone tools that were much sharper and easier to handle. They also fashioned tools from previously neglected materials, working antlers, bones, and ivory into various implements and inventing the needle, which made sewing possible. With these tools, they hunted, cut meat off bones, scraped skins, shaped wood, and turned dried tendons into strings. They used their increasingly ingenious creations to prepare food and to make clothing, shelter, and weapons. They turned shells into personal jewelry and began to fashion art. In short, increasingly sophisticated tools expanded their ability to manipulate the environment, which made possible the emergence of human society and culture.

Evolving Stone Tools

The development of tools, especially those of stone, which have survived much better than others, tells archaeologists about important changes in the technological abilities of human ancestors and early humans. The Oldowan tool shown here (left), used between 2.6 and 1.7 million years ago, was only slightly altered from the original rock in the effort to sharpen it. In contrast, the Acheulian ax (right), used between 1.65 million and 250,000 years ago, shows how its maker carefully flaked off pieces all over the original stone to turn it into a versatile hand tool. (National Museum of Tanzania, Dar es Salaam, ©1985 David L. Brill (left) and Werner Forman/Art Resource, NY (right).)

For the entire Paleolithic era, humans foraged for their food—that is, they gathered and hunted edible resources in their surroundings. The common idea that early humans were great hunters is a myth. Indeed, until *Homo sapiens*, they probably obtained meat only by competing with other scavengers for the flesh of dead animals. The earliest tools often occur near collections of bones from which meat was cut, indicating that Paleolithic peoples discarded tools after use. *Homo sapiens* dared to attack large animals only after they had developed a growing arsenal of tools—including sharp spears, bows, and arrows with stone tips—and could communicate through language.

Once early hominins had learned how to build and maintain fires some 1.5 million years ago, they cooked meat, making it much easier to chew. Much of their diet, however, consisted of other natural resources, including seeds, nuts, fruits, roots, small animals, fish, and seafood, depending on the area. They gathered food daily, but such work was not necessarily arduous, and Paleolithic gatherer-hunters probably had much more free time than many people today. The gatherer-hunters who still inhabit parts of Africa today collect all they need in a few hours, spending the rest of the day in leisure. Foraging was in many ways a very successful livelihood (see Counterpoint: Gatherer-Hunters by Choice: Aborigines of Australia). Observations of modern gatherer-hunters also show that women collect most foods, so world historians increasingly place woman, the gatherer, not man, the hunter, at the center of the Paleolithic economy.

Paleolithic Foragers

Life in Paleolithic Communities

Paleolithic gatherer-hunters typically lived in groups of fifteen to forty members, including several adult males, as well as females and children. Larger groups would have needed more resources than the surroundings could provide. Males probably supplemented gathered resources by providing food for the mothers of their children, strengthening emotional attachments and encouraging long-term relationships. Close connections developed not only between sexual mates but between parents and children. This may be due in part to the large size of the human head. To pass through the birth canal, humans need to be born earlier in their development than other primates. Because much maturation takes place outside the womb and humans must learn many skills, children need to be nurtured and protected for many years. Not until the ages twelve to fifteen do they become self-sufficient. The presence of children limits the mobility of human groups—babies need to be carried. These various aspects of Paleolithic life led to close-knit communities that stayed together for long periods. Thus, family relationships determined many characteristics of Paleolithic life. Such relationships would continue to shape the development of all subsequent human societies.

Small, Cohesive Groups

Paleolithic communities were egalitarian in character, largely because constant migration prevented individuals from accumulating much wealth. Because groups were small, conflicts were relatively easy to settle, and all adults, including women, could participate in most activities. When a group became too large for the region to support it, bands separated and found new places to live. Neighboring bands must have collaborated to a degree, determining borders, for example. These bands must have often exchanged reproductive partners to maintain social ties. As populations splintered, the new groups built and maintained connections with one another.

Societies of Equals

Early humans needed shelter, of course, especially when they moved into cold regions. At first they took advantage of natural features such as caves and overhanging rocks, often visiting them year after year for protection from the elements. Members of *Homo erectus* used the Zhoukoudian (choo-koot-jehn) cave west of Beijing in northern China, for example, from 460,000 to 230,000 years ago (see again Mapping the World, page 8). They left behind archaeological deposits 120 feet deep, which included some one hundred thousand artifacts. Ash layers in the cave, some of them eighteen feet deep, strongly suggest the cave dwellers' ability to light fires 460,000 years ago. Fire had many advantages: it made it possible to see in the dark, and it provided warmth and protection against animals. It also encouraged social interaction as people gathered around the fire.

Shelter and Fire

Mammoth Bone Dwelling
Human ingenuity in exploiting local resources is clear from circular huts built from the tusks, leg bones, and jaw bones of mammoths (extinct elephants) in eastern Europe between about 27,000 and 12,000 years ago. This example from Mezhirich in Ukraine included the remains of nearly one hundred animals and dates to about 15,000 years ago. Covered with hides, it allowed people to live outside caves in a cold climate. (C.M. Dixon, Ancient Art and Architecture Collection.)

Paleolithic peoples often improved natural shelters by building screens made of branches at the entrances of caves. They could also construct tent-like temporary shelters. Indeed, *Homo sapiens* showed great ingenuity in this respect. When wood was scarce, they built shelters by digging pits and constructing domes with mammoth bones or tusks, over which they draped animal skins. The earliest freestanding man-made shelters were round or oval with central hearths to keep inhabitants warm. Until agricultural communities arose, this remained the preferred design for huts and houses. Such shelters provided protection from the elements and promoted group interaction and cohesion.

Paleolithic Religious Beliefs

The emotional ties that held communities together also fostered a respect for the dead not found in other primates. Starting one hundred thousand years ago, Neanderthals began to bury their dead, at first in simple shallow pits in caves but with increasingly elaborate graves over time. The Neanderthal described at the start of this chapter may have been buried on purpose in the cave where he was found. Careful excavations at Shanidar cave in the mountains of modern Iraq uncovered a Neanderthal skeleton surrounded by large amounts of flower pollen. The archaeologists who found him believe that survivors covered the buried person with garlands of flowers. Other burials contain small objects such as pendants and beads. This archaeological evidence reveals that the living gave the dead material goods for the afterlife, suggesting that they believed in the survival of some aspect of the individual after death. The evolution of burial rites also suggests a growing sense among humans of the connections between generations. A community was more than its current members; it also included those who had come before, as well as the generations to come.

Paleolithic Art

Like burial rites, Paleolithic art gives us a glimpse of early human values and beliefs. Only humans create decorative objects. When did art first appear, and why? In 2001 C.E., archaeologists in southern Africa found a brown stone deliberately engraved with cross-hatchings on its surfaces and with long lines across the top, bottom, and center. They date the stone to at least sixty-five thousand years ago, which makes it the oldest purposefully decorated object ever found. What did the design mean? Was it merely ornamental, or did the people who carved it want to record something? These questions continue to excite debate.

It is clear, however, that, especially after forty thousand years ago, humans started to embellish objects and shape them to represent some of the living creatures that surrounded them. Typically, the first portable art objects were modified natural items such

Paleolithic Statuettes of Women

Paleolithic peoples of western Eurasia produced carved figurines of women for thousands of years, most abundantly, in the archaeological record at least, between twenty-six thousand to twenty-three thousand years ago. In regions from Spain to central Russia, archaeologists have found numerous individual statues and collections made from materials such as mammoth ivory and soft stones. Among them is what is called the Venus of Willendorf. Discovered in the late nineteenth century C.E., it is 9-3/8 inches tall and made from limestone. The representation focuses clearly on the woman's hips, breasts, and vulva. Other parts of the body, such as arms and legs, are very sketchily fashioned, and the figure has no face at all.

Assessments of these figurines may say more about the interpreter than about the ancient people who made them. To call this statue a "Venus" after the Roman goddess of love suggests a connection to sexuality and religion. When they were first found, most scholars thought these statuettes were magical objects connected to fertility and childbirth. Recent interpretations are more varied and involve other aspects of a woman's life. Some think the statues represent women in different stages of life, not just when pregnant; others stress a role in social negotiations, or think pregnant women carved these statuettes to communicate their experiences. Unfortunately, the archaeologists who found the statuettes did not record what other objects lay nearby and whether there were architectural remains. Such information could have helped to explain the function of these figurines.

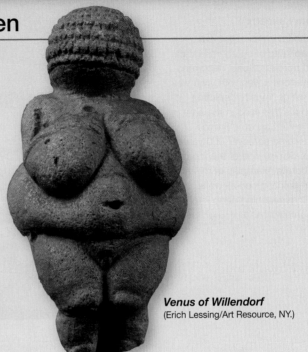

Venus of Willendorf
(Erich Lessing/Art Resource, NY.)

EXAMINING THE EVIDENCE

1. Why has this figurine caused scholars to dispute the name, Venus of Willendorf?

2. How would better archaeological observation have helped in understanding the purpose of such female figurines?

as teeth and shells. People scratched geometric motifs on them and often pierced them with a hole to hang them on a string to wear them as jewelry. Later they shaped stones and bones to resemble living beings. Around twenty-five thousand years ago, people all over western Eurasia sculpted small figurines of women with greatly exaggerated breasts and hips. Although speculation is rife about the meaning of these figurines, their focus on female sexuality has guided most interpretations. Many scholars believe the people who owned them thought they would improve fertility (see Seeing the Past: Paleolithic Statuettes of Women).

Between thirty-five thousand and eleven thousand years ago, people also painted elaborate scenes on walls and ceilings of caves. Archaeologists have found remains of portable art objects all over the modern European continent, but for unknown reasons, cave paintings appear almost exclusively in southern France and northern Spain. Found in almost 250 caves, sometimes miles from the entrance, these paintings are the most dramatic example yet discovered of Paleolithic art. The artists worked by the light of lamps burning animal fat. Archaeological evidence in the Lascaux (la-SKOH) caves in France shows that they even built scaffolding to reach the ceiling. The images in the caves range from small handprints to life-size representations of animals hunted by their communities. Horses and

Paleolithic Cave Art from Lascaux

In the later Paleolithic era, inhabitants of southern France and northern Spain decorated numerous caves with vivid wall paintings, mostly depicting animals that lived in the area. Caves in Lascaux, France, decorated some 17,000 years ago, display one of the most elaborate examples of this art, with paintings on all walls and ceilings reaching deep into the mountainside. (Bridgeman Art Library.)

bison were the most popular subjects, but deer, ibexes, and mammoths were also abundant. Sometimes they even sculpted three-dimensional images of animals in clay against the walls. Whereas the painters represented animals with much realism, their rare depictions of humans are crude stick figures or blend animal and human features. The focus on animal images suggests the central importance of hunting to life in Paleolithic Europe.

Scholars have numerous interpretations of this magnificent artwork. Because the horse and the bison often appear in pairs, some specialists suggest that this pattern reflects male-female symbolism, which they also see in other motifs, including geometric designs. Others consider it very likely that the art expresses complex religious beliefs and theorize that the ideas behind the paintings changed over time because they were made over such a long period. Their subjects are clearly connected to life in the last ice age, because the paintings were no longer made after the climate warmed some eleven thousand years ago. The paintings' simplicity and power clearly reveal the remarkable intellectual abilities of early humans. They also reveal the emergence of a new dimension in human communication. Artwork and the meanings it embodies can survive long after its creator has perished, allowing the artist to connect with future generations. Thus art, like religion, contributed to the increasing sophistication and cohesion of human communities.

The First Neolithic Farmers   9000–4000 B.C.E.

FOCUS

In what ways does the Neolithic agricultural economy reveal humans' increasing intent and ability to manipulate the natural world to their advantage?

The invention of agriculture was one of the most important technological developments in human history. Daily life as we know it today depends on agriculture and the domestication of animals. Yet for most of their existence, human beings obtained their food by collecting what was naturally available. Even today a few populations have not turned to agriculture for their survival, and in many regions some people remained foragers while others farmed.

This novel interaction of humans with nature and agriculture, places them in control of the growth cycle and makes them responsible for the domestication of plants and animals. Those who plant must sow seeds at the right moment, protect plants during growth, harvest them on time, safely store the harvest, and save enough seed for the next season. Those who

TABLE 1.1		
The Rise of Agriculture		
Region	**Main Plant Crops**	**Date**
Southwest Asia	wheat, barley	c. 10,000–9000 B.C.E.
China	rice, millet	c. 8000–6000 B.C.E.
New Guinea	taro, yams, banana	c. 7000–4000 B.C.E.
Sub-Saharan Africa	sorghum	c. 3000–2000 B.C.E.
Mesoamerica	maize, beans, squash	c. 3000–2000 B.C.E.
Andes	potato, manioc	c. 3000–2000 B.C.E.
Eastern North America	squash	c. 2000–1000 B.C.E.

raise animals must protect them against predators and provide fodder. These techniques developed independently in various areas of the world between 10,000 and 1000 B.C.E. and then spread from these core areas to almost all other parts of the globe (see Map 1.3).

The shift to a fully agricultural livelihood began the period scholars call the Neolithic. The shape of stone tools most clearly shows the transition to the Neolithic. Producers elaborately shaped stone flakes to turn them into sharp harvesting tools. Many other technological innovations occurred as well, and the equipment of Neolithic farmers was very different from that of earlier foragers. The processes behind the invention of agriculture are best understood by studying evidence from Southwest Asia, where farming probably originated first, between 10,000 and 9000 B.C.E.

The Origins of Agriculture

Out of thousands of plant species that humans potentially could have domesticated, humans selected very few to become the main staples of their diet. The skills to cultivate these plants developed separately in various parts of the world and at different times. It is difficult to determine where people invented agriculture independently, without influence from other groups, but today many scholars share the view that people developed farming in seven regions: Southwest Asia, China, New Guinea, sub-Saharan Africa, Mesoamerica, the Andes, and eastern North America (see Table 1.1). In each area, people learned to control the growth of local crops, and the technology they developed quickly spread to neighboring areas. The dates by which people in various regions developed farming are subject to much debate, and those provided here are just one of several possible reconstructions. In most places where people learned to control plant growth, they also began to domesticate selected local animals. This was not always the case, however. In New Guinea, for example, the earliest farmers did not keep animals. Most scholars of the rise of agriculture thus focus primarily on the interactions between humans and plants.

The advent of farming involved a long-term change in interactions between humans and naturally available resources, a change so gradual that people at the time probably barely noticed it. Throughout Southwest Asia runs a crescent-shaped belt richly supplied with wild plants and animals. Located at the foothills of mountain ranges, this zone, known as the **Fertile Crescent**, sweeps northward along the eastern Mediterranean coast into present-day southern Turkey and winds south again along the border between modern Iraq and Iran. In around 10,000 B.C.E. it was covered with fields of wild wheat and barley and inhabited by wild sheep, goats, pigs, and cattle. It is these resources that humans first learned to cultivate.

The Fertile Crescent

Fertile Crescent The region of Southwest Asia with rich natural resources arching along the Mediterranean coast and modern southern Turkey and eastern Iraq.

MAP 1.3

The Origins of Agriculture

In places across the globe early humans started to cultivate plants and herd animals, selecting from the locally available species. Most scholars agree that people invented agriculture independently in at least seven distinct regions at different moments in time between about 9000 and 1000 B.C.E. The crops listed here became the main staples of the local diets.

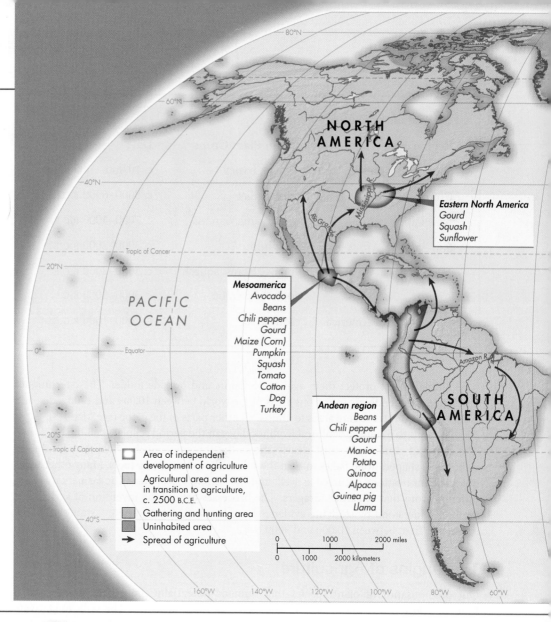

Eastern North America
Gourd
Squash
Sunflower

Mesoamerica
Avocado
Beans
Chili pepper
Gourd
Maize (Corn)
Pumpkin
Squash
Tomato
Cotton
Dog
Turkey

Andean region
Beans
Chili pepper
Gourd
Manioc
Potato
Quinoa
Alpaca
Guinea pig
Llama

☐ Area of independent development of agriculture

▨ Agricultural area and area in transition to agriculture, c. 2500 B.C.E.

▨ Gathering and hunting area

▨ Uninhabited area

➤ Spread of agriculture

| 0 | 1000 | 2000 miles |
| 0 | 1000 | 2000 kilometers |

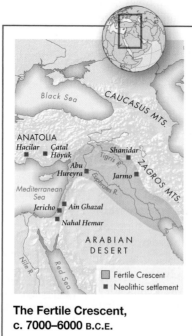

■ Fertile Crescent
■ Neolithic settlement

**The Fertile Crescent,
c. 7000–6000 B.C.E.**

Wild wheat and barley are difficult to gather and consume because of their natural characteristics, such as thick husks. Yet humans did collect their seeds, probably because other foods were insufficient. By doing so, they became familiar with the growth patterns of the plants—and they inadvertently changed the plants' characteristics to allow easier harvests. They favored species with tougher stalks (which could be more easily harvested and would remain upright when harvesters walked through the fields) and thinner husks (allowing easier preparation of food), and over many years these varieties became the only ones remaining in the area. Thus, even before deliberate farming began, humans exerted evolutionary pressure on the natural world, changing the environment and their own societies in the process.

At the same time, humans' relationships with certain animals changed. Whereas hunters continued to pursue deer and gazelles, early farmers nurtured and protected sheep, goats, pigs, and cattle (see Seeing the Past: Saharan Rock Art). Neolithic peoples probably recognized animals' breeding patterns and understood that they required fewer males than females. Farmers selectively slaughtered

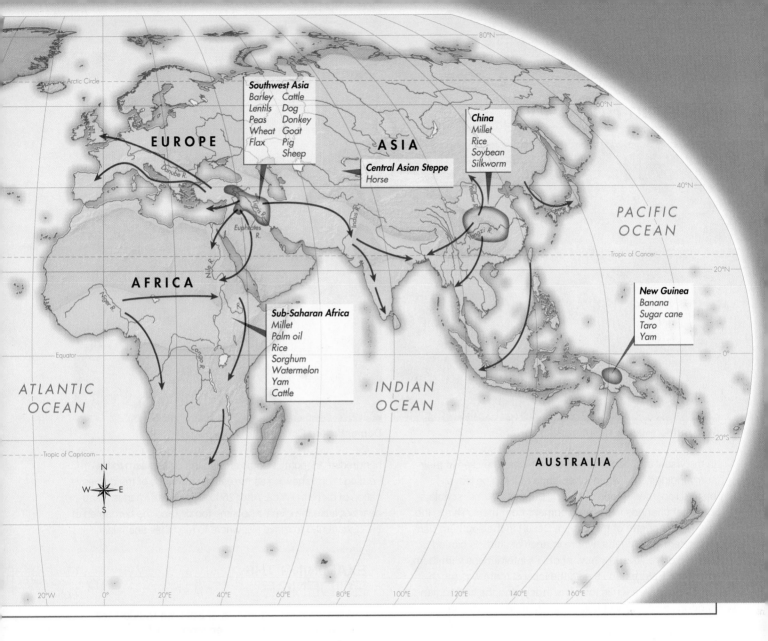

young males for meat and kept females for reproduction and for milk. Like domesticated plants, domesticated animals changed in ways that better suited them to human needs. The protected animals generally became smaller and therefore easier to work with. In the case of goats, the animals' horns changed shape because they were no longer needed for defense, making them less dangerous to their human handlers.

Further, as Neolithic peoples increasingly took their domesticated animals into regions where they did not live in the wild, the animals had to adjust to the new environments; for example, they acclimated to the heat of the lowlands by losing some of their thick coats. Animals were also a convenient way to store calories; farmers could feed them extra plants that would otherwise be discarded, and in times of need slaughter them for their meat. They had many other practical uses, too. Sheep wool and goat hair made protective textiles, milk products were an excellent source of protein, and animal skins, bones, horns, hoofs, and sinews could be turned into a large array of utensils and other items. In a sense, humans learned to use animals as tools, discovering new uses over time and changing the animals themselves to improve their usefulness.

Why Farm?

Although scholars have determined that these changes took place, they are less certain about why humans started to farm. Many suggest that the end of the last ice age around 10,000 B.C.E. brought warmer and drier conditions to Southwest Asia, drastically

Saharan Rock Art

Wild Cattle (Image by Pierre Colombel/Corbis.)

Domesticated Cattle (Jean-Loïc Le Quellec.)

In the visual arts people often depict what they see in their surroundings, and when inhabitants of a region leave behind representations over long periods of time, scholars can infer changes in the environment from them. This is the case in the center of the Sahara Desert in the southern part of modern-day Algeria, where images of animals carved or painted on rocks show how people's interactions with them changed. Before 5000 B.C.E., the local climate was much wetter and more fertile than it is today, and the lush region supported a bounty of animal and human life. The earliest rock carvings in the Tassili region show humans hunting big game with spears and bows. One of the most commonly depicted hunted animals is the wild ancestor of cattle (left), which died out before 5000 B.C.E.

Rock paintings from about 4500 to 2500 B.C.E. show different animals. Instead of wild animals, the artists represented domesticated cattle, individually or in herds of up to one hundred head (right). People around the cattle seem to be herding them, showing us the earliest evidence of the domestication of cattle in Africa. After 2500 B.C.E. these images disappear because the climate became too dry and the herdsmen of the Sahara had to move elsewhere to feed their animals.

EXAMINING THE EVIDENCE

1. What do these examples of Saharan rock art tell us about changes in the environment?

2. How did people's interactions with animals change in this region in around 5000 B.C.E.?

3. Can you speculate why people of the Paleolithic era fashioned such representations?

reducing wild food supplies. According to this theory, humans tried to compensate for losses by moving plants to land where the plants did not reproduce naturally. Other scholars propose that human behavioral changes encouraged the shift to farming. The life of the gatherer-hunter lacked permanence, forcing small groups of people to move around even when women were pregnant or had small children. A desire to stay longer in one place may have pushed early peoples to more closely observe the growth cycles of the plants and animals around them. They may have learned the benefits of storing seeds and planting them for future harvests. Meanwhile, the permanence of their new way of life may have led to larger communities that could survive only if they grew food.

The archaeological record of Southwest Asia shows these processes at work in the period from 10,000 to 9000 B.C.E. The inhabitants increasingly left evidence of plant harvesting and processing in the form of flint and obsidian blades, pestles, mortars, and grinders. Although people still hunted and gathered extensively, by 9000 B.C.E. some lived in fully sedentary communities, where they relied on a combination of foraged and cultivated food.

Once Neolithic people developed agriculture, the technology spread rapidly into regions surrounding the Fertile Crescent, introducing crops and animals that had not existed in the wild. In the north and west, farming spread into the regions that are today Turkey and Europe. By 7000 B.C.E. people in northern Greece farmed, and by 4000 to 3000 B.C.E. the technology had reached Britain and Scandinavia. Wheat and barley cultivation arrived in the Indus Valley by 5000 B.C.E. and somewhat later in Egypt and North Africa. Farmers also moved into regions of Southwest Asia where rainfall was insufficient for farming. Their invention of irrigation agriculture made settlement possible even in the most arid zones (see Chapter 2).

As we saw earlier, not all populations of the world learned farming techniques from Southwest Asia. In China, people developed the skills independently several millennia after agriculture originated in Southwest Asia, focusing on locally available plants. In the middle part of the Yangzi (YANG-zuh) River Valley, where much water is available, wild rice started to grow when the climate became warmer after 8000 B.C.E. At first the local residents collected what was available naturally, but in the period from 8000 to 6000 B.C.E. they gradually used more cultivated rice, and at the end of that period they lived in villages, fully depending on their crops.

Although the crops and techniques used in farming varied from place to place, in every region agricultural life was more difficult than that of the gatherer-hunter. Early farmers had to work many more hours than gatherer-hunters, especially in certain seasons. Furthermore, farmers were more vulnerable to epidemic diseases because they lived together more closely. But farming had advantages. Cultivated crops produced much larger yields than wild plants, so farmers could live in larger communities than foragers. The increased permanence of agricultural communities led to expanded social interactions and a better survival rate for newborn babies. Whatever the reasons for the turn to agriculture, this livelihood became dominant over most of the world in the millennia after it developed. It was only well into the twentieth century C.E. that the majority of the earth's people stopped making a living as farmers.

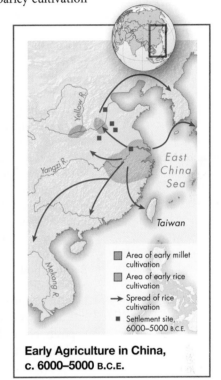

Early Agriculture in China, c. 6000–5000 B.C.E.

Life in Neolithic Communities

As people began living year-round in the same location, the size and number of their material possessions expanded enormously. Their dwellings also changed. The earliest houses, imitating the temporary shelters of migratory foragers, were round or oval. Partly dug into the ground, they contained a central hearth, and floors were paved with stones. As agricultural communities spread over the world, however, the layout of houses evolved into a rectangular form, a layout that remains dominant in residential structures to the present day. This innovation allowed builders to create rooms with specialized functions, such as kitchens and bedrooms. The creation of separate spaces for men and women, for parents and children, and for certain activities reveals the relationships, beliefs, and priorities of the inhabitants. In this light, scholars see increasing complexity of design as a sign that the social organization of communities had become more complex.

New Household Technology

The house became the center of people's activities, the place where they kept the harvest and turned it into food. Because grain must be ground before it can be consumed, grinding stones are common in the archaeological record. Grinding was backbreaking. The first farmers used mortars and pestles, which permitted only small amounts to be ground at a time. Later, they crushed the grain between a flat or convex bottom stone and a smaller, handheld round stone. The millers were mostly women, who rubbed the stone back and forth until the flour was fine enough to use to prepare food. They sat bent over on their knees for such long periods that their wrists, toes, knees, and lower backs became deformed. Skeletons of Neolithic women excavated in the north of modern Syria show those physical injuries. Milling is but one example of a larger trend. As farming developed, the labor associated with farming was increasingly gendered, with some tasks seen as suitable for men and others for women.

Early farmers probably cooked gruel or mash from the flour, but by 3500 B.C.E. people consumed grain principally as bread and beer in Southwest Asia. They were probably invented accidentally. When roasted grains are mixed with water, they form a paste that can easily be baked on a hot stone, and adding other ingredients led to the invention and production of bread. Beer manufacture was very similar to that of bread, except that in brewing the grain mixture was soaked in water to ferment. Thus bread and beer together became essential nutrition to people in many parts of the world. Like milling, cooking and brewing became women's work in many regions.

Pottery and Metalworking

Clay, abundantly available in Southwest Asia, had long been used to form figurines. When early farmers realized the strength of baked clay, they started to create pots for storage and cooking. Pottery was a revolutionary innovation that allowed Neolithic farmers to build on the advantages of settled agriculture. Easily produced from local resources in all shapes and sizes, pottery provides both safe storage of grains against pests and moisture and a means to heat and cook food over a fire. First appearing in Japan around 12,000 B.C.E., pottery was independently invented in Southwest Asia around 6500 B.C.E. Because pottery is also easily decorated with carved incisions or painted designs, and because decorative styles changed rapidly, pottery finds have become the main evidence by which archaeologists date settlements.

The first farmers also liked to make small decorative objects out of metal; natural ore deposits, especially of copper, exist in many parts of Southwest Asia. Although copper ore could be hammered cold, by 5000 B.C.E. people had learned to heat ore to extract pure copper and pour it in liquid form into molds. They later expanded these techniques for use with other metals, and by 4000 B.C.E., people began to mix various metals to make stronger alloys. The most important was bronze, which they manufactured from copper and tin. The development of metallurgy was, in a sense, made possible by farming, because specialization of labor was an important feature of settled communities. Certain people in farming communities could devote themselves to a particular task, such as metalworking, while others went about the job of producing food.

Textile Production

Another vital innovation that agriculture made possible was textile weaving. Domestication made new fibers available, which people learned to twist into threads and wove into clothing, blankets, and many other fabrics. Some fibers derived from domesticated animals—sheep wool and goat hair—and others came from plants grown for the purpose, especially flax, used to make linen thread. The earliest pieces of cloth found so far are from the cave of Nahal Hemar (nak-hal HEY-mar) in modern Israel, dating to around 6500 B.C.E.

The earliest written documents available to us, written long after the invention of agriculture in Southwest Asia, show that women were mostly responsible for turning raw agricultural products into usable goods. They ground cereals and cooked food, and they wove textiles and made pots. They could perform these tasks while staying at home to take care of young children. Scholars assume that this was true in other early agricultural societies as well.

The division of labor along gender lines—with women primarily active around the house and men primarily outside—reflects the growing complexity of interactions in farming communities. Whereas bands of gatherer-hunters were probably egalitarian, in sedentary societies inequalities grew on the basis of wealth, status, and power. Some families accumulated more goods than others because, for example, they were able to harvest more. The greater wealth held by the heads of these families—all men, it seems—may have commanded community respect. Because the communities of the Neolithic period were larger and lived together for prolonged periods, they needed a means to settle conflicts peacefully, and wealthier men may have gained authority over the rest. The archaeological record shows differences in wealth of the inhabitants, albeit on a small scale, as early as 7000 B.C.E. Thus farming and the development of a hierarchical social structure seem to go hand in hand.

Çatal Höyük (cha-TAHL hoo-YOOK) in modern central Turkey is the largest Neolithic settlement yet excavated (see Lives and Livelihoods: The People of Çatal Höyük). Here, archaeologists found stone and clay figurines of women with enormous breasts and thighs, including one seated on a throne flanked by two catlike animals. As with Paleolithic figurines of women, scholars and others understand these statues in different ways, but the idea that they are fertility symbols is very popular. Some interpretations even suggest that they honor a "mother goddess" as the dominant primordial force of nature, but this theory is much disputed. It is possible that early peoples considered women to form the primary line of descent from one generation to the next and that family property passed along the female line—a system called **matrilineal**. But it is risky to conclude that women were in charge and had greater authority than men—a system called **matriarchy**. Nonetheless, a woman's ability to give birth was a force of nature that the people of early agricultural societies depended on for survival, and we can imagine that early farmers honored such forces of nature as being greater than themselves.

Among Paleolithic foragers the nomadic band was the primary social unit; in Neolithic farming communities the unit shifted to single families comprising several generations. The new rectangular form of the house made it possible for settled farmers to live together, close to other families yet separate from them. Neolithic people's burial practices reflect the more intimate family connections. Paleolithic people often buried their dead in caves that they periodically visited, but with the shift to farming people lived in the same house for long periods, and families buried at least some of the dead under the floors of their houses. How they did so varied, but it was common to detach the head from the rest of the body—probably after birds had picked the skeleton clean—and bury it separately. They often placed heads in groups and decorated some of them. Sometimes they filled the eyes with shells and modeled facial features with plaster.

Even more dramatic evidence of the practice of restoring the physical features of the dead comes from Ain Ghazal (ine gahz-AHL) in modern Jordan, a site occupied between 7200 and 5000 B.C.E. There, under floors of some houses, archaeologists found plaster human statues, some more than three feet high, with rudimentary bodies and large heads. The same site also yielded plaster masks modeled on human skulls. The exact interpretation of these practices is not certain, but it seems likely that they are the earliest evidence for a cult of ancestors, a way to preserve their presence in the house. They may even have received food offerings. People of many early cultures in world history maintained similar ties to the deceased.

In short, in religious practices, social structures, and technological and architectural innovations, we see evidence that the advent of settled agriculture produced a set of developments that led to increasingly complex human societies and cultures. This process was not inevitable, however, and not all ancient peoples considered it desirable. The gatherer-hunter lifestyle has certain advantages, and it is in no way obvious that settled agriculture represents a clearly superior alternative.

Growing Social Inequality

Women in the Neolithic Worldview

Neolithic Religious Beliefs

matrilineal A system of family descent that follows the female side of the family.

matriarchy The social order that recognizes women as heads of families and passes power and property from mother to daughter.

The People of Çatal Höyük

One of the most intriguing archaeological sites of the Neolithic era is Çatal Höyük, located in the south of modern Turkey. Occupied between 7200 and 6000 B.C.E., Çatal Höyük was an unusually large Neolithic settlement, some thirty-two acres in size, and it was home to perhaps as many as six thousand inhabitants. Some were farmers, who grew wheat and barley and herded sheep and goats. Numerous bones of wild animals discovered in the houses show that people also hunted the rich wildlife of the surroundings.

Çatal Höyük is remarkable for several reasons. Its mudbrick houses stood side by side without streets in between them and without doors or large windows. Those on the outside of the settlement formed a continuous wall for protection against intruders. The unusual layout forced residents to enter their homes by a ladder through a hole in the roof. The interiors of the houses were even more extraordinary for their time because of their extensive decoration. Many contained a room with paintings, engravings, or modeled reliefs, mostly representing wild animals of the surrounding countryside. Some of the scenes seem bizarre to us, including vultures attacking headless human corpses and women giving birth to bulls. These images must reflect the beliefs and perhaps the anxieties of Çatal Höyük's inhabitants, but their interpretation remains a problem.

We can explain the wealth and size of Çatal Höyük in terms of its location. A nearby volcano provided the hard rock obsidian, which craftsmen chipped and polished into tools and ornaments. Based on chemical analysis of such stone objects excavated all over Turkey, Syria, and Cyprus, archaeologists have determined that they originated at Çatal Höyük and that the town's inhabitants were in contact with people of these distant regions. They bartered the

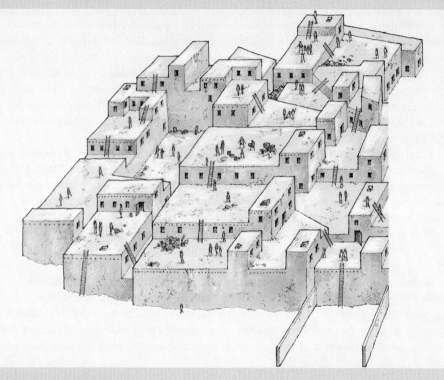

The Houses of Çatal Höyük

Although this reconstruction is hypothetical, it integrates the excavators' ideas about how the people of Çatal Höyük in southern Turkey lived. The remains of the houses suggest that residents entered them from the roofs, and it is clear that they decorated certain rooms with paintings of local animals. (© Dorling Kindersley.)

obsidian products for shells from the Mediterranean Sea and flint from Syria. Çatal Höyük's natural environment was so rich that some inhabitants could focus on obsidian work; others collected and grew food to support them. Given the vivid imagery of their work, the painters of the decorations inside the houses may also have been specialists.

QUESTIONS TO CONSIDER

1. What factors explain the relatively large size of Çatal Höyük for a Neolithic settlement?

2. What material remains reveal information about the inhabitants' ideas?

3. Why did the inhabitants create, from our perspective, such an unusual layout and architecture?

For Further Information:
"Çatal Höyük: Excavations of a Neolithic Anatolian Höyük." http://www.catalhoyuk.com.
Hodder, Ian. *The Leopard's Tale: Revealing the Mysteries of Çatal Höyük*. New York: Thames & Hudson, 2006.
Mellaart, James. *Çatal Hüyük: A Neolithic Town in Anatolia*. New York: McGraw-Hill, 1967.

COUNTERPOINT
Gatherer-Hunters by Choice: Aborigines of Australia

Although agriculture spread rapidly across the globe, it was not universally practiced in ancient times. Until relatively recently, in fact, many people did not farm. Sometimes the local environment necessitated a forager lifestyle; it is impossible to farm in the Arctic Circle, for example. But in locales where *both* livelihoods are possible, people had a choice and they could select the one they preferred. Many of these people had contact with farmers and could have learned agricultural techniques if they had wanted to. In this Counterpoint we consider one such people who continue in a gatherer-hunter way of life to this day: Australian Aborigines.

FOCUS

Why did Australian Aborigines, in contrast to many of the world's other peoples, choose not to farm?

Understanding the History of Aborigines

The largest landmass in which people did not rely on agriculture (until it was forcibly introduced in the modern era) was Australia (see Map 1.4). Before European

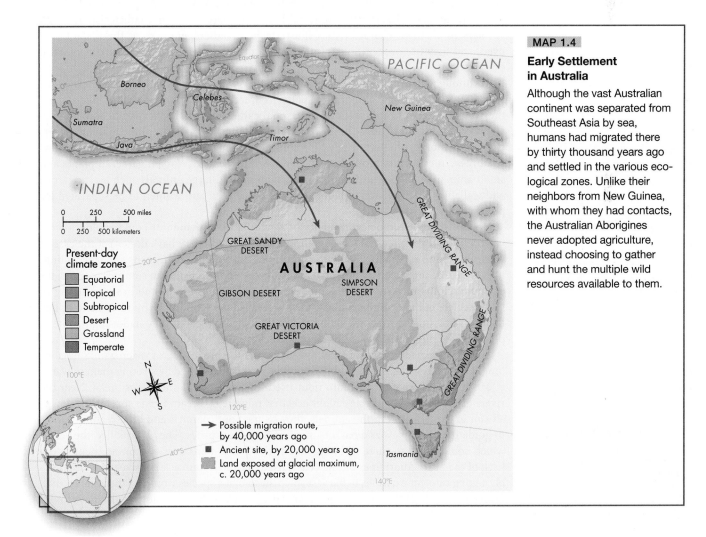

MAP 1.4

Early Settlement in Australia

Although the vast Australian continent was separated from Southeast Asia by sea, humans had migrated there by thirty thousand years ago and settled in the various ecological zones. Unlike their neighbors from New Guinea, with whom they had contacts, the Australian Aborigines never adopted agriculture, instead choosing to gather and hunt the multiple wild resources available to them.

Present-day climate zones
- Equatorial
- Tropical
- Subtropical
- Desert
- Grassland
- Temperate

→ Possible migration route, by 40,000 years ago
■ Ancient site, by 20,000 years ago
▪ Land exposed at glacial maximum, c. 20,000 years ago

settlers first arrived in 1788 C.E., no one in this vast region farmed; the native inhabitants, or **Aborigines**, numbering perhaps 1 million at the time, lived as foragers. We have written descriptions and other sources of information about encounters between the Aborigines and modern Europeans. Reliable information of this sort is lacking for gatherer-hunters of the distant past, but European accounts of Aborigines are heavily biased. Their authors often saw Aborigines as primitive people who lacked the intelligence to farm. When historians took into account the Aborigines' rich archaeological remains and observations of gatherer-hunters who survive today, however, they concluded that Australian Aborigines consciously decided not to practice agriculture, because they knew that foraging was more suitable for their environment.

By thirty thousand years ago, gatherer-hunter immigrants from southeast Asia had settled the whole of the Australian continent. The water level was much lower due to the last ice age, and they had been able to cross the sea by boat—no small feat because even at the lowest sea level they had to sail at least forty miles. The ensuing ice melt, which started around twelve thousand years ago, widened the distance between Australia and adjacent islands and increased its population's isolation. The end of the ice age also caused the climate to dry considerably.

A Lifestyle in Harmony with the Natural World

Despite Australia's enormous variety of natural environments, ranging from tropical rain forests to desolate deserts, the foragers' lifestyles shared certain characteristics. Many scholars think these characteristics illustrate how gatherer-hunters of the distant past lived, and they use observations of modern gatherer-hunters to interpret archaeological evidence.

Although their existence was migratory, they were strongly attached to the regions they inhabited, and their migration patterns were fixed. In fertile regions near water, they maintained huts and shelters at seasonal campsites, where they could stay for several months. In arid regions they moved more often from one water hole to another, setting up temporary shelters. The whole community shared ownership of the land and its resources. In collecting food, they divided labor by gender. Women gathered plants and small animals such as lizards and turtles; men hunted large animals such as kangaroos and wallabies. The division of labor sometimes led men and women to be separated for prolonged periods.

Harvesting Nature's Bounty

So great is the ecological diversity of Australia that inhabitants could exploit a large variety of local resources, as foragers throughout world history have done. Yet the case of Australia shows especially vividly the enormous adaptability of humans and our willingness to take advantage of all potential food sources. In the Australian summer months, for example, moths migrate to the southeastern highlands to escape the heat, gathering in rock crevices in huge numbers. Local people scraped them off by the hundreds and grilled them on hot stones. After removing the moth's inedible parts, they had a high-protein, peanut-sized nugget that tasted like a roasted chestnut.

Another expedient use of local resources was the processing of macrozamia nuts for food. Poisonous when not treated, the kernels must be detoxified by soaking them in water, after which they were ground into flour used to bake a highly nutritious bread. Near the rivers of the southeast, people caught eels that migrate upstream in the spring and downstream in the fall. To trap the animals, they cleaned out channels and built retaining walls to guide them into nets and baskets made of bark and rushes. They then killed the eels—which could be up to three feet long and as thick as a man's arm—by biting them in the back of the head. Aborigines on the coasts used marine resources intensively but responsibly, taking care, for example, to harvest shellfish so that a species would not become extinct. Over time the discarded shells formed large heaps, in which archaeologists also have found

Aborigines Indigenous inhabitants of regions that Europeans colonized starting in the fifteenth century C.E.; the word is used especially in reference to Australia.

bones of birds eaten after they had washed up onto the beach. Coastal people fished in canoes, with men using spears and women using fish lines and hooks. These examples illustrate the resourcefulness of gatherer-hunters, and another important fact: far from being unsophisticated, gatherer-hunters develop highly effective specialized tools to harvest nature's resources.

Beyond collecting what nature provided, Aborigines manipulated the environment to increase the foodstuff available in the wild. In this effort, fire was an important tool. They burned areas with shrubs because they learned that the regenerative process produced a wide variety of edible plants. These plants were useful in their own right but also because they attracted animals that could be hunted. Selective burning also allowed certain desirable plants to grow better and to ripen simultaneously. For example, burning increased production of macrozamia nuts up to eight times. In addition, people replanted fruit seeds on fertile compost heaps near their camps, and when they collected wild yams and other tubers, they did not pull out the entire root but left the part that would regenerate. The Aborigines were thus well aware of the growth patterns of the plants and animals that surrounded them and adjusted natural circumstances so the desired species would thrive.

Increasing Nature's Bounty

The Conscious Choice to Gather and Hunt

Why Aborigines did not go one step further and independently develop agriculture or adopt it from abroad is an interesting question. Australia was not fully isolated before the Europeans' arrival in 1788 C.E.; peoples from neighboring regions such as Indonesia

Gathering Turtle Eggs
Gatherer-hunters ingeniously take advantage of everything nature provides and show great awareness of plants and animal behavior. These Australian Aboriginal women and children know that sea turtles come ashore to bury their eggs, and they collect the eggs before they hatch.
(L. Kuipers.)

and New Guinea visited regularly. Inhabitants of these nearby areas farmed crops, including plants such as yams that can grow in Australia as well. Scholars thus believe that the absence of domestication was a conscious choice. They were content with the resources nature provided, which were adequate and easily available except in rare years of scarcity. Moreover, because much of Australia is dry—droughts can last for years—and has poor soil, farming is difficult in many parts of the continent and does not guarantee a stable food supply.

Moreover, farming is arduous and labor intensive compared with foraging. A woman harvesting and processing macrozamia nuts, for example, can feed herself for the whole day after only two hours of work. The relatively relaxed lifestyle of Aborigines made an impression on some of the earliest Europeans, who observed Australia before they started to settle there. In 1770 C.E., the English explorer James Cook wrote:

> [T]he Natives of New Holland [= Australia] . . . may appear to be the most wretched people upon Earth, but in reality they are far more happier than we Europeans. They live in a Tranquility which is not disturb'd by the Inequality of Condition: The Earth and sea of their own accord furnishes them with all things necessary for life, they covet not Magnificent Houses, Household-stuff &ca, they lie in a warm and fine Climate and enjoy a very wholesome Air, so that they have very little need of Clothing and this they seem to be fully sensible of, for many of who we gave Cloth &ca to, left it carelessly upon the Sea beach and in the woods as a thing they had no manner of use for. In short they seem'd to set no Value upon any thing we gave them, nor would they ever part with any thing of their own for any one article we could offer them; this in my opinion argues that they think themselves provided with all the necessarys of Life and that they have no superfluities.[2]

Religious Life and Social Organization

In contrast to the simplicity of their material culture, Aborigines had a complex religious life and social organization. Their worldview centered on the concept of "Dreaming" or "Dreamtime," which connected past, present, and future. In the distant past, according to Aboriginal belief, mythic beings created the land and its inhabitants and left rules on how humans should interact with one another and with nature. Then they withdrew into the spiritual world, but they continue to send messages through dreams and other altered states of consciousness. Humans needed to maintain contacts with these Dreaming beings through rituals and dances, for which Aborigines donned elaborate clothing, such as cloaks made of possum and wallaby skins. Ritual activity was primarily the domain of initiated men, who often temporarily withdrew from their communities for the purpose.

In Aboriginal society, a person gained respect through ritual knowledge, not wealth, because there was no accumulation of goods. Social interactions, including sexual intercourse and friendship, were allowed only between individuals with a specific family relationship. Marriages, an important way for families to establish ties, were often reciprocal—for example, men exchanged their sisters—and were arranged before those to be married were born. Likewise, gifts of tools, skins, ornaments, and the like were a crucial way to maintain good relations.

Despite these common characteristics, early Australia was culturally diverse, with practices varying from region to region. In the visual arts, for example, stone carvings and paintings on objects and rock surfaces show many regional styles, although treatments of subjects share basic similarities (for example, humans and animals are mostly represented as sticklike figures). The linguistic diversity of Aboriginal Australians was also enormous: in 1788 C.E. more than 250 languages were spoken on the continent.

The history of Australian Aborigines thus reveals that a nonagricultural life is possible, indeed preferable, under certain conditions. Native Australians' gatherer-hunter livelihood led to a distinctive historical development on the continent, with unique technologies and social, economic, and cultural practices.

Conclusion

Neanderthals, with whose discovery we began this chapter, differed greatly from modern humans. Not only did they not look like us, but they also led very different lives from ours. We should remember, however, that they too were a product of millions of years of evolution that had transformed human beings repeatedly.

Four million years ago, our ancestors depended entirely on the natural resources available in their immediate surroundings. They collected and ate plants and animals without tools or fire, relying only on their hands and teeth. But over long spans of time, they adapted to changes in their environments, acquired new skills, and started to modify what was available in their surroundings. Importantly, these developments allowed them to change physically, and they began to walk upright, hold things in their now-agile hands, speak, and think abstract thoughts. Tools and other inventions helped them in their quest for successful livelihoods. After millions of years, some began to domesticate plants and animals and to manage the forces of nature. Others, most notably Australian Aborigines, consciously decided to rely primarily on food available in the wild, for which they foraged.

By 4000 B.C.E., peoples in various parts of the world had learned to manipulate resources so that they could survive periods without naturally available food. They had developed the tools and skills needed to adapt elements of nature to their needs. As they lived in increasingly large communities, their social interactions, means of communication, and working conditions changed. The forces of nature were much more powerful than human abilities, but with a great deal of effort some people had developed the skills needed to spend their entire lives in one place. These early settlers went on to build up other aspects of human culture that are still with us today, such as cities and writing, the focus of our next chapter.

NOTES

1. Charles Darwin, *On the Origin of Species*, ed. Joseph Carroll (Peterborough, Ontario, Canada: Broadview, 2003), 432.
2. J. C. Beaglehole, ed., *The Voyage of the Endeavour 1768–1771: The Journals of Captain James Cook on His Voyages of Discovery* (Cambridge, U.K.: Cambridge University Press, 1955), 1:399.

RESOURCES FOR RESEARCH

Human Origins

The study of the human species draws on an assortment of disciplines, including anthropology, genetics, and linguistics. The literature is extensive, and ideas change rapidly. The selection of books and Web sites is vast; many are extensively illustrated. The book edited by Scarre gives a very up-to-date survey of all the issues discussed in this chapter.

Ardipithecus ramidus. Science, October 2, 2009. http://www.sciencemag.org/site/feature/misc/webfeat/ardipithecus/index.xhtml.

Fagan, Brian. *World Prehistory, A Brief Introduction,* 8th ed. 2010.

Johanson, Donald, and Blake Edgar. *From Lucy to Language,* 2d ed. 2006.

Klein, Richard G. *The Human Career: Human Biological and Cultural Origins*, 2d ed. 1999.

"The New Face of Human Evolution." http://archaeologyinfo.com/.

Scarre, Chris, ed. *The Human Past*. 2005.

"What Does It Mean to Be Human?" Smithsonian National Museum of Natural History. http://www.mnh.si.edu/anthro/humanorigins/.

Stringer, Chris, and Peter Andrews. *The Complete World of Human Evolution*. 2005.

Tattersall, Ian. *The World from Beginnings to 4000 B.C.E.* 2008.

Tattersall, Ian, and Jeffrey H. Schwartz. *Extinct Humans*. 2001.

Thomas, Herbert. *The First Humans: The Search for Our Origins*. 1996.

Paleolithic Food Gatherers, 2,000,000–9000 B.C.E.

Most of the books that treat human origins also discuss the Paleolithic. Additionally, these items more specifically address the art of that era.

Aujoulat, Norbert. "Lascaux: A Visit to the Cave." http://www.culture.gouv.fr/culture/arcnat/lascaux/en/.

Aujoulat, Norbert. *Lascaux: Movement, Space, and Time*. 2005.

Bahn, Paul G., and Jean Vertut. *Journey Through the Ice Age*. 1997.

The First Neolithic Farmers, 9000–4000 B.C.E.

The study of the origins of agriculture can be very technical, and scholars often introduce new ideas in publications of archaeological excavations that require processes or dates to be revised. Scholars often consider how the technology spread worldwide, which they regularly connect to the spread of languages. Several of the books mentioned in previous sections are useful for this period as well, especially Scarre's *The Human Past*. Nissen's somewhat older study provides an excellent survey of developments in Southwest Asia.

Bellwood, Peter. *First Farmers: The Origins of Agricultural Societies*. 2005.

Cauvin, Jacques. *The Birth of the Gods and the Origins of Agriculture*. Translated by Trevor Watkins. 2000.

Nissen, Hans J. *The Early History of the Ancient Near East, 9000–2000 B.C.* Translated by E. Lutzeier and K. Northcutt. 1988.

"Preserving Ancient Statues from Jordan." Arthur M. Sackler Gallery, Smithsonian Institution. July 28, 1996–April 6, 1997. http://www.asia.si.edu/jordan/html/jor_mm.htm.

Smith, Bruce D. *The Emergence of Agriculture*. 1995.

Wenke, Robert J., and Deborah I. Olszewski. *Patterns in Prehistory: Humankind's First Three Million Years*, 5th ed. 2006.

COUNTERPOINT: Gatherer-Hunters by Choice: Aborigines of Australia

The study of Australian aboriginal life involves a mixture of archaeological and ethnographic research, and many of the books discuss the people both before and after European settlement in 1788.

Chaloupka, George. *Journey in Time: The World's Longest Continuing Art Tradition*. 1993.

Flood, Josephine. *Archaeology of the Dreamtime: The Story of Prehistoric Australia and Its People*. 1989.

Kleinert, Sylvia, and Margot Neale, eds. *The Oxford Companion to Aboriginal Art and Culture*. 2000.

Mulvaney, D. J., and J. Peter White, eds. *Australians to 1788*. 1987.

▶ **For additional primary sources from this period**, see *Sources of Crossroads and Cultures*.

▶ **For Web sites, images, and documents related to topics in this chapter**, see Make History at bedfordstmartins.com/smith.

The major global development in this chapter ▶ The adaptation of early humans to their environment and their eventual domestication of plants and animals.

IMPORTANT EVENTS

c. 7 million years ago (mya)	Oldest hominid on record, *Sahelanthropus tchadensis*, lives in central Africa
c. 4.4 mya	*Ardipithecus ramidus* lives in the region of modern Ethiopia
c. 3.2 mya	*Australopithecus afarensis* (Lucy) lives in the region of modern Ethiopia
c. 2 mya	First hominin and first stone tools
c. 1 mya	Ancestors of *Homo erectus* enter Asia
c. 500,000 B.C.E.	Ancestors of Neanderthal enter western Eurasia
c. 400,000–30,000 B.C.E.	Neanderthal lives in western Eurasia
c. 400,000 B.C.E.	First evidence of *Homo sapiens* in Africa
c. 100,000 B.C.E.	Some *Homo sapiens* leave Africa
c. 35,000–10,000 B.C.E.	Paleolithic cave paintings
c. 30,000 B.C.E.	*Homo sapiens* becomes the only human species
c. 15,000 B.C.E.	*Homo sapiens* enters the Americas
c. 10,000–8000 B.C.E.	Development of agriculture in Southwest Asia

KEY TERMS

Aborigines (p. 32)	**matriarchy** (p. 29)
Fertile Crescent (p. 23)	**matrilineal** (p. 29)
hominid (p. 11)	**Neanderthal** (p. 15)
hominin (p. 15)	**Neolithic** (p. 17)
Homo sapiens (p. 15)	**Paleolithic** (p. 17)

CHAPTER OVERVIEW QUESTIONS

1. What caused humans to introduce technological and other innovations?
2. How did these innovations increase their ability to determine their own destinies?
3. How did the relationship between humans and nature change?
4. How have historians and other scholars reconstructed life in the earliest periods of human existence despite the lack of written records?

SECTION FOCUS QUESTIONS

1. What physical and behavioral adaptations and innovations characterized human evolution?
2. In the absence of written sources, what have scholars learned about the Paleolithic economy, adaptations to the natural world, and technological innovations?
3. In what ways does the Neolithic agricultural economy reveal humans' increasing intent and ability to manipulate the natural world to their advantage?
4. Why did Australian Aborigines, in contrast to many of the world's other peoples, choose not to farm?

MAKING CONNECTIONS

1. What hominid species migrated across the globe, and for what reasons? How did natural conditions influence their migrations?
2. How did Neolithic peoples' livelihoods and daily lives compare with those of Paleolithic peoples?
3. What gender-specific roles can we discern in early human history, and how did they emerge?

AT A CROSSROADS ▲

Unassuming clay objects such as this one show human beings' earliest ability to record information for the future. Dating to around 3200 B.C.E., this tablet from southern Mesopotamia is impressed with cuneiform signs that record the transfer of goods in the city of Uruk. Writing was one of many Uruk innovations that announced the birth of the first urban society in world history. (Science Source/PhotoResearchers.)

Temples and Palaces: Birth of the City

5000–1200 B.C.E.

In around 1800 B.C.E., scribes from Sumer, in the south of modern Iraq, wrote down the tale of Enmerkar and the Lord of Aratta. This Sumerian epic recounts the rivalry between Enmerkar, king of the Sumerian city of Uruk, and his unnamed counterpart in Aratta, a legendary city in what is today Iran. Both men wanted to be the favorite of the goddess Inanna, one of the many deities whom the people of this ancient world honored. The two kings communicated through a messenger, but at one point the message became too difficult for him to memorize, so the tale says:

> His speech was very great, its meaning very deep.
> The messenger's mouth was too heavy; he could not repeat it.
> Because the messenger's mouth was too heavy, and he could not repeat it,
> The lord of Uruk patted some clay and put the words on it as on a tablet.
> Before that day, there had been no putting words on clay;
> But now, when the sun rose on that day—so it was.
> The lord of Uruk had put words as on a tablet—so it was![1]

This passage describes in mythical terms the invention of the first writing system on earth, **cuneiform**, in which the writer used a reed to press wedge-shaped marks on a moist clay tablet. The invention of writing marked a major turning point in world history: it

BACKSTORY

As we saw in Chapter 1, people in Southwest Asia were the first in world history to invent agriculture, which allowed them to live in the same place for prolonged periods. The abundant natural resources of the Fertile Crescent, which runs from the eastern Mediterranean shore to the mountains between modern Iraq and Iran, allowed people to live in larger communities, in which social interactions became increasingly complex. In short, settled agriculture in Southwest Asia led to the birth of the city and the state.

In time, cities became major crossroads for peoples, goods, and ideas. It was in cities that the inhabitants of Southwest Asia developed a number of innovative concepts and technologies, including new forms of communication and political organization that remain important to this day. These changes did not happen in the Fertile Crescent itself, however, but in the adjacent river valleys, where natural challenges were much more severe. In this chapter we examine the origins and implications of urbanization, exploring the new patterns and connections that emerged as cities became central to Southwest Asian society and government.

cuneiform The dominant writing system of ancient Southwest Asia, which uses combinations of wedge-shaped symbols for words and syllables.

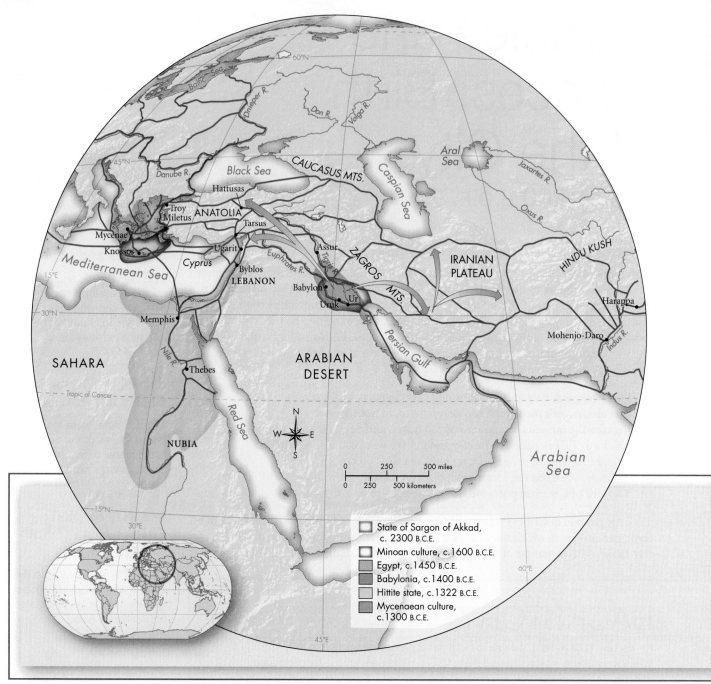

State of Sargon of Akkad, c. 2300 B.C.E.

Minoan culture, c. 1600 B.C.E.

Egypt, c. 1450 B.C.E.

Babylonia, c. 1400 B.C.E.

Hittite state, c. 1322 B.C.E.

Mycenaean culture, c. 1300 B.C.E.

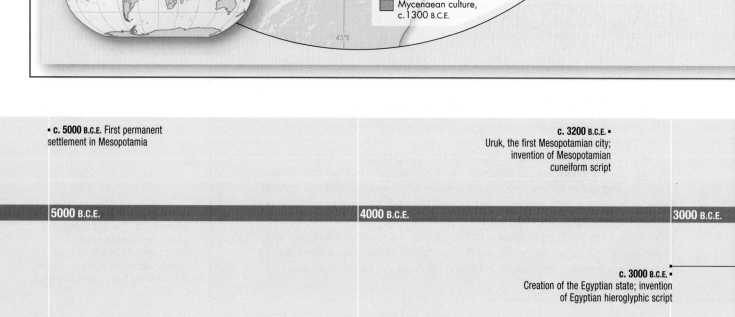

- **c. 5000 B.C.E.** First permanent settlement in Mesopotamia

c. 3200 B.C.E. ▪
Uruk, the first Mesopotamian city; invention of Mesopotamian cuneiform script

| 5000 B.C.E. | 4000 B.C.E. | 3000 B.C.E. |

c. 3000 B.C.E. ▪
Creation of the Egyptian state; invention of Egyptian hieroglyphic script

reflected profound social and cultural developments and created a myriad of new connections, including connections between the present and the distant past. Hundreds of thousands of cuneiform tablets have survived, giving scholars the first written evidence and enormously expanding their access to the lives and thoughts of peoples from the past.

The written and archaeological evidence from ancient Sumer reveals the origins of the world's first urban culture and sheds light on its earliest characteristics. Before we begin exploring that evidence, however, we need to define what we mean by "city." Scholars characterize a **city** not just in terms of its size and large population, but by its role in the life of the region, which extends beyond its boundaries. Thus, the inhabitants of outlying areas relied on the cities of antiquity to meet important needs. People who lived many miles away may have venerated a god in the city temple, for instance, or they may have traveled there to obtain tools. At the same time, inhabitants of cities relied on nearby rural areas for basic needs, such as food, which they could not grow themselves. City dwellers tended to have specialized economic and social roles, such as metalworker, shopkeeper, or priest, and political elites usually controlled their interactions through rules and regulations. In ancient times, the growth of cities often led to a type of political organization we call the **city-state**: an independent urban center that dominates the surrounding countryside. Thus, as cities developed their own distinct economic, social, and political structures, they functioned as regional crossroads, connecting people with communities.

Throughout history, cities and city-states appeared in almost every part of the world as people decided to live together in denser concentrations. This arrangement often arose independently, centuries after cities first appeared in Southwest Asia, and the urban environments varied from place to place. Compared to Southwest Asian cities, for example, Chinese cities had similar numbers of residents but covered much larger areas. Some early cities in Mesoamerica were primarily ceremonial—their purpose

city A center of population, commerce, and culture that provides specialized services to people from surrounding areas.

city-state A form of political organization that incorporates a single city with its surrounding countryside and villages.

MAPPING THE WORLD

Southwest Asia and the Eastern Mediterranean, c. 5000–1200 B.C.E.

The earliest urban societies and states in world history arose in Southwest Asia. Southern Mesopotamia and Egypt were the leaders in urbanization and state creation, and with their extensive trade contacts they influenced adjacent regions and beyond. The use of cuneiform, the world's first writing, for example, spread from Mesopotamia to Iran, Anatolia, and Syria. By 1200 B.C.E., the area was home to a set of territorial states in constant contact—sometimes in peace and sometimes in military conflict.

ROUTES ▼

⇨ Spread of cuneiform writing, c. 3200 B.C.E

— Major trade route

- c. 2550 B.C.E. Khufu's pyramid at Giza

c. 1800–1700 B.C.E. Hammurabi's unification of southern Mesopotamia

▪ c. 1800 B.C.E. Development of alphabetic script in Syria

2000 B.C.E.   **1000 B.C.E.**

c. 3000–2350 B.C.E. Competing city-states in Mesopotamia

c. 1600–1200 B.C.E. First international order in the eastern Mediterranean

▪ c. 1650 B.C.E. End of the Minoan culture

c. 2350–2200 B.C.E. Dynasty of King Sargon of Akkad dominates Mesopotamia

▪ c. 1450 B.C.E. Mycenaean expansion throughout the Aegean

FIRST APPEARANCE OF CITIES

c. 3200 B.C.E.	Southwest Asia
c. 3000 B.C.E.	Egypt
c. 2600 B.C.E.	Indus Valley
c. 2000 B.C.E.	Northern China
c. 1500 B.C.E.	Nubia
c. 1200 B.C.E.	Mesoamerica
c. 100 C.E.	Sub-Saharan West Africa
c. 1000 C.E.	Sub-Saharan East Africa

was apparently not to house people. But regardless of their size and purpose, all cities serve as important focal points for their society's activities.

Accordingly, it is not surprising that starting with the earliest city dwellers, many people have equated cities with civilization, seeing nonurban people as inherently backward and unsophisticated. Formerly, historians also equated urban societies with civilization, but we now realize we must be more flexible in applying terms. Although complex social and economic interactions and technological and cultural innovations often developed in cities, the many other forms of social and economic organization that have evolved over world history cannot be considered static or "uncivilized." As we examine developments in Southwest Asia, it is important to recognize that we are exploring the rise of cities, *not* the rise of civilization.

Moreover, although cities were the focus of cultural development in many regions, that was not universally true. In South Asia, for example, after a period of early urbanization people reverted to village life (see Chapter 3). In Egypt, bordering on Southwest Asia, a state with cities developed very early, but as the Counterpoint to this chapter will show, cities there had a limited role. The king was at the center of political, economic, and cultural life, and from the beginning of the Egyptian state, its inhabitants considered their status as royal subjects more important than their residence in a particular city. Thus, the central role of cities in Southwest Asia reflected a specific set of historical and environmental circumstances; it was not the product of a universal pattern followed by all complex societies.

The rise of cities in Southwest Asia was a long-term process marked by many social, economic, and technological advances that combined to fundamentally alter living conditions and livelihoods. The tale that begins this chapter reflects several elements of urban life that are still part of modern culture today: cities, communication by writing, political institutions, social hierarchies, and long-distance contacts. Once cities had developed, they became the sites of the characteristic culture of ancient Southwest Asia and provided the basis for further developments in every aspect of life.

OVERVIEW
QUESTIONS

The major global development in this chapter: The rise of urban society and the creation of states in Southwest Asia.

As you read, consider:

1. What types of political and social organization appeared in the early history of Southwest Asia?

2. What new technologies appeared, and how did they affect people's livelihoods?

3. How do urban societies differ from village societies?

4. How did the early states of Southwest Asia interact with one another?

Origins of Urban Society:
Mesopotamia 5000–3200 B.C.E.

Sumer, the land where the tale of Enmerkar and the Lord of Aratta took place, was located in southern Mesopotamia, an ancient region that occupied much the same territory as modern Iraq. It was in Mesopotamia that the first urban cultures arose. Abundant archaeological findings provide evidence of the earliest processes in city development, and many cuneiform tablets provide information on later stages. Together these sources allow scholars to reconstruct the development of an urban society, an evolution that occurred over several millennia.

FOCUS

How do historians explain the rise of cities?

The Environmental Challenge

Southern Mesopotamia is an extremely arid region where rain alone is insufficient to grow crops. It is also very hot—regularly more than 120 degrees Fahrenheit in the summer—and lacks certain basic natural resources, including trees, metal, and hard stone for building. So southern Mesopotamia may seem like an unlikely region to develop the world's first urban culture—but it did, mainly due to the inhabitants' ingenuity in facing the region's challenges. Two major rivers ran through the countryside, the Tigris and Euphrates, and people invented irrigation agriculture to use them to water fields (see Map 2.1).

Geography and Climate

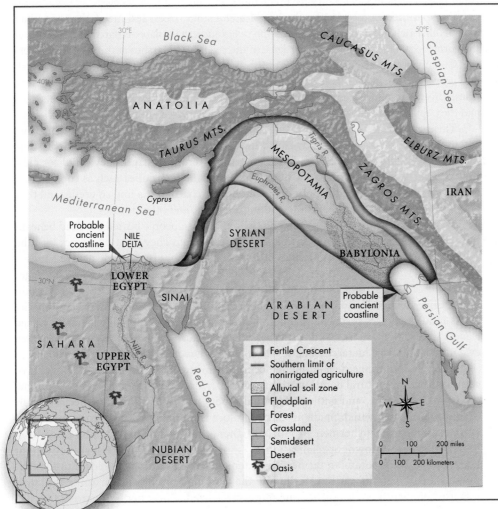

MAP 2.1

The Ecology of Southwest Asia

Southwest Asia, home to the earliest urban societies, includes many different ecological landscapes. In this map, the heavy line labeled "southern limit of non-irrigated agriculture" makes a critical distinction between zones that have enough rainfall for agriculture and zones where agriculture requires irrigation. In actuality, this boundary varies, depending on annual rainfall. It is clear, however, that the cultures of early Mesopotamia and Egypt developed where irrigation was always needed; ultimately, then, their rise depended on the Nile, Tigris, and Euphrates rivers.

By 8000 B.C.E., people in the Fertile Crescent zone of Southwest Asia had developed agriculture. The area had rich plant and animal life and rainfall sufficient to grow crops of wheat and barley. The early farmers kept domesticated animals such as cattle, sheep, goats, and pigs, which enabled them to reside year-round in villages with a few hundred inhabitants. Scholars speculate that some of them visited the arid areas nearby to graze herds and saw the opportunities this region provided—although rain was inadequate in Mesopotamia, the soil is extremely fertile. People discovered that when they guided water from the rivers into fields, barley grew abundantly. This simple innovation allowed farmers using irrigation to establish small villages throughout the southern Mesopotamian plain starting in around 5000 B.C.E.

Irrigation and Its Impact

Once they had invented the basic concept of irrigation, farmers dug canals to carry water over greater distances. But the construction and use of irrigation canals required planning and coordination. If farmers with fields near the head of the canal used too much water, those farther downstream could not irrigate their crops. Moreover, because flooding was a serious threat in the extremely flat Mesopotamian countryside, the canals and fields needed to be lined with strong dikes, which required maintenance. Such tasks demanded organization and cooperation in villages, as well as a system to resolve conflicts over water rights. From the very beginning, irrigation farming stimulated development of new forms of social organization and new connections among members of ancient communities.

Cooperation and Community Growth

Cooperation brought substantial benefits. In southern Mesopotamia, irrigation farmers could reap enormous yields and earn much more income than farmers elsewhere who relied on rainfall. Moreover, despite the absence of useful stone, trees, and metal, the region had several other rich natural resources. Near the rivers and canals, date orchards flourished, and they provided shade for vegetable gardens. In the rivers and marshes at the head of the Persian Gulf, inhabitants could catch loads of fish, as well as turtles, crabs, and water rats, which also provided protein. Herdsmen guided large flocks of sheep and goats to seasonal pastures. These diverse resources fueled the growth of larger communities and attracted outsiders, and the population of southern Mesopotamia rapidly increased after 5000 B.C.E.

Village Life and Social Development

The earliest settlers of Mesopotamia established villages like those of the surrounding Neolithic societies (see Chapter 1). All family members worked at agricultural tasks, some focusing on herding animals and others on growing crops. Because they cared for children, women were more tied to the house than men and had duties such as cooking and grinding grain. They made the pottery that modern archaeologists find so useful, and they wove sheep wool and goat's hair into clothing, blankets, and other textiles.

To maintain a close relationship with their ancestors, people buried the dead beneath the house floors and gave them food and drink offerings. They even dug pipes into the floors of houses to pour these offerings into the tombs. They also provided grave goods—items buried with the dead. These goods provide evidence of social change in the villages during the centuries from 5000 B.C.E. to the time of the origin of cities, 3200 B.C.E. Certain tombs came to include more and richer goods, indicating that their owners had a special status in life. Scholars speculate that communities gave these distinctive goods to village leaders who settled disputes and coordinated labor. Thus, even at this early stage, we see evidence of the social hierarchy that would come to characterize Mesopotamian cities.

Specialization of Labor

Another important development occurred during the same period. As we have seen, in early agricultural communities families performed all the tasks needed to grow crops, raise livestock, and gather additional food. Over time, however, **specialization of labor** developed, which made production more efficient. Specialist farmers, gardeners, herdsmen, and fishermen produced higher yields than families who undertook these tasks on their own. Specialization of labor also led to technological innovation. For example, Mesopotamian farmers invented a plow that dropped seeds into the furrows as it cut open the earth, speeding up the work of planting and ensuring that seed was used efficiently. As labor became more specialized, a new necessity arose: families

specialization of labor The organization of work such that individuals concentrate on specific tasks rather than engage in a variety of activities.

that were formerly self-sufficient had to trade to meet some of their basic needs. This crucial need for exchange was a major stimulus to the development of cities. People needed a central place to meet, a crossroads where they could connect with potential trading partners and exchange goods.

Many of the world's early urban cultures grew up in the valleys of mighty rivers, most notably in Mesopotamia along the Tigris and Euphrates, in Egypt along the Nile, in South Asia along the Indus, and in China along the Yellow (Huang He) and Yangzi rivers. With this in mind, many historians make a connection between irrigation agriculture and the centralized authority and social hierarchy typical of many ancient urban cultures. This line of argument suggests that irrigation depends on a strong central authority to coordinate its construction, use, and maintenance. Archaeological research does not, however, support this argument. Rather, the evidence shows that small communities initiated and maintained irrigation projects; centralized authority developed only long after such projects had begun. Nonetheless, it was the rich agricultural potential of the river valleys that led people in many parts of the world to establish densely populated urban centers.

River Valley Cultures

The First Cities   3200–1600 B.C.E

As we saw earlier, a crucial element in the definition of a city is that it serves communities in the surrounding countryside and that these communities provide goods to people in the city. The city is the center for many activities, including exchange of goods. Archaeological remains throughout Mesopotamia show that during the fourth millennium B.C.E. such central places grew increasingly large. This process culminated in around 3200 B.C.E. at Uruk—the home of Enmerkar in the Sumerian tale quoted at the start of the chapter (see again Mapping the World, pages 40 and 41). The population there became so large (perhaps thirty thousand individuals or more) and provided so many services to the surrounding region that we can consider it the first true city in world history.

> **FOCUS**
> How and why did the rise of the city lead to a more hierarchical society in early Mesopotamia?

Uruk exerted its influence in many ways. It was the economic hub for the exchange of goods and services. It was the religious center with temples for the gods. It was home to political and military powers who governed people, represented them in relations with others, and protected and controlled them.

Soon similar centers arose throughout southern Mesopotamia, organizing the inhabitants of cities and surrounding villages into the political structure historians call the city-state. In later centuries this form of political organization spread from Mesopotamia to the rest of Southwest Asia, characterizing the early history of the region from 3200 to 1600 B.C.E.

The Power of the Temple

What motivated the residents of Uruk and its surroundings to embrace the city as a hub of exchange? Dealing with the city could be inconvenient—for instance, the farmers, herders, fishermen, and others who delivered part of their products to the city sometimes had to wait several months for compensation. One reason they accepted the exchange arrangement was that it had the support of an ideology—that is, a set of ideas and values—to explain and justify it. That ideology was Mesopotamian religion.

In the center of Uruk was a gigantic temple complex, which must have required many community members to build and decorate. Not only did it house the city's gods and goddesses, but its staff also administered the economy. People contributed the products of their labor to the gods, whom they trusted to give something in return in the near or distant future. The head of the temple organization was the priest-king, the gods' representative on earth. A stone vase of the period, known as the Uruk vase, depicts the guiding

The Temple and Its Functions

The Uruk Vase

© Marc Van De Mieroop.

Archaeologists found this alabaster vase in the ruins of the Sumerian city of Uruk. It is over three feet high and dates to about 3200 B.C.E. Its surface is completely carved in an elaborate relief. Images in the bottom section represent the agriculture of the region; in the middle frame, a procession of naked men carry agricultural products in bowls, vessels, and baskets. The high point of the relief's story occurs in the top section, where a female figure faces the city's ruler. At some later date the ruler's depiction was cut out of the scene, but we can reconstruct his appearance from contemporaneous representations on other objects.

The female figure is the goddess Inanna, identified by the two symbols standing behind her, which were the basis for writing Inanna's name in later cuneiform script. Beyond those symbols are three animals amid storage jars for liquids and solid foods. Two small human figures, probably statues, stand on pedestals. The statue of the woman has the symbol of Inanna behind her. The statue of the man holding in his hands a stack of bowls and something like a box; bowls and box together form the shape of the cuneiform sign for "lord" in Sumerian. Scholars believe that sign, the most common in tablets from the period, indicates the highest temple official.

Uruk Vase (Bildarchiv Preussischer Kulturbesitz/Art Resource, NY.)

EXAMINING THE EVIDENCE

1. What does the relief on the vase tell us about the resources of the Uruk region?

2. What is the relationship among common people, secular ruler, and deity as expressed in this relief?

3. How can we interpret this relief as representing the ruling ideology of the time?

Ubaid and Uruk Pottery

Because archaeologists can see clear distinctions among pottery vessels from different periods, they rely on pottery to date the other remains they excavate. Production techniques can reveal other features of the potter's culture as well. Compare the two bowls here. The potter used great care to shape and decorate the one on the left, from the Ubaid period in the fifth millennium B.C.E. The bowl on the right, from the later Uruk period of the fourth millennium B.C.E., was made very quickly and left undecorated, demonstrating the ancient origin of mass production. (Réunion des Musées Nationaux/Art Resource, NY (right) and Image copyright © The Metropolitan Museum of Art/Art Resource, NY (left).)

ideology (see Seeing the Past: The Uruk Vase). Uruk's main goddess, Inanna, received the agricultural products of her people with the city-ruler as intermediary. In return, as the goddess of procreation, Inanna was expected to guarantee fertility and bountiful crops. Thus, city and country were connected by a divine cycle of exchange that benefited both.

Like almost all other ancient peoples, the Mesopotamians honored numerous deities, a system we call **polytheism**. Their gods and goddesses mostly represented aspects of the natural environment. There was a god of the sky, An; of the moon, Nanna; of grain, Ashnan; and many more. Some deities were the patrons of occupations, such as Dumuzi, the god of herding. Others were responsible for abstract concepts: the sun god, Utu, oversaw justice, and Inanna was the goddess of fertility, love, and war.

Every important deity was the patron of a specific city, which was the god or goddess's residence on earth. The Mesopotamians believed the gods controlled every aspect of their lives and were the source of all good and bad fortune. Literary compositions from later centuries sometimes expressed much pessimism about the gods' plans for humans. Their decisions were inscrutable, and life often seemed meaningless. Yet the Mesopotamians also believed they could encourage the gods to be kind through offerings and prayers, and one of their great preoccupations was to discover divine plans for the future (see Chapter 4).

The rise of the city had fundamental consequences for all the local people living in the vicinity; every aspect of life became more complex. In economic terms, specialization of labor soon extended beyond agriculture. The farming sector produced a surplus that could support people who were not farmers. Previously, for example, women had woven clothing for their families, but this task became the full-time occupation of teams of women who received food as compensation. Artisans in temple workshops worked faster and turned out standardized products. We see this in Uruk's pottery—archaeologists have excavated thousands of vessels produced by stamping clay into a mold and baking it. These simple bowls are very different from the wheel-made and painted vessels of the preceding centuries, which took much longer to make and varied in size and decoration. Thus, urbanization and the labor specialization changed the focus of Mesopotamian economic life. Instead of working to meet the needs of a self-sufficient family, people increasingly produced goods and services for a growing commercial marketplace.

Mesopotamian Gods and Goddesses

Expanded Specialization of Labor

polytheism A religious system that accepts the existence of many gods.

Crafts and Trade

Mesopotamian crafts and trade reflected this trend toward expanding economic connections. Artisans manufactured not only practical items but also luxury products using exotic materials from abroad. Merchants attached to the temple sometimes imported these materials from very distant regions. Mesopotamians prized the semiprecious blue stone lapis lazuli (LAP-is LAZ-uh-lee) for their jewelry. They could obtain it only through trade contacts with the mountain regions of modern Afghanistan, more than fifteen hundred miles away, yet substantial amounts appear in the archaeological record. They also imported copper from what is today the country of Oman in the Persian Gulf and tin from present-day Iran (see Map 2.2). Mixed together, copper and tin produce bronze, which is much more durable and versatile than the stone and copper earlier people had used to make tools. That this new metal was invented soon after the first cities arose is no surprise. Only cities had the collective resources to coordinate the import of ingredients from two separate distant sources. Cities became crossroads not only for their immediate surroundings, but for the people and products of different societies.

Uruk at Its Height

By 3200 B.C.E. Uruk was a fully developed city. It had many inhabitants, some of whom had great power over others and controlled much wealth. Its temple buildings were monumental in size, and its artisans had sophisticated skills that required much training. Uruk's residents greatly valued the building projects and the splendor of the city's art. In that sense they resembled many other people throughout history, who devoted much energy and wealth to show off their success. Other regions in Mesopotamia quickly developed cities as well. In their early history, the temple was the center of power, but this was soon to change.

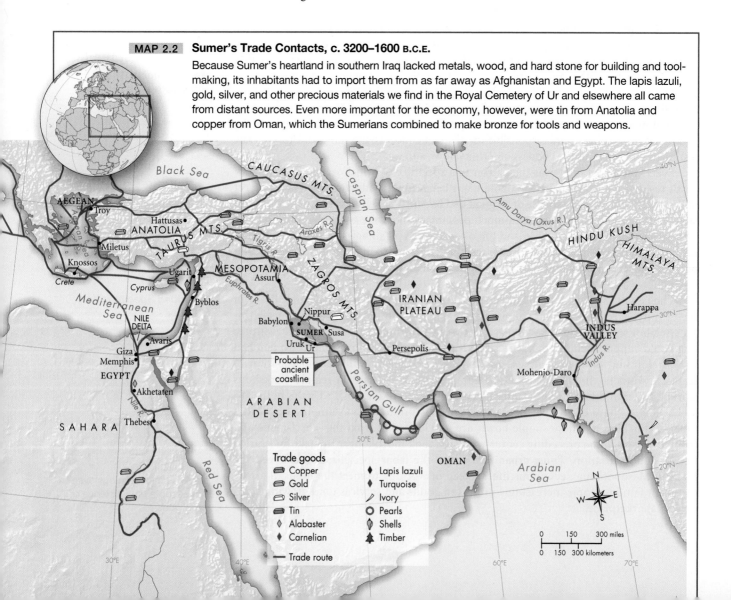

MAP 2.2 **Sumer's Trade Contacts, c. 3200–1600 B.C.E.**

Because Sumer's heartland in southern Iraq lacked metals, wood, and hard stone for building and tool-making, its inhabitants had to import them from as far away as Afghanistan and Egypt. The lapis lazuli, gold, silver, and other precious materials we find in the Royal Cemetery of Ur and elsewhere all came from distant sources. Even more important for the economy, however, were tin from Anatolia and copper from Oman, which the Sumerians combined to make bronze for tools and weapons.

Royal Inscriptions from Early Mesopotamia

Inscriptions carved on stone or pressed into clay first appeared in southern Mesopotamia in around 2500 B.C.E. They honor the king's military feats and his patronage of public works, such as the construction of temples and irrigation canals. The inscriptions tie the king closely to the gods of the city, who are sometimes represented as his physical parents or as his caretakers in his youth. One such king was Eanatum of Lagash, who in around 2450 B.C.E. left several such inscriptions, among them the following example.

> For the god Ningirsu—Eanatum, ruler of Lagash, whom the god Enlil named, whom the god Ningirsu gave strength, whom the god Nanshe selected, whom the goddess Ninhursag nourished with good milk, whom the goddess Inanna gave a good name, whom the god Enki gave wisdom, whom the god Dumuzi'abzu loves, whom the god Hendursag trusts, son of Akurgal, ruler of Lagash, restored the city Girsu for the god Ningirsu and built the wall of the city Uruku for him. For the god Nanshe he built the city Nina.
>
> Eanatum . . . defeated the city Umma, and made twenty burial mounds for it. He gave back to the god Ningirsu the Gu'edena, his beloved field. He defeated the city Uruk, he defeated the city Ur, and he defeated the city Kiutu. He sacked the city Uruaz and killed its ruler. He sacked the city Mishime and he destroyed the city Arua. All the foreign lands trembled before Eanatum, named by the god Ningirsu. When the king of the city Akshak rebelled, Eanatum, named by the god Ningirsu, removed him from the Antasura-field of the god Ningirsu and destroyed the city Akshak.
>
> After all that, Eanatum dug a new canal for the god Ningirsu.

Source: J. S. Cooper, trans., *Sumerian and Akkadian Royal Inscriptions* (New Haven: American Oriental Society, 1986), 1:42–43.

EXAMINING THE EVIDENCE

1. How does King Eanatum establish his relationship with various gods?

2. What are his achievements, according to this text?

3. What does the inscription reveal about the relationship among Mesopotamian city-states?

The Might of the Palace

Rise of Militarism

From its beginnings, the ideology of urban power had a military dimension, as evidenced by early art that shows the priest-king in battle or inspecting bound prisoners. But before 3000 B.C.E., artists emphasized nonmilitary functions. That imagery changed, however, as multiple urban centers emerged alongside Uruk, often as little as twenty miles apart. These cities housed fast-growing populations who needed ever-larger agricultural zones for food, and when both sides claimed an area their demands led to battles. In around 3000 B.C.E., the basis of power in cities began to shift from religion to the military. Neighboring city-states fought wars over territory and resources, and military leaders gained prominence, finally taking full control over political life; they absorbed some earlier religious functions as well. In archaeological sites, we see this change in the appearance of palaces next to temples and in massive walls built to protect cities. Increasingly, Mesopotamian cities were connected to one another primarily by conflict and war.

Royal Dynasties

Temples remained important institutions in Mesopotamian cities, and military leaders used them to legitimize their own rule. They created hereditary **dynasties**, that is, successions of rulers who belonged to different generations of the same family, claiming that the gods had chosen them to lead their city. In around 2450 B.C.E. Eanatum (AI-an-na-TOMB), king of Lagash, for example, declared that several gods had selected and nurtured him to lead his city in war, especially against the neighboring city of Umma. Both cities wanted control of an agricultural zone and repeatedly fought wars over it. Eanatum claimed his victory was a result of the gods' favor (see Reading the Past: Royal Inscriptions from Early Mesopotamia).

dynasty A succession of rulers from the same family.

Militarism thus became a fundamental element of political power and a driving force behind historical change in Mesopotamia. Many other ancient cultures repeated this pattern, including China and Rome. Each Mesopotamian city-state had an army commanded by its king, who consolidated his power at home and abroad through warfare. Some rulers grew so powerful that they could claim the lives of others for their own benefit. In around 2400 B.C.E., members of the royal house of Ur demanded that human attendants and soldiers accompany them to the afterlife. In a few tombs of the Royal Cemetery of Ur, occupants were surrounded by incredible luxuries, such as golden helmets, daggers, and inlaid musical instruments—and by the bodies of dozens of sacrificed men and women. Other rulers took their special connections to the divine world to a different extreme, professing to be gods themselves. Some kings had temples constructed in their own honor. These practices of human sacrifice and divine kingship were short-lived, however, and for most of Mesopotamian history kings were considered mortal representatives of the gods on earth. Nonetheless, these examples of extreme claims to power reflect a general trend toward the concentration of political authority in the hands of a single individual or family.

The political situation became more complex throughout Southwest Asia as a variety of peoples with different cultures and languages developed city-states. People who spoke Sumerian lived primarily in the far south of Mesopotamia. In the rest of the region they spoke mostly Akkadian, a Semitic language related to Hebrew and Arabic, and in Syria and western Iran people communicated in other Semitic and non-Semitic languages. For close to fifteen hundred years, from 3000 to 1600 B.C.E., the city-states of Southwest Asia were regularly in conflict. Some energetic rulers and dynasties gained great fame for conquering large territories. The dynasty of Akkad, the Akkadian-speaking ruler Sargon and his successors, dominated Mesopotamia from about 2350 to 2200 B.C.E. According to later traditions, the conquests of glorious Akkadian warriors reached the edges of the earth. The Sumerian dynasty of Ur was also famous; in the twenty-first century B.C.E. it imposed its rule over all of southern Mesopotamia.

Attempts at unification through conquest culminated in the eighteenth century B.C.E., when Hammurabi (r. 1792–1750 B.C.E.) created a large state around the city of Babylon. He molded southern Mesopotamia into a single political unit, which fundamentally shifted the base of power from the city-state to the territorial state. Although Hammurabi's kingdom soon disintegrated, the territorial state, not the city, would be the most important unit of political power in Southwest Asia during the second half of the second millennium B.C.E.

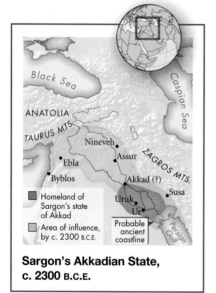

Sargon's Akkadian State, c. 2300 B.C.E.

The New Order of Society

Social Divisions and Political Centralization

Throughout history urban societies have differed radically from village communities in terms of social structure. Urban societies have a hierarchy of power based on professional specialization, with a small, but powerful elite. In the earliest Mesopotamian cities, as we have seen, priests monopolized political power. After 3000 B.C.E. military leaders, whom we call kings, replaced priests as city leaders. Palace households, including military commanders and administrators, supported the kings.

As in any ancient society, the great majority of people in Mesopotamia spent most of their energy producing food: they farmed, herded, hunted, and fished and often lived in outlying villages. But because they depended on the city's central institutions, its temples and palace, their lives differed from those of their ancestors who never experienced cities. As part of a large social structure, they had both responsibilities and benefits. They had to provide assistance to the state, usually through agricultural labor, but also through participating in building projects and military campaigns. In return, they counted on material support from the state.

A special characteristic of early Mesopotamian society is the ration system. Every man, woman, and child who depended on the central institutions received predetermined amounts of barley, oil, and wool. The amounts depended on one's status and gender. Leaders received larger payments than their supporters, and men received more than women. Despite its inequities, the system offered a safety net for individuals in economic trouble. It also helped widows and orphans who had no family support. Everyone but the old had to work, however, to qualify for these rations. This system of rations thus reflected both Mesopotamian social structure and Mesopotamian religious beliefs, with their emphasis on cycles of offerings and rewards. People worked for the city and, in exchange, the city rewarded them in proportion to their perceived contribution to the general well-being.

Kings came to play a key role in maintaining the health of this exchange society. If the powerful completely ignored the needs of those below them in society, the whole system would collapse. In early Mesopotamia, priests helped to prevent such imbalance by controlling the cycle of exchange, which centered on temples. With the growth of secular power (that is, worldly rather than religious authority), it became part of royal ideology that kings should protect the weak. The earliest written records of royal activities already express this idea. King Uruinimgina (ou-ROU-e-NIM-ge-na) of Lagash, for example, stated that he "promised the god Ningirsu [NEHN-gihr-su] that he would never subjugate the orphan and the widow to the powerful." He also gave examples of how he protected the rights of his subjects:

> When the house of a member of the elite borders on the house of a royal servant, and the member of the elite says to him: "I want to buy it from you," whether he answers: "When you buy it, pay me the price that I want" or "You cannot buy it," the member of the elite cannot hit the royal servant in anger.[2]

Treasure from the Royal Cemetery of Ur

The treasures from the royal cemetery of Ur show the massive wealth of those buried in the tombs as well as the superior craftsmanship of Sumerian artisans. This eighteen-inch-tall ram is standing on its hind legs to eat the leaves of a tree. Its creator used gold leaf for the head and legs, copper for the ears, lapis lazuli for the horns and shoulder fleece, and shells for the body fleece. These precious materials were imported from distant regions. (© The Trustees of The British Museum/Art Resource, NY.)

The idea that a good king guaranteed justice to his people remained part of Mesopotamian ideology for many centuries. Its most elaborate expression appeared in the laws of Hammurabi of Babylon. Carved on a seven-and-a-half-foot tall stone stele are some three hundred laws, all phrased in the same two-part form: an "if" action followed by consequences. The phrasing of the statements suggests general rules that judges needed to follow in court cases, but they are not abstract statements of principles. In cases of physical injury, for example, several laws describe distinct body parts:

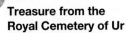

Laws of Hammurabi

> If a member of the elite blinds the eye of another member of the elite, they shall blind his eye. If he breaks the bone of another member of the elite, they shall break his bone (§§ 196-197).[3]

The concept underlying this system of justice is one of retribution: an eye for an eye, a tooth for a tooth. Hammurabi's law code was more complex than this, however, and penalties were related to the social structure. Only when a victim and a transgressor were of the same social level was the punishment equal. When the victim was of a lower class, a monetary fine was imposed:

> If a member of the elite hits an elite woman, and causes her to miscarry her fetus, he shall pay 80 grams of silver for her fetus. Should that woman die, they will kill his daughter. If he causes a woman of the commoner class to miscarry her fetus, he shall pay 40 grams of silver. Should that woman die, he shall pay 240 grams of silver. If he hits a slave woman, and causes her to miscarry her fetus, he shall pay 16 grams of silver. Should that slave woman die, he shall pay 160 grams of silver. (§§ 209–214)[4]

If the victim was of a higher status than the transgressor, the punishment was more severe:

> If a member of the elite strikes the cheek of a member of the elite who is of a higher social status than him, he shall be flogged in public with sixty strikes of an ox whip. (§ 202)[5]

Hammurabi's laws and other contemporary sources indicate clearly that Mesopotamian society was a **patriarchy**: women were always subject to a man, at first their father, and then their husband. They moved from the father's house to the husband's upon marriage. A man could even sell his wife into servitude to pay off a debt. Women were somewhat protected, however. The wife's dowry was her own and could not be taken away upon divorce. A man could marry several women, but the woman's wealth went to her natural children alone. When a soldier went missing during a military campaign, his wife could remarry if she was unable to support herself. Some Babylonian women had considerable property that they could manage without the interference of their fathers or husbands. While their status was certainly below that of men, they had more rights and protection than women in many other ancient societies.

When Hammurabi set up his stele, he wanted to express how just his rule was. He stated its purpose as follows:

> In order that the mighty not wrong the weak, to provide just ways for the orphan and the widow, I have inscribed my precious pronouncements upon my stele and set it up before the statue of me, the king of justice, in the city of Babylon, the city which the gods Anu and Enlil have elevated, within the Esagila, the temple whose foundations are fixed as are heaven and earth, in order to render the judgments of the land, to give verdicts of the land, and to provide just ways for the wronged.[6]

Although protecting the weak was a central part of the ideology of power in Hammurabi's Babylon, that does not mean it was a society of equals. As we have seen, Babylonian law recognized and codified great inequalities rooted in gender and social status. When the number of people living together increased, social inequalities increased, and the new urban society that developed in Mesopotamia had a clear social hierarchy.

Hammurabi's Stele

This tall stone pillar is one of several that Hammurabi set up throughout his kingdom to proclaim his famous laws. The top of the monument shows the king receiving symbols of justice from the seated sun god. More striking is the lengthy, carefully carved inscription, which lists some three hundred laws and presents Hammurabi as a just ruler who protects the people of his land. (Réunion des Musées Nationaux/Art Resource, NY.)

City Life and Learning

FOCUS

Why did ancient peoples develop writing systems, and what has been the enduring impact of this invention on intellectual expression?

The rise of cities also fundamentally changed how humanity expressed itself intellectually. The invention of writing—the ability to express thoughts in a permanent form—was an enduring contribution of the first citizens of Mesopotamia. Because writing and reading required a group of well-trained specialists, it remained an urban phenomenon for all of Mesopotamian history. These specialists were relatively few in number, but they left us innumerable rich examples of the literature and scholarship of the time.

The Invention of Writing

Probably the most famous writings from ancient Mesopotamia today are the Laws of Hammurabi we just discussed, or tales such as the *Epic of Gilgamesh* (see page 55), but script was not invented to write down those types of texts. The need for writing derived from the urban economy, which had become increasingly complex and required a system of record keeping. Administrators had to keep track of income and expenditures, and they needed a means of reviewing transactions that involved large quantities of goods. To address this need, an anonymous group (or perhaps even an individual) in Sumer developed a revolutionary invention: writing. Writing requires a connection between spoken language and the symbols written down. It enables someone who was not present to reconstruct events from the written account alone. The challenge to its inventors was to represent oral expression in graphic form.

The Sumerian epic tale about the origins of writing at the beginning of this chapter does not address this challenge of translating spoken words into written symbols. It merely explains in mythic terms the physical characteristics of writing: the clay tablet into which cuneiform signs were pressed. Clay tablets did indeed appear with the emergence of the first city, Uruk, around 3200 B.C.E. They were pillow-shaped objects a person could hold in one hand. Scribes traced two types of signs with a reed stylus on them: numbers and word-signs.

The earliest scribes were mainly accountants, and it is no surprise that numbers were the most common characters on the first tablets. The tablets demonstrate that the Sumerians knew how to work with very large numbers and that they had a fully developed system of weights and measures. They counted, weighed, and indicated the values of a great variety of items, registering the names with a set of signs understood by everyone who handled the records. In the earliest stage of writing, each word was represented with one sign. It could be a graphic representation of the entire item, such as a drawing of a fish for the word *fish*, or of an emblematic part, such as the head of an ox for the word *ox*. The sign could also be purely abstract, such as a circle with a cross for *a sheep*. It was also crucial that written records express actions. For this purpose, the writers logically extended the meaning of items that they could draw. For example, the foot could communicate the verb *to go*. Sometimes they used similarities in sounds to make the drawing of an object represent an action. A word pronounced *ti* meant both *arrow* and *to receive* in Sumerian. Scribes thus could use the arrow sign to indicate the action of receiving.

The inventors of the script used these techniques to develop an inventory of signs that reproduced the Sumerian language they spoke. The earliest version of the script had some 950 signs and was difficult to use because each sign represented a separate word. In succeeding centuries, the script changed to make it easier to use and more adaptable to the spoken language. The signs developed from elaborate drawings to a handful of straight lines made by pushing a small piece of reed into the clay. The use of reeds created the impression of a wedge, a triangular head joined to a thin line, which inspired the modern name of the script, *cuneiform*, wedge-shaped (see Figure 2.1).

Soon the scribes invented signs that represented not only entire words but the sounds of syllables. This allowed them to reduce the number of signs in the script, because a limited number of syllable signs could be used to form many words; each word no longer required a distinct sign. A further benefit of the increased flexibility of script was that scribes could write down languages other than Sumerian. Throughout the long history of cuneiform, people used it to record many languages, not only in Mesopotamia but in neighboring regions. The cuneiform script was undoubtedly one of Sumer's most influential cultural exports, and it dominated written culture in Southwest Asia for some three thousand years.

After the Sumerians invented script in around 3200 B.C.E. other cultures independently came up with different writing systems: the Egyptians in around 3000 B.C.E., the Chinese after 2000 B.C.E., the Zapotecs (sah-po-TEHK) after 400 B.C.E., and many others

patriarchy A social system in which men hold all authority within the family and transfer their powers and possessions from father to son.

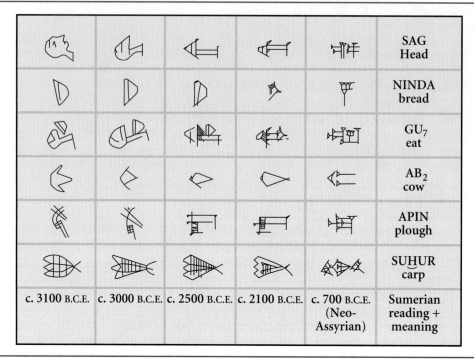

FIGURE 2.1

Cuneiform Writing

The earliest known form of writing originated in Sumer around 3200 B.C.E., when people began linking meaning and sound to signs such as these. Cuneiform was used for numerous ancient Middle Eastern languages and continued to be written for three thousand years.

					Sumerian reading + meaning
					SAG Head
					NINDA bread
					GU₇ eat
					AB₂ cow
					APIN plough
					SUHUR carp
c. 3100 B.C.E.	c. 3000 B.C.E.	c. 2500 B.C.E.	c. 2100 B.C.E.	c. 700 B.C.E. (Neo-Assyrian)	Sumerian reading + meaning

throughout history. Often they started out with very pictorial systems that became more schematic over time. Scholars in each case debate what motivated people to invent writing. Some say the Egyptians intended to honor their kings and the Chinese were primarily concerned with oracles, for example, but the economic needs that arose with the birth of urban societies seem to have been the main inspiration in most cases. Whatever the motivation for its invention, writing vastly increased the power of communication in the societies that possessed it. Written documents allowed ideas and information to be preserved and disseminated in ways that were previously impossible. Further, they created a community of readers who shared a familiarity with common texts, texts written by authors of both their generation and generations before. In this way, written documents created connections that were crucial to the expansion of knowledge.

INVENTION OF WRITING SYSTEMS

c. 3200 B.C.E.	Mesopotamian cuneiform
c. 3000 B.C.E.	Egyptian hieroglyphs
c. 2600 B.C.E.	Indus Valley script
c. 2000–1200 B.C.E.	Chinese writing
c. 1850 B.C.E.	Cretan Linear A
c. 1800 B.C.E.	Earliest alphabetic script, western Syria
c. 400 B.C.E.	Mesoamerican glyphs

The Expansion of Knowledge

Although scribes originally wrote for the practical purpose of administering the complex economies of urban societies, they soon extended writing into all spheres of life. Kings commissioned inscriptions

First Literature   carved in stone to proudly proclaim their accomplishments as military leaders, builders, and caretakers of their people. Hammurabi's law code is a prime example. They also encouraged the creation of poetry, at first to sing praise to themselves and to the gods and heroes of the past. In the third millennium B.C.E. poetry was almost exclusively written in Sumerian, which people of the time regarded as the language of high culture. Most authors remain unknown because they did not sign their works, but there are a few remarkable exceptions. The earliest known author of world literature is Princess Enheduanna (ehn-hoo-DWAHN-ah), the daughter of King Sargon. In the twenty-fourth century B.C.E. she composed a long plea to the goddess Inanna to reinstate her as high priestess of the city Ur after her father's enemy had deposed her:

> He stood there in triumph and drove me out of the temple. He made me fly like a swallow from the window; I have exhausted my life-strength. He made me walk through the thorn bushes of the mountains. He stripped me of the rightful crown of the *en* priestess. He gave me a knife and a dagger, saying to me: "These are the appropriate ornaments for you."[7]

Inanna accepted her prayer and restored Enheduanna to her former status:

> The powerful lady, respected in the gathering of rulers, has accepted her offerings from her. Inanna's holy heart has been assuaged. The light was sweet for her, delight extended over her, she was full of fairest beauty. Like the light of the rising moon, she exuded delight.[8]

Students, mostly the sons of priests but also some girls, copied out these poems and many others. Archaeologists have found thousands of tablets containing their work, including some that described a typical schoolboy's day. A master and his assistant (who did not spare the cane) closely supervised the student, who copied out increasingly difficult and long texts: lists of cuneiform signs, words, short compositions, and excerpts and finally the full text of literary compositions.

We have a detailed view of the teaching profession from a set of cuneiform tablets dated from 1821 to 1789 B.C.E. that document the activities of Ku-Ningal, a schoolmaster who taught in his house near the main temple in the city Ur. He lived in a neighborhood densely populated with people attached to the temple as priests and administrators. Ku-Ningal's family were the temple archivists for at least three generations. In addition to working as an archivist, Ku-Ningal taught his neighbors' children to write. His house was small, with less than eleven hundred square feet of living space, so he probably offered instruction to only a few students at a time. He was relatively wealthy, however, and documents found in the house reveal that he acquired meadows outside the city and expanded his dwelling slightly by buying parts of his next-door neighbor's house. In his home he kept literary manuscripts, copies of royal inscriptions, mathematical texts, and lists of words students had to reproduce. Ku-Ningal may have had literary talents himself and probably composed a hymn in honor of the king, copies of which were found in his house. Thus, writing was the central activity of Ku-Ningal's profession, a skill he passed on to others, and a means of self-expression.

The early second millennium B.C.E. brought the beginnings of literature written in Akkadian, including compositions that would later become famous. Among them was an early form of the *Epic of Gilgamesh*, which describes the hero's search for immortality. Gilgamesh (GIHL-gah-mehsh) was a king of Uruk—the third successor of Enmerkar of the epic at the start of this chapter—who saw his friend Enkidu die and refused to accept that fate for himself. He traveled to the edge of the world to find the only humans to whom the gods had given immortality: Utnapishtim (UHT-nuh-PISH-teem) and his wife, who had

Mesopotamian Mathematical Tablet

Mesopotamian mathematical knowledge, famous in its day, was highly developed, as tablets used in teaching show. This one, from around 1800 B.C.E., asks the student to find the length and width of a rectangle, given the diagonal and area. Students who graduated became the accountants needed to keep track of Mesopotamia's extensive economic activity. (David Lees/CORBIS.)

survived a universal flood. A woman he met on his travels told Gilgamesh, "When the gods created humankind, they gave death to humans and kept life for themselves."

Gilgamesh's search was ultimately futile because physical immortality cannot be attained. But eternal fame is possible. If one's deeds are recorded, they will be remembered forever, something that writing can assure. In that way, Gilgamesh did succeed.

Mesopotamian Mathematics

Schoolboys also had to study mathematics, and they did so in the same way they learned language, by copying out increasingly complex texts. They started with standard lists of capacity, weight, area, length, division, and multiplication. Then they moved to mathematical problems formulated in words, such as how to determine the height of a pile of grain based on its circumference and shape. Early Mesopotamian mathematics was highly developed and had a lasting impact on world history. Its basis was a mix of the decimal (base-10) and sexagesimal (base-6) systems. The numbers 6, 60, 360, and so on, indicated new units of measure. This convention still influences us today; it is why, for example, 60 minutes make an hour and 360 degrees a full circle.

The First International Order 1600–1200 B.C.E.

FOCUS

What were the main features of the first international order, and what developments explain its rise and fall?

No state exists in isolation. Throughout world history we see many moments when contacts between neighboring states produced similarities in political and social structures. Such was the case from 1600 to 1200 B.C.E. in Southwest Asia and adjacent regions, where an international system of states developed. Although these states had similar social organization and culture and exerted increasing influence on one another, they remained distinct. Their close connections did not end their capacity to produce independent innovations.

From City-States to Territorial States in the Eastern Mediterranean

As we have seen, from the beginning of urbanism in 3200 to 1600 B.C.E., the city-state had been the dominant form of political organization throughout Southwest Asia. After 1600 B.C.E., however, a new political order emerged in the region, one characterized by **territorial states**. Territorial states controlled much larger landmasses and included several dependent cities. The king controlled his territory through a hierarchy of officials, governors, and others, who were personally beholden to him. The fact that kings could, and did, move their capitals from city to city within their realms underscores the political shift that had taken place. The primary focus of political loyalty was now the ruler, not the city.

In the centuries between 1600 and 1200 B.C.E, territorial states existed from western Iran to the Aegean Sea and from the Black Sea to south of Egypt (see Map 2.3). The elites who ruled these states knew they belonged to a collective system and maintained constant contact with one another. The development of their individual states became intertwined and an international system emerged that bound them in a shared history. Yet as we will see, the region was very diverse in every respect, including ecology, economy, political organization, and culture.

The Minoans and the Mycenaeans

On the western edge of this international system was the Bronze Age Aegean world, which historians know primarily from archaeological material. Since about 7000 B.C.E. agricultural societies had populated the Greek mainland and the Aegean islands. For millennia, people from the region had traded materials such as the volcanic stone obsidian, which could be made into cutting tools. Different regions had held on to their own cultural traditions, however, and in the second millennium B.C.E. these traditions coalesced into two main cultures: the Minoan, centered on the island of Crete, and the Mycenaean, which flourished in southern mainland Greece.

Minoan Cretan society revolved around palaces, which served as the economic hubs of larger regions. Best known is the palace at Knossos (K-NOSS-oss), a sprawling building centered on a large open court and decorated with colorful wall paintings. Unlike

territorial state A centralized form of political organization that unites inhabitants of an often large geographical area.

Linear A The administrative writing system of the Minoans, which is still not deciphered.

The Minoan Palace at Knossos

This is the throne room from the palace at Knossos, built in around 1450 B.C.E., and much restored after excavations by Sir Arthur Evans at the start of the twentieth century. It vividly illustrates aspects of Minoan culture. The colorful wall paintings show mystical creatures, griffins, beside an alabaster throne in front of a central fireplace. Scholars debate the function of this room, but all agree it must have been central to palace life at the time. (David Porges/Peter Arnold Images/Photolibrary.)

Mesopotamian palaces, the Knossos building and other Cretan palaces lacked defensive structures, which suggests that warfare played a small role in this society. The palaces did share important qualities with Mesopotamian cities, however. Like those cities, Cretan palaces served as crossroads, places where people collected and exchanged resources such as grain, wine, and oil. The Cretans kept track of the exchanges that took place in the palace with an as-yet-undeciphered writing system called **Linear A**. Although the signs in the Linear A system do not resemble those of Southwest Asia at all, they were traced onto clay tablets in imitation of the cuneiform records. Crete's central location in the northeastern Mediterranean gave it a prominent role in maritime trade, making it a regional crossroads. People of the island shipped goods as far away as Sicily and Egypt.

But its apparent prosperity did not protect Crete from disaster. Although it was spared the endemic warfare that characterized Mesopotamia, Crete fell victim to a natural catastrophe. Around 1650 B.C.E. a volcanic eruption on the island of Santorini (ancient Thera) created a tsunami that may have destroyed most of the palaces on Crete.

On the southern and eastern mainland of Greece a very different tradition developed. People here built fortresses, such as Mycenae (my-SEE-nee) and Tiryns (TIHR-ihnz), constructed with stones so large that later Greeks thought only giants could have built them. Nearby burials contained great riches, including weapons, golden masks, and jewelry. Around 1450 B.C.E., the people of this world, the Mycenaeans, expanded their influence throughout the Aegean Sea, including Crete, where all the palaces except Knossos had disappeared. The regional economic activity of the Mycenaeans was focused on fortresses, from which officials

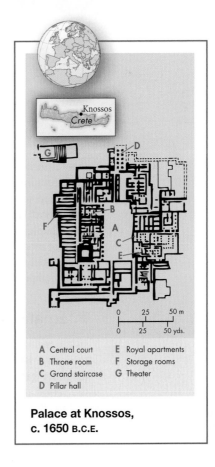

A Central court	E Royal apartments
B Throne room	F Storage rooms
C Grand staircase	G Theater
D Pillar hall	

Palace at Knossos, c. 1650 B.C.E.

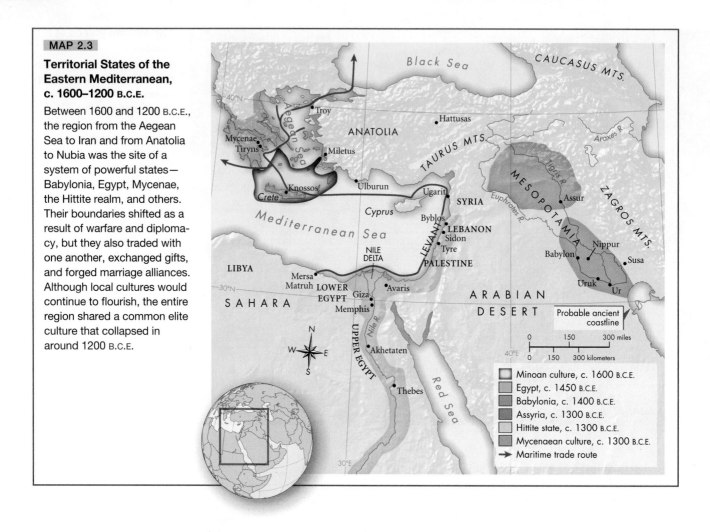

MAP 2.3

Territorial States of the Eastern Mediterranean, c. 1600–1200 B.C.E.

Between 1600 and 1200 B.C.E., the region from the Aegean Sea to Iran and from Anatolia to Nubia was the site of a system of powerful states—Babylonia, Egypt, Mycenae, the Hittite realm, and others. Their boundaries shifted as a result of warfare and diplomacy, but they also traded with one another, exchanged gifts, and forged marriage alliances. Although local cultures would continue to flourish, the entire region shared a common elite culture that collapsed in around 1200 B.C.E.

controlled agriculture and craft production. Scribes recorded activities on clay tablets incised with a script that scholars call **Linear B**.

Linear B tablets do not reveal much about the social and political organization of this area, but they do mention a number of political and military titles, including one, *wanax*, that historians interpret as "ruler." The fortresses probably housed military leaders and their entourages, and Mycenae probably had several coexisting rulers. It seems likely, too, that rulers joined in alliances and accepted one man among them as overlord. The famous Greek poet Homer portrayed this world in the epics he wrote in the eighth century B.C.E. (see Chapter 5). His *Iliad* tells how Greeks joined forces to attack Troy, a city on the west coast of modern Turkey, under the leadership of Agamemnon. Although Homer certainly interpreted what were even in his time events from a distant past, his depiction may reflect the actual political situation in the Mycenaean world.

International Relations

In the regional system of the eastern Mediterranean, state relations ranged from peaceful to hostile. Because power in all of these states was based on military achievement, campaigning was a normal part of every king's career. Scholars could write the entire history of the period as a sequence of battles and conquests, because these are the focus of the ancient record. But kings, courtiers, and others had peaceful international contacts as well. The region's states were connected by competition and conflict, but they were also bound together by important diplomatic and economic ties.

Linear B The administrative writing system of the Mycenaeans, used to record an early form of the Greek language.

In around 1600 B.C.E., the introduction of the horse-drawn chariot fundamentally changed warfare in Southwest Asia. Previously, chariots had been heavy and slow, pulled by oxen and donkeys, but the use of fast, light vehicles allowed warriors to move rapidly over the battlefield. The equipment was expensive, however, and charioteers needed special training. The mass of the armies consisted largely of infantrymen, mostly farmers and others who performed military service for their states. Official inscriptions report on numerous battles and regularly boast about how many opponents were killed and captured. They glorify the king's success in war, but historians should remember that warfare caused misery for many. The official inscriptions and new nature of warfare both reflect the increasingly hierarchical nature of militarized Southwest Asia.

At the same time, however, diplomatic activity thrived. Kings exchanged letters, which scribes all over Southwest Asia wrote in Mesopotamian cuneiform on clay tablets. The letters show that the kings traded valuables to reinforce friendly relations based on mutual respect. The Egyptians mostly offered gold, on which they had a monopoly. In return, they received expensive items from other countries, such as copper from Cyprus or lapis lazuli that the Babylonians imported from Afghanistan. They also exchanged women, and many princesses married foreign kings. The Egyptians did not reciprocate in this respect, however. They loved to receive princesses from abroad but never gave one of their own in return. This angered other kings, who complained bitterly about it in writing.

Women of the courts, especially queens, were also in contact with one another during this era. We know of several letters that Egypt's Queen Nefertari (nehf-uhr-TAHR-ee) wrote Queen Puduhepa (Poo-doo-KHE-pa) in the thirteenth century B.C.E. Puduhepa was queen of the Hittite state that dominated modern-day central Turkey and northern Syria. Both writers were powerful women, and it is no surprise that they conducted their own diplomacy. They called each other "sister" to indicate their equal status, as if they were all part of the same large family.

> Thus speaks Nefertari, the great queen of Egypt, to Puduhepa, the great queen of the Hittites: My sister, I am well and my country is well. May you, my sister, be well and may your country be well. I have heard that you, my sister, have written to me to inquire about my well-being and that you write to me because of the peaceful relations and the good brotherhood that exists between the great king, king of Egypt, and the great king, king of the land of the Hittites, his brother.
>
> The sun god and the storm god will raise your head and the sun god will let goodness flourish and he will preserve the brotherhood between the great king, king of Egypt, and the great king, king of the Hittites, his brother. I am in peace and in brotherhood with you, my sister. Now I send you a present for well-wishing to my sister, and you, my sister, should know about the present I send to you with the royal messenger: 1 multicolored necklace of good gold made up of 12 strings and weighing 801 grams; 1 multicolored linen garment from the city Byssos; 1 multicolored linen tunic from the city Byssos; 5 multicolored linen garments with good thin weave, 5 multicolored linen tunics with good thin weave, a total of 12 linen textiles.[9]

This letter exemplifies how the elites of eastern Mediterranean societies saw themselves as equals with a shared culture and ideology. Both queens communicated in Akkadian, a language neither of them spoke, and appreciated luxuries that often could only be obtained in foreign countries.

Alongside court exchanges, a lively trade in luxury goods connected the societies of the eastern Mediterranean. From the Aegean, for example, people from Egypt and Syria imported wine and olive oil in typical Mycenaean jars. Seafaring merchants conducted much of this trade, and some shipwrecks reveal what they carried. A prime example is a ship found on the south coast of Anatolia (modern Turkey) at Uluburun, dating to around 1300 B.C.E (see again Map 2.3). The array of goods the ship carried was so diverse that it is impossible to identify its origin. The main load consisted of

Charioteers and Diplomats

Women of the Royal Courts

Thriving Trade

ten tons of copper and one ton of tin. The merchants probably picked up these metals in Cyprus and southern Anatolia, intending to exchange them for other goods in various harbors along the route. The ship contained tropical African ebony logs, obtained in Egypt, and cedar logs from Lebanon. The cargo's ivory tusks came from Egypt, and marine snail shells, prized for the dye they contained, were a special product of Syria. The ship also carried manufactured goods, such as Syrian jewelry, Cypriot pottery, and beads of gold, agate, and colored glass, each type from a different source. There was even a jeweler's hoard on board, with scraps of gold and silver and an amulet with the name of the Egyptian queen Nefertiti. The cargo was truly cosmopolitan in origin and reflected the desire for luxury items of elites throughout the region.

Influence of Mesopotamian Culture

The frequent contacts and shared interests extended to culture and art as well. Although each state had its own traditions, often many centuries old, the elites imported the literate culture of Mesopotamia. Earlier, cuneiform script had spread throughout Southwest Asia, inspiring writing in other languages. But now international correspondence was written in Akkadian, even if it involved two states where the language was not native, as we saw in the queens' correspondence. Palaces all over the region employed scribes who could read and write Akkadian. Their libraries contained works of Mesopotamian literature, sometimes adapted to local tastes. In the Hittite capital, for example, the *Epic of Gilgamesh* was read in both a Mesopotamian version and an abbreviated translation in the local Hittite language. Even in Egypt, which had an ancient and very distinct literate culture, some literature was written in Akkadian.

Alphabetic Script

The spread of Mesopotamian culture did not destroy local traditions; rather, a multiplicity of languages, scripts, and literatures flourished. In western Syria a new type of script had developed in around 1800 B.C.E., and its use expanded at this time. The writing was **alphabetic**. Instead of using signs to indicate entire words or syllables, a sign represented each consonant of the language. Vowels were not indicated. This type of writing required fewer than thirty characters. Various alphabetic scripts coexisted, but the system that survived into later periods had a set of characters whose pronunciation was based on a simple principle: each character was a drawing of an item, and the first sound of that item's name gave the character its pronunciation. For example, a drawing of a house represented the sound /b/, the first sound in the Semitic word for house, *baytu*. We know only a handful of such alphabetic inscriptions from the second millennium B.C.E., but this system of writing would spread enormously in the first millennium B.C.E. It is the basis of alphabetic scripts in use today all over the world.

Kings and Commoners: An Unequal System

The flourishing local traditions of the eastern Mediterranean were matched by strong interconnections throughout the region. The rulers knew that they were joined together in a system. The heads of the leading states were like members of a club whose membership was restricted to "Great Kings," the term they used to refer to one another. Always included in this elite group were the kings of Babylonia, the Hittite state, and Egypt. Other rulers joined when resources and fortune enabled them to do so. In around 1350 B.C.E., for example, the king of the Mediterranean island of Cyprus was included on the basis of his control of copper mines.

Growing Social Inequality

Throughout this world there was a similar social structure, one with greater inequality than in the past. The leading elites accumulated enormous wealth, whereas the general population lived in poverty. This social disparity was reflected in the contents of elite tombs. Treasures such as those of King Tutankhamun (tuht-uhnk-AH-muhn) in Egypt (r. 1333–1323 B.C.E.) show the amazing wealth reserved for a tiny ruling class. During their lifetimes, too, the elites basked in luxury, which they enjoyed in palaces in secluded walled sections of their cities. Kings often ordered their subjects to build entirely new, and often gigantic, cities for themselves and their entourages. Removed from the masses of the lower classes, they restricted their company to the palace household. Thus, just as kings emphasized

alphabetic A type of writing with a limited number of characters, each one representing a single sound.

King Tutankhamun's Mask

The contents of the tomb of the king Tutankhamun are a prime example of the vast wealth of Egyptian pharaohs. This mask is one of several found among thousands of objects of gold, silver, and other precious materials. It was made of gold and inlaid with lapis lazuli, quartzite, and colored glass. The combination of materials gives the king's face a vivid, colorful allure. (François Guenet/Art Resource, NY.)

their membership in an exclusive elite in their diplomatic relations with other kings, they built walls around themselves in their day-to-day lives to underscore the vast distance between the powerful and the powerless.

The rulers' lavish lifestyles were funded, in part, by the spoils of military conquest. Egyptians, for example, mined large amounts of gold in Nubia, which they conquered in the sixteenth century B.C.E. Yet it was local populations that bore the brunt of the unequal social system. Primarily farmers, the lower social classes throughout the eastern Mediterranean were compelled to produce surpluses for their urban ruling elites. Although they were not slaves, they were tied to the land and forced to hand over much of their produce. They were not free to leave their land to take up a new life elsewhere—many international agreements between kings stipulated that people fleeing a state should be returned. The kings of this era may have been engaged in almost constant warfare, but they recognized a common interest in maintaining strict control over their subjects, who were the true source of their wealth and power.

Western Syrian Cities at the End of the Bronze Age, c. 1200 B.C.E.

The inequality that characterized the international system may have been the primary cause of its collapse, in around 1200 B.C.E. The success of the system had relied on collaboration and sustained contacts among the various states, even if those interactions involved warfare. After 1200 B.C.E. individual states gradually failed to sustain their social and political systems, and they grew increasingly isolated from one another. Historians have difficulties determining what happened, but revolts from the lower classes seem to have initiated the process. Documentation from Egypt attests to the earliest workers' strikes on record in world history.

Increasing numbers of people seem to have left their villages, fleeing the control of urban elites. These uprisings prompted outsiders from the northern shores of the Mediterranean to immigrate to the unstable kingdoms. Their attacks on coastal cities made sea travel unsafe and unraveled the connections among the various states. Reports of these attacks speak of "Sea Peoples," migrants who forced their way into the rich areas of the eastern Mediterranean. The chaos that ensued changed life fundamentally all over this region. Archaeology shows that several cities disappeared forever. People of the Aegean abandoned their Mycenaean fortresses, and the Hittite state disintegrated. Many cities along the Syrian coast were destroyed, and states such as Egypt and Babylonia lost influence outside their borders and went into economic decline. The rapid and simultaneous decline of the region's states reflects the vital nature of their close connections. Just as these states rose together, creating a system of diplomatic, military, and economic connections that sustained them all, the disintegration of connections brought with it the collapse of the states themselves.

Not all was lost, however. Several places, such as the harbors of Lebanon, remained relatively unscathed, and they would carry second millennium traditions into the first millennium. But as we will see in Chapter 4, the Southwest Asian world after 1000 B.C.E. was very different from the one that gave rise to the first urban societies.

COUNTERPOINT
Egypt's Distinct Path to Statehood

FOCUS

In what ways did the early history of Egypt contrast with that of the ancient states of Southwest Asia?

In the evolution of societies documented in Southwest Asia, the city played a decisive role. It was the earliest unit of social and political organization, and cities dominated all aspects of life in the region for more than fifteen hundred years. The city-state was a stepping-stone to the formation of larger political units. This was the case in nearly all the regions Mesopotamia was in contact with, with one notable exception: Egypt. Egypt never had city-states. It was a highly centralized territorial state from the very beginning.

Egypt's Geography and Early History

The Nile River   Settled agriculture began in Egypt in around 5400 B.C.E. Egypt's farmers, like their counterparts in Mesopotamia, China, and elsewhere, had to rely on river water to grow their crops, because the region receives almost no rain. They were more fortunate than others, however. Every year the Nile rose at just the time when the crops needed water, turning large areas of land along its banks into rich and extremely fertile fields (see Map 2.4). Egypt was truly the gift of the Nile. By monitoring the height of the annual flood, the Egyptians could determine exactly how much land could be farmed each year. The predictability of Egyptian agriculture gave its people an enormous advantage, freeing them from the constant uncertainty about food supplies that plagued other peoples.

Egypt's territory along the Nile River, seven hundred miles long, comprises two regions, which the ancient Egyptians clearly distinguished. In the northern delta area the Nile separates into numerous branches in a flat countryside. Scholars call this region Lower Egypt because it lies where the river drains into the sea. To the south the river runs through a narrow valley in a clearly demarcated basin, the region called Upper Egypt. Prior to 3000 B.C.E., these visibly distinct geographical zones were not part of a single territorial state or dominated by powerful city-states. Instead, the long country stretching beside the Nile was dotted with villages, whose inhabitants farmed the fertile soil the annual floods created.

Then, quite suddenly in around 3000 B.C.E., a state arose that was very different from the city-states that emerged in Mesopotamia at about the same time. Instead of a small area centered on a city, the earliest state in Egypt incorporated a large territory from the Mediterranean Sea to the northernmost place where rapids interrupt the Nile River, preventing travel by boat. The Egyptians portrayed the emergence of the Egyptian state as the result of a campaign of military conquest. The earliest Egyptian historical document shows the victory of a king of Upper Egypt, Narmer, over his Lower Egyptian counterpart (see Seeing the Past: The Palette of Narmer). The document reflects an ideal that would survive throughout Egyptian history: the king held the two parts of the country together through his military might. Modern historians distinguish two types of periods in the three-thousand-year history of the country: when Upper and Lower Egypt were united, they speak of Kingdoms (Old, Middle, and New), and when political fragmentation existed, they speak of Intermediate Periods (First, Second, and Third).

Egyptian Ideology of Kingship

Cities did arise in Egypt, but unlike those in Mesopotamia, they did not become the center of political life and cultural development. Instead, the king played that role. He guaranteed the success and welfare of the country, and in return the entire population supported him and his entourage. This was true from the very beginning of the Egyptian state. The earliest monumental remains are massive tombs from around 3000 B.C.E. with offerings that show that the persons buried in them, the earliest kings, received grave goods that originated from all over the country. The wealth of these and later tombs show a tremendous concentration of Egypt's economic resources in the ruler's palace.

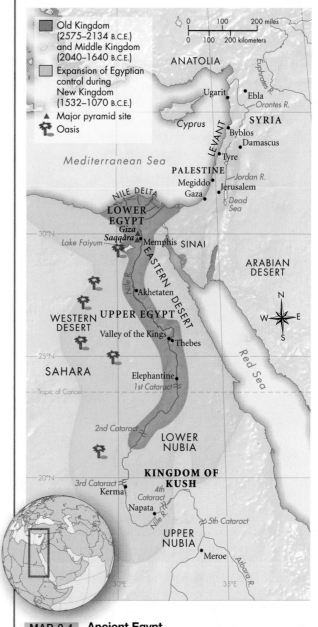

MAP 2.4   **Ancient Egypt**

Egypt stretches along the Nile River for some seven hundred miles and has depended on it from the start of its history to the present. When the ancient state was strong and unified, its influence reached out from its heartland in the Nile Valley and the Delta to the deserts nearby, and to areas in western Asia and Nubia. Its armies sometimes reached places thousands of miles from home.

The Palette of Narmer

Narmer Palette (front and back) (The Art Archive/Egyptian Museum Cairo/Dagli Orti (left) and The Art Archive/Egyptian Museum Cairo/Dagli Orti (right).)

In 1898 c.e., at the Egyptian site of Hierakonpolis, archaeologists excavated a number of sculpted stone objects dating to about 3000 b.c.e. Among them was a thin, flat slab a little over two feet high, known as the Narmer palette, bearing carved representations on both sides, as well as a few hieroglyphic signs.

The front (left) shows a king wearing the high crown of Upper Egypt beating another man with a mace. Above the king is a square that contains two hieroglyphs, which scholars read as "Nar" and "mer." Over the image of the subdued man sits a falcon on a papyrus plant holding a rope around a man's neck. This we can interpret as the god Horus (usually represented as a falcon) handing over the conquered Nile Delta to the king.

On the back of the palette (right), the same king wearing the square crown of Lower Egypt reviews troops holding standards. Beside them are two rows of decapitated bodies with heads at their feet. Two hieroglyphs record the name Narmer both in front of the king's face and on the top of the palette. In other contemporary images, the same King Narmer appears with a double crown, a combination of the crowns of Upper and Lower Egypt, which in later Egyptian history characterizes the unified country.

EXAMINING THE EVIDENCE

1. How do the hieroglyphic signs and the visual elements of the palette combine to convey a message?

2. What message did Narmer hope to communicate with this palette?

3. How do the images on the palette of Narmer compare with the relief on the Uruk vase (see p. 46)?

Egyptian Women Weaving

Images such as this one from an Egyptian tomb represent an idealized view of daily life, yet they show that weaving was an important activity performed by women. The two weavers depicted here use a horizontal loom. Because the Egyptian artistic convention was to show all the important elements of an object, regardless of perspective, the painter depicted the loom from above, allowing us to see the weavers' tools and techniques. (Image copyright © The Metropolitan Museum of Art/Art Resource, NY.)

The difference between the role of cities in Egypt and in Mesopotamia is reflected in the palaces of the two societies. As in Egypt, the palaces of Mesopotamia were sites where great wealth was concentrated. However, their wealth and prominence came from their connection to the cities in which they were located. In contrast, the palaces of Egyptian rulers gained prominence through their connection to the king. This linkage of the palace with the king led the Egyptians to use the term for palace, *per-o*, for the title of king—hence our use today of the term **pharaoh** to refer to the ancient Egyptian king.

Gods and Kings

The Egyptians' ideology of kingship was closely tied to their religious ideas. Like the Mesopotamians, they honored a large number of gods, many of whom represented aspects of the universe. For example, Geb was the earth, Nut the sky, and Re the sun. The Mesopotamian gods had human forms, but the Egyptians visualized many gods as wholly or partly animal. The goddess Hathor was a cow or woman with a cow's head, the god Horus a falcon or falcon-headed man, and so on. Why this was the case we do not know, but many animals became objects of cults.

The king fit into this system, in that he was considered the earthly embodiment of the god Horus, who in mythology had inherited the throne from his father Osiris. To the Egyptians, history was the sequence of kings, each of whom was related to his predecessor just as Horus had been related to Osiris. The Egyptian king was not a god, nor was he a simple human; his status was somewhere in between. As such, he served as a connection between his people and the divine.

The majority of the Egyptian population seems to have accepted this system without much difficulty. Food and other resources were plentiful along the Nile, and they saw the king as a source of stability and peace who would help preserve their fortunate circumstances. In return for his safeguarding the country, they contributed their labor to the great monuments that today remain the greatest testimonies of Egypt's past. They built the

pharaoh The ancient Egyptians' title for their king.

The Pyramid Builders of the Pharaohs

The Pyramids at Giza

To build the Giza pyramids the ancient Egyptians transported, carved, and set into place massive amounts of stone, using tools that were themselves made of stone or of the soft metal bronze. Archaeologists wonder how they managed to accomplish this work in less than a century. It is no surprise that the greatest of the three pyramids—the tomb of King Khufu—was considered one of the wonders of the ancient world. (Fuste Raga/Corbis.)

The three pyramids of Giza on the outskirts of modern Cairo are among the most awe-inspiring monuments of early world history. Archaeologists estimate that the largest of the three, the tomb of King Khufu, contained 2,300,000 blocks of stone with an average weight of $2\frac{3}{4}$ tons, some weighing up to 16 tons. Khufu ruled for twenty-three years, which meant that throughout his reign 100,000 blocks had to be quarried, transported, trimmed and finished, and put in place every year. That comes to about 285 blocks a day, or one for every two minutes of daylight.

The pyramids themselves are just one part of a much larger burial complex that included temples for offerings to the dead king, a ramp to transport the body to the pyramid, secondary burials for queens and others, and statuary. The latter could be as monumental as the Great Sphinx of Giza, the largest monolith (made from a single large block of stone) sculpture in the world.

pyramids and temples tourists see everywhere when they visit the country (see Lives and Livelihoods: The Pyramid Builders of the Pharaohs).

Most Egyptians lived in simple circumstances in villages. They farmed plots of land, which often belonged to the palace or a temple, and they paid part of their harvests as a rental fee. The Nile provided them with fish, and they hunted small animals and caught birds for food as well. Unlike in Southwest Asia, where people made their clothes from the wool of sheep they raised, Egyptians wore mostly linen textiles, which they made from the flax plant that grew throughout the country. Artistic representations show women weaving the cloth. As in Mesopotamia, weaving was an important domestic task in Egypt.

The New Culture of Statehood

Hieroglyphic Script

With the creation of the Egyptian state, new elements of culture appeared around the person of the king. These included monumental buildings, especially temples and tombs, as

Because the logistical requirements for these gigantic projects were daunting, the question of manpower is especially intriguing. Every district of Egypt had to supply laborers, which meant that some had to travel hundreds of miles. They were probably mostly men, but some women may have worked in auxiliary tasks. Scholars now estimate that about twenty-five thousand workers were active at a time, and they infer from later records of state enterprises that they worked three-month stints. The workers needed housing, food, and tools. They left their families behind and slept in crammed dormitories, each laborer being assigned a narrow space. They received rations of bread and beer, which were prepared on a massive scale in kitchens. Archaeologists have found some of the kilns used for baking, and also remains of workshops where tools were manufactured and repaired. Metal tools were mostly made of copper, which is soft, and they must have been sharpened very regularly.

Although no ancient Egyptian description exists of how the pyramids were built, the massive stones could only have been moved into place by dragging them on ramps constructed from wooden beams, stone rubble, and mud. The Giza plateau has little open space, so the architects must have laid out the ramps in circles around the pyramid base. They had to construct new ramps for every pyramid, and space must have become increasingly cramped as temples and secondary tombs surrounded earlier pyramids. We can imagine that workers suffered injuries and even died on the job, but no evidence of that has survived.

The labor must have been grueling, considering the weight of the stones and the height of the pyramids, let alone the heat and other conditions. The workers participated willingly, however, and were not slaves, foreign or Egyptian. We know that it would have been impossible to force them. They used axes, chisels, and other tools that were not much different from the weapons of the time. If workers had wanted to rebel, they could easily have overwhelmed whoever was in charge.

The willingness of Egyptians to participate in this massive enterprise tells us much about the king's position in society. The inhabitants of the entire country regarded him with so much respect that they willingly undertook these tasks. The projects required many years of work, and people had to forsake other responsibilities to work on them. After finishing their stint of pyramid building, these workers would resume their livelihoods as farmers, fishermen, or some other occupation, but with the memory of having contributed to the glory of their king.

QUESTIONS TO CONSIDER

1. How do scholars estimate the number of people involved in constructing Khufu's pyramid?

2. What were the logistical problems of the project?

3. Where did the workers come from, and how were they convinced to participate?

For Further Information:

For general information on Egyptian pyramids: Pyramids. http://www.pbs.org/wgbh/nova/pyramid/excavation.
Lehner, Mark. *The Complete Pyramids*. London: Thames & Hudson, 1997.

---

well as specialized craft products and writing. The Egyptians developed their own script, which we call **hieroglyphics**. The signs were distinct in form from those of Mesopotamian cuneiform, but they shared the same principles in how they rendered words. Hieroglyphic signs were pictorial and were painted on papyrus and pottery or carved in stone. Their meaning derived from accepted convention, and although scholars have identified over six thousand signs, in any period fewer than a thousand were in use. The script stayed in use from about 3000 B.C.E. to 400 C.E. and never lost its basic characteristics (see Figure 2.2). However, because hieroglyphs were very elaborate and cumbersome to write, over time the Egyptians developed derivative scripts.

As in Mesopotamia, the first writings Egyptians produced were limited to business transactions and short inscriptions celebrating the deeds of kings. Then people started to write down compositions, such as hymns and prayers to the gods. In around 2000 B.C.E. creativity flourished as authors composed the tales considered classics of Egyptian literature for centuries afterward. In their literature the Egyptians recorded their

hieroglyphics The writing system of ancient Egypt, which used detailed pictorial symbols to indicate words and syllables.

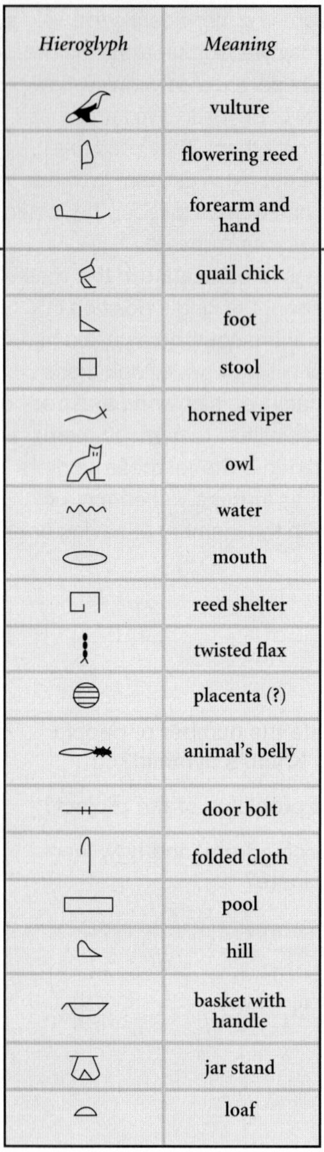

Hieroglyph	Meaning
	vulture
	flowering reed
	forearm and hand
	quail chick
	foot
	stool
	horned viper
	owl
	water
	mouth
	reed shelter
	twisted flax
	placenta (?)
	animal's belly
	door bolt
	folded cloth
	pool
	hill
	basket with handle
	jar stand
	loaf

FIGURE 2.2

Egyptian Hieroglyphs

Ancient Egyptians used pictures such as these to create their own system of writing around 3000 B.C.E. Because Egyptians used this formal script mainly for religious inscriptions, Greeks referred to it as *hieroglyphica* ("sacred carved letters"). Eventually Egyptians also developed the handwritten cursive script called demotic (Greek for "of the people"), a much simpler and quicker form of writing.

thoughts on the subjects most important to them, giving historians insight into their values, priorities, and beliefs. Among the most notable early Egyptian compositions are texts on death and burial.

The Egyptians viewed death not as an end, but as the beginning of a new existence that resembled life in many respects, one that required material goods such as food if the dead were to thrive. Thus, a tomb was more than a depository for the body—it also contained a chapel where surviving family members offered food to the dead. Unlike in Southwest Asia, where tombs were often placed beneath houses, in Egypt they were located apart from settlements in the desert. Egyptians expected to use their bodies after death, so they had to be preserved intact. To achieve this goal, the Egyptians developed mummification. They removed all perishable parts (lungs, intestines, etc.) and treated the other remains in such a way that they maintained their shape. Then they wrapped the bodies in linen and deposited them in coffins to protect them against possible damage. The dryness of the desert aided in preservation as well.

From the start of Egyptian history kings had enormous tombs, a practice that culminated in the great pyramids of Giza, built between 2550 and 2500 B.C.E. (see again Lives and Livelihoods: The Pyramid Builders of the Pharaohs). The masses of stone eloquently demonstrate how much energy the Egyptians would expend to guarantee the king a safe and impressive burial. Common people had the same hopes; they too wanted to be buried safely and to receive gifts into eternity. Royal cemeteries such as the one at Giza reflect the distinct nature of the early Egyptian state. The royal pyramids lie in the center, massive in size and bordered by temples for the cults of the dead kings. Numerous tombs of officials and others surround them. Just as the king was the center of power in life, it was desirable to be near him in death. Even many centuries later common people dug simple tombs near the old royal ones, hoping to benefit from the king's presence.

Although Egypt became part of the international system in the eastern Mediterranean after 1600 B.C.E., its earlier history contrasted notably with that of its neighbors. The king of Egypt was the center of power over the entire territorial state, which he personally held together. The strong unity of Egypt's territorial state led it to become the earliest empire in this part of the world, which we will discuss in Chapter 4.

Conclusion

After the rise of agriculture, the historical development of the world's peoples continued to unfold in Southwest Asia and North Africa, where the Eurasian and African continents meet. We have focused in this chapter on Mesopotamia and Egypt, which rapidly developed socially and economically complex cultures that left behind many remains for historians to study. Their invention of writing, which the mythical tale at the start of the chapter portrayed as a simple act to aid a messenger, had a fundamental impact on our understanding of people's lives in that era. These are the first cultures in history we can study at least in a limited way through the written expressions of the people themselves. We see a clear difference between these two regions: in Mesopotamia (and many other ancient cultures) the city was crucial to political life; in Egypt, it was the king.

After hundreds of years of separate developments, from about 3200 to 1600 B.C.E. the countries of Mesopotamia and Egypt united with others in the eastern Mediterranean region to form a much larger system of exchange in diplomacy, trade, and culture. From 1600 to 1200 B.C.E. states simultaneously competed and joined in a network of interdependence. Their fortunes were intertwined, and in around 1200 B.C.E. they all suffered decline. In the new world that would develop after 1000 B.C.E., the balance of power that undergirded the first international system no longer existed. The inhabitants of Southwest Asia and North Africa were the first in world history to develop the elements of culture we studied in this chapter, but soon afterward peoples elsewhere in Asia also did so. We will turn to these peoples living farther east in the next chapter.

NOTES

1. H. L. J. Vanstiphout, ed. *Epics of Sumerian Kings: The Matter of Aratta* (Atlanta, Ga.: Society of Biblical Literature, 2004), 85.
2. J. S. Cooper, *Sumerian and Akkadian Royal Inscriptions* I (New Haven: American Oriental Society, 1986), 72.
3. Martha T. Roth, *Law Collections from Mesopotamia and Asia Minor* (Atlanta, Ga.: Society of Biblical Literature, 1997), 121.
4. Ibid., 122–123.
5. Ibid., 121.
6. Ibid., 133–134.
7. J. A. Black, et al. *The Literature of Ancient Sumer* (Oxford: Oxford University Press, 2004), 319.
8. Ibid., 320.
9. Translated from Edel, E. *Die ägyptisch-hethitische Korrespondenz aus Boghazkoy.* 1994, 40–41.

RESOURCES FOR RESEARCH

Origins of Urban Society: Mesopotamia, 5000–3200 B.C.E.

Early developments in Mesopotamia interest historians, archaeologists, and anthropologists because Mesopotamia provides the first case in world history of the rise of a city-state. They are often studied using a long-term perspective. Pollock's book devotes special attention to issues of the economy and gender.

Nissen, Hans. *The Early History of the Ancient Near East 9000–2000 B.C.* Translated by E. Lutzeier and K. Northcutt. 1988.

Oates, David, and Joan Oates. *The Rise of Civilization.* 1976.

Pollock, Susan. *Ancient Mesopotamia: The Eden that Never Was.* 1999.

Roaf, Michael. *Cultural Atlas of Mesopotamia and the Ancient Near East.* 1990.

Wenke, Robert J., and Deborah I. Olszewski. *Patterns in Prehistory: Humankind's First Three Million Years,* 5th ed. 2006.

The First Cities, 3200–1600 B.C.E.

The origins of cities and the fundamental effects of urbanization on human society also attract the interest of scholars with varied approaches. Several of the books listed for the previous section are relevant as well to the early history of Southwest Asia.

Chadwick, Robert. *First Civilizations: Ancient Mesopotamia and Ancient Egypt,* 2d ed. 2005.

Liverani, Mario. *Uruk: The First City.* Translated by Z. Bahrani and M. Van De Mieroop. 2006.

Postgate, J. N. *Early Mesopotamia: Society and Economy at the Dawn of History.* 1992.

*Roth, Martha T. *Law Collections from Mesopotamia and Asia Minor,* 2d ed. 1997.

Van De Mieroop, Marc. *A History of the Ancient Near East ca. 3000–323 B.C.* Rev. ed. 2007.

City Life and Learning

The literature of early Mesopotamia, in both Sumerian and Akkadian, presents many challenges for the translator. A few famous works, especially the *Epic of Gilgamesh*, have been translated repeatedly in recent years, each version reflecting a somewhat different approach.

Black, Jeremy, and Anthony Green. *Gods, Demons and Symbols of Ancient Mesopotamia*. 1992.

*Cuneiform Digital Library Initiative. http://www.cdli.ucla.edu/.

*Dalley, Stephanie. *Myths of Mesopotamia: Creation, The Flood, Gilgamesh, and Others*. 1991.

The Electronic Text Corpus of Sumerian Literature. http://etcsl.orient.ox.ac.uk/.

*George, Andrew. *The Epic of Gilgamesh*. 2000.

Van De Mieroop, Marc. *The Ancient Mesopotamian City*. 1999.

*Vanstiphout, H. L. J. *Epics of Sumerian Kings: The Matter of Aratta*. 2004.

The First International Order, 1600–1200 B.C.E.

Many cultures of the international system in the eastern Mediterranean have received detailed attention, and their diplomatic and trade relations are a favorite topic of study. Studies of the demise of the system often focus on the Sea Peoples.

Aruz, Joan, ed. *Beyond Babylon: Art, Trade, and Diplomacy in the Second Millennium B.C.* 2008.

*Beckman, Gary. *Hittite Diplomatic Texts*, 2d ed. 1999.

Bryce, Trevor. *The Kingdom of the Hittites*, rev. ed. 2005.

Institute of Nautical Archaeology. http://ina.tamu.edu/vm.htm

*Moran, William L. *The Amarna Letters*. 1992.

Preziosi, Donald, and Louise A. Hitchcock. *Aegean Art and Architecture*. 1999.

Van De Mieroop, Marc. *The Eastern Mediterranean in the Age of Ramesses II*. 2007.

COUNTERPOINT: Egypt's Distinct Path to Statehood

There are innumerable books and Web sites on Egypt, and many cover the country's archaeological and artistic remains. The selection here focuses on the history and writings of the ancient Egyptians. Kemp's work is especially thought provoking.

Ancient Egyptian sites: http://egyptsites.wordpress.com/.

Baines, John, and Jaromír Málek. *Cultural Atlas of Ancient Egypt*, rev. ed. 2000.

Collier, Mark, and Bill Manley. *How to Read Egyptian Hieroglyphs*. 1998.

Digital Egypt for universities. http://www.digitalegypt.ucl.ac.uk.

Egyptian monuments. http://egyptsites.wordpress.com/

Kemp, Barry J. *Ancient Egypt: Anatomy of a Civilization*, rev. ed. 2006.

*Lichtheim, Miriam. *Ancient Egyptian Literature*, 3 vols. 2006.

Morkot, Robert G. *The Egyptians: An Introduction*. 2005.

Resources on Egypt. http://www.digitalegypt.ucl.ac.uk.

Robins, Gay. *Women in Ancient Egypt*. 1993.

Shaw, Ian. *Ancient Egypt: A Very Short Introduction*. 2004.

Van De Mieroop, Marc. *A History of Ancient Egypt*. 2011.

* Primary source.

▶ **For additional primary sources from this period,** see *Sources of Crossroads and Cultures.*

▶ **For Web sites, images, and documents related to this chapter,** see Make History at bedfordstmartins.com/smith.

The major global development in this chapter ▶ The rise of urban society
and the creation of states in Southwest Asia.

IMPORTANT EVENTS

c. 5000 B.C.E.	First permanent settlement in Mesopotamia
c. 3200 B.C.E.	Uruk, the first Mesopotamian city; invention of Mesopotamian cuneiform script
c. 3000 B.C.E.	Creation of the Egyptian state; invention of Egyptian hieroglyphic script
c. 3000–2350 B.C.E.	Competing city-states in Mesopotamia
c. 2550 B.C.E.	Khufu's pyramid at Giza
c. 2350–2200 B.C.E.	Dynasty of King Sargon of Akkad dominates Mesopotamia
c. 1800 B.C.E.	Development of alphabetic script in Syria
c. 1800–1700 B.C.E.	Hammurabi's unification of southern Mesopotamia
c. 1650 B.C.E.	End of the Minoan culture
c. 1600–1200 B.C.E.	First international order in the eastern Mediterranean
c. 1450 B.C.E.	Mycenaean expansion throughout the Aegean

KEY TERMS

alphabetic (p. 60)
city (p. 41)
city-state (p. 41)
cuneiform (p. 39)
dynasty (p. 49)
hieroglyphics (p. 67)
Linear A (p. 56)

Linear B (p. 58)
patriarchy (p. 53)
pharaoh (p. 65)
polytheism (p. 47)
specialization of labor (p. 44)
territorial state (p. 56)

CHAPTER OVERVIEW QUESTIONS

1. What types of political and social organization appeared in the early history of Southwest Asia?

2. What new technologies appeared, and how did they affect people's livelihoods?

3. How do urban societies differ from village societies?

4. How did the early states of Southwest Asia interact with one another?

SECTION FOCUS QUESTIONS

1. How do historians explain the rise of cities?

2. How and why did the rise of the city lead to a more hierarchical society in early Mesopotamia?

3. Why did ancient peoples develop writing systems, and what has been the enduring impact of this invention on intellectual expression?

4. What were the main features of the first international order, and what developments explain its rise and fall?

5. In what ways did the early history of Egypt contrast with that of the ancient states of Southwest Asia?

MAKING CONNECTIONS

1. How did the development of agriculture in Southwest Asia lead to the first urban culture there?

2. What were the roles of cities in political developments in the regions discussed in this chapter?

3. What was the relationship between gods and humans in Mesopotamia and Egypt?

4. What are similarities and differences between Mesopotamian and Egyptian writing systems, and how do they differ from alphabetic writing?

AT A CROSSROADS ▲

The vast expanses of Central Asia opened up when people first domesticated horses around 2000 B.C.E. and could quickly cross large, arid areas. Central Asian horsemen connected the urban cultures at the fringes of Eurasia, and may have introduced technologies such as bronze manufacture into China. This decorated textile, dating to around 500 B.C.E., comes from Pazyryk, on the modern border between Russia and northern China. It depicts a man riding on horseback using a saddle and a bit, tools that revolutionized the use of horses and have not gone out of use since. (The State Hermitage Museum, St. Petersburg, Russia/Bridgeman Art Library.)

Settlers and Migrants: The Creation of States in Asia

5000–500 B.C.E.

round the year 100 B.C.E., the Chinese historian and astrologer Sima Qian (sih-muh chee-en), in a massive work on the early history of his country, wrote these words about nomadic people living on the fringes of the Chinese state whose emperor he served:

> We hear of these people, known as Mountain Barbarians . . . wandering from place to place pasturing their animals. The animals they raise consist mainly of horses, cows, and sheep, but include such rare beasts as camels, asses, mules, and wild horses. . . . They move about in search of water and pasture and have no walled cities or fixed dwellings, nor do they engage in any kind of agriculture. . . . They have no writing and even promises and agreements are only verbal. . . . All the young men are able to use a bow and act as armed cavalry in times of war. It is their custom to herd their flocks in times of peace and make their living by hunting, but in periods of crisis they take up arms and go off on plundering and marauding expeditions. This seems to be their inborn nature.[1]

This is a stereotypically negative portrayal of nomadic people by an author living in an urban society. His perspective has parallels in writings worldwide and across millennia. Settled people provided almost all the written sources with which the historian works, and

BACKSTORY

In Chapter 1 we saw how humans developed, spread across the globe, and invented agriculture, which enabled them to establish permanent settlements. Societies in various parts of the world evolved differently, often in response to varying environmental challenges and opportunities. But wherever large numbers of people started to live together, they needed institutions and social arrangements to regulate their interactions. The peoples of Southwest Asia and Northeast Africa were the first to form large states, in around 3000 B.C.E. This ultimately led to a complex system of states throughout the region interconnected by diplomatic relations (discussed in Chapter 2). Sometime after the founding of Southwest Asian states, peoples in other parts of Asia also created large political and social entities, each in accordance with their particular circumstances. It is to these early states that we turn in this chapter.

Early Agricultural Societies of South and East Asia, 5000–1000 B.C.E.

FOCUS How did Asia's diverse natural environments shape the different lifestyles of its inhabitants?

The Indus Valley Culture, 2600–1900 B.C.E.

FOCUS What were the main characteristics of South Asia's early urban culture?

Indo-European Migrations, 3000–1000 B.C.E.

FOCUS What does the concept "Indo-European" mean, and how important is it for the study of Eurasia?

India's Vedic Age, 1500–500 B.C.E.

FOCUS How did cultural developments in early Indian history shape the structure of society?

The Early Chinese Dynasties, 2000–771 B.C.E.

FOCUS What factors account for the remarkable cultural continuity of early Chinese states?

COUNTERPOINT: The Oxus People: A Short-Lived Culture in Central Asia, 2100–1700 B.C.E.

FOCUS What are the unique characteristics of the Oxus culture in the early history of Asia?

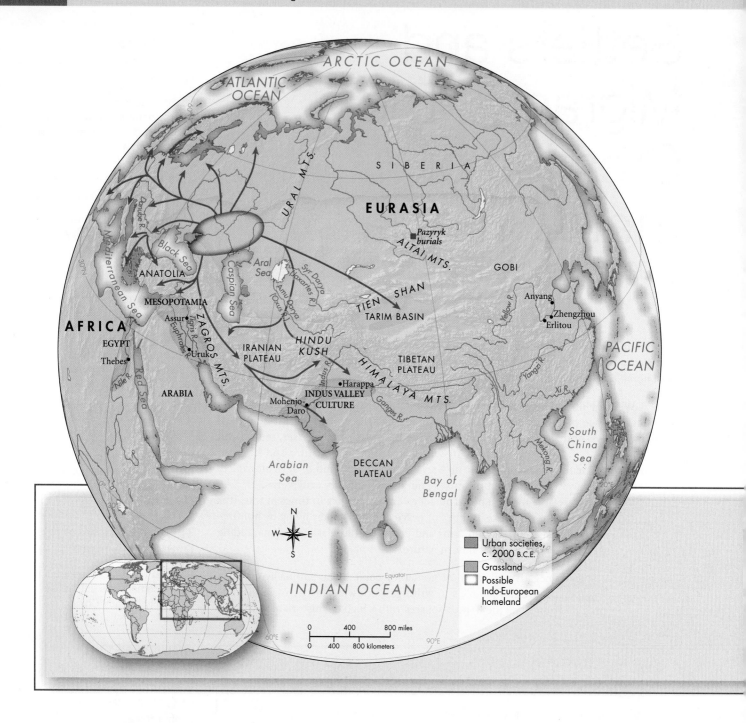

ARCTIC OCEAN

ATLANTIC OCEAN

SIBERIA

EURASIA

URAL MTS.

Pazyryk burials

ALTAI MTS.

GOBI

Black Sea

ANATOLIA

Aral Sea

Caspian Sea

Syr Darya (Jaxartes R.)

TIEN SHAN

Anyang

Yellow R.

Zhengzhou

Erlitou

MESOPOTAMIA

Assur

AFRICA

Amu Darya (Oxus R.)

TARIM BASIN

PACIFIC OCEAN

EGYPT

Euphrates R.

Tigris R.

ZAGROS MTS.

Uruks

IRANIAN PLATEAU

HINDU KUSH

TIBETAN PLATEAU

Yangzi R.

Xi R.

Thebes

Nile R.

Red Sea

ARABIA

Indus R.

Harappa

HIMALAYA MTS.

Mohenjo-Daro

INDUS VALLEY CULTURE

Ganges R.

Mekong R.

South China Sea

Arabian Sea

DECCAN PLATEAU

Bay of Bengal

Equator

Mediterranean Sea

Danube R.

N W E S

INDIAN OCEAN

400 800 miles

400 800 kilometers

60°E

90°E

Urban societies, c. 2000 B.C.E.

Grassland

Possible Indo-European homeland

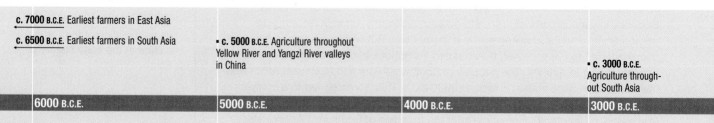

c. 7000 B.C.E. Earliest farmers in East Asia

c. 6500 B.C.E. Earliest farmers in South Asia

▪ **c. 5000** B.C.E. Agriculture throughout Yellow River and Yangzi River valleys in China

▪ **c. 3000** B.C.E. Agriculture throughout South Asia

6000 B.C.E.   **5000** B.C.E.   **4000** B.C.E.   **3000** B.C.E.

typically they did not like, or even understand, those who did not live like themselves. The ancient history of Asia shows, however, that settled and nomadic peoples were connected in numerous and important ways. As alien as nomads may have seemed to urban peoples, the contacts, conflicts, and exchanges among nomadic and settled peoples profoundly influenced world history, shaping the lives of nomads and city dwellers alike.

Asia is a vast landmass with numerous natural environments, which support primarily two types of livelihood: farming and herding. Where sufficient rain fell or rivers allowed for irrigation, farmers worked the soil and lived in the same location year-round. The earliest urban cultures of Asian history arose especially in the river valleys, that is, in Southwest, South, and East Asia. In all these areas people developed large states with urban and literate cultures, but key differences distinguished them. The states of Southwest Asia show continuity from about 3000 B.C.E. to 600 C.E. In South Asia the urban Indus Valley culture, whose script we cannot read, arose around 2600 B.C.E. and ceased to exist after some 700 years. Several centuries later, the new Vedic culture provided the basis of all of the region's later history. In East Asia the Shang (shahng) state of 1570 to 1027 B.C.E. was the first in a long series of Chinese dynasties that continued into modern times. Elsewhere on the Asian continent, such as in the Oxus River Valley, some early urban cultures flourished only temporarily, however, and when people abandoned them, they left few traces for later history.

Whether particular urban cultures were to survive for a short or a long time, their emergence depended on suitable environmental conditions. Beyond Asia's river valleys, however, agriculture was often impossible, and people survived instead as **pastoralists**, nomadic animal herders who moved with their flocks in search of grazing land. The domestication of horses in around 2000 B.C.E. greatly increased the mobility of pastoralists, enabling some to migrate over great distances. These long-distance migrations created links among the urban states of Asia. Especially important were the migrations of speakers of Indo-European languages, whose nomadic lifestyle brought them to western

pastoralist Animal herder who moves around with a flock to find grazing land; the lifestyle of such people is called pastoralism.

MAPPING THE WORLD
The Nomads and Settlers of Early Eurasia

Throughout history, the native migrants crisscrossed the vast grasslands in the center of Eurasia, crucially influencing the urban cultures that arose on the fringes of the steppes. This map shows the situation in around 2000 B.C.E., when the urbanized regions of Egypt, the Middle East, and the Indus Valley, as well as the village culture of China, coexisted with Indo-European migrants, whose spread brought radical changes to Eurasian societies and cultures.

ROUTES ▼

→ Indo-European migration

- **c. 2000 B.C.E.** Spread of domesticated horses throughout Asia

c. 2600–1900 B.C.E. Mature Indus Valley culture

- **1027 B.C.E.** Battle of Muye in China

c. 1500–500 B.C.E. India's Vedic age

| 2000 B.C.E. | 1000 B.C.E. | 0 B.C.E. | 1000 C.E. |

c. 2100–1700 B.C.E. Oxus River culture

1027–771 B.C.E. Early Zhou dynasty in China

c. 2000–1570 B.C.E. Earliest Bronze Age cultures in China

c. 1570–1027 B.C.E. Shang dynasty in China

c. 2000 B.C.E.–100 C.E. Indo-European migrations

China, western Europe, and the Indian subcontinent. Many other nomadic groups flourished as well, and the interactions between settled and pastoral peoples powerfully shaped the history of Asia from its beginning until recent times.

OVERVIEW
QUESTIONS

The major global development in this chapter: The rise of large urban states in Asia and the interactions between nomadic and settled peoples that shaped them.

As you read, consider:

1. How did peoples living in far-flung regions of Asia develop societies that had many similarities?

2. What were the unique characteristics of the cultures studied here?

3. Which features of ancient Indian and Chinese society and culture shaped later developments most fundamentally?

4. What common trends in the interactions between settled and nomadic peoples can you discern?

Early Agricultural Societies of South and East Asia 5000–1000 B.C.E.

FOCUS
How did Asia's diverse natural environments shape the different lifestyles of its inhabitants?

By 8000 B.C.E., people in Southwest Asia had developed agriculture, which made it possible for them to live in the same place for their entire lives. In subsequent millennia, inhabitants of other regions of Asia started to farm as well, especially in river valleys, where the soil was fertile and people could use river water to irrigate crops when rainfall was insufficient. By 5000 B.C.E. farmers had settled throughout the valleys of the Yellow River (Huang He) and the Yangzi River in China, and by 3000 B.C.E. agriculture had spread into parts of the South Asian subcontinent, including the Indus Valley. Out of those communities the earliest urban cultures of East and South Asia would develop. Simultaneously, pastoralists survived by herding animals, grazing them on the continent's steppes, vast areas of semiarid and treeless grasslands. After some pastoralists domesticated the horse, they could cover long distances, which led to their migration over the entire Eurasian continent. These people became the nomads of Central Asia.

Settled Farmers of the River Valleys

The Asian continent has a great deal of natural variety, but most of the regions with agricultural potential lie along mighty rivers whose waters make the adjoining fields very fertile. Besides the Tigris and Euphrates valleys in Southwest Asia, the valleys of the Indus and Ganges in South Asia and those of the Yellow River and Yangzi to the east in China were home to early agricultural societies with intensive food production. The first farmers appeared by 7000 B.C.E. in East Asia and by 6500 B.C.E. in South Asia. Local conditions determined what crops these people could grow. In China they cultivated rice in the southern Yangzi Valley, because the large amounts of water the crop required were available there. In the northern Yellow River Valley, people grew millet, because that hardy grain could survive the region's chronic droughts. In the western Indian subcontinent people cultivated wheat and barley, plants that need a modest, yet annually recurring, amount of water. In each case, environmental conditions determined not only what kinds of crops people grew, but whether settled agriculture was possible at all.

The early farmers lived in villages and produced pottery in which to store produce and liquids and to cook. As we have seen, pottery provides an important key to archaeologists, for shapes and styles of decoration allow them to distinguish cultures and to study their geographical spread. These studies show that the early inhabitants of various regions of modern-day China had distinct customs and practices. On the coast of eastern China, for example, they made delicate vessels on potter's wheels in colored clay, whereas in the central Yellow River Valley they made large bulky vessels by placing bands of clay on top of one another and painting decorations on the upper half. Thus, although each agricultural region may have emerged in response to similar environmental opportunities, each developed distinct cultural characteristics.

Early Agriculture in China

Over time these diverse populations across China increased contacts and started to share cultural elements. Some of the interactions were violent rather than peaceful, so inhabitants of northern China began to protect their villages with walls. They employed a unique building technique that would remain characteristic for many centuries in the region. They filled a wooden frame with layers of earth, which they pounded until the wall became as solid as cement. When the builders removed the boards, straight and strong walls remained.

As in Mesopotamia and Egypt, the construction of such walls and other large projects in early China required organized communal labor and a hierarchical social structure. Again, as in the case of Mesopotamia and Egypt, burial sites provide evidence of this increasing social stratification. By 2000 B.C.E. social differences became evident in people's burials. While the vast majority of people were buried with only a few objects, a small number of elites took many gifts with them to their graves. The goods found in elite graves often had symbolic significance, revealing the owner's special status. That great power went with special status was made very clear by the human sacrifice of people of lower status to serve members of the elite in the afterlife. Archaeologists regularly find skeletons with their feet cut off placed near the principal occupants of rich Chinese graves. Both Mesopotamia and Egypt show evidence of human sacrifice in their early histories as well, but there the practice died out quickly, while in China it continued much longer.

Grave goods are not the only evidence we have of social stratification. As some members of Chinese society grew wealthy, they demanded new and more luxurious products. Highly skilled specialized laborers focused their attention on meeting such demands. One typically Chinese luxury product, silk cloth, provides an example of the specialization of labor that went along with social stratification. Starting in the third millennium B.C.E., Chinese women began weaving cloth from the cocoons of silkworms. They bred the worms and fed them masses of mulberry leaves to make them grow fast. The women unraveled the cocoons to obtain the delicate silk threads and wove them into valuable textiles. The silk trade became a key component of the Chinese economy, and silk production remained a Chinese monopoly until the sixth century C.E., when two Christian monks smuggled some silkworms out of China (see Chapter 10). Thus, silk production both reflected Chinese social structure and helped make China a global trading crossroads.

Similarly, villages appeared by 6500 B.C.E. in the northwestern part of the Indian subcontinent, where farmers grew barley and wheat using techniques probably imported from Southwest Asia. They gradually spread out into regions such as the Indus River Valley,

where the rich soil allowed increased agricultural production and, hence, population growth. Some larger villages may have served as centers of trade. Over time South Asian farmers extended the range of plants they grew and started to cultivate cotton, which they used to weave textiles. By 3500 B.C.E. village life was common in the fertile river valleys of South and East Asia.

Nomadic Herders of the Steppe

Agriculture involves not only farming but also the herding of animals. At the same time that they learned to domesticate plants, the early inhabitants of Asia became responsible for the survival of selected animals. They bred them, protected them against natural predators, milked and sheared them, and guided them to pastureland where they could feed. The search for pasture required herders to move around for at least part of the year, because most natural environments in Asia do not provide sufficient food for herds in the same place year-round. Nomadic herders did not wander at random but moved with their flocks along established routes. These settled patterns of movement reflected knowledge of the region's environment that had been passed down from generation to generation.

From about 3000 B.C.E. on, sheep, goats, and cattle were the most important domesticated animals throughout Asia. The settled farmers and nomadic herders exchanged the specialized goods they each produced. Farmers traded grains, pottery, and other craft goods for the herders' dairy products, wool, and skins. But tensions could arise between the two groups, especially in summer when herders drove their flocks from the dry steppe to the lush river valleys where their animals could graze. At just that time, the farmers' crops were nearly ready for harvest, so allowing flocks near them could prove disastrous. Many ancient accounts focus on these tensions and ignore the cooperation, but both were important. Each group provided the other with goods they could not otherwise acquire, and the need for exchange created a web of connections between nomadic and settled peoples that shaped both cultures. At the same time, the sometimes divergent demands of agriculture and herding led to serious and often violent conflict.

Domestication of the Horse

The pastoral lifestyle originally did not allow people to range over great distances as they moved on foot. A dramatic change happened around 2000 B.C.E., when they started to use horses. People of the Russian steppe may have domesticated the horse as early as 4000 B.C.E., but horses became truly important in world history only when they were hitched to chariots and wagons in around 2000 B.C.E. For both settled and pastoral populations, the two-wheeled horse-drawn chariot was an essential piece of equipment, used in warfare and for other purposes. By 1000 B.C.E., chariot technology had spread throughout Asia, and in pastoral societies charioteers became elites with great wealth and power. Their massive tombs were packed with rich grave goods, including their horses and chariot.

When people started to ride horses using saddles and bits, rather than bareback, their mobility increased even more, and the distances they could cover expanded drastically. By 500 B.C.E., animal herders on horseback roamed the Asian steppes. Their speed and agility made them feared in battle, but the armies of settled populations soon imitated their techniques. The use of the horse revolutionized warfare throughout Asia and beyond.

The mobility of mounted horsemen had a remarkable consequence: during the first millennium B.C.E., shared cultural elements appeared over a vast region, from eastern Russia to western China. From the Black Sea to Siberia, nomadic people used similar burial mounds. They placed the dead in a central chamber of wood or stone, over which they piled an earthen mound. As gifts, they included weapons and sacrificed animals—sheep, goats, cattle, and horses. These burial items reveal the people's preoccupations in life with warfare and animal husbandry.

The best examples of such tombs are found in the Altai Mountains on the modern border between Russia and northern China. At the site of Pazyryk (PA-zee-rick) in that region, Russian archaeologists excavated tomb remains that were extremely well preserved by permafrost, a permanently frozen layer of earth below the surface. The builders covered the tomb chambers with earthen mounds, on top of which they piled loose rocks. The tombs housed the bodies of horses, and of people whose skins had dried naturally, some of them completely tattooed. They also contained textiles (including carpets), leather, and felt, all decorated with images of humans, animals, and other special motifs, as well as weapons and precious goods, including imports from China, India, and Southwest Asia.

The people buried in them were leaders of nomadic groups, who received honors on their deaths. Among them was a young blond woman, covered with body tattoos, who died in around 500 B.C.E. Her tomb shows her special status in society. She was placed in a wooden coffin wearing a blouse imported from India and a three-foot-high felt headdress onto which gilded wooden birds had been sewn. Six horses accompanied her in death,

Burial Practices

Chariot from Pazyryk Burials in Central Asia

The people of Central Asia who relied on the horse for transport invented a new set of tools and equipment to use with the animal, including chariots. Chariots for the elite could be very elaborate. This chariot, found in one of the burials at Pazyryk, was reconstructed from pieces of wood and leather. The distance between the front and back wheels is only 2 inches, which suggests this was a ceremonial object. (The State Hermitage Museum, St. Petersburg. Photograph © The State Hermitage Museum /photo by Vladimir Terebenin, Leonard Kheifets, Yuri Molodkovets.)

which showed that she must have been very wealthy in life, and reflected the profound importance of the horse in the lives of Asian nomads.

Between 5000 and 1000 B.C.E., Asians had thus developed two basic means of survival. Across the wide steppes of Central Asia, they subsisted as nomadic herders who moved with their sheep, goats, cattle, and horses over long distances. In the fertile river valleys, they had become farmers, living in increasingly numerous villages that shared regionally characteristic social structure and agricultural practices. Interactions between the two groups would have an enormous impact on the subsequent history of Asia.

The Indus Valley Culture 2600–1900 B.C.E.

FOCUS

What were the main characteristics of South Asia's early urban culture?

In the third and second millennia B.C.E., the villages of South and East Asia had developed major urban societies in the valleys of the powerful Indus River and the Yellow River. The two regions were strikingly different, however. The Indus Valley had cities earlier than China, but they disappeared after 1900 B.C.E., whereas in China the building of the first cities started a long history of urban life. The Indus culture is also less accessible to us because its script has not yet been deciphered. Scholars thus do not know the names of peoples and places or the language they spoke, and they have no access to verbal expression of their ideas. Further, no later native Indian sources describe Indus elites and their activities. Archaeological remains fill some of the gaps, but uncertainties about their interpretation have led to competing theories about many features of the Indus Valley culture.

Urban Society in the Indus Valley

Archaeological evidence shows that the geographical spread of the Indus culture was enormous, stretching some 1100 miles from the northernmost reaches of the Indus River to the Arabian Sea and some 800 miles from east to west (see Map 3.1). The Indus culture existed in varied natural environments, including fertile agricultural zones with abundant rainfall near the mountains, a large alluvial plain that is naturally fertilized by annual flooding, and a marshy coastal area with islands and peninsulas.

Harappan Cities   Around 3200 B.C.E., villagers in the western part of South Asia started to build larger fortified settlements. This trend culminated suddenly in around 2600 B.C.E. with the creation of the mature Indus culture, which shows amazing shared cultural characteristics over a vast area of some 193,000 square miles. For unknown reasons numerous people moved into cities surrounded by villages. We know of five very large urban centers, whose inhabitants may have numbered thirty thousand (similar to the population of Uruk, discussed in Chapter 2), and more than thirty smaller cities. At the same time, the number of villages remained very high as well: archaeologists have identified more than fifteen thousand of them. Despite the great distances between them, the urban settlements were remarkably similar. Scholars often refer to them as *Harappan*, after the modern name of one of the large cities.

The uniformity is clear from the layout of the cities, although local variations appear. They were surrounded by thick mud-brick walls and contained various sectors. Each of the five large cities had a high sector, set on a mud-brick platform, with monumental buildings, and one or more lower sectors with residences and workshops. The interior layout of each sector was planned on a grid pattern oriented north to south and east to west. In some residential areas, streets up to thirty-three feet wide created city blocks, which were subdivided with narrower streets. Evidence that smaller settlements had the same layout indicates that people consciously planned cities and villages using an established pattern.

Mohenjo-Daro   Mohenjo-Daro (moe-hen-joe-DAHR-oh) in the east of modern Pakistan, the best-known and largest site of the culture, is often taken as the prime example of the layout of

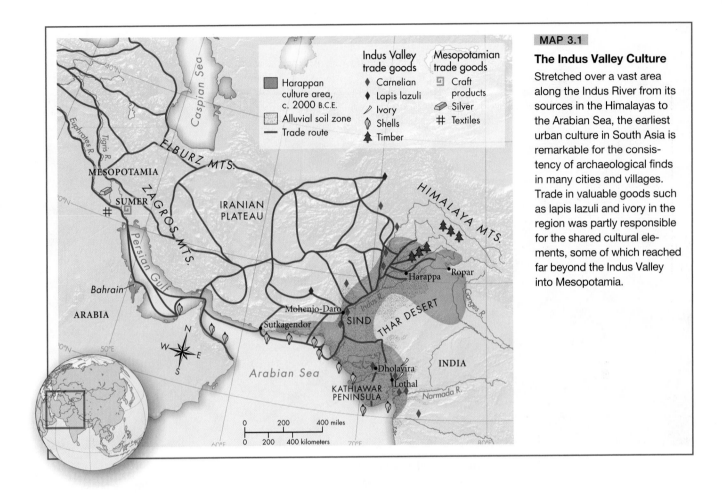

MAP 3.1

The Indus Valley Culture

Stretched over a vast area along the Indus River from its sources in the Himalayas to the Arabian Sea, the earliest urban culture in South Asia is remarkable for the consistency of archaeological finds in many cities and villages. Trade in valuable goods such as lapis lazuli and ivory in the region was partly responsible for the shared cultural elements, some of which reached far beyond the Indus Valley into Mesopotamia.

Indus Valley cities. Its monumental buildings on the high sector are relatively well preserved. They include the Great Bath, 23 feet wide by 39 feet long and 8 feet deep, made of baked bricks and lined with plaster. Around the outside of the bath was a three-inch layer of bitumen, a kind of asphalt used as waterproofing. People may have used the small rooms next to the bath to change clothing. Many scholars think the complex was used for ritual cleansing because it resembles later Indian purification pools. Next to the Great Bath was a vast storehouse for grain, 99 by 99 feet, and the platform also supported a large pillared hall. These structures indicate a communal effort to construct special edifices.

In the residential areas—which also housed the shops and craft workshops—people built their homes using uniformly sized bricks. Most houses had an entrance on a side street and consisted of a courtyard surrounded by rooms on two or three sides. The Harappan cities show a greater attention to sanitation than was seen anywhere else in the ancient world. Houses had private bathrooms and wells, and their sewage systems were connected to main channels underneath the streets. All cities had large artificial basins to collect water. Scholars believe that the Indus people planned these elaborate systems to protect themselves against the flooding of the rivers and heavy rains. They could have used some of the basins as harbors as well.

Although the archaeological remains of Harappan cities are abundant, they present many problems of interpretation. They suggest political and social structures that are very unlike those of other early urban cultures, but the differences may be more apparent than real. Urban societies usually have a hierarchy in which an elite holds power over the mass of the population, often by military means. The remains of the Indus society show no military activity, however. The people never depicted warfare, and none of their tombs con-

Social Structure

The Great Bath at Mohenjo-Daro

This building in the center of Mohenjo-Daro clearly had a use related to water: the bricks are neatly fitted together and sealed with plaster, and the outside is covered with bitumen, a waterproofing substance. Because of the stairs and the benchlike ledge, most archaeologists think it was used for ritual bathing. (Borromeo/Art Resource, NY.)

tained weapons. Further, houses or tombs show no grandiose displays of wealth such as we find in Mesopotamia, Egypt, China, and elsewhere. The archaeological material from the Indus Valley creates the impression (perhaps falsely) that the majority of people shared the existing wealth equally.

Some scholars argue that Harappan society was matriarchal. They think that property passed along the female line of the family rather than the male and that husbands moved into their wives' homes upon marriage. If true, this would make Indus Valley culture very different from other early urban cultures. But the evidence for an Indus matriarchy is far from conclusive.

The existence of massive public works, however, suggests that, as was the case in other urban societies, an elite group did have authority over the rest of the Harappan population. The basis of that authority remains a mystery, as there is no evidence of military control or, as far as we know, of temples that could indicate a religious basis of power. Because, as we will see, long-distance trade was crucial to the Indus Valley economy, many historians propose that a merchant class governed. Other scholars speculate that the Indus Valley culture featured certain people who gained authority by renouncing material goods and luxuries, as people in later Indian history did.

Indus Beliefs   We are as uncertain about Indus religion as we are about Indus society. Scholars have turned to visual and archaeological evidence for insight into Indus beliefs, and many specialists argue that several later Indian practices have their roots in Indus culture. They see the Great Bath at Mohenjo-Daro, for example, as a place for purification with sacred water. Images on the Indus seals regularly show human figures with legs spread in a position resembling later yoga postures. This may indicate that practices such as meditation already existed in the Indus culture. Scholars differ in their acceptance of such ideas, however. Those who see much continuity between the Indus Valley culture and later periods of South Asian history will interpret aspects of the early culture on the basis of later evidence. Those who see little continuity find different explanations.

Political Organization

How do we explain that the five major cities of the Indus Valley culture show an amazing cultural uniformity even though they are located two hundred to four hundred miles apart? The idea that a unified territorial state would have imposed the cultural norms seems improbable, as such a state would have been enormous in size. It seems more likely that each city controlled the territory surrounding it. The cultural similarity, however, indicates that the cities were in close contact with one another. Trade most likely played a key role in creating and reinforcing the contacts and connections that resulted in the uniformity of Indus culture.

Harappan Crafts and Long-Distance Trade

The archaeological evidence is more secure when we look at the role of crafts and trade in the Indus Valley culture. The people seem to have excelled in these activities and devoted much attention to both of them. They imported prized stones, such as carnelian and lapis lazuli, to carve valuable objects, including seals and beads. Wherever archaeologists find such objects, the objects are similar in shape and size, showing that craftsmen throughout the Indus Valley followed standard patterns. Traders also shipped craft items to other cities. All the settlements used a unified system of weights and measures, which greatly facilitated transactions among people of different towns. In every site, archaeologists found sets of stone weights that use the same measuring system. Trade must have been of great importance to the Indus people considering that they devoted so much effort to making it function smoothly and efficiently.

Indus Valley Script

Writing is another indicator that trade was important in the Indus Valley. Although we cannot decipher the texts, all scribes over the vast region of the culture used the same signs and carved them on the same types of objects. Indus script appeared in two contexts that seem connected to trade. People inscribed vessels, probably to indicate who owned the contents; more dramatically, writing appears on stone seals (see Seeing the Past: Inscribed Seals from the Indus Valley). The appearance of these seals throughout the Indus Valley underscores the wide range of the exchanges.

Foreign Trade

Traders also exported Indus Valley craft items to distant places, including Mesopotamia. Although an expanse of some one thousand miles separated Mesopotamia from the Indus River delta, sailors went back and forth by following the Pakistani and Iranian coasts. Archaeological finds in the Persian Gulf show that Indus Valley people traded on their way to Mesopotamia. Inhabitants of the island of Bahrain adopted the Indus system of weights and measures and produced seals in the Harappan style, sometimes inscribing them with signs of the Indus script. Thus Indus cities served as crossroads, connecting communities to one another and to the larger world.

The End of the Indus Valley Culture

How, when, and why did this remarkable urban culture disappear? Around 1900 B.C.E. people throughout the Indus Valley started to leave the great cities and many other settlements, and they abandoned the shared cultural practices, such as weights and measures. Most scholars argue that turmoil forced them to do so. Many of these historians theorize that the arrival of Indo-European-speaking migrants forced the Indus Valley inhabitants to change their lifestyles completely. But there is no clear evidence of conquest. The cities were not burned down or sacked, and there are no signs of violence.

The end of the Indus Valley cities was more likely due to a combination of factors. It is possible that the climate became drier in the early second millennium B.C.E. and that

Inscribed Seals from the Indus Valley

Seals from Mohenjo-Daro (Art Archive/National Museum Karachi/Dagli Orti (left) and Scala/Art Resource, NY (right).)

The people of the Indus Valley used a script that emerged in around 2600 B.C.E., remained in use until around 1900 B.C.E., and then disappeared forever. Some four thousand texts are known, mostly incised on stamp seals, pottery, or pieces of jewelry. People of the Indus Valley used the stone stamps to make an impression on a piece of soft clay, so they cut the inscriptions in mirror image. On these seals the signs often appear next to the image of a single standing animal. Archaeologists have found lumps of clay into which such seals were pressed, often on several sides.

The inscriptions were usually very short, on average containing about five signs. Thus they did not record long sentences or tales, but most likely administrative information, such as the amount of a commodity and the name of the person who supervised the transaction. There are about four hundred signs, which suggests that each sign expressed an entire word.

EXAMINING THE EVIDENCE

1. Although we cannot understand the writing on them, what do these seals tell us about record keeping in the Indus culture?

2. Comparing the two seals, what similarities do you observe? How would you describe the differences?

3. How do the Indus Valley seals differ from the first writings we discussed for other early cultures?

For Further Information:
Kenoyer, Jonathan M. *Ancient Cities of the Indus Valley*. New York: Oxford University Press, 1998.

urban residents could no longer grow enough food to live in large groups. According to this theory, people moved into villages, smaller communities that required smaller concentrations of food, or migrated eastward, where the climate was wetter. This movement disrupted the trade networks that had tied the vast region together, and by 1700 B.C.E. people used a variety of local traditions rather than those that had characterized the mature Indus Valley culture. Some aspects of that culture, such as the possible rejection of material wealth and the beliefs in certain gods, may have inspired later South Asian practices and, in that way, have exerted a deep impact on later history. But the great cities of the Indus Valley ceased to exist, and many centuries passed before urban culture returned to that area of the world.

Indo-European Migrations   3000–1000 B.C.E.

Above we considered the theory that the Indus Valley culture ended because of the immigration of people speaking an Indo-European language. Such migrants may have descended onto the Indian subcontinent and conquered local populations. The scholarly disagreement over exactly what happened illustrates how difficult it is to understand the process by which Indo-European languages came to be spoken over a vast area of Eurasia. However, the fact that by 100 B.C.E. people from western China to western Europe spoke related Indo-European languages certainly was the result of a crucial process in Eurasian history—a process likely connected to the interactions between farmers and pastoralists.

FOCUS

What does the concept "Indo-European" mean, and how important is it for the study of Eurasia?

Indo-European Languages

The term *Indo-European* does not refer to a race or an ethnic group but to a group of languages that are related in vocabulary and grammar. In the eighteenth century C.E., European scholars first observed that people from Britain to South Asia spoke languages that had many similarities. Their discovery of the links between Sanskrit, the sacred language of ancient India, and the European classical languages, Greek and Latin, also showed them that these similarities had existed for many centuries. Note, for example, how English, Sanskrit, Greek, and Latin use the same words to express mother, father, and house (domicile):

English	Sanskrit	Greek	Latin
mother	matar	meter	mater
father	pitar	pater	pater
domicile	dama	domos	domus

Linguists observed that many other European languages and several from South Asia—including Sanskrit and Persian along with their modern derivations, Hindi and Farsi—shared many words and grammatical structures. Hence they reasoned that the languages evolved from an original ancient language that spread when its speakers migrated. They grouped the languages derived from this ancient one under the name *Indo-European*. When Indo-European groups separated, they adjusted to new natural environments and interacted with populations who spoke non-Indo-European languages. Consequently, their languages developed differences, but still maintained clear common Indo-European roots. These roots now help us trace the course of their migrations.

Indo-European Migrations

Speakers of an Indo-European language who called themselves *Arya*, "noble," arrived in South Asia shortly after 2000 B.C.E. and started to displace the local people, who spoke non-Indo-European Dravidian languages. Dravidian languages persist in the southernmost Indian subcontinent today, which together with historical accounts shows that the spread of Indo-European speakers from north to south was gradual. Where the speakers of Indo-European speakers came from and what motivated them to migrate remain unresolved.

The two principal explanations for these migrations show how scholars can interpret the same set of evidence very differently. Some researchers suggest that Indo-European languages spread together with agriculture from the area of modern Turkey where farming originated. Farmers would have migrated east and west from this region starting after 7000 B.C.E. They would have altered not only the local populations' means of survival but also their languages, in a process parallel to that of the Bantu migrations in Africa (see Chapter 8).

Theories of Indo-European Migrations

Other scholars believe the speakers of Indo-European languages were pastoralists who moved into farming areas starting in around 2000 B.C.E. Most believe these migrants originated in the southern Russian steppes, but others argue for a homeland closer to India, and the answer remains elusive. Some suggest that the arrival of Indo-European speakers entailed the conquest and domination of local populations. The conquerors would have benefited greatly from their expertise in horsemanship and their invention of the horse-drawn chariot. It is equally possible, however, that pastoralists often integrated peacefully into existing farming communities.

Indo-European Speakers and Eurasian History

Spread of Indo-European Languages

Although we cannot precisely locate the Indo-European homeland, it is certain that speakers of Indo-European languages spread over Eurasia in the second and first millennia B.C.E., carrying their languages into regions where people spoke other vernaculars. Indo-European languages gradually came to dominate Eurasia. The earliest definitive evidence of an Indo-European language is from what is now Turkey, where, as we saw in Chapter 2, a people called the Hittites had established a powerful state by 1800 B.C.E. whose official court language was Indo-European Hittite. In Greece, evidence of Indo-European first appears in Linear B tablets from 1500 to 1200 B.C.E. that include Greek words. It is possible that Indo-European speakers lived in both Turkey and Greece for many centuries before they started to write.

The presence of Indo-European languages farther west and north in Europe is clear from the earliest written remains found there; that is, from about 500 B.C.E. onward. Although today Indo-European languages are dominant throughout Europe, a few regions remain in which non-Indo-European languages have survived over millennia, such as Finland and the Basque area of Spain.

In Asia, Indo-European speakers did not become as dominant as they were in Europe. In the Middle East outside Turkey (where people today speak Turkish, the non-Indo-European language of later immigrants), people continued to use Semitic languages, such as Akkadian in antiquity and Arabic in more recent times. But migrants speaking Indo-European languages moved into southern Asia, arriving on the Iranian plateau in the second millennium B.C.E. The *Gathas*—songs of the Persian prophet Zoroaster (see Chapter 4)—were probably composed toward the end of that millennium, in around 1300 B.C.E., and their language is Indo-European with close similarities to the Sanskrit of India.

INDO-EUROPEAN MIGRATIONS	
c. 2000 B.C.E.	Aryas arrive in South Asia
c. 1800 B.C.E.	Creation of Hittite state in area of modern Turkey
c. 1500–1200 B.C.E.	Indo-European Greek words appear in Linear B texts
c. 1500–900 B.C.E.	Probable period of composition of the *Rig-Veda* in India
c. 1300 B.C.E.	*Gathas* composed in Iran
c. 1000 B.C.E.	Indo-European languages spoken throughout area of modern Europe

The most easterly evidence of Indo-European languages appears in the Central Asian provinces of modern China, where excavations have uncovered burials with naturally mummified human bodies in the Tarim Basin. Some of the burials date back to 2000 B.C.E., and they continued until 500 B.C.E. The dead people had European physical features, including fair skin and light hair, and some scholars believe that they were Indo-European speakers. They arrived in western China when the chariot first appeared in Shang China, and the two events seem to be related.

Vedas Early collections of Indian hymns, songs, and prayers that contain sacred knowledge; initially preserved in oral form, they were recorded in writing c. 600 B.C.E.

The spread of Indo-European languages was thus one of the most important events in the early history of the entire Eurasian continent. As a result, by the beginning of the Common Era, if not before, peoples from the Atlantic Ocean to the western regions of China spoke a variety of related languages that had a common source. The spread of Indo-European languages is but one example of the profound impact of nomadic peoples on the settled societies of Eurasia.

India's Vedic Age 1500–500 B.C.E.

By 1500 B.C.E. the Aryas had entered the Indian subcontinent from the Iranian plateau. They were probably pastoralists who migrated into the fertile river valleys in search of land, first in the northwest of India and later farther east. During their migrations, the Aryas encountered speakers of the non-Indo-European Dravidian languages. The mixture of peoples, traditions, and languages that resulted led to changes in customs and lifestyles that affected all, and this fusion became the foundation of classical Indian culture (see Map 3.2).

> **FOCUS**
>
> How did cultural developments in early Indian history shape the structure of society?

Vedic Origins

Ancient Indian literature contains many references to the new society that developed when Indo-European speakers migrated into the subcontinent. Unfortunately for historians, the accounts were written down long after the events they describe, raising questions about their accuracy. Historians who use such sources need to keep in mind that they likely tell us as much about the world of their authors as about early Vedic India.

The oldest compositions are the **Vedas**, collections of hymns, songs, prayers, and dialogues. The term *Veda* literally means "sacred knowledge," and the texts are written in a very early form of the Indo-European Sanskrit language. There are four Vedas, the oldest of which is the *Rig Veda*, a collection of 1028 hymns organized in ten books and addressed to various deities. Priests probably composed the *Rig Veda* between 1500 and 900 B.C.E., describing events of that period. The hymns were not written down until around 600 B.C.E., however, and the later authors likely modified their contents.

The authors of the Vedas portrayed a society torn by violent conflict. They depicted the Aryas as light-skinned nomadic warriors who conquered the local dark-skinned population, the *Dasa*, which means "enemy." The Aryas fought on horse-drawn chariots against the Dasa, who often lived in fortified settlements, and also against each other. According to the Vedas, the Aryas greatly valued cattle and needed access to grazing areas for their animals. Although the Vedas focus on military feats, many scholars now believe that they misrepresent actual events. They think it more likely that the Aryas spread throughout India through peaceful interaction and intermarriage with local populations. Thus, instead of the conflict between pastoralists and farmers described in the texts, the Aryas and the local population probably developed slowly and peacefully among people of different lifestyles.

Rise of a New Society: Families, Clans, and Castes

People in early Vedic society belonged to extended families organized along patriarchal lines, the leading men having full control over other members of the family. Women had

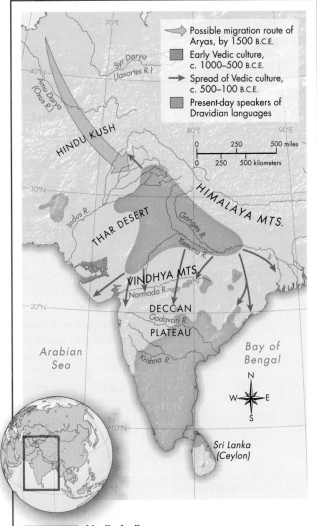

MAP 3.2   **Vedic India**

The migration in around 1500 B.C.E. of Indo-European-speaking Aryas into South Asia introduced radical changes in culture and society, which gradually spread from the northwest throughout much of the subcontinent. The Aryas' new ideas about social hierarchy, religion, and human nature would affect the region's culture for millennia.

Patriarchal Families

little authority and did not inherit family wealth unless there were no male heirs. The *Law-book of Manu*, although written down much later in the first century B.C.E., gives an idea of the low status of women in the Vedic age. The book states:

> I will now propound the eternal laws for a husband and his wife who keep to the path of duty, whether they be united or separated.
>
> Day and night women must be kept in dependence by the males of their families, and, if they attach themselves to sensual enjoyments, they must be kept under one's control. Her father protects her in childhood, her husband protects her in youth, and her sons protect her in old age; a woman is never fit for independence.[2]

Women thus depended on men throughout their lives. As in many other ancient societies, such as Athens in classical Greece (see Chapter 5), a woman's primary duty was to bear children, and her value to the community was measured in these terms.

Political Structure

Extended families joined together in **clans**, groups considered to have descended from the same ancestor. Clans were the basis of the early Vedic political structure. Family heads, all men, met in assemblies and accepted the leadership of a **raja**, a word that corresponds to the Latin *rex*, "king," although a translation of "chief" is more accurate. Clan members shared their resources and maintained strong social ties. Hundreds existed throughout northwest India, some settled in villages, others as pastoral groups. Clashes between clans were frequent, and the rajas had to be great military leaders to gain the respect of their people. This explains the atmosphere of conflict in the Vedas.

Varnas

In early Vedic society among both the indigenous Dasas and the Indo-European Aryas, it was membership in a clan believed to have a common ancestor that primarily determined people's identities. In around 1000 B.C.E., after the composition of the *Rig Veda*, different categorizations arose. One involved the concept of **varna**, which literally means "color." The idea may have originally derived from the division between dark-skinned Dasas and lighter-skinned Aryas, but later the word came to mean something like "class." Originally the varna system had four levels: Brahmans (BRAH-mihn), or priests; Kshatriyas (shuh-TREE-uh), the warriors and aristocrats; Vaishyas (VYSH-yuh), landowning peasants and merchants; and Shudras (SHOOD-ra), by far the largest group, composed of artisans, land-less farmers, and laborers. Later on came the addition of a fifth group, the Untouchables, who worked with materials that others refused to touch, such as animal skins. Entire families, both men and women, belonged to the same varna, and they stayed in the same category over many generations, as people were supposed to marry within their own varna.

This rigorous system of social hierarchy required justification, and a hymn added late to the *Rig Veda* provided it in these terms:

> When the gods spread the sacrifice with the Man as the offering . . .
> When they divided the Man, into how many parts did they apportion him? What do they call his mouth, his two arms and thighs and feet?
> His mouth became the Brahman; his arms were made into the Warrior (Kshatriya), his thighs the People (Vaishya), and from his feet the Servants (Shudra) were born.[3]

clan Group of families related to a real or presumed common ancestor.

raja Chief of Indian clan; the term is related to the Latin word for "king," *rex.*

varna Group identity in early Indian society, related to the concept of class; people belonged to one of four varna as a result of their birth.

jati Division of Indian society that identifies an individual's occupation and social standing.

Just as each part of the human body serves a specific purpose and has a fixed place in the body as a whole, each varna served a specific purpose in society and had a fixed place in the social hierarchy. This social order, like the body itself, had been created by the gods and could no more be questioned or changed than the human body.

Over time the structure of Vedic society became more complex, however. When increasing numbers of people lived together, labor became more specialized, and by 500 B.C.E. subdivisions of the varna system developed. These became known as **jati**. Although varnas continued to determine people's position in the social hierarchy, specific occupations grouped them into jatis. Every specialized occupation could create a new jati, each with its specific tasks and duties. Members of a jati lived together, married each other, and ate together. The designation thus passed on from parents to children, and in fact the term *jati* has the same root as the word for birth.

When Portuguese visitors to the Indian subcontinent in the sixteenth century C.E. observed these social groups, they gave them the name *casta*, which means "breed." That categorization led to the English designations of caste and the **caste system**. The caste system provided a social structure in which everyone had an allotted place. There were clear rules of behavior, which, if broken, would lead to expulsion from the caste—hence the term *outcast*. The upper castes had special rights and access to property, and the system protected their privileges. Social mobility was very difficult in Vedic society. Jatis could improve their lot as a group, but individuals rarely moved into a higher caste. The system had a particular advantage, however: it facilitated the integration of newcomers into Indian society, even those with different faiths. Many immigrants to the subcontinent could establish themselves as a defined jati. The caste system remained a central part of Indian society for thousands of years and still plays a role today.

Caste System

Vedic Religion

The Vedas portray a rich religious system, one that shares ideas and gods described in other Indo-European writings, especially those from Iran and Greece. The atmosphere of conflict dominates in the divine world of the Vedas, and many of the gods represent forces of nature admired because of their strength.

As was true among humans, male gods dominated the Vedic divine world. Their leader was Indra, the war god, often violent and fond of drink. He wielded the thunderbolt and protected the universe against demons. The sky god, Varuna, maintained cosmic order and justice. He punished liars and evildoers, banishing their souls to the miserable netherworld, the House of Clay, whereas the souls of people who had behaved well dwelled in a heaven-like House of the Fathers. The god of fire, Agni, was the intermediary between humans and gods because, as fire, he made it possible for people to give sacrifices. All these gods were strong warriors, but some Vedic hymns emphasized their peaceful aspects as well. They honored the goddess of dawn, Usas, or the lady of the forest, in language that shows deep appreciation for the natural environment. Of dawn, they say, for example:

Gods and Goddesses

> She makes paths all easy, fair to travel, and, rich, has shown herself benign and friendly. We see that you are good: far shines your luster; your beams, your splendors have flown up to heaven.[4]

Humans could communicate with the gods through ritual sacrifice. Trained priests burned offerings to urge the gods to be kind. They slaughtered a variety of animals—horses, cattle, sheep, and goats—while reciting hymns. The priests also drank *soma*, extracted from unknown plants, that gave them divine inspiration. Sacrifice was so central in the Vedic culture that it became connected with creation itself. According to tradition, the gods had created the universe by sacrificing a Lord of Beings, the primeval man who had existed before the universe. Consequently, every time the priests performed a sacrifice, they repeated creation and thus became responsible for the order of the universe.

Ritual Sacrifice

The most important sacrifices, especially those of horses, demanded the presence of the raja. Over time, the raja became the sole patron of sacrifices, and the priests gave him attributes of divinity. In this way a division of authority developed: the priests gained superiority in the ritual world, and the raja became the political, military, and administrative head of the clan. Women were fully excluded from this power structure. Thus Vedic religious practices and beliefs reinforced the social and political order.

The Brahmans' central role in sacrifices confirmed their uppermost status in the caste system and also had a unique effect on the spread of literacy in India. Only they knew the Vedic hymns that were essential during sacrifices. These songs were composed in the upper-class Sanskrit language, which contrasted with Prakrit, the dialect that most people

caste system Indian organization of society that identifies people's position and status on the basis of the group into which they were born.

The Upanishads

At the end of the Vedic period, anonymous mystics and others who rejected the existing social order started to formulate commentaries on the Vedas that reflect evolving religious ideas and speculations in a genre of Indian writing called the Upanishads. The Upanishads are often phrased as dialogues about religious questions between a teacher and a student "sitting in front" (the literal meaning of *Upanishad*). The oldest Upanishads were composed between 800 and 400 B.C.E., but they continued to appear in much later periods. Their main concern is to establish the unity of all things within the Brahman, the eternal entity that binds the universe together. Some Upanishads focus on the practice of meditation. The following passage recommends meditation on the syllable Om (ohm), which was pronounced at the start of every Vedic recitation. Its other designation is *udgitha*. The passage describes what the syllable could mean in the mind of a devotee.

> Let a man meditate on the syllable Om, called the udgitha; for the udgitha is sung, beginning with Om.
>
> The full account, however, of Om is this:
>
> The essence of all beings is the earth, the essence of the earth is water, the essence of water the plants, the essence of plants man, the essence of man speech, the essence of speech the Rig Veda, the essence of the Rig Veda the Sama Veda, the essence of the Sama Veda the udgitha (which is Om).
>
> That udgitha (Om) is the best of all essences, the highest, deserving the highest place, the eighth.
>
> . . .
>
> And that couple is joined together in the syllable Om. When two people come together, they fulfill each other's desire.

Thus, he who knowing this, meditates on the syllable (Om), the udgitha, becomes indeed a fulfiller of desires.

That syllable is the syllable of permission, for whenever we permit anything, we say Om, yes. Now permission is gratification. He who knowing this meditates on the syllable (Om), the udgitha, becomes indeed a gratifier of desires.

By that syllable does the threefold knowledge proceed. When the Adhvaryu priest gives an order, he says Om. When the Hotri priest recites, he says Om. When the Udgatri priest sings, he says Om—all for the glory of that syllable. The threefold knowledge proceeds by the greatness of that syllable and by its essence.

Now therefore it would seem to follow, that both he who knows this (the true meaning of the syllable Om), and he who does not, perform the same sacrifice. But this is not so, for knowledge and ignorance are different. The sacrifice which a man performs with knowledge, faith, and the upanishad is more powerful. This is the full account of the syllable Om.

Source: Nicol Macnicol, trans., *Hindu Scriptures* (London/New York: J. M. Dent & Sons, Ltd., E. P. Dutton & Co., Inc., 1938), 117–118.

EXAMINING THE EVIDENCE

1. How does this passage reflect Vedic ideas?

2. How does it aim to establish unity in the universe?

Brahmans spoke. Brahmans may have had such firm control over the literary tradition that they prevented the written recording of the Vedas and the use of writing in general. This monopoly on literacy strengthened the power of the Brahmans, but it slowed the spread of writing throughout Indian society. Only by 500 C.E. did writing become widespread in India, whereas in other equally complex societies—such as Mesopotamia, where, as we saw in Chapter 2, writing first served administrative functions—it caught on much earlier.

Developments in Vedic Ideas

The Upanishads Early Vedic society was primarily centered in the river valleys of northwest India, and the *Rig Veda* depicts the natural environment of that region. The dense forests farther east in the Ganges plain originally prevented extensive agriculture and herding there. It was only after 1000 B.C.E. when people began to use iron tools, that forests could be cleared. Aryas spread eastward, and during this period of expansion they encountered indigenous traditions that affected their own religious doctrines. Groups of people started to reject the structures of Vedic society and began to formulate new interpretations of the Vedas in a new type of text. Called *Upanishads* (oo-PAHN-ih-shhad), they combined indigenous and Vedic traditions (see Reading the Past: The Upanishads). The texts were only written down around 500 B.C.E., but they express older ideas. They shifted the strong focus on sacrifice that had dominated early Vedic religion toward an emphasis on living a righteous life. This shift was connected to changes in the beliefs about the afterlife and to the concept of **reincarnation**—rebirth in a new form.

The belief arose that every living creature had an immortal essence, something like a soul. Upon death this soul would leave the body and be reborn in another body. When people had behaved well, their souls reincarnated into higher bodies. But when they had misbehaved, they reincarnated into a lower life form, either a lower caste or an animal or plant. The outcome depended on a person's **karma**, his or her behavior in the former life. The idea of reincarnation supported the caste system—a person's position in the hierarchy was the result of earlier behavior and was one's own responsibility. At the same time, it opened up the possibility of upward social movement, even if such movement had to wait for the next life.

The belief in reincarnation tied all forms of life together into a single system, a universal and eternal entity called **Brahman**. Even the gods passed away, and other gods replaced them. The aim of the Upanishads was to make people conscious of their connection to the Brahman. In this view, each being has a Self, called the **atman**, understanding of which liberates people from the constant cycle of reincarnation. They would first attain a state of deep sleep without dreams, unaware of any physical reality. One teacher explained the state as follows:

> Now as a man, when embraced by a beloved wife, knows nothing that is without, nothing that is within, so does this person, when embraced by the intelligent Self (atman), knows nothing that is without, nothing that is within. This is indeed his true form, in which wishes are fulfilled, in which the Self only is his wish, in which no wish is left—free from sorrow.[5]

After achieving deep sleep, an individual could reach a level beyond this dreamless trance, in which he or she realizes that his or her Self is identified with the eternal entity (Brahman). One does not reach the higher stage through active life but by meditating, that is, reflecting on religious questions.

We see, then, that the expansion of the Aryas across India did not result in the simple dissemination of Vedic ideas. Rather, contact with indigenous traditions led to changes in Vedic ideas. A religion that emphasized individual transcendence replaced one that emphasized the role of social elites in divine sacrifice. It is within this later Vedic world that further developments in Indian religious thought would take place (which we will explore in Chapter 6).

Reincarnation

reincarnation Belief system that every living being's soul can be reborn in another life form after death in an eternal cycle of existence.

karma In Indian thought about reincarnation, the consequences of one's behavior in an earlier life that influence events in the present.

Brahman In Indian thought, a universal and eternal soul that binds all life forms together.

atman In Indian thought, the immortal essence of a living creature.

The Early Chinese Dynasties 2000–771 B.C.E.

In India of the second millennium B.C.E., we have seen how the arrival of new people caused sweeping social and religious changes. By contrast, in the region of East Asia that would develop into China, cultures in the early and later periods were linked by continuities. From the start of agricultural life in the vast landmass that constitutes modern China, multiple cultures coexisted, and through increased contacts and exchange they acquired common features. The middle Yellow River Valley was the seat of a succession of dynasties, and archaeological information from that region allows us to study how states governed by a powerful elite developed.

FOCUS

What factors account for the remarkable cultural continuity of early Chinese states?

Re-Creating Early China: Literary Traditions and the Archaeological Record

In around 100 B.C.E., Sima Qian, the court astrologer whom we met at the beginning of the chapter, wrote a history of his country up to his own day. He based his account on existing books that contained anecdotes, speeches, and chronicles of rulers from the beginning of time. His *Records of the Historian* contains historical tales, chronological tables, biographies, and treatises. Because Sima Qian lived in a time when a single dynasty, the Han, ruled China, he depicted the earlier history of his country as a sequence of similar dynasties. According to Sima Qian, after a period in which heroes and sages established the elements of culture, such as agriculture, music, and the arts, three dynasties governed in succession: the Xia (shah), Shang, and Zhou (joe).

For two millennia, Sima Qian and the literary sources he used provided the only evidence of China's early history. Then in the twentieth century C.E., archaeologists unearthed villages, cities, and cemeteries that tell a somewhat different story. The excavations provided evidence that from about 2000 to 771 B.C.E., a sequence of large urban centers flourished in China; they were probably the capital cities of states. In those cities lived elites who surrounded themselves with luxury goods in life and were buried in lavish tombs, similar to those we have seen in Southwest Asia and Egypt.

Oracle Bones   China's early history became clearer with the discovery of the first written material from the region. In the late nineteenth century C.E., farmers from Anyang (ahn-YAHNG) in the Yellow River Valley regularly dug up bones and turtle shells incised with what looked like characters of Chinese script. However, they could not read them. Believing that these "dragon bones" had the power to heal, they ground them into medicinal powders. When scholars saw the bones in 1898, they recognized that the inscriptions contained some of the royal names Sima Qian listed in his history of the Shang dynasty. Further excavations at Anyang revealed large deposits of bones and turtle shells, which scholars refer to as *oracle bones* because of their use in **divination**, that is, the prediction of the future. Some two hundred thousand oracle bones have been discovered, many of them fragmentary, containing mostly short inscriptions. They derive from the reigns of the last nine kings of the Shang dynasty, from about 1200 to 1027 B.C.E. (see Lives and Livelihoods: Chinese Diviners, page 96).

Chinese Writing   The oracle bones are the earliest preserved evidence of writing in China. Other types of records were probably written on perishable materials such as bamboo or silk. The script of the oracle bones uses a principle followed in the cuneiform and hieroglyphic writings we discussed in Chapter 2: a single sign represents an entire word. Some of the characters were pictures of the item they indicated (for example, a kneeling human for a woman), whereas conventional symbols conveyed abstract ideas (for example, a mouth for "to call"). Although many words in Chinese sound alike, each had its own representation in writing, and until the twentieth century C.E. Chinese script did not rely much on syllabic signs. In this respect, it departed from the early scripts of Southwest Asia and Egypt.

The Chinese script has a unique history. After the first emperor, Shi Huangdi (shee huang-dee, discussed in Chapter 6), ordered its standardization, its basic elements and characters did not change, although the shape of the signs evolved over time. The script had a deep effect on Chinese history in that it connected people from a wide geographical area to the same ancient past. As Chinese script spread, its use brought more and more people into a shared history.

The Growth of States 2000–1570 B.C.E.

Soon after 2000 B.C.E. the village cultures that had characterized China for millennia developed into a more uniform culture in which bronze played a major role. Copper had been used for tools since 5000 B.C.E., but around 2000 B.C.E., people started to mix it with tin to produce the much stronger bronze. Scholars disagree about how bronze working arrived in

divination The practice of seeking information about the future through sources regarded as magical.

China. Some argue for an indigenous invention, whereas others believe that Indo-European nomads brought the technology from western Asia to China.

Bronze production in ancient China was unparalleled in the ancient world. The elites valued the metal so much that they commissioned vast numbers of weapons and other items, especially vessels. Demand was so great that in around 1500 B.C.E. large-scale production started. Workers manufactured numerous objects. Many were of giant size—one tomb from around 1200 B.C.E. contained 3520 pounds of the metal, and the largest surviving bronze vessel from antiquity, which weighs 1925 pounds, is also from this era. All the bronze objects were cast in molds with intricate decorations, which were first impressed in clay and later refined by filing the bronze. Mining the metals, transporting them, and casting them required the handicraft of hundreds of workers, many with specialized skills. Thus, like the silk cloth production we discussed earlier in this chapter, the desires of elites stimulated bronze production and required the specialized labor that went along with social stratification.

The earliest large urban site in China is Erlitou (er-lee-toh), dating from around 1900 B.C.E. In its center on top of a pounded-earth platform archaeologists found the remains of a monumental building, measuring about 110 by 117 yards. In later periods of Chinese history, such imposing structures had an official character, and it is thus likely that this was a palace. The objects found at the site of Erlitou resemble those that later clearly showed political control and ritual activity, such as weapons and bronze vessels. Archaeologists also found many animal shoulder blades, and although they were not inscribed, they may have been oracle bones.

The archaeological remains from Erlitou belong to a culture that spread over the central Yellow River Valley and adjacent zones. Scholars used to believe that Erlitou was the capital of the dynasty that Sima Qian called Xia, but today most historians think that the Xia dynasty did not exist and that Sima Qian imposed an image of the state of his day onto an earlier period. Many of Erlitou's cultural elements survived into the succeeding period, which may characterize the start of what Sima Qian called the Shang dynasty. Historians feel that they are on firmer ground in the study of that dynasty, as oracle bones confirm its existence and contain information that archaeology on its own cannot provide.

Shang Dynasty Bronze Vessel

Shang period bronze work is famous for the skill and refinement the artists displayed in their creations. To produce a vessel like this one, they made a clay model of the desired object to create a mold, which they cut into pieces. They cast bronze segments in the clay molds and reassembled them before filling in the details. This process enabled them to produce large items with elaborate decoration. (akg-images/Werner Forman.)

The Shang Dynasty and the Consolidation of Power 1570–1027 B.C.E.

Several major cities in the Yellow River Valley seem to have been successive centers of political power in the second half of the second millennium B.C.E. (see Map 3.3). They differed from early cities in Southwest Asia and the Indus Valley; they covered a much larger area and had zones with clearly distinct functions that housed a hierarchy of social classes. The centers of the early Chinese cities contained large buildings on top of pounded-earth platforms reserved for the elites. Surrounding them were industrial areas with workshops that produced goods for these elites, such as bronze vessels. The common people lived in the outer rings of the cities in small houses partly dug into the ground. This helped inhabitants to keep warm in the winter and cool in the summer, but their living circumstances were generally very poor. On the outskirts of the cities were located the tombs for rulers and other elites, and nearby were sites for rituals related to the dead, such as the reading of oracle bones. Thus, Chinese cities were physical manifestations of Chinese social structure.

Anyang

The city of Anyang shows the culmination of a process of increasing concentration of power and wealth in early China. Located one hundred miles to the north of the Yellow River and stretching over a huge area of some twenty square miles, it most likely was a capital of the Shang state. Anyang's cemetery shows the riches that elites accumulated. It had thirteen large tombs, dug into the ground up to forty-three feet deep and with wooden

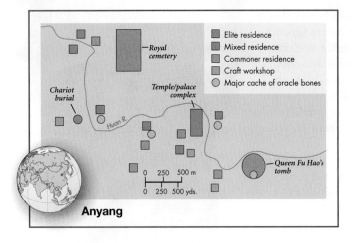

Anyang

burial chambers at the bottom. These monumental tombs certainly belonged to Shang kings and queens, although the fact that all but one were looted prevents us from knowing exactly who was buried in them.

The only remaining intact tomb from Anyang contained dazzling wealth. In 1976 C.E., Chinese archaeologists discovered the tomb of Queen Fu Hao (foo HOW), wife of King Wu Ding, who lived in the thirteenth century B.C.E. Previously known oracle bones had already revealed that she was a highly unusual woman for her time, although she was only one of Wu Ding's many consorts. Some oracle bones state that Fu Hao prepared them, evidence that she took a leading role in divination, which was usually reserved for the king. The oracle bones also indicate that she actively participated in her husband's wars, raising troops and leading them into battle. The finds in the tomb confirmed her unusual status. They included over a hundred weapons—very uncommon for a woman's burial—and some were inscribed with her name. Several bronze vessels were also inscribed with Fu Hao's name or title. The splendor of her tomb goods was magnificent. They included more than 460 bronze objects, some 70 stone sculptures, nearly 705 jade objects, numerous bone hairpins, and some 7000 cowrie shells, which served as currency at the time. Alongside Fu Hao lay six sacrificed dogs and sixteen sacrificed humans. As in other ancient societies, the tombs of the Chinese elites displayed their wealth and power.

Surrounding the royal tombs of Anyang were more than twelve hundred pits containing the remains of people and animals. Human skeletons were the most numerous by far, but there were also twenty pits with horses, and fewer with other animals. Each of two pits held an elephant accompanied by its human attendants. The human sacrifices were usually young men, who were often beheaded or otherwise dismembered, with the heads buried apart from the bodies. Although some of these sacrifices were made at the time of a king's burial, most occurred later, as gifts to the dead. They were part of interactions between the king and his ancestors, which dominated the ritual life of the Shang state.

The cult of ancestors dominated Shang's ritual and religious ideas; the deceased were thought to have enormous powers over the living. A god called *Di* (dee) presided over hierarchically organized powers, which included natural phenomena such as rivers, mountains, and the sun and also people who had lived in the past. These included male and female Shang ancestors of the king, pre-Shang ancestors, and former regional lords. When an important person died, he or she became an ancestor and joined the group of powers. The honors awarded to these people while still alive continued after death and may even have expanded. Ancestors gained even more importance in the later Shang dynasty, at the expense of Di, who may ultimately have come to be considered the first royal ancestor.

The high respect for ancestors also explains the care the Shang gave to burials and the subsequent sacrifices. The living king had to keep ancestors satisfied so that they would not cause harm, and he constantly consulted them through oracle bones to divine the future. Oracle reading evidently took place

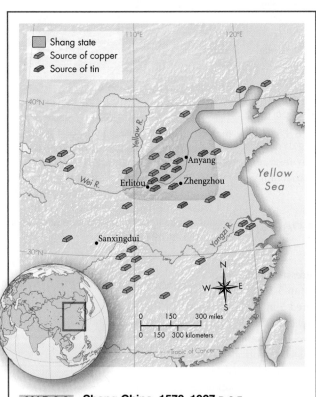

MAP 3.3 **Shang China, 1570–1027 B.C.E.**

The Shang dynasty ruled the Yellow River Valley and its surroundings. They repeatedly moved the capital to sprawling new cities with massive earthwork constructions and impressive royal tombs. Famed for its bronzes, Shang China needed continued access to copper and tin, whose sources the state sought to control.

continuously and required an infrastructure of specialists. These included people to slaughter the animals, which subject regions often provided as tribute; individuals to select and prepare the bones and shells; and scribes to record the questions, predictions, and other information on perishable materials before carving the text on the actual bones or shells (see Lives and Livelihoods: Chinese Diviners). Ancestor worship reinforced the power of kings by connecting them to a host of notable people stretching back through the generations to the beginning of time.

The king enforced his rule through military means as well as rituals. Devotion to warfare was a Shang hallmark. The core of the army fought on chariots pulled by two horses and ridden by a warrior, an attendant, and a driver. The introduction of chariots after 1500 B.C.E. marked a major technological change in Chinese society. Because the earliest chariots in China were fully developed, many scholars think the innovation came from western Asia. Once again, nomads were key to this development. Indo-European-speaking nomads of Central Asia, such as those whose mummified bodies were found in the Tarim Basin, were probably the intermediaries between the two regions.

Besides fighting, the Shang also loved to hunt. Excavations have revealed numerous bones of elephants, bears, rhinoceroses, tigers, leopards, deer, monkeys, foxes, and smaller game. Whereas northern China is now barren and treeless, in ancient times the region was blanketed with dense forests, home to many animals. The Shang hunted them in great numbers, partly for use in the sacrifices that were a major part of their ritual life, but also for sport.

All the monumental remains relate to the top level of Shang society, whose members had access to great wealth and power. A large majority of people, however, lived in poor conditions, working the fields, mining metals, building tombs and monumental residences, and providing other services to their masters. Many were slaves captured during military campaigns, and as we have seen, their lives could be sacrificed to benefit the Shang elites.

Sima Qian's focus on the Shang dynasty, along with Anyang's status as the only city to provide written evidence of this period, creates the false impression that the Shang state was the only important one in late-second-millennium B.C.E. China. Recent archaeological work shows that other regions had their own cultures, which sometimes produced artwork as impressive as that of Anyang, but stylistically distinct. The people of some of these regions must have created states as well. It was one of these centers that ended the Shang dynasty: in the eleventh century B.C.E. the Zhou to the west of the Shang heartland defeated the last Shang ruler, Di Xin.

The Early Zhou Dynasty and the Extension of Power 1027–771 B.C.E.

During the Shang period many distinct groups controlled parts of northern China as either allies or opponents of Shang rulers. According to Sima Qian, the leader of one such group, the Zhou, defeated Di Xin at the Battle of Muye in 1027 B.C.E. King Wen, the Zhou ruler, justified the rebellion with a new ideology: he had received the **Mandate of Heaven** to replace an oppressive ruler. An ode in his honor from the *Book of Songs* states:

Ancestor Worship

Warfare

Social Order

Shang's Neighbors

Statue of a Man from Sanxingdui

Outside the center of Shang rule Chinese artists produced refined bronze work that displays regional styles. One masterpiece is this 8-1/2-foot statue excavated at Sanxingdui to the west of Shang's heartland. Features such as the man's attenuated shape are very unlike the artistic style characteristic of Anyang at the time. (Sanxingui Museum/ChinaStock.)

Mandate of Heaven Concept in Chinese thought that Heaven gave the right to rule to a king or emperor and could withdraw that right were the ruler to behave badly.

Chinese Diviners

Just like other ancient peoples, such as the Mesopotamians, the Chinese were preoccupied with predicting the future. In the Shang period, this stimulated a massive enterprise based on oracle bones. Numerous people were involved, including the preparers of bones or shells, the scribes, and the diviners themselves, a post reserved for noblemen. The Shang king was the principal figure, however, as the questions and interpretations derived their authority from his person. The basic idea behind the divination practice was that ancestors could give guidance about the future and communicate their advice through oracle bones.

In typical practice, the king or his diviners first formulated a statement such as "we will receive millet harvest." The diviner then touched a previously prepared animal shoulder bone or turtle shell with a hot metal point until the bone or shell cracked. He numbered the cracks, and the king interpreted them as being auspicious—that is, indicating a good omen— or not. He then made a prediction such as "Auspicious: We will receive harvest." Next, a scribe carved the original question on the bone or shell, sometimes with the king's prediction and more rarely with a statement of what happened in reality.

The questions posed often involved the success of harvests or whether the queen would give birth to a boy or a girl. They ranged over a wide area of royal activities, however: Whom should the king appoint to a bureaucratic post? When should he make an offering? Will an act of his incur the displeasure of the powers? One group of early diviners often listed alternatives side by side. For example:

Divined: "On the next day, day 31, (we) should not make offering to Ancestor Yi."

Divined: "On the next day, day 31, (we) should make offering to Ancestor Yi."

Some statements contained an appeal for good luck or asked for guidance in the interpretation of an event or a dream. Others aimed to predict disasters, as in this example:

Crack-making on day 30, Que divined: "In the next ten days there will be no disasters." The king read the cracks, and said: "Not so. There will be trouble!" And so it was. On day 31, the king went to hunt buffaloes and the chariot of officer Zi hit the royal chariot. Prince Yang fell to the ground.

Crack-making on day 50, Que divined: "In the next ten days there will be no disasters." The king twice stated:

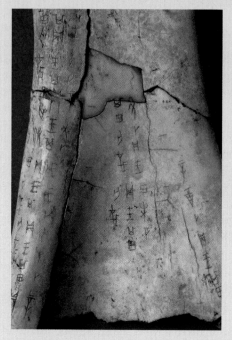

Oracle Bone

Bones inscribed with early Chinese characters present the first examples of Chinese writing dating to the late Shang period, 1200 to 1027 B.C.E. This oracle bone is from the hundreds of thousands that have been found near the Shang capital of Anyang. (Lowell Georgia/Corbis.)

"There will be trouble!" He predicted: "X will have trouble and an affliction." The fifth day came, day 54, X fell from the steps of the sacrificial room. The divination took place in the tenth month.

Oracle bone divination is closely tied to the Shang dynasty. It may have originated earlier in Chinese history, but archaeologists cannot determine from the uninscribed bones and shells they find whether they were consumed for food only or had uses in divination. The Shang dynasty elevated oracle bone divination to a major state enterprise, as the numerous remains show. With the Zhou, however, people turned to other means to find out what the future held in store.

Source: Redouan Djamouri, trans., "Écriture et divination sous les Shang," in *Divination et rationalité en Chine ancienne*, ed. Karine Chemla, Donald Harper, and Marc Kalinowski (Saint-Denis, France: Presses Universitaires de Vincennes, 1999), 19.

QUESTIONS TO CONSIDER

1. What areas of life did Shang divination cover?

2. How did oracle bone reading bolster the king's role in society?

For Further Information:

de Bary, William T., and Irene Bloom, eds., *Sources of Chinese Tradition*, 2d ed., Vol. 1. New York: Columbia University Press, 1999.

Ebrey, Patricia Buckley. *Chinese Civilization: A Source Book*, 2d ed. New York: Free Press, 1993.

Keightley, David N. *Sources of Shang History: The Oracle-Bone Inscriptions of Bronze Age China*. Berkeley: University of California Press, 1978.

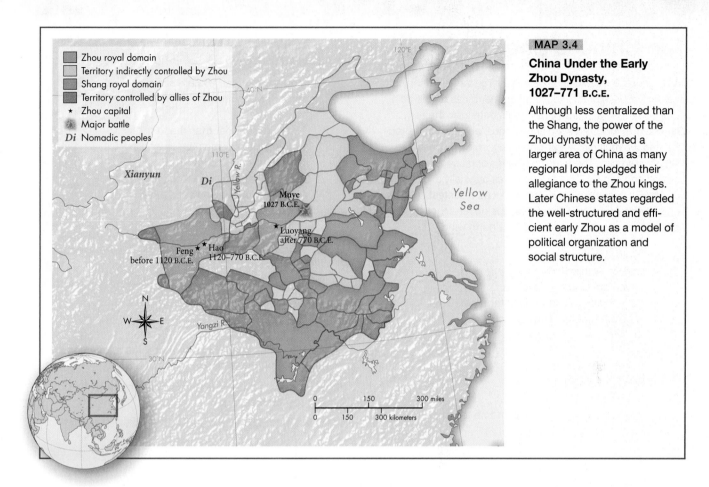

MAP 3.4

China Under the Early Zhou Dynasty, 1027–771 B.C.E.

Although less centralized than the Shang, the power of the Zhou dynasty reached a larger area of China as many regional lords pledged their allegiance to the Zhou kings. Later Chinese states regarded the well-structured and efficient early Zhou as a model of political organization and social structure.

Map legend:
- Zhou royal domain
- Territory indirectly controlled by Zhou
- Shang royal domain
- Territory controlled by allies of Zhou
- ★ Zhou capital
- Major battle
- *Di* Nomadic peoples

August was King Wen,
continuously bright and reverent.
Great, indeed, was the Mandate of Heaven.
There were Shang's grandsons and sons.
Was their number not a hundred thousand?
But the High God gave his Mandate,
and they bowed down to Zhou.[6]

As a supreme divine force, Heaven, called Tian (ty-ehn) in Chinese, gave the right to rule to a just and honorable man. When that man maintained order and harmony on earth, the entire cosmos was harmonious. If he misbehaved, however, Heaven withdrew the mandate, natural disasters occurred, and the people were allowed to rebel. The idea of the Mandate of Heaven thus became a check on rulers and allowed the possibility of political change. All new Chinese dynasties adopted the ideology the Zhou created to justify their rebellion, and even the democracy-seeking protesters at Beijing's Tiananmen Square in May 1989 invoked the rejection of oppressive rulers.

The Zhou was the longest ruling dynasty in Chinese history (1027–221 B.C.E.), although, as we will see, its powers were only nominal after 771 B.C.E. The territory Zhou kings ruled was larger than that of the Shang, stretching beyond the Yellow River Valley, but their control was indirect. Zhou kings did not personally annex and govern all the regions included in the state but appointed family members to do so on their behalf. When it was impossible to subdue a territory fully, they established alliances with local lords who were willing to accept the kings' supremacy. Lords resided in fortified cities and often controlled only a small hinterland. By around 800 B.C.E. there existed some two hundred regional lords in the Zhou state. According to convention, they all belonged to one extended family, with the Zhou king being the oldest brother who deserved the most respect (see Map 3.4).

Political and Social Structure

The Chinese *Book of Songs*

The Chinese *Book of Songs* covers a large variety of topics, including praises of the king and commentaries on the daily life of commoners. Many of its poems date from the early Zhou period. All authors are anonymous, and the voices represented are multiple: kings, noblemen, soldiers, peasants, men, and women. There are love songs and songs about betrayal and sorrow. This example was originally a love song, but later Chinese thinkers interpreted it as a contest song by farmers who urge each other to escape government oppression, metaphorically referred to as the north wind.

> Cold is the north wind,
> the snow falls thick.
> If you are kind and love me,
> take my hand and we'll go together.
> You are modest, you are slow,
> but oh, we must hurry!
>
> Fierce is the north wind,
> the snow falls fast.
> If you are kind and love me,
> take my hand and we'll go home together.

> You are modest, you are slow,
> but oh, we must hurry!
>
> Nothing is redder than the fox,
> nothing blacker than the crow.
> If you are kind and love me,
> take my hand and we'll ride together.
> You are modest, you are slow,
> but oh, we must hurry!

Source: Burton Watson, trans., in Wm. Theodore de Bary and Irene Bloom, eds., *Sources of Chinese Tradition*, 2d ed., vol. 1 (New York: Columbia University Press, 1991), 40.

EXAMINING THE EVIDENCE

1. How can one read this poem both as a love song and as a contest song?

2. How does it use the natural environment to convey its message?

This structure provided a very strict hierarchy to Zhou society. Each local lord and state official had a well-defined rank and position assigned by birth. Sacrifices to ancestors continued. The king made offerings to the ancestors of the royal family, and local lords honored their own ancestors. By participating in these rituals, they reinforced their social ties.

Ritual Practices   Under the Zhou, however, the ritual practices associated with ancestor cults changed. Instead of performing sacrifices, nobles contacted their ancestors by donating bronzes, which they inscribed with short texts listing the names of the donors and sometimes military events. In return, the ancestors were expected to provide favors to the living. The consultation of oracle bones also ended, and in its place kings determined the wishes of ancestors by reading messages in the lines sticks created when thrown down.

Some statements kings made in interpreting cast sticks became part of the major literary works of subsequent Chinese history. Later works, especially the *Book of Songs*, also include poems from the early Zhou period that reflect court life at the time (see Reading the Past: The Chinese *Book of Songs*). Later Chinese extensively edited this early material, however, so modern scholars have trouble determining what is original and what is not. It is clear, however, that many later generations in China saw the Zhou period as very special, with an ideal government and social structure. Just as ancestors provided models for the living to emulate, the Zhou provided a model for the current Chinese state. In this way the image of the Zhou state was fundamental to Chinese thought.

End of the Early Zhou   The Zhou political organization fell apart in 771 B.C.E., when leaders of dependent states started to ignore the king's commands and to fight one another, ushering in a long period of internal warfare. Nonetheless, in the many preceding centuries, a large part of China had become organized culturally and politically along similar lines, and a distinctive Chinese identity had arisen. The cultural developments were the result of indigenous processes, but technological innovations from the nomadic outsiders had played a significant role. Although settled Chinese such as Sima Qian saw these intruders as "barbarians," they had been crucial in the evolution of Chinese culture.

COUNTERPOINT
The Oxus People: A Short-Lived Culture in Central Asia 2100–1700 B.C.E.

The continuity that characterized the settled communities of China and India did not occur everywhere in Asia. In the Central Asian valleys of the rivers Amu Darya and Syr Darya rivers, in present-day Turkmenistan, northern Afghanistan, southern Uzbekistan, and western Tajikistan, a settled society emerged and disappeared over the course of four hundred years. Today's world politics have greatly influenced our knowledge of this region. Archaeological investigations of the area started in the 1970s C.E., when it was part of the former Soviet Union, and the excavators published their results in Russian articles and books that were little known outside the Soviet Union. Only after the end of the Soviet Union in 1991 were these works translated into other languages and these early cultures became known in other parts of the world.

> **FOCUS**
> What are the unique characteristics of the Oxus culture in the early history of Asia?

One culture this archaeological research reveals was highly unusual. Scholars call it either the Oxus (OX-uhs) culture, after the Greek name *Oxus* for the Amu Darya River, or the Bactria-Margiana archaeological complex, derived from the names *Bactria* and *Margiana*, which the ancient Greeks gave to these regions of Central Asia. The rivers there have the special characteristic that they run dry in the desert and do not drain into a sea. These rivers enabled irrigation agriculture, as in other parts of Asia, but only in isolated oases and only when people built a complex system of canals.

It was in these fertile places, around 2100 B.C.E., that people of Central Asia unexpectedly established agricultural settlements in which they could live year-round while farming barley and wheat. They built walled fortresses with guard towers and reinforced gates; a single clan probably inhabited each fortress under a leader who resided in the center. These structures suggest that living conditions were unsafe and that inhabitants needed protection, most likely against neighbors who wanted access to the precious water. They may also have had to resist nomads who roamed the regions north of the Oxus River Valley and may have tried to settle in the oases. Unlike in the contemporary Indus Valley culture, warfare seems to have been a major preoccupation of these people.

One small seal with what may be signs of an unknown script was excavated among the remains of the Oxus culture, but no scholar can read its text. Thus we have no idea what language or languages the people of this culture spoke, but several historians have argued that they were Indo-European migrants who came from areas farther north. They may later have migrated south into Iran and southeast into the Indian subcontinent, where they could have caused the end of the Indus River culture. The creators of the Oxus culture would then have been crucial for the later history of South Asia. Other scholars argue that such theories are highly conjectural because archaeological remains don't tell us the origins and later destinations of this culture's people or what language they spoke.

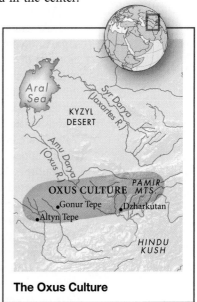

The Oxus Culture

Oxus Culture Fortress

The settlements of the Oxus culture were typically heavily fortified, surrounded by straight rectangular walls with guard towers. This is Gonur Tepe in modern Turkmenistan, which was fully excavated so that its entire plan is visible. The fortress measures 142 by 130 yards and may have contained a temple and a palace. (Kenneth Garrett.)

Whoever the people of the Oxus culture were, archaeological finds show that they created elaborate decorated axes, stamp seals, and vessels, all of which demonstrate very sophisticated metalworking skills. The region's artisans also produced sculptures of women made of a mixture of costly light and dark stones. These works are very distinctive in style and reveal that the society was rich enough to produce luxury goods. The source of this wealth may have been Oxus control of overland trade routes connecting eastern and western Asia. If true, this would show that forerunners of the Silk Road (see Chapter 6) already existed at this early date. In any event, it is clear that inhabitants of the Oxus River Valley were in contact with other regions of Asia by 2000 B.C.E., at which time their craft objects appear all over the Iranian plateau.

But the Oxus culture vanished around 1700 B.C.E., and permanent settlement in the region ceased for some five hundred years. Why? Scholars have come up with various explanations for the culture's demise, ranging from natural causes, such as droughts, to political ones, such as excessive conflict. The region's unusual ecological conditions, which made agriculture possible only in isolated oases, may explain why people saw it as a less-than-ideal environment and abandoned it so suddenly.

The culture shows, however, how people throughout world history sought to exploit whatever ecological niche was available and how their success in doing so depended on forces they could not always control. The circumstances of the Oxus River Valley around

2100 B.C.E. enabled people to live in these kinds of settlements and create a distinctive culture. The conditions that enabled settlement disappeared four hundred years later because of natural changes or for other reasons. People could no longer live in the oases, so they moved elsewhere or turned to a nomadic lifestyle. Whichever was the case, when the environment changed, the settled culture they had created ceased to exist.

Conclusion

The historian Sima Qian, whom we met at the start of this chapter, had a very low opinion of the nomadic people living on the edges of the Chinese state whose ruler he served. His disparaging remarks were misguided, however. Contacts between the settled and the nomadic people of Asia were constant, and throughout the entire history of the continent, the interactions between these two groups with distinct livelihoods were important to both. Their uses of the natural environment were complementary, and cultural exchanges went both ways. The boundaries between the two groups were also not absolute. Many nomadic groups became sedentary, as we saw with the Indo-European speakers in India, just as sedentary people could turn to nomadism, as was possibly the case at the end of the Oxus River culture. To understand the history of the region, we must take both groups into account.

The ancient histories of India and China show how long cultural traditions can last— their influences are still felt today. But historical differences between the two regions are clear. In India, an early urban culture of the Indus Valley ceased to exist before newly arrived Aryas, together with indigenous people, created the foundations of the region's culture. In China the earliest states—the Shang and Zhou—introduced elements such as a script and political ideology that survived into modern times.

Historians do not, however, find such continuity everywhere in Asia. Some ancient cultures, such as that of the Oxus River, disappeared completely. In the next chapter we will return to the western parts of Asia to see how its urban cultures developed new structures, political and otherwise. We will investigate how the first empires in world history evolved.

NOTES

1. Burton Watson, trans., *Records of the Grand Historian by Sima Qian: Han Dynasty II* (New York: Columbia University Press, 1993), 129.
2. *The Laws of Manu*, trans. Georg Bühler (New York: Dover Publications, 1969), 327–328.
3. Wendy Doniger O'Flaherty, *The Rig Veda: An Anthology* (New York: Penguin Books, 1981), 10.90, 30–31.
4. *Rig Veda*, trans. Ralph T. H. Griffith (Benares: E. J. Lazarus and Co., 1896), at sacred-texts.com, book VI, hymn 64.
5. *Hindu Scriptures*, trans. Nicol Macnicol (London/New York: J. M. Dent & Sons, Ltd./E. P. Dutton & Co., Inc., 1938), 93.
6. Burton Watson, trans., Book of Songs in Wm. Theodore de Bary and Irene Bloom, eds., *Sources of Chinese Tradition*, 2d ed., vol. 1 (New York: Columbia University Press, 1999), 38.

RESOURCES FOR RESEARCH

Early Agricultural Societies of South and East Asia, 5000–1000 B.C.E.

Most histories of early India and China include discussions of the periods before written sources appear. For a special focus on the pastoral aspects, see:

Golden, Peter B. "Nomads and Sedentary Societies in Eurasia." In *Agricultural and Pastoral Societies in Ancient and Classical History*, edited by M. Adas, 71–115. 2001.

The Indus Valley Culture, 2600–1900 B.C.E.

The archaeological literature on the Indus Valley culture is often very technical. Some recent overviews appeared in connection with museum exhibitions. Kenoyer's book is the most detailed general survey.

Allchin, Bridget, and Raymond Allchin. *The Birth of Indian Civilization*. 1968.

Aruz, Joan, ed. *Art of the First Cities: The Third Millennium B.C. from the Mediterranean to the Indus*. 2003.

(For the newest discoveries and much more): *The Indus Civilization*. http://www.harappa.com/har/har0.html

Kenoyer, Jonathan M. *Ancient Cities of the Indus Valley*. 1991.

Indo-European Migrations, 3000–1000 B.C.E.

This topic has created much controversy, with scholars disagreeing, especially on the homeland of the Indo-European speakers and on their ways of migrating. Mallory's book provides the broadest survey of the available information.

Encyclopædia Britannica Online, s.v. "Indo-European Languages," http://search.eb.com/eb/article-9109767 (accessed July 30, 2008).

Family Tree of Indo-European Languages. http://www.danshort.com/ie/

Mallory, J. P. *In Search of the Indo-Europeans*. 1991.

Renfrew, Colin. *Archaeology and Language: The Puzzle of Indo-European Origins*. 1990.

India's Vedic Age, 1500–500 B.C.E.

Many general surveys of Indian history include good chapters on the earliest periods. Basham's book, although older than the others cited, contains a particularly readable account.

Avari, Burjor. *India, the Ancient Past: A History of the Indian Sub-Continent from c. 7000 B.C. to A.D. 1200*. 2007.

Basham, A. L. *The Wonder That Was India: A Survey of the Culture of the Indian Sub-Continent Before the Coming of the Muslims*. 1981.

*Goodall, Dominic, ed. *Hindu Scriptures*. 1996.

(For ancient Indian sources): *Internet Indian History Sourcebook*. http://www.fordham.edu/halsall/india/indiasbook.html

The Rig-Veda. http://www.sacred-texts.com/hin/rigveda

Thapar, Romila. *Early India from the Origins to A.D. 1300*. 2002.

The Early Chinese Dynasties, 2000–771 B.C.E.

The literature on the history of China is vast. The works here provide especially accessible introductions.

Ebrey, Patricia Buckley. *The Cambridge Illustrated History of China*. 1996.

Gascoine, Bamber. *A Brief History of the Dynasties of China*. 2003.

Hansen, Valerie. *The Open Empire: A History of China to 1600*. 2000.

Internet East Asian History Sourcebook. http://www.fordham.edu/halsall/eastasia/eastasiasbook.html.

Loewe, Michael, and Edward L. Shaughnessy, eds. *The Cambridge History of Ancient China*. 1999.

Thorp, Robert L. *China in the Early Bronze Age: Shang Civilization*. 2006.

A Visual Sourcebook of Chinese Civilization. http://depts.washington.edu/chinaciv/index.html.

von Glahn, Richard. *The Sinister Way: The Divine and the Demonic in Chinese Religious Culture*. 2004.

COUNTERPOINT: The Oxus People: A Short-Lived Culture in Central Asia, 2100–1700 B.C.E.

Because the Oxus culture became known outside the former Soviet Union only recently, English-language publications on it are still few in number.

Aruz, Joan, ed. *Art of the First Cities: The Third Millennium B.C. from the Mediterranean to the Indus*. 2003.

Lamberg-Karlovsky, Carl C. *Beyond the Tigris and Euphrates: Bronze Age Civilizations*. 1996.

* Primary source.

▶ **For additional primary sources from this period**, see *Sources of Crossroads and Cultures*.

▶ **For Web sites, images, and documents related to topics in this chapter**, see Make History at bedfordstmartins.com/smith.

The major global development in this chapter ▶ The rise of large urban states in Asia and the interactions between nomadic and settled peoples that shaped them.

IMPORTANT EVENTS

c. 7000 B.C.E.	Earliest farmers in East Asia
c. 6500 B.C.E.	Earliest farmers in South Asia
c. 5000 B.C.E.	Agriculture throughout Yellow River and Yangzi River valleys in China
c. 3000 B.C.E.	Agriculture throughout South Asia
c. 2600–1900 B.C.E.	Mature Indus Valley culture
c. 2100–1700 B.C.E.	Oxus River culture
c. 2000 B.C.E.	Spread of domesticated horses throughout Asia
c. 2000–1570 B.C.E.	Earliest Bronze Age cultures in China
c. 2000 B.C.E.–100 C.E.	Indo-European migrations
c. 1570–1027 B.C.E.	Shang dynasty in China
c. 1500–500 B.C.E.	India's Vedic age
1027 B.C.E.	Battle of Muye in China
1027–771 B.C.E.	Early Zhou dynasty in China

KEY TERMS

atman (p. 91)
Brahman (p. 91)
caste system (p. 89)
clan (p. 88)
divination (p. 92)
jati (p. 88)
karma (p. 91)

Mandate of Heaven (p. 95)
pastoralist (p. 75)
raja (p. 88)
reincarnation (p. 91)
varna (p. 88)
Vedas (p. 87)

CHAPTER OVERVIEW QUESTIONS

1. How did peoples living in far-flung regions of Asia develop societies that had many similarities?

2. What were the unique characteristics of the cultures studied here?

3. Which features of ancient Indian and Chinese society and culture shaped later developments most fundamentally?

4. What common trends in the interactions between settled and nomadic peoples can you discern?

SECTION FOCUS QUESTIONS

1. How did Asia's diverse natural environments shape the different lifestyles of its inhabitants?

2. What were the main characteristics of South Asia's early urban culture?

3. What does the concept "Indo-European" mean, and how important is it for the study of Eurasia?

4. How did cultural developments in early Indian history shape the structure of society?

5. What factors account for the remarkable cultural continuity of early Chinese states?

6. What are the unique characteristics of the Oxus culture in the early history of Asia?

MAKING CONNECTIONS

1. How did the development of Indus Valley cities compare with the processes in Southwest Asia (see Chapter 2) and China?

2. How does the social structure of Vedic India compare with those of ancient Southwest Asia (see Chapter 2) and China?

3. In what ways do the interactions between settled and nomadic peoples explain the historical development of Asia?

4. What are the similarities in burial practices of the ancient cultures we have discussed so far, and what do they suggest about attitudes toward class and religion in these societies?

AT A CROSSROADS ▲

In around 500 B.C.E. the Persian emperor Darius started to build a new capital of astonishing magnificence at Persepolis in modern Iran, where he celebrated an annual ceremony of tribute delivery from all subject peoples. The reliefs that decorate the walls show the great diversity of the peoples in his empire, indicating the Persians' awareness of the novelty of this type of political organization. Depicted here are Babylonians on the top level, bringing cups, cloth, and a hump-backed bull, and Phoenicians on the lower level, bringing bracelets, metal vessels, and a horse-drawn chariot. The dress and headgear identify the tribute bearers' origins. (The Art Archive/Gianni Dagli Orti.)

Creation of Empire: North Africa and Southwest Asia

1550–330 B.C.E.

In the late sixth century B.C.E., the Persian king Darius commissioned the carving of a long inscription on a cliff side. In the inscription he described his rise to power as emperor of Persia, the king of twenty-three countries from central Asia to Egypt. He had acquired these territories by defeating a succession of men who, in his words, had falsely claimed kingship over those states. Darius proudly proclaimed:

> Thus says Darius, the king: These are the countries that listen to me—it is under the protection of the god Ahuramazda that I am their king: Persia, Elam, Babylonia, Assyria, Arabia, Egypt, the Sealand, Sardis, Ionia, Media, Urartu, Cappadocia, Parthia, Drangiana, Aria, Choresmia, Bactria, Sogdiana, Gandhara, Scythia, Sattagydia, Arachosia, and Maka, in total twenty-three countries. . . .
>
> Thus says Darius, the king: this is what I have done in one year under the protection of the god Ahuramazda. After becoming king, I have fought nineteen battles in one year, and under the protection of Ahuramazda I won them. I captured nine kings: the Magian named Gaumata, who lied saying: "I am Bardiya, son of Cyrus, king of Persia," and who caused the lands of Persia and Media to rebel; an Elamite called Atrina, who lied saying: "I am the king of Elam," and who caused Elam to rebel; a Babylonian called Nidintu-Bel, who lied saying: "I am Nebuchadnezzar, son of Nabonidus, the king of Babylon," and who caused Babylonia to rebel.[1]

BACKSTORY

In Chapters 2 and 3 we saw how early states developed throughout the Asian continent and in North Africa. From its very beginnings, the state of Egypt incorporated a wide territory centered on the king; in Southwest Asia, India, and China, states first grew around cities and then expanded rapidly. Although a number of these states were quite large, their populations were relatively homogeneous, sharing a common culture and history.

Starting around 1550 B.C.E., however, the rulers of some of these early states began wide-ranging foreign conquests, bringing diverse peoples under their control and creating empires. Imperial rule created a new challenge, one that has confronted empires throughout history: the need to integrate diverse subjects into a single state. As we will see in this chapter, each empire developed its own solutions to this problem.

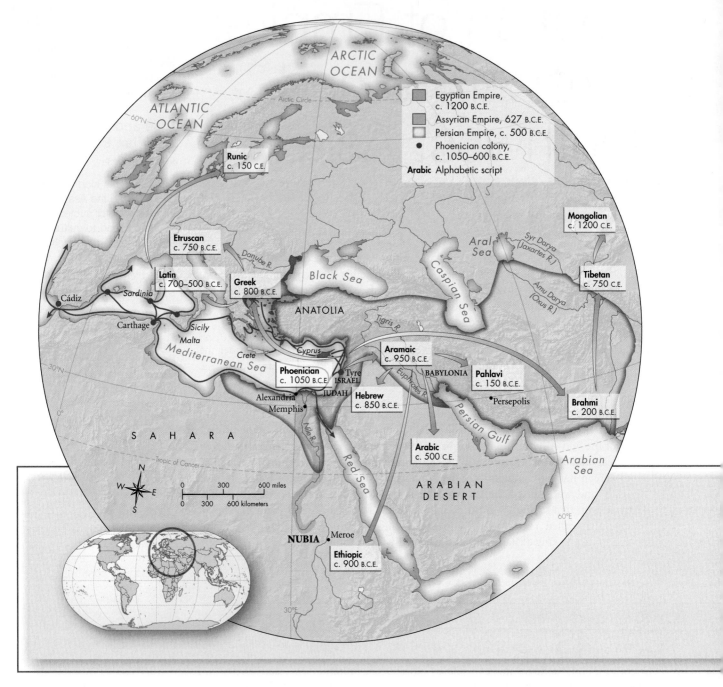

Egyptian Empire, c. 1200 B.C.E.

Assyrian Empire, 627 B.C.E.

Persian Empire, c. 500 B.C.E.

● Phoenician colony, c. 1050–600 B.C.E.

Arabic Alphabetic script

Runic c. 150 C.E.

Mongolian c. 1200 C.E.

Tibetan c. 750 C.E.

Etruscan c. 750 B.C.E.

Latin c. 700–500 B.C.E.

Greek c. 800 B.C.E.

Aramaic c. 950 B.C.E.

Pahlavi c. 150 B.C.E.

Brahmi c. 200 B.C.E.

Phoenician c. 1050 B.C.E.

Hebrew c. 850 B.C.E.

Arabic c. 500 C.E.

Ethiopic c. 900 B.C.E.

ARCTIC OCEAN

ATLANTIC OCEAN

Arctic Circle

60°N

Black Sea

Aral Sea

Caspian Sea

Syr Darya (Jaxartes R.)

Amu Darya (Oxus R.)

Danube R.

ANATOLIA

Tigris R.

Cádiz

Sardinia

Carthage

Sicily

Malta

Crete

Cyprus

Mediterranean Sea

Tyre

ISRAEL

JUDAH

BABYLONIA

Persepolis

Euphrates R.

Persian Gulf

Arabian Sea

30°N

Alexandria

Memphis

Nile R.

SAHARA

Tropic of Cancer

Red Sea

ARABIAN DESERT

0°

60°E

N W E S

0   300   600 miles

0   300   600 kilometers

NUBIA   Meroe

30°E

The following events are part of the timeline at the bottom of the page:

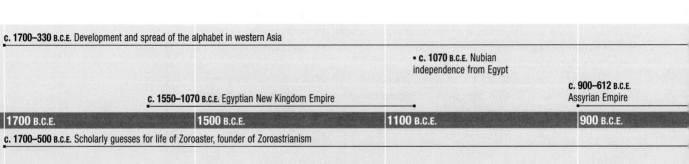

c. 1700–330 B.C.E. Development and spread of the alphabet in western Asia

▪ **c. 1070 B.C.E.** Nubian independence from Egypt

c. 900–612 B.C.E. Assyrian Empire

c. 1550–1070 B.C.E. Egyptian New Kingdom Empire

1700 B.C.E.	1500 B.C.E.	1100 B.C.E.	900 B.C.E.

c. 1700–500 B.C.E. Scholarly guesses for life of Zoroaster, founder of Zoroastrianism

Darius was aware of the cultural and ethnic diversity of his vast empire, a fact he acknowledged by presenting his message in three different languages: his own, Old Persian; Babylonian, the language of Mesopotamia; and Elamite, the language of western Iran. He knew that the Persian Empire had brought together these and other regions in a single unit of unprecedented size. He also knew, however, that it was political and military power that held his empire together. His subjects did not see themselves as Persians, but as distinct peoples.

History has seen many empires, and their diversity makes it difficult to devise a definition of **empire** that encompasses all their variety. A common characteristic is clear, however: empires are very large political units whose leaders impose their rule over diverse countries, peoples, and cultures. Relations between empires and their subjects are complex and influence many spheres of life—political, economic, social, and cultural—so we can study empires from many perspectives. As we will discover in this chapter and others, each empire takes a different approach to the challenge of asserting imperial control. The extent to which the ruling authorities try to impose a single cultural identity on their subjects varies substantially. Moreover, even when a single culture becomes preeminent in an empire, it is not always the conquerors' customs that become dominant. Sometimes imperial powers impose their culture on the conquered territories, but sometimes they permit cultural freedom, and sometimes they embrace the cultures of the people they conquer.

empire A large political unit that imposes its rule over diverse regions, peoples, and cultures; empires can take many different forms.

MAPPING THE WORLD
Rise of the First Empires

The area at the junction of modern Africa, Asia, and Europe was the site of the first empires in world history. They appeared in a long sequence, and as empires rose and fell the sites of imperial centers moved from Egypt to Nubia, Assyria, Persia, and others that followed. Political unification aided the remarkable spread of a new system of writing invented in the heart of this area—the alphabet—but other factors also helped forms of the alphabet reach most of Eurasia and, later, the rest of the world.

ROUTES ▼

⇒ Spread of alphabetic writing
→ Phoenician trade route

c. 730–660 B.C.E. Nubian Empire   **c. 550–330 B.C.E.** Achaemenid Persian Empire

c. 626–539 B.C.E. Neo-Babylonian (Chaldean) Empire

| 700 B.C.E. | 500 B.C.E. | 300 B.C.E. | 100 B.C.E. |

• c. 650 B.C.E. Invention of coinage in Lydia

c. 400 B.C.E.–350 C.E. Kingdom of Meroe

587 B.C.E. Neo-Babylonian sack of Jerusalem

c. 587–530 B.C.E. Judean people in exile

• 330 B.C.E. Alexander of Macedon defeats Persia

OVERVIEW
QUESTIONS

The major global development in this chapter: The rise of empires and the variety and consequences of imperial rule.

As you read, consider:

1. What were the main characteristics of the early empires?

2. How did the empires affect the peoples who created them and their subject populations?

3. How did imperial rulers adapt their control to local circumstances?

4. How did people resist empires?

Because the definition of what constitutes an empire is not simple, it is hard to say when the empires first appeared in world history. Historians agree, however, that a set of large states that incorporated many countries and peoples in much of North Africa and Southwest Asia from 1550 to 330 B.C.E. deserve the title. Thus, in this chapter we focus on the imperial efforts of the Egyptians, Nubians, Assyrians, and Persians. Although all these states constructed empires, their rulers' attitudes toward their subject populations varied. The pharaohs of Egypt showed little respect for the culture of Nubia, for example, whereas Nubian kings and elites eagerly absorbed their Egyptian subjects' cultural traditions and ways of life. Darius and other practical-minded Persian emperors took a middle path, tolerating local beliefs and adopting existing customs, but also demanding full obedience.

As the diverse subjects of empires went about their daily lives, they often started to share cultural habits and build a common cultural tradition. Yet some peoples of these early states, such as the people of Judah, consciously resisted adopting the ways of their conquerors. It is the diversity of interactions between the conquered and the conquerors that led to variation in empires throughout world history.

Imperial Egypt and Nubia   1550 B.C.E.–350 C.E.

FOCUS

How did Egyptians and Nubians interact in the two imperial periods that united them politically?

In northeast Africa, where that continent borders Southwest Asia, the kingdoms of Egypt and Nubia dominated the Nile Valley from around 3000 B.C.E. From about 1550 to 660 B.C.E., first Egypt and then Nubia formed the core of the first empires in this part of the world. Egypt in its New Kingdom period expanded beyond its borders both northward into Asia and southward into Nubia, annexing huge territories. Under a sequence of strong pharaohs, the New Kingdom Egyptian Empire thrived for more than four hundred years.

Several centuries later, Nubia itself became the dominant power in the region, ruling over Egypt for some seventy years. Thus a region once dominated by a powerful neighbor itself developed into a force and overtook its master. Despite this reversal of political fortune, Egyptian culture continued to have a powerful influence in Nubia. The Egyptians had almost completely ignored Nubian culture, but the Nubians promoted Egyptian culture in both the conquered Egyptian state and the Nubian homeland. Similar reversals would occur in other times and places, too (for example, imperial Rome adopted many

assimilation The process by which one group absorbs the cultural traditions of another group.

aspects of Greek culture, as we discuss in Chapter 7). In the case of the Nubian Empire, this **assimilation**—absorption of the cultural traditions of others—produced a unique mix of local and foreign influences that characterized the region for many centuries after Nubia's empire had faded away.

The Imperial Might of New Kingdom Egypt 1550–1070 B.C.E.

Around 1550 B.C.E., the Egyptians started a sustained period of expansion. In the north, they first expelled the Hyksos—foreign rulers who had occupied the Nile Delta for some 150 years—and then marched into the area now occupied by Syria and Palestine. Large armies pushed deep into Asiatic territory, confronting states that belonged to the international system described in Chapter 2. King Thutmose III (r. 1479–1425 B.C.E.) stands out as an especially aggressive empire builder, driving his troops into Syria seventeen times to force local rulers into submission. The resistance remained strong, however, and two hundred years later King Ramesses (RAM-ih-seez) II (r. 1279–1213 B.C.E.) still had to fight massive battles against the Hittites to maintain control over part of the region. The most famous of these clashes was Ramesses's battle at Qadesh (KA-desh) in northern Syria (1275 B.C.E.), which in large relief carvings on several monuments he depicted as a great victory for the Egyptian army.

At the same time, Egypt expanded south into Nubia, occupying some seven hundred miles along the Nile River. There, the opposition was less organized, and once Egypt annexed the region after a century of campaigning, troops were more involved with peacekeeping than with further conquest (see Map 4.1).

Conquest brought tremendous riches to Egypt, allowing its pharaohs to build massive temples, palaces, and tombs stuffed with precious goods. Many pharaohs are famous today because of such monuments. An illustrious example is Queen Hatshepsut (hat-SHEP-soot), who seized power in 1473 B.C.E., when the legitimate heir Thutmose III was still a young boy, and ruled Egypt until 1458 B.C.E., the probable year of her death. To honor her after death, she ordered that a temple be constructed on the west Nile bank of the capital Thebes. Relief sculptures on the walls celebrate her accomplishments.

One depicts a naval expedition to Punt, a fabled land somewhere on the East African coast. The ships sailed down to obtain prized materials needed to construct the temple and worship the gods, such as incense and myrrh, jewels, ivory, and exotic animals and trees. The images show the sailors loading many boats with these goods. Several years after she died, the Egyptians turned against Hatshepsut and defaced the reliefs and statues that depicted her. We do not know why they took these actions, though some scholars think they reflect official opposition to a woman ruler. The Egyptians left her temple standing, however, and its remains today give a glimpse of the grandeur

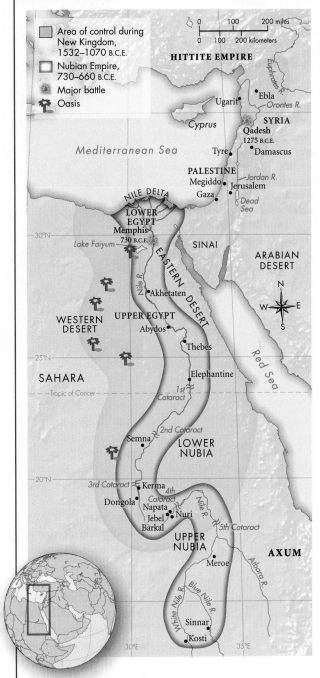

MAP 4.1   **New Kingdom of Egypt and Nubia, 1550–660 B.C.E.**

After ruling supreme in the northern Nile Valley and western Syria in the centuries from 1550 to 1070 B.C.E., Egypt itself was conquered by one of its earlier subjects, Nubia, whose kings extended their power up to the Mediterranean Sea from 730 to 660 B.C.E. Each empire controlled a massive area centered on the Nile, which facilitated constant movement of people and ideas along the river.

Queen Hatshepsut's Expedition to Punt

On the walls of her mortuary temple at Thebes, Hatshepsut had artists illustrate the highlights of her reign. These include an expedition she sent to the distant, fabled land of Punt to obtain exotic materials, including animal skins, incense plants, gold, and other precious materials. The detail here shows the Egyptian boat sailing down the Red Sea. Note the care with which the artist depicted the unusual sea creatures in the foreground; they may have been included to suggest the exceptional nature of the voyage. (Sandro Vannini/Corbis.)

of New Kingdom Egypt. Although Hatshepsut was exceptional in that she became the acknowledged king, she was not the only woman in New Kingdom Egypt who acquired great power. In general, women in this period of Egypt's history seem to have possessed more influence and legal autonomy than anywhere else in the ancient world.

Akhenaten's Religious Reforms

The success of the New Kingdom empire and the wealth it brought the Egyptian elites may have inspired experiments with new ideas about the divine world and the pharaoh's place in it. The most remarkable episode in Egypt's religious history was the reign of King Amenhotep IV (r. 1352–1336 B.C.E.), who early in his rule adopted the name Akhenaten (ah-ken-AHT-en), meaning "servant of Aten." The king abandoned the cults of traditional deities, such as Amun, the highest god, and instead focused all his attention on the god of the sun disk, Aten. In hymns he portrayed Aten as the sole existing deity, and he built an entire city in his honor and made it his capital. Akhenaten depicted himself, his wife Nefertiti, and their daughters as the only humans who could communicate with Aten (see Reading the Past: Akhenaten Praises His God, Aten). Many scholars see in his ideas a form of **monotheism**, belief in the existence of one god only, but Akhenaten did not forbid his people to worship other deities.

Aten was Akhenaten's personal god and the ruler of the universe. This ideology gave the king a unique status, but it came at the expense of the priesthood, which in earlier Egyptian history had held enormous authority (see Chapter 2). Akhenaten's reforms did not last long, however, and soon after his death Amun and his priesthood regained their prominence in Egypt. Akhenaten's failed effort to alter Egypt's religious culture illustrates some of the complexities of cultural change brought about by empire. In this case, an emperor failed to impose long-term cultural change not because he lacked power while he lived, but because the changes he sought challenged the status of another powerful group in his state.

Class and Society in Imperial Egypt

Even during Akhenaten's unusual reign, New Kingdom Egypt was a very unequal society in terms of wealth and status. The empire's success affected people of all social levels, not just the elites. Historians estimate that New Kingdom Egypt had some 3 million inhabitants at its height, with a large proportion of the population serving the state, specifically its kings and its temples. As heads of the religious structure, pharaohs were in

Akhenaten Praises His God, Aten

King Akhenaten produced perhaps the most startling reforms in the long history of Egyptian religion. Whereas Egyptians usually honored a multitude of deities, the New Kingdom ruler focused on one god only: Aten, the sun disk. Akhenaten expressed his exclusive veneration especially through building and the visual arts. He only constructed in honor of Aten, leaving behind several temples and an entire city named Akhetaten after the god, and his artists carved numerous relief sculptures that depicted the king and his family praying to the sun disk. Such material remains leave much room for interpretation about the new ideology, but we have several copies of one long text that expresses Akhenaten's beliefs in words. It is a hymn to Aten praising the god for his beneficent powers. The end of the hymn reads:

> Your rays nurse all fields,
> When you shine, they live and grow for you.
> You made the seasons to foster all that you made,
> Winter, to cool them,
> Summer, that they taste you.
> You made the sky far to shine therein,
> To see all that you make, while you are One,
> Risen in your form of the living sundisk,
> Shining and radiant,
> Far and near.

> You make millions of forms from yourself alone,
> Towns, villages, fields,
> Road and river.
> All eyes behold you upon them,
> When you are above the earth as the disk of daytime.

> When you are gone there is no eye (whose eyesight you have created
> in order not to look upon yourself as the sole one of your creatures),

> But even then you are in my heart, there is no other who knows you,
> Only your son, *Nefer-kheperu-Re Sole-one-of-Re* (Akhenaten),
> Whom you have taught your ways and your might.

> The earth comes into being by your hand as you made it,
> When you dawn, they live,
> When you set, they die;
> You yourself are lifetime, one lives by you.

> All eyes are on beauty until you set,
> All labor ceases when you rest in the west;
> But the rising one makes firm every arm for the king,
> And every leg moves since you founded the earth.

> You rouse them for your son who came from your body,
> The king who lives by Ma'at, the lord of the two lands,
> *Nefer-kheperu-Re Sole-one-of-Re* (Akhenaten),
> The Son of Re who lives by Ma'at,
> The lord of crowns, Akhenaten, great in his lifetime,
> And the great Queen whom he loves,
> The lady of the Two Lands, Nefertiti,
> Who lives and rejuvenates,
> For ever, eternally.

Source: Jan Assmann, *Moses the Egyptian* (Cambridge, MA: Harvard University Press, 1997), 175–177.

EXAMINING THE EVIDENCE

1. What qualities does the hymn assign to Aten?
2. What is the relationship between the king and the god?

---

charge of the temples, to which they assigned massive state resources. A document of the twelfth century B.C.E. indicates that about half a million people worked for temples across Egypt in activities such as farming fields the temples owned. They were not slaves, but people with personal freedom who received food in return for their labor. When the empire flourished, the supplies were guaranteed. Late in the New Kingdom, however, the empire declined, food supplies ran low, and people suffered hardship.

Determined to leave behind magnificent monuments, the pharaohs employed many specially trained craftsmen, including the men who dug and decorated tombs in the Valleys of the Kings and the Queens in the mountains facing the capital, Thebes. We are particularly well-informed about these craftsmen because archaeologists have excavated the village where they lived. The workmen's village, called Deir el Medina (dare uhl meh-DEE-nah) today, was

monotheism A religious system that tolerates the existence of one god only.

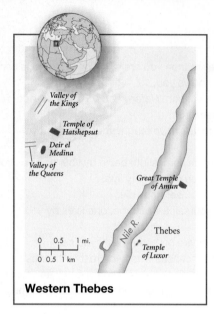

Western Thebes

in the desert between the Nile and the Valley of the Kings. Archaeologists have unearthed numerous writings detailing the lives of inhabitants.

One was a sculptor called Qen, who had two wives and at least ten children. Because the village was in the desert, the family could not grow its own food, which was delivered from the state's storehouses. They received grains, vegetables, fish, oil, and milk, as well as water and firewood. When Qen worked in the tombs, which were several hours by foot from Deir el Medina, he stayed overnight in a camp. Each day he and his colleagues worked two shifts of four hours each, with a lunch break in between. After men had dug and plastered long tunnels and a draftsman had traced the figures, Qen sculpted religious images and hieroglyphic texts to help the king on his way to the underworld, a journey central to the Egyptian religious beliefs discussed in Chapter 2. When Qen died, his children buried him in a tomb near the village. Over the years the pharaoh had rewarded him well for his work, so Qen had acquired precious objects himself, some of which accompanied him in his tomb for his use in the afterlife.

Qen and his coworkers were more privileged than most because of their much-desired skills. Historians cannot know for certain how the majority of people fared because we have no remains from them. We can imagine, however, that all Egyptians benefited to some extent from the empire's existence, at least insofar as it produced internal peace and economic stability. Like Qen, they were all part of an imperial system that connected Egypt to its territories, a system that allowed Egypt's rulers to draw resources from many distant lands to glorify themselves and to enrich their homeland.

Egypt's Attitude Toward Conquered Territories

The New Kingdom empire was so large and included such diverse peoples and countries that the Egyptians were obliged to adjust their attitude toward subjects in response to local conditions. In Southwest Asia, Egypt participated in the eastern Mediterranean system described in Chapter 2, using diplomacy to interact with rulers they considered equals. Vassal rulers, who paid taxes and allegiance to the Egyptian king, governed small kingdoms in the southern part of the Syria-Palestinian area. These vassals were politically dependent on Egypt, but the Egyptians treated them with respect, and sometimes adopted elements of their cultures. For example, New Kingdom Egyptians honored the storm god Baal (bahl) and the goddess of love Astarte (uh-STAHR-tee), both imported from Syria.

In contrast, the Egyptians showed no respect for the cultures and traditions of the Nubians, whom they considered inferior and uncivilized. Their primary interest in Nubia was its gold mines. Egyptian governors ignored the local culture and founded Egyptian-style settlements with administrative buildings and temples devoted to Egyptian gods. Some elite Nubians entered the Egyptian administration, adopting an Egyptian lifestyle to do so. One such man in the fourteenth century B.C.E. was Hekanefer, a prince of the Nubian region of Miam, just south of Egypt. His tomb near his hometown presents him in full Egyptian attire, and the accompanying hieroglyphics call him an admirer of the Egyptian god of the netherworld, Osiris. Interestingly, Hekanefer also features in paintings in a tomb in Thebes, where he appears with Nubian physical features and clothes, prostrating himself in front of an Egyptian official. Clearly, the Egyptians saw Hekanefer very differently than he saw himself. He seems proud to have adopted the dominant Egyptian culture, but for Egyptian elites his most important characteristic was his submission to their rule.

When the eastern Mediterranean system collapsed around 1200 B.C.E., the Egyptian Empire also disintegrated and gradually lost its foreign territories. By 1070 B.C.E. Nubia had become an independent kingdom. Four centuries of Egyptian imperial rule had fundamentally changed Nubia, however, and the kingdom retained the administrative centers the Egyptians had built. The Nubians used the practices they had observed among the

bureaucracy A system of government employing nonelected officials to administer a variety of specialized departments.

Nubian Prince Hekanefer Prostrates Before an Egyptian Official
The Egyptians as a rule depicted the people of Nubia as subjects who owed them allegiance and respect. This painting from the tomb of Tutankhamun's governor of Nubia in the fourteenth century B.C.E. shows local princes in submission, including one named Hekanefer in front of the group. In Hekanefer's own tomb in Nubia, he proudly represents himself in full Egyptian outfit, but here he is shown in Nubian attire, prostrate before the superior Egyptian official. (Francis Dzikowski/akg-images/The Image Works.)

Egyptians to develop a culture distinct from the rest of Africa, continuing such elements as writing and monumental building and maintaining a more centralized state organization than existed elsewhere on the continent.

Nubia's Rise and Rule of Egypt 1000–660 B.C.E.

The Nubians had their capital in Napata (nah-PAH-tuh), which had been the major Egyptian town in the region (see again Map 4.1). Napata was the site of a temple devoted to the leading Egyptian god Amun, whose cult had survived through the centuries. Nubia developed as a strong centralized state shortly after 1000 B.C.E., at a time when Egypt was divided among several competing dynasties and chiefdoms. In Egypt's south, from the area of the religious center Thebes to the Nubian border, the Theban high priest of Amun ruled as if he were a king. In the eighth century B.C.E., political control over Thebes shifted to a new system that centered on the women of the royal court. The highest religious office—which came with control over the vast properties controlled by temples and substantial political power—became that of the high priestess of Amun. She was always a princess of the most powerful political house in Egypt at the time of her selection. To maintain political control over her possessions, she could not marry and have children. Instead, she passed on her office by adopting her successor, again a princess from the strongest dynasty.

The growing power of Nubia in the region became clear when, in 736 B.C.E., its king, Piye (py), gave his sister the office of high priestess. In this way, a Nubian became in effect the ruler of southern Egypt. But northern Egyptian rulers did not accept Piye's authority and threatened to attack Thebes. In response, in around 730 B.C.E., Piye led his troops northward from Napata all the way to Memphis at the tip of the Nile Delta, forcing local rulers to submit. Egypt and Nubia reunited—but this time with Nubia in control. The succession of Nubian kings who ruled this new empire behaved in every respect like the earlier Egyptian pharaohs. They supported Egyptian cults, portrayed themselves as Egyptian rulers with the proper titles, and headed a **bureaucracy**, a group of officials who administered the country.

Although militarily superior to the Egyptians, the Nubians did not attempt to influence Egyptian culture. On the contrary, the Nubian elite absorbed Egyptian customs that they saw as expressions of power and prestige. Nubia's upper classes had imitated Egyptian

Nubia's Conquest of Egypt

Nubian Embrace of Egyptian Ways

culture in the past, but after the conquest they went further, pressing their claim to be the legitimate rulers of Egypt by presenting themselves as Egyptians rather than Nubians.

Nubian kings can be distinguished from native Egyptian rulers only by their retention of Nubian birth names. They used Egyptian titles and promoted Egyptian culture throughout their empire. In the Nubian capital, the cult of the Egyptian god Amun continued to flourish, and the Nubian rulers substantially enlarged and embellished Amun's temple in Napata to rival the one at Thebes, his main sanctuary. Nubian burial customs, inscriptions, and statues also showed a devotion to Egyptian traditions—after the conquest of Egypt, Nubian kings were buried in pyramids rather than the earlier round mounds of earth. Although the Nubian pyramids were smaller and had steeper sides than the older Egyptian structures, the Egyptian examples inspired their shape. Nubians also decorated the tomb chambers with scenes from the Egyptian books of the underworld. As in Egypt, they mummified corpses and set them in human-shaped coffins, placing hundreds of small statuettes in the tombs to assist the dead in the afterlife. The Nubians also used the Egyptian language and hieroglyphic script for their official inscriptions, and in statues of kings the poses matched those of the Egyptian pharaohs. Thus, in a myriad of ways, Nubian rulers demonstrated that their conquest of Egypt was not predicated on a sense of their own cultural superiority. Rather, they saw Egyptian culture as a key source of imperial power and unity, and they sought to use the cultural connections the Egyptians had created to reinforce the legitimacy of their own rule.

Survival of Nubian Traditions

Nonetheless, some local Nubian traditions survived—especially among the commoners of the Nubian state, but even among the elite. For example, in depictions of Nubian kings, artists accurately rendered their African physical features. A very un-Egyptian element in the Nubian burials was the interment of horses along with the king, something that Egyptians never did. The Nubians greatly admired horses, which had contributed to their military victories, and due to Nubian success in battle the horses they bred were in

Statues of Nubian Kings

These statues of Nubian rulers of the first millennium B.C.E., some up to ten feet high, were found in a pit, where they were preserved after a raiding Egyptian king had smashed them in 593 B.C.E. Reassembled, they show that in depicting kings, Nubian artists followed many Egyptian conventions, such as the erect posture, but they also reveal typically Nubian elements, such as indigenous physical features and the royal crown. (Kenneth Garrett.)

high demand in other countries. Thus the Nubians retained the things they valued most in their own culture, while adopting the aspects of Egyptian culture that seemed most useful.

The stability the Nubians brought to Egypt reflects their success in adopting Egyptian ways. The country flourished economically, and in many respects the Nubians oversaw a period of Egyptian prosperity. Although we have no evidence of popular resentment of Nubian rule among Egyptians, some elites, particularly in the north, seem to have wanted independence but lacked the military might needed to resist the Nubians. Then, around 660 B.C.E., the Assyrians of Southwest Asia invaded Egypt and drove the Nubians out of Egypt. When the Assyrians' grip on the country loosened a few years later, a family from the north of Egypt established itself as the new ruling dynasty.

The Nubian Kingdom of Meroe 400 B.C.E.–350 C.E.

Although driven from Egypt, the Nubians continued to rule their homeland. By 400 B.C.E. they moved their political capital to Meroe (MER-oh-ee), some seven hundred miles upstream from Napata. This shift took advantage of the greater fertility of the region surrounding Meroe and of the intersection of trade routes in the city. Those routes reached into regions of Africa farther south, east, and west and made Meroe a major trade crossroads for the continent.

The Kingdom of Meroe, c. 400 B.C.E.–350 C.E.

Over time, the political situation in Egypt changed as first the Greeks (332–30 B.C.E.) and then the Romans (30 B.C.E.–395 C.E.) occupied it. The Meroites had mostly friendly contacts with the Greeks and Romans, who fancied African luxury goods such as gold, ivory, spices, animals, and slaves. During a long period of peace, the enormous Roman appetite for luxury items brought fantastic wealth and a flood of Mediterranean goods into Nubia. Trade with Rome not only made Nubia rich, but also brought Roman influences into Nubian life and culture.

Crossroads of Trade

After the first century C.E., however, Meroe's commercial advantage gradually declined. The kingdom of Axum, to Meroe's east on the Red Sea in what is today Ethiopia, became Rome's preferred center for access to African trade. As Axum's wealth grew, so did its military power, and in 350 C.E., the Axumites conquered Meroe.

After the political separation of Nubia from Egypt in the seventh century B.C.E., Egyptian influences in Nubia remained strong. Even after moving the capital to Meroe, the Nubians continued to honor Egyptian gods such as Amun, to bury kings in pyramids, and to depict themselves in an Egyptian style. Nonetheless, with fewer direct connections to Egypt, local Nubian culture grew more independent, and important changes occurred. In the second century B.C.E., for example, the Meroites started to write their own language, rather than Egyptian. They used two scripts: one based on Egyptian hieroglyphics but with only twenty-three symbols, and the other featuring entirely new sign forms that were much faster to write out. Scholars have not yet deciphered these inscriptions, whose language is unknown.

Culture and Society in Meroe

Women enjoyed a high status in the social structure of Meroe. In royal succession a king was followed by his sister's son, and from the second century B.C.E. on, several women became rulers themselves. Like their male counterparts, they were represented on monuments as defeating enemies and honoring gods. Classical Greek and Roman authors mistakenly concluded from these depictions that queens had always ruled in Nubian society (see Seeing the Past: The Queen of Meroe in Battle). As this example illustrates, the economic connections between Rome and Nubia facilitated cultural exchange and inquiry but did not eliminate misunderstandings and misinterpretations.

The Queen of Meroe in Battle

Naga Temple (front gate) (John Warburton Lee/ AWL Images.)

Queen Amanitare (From *Meroe: A Civilization of the Sudan* by P. L. Shinnie, Thames & Hudson Ltd., London.)

South of the capital Meroe, the Meroites of the late first century B.C.E. or early first century C.E. built a group of temples near a staging post for caravans traveling east. They dedicated one of the temples to the Meroite lion god Apedemak, and built it fully in accordance with an ancient Egyptian plan. Its decoration, however, shows a mixture of ancient Egyptian and local traditions.

The image on the front gate of the temple reveals this mixture. On the right side, the queen is battling enemies with the god's help; she is depicted as equal to her husband, who appears on the left. Both stand in the pose that Egyptian rulers of the distant past used to show their victories, wielding arms over opponents bunched together. Underneath them are rows of bound enemies representing defeated countries. Short Egyptian hieroglyphic inscriptions identify the figures as Queen Amanitare and King Netekamari. Above them, traditional Egyptian gods appear as birds.

These traditional Egyptian motifs are mixed with Meroitic details. The king and queen wield swords rather than the axes or maces that Egyptians would have used. Their dress and jewelry are local, and the lion god Apedemak (unknown in Egypt) assists them. Moreover, unlike Egyptian queens in images, Queen Amanitare is quite chubby, which may have been the local ideal of beauty.

EXAMINING THE EVIDENCE

1. Which decorative features of the front gate would most have startled Egyptians, and which would they have recognized as normal?

2. How does the temple illustrate contacts between Egypt and regions to its south?

For Further Information:

"Naga'a (Middle Sudan)," Poznan Archaeological Museum. http://www.muzarp.poznan.pl/muzeum/muz_eng/nagaa.htm.

The African kingdoms of Egypt and Nubia were thus at the core of the first empires in this part of the world. The Nubian rulers of Egypt showed a clear inclination to absorb the culture of the conquered territory, in sharp contrast with the Egyptians' behavior when they dominated Nubia. The Nubians' adoption of Egyptian culture led to a unique assimilation of local and foreign influences that characterized the region for many centuries after Nubia's imperial period.

Rise and Fall of the Assyrian Empire 900–612 B.C.E.

As we have seen, the Nubians were not driven from Egypt by the Egyptians but by the Assyrians. Waging unrelenting wars of conquest, the Assyrians built the first empire to encompass much of Southwest Asia. Assyria's martial character dominates our modern view of the empire, and the Assyrian state was indeed organized around the demands of warfare. But the Assyrian kings also commissioned engineering projects, built new cities, sponsored the arts, and powerfully influenced cultural developments in the empire. Despite their military successes, structural weaknesses in the empire would ultimately thwart the Assyrian kings' dreams of integrating the conquered territories into a coherent whole. Their conquests did, however, lay the groundwork for later empires in the region.

> **FOCUS**
>
> What kind of power structure did the Assyrians impose on their subjects, and how did it lead to cultural assimilation in the empire?

Assyria: A Society as War Machine

By 1000 B.C.E. Assyria was a state with a long history, but had little influence beyond its heartland in the north of modern-day Iraq. Then, starting around 860 B.C.E., Assyria began a series of wars that would lead to 250 years of dominance in Southwest Asia. The Assyrians defeated all their rivals, and by around 650 B.C.E. their control reached from western Iran to the Mediterranean Sea and from central Anatolia (modern Turkey) to Egypt (see Map 4.2).

The reasons for Assyria's expansion changed as the empire grew. At first, it was a defensive reaction against outside threats, especially those posed by nomads from Syria. But over time, as the Assyrians became used to the wealth that came with conquest, their expansion became more aggressive and more acquisitive. Instead of seeking to defend themselves, they were driven by a desire to seize the wealth and resources of their neighbors, including the Babylonians and the Egyptians.

Assyrian Militarism

The empire's militarism affected every level of Assyrian society. The state was organized as a military hierarchy with the king at the top. All state officers, whatever their responsibilities, had a military rank. The material demands of the Assyrian war machine were enormous. The army required massive amounts of weapons, clothing, and food and vast numbers of horses. But manpower was perhaps in the greatest demand: the central Assyrian state simply could not provide enough soldiers without drawing too many people away from other essential work, such as farming and building.

Deportation

The Assyrians filled their need for manpower through a policy of deporting conquered people. They were not the first empire—or the last—to employ this practice, but they were the most systematic in its use in early times. After the army defeated a region that had resisted Assyrian dominance, the troops forced large numbers of people to resettle elsewhere in the empire, typically hundreds of miles from their homes. These dislocated men, women, and children labored for the Assyrian state, working on farms and construction projects. Some of the men enlisted in the Assyrian army. Besides providing the state with workers, the policy of deportation effectively thwarted opposition to Assyrian expansion and rule. The Assyrians also used the threat of

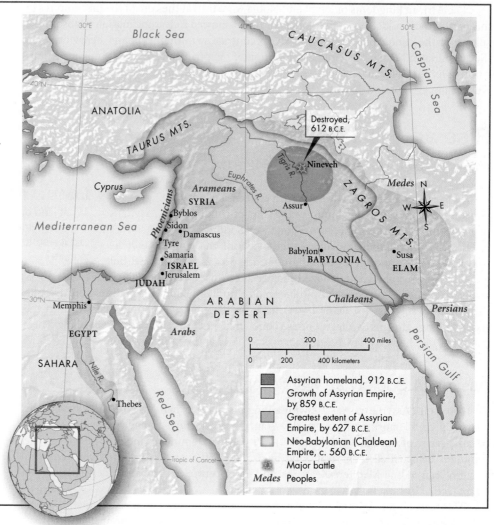

MAP 4.2

The Empires of Assyria and Babylonia, 900–539 B.C.E.

From its small core in northern Mesopotamia, Assyria gradually extended its control over most of the Middle East and at times even Egypt, turning the entire region into a vast land-based empire by 650 B.C.E. By 610, however, the Babylonians had taken over most of Assyria's territory, expanding their empire into parts of the Arabian Desert. Both peoples used the enormous influx of resources to embellish their homelands, creating two of the most impressive cities of the ancient world, Nineveh and Babylon.

deportation as a scare tactic to cow opponents into submission. Moreover, deported people needed the protection of the empire in their new and strange environments. The policy thus aimed both to supply laborers and to reduce the chance of rebellion in the conquered territories.

King and Army

As head of the military hierarchy, the king was supreme commander of the army. The ultimate source of authority, he made all crucial political, military, and administrative decisions. His officials therefore had to be in constant communication with him, which slowed decision making. Couriers had to travel long distances to royal headquarters in the capital to obtain orders on how to proceed in the **provinces**, the territories fully administered by the Assyrians.

The incessant campaigning made the Assyrians seasoned warriors, and their military tactics were undeniably superior to those of their opponents. From about 745 B.C.E. on, the empire had a standing professional army rather than one made up of recruits called up seasonally after they had completed agricultural tasks. Despite the extensive written evidence we have from Assyria, we have little information about the composition and technical support of the army, and we do not know how long men served.

province In an empire, a region or country directly governed by an imperial official answering to the central administration.

Assyria's military culture was dominated by men, allowing most women a limited role in Assyrian society. The available evidence reveals little about ordinary women

Gold for the Assyrian Queen
We get an idea of the wealth of the Assyrian court from the recent find of tombs at the capital Nimrud. Buried with two queens of the ninth and eighth centuries B.C.E. were masses of finely worked gold jewelry, such as these solid gold bracelets decorated with lion heads. (Time & Life Pictures/Getty Images.)

Royal Women

and focuses instead on royal women—queens and princesses. As members of the court, these women led privileged lives and enjoyed fabulous wealth, as the intact tombs of two queens from the ninth and eighth centuries B.C.E. demonstrate. On the two women's bodies together were piled a total of seventy-seven pounds of gold and precious ornaments.

As wives and mothers, royal women could shape political affairs. We saw how Hatshepsut in Egypt rose to the top to become king; in Assyria no woman acquired such power, but certain queens exercised enormous influence. Queen Naqia (na-KEE-ah) married King Sennacherib (sehn-AK-er-ihb) (r. 704–681 B.C.E.) before he ascended the throne, and bore him a son called Esarhaddon (ee-sahr-HAD-in). He was not the first in line for succession, but after Sennacherib's eldest son was murdered, Naqia convinced Sennacherib to declare the young Esarhaddon his heir. Older sons by another wife rebelled, and one (or perhaps several) of them assassinated Sennacherib. This started a civil war, which Esarhaddon won after months of fighting. During Esarhaddon's subsequent rule from 680 to 669 B.C.E., the queen mother Naqia became his staunchest ally. She built a palace for the king, restored temples, and made grand offerings to the gods on his behalf. She corresponded with high officials of the empire, who paid her the same respect they gave the king. Even after Esarhaddon's death she remained prominent. Her last known act was to impose an oath on court officials to obey her grandson as king. As powerful as Naqia was, however, note that it ultimately derived from her status as the mother of a prince, not from her own independent political position. As in many other societies, elite Assyrian women could wield considerable influence, but it was almost always through their connections to powerful men.

Imperial Governance

Indirect Rule

All imperial powers face the challenge of administering territories after conquering them. We saw how the New Kingdom Egyptians used a system of dependent vassals in Southwest Asia, but at the same time they governed Nubian territories directly. The Assyrians were less eager to impose direct rule on defeated countries, however—it would have required large investments in infrastructure and administrators. Moreover, because the empire was centralized around a king who made all decisions, urgent issues in territories far from the king would have been difficult to deal with. Thus, when the military forced a population to submit, they left the local king on the throne but demanded obedience and annual contributions. If the region rebelled—a common occurrence—troops returned to install a pro-Assyrian ruler in the local king's stead. If this arrangement also failed, Assyria annexed the region as a province. The Assyrians usually hesitated to take this drastic step, however. For example, only after repeated rebellions did the Assyrians turn Israel into a province in 722 B.C.E. But they never annexed the state of Judah, south of Israel (see Counterpoint: Assimilation and Resistance: The Peoples of Israel and Judah). As a vassal, Judah provided a useful buffer with Egypt, then part of the rival Nubian Empire.

Motives for Expansion

The Assyrians' preference for indirect rule was linked to their motives for expansion. They were not interested in ruling other peoples, but in acquiring the wealth and resources of other lands. With each conquest, the army captured huge amounts of booty, usually in the form of precious metals and luxury goods, which became palace property. In addition, the empire required yearly contributions, or **tribute**, from conquered territories. In an annual ceremony, ambassadors from Assyria's subject peoples renewed their states' loyalty oaths and brought tribute, often goods that were the region's special assets. Ambassadors from the mountain regions to the north and east of Assyria brought horses, for example, and those from western countries delivered manufactured craft products such as carved ivories and jewelry. In this way, Assyrian palaces became centers for collections of the empire's diverse resources and products.

City Building

Deported subjects gave Assyrian rulers the manpower to construct magnificent cities and to enlarge existing towns to serve as capitals. King Sennacherib, for example, refurbished and expanded the old city of Nineveh (NIN-uh-vuh). Its massive ruins still overlook the modern Iraqi city of Mosul. On these sites the kings erected monumental palaces and temples and decorated them with such materials as cedar wood, ivory, gold, and silver gathered from the entire empire. Although not the largest in the world at that time—Chinese cities were spread over vaster areas—the new Assyrian cities were too gigantic for the surrounding countryside to support. Because agriculture in the Assyrian core produced too little food to feed the city, products from elsewhere in the empire had to be imported. Assyria thus became an enormous drain on the resources of the conquered territories.

Independence Preserved: Phoenicians in the Assyrian Empire

As we have mentioned, the Assyrians shrewdly recognized that it was often preferable to grant independence to their subject peoples so that they could freely carry on activities that would benefit the empire economically. One such people was the Phoenicians, the inhabitants of Mediterranean port cities including Sidon (SIE-duhn), Byblos (BIB-loss), and Tyre (TY-er), which had been important hubs of trade for thousands of years. These cities occupied the thin ribbon of land between the sea and the high Lebanon Mountains. In addition to serving as a Mediterranean crossroads, Phoenician cities were famous for their craftwork, especially production of purple cloth dyed with extracts from the rare murex marine snails.

Phoenician Sea Trade

Benefiting from their extensive maritime trade, the Phoenicians had survived the devastation of the eastern Mediterranean system in the twelfth century B.C.E. In the tenth century B.C.E. they had begun to establish settlements overseas, first on the island of Cyprus and then along the Mediterranean coast in North Africa, in Spain, and on the islands of Malta, Sicily, and Sardinia, near Italy. From the territories surrounding these colonies, the Phoenicians collected metals and other valuable resources and shipped them to the East.

The westernmost Phoenician **colony** was Cádiz on the Atlantic coast of Spain, beyond the Strait of Gibraltar (see again Mapping the World, page 106). There the Phoenicians established a fortified city that was completely Phoenician in character, with temples to Syrian gods such as Astarte and Baal. The settlers were interested in the nearby Spanish mines, which yielded gold, silver, copper, tin, and iron. Local populations extracted

tribute Payment made from one state to another as a sign of submission.

colony A settlement or administrative district in a foreign country established and governed by people who intend to exploit the resources of that country.

precious metal from ore and smelted it into bars that could be shipped east. This same pattern was repeated elsewhere in the Mediterranean. Everywhere they went, the Phoenicians established coastal outposts from which they sent local goods to their home cities.

The Phoenician system of trade was well established by 750 B.C.E., when Assyrian armies reached the Mediterranean coast. The encounter brought both sides mutual gain. For Phoenician traders, Assyria represented an enormous new market. For the Assyrians, Phoenicia provided access to goods they could not otherwise obtain. For example, the Phoenicians traded with Egypt, Assyria's rival at the time, to obtain papyrus, which scribes used for writing alphabetic scripts. So much papyrus entered the Mediterranean region through Phoenicia that the Greeks based the word for book, *biblion*, on the Phoenician city named Byblos, and this term has come down to us in the word *bible*.

Phoenician independence helped the Phoenicians preserve their cultural traditions from the second millennium B.C.E. into the first millennium. A fundamental element of that culture was the alphabet, a script with just twenty-two characters, used to indicate consonants only. The Phoenicians developed this script to record daily transactions on papyrus and parchment, now all decayed, and to chisel inscriptions on stone. Because the Phoenicians had extensive trade contacts, many foreign peoples adopted their alphabet to write their languages (see Figure 4.1). To the east of Phoenicia, these included speakers of the Semitic languages Aramaic and Hebrew, and to the west, the Indo-European-speaking Greeks also adopted it. Because both Aramaic and Greek adopters of the Phoenician alphabet later had broad cultural influence in the Mediterranean and Middle Eastern worlds, that script gained enormous reach. Today the Phoenician alphabet is the basis of all alphabetic scripts in the world.

SPREAD OF THE ALPHABET IN WESTERN EURASIA

c. 1700 B.C.E.	Earliest alphabetic inscriptions in Palestine
c. 1400–1200 B.C.E.	Various alphabetic scripts in western Syria
c. 1050 B.C.E.	Early Phoenician alphabet
c. 950 B.C.E.	Earliest Aramaic alphabetic inscriptions
c. 850 B.C.E.	Earliest Hebrew alphabetic inscriptions
c. 800 B.C.E.	Earliest Greek alphabetic inscriptions
c. 750 B.C.E.	Earliest alphabetic writing in Italy
700–500 B.C.E.	Earliest Latin alphabetic inscriptions
c. 520–330 B.C.E.	Use of Old Persian cuneiform alphabet

The Phoenician Alphabet

Semitic name of letters	Phoenician	Hebrew	Greek name of letters	Greek	Roman
alef	𐤀	א	alpha	A	A
beth	𐤁	ב	beta	B	B
gimel	𐤂	ג	gamma	Γ	C, G
daleth	𐤃	ד	delta	Δ	D

FIGURE 4.1   **Comparative Alphabets**
In the Phoenician alphabet we can find the roots of our own. Our alphabet is based on that of the Romans, who borrowed their letter forms from the Greeks, who in turn adapted the Phoenician alphabet.

Culture and Identity in the Assyrian Empire

Through its far-reaching conquests, the Assyrian Empire brought people from a wide territory together under the same political structure. They spoke a variety of languages, followed different religious systems and customs, and must have been visually distinguishable to the people of the time. The Assyrians displayed different attitudes toward this cultural variety, depending on the region.

Cultural Assimilation

In the core of the empire, the Assyrians enforced assimilation. They relabeled existing cities with Assyrian names, built public buildings in the Assyrian style, and forced the people to support the cult of their leading god, Assur, the divine commander of the army, whose only temple was in the city of Assur on the Tigris River. But beyond this central zone, the Assyrians did not demand that people change their ways of life. Their only concern was that the subjects provide tribute and pay taxes.

Naturally, assimilation occurred because of the imperial deportation policy. When the Assyrians resettled an entire population in a foreign part of the empire, these immigrants maintained their identity for a while, but over generations they adopted local customs. Yet they also influenced the customs of their conquerors, leaving a cultural imprint on Assyria, especially in the realm of language. Many of the deportees came from the west and spoke Aramaic, which may have become the primary spoken language in the empire.

Babylonian and Syrian Influences

The Assyrians willingly accepted cultural influences from the conquered territories, especially when they felt those influences to be superior to their own traditions. This openness to foreign ways is most notable in literature and scholarship, but outsiders also influenced architecture, crafts, and religion. In the second millennium B.C.E., the country of Babylonia to the south of Assyria had been the center of literary and scholarly creativity in Southwest Asia. When the Assyrians conquered it in the late eighth century B.C.E., Babylonian scribes were still very actively composing and duplicating cuneiform texts. King Assurbanipal (ah-shur-BAH-nee-pahl) (r. 668–627 B.C.E.) used their output to build up the richest library of ancient Southwest Asia in his palace at Nineveh. He ordered his officials in Babylon to search for early, well-preserved manuscripts of texts of literary and scholarly character. He was especially interested in omen literature, the texts that guided scholars in interpreting the signs of the gods regarding the future, but all literary genres flourished in his reign. With its thousands of manuscripts, Assurbanipal's library gives us the most complete record of the Babylonian written tradition. Among its many treasures are multiple manuscripts of the *Epic of Gilgamesh* (see Chapter 2).

The literary Babylonian language influenced the Assyrian language used for official inscriptions. Kings commissioned increasingly lengthy records of their military campaigns. Although much of the phrasing in these accounts is repetitive (there are only so many ways to describe crushing an enemy), the authors regularly composed passages of high literary merit. For example, Sargon II (r. 721–705 B.C.E.) used these words to narrate his victory over an enemy army in the mountains:

> I massacred them in great numbers, the corpses of his warriors I spread out like grain, and I filled the mountain plains with them. Their blood I let rush like a river down the mountain gorges, and I dyed the fields, plains, and open country red. I slaughtered his fighters, the force of his army carrying bows and lances, like sheep and I chopped off their heads.[2]

In other forms of cultural expression, too, the Assyrians readily accepted outside influences. In architecture they imitated the palaces they saw in Syria. Assyrian craftwork showed a strong Syrian influence: the jewelry and ivory carvings found in Assyrian palaces were either produced in Syria or made locally using Syrian designs. These designs mixed motifs from the various cultures of the region, including Syria and

Egypt. The influx of expensive goods from foreign sources reflects not only that the Assyrian court was a rich market but that the Assyrians were very willing to accept foreign styles.

In religion, the Assyrians remained true to their old cults, but they attempted to harmonize them with Babylonian ideas. In Babylonian religion, the god Marduk was supreme, and common belief credited him with creating the universe. This event was the subject of a myth, the *Babylonian Creation Story*. It describes how Marduk defeated the forces of chaos and organized the universe, and how the other gods rewarded him by making him their king. The myth was an important element of the Babylonian New Year's festival, which intended to recreate the moment of creation. The Assyrians wanted to integrate their leading god Assur into this myth, and they either made him a forefather of Marduk or directly equated Assur with Marduk. They imported many other Babylonian gods and rites as well. Thus, in many ways, the Assyrian attitude toward foreign cultures mirrored their attitude toward foreign wealth and resources: they were interested in taking anything, and everything, that seemed valuable.

Failure of the Assyrian System

In 663 B.C.E., King Assurbanipal invaded Egypt and looted its rich cities, and in 647 he defeated the long-time rival state of Elam in western Iran. By this time, the Assyrian Empire encompassed an enormous territory, and huge amounts of wealth flowed from dependent peoples to the Assyrian homeland. Just forty years later, however, it would no longer exist. The collapse of the empire was precipitated by attacks launched by previously subjected peoples, but its causes lay in the structure of the system itself.

The military events are clear: after the death of Assurbanipal in 627 B.C.E., Babylonia regained its independence under a local dynasty, which we call Neo-Babylonian or Chaldean (chal-DEE-uhn). Chaldean troops joined the Medes, an Iranian people from the eastern mountains, in an attack on the Assyrian heartland, and in 612 B.C.E. the combined armies destroyed the Assyrian capital, Nineveh. The Assyrians would resist a few years longer in northern Syria, but soon the Chaldeans had taken over almost their entire territory.

Structural Weakness and Military Defeat

At the heart of Assyria's failure to rise to the military challenge from the Chaldeans and the Medes was a serious structural weakness. The centralized power structure required a strong king at the helm, and after Assurbanipal no such person stepped forward. Internal struggles for the throne produced instability and uncertainty. Moreover, the empire relied heavily on the conquered territories to sustain itself—it could not survive without their goods and manpower. Historians believe that when the pressures on the empire's core mounted, the subject states, which always had taken any opportunity to withhold tribute, probably cut off those supplies, and the empire fell apart. The exploitative economic policies on which Assyria depended could be sustained only when backed up by military might. When Assyria's military power faltered, the sources of Assyrian wealth dried up, further undermining the state and leading to collapse of the imperial system.

The Neo-Babylonian Empire

Assyria's successor, the Neo-Babylonian dynasty, soon restored order and extended the empire by annexing more territory (see again Map 4.2). The most famous Neo-Babylonian ruler was King Nebuchadnezzar II (NAB-oo-kuhd-nez-uhr) (r. 604–562 B.C.E.), who captured the kingdom of Judah in 587 B.C.E. Like his Assyrian predecessors, Nebuchadnezzar used the resources of conquered territories to embellish the cities of his homeland. Under Nebuchadnezzar's direction, Babylon became the most fabulous city in the western Eurasian world. We can still see remains from his time on the site or in museums around the world (see Lives and Livelihoods: Mesopotamian Astronomers). The Neo-Babylonian empire did not last long, however. Less than one hundred years after its creation, it was conquered by a far mightier force—the Persian Empire.

Mesopotamian Astronomers

Like the Chinese in the Shang period (see Chapter 3), the Mesopotamians were obsessed with predicting the future. But instead of asking specific questions and finding the answers in the cracks of oracle bones as the Chinese did, the Mesopotamians saw signs from the gods everywhere: in the birth of a malformed animal, the appearance of a large flock of birds, the occurrence of a lunar eclipse, and so on. The challenge to the people was to know how to read these omens.

From early in Mesopotamian history, scholars had compiled lists of guidelines for interpreting omens. The items were phrased in the same way as the Laws of Hammurabi (see pages. 51–52), as "if-then" statements. The "if" part could be any observable phenomenon or an effect produced through a special procedure. The second part indicated what the observation foretold. For example, "If a white cat is seen in a man's house, then hardship will seize the land." Often observations involved slaughtering a sheep to investigate the liver, an organ with many variations in color and shape, any of which could present a sign. For example, "If the left lobe of the liver is covered by a membrane and it is abnormal, the king will die from illness."

In the first millennium B.C.E., astronomical observations became very important to the Mesopotamians, and the longest lists of omens relate to events in the sky, such as planetary alignments, eclipses, and the appearance of stars. One series of omens, *Enuma Anu Enlil* (meaning, "When the gods Anu and Enlil"), was copied out on seventy clay tablets and included some seven thousand entries. It described omens dealing with the moon, including its visibility, eclipses, and conjunction with planets and fixed stars; with the sun, including aspects such as sunspots or a ring around

Assyrian Astronomy

The best evidence of the Assyrian reliance on the stars and other heavenly bodies to predict the future is written lists of astronomical omens, but their art reflects the same interest. This stele from Adad-nirari III in around 800 B.C.E. shows the king under the protection of the moon, Venus, and the Pleiades (seven stars). In front of him are other symbols of leading gods of the Assyrian pantheon. (Art Archive/Archaeological Museum Baghdad.)

The Persian Empire 550–330 B.C.E.

FOCUS

What imperial vision and style of government marked the rise of the vast Persian Empire and allowed it to endure for more than two hundred years?

In the sixth century B.C.E. the Persians, starting from what is today southern Iran, united all the existing empires and states from the Mediterranean coast to the Indus Valley. Remarkably, they were able to integrate an enormously diverse group of peoples and cultures into an imperial whole. Although they demanded obedience to their king, the Persians respected local cultures and identities, and this respect was key to their success. The Persians did encounter resistance from their subject peoples, but their empire—unprecedented in its scale—survived for more than two hundred years partly because of their tolerance. Although others replaced the Persians, the practices of government they initiated survived for many centuries after the empire's disintegration.

the sun; the weather—lightning, thunder, and clouds; and the planets, including their visibility, appearance, and stations. For example, one omen warned: "If the moon makes an eclipse in Month VII on the twenty-first day and sets eclipsed, they will take the crowned prince from his palace in fetters."

Although every Mesopotamian consulted omens, most of those recorded in writing deal with the king. They cover everything important to him personally and to his rule: the outcome of battles, deaths, births, illnesses, the success of the harvest, and many more concerns. Kings ordered scholars from all over the empire to examine anything that could be an omen and to report it to them. From their constant observation of phenomena in the sky, astronomers became aware of cyclical patterns. For example, they learned to calculate when events such as eclipses would occur and when a specific star would appear on the horizon. Ancient Mediterranean peoples thus regarded astronomy as a Mesopotamian science, and they considered the Babylonians its greatest experts.

The observation and interpretation of astronomical and other omens were not goals in themselves, however. Rather, Mesopotamians believed it was possible to change a predicted negative outcome. They aimed to produce this change mostly by appeasing the gods with prayers and offerings. But when an omen foretold the death of the king, the people would place a substitute on the throne and hide the real king in a safe place. They enacted a ritual in which the substitute was crowned, dressed in royal garb, and even provided with a queen. When they considered that the evil had passed, they removed the substitute (most often killing him to indicate that the prediction had been accurate) and restored the real king to the throne.

Omen readers, and especially astronomers, were thus very important, highly respected people in ancient Mesopotamia. They probably had to study for long periods to become familiar with the extensive writings that guided the interpretation of signs, and they had to thoroughly understand the intricacies of the cuneiform script and of Babylonian mathematics, which were at the basis of the analysis. The astronomers' accomplishments as observers of planetary behavior were remarkable, and their predictions of eclipses and the like were accurate. They were also meticulous record keepers, and to this day we identify many of the constellations they were the first to discern.

QUESTIONS TO CONSIDER

1. What was the purpose of omen reading in ancient Mesopotamia?

2. How did astronomers obtain their data?

3. What was the relationship between political rule and omen reading?

For Further Information:

Baigent, Michael. *From the Omens of Babylon: Astrology and Ancient Mesopotamia*. 1994.
Bottéro, Jean. *Mesopotamia: Writing, Reasoning, and the Gods*. Translated by Z. Bahrani and M. Van De Mieroop. Chicago: University of Chicago Press, 1992.
Rochberg, Francesca. *The Heavenly Writing: Divination, Horoscopy, and Astronomy in Mesopotamian Culture*. Cambridge, U.K.: University of Cambridge, 2004.

The Course of Empire

The Persian Empire was established by Cyrus the Achaemenid (a-KEY-muh-nid) (r. 559–530 B.C.E.), who in the sixth century rapidly annexed his neighbors' territories, including the large Neo-Babylonian Empire and the states of central Iran. His son and successor, Cambyses (kam-BIE-sees) (r. 530–522 B.C.E.), added Egypt to the empire, and for another fifty years the Persians campaigned in all directions to conquer new lands. By 480 B.C.E., the Achaemenid Empire incorporated the area from western India to the Mediterranean coast and from Egypt to the Black Sea and the fringes of Central Asia. Indeed, for more than a millennium, four ruling dynasties—the Achaemenids (559–330 B.C.E.), Seleucids (323–83 B.C.E.), Parthians (247 B.C.E.–224 C.E.), and Sasanids (224–651 C.E.)—maintained imperial rule over much of Southwest Asia (see Maps 4.3 and 4.4).

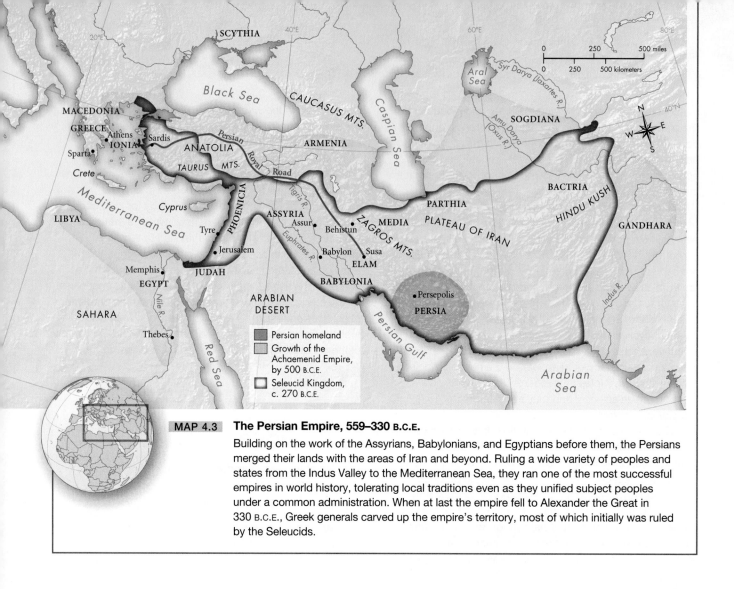

The Persian Empire, 559–330 B.C.E.

Building on the work of the Assyrians, Babylonians, and Egyptians before them, the Persians merged their lands with the areas of Iran and beyond. Ruling a wide variety of peoples and states from the Indus Valley to the Mediterranean Sea, they ran one of the most successful empires in world history, tolerating local traditions even as they unified subject peoples under a common administration. When at last the empire fell to Alexander the Great in 330 B.C.E., Greek generals carved up the empire's territory, most of which initially was ruled by the Seleucids.

Although they were foreign occupiers, the early Persian kings presented themselves as legitimate heirs to local thrones. Thus Cyrus became king of Babylon and continued local traditions of rule. When Cambyses became king of Egypt, he adopted an Egyptian throne name and was represented with traditional Egyptian royal garments and crowns. These men had to be strong individuals to assert their authority over various conquered peoples, who yearned for independence and the return of a native ruler. These feelings boiled over at the death of Cambyses in 522 B.C.E., and only after much campaigning—described in the passage at the beginning of this chapter—did the new Persian king, Darius (r. 521–486 B.C.E.), gain full control of the empire.

Imperial Structure

The difficulties Darius faced led him to undertake a program of reorganization and reform. In place of a collection of states held together by the person of the king, Darius created an imperial structure comprising twenty provinces, called **satrapies** (SAY-trap-eez), thereby extending a uniform system of government over an area of unprecedented size. Each satrapy had a Persian administrator (satrap) and was forced to provide tribute and troops to meet the empire's ever-increasing need for men and resources to control conquered territories. Imperial authorities exploited the skills of their subject peoples: Phoenicians manned the navy along with Cypriots and Ionians; in the army, Arabian camel drivers fought next to North African charioteers.

Greek Resistance

satrapy A province in the Achaemenid Persian Empire, administered by a satrap.

Despite Persia's enormous power and military success, there were limits to its ability to expand. Most famous is the empire's failure to conquer Greece. Between 490 and 479 B.C.E., Darius and his son and successor Xerxes (r. 486–464 B.C.E.) invaded Greece twice, but the Greek city-states defeated the Persian army on land and at sea (as we will see in

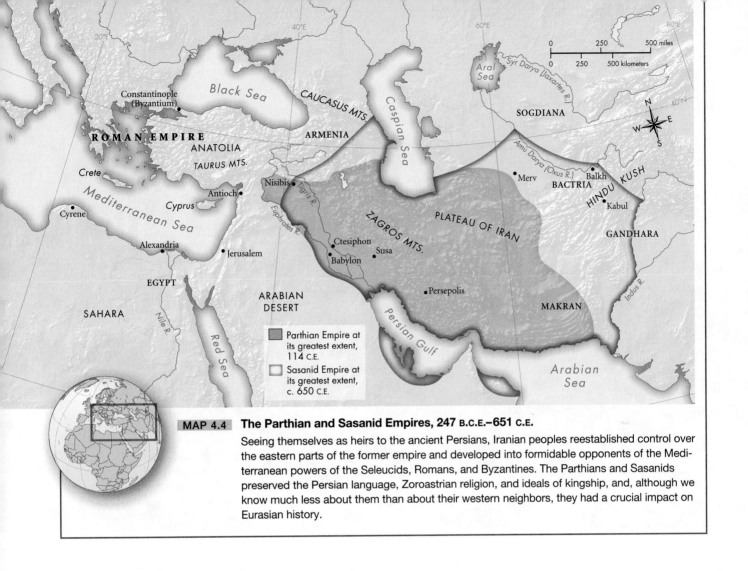

MAP 4.4 **The Parthian and Sasanid Empires, 247 B.C.E.–651 C.E.**

Seeing themselves as heirs to the ancient Persians, Iranian peoples reestablished control over the eastern parts of the former empire and developed into formidable opponents of the Mediterranean powers of the Seleucids, Romans, and Byzantines. The Parthians and Sasanids preserved the Persian language, Zoroastrian religion, and ideals of kingship, and, although we know much less about them than about their western neighbors, they had a crucial impact on Eurasian history.

Chapter 5). Resistance to Persia continued throughout the empire's history, and Egypt, for example, was able to gain independence from 404 to 343 B.C.E.

Yet these rebellions did not destroy the empire. That occurred only with the arrival of a young ruler, Alexander the Great, from Macedonia, the region just north of Greece. With his highly skilled troops, Alexander defeated the Persian King Darius III in three crucial battles, after which some of the king's noblemen killed him and delivered his body to Alexander. These events did not allow Alexander to inherit the entire empire at once, however. Victory came only after he led his troops on a long series of campaigns from Egypt to Iran and farther east, to claim control over these territories. In 324 B.C.E., Alexander set up his capital in Babylon, where, as we will see in Chapter 5, he died three years later.

Macedonian Conquest of Persia

Administering a Multicultural Empire

At Persepolis, in the heartland of Persia, Darius constructed a magnificent city where he annually celebrated the delivery of tribute. Persepolis's ruins still impress us by their grandeur and refinement. The emperor received an enormous tribute. Babylonia, for example, had to deliver 1000 talents (about 60,000 pounds) of silver. India paid 360 talents (about 21,600 pounds) of gold dust. The Persian treasuries were so rich that when later Macedonian conquerors put their contents into circulation, the value of gold and silver dropped steeply due to oversupply. The annual ceremony of tribute delivery had an ideological as well as economic value, for it showed the ruler as master of the subject regions, each dependent people offering him the specialties of their lands. Bactrians, for example, brought camels; Armenians, gold vessels; and Nubians, ivory tusks.

View of Persepolis

The imperial city of Persepolis (the Greek name meaning "the Persian City") dominated the countryside, to be seen from afar and stand as a symbol of the empire's power. Huge palaces with high stone pillars and walls decorated with relief sculptures provided a background for the annual ceremony in which representatives from all parts of the empire came to deliver their tribute as a sign of their submission (see "At a Crossroads," page 104). (akg-images/Suzanne Held.)

Communication with the Provinces

Because communication was of utmost importance in administering this colossal empire, the Persians developed an extensive road system to connect the capital to the provinces. Royal emissaries and trade caravans traveled along these routes to bring messages and goods over great distances. The king used messengers, known as "the eyes and ears of the king," to inspect his provincial officials and to make sure they obeyed his orders. The most famous road was the Royal Road from Susa in western Iran to Sardis in western Turkey, covering a distance of sixteen hundred miles, which a traveler could cover in ninety days. Rest houses along its route accommodated the king's representatives.

Given the empire's vast size and enormous bureaucracy, the efficiency-minded Persians readily adopted existing practices in the conquered territories, including writing and language. In Babylonia they continued to record on clay tablets; in Egypt they wrote on papyri. For affairs that crossed the borders of these earlier states, they used Aramaic language and script. Most people in Syria-Palestine already spoke that language, and the Aramaic alphabetic script was easier to use than the ancient scripts of Mesopotamia and Egypt. Unfortunately, Aramaic records were written on papyrus or parchment, which easily disintegrate, and therefore few such documents have survived.

The Persians' adoption of the Aramaic alphabet spread that system's use far to the east, and it inspired later alphabets as far east as India. Before their empire, the Persians did not have a script. They spoke an Indo-European language, Old Persian, in which they may have had a flourishing oral literature. When Darius became king, he instituted the use of a new script to write Old Persian, an alphabetic cuneiform intended for royal inscriptions. Like Darius's proclamation at the beginning of the chapter, these inscriptions appeared in three languages—Old Persian, Babylonian, and Elamite, the last being the official language of the Elamite state that had ruled western Iran for centuries until about 700 B.C.E. Sometimes scribes added translations into Egyptian as well. The intent was to show that the empire integrated several great literate cultures, and that the ruling Persians themselves also had a written tradition. At the same time, the use of multiple languages ensured that the desires of Persian rulers would be understood by all.

An innovation that simplified trade and spread widely over the empire was the use of coins—small, portable disks of precious metal stamped by official mints to guarantee their value. In around 650 B.C.E., before the Persian Empire, people from the country of Lydia in western Anatolia had invented coinage. They made the earliest coins of electrum, a locally available mixture of silver and gold. Sometime later, others minted coins of pure gold and silver; each region or city could produce its own coins with distinctive stamps. Coins facilitated trade by providing an easily portable, guaranteed means of exchange. They were also used to pay soldiers and taxes.

Because the empire encompassed a vast area with no political boundaries, traders could travel safely and easily throughout Southwest Asia. Kings also encouraged trade through public projects, such as digging a canal from the Nile River to the Red Sea, and they may have sponsored exploration to expand trade contacts. The Persians controlled the Phoenician harbors, giving them access to the resources of the entire Mediterranean. Records show that ships from Anatolia docked in Egypt and that Babylonian merchants traveled in Iran. Taxes collected on trade became another major source of income. Thus, although the Persians extracted tribute as the Assyrians had before them, they took pains to ensure the overall economic health of the empire by promoting and protecting robust trade throughout their domain.

Coinage and Trade

The First Coins

Because people who received payment in gold, silver, or other precious metals ran the risk of receiving inferior metal, in around 650 B.C.E. inhabitants of Lydia developed the idea of casting pieces with a mark stamped on them. Recipients would recognize the distinctive image from an authority that guaranteed the value. The earliest coins were of electrum, as are the examples shown here, but soon gold and silver were more common. The Persian Empire's need to pay soldiers promoted the use of coinage all over its vast territory and beyond. (Charles O'Rear/Corbis.)

Tolerance of Local Traditions

As the empire's network of roads and trade routes eased the movement of people and resources, they helped disseminate Persian culture. Some local elites adopted Persian customs and artistic styles, but Persia's empire had a distinctive attitude toward local traditions and beliefs. Other imperial elites, such as the New Kingdom Egyptians and the Assyrians, were confident that their culture was superior, and their appearance and behavior always reflected that culture. By contrast, the Persians adopted the lifestyles and ideologies of the territories they annexed and integrated themselves into existing structures. As we have seen, the Persian king assumed the role of descendant of the native dynasties. He behaved as a local ruler, participating, for example, in traditional rituals to local gods. Further, the Persians restored local traditions that their imperial predecessors had recently disrupted. Most famous is Cyrus's decision to allow Judean deportees to return from Babylonia to Jerusalem and his promise of monetary support to rebuild the temple there (see Counterpoint: Assimilation and Resistance: The Peoples of Israel and Judah). The Hebrew Bible depicts Cyrus as the savior of the Judean people sent by their god Yahweh (YAH-way). Other literatures, too, presented the Persians as more devoted to the local gods than the rulers they replaced. Such observations may have been propagandistic, but they did contain a grain of truth. By respecting local identities and adopting local customs, the Persians reduced resistance to their rule and claimed political legitimacy in terms the local population understood. They saw themselves as heads of a multicultural empire and did not seek to impose a common Persian identity on their subject peoples.

Zoroastrianism in a Polytheistic World

The local religious practices the Persian kings promoted differed significantly from those of the Persians themselves. Persian religion followed the teachings of Zoroaster (the Greek rendering of the Iranian name Zarathushtra), and Zoroastrianism is still practiced today. He taught through **Gathas** (Songs), which are contained in the Avesta, a collection of writings recorded in around 500 C.E. The Gathas depict a world inhabited by pastoralists, probably located in eastern Iran, similar to the world described in the Indian Vedas (see Chapter 3). The languages of the Gathas and Vedas are closely related, and they both belong to the Indo-Iranian branch of Indo-European.

Zoroaster's Teachings

It is unclear when Zoroaster lived; scholars have suggested dates from 1700 to 500 B.C.E. Persian religion was **polytheistic**—they believed in the existence of many gods—but Zoroaster molded them into a structure that emphasized dualism. According to Zoroaster, the universe is divided into the two opposing forces, good and evil, which were represented by two spirits. A line in his teachings says: "Yes, there are two fundamental spirits, twins which are renowned to be in conflict. In thought and in word, in action, they are two: the good and the bad. And between these two, the beneficent have correctly chosen, not the maleficent."[3] Everything in the Zoroastrian world was characterized by this parallel dualism—good versus evil, truth versus untruth, light versus darkness—and all humans had to choose between them. Zoroastrians worshiped one god only, Ahuramazda (ah-HOOR-uh-MAZZ-duh) ("wise lord"), who was the father of both the beneficent and the hostile spirit and the force for keeping evil in check. The creator of heaven and earth, day and night, light and darkness, Ahuramazda provided ethical guidance to humans to seek truth, goodness, and light.

Gathas The songs that contain the prophet Zoroaster's teachings.

polytheism A religious system's belief in the existence of many gods.

Hebrew Bible The sacred books—in prose and poetry—that document the monotheistic religious ideas of the peoples of Israel and Judah.

Because Zoroaster's teachings stressed that individuals had to seek purity in nature, the cult focused on the pure forces of fire and water. Unlike other peoples of Southwest Asia and neighboring regions, Zoroastrians did not build temples, and they burned sacrifices on altars standing in the open. As in Vedic India (see Chapter 3), priests, called Magi in Greek texts on Persia, played a key role in the sacrifices, and they drank a stimulant, haoma (HOW-muh), that was related to the Vedic drink soma.

It is unclear whether the Persian rulers were Zoroastrians, but historians know that they recognized Ahuramazda as the god who placed them on the throne and guided them in their search for truth. Representations of the king commonly show him next to a winged sun disk containing the upper body of a man, most likely the god Ahuramazda. The altars built near the royal tombs also suggest that kings adhered to Ahuramazda's cult.

Zoroaster's teachings became the basis of the official religion of later Iranian dynasties (the Parthians and the Sasanids, as we will see in Chapter 7). But the ancient Persians did not force their subjects to honor Ahuramazda or adopt Persian cult practices, and Zoroaster's ideas probably had little impact on the general population of the empire. The focus on choosing between good and evil and on worshiping only the god Ahuramazda had a significant impact on Judaism, however, and through it on Christianity and Islam. With the spread of Islam (discussed in Chapter 9), Zoroastrianism became a minority religion in Iran, and its worshipers moved to India, where they are referred to today as Parsees.

Zoroastrianism's Lasting Influence

COUNTERPOINT
Assimilation and Resistance: The Peoples of Israel and Judah

By their very nature, empires produce a degree of assimilation as diverse populations come together and absorb aspects of one another's cultures and lifestyles. The empires discussed in this chapter exposed people everywhere to foreign influences—voluntary or forced movement to new locations, new bureaucratic practices, and novel imperial dress and customs—and local people adopted some new practices. Even in empires that allowed local lifestyles and customs to persist, common practices arose, such as the use of Aramaic script in the Persian Empire. People subjected to mass deportations, such as those the Assyrians used systematically, had to adapt to their new environment, learn how to work the new land, and communicate with the local populations, and in so doing they lost part of their own identities.

In this Counterpoint we examine the effects of this process of assimilation —and resistance to it—in the two small states of Israel and Judah, strategically located in Syria-Palestine, where Asia and Africa meet. All the empires we discussed in this chapter sent armies to these territories in the effort to dominate Israel and Judah.

> **FOCUS**
>
> To what degree and in what ways did the peoples of Israel and Judah accept or reject the influences of the empires they confronted?

Reconstructing the Histories of Israel and Judah

Located in the south of the region between the Mediterranean coast and the Jordan River, Israel and Judah were surrounded by Philistine city-states on the southern coast, Phoenicia on the northern coast, the Aramaic kingdom of Damascus to the north, and the states of Ammon, Moab, and Edom to the east. All were small kingdoms centered on a capital city. For Israel that city was Samaria; for Judah, Jerusalem. The populations throughout the region spoke related languages. In Israel and Judah the language was Hebrew, which the people recorded in an alphabetic script derived from Phoenician.

Scholars reconstruct the histories of Israel and Judah on the basis of a monumental literary work of antiquity, the **Hebrew Bible**, which Christians call the Old Testament. The Bible provides a rich narrative

Ancient Israel and Judah

The Bible as a Historical Source

starting with the creation of the universe, but it is a very challenging historical source. A religious tract, the Hebrew Bible honors the god Yahweh and tells of his interactions with peoples of Israel and Judah. It contains, among much else, the Torah, a set of laws on how people should behave. Anonymous writers and adapters composed the Bible by combining existing myths and tales, historical narratives, king lists, poems, and laws, some of which tradition credits to figures, such as Moses. Judeans in exile in Babylonia probably wrote down the core of the Hebrew Bible in the fifth century B.C.E., but it was later reworked and expanded, and multiple versions circulated. The early Christians added New Testament books to the Old Testament, extending the narrative to include the teachings of Jesus (see Chapter 7). Today Jews and Christians consider the Bible their sacred text, but they diverge in what books they see as integral parts of the work.

Historians' Debate over the Bible

Historians hold a wide range of opinions about the historical value of the Bible. Some regard it as fundamentally factual with some inconsistencies arising from different traditions contained in it, but others question the accuracy of any statement not confirmed by sources other than the Bible. Archaeology has failed to provide much help. It can demonstrate the existence of the cities mentioned, but it cannot, for example, ascribe a building to a particular king. A remarkable aspect of the cultures of Israel and Judah is the rarity of monumental royal inscriptions of the type that existed in the neighboring states. Were such inscriptions destroyed on purpose in Israel and Judah? The reality of the individuals and events described in the Bible is mostly from external sources, especially Assyria.

Peoples Uprooted: Deportation and Exile

Israel and Assyria

The state of Israel arose at the turn of the second millennium B.C.E. when, archaeology shows, newcomers disrupted the existing political structures of Syria-Palestine. At this time, the Philistines settled on the southern coast, and Aramaic kingdoms appeared throughout Syria. Tension was rife. Possibly after a period of union in the tenth century under kings David and Solomon, Israel split into two kingdoms, Israel and Judah, which regularly clashed with each other and with other nearby states. Assyrian pressure, however, caused all of these states to join forces. When the Assyrians campaigned west of the Euphrates River in the ninth and eighth centuries B.C.E., they regularly engaged coalitions that included Israel and Judah. The only existing representation of an Israelite king is a relief of Jehu submitting to the Assyrian King Shalmaneser III (shal-muh-NEE-zer) (r. 858–824 B.C.E.). The Assyrians tried to control the Syrian-Palestinian states by installing pro-Assyrian locals on the throne, but rebellions and refusals to pay tribute were common. Thus, in 722 B.C.E., the Assyrian king Sargon II sacked Israel's capital Samaria, turned the region into a province, and deported most of the population of Israel to other parts of the empire. These deportees soon assimilated to their new surroundings and never emerged as a discernible entity again. Meanwhile Sargon settled people from the east of Assyria in the land of Israel.

Judah and Babylonia

The Assyrians allowed Judah to remain a separate state, although they raided much of its territory to enforce obedience. But the Neo-Babylonians, who replaced the Assyrians as the leading power in Southwest Asia in around 610 B.C.E., sealed Judah's fate. In 587 B.C.E., Nebuchadnezzar II sacked Jerusalem, deported a large proportion of the inhabitants, and imposed a governor on the region. When this governor was assassinated, Nebuchadnezzar returned to Judah in 582 B.C.E. and deported even more Judeans. This period became known as the Babylonian captivity, or the **Exile**.

Nebuchadnezzar settled the displaced people of Judah in the core of the empire near Babylon, where they experienced a very cosmopolitan culture. Babylon's inhabitants came from all over Southwest Asia and beyond, the city was a center of culture, and its ancient religious cults flourished under royal patronage. The Babylonian countryside where the Judeans lived prospered as the result of public works such as the digging of irrigation

Exile In the history of ancient Judah, the period when the Neo-Babylonians deported the Judeans to Babylonia, c. 587–530 B.C.E.

King Jehu of Israel

In contrast to the rulers of neighboring Egypt and Mesopotamia, those of Israel and Judah are not known to us from statuary and other representations. The exception is the ninth-century-B.C.E. King Jehu of Israel, who appears prostrate on a monument the Assyrian Shalmaneser III had carved showing Israel's submission. Why no other representations of the kings of Israel and Judah survive or were ever made remains a mystery. (Erich Lessing/Art Resource, NY.)

canals. The temptation to assimilate and to make the region a new home was great, and many of the deportees yielded to it.

Judean Resistance and Dispersal

Some Judeans reacted against this process by stressing a separate identity rooted in their relationship with their god, Yahweh. His only temple had been in Jerusalem, and the Babylonians had demolished it. Before the Exile, the cult of Yahweh had been central to the states of Israel and Judah, but not exclusive. Other cults flourished as well, especially those devoted to the Syrian gods Baal and Astarte. Debate over which god was supreme, Yahweh or Baal, seems to have taken place for centuries, but over time, most likely during the Exile, the veneration of Yahweh became a monotheistic creed. Yahweh was not only the supreme god, he was the only god. No other gods existed, and the people who revered other gods worshiped idols. Unlike the ideas of Akhenaten or Zoroaster, which allowed for the existence of divine beings alongside Aten or Ahuramazda, Judaism held that Yahweh was the one and only god.

When the Persian king Cyrus conquered Babylonia, his tolerance for local customs led him to issue an edict that allowed the Judeans to return home after some fifty years of exile. Some Judeans chose to remain in Babylon, but others felt that their duty to Yahweh demanded that they return home. They argued that a **covenant**—an agreement between Yahweh and the "people of Israel"—guaranteed Judeans success and a country in return for obedience to God (see Reading the Past: The God Yahweh and the People of Israel Form a Covenant). Yahweh could be worshiped only in the temple at Jerusalem, and it was the people's obligation to return home and rebuild that temple, a project for which Cyrus promised government funds.

Return to Judah

covenant In the Hebrew Bible, Yahweh's promise of success and a homeland in return for his people's obedience.

The God Yahweh and the People of Israel Form a Covenant

The monotheistic religion that developed among the Judeans was based on a covenant, an agreement between the people and their God. The terms of the covenant resembled those of treaties between a human emperor and his subjects. The Hebrew Bible stated this agreement several times; in this passage, Yahweh addresses the patriarch Abraham, who, according to the Book of Genesis, had first arrived in the region that would become the states of Israel and Judah.

When Abram was ninety-nine years old the Lord appeared to Abram, and said to him, "I am God Almighty; walk before me, and be blameless. And I will make my covenant between me and you, and will multiply you exceedingly." Then Abram fell on his face; and God said to him, "Behold my covenant is with you, and you shall be the father of a multitude of nations. No longer shall your name be Abram, but your name shall be Abraham; for I have made you the father of a multitude of nations. I will make you exceedingly fruitful; and I will make nations of you, and kings shall come forth from you. And I will establish my covenant between me and you and your descendants after you throughout their generations for an everlasting covenant, to be God to you and your descendants after you. And I will give to you, and to your descendants after you, the land of your sojournings, all the land of Canaan, for an everlasting possession; and I will be their God."

Source: Genesis 17:1–8, Revised Standard Version.

EXAMINING THE EVIDENCE

1. **What are the terms of the covenant between Yahweh and the people of Israel?**
2. **What relationship between God and Abraham does this passage indicate?**

Judaism as an Identity

The Judeans who returned to Judah adopted firm rules that set them apart from other people in the region. Now known as Jews, they relied on teachers (rabbis) to guide them in their faith and lives and gathered in meeting places (synagogues) to pray as a community. The exclusive belief in one god was essential and strictly enforced. It was very important to observe the Sabbath (literally meaning "seven"), one day a week for rest from work, because God had rested after six days of creation. The Jews established dietary rules, prohibiting the consumption of foods such as pork and shellfish and the combination of dairy products with meat. Women were required to take baths after menstruation to renew ritual purity. These and other distinctive laws, such as a ban on marriage to non-Jews, produced a strong separate Jewish identity.

Jews Outside Judah

But not all Jews lived in Judah. Some remained in Babylonia, and others dispersed over the Persian Empire in a process known as the **Diaspora**. One such emigrant community lived on the Nile island of Elephantine on the southern border of Egypt. The residents left papyri, written in Aramaic, that detail their lives. Mercenaries (soldiers for hire) for the Persian king adhered to the faith in Yahweh and kept in constant contact with Jerusalem. They built their own temple, but the Jerusalem priesthood did not approve of it, and Egyptian opponents destroyed it. Because of the Diaspora, an identity based on a Jewish faith rather than a Judean people developed, with many adherents living abroad. The emigrants focused strictly on one god, but the world was predominantly polytheistic. Thus, regardless of where they lived, Jews maintained a sense of connection to a community, albeit a community of believers rather than of inhabitants of a particular city, state, or region.

Throughout the Hellenistic and Roman periods (see Chapters 5 and 7), the idea of monotheism would further develop. For a time, different interpretations of Judaism existed. These were consolidated, however, after the Jews were forced to leave Judah when the Romans destroyed the second temple of Jerusalem in 70 C.E. In the first cen-

Diaspora Dispersal of people from their homeland; the term originally referred to the Jews who left Palestine after the Babylonian and Roman sacks of Jerusalem, but it is now used for many other peoples as well.

tury C.E. a Jewish sect following the teachings of Jesus of Nazareth would develop Christianity, which would have its immense impact on world history through its influence on the Roman Empire.

Conclusion

In North Africa and Southwest Asia, the earliest empires in world history arose beginning in the second millennium B.C.E. A sequence of political masters accumulated vast territories by defeating previously independent states and forcing their populations to contribute labor and goods to the empire. The emergence of empires prompted peoples with separate cultures and habits to interact, and they exchanged ideas and influenced one another in enduring ways.

The degree to which they assimilated and the sources of the most influential traditions varied enormously. Political domination could lead to cultural supremacy, as when Egypt conquered Nubia, but sometimes rulers eagerly adopted the practices and ideas of their subject people, as when Nubians ruled Egypt. Some imperial powers permitted their subjects to continue cultural practices and even promoted them; in the inscription quoted at the start of the chapter, the Persian King Darius depicted himself as a king of many countries. Others, such as Assyria, did not interfere with cultural matters and local customs as long as their subjects obeyed them. Some subject peoples consciously rejected assimilation, most notably the Judeans. Thus the cultural consequences of imperial rule took a wide variety of forms. This variation would continue throughout world history, and in the next chapter we will see how it emerged in the early empires of Eurasia.

NOTES

1. Translated from Florence Malbran-Labat, *La version akkadienne de l'inscription trilingue de Darius à Behistun* (Rome: GEI, 1994), 93–103.
2. Translated from F. Thureau-Dangin, *Une relation de la huitième campagne de Sargon* (Paris: Geuthner, 1912), lines 131–136.
3. Yasna 30:3. In S. Insler, *The Gathas of Zarathustra* (Leiden: Brill, 1975), 33.

RESOURCES FOR RESEARCH

Imperial Egypt and Nubia, 1550 B.C.E.–350 C.E.

In their general surveys of the culture, many of the books on ancient Egypt treat the New Kingdom's imperial period and the period when Nubians ruled Egypt. A number of works focus on Nubia, often looking at its entire ancient history.

Ancient Egypt Web site. http://www.ancient-egypt.co.uk.
Manley, Bill. *The Penguin Historical Atlas of Ancient Egypt*. 1996.
Morkot, Robert G. *The Black Pharaohs: Egypt's Nubian Rulers*. 2000.
Morkot, Robert G. *The Egyptians: An Introduction*. 2005.
O'Connor, David. *Ancient Nubia: Egypt's Rival in Africa*. 1993.
Romer, John. *Ancient Lives: The Story of the Pharaohs' Tombmakers*. 2003.
Taylor, John H. *Nubia and Egypt*. 1991.

Theban Mapping Project. http://www.thebanmappingproject.com.
Van De Mieroop, Marc. *A History of Ancient Egypt*. 2010.
Welsby, Derek A. *The Kingdom of Kush: The Napatan and Meroitic Empires*. 1996.

Rise and Fall of the Assyrian Empire, 900–612 B.C.E.

The Assyrians left extensive archaeological and written remains, which have been the subject of many specialized studies. General descriptions of the empire often appear in surveys of Mesopotamian history, as well as in more specialized books.

The British Museum. http://www.mesopotamia.co.uk.
Chadwick, Robert. *First Civilizations: Ancient Mesopotamia and Ancient Egypt*, 2d ed. 2005.

Curtis, J. E., and J. E. Reade. *Art and Empire: Treasures from Assyria in the British Museum.* 1995.

Joannès, Francis. *The Age of Empires: Mesopotamia in the First Millennium B.C.* Translated by A. Nevill. 2004.

Kuhrt, Amélie. *The Ancient Near East, c. 3000–330 B.C.* 1995.

Leick, Gwendolyn. *The Babylonians: An Introduction.* 2003.

Markoe, Glenn E. *Phoenicians.* 2000.

Oppenheim, A. Leo. *Ancient Mesopotamia,* 2d ed. 1977.

Saggs, H. W. F. *The Might That Was Assyria.* 1990.

Van De Mieroop, Marc. *A History of the Ancient Near East, ca. 3000–323 B.C.* 2d ed. 2007.

The Persian Empire, 550–330 B.C.E.

Much early work on the Persian Empire was based on Greek sources, which depicted the empire through the eyes of one of its greatest enemies. More recently, scholars have turned to sources from the empire itself, especially those from Mesopotamia and Egypt, to study how the empire functioned.

Allen, Lindsay. *The Persian Empire: A History.* 2005.

Briant, Pierre. *From Cyrus to Alexander: A History of the Persian Empire.* Translated by P. Daniels. 2002.

Brosius, Maria. *The Persians: An Introduction.* 2006.

Curtis, John. *Ancient Persia,* 2d ed. 2000.

*Kuhrt, Amélie. *The Persian Empire: A Corpus of Sources from the Achaemenid Period.* 2007.

Musée Achéménide. http://www.museum-achemenet.college-de-france.fr/.

Wiesehöfer, Josef. *Ancient Persia from 550 B.C. to 650 A.D.* Translated by A. Azodi. 1996.

COUNTERPOINT: Assimilation and Resistance: The Peoples of Israel and Judah

The literature on the ancient history of Israel and Judah is vast. In their use of the Hebrew Bible as a historical source, surveys vary from fully accepting the accuracy of the information to rejecting most of it as historically unreliable. The books below cover a spectrum of approaches, from heavy reliance on the biblical text (Bright; Miller and Hayes) to a critical attitude (Liverani, Soggin).

Bright, John. *A History of Israel,* 4th ed. 2000.

Kamm, Antony. *The Israelites: An Introduction.* 1999.

Liverani, Mario. *Israel's History and the History of Israel.* Translated by C. Peri and P. Davies. 2005.

Miller, J. Maxwell, and John H. Hayes. *A History of Ancient Israel and Judah,* 2d ed. 2006.

Moorey, P. R. S. *Biblical Lands.* 1975.

Soggin, J. Alberto. *An Introduction to the History of Israel and Judah,* 3d ed. Translated by J. Bowden. 1999.

* Primary source.

▶ **For additional primary sources from this period,** see *Sources of Crossroads and Cultures*.

▶ **For Web sites, images, and documents related to topics in this chapter,** see Make History at bedfordstmartins.com/smith.

The major global development in this chapter ▶ The rise of empires and the variety and consequences of imperial rule.

IMPORTANT EVENTS

c. 1700–500 B.C.E.	Scholarly guesses for life of Zoroaster, founder of Zoroastrianism
c. 1700–330 B.C.E.	Development and spread of the alphabet in western Asia
c. 1550–1070 B.C.E.	Egyptian New Kingdom Empire
c. 1070 B.C.E.	Nubian independence from Egypt
c. 900–612 B.C.E.	Assyrian Empire
c. 730–660 B.C.E.	Nubian Empire
c. 650 B.C.E.	Invention of coinage in Lydia
c. 626–539 B.C.E.	Neo-Babylonian (Chaldean) Empire
587 B.C.E.	Neo-Babylonian sack of Jerusalem
c. 587–530 B.C.E.	Judean people in exile
c. 550–330 B.C.E.	Achaemenid Persian Empire
c. 400 B.C.E.–350 C.E.	Kingdom of Meroe
330 B.C.E.	Alexander of Macedon defeats Persia

KEY TERMS

assimilation (p. 109)
bureaucracy (p. 113)
colony (p. 120)
covenant (p. 133)
Diaspora (p. 134)
empire (p. 107)
Exile (p. 132)
Gathas (p. 130)
Hebrew Bible (p. 131)
monotheism (p. 110)
polytheism (p. 130)
province (p. 118)
satrapy (p. 126)
tribute (p. 120)

CHAPTER OVERVIEW QUESTIONS

1. What were the main characteristics of the early empires?
2. How did the empires affect the peoples who created them and their subject populations?
3. How did imperial rulers adapt their control to local circumstances?
4. How did people resist empires?

SECTION FOCUS QUESTIONS

1. How did Egyptians and Nubians interact in the two imperial periods that united them politically?
2. What kind of power structure did the Assyrians impose on their subjects, and how did it lead to cultural assimilation in the empire?
3. What imperial vision and style of government marked the rise of the vast Persian Empire and allowed it to endure for more than two hundred years?
4. To what degree and in what ways did the peoples of Israel and Judah accept or reject the influences of the empires they confronted?

MAKING CONNECTIONS

1. How would you describe the different attitudes of the imperial elites discussed in this chapter toward the cultures of the conquered?
2. What languages and scripts were used in the different empires described in this chapter?
3. How did imperial policies and trade contacts influence the spread of writing systems?
4. What characteristics make these empires different from the earlier political structures we have studied?

AT A CROSSROADS ▲

The remains of the Acropolis ("top of the city") of Athens, towering over the modern city, include the majestic temple to Athena, divine protectress of the city, and the elaborate entrance gate on the left. Built under the world's first democratic government system, the Acropolis stands as a symbol of the Greeks' accomplishments in the first millennium B.C.E. (The Art Archive/Gianni Dagli Orti.)

The Greeks and the Wider World

1200–30 B.C.E.

Around 300 B.C.E., the Athenian Clearchus traveled to a city, now called Ai Khanoum, that Greeks had recently founded on the northern border of modern Afghanistan. On foot and horseback, he covered a distance equivalent to crossing the continental United States. At some point after he arrived, Clearchus inscribed on a rock sayings he had brought with him from the god Apollo's sanctuary at Delphi back home. He wrote:

> When a child, show yourself well behaved;
> When a young man, self-controlled;
> In middle age, just;
> As an old man, a good counselor;
> At the end of your life, free of sorrow.[1]

The inscription shows us that Clearchus actually visited Ai Khanoum and that he brought wisdom from his homeland with him, reflecting the spread of characteristic Greek values over a vast area. All we know about his life otherwise comes from quotes of his writings by later authors, and they show him as a typical Greek intellectual of his time. Born on the island of Cyprus, he had moved to Athens on the Greek mainland to study with the famous philosopher Aristotle. He wrote scholarly treatises on a wide variety of subjects, from water animals to human love. He was especially interested in Persia and India; recent conquests by Alexander the Great of Macedonia had connected Greece to the distant eastern places, which is why Clearchus could visit them. In his curiosity about

BACKSTORY

The historical developments we have studied so far took place primarily outside western Eurasia, the region of modern Europe. Nonetheless, through migration and cultural transmission, these developments did influence western Eurasia. *Homo sapiens*, for example, migrated from Africa to Southwest Asia and then to Europe about forty thousand years ago, and agriculture and Indo-European languages spread into the region after 7000 B.C.E. Central Asian horsemen reached this far west as well. By the second millennium B.C.E., part of Europe had joined the international order.

In the first millennium B.C.E., the first empires of Southwest Asia and North Africa still dominated the eastern Mediterranean. To the west, however, the inhabitants of Europe initiated changes—especially in politics and culture—that would have far-reaching effects on the rest of world history. We now turn our attention to these developments.

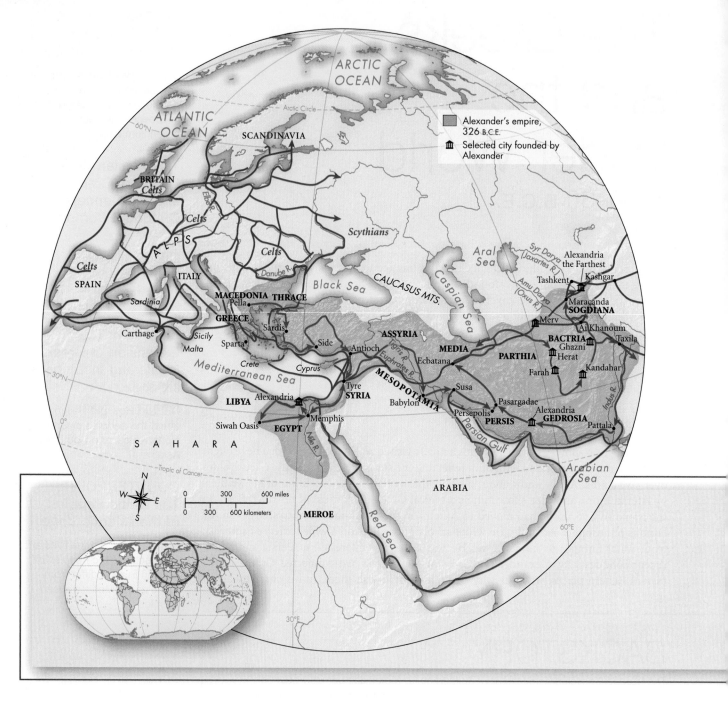

Alexander's empire, 326 B.C.E.

Selected city founded by Alexander

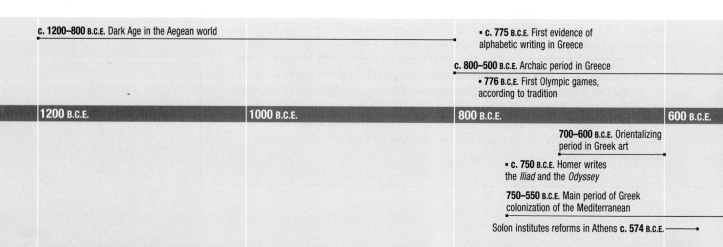

the larger world, he was following an established Greek tradition. For centuries, Greeks had been exploring the Mediterranean region and beyond as merchants and travelers, observing foreign cultures and disseminating novel Greek ideas.

Although the large states and empires considered in previous chapters were forces for political unification and influenced broad territories, they tended to stress stability and generally avoided initiating fundamental political and cultural change. In this chapter we focus on a territory that was at first marginal in terms of political and military power but became a center of cultural and technological innovation: Greece in western Eurasia. In close contact with the nearby empires of Southwest Asia and North Africa, yet politically independent, the Greeks stimulated many political and cultural developments during the first millennium B.C.E. These groundbreaking innovations touched almost every aspect of life: government, human rationality, literature, visual art, and much more. Although Greek city-states were in almost perpetual military competition with one another, people throughout the region shared a common culture, and all experimented with new intellectual endeavors. After several centuries, the military successes of one state, Macedonia, which itself was originally secondary to the Greek world, propelled the spread of these innovations over a vast area, merging them with a host of local traditions.

The ancient Greeks are more accessible to historians than many of the peoples we studied earlier, for a remarkable number of their writings survived through the ages. Because later peoples studied them, at first mostly in the Middle East and Europe and more recently worldwide, these writings had an enormous impact. They give us insight into many later intellectual developments in human history.

Greece was not characteristic of all of western Eurasia, however. Other cultures, notably the Celtic peoples of the Atlantic zone, adhered to their own traditions despite contact with Greece. As we will see in the Counterpoint to this chapter, Celtic culture influenced parts of Europe for many centuries, and Celtic traditions are important to this day.

MAPPING THE WORLD

The Spread of Hellenism

In a rapid sequence of major battles, Alexander the Great conquered a vast empire that brought peoples from Greece to the Indus River Valley under his rule. Through the policy of establishing new cities of Greek immigrants alongside local peoples, he and his successors initiated the merging of cultural traditions known as Hellenism (from "Hellas," the native term for Greece). Hellenism shaped the histories of these regions for many centuries.

ROUTES ▼

— Trade route

→ Campaign of Alexander, 334–324 B.C.E.

- **500–479 B.C.E.** Persian Wars
- **338 B.C.E.** Philip of Macedonia conquers Greece

443–429 B.C.E. Pericles leads Athens

- **331 B.C.E.** Alexander defeats Persia; Alexandria founded in Egypt

431–404 B.C.E. Peloponnesian War

- **30 B.C.E.** Romans conquer Egypt

| **400 B.C.E.** | **200 B.C.E.** | **0** |

c. 500–323 B.C.E. Classical Age of Greece

323–30 B.C.E. Hellenistic period

- **404 B.C.E.** Spartan hegemony in Greece

- **390 B.C.E.** Celts capture Rome in Italy

- **323 B.C.E.** Death of Alexander

OVERVIEW QUESTIONS

The major global development in this chapter: The cultural and political innovations of the ancient Greeks and the expansion of Greek ideals and institutions.

As you read, consider:

1. How did geography and contacts with other peoples shape Greek institutions and values?

2. What were the cultural and political innovations of the Greeks, and how have they proved enduring?

3. To what extent did these innovations affect the lives and livelihoods of ordinary Greeks?

4. How did the spread of Hellenism affect the Greeks and the other peoples of Eurasia and North Africa?

The Development of Ancient Greek Culture 1200–500 B.C.E.

FOCUS

What significant political and cultural developments emerged in Greece in the early first millennium B.C.E.?

Despite their unparalleled size, the empires of Southwest Asia and Egypt (see Chapter 4) had much in common with the states that preceded them. Like their predecessors, they were essentially kingdoms with centralized authority and clear distinctions between rulers and subjects. In contrast, the Aegean world took an entirely new trajectory in the first millennium B.C.E., launching bold experiments in politics, culture, and social organization. Energized by Eastern influences but operating in a different physical environment, the people of the Aegean created a unique culture that would have a great and lasting impact on world history.

A Dark Age in Aegean Life and Culture 1200–800 B.C.E.

Greek Geography

The Aegean people inhabited a world dominated by mountains that made overland travel difficult. The river valleys and plains where they settled allowed only limited agriculture; the climate was dry, but unlike in Mesopotamia and Egypt irrigation was impossible. The sea, however, was dotted with many small islands. By sailing small ships that almost never lost sight of the coastline, the inhabitants maintained contacts among the Greek mainland, the Aegean islands, and the west coast of Anatolia (modern Turkey). Poor agricultural conditions, limited natural resources, and a strong maritime tradition combined to prompt Aegean people to look outward. They turned to trade and migration to meet their challenges (see Map 5.1).

The Aegean Dark Age

The Mycenaean culture of the Aegean disappeared in the twelfth century B.C.E. during that era's general disruptions in the eastern Mediterranean (see Chapter 2). The palace cultures of the past ceased to exist. For centuries, written expression dried up and artistic production slowed to a trickle, prompting scholars to refer to the period from 1200 to 800 B.C.E. as the Aegean Dark Age. During the Dark Age, people deserted large settlements and seem to have survived in small, poor communities of farmers and migratory herders. They continued to produce pottery, however, and Mycenaean wares gradually gave way to what archaeologists call geometric pottery, vessels with intricate geometric patterns covering their entire surface. Inhabitants throughout the Aegean islands used this style of pottery. From this Aegean-wide tradition we can infer that although Dark Age conditions reduced settlement size and limited cultural activities, Aegean communities sustained their interconnections. Despite their hardships, the Aegean people continued to participate in a shared culture.

Greek Colonization of the Mediterranean 800–500 B.C.E.

The Aegean people abandoned rural life relatively suddenly around 800 B.C.E. Demographic growth, internal and external factors, and renewed contacts with the East produced radical social changes. Historians call this new era in Aegean history the Archaic period (c. 800–500 B.C.E.).

Archaeological evidence shows that the settled population of Greece dramatically increased in the eighth century B.C.E. More settlements appeared, and their populations rose substantially. The mushrooming of settled communities may reflect a change in attitudes—a desire to live in large settlements instead of moving around—rather than improvements in farming methods. Indeed, the dry, mountainous land could not support dense populations, and so many Greeks left their homeland, establishing colonies all around the Mediterranean and creating new communities modeled on those in Greece.

MAP 5.1

Greeks and Phoenicians in the Mediterranean

Throughout most of the first millennium B.C.E. Phoenician and Greek traders sailed the Mediterranean Sea, competing to bring natural resources from the west to urban centers in the east. Both peoples established trading posts on the coast as transit points for materials brought from farther inland. The Phoenicians focused especially on the south coast and the far west, while the Greeks settled mostly in the northern Mediterranean and explored the Black Sea coast.

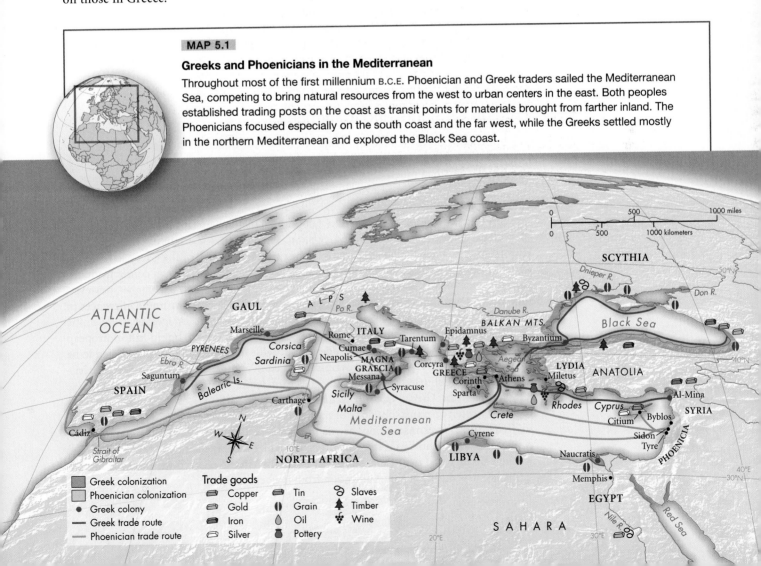

Colonization and Trade

The period of Greek colonization spanned more than two centuries, with most colonies originating between 750 and 550 B.C.E. Migrants fanned out in all directions from the Greek mainland: eastward to the modern Turkish coast and the Black Sea and westward to southern Italy, Sicily, southern France, and Spain. They also settled on the Libyan coast in North Africa.

In this widening circle of expansion, the Greeks competed with the Phoenicians, who had already colonized large parts of the western Mediterranean (see again Map 5.1). The Greeks settled eastern Sicily, for example; Phoenicians already controlled the western part of the island. The Greek colonies' economic bases varied, as did their importance to their home cities. Settlements in fertile agricultural zones shipped grain back home, while other outposts provided commodities such as timber and tin. Some special trading ports facilitated commerce with the great states of Assyria and Egypt; these typically were already established centers where Greeks simply set up business. Hence, in numerous ways, but most directly through trade, colonization strengthened the connections between Greeks and the larger world.

What did the Greeks have to offer areas that were richer in resources? The Greeks produced fine wines and olive oil, but the goods their artisans produced were especially in demand—in particular, pottery. Throughout ancient history Greek potters and painters manufactured exquisitely decorated ceramics, depicting with unprecedented liveliness scenes from epics and other literature. Because each city had its distinct style, modern scholars can easily determine where a vessel was made. Every city shipped large quantities of pottery abroad, either as empty vessels or as containers for wines and oil. People everywhere regarded them as the height of artistic accomplishment and proudly displayed them. Fancy banquets in Italy or France, for example, featured wine cups made in Greece, and the hosts were willing to trade their local resources to obtain them, increasing the wealth of the Greek cities that produced them. Thus, from the beginning, one of the most important Greek exports was their innovative and creative culture.

Foreign Contacts and Influences

The presence of Greeks abroad and visits by Phoenician traders in the Aegean world naturally led to a brisk exchange of ideas, practices, and people in the eighth century B.C.E. Because the East had much older and more developed traditions than the West, most of the inspiration went from east to west, and various Eastern cultural elements entered the Greek world.

Greek Alphabet

Most consequential was the Greeks' adoption of the Phoenician alphabet (see Chapter 4), perhaps as early as the ninth century B.C.E. The Phoenician origin of Greek letters is clear from the names, which are Semitic. For example, the name of the Greek letter *alpha* derives from the Semitic word *aleph*, meaning "ox-head"; the Greek *beta* comes from *bet*, "house"; and so on. The Greeks introduced a crucial innovation in the alphabet, however: they wrote down the vowels, which were not expressed in Semitic writing. Differences in the Greek and Semitic languages made this innovation essential. A speaker of a Semitic language knows what vowels to use from the grammatical context, but in Indo-European languages such as Greek, the context does not provide this clue and the vowels need to be explicitly expressed. Over time the scripts diverged in another way: whereas Semitic writing goes from right to left, Greek writing goes from left to right.

Why did the Greeks start to write again? Scholars assume that economic growth required written accounts, but none of the preserved earliest writing deals with business or trade. The first Greek inscriptions are names, short dedications, or curses. Often the writers state, "X wrote this," as if showing off a rare skill. Probably the majority of early Greek writings disappeared over time, and most likely the Greeks realized the multiple uses of script as a new means of communication from the beginning.

In the eighth to sixth centuries B.C.E., increasing prosperity from manufacturing and trade enabled the Greeks to buy art from foreign regions such as Phoenicia and Syria. Such art inspired Greek potters, painters, and other artists to include Eastern scenes and styles in their work. Sculptors carved human figures in imitation of Egyptian statues, and architects borrowed from Egypt techniques for constructing large buildings in stone. Given these Eastern influences, art historians refer to the seventh century B.C.E. in Greek art as the Orientalizing period, after the word *Orient*, meaning "East."

In the other direction, west to east, the Greeks provided manpower. Foreign empires greatly valued skilled Greek warriors. Greek mercenaries appeared in Egypt in the seventh century B.C.E. and soon afterward in Southwest Asia, where they remained a fixture for centuries. How and why had the Greeks developed such fighting skills? We find the answer in the emergence of powerful Greek city-states.

Growth of the City-State in Archaic Greece   800–500 B.C.E.

Population growth in the mid-eighth century B.C.E. led to fundamental changes in the political organization of the Aegean region. Village communities expanded or merged to form city-states, which became the characteristic political unit of Greek society. The Greeks referred to the city-state using the word **polis**, from which the modern term *politics* derives.

The polis was a self-governing community of citizens. It was administered by officials (who were themselves citizens) with defined responsibilities. There were numerous poleis, each controlling a relatively small territory comprising the city and its immediate surroundings. Although poleis were self-governing, they could be part of a larger political unit. In the fifth and fourth centuries B.C.E., for example, most Greek city-states fell under the hegemony of Sparta or Athens, and the poleis of western Turkey were subjects of the king of Persia for long periods. We have encountered city-states before—in Mesopotamia, for example (see Chapter 2)—but the Greeks added a further ideal to this concept. The citizens of the polis shared power rather than depended on a king. It must be emphasized, however, that most inhabitants of a polis were not citizens, a status reserved in most cases for native-born, male landowners. Women, the landless, slaves, and foreigners were all excluded from Greek government.

Like Mesopotamian city-states, neighboring Greek poleis often competed with one another over scarce resources. As a result, one of the most important duties of the citizen was to fight in the army. The eighth century B.C.E. saw radical changes in military tactics. Instead of a few heavily armed men riding to battle in chariots, from which they dismounted for individual combat, the soldiers formed **phalanxes**. Fighting on foot, these tightly organized groups relied on strict cooperation, every man holding a shield in his left arm to protect the right side of his neighbor. Each soldier, called a *hoplite*, was

Orientalizing Period

Woman's Statue in the Orientalizing Style

This statue, sculpted in Crete between 640 and 620 B.C.E., shows how much styles from Egypt and the Middle East influenced early Greek art. The woman's posture, dress, and hairstyle resemble those that Egyptian or Syrian sculptors of the same period would have shown (compare her to the Ptolemaic statues on page 162). The whole is distinctly Greek, however, and work like this lay at the basis of classical Greek sculpture. (Erich Lessing/Art Resource, NY.)

The Polis

polis The Greek city-state; in the ideal, a self-governing community of citizens.

phalanx A formation of soldiers who overlap their shields and swords to protect one another; developed in ancient Greece.

responsible for acquiring his own equipment: helmet, breastplate, leg armor, spear, and shield. Although much of the gear was made of iron, a cheaper metal than the previously used bronze, hoplites still faced considerable expense, and only landowners could serve. This common obligation, however, along with battle tactics relying on cooperation, created the strong sense of community that characterized the ideal of the polis. The way citizens fought on behalf of their communities mirrored the political connections that bound them to one another.

Shared Ideals

Despite frequent military conflicts among poleis, their inhabitants shared many cultural traits and ideals. They spoke dialects of the same Greek language, honored the same gods, and appreciated similar artistic styles. Sometimes they showed their competitive spirit in peaceful ways during festivals, including musical and literary contests. Most famous are the athletic competitions of the Olympic games. According to tradition, in 776 B.C.E. delegations of various city-states first met to compete in foot races, boxing, discus throwing, and other events in Olympia in southern Greece. The games continued in their original form for more than a thousand years, with cities from all over the Mediterranean sending athletes every four years. So strong were the cultural connections among the Greeks that even during the ruinous Peloponnesian War (discussed later in this chapter) cities of opposing factions participated in the games.

Political Diversity

Despite the shared characteristics of the city-states, their political organizations varied. The early city-states were dominated by aristocrats, a small group of people from wealthy families who inherited their status and made most of the important decisions for the community. When more people acquired wealth, the base of politically engaged men gradually expanded to include all citizens, with elected officials administering the state. These officials could reduce the power of the aristocratic families by issuing laws to regulate social and economic matters. Flouting the ideal of elected officials, from around 650 to 500 B.C.E. individuals seized power in many city-states. The Greeks called these men *tyrants*, which was at first a value-neutral term indicating "lord." People grew to resent this form of government, and rule by **tyranny** gave way to two new types of political organization. Many cities were controlled by an **oligarchy**, a small group of men who were usually wealthy, but not always from the old aristocratic families. Other cities embraced a more radical political system—the ideal of **democracy**, or rule by the people.

Athenian Democracy

Athens and Sparta, the two most prominent Greek city-states of the sixth and fifth centuries B.C.E., illustrate how geography shaped political developments in Greece. Athenians lived near the coast and relied on the sea for much of their livelihood. Starting in the seventh century B.C.E., many Athenians grew rich from maritime trade. They used this wealth to acquire land and built up large estates, dispossessing farmers in the countryside around Athens. As a result, small landowners often became indebted to wealthy city dwellers, and in the seventh century their discontent threatened the city's unity.

The tensions between classes weakened Athens, and various reformers—all aristocratic men themselves—introduced new policies intended to reduce conflict. The first measures were the work of Solon (c. 639–559 B.C.E.). Given full powers as lawgiver in 594 B.C.E., he cancelled all outstanding debts, freed all enslaved citizens, and made it illegal to force debtors into slavery. At the same time he resisted popular pressure to redistribute the lands of aristocrats and instead tried to increase wealth throughout Athenian society. Later reformers included Cleisthenes, who made all citizens equal before the law in 508 B.C.E., and—perhaps the most popular and influential of all—Pericles, who led Athens from 443 to 429 B.C.E. Pericles' many public works projects reduced unemployment, and his political initiatives brought more Athenians into the city's political structure. Collectively, these reforms turned Athens into the most developed democratic system of government in the ancient world (see Reading the Past: Pericles Praises the Democratic Ideal).

The basic principle of Athenian democracy was that all citizens—in the Greeks' limited sense of the term—could and should participate in government. All men over the age of eighteen decided on policy in an assembly that met four times every month. They debated laws, military strategy, diplomatic relations, and religious topics. They considered

tyranny A political system in which one person holds absolute power; originally value-neutral, the term has acquired the negative connotation of severe abuse of power.

oligarchy A political system in which a small group of people holds all powers.

democracy The political ideal of rule by the people.

Pericles Praises the Democratic Ideal

The ancient Greeks greatly admired the power of rhetoric, and certain speeches recorded from the time have become classics emulated to this day. Athens's leader Pericles delivered one such speech at the end of the first year of the Peloponnesian War, in 431 B.C.E. When he honored those who had fallen in battle, he extolled the virtues of the city of Athens and the institutions in whose defense they had died. This speech is the most eloquent description of the democratic ideal in world literature.

Let me say that our system of government does not copy the institutions of our neighbors. It is more the case of our being a model to others, than of our imitating anyone else. Our constitution is called a democracy because the power is in the hands not of a minority but of the whole people. When it is a question of settling private disputes, everyone is equal before the law; when it is a question of putting one person before another in positions of public responsibility, what counts is not membership of a particular class, but the actual ability which the man possesses. No one, so long as he has it in him to be of service to the state, is kept in political obscurity because of poverty. And, just as our political life is free and open, so is our day-to-day life in our relations with each other. We do not get into a state with our next-door neighbor if he enjoys himself in his own way, nor do we give him the kind of black looks which, though they do no real harm, still do hurt people's feelings. We are free and tolerant in our private lives; but in public we keep to the law. This is because it commands our deep respect.

Source: From *Thucydides, History of the Peloponnesian War*, ed. M. I. Finley, trans. Rex Warner (London: Penguin Classics, 1972), 145.

EXAMINING THE EVIDENCE

1. What characteristics of the Athenian political system does Pericles praise? Do you think his claims reflect the reality of life in ancient Athens?

2. Why was this speech pertinent in a period of war?

3. How do the ideals expressed here still echo in political discourse today?

the most important matters of state, listened to one another's arguments, and truly governed as a people. They even stood in judgment over one another—each citizen had the right to be judged by his peers.

Because the Athenian assembly was too large to manage daily business, they created a smaller body for this purpose. Each year five hundred men who were at least thirty years old were selected by lot to join a council, and they served in groups of fifty for a period of thirty-six days each. The council prepared laws for consideration by the assembly and executed the assembly's decisions. To prevent a small group of men from gaining a monopoly on executive power, no man was allowed to serve on the council for more than two years, and these years had to be nonconsecutive. Thus executive power was spread over the entire citizenry.

The ideal of the democratic system was clear: every citizen had the ability to make intelligent decisions and perform official duties. But not everyone thought this was true or that democracy was a good idea. Ancient philosophers such as Plato (see page 152) doubted that all men were equally capable of governing, and modern scholars often depict an Athenian assembly that was easily swayed by the false arguments of great orators. Yet despite the shortcomings Athenian democracy displayed in practice, its ideals have inspired political thinkers throughout world history, especially in modern times.

Sparta's geographical setting was very different from Athens's. In the eighth and seventh centuries B.C.E. the city conquered the fertile regions that surrounded it. The Spartans used this land, farmed by the forced labor of its inhabitants, to support its citizens. This enabled all Spartan citizens—again, the male inhabitants of the city—to sit in an assembly, unencumbered by agricultural work. The institution had much less power than the Athenian assembly, however, because it had to work in concert with an elected council

Spartan Oligarchy

of thirty men, all over sixty years old. A group of five officials, annually elected from among all citizens, held executive power. In practice wealthy families had more influence than poorer ones, because they could bribe officials. The highest Spartan officials were two kings, men from two wealthy families, who ruled simultaneously for life. Their primary role was to lead the army in war, but they had much influence at home as well. Real power in Sparta was thus in the hands of an oligarchy.

Spartan oligarchy and Athenian democracy thus shared several elements, but to us today their ideals seem very different. Athenians declared that citizens, however restricted that group was, could and should be involved in politics, whereas Spartans believed that only select men had the ability to govern. The Spartan economy depended on the control and exploitation of the nearby land and population. Athenians, in contrast, emphasized the sea and trade. The opposition of the two systems would grow over time and, as we shall see, lead to conflict.

A Cultural Reawakening

Homer and Sappho   During the Archaic period many Greek writers turned to poetry. Some of the earliest works had an enormous impact, influencing Western literature until the modern period. Of these early poets, Homer and Sappho stand out because of the beauty of their poetic language and their ability to depict human emotions.

Later Greeks regarded Homer as the greatest poet of their past and the authority on peoples, countries, gods, and events. He composed his two epics, the *Iliad* and the *Odyssey*, probably around 750 B.C.E. Models for all subsequent Western epic poetry, these lengthy poems (c. sixteen thousand and twelve thousand lines, respectively) use highly metaphoric language and a strict metric form. The *Iliad* depicts Greek and Trojan heroes engaged in a ten-year struggle; the *Odyssey* relates the adventures of one Greek warrior on his return home. Homer's intricate stories show acts of heroism, cunning, kindness, and cruelty. The Trojan War provides the background for a novel exploration of the sentiments, strengths, and weaknesses of the men and women involved: the anger of Achilles, the foolish pride of Agamemnon, the longing of Odysseus for his home and his wife, the steadfast love of Penelope. These characters lived a courtly life in which honor, hospitality, proper social behavior, and especially personal excellence were crucial

Sappho (c. 630–570 B.C.E.) was the first known woman poet of Greek literature. She led a community of young women on the island of Lesbos, near the modern Turkish coast. The strength of her poetry lay in her ability to describe human passions, especially love and friendship, often in the context of the religious festivals that occupied young women's lives before marriage. The literary quality of her writings earned her respect in her own lifetime, and her fame grew after her death. With her focus on women and their emotions, Sappho addresses a world that is different from Homer's, but they share an interest in human sentiments as well as the ability to write beautiful poetry.

Greek Temple in Agrigento, Sicily

Some of the best-preserved classical Greek temples are on the island of Sicily, where the Greeks had established colonies. This temple is one of seven built near the city of Agrigento in the sixth and fifth centuries B.C.E. and devoted to gods such as Zeus and his consort Hera. Its layout and the shape of its columns display one of the main styles of Greek architecture, the Doric order. (© DeA Picture Library/Art Resource, NY.)

Greek bards recited poems for entertainment, especially at religious festivals. Like the Mesopotamians, Egyptians, and others, the Greeks believed their gods to be immortal, but they saw them in far more human terms than did peoples elsewhere. The Greek gods loved, fought, lied, ate, drank, and behaved like humans in other ways, regularly interacting with mortals. Zeus, the ruler of heaven, had many affairs with women, divine and human, and sired numerous children.

Religious Ritual

Thus, in many ways the Greek gods simply reflected the Greeks themselves, but there was one crucial difference. The gods, of course, had the power to shape the universe and influence the fate of human beings. Accordingly, the Greeks were careful to appease them through established religious rites, rites in which women often played a major role. Citizens of Greek city-states had a civic duty to participate in public festivals, and the shared experience intensified their feeling of community. In their collective appeasement of the gods, Greek citizens shared the task of protecting and promoting their polis.

The most imposing monuments remaining from the Greeks are their temples, which display remarkable architectural and artistic skill. The temple of Athena, the goddess of wisdom, still defines the skyline of Athens. The basic structure was simple: a central room that held the cult statue (Athena's statue was made of ivory, silver, and gold and measured about forty-one feet high) and was surrounded by a wall and a row of columns. Mythological scenes carved in relief decorated the façades above the columns. In different parts of the Greek world various styles developed, but all Greeks on the mainland and in the colonies regarded the temple as an important sign of their city's wealth and grandeur.

Greek Temples

Although many elements of their culture received inspiration from the East, by 500 B.C.E. the Greeks had developed their own highly original literature, religion, art, and architecture, creating a distinct Greek cultural identity. Subsequent political events would sharpen the contrast between Greeks and other peoples even more.

The Persian Wars, Classical Greece, and the Concept of Cultural Difference 500–338 B.C.E.

For the Greeks, the fifth and fourth centuries B.C.E. were times of both endemic warfare and intellectual and cultural achievement. During this period, people all over the Greek world, but especially in Athens, produced revolutionary innovations in intellectual life. They developed new forms of scientific inquiry and artistic expression and experimented with political structures. Their accomplishments imbued the Greeks with pride and self-confidence, which they expressed in a worldview that made sharp distinctions between Greeks and outsiders. These developments took place against a backdrop of military conflict, both between Greeks and foreigners and among the Greeks themselves. Scholars refer to this period as Greece's Classical Age because it shows the culmination of earlier developments and because later Greeks and others in Western history saw its achievements as the height of human ingenuity in antiquity (see Map 5.2).

> **FOCUS**
>
> What cultural innovations appeared in Greece during its Classical Age?

Struggle Between Persia and Greece 500–479 B.C.E.

While the Greeks developed new political institutions in the city-states, the ideal of kingship, with inherited power held by one man, continued in Southwest Asia. As we saw in Chapter 4, increasingly large political units succeeded one another there, culminating in the late sixth century B.C.E. in the Persian Empire. By 500 B.C.E., Persian power extended from the Indus Valley to the Mediterranean Sea and from Central Asia to Egypt.

To the mighty Persian Empire, conquest of the small and divided city-states of Greece must have seemed like a minor challenge. Successive invasions, however, ended in disaster

Persian Wars

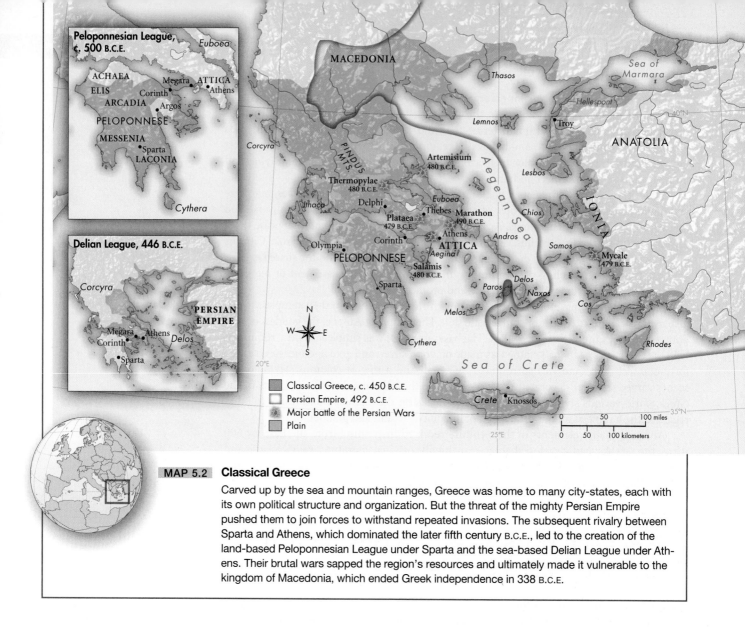

Classical Greece

Carved up by the sea and mountain ranges, Greece was home to many city-states, each with its own political structure and organization. But the threat of the mighty Persian Empire pushed them to join forces to withstand repeated invasions. The subsequent rivalry between Sparta and Athens, which dominated the later fifth century B.C.E., led to the creation of the land-based Peloponnesian League under Sparta and the sea-based Delian League under Athens. Their brutal wars sapped the region's resources and ultimately made it vulnerable to the kingdom of Macedonia, which ended Greek independence in 338 B.C.E.

for Persia. In 490 B.C.E., the Athenians defeated the Persians soundly at the Battle of Marathon, relying on their heavy armor and tight battle formation. Ten years later, the Persian King Xerxes (r. 486–465 B.C.E.) invaded Greece on land and by sea with a gigantic army—the Greek historian Herodotus implausibly claims it included more than 2 million men. At a pass called Thermopylae, three hundred Spartans under King Leonidas stood firm to slow the Persian advance. Every Spartan died in several days of heavy fighting. Xerxes entered central Greece and burned down the temples and monumental buildings of Athens, which its citizens had evacuated without trying to resist a siege.

Despite the destruction of their city, the Athenians continued the fight at sea. They lured the massive Persian fleet into the narrow bay at Salamis, where, unable to maneuver, it fell prey to the smaller Greek ships. The playwright Aeschylus, who participated in the war and perhaps even fought in this battle, ascribes these words to the Persian messenger who reported the rout:

> First the floods of Persians held the line,
> But when the narrows choked them, and rescue hopeless,
> Smitten by prows, their bronze jaws gaping,
> Shattered entire was our fleet of oars.
> The Grecian warships, calculating, dashed
> Round, and encircled us; ships showed their belly:

> No longer could we see the water, charged
> With ships' wrecks and men's blood.
> Corpses glutted beaches and the rocks.
> . . . never in a single day
> So great a number died.[2]

The next year, in 479 B.C.E., the Greeks defeated the remainder of the Persian force and ended further threats of invasion.

The Persian Wars had tremendous consequences for the Greeks. Some thirty city-states had formed an unprecedented coalition, and for the rest of the fifth century B.C.E. Sparta and Athens, which had distinguished themselves militarily, used their fame to command the respect and gratitude of the other Greek city-states. The wars also raised the Greek self-image. A sense of superiority permeated political, social, and cultural life, and the Greeks came to believe that they were the only people capable of achieving the ideal of freedom.

The coalition of states built to resist the Persians did not outlast the war, and political fragmentation returned after 479 B.C.E. Nevertheless, Athens and Sparta used their special status to gain allies, by free will and by force. Each formed a league of allies (see again Map 5.2). Sparta, which had risen to power by exploiting land resources, allied itself primarily with states on the Greek mainland that had strong infantries and few ships. The Spartans dominated most of the city-states of the Peloponnese, that is, the southern Greek peninsula. Their coalition was called the Peloponnesian League. Athens, in contrast, looked outward to the sea, where its navy had crushed the Persians. The Athenians allied themselves with states on the Greek islands and the Ionian coast. They created the Delian League, so named because the coalition originally kept its treasury on the island of Delos. At first, members delivered contributions mainly in the form of ships and their crews, but over time this arrangement developed into silver payments to Athens, which used the money to build and crew ships of its own. Soon Athens had by far the region's largest navy, with which it imposed its will on the members of the Delian League, presenting itself as the protector of democracy against the oligarchic regimes of the Peloponnesian League.

Peloponnesian and Delian Leagues

Athens's Golden Age 500–400 B.C.E.

In the fifth century B.C.E., the substantial contributions that Delian League members made in lieu of ships and crews filled Athenian state coffers. Moreover, Athenian traders shipped pottery, wine, and oil from Greece to ports all along the eastern Mediterranean coast, turning the Athenian harbor, Piraeus, into the dominant commercial center of the region. Thus, political and economic connections dramatically increased Athenian power and wealth, which in turn made possible remarkable innovations in the city's political, scientific, and cultural life.

As we have seen, in the sixth century B.C.E. the Athenians took important steps toward democracy. In the fifth century B.C.E. Athenian democracy reached its zenith under the leadership of Pericles. Pericles sought to ensure that all Athenian citizens, rich or poor, were able to take an active role in government. Hence, he arranged for men who sat in council or on a jury to receive a daily stipend from the state so that poor citizens could take time off from work to fulfill their civic duties. As important as Pericles' policies were, we must remember that they aimed to increase the number of citizens who took part in civic life, not to increase the total number of citizens. Out of a mid-fifth-century population of between three and four hundred thousand, only about fifty thousand Athenians had any political rights.

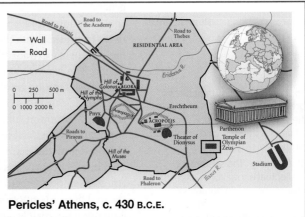

Pericles' Athens, c. 430 B.C.E.

Sophists

Those Athenians with political rights obviously wanted to present convincing arguments in the assembly. As a result, the art of rhetoric, or public speaking, gained importance unprecedented in world history. The need to speak persuasively created a niche for a new type of teacher, called a **sophist** ("wise man"), who offered instruction in rhetoric for a fee. Because of the sophists' focus on oratory technique and the payments, the term *sophist* has a negative connotation today, suggesting someone who makes an invalid argument with the appearance of truth. But in ancient Athens, these men were highly respected and considered much more than mere political "coaches" for hire. Many explored innovative ideas, subjecting Greek intellectual and religious traditions to a rigorous examination that pushed Greek thinking in new directions. Above all, the sophists believed in the power of human reason. Although many were religious and believed in the power of the gods, they saw human rationality as *the* crucial tool for explaining the workings of the universe. Many sophists came from outside Athens. Because of its wealth and vibrant cultural life, the city became an intellectual crossroads and the center of the new field of **philosophy**, a word literally translated as "love of wisdom."

Philosophers

The three most famous and influential Greek philosophers of antiquity were Socrates, Plato, and Aristotle. Although they distanced themselves from the sophists, their ideas and inquiries were made possible by the general atmosphere of intellectual curiosity that the sophists helped create in Athens. The three philosophers investigated all aspects of life and the physical environment using techniques that are still influential today. Although the three men were closely linked (Socrates taught Plato, who in turn taught Aristotle), each made distinctive contributions to Greek philosophy. Socrates developed a mode of questioning designed to help separate truth from assumption. Plato developed the notion of universal ideals. Aristotle analyzed everything from literature to the natural environment by classifying their elements. Together they laid the foundation of education and scientific investigation as practiced in the Middle East and Europe until the modern period (see Lives and Livelihoods: Philosophers of Athens's Golden Age).

Historians

Whereas philosophers investigated general principles, other Athenians explored the events that shaped Greek life, notably the wars that occupied much of fifth-century B.C.E. Greece. As we have seen, Herodotus (c. 485–425 B.C.E.) wrote on the Persian Wars, which ended when he was a young boy, and Thucydides (c. 460–400 B.C.E.) documented the Peloponnesian War between Athens and Sparta (discussed later in this chapter), in which he had fought. The elder of the two, Herodotus, became known in the West as the Father of History ("inquiry" in Greek) because he was the first who studied the past to find the causes of historical events.

Thucydides explained the war between Athens and Sparta as an unavoidable clash between two expansionist states, the former focusing on sea power, the latter on control of land. He used his work as a vehicle to express his support for democratic rule under a strong leader, connecting Athens's problems to deviations from this ideal. The works of Herodotus and Thucydides were revolutionary because they presented historical events as the consequences of human actions, rather than as the result of divine intervention. Moreover, they personified the general curiosity about the structure and causes of things that swept Athens in its Golden Age.

Playwrights

Herodotus and Thucydides had great literary skills and wrote engaging prose narratives. In these talents they were far from alone, for in the fifth century B.C.E. Athens was the hub of an extraordinary literary production including, most prominently, works of drama. The playwright's emphasis was not on action but on the beauty of poetic language. The most famous tragic authors—Aeschylus (525–456 B.C.E.), Sophocles (c. 496–406 B.C.E.), and Euripides (c. 485–406 B.C.E.)—examined human nature and society in all their aspects. A common subject was human *hubris*, the Greek term for excessive pride and self-confidence, which led to the hero's downfall. For example, in *Oedipus the King*, Sophocles explored how the main character's certainty that he could uncover the truth through his own intellect caused his utter ruin: he blinded himself and his mother committed suicide. Another emotion regularly depicted was the desire for vengeance. In *Medea*, Euripides showed how this emotion pushed a slighted wife, Medea, into killing her children to inflict pain upon her former husband. In the *Oresteia*, three plays that form a narrative sequence,

sophist Originally an ancient Greek teacher of rhetoric; today the term has the negative connotation of someone who convinces through false arguments.

philosophy The systematic intellectual endeavor of explaining basic concepts in human existence, such as truth, knowledge, reality, and ethical behavior.

Aeschylus demonstrated how vengeance becomes an endless cycle, as Clytaemnestra killed her husband Agamemnon because he had slaughtered their daughter. In retaliation, their son Orestes murdered her. The cycle ended only when a jury in Athens's law court decided guilt. The *Oresteia* explained how a new institution based on the judgment of humans superseded the older system of never-ending revenge. Indeed, the Golden Age dramatists probed into all aspects of society. In so doing they frequently criticized those characteristics of classical Greece that we now so often praise, such as rationality and self-confidence.

While the characters in the Greek tragedies were almost always figures from the ancient past, comedies featured living people and current events. Greek comedies used bawdy jokes and verbal puns to mock Athens's leaders and to make fun of their society's shortcomings. For example, actors often stood on stage wearing large leather phalluses, and sex and other bodily functions dominated the insults that the characters hurled at each other.

The best-known comic author was Aristophanes (c. 455–385 B.C.E.), whose barbed attacks spared no one. He depicted the philosopher Socrates as hanging in a basket staring at the sky, collecting fees from spoiled young men for teaching them how to win every argument. In the play *Lysistrata* Aristophanes has the women of Athens and Sparta withhold sex to force their husbands to recognize the senselessness of the Peloponnesian War. These plays were performed for a public that understood the allusions and were willing to see their political and intellectual leaders portrayed as buffoons.

Remarkably for a society that treated women as inferior, women were often the central characters of Greek tragedies. Sophocles' heroine Antigone, for example, stood against her uncle's decree that her brother should not be buried. She proudly obeyed divine laws and was willing to die for doing so:

> And so, for me to meet this fate, no grief.
> But if I left that corpse, my mother's son,
> dead and unburied I'd have cause to grieve
> as now I grieve not.
> And if you think my acts are foolishness
> the foolishness may be in a fool's eye.[3]

These female characters, fully developed by the genius of the playwrights, do not fight their inferior status but often uphold values that are more personal than those of the publicly oriented men.

The cultural and intellectual flourishing of Athens in the fifth century B.C.E. derived from the presence of great creative minds in a society that gave some of its people the freedom to explore everything. Out of this environment came a sense of Athenian superiority to the rest of the world. They scorned those who did not speak Greek as "barbarians," a term derived from "bar bar," after the sound of foreign languages to Greek ears. The Greeks depicted non-Greeks as lacking the sense to have proper political institutions, customs, and social behavior. Indeed, outsiders were presented as holding the opposite of Greek values: they tolerated despots, indulged in excess, and committed

Poking Fun at Greek Gods

The ancients took their gods very seriously, but they saw a comic side to them as well. This vase from about 350 B.C.E. shows Zeus (left), father of all the gods, as an old man carrying a ladder, assisted by Hermes (right), herald for the other gods. Zeus is attempting to visit the young Alcmene (in the window), who was thought to be the most beautiful mortal woman on earth. According to myth, Zeus and Alcmene's child was the Greek hero Heracles. (Scala/Art Resource, NY.)

Philosophers of Athens's Golden Age

Three Athenians of the fifth and fourth centuries B.C.E. stand out as giants in the history of Western philosophy: Socrates, Plato, and Aristotle. For some one hundred years their teaching and writing inspired intellectual life in the city and beyond, and ever since their ideas have engaged philosophers. Socrates (c. 470–399 B.C.E.) did not leave any written work; we know of his teachings primarily through his student Plato. Socrates' chief aim was to find justice, which he equated with truth. Questioning people who claimed to be wise in such a way that they realized the limitations of their knowledge, Socrates sought ways to discover true wisdom. Probably because he was, as he himself said, a gadfly constantly reproaching the Athenians, he was condemned to death in 399 B.C.E., ostensibly because he corrupted youth.

Aristotle in Medieval Islamic Tradition

The great classical Greek philosophers were remembered long after antiquity. In the Middle Ages they were especially treasured in the Islamic world, where scholars translated their works into Arabic and interpreted their ideas. This manuscript from the thirteenth century C.E. depicts the philosopher Aristotle teaching Alexander the Great. The manuscript contains a work by a physician of the Abbasid court called "The Usefulness of Animals," which draws from classical works such as Aristotle's. (British Library, London/British Library Board. All Rights Reserved/Bridgeman Art Library.)

incest. This contrast had a political value, for as we have seen, it enabled the Greeks to unite against the Persians. But it led to a skewed view in the historical record of the relationship between Greeks and foreigners. Stressing their own uniqueness, the Greeks downplayed the significant role that Southwest Asia and Egypt played in inspiring many of their cultural achievements.

He chose to commit suicide by drinking hemlock, rather than flee from prison as his friends had arranged for him.

It is hard to determine how much of Plato's (c. 428–348 B.C.E.) writing reflects Socrates' teaching and how much records his own philosophy. Plato used the dialogue form to communicate his ideas. He portrays Socrates as questioning persons in such a way that his ideas were arrived at as the only logical conclusion. The dialogues assume that all knowledge was innate in human beings and could be revealed by asking the right questions, through the so-called Socratic method. In one dialogue, Socrates takes a young slave of his friend Meno through a geometrical proof as if the boy knew the answer all along. In this view, the soul naturally possesses all knowledge; the philosopher needs only to find the key to unlock it. The Socratic method can be used to investigate all aspects of life, from mathematics to love.

Plato stressed the distinction between the physical, which he saw as imperfect, and the spiritual, which he viewed as perfect. Only the immortal human soul knows the spiritual, Plato believed. He also commented on political life in his dialogue, *Republic*, in which he questioned the democratic ideal on the grounds that not all men have the skills needed to make the right decisions. He proposed a hierarchy instead: on top would be "guardians," who are wise and well educated; in the middle, "auxiliaries" would provide protection; on the bottom, "producers" would provide food and manufactured goods. Laws would be the instruments to enable the guardians to carry out their decisions.

Plato founded a school, the Academy, that drew students from all over Greece, including his most famous pupil, Aristotle (384–322 B.C.E.). On Plato's death Aristotle tutored the young Alexander of Macedonia. He returned to Athens in 335 B.C.E. to found his own school, the Lyceum. Aristotle taught a vast array of subjects, from the natural sciences to literary criticism. He collected and analyzed biological samples and wrote about physics, chemistry, anatomy, and medicine, believing that one could classify every thing by analyzing its properties. He abandoned Plato's distrust of the physical, focusing instead on observing particulars, from which one could derive general conclusions through logical induction. Aristotle wrote many analytical treatises, including the famous work *Politics*, in which he described a state in which the virtues of people guided government. He disapproved of tyranny and rule by the masses and wanted a middle road with an assembly directed by able experts. Aristotle thought that slavery was a natural condition for some people and that these individuals should be captured for the benefit of the state. In the field of ethics, Aristotle warned against extremes and argued that people should strive for balance. He also wrote analyses of Greek literature in which he formulated the principles of poetry, using the great tragedies of the fifth century B.C.E. as models.

Because the three philosophers sought rational explanations and (especially Aristotle) formulated ideas very systematically, they became the models for scholarly investigation in the Hellenistic world. Philosophers in Alexandria and elsewhere turned to them for inspiration for centuries. When Christianity and Islam emerged, the thinkers who laid their intellectual foundations merged classical Greek philosophical ideas with biblical concepts. The works of Plato and Aristotle were translated into other languages, notably Arabic, which is how they survived, and for centuries they provided the foundation of scientific investigation in Europe and the Middle East. Even today no philosopher working in the Western tradition can ignore these thinkers.

QUESTIONS TO CONSIDER

1. How and why did approaches to philosophical inquiry differ among Socrates, Plato, and Aristotle?

2. Why did these three philosophers have such influence on later intellectual history?

For Further Information:
Ancient Greek philosophy: http://www.iep.utm.edu/greekphi/.
Annas, Julia. *Plato: A Very Short Introduction*. New York: Oxford University Press, 2003.
Barnes, Jonathan. *Aristotle: A Very Short Introduction*. New York: Oxford University Press, 2000.
Dean-Jones, Lesley. "Philosophy and Science." In *Cambridge Illustrated History of Ancient Greece*. Edited by Paul Cartledge, 288–319. Cambridge, U.K.: Cambridge University Press, 1998.
Taylor, Christopher. *Socrates: A Very Short Introduction*. Oxford, U.K.: Oxford University Press, 2000.

Greeks and Foreigners

Greek city-states were part of a larger Mediterranean economic system. The Greeks may have disliked foreigners, and contacts between Greeks and outsiders were often hostile, but trade never ceased. Their colonies throughout the Mediterranean and Black seas put the Greeks in contact with foreign people from Spain to Scythia. Greek merchants continued to trade with Egypt even when that country was under Persian rule. People everywhere wanted Greek decorated pottery and other luxury products. Moreover, foreign traders prized the silver that the Greeks paid for imported goods. Some Greeks observed foreign cultures firsthand and came to appreciate their unique characteristics, even if such encounters did not shake their confidence in Greek superiority. Herodotus, for example, was fascinated by Egypt, although he considered its culture to be almost the exact opposite of his own:

> For instance, women attend market and are employed in trade, while men stay at home and do the weaving. In weaving the normal way is to work the threads of the weft upwards, but the Egyptians work them downwards. Men in Egypt carry loads on their heads, women on their shoulders; women pass water standing up, men sitting down. To ease their bowels they go indoors, but eat outside in the streets, on the theory that what is unseemly but necessary should be done in private, and what is not unseemly should be done openly.[4]

The Peloponnesian War and the End of Athenian Supremacy 431–404 B.C.E.

Peloponnesian War

Athens's international trade and its control over the Delian League had funded the city's Golden Age. Over time, however, its ever-expanding power led to resentment among its rivals, especially Sparta, the leading city-state of the Peloponnese. The tensions between Athens and Sparta erupted in a generation-long conflict known as the Peloponnesian War (431–404 B.C.E.), which impoverished Greece and undermined its society. During the war years, the Athenians became increasingly authoritarian, extracting ever higher contributions from members of the Delian League, forcing other cities to choose sides, and punishing those who refused to join. They could be ruthless. When the inhabitants of the island of Melos asked to remain neutral, Athens massacred all the men and enslaved all the women and children. Despite such desperate acts, Athens failed to defeat its enemies, and in 404 B.C.E. Sparta prevailed. For the moment, Sparta was the dominant power in Greece.

Rise of Macedonia

Sparta's hegemony, however, did not last long, and the fourth century B.C.E. saw fierce struggles among Greek cities for preeminence. The power that ended this period of civil strife was Macedonia, a territory to the north of Greece that the Greeks had long regarded as backward. Macedonia was a kingdom, and in many respects its relationship to Greece was like that of Nubia to Egypt (see Chapter 4): it owed much of its culture to Greece, yet ultimately it came to dominate its neighbor. Inspired by Greek practices, the Macedonian King Philip II (r. 359–336 B.C.E.) greatly improved his army's strength and tactics by arming his phalanx of foot soldiers with 10-foot-long spears and coordinating their actions with those of the horse-mounted cavalry. With this military advantage, in 338 B.C.E. Philip defeated the city-states of southern Greece and forced them into an alliance under Macedonian leadership. The age of independent Greek poleis was over. Greek culture had reached its highest point after its city-states had united to oppose the might of Persia. When the connections among Greek city-states that had helped produce this vital unity deteriorated, the Greeks were left weak and divided, easy prey for a powerful and determined neighbor.

Macedonia, 359 B.C.E.

Territorial gains, by 336 B.C.E.

Macedonian dependencies and allies, 336 B.C.E.

Major battle

Macedonia Under Philip II, 359–336 B.C.E.

Daily Life in Classical Greece

Athens's acropolis, its famous hilltop covered with monumental marble buildings (see again At a Crossroads, page 138), was a physical expression of the city's wealth and power. Although many Athenians probably took pride in the acropolis, very few enjoyed the wealth and luxury suggested by the city's public spaces. As was the case elsewhere in the ancient world, social inequality was the norm in Greece. Most Greeks were poor and powerless, although conditions varied from place to place. A comparison of Athens and Sparta illustrates the range of social conditions that existed in classical Greece.

In Athens, most people were slaves, landless poor, or resident aliens (called *metics* in Greek), none of whom enjoyed political rights. The last group was especially large. Many metics came to Athens voluntarily, because it was the center of Greek economic and intellectual life. Because they could not own land, they often practiced crafts and trade, activities scorned by Athenian citizens. Slaves were always foreigners. The Athenian state used some of them in public works, such as mining, which was grueling and deadly work. Many slaves worked in private households. Slaves who managed to save money could buy their freedom, although they could not become citizens. Of an estimated total population of three to four hundred thousand people, fifth-century-B.C.E. Athens was home to perhaps one hundred thousand slaves.

Athenian Society

Women, even those of the elite class, had second-class status and little personal freedom. As in Vedic India (see Chapter 3), they were tied to households dominated by men. A father fully controlled a young girl's life and arranged her marriage in her teen years to a suitable man of around thirty years old. Once a wife entered her husband's house, she was responsible for its management but had little control over the property. Her father, husband, or brother acted in public on her behalf, and she could not go out without wearing a veil. When a man died, his sons inherited all he owned; if he left only a daughter, a male relative married her and took charge of the property she inherited (see Reading the Past: Semonides Catalogues the Evils of Women). Prevented from acquiring financial independence, women were defined entirely by their subordinate relationship to men as daughters and wives.

Meanwhile, Athenian men spent most of their time away from home for work or leisure. They often ate and drank with their friends until late at night while female musicians and dancers entertained them. Some women, mostly foreigners, attended those dinners to provide witty conversation, music, and sometimes sexual favors. Many prominent Athenians kept such women in luxurious circumstances as concubines. We should not, however, romanticize such women's lives. The story of Neaira (neh-EYE-ruh), a highly successful courtesan with many rich and influential clients, demonstrates the vulnerability of all Athenian women, regardless of their circumstances. We know her life in detail from the record of a trial involving her in mid-fourth-century-B.C.E. Athens. When Neaira was about ten she joined a brothel with an elite clientele in the city of Corinth. In 376 B.C.E. two men bought her and later offered her the chance to buy her own freedom. A third man gave her the funds and took her to Athens, where she was the victim of his abuse. When she fled to live with yet another man, her original benefactor forcibly reclaimed her, and the two men agreed to share her. Although Neaira was admired by many men, her freedom was always limited and her status depended on the whims of her lovers, who—as in many other ancient societies—could dispose of her as they saw fit.

Greek women from all walks of life shared Neaira's vulnerability. For the Greeks, the purpose of a marriage was to produce children, preferably boys. If a woman could not produce children, she had failed in her primary function and her husband often divorced her. Moreover, childbearing was dangerous in early societies, and scholars blame it for the high death rate of women in Athens. Studies of skeletons show that the life expectancy of women was thirty-six, whereas for men it was forty-five.

Seeing their wives as little more than the mothers of their children, Athenian men looked outside of the home for companionship and pleasure. Women like Neaira provided sexual favors to men, but male homosexual intercourse was also considered normal and acceptable in ancient Athens. Adolescents attached themselves to older men who became their guardians and taught them how to behave as adults.

The Spartan situation—although similarly unequal—was different from that in Athens. The Spartan state owned a large group of dependent laborers, who worked the land. These

Spartan Society

Semonides Catalogues the Evils of Women

Women's inferior status in Greek society is clear from actual practice, but many literary works also display misogynist attitudes. The Greeks accepted the superiority of men in every respect. Aeschylus's *Oresteia*, for example, presents women as mere incubators for the male semen, which they believed determined all of a child's characteristics. Murdering a mother was a lesser crime than killing a father. A number of literary passages lament the very existence of women, as does this poem, "On Women," by the sixth-century B.C.E. satirist Semonides of Amorgos.

For Zeus designed this as the greatest of all evils:

Women. Even if in some way they seem to be a help;

To their husbands especially they are a source of evil.

For there is no one who manages to spend a whole day

In contentment if he has a wife.

Nor will he find himself able to speedily thrust famine out of his house,

Who is a hateful, malicious god to have as a houseguest.

But whenever a man seems to be especially content at home,

Thanks either to good fortune from the gods or to his good relations with the rest

Of mankind, she'll find fault somewhere and stir up a dispute.

For whosoever wife she is, she won't receive graciously

Into the house a friend who comes to visit.

And you know, the very one who appears to be moderate and prudent

Actually turns out to be the most outrageous and shameful.

And when her husband is still in shock from finding out about her, the

Neighbors have a good laugh because even he made a mistake in his choice.

For each man likes to regale others with stories of praise about his own wife,

While at the same time finding fault with any other man's wife.

We don't realize that we all share the same fate.

For Zeus designed this as the greatest of all evils

And bound us to it in unbreakable fetters.

Source: M.L. West. *Greek Lyric Poetry* translated by M. L. West (1994), p. 19 'On Women' (21 lines of poetry). Used by permission of Oxford University Press.

EXAMINING THE EVIDENCE

1. What attributes does Semonides ascribe to women?

2. Why does he consider women to be the curse of all men?

3. What does this satirical poem suggest about the Greeks' attitude toward women?

---

slaves, called helots, were the descendants of the original population of the territory Sparta had conquered early in its history. Unlike slaves elsewhere in Greece, the helots were Greeks rather than foreigners, and at times they tried to rebel. The Spartans used terror tactics to try to keep them in their place. For example, they sent young men into the countryside at night to kill any helot they encountered for sport.

We use the word *Spartan* today to indicate an existence that is frugal, austere, and disciplined. That notion derives from ancient Sparta's education of its boys. The state took them from their mothers at age seven to train in military techniques and gymnastics. Between the ages of twenty and thirty, men lived in communal barracks, even if they were married, and in later life they had to dine with their peers rather than at home. Spartan citizens did not admire individualism; they wanted all men to share the same bravery and devotion to the state. They honed their military skills while helots provided their food.

Spartan women had greater freedom than those in Athens. Relieved of domestic duties by helots, they were responsible for household property, some of which they owned. Some women had large dowries, which husbands could not take away. According to Aristotle, women owned two-thirds of the land in Sparta. To learn how to protect the household, Spartan girls received physical training and exercised naked in public (as did boys). Although far from emancipated, they enjoyed more respect and greater independence than Athenian women.

In both societies, and throughout Greece, life for most people was difficult and dangerous. The wars of the fifth century B.C.E. brought ruin to the Greek countryside and sent many men to fight in distant conflicts. Thucydides describes brutality by all sides in the Peloponnesian War, including indiscriminate slaughter of men, women, and children, as we saw in the case of Melos. Civil wars erupted constantly between different political factions, and opponents received little mercy. The predominance of war in the fifth century B.C.E. explains why so many Greek men later hired themselves out as mercenaries to anyone willing to pay. When the wars ended, young Greek men were left with nothing but their hard-won military skills.

Hellenism: The Expansion of Greek Ideals and Institutions 323–30 B.C.E.

After establishing dominance over Greece, the new power of Macedonia conquered the vast Persian Empire and created in its stead a system of kingdoms ruled by Greeks. As the Greeks moved into Egypt, Southwest Asia, and beyond, contacts between Greeks and local populations led to a cultural fusion known as **Hellenism**, from *Hellas*, the native term for Greece. Although the precise mix of Greek and local culture varied from place to place, people throughout the Hellenistic world were connected through exposure to common language, literature, and intellectual and political ideas. Historians date the Hellenistic age from the death of Alexander in 323 B.C.E. to 30 B.C.E., when the Roman Empire (discussed in Chapter 7) conquered Egypt, the last major Hellenistic state. For most people, day-to-day life in the Hellenistic age was much the same as life in previous centuries. However, the blending of traditions that was the heart of Hellenism exposed men and women to a new and more varied set of beliefs and ideas. Those ideas would be at the center of many cultural developments in the later Mediterranean world.

FOCUS
How did Hellenism affect the peoples of Greece, North Africa, and Southwest Asia?

Creation of the Hellenistic Empires 323–275 B.C.E.

In 336 B.C.E., twenty-year-old Alexander succeeded his father Philip as king of Macedonia and leader of the league of Greek states. As we saw in Chapter 4, almost immediately he invaded the Persian Empire, which for two hundred years had dominated an enormous territory stretching from the Mediterranean coast to India. Defeating the Persians in a quick succession of battles, Alexander proclaimed himself the new master of the empire. The swift military successes earned him the title "the Great" in later tradition.

To thwart challenges to his rule, however, Alexander had to take his troops to every corner of his realm (see again Mapping the World, pages 140 and 141). When he finally reached the eastern border of the Persian Empire and the Indus Valley in 326 B.C.E., his troops rebelled and refused to go farther. Alexander settled in Babylon, where soon afterward, in 323 B.C.E., he died at the age of thirty-three. Did he succumb to the illnesses and wounds he had endured during his campaigns, or did his courtiers tire of the habits he acquired as emperor and assassinate him? Scholarly theories about the cause of his death abound, but it is certain that Alexander's role was paramount in bringing Greece into closer cultural contact with the wider world than ever before.

Because Alexander died without an heir, his generals fought over the giant territory he had conquered. They ultimately carved it into several states, each ruled by a former general

Hellenism The culture that derived from the merger of Greek, Southwest Asian, and Egyptian ideas through the creation of Alexander the Great's empire.

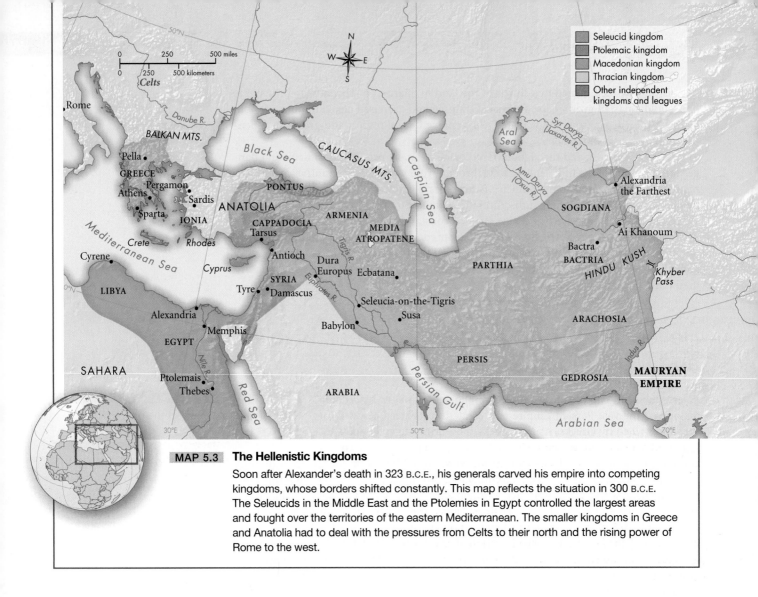

MAP 5.3 **The Hellenistic Kingdoms**

Soon after Alexander's death in 323 B.C.E., his generals carved his empire into competing kingdoms, whose borders shifted constantly. This map reflects the situation in 300 B.C.E. The Seleucids in the Middle East and the Ptolemies in Egypt controlled the largest areas and fought over the territories of the eastern Mediterranean. The smaller kingdoms in Greece and Anatolia had to deal with the pressures from Celts to their north and the rising power of Rome to the west.

Alexander's Successors

(see Map 5.3). The two largest kingdoms were the Seleucid Empire, which initially included lands from Syria to the Indus, and the Ptolemaic Empire, which controlled Egypt and the Libyan coast. To gain acceptance as legitimate rulers, the generals married local women and started dynasties of mixed descent, which governed the Seleucid and Ptolemaic empires for some three hundred years. Seeking legitimacy as kings within the local traditions, they celebrated local religious festivals, supported cults, and commissioned inscriptions in cuneiform (Seleucids) and hieroglyphics (Ptolemies). They also maintained the existing bureaucracies, although Greek gradually took over as the language of administration.

For common Egyptians and Babylonians, little changed. They worked the land and produced goods, interacting with their new authorities only through local government agents; the ruling elite remained mostly in the region's large cities. The Greeks, however, faced fundamental changes both at home and in the new empires. Before they had belonged to small political and social groups in which (ideally) everyone knew each other, but they now lived in immense empires and regularly mingled with people with whom they at first could barely communicate. They maintained the belief that Greek culture was superior, but over time they absorbed the ideas and traditions of the ancient cultures they encountered. The Greeks' political system also changed fundamentally: kingdoms in which absolute power passed from father to son (and also to daughters in the case of the Ptolemies) replaced city-states ruled by citizens. The ideal of the polis survived, however; many new city-states were founded all over the Hellenistic world. They were subject, however, to a king who dictated international affairs and imposed taxes and other obligations.

Statue of Philosopher from Ai Khanoum
Although located several thousand miles east of Greece, Ai Khanoum in modern Afghanistan felt the Hellenistic influence so strongly that this statue from the second century B.C.E. looks as though it could have been carved in Greece itself. The image of the pensive old man suggests that he was a philosopher, and evidence shows that the writings of Aristotle were known in Ai Khanoum. (Getty Images.)

The new political order facilitated intensified cultural exchange. Greek hegemony made travel safer, easier, and more common. Greeks settled throughout the Hellenistic world, looking for new opportunities in distant Hellenistic kingdoms. At the same time, many foreigners moved to Greece and actively participated in Greek intellectual and cultural life.

The Hellenistic City

In his march through the former Persian Empire, Alexander founded some seventy cities, which he used to help establish his local dominance. As his successors continued the policy, new cities took root across the Hellenistic world. Taking the form of city-states, they resembled Greek cities in layout, buildings, and government structures. The new city-states were often built in strategic locations. When they were established in previously urbanized areas, such as Mesopotamia and Egypt, they overtook the old centers in importance.

One such outpost was the city whose ruins are called Ai Khanoum (eye KHA-nuum) today. Built to defend the northeastern border at the Oxus River, until 100 B.C.E. the city successfully kept out tribal people encroaching from Central Asia. The city had a Greek-style palace, a gymnasium, administrative buildings, and a Greek theater, and it was adorned with a Greek-style statuary. It was here that Clearchus, whom we met at the beginning of this chapter, arrived around 300 B.C.E., bringing with him wise sayings from Delphi. Clearchus was not the only philosopher who visited. When archaeologists excavated the palace, they found imprinted on its floor the ink text from a decayed papyrus. It contained an extract from a philosophical dialogue that Aristotle may have written.

In the countries along the eastern Mediterranean coast, the cities were even grander than Ai Khanoum and drew more visitors. The most prominent was Alexandria, which Alexander had founded as the new capital of Egypt in 331 B.C.E. and whose population soon rose to half a million. Located on the Mediterranean Sea, Alexandria dazzled both in appearance and as a center of learning and culture. When Arab forces invaded the city in 642 C.E., they supposedly had to shield their eyes from the sunlight reflected off the city's marble buildings. Alexandria was laid out on a plan of straight streets that intersected at right angles. Palaces, temples, theaters, and an enormous library lined the streets; these were constructed in the Greek style, but the city was also clearly Egyptian. Kings and queens followed traditional styles as they filled the city with monumental statues of themselves as rulers. They also brought in statues from all over Egypt of earlier kings, such as the famous Ramesses II (see Chapter 4).

Alexandria and other cities were set up as Greek poleis, and

Alexandria in Egypt

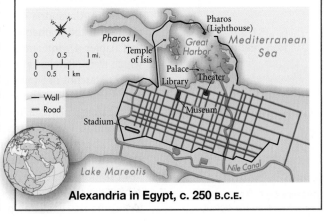

Alexandria in Egypt, c. 250 B.C.E.

Statues of Ptolemaic Royalty

Although the Ptolemies descended from Greek invaders of Egypt, spoke Greek, and promoted Greek culture in such institutions as the Library of Alexandria, they also were Egyptian rulers and had themselves represented in traditional Egyptian style. These statues from the third century B.C.E. show King Ptolemy II, his wife Arsinoe II, and an unknown princess. Nothing in the representations suggests that they are not typical Egyptian rulers. (Scala/Art Resource, NY.)

originally only Greeks and Macedonians qualified for citizenship and the political privileges that went with it. At first, accordingly, only Greeks could serve as administrators, but as natives learned the Greek language and adopted Greek cultural habits, they became eligible for offices and gradually gained civic rights as well. Documents from the period show that some local people took Greek names besides their own to conduct government business. For example, the Egyptian administrator Menches (Men-khez) also called himself Asklepiades (Ass-clay-pee-ja-dez). Over time, Greek and non-Greek populations mixed and intermarried. Alexandria became a melting pot that attracted people with diverse native languages, customs, and religions. Thus Alexandria, like cities throughout the Hellenistic world, became a crossroads, a place that attracted Greek migrants and served as a site of cultural exchange and transformation.

Hellenistic Learning and Livelihoods

Royal patronage drew scholars and artists from all over the Greek-speaking world and beyond to Alexandria. The city became a center of learning, which it actively promoted through the Library and Museum (literally, "House of the Muses"; the Muses were nine sister goddesses who presided over poetry, history, science, and the arts). The Museum housed poets and scientific researchers in all fields. The Library's aim was to collect copies of every known work of Greek literature. Because copyists had made errors over time, librarians also sought to establish an accurate original text for each work by comparing manuscripts. At one point, the Library borrowed from Athens the official copies of the works of the great authors of tragedies from the fifth century B.C.E. It paid an enormous deposit of silver as security, but when the texts arrived, the king willingly gave it up and kept the manuscripts. Alexandria's Library held 490,000 volumes, probably the largest collection of writings in the ancient world.

Hellenistic Scholarship   The promotion of learning epitomized by the Library at Alexandria stimulated intellectual innovation. Scientific inquiry relied on older traditions, and mathematics and astronomy, well-developed sciences in Babylonia (as seen in Chapter 4), influenced Greek science anew. Researchers made remarkable advances, which were often lost after antiquity and rediscovered only in more recent times. For example, Aristarchos of Samos (c. 310–230 B.C.E.) correctly recognized that the planets revolved around the sun, not the earth.

Eratosthenes (c. 276–194 B.C.E.) is a good example of the life of a scholar whose career took him to various parts of the Hellenistic world. He was born in Cyrene in northern Libya, where he received his basic training. After continuing his education in Athens, he accepted at the age of thirty-six the invitation of Egypt's king to become royal tutor and head of the Library in Alexandria. He was enormously erudite and wrote on numerous subjects, including literary criticism, philosophy, history, geography, and mathematics. He also composed epics and poems, which are known only from fragments today. In a treatise,

mystery cult A religious practice with a focus on the occult.

On the Measurement of the Earth, now lost but quoted by later authors, Eratosthenes calculated the earth's circumference with high accuracy. He compared the lengths of noon shadows cast at midsummer in places at the extreme ends of Egypt and so measured the curvature of the globe between them. He calculated that the distance between the two spots had to be multiplied fifty times to constitute a full circle. To determine this distance, the king gave him a group of men who walked with equal paces; they measured the length of Egypt to be about five hundred miles. Because of his versatility scholars often criticized Eratosthenes as only second best, although in every subject. Others likened him to Plato, however, recognizing his great knowledge.

Philosophy flourished in the Hellenistic world. When the polis disappeared as the center of political and social life, philosophers focused more on the individual, exploring ways to live a good and proper life. They presented a wide range of options. The Epicurians, for example, taught that one should enjoy every moment in the pursuit of simple pleasures and a quiet life. Cynics urged the rejection of social norms and conventional behavior, often living as beggars without any physical comfort. The Stoic school was the most influential throughout Greek and Roman antiquity. It granted women more consideration than earlier male-dominated philosophies, enabling some elite women to become involved in intellectual activities. Stoics encouraged intellectual inquiry to provide guidance in moral behavior, which would eliminate the anxieties of daily life and desire. "Freedom is secured not by the fulfilling of one's desires, but by the removal of desire," a Roman Stoic wrote. Such words resemble the somewhat earlier teachings of men like the Buddha and Laozi in India and China (discussed in Chapter 6). Although we cannot know if Hellenistic philosophers encountered these teachings directly, we can say that similar ideas developed in various parts of the ancient world.

Hellenistic Philosophy

While Hellenistic philosophies provided guidance to educated elites, many people, rich and poor, sought comfort and direction from religion. The Hellenistic world brought together an enormous variety of religious traditions and their gods. Although they maintained their cults, the Greeks lost faith in the old gods of the past and were drawn to the divine personification of Fortune—Tyche (TEE-chee) in Greek—in their efforts to deal with life's unpredictability. The ancient Egyptian goddess Isis became very popular outside Egypt in a different form: she was considered all-powerful, even surpassing Tyche. **Mystery cults** based on secret knowledge were very widespread. The Greek god of heaven, Zeus, was equated with leading deities elsewhere: Amun in Egypt, Marduk in Babylonia, Baal in Syria, and Yahweh in Judah. Exposure to Hellenistic culture in turn deeply influenced other religions. Many Jews who lived outside Judah absorbed the new ideas. They even forgot the Hebrew language for a time, and in the early third century B.C.E. the Ptolemaic ruler (Ptolemy II) commissioned a Greek translation of the Hebrew Bible.

Hellenistic Religion

Historians debate how much all this cultural mixing influenced the majority of the people. A Persian, Babylonian, Egyptian, or Greek farmer would still have been illiterate and would have adhered to old traditions and ideas. Even so, gods could and did achieve an unprecedented popularity outside their original place of worship, and people throughout the Hellenistic world were exposed to new ideas. Hellenism left no one totally unaffected.

COUNTERPOINT
The Celtic Peoples of the Atlantic Zone

Historians studying western Eurasia in the first millennium B.C.E. focus primarily on developments in Greece (and somewhat later in Roman Italy, discussed in Chapter 7) because sources are abundant and momentous developments occurred there. The Greeks expressed political ideals, ideas about self-governance, and concerns for aspects of the human condition in very explicit terms and in a rich textual record, inspiring a millennia-long tradition of

FOCUS

How did the lives and livelihoods of the peoples of Atlantic Europe differ from those of the Mediterranean peoples?

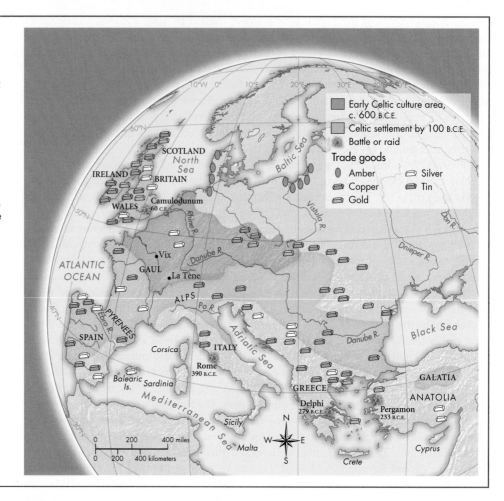

Celtic Peoples, c. 600–100 B.C.E.

Spread over much of the west and center of modern-day Europe, the Celtic peoples controlled natural resources of interest to Greece and Rome. Although at first Celtic warriors could threaten such places as Rome and Delphi and invade Galatia in Anatolia, in the first century B.C.E. Rome successfully annexed most Celtic territories.

intellectual development. These advances were restricted to a tiny part of the modern European continent, however. In the wide areas north and west of Greece, a different world existed. Although the inhabitants of these regions were in contact with the Greeks, they had different lifestyles and ideologies. They did not write much, except for short dedications scratched onto pots and metal strips using the Greek or Latin alphabets. Historians thus turn to archaeological remains to understand them. These peoples' oral literature depicted aspects of their world, and it survived for centuries in Ireland and elsewhere. Moreover, Greek and Roman Mediterranean authors provided useful information, although their writings were often biased. The Romans called them "Celts," a term many scholars and others still use today (see Map 5.4).

Who Were the Celts?

When in the first century B.C.E. and first century C.E. the Romans conquered much of the Atlantic region (see Chapter 7), their historians described the local peoples and their interactions with the new rulers. Like the Greeks, the Romans paid little attention to cultural distinctions among foreign peoples, and the term *Celts* covers a variety of groups and cultures. There was a unity among peoples of the Atlantic region in one sense, however: they all spoke languages that belong to the Celtic branch of Indo-European. Although they have changed greatly with time, some of the languages are still spoken in Ireland, Scotland, Wales, and Brittany (a region of northwestern France to which immigrants from the British

Isles introduced the language between 300 and 600 C.E.). The ideologies of these peoples also seem to have survived in the oral literary traditions of these regions.

Celtic Livelihoods

Warrior Aristocracy

Throughout western Eurasia, from north of the Mediterranean to the Atlantic coast and the British Isles, the Celtic peoples of the first millennium B.C.E. were farmers living in small settlements and villages. The societies greatly valued warrior skills and were ruled by a military aristocracy. The elites inhabited fortresses on natural hills, which they encircled with moats and walls of earth, stone, and timber; they were buried in tombs with their swords, shields, and chariots. The Romans noted that these military leaders treated the general population as if they were slaves.

The warlike culture is prominent in Celtic oral literature. The preserved tales recount how people raided, defended their honor in single combat, and bonded through feasts and hospitality. Unlike in Greece and most of the ancient societies discussed earlier, women actively participated in military life and could themselves become war leaders. Roman historians wrote in awe about Queen Boudicca (BOO-dee-kah), who led an army against them in the year 60 C.E. Goaded by the mistreatment her people suffered, including the rape of her own daughters, she rallied her own and neighboring groups in battle with these words:

> Look round, and view your numbers. Behold the proud display of warlike spirits, and consider the motives for which we draw the avenging sword. On this spot we must either conquer, or die with glory. There is no alternative. Though a woman, my resolution is fixed: the men, if they please, may survive with infamy, and live in bondage.[5]

Her troops lost the battle and she committed suicide, but in the nineteenth century C.E. British people revived Boudicca's memory as a symbol of resistance and woman's valor.

Like most ancient peoples, the Celts honored a multitude of gods who were closely connected to forces of nature. Roman authors provide some information on early religious practices and gods. They say, for instance, that the Celts called the goddess of wells and springs Coventina, and treated priests—whom the Romans called Druids—as the most honored group in Celtic society, equal to warriors. Religious ceremonies included human sacrifice. Throughout the Atlantic world archaeologists have discovered "bog people," men and women executed by strangulation or other means and buried in bogs as offerings to the gods. The Romans regarded Celtic religious practices as so uncivilized that they tried to ban them—without success.

Contacts with the Mediterranean

The Celtic peoples did not live in isolation, however. Starting in the early first millennium B.C.E., contacts with the Mediterranean world were extensive, and they grew over time (see again Map 5.4). The Phoenician and Greek colonies in the western Mediterranean were places of exchange between the Atlantic and Mediterranean worlds. The Greeks obtained silver, tin, and copper from as far as Britain. Atlantic peoples transported amber, a fossilized resin popular in jewelry, all the way from the Baltic Sea to supply the Greeks. In return the Greeks and other Mediterranean peoples provided luxury goods such as drinking vessels. Wine was also an important export to the Celts, who were

Gaul Killing Himself and His Wife

Although ancient Greeks and Romans considered the Gauls to be barbarians, they also could credit them with a great sense of nobility and honor. The statue here is a marble Roman copy of a work originally created in Anatolian Pergamon around 220 B.C.E. It shows the defeated Gaul warrior choosing to kill his wife and himself rather than face capture. (Museo Nazionale Romano/Giraudon/Bridgeman Art Library.)

notorious for their heavy drinking of undiluted wine. A Greek author wrote that a trader could get a slave in return for one jar of wine.

These contacts gave some local Celtic elites access to Mediterranean luxury goods. For example, a woman buried in the late sixth century B.C.E. in a tomb at Vix in eastern France was honored with a massive bronze wine crater and other fancy Mediterranean goods (see Seeing the Past: The Vix Crater: A Greek Vessel in Northern France). Few Celtic people were able to acquire such luxuries, however, and most lived simple lives as farmers. As in the Greek world, social inequality was the rule.

The wealth of the Mediterranean may have inspired Celtic military forays and a desire among some Celts to establish settlements in the region. Several times Celtic groups raided deep into Italy and Greece. In 390 B.C.E., they captured most of Rome, and it took the Romans two centuries to fully drive them from Italy. In 279 B.C.E., one Celtic group tried to ransack the Greek sanctuary at Delphi. Also in the third century B.C.E., other Celts

SEEING THE PAST

The Vix Crater: A Greek Vessel in Northern France

Vix Crater
(Musée Archeologique, Chatillon Sur Seine, France/Giraudon/ Bridgeman Art Library.)

Around 530 B.C.E. a woman about thirty years old was buried in a tomb beneath an earthen mound 138 feet in diameter and 16 feet high. The tomb, near the modern town of Vix, east of Paris, is one of the richest in Atlantic

Europe. It contained jewelry of gold (including a bracelet weighing 1.06 pounds) and of bronze, sometimes decorated with amber.

The most impressive goods were accessories for a drinking party: ceramic cups made in Athens, bronze basins and a jug for pouring made in Italy, and the largest metal vessel of Greek manufacture ever recovered, a crater to mix wine, shown here. This Vix crater, made of bronze, is nearly 5.5 feet tall and weighs 458 pounds. Its rim is decorated with a band of Greek hoplites on foot and on chariots. The handles contain images of the Greek female monster, the Gorgon. The creators of the crater were probably Greek colonists in southern Italy, and it took great effort to transport the heavy object to northern France. European elites could only afford such imported goods only because they controlled one of the metals people of the Mediterranean much desired: tin, which was indispensable in producing bronze.

EXAMINING THE EVIDENCE

1. How does the decoration of this vessel reveal contacts between the people of northern France and Greeks of the Mediterranean?

2. What does it and other burial goods tell us about the woman's social status?

3. Why would the scene on this crater have appealed to the Celts? Keep in mind the chapter discussion in considering this question.

migrated into central Turkey, where they were long known as Galatians, a name derived from one of the peoples of western Europe, the Gauls.

Military Encounters

These raids and other clashes led authors from Greece and Rome to emphasize the physical strength and martial behavior of Celts. But they also saw them as noble savages. When in the late third century B.C.E. a Hellenistic king erected a monument in the city of Pergamon to celebrate his victory over the Galatians, he depicted them as honorable fighters who would rather commit suicide than be captured, mirroring the Roman portrayal of Boudicca.

Thus, at the edge of the Greek world lived a people with fundamentally different traditions. Their history has been overshadowed by that of their more powerful neighbor, whose culture has attracted the attention of scholars for more than two millennia. The Celts were connected to a larger world, however, and their influences on later periods, though less obvious than those of the Greeks, were no less real.

Conclusion

Between 800 and 300 B.C.E., a very small part of the world's population, living in Greece, developed a new set of ideas about every aspect of their lives. Earlier traditions, both domestic and foreign, certainly inspired these ideas, but in questioning inherited practices and beliefs the Greeks created an environment that was unique in every respect: politically, socially, culturally, and intellectually. The benefits were restricted to the very few, but they expressed themselves in writings that were preserved and admired later on, and their thoughts dominate our understanding of this era.

When the Greeks conquered the Persian Empire to the east, their ideas spread over a wide area, enormously expanding their impact. This geographic diffusion explains how wise sayings from mainland Greece, such as those of Clearchus, came to be inscribed on stone as far away as northern Afghanistan. Greek intellectual influence was far reaching and long lasting. Not only did the Romans, whom we will discuss in Chapter 7, build purposely on Greek foundations, but the emperor of India, Ashoka, used the Greek language to spread Buddhist ideals, as we will see in the next chapter. And in many ways, still today, we hearken back to ideals that the Greeks first formulated in the distant past.

NOTES

1. Susan Sherwin-White and Amélie Kuhrt, *From Samarkhand to Sardis: A New Approach to the Seleucid Empire* (Berkeley: University of California Press, 1993), 179.
2. *Aeschylus II*, trans. Seth G. Bernadete (Chicago: University of Chicago Press, 2d ed., 1991), 62–63.
3. *Sophocles I*, trans. Elizabeth Wyckoff (Chicago: University of Chicago Press, 1954), 174.
4. *Herodotus: The Histories*, Book 2:35, ed. John M. Marincola, trans. Aubrey De Selincourt (London: Penguin Classics, 1996).
5. Tacitus, *Annals*, Book 14, Ch. 35. Quoted from http://www.athenapub.com/tacitus1.htm.

RESOURCES FOR RESEARCH

General Works

There are many books on ancient Greek history and culture, and new ones continue to be published. Ranging from broad surveys to detailed studies of specific topics, they take many different approaches to the subject, from chronological surveys to discussions of select topics. Here is a sample.

Cartledge, Paul, ed. *Cambridge Illustrated History of Ancient Greece.* 1998.

(For women in ancient Greece): Diotima: Materials for the Study of Women and Gender in the Ancient World. http://www.stoa.org/diotima/.

Grant, M., and R. Kitzinger, eds. *Civilization of the Ancient Mediterranean.* 1988.

(For translations of Greek literature and other writings): Internet Ancient History Sourcebooks: Full Texts. http://www.fordham.edu/halsall/ancient/asbookfull.html#Greece.

Morris, Ian, and Barry Powell, eds. *The Greeks: History, Culture, and Society.* 2006.

Osborne, Robin. *Greek History.* 2004.

(For translations and Greek text of literature and other writings): Perseus Digital Library. http://www.perseus.tufts.edu.

Pomeroy, Sarah. *Goddesses, Whores, Wives, and Slaves: Women in Classical Antiquity.* 1995.

Pomeroy, Sarah B., Stanley M. Burstein, Walter Donlan, and Jennifer Tolbert Roberts. *A Brief History of Ancient Greece: Politics, Society, and Culture.* 2004.

The Development of Ancient Greek Culture, 1200–500 B.C.E.

The period of the formation of Greek culture is the subject of many specialized studies, including these accessible works.

The British Museum: Ancient Greece. http://www.ancientgreece.co.uk/.

Coldstream, J. N. *Geometric Greece, 900–700 BC.* 2d ed. 2003.

Fischer, N., and H. van Wees, eds. *Archaic Greece: New Approaches and New Evidence.* 1998.

Hall, Jonathan M. *A History of the Archaic Greek World.* 2007.

Osborne, Robin. *Greece in the Making, 1200–479 BC.* 1996.

*Rhodes, P. J. *The Greek City States: A Source Book.* 1986.

The Persian Wars, Classical Greece, and the Concept of Cultural Difference, 500–338 B.C.E.

The Classical Age, the height of ancient Greek culture, is one of the best-studied eras in world history. Scholars have taken many approaches to a wide range of subjects. Hamel uses the life of Neaira as a gateway into many aspects of classical Greece.

The Ancient City of Athens. http://www.stoa.org/athens/.

Hall, Edith. *Inventing the Barbarian: Greek Self-Definition Through Tragedy.* 1989.

Hamel, Debra. *Trying Neaira: The True Story of a Courtesan's Scandalous Life in Ancient Greece.* 2003.

Hornblower, Simon. *The Greek World, 479–323 BC.* 1991.

Kagan, Donald. *The Peloponnesian War.* 2003.

Kinzl, Konrad H., ed. *A Companion to the Classical Greek World.* 2006.

Munn, Mark. *The School of History: Athens in the Age of Socrates.* 2000.

Osborne, Robin. *Classical Greece, 500–323 BC.* 2000.

Powell, Anton. *Athens and Sparta: Constructing Greek Political and Social History, 478 BC.* 1988.

Rhodes, P. J. *A History of the Classical Greek World.* 2006.

Hellenism: The Expansion of Greek Ideals and Institutions, 330–30 B.C.E.

Hellenism also has been studied in great detail, but until recently the work focused on Greek sources. The work of Sherwin-White and Kuhrt has started to rectify that situation by integrating information on the well-documented cultures to the east.

Cartledge, Paul. *Alexander the Great: The Hunt for a New Past.* 2004.

Errington, Malcolm. *A History of the Hellenistic World.* 2008.

Erskine, Andrew, ed. *A Companion to the Hellenistic World.* 2003.

Green, Peter. *Alexander to Actium: The Historical Evolution of the Hellenistic Age.* 1990.

Sherwin-White, Susan, and Amélie Kuhrt. *From Samarkhand to Sardis: A New Approach to the Seleucid Empire.* 1993.

COUNTERPOINT: The Celtic Peoples of the Atlantic Zone

Much more archaeological in nature are studies of the Atlantic peoples, who left no writings of their own.

Cunliffe, Barry. *The Ancient Celts.* 1997.

Cunliffe, Barry. *The Celts: A Very Short Introduction.* 2003.

Ellis, Peter Beresford. *The Ancient World of the Celts.* 1998.

James, Simon. *Exploring the World of the Celts.* 1993.

* Primary source.

▶ **For additional primary sources from this period,** see *Sources of Crossroads and Cultures*.

▶ **For Web sites, images, and documents related to topics in this chapter,** see Make History at bedfordstmartins.com/smith.

The major global development in this chapter: ▶ The cultural and political innovations of the ancient Greeks and the expansion of Greek ideals and institutions.

IMPORTANT EVENTS

c. 1200–800 B.C.E.	Dark Age in the Aegean world
c. 800–500 B.C.E.	Archaic period in Greece
776 B.C.E.	First Olympic games, according to tradition
c. 775 B.C.E.	First evidence of alphabetic writing in Greece
c. 750 B.C.E.	Homer writes the *Iliad* and the *Odyssey*
750–550 B.C.E.	Main period of Greek colonization of the Mediterranean
700–600 B.C.E.	Orientalizing period in Greek art
c. 574 B.C.E.	Solon institutes reforms in Athens
c. 500–323 B.C.E.	Classical Age of Greece
500–479 B.C.E.	Persian Wars
443–429 B.C.E.	Pericles leads Athens
431–404 B.C.E.	Peloponnesian War
404 B.C.E.	Spartan hegemony in Greece
390 B.C.E.	Celts capture Rome in Italy
338 B.C.E.	Philip of Macedonia conquers Greece
331 B.C.E.	Alexander defeats Persia; Alexandria founded in Egypt
323 B.C.E.	Death of Alexander
323–30 B.C.E.	Hellenistic period
30 B.C.E.	Romans conquer Egypt

KEY TERMS

democracy (p. 146)
Hellenism (p. 159)
mystery cult (p. 163)
oligarchy (p. 146)
phalanx (p. 145)

philosophy (p. 152)
polis (p. 145)
sophist (p. 152)
tyranny (p. 146)

CHAPTER OVERVIEW QUESTIONS

1. How did geography and contacts with other peoples shape Greek institutions and values?
2. What were the cultural and political innovations of the Greeks, and how have they proved enduring?
3. To what extent did these innovations affect the lives and livelihoods of ordinary Greeks?
4. How did the spread of Hellenism affect the Greeks and the other peoples of Eurasia and North Africa?

SECTION FOCUS QUESTIONS

1. What significant political and cultural developments emerged in Greece in the early first millennium B.C.E.?
2. What cultural innovations appeared in Greece during its Classical Age?
3. How did Hellenism affect the peoples of Greece, North Africa, and Southwest Asia?
4. How did the lives and livelihoods of the peoples of Atlantic Europe differ from those of the Mediterranean peoples?

MAKING CONNECTIONS

1. How do the political systems of the Greek city-states Athens and Sparta compare with those of contemporary empires in Asia and North Africa (see Chapter 4)?
2. How would you describe the cultural interactions between Southwest Asia and Greece from the Archaic to Hellenistic periods?
3. What ideals of classical Greece influenced later developments in world history?

6

AT A CROSSROADS ▶

The Kushan emperors
promoted a cross-cultural
art form that combined
Hellenistic Greek styles with
South Asian motifs. Known
as "Gandharan" from the
Kushan capital of Gandhara
in modern northwest
Pakistan, a typical example
is this statue of the Buddha,
dated sometime in the first
to third centuries C.E. It
shows an iconic South
Asian figure, the Buddha,
seated in a traditional pose
of meditation. The realism
and detail reflect Hellenistic
art, especially in the carving
of the folds of his dress.
(Fitzwilliam Museum, University
of Cambridge, UK/Bridgeman
Art Library.)

Peoples and World Empires: Classical India, the Kushan Empire, and China

500 B.C.E.–500 C.E.

On the Indian peninsula sometime in the second century C.E., a man named Dashafota carved an inscription on a stone left by a well. The short text in the Sanskrit language reads:

> During the reign of the Maharaja, Rajatiraja, Devaputra, Kaisara Kanishka, the son of Vajheshka, the 41st year, on the 25th day of the month Jyaishtha, on this day a well was dug by Dashafota, the son of Poshapuri, in honor of his mother and father, in order to confer benefit on himself together with his wife and his son, for the welfare of all beings in the various births. And here I throw in 100,000 coins as a religious gift.[1]

Dashafota was a subject of Emperor Kanishka II, whose Kushan dynasty had conquered large parts of Central Asia and the Indian peninsula. The king's titles, taken from those of the great empires of Eurasia, show him to be an equal of the powerful rulers whose realms surrounded him. Those titles included the Indian *maharaja*, "Great King," and the Chinese *devaputra*, "son of God." *Rajatiraja*, "king of kings," is from the Parthian emperor, and *kaisara*, "Caesar," is from the Roman. Kanishka's empire was at the crossroads of large states that stretched from the China Sea to the Atlantic Ocean. His assumption of these titles

BACKSTORY

We left the discussion of Asia in Chapter 3 in 500 B.C.E. By this point, centuries of development in India and China had laid the foundations for the two regions' subsequent histories. In India, many had accepted the Vedic traditions and the caste system, whereas in China the ideal of political unification and dynastic rule had been firmly established. In other parts of Asia, such as the Oxus River Valley, early cultural developments had suddenly ended, and the people had abandoned the regions they formerly occupied. We return now to Asia to study how the peoples of China and India both built on and challenged their cultural inheritance.

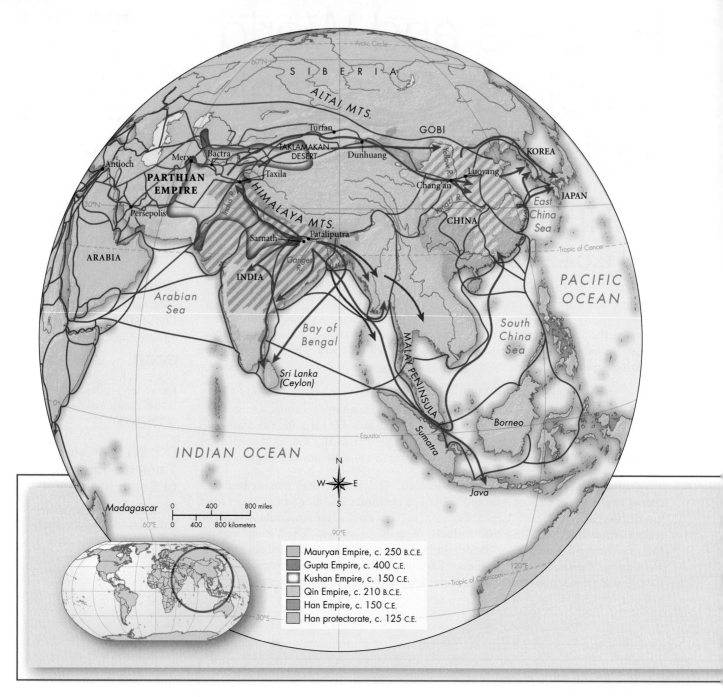

Mauryan Empire, c. 250 B.C.E.
Gupta Empire, c. 400 C.E.
Kushan Empire, c. 150 C.E.
Qin Empire, c. 210 B.C.E.
Han Empire, c. 150 C.E.
Han protectorate, c. 125 C.E.

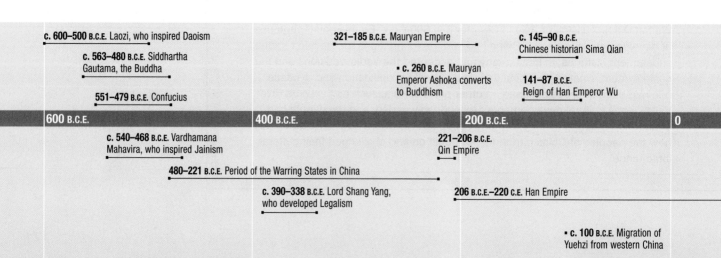

c. 600–500 B.C.E. Laozi, who inspired Daoism

c. 563–480 B.C.E. Siddhartha Gautama, the Buddha

551–479 B.C.E. Confucius

c. 540–468 B.C.E. Vardhamana Mahavira, who inspired Jainism

480–221 B.C.E. Period of the Warring States in China

c. 390–338 B.C.E. Lord Shang Yang, who developed Legalism

321–185 B.C.E. Mauryan Empire

c. 260 B.C.E. Mauryan Emperor Ashoka converts to Buddhism

221–206 B.C.E. Qin Empire

c. 145–90 B.C.E. Chinese historian Sima Qian

141–87 B.C.E. Reign of Han Emperor Wu

206 B.C.E.–220 C.E. Han Empire

c. 100 B.C.E. Migration of Yuehzi from western China

600 B.C.E.   400 B.C.E.   200 B.C.E.   0

shows that he and his people knew of the other empires and their rulers, the result of frequent interactions through trade. Kanishka's empire was indeed equal to the others, and because of its central location in Asia, it acted as a conduit for their goods and ideas.

Dashafota's inscription acknowledges that the Eurasian world of the time was one of territorial empires. This was true for the entire period from 500 B.C.E. to 500 C.E., when centralized states incorporated varied regions and cultural traditions and established a degree of uniformity over them. In the east of this vast area, India, Central Asia, and China each saw a succession of such empires, including the Mauryan, Gupta, Kushan, Qin, and Han. As we will see, these imperial dynasties were interrupted by periods of political fragmentation, and some regions, such as the Tamil area in southern India, were never incorporated into an empire. The empires that did arise were in close contact with one another, bound together by trade that moved along the land and sea routes connecting the eastern and western borders of Asia.

These centuries saw a profuse cultural flowering that fed intellectual and artistic traditions for millennia. Like their Greek contemporaries, great thinkers in India and China developed new ideas about life and government that affected all levels of society. Their teachings launched religious and philosophical trends that were fundamental to the later histories of these countries and spread far beyond their borders. This creativity expressed the will and passion of untold individuals, often reacting against the political circumstances of their time. The intellectual currents these peoples engendered were spread through integration into imperial ideologies, but the ideas long outlived the empires that promoted them. Indeed, they shaped all subsequent thought in Asia. Thus we refer to the eras of their creation as the **classical** periods of both India and China.

classical The traditional authoritative form of a culture.

MAPPING THE WORLD

Empires and Exchange in Asia, 500 B.C.E.–500 C.E.

For a thousand years, the vast territories of Asia were connected through a vibrant trade in goods and ideas regardless of the political powers that dominated parts of the region. Qin and Han China in the east and the Mauryan, Kushan, and Gupta empires in South and Central Asia were hotbeds for the development of new ideas and technologies, many of which subsequently spread throughout Asia and beyond into the Parthian and Roman worlds.

ROUTES ▼

— Silk Road
— Other trade route
➔ Spread of Buddhism
➔ Spread of Hinduism

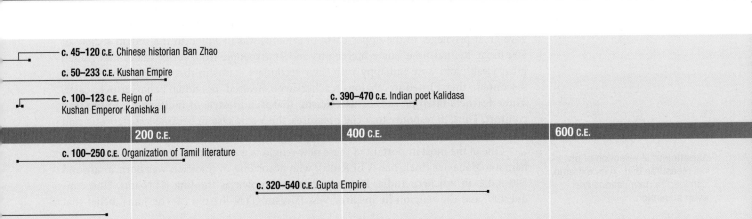

c. 45–120 C.E. Chinese historian Ban Zhao

c. 50–233 C.E. Kushan Empire

c. 100–123 C.E. Reign of Kushan Emperor Kanishka II

c. 390–470 C.E. Indian poet Kalidasa

200 C.E.   **400 C.E.**   **600 C.E.**

c. 100–250 C.E. Organization of Tamil literature

c. 320–540 C.E. Gupta Empire

OVERVIEW
QUESTIONS

The major global development in this chapter: The revolutionary religious and cultural developments in India and China that took place between 500 B.C.E. and 500 C.E. and remained fundamental to the history of Asia.

As you read, consider:

1. How did new social circumstances stimulate changes in religious beliefs and cultures?

2. What processes encouraged close connections among the various regions of Asia?

3. In what ways did the revolutionary thinkers discussed here have a lasting impact on the histories of the regions they inhabited and beyond?

India: Thinkers, Traders, and Courtly Cultures 500 B.C.E.–500 C.E.

> **FOCUS**
>
> How did the new religious ideas of the last centuries B.C.E. suit the social and political structures of India?

In around 500 B.C.E., Indian culture and society started to undergo fundamental changes that continued for almost a millennium. The teachings of several influential thinkers radically affected prevailing religious currents, changing the nature of the caste system (see Chapter 3) and stressing individual responsibility for all people. Politically the region saw the successive rise of the Mauryan and Gupta empires, which placed large parts of South Asia under centralized control. Culturally, Indian arts and scientific investigation blossomed. Exchanges of all kinds occurred between India and the larger world. People from China, Central Asia, and the Mediterranean came to India, often as traders, sometimes as conquerors, and people from India traveled far and wide as merchants and missionaries. India became a crossroads of connections that spread across the Asian continent, bringing outside influences to India and bringing Indian culture, ideas, and products to the rest of Asia.

Religious Ferment: The Rise of Jainism, Buddhism, and Hinduism

The rigor of the Vedic caste system, which assigned people a place in society at birth and gave great privileges to the upper-caste Brahmans, was ill suited to the Indian society of 500 B.C.E. By that time, some merchants and craftspeople from lower castes had gained great wealth and were unhappy with their secondary status in the caste system. In their discontent, they turned to religious teachers who stressed individual behavior over caste. These teachers often prescribed **asceticism**, that is, a lifestyle of indifference to physical comfort. Thus, in response to social pressures, the Vedic system became less rigorous, and a variety of new and profoundly influential religions emerged.

One of the most important of these new religions was based on the teachings of Vardhamana Mahavira (mah-hah-VEER-uh), who according to tradition was born in around 540 B.C.E. in northern India. Mahavira became known as the Jina (JYN-uh), "the conqueror," and the religion he inspired was Jainism (JYN-ihz-uhm). The Jains' belief that

asceticism A rejection of physical pleasures that, in its extreme, can lead to deprivations and even starvation.

Jainism

everything—humans, animals, plants, and inanimate objects—had a soul led devotees to complete nonviolence. They believed that no creature whatsoever should be killed, even accidentally. Jains call the moral virtue that inspires such behavior **dharma**. In an extreme form of the religion, followers filtered their water to avoid swallowing small insects. They also tried to end the cycle of reincarnation (rebirth in a different form), which bolstered the caste system, and to free the soul from the body through ascetic behavior such as fasting. Because Mahavira himself had discarded clothing in his life, some of his followers insisted that devotees should be completely naked; others allowed only simple white robes.

Few could adhere fully to such a rigorous lifestyle, but Jainism was especially popular among urban merchants and artisans who were attracted to its rejection of castes. Its pacifism also had great appeal, inspiring men and women ever since its inception, including the twentieth-century Indian statesman Mahatma Gandhi, who grew up in a region where Jainism was widespread. Some political elites promoted Jainism, but the religion never spread beyond India.

In sharp contrast, another religion that originated in India, Buddhism, had a powerful impact on the entire Asian continent. Buddhism is based on the teachings of the Buddha, "the Awakened One"—that is, the one who awakened from a sleep of ignorance to find freedom from suffering. According to traditions written down centuries after his death, the Buddha was Prince Siddhartha Gautama from southern Nepal, who lived from about 563 to 480 B.C.E. Gautama's father shielded him from the evils of life, giving him access to all possible pleasures in his luxurious palaces. But when Gautama was twenty-nine years old, he insisted on going outside, and he was shocked to finally witness old age, illness, and death. When his father told him these conditions were inescapable, he moved into the forest to search for a state beyond birth and death. At first he joined other ascetics, but he realized self-mortification was not the answer. After weeks of meditation, resisting the temptations the god of desire showered upon him, he formulated the idea of "the middle way." A balanced way of life between the extremes of luxury and asceticism was the answer to human suffering. Having thus become the Buddha, he established the Four Noble Truths: (1) existence is suffering, (2) the cause of suffering is negative deeds of the body inspired by desire, (3) desire can be eliminated, and (4) the way to end desire lies in the eightfold path—right belief, resolve, speech, behavior, occupation, effort, contemplation, and meditation.

The Buddha and His Teachings

Buddhism's appeal relied on three elements, the "three jewels": (1) the charismatic teacher, the Buddha; (2) his teachings, the Buddhist interpretation of dharma; and (3) the community, **sangha**. For forty-five years after his awakening, the Buddha traveled throughout northeastern India to teach the religion. Most followers remained laypeople, but some devoted their lives to Buddhism, becoming monks and nuns and founding **monasteries**, communities reserved for followers. There they renounced material goods and led a life of moderation and meditation, supported by the donations of local populations. They strove to reach **nirvana**, a state without desire, hatred, and ignorance and, ultimately, without suffering and rebirth, in which the physical was completely removed from the spiritual.

After the Buddha died, followers cremated his remains and distributed them over large parts of India, where they were buried underneath earthen mounds called **stupas**. According to tradition, the emperor Ashoka built eighty-four thousand stupas after he converted to Buddhism in 260 B.C.E., giving the Buddha a physical presence throughout India. Pilgrims visited sites that had been important in the Buddha's life and spread the new religion, reaching a wide audience by using vernacular dialects rather than the obscure literary Sanskrit of the Brahmans. By promising an escape from the cycle of reincarnation and by rejecting the caste system, Buddhism appealed powerfully to the new wealthy mercantile class. Moreover, its "middle way" was an easier practice than the stricter Jainism.

As followers interpreted the Buddha's teaching, different schools of thought emerged. The most popular tradition, Mahayana Buddhism, became the "Greater Vehicle" to salvation; it was open to more people than the more restrictive Hinayana ("Lesser Vehicle") Buddhism, which more closely adhered to the Buddha's original dharma. Mahayana Buddhism portrayed

dharma A term with slightly different meanings in various Indian religions, it refers in Jainism to moral virtue, in Buddhism to the teachings of the Buddha, and in Hinduism to duty.

sangha In Buddhism, the community of monks and nuns who see themselves as the successors of the people who traveled with the Buddha in his lifetime.

monastery A community of adherents to a particular religion, who often live in seclusion from general society.

nirvana In Buddhism, the goal of religious practice, a state of existence without desire, hatred, ignorance, suffering, and, ultimately, reincarnation.

stupa A Buddhist monument built to hold a part of the Buddha's remains or an object connected to him.

The Great Stupa of Sanchi, India

According to tradition, in 260 B.C.E. Emperor Ashoka built thousands of stupas across India to cover ashes of the cremated Buddha. This example from Sanchi is known to have a simple hemispherical brick core to hold the remains. In later centuries people turned the stupa into an elaborate construction with a large stone mound and entrance gates. The monument is still in use today. (Frédéric Soltan/Corbis.)

the Buddha as a divine being people could worship. Any man or woman who acquired freedom from suffering and postponed nirvana to teach it to others was a called a ***bodhisattva***, an "enlightened being," who in turn became an object of veneration. The two schools coexisted, sometimes within the same monastery.

Spread of Buddhism

Royal support greatly facilitated the spread of Buddhism. Particularly important was the emperor Ashoka, a skillful military leader whose campaigns greatly expanded the Mauryan Empire (discussed later in this chapter). Sickened by the death and destruction of his conquest of Kalinga in 260 B.C.E., he converted to Buddhism, hoping to bring the various peoples in his empire together under the common ideal of humanity and virtue. Ashoka proclaimed his aspirations by inscribing them on rock surfaces and stone pillars in an assortment of languages and dialects. For example:

> This world and the other are hard to gain without great love of Righteousness [dharma], great self-examination, great obedience, great circumspection, great effort. Through my instruction respect and love of Righteousness daily increase and will increase. . . . For this is my rule—to govern by Righteousness, to administer by Righteousness, to please my subjects by Righteousness, and to protect them by Righteousness.[2]

bodhisattva In Buddhism, a person who found enlightenment and teaches others.

Thus, by promoting a universal religion, establishing precepts to govern all of his people, and translating his precepts into many languages so that all could understand them, Ashoka consciously sought to strengthen connections among the peoples and communities of his empire.

Ashoka's efforts to promote Buddhism were not confined to the Mauryan Empire. He sent missionaries to spread Buddhism beyond India, and later traditions regularly attribute the religion's arrival to his initiatives. In Sri Lanka, for example, they say that Ashoka's son Mahendra converted many people through acts of kindness and piety. Buddhism's spread also benefited from the support of merchants, who especially in early centuries C.E. traveled widely from India to other parts of Asia, as we will see. They carried Buddhist manuscripts to distant places, where scholars translated them into local languages and adapted them to local tastes. The spread of Buddhism beyond India proved crucial to the religion's survival. Hinduism eventually replaced Buddhism as India's dominant religion, but Buddhism continued to flourish abroad.

Buddhism and Jainism challenged the Vedic tradition and drew believers away from the older religion. But the Vedic tradition evolved rather than withered away. After 500 B.C.E. the Vedic tradition widened its appeal by abandoning its special treatment of the Brahmans and its rigorous adherence to the caste system. These developments coincided with the production of written Sanskrit versions of the Vedas, as well as of a large literature, both secular and religious. Although scholars call the new religion "Hinduism," that term did not appear until the eleventh century C.E., when India's Muslim conquerors used it to refer to the religious practices of the people of India in general. Influenced by Jainism and Buddhism, Hinduism found ways to emphasize the value of the individual within a caste framework. All people had an obligation to carry out the activities and duties of their caste, but proper behavior could free any individual from the cycle of reincarnation. Hence, Hinduism combined essential elements of the Vedic tradition with some of the beliefs and ideals of the tradition's critics, creating a stronger and more popular religion.

Hinduism honors many gods and goddesses, and their worship is an important duty. The major division in Hinduism is between devotees of the two most prominent male gods, Vishnu and Shiva. Both had been minor gods in Vedic times. Shiva was of Dravidian origin and remained more popular in the south of India, whereas Vishnu had an Indo-European background and was more popular in the north. Vishnu was a benevolent god who preserved and protected the universe. Shiva, however, had warlike characteristics and was present in places of disaster. Vishnu could appear in numerous incarnations, which linked him to the gods and heroes of other traditions. Thus, in one incarnation Vishnu could be Krishna, a warrior god and a shepherd; in another incarnation he was the Buddha. This flexibility was a key consequence of the Vedic tradition's evolution into Hinduism. One of Hinduism's strengths was its ability to incorporate elements from many religious traditions and to thrive in diverse communities across India.

The Hindu way of life encouraged a balanced pursuit of devotion and pleasure. People should seek righteousness, virtue, and duty, but they could also pursue material gain, love, and recreation. Correct balance among these pursuits would lead to liberation from worldly life. The poem known as the *Bhagavad Gita* ("Song of the Lord") explains how a person could attain the ideal balance in an active life. The poem is a dialogue between the hero

Image of a Bodhisattva

The bodhisattva—an individual who, through wisdom, moral behavior, and self-sacrifice, guided people to awakening—became a popular figure in Buddhist art and literature. This depiction of one comes from the Ajanta caves in western India, where Buddhist temples famous for their frescoes were excavated in the rock between the first century B.C.E. and the seventh century C.E. The bodhisattva is shown in a posture typical for meditation. (Frédéric Soltan/Corbis.)

Hinduism

Arjuna and his charioteer, Krishna, who is the incarnation of Vishnu. When Arjuna is reluctant to fight his family members and friends, Krishna convinces him that he will hurt only their bodies, which are renewable, and not their souls, which are immortal:

> Just as man, having cast off old garments, puts on other, new ones, even so does the embodied one, having cast off old bodies, take on other, new ones.
> Weapons do not cleave him, fire does not burn him; nor does water drench him, nor the wind dry him up.
> He is uncleavable, he is unburnable, he is undrenchable, as also undryable. He is eternal, all pervading, stable, immovable, existing from time immemorial.[3]

As a warrior, Arjuna has a specific role in society, just as everyone does, whatever their place in society. The idea of specific roles reinforced the caste system, in which the duty of the Brahman was to provide wisdom; of the warrior, valor; of the Vaishya, industry; and of the Shudra, service.

The centuries after 500 B.C.E. thus witnessed remarkable intellectual activity in India as thinkers reinterpreted the ancient Vedic ideals and sought to make them accessible to all people. Hinduism continued to stress the caste system, but people on every level could find spiritual liberation. In contrast, Buddhism and Jainism focused on the individual quest for salvation outside the caste system. All three religions proved to have widespread and long-lasting appeal, and they continue to inspire millions of people to this day.

Unity and Fragmentation: The Mauryan and Gupta Empires

With its vast size and varied ecology of forests, deserts, mountain ranges, and river valleys, it was not easy to bring the Indian subcontinent under central political control. Further, its population had varied cultural traditions, languages, and scripts. Nevertheless, between 500 B.C.E. and 500 C.E., a series of empires, including those of Persians, Macedonians, Mauryans, and Guptas, controlled large parts of India. Their leaders came from diverse backgrounds: some were from India itself, but others were outsiders who conquered parts of the subcontinent. All encouraged the merging of traditions throughout their realms, and some used the new religions to inspire a regional sense of community.

Rise of the Mauryan Empire

When the Aryas moved into the eastern Indian Ganges Valley sometime before 1500 B.C.E. (see Chapter 3), they established a number of kingdoms. In later centuries, these kingdoms were often at war with one another, but eventually these civil struggles ended, perhaps in part due to outside pressures. In 326 B.C.E. Alexander of Macedonia crossed the Indus River and confronted Indian armies. Greek sources say that a rebellious Indian prince, whose name they render in Greek as Sandracottos (san-droh-KOT-uhs), met Alexander and urged him to conquer the kingdom of Magadha in the Ganges Valley. Alexander's men refused to go farther east, however, and retreated. This, according to some, was Alexander's greatest mistake: "Sandracottos, when he was a stripling, saw Alexander himself, and we are told that he often said in later times that Alexander narrowly missed making himself master of the country, since its king was hated and despised on account of his baseness and low birth."[4]

Later Indian sources do not mention Alexander, but they do describe the Indian prince, using his Indian name, Chandragupta. He started out as a penniless servant but established himself as ruler of the kingdom of Magadha. Through conquest and clever diplomacy, he created the largest empire in Indian history—called Mauryan after the name of Chandragupta's dynasty—bringing the entire subcontinent except for the Tamil south under his control (see Counterpoint: Tamil Kingdoms of South India). By 321 B.C.E., Chandragupta had annexed the Indus Valley. He later acquired the Greek-controlled region of Bactria—northern Afghanistan today—from the Seleucid Empire in exchange for five hundred elephants (see Map 6.1).

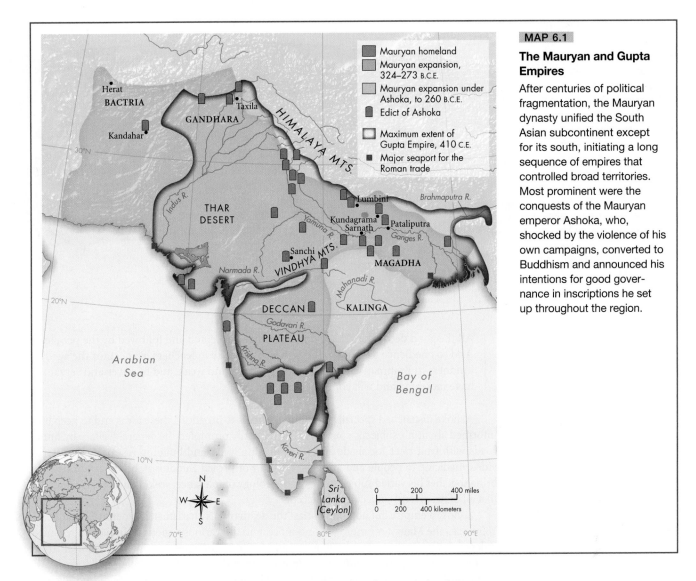

MAP 6.1

The Mauryan and Gupta Empires

After centuries of political fragmentation, the Mauryan dynasty unified the South Asian subcontinent except for its south, initiating a long sequence of empires that controlled broad territories. Most prominent were the conquests of the Mauryan emperor Ashoka, who, shocked by the violence of his own campaigns, converted to Buddhism and announced his intentions for good governance in inscriptions he set up throughout the region.

Chandragupta relied on his chief adviser, Kautilya, to create the empire's administration, which became famous for its efficiency. Kautilya left behind a handbook on government, the *Arthasastra*, or "Treatise on Material Gain," as a guideline for future officials. He presented the figure of the king as the center of the state and the source of people's wealth and happiness. The king was the sole guarantee against disorder and could use any means necessary to avoid it, including spies and political assassination. For much of his reign, Chandragupta followed Kautilya's advice, consolidating his own power and eliminating potential sources of opposition. It is possible, however, that he came to regret his ruthless policies, because in around 297 B.C.E. Chandragupta abdicated the throne, became a Jain monk, and starved himself to death in absolute asceticism.

The religious climate of his day also deeply influenced Chandragupta's grandson and successor, Ashoka. As we have seen, the human cost of his wars of conquest prompted him to convert to Buddhism in around 260 B.C.E. Buddhist ideals inspired his government, and he announced his reforms publicly throughout the empire through the use of the carved inscriptions described earlier in this chapter. Ashoka's inscriptions are the oldest preserved writings from India, after the Indus Valley texts (see Chapter 3).

Ashoka ruled his empire in a way that was unique for his time. He urged nonviolence, humane treatment of servants, and generosity to all. He did not force his views on his people, instead leading through example. One of his statements was:

King Ashoka

Inscription of King Ashoka
After his conversion to Buddhism in around 260 B.C.E., King Ashoka broadcast his message of tolerance and care for the people in his land in a series of inscriptions on pillars and rock façades. He used local languages and scripts to do so, and these inscriptions are the earliest evidence of writing in India after the Indus Valley script. This fragment of a pillar is inscribed in the Brahma script, the ancestor of all modern Indian scripts. (© The Trustees of The British Museum/Art Resource, NY.)

> All the good deeds that I have done have been accepted and followed by the people. And so obedience to mother and father, obedience to teachers, respect for the aged, kindness to Brahmans and ascetics, to the poor and weak, and to slaves and servants, have increased and will continue to increase.[5]

Ashoka dispatched specially appointed officers to broadcast these ideas and to keep him informed about his subjects' concerns. The emperor promoted the general welfare by lining roads with fruit trees for shade and food, digging wells, and building rest houses. He provided medicine to people and animals. He did not preach Buddhism, but instead hoped to bring together his varied subjects under an ideology of tolerance, seeking universal principles that all of his diverse subjects could accept.

Ashoka's empire did not long outlast the death of this charismatic leader in 232 B.C.E. By 185 B.C.E., the Mauryan Empire was no more, and the various regions of India had regained independence. Between about 200 B.C.E. and 300 C.E., foreigners such as the Central Asian Kushans annexed parts of India. Foreign invasion and political fragmentation did not, however, end India's cultural flowering. India's religious and intellectual vitality did not depend on political unity, and the arrival of outsiders created new conduits for the spread of Indian culture abroad.

Gupta Empire   The breakup of India was temporarily reversed when a dynasty from the Ganges Valley, the Guptas, unified the north and parts of the center between about 320 and 540 C.E. (see again Map 6.1). The dynasty's founder took the name Chandra Gupta to recall the Mauryan Empire of the past, but his state was smaller and much less centralized. The Guptas replaced the direct administration of the Mauryans with a system that relied on the cooperation of allies and vassals. Much of the conquest was the work of Chandra Gupta's son, Samudra Gupta (c. 330–380 C.E.). Later Indians saw him as the ideal king because he was a great warrior as well as a poet and musician.

Unlike Ashoka, who had sought to inspire the loyalty of his people through good works, Samudra Gupta used violence and the threat of violence to hold his empire together. This strategy proved effective, and he could control his subjects while expanding his empire. Inscriptions from his reign claim that he received tribute from places as distant as Central Asia in the north and Sri Lanka in the south. The Gupta Empire gradually came under increasing pressure from Central Asian nomads, who raided northwest India throughout the fifth century C.E. The expense and effort to keep these raiders out proved so great that by 540 C.E. the Gupta Empire had disappeared. Not until the Mughal dynasty in the sixteenth century C.E. would empire return to India.

A Crossroads of Trade

Like people all over the ancient world, most Indians devoted their lives to agricultural tasks. They lived in small villages, enjoying few if any luxuries. The work of this rural labor force was nonetheless crucial to India's cultural and material development. Food produced in the countryside made possible the growth of cities, which were at the heart of both internal and external trade. Indian urban artisans created products that appealed to elites all over India. Moreover, its location at the crossroads of land and sea trade routes across Asia and beyond placed India at the center of an enormous and dynamic international trading system. Despite the region's political turmoil from 500 B.C.E. to 500 C.E., long-distance trade continued to grow. India was in contact with far-flung lands, from China and Southeast Asia to East Africa and the Mediterranean world. As both importers and exporters of luxury goods, its merchants accumulated enormous wealth. Indian rulers, who also benefited financially from this trade, sent ambassadors to distant lands, promoting an exchange of ideas and styles as well as goods.

Silk Road

India's merchants looked both east and west to trade with Asia's great empires. Caravans to and from China took advantage of the age-old trade routes that crossed Asia to India's north, which later became known as the **Silk Road** or, sometimes, the "Silk Roads," as it was not a single route but instead incorporated various parallel branches. Leading four thousand miles through lush regions, deserts, and mountain ranges, it connected China to western Asia and the Mediterranean coast in ancient and medieval times (see again Mapping the World, page 172). The name derives from the Chinese monopoly on silk, which lasted until the fifth century C.E. People throughout Eurasia coveted the cloth so much that they shipped large amounts of gold, silver, and other products east to obtain it. Few traveled the entire Silk Road, instead passing goods on to others in trading stations in oases, near mountain passes, and in other strategic locations. Ideas as well as material goods moved along the road; it was the route by which Buddhism and Christianity spread into China.

Reliance on the Silk Road connected the fortunes of far-flung peoples. The empires of Rome and Byzantium in the Mediterranean area (discussed in Chapter 7) provided enormous markets for the products shipped along the Silk Road. While these empires thrived, so did the Asian trading cities along the western portion of the Silk Road, but when Rome and Byzantium declined, many of these cities were abandoned. In the thirteenth and fourteenth centuries C.E. the arrival of the Mongols in western Asia revived this region and enabled Marco Polo, a merchant from Venice, to reach the Chinese court and write one of the great works of travel literature. In time, trade with the East would enable Venice to build a maritime empire and become in its own right a crossroads for exchanges between Europe and Asia.

Trade with Rome

While traders from north India traveled the Silk Road, those from the south sailed the seas to gain access to goods and foreign markets. In Southeast Asia they obtained spices and semiprecious stones, luxury goods for which Indians found a large market among the Roman imperial elite. The Romans paid with gold coins, wine, copper, tin, and lead. An anonymous Greek traveler of the first century C.E. described ports and marketplaces from Egypt to the Indian Ocean, including various harbors on the Indian coast. Archaeologists have uncovered Roman objects in India that suggest the presence of Roman settlers. But more Indians sailed to the west than Romans to the east, as evidenced by the names that appear in Indian scripts on potsherds excavated in Red Sea ports. Situated between major empires, Indian traders could obtain goods in the empires of the east and sell them in the empires of the west. International trade brought many outside influences to India and helped disseminate Indian religions, ideas, and goods throughout Asia and beyond.

The rulers of many Indian states taxed international trade and so had a substantial stake in it. Hence it was in their interest to facilitate and encourage long-distance commerce through embassies. In about 25 B.C.E., one such Indian trade mission traveled to Rome. According to the Greek historian Nicholas of Damascus, they brought as gifts to the Roman emperor Augustus tigers, pheasants, snakes, giant tortoises, and an armless boy who could shoot arrows with his toes. Missions of this type presented exotic eastern products to an eager Roman clientele.

Silk Road The caravan route with various branches that connected China in the east to the Mediterranean Sea in the west, passing through regions such as South and Southwest Asia.

The economies of Asia were thus joined by an exchange of luxury products. For centuries, political changes in any region could affect the trade, but they did not fundamentally alter it. The decline of the Western Roman Empire in the fourth century C.E. and the end of the Gupta Empire soon thereafter, however, were a major blow to India's long-distance trade. Only in the ninth century C.E. did it revive.

Literary and Scientific Flowering

At around the time that Greece's culture reached new heights in its Classical Age, a period of great literary production began in India. It was to last from 500 B.C.E. to 500 C.E., India's own classical period. This flowering, which continued despite the region's shifting political circumstances, involved religious and secular poetry, drama, and prose. The Brahmans' control over literature through their teaching of the Vedas in memorized form weakened in the Mauryan period, when scribes started to write down the Vedas and their interpretations in the Upanishads. Ashoka's use of various languages and scripts in the third century B.C.E. encouraged the use of spoken dialects in writing and indicates that different literate traditions coexisted in his empire.

The language of the Vedas inspired the primary literary language of ancient India, Sanskrit. Although it was probably little spoken, it was used for much of Indian literature until the nineteenth century C.E. Sanskrit texts fall into a wide range of genres, but most prominent are the epics, or warrior songs. Previously passed down orally, epics began to be recorded in writing after 100 B.C.E. Although the epics represent the traditional values of Hinduism, their engaging stories fascinated people of varied religions all over India and Southeast Asia, and they became the basis for multiple interpretations in many languages and formats, including modern film.

Perhaps the longest single poem in world literature is the *Mahabharata*, the "Great Epic of the Bharata Dynasty," with one hundred thousand stanzas written in Sanskrit. It describes the contest between two branches of the same royal family, which culminated in an eighteen-day-long battle that involved all the kings of India and also Greeks, Bactrians, and Chinese. The epic showed how people of all ranks, including kings and warriors, should behave, following the rules of dharma, which in Hindu thought refers to "duty."

A shorter epic, the *Ramayana*, the "Story of Prince Rama," shows the adherence to dharma in practice. A plot against the prince forced Rama to flee to the forest with his wife Sita. Sita was kidnapped, taken to the island of Sri Lanka, and compelled to reside in the house of another man. After many adventures, Rama freed her with the help of monkeys, but because people doubted her chastity, he had to force her to live in the forest despite his great love for her. There she gave birth to

Delhi's Iron Pillar

Near Delhi in modern India stands an iron pillar whose characteristics demonstrate the great technical skills of Gupta craftsmen. Probably erected in around 400 C.E., the pillar is more than 13 feet tall and weighs about 6 tons. The iron is 98 percent pure, which is possible only when extremely high heat has been applied. The ability to work this enormous mass of metal was unparalleled in early world history and was not attained in Europe until the nineteenth century C.E. (Dinodia Photos.)

Rama's twin sons. In the end, the family was reunited, but Sita asked to be returned to her mother, the goddess Earth. The *Ramayana* and the *Mahabharata* enjoyed great popularity across India, providing common cultural touchstones for the continent's diverse peoples.

Indian poetry was not limited to sweeping epics. Most notable are the works of Kalidasa, who probably lived in the Gupta period between 390 and 470 C.E. In one short poem, the "Cloud Messenger," he describes how an exiled man asks a cloud to carry a message to his wife, whom he misses deeply. He declares:

Sanskrit Poetry and Plays

> In the vines I see your limbs, your look
> in the eye of a startled doe, the loveliness
> of your face in the moon, in the peacock's plumage your hair,
> the playful lift of your brows in the light ripples
> of rivers, but, O, sadly, nowhere, my passionate girl,
> is the whole of your likeness in any one of these.[6]

Kalidasa was also famous for his dramatic works, which were very popular as court entertainment. The stories featured gods, heroes, and courtiers who suffered a good deal of intrigue and hardship but always prevailed in the end.

Scholarship also flourished during India's classical period. In linguistics, Panini developed a grammar of the Sanskrit language in around the fifth century B.C.E., recording more than four thousand grammatical rules. His work impressed later generations so much that they used it as the absolute standard of the language, inhibiting change. Consequently, Sanskrit grew increasingly distant from the commonly spoken Prakrit.

Scholarship

Investigations in astronomy, medicine, physics, and chemistry brought technological wonders. Probably in about 400 C.E., ironsmiths set up a pillar 13 feet 8 inches tall near Delhi that was made of a single piece of iron so chemically pure that it has not rusted in sixteen hundred years. And Indian mathematicians would have a great impact on the world by inventing the concept of zero. The Indian number system, with its symbols from 0 to 9, spread east and west in the seventh century C.E., and western Europeans adopted it from the Middle East as "Arabic" numerals in around 1000 C.E.

The Kushan Peoples of Central Asia 100 B.C.E.–233 C.E.

As we saw in Chapter 3, in ancient times the vast treeless steppe of Central Asia was home to nomadic groups whose livelihood depended on animal husbandry. The settled inhabitants along the steppe's borders lived in fear of these horse-riding warriors. At various times, nomads entered the urbanized states, seized power, and created empires. The nomads ruled such empires through existing political and social structures, absorbing the customs and cultures of the sedentary peoples in the process.

> **FOCUS**
> How did the geographical location and trade relations of the Kushan Empire affect its cultural traditions?

An early example of this dynamic occurred from around 50 to 233 C.E., when tribes originally from the western borderlands of China built an empire that included large parts of south-central Asia and India. These people, the Kushans, ruled a thriving multicultural empire that lasted for nearly two centuries. As the inscription at the beginning of this chapter indicates, the Kushan ruler considered himself equal to the great emperors of his time who ruled large urbanized territories, both to his east (China) and to his west (Parthia and Rome). That was not an idle boast—the Kushan Empire rivaled the other great empires of Eurasia in political power, wealth, and cultural production. The Kushan peoples are an excellent example of how nomads of Central Asia shaped the history of Eurasia.

Foundations of Empire

The introduction of horses (discussed in Chapter 3) increased the mobility of nomadic herders, which brought them in contact with various urbanized regions at the edges of the Central Asian steppe. Because they did not leave any writings themselves, we must rely on descriptions from sedentary neighbors to reconstruct their histories. Chinese sources report on the early history of one of these peoples, who would become known as Kushans. They describe struggles between nomadic groups on the western border of the Han state in around 100 B.C.E. The previously dominant Yuehzi (YOU-EH-juh) came under attack by another group, the Xiongnu (SHE-OONG-noo), who killed their king. The Yuehzi subsequently migrated westward, where one faction, the Great Yuehzi, occupied the region north of the Oxus River Valley that had only recently been resettled. The Great Yuehzi remained organized as five nomadic tribes, although they controlled cities in the Oxus River Valley whose inhabitants practiced irrigation agriculture (see Reading the Past: A Family of Chinese Historians Trace Early Kushan History).

The social and political organization of the Yuehzi did not change for more than a century, until one tribe gained supremacy over the other four in about 50 C.E. The Chinese called these people Kuei-shuang, a Chinese rendering of the name *Kusana* from Indian sources; today we use the name *Kushan*. Soon after dominating the other tribes, the Kushans conquered the regions to their south: Parthia, Bactria, and Gandhara. At the height of its power, the empire incorporated modern-day Afghanistan, Pakistan, and

READING THE PAST

A Family of Chinese Historians Traces Early Kushan History

In around 80 to 100 C.E., Ban Biao, Ban Gu, and Ban Zhao wrote the *History of the Former Han Dynasty*, which includes an account of the early history of the Kushan Empire. Information about the distant country came from envoys of the Han court, who visited the region to establish alliances against the Xiongnu on the northern border.

The king of the country of the Great Yuehzi resides at the city of Chien-shih, at a distance of 11,600 *li* [about 3850 miles] from Changan. It is not controlled by the [Chinese] governor-general [in Central Asia]. It has a population of 100,000 households, with 400,000 people and 100,000 excellent soldiers. . . . Its soil, climate, products, prevailing popular customs and money are the same as those of the An-hsi [Parthia]. [This country] produces one-humped camels. The Great Yuehzi originally formed a nomadic state; they moved about following their cattle, and had the same customs as the Xiongnu. As their archers numbered more than a hundred thousand, they were strong and treated the Xiongnu with contempt. Originally they lived between Tunhuang and Ch'i-lien. But when Mao-tun [Xiongnu leader, c. 209–174 B.C.E.]

had attacked and defeated the Yuehzi, and when Lao-shang [Xiongnu leader, c. 174–161 B.C.E.] had killed the Yuehzi [king] and had made a drinking vessel from his skull, then the Yuehzi went far away. They passed through Ta-yüan [Ferghana] and to the west [of that country] they smote Ta-hsia and subdued it. They had their capital north of the Kuei [Oxus] River and [this] they made their royal court.

Source: E. Zürcher, trans., "The Yüeh-chih and Kaniska in the Chinese Sources," *Papers on the Date of Kaniska*, ed. A. L. Basham (Leiden, Netherlands: Brill, 1968), 364–365.

EXAMINING THE EVIDENCE

1. How do the authors explain the migration of the Yuehzi, the Kushans' ancestors?

2. What is the lifestyle of the Yuehzi and their opponents, the Xiongnu?

northwest India (see Map 6.2). These were very wealthy lands, densely urbanized and home to multiple flourishing cultural traditions that the Kushan rulers readily absorbed.

A Merging of Cultural Influences

The Kushan Empire brought together regions with manifold traditions, and its far-reaching contacts with peoples abroad helped make it a culture that embraced an enormous diversity of influences. Like the leaders of the Persian Empire (see Chapter 4), Kushan rulers did not seek to impose a uniform identity on their subjects, but instead embraced the diverse cultures of their domain.

When the Yuehzi first arrived in the Oxus River region in the first century B.C.E., the people there worshiped a mixture of Iranian and Greek gods. The Iranian tradition was Zoroastrian, whereas the descendants of the Seleucid Empire worshiped Greek gods. The two traditions had already partly merged in that Iranian gods were equated with Greek deities. Indian influences were also present, representing both the Buddhist and Brahmanist traditions. When the Kushan Empire took over the region in around 50 C.E., its leaders sought to reinforce the legitimacy of their rule by using Greek, Iranian, and Bactrian imagery and ideas to explain and define their royal status.

The Kushans promoted Indian religious practices as well; later tradition honored the Kushan ruler Kanishka II as a great supporter of Buddhism. (The dates of the reign of

Multicultural Religion

MAP 6.2   **The Kushan Empire**

After migrating from western China to the Oxus River region of Central Asia, the Yuehzi created the Kushan Empire (50–233 C.E.), which by 150 C.E. controlled a large area of Central Asia as well as territories in modern-day Afghanistan, Pakistan, and India. Tolerant of existing traditions, the Kushan rulers promoted the merging of cultures, drawing inspiration from Iran and the Hellenized Roman world, with which they maintained a lively trade.

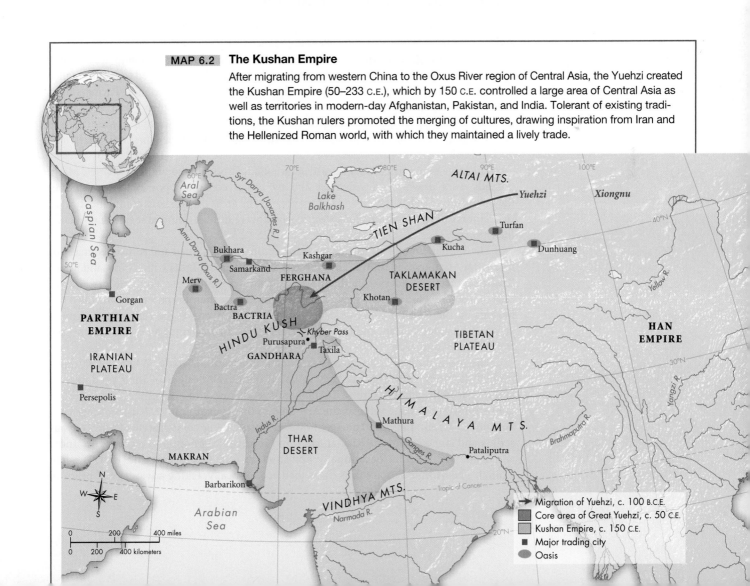

Migration of Yuehzi, c. 100 B.C.E.
Core area of Great Yuehzi, c. 50 C.E.
Kushan Empire, c. 150 C.E.
Major trading city
Oasis

Kanishka II are contested, but scholars agree that he ruled for twenty-three years starting sometime between 78 and 144 C.E.) One story relates that after he defeated the Indian state of Pataliputra, he chose the alms bowl of the Buddha rather than massive tribute as the price for his victory. Kanishka II built many Buddhist stupas and monasteries, and he sponsored the study of Buddhist texts. Because he encouraged contacts with China, Buddhism spread into that country; the earliest evidence for Chinese Buddhism dates to the second century C.E.

Gandharan Art and Writing

Art and literature also reflected the Kushan embrace of multiple cultural traditions. The Gandharan art style, which used Greek styles to portray traditional Indian figures such as the Buddha, flourished under the Kushans (see again At a Crossroads, page 170). Many Gandharan statues represent women with much sophistication and detail, and the art was a favorite of wealthy merchants. At the same time, imperial art represented the king in heavy robes and tall boots, based on Central Asian traditions. Local artistic practices in various regions of the Kushan Empire continued as well.

Likewise, many scripts and languages were in use. The Kushans used the Greek alphabet to write Greek and local languages. From India came two scripts called Brahmi and Kharosthi and the Prakrit and Sanskrit languages. The Kushans probably employed Indians as their administrators, and under them Buddhist monks spread Indian languages and scripts, which can be seen on coins and in official inscriptions. Sometimes they presented texts in several languages.

Farmers and Traders: The Kushan Economy

Farmers

The region north of the Oxus River receives too little rainfall for agriculture, but the river and its tributaries allow irrigation. People practiced irrigation before the Yuehzi arrived, and the Kushans greatly expanded and systematized the existing technology throughout their Central Asian provinces. They lengthened earlier canals and merged separate smaller systems into a network that covered mountain regions as well as lowlands. Farmers used plows with iron shears, which enabled more land to be cultivated than ever before. They grew highly varied crops, including cereals, fruits, and cotton. Animal husbandry was vitally important to the economy as well; the two-humped Bactrian camel was prized as a pack animal.

The large-scale agricultural infrastructure made it possible to build new cities. Many nomads were drawn to a sedentary life by urban economic possibilities, including the manufacture of household and luxury goods. The areas the Kushans commanded were rich in minerals and semiprecious stones, which were in high demand inside and outside the empire.

Traders

The Kushan Empire lay astride the transcontinental Silk Road and controlled many of its central Asian trading routes. The empire's territory linked India with China, and under Kushan protection traders from the Indian subcontinent spread out along the Silk Road to establish stations to the east. At its fullest extent, the Kushan Empire also controlled the harbors on the west Indian coast, leaving Kushan merchants at the center of exchanges among China, India, Iran, and the Mediterranean. The state gained an enormous income from taxes on this trade.

The production of coins greatly facilitated international trade. When the Kushans minted their first official coins, they imitated the Greek designs of their predecessors and inscribed the coins in Greek. To allow easy exchange with the Romans, they struck a gold coin with the same value as the one used in the Roman Empire. Kushan kings later abandoned Greek usages in coinage, however, introducing coins inscribed with various scripts and languages of the Kushan state and representing non-Greek gods from India and Iran. The Buddha occasionally appeared as well (see Seeing the Past: Kushan Coins). The Kushan Empire thus flourished economically, taking advantage of peaceful

Kushan Coins

Kushan Coin, c. 100 C.E. (Classical Numismatic Group, Inc.; http://www.cngcoins.com/.)

The Kushan emperors minted coins to facilitate trade with their neighbors. They provide a series of portraits of the various kings, who had themselves represented with inscriptions giving their names and titles and with religious figures whom they considered important. These coins vividly show how multiple cultures influenced the Kushans.

The gold coin shown here has the portrait of King Kanishka II on the front (left). He appears in clothing typical of horsemen of Central Asia—a heavy robe and thick boots—and he places an offering on a small altar to his right. His left hand holds a staff. The flames from his shoulders indicate his superhuman status. The inscription at the edge of the coin is in the Bactrian language using the Greek alphabet, to which a letter was added to render the sound /sh/. It reads "King of

Kings, Kanishka, the Kushan." On the back (right) appears an image of the Buddha, with his name written in Greek letters as "Boddo." Other coins of Kanishka depict Greek, Indian, and Iranian deities.

EXAMINING THE EVIDENCE

1. Judging from this example, in what ways do Kushan coins reflect the multiple religious influences on the empire?

2. What do these coins tell us about languages and scripts in the Kushan Empire?

conditions, the unification of diverse regions with different resources, and control over the trans-Asian trade routes.

The Kushans are one in a sequence of nomadic peoples from Central Asia whose interactions with surrounding urbanized areas profoundly influenced the histories of these regions. Through their wide-ranging contacts, the Kushans contributed to the development of all of Asia. Their acceptance of varied traditions led to a remarkable multiculturalism and the creation of dynamic new hybrid cultures. Although the nearly two-hundred-year Kushan supremacy ended with the rise of a new empire to the west, Sasanid Iran, remnants of a Kushan state survived into the ninth century C.E. In India, the disappearance of the Kushans gave the Guptas the freedom to create their own empire.

China's First Empires: The Qin and Han Dynasties 221 B.C.E.–220 C.E.

FOCUS

How did the early Chinese philosophers come to have a long-lasting influence on the intellectual development of the region?

In the east of Asia, the unified Shang and Zhou (joe) kingdoms of the second and early first millennia B.C.E. started to disintegrate in around 800 B.C.E. (see Chapter 3). Historians still see the period from 770 to 221 B.C.E. as part of the Zhou dynasty, but the political situation differed greatly from those of earlier centuries, when unity rather than fragmentation prevailed. The later Zhou dynasty is divided into the Spring and Autumn Period (770–481 B.C.E.) and the Period of the Warring States (480–221 B.C.E.). The name "Spring and Autumn Period" derives from a book called *The Spring and Autumn Annals*. It depicts a world of more than one hundred states routinely involved in wars, both among themselves and with inhabitants of the surrounding regions. Conflicts increased even more in the Period of the Warring States.

Perhaps inspired by the volatility of the time, revolutionary thinkers such as Confucius, Mencius (mehng-tsi-uz), Laozi (low-ZUH), and Lord Shang Yang founded intellectual movements that questioned human nature, the state, and political behavior. The implementation of their ideas led to a reconfiguration of political life that paved the way for the first Chinese empires, the Qin (chin), which was followed by the Han (hahn). These empires controlled a huge territory that at times stretched into Central Asia and southern China. Qin and Han rulers centralized and unified administrative practices. From about 500 B.C.E. to 200 C.E., culture flourished in China, especially scholarly writings. Scribes produced numerous copies of a wide variety of texts on law, medicine, divination, philosophy, and many other topics. In contrast to Indian thinkers, who generally focused on religious issues, Chinese scholars turned their attention to secular subjects and concerns. Therefore, we tend to label their teachings as philosophy—as we do for Greek thinkers of the time—rather than religion. Nonetheless, Indian, Chinese, and Greek thinkers were engaged in a common project. They all sought to understand and improve the societies in which they lived.

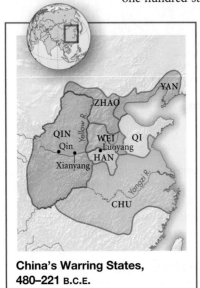

China's Warring States, 480–221 B.C.E.

Intellectual Churning: Confucians, Daoists, and Legalists

Confucius

Confucius (551–479 B.C.E.) dominates the intellectual history of this period, and his teachings have crucially influenced Chinese society and political life to this day. His own life, however, was rather uneventful. The son of an impoverished aristocrat from a small state of the later Zhou period, Confucius (from the Chinese name Kongfuzi, "Master Kong") was a good student and sought out teachers to learn new subjects. He obtained a minor government post in his native state, but in his thirties he turned to education, supporting himself by tutoring young aristocrats. Later in life he held higher government positions, but he fell out of favor with his local overlord because of his uncompromising support of the Zhou king. After traveling for twelve years to find employment in other states, he returned home to teach. During this time his fame grew as one who awakened the people from their ignorance. His followers grew in number, and the Han historian Sima Qian claims that, when Confucius died at the age of seventy-three, three thousand followers were studying with him.

It was these students who wrote down their conversations with him and thus preserved his teachings; Confucius himself did not write down his ideas. Probably compiled by 100 B.C.E. in the form known today, Confucius's *Analects* document the philosopher's ideas about human nature, behavior, and the state. He taught that proper conduct in all social interactions instilled in individuals a humaneness that emphasized benevolence and kindness. Like Indian thinkers of around the same time, Confucius urged that behavior adhere to a moral code: "For the gentleman integrity is the essence; the rules of decorum are the way he puts it into effect; humility is the way he brings it forth; sincerity is the way he develops it. Such indeed is what it means to be a gentleman."[7] As a former administrator, Confucius especially stressed respect for parents and superiors. He urged children to take care of their parents in old age and to mourn them after death for a three-year period, and he encouraged people to obey those above them in the social hierarchy.

Proper behavior, Confucius believed, should also be taught to highborn men who desired to become good rulers. He did not want to institute a new political system but to return to the centralized rule of the Zhou dynasty (see Chapter 3). He stressed that doing good would stop the forces of evil, including war. Confucius renounced coercion in government because it produced resentment among subjects rather than respect. Thus his teachings went beyond establishing moral guidelines for individuals. He believed that proper behavior by all men and women could help produce a more peaceful and prosperous society.

After Confucius's death, a number of different philosophers interpreted and further developed his teachings. Among the most influential was Mencius (c. 372–289 B.C.E.), who stressed the basic goodness of human nature. Mencius emphasized the importance of human compassion and believed all human beings shared the capacity to empathize with one another. The philosopher Xunzi (shoon-zuh) (c. 300–230 B.C.E.), by contrast, saw humans as basically greedy and selfish, and he urged leaders to adopt strict rules to prevent their subjects from doing evil.

Confucian Interpretations

Confucius taught that proper behavior involved active participation in society. In contrast, those who came to be known as Daoists urged people to seek a simple and honest life. They should withdraw from society and meditate, forsaking the pursuit of wealth and prestige and seeking a peaceful inner life. If many people behaved well, the world would be in harmony and follow its natural course, which was far superior to a world that people tried to actively control. These teachings are ascribed to a sixth-century B.C.E. sage, Laozi, but they probably represent the work of more than one philosopher collected in the third century B.C.E. under Laozi's name. In the Later Han period after 25 C.E., Daoism became an official religion, closely associated with Buddhism, with which it shared many ideas, and Laozi was depicted as a god.

Daoism

Rather than stressing practical guidance to rulers and officials, Daoism focused on personal introspection. On the opposite end of the spectrum was a school of thought called Legalism, which focused on the ruler, the social hierarchy, and practical aspects of government. At the height of the political turbulence of the Warring States period, Lord Shang Yang (c. 390–338 B.C.E.) put legalistic ideas into practice in the then small state of Qin, paving the way for the later unification of China. He believed every man should have an occupation that benefited the state, so he introduced compulsory military service and forced others to become farmers, whose activities government administrators monitored closely. He introduced strict laws—hence the name *Legalism*—that harshly punished even the smallest crime. Leaving trash on the street, for example, could lead to the amputation of a hand or foot. He assumed that fear would prevent people from wrongdoing; the only reward they could expect for correct behavior was absence of punishment. Lord Shang also introduced the principle of collective responsibility. If a soldier disobeyed, his entire family was executed. When the Later Qin state forced Lord Shang's ideas onto the entire population of China, its ruler became so unpopular that the people rebelled and overthrew the government.

Legalism

Unification and Centralization: The Worlds of Qin and Han

The great philosophers of ancient China lived in a period of political turmoil and fragmentation. Although the Zhou kings nominally ruled the entire region, after 771 B.C.E. China was actually carved into numerous small principalities. It was only after five hundred years of fragmentation that rulers, inspired by the teachings of Confucius, Lord Shang, and others, restored China's political unity (see Map 6.3).

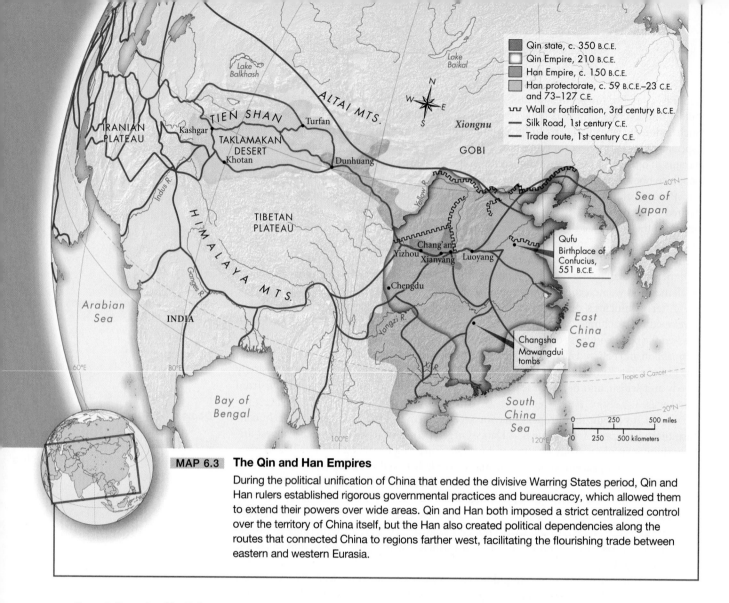

MAP 6.3 **The Qin and Han Empires**

During the political unification of China that ended the divisive Warring States period, Qin and Han rulers established rigorous governmental practices and bureaucracy, which allowed them to extend their powers over wide areas. Qin and Han both imposed a strict centralized control over the territory of China itself, but the Han also created political dependencies along the routes that connected China to regions farther west, facilitating the flourishing trade between eastern and western Eurasia.

Foundations for Qin Rule: Changes in Warfare and Administration

Two innovations dramatically changed the nature of warfare in the period of political fragmentation. First, chariotry had been the core of the Shang army, but it lost its effectiveness in mountainous or marshy terrain. In its place, infantry rose in importance, requiring local leaders to force thousands of farmers and other commoners to fight. The chariot-based aristocracy disappeared in favor of a more meritocratic army in which a soldier from any social background could rise up the military ranks, similar to what we saw in ancient Greece (discussed in Chapter 5). Second, after Central Asian nomads introduced iron technology into China, iron became the preferred metal for weapons. Not only were iron weapons much stronger than bronze, but iron ore was much more widely available than copper and tin. More and better weapons were thus produced more cheaply.

As the military aristocracy declined and family ties became less important in determining social status, bureaucracies arose to administer the states. Inspired by Legalism, lords instituted centralized systems of taxation and a military draft. Over time, some ten dominant states developed from the multitude of smaller ones, absorbing neighbors and adding new territories. Although they warred against one another regularly, they also traded goods, especially luxury items such as silk and craft products. A new educated elite arose among the administrators, trained in the ideas Confucius had introduced.

Shi Huangdi, First Emperor of China

The state that most successfully applied Legalism was Qin in western China, where Lord Shang had been minister of state. In 237 B.C.E., the Qin ruler started an all-out war, and after fifteen years he had unified an immense part of China (two-thirds of today's territory) under his rule. He succeeded because his state had a strong economic base and he could raise numerous troops and arm them with iron weapons. In 221 B.C.E., proclaiming himself Shi

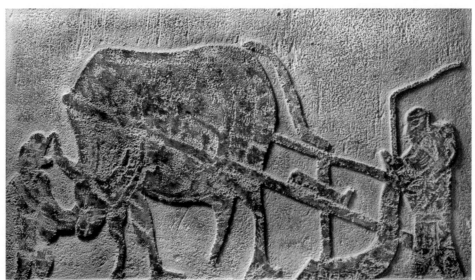

Han Farmers at Work

Like that of all ancient states, imperial China's success depended to a great extent on agricultural development. The first emperor, Qin ruler Shi Huangdi, instituted reforms that expanded China's farming capabilities. Shown here is a stone relief from the Han dynasty of two men plowing with an ox-drawn plow. The relief was originally part of the decoration of a tomb built sometime between 200 B.C.E. and 200 C.E. (Werner Forman Archive/Topham/The Image Works.)

Huangdi (shee huang-dee), "First August Emperor," he began a series of reforms that would determine the political organization of China for more than four hundred years and inspire the norms of centralized rule in China up to the early twentieth century C.E. The modern name *China* derives from *Qin*.

Shi Huangdi (r. 221–210 B.C.E.) considered the expansion of China's agriculture the basis of progress, and, like the Babylonians, Kushans, and others we have discussed, he ordered large irrigation canals to be dug. He also sponsored the exploitation of new territories by giving land to farmers, whom the state closely supervised. Shi Huangdi first and foremost sought political centralization through three branches of government: taxation authorities, the military, and supervisors of officials. The Qin Empire was subdivided into provinces (at first thirty-six and later forty-two), and he and his successors governed it rigidly. They forced people to construct four thousand miles of roads to connect the provinces to one another and to the capital Xianyang (shan-yahng). Another large-scale public work, the result of backbreaking labor by three hundred thousand men, was the building of defensive walls at the northern border of the state, the forerunner to the Great Wall of China. Shi Huangdi also standardized the script his bureaucrats used. Instead of preserving the local variants that had developed out of Shang writing, he used a unified script to record the variety of languages spoken in the empire. He also imposed a single system of weights and measures and of coins.

The First August Emperor did not tolerate dissent. Indeed, according to late Han sources, Shi Huangdi assassinated 460 Confucian scholars who had criticized him, and in 213 B.C.E. he ordered that all books be burned except practical works on agriculture, medicine, and divination. The great classics of Chinese literature and philosophy would have disappeared had copies not been hidden or memorized by people who transmitted them orally. Thus Shi Huangdi sought to unify his people through very different policies than those of the Kushans or the Persians. They had seen diversity as a source of strength, but Shi Huangdi saw in it the potential for disorder, chaos, and rebellion. Suppressing difference and dissent, he sought to impose a unified culture on China, one in which all aspects of Chinese life served the interests of the centralized state.

One of the most massive building projects of Shi Huangdi's reign reflects the concentration of power in his hands. This is his tomb near his capital at Xianyang, which archaeologists have been excavating carefully since the 1970s. Only a small part has been uncovered so far, but what we already know is astounding. The emperor created an underground palace, surrounding himself with an army of seventy-three hundred life-size terra cotta statues. They depict footmen, archers, charioteers, and cavalry, and although the bodies were mass-produced, the faces show individual characteristics, as if real soldiers had posed for them.

Sima Qian described the central tomb (so far unexcavated) and claimed that it had a bronze foundation to protect against underground water, representations of seas and rivers composed of mercury made to flow by special mechanisms, and crossbow traps that the motion of an intruder would trigger. According to legend, seven hundred thousand men built the tomb and were imprisoned in it when they finished. Childless royal concubines also accompanied their master in death. Moreover, the tomb was filled with treasures from all over the land. Pearl-inlaid representations of the constellations of the sky covered the ceiling, and the floor displayed the extent of the empire. The entire complex seems to have been intended to continue the emperor's rule in the afterlife.

Rise of the Han Empire

The death of Shi Huangdi in 210 B.C.E. effectively meant the end of his dynasty, as subsequent palace intrigues weakened the central hold of the state and made peasant rebellions possible. Resentful of the Qin's harsh rule, mobs sacked the court and killed imperial officials. But China did not once again fall into pieces—a determined and popular rebel leader, Liu Bang (lee-OO bangh), managed to establish full dominance in 206 B.C.E. Liu Bang created a new nobility by giving two-thirds of the empire as kingdoms to relatives and supporters, keeping only one-third under direct state administration. His generosity generated support for himself and his dynasty, which he named Han after his home region (see again Map 6.3). The Han Empire governed China for four hundred years (206 B.C.E.–220 C.E.) with only a short interruption (9–24 C.E.). Historians refer to the first half of the Han period, in which the capital was at Chang'an in the west, as Former Han (206 B.C.E.–25 C.E.); they call the second half, in which the capital was at Luoyang farther east, Later Han (25–220 C.E.).

Although Liu Bang had moderated the Qin concentration of power by reestablishing the earlier system of inherited domains under aristocrats, the forces of centralization remained strong. The most prominent ruler of the Former Han, Emperor Wu, held the throne from 141 to 87 B.C.E.; he greatly expanded the government's powers and ruled with an iron fist. Wu needed a large bureaucracy administered by men with the proper skills to perform their tasks. Although local noble families recommended those who became officials, Wu introduced a **civil service examination** to determine where to place each appointee. He also centralized the education system. Whereas previously, private tutors (such as Confucius) had taught young men, Wu created a central school whose core was composed of five so-called Erudite Scholars, each a specialist in an aspect of Confucius's teaching. At first each scholar had fifty students apiece, but soon the student population swelled to three thousand, a number that grew larger over time. The graduates, who became the empire's officials, in turn formed a new class of educated men more loyal to the state than to the aristocratic families. Because Confucian ideas formed the basis of their education, the central role of these ideas in formal training was confirmed for two millennia. Emperor Wu's state thus combined the pragmatism of Legalism with an intellectual training based on Confucian traditions. In the process, he created a Chinese elite connected by their participation in a shared intellectual tradition.

Highly centralized and well organized, the Former Han state relied on agricultural resources for its support. In addition, a state monopoly on iron and salt allowed the emperor to charge artificially high prices for these vital products. Trade of luxury goods, especially silk and lacquer ware, also brought substantial income to the empire. But the harsh system of government stirred the people's anger.

Shi Huangdi's Terra Cotta Army

The tomb of the first emperor of China near his capital at Xianyang is one of the greatest archaeological sites of the ancient world, and it is still mostly unexcavated. A massive army of soldiers surrounds the tomb, each life-size figure made from baked clay and shaped to show the individual warrior's features. Created shortly before 200 B.C.E., the complex reveals a commitment to the dead emperor on a par with what we see in Egypt and other ancient cultures. (Alfred Ko/CORBIS.)

A combination of causes led to the collapse of the Han Empire. By the end of the first century B.C.E., a few local families had acquired huge estates and reduced the population to the status of slaves. A usurper seized the throne in 9 C.E., temporarily discontinued the Han dynasty, and freed the slaves. When the Han regained the throne by 25 C.E., the local landed gentry became even more powerful than before. In consequence, large numbers of peasants from several provinces rose in rebellion. Although the state crushed the uprisings, they weakened the central government, and by 220 C.E. the Han dynasty fell, leaving China politically fragmented once again.

The leaders of both the Qin and Han empires were driven by a desire to centralize power. In both dynasties, a government bureaucracy applied uniform practices throughout the empire. State-trained officials, chosen for their abilities rather than family connections, staffed the administration. Their allegiance to the state created a powerful unifying force. The pressures of decentralization remained strong, however—especially the resilience of aristocratic families, whose wealth allowed them to control local populations. The competing forces of centralization and decentralization led those in power to exploit the general population, who, pushed to the limit, grew to resent all authority and ultimately overthrew both empires.

Preserving and Spreading the Written Word

The Chinese political elite, interconnected by its education and intellectual training, placed special value on the written word. That written texts were important in Qin and Han China has been amply demonstrated in recent years through the excavation of elite tombs. Members of the bureaucracy buried themselves with their libraries, which consisted of manuscripts written on bamboo and silk. The physical objects themselves were very valuable. The use of bamboo forced the scribes to write the characters in long vertical columns, a layout that survived in Chinese writing until the twentieth century C.E., when writers began to use horizontal lines in letters and books (see Lives and Livelihoods: Papermakers).

Three tombs excavated in the 1970s at Mawangdui in the Hunan province of southern China reveal the high value that the Chinese elite accorded manuscripts. They belonged to a local lord who had supported the Han dynasty, his wife, and a man who died in his thirties, probably their son. Whereas the woman's burial stands out because of the perfect preservation of the tomb gifts, including clothing, lacquer ware, ceramics, and food, the son's burial is astonishing for its extensive library. On bamboo strips appear numerous medical treatises, including recipes to enhance sexual pleasure. The silk manuscripts uncovered in this tomb include several of the classic works of ancient Chinese philosophy, as well as books on astronomy, astrology, fortune-telling, calendar making, politics, military affairs, ideology, culture, science, and technology. Moreover, the earliest preserved maps from China come from this tomb: one shows the region around the tomb; another, the borderland with the south; and the third, the location of military garrisons. The fact that the dead man had his library buried with him suggests that he wanted to show off his ability to read and write, a rare skill that was the hallmark of the upper levels of Chinese society.

The Former Han period was crucial to the preservation of the Chinese literature of the earlier Zhou and Warring States periods—works that would determine the form of literary production for millennia. The great philosophers of early China were closely connected to this literary flowering. A tradition developed that Confucius, who left no writings of his own, had edited earlier literary works, such as the *Book of Songs* (see Chapter 3). When Emperor Wu made Confucius's teachings the basis of education, these works became mandatory reading for all Chinese bureaucrats. They memorized, for example, the 305 poems of the *Book of Songs*, whose rhyming format later Chinese poets imitated. Tradition credits the founder of Daoism, Laozi, as the author of the *Classic of Integrity and the Way*, a discussion in verse of a tranquil and harmonious life. The work uses a vivid and powerful poetic imagery that has inspired many later writers both in China and abroad. It has been translated more often than almost any other work in world literature, with some forty English translations published since 1900. *Classic of Integrity and the Way* is a rather short

civil service examination First instituted in Han China, a centrally administered test for applicants to government jobs that measures their qualifications; the goal was to base appointments on merit rather than political or other connections.

Papermakers

Early Chinese Paper
The invention of paper made writing materials much cheaper in China. This early example of paper was used for administrative purposes. Meant to be read from right to left and from top to bottom, it gives accounts of grain with the prices at the end of each line. (© 2011 The British Library (Or. 8212/499, recto).)

History shows us countless instances of one region's invention spreading worldwide over the centuries and becoming so common that we now take it for granted. One such invention was paper, developed in China in around 100 C.E. According to Chinese tradition, a courtier named Ts'ai Lun (tsy loon) invented paper and presented it to the Han emperor in 105 C.E. Earlier Chinese had written on bamboo strips or on expensive materials such as silk. Ts'ai Lun produced his new writing material from vegetable fibers, as well as tree bark, hemp, rags, and fishing nets, all of which were relatively cheap.

The making of paper involved several steps. The raw materials were ripped into fibers that were washed, cooked, and mixed into a thick liquid. Workers then dipped rectangular wooden frames into the liquid to form thin sheets, which they left to dry on the moulds before removing the resulting sheets and bleaching and cutting them. We know little of the individual workers involved, but they clearly had very specialized skills. Chinese sources praise several of them for having refined the product over the centuries. One gave paper a shining appearance, for example, and another discovered that using a special tree bark made the paper ideal for calligraphy, the art of writing that Chinese much admired. Production by Chinese papermakers was enormous: in around 800 C.E. the finance ministry alone required half a million sheets annually.

At first, the Chinese carefully guarded the technique of papermaking, but they could not contain its spread. Traveling monks took it to Korea and Japan, where people started to produce the material in the early seventh century C.E. Later that century, people in India read paper books written in Sanskrit. Chinese prisoners captured in the 793 C.E. Battle of Talas River (discussed in Chapter 9) taught people of the Middle East how to manufacture paper, and one year

Sima Qian, Father of Chinese Dynastic History

text, only about some five thousand Chinese characters long, but its influence on later Chinese and world literature has been immense.

The writing of history in prose flourished under the Han dynasty. China's counterpart to Greece's Herodotus was Sima Qian (c. 145–90 B.C.E.), whose *Records of the Historian* has defined our modern understanding of early Chinese history. The work ends with an autobiographical section in which Sima Qian dramatically recounts how he fell from the emperor's favor for backing a disgraced general. He refused to commit suicide, which would have been considered honorable, accepting instead the punishment of castration so that he could continue his writing. So massive that no full translation in a European language exists, Sima Qian's history has 130 chapters containing more than half a million characters.

Whereas Herodotus had to rely heavily on secondary accounts from such sources as Egyptian priests, Sima Qian could base his work on earlier Chinese writings, including

later Baghdad opened its first paper mill. Because the Middle East lacked the plant materials used in China, papermakers found substitutes, mostly linen rags. Middle Eastern craftsmen produced increasing supplies of the paper, which was useful for writing but also for wrapping and as decoration. Europeans at first imported the material from Middle Eastern centers of production such as Damascus, but by the fourteenth century they had founded paper mills of their own. The earlier materials for writing—tree bark in India and parchment in the Middle East and Europe, for example—had long-lasting popularity, but the relative cheapness of paper and its ease of use finally made it the dominant medium for writing. When Europeans invented the printing press in around 1450, paper's success as a writing tool was guaranteed.

For centuries, paper manufacture was the domain of artisans who worked in small workshops and produced sheets individually. In around 1800 two inventions revolutionized production. The primary basic material became wood pulp, which is much more abundant than the rags and bark in use earlier, and in 1798, the Frenchman Nicholas-Louis Robert invented a machine that combined all production steps. Once a time-consuming and expensive process, papermaking became relatively quick and cheap.

Paper's effect on culture was far reaching. Its use allowed the written word to spread much more widely, and the increased access to writing encouraged literacy. The use of paper for pamphlets and newspapers in the modern period made it possible for political ideologies to reach large audiences. Even today, when we rely on our computers for so much of our communication, it is hard to imagine a world without paper.

PAPERMAKING

c. 100 C.E.	Paper invented in China
300–400 C.E.	Paper becomes the dominant writing material in China
600–610 C.E.	First paper in Korea and Japan
751 C.E.	First paper in Central Asia
793 C.E.	First paper in the Middle East
1300–1400 C.E.	First paper mills in Europe
c. 1450 C.E.	European invention of the printing press
1798 C.E.	Frenchman Nicholas-Louis Robert invents the papermaking machine

QUESTIONS TO CONSIDER

1. What writing materials existed before the invention of paper?

2. How long did it take for papermaking to spread all over Eurasia?

3. What explains the success of paper over other writing materials?

For Further Information:
Bunch, Bryan H. *The History of Science and Technology: A Browser's Guide to the Great Discoveries, Inventions, and the People Who Made Them, from the Dawn of Time to Today*, 2004.
Tsuen-Hsuin, Tsien. "Paper and Printing." In vol. 5, *Science and Civilisation in China*. Edited by Joseph Needham, 1985.
Twitchett, Denis. *Printing and Publishing in Medieval China*. New York: Frederick C. Beil, 1983.

records of speeches and events, lists of rulers, and similar documents. From these sources, he developed the idea that a sequence of dynasties had always ruled all of China, a tradition that has continued in Chinese historical writing until modern times. He started with a mythological distant past, when sages brought civilization to humanity. Afterward the Xia, Shang, and Zhou dynasties (discussed in Chapter 3) ruled the country as a whole. He even calculated the dates when kings ruled and gave details on battles and other events. By suggesting that unified centralization under a dynasty was normal for the region, Sima Qian wanted to show that Han efforts at empire building were in keeping with tradition.

Sima Qian's history stops at around 100 B.C.E., but a family of scholars from the first century C.E. carried on the tradition of dynastic history. The father, Ban Biao (bahn bi-ah-ow), started a work called *History of the Former Han Dynasty*, and his son, Ban Gu (bahn gu), continued it. Finally, the emperor ordered Gu's sister, Ban Zhao (bahn jow), to finish the work,

Ban Zhao

giving her access to the state archives. Ban Zhao took the narrative up until the interruption of the Han dynasty in the first decade C.E. Others continued the genre of dynastic history, and in 1747 C.E. the combined work of this family and subsequent authors amounted to 219 volumes, an unparalleled continuous record of the history of a country.

Ban Zhao (c. 45–120 C.E.) was a remarkable woman in a period when most families saw their daughters as little more than economic burdens. Coming from a scholarly family, she was well educated before her marriage at the age of fourteen. Still young when her husband died, she joined her brother at court at age thirty, an unusual step when widows of the time were expected to stay with their husbands' families. At court she gained influence with the empress Dou, who in 92 C.E. was accused of treason; her supporters, including Zhao's brother Ban Gu, were exiled or executed. As a woman, Zhao escaped severe punishment, and she was given the task of finishing the official history of the Han dynasty. At the same time she taught young women, including a girl called Deng, who later went on to become empress. Zhao's political influence was enormous. She also wrote numerous literary and scholarly works, which her daughter-in-law collected after Zhao's death. At first, her fame derived primarily from her *History*, but from about 800 C.E. on, her *Lessons for Women* gained enormous popularity (see Reading the Past: Women in Han China). Men used it to justify the inferior role of women in society, but in

READING THE PAST

Women in Han China

Ban Zhao's *Lessons for Women* of the early second century C.E. made her the most famous female author in Chinese history. Although she wrote the work as personal advice to women, men later used the book to prescribe how women ought to behave in relation to men.

A woman ought to have four qualifications: 1. womanly virtue, 2. womanly words, 3. womanly bearing, and 4. womanly work. Now what is called womanly virtue need not be brilliant ability, exceptionally different from others. Womanly words need be neither clever in debate nor keen in conversation. Womanly appearance requires neither a pretty nor a perfect face and form. Womanly work need not be work done more skillfully than that of others.

To guard carefully her chastity, to control circumspectly her behavior, in every motion to exhibit modesty, and to model each act on the best usage—this is womanly virtue.

To choose her words with care, to avoid vulgar language, to speak at appropriate times, and not to weary others with much conversation may be called the characteristics of womanly words.

To wash and scrub filth away, to keep cloths and ornaments fresh and clean, to wash the head and bathe the body regularly, and to keep the person free from

disgrace and filth may be called the characteristics of womanly bearing.

With wholehearted devotion to sew and to weave, to love not gossip and silly laughter, in cleanliness and order to prepare the wine and food for serving guests may be called the characteristics of womanly work.

These four qualifications characterize the greatest virtue of a woman. No woman can afford to be without them. In fact they are very easy to possess if a woman only treasure them in her heart. The ancients had a saying: "Is Love far off? If I desire love, then love is at hand." So can it be said of these qualifications.

Source: Victor H. Mair, ed., "Pan Chao, *Lessons for Women*," *The Columbia Anthology of Traditional Chinese Literature* (New York: Columbia University Press, 1994), 537–538.

EXAMINING THE EVIDENCE

1. What are the basic tenets of Ban Zhao's advice to women?

2. Why can this passage from the independent and politically influential Zhao be interpreted as an argument for women's secondary role in society?

reality Zhao had written practical advice to her daughters on how to survive in their husbands' family homes. When Zhao died shortly before 120 C.E., Empress Deng officially mourned her, an unusual honor for a commoner.

From 500 B.C.E. to 200 C.E., then, the foundations of Chinese culture were established in arts and sciences as well as politics. The chaos and disorder of the Spring and Autumn Period and the Warring States period inspired many of these developments. Hoping to stabilize their society, scholars developed philosophies with long-lasting influence, and politicians gave these philosophies practical applications in statecraft. Politically, imperial administrations were highly centralized and harsh, but the forces of decentralization also remained strong. Both the central administration and the local elites demanded much from the general population, and in the end their excessive demands may have led to the collapse of the entire system.

COUNTERPOINT
Tamil Kingdoms of South India

The development of large, highly centralized empires characterized much of Eurasian history in the centuries from 500 B.C.E. to 500 C.E. But imperial states were not universal in Asia. On the fringes of the empires in this chapter were societies with very different social and political structures whose populations created their own classical traditions. One such nonimperial region is the south of the Indian peninsula, the Tamil regions, which preserved ancient cultural traditions from southern India that differed significantly from those of the Aryas in the north.

FOCUS

How did southern Indian developments differ from those in other parts of Asia?

Rise of the Tamil Kingdoms

In around 250 B.C.E., the Mauryan emperor Ashoka referred to people in the Tamil regions as Cholas, Cheras, and Pandyas. At that time they were still organized as chiefdoms—that is, social hierarchies whose leaders had authority over small clan groups. Despite their relatively simple social and political organization, the archaeological remains show that these societies had far-reaching trade contacts. Megalithic burials appear throughout southern India. These large stone monuments take a variety of forms, including dolmen (two or more vertical stones supporting a horizontal slab), single standing stones, stone circles, and rock-cut chambers. This variety suggests that the builders had different cultural traditions, but the burials all contained iron tools and the same type of pottery. The tombs contained the bodies of one or more persons, each with small amounts of valuables such as carnelian beads and gold objects. They date from the entire first millennium B.C.E.; the most recent ones contain Roman coins from the last century B.C.E. The coins show that Tamil areas benefited as much from long-distance trade as the regions under imperial control to the north. South India's main export was pepper, which people used as condiment, food preservative, and medication for digestive problems. The Romans imported so much pepper that in around the year 77 C.E. the writer Pliny claimed it drained the empire's cash resources. He grumbled, "Pepper has nothing to recommend it in either fruit or berry. To think that its only pleasing quality is pungency and that we go all the way to India to get this!"[8]

Probably because a more centralized political structure benefited trade, small kingdoms with a limited number of cities arose in southern India. No empires developed, but competition among these kingdoms was fierce and warfare was a regular aspect of people's lives.

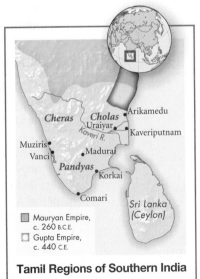

Mauryan Empire, c. 260 B.C.E.

Gupta Empire, c. 440 C.E.

Tamil Regions of Southern India

Dolmen in Southern India
The cultures of southern India were distinct from those in the north. Among the unique southern features is the use of megalithic constructions for burial, such as these dolmen from Marayoor in the state of Kerala, each made from four massive standing stone slabs with a fifth slab on top. Dolmen were used for burial for several centuries during the first millennium B.C.E., probably for the leaders of the communities who built and maintained them. (Dinodia Photos.)

Tamil Culture and Society

As in Archaic Greece, war inspired a literature that praised valor and glory in battle. Like Greek poets, Tamil poets composed works dealing with human emotions, such as love and friendship. Tamil poetry of the early centuries C.E. represents a rich South Asian tradition very distinct from the Sanskrit tradition of northern India, and it is still the pride of the region today. Tamil is a Dravidian language, fully distinct from the Indo-European languages of northern India. Although they had contacts with the north, until 250 C.E. Tamil writers resisted the influence of Sanskrit. The poets were mostly men, but thirty-two women have also been identified as authors. All belonged to the educated upper class, and some traveled from court to court to recite their work. One of the most renowned was the poet Auvaiyar. Fifty-nine of her poems are preserved, many of them in praise of King Atiyaman, at whose court she resided.

Contemporary Indians from the north saw the Tamils as unsophisticated barbarians, and modern scholars long ignored their literature. But today, scholars appreciate Tamil poetry's sophistication and its portrayals of the strength and nobility of human emotions under the hard conditions of incessant warfare. In this example, a wife mourns a dying warrior:

> I cannot cry out,
> I'm afraid of tigers,
> I cannot hold you,
> your chest is too wide
> for my lifting.
>
> Death
> has no codes
> and has dealt you wrong,
> may he
> shiver as I do!
>
> Hold my wrist
> of bangles,
> let's go to the shade
> of that hill.
> Just try and walk a little.[9]

The poems shed light on the position of women in Tamil society. They assign married women with children a positive role, representing them as a great asset to their husbands.

The poems portray widows, however, in a negative way. Widows were forced to lead an ascetic life to reduce the threat to others they were believed to pose. Poems suggest that they shaved their heads, slept on stone beds, and ate poor food.

The poems also clearly distinguish the various livelihoods practiced in southern India. Each depended on a specific natural environment—some groups gathered and hunted, others fished, others herded animals, and some farmed the fields. A fifth group made a living from trade. All the groups started out organized as clans, but as trade grew and cities developed, clans gave way to urban social hierarchies.

Political leaders in southern India seized control of the trade because of the wealth it produced. The poetry they sponsored in their courts celebrated their rule as kings, placing them at the center of society and honoring their military valor. Their power is reflected in the enormous size of their megalithic burial tombs, which required massive construction efforts. Although Tamil culture was exposed to influences from the north, it maintained its independence for centuries. In many ways, the grandeur of its culture equaled that of the great empires of Asia, but the kingdoms that produced Tamil culture were much less centralized and complex. Because great empires tend to dominate our view of the past, we sometimes get the false impression that only empires can develop enduring and influential cultural traditions. The Tamil kingdoms of ancient India prove this impression wrong.

Conclusion

When Dashafota carved the second-century-C.E. inscription translated at the start of this chapter, he knew that his king, Kanishka II, ruled one of a string of empires in Eurasia. In the east, the empires covered large parts of India, Central Asia, and China, and in each of these regions the teachings of great thinkers from the fifth to first centuries B.C.E. profoundly influenced later history. The Buddha and Confucius, among many others, had reacted to the tumultuous social and political conditions of their lifetimes, focusing on personal behavior and responsibility. The empires that arose after their deaths integrated their revolutionary religions and philosophies into ideas about the state, introducing a common ruling ideology to vast territories with multiple cultural traditions. Prescriptions for proper individual behavior and personal development could spread into regions with very different environments: nomads from the Central Asian steppe, for example, adopted teachings the Buddha had developed in the forested regions of northern India. Because every individual was part of a large state, new ideologies could define each person's role and responsibilities.

Although empires promoted the spread of new teachings, political centralization was not a precondition for cultural flowering. In south India too competing Tamil kingdoms developed enduring cultural traditions. Also, while the great empires of this period succumbed to the forces of decentralization, the traditions they had promoted survived and spread over all of Asia, a process aided by the continent's commercial connections. The multiplicity of ideas and traditions was never abandoned, and a myriad of religious teachings and philosophies coexisted in this world. When we turn next to the spread of the Roman Empire in western Eurasia, we will see similar cultural and religious innovations whose impact also persists today.

NOTES

1. Sten Konow, "The Ara Inscription of Kanishka II: The Year 41," *Epigraphica Indica* 14 (1917): 143 (with slight changes).
2. Ainslee T. Embree, ed., *Sources of Indian Tradition*, 2d ed. (New York: Columbia University Press, 1988), 1:144.
3. Ibid., 1:282.
4. Plutarch, "Life of Alexander," 62, 4.

5. *Sources of Indian Tradition*, 1:148.
6. Leonard Nathan, *The Transport of Love* (Berkeley: University of California Press, 1976), 83.
7. Confucius, *Analects* 15, 17, *Chinese Civilization: A Sourcebook*, 2d. ed., trans. Patricia Buckley Ebrey (New York: The Free Press, 1993), 18.
8. Pliny, *Natural History* 12.14, trans. H. Rackham (Cambridge, MA: Harvard University Press, 1968), 4:21.
9. Paul Davis et al., eds., *The Bedford Anthology of World Literature* (Boston: Bedford/St. Martin's, 2004), Book 2, 222–223.

RESOURCES FOR RESEARCH

India: Thinkers, Traders, and Courtly Cultures, 500 B.C.E.–500 C.E.

This period is discussed in numerous historical surveys of India. Because Buddhism and Hinduism had a long and continuing influence, many books treat the early developments of these religions within a long-term context.

Avari, Burjor. *India, the Ancient Past: A History of the Indian Sub-continent from c. 7000 B.C. to A.D. 1200*. 2007.
Basham, A. L., ed. *A Cultural History of India*. 1997.
Basham, A. L. *The Wonder That Was India: A Survey of the Culture of the Indian Sub-continent Before the Coming of the Muslims*. 1981.
*Embree, Ainslee T., ed. *Sources of Indian Tradition*, 2d ed., vol. 1. 1988.
* Internet Indian history sourcebook: http://www.fordham.edu/halsall/india/indiasbook.html.
Keown, Damien. *Buddhism: A Very Short Introduction*. 1996.
Knott, Kim. *Hinduism: A Very Short Introduction*. 1998.
Kulke, Hermann, and Dietmar Rothermund. *A History of India*, 3d ed. 1998.

The Kushan Peoples of Central Asia, 100 B.C.E.–233 C.E.

The Kushan Empire is often discussed within the wider context of the histories of India or Central Asia.

Frye, R. *The Heritage of Central Asia: From Antiquity to the Turkish Expansion*. 1996.
Harmatta, János, ed. *History of Civilizations of Central Asia*. Vol. 2, *The Development of Sedentary and Nomadic Civilizations: 700 B.C. to A.D. 250*. 1994.
Liu, Xinru. *Ancient India and Ancient China: Trade and Religious Exchanges A.D. 1–600*. 1988.
(A rough guide to Kushan history): http://www.kushan.org.
(For a selection of Kushan artworks): Heilbrunn timeline of art history. http://www.metmuseum.org/toah/hd/kush/hd_kush.htm.

China's First Empires: The Qin and Han Dynasties, 221 B.C.E.–220 C.E.

As is true for India, discussions of this period appear in various general histories of China. Because of the continuing impact of ancient Chinese philosophers, their ideas are often discussed in a long-term context.

Clements, Jonathan. *Confucius: A Biography*. 2004.
*de Bary, Wm. Theodore, ed. *Sources of Chinese Tradition*. 1999.
*Ebrey, Patricia Buckley, ed. *Chinese Civilization: A Sourcebook*, 2d ed. 1993.
Gascoine, Bamber. *A Brief History of the Dynasties of China*. 2003.
Hansen, Valerie. *The Open Empire: A History of China to 1600*. 2000.
(For a collection of ancient Chinese textual sources): Internet East Asian sourcebook. http://www.fordham.edu/halsall/eastasia/eastasiasbook.html.
*Mair, Victor H., ed. *The Columbia Anthology of Traditional Chinese Literature*. 1994.
Portal, Jane, ed. *The First Emperor: China's Terracotta Army*. 2007.
*Sima Qian. *The First Emperor: Selections from the* Historical Records. Edited by K. E. Brashier. Translated by Raymond Dawson. 2007.
Wei-ming, Tu. "Confucius and Confucianism," in the *New Encyclopaedia Britannica*, 15th ed., vol. 16. 1997.

COUNTERPOINT: Tamil Kingdoms of South India

Many books on India also discuss the Tamil area. The first two listed here translate numerous Tamil poems.

*Hart, George L., and Hank Heifetz, trans. and eds. *The Four Hundred Songs of War and Wisdom*. 1999.
*Ramanujan, A. K. *Poems of Love and War*. 1985.
Ray, H. P. *The Archaeology of Seafaring in Ancient South Asia*. 2003.
Thapar, Romila. *Early India from the Origins to A.D. 1300*. 2002.

* Primary source.

▶ **For additional primary sources from this period**, see *Sources of Crossroads and Cultures*.

▶ **For Web sites, images, and documents related to topics in this chapter**, see Make History at bedfordstmartins.com/smith.

The major global development in this chapter ▶ The revolutionary religious and cultural developments in India and China that took place between 500 B.C.E. and 500 C.E. and remained fundamental to the history of Asia.

IMPORTANT EVENTS

c. 600–500 B.C.E.	Laozi, who inspired Daoism
c. 563–480 B.C.E.	Siddhartha Gautama, the Buddha
551–479 B.C.E.	Confucius
c. 540–468 B.C.E.	Vardhamana Mahavira, who inspired Jainism
480–221 B.C.E.	Period of the Warring States in China
c. 390–338 B.C.E.	Lord Shang Yang, who developed Legalism
321–185 B.C.E.	Mauryan Empire
c. 260 B.C.E.	Mauryan Emperor Ashoka converts to Buddhism
221–206 B.C.E.	Qin Empire
206 B.C.E.–220 C.E.	Han Empire
c. 145–90 B.C.E.	Chinese historian Sima Qian
141–87 B.C.E.	Reign of Han emperor Wu
c. 100 B.C.E.	Migration of Yuehzi from western China
c. 45–120 C.E.	Chinese historian Ban Zhao
c. 50–233 C.E.	Kushan Empire
c. 100–123 C.E.	Reign of Kushan emperor Kanishka II
c. 100–250 C.E.	Organization of Tamil literature
c. 320–540 C.E.	Gupta Empire
c. 390–470 C.E.	Indian poet Kalidasa

KEY TERMS

asceticism (p. 174)
bodhisattva (p. 176)
civil service examination (p. 192)
classical (p. 173)
dharma (p. 175)

monastery (p. 175)
nirvana (p. 175)
sangha (p. 175)
Silk Road (p. 181)
stupa (p. 175)

CHAPTER OVERVIEW QUESTIONS

1. How did new social circumstances stimulate changes in religious beliefs and cultures?

2. What processes encouraged close connections among the various regions of Asia?

3. In what ways did the revolutionary thinkers discussed here have a lasting impact on the histories of the regions they inhabited and beyond?

SECTION FOCUS QUESTIONS

1. How did the new religious ideas of the last centuries B.C.E. suit the social and political structures of India?

2. How did the geographical location and trade relations of the Kushan Empire affect its cultural traditions?

3. How did the early Chinese philosophers come to have a long-lasting influence on the intellectual development of the region?

4. How did southern Indian developments differ from those in other parts of Asia?

MAKING CONNECTIONS

1. What ideas that emerged in classical India and China remained fundamental to the later histories of these countries?

2. How would you describe the cultural and intellectual interactions among the various Asian cultures discussed in this chapter?

3. How did the cultural innovations in India and China compare with those in Greece of the first millennium B.C.E. (see Chapter 5)?

7

AT A CROSSROADS ▲

Over the centuries from 500 B.C.E. to 500 C.E., Rome grew from a small village in the heart of the Italian peninsula into the crossroads of a vast empire dominating all of western Eurasia. Pictured here is the Roman Forum, the ancient square that was for centuries the center of Roman public life. Temples and government buildings surround the Forum, and looming in the background is the Colosseum, a massive amphitheater constructed for gladiatorial contests and other public spectacles. Completed in 80 C.E., the Colosseum is now one of imperial Rome's most iconic symbols. (Raimund Koch/Getty Images.)

The Unification of Western Eurasia

500 B.C.E.–500 C.E.

In around 100 C.E., the Roman historian Tacitus (c. 56–117 C.E.) described how inhabitants of Britain, encouraged by the Roman governor Agricola, took on the habits of their Roman occupiers:

> To induce a people, hitherto scattered, uncivilized and therefore prone to fight, to grow pleasurably inured to peace and ease, Agricola gave private encouragement and official assistance to the building of temples, public squares, and private mansions. He praised the keen and scolded the slack, and competition to gain honor from him was as effective as compulsion. Furthermore, he trained the sons of the chiefs in the liberal arts and expressed a preference for British natural ability over the trained skill of the Gauls. The result was that in place of distaste for the Latin language came a passion to command it. In the same way, our national dress came into favor and the toga was everywhere to be seen.[1]

The Romans built their empire through military conquest, taking over new lands in order to dominate them. Roman expansion spread Roman culture, for, as this passage from Tacitus makes clear, conquered peoples were often as eager to adopt Roman practices as the Romans were to encourage their adoption. From North Africa to Britain and from the Atlantic coast to the Euphrates River, numerous peoples were "Romanized" to some degree, leaving behind aspects of their previous cultural identities to acquire the benefits of participating in the empire. This process worked both ways, because incorporating new cultures into the empire changed what it meant to be Roman.

The impact of the interactions between Romans and the peoples they conquered was all the more profound because the Romans sought to transform the territories they acquired. After each new conquest, they reorganized the subject region by introducing Roman administration, politics, social practices, and technology. Conquered territories were thus fully

BACKSTORY

As the Mauryan, Gupta, Kushan, Qin, and Han empires were bringing vast areas of Asia under one rule (see Chapter 6), a similar political unification occurred in western Eurasia, merging two regions with previously separate histories. In the Middle East and eastern North Africa, empires had existed since the second millennium B.C.E. New Kingdom Egypt, Nubia, Assyria, and Persia, for example, had all brought large and diverse populations under their rule (see Chapter 4). However, the peoples of the western Atlantic zone of modern-day Europe and the Mediterranean areas to its south had never known political union. The citizens of Rome would fundamentally change that situation, creating an empire that would profoundly influence the history of the world.

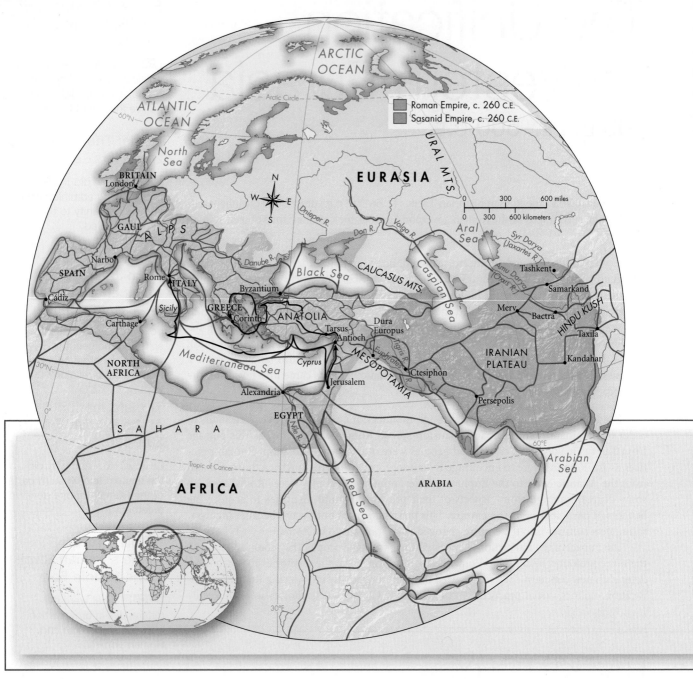

Roman Empire, c. 260 C.E.
Sasanid Empire, c. 260 C.E.

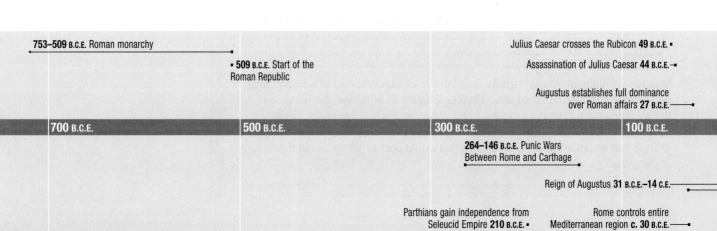

753–509 B.C.E. Roman monarchy

▪ **509 B.C.E.** Start of the
Roman Republic

Julius Caesar crosses the Rubicon **49 B.C.E.** ▪

Assassination of Julius Caesar **44 B.C.E.** ▪

Augustus establishes full dominance
over Roman affairs **27 B.C.E.**

700 B.C.E.   **500 B.C.E.**   **300 B.C.E.**   **100 B.C.E.**

264–146 B.C.E. Punic Wars
Between Rome and Carthage

Reign of Augustus **31 B.C.E.–14 C.E.**

Parthians gain independence from
Seleucid Empire **210 B.C.E.** ▪

Rome controls entire
Mediterranean region **c. 30 B.C.E.**

integrated into Roman political and administrative structures. In time, subject peoples gained the opportunity to become Roman citizens. Men from the provinces could even become emperors, which has no parallel in the earlier empires we have studied. Only eighty-four years after the death of the first emperor, Augustus, a man from Spain, Trajan (r. 98–117 C.E.), took the highest office in Rome, and many other provincials later attained the same position.

At the heart of the vast empire was the city of Rome. From its foundation—traditionally said to be in 753 B.C.E.—to its establishment as an imperial capital, Rome underwent a remarkable political evolution. After a period of rule by kings, the most common type of government in the ancient world, the Romans set up institutions, which were republics with the aim of preventing one man from holding all power. These included a Senate as a place of deliberation, rotating officials with executive powers, term limits, and other safeguards against tyranny. In spite of these carefully crafted institutions, the Roman Republic failed and descended into the chaos of civil wars until one man, Augustus, assumed full control in around 27 B.C.E.

Because the Romans were so successful and left behind so much evidence of their activities, Rome has become the foremost example of an ancient empire. Indeed, the term *empire* itself derives from the Romans' designation, *imperium*, which means "rule." Many Republican institutions are still held up today as ideals of representative government. Even though Roman history itself shows how these institutions can fail, the principles behind them continue to inspire admiration.

The standardization of imperial practices that Tacitus evokes in this chapter's opening lines also explains the success of a new religion, Christianity. Christianity originated in a small community in the Roman Middle East, finding its early adherents among the lower classes and the powerless. Spreading from the Middle East via the empire's network of roads

MAPPING THE WORLD

The Roman and Sasanid Empires, c. 260 C.E.

In around 260 C.E., nearly all of western Eurasia was in the hands of two large imperial powers, Rome and Sasanid Persia. The two empires had risen through very different processes: the citizens of Rome had annexed more territory over the centuries, whereas the Sasanids inherited the territories of the Parthians and earlier empire builders. Both controlled numerous peoples with varied cultures and histories, however, and both were home to intellectual and religious innovations that would radically affect the later histories of the regions. Despite their often hostile interactions, Rome and Sasanid Persia sustained a flourishing trade, one that included many luxury products from countries farther afield. Thus, although their rivalry was intense, they together forged a large exchange network for goods and ideas.

ROUTES ▼

— Major Roman road

— Caravan route

— Maritime trade route

→ Travels of Paul, c. 40–70 C.E.

100–200 C.E. Pax Romana; height of the Roman Empire

• **313 C.E.** Constantine issues Edict of Milan, legalizing Christianity

• **410 C.E.** German tribes sack Rome

100 C.E.   **300 C.E.**   **500 C.E.**

c. **4 B.C.E.–30 C.E.** Life of Jesus   • **224 C.E.** Sasanids overthrow Parthians

• **395 C.E.** Roman Empire divided into eastern and western parts

• **212 C.E.** Caracalla grants citizenship to nearly all free inhabitants of the empire

• **476 C.E.** German leader Odoacer forces last western Roman emperor to step down

and sea routes, it eventually became the official state religion, and its institutions merged with those of the state. Once this happened, the power of the state helped bring Christianity to all of the empire's peoples.

As powerful and important as the Roman Empire was, it was not without its peers, and ultimately it could not defeat its rivals to the east, the Parthians and Sasanids from Iran. Although in the history of Europe the Roman Empire was a watershed, in a global perspective it was one of a series of world empires that stretched across Eurasia from around 500 B.C.E. to 500 C.E. It is worth remembering that the Kushan emperor, Kanishka II (discussed in Chapter 6), placed the rulers of China, India, and Parthia on the same level as the emperor of Rome.

OVERVIEW
QUESTIONS

The major global development in this chapter: The unification of western Eurasia under the Roman Empire.

As you read, consider:

1. How are Roman political institutions still important to us today?

2. How did the Romans face the challenges of creating and maintaining an empire?

3. What impact did Rome have on the lives of the people it conquered?

4. How did Christianity's rise benefit from the Roman Empire?

5. What were the limits of Roman imperialism?

Rome: A Republican Center of Power 500–27 B.C.E.

FOCUS

What were the political ideals of Republican Rome, and how did some outlive the Republic itself?

In a sequence of increasingly far-ranging campaigns that started in the fifth century B.C.E. and continued into the second century C.E., Rome established military dominance over a large territory encircling the Mediterranean Sea and extending far inland into Atlantic Europe. Unlike Alexander of Macedonia, who had subdued the populations of an enormous landmass in one fell swoop (see Chapter 5), the Romans engaged in a long series of wars against neighbors ranging from tribal leagues to powerful unified states. The wars were ruthless, and more than once Rome seemed close to annihilation. But the perseverance and skill of Roman soldiers always won out in the end.

Rome's initial military success arose under a political system different from that of surrounding states. After an initial period of monarchy, traditionally said to have lasted from the founding of Rome in 753 to the expulsion of the last king in 509 B.C.E., Rome was officially a republic in which citizens shared power and elected their officials. In theory, all citizens represented Rome, so it was unimportant who held positions of power. In reality, however, social tensions created political division and conflict in Republican Rome. The acquisition of foreign territories and their wealth only exacerbated these problems, because social and economic inequality increased and military leaders played an ever greater role in domestic politics. These tensions underlay the entire Republican period and ultimately led to the collapse of Republican institutions and establishment of an imperial government.

From Village to World Empire

The origins of Rome are shrouded in mystery, but we know that in the eighth to fifth centuries B.C.E. various Latin-speaking people inhabited the center of Italy, a mountainous peninsula where a variety of groups shared power. In the north Celtic speakers dominated, just south of them the Etruscans had a powerful kingdom, and elsewhere tribal leagues held sway. Outsiders had also established colonies in Italy, especially in the south. Some were Greek, and others were settlements of the important North African city of Carthage, itself a colony of the Phoenicians.

In the late fifth century B.C.E., Rome—still a small settlement then—took advantage of Etruscan decline to start a sustained period of expansion fueled by the fighting skills of its landowning citizens. Progress was initially slow, but by 264 B.C.E. Rome was master of most of Italy (see Map 7.1). The successes altered the city's strategic position. Like the Spartans in Greece, the Romans originally concentrated on acquiring nearby territory. The conquest of Italy led the Romans to look across the sea to Sicily. There they faced a major foreign power, North African Carthage, which owned colonies on the island. Understanding that Carthage's power derived from its navy, the Romans built a fleet to confront their rival. They did so with great technological ingenuity, equipping battleships with platforms where foot soldiers could fight using the same techniques they used on land. Thus, they applied a Roman strength, their infantry, to an arena in which Carthage had the seeming advantage.

Punic Wars

Rome and Carthage fought three long wars between 264 and 146 B.C.E., called the Punic Wars after the Latin word *Poeni*, Phoenician. Rome won the First Punic War (264–241 B.C.E.), but imposed such harsh penalties that Carthage felt compelled to react. At the start of the Second Punic War (218–201 B.C.E.), its general, Hannibal, led an army to Italy through Spain, famously crossing the Alps with two dozen elephants, and ransacked the countryside, defeating Roman opposition repeatedly. He spent sixteen years in Italy but could not attack Rome itself because of the staunch resistance by the inhabitants of the surrounding area. The delay caused by this resistance allowed Rome's citizens to regroup, and after many bloody battles the Roman general Scipio Africanus crushed Hannibal on North African soil in 202 B.C.E. Following the Third Punic War (149–146 B.C.E.), Rome gained control over all of Carthage's territories on the Mediterranean islands, in North Africa, and in Spain. Thus Rome became the dominant military power in the western Mediterranean by 146 B.C.E.

Wars in the East

Meanwhile, in the eastern Mediterranean, the great empire of Alexander of Macedonia had split into rival kingdoms. Rome entered the region partly because some of the rival states sought the support of the Roman armies' superior fighting skills. Rome showed its ruthlessness in 146 B.C.E. by annihilating both Carthage and the Greek city of Corinth, slaughtering the men and enslaving the women and children. The whole Greek world was shocked by Rome's violence. By 100 B.C.E. much of Greece and Anatolia had become Roman territory.

Continued Expansion

Inspired by the wealth and glory that incessant campaigns could bring, ambitious Roman military leaders looked for new territories to conquer. One such leader, Julius Caesar (100–44 B.C.E.), marched his troops into Gaul, the region north of the Alps as far as Britain, turning the Atlantic zone into his personal power base. Soon afterward, in 31 B.C.E., the general and future first Roman emperor, Octavian (Augustus, 63 B.C.E.– 14 C.E.), annexed Egypt and pushed Roman territory until it reached natural borders that his armies could more easily defend. In the south the Sahara Desert provided such an impassable barrier, and in the east the Euphrates River and Syrian Desert formed another natural border. In the north, Octavian conquered the passes through the Alps to

MAP 7.1

Roman Expansion Under the Republic, 500 B.C.E.–14 C.E.

From a village founded in around 500 B.C.E. in the center of Italy, over the next five hundred years Rome grew into a world power that encircled the Mediterranean and reached far into modern western Europe. At first, the expansion took place under the leadership of the Republic, with elected officials and generals. However, especially in the last century B.C.E., it gave ambitious men an opportunity to build power bases, which they used to force their will upon the people and institutions of Rome. This process ended when Octavian, who annexed the wealthy country of Egypt, acquired every powerful office and became Rome's first emperor, Augustus (r. 27 B.C.E.–14 C.E.).

the Danube so that the river could serve as a frontier. Along the Atlantic coast in the west, Rome's territory extended from Gibraltar to the Rhine (see again Map 7.1). Its control established, the Roman Empire would turn the regions within these borders into a coherent political whole, dominated by Roman culture, lifestyles, and livelihoods.

Society and Politics in the Republic

The essential unit of Roman society was the family, whose head was the oldest man, the **pater familias**. Groups of families considered themselves to be descendants of a common ancestor, and each such group had its own religious and social practices. The family incorporated not only those related by blood but also slaves and what the Romans called **clients**. The latter

pater familias The head of a Roman household, with full power over other family members and clients.

client Within the early Roman social structure, a person who was economically dependent on an influential family head.

208

were persons of a lower social rank who were economically attached to the family and received assistance from the pater familias. In return he expected clients to support him, by voting for him in an election, for example, or even serving in his private militia. The pater familias had unrestricted powers over the other members of the family. Adult sons with children of their own did not have an independent legal status and could not own property. Thus, some men with very prominent official positions could be excluded from legal transactions while their fathers were still alive. Hence, the Roman family was like a miniature society, with the eldest male holding absolute authority over all of his dependents.

Women had a secondary role, although over time they gained financial power. At first, in the usual marriage a woman entered her husband's family and was under full control of its leader. But in the second century B.C.E. so-called free marriages became common: a married woman remained a member of her father's family and inherited a share of his property. Upon her father's death she became financially independent, and several affluent women acquired much influence in this way.

Wealthy family heads formed a hereditary aristocratic class, the **patricians**, who in Rome's early days held all political power. Most people did not belong to patrician families, however, especially the increasing number of people from conquered territories who had moved to Rome. These other folk, the **plebeians**, could not claim descent from the ancestors of the patrician families or participate in their religious rites. In the first two centuries of the Republic the plebeians' struggle to acquire political influence and their share of public assets dominated Rome's political and social life.

When the Romans ended the monarchy and created the Republic in 509 B.C.E., they sought a balance of power between the people and government officials, or **magistrates**. But the resulting system was less representative than that of classical Athens (see Chapter 5). Although all citizens sat in various assemblies and had the right to elect magistrates, real power was in the hands of the **Senate**, whose members were mostly patricians with lifelong terms. Senators voted on laws, represented Rome in foreign affairs, and appointed the governors of provinces. Because they nominated men for election by the assembly, they controlled access to the highest offices. Thus the Senate was a representative body only in the sense that it represented the interests of Rome's political and social elites.

The Romans were, however, more generous in granting citizenship than the Greeks, who limited citizenship to male landowners. Originally, only free inhabitants of Rome could become citizens, but in the early period of the Republic, people of conquered Italian territories, freed slaves, and others regularly became citizens. Only men were full citizens, because the status involved military service and political participation, and women could not participate in either of these spheres.

To limit the power of magistrates, the Romans restricted them to one-year terms and placed two men in each office. The two most prominent magistrates were the **consuls**. Patricians monopolized the office of consul until 367 B.C.E., when plebeians forced passage of a law requiring one consul to be from their ranks. As the state and the number of people governed expanded, other magistracies had to be created to carry out special tasks, but the concept of power sharing between two men remained a firm rule. The only exception occurred in times of crisis, when the Senate gave absolute power to a single magistrate, the dictator. The term *dictator* did not have the negative meaning then that it has today. He was someone who could make decisions on his own, and he returned to his former status after six months or when the emergency had passed, whichever came first.

In the struggle between plebeians and patricians, Rome's expansion tilted the balance of power in the plebeians' favor. Rome's wars of conquest and the need to control conquered territories continually increased reliance on the military. The growing army depended on plebeian recruits, and the plebeians used this to extract concessions from patricians. They forced the Senate to create the new government office of **tribune** to protect plebeians from arbitrary decisions by patrician magistrates. Tribunes could veto (a Latin term that means "I prohibit") acts by consuls and the Senate. At this time the plebeians also received their own temples, as well as their own assembly.

The Roman Family

Political Structure

patrician The Roman aristocratic class.

plebeian The Roman class of commoners.

magistrate A Roman government official.

Senate The Roman assembly of elderly men, usually patricians, whose main function was to deliberate important issues of state and give advice.

consul In the Roman Republic, one of the two highest magistrates.

tribune The Roman magistrate whose role was to protect the interests of the plebeians.

Statue of a Roman Patrician

In this typical example of Roman sculpture dating from around 25 B.C.E., the subject wears a toga that identifies him as a senator. Because family was so crucial for patrician leaders' social status, he holds the busts of his ancestors in his hands. (Scala/Art Resource, NY.)

Greek Cultural Influences

This increase in the political and economic power of the plebeians did not, however, lead to social equality in Rome. In fact, inequality actually increased. Some businessmen became extremely rich from state contracts to construct Rome's enormous public works. Private contractors built roads, equipped the army, exploited mines, and even collected taxes. Their wealth enabled them to join the order of **equestrians**, officially cavalrymen but in reality men with a certain amount of property who were not in the Senate. Many Romans, however, did not fare so well. The wars on Italian soil had ruined the livelihood of countless farmers. Rich men—patricians and equestrians—bought up their lands and turned them into *latifundia*, large estates on which they raised cattle and produced cash crops (wine, olive oil, and various fruits). After the conquest of Sicily and North Africa, wheat from their rich farmlands was shipped to Rome rather than being produced near the city. Italian farmers who stayed on the land did so as tenants or day laborers, not as owners. Other farmers left the land and joined the ranks of the urban poor or the army. Thus, as Rome grew, becoming the crossroads of the Mediterranean, one result was social and economic dislocation in Italy. The same dynamic that made Rome rich and powerful impoverished many of its Italian citizens.

To make matters worse, free Romans had to compete for jobs with foreign slaves. Because defeated peoples were often sold into slavery, each new conquered territory added to the flood of slaves that saturated the labor market. The market on the Greek island of Delos reportedly processed several thousand slaves a day. Scholars estimate that of the 6 million people in Italy in around 100 B.C.E., 2 million were slaves. Some were domestic servants in rich Roman households. Such slaves were often freed by their masters, although they remained clients. The majority of slaves were less fortunate, however. They worked in silver mines and stone quarries, farmed the latifundia, and manned workshops. Because slaves were so plentiful and so cheap, they were often treated harshly. It is not surprising, therefore, that the period from 150 to 70 B.C.E. witnessed several slave revolts. The most famous took place between 73 and 71 B.C.E. Led by a fugitive slave named Spartacus, tens of thousands of slaves rose in a revolt that devastated the Italian countryside. They defeated three Roman legions before they were crushed and Spartacus was killed.

Bloody slave revolts were one aspect of the relationship between the Romans and conquered peoples. It would be a mistake, however, to conclude that the Romans and their subjects were connected only by mutual animosity. Roman expansion created new cultural connections throughout the Mediterranean, and the peoples of the empire had a profound and multifaceted impact on Roman life. Among the slaves the Romans brought to Italy were educated Greeks who became physicians, secretaries, and tutors. The Romans were skilled warriors, but they had given little attention to intellectual pursuits such as philosophy and the arts. Thus, when they encountered Greek culture, first in Greek colonies in Italy and later in Greece itself and the Hellenistic world, they eagerly absorbed many elements of it. A Roman poet of the first century B.C.E. wrote: "Greece was captured but it captivated its wild conqueror."[2] The Romans imitated Greek styles in their buildings and artwork. They equated Roman gods with Greek ones: the Roman Jupiter with the Greek Zeus, the Roman goddess Minerva with the Greek Athena, and so on. They adopted Greek religious rites. Elite Roman children learned the Greek language, and Greek scholars came to Rome to form philosophical schools of the type that had existed earlier in the Hellenistic world. The Stoics especially had great success (see

Chapter 5). Not all Romans appreciated these influences, and some wrote that they inspired weakness and decadence. But the trend could not be stopped, and familiarity with Greek culture became a hallmark of Roman education. At the same time that the Romans transformed the political institutions and physical infrastructure of their provinces, contact with the Greek world forever altered Roman culture.

Thus expansion brought a host of changes in Roman life. Military success, however, did not bring economic equality or political stability. By 150 B.C.E., a small number of wealthy land-owners, merchants, and entrepreneurs shared power, whereas the mass of the population was landless and had little political representation. A few politicians took up the cause of the poor, most famously Tiberius Gracchus (c. 163–133 B.C.E.). In 133 B.C.E. he became a tribune and tried to enforce an old law that no individual could cultivate more than about 300 acres (120 hectares) of land. The patrician owners of huge estates would not tolerate this, and a group of senators lynched Gracchus. This was the first in a long string of political assassinations, indications of the power struggles that would ultimately trigger the end of the Roman Republic.

Failure of the Republic

By 100 B.C.E. social tension and political intrigue pervaded Roman society. Individuals and families bought political influence with the wealth they looted from conquered regions. They broke the ancient rules on who could hold offices and for how long. Military men interfered in politics. Armies were often more loyal to their commanders than to the state, and commanders did not hesitate to use their armies to advance their personal political ambitions. Several civil wars broke out in the first century B.C.E., bringing enormous devastation and loss of life and draining the energy of the Roman people. By the end of the century, they were so war-weary that they granted one man, Octavian, supreme power.

Julius Caesar, who lived from 100 to 44 B.C.E., is a good example of the famous men—and some women—who struggled for power in the first century B.C.E. A member of an old, albeit not wealthy, Roman family, he started his political career by allying himself with powerful men to win a number of offices. He managed to gain the governorship of northern Italy, which he used as a springboard for the conquest of Gaul. His wars there from 58 to 50 B.C.E. were merciless—he exterminated entire tribes—and brought him unparalleled personal wealth.

Caesar used this wealth to broaden his political influence in Rome and to remain in elected offices despite legal restrictions. Others opposed him, however—at one point the Senate ordered him to lay down his army command. In response, on January 10, 49 B.C.E., Caesar led his troops across the Rubicon River, the northern border of Italy, which was an act of treason as no provincial army was allowed to pass that point. The ensuing civil war took Caesar and his army to distant Roman territories, and it was four years before he won the often brutal conflict. Back in Rome in 44 B.C.E., he tried to restore order, but he did not have time. On March 15—known in the Roman calendar as the Ides of March—opponents assassinated Caesar on his way to the Senate.

Not all people who lost their lives in these conflicts were leading politicians and military men. Another career steeped in intrigue was that of Marcus Tullius Cicero (106–43 B.C.E.). He was famous in his own day for the speeches he gave in prosecution or defense of public figures caught in political disputes. He devoted himself to philosophy, adopting Stoic values, and to poetry, and he wrote numerous letters (nine hundred of which are preserved). His speeches stand today as examples of great oratory, and already in antiquity people studied them to learn how to argue forcefully.

Roman Slave Tag

Roman slaves were clearly identified as someone's personal property and wore metal collars with tags attached such as the one shown here, dating to the fourth century C.E. The text written on it reads: "Stop me from running away and return me to my master, Viventius, who lives in Callistus's court." (©The Trustees of the British Museum/Art Resource, NY.)

Power Struggles and Civil Wars

equestrian The class of wealthy businessmen and landowners in ancient Rome, second only to the patricians in status and political influence.

latifundia Vast rural estates in ancient Rome whose owners employed a large number of tenant farmers and sometimes slaves.

Cicero's unhappy fate was the result of political misjudgment. After Caesar's death he attacked members of the powerful new coalition that grew around Octavian. They had him assassinated and displayed his head and hands on the speaker's platform in Rome.

Octavian (Augustus)

Caesar's assassination in 44 B.C.E. led to another thirteen-year-long civil war, fought in various battlefields throughout the Mediterranean. The population grew so tired of war and chaos that they did not object to one man taking control, as long as it would bring peace and stability. That man was Octavian, the creator of imperial rule in Rome. After crushing his opponents in 31 B.C.E., he developed a system in which he and his successors would exercise absolute control in practice, yet in theory would respect the old political institutions of the Roman Republic. Octavian obtained overall command of the army and of the provinces with the most important legions. He could propose and veto any legislation, overrule provincial governors, and sit with the highest magistrates, the consuls. In 27 B.C.E. the Romans awarded him the title *Augustus*, "noble one," suggesting he was closer to the gods than to humans.

Augustus's dominance of government was unprecedented in Roman history, but he cloaked his ambition by appearing to accumulate traditional Republican offices, which he held without the usual term limits. He called himself *princeps*, "the first citizen," not "king" or another title that would have indicated absolute rule. In that sense, Augustus was a master of diplomacy: he offered the war-weary people of Rome a new and efficient system of government without casting it as the monarchical system they had traditionally rejected.

Augustus's tactics won him the people's support and admiration, and in 2 B.C.E. they named him "father of the country," although he still claimed to be merely a consul. When he died in 14 C.E., he had ruled Rome as de facto emperor for forty-two years, and few Romans remembered life without him. Augustus's political acumen and the length of his reign contributed to the durability of the system of government he created. His successors would maintain it for the next two hundred years.

Rome: The Empire 27 B.C.E.–212 C.E.

FOCUS

How did the Roman Empire bring administrative and cultural unity to the vast territory it ruled?

Starting with Augustus, a succession of powerful Romans ruled an enormous territory that brought together numerous peoples with a variety of cultural backgrounds and traditions. A massive army enforced imperial control, but in a process known as Romanization, universal administrative and economic practices fused the regions of the Roman Empire into a cohesive whole. Retired Roman soldiers routinely moved to the provinces, as did others, and people from the provinces moved to Rome to work at running the empire. The system of government that dominated Roman life for several centuries became the archetype of an empire. Even though its structure contained weaknesses that would lead to its decline in the west, the Roman Empire was highly successful and fundamentally changed the histories of all the regions it controlled.

Emperors and Armies

With an emperor dominating a government that was still attached to its Republican roots, the Romans had to reorganize the other institutions of state. The Roman Senate lost its decision-making powers, but it retained important functions: senators filled the highest government and military offices, and the Senate acted as a court of law. The emperor decided who would receive magistracies, however, and the Senate always approved his choices.

The Emperor

The emperor exercised both military and civilian authority. As in the Republic, the military played a substantial role in Roman imperial politics. Thus the emperor's relationship to the army was pivotal, and most Roman emperors were active soldiers. The continuous campaigns sometimes extended the empire beyond its Augustan borders—in 43 C.E.,

MAP 7.2

Roman Expansion Under the Empire, 14–212 C.E.

Roman emperors attempted to enlarge the empire through repeated campaigns, but mostly they only succeeded in securing the borders along natural boundaries, such as the Sahara Desert and the Rhine and Danube rivers. Their activities consolidated Roman rule over the territory, however, and increased the integration of non-Italians into the imperial governmental structure. In certain periods, such as the second century C.E., Roman rule brought great stability and prosperity to a wide area.

for example, Claudius (r. 41—54 C.E.) annexed much of Britain—which could bring the emperor great wealth and glory (see Map 7.2). War could also lead to disaster, as when the Sasanid Persians captured the emperor Valerian (r. 253–260 C.E.) in 260 C.E. and tortured him to death (see Counterpoint: Rome's Iranian Rivals in the Middle East).

The emperor's civilian duties required his constant attention. He was flooded with requests for guidance and favors, and his answers, communicated by letter, had the force of law. The emperor controlled a massive treasury, which received income mostly from customs duties and taxes on sales, land, and agricultural products. The emperor also had enormous personal wealth, from his own estates, which he could extend by confiscating property, and from gifts by those who wished to obtain his favor. As the center of an imperial government that connected Rome to its provinces, the emperor had an unparalleled ability to shape the lives of Rome's citizens and subjects.

One way Roman emperors shaped Roman life was by commissioning extensive public works, many of which still stand today (see Lives and Livelihoods: Roman Engineers). They built majestic theaters and huge amphitheaters and erected triumphal arches to celebrate their military victories. They laid out forums—open places with temples, shops,

Public Works

Roman Engineers

Pont du Gard

The Romans are rightly famous for their engineering skills. A key concern was guaranteeing the water supply to cities throughout the empire, and several of their aqueducts still stand as major signs of their accomplishment. This is the Pont du Gard, part of an aqueduct in the south of modern France that was built in the first century C.E. The structure remained in use as a bridge into the eighteenth century. (akg-images/ Bildarchiv Steffens.)

Throughout the territory of the former Roman Empire, we can still see the impressive remains of constructions put up some two thousand years ago. Numerous landmarks in the modern city of Rome date to ancient times. Visitors admire monuments such as the Colosseum, the giant amphitheater opened for gladiatorial games in 80 C.E. (see again At a Crossroads, page 202), and the Pantheon, whose present form dates to around 120 C.E. A temple for the veneration of all Roman gods, the Pantheon had the largest dome on earth until modern times, 142 feet wide. In the former provinces still stand Roman bridges, watermills, aqueducts, and other monuments equally old and sometimes still functional.

Roman engineers are famous not because of their originality—they mostly continued to use Greek inventions—but because they developed techniques to their fullest extent. They also left behind the most detailed writings on and public buildings in which citizens conducted government business. An elaborate road system extended from Scotland to the Sahara Desert. The roads ran straight for miles, extending over stone bridges when needed, and their surfaces were carefully paved to resist all weather. If two cities were more than a day's journey apart, they provided rest houses. At first the roads had military functions, but wheeled vehicles and messengers also used them. By building and improving the empire's transportation network, the emperors connected their provinces to Rome, making their capital the crossroads of the Mediterranean.

Imperial Succession   Because of the emperor's pivotal role in the political system, the empire's power centers viewed the choice of emperor with the utmost concern, and succession was highly contested. Rarely did a natural son succeed his father as emperor. This was true from the start of the empire: Augustus had no sons, so he groomed several relatives, including his daughter's sons, to succeed him. When they all died before him, he reluctantly chose Tiberius, his last wife's son from a previous marriage, as heir and adopted him as a stepson (see Seeing the Past: The Augustan Cameo Gem).

engineering in the ancient world. Most elaborate is the work of Vitruvius from the first century C.E. His *On Architecture* is ten volumes of information on materials, construction methods, water management, town planning, and many other subjects.

Engineers and skilled builders were organized in associations that grouped together specialists. The variety of these associations shows that skills were highly specialized: stonemasons, demolition experts, brickmakers, plasterers, painters, and many others had their own associations. Only people who belonged to the association could do the job. Access was restricted, however, and often only the sons of existing members could join. Young workers had to undergo a long apprenticeship before they could work independently. The associations also provided assistance to their members—for example, to pay for funerals or tombs. They worked under the supervision of architects, who were highly respected.

As groups of engineers traveled and worked in different regions, they contributed to the unity of the empire. They used the same techniques to create Roman buildings and monuments of similar appearance everywhere, from modern-day Britain to Syria. Among the most impressive Roman remains still standing are aqueducts—man-made channels that brought water from distant sources. Constructed in stone and concrete (lime, sand, and water poured into molds to obtain the desired shape), the aqueducts relied on gravity to move the water. Their builders sometimes used massive constructions to bypass natural obstacles. One amazing example is the Pont du Gard ("Bridge over the Gard") in the south of modern France. To allow passage over the Gard River valley, Roman engineers built three tiers of stone arches rising 180 feet above the riverbed. The water runs through a channel on top that is 4.5 feet wide and 5.5 feet deep, covered with stone slabs to protect against the sun and pollution. Many aqueducts supplied Rome with water, and some still feed fountains in the city today, including the landmark Trevi Fountain.

Military engineers were especially important in Rome's extensive wars. They devoted much effort to the development of artillery. One typical Roman piece of equipment was the ballista, a large crossbow, mounted on wheels, that could propel a projectile for one thousand feet or more with a high degree of accuracy.

Many of the techniques Roman engineers used were forgotten after the end of the empire, but once Europeans of the fifteenth and later centuries C.E. rediscovered the writings of Vitruvius and others and investigated the remains still standing, they used them as the basis for their constructions. Roman engineering is thus another connection between antiquity and modern times.

QUESTIONS TO CONSIDER

1. How did Roman engineers serve the needs of the empire?

2. How did they contribute to the spread of Roman culture?

3. How did their organization contribute to their success?

For Further Information:
Hodge, A. Trevor. *Roman Aqueducts and Water Supply*, 2d ed. London: Duckworth, 2002.
Landels, J. G. *Engineering in the Ancient World*, 2d ed. Berkeley: University of California Press, 2000.

From the early history of the empire, generals contested succession, relying on armies to enforce their claims. When Augustus's dynasty ended with the suicide of the childless Nero (r. 54–68 C.E.), four men in quick succession claimed the throne, each with the support of provincial troops. Finally Vespasian (vehs-PAYZ-ee-an) (r. 69–79 C.E.), backed by the troops in the east, seized full control.

The army sometimes sold the throne to the highest bidder. Because real power now derived from military support, the emperor's direct connection to the city of Rome and its aristocratic families vanished. Vespasian was not born in Rome, but in provincial Italy to humble parents. Ten years later a Spaniard, Trajan (r. 98–117 C.E.), became emperor. Soon afterward the rulers began to come from other regions of the empire—Gaul, North Africa, Syria, and the Balkans.

Nonetheless, because it was the capital of the empire, many emperors focused attention on the city of Rome, spending enormous amounts to construct fountains, theaters, stadiums, baths, and other monuments. The Roman historian Suetonius (c. 69–140 C.E.) quotes Augustus's boast that he found Rome a city of brick and left it a city of marble.

The City of Rome

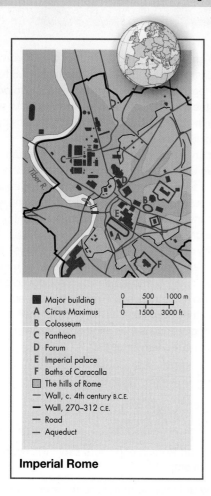

Major building
A Circus Maximus
B Colosseum
C Pantheon
D Forum
E Imperial palace
F Baths of Caracalla
The hills of Rome
— Wall, c. 4th century B.C.E.
— Wall, 270–312 C.E.
— Road
— Aqueduct

Imperial Rome

Workers and artisans from all over the empire flocked to the city to provide labor and craftsmanship. Its population grew to around a million. Most were poorly paid laborers and servants, but there were also numerous shopkeepers, bakers, fishmongers, and others who provided goods and services. Many inhabitants lived in terrible conditions, in city blocks packed with multiple-story wooden buildings. When in July 64 C.E. a fire erupted, it took almost a week to put it out; ten of the fourteen urban districts were damaged, and three were burned to the ground.

Because many Roman residents were poor and unemployed, emperors sought to ward off restlessness with "bread and circus games": food handouts, performances, races, and contests between gladiators, that is, enslaved men fighting to the death for public entertainment. (Spartacus had been a gladiator before leading his slave rebellion.) The Roman Colosseum, built in the first century C.E. for such games, could seat fifty thousand spectators. The games and food handouts diverted people's attention and made them feel as if the emperor cared about them.

In return for such benefits, the people awarded the emperor divine status. The Senate had declared Augustus a god after his death, and soon the idea took hold that the living emperor was a deity. The rulers themselves liked the idea; Emperor Domitian (r. 81–96 C.E.), for example, insisted that he should be addressed as "master and god." Other members of the imperial family were likewise deified to exalt their status. Visual imagery such as statues, relief sculptures, and coins that appeared throughout the empire broadcast the idea that the emperor was a god, and in the provinces temples existed for his cult.

The army was the central institution in Roman society, the backbone of the empire. It was enormous, although enlistments varied over time. Scholars estimate that more than 10 percent of the adult male population typically served in active duty at one time. In theory it was an army of landowning Romans: in the early Republic only men who could pay for their equipment were allowed to join, as had been the case with the Greek hoplites (see Chapter 5). Reforms enacted in 107 B.C.E. allowed landless poor men to enlist, and these recruits received farms when they returned to civilian life after many years of service.

The Roman Army

The core of Rome's army consisted of **legions**, infantry units of six thousand men each, divided into ten cohorts of six centuries—one hundred men—each. The legionaries of the empire were predominantly non-Italians, who received Roman citizenship when they enlisted. They trained hard to fight in unison and were well armed. Alongside the legionaries fought auxiliaries, non-Roman soldiers who often excelled in a special skill such as archery. They fought under a Roman officer in cohorts of five hundred or one thousand men each. Upon retirement they, too, as well as their sons, became Roman citizens, and their female family members acquired the rights of Roman women. Thus the army facilitated the fuller integration of provincials into Roman life.

Military service was long and arduous. A legionary served twenty years, an auxiliary twenty-five. Until the late second century C.E., soldiers were not allowed to marry, although they could have long-term relationships. The army's maintenance took up a major part of the state's finances. To keep soldiers loyal, their salaries were regularly increased, and they received a share of the booty, as well as special gifts (for example, to gain their allegiance when a new emperor took office) and a retirement bonus. Over time, the growing cost of maintaining the army, and through it control over the empire, would put a great strain on the imperial system.

legion A military unit in the Roman army consisting of six thousand infantry soldiers.

Despite the frequent changes of emperors and their often erratic behavior and military adventures, the peoples of the empire enjoyed substantial periods of peace and prosperity.

The Augustan Cameo Gem

(Erich Lessing/Art Resource, NY.)

Probably in around 50 C.E., an anonymous artist cut this stone ($7\frac{1}{2}$ inches high, 9 inches wide) in honor of Augustus, visually expressing the new idea of rule introduced by the first emperor of Rome. Although officially Augustus was only "a first citizen," in this piece the artist conveys the idea that he was a king linked to the gods. It may have been possible only after Augustus's death in 14 C.E. to express such an idea.

In the center of the top register we see the goddess Roma, along with Augustus as a heroic seminude; his image is based on that of statues representing Jupiter, head of the Roman pantheon. To the right are Gaia, the goddess of the earth, and Neptune, the sea god, to express the idea that Augustus's rule encompassed both land and sea. Oikumene (oy-ku-MEHN-ay), the personification of the civilized world, holds a crown over the emperor's head. On the left is Tiberius, Augustus's designated successor, descending from his chariot after he defeated the barbarian threat represented on the bottom register. Next to Tiberius stands a young man in military dress; he represents Germanicus, Tiberius's adopted son, who had died before Tiberius. The image thus represents the idea of a royal dynasty in which generations of the same family rule in succession.

EXAMINING THE EVIDENCE

1. What ideals of rule does the artist express in this piece?

2. How does this representation of Augustus diverge from his official status in society as *princeps*, "the first citizen"?

In particular, the second century C.E. was a time of ***Pax Romana***, or Roman peace: a sequence of competent rulers held power, the borders were secure, and internal tranquility generally prevailed. In this climate of peace and prosperity, Roman culture spread rapidly throughout the empire. This process of cultural exchange was accelerated by a shift in the role of the Roman army as the wars of conquest came to an end.

> **Pax Romana**

The Provincial System and the Diffusion of Roman Culture

The Roman legions were stationed in the border areas, which initially functioned as sites to launch further expansion. From the late second century C.E. on, however, the legions took on a defensive role, protecting the borders against foreign invaders. The presence of legionaries and Roman bureaucrats fundamentally altered the local societies, especially in the west. The impact of this process is still visible today. Modern inhabitants of places that were once Roman provinces speak Romance languages—languages that developed from Latin—rather than Germanic and Slavic tongues. This is why the people of modern Romania still speak a language derived from Latin, whereas their neighbors, whose territories never became Roman provinces, use Slavic languages. Moreover, many ancient Roman settlements are important western European cities today, including

> **Pax Romana** Literally, "Roman peace," the period in the second century C.E. when the empire was stable and secure.

London and Paris. In these and myriad other ways, Rome had a permanent impact on its territories.

Roman Settlements

The Romans influenced occupied territories most directly by creating various types of settlements. On the empire's borders, the Romans built military camps that became centers of trade and attracted the local populations. They turned existing settlements into Roman cities or founded new cities. These contained public baths, triumphal arches, temples, theaters, and amphitheaters, all patterned on those in Rome itself.

The new cities structured their governments on the Roman model. The local elite ran for election to high offices and sat on councils from which senators were often chosen. Like the emperor in Rome, these men were expected to lavish gifts upon the cities by constructing public monuments and buildings, organizing spectacles, and giving food handouts. At first they exercised a great deal of autonomy, and the Roman bureaucracy did not attempt to rule the empire directly. Over time, however, Roman emperors intervened more often in provincial affairs. Moreover, the great expense associated with holding office led to a shortage of local candidates. As a result, in the second century C.E. local autonomy gave way to direct rule by the emperor's representatives.

Romanization

Although Roman customs and lifestyles were not officially enforced, provincials who wanted to participate in the empire's business had to learn Latin in the west and Greek in the east and to dress and behave like Romans. Their material goods and houses reflected Roman styles. For example, floor mosaics such as those favored in Rome decorated houses built from North Africa to Britain, and provincial craftsmen produced items that imitated Italian products, such as clay lamps, for local consumption.

But **Romanization**, the process through which Roman culture spread into the provinces, was not wholesale adoption of Roman practices. Rather, local and imperial traditions merged as people retained the parts of their own culture they valued most while

A Roman Mosaic in England

With the military expansion of the Roman Empire throughout western Eurasia came the spread of Roman culture. The mosaic shown here, dating to around 350 C.E., is a typical example of Roman floor decoration. Not only is the style Roman, but so is the story illustrated, the tragedy of Dido and Aeneas, two lovers separated by the gods, as told in Virgil's *Aeneid*. The mosaic shows that the poem was known at the edges of the empire. (Somerset County Museum, Taunton Castle, UK/Bridgeman Art Library.)

Romanization The process by which Roman culture spread across the empire.

adopting aspects of Roman culture. Consequently, the east and the west of the empire were very different. Much of the western empire had been inhabited by nonliterate societies with few cities, and when the Romans annexed these regions, they introduced urban life, which naturally had a strong Roman character. In contrast, in the eastern territories, Hellenistic cultures had flourished before the Roman conquest, and many inhabitants were urban, literate, and educated (see Reading the Past: A Young Woman Laments Her Premature Death). Cities in the eastern empire remained Greek in character but prospered under Roman rule. Alexandria in Egypt was the second largest city of the empire after Rome, and its economy boomed because vast amounts of Egyptian grain were shipped through its harbor to Rome. Culturally it may have surpassed Rome itself, with its multitude of scholars and artists from all over the eastern world.

Spread of Citizenship

The diffusion of Roman culture coincided with the spread of citizenship. Only citizens could hold office, so non-Romans who wanted to participate in government had to become citizens. Over time the empire granted citizenship to more and more people, including other Italians, officials from the provinces, and former soldiers of foreign origin. Finally, in 212 C.E., Emperor Caracalla (cahr-ih-CAHL-ah) (r. 211–217 C.E.) gave nearly all free men in the empire Roman citizenship and all free women the same rights as Roman women. This created a new sense of unity, but at the same time it reduced the appeal of citizenship because it became less exclusive. Moreover, men from the provinces no longer needed to enlist in the army to become citizens, so to meet the constant demand for soldiers, the army increasingly turned to Germanic mercenaries.

The expansion of citizenship was part of a larger trend toward increased opportunities for provincials within the empire. Once the empire was established, ambitious men could move from one end to the other of a vast territory in pursuit of a career. Inscriptions honoring these men after their deaths report many such careers. In one example, Quintus Gargilius started out as a military officer in Britain. He then moved to North Africa, where he led Spanish troops and became responsible for governing two Roman cities in the north of what is today Algeria. After he died in an ambush, city leaders set up a monument to honor their fallen leader:

> To Quintus Gargilius, son of Quintus, member of the Quirina Martialis tribe, Roman equestrian, who was prefect of the first cohort of the Astyres in the province of Britannia, tribune of the Spanish cohort in the province of Mauritania Caesariensis [northern Algeria], after military service, set in charge of the cohort of Moorish aides and mounted detachments acting as protection in the territory of Auzia, decurio of the two colonies Auzia and Rusgunia and provincial patron, on account of his outstanding love for the citizens and his singular affection for the fatherland, and because, through his bravery and watchfulness against the rebel Faraxen, whom he captured with his associates and killed, the college of the colony of Auzia has made for him, at public expense [this monument] after he was deceived [and killed] by the ambush of the Bavares. It was dedicated on March 25 of the provincial year 221 [260 C.E.].[3]

Roman Law

Another means of unifying the empire was through law, which was evenly applied throughout the territories. From the Republican period on, legal experts had developed comprehensive procedures, mainly for private law, that is, interactions between individuals. Laws laid out rules for transactions in every aspect of life. They stipulated, for example, that a woman who married or divorced retained her property. They determined whether a neighbor could pick fruits from a tree overhanging his garden or collect water that ran off a roof. For transfers of property, they indicated what documentation was needed and whether or not witnesses had to be present.

Several emperors commissioned legal scholars to codify the laws and ensure their consistency. The laws had such an impact that people based their legal practices on them even after the empire's collapse. Roman law is the foundation of the continental European legal system to this day.

A Young Woman Laments Her Premature Death

To reconstruct Roman history we often rely on the extensive writings of ancient historians and official records. But many common people in the Roman Empire left documents as well, including business correspondence, letters, and the like, written on parchments and papyri that have survived only in Egypt, thanks to the region's dry climate. They also carved inscriptions on gravestones. This example of such an inscription comes from Egypt and was written in Greek. In it, a young woman asks passersby to mourn her premature death.

What profit is there to labor for children, or why honor them above all else, if we shall have for our judge not Zeus, but Hades [god of the underworld]?

My father took care of me for twice ten years, but I did not attain to the marriage bed of the wedding chamber,

Nor did my body pass under the bridal curtain, nor did the girls my age make the doors of cedar resound throughout the wedding night.

My virginal life has perished. Woe for that Fate, alas, who cast her bitter threads on me!

The breasts of my mother nourished me with their milk to no purpose at all, and to those breasts I cannot repay the favor of nourishment for their old age.

I wish I would have left my father a child when I died, so that he would not forever have an unforgettable grief through remembrance of me.

Weep for Lysandre, companions of my same age, the girl whom Philonike and Eudemos bore in vain.

You who approach my tomb, I implore you very much, weep for my youth, lost prematurely and without marriage.

Source: Jane Rowlandson, ed., *Women and Society in Greek and Roman Egypt* (Cambridge, U.K.: Cambridge University Press, 1998), 347.

EXAMINING THE EVIDENCE

1. What would have been expected from the deceased Lysandre had she lived longer?

2. What does this inscription tell us about the role of women in Roman society?

3. What does it tell us about the role of children in Roman society?

Christianity: From Jewish Sect to Imperial Religion

FOCUS

Why did imperial policy toward Christianity shift from persecution to institutionalization as Rome's state religion?

Roman culture profoundly influenced life throughout the empire, but as we have seen, cultural diffusion was a two-way process. We have already explored the Roman adoption of Greek culture in the second and first centuries B.C.E. In the first centuries C.E., the teachings of Jesus, a Jewish preacher in Palestine, fundamentally changed the religious outlook of many inhabitants of the Roman Empire, and by 325 C.E. his ideas would become the basis for a new state religion, Christianity. Christianity's absorption of classical Greek philosophical tradition and the merging of the church hierarchy with that of the imperial bureaucracy explain the new religion's remarkable success. These intellectual and bureaucratic foundations enabled the Christian church to survive the collapse of the Roman Empire in the west and to dominate the religious life of Europe for centuries.

Religions in the Roman Empire

The Roman Empire was home to numerous cultural and religious traditions. The Romans readily adopted foreign cults and religions, making no effort to monopolize the religious life of the empire. As a result, foreign gods found new adherents far from the regions where they originated. The Iranian god of light, Mithras, for example, was a favorite of soldiers throughout the empire because he was armed with a knife at birth.

Roman Depiction of the Iranian God Mithras

In the time of the empire, the Romans often adopted the religious cults of conquered peoples and incorporated foreign gods into their pantheon without difficulties. Especially popular was the Iranian god of light, Mithras, whose heroic deeds appealed to soldiers. In this marble relief of the second or third centuries C.E., he slays a bull to guarantee fertility. Overlooking him are images of the sun god and moon goddess, both also deities with eastern origins. (Louvre, Paris/Giraudon/Bridgeman Art Library.)

Mystery Religions

In the first century C.E., eastern mystery religions, or religions of salvation, gained much popularity throughout the empire. Under the new system of government, both ideas and populations could travel more easily over a vast area, which probably increased interest in foreign traditions and left people unsatisfied with their own. The cults of the Egyptian gods Osiris and Isis, which were seen as exotic and mysterious, were particularly popular. At the same time, a strong tendency arose to merge the gods of various cultures. Mithras, for example, came to be equated with the invincible Roman sun god, Sol Invictus. Moreover, that merged god was sometimes placed at the center of Roman religion as if he were the only deity. Thus the process of religious experimentation and exchange produced a Roman tendency toward monotheism, the belief in the existence of only one true deity.

Judaism in the Roman Empire

Although monotheism may have been a new concept to many Romans, in some parts of the empire it had a long history. In Palestine in the east of the empire, the monotheistic religion of Judaism had survived (see Chapter 4) and its temple hierarchy was integrated into the Roman administrative structure. In the capital city of Jerusalem, the aristocracy cooperated with the Romans, who kept them in power and allowed them to practice their faith. Several interpretations of Judaism coexisted, however, some focusing on adherence to established law, others more open to foreign cultural traditions. Certain Jewish groups wanted to overthrow Roman rule, among them the Zealots (originally a Greek term that indicates a zealous follower), some of whom were willing to assassinate Roman sympathizers. Thus in Palestine the process of Romanization was contested, with some Jewish groups choosing to adopt Roman ways and others seeing Roman rule and Roman culture as totally incompatible with the survival of an authentic Jewish identity.

Jesus

It was in this context of competing Jewish interpretations that the teachings of one preacher, Jesus of Nazareth, became popular. Focusing on personal faith, Jesus reached out to the disenfranchised of society, including women and the poor. We know of his teachings through accounts of his followers, whose story of his life situates him in the first decades of the first century C.E. Although the dates are uncertain, scholars estimate that he lived from about 4 B.C.E. to 30 C.E. Accounts of his life, which we call the New Testament gospels today, show that the traditional Jewish urban hierarchy rejected Jesus and that the Romans, who thought he advocated independence from the empire, executed him as a subversive and a rebel.

After his execution, a small community of Jesus's followers preserved his message and identified Jesus with the messiah, the "anointed one," whom earlier prophets had announced as the liberator of the Jews from imperial oppression. Jesus's disciples started to teach his message to other Jews. Initially their greatest appeal was to Jews who had partly assimilated into the Greek-speaking communities of Syria, and the gospels were written in Greek rather than Aramaic, the most common spoken language in the region. They used the Greek term *Christ* for messiah, which led to the word *Christians* for their followers. According to Christian tradition, Jesus's leading disciple, Peter, traveled to Rome to found a Christian community in the empire's capital.

Christianity's Spread Outside the Jewish Community

Travels of Paul

The earliest Christians saw themselves as Jews who could teach only those who obeyed the laws of circumcision and of the Jewish diet. A teacher from Anatolia called Paul especially advocated an end to that restriction, and in around 50 C.E. he began to spread Christianity among non-Jews. Addressing his message to people in Anatolia, Greece, Macedonia, and Rome, Paul established numerous Christian communities throughout the Eastern Roman Empire (see Map 7.3). The Roman communication and transportation network that connected the far-flung communities of the empire greatly facilitated Paul's missionary activities.

Jewish-Christian Split

Initially, Christian communities existed in harmony with the Jewish temple hierarchy in Jerusalem, but when the Christians failed to back a Jewish rebellion against the Romans in the years 66 to 74 C.E., many Jews considered Christians to be traitors. By 90 C.E., the two religions had split apart. At that time, a substantial number of Christian communities prospered in the regions of Syria-Palestine, Anatolia, and Greece. The two largest cities of the empire, Rome and Alexandria, also housed numerous Christians, and some Christian communities sprang up east of the Roman Empire in Parthian territory.

Early Christians

The early Christians were mostly urban merchants and members of the lower classes. They may have been drawn to the church because of its focus on human equality— slaves could hold leading offices—and support for the poor. That equality extended to women, who at first seem to have made up a large part of the congregations and to have held prominent roles. Rich women often made their homes available as gathering places and gave hospitality to traveling preachers. Paul often addressed his letters to women, advising them on how to teach the new religion. When the Christian church became more institutionalized, however, the role of women decreased, and the new church selected its leaders from among old men, the literal meaning of the Greek title given to them, *presbyteros*. By the early second century C.E., each Christian community elected one such elder as "overseer," *episkopos* in Greek, which became the title *bishop*. Various bishops vied for supremacy, which the bishop in Rome finally won by arguing that Peter had founded his church in Rome.

Toward a State Religion   50–324 C.E.

Persecution of Christians

Because they refused to honor other gods and formed close-knit communities, the early Christians grew apart from others in society—a development that made them an easy target for persecution by the authorities. As we have discussed, the Romans were generally tolerant of foreign religions, but not if such religions seemed to inspire rejection of the Roman community and state. At first, acts of persecution were tied to specific events, such as the burning of Rome in 64 C.E. Emperor Nero blamed the disaster on Christians and ordered the execution of those living in Rome. When the empire subsequently encountered military setbacks, the idea that the Christians' refusal to honor traditional gods had caused divine displeasure led to more general persecutions. In the mid-third century C.E., officials traveled across the empire and forced people to make offerings to Roman deities. If they refused, as Christians often did, they were killed. In addition, early Christians were sometimes attacked by non-Christian populations, who resented the isolation of Christian communities. Local governments tolerated such mob violence.

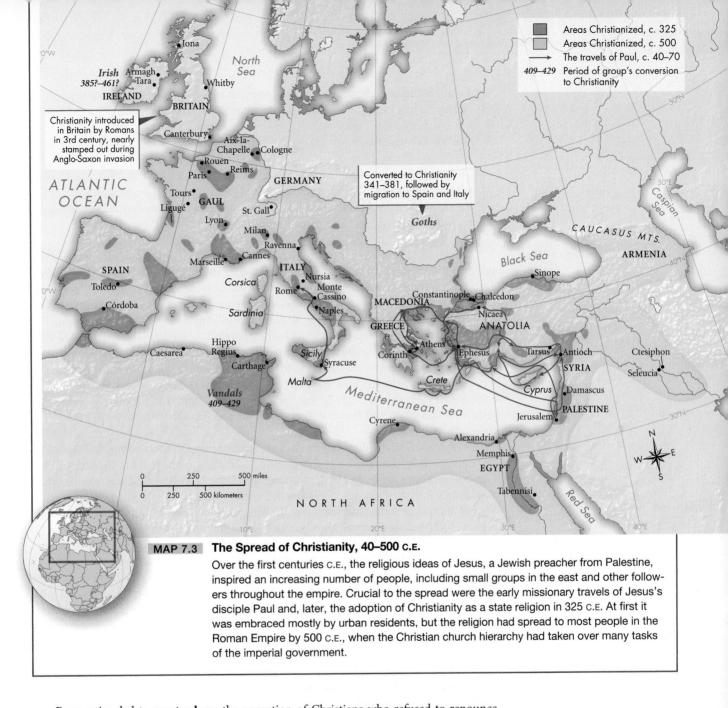

MAP 7.3 **The Spread of Christianity, 40–500 C.E.**
Over the first centuries C.E., the religious ideas of Jesus, a Jewish preacher from Palestine, inspired an increasing number of people, including small groups in the east and other followers throughout the empire. Crucial to the spread were the early missionary travels of Jesus's disciple Paul and, later, the adoption of Christianity as a state religion in 325 C.E. At first it was embraced mostly by urban residents, but the religion had spread to most people in the Roman Empire by 500 C.E., when the Christian church hierarchy had taken over many tasks of the imperial government.

Persecution led to **martyrdom**, the execution of Christians who refused to renounce their faith. Such acts of defiance, even under the greatest tortures, became a sign of great devotion, to be admired and praised. Early Christian writings recount in detail the suffering of the faithful, including women, who through their trials acquired a status equal to men. One early record is the prison diary of Vibia Perpetua (WIHB-ee-ah pehr-PEHTCH-u-ah). The twenty-two-year-old woman described her imprisonment in the city of Carthage in the year 203 C.E. with her baby son, whom she was still nursing. When the child lost interest in breast milk, Perpetua saw this as a sign from God that she was free to go to her death. She and four other Christians were thrown to the animals: a wild cow trampled her, and a soldier killed her with his sword.

Perpetua described three visions she had in prison. In the final vision she saw herself in an arena facing a giant Egyptian. She wrote:

> Then came out an Egyptian against me, of vicious appearance, together with his seconds, to fight with me. There also came up to me some handsome young men to be my seconds and assistants. My clothes were stripped off, and suddenly I was

martyrdom The suffering of death for one's religious beliefs.

a man. My seconds began to rub me down with oil (as they are wont to do before a contest). Then I saw the Egyptian on the other side rolling in the dust.

She was victorious and

The crowd began to shout and my assistants started to sing psalms. Then I walked up to the trainer and took the branch. He kissed me and said: "Peace be with you, my daughter!"... I awoke. I realized that it was not with wild animals that I would fight but with the Devil, but I knew that I would win the victory.[4]

Edict of Milan

In 313 C.E., about a century after Perpetua's death, Emperor Constantine issued the Edict of Milan, which allowed Christians to practice their faith openly. Now that martyrdom was no longer necessary, early Christians focused on an ascetic lifestyle to express devotion to the faith. They saw the body as merely a temporary container of the soul, and they believed that rejecting physical pleasure would stimulate the soul's perfection. The dislike of the body was especially acute in the domain of sexuality. The teachings of Paul already had celebrated celibacy as a virtue, but abstinence from sexual relations, especially for women, became an obsession in the second century C.E. Women who remained virgins were thought to carry an intact soul in an intact body. Sexual abstinence was encouraged even in marriage. At this time the church started to promote the idea that Jesus's mother Mary had been a perpetual virgin and removed references to his siblings from official literature.

How could Christianity, with its focus on austerity, appeal to a wide public? Although there are no definitive answers to this question, some historians point to the humanity of Christ's teachings: unlike the distant Roman gods, the Christian God was so concerned with humans that he sacrificed his son for their salvation. In Christian doctrine, God became human in Jesus, and Jesus was the force through which God influenced human history. Such closeness between humans and god was absent in other religions.

Moreover, Jesus preached love and compassion for one's peers, and his followers actively built a sense of community that transcended social and cultural boundaries and was much stronger than that of other religious groups. The new community served very well in a Roman world in which people moved around and often ended up in large cities with mixed populations. Furthermore, the early Christian church was well organized to provide services otherwise missing. It protected widows, fed the poor, and gave an education to some. Many of the empire's bureaucrats were Christians who knew how to read and write. Some historians see the church's organizational skills as its major strength. Those skills may have been the reason that Christianity became the empire's official religion.

Conversion of Constantine

Christianity's guarantee of success came under Emperor Constantine (r. 307–337 C.E.). Early in his reign Constantine fought rival contenders to the throne, and when he won a crucial battle in 312 C.E., he credited his victory to the Christian god and converted to Christianity. According to tradition, he did so because he saw a vision of Christ before the battle. Historians today debate whether Constantine was spiritually motivated or a pragmatist who recognized the growing influence of the religion in the empire and sought to win the support of its adherents.

In any case, Constantine's embrace of Christianity was of enormous historical significance. A year after his military victory, he promulgated the Edict of Milan, guaranteeing freedom of worship to Christians and all others. When Constantine became sole ruler of the Roman Empire in 324 C.E., he used the Christian church as an institution to unify the empire. He granted land to build churches, especially in places significant to the religion's history. In this cause, his mother, Helena, traveled through Palestine and financed the building of memorials in locations where, according to the gospels, crucial events in Jesus's life had taken place. A story developed that while supervising the construction of the Church of the Holy Sepulcher in Jerusalem she even found the cross on which he was crucified. Thus, in the early days of Christianity, Christians used the

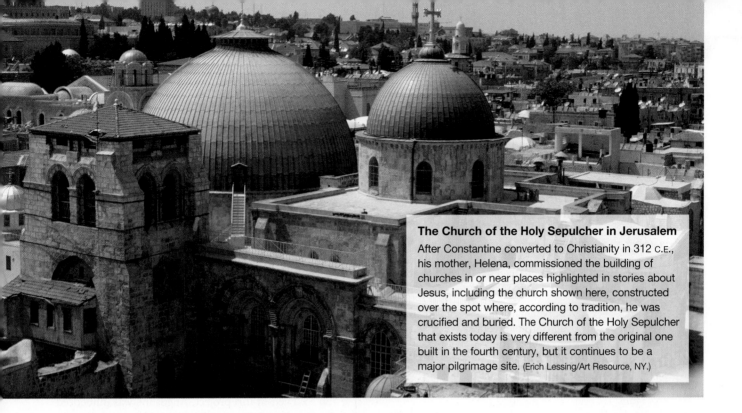

The Church of the Holy Sepulcher in Jerusalem
After Constantine converted to Christianity in 312 C.E., his mother, Helena, commissioned the building of churches in or near places highlighted in stories about Jesus, including the church shown here, constructed over the spot where, according to tradition, he was crucified and buried. The Church of the Holy Sepulcher that exists today is very different from the original one built in the fourth century, but it continues to be a major pilgrimage site. (Erich Lessing/Art Resource, NY.)

roads and sea routes that connected the empire to spread their message and establish new outposts for their religion. By Constantine's day, Christianity had grown to such an extent that the empire turned to Christian institutions and networks to reinforce imperial unity.

Institutionalization of the Christian Church

After Constantine, the institutions of the empire and Christian church were increasingly intertwined, and the power of the church within the empire was irreversible. Changes in the imperial administration, which had become fully focused on the emperor's authority, confirmed the religion's grip. Whereas the empire's earlier administration had been decentralized, the concern of provincial governors and local wealthy citizens, by 300 C.E. the emperor's court had taken over most administrative tasks. Government offices were assigned with careful attention to rank and responsibilities. According to one estimate the imperial court controlled thirty to thirty-five thousand such offices by 400 C.E. The Christian church mirrored the centralized imperial bureaucracy when it stabilized its structure and hierarchy. The imperial and Christian administrative structures coincided, and soon religious leaders also adopted civilian roles.

Doctrinal Debates

As Christianity spread over the wide empire with its multiple cultural traditions, differences of opinion about aspects of the religion emerged. Especially controversial in Constantine's time was the question of the relationship between Jesus's divine and human natures. A doctrine called Arianism (AYR-ee-an-ihz-uhm), which originated with Arius, a priest of Alexandria, claimed that Jesus could not have been divine because he was born from the will of God and had died. Only God, the father, was eternal and divine. Constantine, to whom religious disagreement meant civil disorder, called a council of bishops at Nicaea in Anatolia in 325 C.E. to determine the official doctrine. The council rejected Arianism, but disagreements remained over such questions as exactly when in the year Jesus died and whether priests should remain celibate, among many others. Over the next centuries several councils followed, as we will see in Chapter 9. Opinion differed especially between eastern and western church leaders, who became more distant from each other as the eastern and western halves of the empire increasingly diverged.

Augustine's Influence

At the same time, intellectuals refined the philosophical basis of the Christian creed. Particularly important in this context was the North African bishop Augustine

RISE OF CHRISTIANITY

c. 20–30 C.E.	Jesus teaches in Palestine
c. 40–70 C.E.	Paul spreads Christianity in the Mediterranean
64 C.E.	Nero persecutes Christians in Rome
c. 90 C.E.	Split between Judaism and Christianity
312 C.E.	Constantine converts to Christianity
313 C.E.	Edict of Milan establishes freedom of worship for Christians
324 C.E.	Constantine makes Christianity the official state religion
325 C.E.	Council of Nicaea labels Arianism a heresy
c. 340–420 C.E.	Life of Jerome
354–430 C.E.	Life of Augustine
c. 400–500 C.E.	The Roman imperial and Christian church bureaucracies merge

(354–430 C.E.), who connected Christian thought to Plato's notions of universal ideals (see Chapter 5). Just as Plato believed that rigorous intellectual searching revealed the ideal form of the good, Augustine saw reading the Bible as a way to comprehend God's goodness. Thus the cultural exchanges that shaped the Roman Empire also shaped Christianity. Through the work of Augustine, the Greco-Roman intellectual tradition became embedded in Christian religious thought.

To explain the military difficulties Rome encountered in his lifetime, Augustine reinterpreted the history of the world in his *City of God* (written between 413 and 425 C.E.). He contrasted the "city of man," in which people pursue earthly pleasures, with the "city of God," in which they dedicate their lives to the promotion of Christian ideals. Roman gods and non-Christian philosophers had failed to provide true happiness to humanity; only the Christian God could do so. Even in this project, Augustine was influenced by Greek and Roman thought. Although Augustine attacked earlier philosophers, he was very familiar with their works and used their systems of reasoning. By helping to merge the Roman and Christian traditions, Augustine did much to help cement the place of Christianity in Roman life.

Jerome's Translation of the Bible Others promoted the development of Christianity by making it more accessible. Jerome (c. 340–420 C.E.), who was born in the area of modern Slovenia but moved to Rome, translated the Bible from Hebrew and Greek into Latin. The Latin speakers of the western empire found his translation much easier to comprehend, which greatly facilitated conversion in that region.

The merger of Christian ideas with Roman imperial ideology and bureaucracy led to ultimate success for the religion, even while the empire collapsed in the west. Emperors credited military victories to Christianity and became the upholders of the faith, persecuting non-Christians and dissenting voices within the church. Civil and religious bureaucracies were combined—bishops were also judges, for example. Thus, to understand fully the success of Christianity, we must further explore political developments in the late Roman Empire.

Transformation of the Roman Empire 200–500 C.E.

FOCUS

How and why did the eastern and western parts of the Roman Empire develop differently?

The emperor Caracalla's edict of 212 C.E., which gave citizenship to nearly all free people in the Roman Empire, was the culmination of a long process that changed life for the masses. During the Pax Romana of the second century C.E. in particular, they had enjoyed a long period of stability and economic growth. In the third century C.E., however, severe social and economic crises gripped Rome. Divisions between the eastern and western parts became more acute, and after attempts to keep the empire together, a definitive partition took place in 395 C.E. In the following century, the pressures on the Western Roman Empire became too great, and it collapsed. To this day scholars debate the causes of Rome's collapse in the west. What is undeniable is that fundamental changes took place, and that western Eurasia in 500 C.E. was a very different place from that of 200 C.E.

Division Between East and West

The peace and stability of the Pax Romana was shattered when, in the third century C.E., generals using their legions in fights over the imperial throne devastated the land. Outsiders took advantage of the disarray to raid the empire, and in many places the economy collapsed. It was during this chaotic period that the eastern and western parts of the empire split—they had often served as distinct power bases for contenders to the throne. As we have seen, they had very different cultural histories, and in religious terms they grew further apart because their inhabitants interpreted Christianity differently.

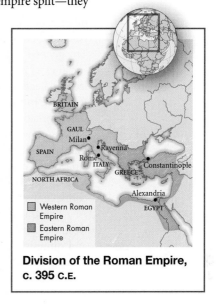

In 324 C.E., Emperor Constantine turned the old city of Byzantium in the eastern part of the empire into a majestic new capital, which he called Constantinople ("city of Constantine"). He filled it with magnificent buildings and established a senate, calling his capital the "new Rome." Strategically located near the empire's borders and situated on major trade routes, Constantinople soon became the most important city of the east. Its rise exacerbated the growing division between the two parts of the empire, however, and by 395 C.E. a single ruler could no longer govern the Roman Empire. Rather, one emperor resided in Constantinople in the east; in the west another emperor ruled, at first from Rome and later from the Italian cities Milan and then Ravenna. The two halves had different histories thereafter: the western part declined and fell prey to Germanic invaders, but the eastern part remained an imperial power for centuries.

Division of the Roman Empire, c. 395 C.E.

Economic Strains and Social Tensions

Throughout its existence, the costs of running the Roman Empire had been enormous. In the third century C.E., the army, which had always been large, grew massive, and emperors gave soldiers increasingly high pay to gain their support. Already expected to

Growing Costs of Empire

Emperor Theodosius's Monument in Constantinople

Work to embellish Constantinople began soon after it became the capital of the Eastern Roman Empire. In 390 C.E. Emperor Theodosius I set up the oldest monument preserved today, an ancient obelisk taken from Egypt and placed on a platform decorated with reliefs carved in his time. This relief shows the emperor ready to hand the laurels of victory to the winner of a chariot race, an image befitting the location of the monument in the city's hippodrome, an arena for equestrian events. (The Art Archive/Gianni Dagli Orti.)

commission public works and monumental buildings, after the official conversion to Christianity, emperors were also obliged to build numerous churches and donate property to the church and its clergy. The imperial administration thus grew increasingly concerned over finances.

Social Impact

To guarantee state income and promote economic stability, the emperors took steps to limit economic and social mobility. Peasants were tied to the land, unable to leave to pursue other economic opportunities. Artisans were similarly tied to their workshops and had to pass on their occupations to their sons, and when soldiers retired their sons replaced them. The general population of the empire thus became tied to the land and fixed in a particular social class from which they could not advance. This new arrangement facilitated tax collection, because social class determined the level of taxation, but it severely limited people's freedom. In the country, peasants sought protection against the state from the landowners they worked for. In the cities, the poor turned to bishops, who had gained special prominence and who could act as people's patrons—in the fifth century C.E., bishops became the masters and protectors of entire cities, especially in the western empire. Thus, as the problems of the empire intensified, its inhabitants increasingly saw the imperial government as a threat rather than a protector, and they tried to establish a new set of social and political connections to guarantee their safety and security.

This transformation was accelerated by the decline of cities and towns in the west. They were victims of insufficient funds for public works, a disappearing imperial administration, and diminished trade. Economic power shifted to the landed estates, whose owners were masters over the people working for them and produced all they needed by themselves. This greatly reduced the western emperor's powers, and many regions became virtually autonomous. By contrast, in the east the cities were more resilient, and the peasants resisted forced settlement and retained their independence.

Collapse in the West and Revitalization in the East

After 200 C.E., outside pressures exacerbated the internal problems of the Roman Empire. In the east, the empire fought over border territories with the centralized states of Parthia and, after 224 C.E., Sasanid Persia. Because these wars involved two equal powers, they regularly ended in negotiated settlements. In the west, Rome confronted various Germanic tribal groups, which acted independently of one another. In time these groups breached the Rhine and Danube frontiers.

The Western Empire

The tribal threat had loomed since the beginning of the empire, and the Romans had strengthened the western border with a long line of walls and fortresses. Some tribes infiltrated imperial lands, however, and officials allowed them to settle there. Because German tribes themselves were under pressure from Central Asian nomadic Huns, they increased their efforts to enter the empire and broke down Rome's resistance. The Huns entered the fray themselves under their king, Attila, who acquired the epithet "scourge of God." He invaded Gaul in 450 and then assailed Italy, where the bishop of Rome had to pay him off. Although an emperor remained enthroned in the western empire, his influence was minor, and he watched feebly as various German leaders struggled for power. Thus nomadic peoples profoundly influenced the history of the sedentary peoples of the Roman Empire, duplicating a pattern we have seen in other societies around the world.

Despite the Germanic presence, there was much continuity in daily life in the western empire. The older inhabitants kept obeying Roman law, while the Germans followed their own legal traditions. Landed estates remained the focus of economic activities, the difference being that their lords now depended on German kings. Bureaucrats were still needed, and those of the empire continued to serve. Because many Germans converted to Christianity upon entering the empire, religious practices remained the same, and the church even increased its influence. Thus when in 476 C.E. Odoacer (OH-doo-way-sahr), the German king whose territory included Italy, forced the last Roman emperor, Romulus Augustulus, to abdicate, the event did not affect most people's lives. The western empire ceased to exist, and several Germanic kingdoms arose in its place, as we will see in Chapter 9.

The history of the eastern empire was very different from that of the west. Constantinople was a powerful major city and, notwithstanding outside pressures, its emperors governed large territories that remained urban and economically successful. The court saw itself as the protector of the Christian faith and of Roman civilization. A distinct eastern culture of the late world of antiquity developed; today historians call it Byzantine. The eastern empire and its culture would continue into the fifteenth century C.E., when the Turks captured Constantinople. Thus the urban culture of the eastern Mediterranean survived both integration into the Roman Empire in the second and first centuries B.C.E. and the western empire's disintegration some five hundred years later.

COUNTERPOINT
Rome's Iranian Rivals in the Middle East

To ancient Romans, their empire may easily have seemed the strongest power on earth, invincible and unlimited. In reality, however, Rome's dominion of western Eurasia was just one of a string of empires that stretched across Eurasia from the South China Sea in the east to the Atlantic Ocean in the west. We have discussed several of these empires before. The Han Empire in China (206 B.C.E.–220 C.E.) and the Kushan Empire in Central and South Asia (c. 50–233 C.E.) both controlled territories not much smaller than Rome's. Closer to Rome was a Southwest Asian power that never yielded to Roman armies. Centered in Iran and heirs to the ancient Persian Empire, two empires in succession withheld the forces of Roman expansion (see Map 7.4). From the moment Rome started to annex regions of the eastern Mediterranean in the first century B.C.E., it confronted the Parthians, who ruled Iran, Mesopotamia, parts of Syria, and eastern Anatolia. The Sasanids overthrew the Parthians in 224 C.E. and continued the competition with Roman Byzantium until their defeat by Muslim armies in the seventh century (discussed in Chapter 9).

> **FOCUS**
>
> What were the differences in organization between the Iranian and Roman empires?

These Iranian empires demonstrated not only that Rome's military dominance had limits but that the structure of a powerful empire did not have to resemble that of Rome. In contrast to the Roman style of control, which imposed a uniform system over subject territories, the Iranian empires were conglomerates of kingdoms and provinces whose kings and governors owed obedience to a "king of kings." These empires successfully ruled a vast area for more than nine centuries.

The Parthians 247 B.C.E.–224 C.E.

Soon after Alexander of Macedonia's death in 323 B.C.E., the territories he had conquered from the Mediterranean Sea to the Indus Valley had become the Seleucid Empire (see Chapter 5). Gradually, however, various regions of the Seleucid state gained independence. In the north, to the east of the Caspian Sea, was the province of Parthia, where in 247 B.C.E. a new people came to power under a leader called Arsaces (ar-SAY-sez). They may have originally been one of the many nomadic groups who seized control over the cities in the region and assumed rule. The Seleucids recognized Parthia's independence in around 210 B.C.E., and in succeeding decades Parthians annexed parts of Iran and Mesopotamia. When Rome conquered the remains of the Seleucid Empire in the eastern Mediterranean, it found itself faced with a formidable new opponent in the Parthians.

The Euphrates River formed a natural border between the two empires, but several Roman generals sought fame and fortune by leading their forces across the river. The results were often disastrous. In a battle in 53 B.C.E., for example, tens of thousands of Roman soldiers lost their lives. Likewise the Parthians regularly tried to annex Roman-

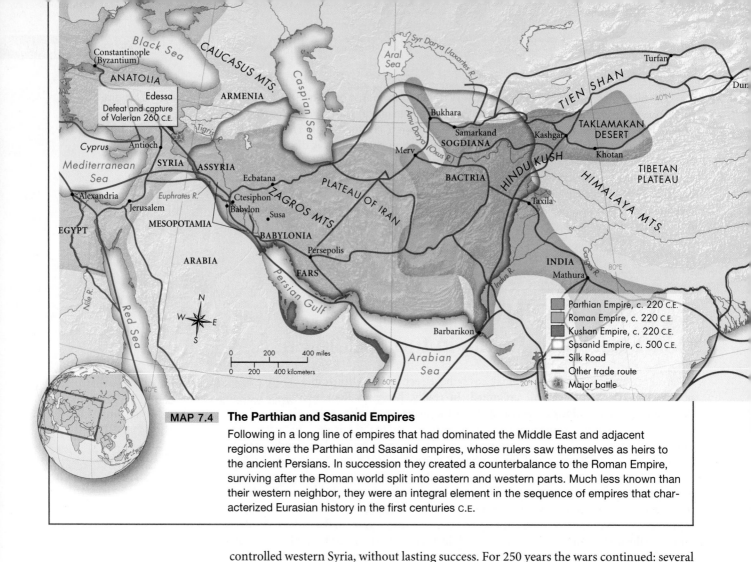

MAP 7.4 **The Parthian and Sasanid Empires**
Following in a long line of empires that had dominated the Middle East and adjacent regions were the Parthian and Sasanid empires, whose rulers saw themselves as heirs to the ancient Persians. In succession they created a counterbalance to the Roman Empire, surviving after the Roman world split into eastern and western parts. Much less known than their western neighbor, they were an integral element in the sequence of empires that characterized Eurasian history in the first centuries C.E.

controlled western Syria, without lasting success. For 250 years the wars continued: several Roman emperors of the second century C.E. made gains in northern Syria and Mesopotamia, but the territories were never truly integrated into the Roman Empire.

Imperial Organization
The Parthians could manage these territorial gains and losses because they saw their ruler as a "king of kings," a master of vassals from various states. This idea had already existed in the Persian Empire, and the Parthians claimed familial descent from these earlier rulers in their efforts to gain acceptance as kings. As in the past, the empire's cohesion depended greatly on the strength of the Parthian ruler; the local kings had a local power base and sufficient independence to switch allegiance at times. The cities, the hubs from which the Seleucids had governed the territory, also maintained the sovereignty they had before, and Greek speakers often preserved political organizations, such as the assembly. Nonetheless, the structure gave flexibility and resilience to the Parthian Empire: the loss of one territory would not have disastrous effects on the whole.

Trade
Despite the numerous wars between Parthians and Romans, the two rivals maintained important economic connections. Parthia controlled a large part of the Silk Road, which, as we saw in Chapter 6, brought luxuries from the East to Rome: Indian pepper, aromatics, perfumes, precious stones and pearls, and Chinese silk. In the first century C.E. the Romans tried to bypass the Parthians by establishing a direct link to India by sea, but the Roman elite's appetite for luxury goods was so great that they still needed overland trade. The Parthians contributed to this trade, exporting foods such as pomegranates and alfalfa to China, as well as Iranian horses, which the Chinese greatly admired.

The Sasanids 224–651 C.E.

In 224 C.E., Ardashir (AR-da-shear), the leader of a Parthian vassal kingdom, defeated the last Parthian king in battle and asserted supremacy over the entire empire. A native of the southwestern Iranian region of Fars, Ardashir claimed descent from a man named Sasan, and his dynasty is thus called the Sasanids. The structure of the Parthian Empire allowed for such a change of ruler; in essence, a new "king of kings" had arisen. The Sasanids developed the idea of "the empire of the Iranians," which the king was destined to rule because he was the descendant of mythical kings and of gods. His line of royal descent ran through the Persian emperors of the sixth to fourth centuries B.C.E. and gave rise to the idea of a history of the country of Iran with a long succession of rulers. The Sasanids thus inherited their concept of kingship from the Parthians, but added increased centralization of power to it.

Diplomatically, the Sasanids carried on as the Parthians had, their trade with Rome being an enormous source of income. Simultaneously, wars with the Romans continued with some notable Sasanid successes: for example, in 260 C.E. King Shapur I defeated the Roman army of Valerian and captured the Roman emperor alive. This was the first time ever that a Roman emperor had been taken captive in battle. The wars did not end with the division of the Roman Empire, and Byzantine and Sasanid forces regularly fought each other, despite threats to both from the Huns of Central Asia. The end of the Sasanid dynasty came from the south, when Muslim armies from Arabia invaded Iran in the seventh century.

Continued Wars with Rome

So for almost a thousand years the Parthians and Sasanids successfully ruled Iran and the surrounding regions, basing their authority on a system of supreme kingship over varied vassals. They enforced control through armies that were especially effective because of the cavalry. The core of the army consisted of mounted archers and heavily armored mounted spearmen, their horses covered with armor as well. The Romans were in awe of these opponents. One soldier wrote in 362 C.E.:

The Iranian Army

> The Persians opposed us with squadrons of mounted armored soldiers drawn up in such serried ranks that their movements in their close-fitting coats of flexible mail dazzled our eyes, while all their horses were protected by housings of leather.[5]

A Tapestry of Cultures and Religions

Like the other empires we have studied, those of the Parthians and Sasanids brought together people with diverse cultural backgrounds and religions, who spoke many languages and used different scripts. Like the Kushans of Central Asia, they tolerated these various

Shapur Celebrates the Capture of Valerian

In 260 C.E. the Sasanid ruler Shapur defeated the Roman army in northern Syria and captured its emperor Valerian alive, a feat unparalleled in Roman history. In this relief, carved on a rock near the tombs of the ancient Persian kings seven miles from Persepolis, the Persians celebrated by depicting the Roman emperor kneeling in submission. According to tradition, after the Roman emperor was killed in captivity, Shapur had him skinned and preserved. (The Art Archive/Gianni Dagli Orti.)

A Sasanid Account of the Wars with Rome

Near the ancient Persian city of Persepolis, the Sasanid king Shapur I (r. 239–270 C.E.) set up an inscription in three languages that described his wars with the Romans. The languages he used were Middle Persian, the language the court spoke at the time; Parthian, the language of the preceding rulers of Iran; and Greek, the language of the eastern Roman Empire. Although he glorifies his own actions in the account and perhaps ignores his military setbacks, his account is a useful balance to the Roman picture of wars in the east. Shapur boasts, for example:

Just as we were ascended to the throne over the lands, the Caesar Gordian gathered in all of the Roman Empire an army of Goths and Germans and marched on Asurestan [Assyria], against Iranshahr and against us. On the border of Assyria, at Misike [where the Euphrates and Tigris rivers are close together], a great frontal battle took place. And Caesar Gordian was killed and we destroyed the Roman army. And the Romans proclaimed Philip Caesar. And Caesar Philip came to us to plead,

and paid us 500,000 denarii as ransom for his life and became tributary to us.

The inscription goes on to describe three wars against the Romans; the last one led to the capture of the Roman emperor Valerian in 260 C.E. Shapur I was so proud of that event that he ordered a large rock-relief carving in which the Roman is shown begging for his life (see page 231).

Source: Translation from Philip Huyse. *Die dreisprachige Inschrift Shabuhrs I. an der Ka'ba-i Zardusht (ShKZ)* (London: School of Oriental and African Studies, 1999), 26–27.

EXAMINING THE EVIDENCE

1. Why would Shapur I have commissioned an inscription in three languages?

2. Why are records of this type especially important for our knowledge of the Roman Empire?

---

traditions and even promoted them. The emperors spoke Aryan languages of Iran (Parthian and Middle Persian), which they used for official inscriptions often carved on rock surfaces and written in alphabetic scripts derived from Aramaic (see Reading the Past: A Sasanid Account of the Wars with Rome). They also used Greek as an official language, often on coins and also for translations of the rock inscriptions. The Semitic Aramaic language, written in its own script, was very important for administration. The use of a variety of Semitic (for example, Hebrew) and Indo-European (for example, Bactrian, Armenian) languages persisted throughout the entire period. Besides administrative and official records, a great variety of writings appeared, including literature translated from Greek and Indian originals.

Religious Toleration   Although the kings relied on Zoroastrianism (see Chapter 4) to support their rule, the variety of religions in the empire was equally great. A Zoroastrian priest wrote in the third century C.E. that the empire housed "Jews, Buddhists, Hindus, Nazarenes, Christians, Baptists, and Manicheans,"[6] that is, followers of the various religions from India and the Eastern Roman Empire, including various Christian sects.

Manichaeism   A new religion that originated in Iran perfectly illustrates a coalescence of various spiritual influences. Its founder, Mani (MAH-nee), was born in 216 C.E. in the Babylonian part of the then Parthian Empire. At age twenty-four, Mani started to preach a religion he hoped would appeal universally. He saw Buddha, Zoroaster, and Jesus as his precursors in a long line of prophets and borrowed from all their teachings. Like Zoroaster, Mani saw a strict opposition between soul and body, good and evil, and light and dark. To him life was painful, and the human soul had succumbed to evil. Only true knowledge would free the soul and return it to its original state of goodness, which it would share with God. Mani urged people to live an ascetic life, but realized that few people could do so at the desired level.

Mani traveled widely to spread his ideas, and he encouraged his followers to do the same. His teachings were so flexible that they could easily merge with existing religions, such as Buddhism, Daoism, Zoroastrianism, and Christianity. In the west they inspired many Christians of the Roman Empire, including Augustine, who followed Manichaean teachings for nine years, but the church hierarchy saw them as heresy. In Iran, too, the original toleration of Manichaeism gave way to persecutions. Mani himself died in prison sometime between 274 and 277 C.E., and his severed head was impaled on a pole for public display. His followers likened his death to Jesus's crucifixion. His religion survived, however, until persecutions in the Roman Empire in the fifth century and in the Middle East in the tenth century almost extinguished it.

Conclusion

When the Roman historian Tacitus wrote in around the year 100 C.E. that the empire he inhabited changed the way people lived as far away as Britain, he was not bragging groundlessly. Rome had created a world in which people from North Africa and Syria to Britain and France shared habits and tastes. A man born in one corner of the empire could make a career hundreds of miles away and end up in Rome as a politician. The cohesion of the Roman Empire explains why the ideas of a small Jewish sect could spread over an enormous area and why the Christian church it inspired could obtain an encompassing structure once it assimilated with the imperial bureaucracy. The Roman Empire was a crucial milestone in the history of western Eurasia, a structure that fundamentally shaped the region with effects still visible today. Its own development is a fascinating story of how strong Republican institutions with elected officials and term limits failed to prevent the consolidation of power in the hands of one man. In European tradition, the Roman Empire became the embodiment of the ancient world, a period of the past that produced great human achievements that needed to be recovered. The ancient Romans left behind so much material—written and nonwritten—that we can recreate their world in great detail and see it as the archetype of empire.

A subject of the empire may have imagined that Rome was unique and dominated the entire world. But students of world history today realize that it was merely part of a system of empires that stretched throughout Eurasia. Although we call them all empires, they had varied organizations and degrees of centralization. For each region, the empire constituted a finishing point of developments that had started thousands of years earlier, as politically united regions grew larger and cultural uniformity increased. These empires represent the culmination of ancient history throughout Eurasia.

NOTES

1. H. Mattingly, trans., *Tacitus on Britain and Germany* (Harmondsworth, Middlesex, U.K.: Penguin Books, 1978), 72.
2. Horace, *Epistles* 2.1, lines 156–157.
3. J. Parrès, http://rambert.francis.free.fr/aumale/aumalehisto/aumalerom3.htm.
4. Herbert Musurillo, ed. and trans., *The Acts of the Christian Martyrs* (Oxford: Clarendon Press, 1972), 119.
5. Ammianus Marcellinus, 24.6.7., qtd. in M. Brosius, *The Persians* (London: Routledge, 2006), 187.
6. Josef Wiesehöfer, *Ancient Persia from 550 B.C. to 650 A.D.* (London: Tauris, 1996), 199.

RESOURCES FOR RESEARCH

General Works

Ancient Rome is the subject of a vast amount of research and writing, and works continue to be published on every aspect of its history and culture. Most of the references listed here relate to this chapter as a whole.

Grant, Michael, and Rachel Kitzinger, eds. *Civilization of the Ancient Mediterranean*, 1988.

*(For quotes from ancient texts on numerous subjects): Internet Ancient History Sourcebook: Rome. http://www.fordham.edu/halsall/ancient/asbook09.html.

(For information on women): Materials for the Study of Women and Gender in the Ancient World. http://www.stoa.org/diotima.

McGeough, Kevin M. *The Romans: New Perspectives.* 2004.

*(For ancient texts in the original and in translation, and other online resources): Perseus Digital Texts. http://www.perseus.tufts.edu.

Woolf, Greg, ed. *Cambridge Illustrated History of the Roman World.* 2003.

Rome: A Republican Center of Power, 500–27 B.C.E.

To reconstruct the earliest history of Rome, modern historians rely on accounts that Romans such as Livy produced in the late Republic and early empire, and on archaeological remains. Some of the main political actors of later Republican times left their own writings—for example, Julius Caesar, whose war accounts are fascinating in their detail and information on the late Republic.

Cornell, T. J. *The Beginnings of Rome: Italy and Rome from the Bronze Age to the Punic Wars (c. 1000–264 B.C.).* 1995.

*Julius Caesar. *The Civil War.* Translated by John Carter. 1997.

*Lewis, Naphtali, and Meyer Reinhold, eds. *Roman Civilization: Selected Readings,* 3d ed. Vol. 1, *The Republic and the Augustan Age.* 1990.

*Livy. *The Early History of Rome.* Translated by Aubrey de Sélincourt. 1961.

Matyszak, Philip. *Chronicle of the Roman Republic: The Rulers of Ancient Rome from Romulus to Augustus.* 2003.

Rome: The Empire, 27 B.C.E.–212 C.E.

Ancient Roman historians such as Tacitus left us detailed biographies of emperors, which are engaging works with stories of court intrigues and other scandals. They have inspired modern fiction, which can represent Roman antiquity very realistically, as in Graves's novels. Because there is so much historical data, we have an enormous volume of publications on every aspect of the empire.

Bunson, Matthew. *Encyclopedia of the Roman Empire.* 1994.

Graves, Robert. *Claudius the God.* 1943.

Graves, Robert. *I, Claudius.* 1934.

*Lewis, Naphtali, and Meyer Reinhold. *Roman Civilization. Selected Reading.* Vol. 2, *The Empire,* 3d ed. 1990.

Online Encyclopedia of Roman Rulers and Their Families. http://www.roman-emperors.org.

Scarre, Christopher. *Chronicle of the Roman Emperors: The Reign-by-Reign Record of the Rulers of Imperial Rome.* 1995.

*Tacitus. *The Histories.* Translated by D. S. Levene. 1977.

Wells, Colin. *The Roman Empire,* 2d ed. 1992.

Christianity: From Jewish Sect to Imperial Religion

The birth and early development of Christianity continues to engage scholars and other writers. A vast literature approaches the subject from multiple angles.

Fox, Robin Lane. *Pagans and Christians.* 1986.

Hopkins, Keith. *A World Full of Gods: Pagans, Jews, and Christians in the Roman Empire.* 1999.

*MacMullen, Ramsay, and Eugene N. Lane, eds. *Paganism and Christianity, 100–425 C.E.: A Sourcebook.* 1992.

Markus, R. A. *Christianity in the Roman World.* 1974.

Stark, Rodney. *The Rise of Christianity: How the Obscure, Marginal Jesus Movement Became the Dominant Religious Force in the Western World in a Few Centuries.* 1997.

Transformation of the Roman Empire, 212–500 C.E.

The study of the later centuries of the Roman Empire is a relatively new academic pursuit that has become very popular because it allows scholars to deal with many traditions and cultures. Brown's book is often regarded as the work that gave rise to this new interest.

Bowersock, G. W., Peter Brown, and Oleg Grabar, eds. *Late Antiquity: A Guide to the Postclassical World.* 1999.

Brown, Peter. *The World of Late Antiquity.* 1971.

Cameron, Averil. *The Late Roman Empire, A.D. 284–430.* 1993.

Garnsey, Peter, and Caroline Humfress. *The Evolution of the Late Antique World.* 2001.

Mitchell, Stephen. *A History of the Later Roman Empire, A.D. 284–641: The Transformation of the Ancient World.* 2007.

COUNTERPOINT: Rome's Iranian Rivals in the Middle East

Until recently, study of the Parthians and Sasanids was a highly specialized academic field. Now, however, several scholars have written more accessible works that place these empires within the sequences of ancient Persian empires and that rely on indigenous as well as Roman sources. The Web site listed here contains an extensive collection of materials, including a massive bibliography.

Brosius, Maria. *The Persians: An Introduction.* 2006.

Garthwaite, Gene R. *The Persians.* 2005.

Harrison, Thomas, ed. *The Great Empires of the Ancient World.* 2009.

The Parthian Empire. http://parthia.com/.

Wiesehöfer, Josef. *Ancient Persia from 550 B.C. to 650 A.D.* 1996.

* Primary source.

▶ **For additional primary sources from this period,** see *Sources of Crossroads and Cultures.*

▶ **For Web sites, images, and documents related to topics in this chapter,** see Make History at bedfordstmartins.com/smith.

The major global development in this chapter ▶ The unification of western Eurasia under the Roman Empire.

IMPORTANT EVENTS

753–509 B.C.E.	Roman monarchy
509 B.C.E.	Start of the Roman Republic
264–146 B.C.E.	Punic Wars between Rome and Carthage
210 B.C.E.	Parthians gain independence from Seleucid Empire
49 B.C.E.	Julius Caesar crosses the Rubicon
44 B.C.E.	Assassination of Julius Caesar
31 B.C.E.–14 C.E.	Reign of Augustus
c. 30 B.C.E.	Rome controls entire Mediterranean region
27 B.C.E.	Augustus establishes full dominance over Roman affairs
c. 4 B.C.E.–30 C.E.	Life of Jesus
100–200 C.E.	Pax Romana; height of the Roman Empire
212 C.E.	Caracalla grants citizenship to nearly all free inhabitants of the empire
224 C.E.	Sasanids overthrow Parthians
313 C.E.	Constantine issues Edict of Milan, legalizing Christianity
395 C.E.	Roman Empire divided into eastern and western parts
410 C.E.	German tribes sack Rome
476 C.E.	German leader Odoacer forces last western Roman emperor to step down

KEY TERMS

client (p. 208)	*pater familias* (p. 208)
consul (p. 209)	**patrician** (p. 209)
equestrian (p. 210)	*Pax Romana* (p. 217)
latifundia (p. 210)	**plebeian** (p. 209)
legion (p. 216)	**Romanization** (p. 218)
magistrate (p. 209)	**Senate** (p. 209)
martyrdom (p. 223)	**tribune** (p. 209)

CHAPTER OVERVIEW QUESTIONS

1. How are the institutions of Republican Rome still important to us today?
2. How did the Romans face the challenges of creating and maintaining an empire?
3. What impact did Rome have on the lives of the people it conquered?
4. How did Christianity's rise benefit from the Roman Empire?
5. What were the limits of Roman imperialism?

SECTION FOCUS QUESTIONS

1. What were the political ideals of Republican Rome, and how did some outlive the Republic itself?
2. How did the Roman Empire bring administrative and cultural unity to the vast territory it ruled?
3. Why did imperial policy toward Christianity shift from persecution to institutionalization as Rome's state religion?
4. How and why did the eastern and western parts of the Roman Empire develop differently?
5. What were the differences in organization between the Iranian and Roman empires?

MAKING CONNECTIONS

1. How did the political and cultural achievements of Republican Rome compare with those of classical Greece (see Chapter 5)?
2. How did the world empires of the centuries from 500 B.C.E. to 500 C.E. facilitate the spread of new ideas and religions? Compare, for example, the Han (see Chapter 6) and Roman empires.
3. How does the level of cultural integration in the Roman Empire compare with that of the Eurasian empires we studied in earlier chapters?
4. In what sense did Christianity merge earlier traditions of the eastern Mediterranean world?

8

AT A CROSSROADS ▲

The ancient populations of South America developed textiles into an art form, experimenting with fiber materials and decorations. In the first millennium B.C.E., the people of Paracas in the southern Andes revolutionized textile production by introducing tapestry weaving and new techniques of dyeing. The fragment shown here, part of a mummy wrapping produced in the first century B.C.E., depicts a mythical monster we call the "Decapitator." (Private Collection/Boltin Picture Library/Bridgeman Art Library.)

Reading the Unwritten Record: Peoples of Africa, the Americas, and the Pacific Islands

3000 B.C.E.–500 C.E.

I n 1769 C.E., Sir Joseph Banks visited the Polynesian islands in the South Pacific in his ship, the *Endeavour*. In describing the inhabitants in his journal, the English explorer remarked on their navigational skills:

> The people excell much in predicting the weather, a circumstance of great use to them in their short voyages from Island to Island. They have many various ways of doing this but one only that I know of which I never heard of being practisd by Europaeans, that is foretelling the quarter of the heavens from whence the wind shall blow by observing the Milky Way . . . in this as well as their other predictions we found them indeed not infallible but far more clever than Europaeans. In their longer voyages they steer in the day by the Sun and in the night by the Stars. Of these they know a very large part by their Names and the clever ones among them will tell in what part of the heavens they are to be seen in any month when they are above their horizon; they know also the time of their annual appearing and disapearing to a great nicety, far greater than would be easily believed by an Europaean astronomer.[1]

BACKSTORY

At the start of this book we looked at the evolution of the human species and our ancestors' migration throughout the globe. As the setting for the lives of the earliest humans, Africa played a major role in these events. Vast oceans separated Africa and its original human inhabitants from places such as the Americas and the islands of the Pacific Ocean. But over broad expanses of time, the significance of these gaps between the earth's far-distant realms diminished as African peoples responded to changes in their physical environment and migrated to other parts of the world. In this chapter, we shift our focus from the ancient cultures of Eurasia to Africa, the Americas, and the Pacific in the period 3000 B.C.E. to 500 C.E. In so doing, we explore a unique challenge these regions present to the historian: reconstructing the history of societies that did not leave a written record.

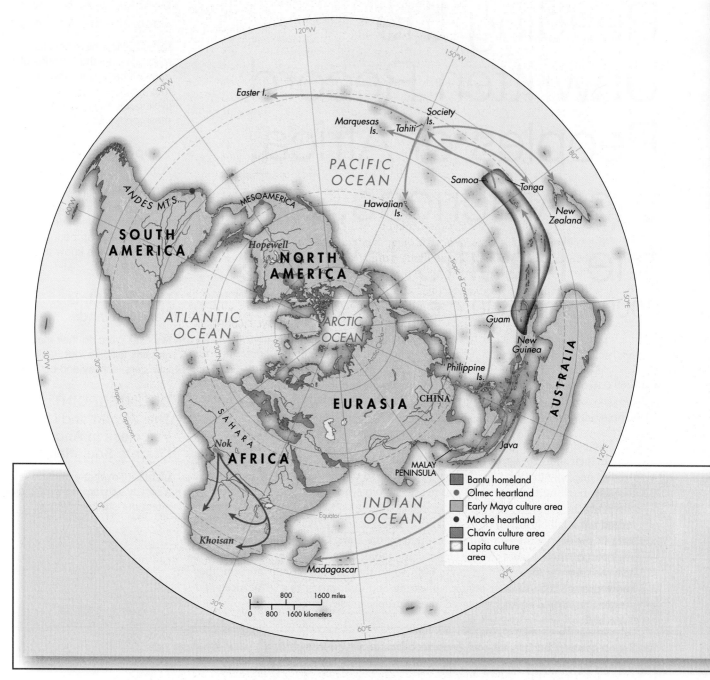

Bantu homeland
Olmec heartland
Early Maya culture area
Moche heartland
Chavín culture area
Lapita culture area

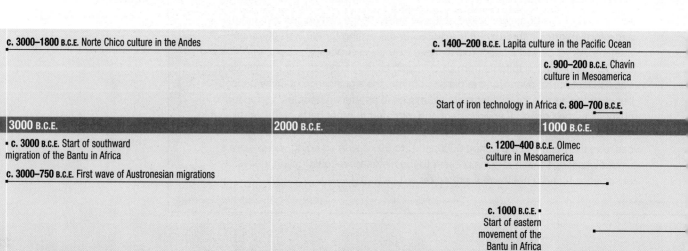

c. 3000–1800 B.C.E. Norte Chico culture in the Andes

c. 1400–200 B.C.E. Lapita culture in the Pacific Ocean

c. 900–200 B.C.E. Chavín culture in Mesoamerica

Start of iron technology in Africa **c. 800–700 B.C.E.**

3000 B.C.E.   **2000 B.C.E.**   **1000 B.C.E.**

• **c. 3000 B.C.E.** Start of southward migration of the Bantu in Africa

c. 3000–750 B.C.E. First wave of Austronesian migrations

c. 1200–400 B.C.E. Olmec culture in Mesoamerica

c. 1000 B.C.E. •
Start of eastern movement of the Bantu in Africa

Savvy seafarers, the ancestors of these Polynesians had boldly spread over the myriad of islands in the Pacific Ocean, but they had maintained many of their original customs. Thus Banks stated:

> From the similarity of customs, the still greater of Traditions and the almost identical sameness of Language between these people and those of the Islands of the South Sea there remains little doubt that they came originally from the same source: but where that Source is future experience may teach us, at Present I can say no more than I firmly believe that it is to the Westward and by no means to the East.[2]

Banks was among the handful of early European explorers who drew the peoples of Polynesia into history by recording some of their customs, practices, and languages. Because these people did not write, our only records of their early histories are the accounts of literate visitors. Banks's efforts are all the more valuable because he carefully observed the Polynesians and willingly acknowledged their intelligence and skills. More often, however, European observers' comments were derogatory or patronizing, depicting the peoples of Africa, the Americas, and the Pacific Islands as savages without culture.

All peoples of the world have a history, but in ancient times very few people wrote. Historians today work primarily with written evidence that provides direct access to peoples of the past. Thus there are limits to what they can say about people who left no written documents, such as the early Polynesians whom Sir Joseph Banks described, or about cultures such as the Olmec of Mesoamerica, whose writings they do not comprehend. To explore the lives of such populations, researchers must rely on material remains, which can be anything from a massive city to a simple ax or knife used to build a boat or to harvest fruit. Scholars usually refer to this type of archaeological study as **prehistory**, a discipline that focuses on the remains of nonliterate peoples or peoples with early writing systems that are still not fully deciphered. Their artifacts can reveal developments as complex as those recorded by ancient literate cultures.

prehistory The scholarly discipline that studies peoples' histories before they left behind written evidence; also the time period during which cultures had no writing.

MAPPING THE WORLD

Peoples of Africa, the Americas, and the Pacific Islands, c. 3000 B.C.E.–500 C.E.

Throughout the ancient world, peoples without writing—and hence outside the traditional historical record—established vibrant cultures, which are known to us mostly from archaeological remains. In Africa and the Pacific Islands, migrants spread aspects of these cultures over wide areas and into different natural zones, whereas in the Americas, cultures developed distinctive elements in relative geographic isolation. Everywhere ancient peoples created traditions of lasting impact.

ROUTES ▼

→ Bantu migrations, c. 3000 B.C.E.–400 C.E.

→ Austronesian migrations, c. 3000 B.C.E.–1000 C.E.

c. 200–600 c.e. Moche culture in the Andes

• c. 400 c.e. Bantu arrival in southern Africa

| 0 | 1000 c.e. | 2000 c.e. |

c. 100 B.C.E.–400 C.E. Hopewell culture in eastern North America

c. 400 B.C.E.–250 C.E. Early Maya culture in Mesoamerica

c. 800 B.C.E.–200 C.E. Nok culture in West Africa

c. 400–1200 c.e. Second wave of Austronesian migrations

In this chapter we consider prehistoric cultures from various parts of the world as examples of historical developments in such societies. Literate observers often used to dismiss them as "peoples without history," but in the 1980s the anthropologist Eric Wolf laid the groundwork for a new attitude by showing how prehistoric cultures actively shaped world history. The examples in this chapter show that such societies could reach high levels of social and technological development and acquire many features of what we call civilization, including cities.

This is not to say that these societies closely resembled those of Eurasia in the same period. Some purposely rejected technologies that were almost universally used elsewhere in the ancient world, such as pottery. Members of these societies lived in smaller communities than their contemporaries in Eurasia, and they did not create the large states that emerged there. The prehistoric peoples we study here were more physically isolated from other cultures than those treated before, and local conditions had more impact than outside influences on their cultural development. Geographical features such as high mountain ranges and dense forests were harder to cross than in Eurasia, where transcontinental routes existed. Yet some of these small groups—especially among the Polynesians and Africa's Bantu speakers—migrated vast distances by water or land and in this way spread technologies and cultural traditions to a range of new environments.

As in Eurasian societies, in this period the inhabitants of Africa, the Americas, and the Pacific Islands laid the groundwork for later developments. In a sense, they are the voiceless peoples of early world history, for the absence of writing that we can comprehend makes them less approachable than other cultures we have studied. But it is important to remember that throughout the ancient world, very few people speak to us directly—as in every society we have discussed so far, the great majority of people were illiterate and remain equally voiceless.

OVERVIEW
QUESTIONS

The major global development in this chapter: The evolution of ancient cultures without writing and their fundamental role in world history.

As you read, consider:

1. How does the presence or absence of writing influence how we study ancient cultures?

2. Why did the ancient cultures of Africa, the Americas, and the Pacific often show similar developments in spite of their isolation from one another?

3. How is the spread of peoples, languages, and technologies interrelated, and in what ways can we study these processes?

Peoples of Sub-Saharan Africa

FOCUS

How have scholars reconstructed the histories of early Africans, and what do their sources reveal about the livelihoods and cultures of these peoples?

The human species originated in Africa, the continent with the longest history in the world. But except in northern Africa, the study of early African history must be based primarily on material remains, because there were no native writing systems, and accounts by foreign visitors are scarce until European reports from the seventeenth century C.E. Thus, we mainly reconstruct developments in sub-Saharan Africa in ancient times through archaeology, with some help from linguistics. These sources show a long-term process during which the livelihoods of most people changed from gathering and hunting to agriculture, as was the case in the Eurasian regions we studied before. In many parts of Africa, migrations by peoples speaking Bantu languages were responsible for the shift to settled farming. Geography and climate combined to keep these farming communities small, however, and large urban centers did not emerge in Africa in this period.

Early Hunters and Herders

The earliest inhabitants of Africa, as elsewhere, survived by gathering and hunting local resources. Animals and plants were abundant enough that small groups of people could comfortably survive throughout most of the continent. Africa has several ecological zones that provide a diversity of wild resources (see Map 8.1).

African Ecology

Around the equator lies a tropical rain forest. The area has few food sources and the climate promotes tropical diseases such as malaria, so in ancient times human occupation was very limited there. But **savannas**—tropical or subtropical grasslands with scattered trees and shrubs where plenty of animals reside and plant life is rich—cover large parts of Africa. These grassy expanses have drawn gatherers and hunters throughout history. Wild food supplies were especially plentiful near lakes, and ancient peoples who lived near them could spend most of the year in the same settlement without farming. Instead, they subsisted largely by fishing, hunting, and collecting plants and nuts.

Soon after 5000 B.C.E., some people in northern Africa moved from gathering and hunting to herding animals. This transition is vividly documented in cave paintings in the Tassili (TAH-sihl-ee) region, located in the midst of the Sahara Desert in southern modern-day Algeria (see again Chapter 1's Seeing the Past: Saharan Rock Art, page 21). Before 5000 B.C.E., the climate there was much wetter than it is today, and it supported a bounty of animal and human life. The earliest paintings, whose exact date we cannot establish, show humans hunting big game with spears and bows. But those painted from perhaps 4500 B.C.E. to 2500 B.C.E. depict people as herders of cattle, sheep, and goats. Wild cattle were native to the Sahara. Sheep and goats were not, however, so the Saharan people must have imported them from the Middle East, where these animals had been herded since 8000 B.C.E. Later art shows attempts to domesticate other native animals, such as giraffes and ostriches, a sign of the people's greater reliance on domesticated resources. Simultaneously, early Africans collected and cared for plants more intensively. Thus we can say that from 4500 B.C.E. to 2500 B.C.E., a widespread pastoral culture flourished in Africa north of the rain forest.

Bantu Migrations

Today some 85 million people in Africa speak a myriad of closely related languages that originate from one common source. Scholars call the linguistic group they belong to **Bantu**, after a native term for "persons" or "people." The expansion of Bantu languages all over the continent is related to the spread of agriculture and is fundamentally important to African history. The processes involved parallel those of the spread of Indo-European languages discussed in Chapter 3, and scholars study them in the same way. Linguistic analysis identifies similarities and differences among the various languages to determine how closely they are related and to estimate when their speakers became separated. As these examples from four central African languages show, the similarities are great, but there are clear differences.

savanna Tropical or subtropical grassland with scattered trees and shrubs.

Bantu The name for some five hundred closely related languages spoken in sub-Saharan Africa, and for the speakers of these languages.

English	Asu	Bemba	Koyo	Yao
husband	ume	lume	lomi	lume
house	umba	nganda	ndago	njuumba
cattle	ngombe	ngombe	(not used)	ngoombe

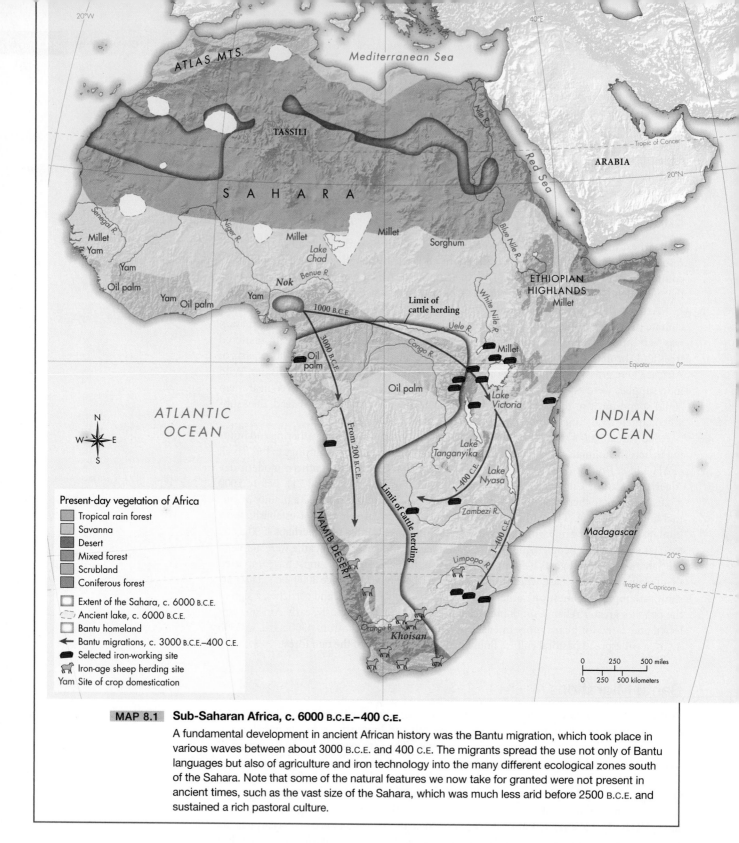

MAP 8.1 **Sub-Saharan Africa, c. 6000 B.C.E.–400 C.E.**

A fundamental development in ancient African history was the Bantu migration, which took place in various waves between about 3000 B.C.E. and 400 C.E. The migrants spread the use not only of Bantu languages but also of agriculture and iron technology into the many different ecological zones south of the Sahara. Note that some of the natural features we now take for granted were not present in ancient times, such as the vast size of the Sahara, which was much less arid before 2500 B.C.E. and sustained a rich pastoral culture.

The roughly five hundred Bantu languages differ from one another to varying degrees. Most scholars accept that the first Bantu speakers had a single homeland in the southern region of modern-day Cameroon and eastern Nigeria. From this core, people migrated in successive waves south and east in a long-term process, until their descendants inhabited most of sub-Saharan Africa (see again Map 8.1). Scholars debate the dates of the migrations, but many agree that a first southward movement began in the west of Africa in about 3000 B.C.E. Another wave began in around 1000 B.C.E. and swept east to the region of the

Great Lakes in modern Kenya and Tanzania. This second wave moved into southern Africa and merged with the descendants of the first southward migration, a process that may have been completed by 400 C.E.

The speakers of Bantu languages had very diverse forms of social, political, and economic organization, but all based their economic lives on agriculture. The Sahara Desert had dried up after 5000 B.C.E., pushing people into the sub-Saharan savanna, and it was probably on the edges of the rain forest that they learned how to farm crops. The yam, the root of a tropical vine, proved especially important. The knowledge of how to cultivate yams probably arose accidentally as people observed that plants growing on rubbish heaps near settlements flourished more than fully wild plants. After the men cut down trees and other large plants, leaving some remains to screen the soil from heavy rains, the women made narrow furrows in the earth in which they planted yam cuttings. Similarly, the inhabitants of the savanna learned to farm sorghum and millet, local grasses that produce grains, and they promoted the growth of a palm tree whose nuts they could press for oil. The earliest farmers in sub-Saharan Africa also raised cattle.

In around 3000 B.C.E. these agriculturalists started to migrate. It was a slow process, and it did not begin for any one reason. Probably the most common cause was that a community grew too large for the local area to support, so part of the population had to leave. But other motivations existed—sometimes adventurous individuals set out on long journeys, or a community could expel people they considered undesirable. The migrants traveled on foot or by boat, searching for new areas suitable to their agriculture.

Wherever the Bantu migrants settled, their villages became the focal point for the smaller groups of gatherer-hunters in the area. These local groups were probably most attracted by the settlers' use of pottery, which made cooking easier (see Lives and Livelihoods: Potters of Antiquity). The gatherer-hunters exchanged their fish or meat with the settlers for farmed food, and Bantu languages were probably crucial to their interactions. Over time, the gatherer-hunters introduced the Bantu to the rain forest. This development may have harmed the local populations, because the forest clearance needed for the cultivation of yams drew malaria-bearing mosquitoes. In any event, the encounters between the original people and the newly arrived Bantu speakers led to cultural exchange and assimilation. Bantu speakers started to adopt non-Bantu words and expressions, and the original populations adopted agriculture and other Bantu practices.

Bantu speakers moved everyplace in eastern and southern Africa where farming was possible, but they did not enter zones too dry to cultivate their crops. Into these areas they pushed people who maintained a gathering and hunting lifestyle until modern times. Prominent among them were the Khoisan (KOI-sahn), gatherer-hunters and pastoralists from southern Africa who spoke languages in which a clicking sound is used for consonants. Although the Bantu displaced the Khoisan in many parts of southern Africa, Khoisan gatherer-hunters survived in desert areas into the modern period.

Farming became more efficient with the arrival of iron technology, which deeply influenced Bantu society and agriculture. Iron has several advantages over other metals: iron ore is found in numerous locations, and the metal is stronger than the bronze that many cultures used before iron. The first evidence for working iron ore in world history comes from about 2000 B.C.E. in the Middle East, but people in the region started to use the metal extensively to arm soldiers and make tools only in about 800 B.C.E. Soon afterward, iron technology appeared in sub-Saharan Africa. Most scholars think it arrived from the Middle East, because to work iron one must know how to regulate air flow in furnaces; people in sub-Saharan Africa did not melt any metals before, and without experimenting with softer metals it seems unlikely that they would have developed the skills to work iron. It remains unclear how the technology reached sub-Saharan Africa, however, and other scholars argue that people developed it locally. In any case, the replacement of stone tools with iron tools had a great impact on agriculture. It became much easier to clear trees in the previously impenetrable rain forest, rendering new areas fit for farming.

Those who could work iron could make much better weapons than the stone arms others used. This military advantage may have encouraged them to drive out gatherer-

Farmers and Migrants

Bantu Relations with Gatherer-Hunters

Iron Technology

Potters of Antiquity

With very few exceptions, people in agricultural societies produce pottery, that is, containers made of clay that have been baked to keep their shape. In antiquity all pottery was fired at a relatively low temperature, between 1652° and 2192° F, and needed to be glazed (coated with a special layer) to become waterproof. Archaeologists find broken and whole pots in large quantities in almost every excavation. These remains are crucially important to our understanding of ancient societies because of their enormous variety in shape and decoration.

Pottery manufacture began in Japan in around 12,000 B.C.E. From the start, people shaped pots in different ways and decorated them according to local tastes. They molded them into countless forms, painted them with various pigments, and incised them or added such elements as knobs. Shapes and decorations changed rapidly, giving the archaeologist an effective means for dating. Variations in the quality and care of pottery decoration inform historians about class differences, and the presence of foreign pottery in certain places reveals trade contacts. Beyond their importance to the modern scholar, potters were crucial contributors in ancient societies, creating valuable utensils as well as expressing ideologies and aesthetic values.

Pottery revolutionized cooking, allowing people to heat liquids and other food products such as fats and store them for prolonged periods. This feature of pottery had the greatest effect on women's lives. It is likely that pottery was mainly the work of women who shaped, decorated, and baked basic pots as part of their domestic chores. Because basic pots are easy to make, the earliest potters worked at home or in simple communal installations. From the beginning, these women showed imagination and the desire to make something beautiful. The creative possibilities of working with clay are almost limitless because it is flexible and easy to decorate, and so for peoples all over the world, pots are often the most prominent and plentiful art forms.

Many of the cultures discussed in this chapter had especially skilled potters. The Moche potters of the Andes, for example, fashioned vessels in the shape of human heads, creating what may have been portraits of their patrons. At the same time, people living in southern Peru used the patterns of Paracas textiles to adorn their pots in colorful ways. Although the meanings of these decorations are mysterious to us, they may have had great symbolic importance to the pots' owners. Unfortunately, we do not know the identities of the individual potters. In ancient literate societies where pottery remained valuable, we do

Moche Vessel

Once baked, clay survives extremely well in most climates, and the potters of antiquity left much remarkable artwork for us to study. Particularly famed for the skills of their potters are the Moche from the South American Andes, whose state lasted from about 200 to 600 C.E. Many vessels represent human heads, probably those of the men who commissioned them. They show the men as warriors, strengthening the view that the Moche were a militaristic society. (Private Collection/Paul Maeyaert/AISA/Bridgeman Art Library.)

sometimes know the maker. A Greek vase from around 530 B.C.E. contains the remark, "Exekias made and painted me," but such signatures are rare. Roman potters regularly impressed a stamp that identified their workshop.

Artistic experimentation with pottery inspired other forms of creativity. The earliest preserved sculptures of sub-Saharan Africa are the terra cotta heads of the Nok culture in Nigeria (see page 246). Potters' work with clay must have been instrumental in teaching the sculptors of these striking figures what shapes they could obtain.

Thus, the potters of antiquity were not mere artisans who provided for basic needs. They were also artists who imaginatively expressed their societies' ideas and tastes, which we can study today through their enduring creations.

QUESTIONS TO CONSIDER

1. In what ways is pottery useful to the scholar?

2. How can pottery reveal the social conditions of an ancient society?

For Further Information:

Barnett, William K., and John W. Hooper, eds. *The Emergence of Pottery: Technology and Innovation in Ancient Societies*. Washington, D.C.: Smithsonian Institution Press, 1995.
Orton, Clive, Paul Tyers, and Alan Vince. *Pottery in Archaeology*. Cambridge, U.K.: Cambridge University Press, 1993.

hunters by force. Iron weapons were also better for hunting large animals. Further, iron had a powerful social impact, because people used the metal as a measure of value for exchange. Objects of high-quality iron brought prestige to those who possessed them.

Matrilineal descent was the cornerstone of Bantu social organization. Status, goods, and political office were inherited from mothers, and a man usually moved to his wife's village upon marriage. Adolescent boys were initiated into adult life in circumcision rituals, secret ceremonies that could last for several weeks. Circumcision rituals inducted young men into community-wide fraternities that shouldered many of the collective tasks of the village, both in peace and in war.

In these societies, marriage was a less significant rite of passage into adult society than it was in the Eurasian societies we have studied. Childbearing, not marriage, signified a woman's entry into full adulthood. Although men cleared forests for cultivation, women did virtually all the farming. This division of labor encouraged polygamy. Women's labor made valuable contributions to household wealth, and a man with several wives could farm more land, produce more food, and raise more children. Despite the prevalence of matrilineal descent and the central place of women in production as well as reproduction, decision-making authority within families was usually a male privilege.

With the migrations, Bantu social and political institutions changed significantly, especially in East Africa. The dislocations of migration and the intermarriage with indigenous peoples caused a steady shift away from the Bantu tradition of matrilineal descent and inheritance to patrilineal descent and strict gender roles in food production. This change also resulted from the growing importance of herding, especially cattle raising. Cattle became the crucial form of wealth in East African societies, and this wealth went to the men who tended the cattle. Agriculture remained a woman's task with little prestige. As cattle herds increased in size, ownership of cattle conferred status as well as wealth. Men who owned large herds of cattle could attract many followers and dependents and assume positions of leadership in their communities. Moreover, the authority of chiefs derived increasingly from wealth; previously, it had depended heavily on ties to the spirits of their ancestors residing at the ancestral burial grounds. Thus, the cultural exchanges that accompanied Bantu migrations changed the societies of both the Bantu migrants and the peoples they encountered. Encounters with Bantu speakers introduced new languages, technologies, and forms of subsistence to local populations, and the connections between Bantu speakers and their new neighbors led to a significant reorganization of Bantu society.

Because sub-Saharan Africans did not write until their encounters with Europeans in the modern period, we have no texts on Bantu religious beliefs. Accordingly, to reconstruct early Bantu ideas, historians of religion use tales and customs that exist today or that earlier visitors recorded. Just as scholars use similarities in language to trace Bantu migrations, they use similarities in myths and beliefs among distant African peoples to identify the original, common set of religious ideas. For example, many modern Bantu speakers think that proper human conduct was part of the natural order established at the time of creation, but that the creator has remained distant ever since. They believe that natural disasters and evil arise from human transgressions that disturb the cosmic order. To restore the essential positive nature of things, mortals must perform rituals to clear away anger and calm the spirits. Although these views are widespread and probably originated with the earliest Bantu, scholars accept that ideas and rituals change over time, so they cannot firmly establish what the Bantu speakers of antiquity believed and how they expressed those beliefs.

The archaeological remains of ancient Africa—mostly tools, pottery, and dwellings—are largely devoted to basic human needs such as food and housing. But the early sub-Saharan Africans also produced nonutilitarian goods. From around 800 B.C.E. to around 200 C.E., for example, people of the Nok culture in modern northern Nigeria created remarkable artwork in terra cotta. Their baked clay human heads, often life-size, show unique skills of representation. Throughout their history, the Khoisan people of southern Africa produced many cave paintings, representing their lives as hunters of local animals such as giraffes and elands. People from sub-Saharan Africa undoubtedly fashioned many other objects of art as well, but they were often made of materials that have now decomposed.

Bantu Society

Bantu Religion

Bantu Art

A Nok Figurine

In the centuries between 800 B.C.E. and 200 C.E., the Nok culture of western Africa produced impressive statues of terra cotta (baked clay), the oldest known figurative sculpture south of the Sahara. Made, like the culture's pottery, from coils of clay, these statues are hollow. Most of the remains are heads or other body parts from large statues, which were close to life-size when complete but often broke over time. For reasons scholars continue to debate, Nok artists tended to emphasize certain elements of the person's appearance—in this example, the woman's eyes and jewelry. (Museum of Fine Arts, Houston/Funds from the Brown Foundation Accessions Endowment Fund/ Bridgeman Art Library.)

Thus, ancient Africa produced diverse and dynamic communities, connected by a common thread of Bantu culture, society, and technology. The cultural richness of sub-Saharan Africa in ancient times had parallels in other parts of the world where prehistoric cultures flourished. Those of the Americas will draw our attention next.

Peoples of the Americas

FOCUS

What kinds of evidence have scholars used to recreate the experience of ancient American peoples, and what do we know about these cultures?

As we saw in Chapter 1, the most widely accepted theory about the peopling of the world holds that migrants crossed into North America from northeastern Asia during the last Ice Age about fifteen thousand years ago and then spread throughout the Americas. When the glaciers gradually melted, rising sea levels cut off the Americas from the rest of the world. Although sailors from Europe and perhaps from Africa could still reach American shores, these visits did not introduce lasting changes until the sixteenth century C.E. Thus, all technological and social developments after people arrived in the ancient Americas were due to internal processes until European contact.

In Central and South America, societies developed first into states and later into empires. Mountain ranges created separate areas with distinct natural conditions. Despite the difficulties of overland contacts and the region's enormous ecological diversity, cultural similarities developed over wide areas, and a number of populations seem to have shared ideologies and religious beliefs. In Central America, or Mesoamerica, and the Andes Mountains of South America, archaeological evidence reveals a variety of advanced cultures. By contrast, the peoples of North America remained mostly isolated from their southern neighbors and pursued a gatherer-hunter lifestyle for much longer. As we explore the cultures of ancient America, we will look at societies in both regions to illustrate key historical developments in this part of the world.

The Olmecs 1200–400 B.C.E.

Volcanoes in the narrow strip of land that connects North and South America created high mountain barriers between numerous valleys and coastal zones. Because these natural barriers created relatively isolated areas with distinct natural environments, it is no surprise that several centers of cultural development arose (see Map 8.2). One such area occupies the modern Mexican states of Tabasco and Veracruz, south of the Gulf of Mexico. Between 1200 and 400 B.C.E., this region had a flourishing common culture that influenced others for hundreds of miles beyond its heartland. Scholars today call the culture in Tabasco and Veracruz *Olmec*, after the name Spanish conquerors in the sixteenth century C.E. gave the region's people.

Olmec Livelihoods

The Olmecs, or their ancestors, were one of the few peoples on earth who invented agriculture independently, sometime between 3000 and 2000 B.C.E. Their crops differed from those of Eurasia and North Africa, however, because their indigenous plants were different. The cereal they cultivated was maize (corn), and beans and squash were also very important. Moreover, unlike Eurasia and Africa, the Americas had no large native mammals that could be domesticated for food. So before the arrival of the Spanish in the sixteenth century C.E., the main sources of protein for all Mesoamerican people were hunted animals (rabbits, deer, and iguanas), domesticated turkeys and dogs, and fish, which supplemented the crops they grew.

Olmec Ceremonial Centers

Although agriculture was not as productive in Mesoamerica as in the river valley cultures of South Asia and northern Africa, the Olmecs could concentrate enough resources to construct elaborate ceremonial centers. The earliest such center, San Lorenzo, was inhabited beginning in 1500 B.C.E. In around 1200 B.C.E., the people leveled the mountain top where the settlement was situated and created a platform some 2500 by 3300 feet in size and 165 feet higher than the surrounding countryside. On top of this platform they built podiums and pyramids of clay and erected numerous sculptures, including ten massive stone heads. These sculptures were made of the volcanic rock basalt, which the Olmecs could have obtained only in mountains some fifty miles away; they probably placed the rocks on rafts to float downriver to the ceremonial center. The stone heads represented men who must have been important to the people of San Lorenzo, but scholars do not

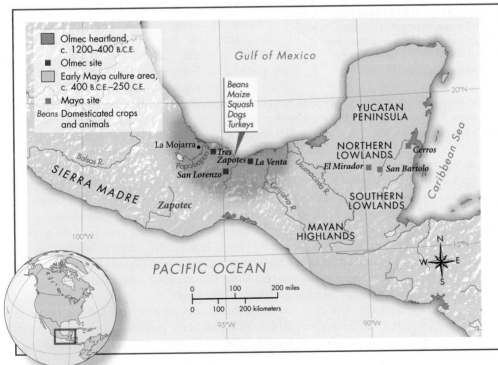

MAP 8.2

Mesoamerica, c. 1200 B.C.E.–250 C.E.

Mesoamerica forms a land bridge between North and South America, yet is itself fragmented by mountain ranges and valleys. It was home to a variety of highly developed cultures between 1200 B.C.E. and 250 C.E., Olmec and Maya prominent among them. Both cultures left behind impressive buildings and monumental artwork, which shed light on elaborate ceremonial activity, including blood sacrifices and ballgames. These traditions would survive in the region after ancient times.

An Olmec Colossal Head

The Olmec had a centuries-long tradition of setting up colossal heads of men with helmetlike headgear, which may indicate that they were warriors or participants in ceremonial ballgames. The example shown here is 10 feet high and 7 feet wide and made of basalt, a volcanic rock imported from distant mountains. This head is one of the earliest from San Lorenzo, the largest city in Mesoamerica and the leading Olmec site from about 1200 to 900 B.C.E. (Art Archive/Xalapa Museum Veracruz Mexico/Gianni Dagli Orti.)

know their identity. They could have been kings, chiefs, or participants in the ballgames characteristic of later Mesoamerican culture.

In around 900 B.C.E., the Olmecs shifted the focus of their building activity fifty-five miles to the northeast to the site that is now called La Venta. Between 800 and 400 B.C.E., they developed the locale into their most elaborate ceremonial center. At its core stood a clay pyramid (badly destroyed today) with a base measuring 420 by 240 feet and a height of over 108 feet. Bordering the pyramid to the north and south were plazas that contained magnificent stone monuments: colossal heads, massive thrones, stelae decorated with carved relief sculptures, and statues. Also carved from imported stone, the heads in some cases are 11 feet high and weigh 20 tons. The complex at La Venta contained a jaguar mask of green serpentine stone and what seems to be a tomb chamber filled with jade.

The remains at La Venta tell an intriguing and puzzling story. The stone sculptures were regularly damaged on purpose: faces were erased, arms and heads cut off, and pieces removed. The Olmecs then buried the sculptures and displayed new ones, which indicates that they were responsible for the mutilations. It is possible that the monuments' destruction was part of a ceremony performed at the death of the person portrayed. Speculation about the reasons for these acts continues, however. The size, complexity, and artistry of Olmec ceremonial centers speaks to the sophistication of Olmec culture, but like so much else about prehistory, we have more questions than answers about the Olmecs and their practices.

Just as we cannot offer verified explanations of Olmec practices, the absence of written evidence makes it difficult to explain the overarching purpose of the complexes at San Lorenzo and La Venta. Although they share certain elements with the cities of Eurasia, such as monumental buildings, they seem not to have been large population centers, as those cities were. They appear instead to have been primarily ceremonial in character, and ideas about what ceremonies took place there often depend on theories about the relationship between the Olmecs and later Mesoamerican cultures, especially the better-known Maya. Ceremonial centers with pyramids and intricate sculptures remained a part of Mesoamerican culture until the Spanish conquest in the sixteenth century C.E., and later practices are easier to understand because we have early European accounts and some written Maya evidence. For example, in the classical Maya period of 250–900 C.E. (discussed in Chapter 11), the ballgame ritual was very important; it ended in a blood sacrifice to renew the life-giving powers of the gods. It appears very likely that the Olmecs played the ballgame, as a dozen rubber balls were found as ritual deposits in a spring to the east of San Lorenzo, together with Olmec wooden sculptures. Because the game may have been important to the Olmecs, some scholars interpret the culture's colossal sculpted heads as representations of ball players.

Olmec Society and Ideology

It is clear that Olmec society was hierarchical, with an elite who had the power to demand labor from the general population. Based on Maya parallels, many archaeologists believe that the elites could even claim the lives of commoners and that they regularly practiced human sacrifice. The source of the elite's authority is debated. Many Olmec representations show men involved in rituals, which, along with their interpretations of Maya culture leads some scholars to suggest that Olmec leaders derived power from their role as **shamans**, individuals who have the ability to communicate with nonhuman powers and who safeguard the community's prosperity. The shaman's consumption of hallucinogenic drugs, such as extracts from toads, facilitated the dialogue with supernatural forces. Shamans appear in many parts of the world, and throughout history various societies have seen certain persons, often with unusual physical characteristics, as crucial to communication with greater powers, and the Olmecs may indeed have been among the peoples with this view. The leaders' powers probably had more secular aspects as well. The ceremonial centers gave prominence to stones imported from distant places, and it is likely that only elites could obtain them. This privilege must have confirmed their special status.

The validity of these scholarly interpretations of Olmec culture and ideology depends strongly on the Olmecs' connection to later Mesoamerican societies. Because their monuments are similar, many scholars see Olmec as the "mother culture" and inspiration of all subsequent Mesoamerican cultures. In this interpretation, the Olmecs would have spread their ideas and practices through trade to regions as distant as the Mexican west coast and El Salvador to the south, where later Mesoamerican cultures flourished. The appearance of Olmec objects and artistic motifs in these regions supports this view. Others disagree, however, and consider the various cultures of Mesoamerica to be of local origin, the result of internal developments.

The Early Maya 400 B.C.E.–250 C.E.

Olmec culture had disappeared by 400 B.C.E., for reasons that are unclear to us, and several major Mesoamerican cultures developed to the east and west of the Olmec heartland. In some of these cultures, people such as the Zapotecs (sah-po-TEHK) started to write, typically carving a few **glyphs**—symbolic characters used to record a word or a syllable in writing—beside the image of a person. Scripts survive in a variety of languages, but scholars can read none of them. The highly pictorial glyphs suggest that the content of the inscriptions resembles that of later Maya texts and deals with sacrifice, war, and the capture of enemies. The texts also use the calendar of the classic Maya, which allows scholars to date the inscriptions very accurately. Most of the inscriptions derive from western Mexico, with a few from the east coast (see Reading the Past: The La Mojarra Stele). Our inability to read Zapotec writing leaves us guessing about much of their early history; we know more about another Mesoamerican society, the Maya.

One of the best-documented Mesoamerican cultures in the archaeological record was that of the Maya, centered in the Yucatan Peninsula in the southeast corner of the Gulf of Mexico (see again Map 8.2). Although the culture achieved its height after 250 C.E., it originated earlier, in a time when various early Maya kingdoms existed side by side. Beginning in around 800 B.C.E., in an area of dense forest, the early Maya developed a number of complexes that included massive stone buildings, pyramids, and platforms. Throughout the first millennium B.C.E. and early first millennium C.E., they established several ceremonial centers. The largest was at El Mirador in the remote jungle of Guatemala, where between 150 B.C.E. and 50 C.E. the inhabitants built numerous tall pyramids, plazas, platforms, causeways, and elite houses in stone, decorating them with stone reliefs. How such a complex came to be constructed in such surroundings remains a mystery, because the area has insufficient agricultural land to support a large labor force.

El Mirador was not the only large Maya religious complex. In around 50 B.C.E., the site of Cerros (SEHR-roh), in a more hospitable environment near the sea, suddenly grew from a small village into a major center. The inhabitants leveled existing houses and shattered their contents—pottery, ornaments, and other objects. On top of the rubble they

Maya Ceremonial Centers

shaman A tribal member who acts as an intermediary between the physical and spiritual worlds.

glyph A figurative symbol, usually carved in stone, that imparts information.

The La Mojarra Stele

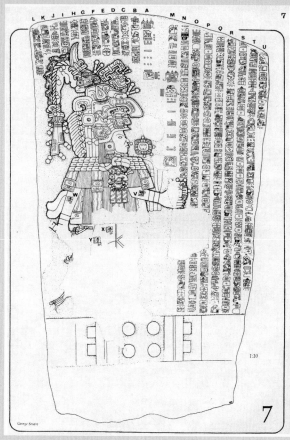

The La Mojarra Inscription, c. 160 C.E.
(Courtesy of George Stuart.)

Although the first Mesoamerican writing dates to about 400 B.C.E., historians cannot read the earliest inscriptions with certainty, because they often do not know what language the texts record. Yet scholars do find continuity between the earliest scripts and the later, better-known classic Maya script (discussed in Chapter 11). For example, many topics addressed in classic Maya inscriptions, such as warfare and the glorification of the leader, also appear much earlier. Moreover, the calendar used was the same, which allows scholars to date inscriptions with confidence.

In 1986 archaeologists discovered one early inscription on this stele, or stone tablet, at La Mojarra (la moh-HAH-rah), in the province of Veracruz in eastern Mexico, a region the Olmecs had occupied before the inscription was carved (see again Map 8.2). It contains two dates, 143 and 156 C.E., and seems to have been carved soon afterward. The language of the inscription is a matter of debate among scholars, as is the exact content, but all agree that the man with the elaborate cloak and headdress must be some kind of leader. They speculate that the stele deals with issues of sacrifice and war in parallel with later Maya inscriptions, which often deal with these concerns. The man's elaborate headdress resembles that of Maya war leaders. The La Mojarra inscription raises various puzzling questions, however. Why is this the only lengthy inscription from early Mesoamerica so far discovered? Is its language related to that of the Olmecs? And what is the relationship between this script and the later Maya?

EXAMINING THE EVIDENCE

1. In the absence of knowledge of the language, how have scholars sought to interpret the La Mojarra inscription?

2. What enables scholars to relate the inscription to the Olmecs?

---

erected a temple, surrounding it with plazas, pyramids, causeways, and other monuments characteristic of Maya settlements. The transformation occurred so abruptly that it must have resulted from the arrival of some powerful authority, who ordered the construction of a new settlement.

Maya Script   Early Maya sites contain a few glyphs that scholars can connect to a later stage of the Maya script. Much of the interpretation of the early inscriptions remains uncertain, but they clearly focus on the deeds of kings, especially in war. By understanding the calendar, scholars can assign precise dates to some early Maya monuments. For example, one stele was carved in the year 197 C.E. It shows a leader, whose name in the accompanying text is expressed by the combination of a bone and a rabbit skull, which scholars read as Bak T'ul. He is dressed as the rain god and surrounded by scenes of human sacrifice, fertility, and renewal. Beneath his hand are the severed bodies of three victims going down into the underworld.

Maya Society and Ideology

As in Eurasia, all of the evidence indicates that a political and social elite in Mesoamerica held power over the mass of the population whose labor they commanded. The leaders of these societies commissioned representations showing them participating in rituals that often involved bloodletting and human sacrifice. Those rituals probably gave them a special connection to the gods: they were not methods of punishment but rather events that gave prestige to their participants. Men and women pierced themselves with stingray spines, thorns, or lancets, especially through the tongue, ears, and genitals. They usually collected the blood on clothlike paper, which they burned so that the gods could consume the blood in the form of smoke (see Seeing the Past: Early Maya Frescoes).

The early Maya cultures arose in a range of natural environments, as Map 8.2 reveals, and people's choice of a particular location for settlement was probably connected to their ideas about the universe and the king's role in connecting the human and supernatural worlds. We can scarcely imagine the massive amounts of labor and coordination involved in early Maya building projects; they were undertaken either without bureaucratic accounting records or with documents that have been lost over time, if indeed they ever existed. Such accomplishments as these led to the network of Maya city-states in the classical age, which we will study in Chapter 11.

Andean Peoples 900 B.C.E.–600 C.E.

Andean Ecology

Along the west coast of South America runs a narrow finger of land that contains an amazing variety of ecological zones (see Map 8.3). Here the Pacific Ocean and the tops of the Andes Mountains, which can reach heights of over four miles, are only sixty miles apart.

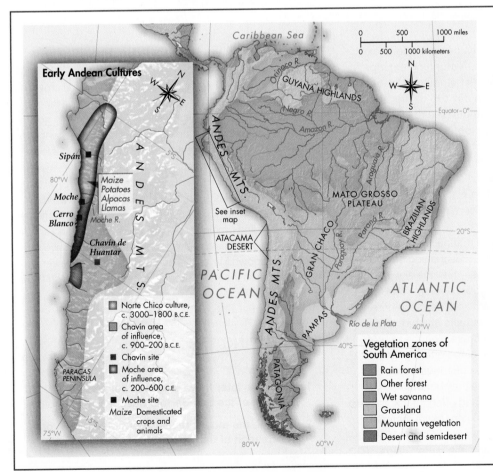

MAP 8.3

South America, c. 3000 B.C.E.–600 C.E.

Perched on steep mountain slopes overlooking the Pacific Ocean, inhabitants of the Andes Mountains established a sequence of cultures, each one characterized by unique remains. After a period of diversity, the Chavín culture unified the region from around 900 to 200 B.C.E., apparently on the basis of shared ideology. The subsequent Moche state, flourishing from around 200 to 600 C.E., used military might to impose itself upon multiple populations.

Early Maya Frescoes

Fresco from San Bartolo, c. 100 B.C.E. (Kenneth Garrett.)

In archaeology, chance discoveries can provide unexpected insights into past cultures. A stunning example is a find in 2001 by an archaeologist studying Mesoamerican culture. When making a day trip to the site of San Bartolo in the Guatemalan jungle (see again Map 8.2), he rested in a tunnel dug by looters. His flashlight revealed a chamber with traces of early Maya frescoes. Subsequent excavations of the entire room uncovered remarkable paintings on all the walls. The Maya artists who created them in around 100 B.C.E. displayed skills that scholars previously thought were not achieved until some four hundred years later.

The murals tell the story of the original creation of order in the world. They show four gods making offerings next to four trees that connect the earth to the sky in the Maya view of the universe. Each god's offering relates to an aspect of the universe. The third god, depicted here, offers an elaborate creature with aspects of a bird and a snake (in the lower right corner) representing the sky. At the same time, the gods provide a blood offering by piercing their penises with a lance. Blood offerings were very important in Maya religion, because they guaranteed renewal. The ideas about creation and offerings expressed here are the same as those in much later Maya material, including the *Popul Vuh*, written between 1554 and 1558 C.E. to tell local traditions about creation, the gods' deeds,

and the history of the people and kings of the region of modern Guatemala.

Another scene in the room depicts the original crowning of the maize god alongside the crowning of a Maya king, who thereby obtained legitimacy for his rule from the god. Before this image was found, there was no firm evidence that the early Maya people had a fully developed ideology of kingship under divine protection.

Originally located next to a pyramid from about 100 B.C.E., the painted room was soon thereafter buried below a larger pyramid. The complex was part of a settlement with some one hundred buildings, including a palace, a ball court, and another small pyramid, underneath which archaeologists excavated the earliest known Maya royal tomb. Overall, people seem to have developed the site in around 600 B.C.E. and stayed there at least until 100 C.E.

EXAMINING THE EVIDENCE

1. How does later Maya evidence help clarify the meaning of the San Bartolo frescoes?

2. What do the murals reveal about Maya ideas on the creation of the universe?

Between them is a diverse array of environments, including a coastal area that is arid except where rivers run through it. Marine resources are abundant, however, because the current that brings cold water from the South Pole carries vital nutrients that feed a wide variety of fish, shellfish, and sea mammals. Thanks to this sea life, early Andean coastal residents did not need to practice agriculture.

At irregular intervals this cold-water current is reversed by a global climatic event called **El Niño** (ehl NEEN-yoh) (Spanish for "the Christ Child," as the name derives from its occurrence around Christmas). When El Niño appears, warm water from the north chases away the marine life, while rainstorms sweep across and devastate the countryside. The unpredictable disruptions of El Niño take years to repair, and these times of crisis may have led to social and political upheaval among Andean peoples throughout history.

Perhaps to offset the uncertainties of marine supplies, the peoples of the Andes started to farm plants on the mountain slopes, potatoes possibly as early as 4400 B.C.E. and maize after 1500 B.C.E. Farther up the mountains they herded the alpaca and the llama, the only domesticated beasts of burden in South America. The tops of the Andes Mountains are so high that only people who have physically adjusted to the scarcity of oxygen can be active there. Thus in the Andean peoples we see a clear example of the profound impact of ecology on social development. As the peoples of the Andes adapted to local conditions and environmental change, unique communities evolved that reflected the challenges and opportunities the region's ecology presented.

Norte Chico Culture

As they adapted to their region's ecological diversity, early Andean peoples developed complex societies with a large array of intricate cultural expressions. One such local culture emerged in valleys of the Norte Chico region on the coast some one hundred miles north of Peru's modern capital, Lima, where between 3000 and 1800 B.C.E. people constructed large ceremonial centers, apparently for religious purposes. In some twenty centers, they built platforms on artificial mounds with circle-shaped plazas partially sunken into the ground. Buildings surrounded these platforms. The people of this culture did not yet make pottery, but they used gourds as containers, sometimes decorated with the image of a god holding a staff. They lived off the resources from the sea and practiced agriculture inland, including cotton, which they grew with irrigation.

Chavín Culture

In around 900 B.C.E., the cultural diversity of the Andes gave way to relative uniformity when a new culture, called Chavín (cha-BEAN), came to dominate a wide area of north and central Peru. In the Chavín culture, people used the same style of pottery decoration, similar artifacts, and the same architecture for about seven hundred years. The ceramics of Chavín show remarkable skill; the artisans shaped the vessels in many different forms, including elaborately decorated human and animal figures. They often depicted hybrid creatures, combining human and animal attributes, as well as snakes, birds, crocodiles, and fish. These animals came from different ecological zones within the region, including the Amazon forest on the east side of the Andes, which indicates that the Chavín people traveled widely. They also refined metalworking techniques, using pure gold or alloys of gold with silver or copper. Chavín artisans knew how to solder pieces together and how to shape them into three dimensions. At the site that gave the culture its name, Chavín de Huantar, 170 miles north of Lima, stood a stone temple complex with galleries, stairs, and ramps looking out over a plaza that was partly sunken into the ground. Fantastical stone carvings decorated the complex, including sculpted heads of humans, birds, and canines, as well as reliefs of felines, serpents, and supernatural beings made up of the body parts of various creatures. Once again, as we saw in Africa and other American societies, isolation and the challenges presented by geographical boundaries by no means inhibited creativity and innovation.

The Chavín culture inspired peoples over a wide stretch of the Andean region, including those of the south-central Peruvian peninsula of Paracas (pah-RAH-kas), 150 miles south of Lima. This area is especially famous for its long history of textile production. Even before the introduction of agriculture, people in this region wove fibers from cacti, grasses, and other

El Niño A periodic change in the sea current in the Pacific Ocean west of South America, which brings about severe climatic change in regions in and near the Pacific.

Weavers of Paracas

plants into textiles. When they domesticated cotton in around 3500 B.C.E., it became the main vegetable fiber for weaving, but people also used alpaca and llama hair.

In the late first millennium B.C.E., the introduction of tapestry weaving and new techniques of dyeing revolutionized textile production. The weavers produced intricate patterns and figures using multicolored threads and further decorated the cloth with feathers, metal strips, and other embellishments. The textiles had great importance in people's lives, especially at crucial events such as birth, marriage, and death, when individuals received special cloth. The most remarkable textiles produced by the inhabitants of Paracas are those used in the burials of wealthy people. The dead sat in a fetal position, wrapped in thick layers of multicolored cotton garments. These included embroidered mantles, tunics, and headbands that depicted mythical creatures and humans in ornate dress. Some of the dead were wrapped in more than one hundred such garments. The resulting mummy bundles were covered with white cotton sheets and placed in an underground vault, with up to forty individuals in one vault.

The Militaristic Moche State

The shared artistic motifs in the Chavín area and beyond suggest the region shared a common belief system that accorded great significance to animals and the forces of nature. Because there is no evidence of military conquest, it was evidently ideology rather than conquest that produced this cultural unity. In around 200 B.C.E., however, this unity ended, and the appearance of massive defensive structures around settlements suggests that wars may have torn the different peoples apart. After a period of disintegration, a new set of states arose, but the basis for control differed dramatically from that of the Chavín culture. One such state, in northern Peru, is called Moche (MOH-che) today, after the river in its center (see again Map 8.3). Flourishing from around 200 to 600 C.E., the Moche state was highly militaristic and hierarchical, as evidenced by its art, which teems with brutal images of warfare, torture, and other forms of violence.

The Moche economy was based on an elaborate system of irrigation agriculture. The people laid out a large network of mud canals on the mountain slopes, guiding the water for miles into the valleys. The farmers cultivated a mixed crop of maize, beans, squash, and chili peppers and fertilized the fields with guano (bird dung). With increased resources gained through agricultural development and military muscle, more people could live in cities, where they constructed huge ceremonial complexes.

At the Moche capital in Cerro Blanco, a few miles south of the modern city of Trujillo in northwestern Peru, the people built two enormous mud-brick temples in pyramid shapes. One of the largest solid structures in the Americas, the Pyramid of the Sun stood at least 130 feet high, measured 1115 feet by 525 feet at its base, and contained some 143 million bricks. Nearby rose the slightly smaller Pyramid of the Moon, made up of three separate platforms. The leaders of Moche society lived on top of these giant pyramids. But the structures also formed a ceremonial complex in which human sacrifice was central, as was the case in Maya culture. Excavations of nearby plazas have revealed the remains of seventy individuals who were killed and dismembered, their body parts having been thrown off the platforms. Human sacrifice is also prominent in the representational arts of the Moche. Humans in bird costumes slit the throats of prisoners, drank their blood, and cut off their heads, feet, and hands. The goal of the many wars the Moche

A Mummy from Paracas

Mummies are found not only in Egypt but also in many parts of the ancient world. Examples like this one from Paracas in the southern Andes show how much attention the people there paid to burial, dressing the dead with finely woven textiles and adorning them with jewelry made from bones. These mummies were usually placed in a seated position and wrapped with multiple layers of decorated textiles, such as those shown here and in At a Crossroads on page 236. (Museo del Oro, Lima, Peru/Bridgeman Art Library.)

appear to have waged was probably not to kill enemies on the battlefield but to capture them and bring them home for these sacrifices.

Other Moche archaeological sites had similar ceremonial complexes. At Sipán (SHEE-pan) in northern Peru, archaeologists in 1987 C.E. discovered tombs that were also connected with human sacrifice. So far, these excavations have uncovered twelve tombs, three of them beneath large pyramids. The occupants of the pyramid tombs were buried with enormous amounts of grave goods—including pottery, jewelry, and textiles—as well as other humans (see again Lives and Livelihoods: Potters of Antiquity). In the richest tomb, said to be of "the lord of Sipán," eight individuals accompanied the dead, including three adult men, one adult woman, three young women, and one child. On top of the burial chamber lay the body of a young man whose feet had been amputated, seemingly to prevent his escape. The garments of the tomb occupants suggest that they were the central figures in the sacrificial ceremonies, as represented in Moche art.

The Moche state went into decline in the sixth century C.E., probably due to natural disasters, including a long drought. By 800 C.E. other states would arise to replace it. In around 1400 the entire Andean zone would be incorporated into the Inca Empire, which would continue some of the practices the Moche people had begun.

Ritual and Human Sacrifice

Gatherer-Hunters of North America 800 B.C.E.–400 C.E.

The vast North American continent contains many varied natural environments, and for millennia after humans arrived the relatively few inhabitants survived by hunting and collecting wild resources (see Map 11.3, page 357). Hunters in the Great Plains, for example, killed large bison herds after driving them into closed-off canyons. At times the meat was so abundant that they butchered only the best parts. These folk also gathered plants and hunted small game, however; the bison were caught mostly in the fall to provide meat for the winter months.

Eastern North America, between the Great Plains and the Atlantic Ocean, was a vast wooded region with a network of rivers centered on the Mississippi Valley, an area the size of India. Although this region had great agricultural potential because of its rich alluvial soils, until 400 C.E. most inhabitants survived by hunting and gathering the rich wild resources. They made simple pottery and crafted artwork, often using materials that had to be imported from distant regions. These materials were items of exchange among the small communities that lived throughout the region. The men who arranged for the exchange became community leaders and settled disputes in the mostly egalitarian societies. They or others may also have been shamans.

The people of these communities joined forces to construct large earthworks, mostly low mounds that covered tombs, but also fortifications and platforms for buildings. The areas inside these fortifications were used for ceremonial rather than residential purposes. The largest known site of the period, at Newark in modern Ohio, belonged to what archaeologists call the Hopewell culture, which lasted from about 100 B.C.E. to 400 C.E. This site includes a large rectangular enclosure,

Great Plains Hunters

Eastern Woodlanders

The Hopewell Shaman

This small stone figure was discovered near a burial mound of the Hopewell culture, which flourished from 100 B.C.E. to 400 C.E. along rivers in northeastern and midwestern North America. The figure wears a bearskin and appears to be holding a decapitated head in its lap. It probably represents a shaman, a man or woman who acted as an intermediary between humans and the forces of nature and the gods. (Ohio Historical Society.)

**The Hopewell Culture,
c. 100 B.C.E.–400 C.E.**

one hundred acres in size, that surrounded forty mounds. Those mounds contained many crafted objects, often in hoards. The materials came from distant sources: shell from the Gulf of Mexico, copper from the Great Lakes, mica from the Carolinas, and obsidian (a glass-like volcanic rock) from the Rocky Mountains. The mound-building culture continued in the eastern woodlands after 400 C.E., when the introduction of agriculture fundamentally changed its social and economic structures (see Chapter 11). Even in this early period, however, we see evidence of sophisticated social organization and long-distance economic connections.

Thus, in ancient times various regions in the Americas developed cultures of different levels of complexity. All this took place without an extensive written tradition—in Mesoamerica the few examples of writing are brief official statements regarding wars and kingship, and in the Andes and North America no documents are preserved for this period. Although the absence of writing denies us access to many aspects of these cultures, archaeology provides us with abundant evidence of the energy and diversity of ancient American societies.

Peoples of the Pacific Islands

FOCUS

What do their material remains tell us about the Pacific Islanders' society and culture?

The Pacific Ocean, stretching 12,500 miles along the equator, covers much of the globe's tropical zone. This expanse is dotted with a myriad of small islands, mostly of volcanic origin or taking the form of **atolls**, rings of coral that grew up around sunken islands (see Map 8.4). Although their natural resources are limited to a few native plants, humans inhabit some fifteen hundred of the twenty-five thousand islands, the result of a colonization process that spanned millennia. These people did not create scripts, so their written histories begin with European descriptions from the eighteenth century C.E., such as the account by Sir Joseph Banks quoted at the start of this chapter.

Archaeology has helped to fill gaps in the study of these peoples' ancient past. Because archaeological exploration of the islands started only in the 1950s, it is still in its early phases, and many conclusions about the islands' early history are tentative. They do demonstrate, however, that people in this part of the world had the initiative and courage to sail across enormous distances to discover new lands—and that they brought their agricultural lifestyle with them.

Agricultural Livelihoods

Fishers, Farmers, and Herders

The early inhabitants of the Pacific Islands derived much of their food from the sea. Archaeological finds of food remains and simple agricultural tools show that they also cultivated plants and herded animals that their ancestors brought with them during migrations. Only a few native plants and fruits of the Pacific Islands became important foods; the islanders' main crops—coconut, taro, yam, banana, and breadfruit—were not native, and farmers had imported them from elsewhere. The peoples of the Pacific Islands promoted their growth using simple yet efficient techniques. For example, taro, a plant with an edible root, requires a very wet soil, so in some places the islanders created irrigation systems. By contrast, the yam, another root plant, needs a much drier soil, and the people drained marshes to grow it. Their domesticated animals were few—chickens, pigs, and dogs—but they were found on all inhabited islands. We see, then, that human needs profoundly shaped the ecology of the Pacific Islands. Islanders introduced new plant and

atoll A small ringlike island made of coral.

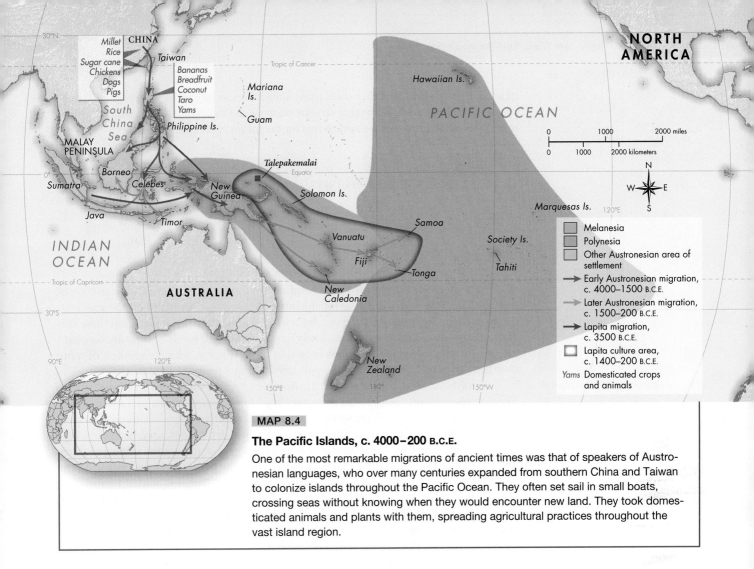

MAP 8.4

The Pacific Islands, c. 4000–200 B.C.E.

One of the most remarkable migrations of ancient times was that of speakers of Austronesian languages, who over many centuries expanded from southern China and Taiwan to colonize islands throughout the Pacific Ocean. They often set sail in small boats, crossing seas without knowing when they would encounter new land. They took domesticated animals and plants with them, spreading agricultural practices throughout the vast island region.

animal species and altered the land itself to create environments capable of sustaining their communities.

Scholars believe that much of the colonization of new islands was deliberate, displacing the earlier theory that drifters settled the islands by accident. As with Bantu migrants in Africa, Polynesian peoples set out with the plants and animals they intended to grow and breed, and they established permanent dwellings soon after arriving in the new land. In Africa the Bantu speakers moved on land or traveled along rivers in boats; in the Pacific, migration required sailing, sometimes across great distances. Because the supply of food was steady, Polynesians did not decide to move because the natural resources of their original islands were insufficient. More likely, younger sons initiated the adventures to find places where they could head their own families, a status that was denied them in hierarchical systems that gave precedence to the eldest son.

Colonization of Islands

Peopling the Islands

Analysis of the migrations that populated the Pacific Islands uses the same methodologies as studies of Bantu and Indo-European migrations, and it faces the same uncertainties. All reconstructions of migrations rely on a mixture of linguistic and archaeological evidence to determine what modern populations share common ancestors and when they became separated from one another. The dating of events is especially problematic, because it relies on scant archaeological evidence.

The peoples of the Pacific Islands speak languages that belong to the Austronesian family, which also includes modern Malayan and Indonesian. Some one thousand Austronesian languages exist, and they show many similarities, as Joseph Banks recognized in the passage at the beginning of the chapter. For example, the inhabitants of three island groups in Polynesia use almost all the same terms for the following English words:

English	Society Islands (includes Tahiti)	Tonga	New Zealand
two	rooa	looa	rooa
five	reema	neema	reema
eye	matta	matta	matta
to drink	ainoo	ainoo	ainoo

The indigenous peoples of Taiwan and of some areas in southern China also speak Austronesian languages, as do the inhabitants of Madagascar, an island off the southeast coast of Africa. By comparing the vocabularies and grammatical features of all these languages, linguists can determine how closely they are related. If two languages are very similar, the peoples speaking them must have split quite recently, whereas speakers of more divergent languages must have lived separately for longer periods.

Austronesian Migrations

Linguistic analysis indicates that Austronesian speakers migrated in several waves. The first speakers of Austronesian languages lived in southern China and Taiwan, where the largest variety of such languages exists today. These early Austronesians were farmers who grew millet, rice, and sugar cane; they lived in wooden houses, used boats, and kept pigs, dogs, and chickens. They knew how to make pottery but did not use metals, and they had a typical Neolithic lifestyle that they shared with the people of farther inland China (see Chapter 3). In around 3000 B.C.E. this homogenous population started to break up, and some people migrated south by sea to the Philippines, where they discovered tropical plants for cultivation, such as breadfruit, coconut, bananas, yams, and taro (see again Map 8.4). They improved the canoes they used, probably by adding sails and outriggers (beams on the side that greatly increased stability).

These new technologies enabled the people to spread rapidly and widely. In subsequent centuries Austronesian speakers settled on the islands of Southeast Asia to the west and of Melanesia and western Polynesia to the east, a process that seems to have ended around 750 B.C.E. Then there was a pause of about a thousand years before further expansion occurred in around 400 C.E., as we will see in Chapter 11. Many of the islands at which the Austronesians arrived had only small gatherer-hunter communities that were easily displaced, and members of these communities gradually learned how to farm. On the large island of New Guinea, however, indigenous people had developed agriculture in the highlands long before the arrival of the Austronesians, and with their larger numbers they restricted Austronesian settlement to areas on the shores.

Lapita Culture

The migrating Austronesians took with them a mixture of technologies and styles that gives us another means of using the archaeological record to trace their movements. From 1400 to 200 B.C.E., those living in Melanesia surrounded themselves with material goods that archaeologists identify as belonging to the Lapita (lah-PEE-tah) culture. Most distinctive is the pottery—although the pots were poorly made and not well fired, they were extensively decorated by incising lines or impressing comb-like toothed instruments, which left a series of dots. The lines formed geometric motifs and occasionally human features such as faces, and they were probably filled with lime and other white substances. The designs resembled the body tattoos popular among Austronesian speakers.

The pottery, fishhooks, and other implements of the Lapita culture spread eastward from Melanesia into western Polynesia by 1000 B.C.E. The migration was amazingly

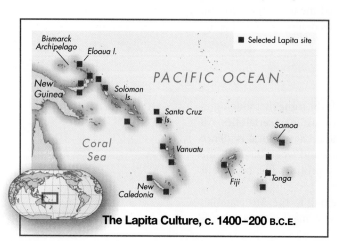

The Lapita Culture, c. 1400–200 B.C.E.

fast: scholars estimate that they explored 2800 miles of the ocean over as few as fifteen to twenty-five human generations. In the end, Lapita culture appeared across 4050 miles, from northeastern New Guinea to Samoa. Although some pots were traded among islands, local artisans produced most pottery using the same techniques as their forebears. After 750 B.C.E. the quality of their pottery declined even further, however, and by the beginning of the common era some Polynesians stopped producing pottery altogether.

The Polynesians' decision to abandon the use of pottery is unique in world history. Everywhere else, people considered the technology superior because pots could be used to store and cook foods (see again Lives and Livelihoods: Potters of Antiquity). The absence of pottery in Polynesia is easily understandable, however, because atolls lack the clay needed to make it. On other islands, however, people consciously decided to stop using pots even when clay was present. Instead of boiling foods, they baked them in underground ovens, and for storage, drinking cups, and the like, the islanders used coconut shells, which were readily available. In short, they had no need to continue using advanced pottery technology.

The people of the Lapita culture inhabited small villages, living in houses they sometimes built on stilts. They grew taro, yams, and other tropical plants and kept dogs, pigs, and chickens. They were mostly self-sufficient, with trade in obsidian for stone tools the only essential link among the islands. Because of their self-sufficiency, and the influence of the indigenous populations on the settlers, Lapita communities developed many local characteristics, making Melanesia a highly diverse world.

Lapita Lifestyles

When the descendants of the Austronesian migrants came into contact with Europeans in the eighteenth century C.E., the islanders may still have adhered to practices that dated back many centuries. But we must take care not to imagine these societies as static and unchanging. Rather, we should acknowledge that throughout history the peoples of this region were experts at adapting their lifestyles to the local circumstances of numerous islands. As members of small communities, they did not need writing, instead passing on their knowledge, skills, and beliefs orally, from person to person, over many centuries.

COUNTERPOINT
The Voiced and Voiceless in Ancient Literate Societies

When we study peoples of the ancient past, we find a wealth of visible, physical artifacts, which can be astonishingly rich and appealing. In this chapter we have seen Nok sculptures, Olmec colossal heads, Andean textiles, and many other examples of human ingenuity that tell us much about their creators. But historians are especially attracted to written documentation, because it can reveal elements of ancient cultures about which there is no other evidence, such as the languages people spoke, the names they gave themselves and the things that surrounded them, their literary creativity, and much more. The advent of writing in the various cultures of the world is thus an important turning point, because it opens new pathways for us to approach the peoples of the past.

FOCUS

To what extent does a society's literacy or nonliteracy affect our study of it?

The first humans to invent writing lived some 5300 years ago in the Middle East, as we saw in Chapter 2. Others developed new writing systems independently, such as the people in Shang China, discussed in Chapter 3, or the Zapotecs in Mesoamerica, considered in this chapter. More often, however, cultures eagerly adopted writing technology from neighboring societies, adjusting it to suit their languages. Almost everywhere, writing emerged as a tool when societies reached a level of complexity that made the memorization of important information impossible.

We should not, however, overestimate the impact of writing on ancient societies. In all the cultures we have studied so far, only a very small segment of the population used writing, and these people were mostly wealthy, male, and urban. Before modern times, literacy remained a rare skill. The inequality of access to literacy can distort the historian's picture of the past, because the voices of those who wrote are so much clearer and so much louder than the voices of those who did not.

Uses of the Written Record

The earliest known written records vary considerably in their nature and purpose. In Babylonia, where script appeared around 3200 B.C.E., its primary purpose was to record the exchange of goods. The Egyptians soon afterward also noted down economic information, but they used script mainly to commemorate the deeds of kings. In China, the earliest preserved written sources were the oracle-bone inscriptions that kings started to commission in around 1200 B.C.E. as a way to determine future events. In Mesoamerica, where writing appeared in the last centuries B.C.E., the Zapotec and early Maya inscriptions on stone—still not fully deciphered—dealt with the heroic acts of kings. These are the purposes of writing that we can ascertain from the preserved records. But it is likely that much of the earliest writing in these and other cultures appeared on materials that have since disintegrated and are thus lost from the historical record. The earliest manuscripts from Central Asia, for example, were made of tree bark, and that material survives only in very unusual circumstances.

Despite these differences in focus of the earliest preserved writings, many scholars believe that economic needs everywhere inspired the desire to keep records. Those needs began when people started to live together in large communities and were involved in so many transactions that it was impossible to keep track of them without written records. After the technology to record the spoken language in written form had been invented for administrative purposes, people could write down anything, including tales, accounts of military accomplishments, consultations with their gods, and much more. In most cultures the purposes of writing multiplied quickly after script came into use.

The Voiceless Many

As we have discussed, however, literacy was never very widespread in ancient cultures. To learn how to read and write required training from which most people were excluded. Moreover, there are degrees of literacy that require different periods of training. In a culture such as that of classical Greece, for example, many citizens of Athens may have been able to read basic words such as signs and the names of people. But they may not have managed to comprehend a treatise of Aristotle, and they would not have known how to compose a long letter. And consider this: the citizenry of Athens was a highly select group of landowning men. Among those excluded from citizenship, literacy was even more restricted.

Whether a person was included in or excluded from literate life depended mostly on economic factors. Only those who were involved with activities beyond a subsistence level would have needed to record anything in writing. Such people would usually have been city residents with substantial economic assets: landowners who received accounts from their estates, financiers who had to keep track of the loans they issued, merchants with goods in transit to foreign destinations, and so on. These people would join large-scale organizations such as palaces, temples, and monasteries that kept accounts of their holdings. Furthermore, some of those propertied individuals, or people supported by them, could engage in activities that did not produce economic benefit, such as composing plays and epics. The large majority of these people were men because, for the most part, males alone received an education.

For a woman in an ancient society to become literate, a good deal of luck and probably a very strong will were essential. In all early literate societies some women did write, however, and their writings constitute a small portion of the material that historians use as sources. In ancient Mesopotamia, women scribes recorded economic transactions, usually for institutions that provided services to women. For example, some Babylonian cities had **cloisters**, places devoted to religious observation in which rich families housed daughters they did not want to marry off. Were they to marry, these girls would take a share of the family property with them, and the family's total assets would correspondingly shrink. Although these girls were kept in seclusion, they engaged in financial activities and used the services of women scribes.

A small number of the earliest figures in world literature are women. The first known author in history is Enheduanna, a Babylonian princess. Living in around 2400 B.C.E., she was a priestess of the moon god in the city of Ur, and we know that she composed several poems in the Sumerian language (see Chapter 2). Likewise, in China of the first century C.E., the historian Ban Biao gave his daughter a literary education. As we saw in Chapter 6, Ban Zhao finished her father's *History of the Han Dynasty* and wrote other works of literature.

One of the most renowned poets of Greek antiquity was Sappho (c. 630–570 B.C.E.), whom we met in Chapter 5. The daughter of an aristocratic family, Sappho wrote poetry about religious festivals, military celebrations, and life at court. In her moving poems she focused on her emotions, which often involved the young women who were her friends and companions. Due to a military coup, her family was forced to leave their home on the Aegean island of Lesbos for a period of exile in Sicily, which she described with anger. But she was already so famous that the inhabitants of Sicily welcomed her with great ceremony.

Much of Sappho's poetry has been lost through the ages, but the pieces that remain show a remarkable sensitivity and ability to describe human feelings. Fortunately, scholars continue to discover some of her poems on fragmentary manuscripts preserved in the dry sands of Egypt. One such discovery on a papyrus from the third century B.C.E., made in 2004, contains a description of old age. Because the beginning of the papyrus is damaged, the words in parentheses are the translator's conjecture:

> (You for) the fragrant-bosomed (Muses') lovely gifts
> (be zealous,) girls, (and the) clear melodious lyre:
> (but my once tender) body old age now
> (has seized;) my hair's turned (white) instead of dark;
> my heart's grown heavy, my knees will not support me,
> that once on a time were fleet for the dance as fawns.
> This state I oft bemoan; but what's to do?
> Not to grow old, being human, there's no way.
> Tithonus once, the tale was, rose-armed Dawn,
> love-smitten, carried off to the world's end,
> handsome and young then, yet in time grey age
> o'ertook him, husband of immortal wife.[4]

Women such as Enheduanna, Ban Zhao, and Sappho were exceptional, however. In general, most known and unknown writers of ancient societies were men.

Outside the urban centers, in the villages and temporary settlements where most ancient peoples lived, very few were literate, if any. Thus their lives are often not revealed to us, or we view their experience only through the eyes of urban dwellers with very different concerns and lifestyles. One notable nonliterate group was the pastoral nomads who cared for herds of animals, which they led to various pastures at different times of the year—often the mountains in the summer when the snow melted and the valleys in the winter. Only in the winter would they interact with people living in cities, exchanging goods with them. Some of these interactions are reported in the writings of urban residents who did not look upon the pastoralists positively; they typically found the herders

cloister A place, usually a monastery or convent, in which people live in seclusion to concentrate on religious observation.

A Fragment of Sappho's Poetry

The dry climate of Egypt allowed numerous papyri to be preserved, including many that contain literature from Greek antiquity. The fragmentary papyrus shown here, dating from the third century B.C.E., contains the text of a poem that Sappho wrote in around 600 B.C.E. It was only in 2004 that a scholar recognized that the fragment recorded a previously unknown work from the famed Greek poet. (Papyrus Collection, The Institute for Ancient Studies, University of Cologne.)

uncivilized and dangerous. Sima Qian's quote at the beginning of Chapter 3 is just one of the many statements of this nature.

These exclusions from the technology of writing limit modern historians' view of the peoples of the past. Scholars can rarely close this gap through the archaeological record: archaeologists seldom excavate the remains of villages, and the temporary camps of nomads left virtually no traces. In investigations of urban remains, historians can focus on aspects traditionally associated with women, such as kitchens in the houses. But they must be careful not to impose a presumed gender division of labor upon all peoples of the past. Within ancient literate societies there are always large numbers of people whose voices we cannot hear.

Conclusion

Were we to imagine a woman making a tour around the world in the year 1 C.E. (an improbable adventure), we could reconstruct who her hosts would have been and how she would have been received for many stages of the voyage. She would have stayed in a city only very rarely, but when she did we can picture her as the guest of a courtier of the Roman, Parthian, Kushan, and Han emperors as she made her way across Eurasia, and we could even think of a name for that courtier. In Mesoamerica she might have seen the ceremonial centers of the early Maya, people whose names we do not know. Most days, however, she would have visited people in small villages or in temporary settlements whose names we cannot even guess. Many of her hosts in Eurasia, Africa, the Pacific Islands, and the Americas would have been farmers, but others would have foraged or raised herds of animals to feed themselves.

At a distance of more than two thousand years, the details of the histories of most of the world's inhabitants in the year 1 C.E. are vague to us, but there is much that we do know. A crucial distinction in our ability to study the peoples of that past is whether or not they wrote down information that tells us their names, their activities, and the languages they spoke. Few literate cultures existed. The archaeological remains of cultures without writing show us, however, how much they could accomplish, even in areas where in other cultures writing was crucial. The Polynesian sailors Joseph Banks described at the start of this chapter could navigate without the written records or maps that were indispensable to that eighteenth-century European explorer.

All over the world, the foundations of later histories developed in the long period from the evolution of the human species to 500 C.E. They settled most parts of the globe; they invented most of the tools we consider part of civilization, such as agriculture, writing, cities, and metalwork; and they developed elements of culture that were not utilitarian, such as literature, philosophy, and the visual arts. In many parts of the world, these innovations were fundamental to later historical developments. For their cultural and intellectual lives, people in Europe, the Middle East, and South and East Asia still rely on the creations of their ancestors. So, too, do people whose ancestors did not write. In ancient times, people all over the globe contributed to the world that we live in today.

NOTES

1. *The Endeavour Journal of Joseph Banks, 1768–1771*, ed. J. C. Beaglehole (Sydney, Australia: Halstead Press, 1962), 1:368, 2:37. Spellings from the original source.
2. Ibid.
3. Eric R. Wolf, *Europe and the People Without History* (Berkeley: University of California Press, 1982).
4. Martin West, trans., "A New Sappho Poem," *The Times Literary Supplement*, June 24, 2005.

RESOURCES FOR RESEARCH

General Works

In the absence of written sources, historians draw deeply on works from the archaeological perspective. Milleker's book gives an interesting idea of what high art a traveler would encounter on a trip around the world in the year 1 C.E.

Milleker, Elizabeth J., ed. *The Year One: Art of the Ancient World East and West*. 2000.

Scarre, Chris, ed. *The Human Past: World Prehistory and the Development of Human Societies*. 2005.

Wenke, Robert J., and Deborah I. Olszewski. *Patterns in Prehistory: Humankind's First Three Million Years*, 5th ed. 2006.

Peoples of Sub-Saharan Africa

Works that treat the history of the continent until European colonization in the eighteenth century often include studies of Africa's early history. Vansina's book excels in its use of linguistic data for historical reconstructions.

(For archaeological sites in Africa): African Archaeology, http://www.african-archaeology.net/, and Society of Africanist Archaeologists, http://safa.rice.edu/links.cfm.

Ehret, Christopher. *The Civilizations of Africa: A History to 1800*. 2002.

(For sources of African history): H-Africa. http://www.h-net.org/~africa/.

Stahl, Ann, ed. *African Archaeology: A Critical Introduction*. 2005.

Vansina, Jan. *Paths in the Rainforests: Toward a History of Political Tradition in Equatorial Africa*. 1990.

Peoples of the Americas

Many works focus on just one of the many cultures of the early Americas. They usually concentrate on either archaeological research or the fine arts of these cultures.

Burger, Richard L. *Chavín and the Origins of Andean Civilization*. 1995.

Fagan, Brian. *Ancient North America*, 4th ed. 2005.

(Hopewell culture): Ohio History Central. http://www.ohiohistorycentral.org/entry.php?rec=1283.

(Moche culture): http://www.huacas.com/.

(Norte Chico culture): http://www.fieldmuseum.org/research_Collections/anthropology/anthro_sites/PANC/default.htm.

Pillsbury, Joanne, ed. *Moche Art and Archaeology in Ancient Peru*. 2001.

(San Bartolo frescoes): http://www.sanbartolo.org/research.htm.

Peoples of the Pacific Islands

Because the archaeological exploration of this vast region is still in its infancy, relatively few books providing general overviews have been published.

Bellwood, Peter. *Man's Conquest of the Pacific*. 1979.

Kirch, Patrick V. *The Lapita Peoples*. 1997.

Kirch, Patrick V. *On the Road of the Winds: An Archaeological History of the Pacific Islands Before European Contact*. 2000.

(Lapita culture): Report of the 1997 Lapita Project. http://www.sfu.ca/archaeology/museum/tonga/toc.html.

Spriggs, Mathew. *The Island Melanesians*. 1997.

COUNTERPOINT: The Voiced and Voiceless in Ancient Literate Societies

Issues of ancient literacy are usually addressed in studies that focus on a specific culture.

Harris, William V. *Ancient Literacy*. 1989.

Houston, Stephen D., ed. *The First Writing: Script Invention as History and Process*. 2004.

▶ **For additional primary sources from this period**, see *Sources of Crossroads and Cultures*.

▶ **For Web sites, images, and documents related to topics in this chapter**, see Make History at bedfordstmartins.com/smith.

The major global development in this chapter ▶ The evolution of ancient cultures without writing and their fundamental role in world history.

IMPORTANT EVENTS

c. 3000 B.C.E.	Start of southward migration of the Bantu in Africa
c. 3000–1800 B.C.E.	Norte Chico culture in the Andes
c. 3000–750 B.C.E.	First wave of Austronesian migrations
c. 1400–200 B.C.E.	Lapita culture in the Pacific Ocean
c. 1200–400 B.C.E.	Olmec culture in Mesoamerica
c. 1000 B.C.E.	Start of eastern movement of the Bantu in Africa
c. 900–200 B.C.E.	Chavín culture in Mesoamerica
c. 800–700 B.C.E.	Start of iron technology in Africa
c. 800 B.C.E.–200 C.E.	Nok culture in West Africa
c. 400 B.C.E.–250 C.E.	Early Maya culture in Mesoamerica
c. 100 B.C.E.–400 C.E.	Hopewell culture in eastern North America
c. 200–600 C.E.	Moche culture in the Andes
c. 400 C.E.	Bantu arrival in southern Africa
c. 400–1200 C.E.	Second wave of Austronesian migrations

KEY TERMS

atoll (p. 256)
Bantu (p. 241)
cloister (p. 261)
El Niño (p. 253)

glyph (p. 249)
prehistory (p. 239)
savanna (p. 241)
shaman (p. 249)

CHAPTER OVERVIEW QUESTIONS

1. How does the presence or absence of writing influence how we study ancient cultures?

2. Why did the ancient cultures of Africa, the Americas, and the Pacific often show similar developments in spite of their isolation from one another?

3. How is the spread of peoples, languages, and technologies interrelated, and in what ways can we study these processes?

SECTION FOCUS QUESTIONS

1. How have scholars reconstructed the histories of early Africans, and what do their sources reveal about the livelihoods and cultures of these peoples?

2. What kinds of evidence have scholars used to recreate the experience of ancient American peoples, and what do we know about these cultures?

3. What do their material remains tell us about Pacific Islanders' society and culture?

4. To what extent does a society's literacy or nonliteracy affect our study of it?

MAKING CONNECTIONS

1. Consider the agricultural techniques and resources of the inhabitants of Africa, the Americas, and the Pacific. What do the similarities and differences reveal about the development of their cultures?

2. Why did Eurasian societies develop the features we associate with civilization before their counterparts elsewhere in the world?

3. What are the similarities and differences between the major cities of Eurasia and the ceremonial centers of the Americas?

PART 2

The Formation of Regional Societies

500–1450 C.E.

CH 9

ALTHOUGH NO SINGLE LABEL adequately reflects the history of the world in the period 500–1450, its most distinctive feature was the formation of regional societies based on common forms of livelihoods, cultural values, and social and political institutions. The new age in world history that began in around 500 C.E. marked a decisive break from the "classical" era of antiquity. The passing of classical civilizations in the Mediterranean, China, and India shared a number of causes, but the most notable were invasions by nomads from the Central Asian steppes. Beset by internal unrest and foreign pressures, the empires of Rome, Han China, and Gupta India crumbled. As these once-mighty empires fragmented into a multitude of competing states, cultural revolutions followed. Confidence in the values and institutions of the classical era was shattered, opening the way for fresh ideas. Christianity, Buddhism, Hinduism, and the new creed of Islam spread far beyond their original circles of believers. By 1450 these four religious traditions had supplanted or transformed local religions in virtually all of Eurasia and much of Africa.

The spread of foreign religions and the lifestyles and livelihoods they promoted produced distinctive regional societies. By 1000, Europe had taken shape as a coherent society and culture even as it came to be divided between the Roman and Byzantine Christian churches. The shared cultural values of modern East Asia—rooted in the literary and philosophical traditions of China but also assuming distinctive national forms—also emerged during the first millennium C.E. During this era, too, Indian civilization expanded into Southeast Asia and acquired a new unity expressed through the common language of Sanskrit. The rapid expansion of Islam across Asia, Africa, and

CH 10

266

CH 11

CH 12

even parts of Europe demonstrated the power of a shared religious identity to transcend political and cultural boundaries. But the pan-Islamic empire, which reached its height in the eighth century, proved unsustainable. After the authority of the Abbasid caliphs ebbed in the ninth century, the Islamic world split into distinctive regional societies in the Middle East, North Africa, Central and South Asia, and Southeast Asia.

We also see the formation of regional societies in other parts of the world. Migrations, the development of states, and commercial exchanges with the Islamic world transformed African societies and brought them into more consistent contact with one another. The concentration of political power in the hands of the ruling elites in Mesoamerica and the Andean region led to the founding of mighty city-states. Even in North America and the Pacific Ocean—worlds without states—migration and economic exchange fostered common social practices and livelihoods.

Nomad invasions and political disintegration disrupted economic life in the old imperial heartlands, but long-distance trade flourished as never before. The consolidation of nomad empires and merchant networks stretching across Central Asia culminated in the heyday of the overland "Silk Road" linking China to the Mediterranean world. The Indian Ocean, too, emerged as a crossroads of trade and cultural diffusion. After 1000, most of Eurasia and Africa enjoyed several centuries of steady economic improvement. Rising agricultural productivity fed population expansion, and cities and urban culture thrived with the growth of trade and industry.

Economic prosperity and urban vitality also stimulated intellectual change. Much of the new wealth was channeled into the building of religious monuments and institutions. New institutions of learning and scholarship—such as Christian Europe's universities, the madrasas of the Islamic world, and civil service examinations and government schooling in China—spawned both conformity and dissent.

Cross-cultural interaction also brought conflict, war, and schism. Tensions between Christians and Muslims erupted into the violent clashes known as the Crusades beginning in the late eleventh century. The boundaries between Christendom and the House of Islam shifted over time, but the rift between the two

CH 13

faiths grew ever wider. The rise of steppe empires—above all, the explosive expansion of the Mongol empires—likewise transformed the political and cultural landscape of Asia. Historians today recognize the ways in which the Mongol conquests facilitated the movement of people, goods, and ideas across Eurasia. But contemporaries could see no farther than the ruin sowed by the Mongols wherever they went, toppling cities and laying waste to once-fertile farmlands.

After 1300 the momentum of world history changed. Economic growth slowed, strained by the pressure of rising populations on productive resources and the effects of a cooling climate, and then it stopped altogether. In the late 1340s the Black Death pandemic devastated the central Islamic lands and Europe. It would take centuries before the populations in these parts of the world returned to their pre-1340 levels.

By 1400, however, other signs of recovery were evident. Powerful national states emerged in Europe and China, restoring some measure of stability. Strong Islamic states held sway in Egypt, Anatolia (modern Turkey), Iran, and India. The European Renaissance—the intense outburst of intellectual and artistic creativity envisioned as a "rebirth" of the classical civilization of Greece and Rome—flickered to life, sparked by the economic vigor of the Italian city-states. Similarly, Neo-Confucianism—a "renaissance" of China's classical learning—whetted the intellectual and cultural aspirations of educated elites throughout East Asia. Maritime Asia, spared the ravages of the Black Death, continued to flourish while

CH 14 →

	500		750	
Americas	• 500 First permanent settlements in Chaco Canyon		800–900 Collapse of the Maya city-states	
	500–1000 Andean state of Tiwanaku			Rise of Chimu state 900
	550–650 Collapse of Teotihuacán		700–900 Heyday of Andean state of Wari	
Europe	• 507 Clovis defeats Visigoths and converts to Christianity	Charles Martel halts Muslim advance into Europe 732 •	• 793 Earliest record of Viking raids on Britain	
	590–604 Papacy of Gregory I	Charlemagne crowned emperor 800 •		
Middle East	527–565 Reign of Byzantine emperor Justinian I	• 680 Permanent split between Shi'a and Sunni Islam		
	570–632 Life of Muhammad	661–743 Umayyad caliphate	750–850 Abbasid caliphate at its height	
Africa	• 500 Spread of camel use; emergence of trans-Saharan trade routes	• 750 Islam starts to spread via trans-Saharan trade routes		
Asia and Oceania	581–618 Sui Empire	• 668 Unification of Korea under Silla rule		
	618–907 Tang Empire	755–763 An Lushan rebellion		
	600–1000 Polynesian settlement of Pacific Islands			

Eurasia's major land-based economies struggled to regain their earlier prosperity.

In 1453 Muslim Ottoman armies seized Constantinople and deposed the Byzantine Christian emperor, cutting the last thread of connection to the ancient world. The fall of Constantinople symbolized the end of the era discussed in Part 2. Denied direct access to the rich trade with Asia, European monarchs and merchants began to shift their attention to the Atlantic world. Yet just as Columbus's discovery of the "New World" (in fact, a very ancient one) came as a surprise, the idea of a new world order centered on Europe—the modern world order—was still unimaginable.

CH 15

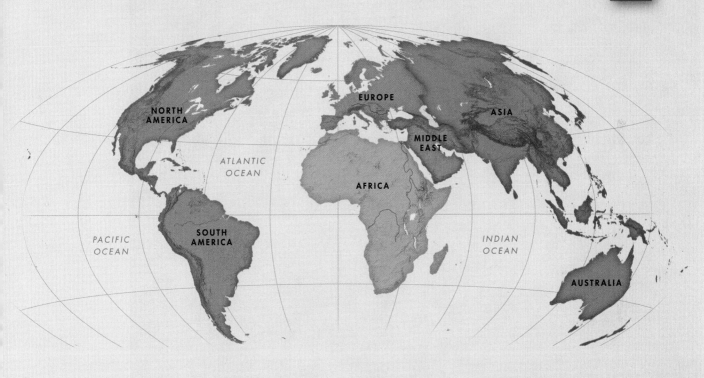

1000	1250	1500

950–1150 Height of Toltec culture ▪ 1200 Incas move into Cuzco region Columbus reaches the Americas 1492 ▪
▪ 1050 Consolidation of Cahokia's dominance ▪ 1150 Abandonment of pueblos in Chaco Canyon ▪ 1325 Aztecs found Tenochtitlán 1430–1532 Inca Empire
1250–1300 Collapse of Cahokia

▪ 988 Rus prince Vladimir converts to Christianity ▪ 1066 Norman conquest of England ▪ 1150 Founding of first university at Paris 1347–1350 Outbreak of Black Death 1400–1550 Italian Renaissance
1150–1300 Heyday of the Champagne fairs 1337–1453 Hundred Years' War Reconquista
Mongol conquest of Kiev 1240 ▪ 1270–1300 Introduction of overseas navigational aids completed 1492 ▪

First Crusade ends with Christian capture of Jerusalem 1099 ▪ ▪ 1120 Founding of order of Knights of the Temple ▪ 1291 Mamluks recapture Acre, last Christian stronghold in Palestine
▪ 1258 Mongols sack Baghdad 1347–1350 Outbreak of Black Death ▪ 1453 Fall of Constantinople to the Ottomans
Saladin recaptures Jerusalem 1187 ▪

▪ 969 Fatimids capture Egypt Reign of Sunjata, founder of 1250–1517 Mamluk dynasty
Fall of kingdom of Ghana 1076 ▪ Mali Empire 1230–1255 ▪ 1250 Kingdom of Benin founded
1100–1500 Extended dry period in West Africa prompts migrations

850–1267 Chola kingdom 1100–1500 Easter Island's stone monuments 1336–1573 Ashikaga Shogunate
939 Vietnam achieves independence from China Formation of first Hawaiian 1206–1526 Delhi Sultanate 1368–1644 Ming Empire
960–1279 Song Empire chiefdoms 1200–1400 1271–1368 Yuan Empire 1392–1910 Korean Yi dynasty

AT A CROSSROADS ▲

The emperors of Constantinople had grand ambitions to rebuild the Roman Empire on new foundations of Christian faith. They displayed special devotion to the Virgin Mary, the patron saint of their capital. This mosaic in the Hagia Sophia, Constantinople's greatest Christian church, shows Emperor Constantine (right) offering a model of the city to Mary and the infant Jesus. Emperor Justinian I (left) presents a model of the Hagia Sophia, which he rebuilt in 562. (Erich Lessing/Art Resource, NY.)

The Worlds of Christianity and Islam

400–1000

In 550, Médard, the bishop of Noyon, northeast of Paris, faced a dilemma. Radegund, the pious wife of the Germanic king Clothar, had come to him seeking to become a nun. But Médard was reluctant to offend Clothar, his patron and benefactor, and the king's men had threatened to drag him from his church should he attempt to place a nun's veil on their queen. According to her biographers, Radegund, sizing up the situation, entered the sacristy, put on a monastic garb, and proceeded straight to the altar, saying, 'If you shrink from consecrating me, and fear man more than God, pastor, He will require His sheep's [Radegund's] soul from your hand.'" Chastened, Médard laid his hands upon Radegund and ordained her as a deaconess.

Radegund (520–587) was the daughter of a rival German king who was a bitter enemy of Clothar's tribe, the Franks. When Radegund was eleven, the Franks slaughtered her family and took her prisoner. Later she was forced to marry Clothar and became, in her words, "a captive maid given to a hostile lord." Raised a Christian, Radegund took refuge in religion. Even before renouncing secular life, "she was more Christ's partner than her husband's companion."[1] Her biographers describe in great detail the physical torments she inflicted on herself, her ministrations to the poor and the sick, the miracles she performed, and the rich gifts she bestowed on the church and the needy. After Clothar's death, Radegund founded a convent at Poitiers and took up a life of full seclusion. But she continued to play the role of Christian queen, maintaining a vigorous correspondence with the leading clergy of the day and trying to act as peacemaker between feuding Frankish kings.

BACKSTORY

As we saw in Chapter 7, the Roman Empire enjoyed a period of renewal in the early fourth century under Constantine, who reinvigorated imperial rule and adopted Christianity as an official religion. But the western part of the empire, wracked by internal conflicts and Germanic invasions, crumbled in the fifth century. By contrast, the emperors at Constantinople, buoyed by the diverse and resilient economy of the eastern Mediterranean, continued to preside over a strong state, which historians call the Byzantine Empire. The resurgent Persian Empire of the Sasanid dynasty struggled with the Romans for control of Syria, Mesopotamia, and Armenia. The rise of Islam in the seventh century would transform political, religious, and economic life from the Mediterranean to Persia.

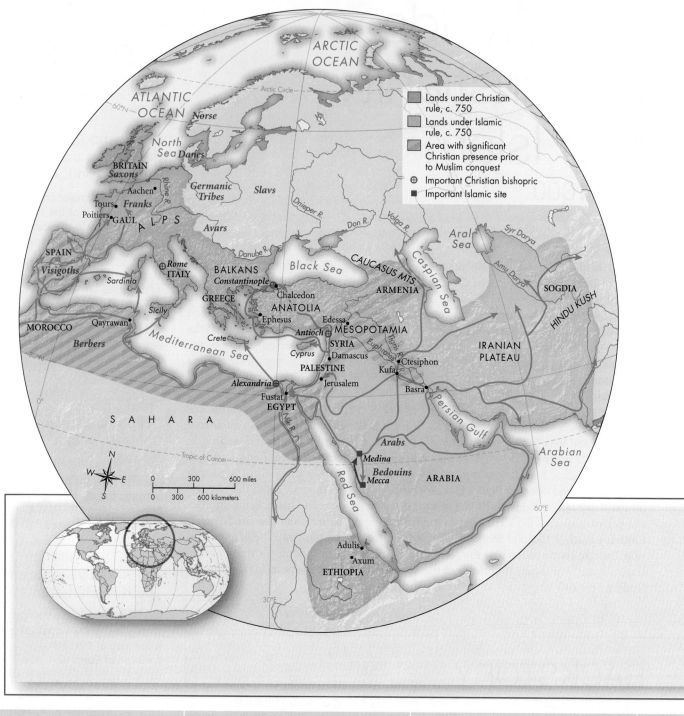

410 Visigoth sack of Rome

· 507 Clovis defeats Visigoth invaders and converts to Christianity

· 431 Council of Ephesus denounces Nestorianism as heresy

Muslim invasion and conquest of Visigoth-ruled Spain **710–711**

570–632 Life of Muhammad, founder of Islam

661–743 Umayyad caliphate

500

600

700

527–565 Reign of Justinian I as Byzantine emperor

590–604 Papacy of Gregory I

Split between Shi'a and Sunni Islam **680 ·**

· 589 Conversion of Visigoths to Roman Christianity

· 622 Muhammad's hijra to Medina, marking the beginning of the Islamic calendar

By Radegund's day, Christianity had become deeply entrenched in all of the Roman Empire's former territories and had spread beyond to Iran, Armenia, and Ethiopia. Pagan societies on the fringes of the old empire, such as the roving Germanic tribes and the Slavic peoples of Eastern Europe, gradually adopted the Christian religion as well. Even the Norse Vikings, at first reviled as the mortal enemies of Christianity, remade themselves into models of Christian piety.

Unity proved elusive in Christendom (the realm of Christianity), however. Radegund's contemporary Justinian I (r. 527–565), the emperor at Constantinople, tried to reunify the old Roman Empire through military conquest. But Justinian's triumphs barely outlasted his death in 565. New adversaries in the east—above all, the rising religion of Islam—drew the emperors' attention away from the western provinces of the old empire. The rulers of Constantinople began to identify themselves exclusively with their capital's Greek heritage, spurning Roman traditions and replacing Latin with Greek as the official language of the empire. By 600 the religious and cultural gulf between the Latin west and the Greek east had so widened that historians speak of the latter as the Byzantine Empire (from *Byzantium*, the Greek name for Constantinople).

At the same time that the Latin west and the Greek east took increasingly divergent paths, a new and powerful culture arose that would challenge both. The emergence and spread of Islam in the 600s occurred with astonishing speed and success. The Muslim conquests sowed the seeds of Islamic faith and Arab social institutions in diverse societies in Africa, Europe, and Asia. The pace of conversion to Islam varied greatly, however. Islam quickly made deep inroads among urban merchants and among pastoral nomads such as the Berbers of North Africa. In agrarian societies such as Syria, Mesopotamia, and Spain, the Arabs long remained a tiny elite ruling over Christian majorities, who only gradually accepted Islam. In regions hemmed in by the expansion of Islam, such as Armenia and Ethiopia, the Christian faith became the hallmark of political independence. Thus Islamic expansion did not impose a uniform culture over a vast empire. Local conditions in each

MAPPING THE WORLD

Christian and Islamic Lands, c. 750

By 750, the old Roman Empire had been partitioned between two faiths, Christianity and Islam. Christendom itself was increasingly becoming a house divided between two rival churches centered at Constantinople and Rome. The Abbasid caliphate had deposed the Umayyad dynasty of caliphs, based at Damascus, in 747. The new Abbasid capital at Baghdad soon eclipsed Damascus and the holy cities of Mecca and Medina as the political and religious center of the Islamic world.

ROUTES ▼

→ Major campaign of Islamic forces, 625–732

→ Muhammad's hijra, 622

868–883 Zanj revolt against the Abbasid regime

793 Earliest record of Viking raids on Britain

988 Vladimir, the Rus prince of Kiev, converts to Christianity

870–930 Vikings colonize Iceland

800   900   1000

747–1258 Abbasid caliphate

800 Coronation of Charlemagne as emperor by Pope Leo III

909 Fatimid dynasty founded

732 Charles Martel halts Muslim advance into Europe

Muslim territory shaped the terms and consequences of cultural exchange among Muslim conquerors, subject peoples, and neighboring states.

However, like Christianity, Islam claimed to be a universal religion. Both religions offered a vision of common brotherhood that brought a new religious sensibility to daily life and integrated disparate peoples into a community of faith. Although Christianity and Islam spread along different paths, both were beset by an abiding tension between sacred and secular authority. The Christian church preserved its autonomy amid political disorder in the Latin west, whereas the Byzantine emperors yoked imperial power and clerical leadership tightly together. The vision of a universal Islamic empire combining spiritual faith with political and military strength was crucial to the initial expansion of Islam. In the ninth and tenth centuries, however, the Islamic empire fragmented into numerous regional states divided by doctrine, culture, and way of life. Nonetheless, the economic vibrancy and religious ferment of the far-flung Islamic world created a vast territory through which Muslim merchants, missionaries, and pilgrims moved freely, drawing together the separate worlds of Asia, Africa, and Europe. Islamic cities and ports became global crossroads, centers for the exchange of goods and ideas that helped create new cultural connections stretching from the Iberian peninsula to China.

OVERVIEW QUESTIONS

The major global development in this chapter: The spread of Christianity and Islam and the profound impact of these world religions on the societies of western Eurasia and North Africa.

As you read, consider:

1. How and why did the development of the Christian church differ in the Byzantine Empire and Latin Christendom?

2. In what ways did the rise of Christianity and Islam challenge the power of the state?

3. Conversely, in what ways did the spread of these faiths reinforce state power?

4. Why did Christianity and Islam achieve their initial success in towns and cities rather than in the rural countryside?

Multiple Christianities 400–850

FOCUS

In what ways did Christianity develop and spread following its institutionalization in the Roman Empire?

In the century following the Roman emperor Constantine's momentous conversion to Christianity in 312, Christian leaders were confident that their faith would displace the classical Mediterranean religions (see Chapter 7). Yet the rapid spread of the Christian religion throughout Roman territories also splintered the Christian movement. Their fierce independence honed by hostility and persecution, Christian communities did not readily yield to any universal authority in matters of doctrine and faith. Efforts by the Byzantine emperors to impose their will on the Christian leadership met strong resistance. The progress of conversion throughout the territories of the old Roman Empire came at the cost of increasing divisions within the church itself.

The Christian Church in Byzantium

In the eastern Mediterranean, where imperial rule remained strong, the state treated the Christian church and clergy as a branch of imperial administration. Although the Christian communities of the eastern Mediterranean welcomed imperial support, they also sought to preserve their independence from the emperors' direct control. For example, bishops elected by their local followers exercised sovereign rule over religious affairs within their jurisdictions. In the late fourth century a council of bishops acknowledged the special status of the bishop of Constantinople by designating him as patriarch, the supreme leader of the church. But the bishops of Alexandria in Egypt and Antioch in Anatolia (modern Turkey) retained authority and influence nearly equal to that of Constantinople's patriarch (see Map 9.1). Thus, although Byzantine emperors sought to use the Christian church as a vehicle to expand and reinforce their power, church leaders contested this agenda throughout the empire.

Tensions between secular and religious officials were not the only source of division in eastern Christianity. The urban elite of imperial officials and wealthy merchants adopted the new religion, but alongside such new Christian practices as prayer, repentance, and almsgiving they often continued to uphold the old forms of Greek religion. Their vision of Christianity reflected the strong influence Greek culture continued to exert on Byzantine city life. These were urban people, and their religious beliefs and practices grew out of a cosmopolitan urban context.

The Ascetic Movement

In Syria and Egypt, however, rural inhabitants embraced a more austere form of Christian piety. Some of the most impassioned Christians, deploring the persistence of profane Greco-Roman culture in the cities, sought spiritual refuge in the sparsely inhabited deserts, where they devoted themselves to an ascetic life of rigorous physical discipline and contemplation of the divine. Perhaps the most famous of these ascetics was Symeon the Stylite, who for many years lived and preached atop a sixty-foot pillar. After his death in 459, thousands of pilgrims flocked each year to Symeon's shrine in northern Syria.

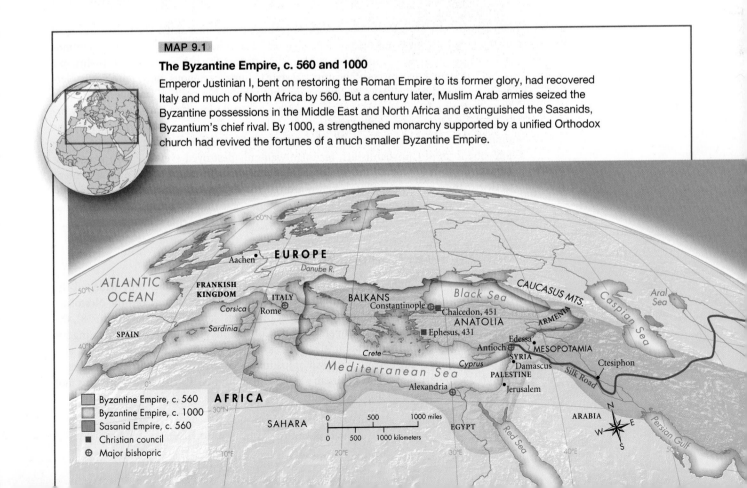

MAP 9.1

The Byzantine Empire, c. 560 and 1000

Emperor Justinian I, bent on restoring the Roman Empire to its former glory, had recovered Italy and much of North Africa by 560. But a century later, Muslim Arab armies seized the Byzantine possessions in the Middle East and North Africa and extinguished the Sasanids, Byzantium's chief rival. By 1000, a strengthened monarchy supported by a unified Orthodox church had revived the fortunes of a much smaller Byzantine Empire.

Byzantine Empire, c. 560
Byzantine Empire, c. 1000
Sasanid Empire, c. 560
■ Christian council
⊕ Major bishopric

Rise of Christian Monasteries

While also serving as spiritual guides for the Christian population at large, other ascetics founded monasteries that attracted like-minded followers. The monastic movement began sporadically in Egypt and Syria in the late third century and surged in the fourth and fifth centuries. The austerity of monastic life endowed monks with an aura of holiness and sacred power that outshone the pomp and finery of church leaders in the cities. Whether hidden away in the monasteries or preaching their convictions among the people, these holy men became alternative sources of sacred authority independent of the official church hierarchy.

Disputes over Doctrine

The divisions within eastern Christianity went beyond differences in style and presentation to disagreements over basic Christian beliefs. Straying from orthodoxy—established church doctrines—became common among recluses, itinerant preachers, and even those in the church's highest ranks. Already in the time of Constantine, the bishops had been locked in debate over the divinity of Jesus (see Chapter 7). Nestorius (neh-STORE-ee-us), elected patriarch of Constantinople in 428, renewed this controversy by proclaiming that Jesus had two natures, one human and one divine. Nestorius especially objected to the idea that a human woman, Mary, could give birth to the son of God. But Nestorius's views outraged Cyril, the bishop of Alexandria, who insisted that Jesus had a single, fully divine nature, a principle that became known as the Monophysite ("single nature") doctrine. Councils of bishops held at Ephesus (431) and Chalcedon (KAL-suh-dahn) (451) denounced Nestorius's views as heresy (see again Map 9.1). To counter the claims of Nestorius, the Ephesus council formally declared Mary "mother of God" (see Seeing the Past: Mary as Mother of God). The Chalcedon council, in an effort to heal the split among the clergy, adopted a compromise position, that Jesus was both "fully divine and fully human." But the bishops of Alexandria remained committed to their Monophysite views, whereas the Nestorian doctrine gained a considerable following among local clergy in Syria and Mesopotamia. This debate may seem esoteric to modern observers, but it is important to remember that, from the point of view of the participants, the stakes could not have been higher. At issue was the very nature of Jesus and, thus, the essential nature of Christianity. It is, therefore, not surprising that this debate led to long-lasting divisions within the Christian community.

Justinian's Imperial Orthodoxy

There were, however, countervailing pressures for Christian unity. The pressure exerted by the Germanic invasions discussed in Chapter 7 compelled the emperors at Constantinople to shore up religious solidarity as a defense against the pagan onslaught. Justinian I (r. 527–565) used the powers of the imperial state to impose religious unity, refusing to tolerate heretics and nonbelievers. Born a peasant but schooled in political intrigue while rising through the ranks of the palace guard, Justinian believed himself to have been divinely ordained to restore order to the Roman world. He began his campaign to impose religious uniformity on his empire soon after his coronation. "His ambition being to force everyone into one form of Christian belief, Justinian wantonly destroyed everyone who would not conform," wrote Procopius, the great historian of Justinian's reign.[2] He also put the content of Christianity in service of his drive toward religious orthodoxy as a means of promoting political unity. The theology elaborated at Constantinople during the next several centuries reiterated the principles of order and hierarchy on which the imperial state was built.

Christianity in Asia and Africa

Far from restoring unity, though, Justinian's often strong-arm tactics only widened the fractures within the church. Alexandria resisted imperial domination, and the Nestorian heresy became entrenched in the easternmost provinces. Jacob Baradaeus (died 578), the Monophysite bishop of Edessa, openly defied Constantinople's authority by forming his own separatist church (what became known as the Jacobite movement) in Anatolia and Syria. Christians living beyond the reach of Justinian's control were even more reluctant to submit to imperial dictates. Justinian's vision of a unified Christian empire was not matched by the power to impose his will.

Mary as Mother of God

The Virgin of Vladimir **(artist unknown):** This icon, sent to the Rus prince of Kiev from Constantinople in 1131, became renowned for its miracle-working powers. (Scala/Art Resource, NY.)

over the question of Jesus's divinity that reached a climax at the 431 Council of Ephesus elevated Mary to a position in Christian devotion second only to Jesus himself.

Devotion to Mary intensified through a proliferation of festival days, liturgies, miracle stories, and visual images. When Constantinople's patriarch renovated the city's principal Christian church, Hagia Sophia, after the defeat of the iconoclasm movement in the mid-ninth century (see page 281), the mosaic shown at the start of this chapter of an enthroned Mary and the child Jesus flanked by two haloed Byzantine emperors was placed prominently over an entrance to the church's nave.

Icons intended for personal, private devotion depicted the Virgin and Child in a very different manner. The example reproduced here, known as the Virgin of Vladimir (the Kievan prince who commissioned it), portrays the Virgin and Child locked together in a tender maternal embrace, faces touching. The tiny head and hands of Jesus accentuate his infantlike helplessness. In contrast to her public portrayal as the enthroned Mary, in this personal icon Mary's gaze is fixed on the viewer, with her left hand upraised in a gesture of prayer that likewise beckons toward the viewer. Many icons of this type also were brought to Italy and had a strong influence on the religious art of the early Renaissance, a European cultural movement that we will discuss in Chapter 15.

Source: Maria Vassilaki, ed., *Mother of God: Representations of the Virgin in Byzantine Art* (Milan: Skira editore, 2000), plates 61, 24.

There is little scriptural authority for the central place that Mary, mother of Jesus, eventually came to occupy in Christian beliefs and rituals. The few references to Mary in the Gospels make no mention, for example, of her lifelong virginity or her ascent to heaven. Nonetheless, early Christian writings singled Mary out as a role model for women, stressing her obedience and virginity in contrast to the biblical Eve. The virginity of Mary also provided inspiration for the ascetic and monastic movements that began to flourish in the third and fourth centuries. Ultimately, the theological controversy

EXAMINING THE EVIDENCE

1. How does the "At a Crossroads" mosaic from Hagia Sophia (see page 270) and the icon shown here differ in their depiction of Mary as a maternal figure? What do these contrasts tell us about the differences between public and private devotion to Mary?

2. How does the Byzantine conception of imperial authority expressed in the mosaic from Hagia Sophia compare with the Roman conception as evidenced in the image of Augustus on page 217?

Christianity in Armenia

Armenia, at the frontier between the Roman Empire and the Persian Sasanid Empire, nurtured its own distinctive Christian tradition. Christianity had advanced slowly in Armenia following the conversion of its king in the early fourth century. But after Armenia was partitioned and occupied by Roman and Sasanid armies in 387, resistance to foreign rule hardened around this kernel of Christian faith. With the invention

Byzantine Emperorship

This mosaic from the San Vitale church in Ravenna, Italy, depicts Justinian surrounded by his civil, military, and ecclesiastic officials—a clear effort to project the emperor's identity as head of both state and church. The mosaic was commissioned in around 550 not by Justinian, however, but by Maximian, archbishop of Ravenna in Italy, the only figure labeled by the artist. (Giraudon/Bridgeman Art Library.)

of the Armenian alphabet in around 400 came a distinctive Armenian literary heritage of Christian teachings. Christianity had become the hallmark of Armenian independence, and the Armenian clergy also repelled Justinian's attempts to impose religious orthodoxy.

Sasanid Toleration of Christianity

Except in Armenia, where Christians suffered political persecution, the Sasanids generally tolerated Christianity, which along with Judaism was well entrenched in Mesopotamia. The Nestorian church enjoyed a privileged position at the Sasanid capital of Ctesiphon (TEH-suh-fahn), south of modern Baghdad, and a number of Nestorian clergy attained high office at court. Nestorian Christians celebrated the Sasanid seizure of Jerusalem from Constantinople in 618 as a triumph over heresy. Nestorian missionaries traveled eastward and established churches along the trade routes leading from Persia to Central Asia. Merchants from the caravan settlements of Sogdia carried their adopted Nestorian faith eastward along the Silk Road as far as China, as we will see in Chapter 10. In this way, Sasanid political policies and economic connections facilitated the growth and spread of a distinctive form of Christianity.

Christianity also gained a foothold in Ethiopia, at the northern end of the Rift Valleys in eastern Africa, and once again trade played a key role. Long a bridge between sub-Saharan Africa and the Mediterranean, Ethiopia also became the main channel of trade and cultural contact between the Roman world and the Indian Ocean. Both Jewish and Christian merchants settled in the Ethiopian towns that served this trade, chief of which was Axum (AHK-soom).

Rise and Fall of Axum

By the first century C.E., Axum was a thriving metropolis connected to the Mediterranean trade network through the Red Sea port of Adulis (ah-DOOL-iss). Axum was the chief marketplace for exotic African goods such as ivory, gold, precious stones, and animal horns and skins. Although the majority of the population consisted of herders and farmers, townsmen made pottery, worked leather and metal, and carved ivory. The use at the Axum court of Greek and Syriac, along with Ge'ez (geeze), the native written language of Ethiopia, reflected the multinational character of the merchant and official classes.

Commercial wealth led to the creation of a powerful monarchy. During the early fourth century the rulers of Axum officially recognized Christianity as their state religion. Intolerance of other creeds hardened as the pace of conversion to Christianity accelerated.

Axum's Jews emigrated farther inland, where they formed the nucleus of their own independent state, which would later be known as Falasha.

But the Islamic conquests in the seventh century disrupted the lucrative trade on which Axum's vitality depended. Trade routes shifted away from the Red Sea to Syria, and Damascus became the new commercial capital of the eastern Mediterranean. When the Axum monarchy declined, a class of warrior lords allied with Christian monasteries gained both economic and legal control of the agrarian population. As in Europe, most of the population was reduced to servile status, and much of the produce of the land supported Christian monasteries, which remained the repositories of learning and literate culture. In this way, trade brought Christianity to Axum and created the wealth that built its Christian monarchy. When regional trade patterns changed, Christianity in Axum changed as well.

In the twelfth and thirteenth centuries, new royal dynasties arose in the highlands of Ethiopia that became great patrons of Christianity. These dynasties claimed direct descent from the ancient kings of Israel, but they also drew legitimacy from African traditions of sacred kingship. Ethiopia endured as a Christian stronghold down to modern times, although hemmed in by the hostile pastoral nomads of the coastal lowlands, who converted to Islam. Not surprisingly, isolated as it was from the larger Christian world, the Ethiopian church developed its own distinctive Christian traditions.

Ethiopia, Christian Stronghold

Christian Communities in Western Europe

While the Christian movements in Asia and Africa strove to maintain their independence from Constantinople, the collapse of the imperial order in the west posed different challenges for the Christian faithful. In the absence of the patronage (and interference) of the Byzantine emperors, a variety of distinctive Christian cultures emerged throughout the former western provinces. With imperial Rome in ruins, local communities and their leaders were free to rebuild their societies on the pillars of Christian beliefs and practices. When the Frankish king Charlemagne achieved military supremacy in western Europe at the end of the eighth century, his contemporaries heralded their new emperor as having been chosen by God "to rule and protect the Christian people."[3]

When imperial Rome fell, Christianity in the west was largely an urban religion. Amid ongoing warfare and violence, the beleaguered Christian towns in Gaul and Spain turned for leadership to provincial notables—great landowners and men of the old senatorial class. The bishops of Rome proclaimed their supreme authority in doctrinal matters as popes (from *papa*, or "grand old man"), the successors of St. Peter, who represented the universal ("Catholic") church. But Christian communities in the provinces of western Europe entrusted their protection to local men of wealth and family distinction, whom they elected as bishops. Bred to govern in the Roman style, these aristocrats took firm control of both secular and religious affairs. Although many of these men had been born to luxury and comfort, they embraced the austerity of monastic life, which further enhanced their aura of holiness. In time, with the assistance of zealous Christian missionaries, they negotiated settlements with their new Germanic overlords—the Franks in Gaul, the Visigoths in Spain, and the Saxons in Britain—that fully welcomed the Christian religion.

Bishops of the West

In an increasingly uncertain and violent world, the bishops of the west rallied their followers around collective religious ceremonies and the cults of saints. From at least the second century, Christians had commemorated beloved and inspiring martyrs and bishops as saints. Later, hermits, monks, and outstanding laypeople, both men and women, were also honored as saints. Christians viewed saints as their patrons, persons of power and influence who protected the local community and interceded on its behalf for divine blessings. They regarded the bodily remains of saints as sacred relics endowed with miraculous potency. Thus, worship of saints at the sites of their tombs became a focal point of Christian life. Just as Christian communities turned to provincial elites for protection, Christians looked to the saints to keep them safe in a hostile world.

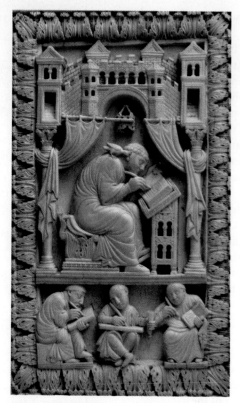

Pope Gregory I

Pope Gregory I exercised firm personal leadership over the Latin Christian church through his voluminous correspondence with bishops, missionaries, and noble laypeople. At least twenty thousand letters were dispatched from Rome under his name during the fourteen years of his papacy. This ivory carving shows the pope at his writing desk, with scribes below copying his writings. (Erich Lessing/Art Resource, NY.)

In the 460s, the bishop of Tours built a huge and ornate basilica at the site of the grave of the martyr St. Martin (335–397). Its reputation swelled by a flood of reports of miracles, it became a fortress of Christian faith and attracted pilgrims from throughout Gaul and beyond. When the Frankish king Clovis challenged the Visigoth ruler Alaric for control of southern Gaul in 507, he sought (and reportedly received) divine blessing at St. Martin's shrine. After defeating the Visigoths, Clovis returned to Tours laden with booty that he donated to the shrine. Similar cults and networks of pilgrimage and patronage sprung up around the relics of other saints.

Pope Gregory I (540–604) typified the distinctive style of leadership in the western Christian church. Born into a prominent Roman aristocratic family, Gregory entered the imperial service in 573 as the governor of Rome. Pulled by a strong religious calling, however, he soon retired to become a monk. After achieving fame for his devotion to learning and ascetic lifestyle, Gregory yielded to repeated summons to return to public service. He spent a decade as the papal envoy to the Byzantine court before returning to Rome upon his election as pope in 590. Keenly aware of the divisions within the Christian world, Gregory strove to make the papacy the centerpiece of a church administration that stretched from Britain to North Africa. Mindful, too, of the limited penetration of Christian religion in the countryside, he worked tirelessly to instill a sense of mission among the Christian clergy. "The art to end all arts is the governing of souls," wrote Gregory, insisting that the contemplative life of the monastery must be joined to the pastoral duty of saving sinners.[4]

Slowly but surely, Gregory's vision of the Christian clergy as the spiritual rulers of the humble peasantry gained converts. By the eighth century, social life in the western European countryside revolved around the village church and its liturgies. Christian sacraments marked the major stages of the individual's life from birth (baptism) to death (last rites), and the religious calendar, with high points at the celebrations of Christ's birth (Christmas) and resurrection (Easter), introduced a new rhythm to the cycle of the seasons.

Still, Latin Christendom was far from united. Distinctive regional Christian churches and cultures had emerged in Italy, Gaul, Britain, and Spain; indeed, we can think of these as a cluster of micro-Christendoms clinging to the fragments of the former Roman Empire. During the eighth century, however, the rise of the Carolingian dynasty and its imperial aspirations would bring these regional Christendoms into a single European form.

Social and Political Renewal in the Post-Roman World 400–850

FOCUS

What major changes swept the lands of the former Roman Empire in the four centuries following the fall of imperial Rome?

The Byzantine emperors in the east and the Germanic chieftains who ruled the empire's former western European provinces shared a common heritage rooted in the Roman imperial past and Christian religion. The Byzantine Empire faced a profound crisis in the sixth and seventh centuries. Protracted wars with the Sasanids, the Slavs, and the Avars were followed by the loss of two-thirds of Byzantium's realm to the rapid advance of Muslim Arab armies. Yet the Byzantine Empire survived, thanks to the revitalization of the imperial state and a resilient economy. Byzantine political institutions and especially its distinctive version of Christianity also exerted a powerful influence on the Slavic peoples and led to the formation of the first Rus state. Although Byzantium regained its political and cultural vigor in the ninth century, their fellow Christians, the Frankish empire of the Carolingian dynasty, proved to be more a rival than an ally.

Crisis and Survival of the Byzantine Empire

Justinian I's conquests in Italy and North Africa had once again joined Constantinople and Rome under a single sovereign, but this union was short-lived. Lengthy wars and the enormous costs of Justinian's building programs sapped the fiscal strength of the empire. Although the Byzantine forces repulsed a Sasanid-led attack on Constantinople in 626, this victory was eclipsed within fifteen years by the loss of Syria, Palestine, and Egypt to Muslim armies, as we shall see. By 700 the Byzantine Empire was a shrunken vestige of Justinian's realm, consisting essentially of Constantinople and its immediate environs, a few territories in Greece, and Anatolia. Once-flourishing commercial cities lost much of their population and were rebuilt as smaller, fortified towns to defend the local bishop and his church.

Constantinople alone stood out as a thriving crossroads of trade, learning, and aristocratic culture. Home to a dense mosaic of languages and nationalities united by the Christian faith, Constantinople numbered five hundred thousand inhabitants at its peak in Justinian's age. Social frictions frequently ignited outbursts of violence, such as the Nika (Greek for "conquer") Revolt of 532, a weeklong protest against Justinian's high-handed officials that left nearly half of the city burned or destroyed. To soothe these tensions, the emperors staged an elaborate cycle of public rituals—military triumphs, imperial birthdays, and Christian festivals—that showcased their essential role in fostering unity and common purpose among Constantinople's populace.

Accompanying Byzantium's declining power and prestige were worsening relations with Rome. Emperor Justinian II (r. 685–695) convened a council of bishops at Constantinople in 692 that granted the emperor greater control over the church and its clergy. The council rejected Latin customs such as priestly celibacy and affirmed the independence of the patriarch of Constantinople from the Roman pope in matters of religious doctrine. This rupture between the emperor and the pope was partially mended in the later years of Justinian II's reign, but over the course of the eighth century the religious **schism** widened. The Frankish king Charlemagne's coronation as emperor by Pope Leo III in 800 in effect declared Charlemagne to be the protector of the church, usurping the Byzantine emperor's role. Although Charlemagne negotiated a compromise in 813 that recognized the Byzantine monarch as "emperor of the Romans" and pledged friendship between the two rulers, Latin Christendom had clearly emerged as a separate church.

Within Byzantium, debate raged over the proper conduct of life and religion in a Christian society, especially concerning the veneration of icons—painted images of Jesus, Mary, and the saints. The powerful new faith of Islam denounced any representation of the divine in human form as idolatry. This radical **iconoclasm** (Greek for "image-breaking") struck a responsive chord among the many Byzantines who saw the empire's political reversals as evidence of moral decline. Throughout the eighth century a bitter struggle divided Byzantium. On one side were the iconoclasts, who sought to match Muslim religious fervor by restoring a pristine faith rooted in Old Testament values. On the other side were the defenders of orthodoxy, who maintained that the use of explicitly Christian images of Jesus and Mary was an essential component of the imperially ordained liturgy on which social unity depended. In the mid-ninth century the proponents of orthodoxy prevailed over the iconoclasts. Henceforth Byzantine Christianity became known as the Orthodox Church, in which religious authority became tightly interwoven with imperial power.

In the second half of the ninth century the Muslim threat abated, and the Byzantine Empire enjoyed a rebirth. Resurgent economic strength at home fueled military success against the Muslims and the Slavs. The church and the army supported efforts to enhance the power and authority of the emperor and the central state. Yet as the leading classes of Byzantine society rallied around a revitalized imperial institution, the estrangement between the churches of Constantinople and Rome intensified. The split between the two churches was about more than conflicts over theology and church hierarchy. The peoples of the Latin west and the Greek east, who had once shared a common history and culture as subjects of the Roman Empire, were moving in different directions.

Schism Between Constantinople and Rome

The Iconoclastic Controversy

schism A split in any organized group (especially a church or religious community) resulting in a formal declaration of differences in doctrine or beliefs.

iconoclasm Literally, "destruction of images"; the word originates with the movement against the veneration of images in the Byzantine Empire in the eighth and ninth centuries.

Christ Pantokrator

Following the final defeat of iconoclasm, images of Christ Pantokrator (Greek for "ruler of all") became a standard feature of Byzantine church decoration. Typically placed on vaulted domes, these images emphasized Jesus's transcendent divinity. This version of the Pantokrator, which portrays Jesus as a teacher, was created in 1148 by Byzantine mosaic artists hired by Roger II, king of Sicily, to decorate his newly built Cefalu Cathedral. (Corbis.)

The Germanic Successor States in Western Europe

At the peak of the Roman Empire, its northern frontier stretched three thousand miles, from the British Isles to the Black Sea. From the vantage point of Rome, this frontier marked a sharp boundary between civilized and barbarian peoples. But as we saw in Chapter 7, provincial Romans had frequent social and economic interactions with their Celtic and Germanic neighbors. Many Germanic chieftains who became overlords of the empire's western provinces in the fifth and sixth centuries had previously served as mercenaries defending the territories they now ruled. In a sense, they were at least partially Romanized before they conquered Rome (see Map 9.2).

Livelihoods of the Germanic Peoples

Similar patterns of livelihood prevailed among the Germanic peoples—and indeed among all the peoples of northern and eastern Europe. In most of the region, small, patriarchal farming communities predominated, in which men had full authority over members of their families or clans. The most important crop was barley, which was consumed as porridge, bread, and beer. Cattle-raising also was important, both to feed the community and as an index of positions in the social hierarchy. The number of cattle a household possessed determined its wealth and prestige, and acquiring cattle was a chief objective of both trade and warfare.

Valor and success in warfare also conferred prestige. Village communities organized themselves into warrior bands for warfare and raiding, and at times these bands joined together to form broad confederations for mutual defense and campaigns of plunder. These groups were primarily political alliances, and thus they constantly dissolved and reformed as the needs and interests of their constituent tribes shifted. Kinfolk found solidarity in their common genealogical descent, but marriage ties, gift giving, and sharing food and drink at feasts helped nurture bonds of fellowship and loyalty. Contact with the Roman world, through both trade and war, magnified the roles of charismatic military leaders, men skilled at holding together their fragile coalitions of followers and negotiating with the Roman state. As we saw in Chapter 7, Rome's eagerness to obtain the military services of these confederations further encouraged the militarization of Germanic society.

The Goths

One such confederation, the Goths, arrived in Italy and Gaul as refugees, driven westward by the invasions of the Hun nomads from Central Asia in the fifth century (see Chapter 7).

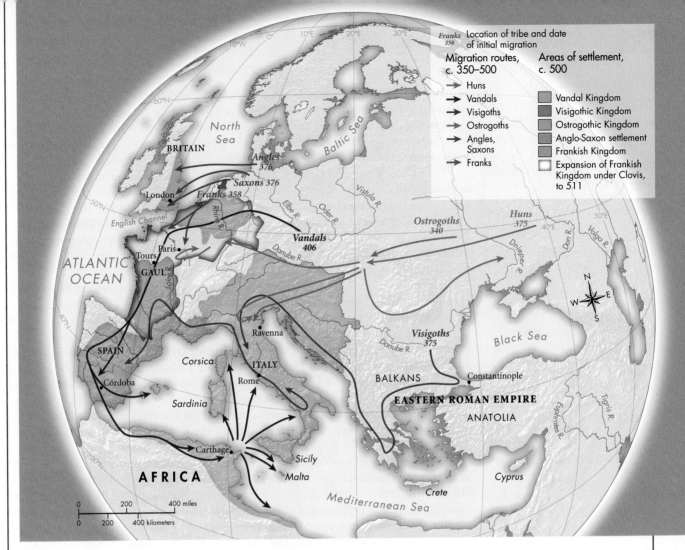

MAP 9.2 **Conquests and Settlements of the Germanic Tribes, c. 350–500**

The Germanic peoples had long inhabited the lands along the Roman Empire's frontiers in northern and eastern Europe. In the fourth and fifth centuries, as Rome's authority disintegrated, Germanic chieftains led their followers to invade and occupy Roman territories. The new Germanic rulers such as the Franks and the Goths cultivated alliances with local leaders and the Christian church and restored a measure of stability.

Expelled from their homeland in the lower Danube region, the Visigoths (Western Goths) followed their king Alaric into the Balkans and Italy. Driven more by desperation and hunger than by greed, Alaric's army captured and plundered Rome in 410. In 418 the Visigoths negotiated an alliance with the Byzantine emperor that allowed them to occupy southern Gaul—the first Germanic people to complete the transition from confederation to kingdom.

The Ostrogoths (Eastern Goths) emerged as an independent force in the late fifth century, following the death of the Hun leader Attila, whom the Ostrogoths loyally served. After Attila's empire disintegrated, the Ostrogoths shifted their allegiance to Constantinople. In 488 the Byzantine emperor dispatched the Ostrogoth leader Theodoric to subdue Odoacer, the German king who had seized Rome and deposed its last emperor in 476. Theodoric conquered the Italian peninsula in 493 but refused to relinquish control to Constantinople. The Ostrogoths ruled Italy until they were overwhelmed by Justinian's armies in 553.

Only a small number of the Goths entered Gaul and Italy as members of the warrior ruling elite, entitled to the privileges of "Gothic freedom." Most were farmers whose livelihood scarcely differed from that of their Roman neighbors. Sensational images of "barbarian invasions" obscure the fact that many Germans wanted to assimilate into the Roman world. The Romans likewise welcomed the peace and security brought by the German

283

kings. Acceptance of "barbarian" rule accelerated most rapidly where the German rulers converted to Roman Christianity. We should not think of the fall of the western empire as the destruction of one culture and its replacement by another. What took place, instead, was a complex process of cultural exchange shaped by changes in the political and economic fortunes of the empire and by the needs and ambitions of nomadic peoples.

The Franks

The Franks, a league of German tribes in the lower Rhine River Valley, had long lived in close proximity to the Roman world. So thoroughly had the Franks been assimilated into Roman life that their own legends about their ancestry had faded by 600, the approximate date of the earliest Latin accounts of their history and origins. The "long-haired kings"—as the Romans called them—of the Franks gained power through loyal military service to the empire. When the Roman state collapsed, the Frankish kings allied with Christian bishops in the interest of preserving local order.

Under the leadership of Clovis (r. 482–511), the Franks consolidated their control over the Rhineland and Gaul. Although the circumstances of Clovis's conversion to Roman Christianity are murky, we have seen that he credited to St. Martin his decisive victory in 507 over the Visigoths in southern Gaul. Clovis also issued a law code, Roman in form but German in substance, of rules governing crime and property, including the principle, later widely adopted in Europe, that "no portion of the inheritance [of land] shall come to a woman."[5] When Clovis died in 511, his kingdom was divided among his four sons, including Clothar, future husband of Radegund (whom we met at the beginning of this chapter). But the fundamental unity of the Frankish kingdom endured, held together by Frankish law, Christian faith, and the unwavering allegiance of the old Roman aristocrats.

The Carolingian Dynasty

The Franks added new conquests during the sixth and seventh centuries, but the pattern of decentralized rule continued. The lightning conquest of Spain by Muslim armies in 710–711 triggered a crisis that reversed this erosion of royal power. When the Muslim forces subsequently invaded southern Gaul, local nobles turned to a Frankish warlord, Charles Martel, for protection. Martel's decisive victory over the Muslims at Tours in 732 made him the undisputed leader of the Franks; his descendants would rule as the Carolingian (from *Carolus*, Latin for "Charles") dynasty of kings.

Frankish political power reached its height under Martel's grandson Charlemagne (r. 768–814). Drawing on the Roman Empire as a model, Charlemagne's conquests added substantial territories to the Frankish empire, extending from the Baltic Sea to the Adriatic Sea. Charlemagne incorporated these new dominions into his empire by sharing power with local rulers and allowing their peoples to be governed in accordance with their own laws and customs. This policy also allowed colonists who migrated to newly conquered regions of the empire to preserve their distinct legal status and autonomy. Thus the Carolingian Empire created new ethnic identities among its diverse subjects.

Charlemagne sought to elevate himself and his empire to the imperial dignity enjoyed by Byzantium. He made protection of the pope and Roman orthodoxy an essential component of his mandate. The culmination of his efforts took place on Christmas Day, 800, when Pope Leo III placed a crown on Charlemagne's head and proclaimed him Augustus, the title of the first Roman emperor. Although recognition of Charlemagne and his successors as "emperors" only partially reversed the political fragmentation of post-Roman Europe, it forged a lasting bond between the papacy and the secular rulers of Latin Christendom. Compared with Byzantium, church and state remained more independent of each other in western Europe. Nonetheless, Charlemagne established a new ideology of Christian kingship.

Frankish Kingdom, 768
Areas conquered by Charlemagne, to 814
Tributary peoples
Byzantine Empire

Empire of Charlemagne, 814

Economic Contraction and Renewal in Christendom

The Manorial Order

Although the Franks preserved the rural aristocracy's control over the land and patronized the Christian church and monasteries, the urban culture of the Roman world withered. The nobility retreated to the security of their rural estates, and the great monasteries in the countryside, enriched by royal land grants, began to overshadow the urban bishops. The Carolingian monarchs, too, abandoned the old Roman towns, preferring to hold court at rural villas such as Charlemagne's capital at Aachen, along the modern border between Germany and Belgium. Both secular lords and monastic abbeys built up vast estates; for labor, they subjected the rural population to increasingly servile status. Throughout the Carolingian realm this new institution, the **manor**, was widely adopted. The tenants became **serfs**, tied to the land and subject to the legal authority of the lord. The obligations of serfs could vary significantly, but in general they owed labor services to the lord, as well as rents and fees for the right to graze animals and collect firewood. Women provided labor as well, either in the manor's workshops or by making cloth in their own homes.

Decline of Towns and Commerce

Whereas the expansion of the Carolingian Empire stimulated commercial exchange with Saxon lands in Britain and Denmark, elsewhere industry and trade diminished. Towns and commerce in Europe declined in part from the rise of the new rural manors, but more fundamental was the contraction of the international trading system centered on Constantinople. A terrible plague that swept across the Mediterranean from Egypt to Europe in 541–542 dealt a devastating blow to the urban network of the Roman world, which had survived the decline of the empire itself. Byzantine officials reported that 230,000 died in Constantinople alone, and Mediterranean cities from Antioch to Alexandria also suffered huge losses. Slav and Avar raids decimated the once-thriving cities of the Balkans, and the Sasanid and Muslim conquests of the seventh century deprived the empire of its richest domains. These cumulative demographic and territorial losses greatly reduced economic productivity. Egypt no longer delivered the ample grain tribute upon which the Byzantine state depended to feed its cities and armies, and in much of Anatolia farmland reverted to sheep pasture for lack of labor to grow cereal crops.

Political setbacks, the decline of towns, and the shrinking population led to a downturn in the Byzantine economy. The circulation of money slowed and in many parts of the empire disappeared altogether between the mid-seventh and early ninth centuries. Yet the Byzantine state still appropriated a significant share of agricultural surpluses, which it distributed as salaries to its officials and soldiers. Hit hardest by the waning economic fortunes of the empire was the provincial landowning aristocracy. Peasants who owned their own land increased in numbers and importance, and the state benefited from the taxes they paid.

Economic Recovery in Byzantium

Yet even as it hit bottom, the Byzantine economy displayed far more vigor than that of the Germanic kingdoms. During the sixth and seventh centuries, the Italian cities under Byzantine rule were the major exception to the pervasive decline of urban population and economic activity throughout Europe. Throughout the empire, political stability rekindled population growth in both town and countryside, especially in the long-settled coastal regions. By 800 unmistakable signs of economic prosperity had reappeared: the demand for coinage increased, new lands were put under the plow, and reports of famine became less frequent and less desperate. The Mediterranean trade network centered on Constantinople began to recover as tensions with Islamic rulers eased. A Muslim scholar writing in around 850 listed among Baghdad's imports from the Byzantine Empire "gold and silver wares, coins of pure gold, medicinal plants, gold-woven textiles, silk brocade, spirited horses, female slaves, rare copperware, unpickable locks, lyres, hydraulic engineers, agrarian experts, marble workers, and eunuchs."[6]

The quickening prosperity of the Byzantine economy promoted commerce across the Mediterranean. Silks produced in Constantinople's workshops ranked among the most prized luxury goods in the Carolingian world (see Lives and Livelihoods: Constantinople's

manor A great estate, consisting of farmlands, vineyards, and other productive assets, owned by a lord (which could be an institution, such as a monastery) and cultivated by serfs.

serf A semifree peasant tied to the land and subject to the judicial authority of a lord.

Constantinople's Silk Producers

During the heyday of the Roman Empire, when silk was said to be worth its weight in gold, Romans depended entirely on imports of silk from China. According to the historian Procopius, sericulture—the raising of silk-worms to make silk—first appeared in the Byzantine Empire in his own time, during the reign of Emperor Justinian I (r. 527–565). Several Indian monks arrived at Constantinople offering to reveal the secrets of sericulture:

> When the Emperor questioned them very closely and asked how they could guarantee success in the business, the monks told him that the agents in the production of silk were certain caterpillars, working under nature's teaching, which continually urged them to their task. To bring live caterpillars from that country would be impracticable indeed, but . . . it was possible to hatch their eggs long after they had been laid by covering them with dung, which produced sufficient heat for the purpose.[1]

The monks delivered the eggs as promised, and silk manufacture subsequently became a pillar of the Byzantine economy.

Since Roman times, silk clothing had become a conspicuous mark of wealth and social distinction. The Byzantine government issued numerous decrees restricting the wearing of certain kinds of silk to the nobility. Purple-dyed silks—the "royal purple," a pigment derived from a tropical sea snail—were reserved for the emperor alone. Silk also served as a valuable tool of diplomacy. The Byzantine emperors regularly sent gifts of silk fabrics to the Frankish kings and the Islamic caliphs. In the Carolingian Empire, Byzantine silks were coveted luxury goods, flaunted by male aristocrats and well-born nuns no less than by royal princesses. The prominence of silk garments, furnishings, and liturgical vestments in wills, dowry and marriage contracts, and church inventories attests to both their economic value and their social prestige.

Emperor Justinian I restricted silk manufacture to imperial workshops, but the Islamic conquests deprived the Byzantine state of its monopoly on silk production. Muslim

Byzantine Silk Shroud
Byzantine silk fabrics were highly prized in Latin Christendom. Tradition has it that this piece was placed in the tomb of the Frankish ruler Charlemagne after his death in 814. The design features a charioteer—probably an emperor—driving a four-horse chariot. Attendants in the background hold out crowns and whips; those at the bottom pour coins onto an altar. (Erich Lessing/Art Resource, NY.)

entrepreneurs took over the flourishing silk industry in Syria and introduced sericulture to Sicily and Spain. Then, as the demand for luxury silk goods surged, in the ninth century the Byzantine court allowed private merchants to manufacture and trade silk. At the same time the imperial government imposed tight controls on the private silk trade. These laws have been preserved in the *Book of the Prefect*, a set of commercial regulations issued by the chief magistrate of Constantinople in around 912.

Silk manufacture involves a complex series of operations, ranging from low-skilled tasks such as raising silk-worms and reeling yarn to those requiring high technical proficiency, such as weaving, dyeing, and embroidery. In late Roman times, imperial textile workers, both men and

Silk Producers). Significant economic growth, however, would not return to the European heartland until the late tenth century, well after the expansion of the Byzantine economy was under way.

Origins of the Slavs and the Founding of Rus

During its crisis of the sixth and seventh centuries, the Byzantine empire confronted a new people on its borders, the Slavs. Today nearly 300 million people in Eastern Europe

women, had been reduced to hereditary occupational castes. By Justinian's day, the standing of skilled silk artisans had risen appreciably, and government employment was considered a privilege, not a burden. In the tenth century shortages of skilled labor grew so acute that the government prohibited private merchants from offering artisans wage advances or contracts of more than one month's duration. The intent behind this rule was to ensure that all firms had competitive access to the best craftsmen. Further, the government required these private craftsmen to belong to one of five separate guilds.

This kind of intervention in the marketplace exemplified the Byzantine state's economic philosophy. By splitting the private silk industry into separate guilds, the state enforced a strict division of labor that prevented a few large firms from consolidating control over silk manufacture and trade. Thus, the reeling workshops had to purchase raw silk from middlemen dealers rather than from the producers themselves; after the raw silk was reeled into yarn, it had to be sold back to the middlemen, who in turn marketed the yarn to the silk clothiers. The clothiers produced finished cloth but could sell it only to wholesale merchants, not directly to retail customers.

Yarn production was largely a family business. The silk clothiers, in contrast, combined weaving, dyeing, and tailoring workshops under one management, relying mostly on hired labor but employing household slaves as well. Slaves also operated workshops as agents for their masters. Government workshops employed skilled craftsmen divided into guilds of clothiers, purple dyers, and gold embroiderers, who made richly decorated fabrics for the emperor and his officials. Menial tasks were relegated to servile labor, including foreign slaves.

Although keen to profit from the high prices its silks commanded in foreign markets, the Byzantine government also sought to protect the domestic industry from international competition. The Byzantine rulers kept foreign silk importers, chiefly Muslims and Jews, under close surveillance. After depositing their goods in a government warehouse, foreign merchants were sequestered in special lodgings, where they were permitted to remain for a maximum of three months. Domestic silk importers could not deal directly with foreign merchants. Instead, they negotiated collectively for the purchase of imported wares. This practice, too, ensured that all firms, small and large, had some access to imported products.

The Byzantines also feared the loss of trade secrets to foreign competitors. Foreign merchants were prohibited from taking certain silk goods and unsewn fabrics out of Constantinople, and their cargoes were carefully inspected before they could leave the city. The city magistrate decreed that "every dyer who sells a slave, a workman, or a foreman craftsman to persons alien to the city or the Empire shall have his hand cut off."[2] But these efforts to monopolize technological know-how proved futile. By 1000, technical mastery of silk manufacture had become widely disseminated. Surviving silk specimens show that Byzantine and Muslim artisans freely borrowed weaving techniques, artistic motifs, and color patterns from each other, to the point where it is nearly impossible to distinguish their handiwork.

---

1. Procopius, *The History of the Wars*, 4:17.
2. *Book of the Eparch*, Chapter 8, in E. H. Freshfield, *Roman Law in the Later Roman Empire: Byzantine Guilds, Professional, Commercial; Ordinances of Leo VI, c. 895, from The Book of the Eparch* (Cambridge, U.K.: Cambridge University Press, 1938), 26.

QUESTIONS TO CONSIDER

1. Did the Byzantine government's measures to regulate the silk industry stimulate or discourage competition among producers?

2. Did guild organizations in the Byzantine silk industry exist primarily to promote the interests of artisans, merchants, or the government?

For Further Information:

Laiou, Angeliki E., and Cécile Morrisson. *The Byzantine Economy.* Cambridge, U.K.: Cambridge University Press, 2007.

Laiou, Angeliki E., ed. *The Economic History of Byzantium from the Seventh Through the Fifteenth Century.* 3 vols. Washington, DC: Dumbarton Oaks Research Library and Collections, 2002.

and Russia speak a Slavic language. They trace their ancestry back to peoples known as *Sclavenoi* in Greek, who first appear in sixth-century Byzantine chronicles. As the Goths migrated westward into the former Roman territories, they abandoned their homelands to the Slavs, small, independent communities who rejected the imperial order of Byzantium. As contact with the Roman world declined, the material culture beyond the eastern frontiers of the old empire became more impoverished. Early Byzantine accounts classified the Slavs, together with the Avars and the Goths, as pagan savages and mortal enemies of Christendom. Between the fifth and tenth centuries, however, Byzantine interaction with

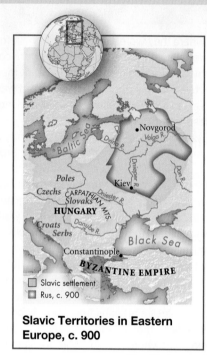

Slavic Territories in Eastern Europe, c. 900

Slavic settlement

Rus, c. 900

both settled and nomadic Slavic populations led to the crystallization of an identifiable Slavic culture with its own written languages and to the assimilation of the Slavs into a larger Christian civilization.

Like the Germanic peoples, most Slavs lived in small farming settlements consisting of several extended related families: "each living with his own clan on his own lands," in the words of a Russian chronicler.[7] The Slavs practiced shifting cultivation, regularly moving into wilderness areas and cutting down virgin forest to plant barley and millet, using the nitrogen-rich ash of burnt trees as fertilizer. Procopius portrayed the Slavs as leading "a primitive and rough way of life. . . . They are neither dishonorable nor spiteful, but simple in their ways, like the Huns."[8] Another Byzantine writer complimented Slavic women as "chaste beyond all measure," willing to kill themselves upon the death of their husbands because they "regard widowhood as no life at all."[9]

Social stratification increased by the eighth century; chiefs and their retinues crowned the social order, and hilltop strongholds with timber fortifications proliferated. Distinctive Slavic forms of pottery and silver jewelry appeared, but the material culture of the forest-dwelling Slavs was dominated by wood products and has mostly vanished. Trading posts for bartering furs and slaves sprang up near major crossroads, and craftsmen such as blacksmiths and silversmiths wandered from place to place offering their services.

Slavic Conversion to Christianity

In the ninth and tenth centuries the Slavic peoples were strongly influenced by Byzantine and Frankish models of government, law, and religion. The uniform Slavic culture divided into separate societies and political allegiances, leading to the emergence of Serb, Croat, Polish, and other Slavic national identities. The most far-reaching change was the conversion of most Slavic peoples to Christianity. Slav rulers, pressured by hostile Christian adversaries, were the first to convert. The Slavic adoption of Christianity only heightened frictions between Rome and Constantinople, however, because the southern and eastern Slavs adhered to Byzantine rites and beliefs, whereas Latin teachings prevailed among western Slavs.

Emergence of Rus

According to later (and not wholly reliable) Russian chronicles, the first state of Rus was formed in 862 when Scandinavian communities in the Novgorod region elected a Viking chieftain as their ruler. But a Rus confederation of Viking settlements engaging in slave raiding and fur trading had already emerged some decades before. Lured by the riches of the Mediterranean world, the Rus pushed southward toward the Black Sea along the Dnieper and the Volga rivers. A major assault by the Rus on Constantinople in 911 forced the Byzantine emperor to sue for peace by conceding generous trading privileges. At some point, probably in the 930s, the Rus princes shifted their capital to Kiev in the lower Dnieper valley.

By the late tenth century Kievan Rus had emerged as the dominant power in the Black Sea region. Prince Vladimir (r. 980–1015) consolidated Rus into a more unified state and adopted the Christian religion of Byzantium. Conversion to Christianity and deepening commercial and diplomatic ties with Byzantium marked a decisive reorientation of Rus away from its Scandinavian origins. Drawn south by Byzantine wealth, Rus invaders did not destroy the culture they encountered but instead became part of it, adding their own cultural heritage to that of the eastern Christian world.

Thus the middle centuries of the first millennium C.E. saw both the growth and the splintering of Christianity, as competing visions of Christianity emerged. This competition would soon become more complex with the arrival of a new religion. Although the Latin and Orthodox churches continued to win new converts in eastern and northern Europe, the sudden emergence of Islam in the seventh century transformed the religious landscape of the Mediterranean world. Even though large Christian communities persevered under Muslim rule in regions such as Syria, Iran, and Spain, the Mediterranean Sea took on new significance as a boundary between religious faiths.

The Rise and Spread of Islam 610–750

In the early seventh century, the Arab prophet Muhammad (c. 570–632) founded what became a new religion, Islam, rooted in the Judaic and Christian traditions but transformed by the divine revelations he proclaimed. Muhammad was more than a religious teacher, however. He envisioned the community of believers as a tight-knit movement dedicated to propagating the true faith, and his successors fashioned Islam into a mighty social and political force. Within a century of Muhammad's death in 632 an Islamic empire had expanded beyond Arabia as far as Iran to the east and Spain to the west. As in Christendom, tensions arose between political rulers and religious authorities. During the tenth century the united Islamic empire fractured into a commonwealth of independent states. Yet the powerful inspiration of Muhammad's teachings and Islam's radical egalitarian ideals sustained a sense of community that transcended political and ethnic boundaries.

> **FOCUS**
>
> In what ways did Islam instill a sense of common identity among its believers?

The Prophet Muhammad and the Faith of Islam

The Arabian Background

Muhammad's call for a renewal of religious faith dedicated to the one true God must be seen in the context of social and religious life in the Arabian peninsula. The harsh desert environment of Arabia could sustain little more than a nomadic pastoral livelihood. Domestication of the camel since about 1000 B.C.E. allowed small, clan-based groups known as Bedouins to raise livestock. During the summer the Bedouins gathered at oases to exchange animal products for grain, dates, utensils, weapons, and cloth. Some of these oases eventually supported thriving commercial towns, of which the most prosperous was Mecca.

The Bedouin (BED-uh-wuhn) tribes regularly came to Mecca to pay homage at the Ka'aba (KAH-buh) shrine, which housed the icons of numerous gods worshiped throughout the region. Mecca thus served as a sanctuary where different tribes could gather to worship their gods in peace. The religious harmony that prevailed at Mecca also offered opportunities to settle disputes and conduct trade. The Meccan fairs gave birth to a common culture, language, and social identity among the leading clans of Arabia.

Building on its status as an Arabian crossroads, Mecca developed economic connections with the larger world. During the sixth century, it blossomed into a major emporium of international trade between the Mediterranean and the Indian Ocean. Yet urban growth was accompanied by social tensions. Clan solidarity remained paramount, and the gap between rich and poor widened. No single ruler presided over Mecca, and economic inequality sowed dissension. It was here that Muhammad, the founder of Islam, was born in around the year 570.

Muhammad's Life and Message

Muhammad belonged to a once-prominent clan whose fortunes were in decline. As a young man he worked as a caravaner for a woman named Khadija, a rich widow older than Muhammad, whom he married when he was twenty-five. Although Muhammad seemed to have gained a secure livelihood, moral doubts and growing contempt for what he regarded as the arrogance and greed of his fellow Meccans deeply troubled him. Beginning in around 610 he experienced visions of a single, true God ("Allah") who did not cater to the worldly wishes of worshipers as the pagan gods of his countrymen did but instead imposed an uncompromising moral law upon all peoples. Muhammad's revelations were suffused with a deep sense of sin inspired by Christianity. From Judaism Muhammad incorporated devotion to the one true God, a sense of personal mission as a prophet sent to warn the world against impiety, and a regimen of ritual prayer intended to instill rightful thought and conduct. Thus Muhammad's message was shaped by both the social and economic conflicts of his day and the long religious history of the region.

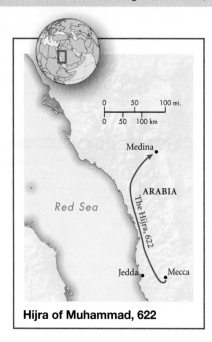

Hijra of Muhammad, 622

Initially, Muhammad communicated his visions only to a small group of confidants. In 613, however, a revelation instructed him to "rise and warn," and he began to preach publicly. Muhammad's egalitarian vision, in which all believers were equal before God, directly challenged tribal loyalties and clan leaders. Like Jesus, his teachings won favor among the lower classes, the poor and propertyless, while making him a pariah among the affluent and powerful clans. Persecution forced Muhammad and his followers to seek sanctuary in Medina, a nearby oasis town, in 622. Muhammad's move to Medina, known as the **hijra** (HIJ-ruh) ("migration"), subsequently marked the beginning of the Muslim calendar.

In Medina, Muhammad's reputation for holiness and fairness and his vision of a united community bound by a single faith elevated him to a position of leadership. The primary obstacle to the consolidation of his power in Medina was the town's large Jewish population, which rejected Muhammad's claims of prophethood and allied with his Meccan enemies. Muhammad began to issue new revelations accusing the Jews of breaking the covenant with God and declaring that he himself was the direct successor of the first and greatest prophet, Abraham. Muhammad vowed that his own creed of Islam ("submission") would supersede both Judaism and Christianity. Backed by Medina's clan leaders, Muhammad executed or exiled the town's leading Jewish citizens, thereby securing unchallenged authority in political as well as spiritual matters.

Subsequently Muhammad and his followers warred against Mecca—the first instance of a **jihad** ("struggle") of the sword, a holy war fought against those who persecute believers. In 630, the Meccans surrendered their city to Muhammad, who destroyed the idols of pagan gods in the Ka'aba and instead established it as the holiest shrine of Islam. Most Bedouin tribes soon capitulated to Muhammad as well. Preparing in 632 for an invasion of Syria, Muhammad was struck down by an illness and died in Medina. By the time of his death, he had created the basis for a new political order founded on a universal religion and a faith in the oneness of God that transcended clan, ethnic, and civic identities.

The Five Pillars of Islam

The revelations of Muhammad were written down in Arabic in the **Qur'an**, which Muslims regard as the completion of earlier revelations from God set down in the Jewish Torah and the Christian Gospels. The Qur'an elaborates the "five pillars of faith": (1) bearing witness to the unity of God and the prophethood of Muhammad; (2) daily prayers while facing the direction of Mecca; (3) fasting during Ramadan, the ninth month of the Islamic calendar; (4) giving alms to the poor; and (5) for those physically able and with the financial means, the obligation to make a pilgrimage (*hajj*) to Mecca. Performance of the "five pillars" gave public expression to membership in the **umma**, the community of the faithful. The daily regimen of prayer, the annual observation of Ramadan, and the duty to complete the hajj at least once during one's lifetime transformed the rhythms and purpose of life for herders and townfolk alike. All of these practices were joyous public ceremonies that served as visible symbols of submission to divine will. In the absence of a formal priesthood, the **ulama**—scholars and teachers steeped in study of the Qur'an—acted as the custodians and interpreters of divine teachings.

Several principles set Islam apart from the earlier monotheistic traditions of Judaism and Christianity: the stress on complete subjugation to God's commands—the fundamental tenet of Islam; the subordination of all other identities and loyalties to the community of believers; and dedication to defending the community and spreading the true religion. Although the Qur'an modified some of the prevailing norms of Bedouin society—for example, by recognizing women and children as individuals with their own needs and some limited rights—on the whole it reinforced the patriarchal traditions of clan society (see Reading the Past: Women and Property in Islam). At the same time, the charismatic leadership of clan elders yielded to the higher authority of divine will. Aspects of Islam were rooted in Bedouin culture, but the

hijra Muhammad's move from Mecca to Medina in 622, which marks year 1 of the Islamic calendar.

jihad Literally, "struggle"; a key concept in the Qur'an, which can refer to the individual's spiritual effort to follow "the path of God" (jihad of the soul) or to a holy war (jihad of the sword) against those who persecute Islam.

Qur'an The book recording the revelations of the Prophet Muhammad; regarded as the most sacred scripture in Islam.

umma The worldwide community of believers in Islam.

ulama Scholars learned in Islamic scripture and law codes who act as arbiters of Islamic teachings.

Women and Property in Islam

Under laws that prevailed in Latin Christendom until the nineteenth century, women had no right to inherit property, even from their deceased husbands. The Jewish legal tradition allowed only limited inheritance rights to women, generally for unmarried daughters or to perpetuate the family line when a man had no male heirs. Islamic law, by contrast, explicitly granted women certain property rights and control over their own earnings. In practice, however, the property rights of Islamic women and their access to gainful employment have been shaped and in some cases curtailed by social practices and scriptural interpretation.

Islam establishes men as the guardians of women, responsible for both their material welfare and their moral conduct, obligations that entail the right to punish women for their moral failings. At the same time, in keeping with the commandment against coveting the wealth and property of others, women are entitled to whatever earnings they receive from their work, trade, or property.

> Men are the ones who support women since God has given some persons advantages over others, and because they should spend their wealth on them. Honorable women are steadfast, guarding the Unseen just as God has it guarded. Admonish them, foresake them in beds apart, and beat them if necessary. If they obey you, do not seek any way to proceed against them.
> Qur'an, 4.34

> In no way covet those things in which God has bestowed his gifts more freely on some of you than on others: to men is allotted what they earn, and to women what they earn.
> Qur'an, 4.128

In both the Jewish and Islamic traditions, at the time of marriage the husband must provide the wife with a dowry that becomes her irrevocable personal property. Whereas the husband has free use of this property during the marriage under Jewish law, Islamic law places the dowry entirely at the disposal of the wife. The Qur'an also guarantees women an inheritance from their parents and close kin, though their share is usually less than the portion received by male heirs.

> [Upon marriage], give women their dowry as a free gift. If they of their own good wish remit any part of it to you, take it and enjoy it with good cheer.
> Qur'an, 4.4

> From what is left by parents and near relatives there is a share for men and a share for women, whether the property be small or large.
> Qur'an, 4.7

> God instructs you concerning your children's inheritance: a son should have a share equivalent to that of two daughters: if you have only daughters, two or more, their combined share is two-thirds of the inheritance; if only one, her share is a half.
> Qur'an, 4.11

Under Jewish law, both men and women could initiate a divorce, but one of the radical reforms of Christianity was to abolish divorce. Islamic law granted the right of divorce to men but not to women. The Qur'an allows the husband to divorce a wife without her consent, but it also requires that he provide financial support for a divorced wife, as well as a widow. Following a period of mourning, widows are free to leave their husband's household together with their property and remarry if they wish.

> A divorce may be pronounced twice [to give the parties a chance to reconcile]: after that, the parties should either hold together on equitable terms, or separate with kindness.
> Qur'an 2.229

> Those of you who die and leave widows should bequeath for their widows a year's maintenance and residence.
> Qur'an, 2.240

> For divorced women, maintenance should be provided on a reasonable scale.
> Qur'an, 2.241

EXAMINING THE EVIDENCE

1. Did Islamic law strengthen or weaken women's economic dependence on men?

2. Did Islamic laws on divorce and women's property correspond more closely to Jewish or to Christian precedents?

Divorce Hearing

Although permitted under Islamic law, divorce was regarded as a last resort. In this illustration from *The Assemblies* of al-Hariti, dated 1237, a man accompanied by his several wives pleads his case before the judge, who sits on a raised platform in front of a curtain of authority. Both the husband and the accused wife are portrayed as stubborn; the judge dismisses the case by giving each a gold coin. (Bibliothèque nationale de France.)

Factions Within Islam

caliph The designated successor to Muhammad as leader of the Muslim faithful in civil affairs.

imam The supreme leader of the Islamic community (especially in the Shi'a tradition), the legitimate successor to Muhammad; or any Islamic religious leader.

Shi'a A branch of Islam that maintains that only descendants of Muhammad through his cousin and son-in-law Ali have a legitimate right to serve as caliph.

Sunni The main branch of Islam, which accepts the historical succession of caliphs as legitimate leaders of the Muslim community.

religion pointed toward a new understanding of community in which membership was defined not by kinship or geography but by assent to a common set of religious principles.

The Islamic Empire of the Umayyad Caliphs 661–743

Muhammad's stature as the Prophet made him unique in the Islamic community. After his death the community faced the thorny problem of choosing his successor. Although Kadijah is said to have borne Muhammad four daughters and two sons, only two of his daughters outlived him. Eventually a compromise was reached that recognized Muhammad's father-in-law, Abu Bakr (AH-boo BOCK-ear), as **caliph** (KAY-luhf) ("deputy"). The caliph would inherit Muhammad's position as leader of the Islamic community, but not his role as prophet. As caliph, Abu Bakr led the community in wars of conquest and submission. The Byzantine and Sasanid empires, weakened by three decades of wars against each other, were no match for the Arabs. The Arabs decisively defeated the Byzantine army in Palestine in 634 and proceeded to capture Syria, Mesopotamia, and Egypt by 641. The Byzantine Empire lost most of its territories in the east but survived. The Sasanid Empire, however, utterly collapsed after Arab armies seized its capital of Ctesiphon in 637.

Abu Bakr and his immediate successors as caliphs ruled by virtue of their close personal relationships to the Prophet Muhammad, but disputes over succession persisted. The third caliph, Uthman (r. 644–656), a Meccan aristocrat of the Umayya (oo-MY-uh) clan, sought to resolve the succession problem by creating a family dynasty. Uthman's grab for power provoked civil war, however, and he was assassinated in 656. Ali, Muhammad's cousin and husband of his daughter Fatima, was elected to replace Uthman, but he failed to unite the warring Arab tribes. In 661 Ali, too, was assassinated. Mu'awiya (moo-AH-we-yuh) (r. 661–680), a cousin of Uthman and governor of Syria, emerged as the most powerful Muslim leader and succeeded in establishing a hereditary dynasty of Umayyad caliphs. Hence politics shaped Islam during Muhammad's lifetime and continued to affect its development long after his death. Just as the expansion of Christianity brought with it divisions and conflicts, Islam's success undermined its unity as factions formed within the Islamic world.

Although Mu'awiya cemented dynastic control over the caliphate and built up an imperial government in his new capital of Damascus, the wounds opened by the succession dispute failed to heal. When Mu'awiya died in 680, Ali's son Husayn (hoo-SANE) launched an insurrection in an attempt to reclaim the caliphacy. The Umayyads defeated the rebels, and Husayn was captured and killed. Nonetheless, a faction of Muslims remained who contended that the only rightful successors to the caliphate were Ali and his descendants, known as the *imam* ("leaders"). This group, which became known as the **Shi'a**, regarded Husayn as a great martyr. Another group, the Khariji, had turned against Ali because of his vacillating leadership and perceived moral failings. The Khariji rejected hereditary succession to the office of caliph in favor of election, insisting that religious devotion and moral purity were the only proper criteria for choosing the caliph. Both the Shi'a and the Khariji emphasized the role of the caliph as an infallible authority in matters of religious doctrine. Supporters of the Umayyad caliphs, known as the **Sunni**, instead regarded the caliph primarily as a secular ruler. Although the Sunni believed that the chief duty of the caliph was to protect and propagate Islam, they turned to the ulama rather than the caliph for interpretation of Islamic doctrine and law. Thus the divisions in Islam that grew out of disputes over the succession evolved into divergent understandings of the nature of the Islamic community and Islamic institutions.

When Abd al-Malik (r. 685–705), following a bloody struggle, assumed the office of Umayyad caliph in 685, the Muslim world was in disarray after a half century of astonishingly rapid expansion. Abd al-Malik succeeded in quelling uprisings by Shi'a and Khariji dissidents and restoring the caliph's authority over Arabia and Iran. He retained much of the administrative system of the Byzantine and Sasanid states, while substituting Arabic for Greek and Persian as the language of government. He also enacted currency reform, replacing images of human rulers with quotations from scripture, thereby providing another powerful symbol of Islamic unity. Abd al-Malik upheld the supremacy of Arabs in

Damascus's Great Mosque
Caliph al-Walid I (r. 705–715) built grand mosques at Medina, Jerusalem, and the Umayyad capital of Damascus to display the power and piety of the Islamic empire. The small octagonal building on pillars at left in the courtyard of the Great Mosque at Damascus served as the treasury for the Muslim community. The mosque's southern entrance at right was reserved for the caliph and led directly to his palace. (Photo by Ketan Gajria.)

Umayyad Reform and Expansion

government as well as faith, but bureaucratic office and mastery of the written word displaced martial valor as marks of leadership. He thus succeeded in creating a powerful monarchy supported by a centralized civilian bureaucracy.

Abd al-Malik and his successors continued to pursue vigorous expansion of ***dar-al-Islam*** ("the House of Belief") through military conquest, extending the Umayyad realm across North Africa and into Central Asia. In 710–711 a coalition of Arab and Berber forces from Morocco invaded the Iberian peninsula and quickly overran the Visigoth kingdom, stunning Latin Christendom. This invasion marked the beginning of a conflict between Christians and Muslims in the Iberian peninsula that would continue for centuries.

At first, to preserve the social unity of the conquerors, the Arabs ruled from garrison cities deliberately set apart from older urban centers. The Arabs thus became an elite military class based in garrison cities such as Basra and Kufa (both in Iraq), Fustat (modern Cairo), and Qayrawan (KYE-rwan) (in Tunisia), living off taxes extracted from farmers and merchants. Regarding Islam as a mark of Arab superiority, they made little effort to convert their non-Arab subjects. "Peoples of the Book"—Jews, Christians, and Zoroastrians, collectively referred to as ***dhimmi*** (DEE-me)—were permitted to practice their own religions, which the Arabs regarded as related but inferior versions of Islam, but under certain restrictions (see Reading the Past: The Pact of Umar). The dhimmi also had to pay a special tax (*jizya*) in return for the state's protection.

The segregation of Arabs from the conquered peoples could not be sustained indefinitely, however. Settlement in garrison towns transformed the lifestyle of the nomadic Arabs, and interactions with native populations led to assimilation, especially in Iran, far from the Arabian homeland. After a century of trying to maintain a distinct Arab-Muslim identity separate from local societies, the Umayyad caliphs reversed course and instead began to promote Islam as a unifying force. Caliph Umar II (r. 717–720) encouraged conversion of local rulers, merchants, and scholars. Although most people remained faithful to their ancestral religions, many members of the local elites were eager to ally with their Arab rulers. They converted to Islam, adopted the Arabic language, and sought places in the military and government service as equals to Arabs on the basis of their shared religion.

From Unified Caliphate to Islamic Commonwealth 750–1000

Umar II's efforts to erase the distinctions between Arabs and non-Arabs and create a universal empire based on the fundamental equality of all Muslims stirred up strong opposition from his fellow Arabs. Although the creation of a unified Islamic state fostered the emergence of a

dar-al-Islam Literally, "the House of Belief"; the name given to the countries and peoples who profess belief in Islam; in contrast to *dar-al-harb* ("the House of War"), where Islam does not prevail and Muslims cannot freely practice their religion.

dhimmi The Arabic term for "peoples of the book" (i.e., the Bible), namely Jews and Christians, who are seen as sharing the same religious tradition as Muslims.

FOCUS
How did the tensions between the ulama and the Abbasid caliphs weaken a unified Islamic empire?

The Pact of Umar

The Pact of Umar purports to be a letter from a Christian community in Syria seeking a truce with their Muslim overlords after the caliph Umar I conquered Syria in 637. Most scholars doubt that this document actually was written by Christians of that era. Rather, it was probably composed in the ninth century by Islamic jurists who wished to prescribe the conditions under which Muslims would tolerate the dhimmi communities, Jews as well as Christians, under their rule. But at least some of these regulations were enacted by the Abbasid caliphs. It has also been suggested that the restrictions on religious activities derived from Sasanid policies toward religious minorities within their empire. Regardless of its true origins, Muslim rulers frequently invoked the Pact of Umar as a model for regulating the conduct of Christians and Jews.

This is a letter to the servant of God Umar, Commander of the Faithful, from the Christians of [specific city]. When you came against us, we asked you for safe-conduct for ourselves, our descendants, our property, and the people of our community, and we undertook the following obligations toward you:

We shall not build, in our cities or in their neighborhood, new monasteries, churches, convents, or monks' cells, nor shall we repair, by day or by night, such of them as fall in ruins or are situated in the quarters of the Muslims.

We shall keep our gates wide open for passersby and travelers.

We shall give board and lodging to all Muslims who pass our way for three days.

We shall not give shelter in our churches or in our dwellings to any spy, nor hide him from the Muslims.

We shall not teach the Qur'an to our children.

We shall not manifest our religion publicly nor convert anyone to it. We shall not prevent any of our kin from entering Islam if they wish it.

We shall show respect toward the Muslims, and we shall rise from our seats when they wish to sit. We shall not seek to resemble the Muslims by imitating any of their garments, the *qalansuwa* [a fez-like cap], the turban, footwear, or the parting of the hair.

We shall not speak as they do, nor shall we adopt their *kunyas* [honorific names].

We shall not mount on saddles, nor shall we gird swords nor bear any kind of arms nor carry them on our persons.

We shall not engrave Arabic inscriptions on our seals. We shall not sell fermented drinks. . . . We shall not display our crosses or our books in the roads or markets of the Muslims.

We shall use only clappers [percussion instruments to accompany singing] in our churches very softly.

We shall not raise our voices when following our dead.

We shall not show lights on any of the roads of the Muslims or in their markets. We shall not bury our dead near the Muslims.

We shall not take slaves who have been allotted to Muslims.

We shall not build houses overtopping the houses of the Muslims.

(When I brought the letter to Umar, may God be pleased with him, he added, "We shall not strike a Muslim.")

We accept these conditions for ourselves and for the people of our community, and in return we receive safe-conduct. If we in any way violate these undertakings for which we ourselves stand surety, we forfeit our covenant, and we become liable to the penalties for contumacy [falsehood] and sedition [treason].

Source: A. S. Tritton, *The Caliphs and Their Non-Muslim Subjects*, by A. S. Tritton (1930): "The Pact of Umar." By permission of Oxford University Press.

EXAMINING THE EVIDENCE

1. In what ways were Christians expected to show deference to the superiority of Islam? Why were these visible expressions of subjugation considered important?

2. What Christian religious activities and symbols were deemed offensive to Muslims? Why?

cosmopolitan society and culture, rebellions by Bedouin tribes and Shi'a and Khariji communities caused the collapse of the Umayyad regime in 743. A new lineage of caliphs, the Abbasids, soon reestablished a centralized empire. But by 850, Abbasid power was in decline, and regional rulers and religious leaders began to challenge the caliphs' authority (see Map 9.3).

Rise of the Abbasid Caliphs

In 747, the Abbasids (ah-BASS-id), a branch of Muhammad's clan that had settled in Khurasan in northern Iran, seized the caliphate in their own name. They based their legitimacy on their vow to restore the caliphacy to the imams descended from Muhammad, a vow that won them the crucial support of Shi'a Muslims. Once securely in power, however, the Abbasids revived Umar II's vision of a pan-Islamic empire. Proclaiming the universal equality of all Muslims, the Abbasids stripped the Arabs of their military and economic privileges while recruiting non-Arab officers and administrators loyal to the new dynasty.

The Abbasid dynasty perpetuated the image of the caliph as a universal sovereign and supreme defender of Islam. When the Abbasid caliph al-Mansur (r. 754–775) began building his new capital of Baghdad on the banks of the Tigris River, near the former Sasanid capital of Ctesiphon, in 762, he claimed to be fulfilling a prophecy that a city would be built at this spot, at "the crossroads of the whole world."[10] Baghdad soon mushroomed into a giant complex of palaces, government offices, military camps, and commercial and industrial quarters.

At the heart of Baghdad, al-Mansur built the so-called Round City, more than a mile in diameter, which housed the caliph's family and the offices of government. At the center of the Round City, the green-domed palace of the caliph and the city's Grand Mosque stood together in the middle of a large open plaza, accentuating the unique majesty of the caliph's authority

The New Capital of Baghdad

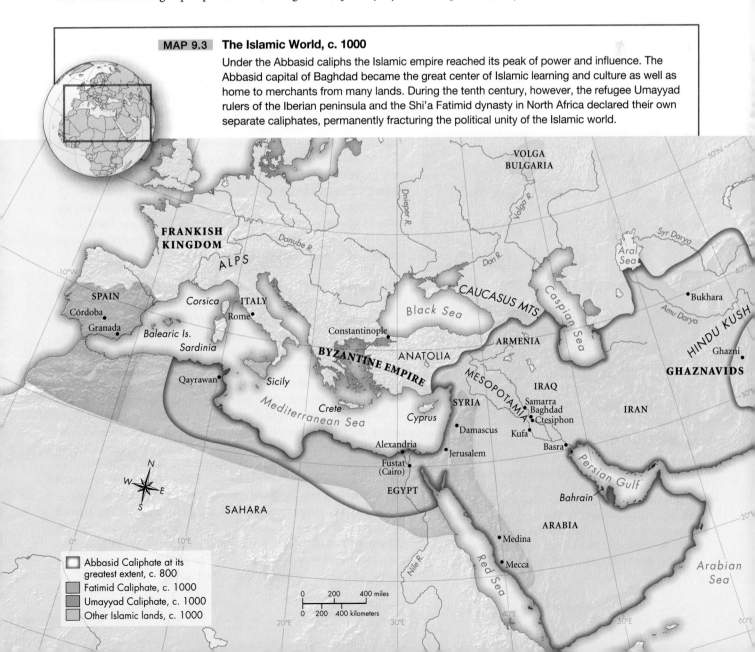

MAP 9.3   **The Islamic World, c. 1000**

Under the Abbasid caliphs the Islamic empire reached its peak of power and influence. The Abbasid capital of Baghdad became the great center of Islamic learning and culture as well as home to merchants from many lands. During the tenth century, however, the refugee Umayyad rulers of the Iberian peninsula and the Shi'a Fatimid dynasty in North Africa declared their own separate caliphates, permanently fracturing the political unity of the Islamic world.

- ☐ Abbasid Caliphate at its greatest extent, c. 800
- ☐ Fatimid Caliphate, c. 1000
- ☐ Umayyad Caliphate, c. 1000
- ☐ Other Islamic lands, c. 1000

over both civil and religious affairs. In Baghdad, as in other Islamic cities, the mosques, bazaars, and public baths became the centers of community life. Baghdad was divided into numerous residential neighborhoods, which acquired some measure of informal autonomy. The caliphs entrusted many tasks of municipal government to quasi-autonomous judicial, police, and fiscal officials, while the ulama dispersed across the city's neighborhoods performed informal but vital roles as community leaders. Well-regarded professionals, such as jewelers, perfumers, and booksellers, opened shops adjacent to the mosques, whereas those in dirty industries, such as tanners and butchers, were banished to the city's outskirts. House architecture and the winding, narrow city streets were designed to render women invisible to the public eye. Open public spaces such as squares and parks were notably absent. But Islamic rulers seldom imposed residential segregation based on ethnicity or religion.

Baghdad's Cosmopolitan Culture

The merchant communities of Baghdad and other cities included a mix of Jews, Christians, Persians, and Central Asians, as well as Muslims. Abbasid policies favoring conversion to Islam isolated Christians and Jews, turning them into ethnic minorities. Nonetheless, Jews and Nestorian Christians enjoyed better opportunities to earn a living and practice their religions in the Muslim world than they had under Byzantine rule.

The Abbasid rulers cultivated a cosmopolitan court life that blended Persian culture and Islamic faith. The court and wealthy officials and merchants in Baghdad became great patrons of scholars, physicians, and poets. Baghdad's scholars translated numerous Greek, Persian, and Indian works on philosophy, science, and medicine into Arabic, the common language of the Islamic world.

Alongside its officials, scholars, merchants, soldiers, and artisans, Baghdad society included a significant number of slaves. According to Islamic law, Muslims could not enslave their fellow Muslims. Thus, slaves were mostly obtained by purchase from Central Asia, the Slavic lands, and Africa. Elite households employed slaves as domestic servants, concubines, guards, and entertainers. Despite their legal status as slaves, they could acquire some measure of social rank in Muslim society, as the example of Arib al-Ma'muniya (797–890) shows. Sold as a young girl to a high Abbasid official, Arib was trained in singing and music, talents that were in great demand in the elite homes of Baghdad. Arib became a leading figure in the capital's musical and literary salons. Through these contacts and her love affairs with high-ranking members of the Abbasid government and army, she acquired powerful friends and patrons. By the end of her life Arib had become a wealthy woman who owned and trained her own slave singers.

The rise of the Abbasid caliphate drew the Islamic world farther from its roots in Arabia. The Umayyad caliphs had been tied to the culture and society of the Arabian deserts. After the founding of the Abbasid caliphate, however, Arabia was no longer at the center of the Islamic world. Mecca and Medina remained the holy cities, where pilgrims from every corner of the Muslim world gathered and intermingled. But religious leadership, like political and economic power, shifted to Baghdad and other commercial centers such as Damascus, Basra, and Cairo.

Iraq, the heartland of the Abbasid caliphate, experienced extraordinary economic and urban development. Building on improvements carried out by the Sasanid Empire, the Abbasid government invested heavily in the irrigation works needed to sustain agriculture. Muslim landowners in southern Iraq imported slaves from the nearby East African region of Zanj to work on sugar cane plantations and to convert the salt marshes into farmland. Foreign trade introduced both exotic goods and new manufacturing technologies. Papermaking, learned from China, displaced the practice of writing on papyrus leaves. Cotton textile manufacture and sugar refining emerged as major industries using techniques imported from India. The Muslim world became part of a vast global trading network, with Baghdad at its center.

Abbasid Court Culture

The Abbasid caliphs favored a cosmopolitan cultural style drawn from Persian and Greek, as well as Islamic, traditions. Frescoes from the ruins of the Abbasid palace at Samarra in Iraq—such as this scene of two dancing girls pouring wine—celebrate hunting, feasting, and the pleasures of court life. But after the caliphs' power began to decline in around 900, human figures disappeared almost entirely from Islamic art for centuries. (bpk/Art Resource, NY.)

Rise of the Religious Scholars

Whereas the power of the caliphs rested on their wealth, their legitimacy ultimately derived from their role as defenders of Islamic orthodoxy. Yet the caliphs did not inherit Muhammad's stature as prophet, and the Qur'an remained the indisputable testament of religious wisdom. Through their commentaries on scripture, the ulama taught how to apply the Qur'an to the conduct of social life. Religious teachers also compiled records of the deeds and words of Muhammad, known as *hadith*, as guides to the proper fulfillment of divine commandments. The caliphs thus occupied an ambiguous space in Islamic religious life. It was their job to defend Islamic orthodoxy, but they lacked the power to define that orthodoxy.

Their position was made even more difficult by the proliferation of scriptural commentaries and hadith, which widened the scope for individual interpretation of Islamic doctrine. In response, the caliphs sought to ensure orthodoxy by creating formal legal codes (*shari'a*) and law courts that combined religious and civil authority. Schools of law sprang up in major seats of Islamic learning such as Baghdad, Basra, Fustat, and Medina (see Chapter 13). However, because no consistent body of law could be applied uniformly throughout the caliphate, this initiative only added to the profusion of scriptural commentary and legal opinion that threatened to splinter the unity of Islamic teachings.

Faced with the potential fracturing of Islam, the ulama largely reconciled themselves to the caliphs' authority to maintain unity and order. Yet beneath this acceptance of Abbasid rule simmered profound discontent. "The best ruler is he who keeps company with scholars," proclaimed a leading religious teacher, "but the worst scholar is he who seeks the company of kings."[11] For the ulama, the special privileges and riches of the caliph and his courtiers betrayed Islam's most basic principles. The fundamental conflict remained. The caliphs sought to merge political and religious authority in a centralized state. The ulama, in contrast, worked to redefine the role of the caliph to establish clear limits to the caliph's power. In their view, the role of the caliph was not to determine Islamic law but rather to ensure the just administration of the shari'a for the benefit of all.

Relations between the caliphate and the ulama sank to their lowest point during the reign of al-Mamum (r. 813–833). Confronted with fierce opposition among the leading ulama and civil officials, al-Mamum launched a harsh campaign to force the ulama to acknowledge the caliph's higher authority in theological matters. His heavy-handed tactics failed, however. The spiritual leadership of the ulama rested securely on the unswerving allegiance of ordinary citizens, which the caliph was powerless to usurp.

Islamic Teachings and Law Schools

Tensions Between the Caliphs and the Ulama

Collapse of the Unified Caliphate

Unable to command the loyalty of its subjects and with its very legitimacy in question, the Abbasid regime grew weaker and ultimately collapsed. Al-Mamum's brother and successor as caliph, al-Mutasim (r. 833–842), faced growing dissent among both his officials and the ulama. He withdrew from Baghdad and took up residence at a new capital he built at Samarra, seventy miles to the northwest. Al-Mutasim also made the fateful decision to recruit Turkish slaves from Central Asia to form a new military force loyal to the caliphate. The slave soldiers soon ousted civil officials from the central government and provincial posts. In 861 a regiment of Turkish troops revolted and murdered the caliph, plunging the caliphate into anarchy. In 868 a renegade imam roused the Zanj slaves and other disaffected people in southern Iraq to revolt, promising "to give them slaves, money, and homes to possess for themselves."[12] The Zanj rebellion lasted fifteen years, claiming many thousands of lives and draining the fiscal and military resources of the Abbasid regime. Some measure of stability was restored in 945, when a Persian military strongman took control of Baghdad, reducing the Abbasid caliph to a mere figurehead. But by then rulers in Spain and North Africa had claimed the mantle of caliph for themselves.

In the early years of the Abbasid caliphate, the sole survivor of the Umayyad clan, Abd al-Rahman (ahbd al-rah-MAHN) (r. 756–788), had assembled a coalition of Berber and Syrian forces and seized power in Muslim Spain. Too far removed from the Muslim heartland

Rival Caliphates

to pose a threat to the Abbasids, the Umayyad regime in Spain coexisted uneasily with the Baghdad caliphate. In 931, as Abbasid authority ebbed, the Umayyad ruler Abd al-Rahman III (r. 912–961) declared himself the rightful caliph in the name of his forebears.

Another claim to the caliphacy arose in North Africa, a stronghold of a messianic Shi'a movement known as the Ismaili. The Ismaili believed that soon the final prophet, the true successor to Muhammad and Ali, would appear in the world to usher in the final judgment and the resurrection of the faithful. Hounded from Baghdad, Ismaili evangelists had instigated secessionist movements in North Africa, Bahrain, and the Caspian region. In 909, an Ismaili leader in Algeria proclaimed himself caliph, founding what came to be called (in homage to Muhammad's daughter Fatima) the Fatimid dynasty. In 969 the Fatimids captured Egypt and made Cairo the capital of their caliphate.

Flowering of Islamic Culture

By the middle of the tenth century, then, the unified caliphate had disintegrated into a series of regional dynasties. The collapse of political unity, however, did not lead to decline of Islamic social and cultural institutions. On the contrary, the tenth century was an age of remarkable cultural flowering in the Islamic world. The sharpening doctrinal disputes of the age produced an outpouring of theological scholarship and debate, and conversion of non-Arabs to Islam accelerated. Sufism, a mystical form of Islam based on commitment to a life of spirituality and self-denial, acquired a large following (see Chapter 13). Despite its political fragmentation, the Islamic world retained a collective identity as a commonwealth of states united by faith. The networks of travel and communications formed during the heyday of the Umayyad and Abbasid caliphates continued to help the circulation of people, goods, ideas, and technology throughout the Islamic lands.

COUNTERPOINT
The Norse Vikings: The New Barbarians

FOCUS

How did the Vikings' society and culture contrast with those of the settled societies of Europe?

The Norse Vikings ("sea raiders") who terrified Latin Christendom for more than two centuries can be seen as the maritime equivalent of the steppe nomads of Central Asia. The Vikings operated as independent bands of pirates and rarely acknowledged any authority other than the captains of their ships. Their Nordic homelands did not shift to formal centralized authority until the mid-eleventh century. Ultimately, however, the Vikings, like the nomadic peoples of the Central Asian steppes, were transformed by their interactions with the settled peoples whose goods they coveted.

The Viking Raids 790–1020

The earliest record of the Vikings relates that in the year 793 strange omens appeared in the skies over northeastern England, followed by a dire famine; then, "on June 8th of the same year, merciless heathens laid waste the Church of God in Lindisfarne [in northeast England], with plundering and killing."[13] By 799 the Vikings were launching raids along the coast of France. They would return to plunder the peoples to their south virtually every spring thereafter until the early eleventh century. The leaders of Christendom were aghast at what they interpreted as a brutal assault on the church and true religion. The Vikings were not, however, motivated by hatred of Christianity. They wanted money, goods, and slaves, and they were just as likely to prey on their fellow pagans as on Christians.

The Viking marauders originated from the Nordic, or Scandinavian, lands ringing the Baltic and North seas, whose thick forests, thin soils, and long winters discouraged agriculture (see Map 9.4). Like the Germans, the Norse prized cattle. Pasture was scarce, though, and in many places overgrazing had forced the inhabitants to replace cattle with less demanding sheep. Given this harsh and unpromising environment, it is not surprising that many Vikings turned to military raids to acquire what they could not produce themselves.

Viking Warriors

Warfare had a long history in this region, but Nordic settlements rarely were fortified. The object of war was booty rather than seizing land, and the evolution of Viking military technology reflected this goal. Instead of developing the castles and stone fortifications that proliferated in northern Europe, the Vikings concentrated on improving their ability to launch seaborne raids. Between the fifth and eighth centuries, Norse shipbuilders developed larger and more seaworthy longboats, equipped with keels and powered by sails and by crews of thirty to sixty oarsmen. Using these vessels, roving Viking bands crossed the North Sea to pillage the unsuspecting coastal communities of Britain and France.

During the eighth century local chieftains all around the Nordic coasts constructed great halls, the "mead halls" celebrated in *Beowulf*, a tenth-century epic recounting the feats of a heroic Norse warrior. (Mead is a potent alcoholic beverage made from fermented honey and water.) Yet the great halls typically housed no more than thirty warriors and their families, and outfitting a single longboat required recruiting additional men beyond the chieftain's immediate retinue. For raiding expeditions, convoys of longboats were assembled under the leadership of a king, or paramount chief. Although these alliances were often renewed from season to season, the captains of these expeditions exercised little control over the subordinate chieftains, except in war and plunder. Such alliances did not reflect permanent connections among Viking groups or the beginnings of durable political institutions. Rather, they were arrangements of convenience, kept in place only as long as all involved profited from them.

Viking Kings

As a result, amid the conflict and rivalries of this warrior class few families could uphold their claim to royal authority for more than a couple of generations. The Christian missionary Ansgar, traveling in southern Sweden in around 865–875, observed that although the king at Uppsala led armies overseas and conducted diplomatic negotiations with the Franks, in civil matters he deferred to an assembly of chieftains and landowners. The anonymous author of *Beowulf* boasted of a mighty Danish king who "shook the halls, took mead-benches, taught encroaching foes to fear him . . . until the clans settled in the seacoasts neighboring over the whale-road all must obey him and give tribute."[14] Yet outside of the epics and sagas, few kings commanded such awe and allegiance.

The Norse kings did not levy taxes in coin or grain. The king's role was not to accumulate wealth, but to distribute it. Extravagant banqueting in the mead halls—occasions of majesty in lands of meager and monotonous diets—lay at the heart of social and ritual life. Feasting enabled kings and chieftains to renew friendships and allay rivalries, while bestowing gifts of gold and other treasures allowed them to display their liberality and lordship.

In contrast to the settled peoples of Christendom and the Islamic world, the Vikings were indifferent town builders and traders. Few merchants ventured into hostile Viking waters. Those who did briefly disembarked at seaside trading posts during the summer but did not settle permanently in the region. In the ninth and tenth centuries a few of these seasonal markets—including Ribe and Hedley in Denmark and Birka in Sweden—grew into towns, with their own Christian bishops and mints, and attracted colonies of foreign merchants. But these towns remained small enclaves of at most two thousand inhabitants. Only after 1000 did Nordic iron, furs, and slaves gain a foothold in European markets.

Islamic silver coins imported from the Black Sea began to appear in the Baltic region at the close of the eighth century. Silver was made into jewelry, used to pay legal fines, and offered as gifts to win allies and favors. The abundance of Islamic coins found in Viking hoards should not be taken as a measure of commercial activity, however. The richest hoards of Islamic coins have been discovered on the island of Gotland, midway between Latvia and Sweden. Yet Gotland lacked good harbors and towns. Most likely the islanders obtained their troves of silver from piracy rather than trade. Despite their treasure, they rigidly adhered to their traditional ways of life, to judge by the evidence of their small farms and the conservative dress and ornaments of their women.

Norse Emigration and Colonization

In the ninth century the Norse chieftains began to conduct expeditions aimed at conquest and colonization. Danish marauders seized lands in eastern England and imposed their own laws and customs on the Anglo-Saxons. By about 1000, the Danes had extended their control to parts of Norway, Sweden, and, under King Cnut (Keh-NEWT) (r. 1017–1035), all of England. Vikings also occupied parts of Ireland and coastal lands on the European continent from Normandy to Denmark.

Legends relate that the island of Iceland was first colonized during 870–930 by hundreds of families fleeing the tyranny of the Norwegian king Harald Fair-haired. More likely the immigrants were driven by hunger for land. Iceland, with its relatively mild winters, ample pasture for cattle, and abundant game, must have seemed a windfall. But human settlement soon upset the island's fragile ecology. Forests and fields were ruined by timber cutting, erosion, and overgrazing, while the game was hunted to extinction. By 1000 the settlers were desperately short of fuel and timber, and fishing had become the staple of their livelihood.

In around 980 Icelanders in search of virgin territories made landfall on Greenland, only to discover that this new world was even less well endowed with forests, pasture, and arable land. Subsequent foraging expeditions took them to Newfoundland, but there, too, the prospects for farming and stock raising were dim, and settlements were short-lived.

The maritime conquests of the Vikings proved to be more fleeting than the far-flung empires of the Central Asian nomads. Prolonged contact with Latin Christendom eventually eroded the Viking way of life. From about 1000 on, towns and merchants proliferated, local chieftains yielded to the rule of royal dynasties, and kings submitted to baptism and the Christian church's authority. As these new forms of economic, religious, and political

Viking Memorial Stone

Viking picture stones such as this eighth-century one from the island of Gotland off the coast of Sweden are believed to have been memorials dedicated to dead warriors and chiefs. Scholars disagree about the precise meaning of the scenes shown on this stone. One interpretation suggests that the stone depicts the death of a warrior in battle and his final journey to the underworld on the Viking longboat at bottom. (Courtesy of The Bunge Museum, an open air museum in Gotland, Sweden, displaying 8th century picture stones, and allowing visits to 17th, 18th and 19th century homes, mills, gardens, and workshops. www.bungemuseet.se.)

life permeated the Nordic world, the Vikings' plundering ceased. Yet even as the Norse peoples were pulled into the orbit of Latin Christendom, their songs and legends continued to celebrate the deeds of their pagan ancestors.

Conclusion

By the year 1000 the classical civilizations of western Eurasia had been reshaped by their new dominant religious cultures, Christianity and Islam. Christianity had spread throughout the European provinces of the old Roman Empire, whereas Islam prevailed in the heartlands of the ancient Persian and Egyptian empires and among the pastoral desert tribes of Arabia and North Africa. Christianity and Islam both flourished most vigorously in the cities. By 1000 the Christian church had made a concerted effort to extend its reach into village society through its legions of parish priests, and monastic orders ranked among the greatest landowners of Europe. The penetration of Islam into the countryside in long-settled areas such as Syria, Iraq, and Iran came more slowly.

The Christian communities allied with their secular rulers, whether they were Roman aristocrats, German chieftains, or the Byzantine emperor. From its inception, Islam became a political force as well as a religious movement, and the Umayyad caliphs created a vast Islamic empire. Despite efforts by the Byzantine emperors and the Muslim caliphs to impose religious orthodoxy, however, both Christendom and the Islamic empire fractured into competing religious traditions and a multitude of states.

At the same time, these religious faiths advanced into new frontiers. German kings and warriors followed in the footsteps of our chapter-opening heroine Radegund in embracing Christianity. Cultural, economic, and political interaction with the Byzantine Empire brought most Slavic peoples into the Christian fold. The arrival of Christianity in the Norse lands of northern Europe brought an end to the Viking menace. Although the prospects for a unified Muslim empire receded, Islamic religion and culture had become deeply implanted in a vast territory stretching from Iran to Spain. Starting in around 1000, Islam again underwent rapid expansion, notably in Africa and Asia, where, as we shall see in the next chapter, the Indian religions of Buddhism and Hinduism had shaped many diverse societies.

NOTES

1. Jo Ann McNamara and John E. Halborg, eds. and trans., *Sainted Women of the Dark Ages* (Durham, NC: Duke University Press, 1992), 65, 72, 75.
2. Procopius, *The Secret History*, trans. G. A. Williamson (London: Penguin, 1966), 106.
3. Alcuin, "Letter 8" (to Charlemagne), in Stephen Allott, *Alcuin of York, c. A.D. 732 to 804: His Life and Letters* (York, U.K.: Sessions, 1974), 11.
4. Gregory, *Pastoral Care*, 1.1, trans. Henry Davis, in *Ancient Christian Writers* (New York: Newman Press, 1950), 11:21.
5. Roy Cave and Herbert Coulson, eds., *A Source Book for Medieval Economic History* (New York: Biblo and Tannen, 1965), 336.
6. Al Djahiz, *A Clear Look at Trade*, quoted in Michael McCormick, *Origins of the European Economy: Communications and Commerce, A.D. 300–900* (Cambridge, U.K.: Cambridge University Press, 2001), 591.
7. S. H. Cross and O. P. Sherbovitz-Wetzor, *The Russian Primary Chronicle, Laurentian Text* (Cambridge, MA: Mediaeval Academy of America, 1953), 53, referring to the Poliane people inhabiting modern-day Ukraine.
8. Procopius, *History of the Wars*, trans. H. B. Dewing (Cambridge, MA: Harvard University Press, 1924), 7:14, 22–30.
9. Pseudo-Maurice, *Strategikon*, 11.4, quoted in P. M. Barford, *The Early Slavs: Culture and Society in Early Medieval Eastern Europe* (London: British Museum Press, 2001), 68.
10. Quoted in Gaston Wiet, *Baghdad: Metropolis of the Abbasid Caliphate* (Norman: University of Oklahoma Press, 1971), 11.
11. Sufyan al-Thawri, quoted in Francis Robinson, ed., *The Cambridge Illustrated History of the Islamic World* (Cambridge, U.K.: Cambridge University Press, 1996), 22.
12. *The History of al-Tabari* (Albany: State University of New York Press, 1992), vols. 36, 38.
13. Charles Plummer, ed., *Two of the Saxon Chronicles* (Oxford: Clarendon Press, 1892), 57.
14. *Beowulf*, lines 4–11, from *Beowulf: A Verse Translation*, trans. Michael Alexander (London: Penguin, 1973), 3.

RESOURCES FOR RESEARCH

Multiple Christianities, 400–850

Spearheaded by the pathbreaking work of Peter Brown, scholars now emphasize the continuation of the culture and institutions of the Roman Empire in the worlds of both Latin and Byzantine Christianity, as well as the multitude of distinct forms that Christianity took in different societies. MacMullen and the essays in Kreuger's volume focus on the religious experiences of ordinary people.

Brown, Peter. *The Rise of Western Christendom*, 2d ed. 2003.

Burstein, Stanley, ed. *Ancient African Civilizations: Kush and Axum*, rev. ed. 2009.

Kreuger, Derek, ed. *Byzantine Christianity*. 2006.

MacMullen, Ramsay. *Christianity and Paganism in the Fourth to the Eighth Centuries*. 1997.

McNamara, Jo Ann, and John E. Halborg, eds. and trans. *Sainted Women of the Dark Ages*. 1992.

Social and Political Renewal in the Post-Roman World, 400–850

In contrast to the conventional images of the Germans and Slavs as alien barbarians, recent studies—such as Geary's work—emphasize the fluidity of social and cultural identity and the dynamic interactions among peoples in post-Roman Europe. Angold provides a brief but compelling portrait of the early Byzantine Empire in relation to both Latin Christendom and the Islamic world.

Angold, Michael. *Byzantium: The Bridge from Antiquity to the Middle Ages*. 2001.

(Byzantium): Byzantine Studies on the Internet. http://www .fordham.edu/halsall/byzantium/index.html.

Franklin, Simon, and Jonathan Shepard. *The Emergence of Rus, 750–1200*. 1996.

Geary, Patrick J. *Before France and Germany: The Creation and Transformation of the Merovingian World*. 1988.

McKitterick, Rosamond, ed. *The Early Middle Ages: Europe, 400–1000*. 2001.

Treadgold, Warren. *A History of the Byzantine State and Society*. 1997.

Worlds of Late Antiquity. http://www9.georgetown.edu/faculty/ jod/wola.html.

The Rise and Spread of Islam, 610–750

Gordon's highly accessible text is a useful introduction to the origins and early history of the Islamic movement. Berkey's book combines narrative and thematic approaches to the development of Islam in the Middle East before modern times. Muhammad remains an elusive biographical subject; Rodinson's study, though dated (originally published in 1961), is still regarded as reliable.

Berkey, Jonathan. *The Formation of Islam: Religion and Society in the Near East, 600 to 1800*. 2003.

Bulliet, Richard. *Islam: The View from the Edge*. 1994.

Crone, Patricia. *Meccan Trade and the Rise of Islam*. 1987.

Gordon, Matthew S. *The Rise of Islam*. 2005.

Rodinson, Maxime. *Muhammad*, 2d ed. 1996.

From Unified Caliphate to Islamic Commonwealth, 750–1000

Lapidus's encyclopedic survey is especially valuable for its detailed regional-focused reviews of the varieties of Islamic society and culture. Hodgson remains a classic work in terms of both its erudition and its emphasis on the world-historical context of the rise and development of Islam. Daftary provides an authoritative introduction to the history, doctrines, and practice of one of the most important branches of Shi'a Islam.

(Byzantium): Byzantine Studies on the Internet. http://www .fordham.edu/halsall/islam/islamsbook.html.

Daftary, Farhad. *A Short History of the Ismailis: Traditions of a Muslim Community*. 1998.

Hodgson, Marshall. *The Venture of Islam: Conscience and History in a World Civilization*. Vol. 1, *The Classical Age of Islam*. 1974.

Kennedy, Hugh. *The Court of the Caliphs: The Rise and Fall of Islam's Greatest Dynasty*. 2004.

Lapidus, Ira M. *A History of Islamic Societies*, 2d ed. 2002.

Lewis, Bernard, ed. *Islam: From the Prophet Muhammad to the Capture of Constantinople*. 2 vols. 1974.

COUNTERPOINT: The Norse Vikings: The New Barbarians

Recent archaeological research—as exemplified by Christiansen's meticulous study—challenges many of the prevailing assumptions about the Vikings' society and livelihood. The Sawyers chronicle the transformation of Norse life and culture after the conversion to Christianity. Jochens, drawing primarily on Icelandic sources, argues that conversion brought few changes to the lives of Norse women.

Christiansen, Eric. *The Norsemen in the Viking Age*. 2002.

Jochens, Jenny. *Women in Old Norse Society*. 1995.

Logan, F. Donald. *The Vikings in History*, 3d ed. 2005.

Page, R. I. *Chronicles of the Vikings: Records, Memorials, and Myths*. 1995.

Sawyer, Birgit, and Peter Sawyer. *Medieval Scandinavia: From Conversion to Reformation, circa 800–1500*. 1993.

▶ **For additional primary sources from this period**, see *Sources of Crossroads and Cultures*.

▶ **For Web sites, images, and documents related to topics in this chapter**, see Make History at bedfordstmartins.com/smith.

The major global development in this chapter ▶ The spread of Christianity and Islam and the profound impact of these world religions on the societies of western Eurasia and North Africa.

IMPORTANT EVENTS

410	Visigoth sack of Rome
431	Council of Ephesus denounces Nestorianism as heresy
507	Clovis defeats Visigoth invaders and converts to Christianity
527–565	Reign of Justinian I as Byzantine emperor
570–632	Life of Muhammad, founder of Islam
589	Conversion of Visigoths to Roman Christianity
590–604	Papacy of Gregory I
622	Muhammad's hijra to Medina, marking the beginning of the Islamic calendar
661–743	Umayyad caliphate
680	Split between Shi'a and Sunni Islam
710–711	Muslim invasion and conquest of Visigoth-ruled Spain
732	Charles Martel halts Muslim advance into Europe
747–1258	Abbasid caliphate
793	Earliest record of Viking raids on Britain
800	Coronation of Charlemagne as emperor by Pope Leo III
868–883	Zanj revolt against the Abbasid regime
870–930	Vikings colonize Iceland
909	Fatimid dynasty founded
988	Vladimir, the Rus prince of Kiev, converts to Christianity

KEY TERMS

caliph (p. 292)
dar-al-Islam (p. 293)
dhimmi (p. 293)
hijra (p. 290)
iconoclasm (p. 281)
imam (p. 292)
jihad (p. 290)
manor (p. 285)

Qur'an (p. 290)
schism (p. 281)
serf (p. 285)
Shi'a (p. 292)
Sunni (p. 292)
ulama (p. 290)
umma (p. 290)

CHAPTER OVERVIEW QUESTIONS

1. How and why did the development of the Christian church differ in the Byzantine Empire and Latin Christendom?

2. In what ways did the rise of Christianity and Islam challenge the power of the state?

3. Conversely, in what ways did the spread of these faiths reinforce state power?

4. Why did Christianity and Islam achieve their initial success in towns and cities rather than in the rural countryside?

SECTION FOCUS QUESTIONS

1. In what ways did Christianity develop and spread following its institutionalization in the Roman Empire?

2. What major changes swept the lands of the former Roman Empire in the four centuries following the fall of imperial Rome?

3. In what ways did Islam instill a sense of common identity among its believers?

4. How did the tensions between the ulama and the Abbasid caliphs weaken a unified Islamic empire?

5. How did the Vikings' society and culture contrast with those of the settled societies of Europe?

MAKING CONNECTIONS

1. How did the political institutions and ideology of the Islamic empire of the Umayyad and Abbasid caliphates differ from those of the Roman Empire (see Chapter 7)?

2. In what ways did the spiritual authority of the Islamic ulama differ from that exercised by the Christian popes and bishops?

3. How does the Islamic conception of the community of the faithful compare with Jewish and Christian ideas of community?

4. What were the causes and effects of the Viking raids and invasions in Europe in the eighth through tenth centuries, and how did these compare with the early invasions of the Roman Empire by the Germanic peoples (see Chapter 7)?

AT A CROSSROADS ▲

The Chinese monk Xuanzang's epic journey to India epitomized the cross-cultural exchanges that took place across Asia during the heyday of the Silk Road. In this Japanese painting commemorating Xuanzang's life, the pilgrim monk parades in triumph through the Chinese capital of Chang'an, preceded by horses bearing the precious Buddhist scriptures he brought back from India. The painting was commissioned in around 1300 by the Kofukuji Monastery in Nara, the headquarters of a Buddhist school dedicated to Xuanzang's teachings. (From the Collection of the Fujita Museum, Osaka, Japan. First section, tenth chapter of the painted scroll, *Genjo sanzo e* (Japanese National Treasure).)

Religion and Cross-Cultural Exchange in Asia

400–1000

In 642, a Chinese Buddhist pilgrim named Xuanzang (shoo-wen-zhang) (c. 602–664) was enjoying a leisurely stay at the court of the king of Assam, in the Himalayan foothills of northern India. Thirteen years before, Xuanzang had left China, where he had studied Buddhist scriptures and Indian languages at Chang'an, capital of the recently founded Tang dynasty (618–907). As his studies progressed, however, Xuanzang concluded that he could obtain authentic scriptures that preserved the Buddha's original teachings only by traveling to India, homeland of the Buddha, "the Awakened One." Defying an imperial decree that forbade travel abroad, Xuanzang embarked across the deserts and mountain ranges of Central Asia and spent years retracing the footsteps of the Buddha. It was these travels that had brought him to the court of Assam.

Xuanzang's visit, however, was interrupted by an urgent summons from King Harsha (r. 606–647), the most powerful Indian monarch at the time. During his time in India, Xuanzang had acquired a reputation as a great philosopher and skilled orator, and he had come to the attention of King Harsha, a pious man and an earnest patron of both Hindu Brahman priests and Buddhist monks. "He divided the day into three parts," commented Xuanzang, "the first devoted to affairs of state, and the other two to worship and charitable works, to which he applied himself tirelessly, as there were not enough hours in the day to complete his ministrations."[1] Harsha now wished to host a grand philosophical debate featuring his Chinese guest.

On the appointed day King Harsha led a vast procession of princes, nobles, soldiers, and priests to a parade ground on the banks of the Ganges River. Xuanzang wrote, "In the

Steppe Peoples and Settled Societies of Central Asia

FOCUS What strategies did nomadic steppe chieftains and the rulers of agrarian societies apply in their dealings with each other?

The Shaping of East Asia

FOCUS How did the spread of Buddhism transform the politics and societies of East Asia?

The Consolidation of Hindu Society in India

FOCUS Why did the religious practices of Hinduism gain a broader following in Indian society than the ancient Vedic religion and its chief rival, Buddhism?

The Diffusion of Indian Traditions to Southeast Asia

FOCUS What aspects of Indian religions had the greatest influence on the societies and cultures of Southeast Asia?

COUNTERPOINT: Sogdian Traders in Central Asia and China

FOCUS How did the social and economic institutions of the Sogdian merchant network differ from those of the nomadic confederations and the agrarian empires?

BACKSTORY

In China as in the Roman world, invasions and migrations by "barbarian" peoples followed the collapse of the empire. After the Han Empire fell in the third century C.E. (see Chapter 6), endemic fighting among regional warlords weakened China and made it possible for steppe nomads to conquer the north China heartland in the early fourth century. Pressure from central Eurasian nomads also contributed to the demise of the Gupta Empire in northern India at the end of the fifth century (see Chapter 6). Yet political turmoil and the fragmentation of India and China into smaller rival kingdoms did not breed isolation. On the contrary, the Silk Road flourished as a channel of trade and cultural exchange during these centuries. Traversing both overland and overseas trade routes, missionaries and merchants carried Indian religions to China and Southeast Asia, where they profoundly influenced not only religious beliefs and practices but political and social institutions as well.

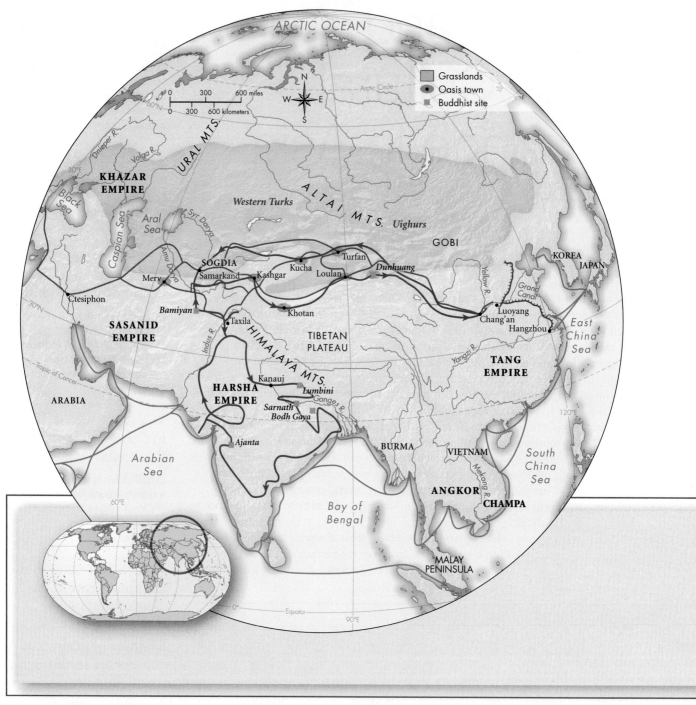

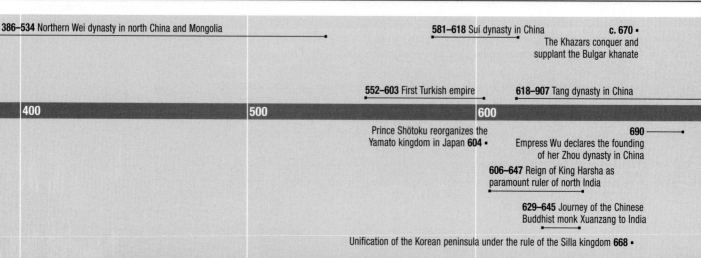

386–534 Northern Wei dynasty in north China and Mongolia

581–618 Sui dynasty in China

c. 670 •
The Khazars conquer and
supplant the Bulgar khanate

552–603 First Turkish empire

618–907 Tang dynasty in China

400

500

600

Prince Shōtoku reorganizes the
Yamato kingdom in Japan 604 •

690 —
Empress Wu declares the founding
of her Zhou dynasty in China

606–647 Reign of King Harsha as
paramount ruler of north India

629–645 Journey of the Chinese
Buddhist monk Xuanzang to India

Unification of the Korean peninsula under the rule of the Silla kingdom 668 •

center strode a huge, elaborately caparisoned elephant bearing a golden statue of the Buddha more than three feet high. On the left went King Harsha, dressed as [the Hindu god] Indra and holding aloft a jeweled parasol, while on the right was the King of Assam, wearing the regalia of [the Hindu god] Brahma and grasping a white fly-whisk."[2] The theological tournament lasted five days, during which the rhetorical clashes grew increasingly fierce. When Harsha declared Xuanzang the victor, his Brahman opponents allegedly set fire to the shrine housing the Buddha's image, and one of them tried to assassinate the king. Harsha, keen to avert religious strife among his subjects, punished the ringleader but pardoned the rest of the disgruntled Brahmans.

Four months later, Xuanzang departed for home. Although he had left China illegally, he returned in triumph. The Tang emperor anointed him "the jewel of the empire" and built a magnificent monastery to house the precious Buddhist icons, relics, and books that he had brought back from India. A legend in his own lifetime, Xuanzang devoted the last twenty years of his life to translating Buddhist texts and to seeking refuge from his admirers.

Xuanzang's remarkable experiences were part of the larger pattern of cross-cultural encounters and exchanges that shaped Asia in the second half of the first millennium C.E. Since the inception of the Silk Road route in the first century C.E. (see Chapter 6), Buddhist missionaries had accompanied the caravans setting out from the frontiers of India to seek the fabled silks of China. As we will explore in this chapter, in later centuries others traveled between India and China bearing goods and ideas that fertilized cross-cultural exchange, including nomad warriors from Central Asia, long-distance traders such as the Sogdians, and missionaries and pilgrims. A similar interweaving of commerce and evangelism also drew Southeast Asia into sustained contact with India, and to a lesser extent with China.

The resulting spread of Buddhism and Hinduism from India provided the foundations for distinctive regional cultures across Asia. Political and social crises in China and India prompted serious questioning in those countries of traditional beliefs and values, creating a climate more receptive to new ideas. At the same time, the leaders of newly emerging states

MAPPING THE WORLD

Cross-Cultural Exchange in Asia

Both goods and ideas flowed across the Silk Road, the name given by a nineteenth-century German geographer to the network of caravan routes crossing Central Asia from China to Iran. During the peak of the Silk Road from the fourth to the eighth century C.E., Sogdian merchants dominated East-West trade. Buddhist missionaries journeyed from India to China by following the overland Silk Road, as did the Chinese monk Xuanzang on his pilgrimage to India in the early seventh century.

ROUTES ▼

— Silk Road, c. 600

— Maritime trade route, c. 600

➔ Travels of Xuanzang, 629–645

755–763 A Lushan rebellion in north China severely weakens the Tang dynasty

802 Consolidation of the Angkor kingdom in Cambodia by Jayavarman II

939 Vietnam achieves independence from China

800   **900**   **1000**

c. 760 Sailendra kings in Java begin construction of the Borobudur monument

965 Rus invaders destroy the Khazar khanate

861 Conversion of the Khazars to Judaism

792 Kyoto established as Japan's new capital

in East and Southeast Asia looked toward China and India for models of political institutions and cultural values. A common civilization inspired by Chinese political, philosophical, and literary traditions and permeated by Buddhist beliefs and practices emerged in East Asia. In Southeast Asia, a more eclectic variety of societies and cultures developed, one that blended Indian influences with native traditions. In time, the emergence of new societies throughout Asia would give rise to new trade patterns. By the tenth century the maritime realm stretching from Korea and Japan to Java and Malaysia had supplanted the overland Silk Road as the major channel of economic and cultural interaction within Asia.

OVERVIEW
QUESTIONS

The major global development in this chapter: The cultural and commercial exchanges during the heyday of the Silk Road that transformed Asian peoples, cultures, and states.

As you read, consider:

1. In what ways did Asian societies respond to cross-cultural interaction during the period 400–1000?

2. What strategies did pastoral nomads adopt in their relations with settled societies, and why?

3. What patterns of political and cultural borrowing characterized the emerging states in East and Southeast Asia?

4. Why did India and China experience different outcomes following the collapse of strong and unified empires?

Steppe Peoples and Settled Societies of Central Asia

FOCUS

What strategies did nomadic steppe chieftains and the rulers of agrarian societies apply in their dealings with each other?

Neither the fall of the Han dynasty in China in the early third century nor the collapse of the Roman Empire in the West in the fifth century resulted directly from invasions by pastoral nomads from the steppes of Central Asia. In both cases, imperial decline was the cause rather than the consequence of nomadic invasions. Political instability following the demise of the Han encouraged raids by nomadic groups on China's northern frontiers. During the fifth century, one of these groups, the Tuoba confederation, gradually occupied nearly all of northern China, as well as Manchuria and Mongolia.

Despite the political instability on the Eurasian steppe in this era, trade and cultural exchange flourished as never before. The heyday of the Silk Road between the fifth and the eighth centuries witnessed major changes in the societies and cultures of Asia. No group was more deeply affected by these changes than the pastoral nomads of the Central Asian steppe. The empires of the Tuoba, the Turks, and the Khazars marked a new stage in state formation among the nomadic tribes. The military ingenuity and political skills these nomad confederations developed would later make possible the greatest nomad conquerors of all, the Mongols.

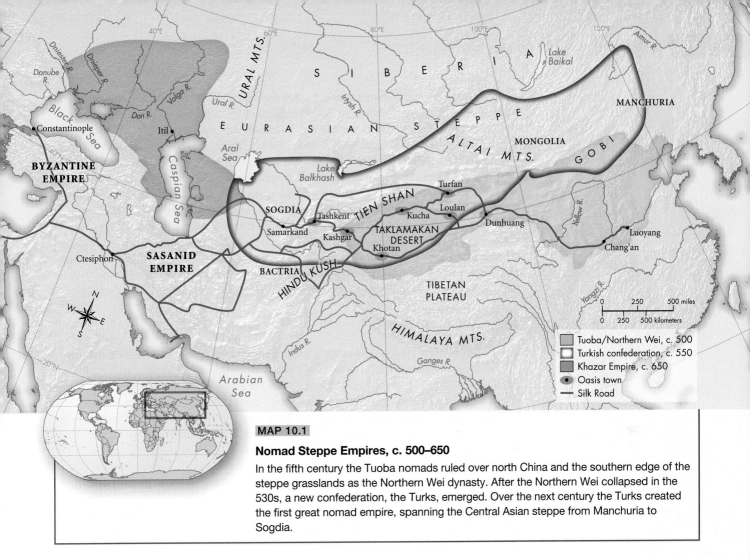

MAP 10.1

Nomad Steppe Empires, c. 500–650

In the fifth century the Tuoba nomads ruled over north China and the southern edge of the steppe grasslands as the Northern Wei dynasty. After the Northern Wei collapsed in the 530s, a new confederation, the Turks, emerged. Over the next century the Turks created the first great nomad empire, spanning the Central Asian steppe from Manchuria to Sogdia.

Nomad Conquerors of China: The Northern Wei 386–534

China had a frontier stretching thousands of miles along the border of the steppe grasslands. Throughout the more than four hundred years of the Han dynasty (202 B.C.E.–220 C.E.), steppe nomads had shifted between a "hard" strategy of invading China and extorting tribute during times of strength and a "soft" strategy of allying with Chinese rulers and symbolically acknowledging their overlordship during times of weakness. The nomads were primarily interested in obtaining scarce resources they could not produce themselves, such as grain. They also sought precious goods, notably gold, metal wares, and silk cloth, which they needed to cement the alliances that held their confederations together. Nomad chieftains had no desire to conquer the agrarian states and adopt their lifestyle. They preferred to acquire the goods they desired through tribute and trade rather than direct rule.

Nomad Conquest of North China

The demise of the Han dynasty in 220 ushered in a century of civil wars that sapped the empire's defenses and left China vulnerable to foreign invasion. In 311, steppe invaders sacked Luoyang (LWAUGH-yahng), the capital of the reigning Jin dynasty. The Jin emperor fled with his court to the Yangzi River delta, leaving the Chinese heartland in the north at the mercy of marauding armies. For the next three centuries, a series of foreign rulers controlled north China; some were wise, and many were rapacious. Then, in the late fourth century, a measure of stability was restored to north China by the rulers of a new confederation of steppe peoples, the Tuoba (TWAUGH-bah).

Northern Wei State

The rise of the Tuoba marked the first attempt by steppe nomads to build enduring institutions for governing agrarian China, rather than merely seeking to extract booty from it. In 386 the Tuoba declared their imperial ambitions by adopting a Chinese-style dynastic name, Northern Wei (way). From 430, when the Tuoba captured the former Han capital of Chang'an, down to the 530s, the Northern Wei reigned virtually unchallenged across a wide swath of Asia from Manchuria to Bactria (see Map 10.1).

309

To reinforce their legitimacy and further their imperial ambitions, the Northern Wei promoted cross-cultural exchange between themselves and their Chinese subjects. The Northern Wei rulers avidly embraced the Buddhist faith that, as we will see, had spread throughout Central Asia. Emperor Xiaowen (SHIAW-when) (r. 471–499) encouraged intermarriage between the Tuoba nobility and the leading Chinese aristocratic clans, as well as adoption of Chinese language, dress, and customs. Xiaowen sought to create a hybrid ruling class that combined the martial traditions of the steppe with the cultural prestige and administrative acumen of imperial China. Ultimately, however, his policies divided the "sinified" Tuoba—those who adopted Chinese ways—within China from the Tuoba nobles based in the steppe grasslands, who staunchly resisted Chinese habits and values. This split widened when purist Tuoba chiefs from the steppes revolted in 524. The Northern Wei state crumbled ten years later. A cultural policy meant to unify the Tuoba and the Chinese and thereby cement Northern Wei rule ended up creating fatal divisions among the Tuoba themselves.

Rise of the Turks

The return of tribal strife to the eastern steppe gave charismatic leaders among the pastoral nomads a chance to forge new coalitions. In Mongolia, a chieftain named Bumin (BOO-min) (d. 552) emerged as the *khan* ("lord") of a new confederation called the Heavenly Turks. Bumin initially allied with the purist Tuoba chiefs, but he soon became their overlord. Bumin's successors extended the Turkic conquests eastward to Manchuria, but they were content to exact tribute from, rather than conquer, the Tuoba-Chinese states that had succeeded the Northern Wei in north China.

Turkic Warriors   Technology played a role in the Turks' rise to prominence. Recent innovations in warfare, such as the use of stirrups, had become widespread in the eastern steppe in the fifth century. The stirrup gave horse-riding archers a steadier posture from which to shoot. Turkic warriors cloaked themselves in mailed armor and wielded large bows and curved sabers. Thus equipped, the Turkic cavalry transformed themselves into a far more deadly force than the mounted warriors of the past.

The Turks' most dramatic advance occurred in the western steppe. They swallowed up the oasis towns and principalities of the Silk Road, reaching as far west as the Black Sea, and negotiated a marriage alliance with the Sasanid king. Like earlier steppe confedera-

Central Asian Horse Riders
The invention of the metal stirrup marked an important advance in warfare, enabling riders to wield bows and swords more effectively. By 200 C.E. Chinese craftsmen were making iron and bronze stirrups like the ones shown in this mural from the tomb of a Chinese general. Widely adopted by the steppe nomads of eastern Asia by 400, the stirrup spread westward and reached Europe in the eighth century. (Shaanxi Museum/ ChinaStock.)

khan The Turkish word for "lord," used especially for rulers of the nomad empires of the central Eurasian steppes.

tions, the Turks preferred tribute and trade as means of obtaining booty. The merchants of Sogdia, in modern Uzbekistan, became key advisers and agents of the Turkic leaders. Control of the entire length of the Silk Road by a single power was a boon to trade, and the Sogdian capital of Samarkand (SAM-mar-kand) flourished as a great crossroads for merchant caravans (see Counterpoint: Sogdian Traders in Central Asia and China). This robust commercial activity also stimulated trade along the lower reaches of the Volga River and opened a route that the Vikings would later exploit.

In diplomatic negotiations with the autocratic empires of Iran and China, the Turkic khans presented themselves as supreme monarchs. Nevertheless, the Turkic confederation remained a loose band of tribes whose chieftains retained considerable autonomy. When, as we will see, a strong empire reemerged in China under the Sui dynasty in the late sixth century, the Turks lacked effective leadership to counter a resurgent China. By 603 the Sui captured the eastern portion of the Silk Road corridor, splitting the Turks into separate eastern and western groups.

Breakup of the Turkic Confederation

A Turkic Khanate in the West: The Khazars

Following the division of the Turkic Empire in 603, local tribal identities once again came to the fore in the western part of the former empire, where few people were of Turkic ancestry. The Khazars (hus-ahr), based in the Caucasus region between the Black and Caspian seas, emerged as an independent khanate allied with the Byzantines against the Sasanids. In around 650 the Khazars conquered the rival Bulgar khanate that had been established northeast of the Black Sea (see again Map 10.1). Later, in the tenth century, the Khazars drove the Magyar chieftains westward into the Danube River basin, where they established a durable state, Hungary, and converted to Christianity.

Khazar Expansion

Following their triumph over the Bulgars, the Khazars moved their capital to Itil in the Volga River delta. In the mid-eighth century the Khazars developed close diplomatic and commercial relations with the Abbasid caliphs. Although Itil consisted of little more than a massed array of felt tents, the Khazar capital attracted merchants from distant regions. Many Muslims resided there, along with a sizable community of Jewish merchants who had fled Constantinople because of the anti-Jewish policies of the Byzantine government. Commercial exchange with the Muslim world was fed by the rich mines of the Caucasus region, the tribute of furs collected from Slavs in the Dnieper River Valley, and the steady flow of slaves seized as war captives. Despite the Khazars' nomadic lifestyle, their capital became a crossroads for trade and cultural exchange.

This openness was dramatically demonstrated when, in around 861, the reigning Khazar khan abruptly converted to Judaism, reportedly after listening to debates among a Muslim mullah, a Christian priest, and a Jewish rabbi. The khan adopted the Jewish Torah as the legal code of the Khazars, although Christians and Muslims continued to be judged according to their own laws. Hebrew became the primary written language of government and religion. Subsequently the head of the Jewish community gained effective power over political affairs, relegating the khan to the role of a symbolic figurehead. The Khazar khanate did not long survive this dramatic shift. In 965 Rus armies overran Itil and other Khazar towns, bringing the khanate to an end and opening the region to settlement by Christian Slavs.

Conversion to Judaism

The Shaping of East Asia

The culture and technology of the Chinese Empire—and of course its political and military muscle—could not fail to have a powerful impact on its neighbors. Chinese agriculture and metalworking were adopted in the Korean peninsula from the eighth century B.C.E. and in the Japanese archipelago after the fourth century B.C.E. Rapid advances in agricultural production and the rise of local and regional chiefdoms followed.

FOCUS

How did the spread of Buddhism transform the politics and societies of East Asia?

The imposition of direct Chinese rule on part of the Korean peninsula and on Vietnam during the Han dynasty left a deep imprint on these regions. Independent Korean states arose after the Han Empire collapsed in the early third century C.E., but Vietnam remained under Chinese rule until the tenth century. In the Japanese islands, contact and exchange with the continent stimulated the progress of state formation beginning in the third century.

Although both Korea and Japan preserved their independence from the resurgent Sui (581–618) and Tang (618–907) empires in China, the societies of both the peninsula and the archipelago were shaped by Chinese political and cultural models and traditions. The farthest-reaching cultural transformation of this era was the adoption of a foreign tradition, Buddhism, as the dominant religion within China, and subsequently in the rest of East Asia. With the waning of Tang imperial might after the mid-eighth century, however, Japan and Korea shifted away from Chinese models and developed their own distinctive political and social identities. After Vietnam gained independence in the early tenth century, the multistate system of modern East Asia assumed definitive form.

The Chinese Transformation of Buddhism

From the first century C.E., Buddhist missionaries from India had crossed the steppe grasslands of Central Asia and reached China. The rise of the kingdom of the Kushans, great patrons of Buddhism, at the intersection of the trade routes linking China with India and Iran had stimulated the spread of Buddhism along these thoroughfares (see Chapter 6). Although the Kushan kingdom disintegrated in the second century, the rulers and inhabitants of the oasis towns of central Eurasia had converted to Buddhism, creating a neat path of stepping-stones for the passage of Buddhist monks and doctrines from India to China.

The collapse of the Han Empire and subsequent foreign invasions prompted many Chinese to question their values and beliefs and to become receptive to alternative ideas and ways of life. Buddhism was well known in Chinese philosophical circles by the third century, but it was not until the fifth century that this nonnative religion began to penetrate deeply into Chinese society.

In its original form, Buddhism could not be readily assimilated into the Chinese worldview. Its rejection of the mundane world and its stress on a monastic vocation conflicted with the humanist goals and family-centered ethics of Confucianism. As we saw in Chapter 6, however, the **Mahayana** school of Buddhism maintained that laypeople in any walk of life had equal potential for achieving enlightenment and salvation. The figure of the **bodhisattva** (boh-dihs-SAHT-vah), an enlightened being who delays entry into nirvana to aid the faithful in their own religious quests, exemplified the Mahayana ideal of selfless compassion and provided a model for pious laypeople and clergy alike. The Mahayana vision of a multitude of Buddhas (of whom the historical Buddha was only one) and bodhisattvas as divine saviors also encouraged the prospect of gaining salvation within a person's present lifetime, rather than after many lives of suffering. It was the Mahayana school of Buddhism, therefore, that made broad inroads in China.

Mahayana Buddhism's compatibility with existing Chinese cultural and intellectual traditions was crucial to its acceptance. The Buddhist doctrine of *karma*—the belief that the individual's good and evil actions determine one's destiny in the next reincarnation—was revised to allow people to earn merit not just for themselves but also for their parents and children. The pursuit of merit and eradication of sin became a collective family endeavor rather than a solitary, self-centered enterprise.

Buddhist Family Shrine

Although the Buddha had presented the pursuit of enlightenment as an individual quest, Mahayana Buddhists in China promoted devotional acts intended to earn karmic merit for the entire family. This stone stele, dated 562, features carvings of numerous Buddhas and bodhisattvas. The name of the donor is inscribed alongside each image. Nearly all the donors were surnamed Chen, suggesting that the monument was a collective family project. (Collected in Shanxi Museum.)

This understanding of karma fit well with the Chinese practice of ancestor worship and the emphasis on the family as the fundamental moral unit. Moreover, the Buddhist regimen of mastery of scripture, lavish donations to support the clergy, and ritual observances governing all aspects of daily life fit readily into the lifestyles of the educated, wealthy, and ritual-bound upper classes in China. Indeed, the lay religious practices of Buddhism served to confirm the Chinese aristocracy's own sense of social superiority. Not surprisingly, Buddhist missionaries in China initially directed their conversion efforts at the rulers and aristocrats, whose faith in Confucianism had been badly shaken by the collapse of the Han.

During the fifth century, devotion to Buddhism spread swiftly among the ruling classes in both north and south China. The Tuoba rulers of the Northern Wei dynasty had long been familiar with Buddhism. Several Northern Wei emperors converted to Buddhism and became avid patrons of Buddhist institutions. Buddhism also served useful political purposes. In a world fractured by warfare and political instability, the universalist spirit of Buddhism offered an inclusive creed that might ease social and ethnic frictions among the Chinese and the diverse foreign peoples who had settled within China. The Northern Wei rulers were especially attracted to the Buddhist ideal of the *chakravartin* (chuhk-ruh-VAHR-tin), the "wheel-turning king" (controller of human destiny) who wages righteous wars to bring the true religion to the unenlightened peoples of the world. The chakravartin ideal was founded on the historical precedent of Ashoka (see Chapter 6), the great Mauryan king of the third century B.C.E., whose imperial dominion was closely tied to his support and patronage of Buddhism.

Chinese rulers in the south also became patrons of Buddhism. The desire to earn religious merit through acts of faith and charity spurred Chinese aristocrats to donate land, money, and goods to support the Buddhist clergy. The profusion of domestic shrines and devotional objects illustrates the saturation of upper-class life in China by Buddhist beliefs and practices.

In the sixth century, two interrelated developments profoundly altered the evolution of Buddhism in East Asia. First, Chinese monastic communities and lay congregations created their own forms of Buddhist theology and religious discipline, forms that were more closely attuned to the concerns of their Chinese audience. Second, these new movements reached well beyond the elite and led to the emergence of Buddhism as a religion of the masses. As a reaction against the exclusivity of earlier forms of Buddhism, two new forms of Buddhism developed—Pure Land Buddhism and Chan (Zen) Buddhism.

Pure Land Buddhism first emerged as a coherent religious movement in China during the sixth century. Born amid the incessant war and deepening poverty that afflicted the Chinese world after the collapse of the Northern Wei state in 534, Pure Land expressed deep pessimism about mortal existence. The formidable burden of sins accumulated over countless lifetimes made the possibility of attaining salvation through one's own merit-earning actions appear hopelessly remote. Yet people of sincere faith could obtain rebirth in the Pure Land, a celestial paradise, through the aid of savior figures such as Amitabha (Ah-MEE-tah-bah), the presiding Buddha of the Pure Land, or Guanyin (GWAHN-yin), the bodhisattva of compassion.

Like the later Protestant Reformation of Christianity, Pure Land Buddhism emphasized salvation through faith alone rather than good works. One did not achieve nirvana by making large donations to Buddhist monasteries, but by fully committing oneself to a spiritual life. Thus, it offered the hope that through sincere piety all persons, no matter how humble, might attain salvation within their present lifetimes. Originating among lay congregations alienated by the luxury and splendor that increasingly enveloped the monastic establishments, Pure Land teachings found favor among poor and illiterate people. Its devotions focused on simple rituals, such as chanting the names of Amitabha and Guanyin, that did not require wealth, learning, or leisure. Because of the universal appeal of its message, the Pure Land movement transformed Chinese Buddhism into a mass religion focused on the worship of compassionate savior figures.

From an Elite to a Mass Religion

Mahayana A major branch of Buddhism that emphasizes the potential for laypeople to achieve enlightenment through the aid of the Buddha and bodhisattvas.

bodhisattva In Mahayana Buddhism, an enlightened being who delays entry into nirvana and chooses to remain in the world of suffering to assist others in their quest for salvation.

chakravartin In Indian political thought, the "wheel-turning king," a universal monarch who enjoys the favor of the gods and acts as a defender of religious orthodoxy.

Pure Land A school of Mahayana Buddhism, originating in China, that emphasizes the sinfulness of the human condition and the necessity of faith in savior figures (the Buddha and bodhisattvas) to gain rebirth in paradise.

Like Pure Land, **Chan Buddhism**—better known by its Japanese name, Zen—reacted against the unseemly wealth and privileges enjoyed by the clergy. Also like Pure Land, Chan Buddhists rejected a religious life centered on what they perceived to be rote recitation of scripture and performance of complex rituals. Chan instead embraced strict discipline and mystical understanding of truth as the genuine path of enlightenment. But in contrast to Pure Land, Chan Buddhism continued to honor the monastic vocation, and as the ultimate goal of its religious quest it emphasized sublime spiritual mastery of Buddhist teachings rather than rebirth in a paradise of material comfort. The Chan movement gained a widespread following among the clergy beginning in the eighth century and subsequently became the preeminent monastic tradition throughout East Asia.

Reunification of the Chinese Empire: The Sui Dynasty 581–618

The collapse of the Northern Wei in 534 once again plunged northern China into anarchic warfare. In 581, Yang Jian (d. 604), a member of the mixed-blood Tuoba-Chinese aristocracy, staged a bloody coup in which he deposed and killed his own grandson and installed himself as emperor. As iron-fisted ruler of the Sui dynasty (581–618), Yang Jian quickly reasserted military supremacy. In 589 he conquered southern China and restored a unified empire.

Yang Jian was determined to resurrect the grandeur of the Han by rebuilding a centralized bureaucratic state. He immediately abolished the entitlements to political office enjoyed by aristocratic families during the centuries of disunion. Although the inner circle of his government would still be drawn from the hybrid aristocracy fostered by the Northern Wei, high office was a privilege the emperor could bestow or take away as he saw fit.

Eleven-Headed Guanyin

Guanyin, the bodhisattva of compassion, became the most popular figure in East Asian Buddhism. This tenth-century banner depicts Guanyin with eleven heads and six arms, symbolizing Guanyin's role as a savior. Guanyin is surrounded by scenes from the *Lotus Sutra* in which the bodhisattva rescues devout followers from perils such as fire and bandits. The donor, dressed as a Chinese official, appears at bottom right. (Arthur M. Sackler Museum, Harvard University Art Museums/Bequest of Grenville L. Winthrop/Bridgeman Art Library.)

China's Grand Canal

Yang also retained the system of state landownership that the Northern Wei had put in place. The Northern Wei rulers, descended from nomad chiefs, had introduced policies designed to simplify the task of administering the unfamiliar agrarian world of China. Under the **equal-field system**, the Northern Wei government allocated landholdings to individual households according to formulas based on the number of able-bodied adults the household had to work the land and how many mouths it had to feed. Each household was expected to have roughly equal productive capabilities, so that the state could collect uniform taxes in grain, cloth, and labor or military service from all households. Although aristocratic families largely preserved their extensive landholdings, this system of state landownership provided the Northern Wei with dependable sources of tax revenues and soldiers.

Yang Jian's son and successor, Yang Guang (r. 604–618), further centralized control over resources by building the Grand Canal. This artificial waterway connected the Sui capital at Chang'an in northwestern China with the rice-growing regions of the Yangzi River delta. With the Grand Canal, the central government could tap the burgeoning agricultural wealth of southern China to feed the capital and the military garrisons surrounding it. As we have seen in previous chapters, ancient cities originally depended on their immediate surrounding rural areas for food and other products. The construction of the Grand Canal was important, because it allowed Chang'an to draw resources from further away in the countryside with greater ease, thereby increasing its size and power.

The Sui rulers differed sharply from their Han predecessors in their commitment to Buddhism rather than Confucianism. Unlike the uniform culture of the Han rooted in Confucian traditions, the Sui realm encompassed a heterogeneous collection of peoples divided by ancestry, language, and customs. A devout believer in Buddhism since childhood, Yang Jian recognized Buddhism's potential to aid him in rebuilding a universal empire. Buddhism was equally entrenched in all of China and could provide a set of common values that would unite his subjects. Yang Jian cultivated his self-image as a chakravartin king and imitated the example of Ashoka by building hundreds of Buddhist shrines and monasteries throughout the empire.

Sui Patronage of Buddhism

Yet the Sui dynasty ended as abruptly as it began. Foreign affairs, rather than domestic problems, proved the dynasty's undoing. From the outset the Sui had tempestuous relations with their Korean neighbors. In 612 Yang Guang launched an invasion of the Korean peninsula that ended in disastrous defeat. When the emperor insisted on preparing a new offensive, his generals revolted against him, and he was assassinated in 618. One of his former generals, Li Yuan (565–635), declared himself emperor of a new dynasty, the Tang.

Chan Buddhism A Buddhist devotional tradition, originating in China, that emphasizes salvation through personal conduct, meditation, and mystical enlightenment; also known as Zen Buddhism.

The Power of Tang China 618–907

The coup that brought the Tang dynasty to power was only the latest in a series of coups led by the Tuoba-Chinese aristocratic clans dating back to the fall of the Northern Wei. Yet unlike its predecessors, the Tang fashioned an enduring empire, the wealthiest and most powerful state in Asia (see Map 10.2). Given their roots in both the Chinese and Tuoba nobilities, the Tang rulers laid equal claim to the worlds of the steppe nomads and settled peoples. They extended Chinese supremacy over the oasis city-states of the eastern steppe, which further fragmented the Turkic confederation. Within China, they revived Confucian traditions while building on the institutional foundations of the Northern Wei and Sui to reestablish a strong bureaucratic state.

equal-field system A system of state-controlled landownership created by the Northern Wei dynasty in China that attempted to allocate equitable portions of land to all households.

At the pinnacle of its political supremacy in the late seventh century, the Tang dynasty was beset by a jarring crisis. During the reign of the sickly emperor Gaozong (r. 650–683), the empress Wu Zhao (625–705) took an increasingly assertive role in governing the empire. Fierce opposition from the aristocrats who dominated the Tang court provoked Empress Wu to unleash a campaign of terror against her enemies. At the same time she carefully nurtured support among lesser aristocrats, expanding the use of civil service examinations to broaden access to bureaucratic office.

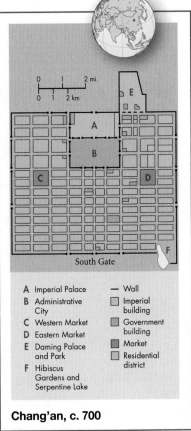

In 690 Wu Zhao set aside the Tang dynasty and declared her own Zhou dynasty, becoming the only woman ever to rule as emperor of China. Although Confucian historians depicted her in the harshest possible light, there is little evidence that the empire's prosperity diminished during her reign. Shortly before her death in 705, however, Empress Wu was forced to abdicate, and the Tang dynasty was restored.

The Tang capital of Chang'an had been built by the Sui founder, Yang Jian, near the site of the ancient Han capital. The Chinese conceived of their capital not only as the seat of government but also as the axis of cosmological order. The capital's design—laid out as a nearly perfect square, with its main gate facing south—expressed the principles of order and balance that imperial rule was expected to embody. Imperial palaces, government offices, marketplaces, and residential areas were symmetrically arranged along a central north-south avenue in checkerboard fashion. Two great marketplaces, enclosed by walls and gates, were laid out in the city's eastern and western halves. The bustling Western Market, terminus of the Silk Road, teemed with foreign as well as Chinese merchants. The more sedate Eastern

South Gate

A Imperial Palace
B Administrative City
C Western Market
D Eastern Market
E Daming Palace and Park
F Hibiscus Gardens and Serpentine Lake

— Wall
▫ Imperial building
▫ Government building
▪ Market
▫ Residential district

Chang'an, c. 700

The Imperial Capital of Chang'an

Market catered to an elite clientele of officials and aristocrats. The cosmopolitan styles of life and culture radiating from Chang'an reverberated throughout East Asia, shaping tastes in fashion, furnishings, and pastimes, as well as music, dance, and art (see Lives and Livelihoods: Tea Drinkers in Tang China). Chang'an was an economic and cultural crossroads of immense importance not just to China, but to all of Asia.

Demise of Tang Power

Yet the gilded glory of Tang civilization masked deepening political and economic divisions. In some ways, the Tang were victims of their own success. Aristocratic factions jockeyed for control of the court and the riches and privileges at its disposal. Economic prosperity and commercial growth unleashed market forces that eroded the foundations of the equal-field landownership system and jeopardized the state's financial stability. The gravest challenge to Tang rule came in 755, when An Lushan (ahn loo-shahn), a Sogdian general who commanded the Tang armies along the northeastern frontier, revolted. Convinced that he was about to fall victim to court intrigues, An rallied other generals to his side and marched on Chang'an. The emperor was forced to abandon the capital and seek sanctuary in the remote southwest. The dynasty survived, but probably only because An Lushan was assassinated—by his son—in 757. The rebellion finally was suppressed in 763, thanks to the crucial aid of Turkic Uighur mercenaries from Central Asia.

Although the Tang dynasty endured for another 150 years, it never recovered from the catastrophe of the An Lushan rebellion. The court ceded much military and civil authority to

MAP 10.2   East Asia, c. 650

The early Tang emperors sought to reassert Chinese dominion over the eastern steppe, including Manchuria and Korea. Tang military assistance helped the Korean kingdom of Silla to topple Koguryo, long the most powerful of the Korean states, in 668. Although Tang China exerted a powerful cultural influence on its East Asian neighbors, Silla and the newly christened emperors of Japan retained their political independence.

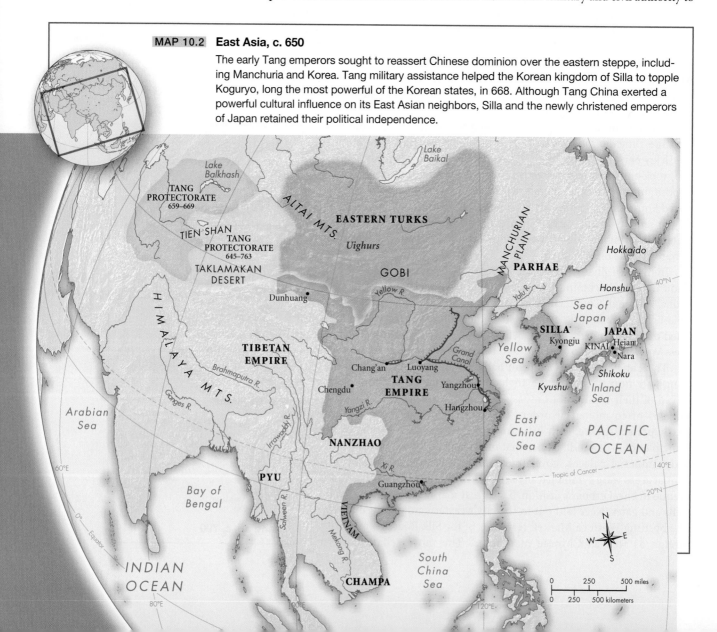

provincial warlords. The rebellion wrecked the empire's finances by forcing the government to abandon the equal-field system and relinquish its control over landholdings. Many of the millions of peasants displaced by marauding armies took refuge in the south, which escaped much of the devastation suffered by the north China heartland. The aristocratic families who had dominated government and society since the Han dynasty were perhaps the major casualties of the rebellion. Tethered to the weakened Tang court, their estates lying in ruin, the old aristocracy clung to its prestige but never regained its power.

China and Its Neighbors

At the height of its power in the late second century B.C.E., the Han Empire had annexed portions of the Korean peninsula and Vietnam and established colonial rule over the native peoples of these regions. The introduction of the Chinese written language, as well as China's political institutions and cultural heritage, exerted a lasting influence on Korea and Vietnam, and later on Japan as well. The rise and fall of the Sui and Tang empires gave birth to East Asia as a common civilization divided into separate national states. Although each state had a unique identity and aggressively asserted its independence, Chinese policies and influences profoundly shaped how each of them developed. Elites in Korea, Vietnam, and Japan all looked to China for political and cultural models, adapting Chinese practices to suit local conditions.

Vietnam

Local rulers continued to resist foreign domination after the Han Empire conquered northern Vietnam in 111 B.C.E. In 40 C.E. a Viet queen, Trung Trac, and her sister led a revolt against the tribute demands of the Han officials. A Han general ruthlessly crushed the rebellion, executed the Trung sisters, and imposed more direct Chinese control over local society. He also erected a pair of bronze pillars along Vietnam's central coast to mark the boundary of Chinese rule—and by extension to symbolize the limits of civilization itself. Vietnam remained under Chinese dominion after the fall of the Han dynasty, but actual authority passed to a landlord class of mixed Chinese and Vietnamese ancestry linked by cultural and literary traditions to the Chinese world.

Korea

Chinese rule in Korea continued until the nomad invasions that overran north China in the early fourth century C.E. In 313 the Chinese-ruled territories in Korea were seized by Koguryo (koh-goo-ryuh), a recently formed confederation based in southern Manchuria. Pressure from nomad invaders soon forced Koguryo out of Manchuria. Koguryo moved its capital to the site of modern Pyongyang, but it became embroiled in conflict with the states of Paekche (pock-CHAY) and Silla (SHEE-lah), which had sprung up in the southern peninsula.

Japan

The earliest reference to the Japanese islands in Chinese records refers to an embassy dispatched to the Chinese court in 238 by Himiko (hee-mee-KOH), queen of the Japanese Wa people. Himiko was described as a spinster sorceress whom the Wa had elected as ruler to instill unity and curb the violent disorder that had wracked the archipelago for generations. Himiko's stature as supreme ruler reflected a pattern of dual-gender rulership that was a distinctive feature of early states in Japan.

At the time that Himiko's envoys arrived in China, influences from the mainland had only recently set in motion what would become a profound transformation in the economy and society of the Japanese islands. Settled agriculture based on rice cultivation had developed in Japan only since the fourth century B.C.E. Bronze and iron wares—chiefly weapons and prestige goods such as bronze mirrors—appeared together in the archipelago, probably in the first century C.E. During the first four centuries C.E., the population of the Japanese islands grew rapidly, in part because of immigration from the continent.

During the fourth century the Yamato kingdom in Kinai, the region around the modern city of Osaka, gained dominance in the Japanese islands. The Yamato "great kings" may or may not have descended from the Wa lineage of Himiko, but their power clearly derived from their success as warrior chiefs. Although the Yamato won the Chinese court's

Tea Drinkers in Tang China

Tea Drinking and Buddhist Hospitality

During the Tang dynasty tea drinking became an indispensable part of Chinese social life. This painting is a sixteenth-century copy of one attributed to the Tang artist Yan Liben (d. 673). It illustrates the story of a scholar who visits an elderly monk, intending to steal a famous work of calligraphy for the Tang emperor. After the monk and the scholar devote several days to lofty talk of art, the monk finally shows the treasured heirloom to his guest, who snatches it away. Here the scholar and the monk converse while two servants prepare tea for them. (National Palace Museum, Taiwan, Republic of China.)

The wild tea plant is native to the mountainous borderlands between China and India. References to drinking an infusion of fresh tea leaves in hot water date back to the first century B.C.E., but the vogue for drinking tea made from roasted leaves became widespread during the Tang dynasty. In the mid-eighth century a Tang scholar-official named Lu Yu wrote *The Classic of Tea*, which became so widely celebrated as a handbook of connoisseurship that tea merchants made porcelain statues of Lu Yu and worshiped him as their patron deity.

In Lu Yu's estimation, the finest teas were produced in Sichuan in western China and in the hilly region south of the Yangzi River, along China's eastern coast. Tea plants flourished best in a humid climate and in stony, well-drained soils on mountain slopes. After the outbreak of the An Lushan rebellion in 755, many peasants fled war-torn northern China and settled in the upland valleys of the south, where the rugged terrain was far better suited to tea cultivation than to rice agriculture. Over the next four centuries, as the popularity of tea drinking rose, tea cultivation

recognition as rulers of Japan, they only gradually extended their authority over the heterogeneous local chiefdoms scattered across the archipelago.

Warrior Rule in Korea and Japan

Meanwhile, in the Korean peninsula, the practice of mounted warfare developed by steppe nomads such as the Tuoba upset the balance of power. Koguryo had quickly imitated the Tuoba style of mounted warfare, in which both warriors and horses were clad in full body armor. At the start of the fifth century, Koguryo decisively defeated the combined armies of Paekche and their Yamato allies. The Paekche king abandoned his capital near modern Seoul and resettled in the southwestern corner of the peninsula. The militarization of the Yamato state in the fourth and fifth centuries was accompanied by a sharp increase in the incidence of warfare in the Japanese islands, fueled by imports of iron weapons from Korea. As in Korea, a warrior aristocracy now dominated in Japan.

spearheaded settlement of the interior provinces of southern China.

Tea was harvested in the spring. Although large tea plantations hired both men and women, in peasant households the task of tea picking fell almost exclusively to women, of all ages. "Tea comes in chopped, loose, powdered, and brick varieties, but in all cases the tea leaves are simply picked, steamed, roasted, pounded, and sealed in a ceramic container,"[1] Lu wrote, but he scrupulously differentiated many types of tea and methods of preparation. In Lu Yu's day, roasted tea leaves usually were pressed into bricks for ease of storage and transport. Fragments of these bricks were crushed or ground into a fine powder before brewing.

Originally, drinking tea was a leisurely pastime of the elite, but over the course of the Tang dynasty, tea became a common staple in all social classes. Lu Yu greatly esteemed tea for its medicinal value:

> Because tea is of "cold" nature it is most suitable as a beverage. A person who ordinarily is moderate in disposition and temperament but feeling hot and dry, melancholic, or suffering from headaches, soreness of the eyes, aching in the four limbs, or pains in the hundred joints should take four or five sips of tea. Its flavor can compare favorably with the most buttery of liquors, or the sweetest dew of Heaven.[2]

Feng Yan, a contemporary of Lu Yu, attributed the rising popularity of tea to Chan Buddhist monks, who drank tea to remain wakeful and alert during their rigorous meditation exercises. Monastic regulations prohibited monks from eating an evening meal but allowed them to drink tea while fasting. The diary of the Japanese Buddhist monk Ennin, who traveled throughout China on a pilgrimage between 838 and 847, contains many references to tea as a courtesy provided to guests, as a gift, and as an offering placed on the altars of Buddhist divinities and saints.

The habit of tea drinking also spread beyond the borders of China. Feng Yan reported that "Uighur Turks who came to the capital bringing herds of fine horses for sale would hasten to the marketplace and buy tea before returning home."[3] The stock-raising nomads of Central Asia and Tibet flavored their tea with butter or fermented milk.

Lu Yu's commentary bristles with sharply worded judgments about the aesthetics of preparing and drinking tea. For example, he observed that it was common to "stew tea together with finely chopped onion, fresh ginger, orange peel, or peppermint, which is boiled until a glossy film forms, or the brew turns foamy."[4] But in Lu's view such vile concoctions were "like water tossed into a ditch."[5] In choosing tea bowls Lu favored the celadon (sea green) hue of the Yue porcelains of eastern China as a fitting complement to the greenish color of tea. Later generations of tea connoisseurs in China and Japan developed complex tea ceremonies that became fixtures of refined social life.

---

1. Translated from Lu Yu, *The Classic of Tea*, Chapter 6.
2. Ibid., Chapter 1.
3. Translated from Feng Yan, *Master Feng's Record of Things Seen and Heard*, Chapter 6.
4. Lu, *The Classic of Tea*, Chapter 6.
5. Ibid.

QUESTIONS TO CONSIDER

1. How did Buddhist religious practices promote tea drinking?

2. Why did the cultivation of tea in China increase dramatically during the Tang dynasty?

For Further Information:
Evans, John C. *Tea in China: The History of China's National Drink*. New York: Greenwood Press, 1992.
Sen Shōshitsu XV. *The Japanese Way of Tea: From Its Origins in China to Sen Rikyū*. Honolulu: University of Hawaii Press, 1998.

Buddhism first arrived in Korea in the mid-fourth century. The Koguryo kings lavishly supported Buddhist monasteries and encouraged the propagation of Buddhism among the people. Paekche and Silla adopted Buddhism as their official religion in the early sixth century. In 552 a Paekche king sent a letter to the Yamato ruler in Japan urging him to adopt Buddhism, which "surpasses all other doctrines," adding that in Korea "there are none who do not reverently receive its teachings."[3] Koguryo and Silla also dispatched Buddhist monks to Japan, and it was a Koguryo monk, Hyeja (tee ay-JUH), who after his arrival in Japan in 595 became tutor to the regent Prince Shōtoku (SHOW-toe-koo) (573–621). Shōtoku subsequently sent missions to China, and their reports inspired him to imitate both the Sui system of imperial government and its fervent devotion to Buddhism. In both Korea and Japan, Buddhist monasteries became far more

Spread of Buddhism to Korea and Japan

Korea, c. 600

powerful institutions than in China, but they still looked to China for innovations in religious doctrines and practices.

The fall of the Sui dynasty did not resolve the tense confrontation between the Chinese empire and Koguryo. The Tang rulers formed an alliance with Silla, the rising power in the southern part of the Korean peninsula. With Chinese support, Silla first defeated Paekche and then in 668 conquered Koguryo, unifying Korea under a single ruler for the first time. Although the Tang court naively assumed that Silla would remain a client state under Tang imperial dominion, the Silla kings quickly established their independence.

The growing power of the Tang was witnessed with great trepidation at the Yamato court. In 645, after a violent succession dispute, sweeping political reforms recast the Yamato monarchy in the image of Tang imperial institutions. Efforts to strengthen the hand of the Yamato king and his government intensified after the Tang-Silla alliance heightened fears of invasion from the mainland. The court issued a law code, based on that of the Tang, that sought to adapt Chinese institutions such as the equal-field landownership system to Japanese circumstances. At the same time, the Japanese court remade its national identity by replacing the dynastic title Yamato with a Chinese-inspired name, Nihon (nee-HOHN) ("Land of the Rising Sun"). Although their concepts of rulership were partly borrowed from Chinese models, the Japanese emperors (as they now called themselves) also asserted their independence from and equality with the Tang Empire.

Tang Influence on East Asian Neighbors

In the early eighth century, Tang China reached the height of its influence on its East Asian neighbors. In Korea, Japan, and Vietnam alike, the Chinese written language served as the *lingua franca*, or common language, of government, education, and religion. Adoption of Chinese forms of Buddhism reinforced Tang China's cultural preeminence. In northern Vietnam, Chinese ways of life became deeply implanted in the fertile plains of the Red River delta around modern Hanoi. Although the Vietnamese inhabitants of the plains chafed under Tang rule, their adoption of rice farming and settled livelihoods in-

Horyuji Monastery
After gaining the patronage of rulers and aristocrats in China in the fourth century C.E., Buddhism soon spread to Korea and Japan. The Horyuji monastery, founded by Japan's Prince Shōtoku in the seventh century, was built in a Chinese architectural style adjacent to the prince's palace. The five-story pagoda, believed to be the world's oldest wooden building, houses a statue of the bodhisattva Guanyin (known in Japan as Kannon). (Vanni/Art Resource, NY.)

creasingly alienated them from the forest-dwelling highland peoples, the ancestors of the modern Hmong (mahng). Thus Chinese culture created connections between all of the states of East Asia. Elites in China, Korea, Vietnam, and Japan were bound together by a common language, similar political ideas and institutions, and shared religious beliefs. East Asian elites outside of China had something else in common, however: they were united in resisting Chinese rule.

By the early tenth century, the political boundaries of East Asia had assumed contours that would remain largely intact down to the present. Silla (supplanted by the new Koryo dynasty in 935) ruled over a unified Korea. Most of the Japanese archipelago acknowledged the sovereignty of the emperor at Kyoto, the new capital modeled on the design of Chang'an and founded in 792. In 939, after the Tang dynasty was finally deposed, local chieftains in Vietnam ousted their Chinese overlords and eventually formed their own Dai Viet kingdom. Although Korea, Japan, and Vietnam achieved lasting political independence, they remained within the gravitational pull of a common East Asian cultural sphere centered on China. At the same time, the decline of the Silk Road caravan trade and the waning popularity of Buddhism in the land of its origin loosened the ties between China and India. Henceforth, the cultural worlds of East Asia and South Asia increasingly diverged.

East Asian Political Boundaries and Common Culture

The Consolidation of Hindu Society in India

The period of the Gupta Empire (c. 320–540) often is regarded as India's classical age. Indian historians portray the Guptas as the last great native rulers of India—a dynasty under which a revived Vedic religion surpassed the appeal of the dissident religions of Buddhism and Jainism. Yet the power of the Gupta monarchs was less extensive than that of the Mauryan emperors they claimed as their forebears. Gupta rule was largely confined to the Ganges River Valley heartland, and by the 480s the Hun invasions had already dealt the dynasty a mortal blow (see Chapter 6).

FOCUS

Why did the religious practices of Hinduism gain a broader following in Indian society than the ancient Vedic religion and its chief rival, Buddhism?

The demise of the Gupta Empire, like that of the Roman Empire in Europe, resulted in the fragmentation of political power and the formation of a system of regional states. Unlike in China, however, political disunity remained the norm in India for centuries to come. Not until the rise of the Mughal Empire in the sixteenth century would India be unified again. The absence of a unified state did not deflect the emerging cultural and social trends of the Gupta era, however. On the contrary, in post-Gupta India, as in post-Roman Europe, common values, social practices, and political institutions penetrated more deeply into all corners of the subcontinent.

Land and Wealth

The Chinese pilgrim Xuanzang, whom we met at the start of this chapter, arrived in India during the heyday of King Harsha (r. 606–647), perhaps the most powerful of the post-Gupta monarchs (see Map 10.3). Yet Harsha's kingdom depended on his own charismatic leadership, and it perished soon after his death. Other dynasties survived longer, but their authority was confined to the ruling families' regional power base. Nonetheless, a strikingly uniform political culture spread throughout India. In addition, regional states expanded their reach into hinterland territories, bringing neighboring hill and forest tribes under their sway and assimilating them to the norms of caste society. Thus, although political ties among Indian peoples were weak, the cultural connections were increasingly strong.

The Gupta monarchs, recognizing that their control over local societies was limited, had started awarding royal lands to their officials and Brahman priests. The Gupta expected the recipients to take charge of settling and cultivating these lands. In post-Gupta

Land Grants and Village Society

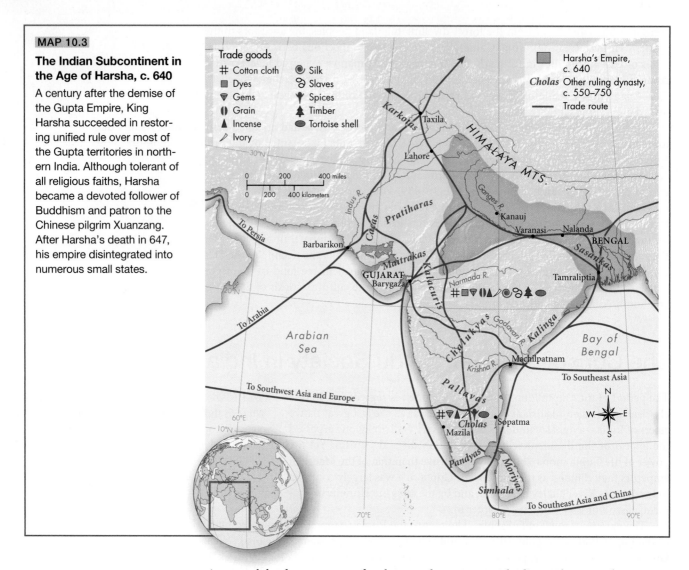

MAP 10.3

The Indian Subcontinent in the Age of Harsha, c. 640

A century after the demise of the Gupta Empire, King Harsha succeeded in restoring unified rule over most of the Gupta territories in northern India. Although tolerant of all religious faiths, Harsha became a devoted follower of Buddhism and patron to the Chinese pilgrim Xuanzang. After Harsha's death in 647, his empire disintegrated into numerous small states.

times, such land grants were often bestowed on corporate bodies such as temples, monasteries, and Brahman communities. Xuanzang observed that "the royal lands are divided into four parts: one portion provides for the needs of the court and sacrificial offerings; the second portion is given as compensation to officers and ministers for their service; the third is awarded to men of intelligence, learning, and talent; and the fourth establishes charitable endowments for religious institutions."[4] In some cases the grants included whole villages and their populations, and the peasants fell under the administrative and legal jurisdiction of the grant recipients (see Reading the Past: A Copper-Plate Land Grant Inscription).

This system of royal land grants stabilized the agricultural base of society and the economy while fostering a landlord class of Brahmans who combined religious authority, caste prestige, and landed wealth. Yet nothing like the large manors or serfdom characteristic of Latin Christendom at this time appeared in India. The peasant household remained the basic unit of work and livelihood. Rural society, especially in the south, typically was governed by village assemblies that enjoyed some measure of independence from their lords.

The practice of royal land grants transferred most wealth to temples and Brahman landlords. These landowners dominated the local economy, garnering tribute from the lands and peasants attached to them and controlling enterprises such as mills, oil presses, and moneylending. Beginning in the tenth century, temples dedicated to gods such as Shiva and Vishnu were built on an unprecedented monumental scale, symbolizing the

A Copper-Plate Land Grant Inscription

This inscription from 753 records a land grant made by the king of the Pallava dynasty in southern India to the king's religious teacher, a local Brahman. The grant was recorded on eleven copper plates that were strung together on a copper wire and stamped with the Pallava royal seal—a bull and the phallic symbol associated with the god Shiva.

The inscription begins with a eulogy written in Sanskrit lauding the king. Details of the land grant, written in the local language, Tamil, follow. This passage from the Tamil portion defines the relationship between the land grant recipient and the local village community.

> Having seen the order . . . we, the inhabitants, went to the boundaries which the headman of the district pointed out, walked around the village from right to left, and planted milk-bushes and placed stones around it. . . . The recipient shall enjoy the wet land and the dry land included within these four boundaries, wherever the iguana runs and the tortoise crawls, and shall be permitted to dig river channels and irrigation channels. . . . Those who take and use the water in these channels by pouring out baskets, by cutting branch channels, or by employing small levers shall pay a fine to be collected by the king. The recipient and his descendants shall enjoy the houses, house gardens, and so forth, and shall have the right to build houses and halls of burnt tiles. The land included within these boundaries we have endowed with all exemptions. The recipient shall enjoy the exemptions obtaining in this village without paying for the oil-mill and looms, the hire of the well-diggers, the share of the Brahmans of the king, the share of shengodi [a plant], the share of figs, the share of lamp black, the share of corn-ears, the share of the headman, the share of the potter, the sifting of [rice] paddy, the price of ghee [clarified butter], the price of cloth, the share of cloth, the hunters, messengers, dancing-girls, the grass, the best cow and the best bull, the share of the district, cotton-threads, servants, palmyra molasses, the fines to the accountant and the minister.

Source: Kasakkudi Plates of Nandivarman, *South Indian Inscriptions,* Archaeological Survey of India, vol. 2, part 3 (Madras: Government Press, 1896), 360–362.

EXAMINING THE EVIDENCE

1. What services—supported by the taxes and fees explicitly exempted from this land grant—did the village community provide to its members?

2. Why did rights to water figure so prominently in this grant?

---

dominance of the temple over community life. In this way, royal land grants established a connection between local elites and institutions and the king, even as they increased the wealth and power of land grant recipients.

Devotional Worship in Hinduism

Beginning in Gupta times, Brahmanical religion regained its primacy, while competing religious movements such as Buddhism and Jainism retreated to the margins of Indian society. The resurgence of Brahmanical religion during this period—in the form now called **Hinduism**—stemmed both from changes in religious practice and from the wealth and power Brahman groups obtained through royal patronage.

The farthest-reaching change in Hindu practice was displacement of the sacrificial rituals only Brahmans could perform by forms of worship all ranks of society could participate in. Personal devotion to gods such as Shiva and Vishnu—whose cults took many distinct forms, depending on regional traditions and even individual imagination—replaced Brahmanical rituals as the core of religious life.

Devotional worship, or *bhakti*, was celebrated as the highest form of religious practice in religious texts known as the **Puranas**. The Puranas instructed believers in the proper forms for worshiping a specific god. Hinduism, like Buddhism and Jainism, centered on the salvation of the individual, regardless of one's caste. At the same time, Hinduism fostered collective worship of the gods enshrined at local village temples. Bhakti worship also encouraged more active participation by women, who previously had been excluded from religious life.

Hinduism The name given (first by Muslims) to the body of religious teachings, derived from the Brahmanical religion of the Vedic era, that developed in response to the challenge of Buddhism.

Puranas Religious writings, derived from oral tradition and written down during the first millennium C.E., that recount the legends of the gods and serve as the canonical texts of popular Hinduism.

Proliferation of Hindu Temples and Deities

Hindu temples joined religious piety to political power. The Puranas constructed genealogical ties between ancient heroes and gods and present-day rulers. Royal inscriptions also celebrated the close relationship between kings and the gods, in some cases asserting that the king was an incarnation of a god such as Shiva or Vishnu.

The focus on worshiping images of the gods that accompanied the spread of Hinduism accelerated the trend of founding temples through royal land grants. Temples grew in size and splendor. Major temples employed large retinues of Brahman priests, students, and caretakers. Many temples also maintained troupes of female attendants—known as *devadasis*—who were "married" to the local god. The devadasis performed rituals that combined music and dance and served as temple wardens. Devadasis at major temples often were highly educated and accomplished artists, respected in local society and accorded a freedom from social convention denied to married women. At poorly endowed temples, however, devadasis sometimes had no choice but to sell their sexual services to support themselves.

The rapid growth of local temples and bhakti devotion spurred intense adoration of a multitude of new or transformed deities. The proliferation of deities resulted from the absorption of local cults into Hindu religion. People worshiped the principal Hindu gods, Shiva and Vishnu, in many different incarnations. Krishna, an incarnation of Vishnu, appeared both as the wise philosopher-warrior of the celebrated philosophical poem *Baghavad Gita* ("Song of the Lord") and as a rustic herdsman, the patron of cowherds and devoted lover of the milkmaid Radha. Kings and warriors particularly venerated Shiva, an icon of sovereign authority and wielder of terrible powers of destruction. The elephant-headed god Ganesh was recast as the offspring of Shiva and his elegant consort (or spouse) Parvati.

Worship of goddesses who originated in local fertility cults marked a significant departure in Hinduism from the older Vedic tradition. Consort goddesses were seen as necessary complements to male gods such as Shiva, whose power and energy could be activated only through union with a female. Yet goddesses such as Lakshmi, the consort of Vishnu, and Shiva's many wives also attracted their own personal followings. Brahman priests condoned these goddess cults, which became a distinctive feature of Hinduism.

As he traveled about India, Xuanzang was appalled by the decayed state of Buddhism in its homeland. Monuments lay in ruin; once-grand monasteries stood desolate. Arriving at Varanasi (the modern city of Benares in northern India), which Buddhists revered as the site of the Buddha's first sermon, the Chinese pilgrim found "a densely crowded city teeming with rich and prosperous inhabitants, their houses filled with great wealth and rare goods." But "few of them revered Buddhist teachings. . . . Of Deva [Hindu] temples there were more than a hundred, and more than ten thousand adherents of the non-Buddhist sects, the great majority professing devotion to Shiva."[5] Popular devotion to Buddhism was fading, and by the thirteenth century it would vanish altogether.

New Economic and Social Trends

The land grant system and the temple-centered economy it spawned stimulated the expansion of agriculture and village settlement into frontier areas. New irrigation and fertilization techniques also promoted the growth of the agricultural economy. The encroaching agrarian states with their caste-based social order incorporated many tribal groups in the forests and hills. An inscription dated 861 celebrated the conquest of a frontier area in western India by a king of the Pratihara dynasty, boasting that he had made the land "fragrant with the leaves of blue lotuses and pleasant with groves of mango and *madhuka*-fruit trees, and covered it with leaves of excellent sugarcane."[6]

The prominence of the temple-centered economy in these centuries also reflected the decline of towns and trade. Xuanzang sadly observed that people had abandoned many of the great cities in which Buddhism had thrived in the past. Archaeological research confirms

The Many Faces of Shiva

Hindus worship the god Shiva in many forms, as both a creator and a destroyer. The faces on this sculpture—which include a bust of Shiva's consort Parvati, the embodiment of feminine composure and wifely devotion—portray Shiva as both a fierce exterminator and a serene ascetic. The four faces encircle a *linga*, an erect phallus symbolizing Shiva's powers of fertility and procreation. (Erich Lessing/Art Resource, NY.)

the decline of urban centers in the Ganges Valley between the seventh and tenth centuries. Circulation of coins ceased in many areas. The proliferation of land grants attests to the growing importance of wealth in the form of landed property and goods rather than money.

As local agricultural economies became more important, international trade declined. Arab seafarers frequented the western coast of the peninsula to obtain spices, pepper, gems, and teak in exchange for horses, but India was largely severed from the lucrative Central Asian caravan trade now in the hands of hostile Turkic and Muslim neighbors. Itinerant traders and local merchants remained active, however, supplying agricultural produce, ghee (clarified butter), betel leaves (a popular stimulant), and cotton cloth to ordinary villagers and procuring ritual necessities and luxury goods for temples and royal courts.

As Brahman religion and social norms became more deeply entrenched in village society and the frontier tribal regions, the structure of caste society underwent profound changes. Many of the upstart regional dynasties came from obscure origins. Although these ruling families strove to invent a noble ancestry in the *Kshatriya* (warrior) caste, status in court society depended more on personal relations and royal favor than caste standing.

The rigid formal hierarchy of the four major caste groups—Brahmans (priests), Kshatriyas (warriors), Vaishyas (merchants and farmers), and Shudras (servile peoples)—could not contain the growing complexity of Indian society, especially with the inclusion of pastoral nomads and forest-dwelling tribes. Social status based on occupation—known as *jati*—often superseded ancestral birth, at least on the lower rungs of the caste hierarchy. Jatis developed their own cultural identities, which were expressed in customs, marriage rules, food taboos, and religious practices. Merchant and artisan jati groups acquired an institutional identity as professional guilds. Leaders of wealthy jatis sometimes became temple wardens and persons of distinction in local society.

Yet the status of merchants and artisans often varied from place to place. In some localities, certain craftsmen jati—for example, butchers, shoemakers, and cloth fullers—were required to live outside the town walls, like Untouchables and other social groups deemed ritually unclean. Blacksmiths and carpenters formed special organizations in an effort to raise their social standing. The court also granted special privileges to groups of artisans who worked for it, such as copperplate engravers, weavers in the employ of the royal family, and masons building royal temples and palaces.

The rights and privileges of women, like those of men, differed according to caste and local custom. As in most cultures, writers and artists often idealized women, but they did so in terms that distinguished feminine from masculine qualities. Whereas the ideal man was described in strongly positive language—emphasizing, for example, ambition, energy, mastery of knowledge and spiritual paths, and skill in poetry and conversation—female virtues were often conveyed through negative constructions, such as absence of jealousy, greed, arrogance, frivolity, and anger. These characterizations reflect prevailing notions of women's weaknesses.

Women were encouraged to marry young and remain devoted to their husbands throughout their lives. The earliest reference to the practice of *sati*, in which a widow commits suicide following the death of her husband, dates from the sixth century. Yet only women of the Kshatriya caste were expected to perform sati, primarily when the husband had died heroically in battle. But the fate of a widow in this patriarchal society was often grim. Unable to inherit her husband's property or to remarry, a widow depended on her husband's family for support. However, women who chose not to marry, such as nuns and devadasis, were accepted as normal members of society.

Court Society and Culture

The gradual unraveling of the Gupta Empire left a multitude of local kings. Each claimed exalted ancestry and strove to shore up his social base by awarding land grants. In this political world—referred to as the "circle of kings" in the *Arthashastra* ("The Science of Material Gain"), a renowned treatise on statecraft—each ruler pursued his advantage through complex maneuvers over war and diplomacy involving numerous enemies and

Decline of Towns and Trade

Upheaval in the Caste System

Women's Status

Post-Gupta "Circle of Kings"

jati In India, a caste status based primarily on occupation.

The Lure of Court Life

The sumptuous splendor of Indian court life drew sharp criticism from Buddhist and Jain ascetics. At the left of this mural, created in around 500 to represent a Buddhist legend, King Mahajanaka, wearing a crown and garlanded with pearls, sits in a stately palace. His wife and palace ladies fail to persuade him to continue his life of ease and luxury, however—at the right the king rides away from the palace, having renounced worldly pleasures. (Frédéric Soltan/Corbis.)

allies. Kings achieved political dominance by gaining fealty and tribute, not by annexing territory, as was usual in China, for example. The consequence was that connections between rulers were of paramount importance.

Given the treachery and uncertainty of the "circle of kings," rulers eagerly sought divine blessings through lavish patronage of temples and their gods. They portrayed themselves as devoted servants of the supreme gods Shiva and Vishnu, and they demanded similar reverence and subservience from their courtiers and subjects. The rituals of the royal court gave monarchs an opportunity to display their majesty and affirm their authority over lesser lords. As we also see in Europe and the Islamic world at this time, royal courts became the main arenas of political intercourse, social advancement, and cultural accomplishment.

Attendance at court and participation in its elaborate ceremonial and cultural life was crucial to establishing membership in the ruling class. Marrying a daughter to a powerful king was the surest means of securing a family's social and political eminence. Important kings had numerous wives, each with her own residence and retinue. Relations within royal households were governed by the same strategies of alliance, rivalry, and intrigue that characterized the political realm of the "circle of kings." In both cases, personal connections played a central role in the distribution and exercise of power.

Kama Sutra

The lifestyle of the courtly elite was exemplified in the *Kama Sutra* ("The Art of Pleasure"), composed during the Gupta period. Most famous for its frank celebration of sexual love, the *Kama Sutra* was intended as a guidebook to educate affluent men in the rules of upper-class social life. It is addressed to a "man about town" who has received an education, obtained a steady source of wealth (whether from land, trade, or inheritance), established a family, and settled in a city populated by other men of good birth and breeding. The book enumerates sixty-four "fine arts" that a cultivated man should master, from dancing and swordsmanship to skill in conversation and poetry. The *Kama Sutra* also dwells on the protocols of courtship and erotic love, although only one of its seven books is devoted to sexual techniques. Above all, the *Kama Sutra* exalts mastery of the self: only through discipline of the mind and senses can a man properly enjoy wealth and pleasure while avoiding the pitfalls of excess and indulgence.

The *Kama Sutra* describes an urbane lifestyle that imitated the worldly sophistication and conspicuous consumption of the king and his court. It dismisses rural society, in contrast, as boorish and stultifying. Village life dulls one's sensibilities and coarsens manners and speech. Village youths, complained a contemporary poet, "cannot grasp facial expressions, nor do they have the intelligence to understand subtle meanings of puns and innuendos."[7] Despite such assertions that a vast cultural gulf separated the court from the countryside, courtly culture and its values permeated the entire ruling class, including local lords and Brahman landowners.

The post-Gupta era witnessed steady cultural integration throughout the Indian subcontinent, even in the absence of political unity. Non-Brahman religions and social values were increasingly marginalized, and by the tenth century Hindu religious culture, as well as the norms of caste society, prevailed in almost all regions.

Cultural Integration

The Diffusion of Indian Traditions to Southeast Asia

Indian culture and religions spread to Southeast Asia before the emergence of indigenous states or literary and philosophical traditions, in a process resembling how China influenced its East Asian neighbors. Thus Indian traditions had a powerful effect on the development of Southeast Asian ideas about kingship and social order and provided a new vocabulary to express cultural and ethical values.

FOCUS

What aspects of Indian religions had the greatest influence on the societies and cultures of Southeast Asia?

Southeast Asian religious beliefs and practices integrated aspects of two Indian religions, Hinduism and Buddhism. As in East Asia, Mahayana Buddhist teachings were readily adapted to local cultures. Hinduism, with its roots in Indian social institutions, especially the caste system, proved less adaptable. Yet some elements of Hinduism, such as bhakti devotional cults and the worship of Shiva, also flourished in Southeast Asia. Given the Brahman priesthood's prominent role in Southeast Asia—despite the absence there of caste societies—it would be more appropriate to refer to this tradition as **Brahmanism** than as Hinduism. Across the mainland and islands of Southeast Asia, aspects of both Buddhism and Brahmanism would intermingle in novel ways, fusing with ancient local traditions to produce distinctive religious cultures (see Map 10.4).

Commerce and Religious Change in Southeast Asia

The spread of Indian religions and cultural traditions to Southeast Asia occurred gradually beginning in the early centuries C.E. Indian influence did not result from conquest or large-scale migration and colonization. Rather, it was carried by Indian merchants and missionaries following the maritime routes from the Bay of Bengal to the South China Sea. Buddhist missionaries were crossing the Southeast Asian seas to China by the second and third centuries C.E. Brahmans, in contrast, lacked the evangelical zeal of Buddhist monks, and Indian law prohibited Brahmans from traveling abroad for fear of jeopardizing their purity of body and spirit. Brahmanism was disseminated to Southeast Asia, therefore, largely via Indian merchant colonies, and also by Southeast Asian natives who traveled to India for study and training and returned as converts.

Historians find evidence for the diffusion of Brahmanism to Southeast Asia in Funan, the first identifiable state in the region, and in Java during the early centuries C.E. The Funan state, based in the lower Mekong River Valley (in present-day Vietnam and Cambodia), flourished during the first to fourth centuries C.E. as the principal trading center between India and China. Contemporary Chinese observers noted that Indian beliefs and practices were prevalent in Funan, as was the use of Indic script in writing. Local lore even attributed the ancestry of the Funan rulers to the marriage of a local princess with an Indian Brahman.

Brahmanism also flourished in central Java, as attested by the presence of Brahman monastic communities and the adoption of many Indian gods into local religion. The

Brahmanism in Funan and Java

Brahmanism The distinctive Hindu religious tradition of Southeast Asia, in which the Brahman priesthood remained dominant despite the absence of a caste system.

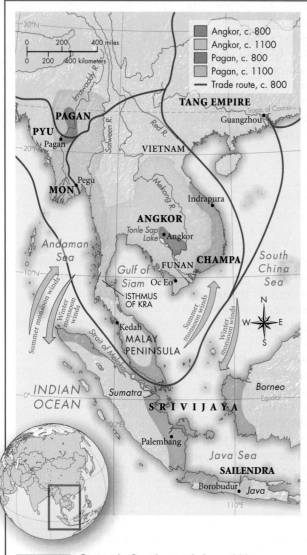

MAP 10.4   **States in Southeast Asia, c. 800**

Many Southeast Asian states, such as Angkor in the lower Mekong River Valley and the Sailendra dynasty in Java, were based in fertile agricultural regions. But the Champa and Srivijaya confederations ruled the seas and derived their power from the profits of trade. During its heyday from the seventh to the twelfth centuries, Srivijaya dominated the maritime trade routes linking China with India and the Islamic world.

Brahmanism in Champa

Brahmanism and Buddhism in Angkor

earliest inscriptions in Old Javanese, dating from the late fourth to early fifth centuries, refer to gifts of cattle and gold to Brahman priests and to royal ceremonies apparently derived from Indian precedents.

As in India, local rulers in Southeast Asia appropriated Hindu religious ideas and motifs that meshed with their own worldviews and grafted them onto ancient local traditions. In Champa (along Vietnam's central coast), the cult of Shiva, centered on the worship of stone phalli, resembled older fertility rituals in which people presented offerings to rough stone icons of local gods. In Java, the high gods of Hinduism came to be identified with the island's fearsome volcanoes, which the inhabitants regarded as the homes of the gods. Mountain symbolism is also striking in the architecture of the Buddhist monument of Borobudur (booh-roe-boe-DOOR) in central Java, and in the temple complexes of Angkor in Cambodia (see Seeing the Past: Borobudur: The World's Largest Buddhist Monument, page 331).

Religion and the Constitution of State Power

From the beginning, Southeast Asia's borrowing of religious ideas from India was closely linked to the ambitions of Southeast Asian rulers. Indian traditions that related kingship to all-powerful gods had obvious appeal to local chieftains seeking to augment their authority and power. Both Buddhism and Brahmanism provided models for divine blessing of royal authority. In the Buddhist tradition, the universal monarch, the chakravartin, achieved supremacy through lavish acts of piety and devotion. In the Brahmanical tradition, by contrast, the king partook of divine power by identifying with the high gods, above all Shiva, and received worship from his subjects much as the gods did. This association of the king with the gods sanctified the king's role as ruler and protector of his people. Although the gods might lend aid to the king, ultimately it was the king's personal charisma that endowed him with sovereign power.

The earliest appearance of the worship of Shiva in Southeast Asia is found in Champa, where a loose confederation of local rulers shared power under a weak royal overlord (see again Map 10.4). One Champa king instituted a Shiva cult at the royal shrine at Mi-son, the ritual center of the Champa confederation, in the fourth century. Yet the Champa chiefdoms never coalesced into a centralized state, perhaps because the small coastal plains yielded only meager agricultural surpluses. The Champa chieftains instead relied on piracy and plunder to obtain wealth. Thus Indian political and religious ideas alone were not enough to create a powerful king. Without the resources to pay soldiers and officials and reward allies, kings could never be powerful enough to dominate their wealthiest subjects.

However, where ample resources were combined with a compelling political ideology, powerful kings did emerge. For example, worship of Shiva aided consolidation of state power in the broad plains around the Tonle Sap Lake in the lower Mekong River Valley. The founder of the Angkor kingdom, Jayavarman (JUH-yuh-vahr-mon) II, was pro-

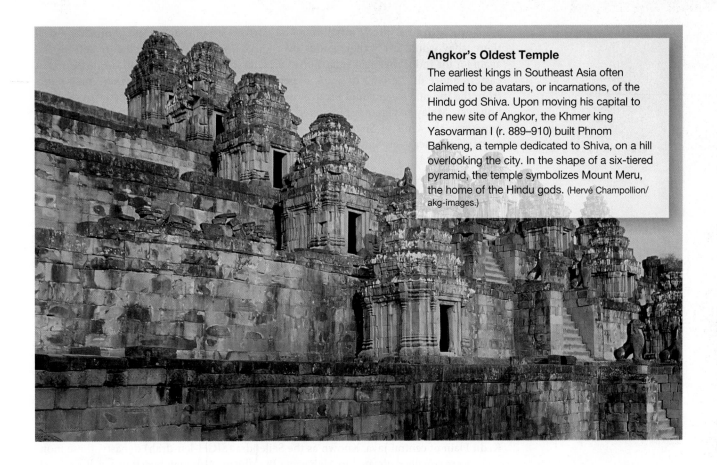

Angkor's Oldest Temple
The earliest kings in Southeast Asia often claimed to be avatars, or incarnations, of the Hindu god Shiva. Upon moving his capital to the new site of Angkor, the Khmer king Yasovarman I (r. 889–910) built Phnom Bahkeng, a temple dedicated to Shiva, on a hill overlooking the city. In the shape of a six-tiered pyramid, the temple symbolizes Mount Meru, the home of the Hindu gods. (Hervé Champollion/akg-images.)

claimed universal monarch by his Brahman advisers in 802; he consolidated his dominion over the region's local lords by combining devotion to Shiva with homage to himself as deva-raja (divine lord).

During the early phase of the Angkor state, kings delegated control over the land and its inhabitants to officials assigned to temples established throughout the realm by royal charter. The Brahman priesthood managed the administrative affairs as well as the ritual ceremonies of these temples. Not until a century later did one of Jayavarman's successors, Yasovarman (YAH-suh-vahr-mon) I (r. 889–c. 910), consolidate royal authority by establishing his capital at Angkor and building the first of its numerous temple complexes. The many temples he founded at Angkor and elsewhere were dedicated primarily to Shiva, Vishnu, and Buddha. Depending on individual inclinations, later Angkor kings sometimes favored worship of Vishnu—the chief deity at Angkor's most famous temple complex, Angkor Wat—or patronage of Mahayana Buddhism, and their temple-building projects reflected these personal religious allegiances.

Apart from Brahmanism, Mahayana Buddhism was the other Indian religious tradition that initially attracted devotion and patronage in Southeast Asia. Chinese pilgrims in the seventh century described the Pyu and Mon city-states of lower Burma, which had ready access by sea to the great Mahayana monasteries in Bengal, as "Buddhist kingdoms." Burmese ambassadors to the Tang court in the ninth century reported that all children were required to spend some time as novices in Buddhist monasteries. Mahayana Buddhism was also enthusiastically welcomed by Malay chiefs in Sumatra, who had begun to capitalize on a major reorientation of maritime trade routes that occurred between the fourth and sixth centuries.

Previously, merchants had avoided the monsoon winds that dictated the rhythms of seafaring in the Southeast Asian seas. Instead of sailing around the Malay peninsula,

**Mahayana Buddhism
in Burma and Sumatra**

Maritime Trade

ships would land at the Kra Isthmus, the narrowest point along the peninsula. From there, they would carry their goods overland to the Gulf of Siam before setting sail again for the Indochina peninsula. Funan used its strategic location on the more protected eastern shore of the Gulf of Siam to become the major crossroads where merchants from the Indian Ocean could meet those from China. Beginning in the fourth century, however, Malay navigators pioneered an all-sea route through the Straits of Melaka, bypassing the Gulf of Siam altogether. Funan's prosperity abruptly ended, and the ports of southeastern Sumatra replaced Funan as the linchpin of maritime trade (see again Map 10.4).

Trade routes shifted in part because of the growing importance of Southeast Asian products in international trade. Earlier, trade between India and China consisted largely of exchanging Chinese silk for products from western Asia (frankincense, myrrh, and other substances used to make perfume and incense). Gradually, cheaper local substitutes, such as Sumatran camphor and sandalwood from Timor, began to enter this trade, and by the seventh century both Arab and Chinese merchants had become avid buyers of Sumatran pepper and the fine spices (cloves, nutmeg, and mace) from the Molucca Islands far to the east. The Sumatran ports were ideally situated to capture this trade.

The Buddhist Kingdoms of Srivijaya and Sailendra

In the late seventh century, the ruler of the Sumatran port of Palembang founded the first of a series of kingdoms known collectively as Srivijaya (sree-vih-JUH-yuh). Our first image of a ruler of Srivijaya comes from an inscription of 683, which tells how the king celebrated his conquest of a rival city-state and gravely admonished his vanquished foe to accept Buddhism. The rulers of Srivijaya became great patrons of Mahayana Buddhism. The large international community of monks that gathered at Palembang included novices from China seeking instruction from Indian monks.

The rise of Srivijaya was soon followed by the emergence of a lineage of kings in the Kedu Plain of central Java. Known as the Sailendra (SIGH-len-drah) dynasty, these monarchs were equally dedicated to Mahayana Buddhism. Although boasting a rich rice agriculture, the Kedu Plain was isolated from the coast by a ring of mountains, and thus did not have direct access to the maritime commercial world. Nonetheless, in the mid-eighth century the Sailendra kings achieved dominance over the Kedu Plain by borrowing heavily from Indian religious and political traditions, probably through the cordial relations they cultivated with Srivijaya.

The Sailendra kings used Sanskrit sacred texts and administrative language to construct a network of religious and political allegiances under their leadership. They also founded many Buddhist shrines, which attracted monks from as far away as Bengal and Gujarat. The massive monument of Borobudur in central Java testifies to the Sailendra kings' deep faith in Mahayana Buddhism (see Seeing the Past: Borobudur: The World's Largest Buddhist Monument).

Allied to Srivijaya by their common faith and intermarriage between the royal families, the Sailendra dynasty flourished from 750 to 850. In around 850, however, the Sailendra were suddenly expelled from Java by an upstart rival devoted to Shiva. The royal house fled to Sumatra, where they joined their Srivijaya kin. Bereft of Sailendra patronage, the Buddhist monasteries in Java plunged into irreversible decline. Henceforth, Brahmanism predominated in Java until a wave of conversions to Islam began in the fifteenth century.

Indian Religions in Southeast Asia: A Summing-up

Indian religions were assimilated in Southeast Asia as the existing cultural and social frameworks adapted foreign ideas. The potent ideologies of the Sanskrit literary heritage and the organizational skills of Buddhist and Brahman holy men stimulated the formation of states based on divinely sanctioned royal authority. Both the Brahmanical and Buddhist traditions contributed to the rise of monarchies in the maritime realm, in the rice-growing plains of the great river valleys, and in central Java. The Angkor kingdom

Borobudur: The World's Largest Buddhist Monument

The Monument at Borobudur (Luca Tettoni/Corbis.)

The Sailendra kings never built palaces or cities for themselves. Instead they devoted their wealth and resources to building vast monuments displaying their devotion to the Buddhist faith. The massive stone edifice they erected at Borobudur in central Java rises from a fertile plain ringed by imposing volcanoes. Construction of Borobudur began in around 760 and took seventy years to complete.

The exact purpose of the Borobudur monument, which was neither a temple nor a monastery, continues to provoke scholarly debate. Borobudur consists of ten concentric terraces of decreasing size crowned by a bell-shaped stupa, a Buddhist shrine used as a repository for relics or other sacred objects. The terraces are adorned with carved reliefs depicting many episodes from the basic scriptures of Mahayana Buddhism and with more than five hundred statues of Buddhas. The carved reliefs provide a virtual

encyclopedia of Mahayana teachings. But they also include many scenes from court life, which spoke more directly of the royal majesty of the Sailendras. Some scholars have suggested that the mountainlike edifice celebrated the Sailendras' exalted stature as "Lords of the Mountains" and marked the dynasty's original home.

By visiting Borobudur, the Buddhist faithful could pass physically and spiritually through the ten stages of devotion necessary to attain enlightenment. Entering from the eastern staircase, they would proceed slowly around each terrace, studying and absorbing the lessons told by the carved reliefs before passing to the next level. To see all the reliefs one must walk around the monument ten times, a distance of three miles. Reliefs at the lower levels retell well-known stories from the life of the Buddha and other holy figures. The higher levels are devoted to the pilgrim Sudhana, who visited 110 teachers in his quest for enlightenment. On the upper levels the narrow galleries of the lower levels give way to three round open terraces surmounted by numerous latticelike stupas enclosing life-size statues of Buddhas. The devotee's ascent of the monument symbolized a spiritual progress from the world of illusion to the realm of enlightenment.

Source: John Miksic, *Borobudur: Golden Tales of the Buddhas* (Hong Kong: Periplus, 1990).

EXAMINING THE EVIDENCE

1. How can we see the architectural design of Borobudur as a physical representation of the world, which in Buddhist cosmology is depicted as a series of circular oceans and continents surrounding a sacred mountain at the center?

2. In what ways does the monument reflect Buddhism's renunciation of worldly life?

represents the most striking case of simultaneous patronage of both Brahmanism and Mahayana Buddhism, but to a lesser degree this eclectic adoption of Indian religions occurred throughout Southeast Asia.

Royal temples and monuments became focal points for amassing wealth in service to the gods, while also serving as testaments to the kings' piety. Local temples likewise accumulated landholdings and stores of treasure, serving as both the economic and the ceremonial hubs of community life. In contrast to Islam, which exercised a powerful centralizing pull and created a common brotherhood of faith across national, ethnic, and cultural boundaries, Indian religions in Southeast Asia—as in India itself—spawned a diverse array of regional religious cultures.

COUNTERPOINT
Sogdian Traders in Central Asia and China

FOCUS

How did the social and economic institutions of the Sogdian merchant network differ from those of the nomadic confederations and the agrarian empires?

The heyday of the overland caravan routes of Central Asia—the Silk Road—was between the fifth and the eighth centuries. Chinese and Persian emperors, nomad chieftains, and kings of oasis city-states all struggled to capture a share of the lucrative Silk Road trade. Yet the great length of the trade routes and the harsh deserts and mountains through which they passed made it impossible for any single political power to dominate the Silk Road. Instead, rulers great and small had to cultivate close ties with those who, in the words of a Moroccan spice merchant turned Christian monk, "to procure silk for the miserable gains of commerce, hesitate not to travel to the uttermost ends of the earth."[8] The Sogdian merchants who linked the steppe lands of the nomads with Asia's great agrarian empires did so through economic enterprise rather than military might or political power.

A Robust Commercial Economy

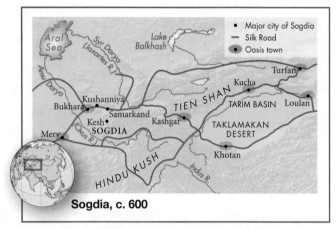
Sogdia, c. 600

Sogdia (SUGG-dee-yah) (now divided between Uzbekistan and Tajikistan) was a fertile agricultural region surrounded by the grassland habitat of the central Eurasian nomads. Persian in language and religion, Sogdian culture was also enriched by contact with the Indian and Greek worlds. Alexander the Great conquered the region in the fourth century B.C.E.

Sogdia's commercial economy began to develop slowly beginning in the first century C.E. Sogdian merchants achieved success by leaving their homeland and traveling to distant regions, especially eastward to China. The dispersion of Sogdian merchants took the form of a **trade diaspora** (*diaspora* was the Greek word for scattering grain), a network of merchant settlements spread throughout foreign lands. These communities remained united by their common origins, religion, and language, as well as by family ties and business partnerships (see Reading the Past: Letters from a Sogdian Castaway).

Nomad incursions in the fifth and sixth centuries ruined many cities in Central Asia, as the Chinese pilgrim Xuanzang observed. Sogdia's city-states were largely spared this devastation and began to enjoy unprecedented prosperity. Agriculture and trade supported ambitious building projects, including an extensive system of irrigation canals and long walls to fend off both nomad attacks and encroaching desert sands.

Sogdian-Turkic Alliance

The creation of the Turkic nomad empire in the mid-sixth century catapulted Sogdian merchants to dominance over the Silk Road trade. Sogdian merchants forged an alliance with the Turks and entered the administration, army, and diplomatic service of the Turkic khan. When the Sasanid king rebuffed the Turkic khan's offer of trade, a Byzantine historian tells us, it was "Maniakh, the leader of the Sogdians" who advised the khan "that it would be better for the Turks to cultivate the friendship of the Romans [i.e., the Byzantines] and send their raw silk for sale to them, because they made more use of it than other people."[9]

Prominent Sogdians intermarried with the Turks, and the Turks adopted the written language of the Sogdians. Under the umbrella of Turkic military power, Sogdian merchant colonies sprouted in Mongolia and on the frontiers of China, and they spread westward as far as the Black Sea. Sales contracts found at Turfan, the principal hub of the Silk Road,

trade diaspora A network of merchants from the same city or country who live permanently in foreign lands and cooperate with one another to pursue trading opportunities.

Letters from a Sogdian Castaway

In 1907, while surveying the ruins of a guardhouse near Dunhuang, the westernmost outpost of the Tang Empire, the British explorer Aurel Stein found a post bag that had been lost in transit. The letters, written in Sogdian and dating from the early fourth century, perhaps had been confiscated by Chinese border officials. Among the contents were two letters written by Miwnay, a Sogdian woman living in Dunhuang—one to her husband, a traveling merchant, and the other to her mother in Loulan, a desert town hundreds of miles farther west.

In the letter to her husband, Nanai-dhat, Miwnay complains that it had been three years since he abandoned her and her daughter in Dunhuang. She implores him to return. Miwnay had appealed to Artivan, a relative of her husband, and Farnkhund, apparently one of his business associates, as well as the leaders of the Sogdian community at Dunhuang, but they refused her requests for help. Here Miwnay describes her plight to her mother:

> I am very anxious to see you, but have no luck. I petitioned the councilor Sagharak, but the councilor says, "Here there is no other relative closer to [my husband] than Artivan." And I petitioned Artivan, but he says: "Farnkhund is . . . [missing text], and I refuse to hurry, . . ." And Farnkhund says, "If [Artivan] does not consent that you should go back to your mother, how should I take you? Wait until . . . comes; perhaps Nanai-dhat will come." I live wretchedly, without clothing, without money. I ask for a loan, but no one consents to give me one, so I depend on charity from the priest. He

said to me, "If you go, I will give you a camel, and a man should go with you, and on the way I will look after you well." May he do so for me until you send me a letter!

In a postscript to the letter to the husband, Miwnay's daughter adds that Farnkhund had run away and the Chinese authorities were holding her mother and herself liable for Farnkhund's debts. Miwnay's closing words convey her bitterness toward her husband:

> I obeyed your command and came to Dunhuang. I did not observe my mother's bidding, nor that of my brothers. Surely the gods were angry with me on the day when I did your bidding! I would rather be wife to a dog or pig than to you!

Source: Nicholas Sims-Williams, "Towards a New Edition of the Sogdian Ancient Letters: Ancient Letter 1," in Étienne de la Vaissière and Eric Trombert, eds., *Les Sogdiens en Chine* (Paris: École française d'Extrême Orient, 2005), 185–187.

EXAMINING THE EVIDENCE

1. What does Miwnay's predicament tell us about the status of women in Sogdian society?

2. What do these letters reveal about the role of the family in the organization of the Sogdian merchant network?

show Sogdian merchants buying and selling silk, silver, gold, perfume, saffron, brass, medicines, and cane sugar. Horses ranked first among the goods they brought to China, while slaves, Siberian furs, and gems and spices from India filled the markets of Samarkand and other Sogdian cities.

The dominance of Sogdians over Silk Road commerce fed stereotypes about their immense wealth and shallow morals. Xuanzang, who passed through Samarkand in 630, pronounced the Sogdians "greedy and deceitful," snidely observing that "fathers and sons scheme for profit, because everyone, noble and commoner alike, regards wealth as the measure of distinction."[10] At the same time, Sogdian merchants living in Chinese cities occupied a prominent place in the cosmopolitan cultural world of Tang China. The popularity of Persian fashions, music, dance, and sports such as polo at the Tang court can be attributed to the influence of Sogdians who settled in Chang'an. Sogdian merchants' homes, as well as temples dedicated to Persian religions, clustered around the Tang capital's Western Market, the gateway to the Silk Road.

Sogdian Communities in Central Asia and China

The Sogdian émigré communities in Central Asia and China drew strength from their strong communal bonds, but as the generations passed, many Sogdians in China began to assimilate to the cosmopolitan Chinese culture. The Sogdian silk merchant He Tuo, who settled in China in the mid-sixth century, joined the entourage of a Chinese prince and amassed a great fortune. His eldest son and nephew became experts at cutting gemstones, and the Sui emperor Yang Jian placed the nephew in charge of the imperial jewelry workshop. The He family is credited with introducing the techniques of glassmaking to China. Another of He Tuo's sons had a brilliant career as a Confucian scholar in service to the Sui court. The Tang emperors also frequently employed Sogdians in important civil and military offices, most notoriously the general An Lushan, whose rebellion nearly brought down the Tang dynasty.

Breakdown of the Trade Network

Muslim Takeover of Sogdia

The Muslim conquest of Sogdia in the early eighth century marked the beginning of the end of Sogdian prosperity. When Samarkand surrendered to an Islamic army in 712, the city's population was forced to pay an indemnity of two million silver coins and three thousand slaves and agreed to submit annual tribute of two hundred thousand silver coins. Unlike many of their neighbors, however, the Sogdians stubbornly resisted both their new Arab overlords and Islamic religion. As a result Sogdia remained isolated from the commercial and cultural worlds of the Islamic empire.

Impact of An Lushan Rebellion

The An Lushan rebellion of 755–763 dealt another major blow to the Sogdian trade network. It severely damaged the Chinese economy, and after the rebels were defeated many Sogdians in China disguised their ancestry and abandoned their culture out of fear of persecution.

Rise of Asian Maritime Trade

Finally, with the rise of maritime trade routes connecting the Islamic world and China, overland traffic across the Silk Road dropped off steeply. By the late tenth century, the Sogdian language and culture were on the verge of extinction in Sogdia itself, and the scattered Sogdian communities had blended into the foreign societies they inhabited. Samarkand, however, would enjoy a brilliant revival in the fourteenth century under the Turkic emperor Timur, when the city was reborn as an Islamic metropolis (see Chapter 15).

Conclusion

Commercial and cultural exchanges across the Silk Road during the first millennium C.E. linked the distant agrarian empires of China, India, and Iran. The interactions that resulted transformed the peoples and cultures along the Central Asian trade routes. Nomad chieftains, for example, developed the political acumen to knit together tribal confederations and pursue profits through trade, plunder, and conquest. The Tuoba, the Turks, and the Khazars all transcended their original predatory purposes by creating empires that spanned both the pastoral nomadic and the settled agrarian worlds. In each case, however, these empires failed to create political institutions that might have perpetuated their dominion over settled societies. The Sogdian merchant communities forged very different commercial and cultural linkages across Asia, but these networks, too, proved vulnerable to shifts in political fortunes and trade patterns.

The movement across the Silk Road of goods and of people such as the Buddhist pilgrim Xuanzang fostered unprecedented cosmopolitan cultural intercourse throughout Asia. The complex intermingling of peoples, cultures, and religious faiths peaked with the rise of the Sui and Tang empires in China. The spread of Buddhism to China and from there to Korea, Japan, and Vietnam provided the foundation for a common East Asian culture. The political dominance of the Chinese empires also spread China's written language, literary heritage, and social values among its neighbors. Correspondingly, the demise of Tang power after the An Lushan rebellion in the mid-eighth century undermined China's cultural dominance. Subsequently a new order of independent states emerged in East Asia that has persisted down to the present.

In India, too, a cosmopolitan culture and a more homogeneous ruling class formed during the first millennium c.e., despite the absence of political unity. This elite culture was based on Gupta political institutions and Hindu religious beliefs and social values expressed through the new lingua franca, or common language, of Sanskrit. Some scholars have dubbed it "the Sanskrit cosmopolis." The royal lineages and noble classes that founded the first states in Southeast Asia during this period participated fully in creating this cosmopolitan culture. Yet by the tenth century, as in East Asia, the common elite culture encompassing South and Southeast Asia had begun to fragment into more distinctive regional and national traditions.

Between the fifth and tenth centuries, regional cultures in East and South Asia were formed by the movement of people and goods across trade routes, the mixture of religious and political ideas, and the spread of common forms of livelihood. The same forces were also at work in the formation of regional societies in the very different worlds of the Americas and the Pacific Ocean, as we will see in the next chapter.

NOTES

1. Translated from Xuanzang, *Record of the Western Regions.*
2. Ibid., Book 5.
3. Translated from *The Chronicles of Japan*, Chapter 19.
4. Translated from Xuanzang, *Western Regions*, Book 2.
5. Ibid., Book 7.
6. Translated in Munshi Debiprasad, "Ghatayala Inscription of the Pratihara Kakkuka of [Vikrama-]Samvat 918," *Journal of the Royal Asiatic Society* (1895): 519–520.
7. Quoted in Daud Ali, *Courtly Culture and Political Life in Early Medieval India* (Cambridge, U.K.: Cambridge University Press, 2004), 197.
8. Cosmas Indicopleustes, *Christian Topography* (c. 547–550) (London: Hakluyt Society, 1897), Book II, 47.
9. R. C. Blockley, *The History of Menander the Guardsman* (Liverpool, U.K.: Cairns, 1985), 115.
10. Translated from Xuanzang, *Western Regions*, Book 1.

RESOURCES FOR RESEARCH

Steppe Peoples and Settled Societies of Central Asia

The centrality of Central Asia to world history has been analyzed from a variety of perspectives. Bentley focuses on the spread of world religions, Beckwith on political interactions and the formation of empires, and Christian on the movements of peoples and social transformations. Liu offers a lively discussion of cultural life across the Silk Road.

Barfield, Thomas. *The Perilous Frontier: The Nomadic Empires and China.* 1989.

Beckwith, Christopher I. *Empires of the Silk Road: A History of Central Eurasia from the Bronze Age to the Present.* 2009.

Bentley, Jerry H. *Old World Encounters: Cross-Cultural Contacts and Exchanges in Pre-Modern Times.* 1993.

Christian, David. *A History of Russia, Central Asia, and Mongolia.* Vol. 1, *Inner Eurasia from Prehistory to the Mongol Empire.* 1998.

Liu, Xinru, *The Silk Road in World History.* 2010.

The Shaping of East Asia

Although he overstates the degree of Chinese influence, Holcombe provides a succinct digest of the formation of a shared East Asian civilization. Adshead likewise exaggerates China's cultural dominance, but his detailed comparison of Chinese, Islamic, Indian, and both Latin and Byzantine Christian civilizations contains many important insights. Farris and Pai offer sure-handed guidance through the thorny debates over foreign influence and cultural identity that have dominated the study of the emergence of the Japanese and Korean states, respectively.

Adshead, S. A. M. *T'ang China: The Rise of the East in World History.* 2004.

Benn, Charles. *Daily Life in Traditional China: The Tang Dynasty.* 2002.

Farris, William Wayne. *Sacred Texts and Buried Treasures: Issues in the Historical Archaeology of Ancient Japan.* 1998.

Holcombe, Charles. *The Genesis of East Asia, 221 B.C.–A.D. 907.* 2001.

Pai, Hyung-Il. *Constructing "Korean" Origins: A Critical Review of Archaeology, Historiography, and Racial Myth in Korean State-Formation Theories.* 2000.

A Visual Sourcebook of Chinese Civilization. http://depts .washington.edu/chinaciv/.

The Consolidation of Hindu Society in India

In contrast to earlier studies that defined post-Gupta India in terms of political and economic regression, recent work argues that the Indian economy and society continued to be vital despite political fragmentation. Thapar's encyclopedic yet accessible survey caps a distinguished career as the most important interpreter of India's early history. Ali's illuminating investigation of court society reconceptualizes the nature of kingship in Indian culture.

Ali, Daud. *Courtly Culture and Political Life in Early Medieval India.* 2004.

Basham, A. L. *The Origins and Development of Classical Hinduism.* 1989.

Champakalakshmi, R. *Trade, Ideology, and Urbanization: South India, 300 B.C. to A.D. 1300.* 1996.

Chattopadhyaya, Bradjadulal. *The Making of Early Medieval India.* 1994.

Thapar, Romila. *Early India: From the Origins to A.D. 1300.* 2002.

The Diffusion of Indian Traditions to Southeast Asia

Hall provides a comprehensive introduction to the impact of maritime trade on the political, economic, and religious transformations of the region during this formative era. Wolters's collection of essays examines conceptual approaches for the study of this highly diverse region. Higham, an archaeologist, admirably synthesizes current scholarship on Angkor.

Hall, Kenneth R. *A History of Early Southeast Asia: Maritime Trade and Societal Development, 100–1500.* 2011.

Higham, Charles. *The Civilization of Angkor.* 2002.

Shaffer, Lynda. *Maritime Southeast Asia to 1500.* 1996.

Tarling, Nicholas, ed. *Cambridge History of Southeast Asia.* Vol. 1, Part 1. 1992.

Wolters, O. W. *History, Culture, and Region in Southeast Asian Perspectives.* 1999.

COUNTERPOINT: Sogdian Traders in Central Asia and China

Little scholarship on Sogdia and its merchants is available in English, but the translation of de la Vaissière's landmark study helps to remedy this omission. Schafer catalogues the impact of the rich material culture of Central Asia on Tang culture and literature.

Schafer, Edward. *The Golden Peaches of Samarkand: A Study in T'ang Exotics.* 1963.

de la Vaissière, Étienne. *Sogdian Traders: A History.* 2005.

▶ **For additional primary sources from this period**, see *Sources of Crossroads and Cultures*.

▶ **For Web sites, images, and documents related to topics in this chapter**, see Make History at bedfordstmartins.com/smith.

The major global development in this chapter ▶ The cultural and commercial exchanges during the heyday of the Silk Road that transformed Asian peoples, cultures, and states.

IMPORTANT EVENTS

386–534	Northern Wei dynasty in north China and Mongolia
552–603	First Turkish empire
581–618	Sui dynasty in China
604	Prince Shōtoku reorganizes the Yamato kingdom in Japan
606–647	Reign of King Harsha as paramount ruler of north India
618–907	Tang dynasty in China
629–645	Journey of the Chinese Buddhist monk Xuanzang to India
668	Unification of the Korean peninsula under the rule of the Silla kingdom
c. 670	The Khazars conquer and supplant the Bulgar khanate
690	Empress Wu declares the founding of her Zhou dynasty in China
755–763	An Lushan rebellion in north China severely weakens the Tang dynasty
c. 760	Sailendra kings in Java begin construction of the Borobudur monument
792	Kyoto established as Japan's new capital
802	Consolidation of the Angkor kingdom in Cambodia by Jayavarman II
861	Conversion of the Khazars to Judaism
939	Vietnam wins independence from China
965	Rus invaders destroy the Khazar khanate

KEY TERMS

bodhisattva (p. 312)
Brahmanism (p. 327)
chakravartin (p. 313)
Chan Buddhism (p. 314)
equal-field system (p. 314)
Hinduism (p. 323)

jati (p. 325)
khan (p. 310)
Mahayana (p. 312)
Puranas (p. 323)
Pure Land (p. 313)
trade diaspora (p. 332)

CHAPTER OVERVIEW QUESTIONS

1. In what ways did Asian societies respond to cross-cultural interactions during the period 400–1000?

2. What strategies did pastoral nomads adopt in their relations with settled societies, and why?

3. What patterns of political and cultural borrowing characterized the emerging states in East and Southeast Asia?

4. Why did India and China experience different outcomes following the collapse of strong and unified empires?

SECTION FOCUS QUESTIONS

1. What strategies did nomadic steppe chieftains and the rulers of agrarian societies apply in their dealings with each other?

2. How did the spread of Buddhism transform the politics and societies of East Asia?

3. Why did the religious practices of Hinduism gain a broader following in Indian society than the ancient Vedic religion and its chief rival, Buddhism?

4. What aspects of Indian religions had the greatest influence on the societies of Southeast Asia?

5. How did the social and economic institutions of the Sogdian merchant network differ from those of the nomadic confederations and the agrarian empires?

MAKING CONNECTIONS

1. How and why did the spread of Buddhism from India to China and Southeast Asia differ from the expansion of Islam examined in Chapter 9?

2. Do you think that the invasions of Germanic peoples into the Roman Empire had more lasting consequences (see Chapter 9) than the invasions in China by steppe nomad peoples? Why or why not?

3. Compare the main values of Hinduism in the post-Gupta period with those of the ancient Vedic religion (see Chapter 3). How had the goals of religious practice changed, and what effect did these changes have on Indian society?

AT A CROSSROADS ▶

The Mesoamerican ball-game, which spread as far as northeastern North America, was charged with powerful ritual and religious meaning. Maya myths associate the ballgame with the Hero Twins' triumph over the gods of the underworld and with the gift of agriculture. This stone disk, which dates from about 590 and once marked the site of a ball court in the modern Mexican province of Chiapas, displays a ballplayer striking the ball with his hip. The headdress and inscriptions suggest that the ballplayer is a royal figure reenacting the feats of the Hero Twins. (Giraudon/ Bridgeman Art Library.)

Societies and Networks in the Americas and the Pacific

300–1200

When Holy Lord Eighteen Rabbit (r. 695–738) became king of the Maya city-state of Copán (co-PAHN) in today's western Honduras, his society was at the peak of its wealth and strength. Eighteen Rabbit's building projects reflected Copán's power. He commissioned an impressive series of stone monuments, adding major new temples in the heart of the city and laying out a Great Plaza to the north. He rebuilt Copán's magnificent ball court, where the warriors reenacted the Maya myth of creation as a gladiatorial contest culminating in the blood sacrifice of captured nobles. At the entrance to the Great Plaza, Eighteen Rabbit erected a stone pillar commemorating his accession as king, and the plaza itself was studded with carved stelae depicting Eighteen Rabbit as a multifaceted deity. One stele shows him as a mighty warrior holding up the sky; others portray him dressed as the Maize God and the spirit of the planet Venus.

After ruling Copán for forty-three years, Eighteen Rabbit was betrayed by one of his followers. In 725 he had installed a man named Cauac (kah-WOK) Sky as ruler of the nearby city of Quiriga (kee-REE-gah). In 738 Cauac Sky captured Eighteen Rabbit and carried the Copán king back to Quiriga, where he was killed as a sacrificial victim. Copán preserved its independence after Eighteen Rabbit's execution; Cauac Sky made no attempt

BACKSTORY

As we saw in Chapter 8, during the first millennium B.C.E. signs of growing social complexity and a hierarchy of villages and towns emerged in both the Olmec culture on Mexico's Atlantic coast and the Chavín culture along Peru's Pacific coast. By 200 B.C.E., however, the Olmec and Chavín societies had been eclipsed by the rising city-states of the Maya and Moche, respectively. These city-states concentrated political and military power by mobilizing massive amounts of labor to build monumental cities and irrigation systems for agriculture. Meanwhile, in North America, agriculture and settled societies did not appear until the first millennium C.E., when native peoples began to adopt Mesoamerican food crops and farming techniques. In the Pacific Ocean, once the Lapita migrations ceased in around 200 B.C.E., many islands remained undisturbed by human occupation. Colonization of the Pacific Islands would not resume until after 500 C.E.

The Classical Age of Mesoamerica and Its Aftermath

FOCUS What common beliefs and social and political patterns did the various local societies of Mesoamerica's classical age share?

City and State Building in the Andean Region

FOCUS How did environmental settings and natural resources shape livelihoods, social organization, and state building in the Andean region?

Agrarian Societies in North America

FOCUS How did the introduction of Mesoamerican crops transform North American peoples?

Habitat and Adaptation in the Pacific Islands

FOCUS In what ways did the habitats and resources of the Pacific Islands promote both cultural unity and cultural diversity?

COUNTERPOINT: Social Complexity in Bougainville

FOCUS Why did the historical development of the Melanesian island of Bougainville depart so sharply from that of contemporaneous societies in the Americas and the Pacific?

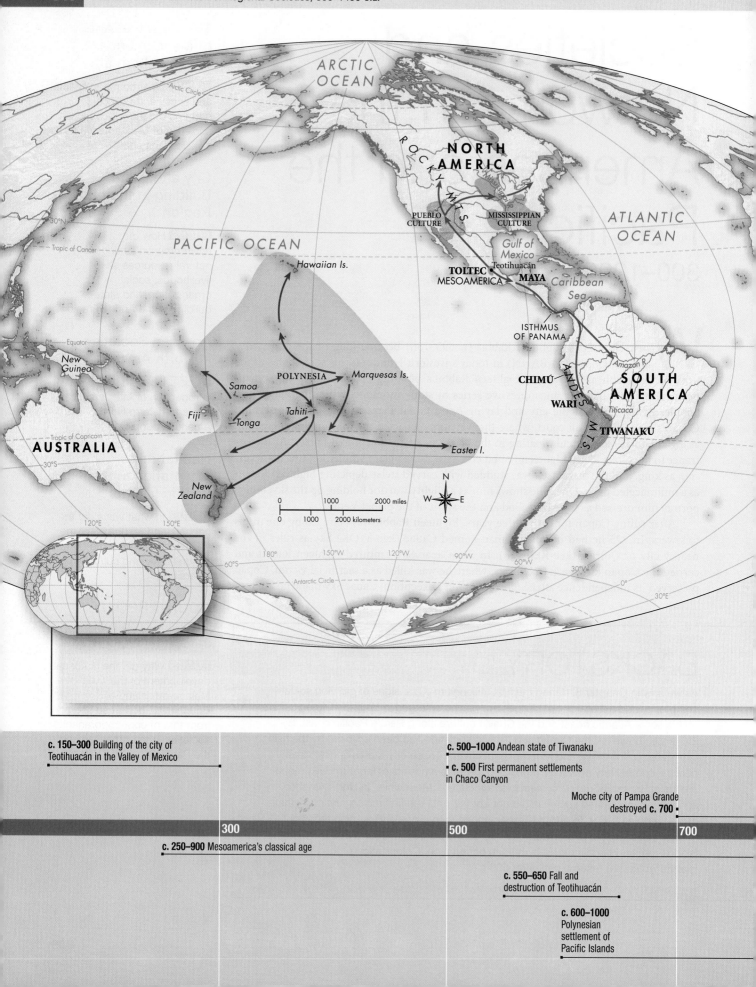

c. 150–300 Building of the city of
Teotihuacán in the Valley of Mexico

c. 500–1000 Andean state of Tiwanaku

c. 500 First permanent settlements
in Chaco Canyon

Moche city of Pampa Grande
destroyed **c. 700**

300

500

700

c. 250–900 Mesoamerica's classical age

c. 550–650 Fall and
destruction of Teotihuacán

c. 600–1000
Polynesian
settlement of
Pacific Islands

to occupy Copán or destroy its monuments. In fact, Eighteen Rabbit's successor as Copán's ruler completed one of his predecessor's most ambitious projects, a pyramid staircase that set down in stone the history of his dynasty. The inscription carved into the staircase steps reaffirmed the power of Copán by celebrating the accomplishments of its ancient warrior kings. The seated sculptures of earlier rulers placed at ascending intervals include an image of Eighteen Rabbit. His death—"his breath expiring in war"—was duly noted, but only as an unfortunate episode in an otherwise heroic history. He received full honors as a noble martyr and sacred ancestor.

The life and death of Eighteen Rabbit recorded in his city's monuments exemplify the obsession with dynastic continuity that was so central to the Maya kings' identity. The rulers of the Maya city-states devoted enormous resources to asserting their godlike power to command their subjects' labor and wealth. Their monuments wove together history and myth to tell the story of conquests, captives, slain enemies, and military alliances. Yet this wealth of historical documentation speaks in a single uniform voice. It is the speech of kings and nobles and sheds little light on the lives of the commoners who toiled under their rule.

As we saw in Chapter 8, the scarcity of written records, especially in comparison to Eurasia, complicates scholars' efforts to recover the histories of peoples of the Americas, the Pacific Islands, and most of sub-Saharan Africa. Only in Mesoamerica, stretching from central Mexico to Honduras, do we find substantial indigenous writings, which are as yet only partly deciphered. But the absence of documentary evidence does not indicate social or cultural isolation. Throughout the period from 300 to 1200, movements of peoples, goods, and ideas had far-reaching influences on these regions of the world. As in Eurasia, cross-cultural interaction played a significant role in shaping peoples and cultures.

The intensity of interaction and degree of cultural convergence varied with time and place. In Mesoamerica, cross-cultural interactions created a set of institutions and ideologies that knitted together local societies and cultures from the highland plateaus of central Mexico to the tropical rain forests of the Maya world. In the Andean region of South

MAPPING THE WORLD

Formation of Regional Societies in the Americas and the Pacific

In the Americas and the Pacific—as in Eurasia and Africa during this era—migration and trade promoted cultural exchange and the formation of regional societies. Complex states based on intensive agriculture arose in Mexico, the Maya region, and the Andes, but the southwestern deserts and eastern woodlands of North America fostered sharply distinct societies. The Polynesian migrations spawned a remarkable cultural unity across the central and eastern Pacific Ocean.

ROUTES ▼

→ Spread of maize cultivation, c. 1000 B.C.E.–700 C.E.

→ Polynesian migration, c. 300–1000 C.E.

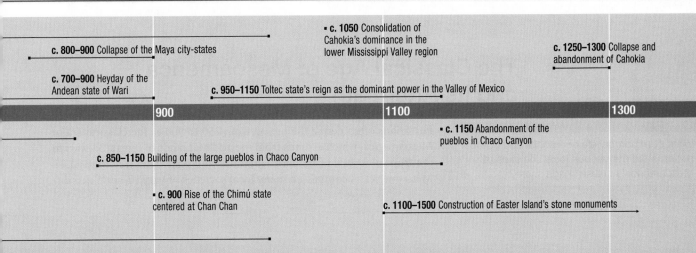

c. 800–900 Collapse of the Maya city-states

c. 1050 Consolidation of Cahokia's dominance in the lower Mississippi Valley region

c. 1250–1300 Collapse and abandonment of Cahokia

c. 700–900 Heyday of the Andean state of Wari

c. 950–1150 Toltec state's reign as the dominant power in the Valley of Mexico

900   1100   1300

c. 1150 Abandonment of the pueblos in Chaco Canyon

c. 850–1150 Building of the large pueblos in Chaco Canyon

c. 900 Rise of the Chimú state centered at Chan Chan

c. 1100–1500 Construction of Easter Island's stone monuments

America, too, inhabitants of the coastal plains and the highlands developed common political and cultural institutions. In contrast, cross-cultural influences touched virtually all of the local societies of North America without producing a shared cultural and political identity. In the Pacific Islands, migration, trade, and social interchange produced both the high degree of cultural uniformity of Polynesia and the remarkable cultural diversity found on the single island of Bougainville.

Equipped only with stone tools, these peoples faced formidable obstacles in their efforts to create stable agricultural economies. Landscapes as diverse as the alpine plateaus of the Andes, the barren deserts of southwestern North America, and the volcanic islands of the Pacific posed daily challenges to farming folk. Their success produced larger surpluses, greater social stratification, and more hierarchical political systems than before. In North America and the Pacific Islands, political and religious authority was dispersed among numerous hereditary chiefs. But in Mesoamerica and the Andean region, where irrigated agriculture supported denser populations, large states emerged. A distinct ruling class governed these states; their authority rested on an ideology that defined the cosmic order and explained the rights and obligations of all members of society, as well as the special status of the ruling class. The rulers of these states, such as Eighteen Rabbit, expressed their ideologies not only in words but in the design of their settlements and cities, in monumental architecture and sacred objects, and in rituals performed on behalf of both their deceased ancestors and their living subjects.

OVERVIEW
QUESTIONS

The major global development in this chapter: The formation of distinctive regional cultures in the Americas and the Pacific Islands between 300 and 1200.

As you read, consider:

1. How did these societies, equipped with only Stone Age technologies, develop the social and political institutions and the patterns of exchange to tame often hostile environments and build complex civilizations?

2. How did differences in environment and habitat foster or discourage economic and technological exchanges among adjacent regions?

3. What were the sources of political power in the societies discussed in this chapter, and how were they similar or dissimilar?

4. How did differences in urban design reflect distinctive forms of political and social organization?

The Classical Age of Mesoamerica and Its Aftermath

FOCUS

What common beliefs and social and political patterns did the various local societies of Mesoamerica's classical age share?

Historians often define the period from 250 to 900 as the classical era of Mesoamerica, which extends from the arid highlands of central Mexico to the tropical forests of modern Honduras and Nicaragua (see Map 11.1). Mesoamerica encompassed many local societies of varying scale and dif-

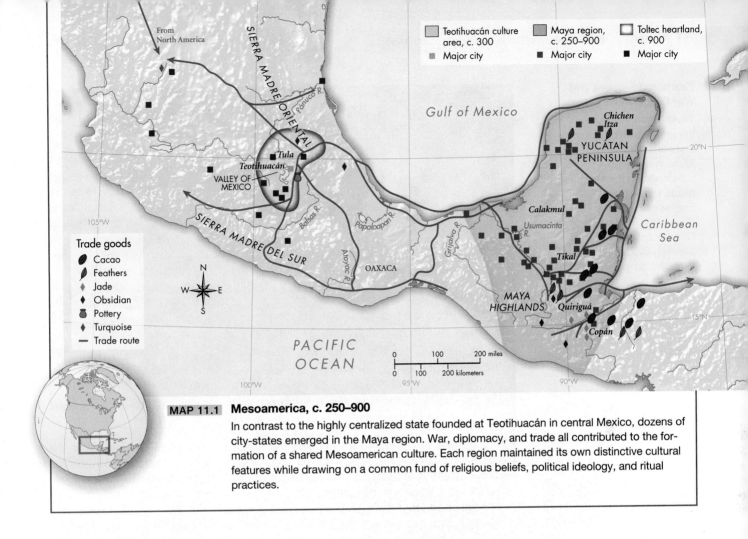

MAP 11.1 Mesoamerica, c. 250–900

In contrast to the highly centralized state founded at Teotihuacán in central Mexico, dozens of city-states emerged in the Maya region. War, diplomacy, and trade all contributed to the formation of a shared Mesoamerican culture. Each region maintained its own distinctive cultural features while drawing on a common fund of religious beliefs, political ideology, and ritual practices.

ferent degrees of integration and complexity. What united it as a regional society was a set of shared ideas about the operation of the cosmos. This common ideology produced similar patterns of elite status, political power, and economic control.

Between the first and ninth centuries, Mesoamerica underwent a remarkable cycle of political consolidation and disintegration. At the beginning of this period, Mesoamerica was home to numerous **chiefdoms**, in which a hereditary chief exercised political and religious authority and military leadership over a group of tribes or villages. By the third century, more complex and more steeply stratified political orders—**city-states**—dominated both the highlands and the lowlands by extracting labor and tribute from their subjects.

Bronze and iron metallurgy were unknown in Mesoamerica during this period. Yet despite the limitations of Stone Age technology, the people built great cities, and their skilled craft industries flourished. Highly productive agriculture based on maize, beans, squash, and chili peppers supported some of the world's densest populations.

The monumental metropolis of Teotihuacán (teh-o-tee-WAH-kahn) in central Mexico and the dozens of Maya city-states testify to the strong control the rulers wielded over their subjects' lives. As was true of the classical ages of Eurasia and Africa, the classical era of Mesoamerica was a time of strife and crisis as well as expanding economic and cultural interchange.

Political Power and Ideology in Mesoamerica

Scholars have traced the origins of Mesoamerican cultural and political traditions to the ancient Olmec civilization (see Chapter 8). Powerful Mesoamerican city-states emerged during the first centuries C.E., and cross-cultural exchange intensified as trade and warfare

chiefdom A form of political organization in which a hereditary leader, or chief, holds both political and religious authority and the rank of members is determined by their degree of kinship to the chief.

city-state A small independent state consisting of an urban center and the surrounding agricultural territory.

Feathered Serpent and War Serpent

Teotihuacán's monuments lack the prolific historical records and portraits of royal figures found in the Maya world. But scholars think the sculpted heads shown here of the Feathered Serpent and the War Serpent on the Temple of Queztalcoatl, constructed between 200 and 250, may represent an expression of power by a single ruler or dynasty. Many of these images were defaced in the fourth century, perhaps as a warning against royal ambitions. (Photolibrary.)

Sources of Political Power and Ideology

among cities forged connections between the Mesoamerican peoples. Throughout the region, people came to recognize a similar array of gods—feathered serpents, lords of the underworld, and storm gods. Knowledge of the Mesoamerican calendar and writing gave rulers important tools for state-building.

In the absence of bronze and iron metallurgy, **obsidian**—a hard volcanic stone used to sharpen cutting tools—was crucial to agricultural production. The two sources of obsidian in the region, the northern part of the Valley of Mexico and highland Guatemala, emerged as early centers of economic exchange and state formation. Poor transportation limited the reach of political control, however; in the absence of draft animals (domesticated beasts of burden) and wheeled vehicles, people could transport only what they could carry on their backs. Long-distance exchange was therefore difficult, and it was restricted to the most highly desired goods. Political power was based more on controlling labor than on accumulating property. Yet the possession of rare and exotic **prestige goods** gave rulers awesome authority, and so items such as jade, gold, jaguar skins, feathers, and cacao seeds (for making chocolate) acquired great value. Rulers of the Mesoamerican city-states constantly warred against each other, vying for control of labor resources and prestige goods and exacting tribute from their defeated enemies.

Mesoamerican political power was explained and legitimated by a political ideology that many scholars argue was rooted in memories of the great rulers and cities of antiquity. The people collectively associated these memories with a mythical city known as **Tollan** ("the place of reeds"), which they saw as a paradise of fertility and abundance, the place where human and animal life began. They believed Tollan was the earthly abode of the god Feathered Serpent (whom the Aztecs would later name Quetzalcoatl [kate-zahl-CO-ah-tal]), the creator and patron of humanity. Mesoamerican myths associated the Feathered Serpent with elemental forces such as wind and fire, and also with the planet Venus, the "morning star" that heralds the arrival of the life-giving sun. Mythological lore credited the Feathered Serpent with creating the sun and moon, inventing the calendar and thus the cycles of time, and bestowing basic necessities such as maize, their staple food.

But Mesoamerican concepts of cosmic order, in which cycles of time are punctuated by violence and death, required that the Feathered Serpent sacrifice his own life to

obsidian A hard volcanic stone used to sharpen cutting tools and thus one of the most valuable natural resources for Stone Age peoples.

prestige good A rare or exotic item to which a society ascribes high value and status.

Tollan In Mesoamerican myths, the name of the place where the gods created human beings, and thus the place of origin for all of humanity.

renew the creative powers of the universe. Human rulers in turn could acquire and maintain political power only through offering frequent blood sacrifices to the gods. These blood sacrifices involved both the execution of war captives and bloodletting rituals by rulers and priests, who used needles of obsidian, bone, or stingray spines to pierce their tongues and ears and extract blood. Human rulers embodied the divine powers of the Feathered Serpent and reenacted his heroic exploits through ritual performance.

Mesoamericans believed that all humans originally spoke a common language and lived under the benign rule of the Feathered Serpent. Gradually, though, groups of people developed their own languages, customs, and beliefs and went their separate ways. By building temples and cities, rulers sought to renew the common community of the original Tollan. Claiming the heritage of Tollan gave legitimacy to new rulers and dynasties and provided a rationale for accepting foreign conquerors. Thus political power in Mesoamerica was rooted in a shared cultural heritage and a vision of cultural unity.

The City-State of Teotihuacán

The rise of Teotihuacán, about thirty miles northeast of present-day Mexico City, as the dominant center in the Valley of Mexico was due largely to its location near the region's major obsidian mines and irrigated farmland. Only a few fragments of Teotihuacán writing have survived, so we have far less direct evidence of Teotihuacán's history than we do for the Maya city-states. We do know that in the first two centuries C.E., Teotihuacán's founders constructed a magnificent city with wide avenues, numerous walled residential complexes, and a massive open plaza anchored by giant pyramids and temples.

Most of the population of the valley, farmers and craftsmen alike, lived in this vast city. To house all these people, apartment-like stone buildings—the first apartment compounds in world history—were constructed. These compounds housed an average of fifty to one hundred persons in a series of apartments built around a central patio, which in some cases had its own ritual mound. The apartments usually housed members of a single kinship group, but some were for craftsmen working in the same trade. This residential pattern suggests that the city's people were divided into groups (probably based on kinship) that shared everyday life, collective rituals, and in some cases specialized trade and craft occupations.

These groups may also have been the basic units of the city's economy. Although the scale of Teotihuacán's buildings and monuments shows that the state could command vast amounts of labor, there is little evidence that its rulers exercised direct control over the inhabitants' ordinary working lives. Even the obsidian tool–making industry, the mainstay of the city's economic dominance, was dispersed among hundreds of small domestic workshops, not centralized in large state-run industrial enterprises.

Despite the extensive centralization of the Teotihuacán state, scholars have not found evidence of a hereditary dynasty of kings. Most believe that in its formative stages, Teotihuacán—like the city-states of Mesopotamia discussed in Chapter 2—was ruled by a cadre of priests rather than a military elite. Ritual action, including blood offerings, dominates the art and imagery of Teotihuacán, but warriors and scenes of warfare rarely appear until the fourth century C.E. Human sacrifice was a notable aspect of Teotihuacán's public culture. Nearly two hundred sacrificial victims, bound and dressed in war regalia, were

Social and Economic Organization

Priestly Rule and Ritual

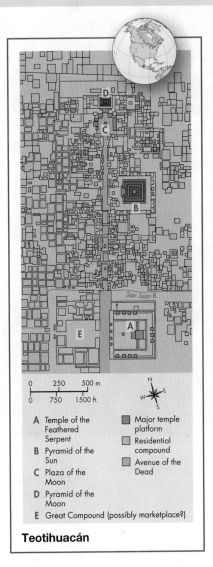

A Temple of the Feathered Serpent
B Pyramid of the Sun
C Plaza of the Moon
D Pyramid of the Moon
E Great Compound (possibly marketplace?)

Major temple platform
Residential compound
Avenue of the Dead

0 250 500 m
0 750 1500 ft.

San Juan R.

Teotihuacán

Teotihuacán

At its peak between 250 and 350, Teotihuacán was one of the largest cities in the world. The Avenue of the Dead stretches for 3 miles from the Pyramid of the Moon (foreground) to the Temple of Queztalcoatl and the residences of the elite; the Pyramid of the Sun stands to the left. Some two thousand apartment compounds housing the city's ordinary inhabitants lined both sides of the avenue. (©Herb Lingl/aerialarchives.com.)

buried beneath the Temple of the Feathered Serpent, the hub of government, when it was constructed in the early third century.

Teotihuacán's precise gridlike layout reflects a paramount desire to impose human order on an unpredictable natural world. The city's planners aligned its pyramids and plazas with crucial astronomical phenomena to provide a consecrated space to perform sacred rituals at the proper times. The Temple of the Feathered Serpent was flanked by twelve platforms, which served as stages for elaborate seasonal rites to ensure abundant harvests, cosmic balance, and social stability. The technologies of architecture, astronomy, and calendrical calculation were essential to maintain the orderly structure of the cosmos. Above all, the city's builders intended Teotihuacán to be seen as the Tollan of its day, a ceremonial complex dedicated to perpetuating the power and authority of its ruling class through awesome public rituals. It was for this reason that centuries later, the Aztecs named the city's massive ruins Teotihuacán, "the place where men become gods." In every way, the city was designed to function as a place of connection between the human and the divine.

Teotihuacán's Power and Influence

By 500 C.E. Teotihuacán's population had swelled to as many as two hundred thousand inhabitants, surpassed probably only by Constantinople among contemporary cities worldwide. The rise of Teotihuacán signaled the ascendancy of the central Mexican highlands as the dominant economic, political, and cultural region in Mesoamerica. Yet Teotihuacán's rulers pursued imperial expansion only fitfully, if at all. The area under their direct control seems to have been fairly limited, perhaps just the Valley of Mexico. Nevertheless, the city's influence radiated to the entire region through the prestige of its artifacts and culture, both of which were widely imitated throughout Mesoamerica. Visiting merchants and diplomatic missions from the Oaxaca (wah-HAH-kah) highlands, the Gulf Coast, and the Maya region inhabited their own special quarters in Teotihuacán. These foreigners' barrios (neighborhoods) were crossroads of cultural and economic exchange that helped disseminate sacred knowledge, ritual culture, political intelligence, and prestige goods throughout Mesoamerica.

By the fifth century, the Teotihuacán state exerted a far-reaching influence over the Mesoamerican world through its splendid monuments, its grand public ceremonies, and the abundant output of its craft workshops. At the same time, Teotihuacán's leaders took a more aggressive stance toward rival chiefs and foreign states. This shift would have crucial consequences for the Maya city-states.

The Maya City-State Network

The Maya city-states developed before the rise of Teotihuacán in central Mexico. Like other Mesoamerican cultures, the Maya inherited many features of the ancient Olmec civilization of the Gulf coast, including its monumental architecture, social institutions, calendar, and ritual art. In contrast to the Mexican highlands, however, where the massive scale of Teotihuacán dwarfed all other cities and polities, the Maya region never had a single dominant power.

In both the highlands near the Pacific coast and the lowland rain forests to the north, the early phase of Maya political and economic expansion was suddenly interrupted in the second and third centuries C.E. Major cities were abandoned, especially in the Pacific highlands, and new building and settlement came to a halt. The causes of this disruption are unknown, but its pervasive effects have led scholars to speculate that it resulted from some ecological catastrophe, perhaps a volcanic eruption. This catastrophe did not bring an end to Maya society, but it did alter the political landscape. By the time economic and demographic growth recovered at the beginning of the fourth century, political power had shifted decisively from the highlands to the city-states of the lowlands, such as Copán and Tikal (tee-KAHL).

The period from 250 to 900, the classical age of Maya civilization, witnessed the founding of nearly forty city-states. During these centuries the **Holy Lords**, as the Maya rulers called themselves, engaged in prodigious building of cities and monuments. But this era was also marked by succession struggles, dynastic changes, and perpetual political insecurity. The Holy Lords of powerful city-states frequently resorted to war to subdue neighbors and rivals. Victors rarely established direct rule over vanquished enemies, however. Unlike the Eurasian rulers we studied in earlier chapters, Maya elites did not dream of creating vast empires.

Instead, they were more likely to seek booty and tribute, and above all to seize war captives. Conquerors often brought back skilled craftsmen and laborers to their home city, reserving captives of high rank, such as the unfortunate Eighteen Rabbit, for blood sacrifices. Maya ceramic art often depicts tribute bearers offering cloth, foodstuffs, feathers, and cacao to enthroned rulers. Thus the Maya nobility may have conceived of war as a sacred ritual, but one that also furthered their ambitions for wealth and power. At the same time, armed conflict resulted in the exchange of people and goods among Maya city-states, contributing to the Maya region's cultural uniformity.

Maya myths about the origins of the gods and humanity have been preserved in the *Popol Vuh*, or "Book of Council." The descendants of a former Maya royal family wrote down these legends in the Latin alphabet after the Spanish conquest of Mesoamerica in the sixteenth century (see Reading the Past: The Maya Hero Twins Vanquish the Lords of the Underworld). The *Popul Vuh* portrays humans as the servants of the all-powerful gods who created them. In return for the gods' gifts of maize and timely rains, humans were obliged to build monuments to glorify the gods, to offer them sacrifices (especially human blood), and to regulate their own lives according to a sacred calendar. The Maya believed that all human beings possess a sacred essence, *ch'ulel* (choo-LEL), which is found in blood. The exalted status of kings and nobles endowed them with more potent ch'ulel, and so they were especially prized as blood sacrifices. Although the Maya kings depicted themselves as

Contraction and Recovery

Warring City-States of the Classical Age

Myths of Origins in the *Popol Vuh*

Holy Lord The title given by the Maya to the rulers of their city-states.

ch'ulel In Maya belief, the sacred essence contained in human blood that made it a potent offering to the gods.

The Maya Hero Twins Vanquish the Lords of the Underworld

The *Popol Vuh* records the myths about the world's creation and the origins of human society as handed down by the Quiché, a late Maya people. Central to the mythology of the Popol Vuh is the struggle between the gods and the Xibalba (shee-BAHL-ba), the lords of the underworld. The narrative focuses mostly on the exploits of the Hero Twins, whose father had been defeated by the Xibalba in a ball-game contest and decapitated. The Hero Twins travel to the underworld, outwit the Xibalba, and avenge their father's death.

In the following passages from the *Popol Vuh*, the Hero Twins inform the defeated Xibalba that as punishment for their heinous deed they will no longer receive blood sacrifices—and thus they will lose their power over mortals. Then the Hero Twins resurrect their father and assure him that in the future he will receive worship from the as-yet-unborn humans. Their triumph complete, the twins become transformed into the sun and moon (or, in other versions, the planet Venus), whose daily progressions through the heavens remind humanity of the triumph of the gods over the lords of death.

Passage 1:

"Here then is our word that we declare to you. Hearken, all you of Xibalba; for never again will you or your posterity be great. Your offerings also will never again be great. They will be reduced to croton [a shrub] sap. No longer will clean blood be yours. Unto you will be given only worn-out griddles and pots, only flimsy and brittle things."

"You shall surely eat only the creatures of the grass and the creatures of the wastelands. No longer will you be given the children of the light, those begotten in the light. Only things of no importance will fall before you." . . . Thus began their devastation, the ruin of their being called upon in worship. . . .

Here now is the adornment of their father by them. . . . His sons then said to him: "Here you will be called upon. It shall be so." Thus his heart was comforted.

"The child who is born to the light, and the son who is begotten in the light shall go out to you first. Your name shall not be forgotten. Thus be it so," they said to the father when they comforted his heart.

"We are merely the avengers of your death and your loss, for the affliction and misfortune that were done to you." Thus was their counsel when they had defeated all Xibalba.

Then [the Hero Twins] arose as the central lights. They arose straight into the sky. One of them arose as the sun, and the other as the moon.

Passage 2:

Now when they came from Tulan Zuyva [Tollan], they did not eat. They fasted continuously. Yet they fixed their eyes of the dawn, looking steadfastly for the coming forth of the sun. They occupied themselves in looking for the Great Star, called Icoquih [Venus], which appears first before the birth of the sun. The face of this Green Morning Star always appears at the coming forth of the sun.

When they were there at the place called Tulan Zuyva, their gods came to them. But it was surely not then that they received their ultimate glory or their lordship. Rather it was where the great nations and the small nations were conquered and humiliated when they were sacrificed before the face of Tohil. They gave their blood, which flowed from the shoulders and armpits of all the people.

Straightaway at Tulan came the glory and the great knowledge that was theirs. It was in the darkness, in the night as well, that they accomplished it. . . .

[Tohil spoke to them]: "You shall first give thanks. You shall carry out your responsibilities first by piercing your ears. You shall prick your elbows. This shall be your petition, your way of giving thanks before the face of god."

"Very well," they said. Then they pierced their ears. They wept as they sang of their coming from Tulan.

Source: Allen J. Christenson. Popol Vuh, *The Sacred Book of the Maya*, translated by Allen Christenson. Copyright © 2003 by O Books. University of Oklahoma Press, 2007. Used by permission of the publisher.

EXAMINING THE EVIDENCE

1. Why did the Maya believe that human beings must offer blood sacrifices to the gods?

2. Why might the Maya have been so deeply interested in the movements of the sun, moon, and planets?

gods, they attained immortality only after death, and the natural death of a king was considered a necessary sacrifice to ensure the renewal of divine blessings. Women of high birth also participated in the political and ceremonial life of the Maya ruling class, and Maya inscriptions record that several women ruled as Holy Lords. Maya elites thus occupied a unique position at the intersection of the human and the divine, ensuring the world's continuity both by demanding labor and sacrifices from the Maya population and by becoming sacrifices themselves.

The Mesoamerican ballgame, which dates back at least to Olmec times, was no mere spectator sport. On important ritual occasions, the ballgame became a solemn restaging of the mythical contest in which the Hero Twins triumphed over the lords of the underworld. When Eighteen Rabbit renovated Copán's ball court, he made it the city's ceremonial centerpiece, surrounding it with the greatest temples and monuments. The object of the ballgame, played by two teams of up to four players each, was to keep a rubber ball up in the air without using hands or feet. The slope-sided arenas represented the crack in the earth leading to the underworld. Allowing the ball to strike the ground risked incurring the wrath of the underworld gods. After the outcome was decided, the ball court became a sacrificial altar where the losers' heads were impaled on a skull rack alongside the court. These blood sacrifices not only commemorated the victory of the Hero Twins but also renewed the life-giving power of the gods.

The intricate Maya calendar determined the timing of war, sacrifice, agricultural work, and markets and fairs. The Maya believed that time and human history moved in elaborate cycles determined by the movements of the sun, moon, and planets—especially Venus, which in Maya belief governed sacrifice and war. To ensure a favorable outcome, the Maya people sought to align major actions in the present, such as attacks on enemies, with heroic events and accomplishments in the past. Thus the Maya took great care to observe and record astronomical phenomena. Maya astronomers calculated eclipses and the movements of planets with astonishing precision: their charts of the movements of Venus, which survive in bark-paper books, are accurate to within one day in five hundred years.

Bloodletting by a Maya Queen

Blood sacrifices offered to the gods occupied a central place in Mesoamerican political life. This stone monument shows the king of Yaxchilan holding a torch over the head of his queen, who is performing a ritual bloodletting by passing a spiked cord through her tongue. The ritual celebrated the birth of the king's son in 709. (Erich Lessing/Art Resource.)

Maya Social Order

Maya society revolved around the activities of the king and the royal clan. Beneath this ruling elite existed a multitiered social order based on class, residence, and kinship. As in many early Eurasian cultures, astrologers, diviners, and especially scribes occupied privileged positions in Maya society. These groups possessed the knowledge crucial to maintaining the royal mystique and to carrying out the tasks of government. The cities also housed large groups of specialized craftworkers in trades such as pottery manufacture, stone and wood carving, weaving, toolmaking, and construction. Urban artisans who made luxury goods for the nobility lived in larger dwellings near the cities' ceremonial centers, which indicates that they had higher socioeconomic status. At Tikal one artisans' compound was reserved for dentists who specialized in inlaying the teeth of the nobility with jade and other precious stones.

In the countryside, three to four families, probably kinfolk, lived in a common compound, each family in its own one-room building. The residential compound included a common kitchen and storage facilities, which they all shared. Clusters of residential compounds formed hamlets of several hundred persons. The considerable differences in the richness of burial goods suggest that the size, wealth, and prestige of the kin groups of commoners varied widely.

Larger outlying settlements, where powerful noble families resided, had paved plazas, pyramids, and temples but lacked the altars and ball courts of royal cities. These local nobles governed the surrounding population and organized the delivery of tribute and labor demanded by the supreme Holy Lords. The burden of labor service—to construct cities and to serve in the military—weighed heavily on the subject population. Like other ancient city-states we have studied, Maya city-states turned to the surrounding area for resources and labor and thereby became local crossroads for people, goods, and ideas.

Maya Family Life

Written records from the Maya classical age say little about family life. Although descriptions of Maya society compiled by the Spanish conquerors in the sixteenth century suffer from biases and misrepresentations, they reveal aspects of Maya culture that cannot be gleaned from archaeological evidence. According to these accounts, children were considered members of their fathers' lineage and took their surnames, but they also acquired "house names" from their mothers. Property and status passed from parents to children: sons inherited from fathers, and daughters inherited from mothers. Upon marriage, the husband usually moved in with his wife's family for a period of service lasting six or more years. Thereafter the couple might live with the husband's family or set up their own separate household.

Maize, usually made into steamed cakes known as *tamales*, was the staple of the Maya diet. The lowland Maya practiced both dry-land and intensive wet-land agriculture, growing maize, cotton, beans, squash, chili peppers, root crops, and many other vegetables. Hunting also provided food, but the only domestic animals the Maya possessed were dogs and turkeys. Maya rulers also received fish and shellfish as tribute from coastal areas.

Population Growth and Long-Distance Exchange

During the prosperous classical era the Maya population grew rapidly. In a pattern we have seen repeated around the world, population growth stimulated regular contact and communication throughout the region, and also the specialized production of agricultural and craft goods. The urban ruling elites, while continuing to war against one another, exchanged prestige goods over long distances. The unusual uniformity in spoken languages and pottery manufacture suggests that ordinary people also interacted frequently.

Influence of Teotihuacán

It was during the classical age, too, that Teotihuacán's influence left a clear imprint on the Maya world. Obsidian tools, ceramics, stone pyramid architecture, and other artifacts imported into Maya city-states show that cultural interaction and trade with Teotihuacán were well established (see again Map 11.1). Long-distance trade between the central Mexican highlands and the Maya lowlands was complemented by reciprocal gift giving and the dispatch of emissaries among rulers. The circulation of exotic goods charged with sacred power—feathers, pelts, and precious stones—reinforced elite status and helped spread religious practices.

In the fourth century Teotihuacán also became a major political force in the Maya region. Teotihuacán trade and diplomatic missions made forays into Maya lands and cultivated local clients, who reaped political and economic benefits from allying with Teotihuacán. The sudden appearance of Teotihuacán building styles, pottery, and tomb goods suggests that some cities, particularly in the coastal plains and highlands of Pacific Guatemala, fell under the rule of governors dispatched from Teotihuacán. At the very least, some Maya elites, especially upstart contenders for power seeking to unseat established royal dynasties, emulated certain features of Teotihuacán's political ideology. At Tikal and Copán, mysterious figures identified as "Lords of the West" overthrew previous rulers and founded new royal dynasties. These foreign regimes quickly assimilated into the native ruling elites of their cities. Economic ties to Teotihuacán, and perhaps adoption of Teotihuacán's more centralized system of administration and tribute collection, enriched Tikal and Copán. Both cities developed their own networks of client cities and exercised at least informal dominance over their local regions.

The Passing of Mesoamerica's Classical Age

Destruction of Teotihuacán

Between 550 and 650 Teotihuacán was destroyed. Sacred monuments were cast down, civic buildings were burned, and at least some portion of the population was slaughtered, leaving little doubt that the destruction was politically motivated. Historians do not know whether the razing of Teotihuacán resulted from foreign invasion or domestic political strife. Clearly, the perpetrators aimed not merely to overthrow the current regime but to obliterate the city's sacred aura. Most of Teotihuacán's population scattered, and the city never regained its preeminence. No successor emerged as the dominant power. For the next three or more centuries, the Valley of Mexico was divided among a half-dozen smaller states that warred constantly against one another.

In 562 an alliance of rival states vanquished Tikal, the most powerful Maya city-state, and sacrificed its king. As was Maya practice, however, the allies did not attempt to establish direct rule over Tikal, and by 700 it had recovered and its kings once again became the paramount lords of an extensive network of allies and trading partners. Interestingly, Maya royal monuments of the eighth century at Tikal (and at Copán during the reign of Eighteen Rabbit and his successors) feature a great revival of Teotihuacán imagery, even though the Mexican city had long been reduced to ruin. The reverence shown to Teotihuacán as a royal capital illustrates the lasting appeal of its ideas and institutions throughout Mesoamerica.

From Ruin to Recovery in Tikal

The brilliant prosperity that Tikal and other Maya city-states enjoyed in the eighth century did not last. Over the course of the ninth century, monument building ceased in one Maya city after another. Although there is evidence of internal struggles for power and of interstate warfare, scholars believe that population pressure or an ecological disturbance triggered a more profound economic or demographic crisis. The collapse of the Maya city-state network not only ended individual ruling dynasties but also dismantled the basic economy of the region. Cities and cultivated fields were abandoned and eventually disappeared into the encroaching jungle. The region's population fell by at least 80 percent. New—but much more modest—cities arose along the Gulf coast of the Yucatan peninsula in the following centuries, but the cities of the Maya classical age never recovered.

Collapse of the Maya City-States

The crumbling of the entire region's political and economic foundations reveals the tight web of interdependence within the Maya city-state network. The Maya peoples were more culturally uniform than peoples in other parts of Mesoamerica, sharing common languages, material culture, ritual practices, aesthetic values, and political institutions. Their diversified regional economy promoted specialized production and reliance on exchange to meet subsistence needs. Yet the competition among many roughly equal city-states also produced an unstable political system rife with conflict. Sharp reversals in political fortunes, booms in monument building followed by busts of destruction and abandonment, and frequent changes of ruling dynasties (which court historians took great pains to conceal) shaped the Maya world. Ultimately the political instability of the Maya city-state network eroded its infrastructure of production, labor, transport, and exchange.

By 900, with the passing of both Teotihuacán and the Maya city-states, Mesoamerica's classical age had ended. Yet the region's cosmopolitan heritage endured in the Toltec state that dominated the central Mexican highlands from around 950 to 1150 (see again Map 11.1). Although descended from nomadic foragers from Mexico's northern deserts, the Toltecs resurrected the urban civilization, craft industries, and political culture of Teotihuacán. The Toltec capital of Tula became the new Tollan. According to Toltec annals written shortly after the Spanish conquest, the founder of Tula bore the name Quetzalcoatl (Feathered Serpent). Images of the Feathered Serpent frequently recur among Tula's ruins. Once again, in a pattern we have seen in other parts of the world, a nomadic people had inherited the culture of an urban society.

Post-Classical Mesoamerica: The Toltecs and Chichen Itza

This era also produced a remarkable synthesis of Mexican and Maya traditions. Chichen Itza (chuh-chen uht-SAH), in the heart of the Yucatan peninsula, dominated the northern Maya region in the tenth century. The art and architecture of Chichen Itza so closely resembles that of Tula that some scholars believe Chichen Itza was a colony of the Toltec state. But Chichen Itza's major monuments are older than those of Tula. Relief carvings on the temples surrounding Chichen Itza's ball court depict the lords of Itza (the name means "sorcerer of water") summoning the Feathered Serpent, who grants them the right to rule this land. Although it is unlikely that the Toltecs ruled over Chichen Itza, there is little doubt that both cities were conceived as reincarnations of ancient Tollan and shared a political ideology centered on the Feathered Serpent. The striking similarities between Tula and Chichen Itza offer compelling evidence of the growing cultural integration of Mesoamerica.

City and State Building in the Andean Region

FOCUS

How did environmental settings and natural resources shape livelihoods, social organization, and state building in the Andean region?

At the height of Mesoamerica's classical age, a series of rich and powerful states, centered on spectacular adobe and stone cities, sprouted in both the northwestern coastal lowlands and the Andean highlands of South America (see Map 11.2). But the narrow land bridge of the Isthmus of Panama, covered by thick tropical forests, hampered communication between North and South America. Despite similarities in art, architecture, ritual, and political ideology, there is scant evidence of sustained contact between Mesoamerican and Andean societies during this era. Indeed, their differences are striking. Metalworking, already highly refined in the Andean region in the first millennium B.C.E., was unknown in Mesoamerica until the seventh century C.E. The massive irrigation systems of the Andean region had no parallel in Mesoamerica, and urbanization and trade networks were far more extensive in Mesoamerica than in the Andes. And although the Andean region was characterized by strong states and powerful rulers, they did not develop the traditions of writing and record keeping that became vital to political life in the Maya city-states.

All along the Pacific coast of South America, the abrupt ascent of the Andean mountain chain creates a landscape of distinctive ecological zones. Low coastal deserts give way to steep valleys and high mountain ranges interspersed with canyons and plateaus. Marked differences in climate and resources within relatively short distances led local populations to practice a variety of subsistence strategies, while also encouraging cooperation and exchange. Still, the formidable geographical barriers and uneven distribution of resources favored social and cultural diversity and inhibited imperial control by highly centralized states.

Nonetheless, Andean rulers strove to forge regional connections, promoting economic integration by bringing together diverse groups, resources, and technologies. These efforts met with some success. Careful use of the region's material wealth produced impressive achievements, most spectacularly in the monumental cities built in both the highlands and lowlands. Yet the challenges of the Andean environment and the resulting fragility of its agriculture continually threatened the social and political institutions that produced these achievements.

States and Societies in the Coastal Lowlands

Demise of the Moche and Rise of the Chimu

As we saw in Chapter 8, the earliest Andean states, Chavín and Moche, were founded in the arid coastal valleys of northern Peru. Moche, which had supplanted the earlier Chavín cultures by the first century C.E., was dominated by a powerful warrior elite who mobilized large numbers of forced laborers to build monumental pyramids and irrigation systems. But Moche was beset by climatic and political upheavals. In the early seventh century the grand ceremonial complex at Cerro Blanco was abandoned. Evidence from tree rings indicates that in the late sixth century the region suffered a drought lasting more than thirty years, followed by decades of unusually heavy rains and severe flooding, which partly destroyed Cerro Blanco's great pyramids in around 635. Scholars speculate that the El Niño currents might have caused these climatic upheavals. The largest late Moche city,

Pampa Grande, was burned to the ground in around 700. Whether the city's destruction resulted from domestic unrest or foreign invasion is unclear.

In the late ninth century a new state, Chimú (chee-MOO), arose in the Moche valley. Chimú's rulers, like the Moche leaders, depicted themselves as godlike figures and dramatized their authority through rituals of human sacrifice. But Chimú achieved far more political control over the coastal region than Moche had. It would thrive for over five centuries before succumbing to the Incas.

At its peak, the Chimú capital of Chan Chan comprised a vast maze of adobe-walled enclosures covering eight square miles. The city included at least nine palace compounds, residences for members of the royal clan who shared paramount rulership. There were also some thirty smaller residences of minor nobility and state officials, and densely packed barrios where the city's artisans, laborers, and traders lived in cramped dwellings made of mud-covered cane. Caravansaries (inns with large courtyards and stables) at the city's center welcomed llama caravans bringing trade goods from the highlands, especially alpaca wool, gold, silver, and copper.

Chan Chan was built on a barren plain near the Peruvian coast. Its inhabitants, and the power of its rulers, were nourished by irrigated agriculture and the construction of a much more extensive network of canals than that of Moche. In the thirteenth and fourteenth centuries the Chimú state expanded into neighboring valleys to tap additional land and water supplies. Military conquest was undoubtedly important in this expansion, but the stability of the Chimú state owed much more to trade and economic integration. Local rulers enjoyed substantial autonomy, and they had access to an enormous range of fine prestige goods produced in Chan Chan's workshops. Centuries later, Inca conquerors relocated large numbers of Chan Chan artisans to their capital at Cuzco after annexing Chimú in the 1460s.

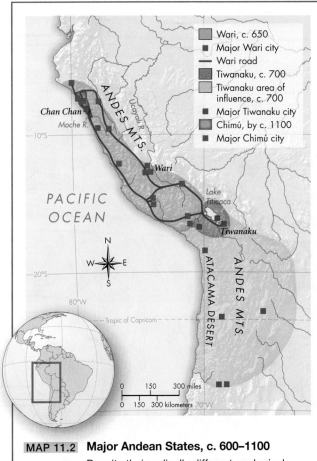

MAP 11.2   **Major Andean States, c. 600–1100**

Despite their radically different ecological habitats, both coastal and highland states of the Andean region relied on sophisticated—but fragile—systems of irrigated agriculture. Coastal Chimú and highland Tiwanaku each developed extensive networks of interregional trade. The highland Wari state, in contrast, imposed its military rule by building a series of fortified towns to control local populations.

States and Societies in the Andean Highlands

Inhabitants of the Andean highlands developed sophisticated agricultural systems to overcome the high altitude, erratic rainfall, and short growing season of the region. Indigenous crops, chiefly potatoes and quinoa (a native cereal), were the staples of the highland diet. Cultivation of raised fields constructed on cobblestone bases and fed by runoff of rain from the surrounding mountains began as early as 800 B.C.E.

Raised-field agriculture relied on an intricate system of irrigation but did not require complex technology, intensive labor, or large-scale organization. Local groups of farmers, known to the Inca as *ayllu* (aye-YOO), constructed the fields well before the appearance of complex political systems. The ayllu were essentially based on cooperative labor, though in some cases they relied on real or invented kinship ties to reinforce group solidarity. Ayllu typically owned lands in different locations and ecological zones (valley floors, hillsides, pasture) to minimize risk of crop failures. Groups of ayllu periodically pooled their labor to construct and maintain extensive networks of fields, canals, and causeways.

Raised-Field Farming

ayllu Groups of farmers (or other specialized occupations) in the Andean highlands who shared claims to common lands and a common ancestry.

Andean Agriculture

Farmers in the arid Andean highlands irrigated their fields with water stored in stone-lined reservoirs. The public benefits of irrigation encouraged the formation of cooperative labor groups known as ayllu. This depiction of Andean raised-field farming was included in a chronicle written by a native Peruvian in around 1615. (Photo: akg-images.)

In contrast to Mesoamerican peoples, who lacked economically useful domesticated animals, Andean peoples used the llama as a beast of burden and the alpaca as a source of meat and wool; the latter was especially important in this bitterly cold environment. Llama caravans traveled up and down the spine of the Andes ranges, trading in local specialties such as woolen cloth, pottery, and bone tools and utensils. Small towns near Lake Titicaca became trading posts that fed this growing interregional exchange. In the fifth century C.E. the city of Tiwanaku (tee-wah-NAH-coo), at the southern end of Lake Titicaca, became the dominant economic and political center of the region, serving as a crossroads connecting the environmentally diverse Andean communities (see again Map 11.2).

Tiwanaku included ceremonial centers with grand temples and public plazas, a large square stone-walled administrative center, and extensive residential barrios. At its peak between 500 and 800 the city may have housed as many as sixty thousand inhabitants, so it was roughly the same size as Chan Chan but less than one-third of Teotihuacán's maximum population. Some scholars believe that by this time Tiwanaku had developed from a major metropolis into a highly centralized state led by a small group of priestly clans or perhaps a royal dynasty. The power of the ruling elite rested on a highly ordered cosmology expressed through the precise spatial layout of the city and its lavish culture of rituals and feasting. The religious symbols and images of gods found at Tiwanaku were clearly ancestral to those of the Incas. As in Mesoamerica, public ceremony was central to religious and political life. The many drinking vessels and snuff tubes, spoons, and trays found among the ruins of Tiwanaku confirm that consumption of alcohol and hallucinogenic plants was important during these ceremonies. The prodigious drinking and eating at these events also provided occasions for rulers to demonstrate their generosity and to strengthen social and political bonds with their subjects (see Seeing the Past: Images of Power in Tiwanaku Art).

Tiwanaku's Broad Influence   The uniformity of Tiwanaku ceramic art and architecture, which came to be widely dispersed throughout the region, suggests that Tiwanaku's political ideology and craft traditions exercised a strong influence over local communities. Some scholars interpret Tiwanaku's pattern of development—intensification of agriculture, specialization of craft manufactures, road building, and resettlement of the population on farmland reclaimed from the lake bed—as evidence of strong state control. Others question the portrayal of Tiwanaku as a centralized empire whose rule rested on colonial domination and extraction of tribute. Although there is ample archaeological evidence of human sacrifice and display of decapitated enemies as trophies, Tiwanaku had no fortifications. Weapons and images of warfare are rare in Tiwanaku art, suggesting that the city's power derived more from its economic strength and religious ideology than from military aggression.

Wari's Militarized State   Tiwanaku was not the only significant political force in the Andean highlands. During the seventh and eighth centuries the city-state of Wari (WAH-ree), four hundred miles to the north, established a far-flung network of walled settlements in the highland valleys to its north and south, extending almost the entire length of modern Peru. In contrast to

Images of Power in Tiwanaku Art

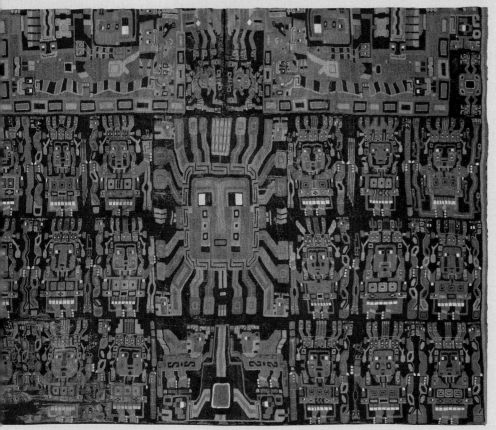

Wool Tunic from Tiwanaku, c. 200–400 (Private Collection.)

The lack of written records leaves us with many mysteries about the composition, character, and even the names of the ruling elites who lived in the sumptuous palaces of the city of Tiwanaku. But artistic and architectural evidence gives important clues about the self-image of Tiwanaku's rulers. Decorated wool garments and tapestries provide us with rich visual materials of a sort rarely found for other ancient civilizations. The extreme dryness of the Andean highland environment preserved organic materials such as textiles that would have quickly disintegrated in humid climates.

Scholars interpret the dense patterns on the wool tunic shown here as a representation of Tiwanaku and its ruling powers. The face of a god, shown as a many-rayed sun, dominates the center. Below the god's face is a stepped structure that resembles the principal shrine at Tiwanaku. On the lowest tiers of this structure stand two winged figures with feline faces (their heads turned back over their

shoulders) and gold ankle bracelets. These figures are probably priests wearing ritual costumes.

Flanking the central images on each side are rows of human figures in elaborate dress holding staffs, arrows, or plants. All of the figures, like the central deity, have vertically divided eyes, which are thought to be a mark of ancestral or divine status. Three upturned animal heads are attached to each headdress, and each figure wears three gold ornaments on its chest. Yet the great variety of headdress styles, facial markings, and garment patterns indicates that each figure represents a specific identity, most likely the heads of the ruling lineages of Tiwanaku or the leaders of subordinate towns and social groups. The array of images suggests a religious festival or procession in which the leaders of human society pay homage to the gods and ancestors.

The Incas who later ruled the Andean region believed that festivals were occasions when the living could connect with their ancestors and invoke divine power to bring life-giving rain to their fields and pastures. The dominant images in Tiwanaku art suggest that the Tiwanaku shared such beliefs.

Source: From Margaret Young-Sánchez, ed., *Tiwanaku: Ancestors of the Inca* (Lincoln: University of Nebraska Press, 2004), 47, Figure 2.26a.

EXAMINING THE EVIDENCE

1. The figures in the wool tunic hold staffs that take the form of hybrid creatures with serpent bodies and feline (perhaps jaguar) heads. Why do you think Tiwanaku's leaders chose these animals to represent their power?

2. What does the emphasis on symmetry and repetition in Tiwanaku art, architecture, and urban design suggest about their rulers' ideas of social and cosmic order?

Tiwanaku, the Wari state set up military outposts to control and extract tribute from local populations.

Wari was located on a plateau at a lower altitude than Tiwanaku, but the region was drier and more dependent on irrigation for agriculture. Wari farmers grew maize along with highland crops such as the mainstays, potato and quinoa, in terraced fields constructed on hillsides and watered by canals. Tiwanaku and Wari shared a common religious heritage but had markedly different forms of religious practice. Wari architecture suggests a more exclusive ceremonial culture restricted to private settings and a small elite, in contrast to the grand temples and public plazas of Tiwanaku.

Decline of the Highland States
Archaeological evidence reveals that by the ninth century Wari's colonial empire had collapsed and new building in the city had come to a halt. In around 1000 the same fate befell Tiwanaku. Prolonged drought had upset the fragile ecological balance of raised-field agriculture, and food production declined drastically. The city of Tiwanaku was abandoned, and political power came to be widely dispersed among local chieftains solidly entrenched in hilltop forts. Highland peoples continued some irrigated agriculture, but they relied heavily on animal herds for subsistence. Incessant warfare merely produced a political standoff among local chiefdoms, with no escalation into conquest and expansion until the rise of the Inca Empire in the fifteenth century.

Agrarian Societies in North America

FOCUS

How did the introduction of Mesoamerican crops transform North American peoples?

North America, like the Andean region, long remained isolated from developments in Mesoamerica. The deserts of northern Mexico impeded movement of peoples and technologies from the centers of Mesoamerican civilization to the vast landmass to the north. Although North American peoples cultivated some native plants as food sources as early as 2000 B.C.E., agriculture did not emerge as a way of life in North America until maize was introduced from Mesoamerica in around 1000 B.C.E. (see again Mapping the World, page 340).

Maize first appeared in North America's southwestern deserts, but the transition to agriculture in this arid region was gradual and uneven. The eastern woodlands had a greater variety of subsistence resources and a longer tradition of settled life, yet here, too, Mesoamerican crops eventually stimulated the emergence of complex societies and expanding networks of communication and exchange (see Map 11.3).

Pueblo Societies in the Southwestern Deserts

Shift to Settled Life
Mesoamerican agriculture penetrated the deserts of northern Mexico and the southwestern United States slowly. Farmers gradually adapted Mesoamerican crops to this hot, arid environment by carefully selecting seeds, soils, and naturally irrigated lands for cultivation. But it was only after 200 C.E. that yields from growing crops encouraged the southwestern desert peoples to abandon gathering and hunting in favor of settled agriculture. Clay pots used for food storage and cooking also first appeared in the Southwest at this time. Another important cause of the shift to farming was, ironically, the bow and arrow, introduced by bison hunters of North America's Great Plains, also in around 200 C.E. By providing more protein from game, use of the bow and arrow made it easier to adopt maize, which supplies ample calories but is very low in protein, as a staple food.

Early agricultural settlements in the southwestern deserts tended to be small, loose clusters of oval pit dwellings. But even these small villages contained special buildings used for ritual purposes. These buildings were the forerunners of the *kivas*, or large ceremonial rooms, of the later pueblo societies in which people lived in large complexes of adjoining adobe buildings.

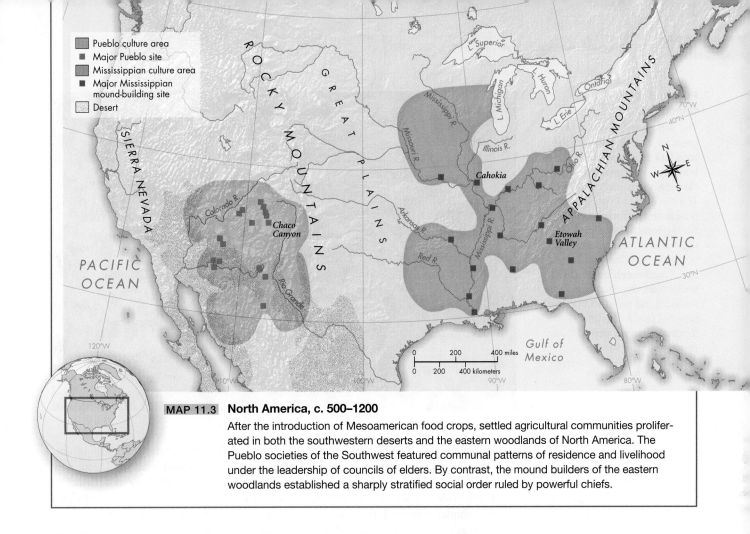

Legend:
- Pueblo culture area
- Major Pueblo site
- Mississippian culture area
- Major Mississippian mound-building site
- Desert

MAP 11.3 North America, c. 500–1200

After the introduction of Mesoamerican food crops, settled agricultural communities proliferated in both the southwestern deserts and the eastern woodlands of North America. The Pueblo societies of the Southwest featured communal patterns of residence and livelihood under the leadership of councils of elders. By contrast, the mound builders of the eastern woodlands established a sharply stratified social order ruled by powerful chiefs.

The limited productivity of the land made self-sufficiency difficult. Farmers often traded to obtain food as well as salt, stone for toolmaking, and prestige goods, including hides and precious stones such as turquoise. After 700 C.E., population growth and increasing dependence on agriculture led to replacement of the pithouse villages with **pueblos**, in which hundreds or even thousands of people lived in contiguous buildings constructed of adobe clay or stone. By 900, pueblo villages had spread throughout much of the northern tier of the southwestern deserts, especially on the Colorado River plateau.

Chaco Canyon, in northwestern New Mexico, dramatically illustrates the transformation of social life in the southwestern deserts as its agricultural livelihood matured. The first villages, along with maize and squash agriculture, appeared in the canyon in around 500 C.E. The largest of these early villages consisted of no more than twenty pithouses. Between 700 and 900, large pueblos replaced the pithouse villages. The dwelling spaces in the pueblos were arranged in semicircular arcs so that each multiroom family unit was equidistant from a central chamber, the **kiva** that served as the community's ceremonial nucleus.

During the tenth century, Chaco Canyon's population exploded. Much larger pueblos with more than two hundred rooms appeared. By the twelfth century the canyon had thirteen of these large pueblos housing a population of approximately six thousand people.

Both large and small settlements in Chaco Canyon contained turquoise workshops that manufactured a wide range of ritual ornaments. Because the nearest sources of turquoise were in the modern Santa Fe area, about one hundred miles to the east, craftsmen had to obtain their raw material through trade or possibly tribute. Exchange networks linked Chaco Canyon with at least seventy communities dispersed across more than ten thousand square miles throughout the Colorado River plateau. These outlying settlements also featured pueblo construction and were connected to Chaco Canyon by a network of

Pueblo Villages

Chaco Canyon

pueblo A communal village built by the peoples of southwestern North America, consisting of adjoining flat-roofed stone or adobe buildings arranged in terraces.

kiva A large ceremonial chamber located at the center of the pueblo.

Pueblo Bonito, Chaco Canyon

The largest of Chaco Canyon's great houses, Pueblo Bonito rose four stories and contained hundreds of rooms and numerous large circular kivas. The diversity of Pueblo Bonito's burials and artifacts—including trade goods from coastal regions and Mesoamerica—suggests that Chacoan society had a moderately developed social hierarchy. Archaeological research has revealed that over time the pueblo's primary function changed from residential complex to ceremonial center. (R. Perron/Art Resource, Art Resource, NY.)

rudimentary roads. Most likely the outlying communities were populated by emigrants forced to leave Chaco Canyon as population growth overburdened local food resources. Although Chaco Canyon may have served as a ritual hub for the entire web of settlements, centralized rule was absent even within the canyon's confines. Each pueblo seems to have pursued similar industrial, trade, and ceremonial activities. Historians generally have concluded that councils of elders coordinated these activities and managed relations with neighboring communities but that no privileged groups of families attained exclusive rights to political office. Hence in Chaco Canyon we see another example of the diversity of historical development. Agriculture led to population growth and large settlements, but, unlike in much of Eurasia, it did not lead to the emergence of kingship or empire building.

Abandonment of Chaco Canyon

In the early twelfth century prolonged drought weakened the canyon's fragile agricultural base. Many inhabitants migrated elsewhere, and others probably returned to foraging. Pueblo societies continued to flourish in other parts of the southwestern deserts where local conditions remained favorable to farming or trade. Although long-distance exchange continued, none of the other pueblo societies developed an integrated network of settlements like that of Chaco Canyon.

Some scholars believe that regional exchange and the founding of pueblo towns were stimulated by long-distance trade with merchants from the central Mexican highlands. Others contend that trade emerged in the southwestern deserts as a practical response to the unreliability of agriculture in this harsh environment. Environmental changes—especially soil exhaustion and increasingly irregular rainfall—may also have led to the abandonment of concentrated pueblo settlements and the return to more dispersed settlement beginning in the twelfth century. However, a similar trend toward concentration of political power and wider networks of exchange during the period 1000 to 1200, followed by a reversion to smaller and more isolated communities in the centuries before European contact, also occurred in the temperate woodlands of the Mississippi Valley, where livelihoods were less vulnerable to climatic change.

Mound-Building Societies in the Eastern Woodlands

Spread of Mesoamerican Agriculture

Beginning in around 700 C.E., the introduction of new technologies radically altered the evolution of eastern woodland societies in North America. The most important innovation was the cultivation of Mesoamerican food crops. The widespread cultivation of maize, perhaps prompted by greater control over labor and resources by a rising class of chiefs, revolutionized agriculture and transformed the woodlanders' economic livelihood. At the same time, the flint hoes that accompanied the spread of maize farming made it possible to construct mounds on a much larger scale, and the introduction of the bow and arrow from the Great Plains led to new hunting tactics.

The spread of Mesoamerican agriculture encouraged migration, regional exchange, and the formation of chiefdoms. Unlike the southwestern deserts, where the founding of settled communities followed the transition to agriculture, the eastern woodlands already had permanent villages. Still, population growth triggered by the capacity to produce more food led to greater occupational specialization and social complexity. Favorably located mound settlements conducted a lively trade in stone tools made from chert (a flintlike rock) and obsidian, marine shells from the Gulf of Mexico, and copper from the upper Great Lakes region, as well as salt, pottery, and jewelry. Population growth also caused friction among neighboring groups competing for land, and farmers displaced foragers from the river valleys best suited to agriculture.

As a result of these developments, the middle and lower reaches of the Mississippi River Valley experienced rapid economic and political changes. Scholars have given the name **Mississippian emergence** to the spread of common technologies, cultural practices, and forms of social and political organization among Mississippi Valley farming societies from the eighth century onward (see Lives and Livelihoods: The North American Mound Builders).

Although most Mississippian societies remained small, in some cases regional trading centers blossomed into powerful chiefdoms. The most famous is Cahokia (kuh-HOH-kee-uh), at the junction of the Illinois and Mississippi rivers just east of modern St. Louis. At its fullest extent, the settlement at Cahokia covered an area of eight square miles. Surrounded by four sets of wooden fortifications, it contained at least ten thousand people, and perhaps as many as thirty thousand. Cahokia's physical size and population thus were comparable to those of the city-states of ancient Mesopotamia, as well as Mesoamerica, in their formative stages of development.

Mound building at Cahokia began in around 900. From 1050 the pace of construction quickly accelerated, and by 1200 Cahokia's inhabitants had erected more than one hundred mounds surrounding a four-tiered pyramid set in the middle of four large plazas oriented north, south, east, and west. Five woodhenges (circles marked by enormous upright cedar posts) enclosed additional ceremonial sites.

Some of Cahokia's mounds were used for elite burials, but most served as platforms for buildings. The height of a mound was an index of prestige. The central pyramid, covering fourteen acres and rising over one hundred feet, was crowned by an enormous pole-and-thatch building covering five thousand square feet, which scholars believe was the residence of Cahokia's paramount chief. As was the case with the monuments of Mesoamerican cities, the placement of Cahokia's mounds was apparently determined by observations of crucial celestial events.

Also as in Mesoamerican cities, Cahokia's impressive mounds, plazas, and woodhenges displayed the power of its rulers to command labor and resources. The Grand Plaza of Cahokia served as a stage from which the chiefs presided over celebratory feasts, fiercely competitive games played with small stone disks known as chunkeys, and solemn death rites in which troops of young women, probably obtained as tribute from outlying areas, were sacrificed. Nonetheless, despite the similarity of Cahokia's plaza-and-pyramid

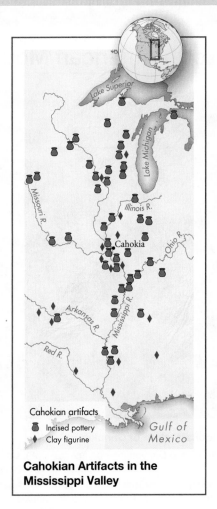

Cahokian Artifacts in the Mississippi Valley

Cahokia

Mississippian emergence The name scholars give to the spread of common technologies, cultural practices, and forms of social and political organization among a wide range of farming societies in the Mississippi Valley of North America, beginning in around 700 and peaking between 1000 and 1500.

The North American Mound Builders

Artist's Reconstruction of Cahokia

Compared to Chaco Canyon (see pages 357–358), Cahokia exhibited a more steeply graded social order. Moreover, in contrast to other mound-building societies—which gradually increased the size of their mounds—construction at Cahokia began with the massive pyramid and great plaza at its core. From the outset Cahokia's rulers displayed an ability to mobilize community labor on a scale unparalleled anywhere else in North America. (Richard Schlecht, National Geographic Image Collection.)

Scholars generally believe that the mounds built by North American woodlands societies symbolized the fertility of the earth and its inhabitants. The idea was that the act of building mounds renewed the fertility of the earth and the welfare of the community. Mound construction strengthened social solidarity by bringing people together in activities intended to ensure the prosperity of all. Moreover, mound building was accompanied by feasting that celebrated communal solidarity. Yet as the woodlands societies grew more complex and stratified, mound-building began to serve other purposes. Paramount chiefs and elite families often appropriated the mounds' symbolic power by reserving them as burial grounds for their exclusive use or by erecting temples on their summits to glorify their ancestors.

The Etowah (EE-toe-wah) River Valley in northwestern Georgia provides evidence of this process of social and political change. Here, as in many parts of the eastern

architecture to Mesoamerican prototypes, there is no evidence of direct Mesoamerican influence at Cahokia or other Mississippian mound-building sites. Indeed, archaeologists have not found imported Mesoamerican manufactured goods anywhere in the eastern woodlands. Although Mesoamerican beliefs and rituals may have had some influence on them, Cahokia's elite generated its own distinctive cosmology and ideology (see Seeing the Past: Symbols of Fertility in Cahokian Sculpture).

Cahokia's Influence   Following the abrupt and dramatic consolidation of power at Cahokia in around 1050, its influence radiated outward throughout the Mississippi Valley. A number of other regional centers, perhaps rivals of Cahokia, emerged from the area of modern Oklahoma to the Atlan-

woodlands, the adoption of maize agriculture led to greater social and political complexity. Etowah, which eventually boasted six mounds, became the region's major political center. It first achieved local prominence in the eleventh century, but over the next five centuries its history showed a cyclical pattern of development and abandonment.

In the eleventh century Etowah was a small settlement with residences, community buildings, and perhaps a small mound and plaza. Ritual life was confined to feasting, and there was a notable absence of prestige goods that would signify a strong social hierarchy. The earliest confirmed evidence of mound building dates from the twelfth century, when several other mound settlements appear in the Etowah Valley. Although these settlements were probably the capitals of independent chiefdoms, archaeological evidence of social ranking at this time is slim. Apparently these settlements were still organized around principles of community solidarity rather than hierarchy and stratification.

In the first half of the thirteenth century, the entire Etowah Valley was abandoned, for unknown reasons. When settlement resumed after 1250, a social transformation occurred. Over the next century mound building expanded dramatically, and a sharply stratified chiefdom emerged that exercised overlordship over at least four neighboring mound settlements. Monuments were built at the site, including a large ceremonial hall and a raised central plaza. In a burial mound reserved exclusively for Etowah's ruling elite, archaeologists have found prestige goods such as engraved shell ornaments, flint swords, embossed copper plates, and copper headdress ornaments. The wide dispersal of these items across the southeastern woodlands in the thirteenth and fourteenth centuries indicates that there were strong networks of regional exchange.

In Etowah and elsewhere in the region, wooden fortifications and ceremonial art featuring motifs of violence and combat testify to increasing political conflict and warfare. Copper plates depicting winged warriors found in Etowah burial mounds were almost certainly imported from the Mississippian heartland, if not from Cahokia itself.

The concentration of power that was evident in the Etowah chiefdom during the thirteenth and fourteenth centuries proved to be unstable. After 1375 Etowah and other large chiefdoms in the southeastern woodlands collapsed. The inhabitants again abandoned the site of Etowah. Regional trade networks became constricted, and the flow of prestige goods diminished. Whether chiefly authority was weakened by enemy attack or internal strife is uncertain. By the time the Spanish explorers arrived in 1540, another trend toward concentration of political power and expansion of territorial control was well under way. At this point, however, the capacity to organize mound building and the possession of prestige goods were no longer sufficient to claim political authority. Warfare had supplanted religious symbolism as the source of a chief's power.

QUESTIONS TO CONSIDER

1. In what ways did the purposes of the North American mound builders resemble those of the builders of monumental cities in Mesoamerica and the Andean region? In what ways did they differ?

2. How did changes in the structure and purpose of mound building at Etowah and Cahokia reflect new developments in social organization and the basis of political power in North American societies?

For Further Information:

King, Adam. *Etowah: The Political History of a Chiefdom Capital*. Tuscaloosa: University of Alabama Press, 2003.

Reilly, F. Kent, III, and James F. Garber, eds. *Ancient Objects and Sacred Realms: Interpretations of Mississippian Iconography*. Austin: University of Texas Press, 2007.

tic coast. Local chiefs imitated the mound building and sacred ceremonies of the Mississippian culture. Control of prestige goods acquired through trade enhanced the charismatic authority of these chiefs. Still, the power of the paramount chiefs at Cahokia and elsewhere rested on their alliances with lesser chiefs, who were the heads of their own distinct communities, rather than on direct control of the settled population. Political power thus remained fragile—vulnerable to shifts in trade patterns, economic fortunes, and political loyalties.

Cahokia declined after 1250 as competition from rival chiefs grew and as its farming base shrank due to prolonged droughts and deforestation. After 1300, Cahokia's inhabitants abandoned its grand ceremonial center and dispersed. Other smaller Mississippian

Cahokia's Collapse

Symbols of Fertility in Cahokian Sculpture

Birger Figurine (Courtesy of the Illinois State Archaeological Survey, University of Illinois.)

Mississippian peoples rarely incorporated images of humans and their activities into their art. Scholars have therefore closely scrutinized a small number of flint clay sculptures in the form of human beings for clues to Mississippian ideas about themselves and their world. These figurines mostly depict men engaged in battle, beheading enemies, and making offerings to ancestors and gods. Only in a few rare cases, such as the so-called Birger figurine shown here, do they include images of women.

Unearthed at Cahokia, the Birger figurine dates to the early twelfth century, the peak of Cahokia's dominance. It depicts a woman kneeling on a coiled snake, her left hand resting on the serpent's feline head (perhaps a puma) and her right hand holding a hoe. On her back she wears a square pack. Vines entwine the woman's body and stretch up her spine, putting forth fruit resembling squash or gourds. The figurine, discovered at a mortuary temple reserved for priests and nobles, was apparently deliberately broken during a ritual dedicated to the dead.

The association with serpents and agricultural tools and crops is typical among the small number of female Mississippian flint clay figures. Scholars generally agree that these symbols link the fertility of women as childbearers to the fertility of the earth. The snake symbolizes the earth itself, which the woman cultivates with her hoe. The plants and fruit wrapped around the woman's body signify both the fertility of women and their prominent role in farming. Images of the land and farming appear only in connection with female figures in Mississippian art.

Some scholars go further to argue that the Birger figurine and similar objects express a mythology in which women are associated with an underworld (symbolized by the serpent) that is the source of water, fertility, and the power of water-dwelling monsters. Male chiefs and warriors, by contrast, appear together with signs of the heavens, such as the sun and birds. The imagery of the Birger figurine also suggests a connection to the Earth Mother or Corn Mother myths that recur frequently in the ceremonial traditions of later eastern woodland peoples. The Earth Mother symbolized the life-giving power of plants and women, as well as the cycles of regeneration in which crops sprung from seeds and the souls of the dead were reborn in children. The Earth Mother thus was a goddess of both life and death.

Mississippian art and mythology exhibit a profound dualism: the underworld associated with women and water is strictly divided from the upper world of men and its motifs of sun, fire, and birds. This rigid gender segregation undoubtedly reflects a society that sharply separated the spheres, activities, and powers of men and women.

Source: Birger Figurine: From Rinita A. Dalan et al., *Envisioning Cahokia: A Landscape Perspective* (DeKalb: Northern Illinois University Press, 2003), 202, Figure 47. (Courtesy of Illinois Transportation Archaeological Research Program, University of Illinois.)

EXAMINING THE EVIDENCE

1. In what ways do Mississippian ideas about female qualities and powers, as revealed in the Birger figurine, differ from the Mesoamerican conception of masculine power expressed by the "At a Crossroads" ballplayer illustration on page 338?

2. Why would the priests break objects such as this figurine during the rituals performed in honor of the dead?

chiefdoms persisted down to the first contacts with Europeans in the sixteenth century and beyond. But in the wake of Cahokia's collapse, long-distance economic and cultural exchanges waned, and the incidence of violence grew. The prevalence of warrior imagery, the concentration of the population in fortified towns, and the ample evidence of traumatic death from excavated cemeteries all point to the emergence of warfare as a way of life.

The scale and complexity of the settlements and ritual complexes at Cahokia were unique in North America. Yet its influence as a panregional cultural force is reminiscent of other urban centers in the Americas. As in Tiwanaku, feasting, sacrifice, and resettlement of rural inhabitants in the urban core forged a distinctive cultural identity at Cahokia. Also like Tiwanaku, Cahokia apparently served as a ritual center for a group of independent chiefdoms that for a time merged into a single political entity. At the peak of its power, Cahokia's culinary habits, pottery styles, and agricultural techniques spread over a vast area. In this sense, as an economic and political crossroads, Cahokia was central to the emergence of a distinctive Mississippian society.

Habitat and Adaptation in the Pacific Islands

The Lapita colonization (see Chapter 8) transformed the landscapes and seascapes of the western Pacific, or Near Oceania. After approximately 200 B.C.E., though, what historians call the "long pause" in transoceanic migrations set in. Subsequently the cultural unity spawned by the Lapita migrations fragmented as local groups adapted to their diverse island habitats. Trade networks collapsed, and pottery making declined everywhere.

> **FOCUS**
> In what ways did the habitats and resources of the Pacific Islands promote both cultural unity and cultural diversity?

The "long pause" may reflect not people's lack of effort, but rather their lack of success in making landfall on the smaller and far more widely dispersed islands of the central and eastern Pacific, or Remote Oceania. But in around 300 C.E. (some scholars would say even several centuries earlier), a new wave of migration began with a leap eastward of more than twelve hundred miles from Samoa to the Marquesas and Society Island archipelagoes. This second wave of exploration brought human colonists to virtually every habitable island in the Pacific Ocean by the year 1000 (see Map 11.4).

In Near Oceania, the interaction of the Lapita peoples with the native Papuan societies had generated extraordinary cultural diversity. In contrast, this second wave of migrations into the farthest reaches of Remote Oceania fostered a culturally unified set of islands known as Polynesia. Still, Polynesian settlers did modify their livelihoods and social and political institutions to suit the resources of their island habitats. **Human ecology**—the ways in which people adapt to their natural environment—was as flexible in the Pacific Islands as in the world's great continental landmasses.

Polynesian Expansion

The Pacific Islands are commonly divided into three parts: Melanesia ("Middle Islands"), Micronesia ("Small Islands"), and Polynesia ("Many Islands"). Yet Melanesia makes sense only as a geographic label, not as a social or cultural unit. In fact, the peoples of Melanesia (if we include New Guinea) make up the most diverse and complex assembly of peoples and cultures on earth. Similarly, Micronesia had at least two major language groups and was populated over the course of four separate periods of immigration.

Polynesian societies, in contrast, share a strong social and cultural identity. Polynesian culture emerged from the Lapita settlements of Tonga and Samoa in the first millennium B.C.E. Following the leap to the Marquesas and Society archipelagoes, Polynesians spread through a chain of migrations westward into Micronesia, northward to the Hawaiian Islands, and eastward as far as Easter Island.

human ecology Adaptation of people to the natural environment they inhabit.

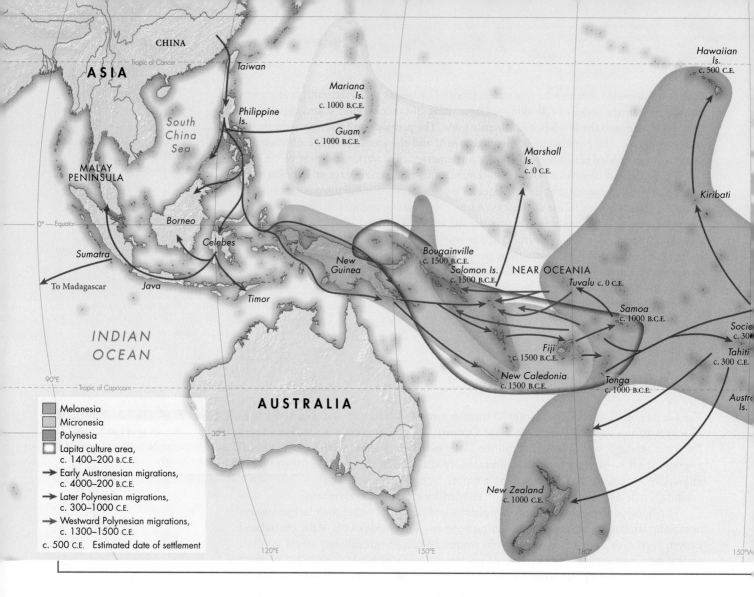

Like the Lapita colonization, the Polynesian expansion included a cycle of vigorous interisland interactions during the initial phase of colonization, followed by progressive isolation and interruption of communication and exchange. The most remote parts of Polynesia, such as Easter Island and the Hawaiian archipelago, became solitary worlds.

The distinctive character of Polynesian societies owes much to their isolation. Fiji was virtually unique in maintaining exchanges of goods, people, and cultural influences with Melanesian societies; Tonga and the rest of Polynesia lost all contact with Melanesia. But however isolated the Polynesian societies of the central Pacific became, their recent common ancestry gave them similar languages, social practices, and forms of livelihood. One striking feature of the Polynesian expansion was the widespread abandonment of pottery manufacture. In contrast to the Lapita peoples, who regarded elaborately decorated pottery as a sign of high social rank, pottery—for reasons still unknown—lost its status as a prestige good among the Polynesians. Pottery was also replaced by coconut shells and wooden bowls for utilitarian purposes such as storing and cooking food.

Although Polynesian settlers had reached all of the habitable Pacific Islands by 1000, migration among settled islands continued. In around the year 1300 Polynesian voyagers would begin to travel westward into Micronesia and the southern parts of Melanesia. On some small islands, such as Tikopia (TEE-co-pi-ah) in Melanesia, Polynesians would wholly replace the native population, but more commonly the migrants mixed with the native peoples to produce hybrid cultures. Micronesian peoples, living in unstable envi-

Polynesia's Cultural Unity

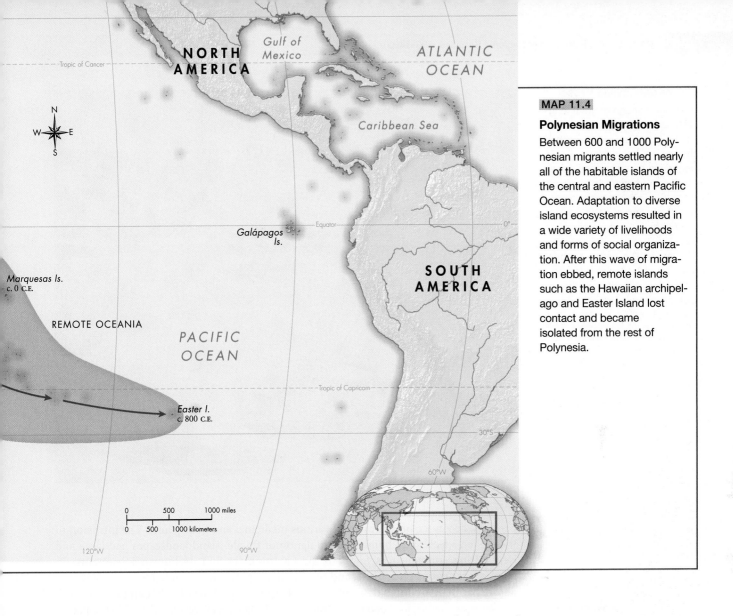

MAP 11.4

Polynesian Migrations

Between 600 and 1000 Polynesian migrants settled nearly all of the habitable islands of the central and eastern Pacific Ocean. Adaptation to diverse island ecosystems resulted in a wide variety of livelihoods and forms of social organization. After this wave of migration ebbed, remote islands such as the Hawaiian archipelago and Easter Island lost contact and became isolated from the rest of Polynesia.

ronments with limited resources, displayed enormous flexibility in changing their ways of life and welcoming strangers into their communities.

Distinctive ecosystems nurtured a wide range of livelihoods and political systems across the Polynesian Pacific. Larger islands with richer and more varied resources, among them Tahiti, Tonga, and Hawaii, gave rise to highly stratified societies and complex chiefdoms with tens of thousands of subjects. The rigid hierarchical structure of the Polynesian chiefdoms was based on command of economic resources. The vast majority in their populations were landless commoners. Local chiefs held title to cultivated lands but owed **fealty** (allegiance to a higher authority) and tribute to paramount chiefs, who wielded sacred power over entire islands (as we will see in Chapter 12's Counterpoint on the Hawaiian Islands, page 398).

Ecosystems and Social Stratification

Subsistence and Survival in the Pacific Islands

Counter to the romantic fantasies of nineteenth-century European travelers and twentieth-century anthropologists, the Pacific Islands were not pristine natural worlds undisturbed by their "primitive" human inhabitants. On the contrary, human hands had radically transformed the island ecosystems. For example, the islands of Remote Oceania originally lacked plant and animal species suitable for human food consumption. Polynesian settlers changed all that by bringing with them pigs, dogs, chickens, yams, taro, sugar cane,

fealty An expression of allegiance to a higher political authority, often verified by swearing an oath of loyalty, giving tribute, and other gestures of submission.

Polynesian Sailing Vessel

Although the age of great long-distance voyaging had ceased by the time Europeans reached the Pacific, Polynesians continued to make open-ocean journeys of hundreds of miles. In 1616 a Dutch mariner drew this illustration of a Polynesian double-hulled canoe sailing between Tonga and Samoa. The largest Polynesian canoes were roughly the same length as the sailing vessels of the European explorers. (*A Chronological History of the Voyages & Discoveries in the South Sea or Pacific Ocean*, London: Lake Hansard & Sons.)

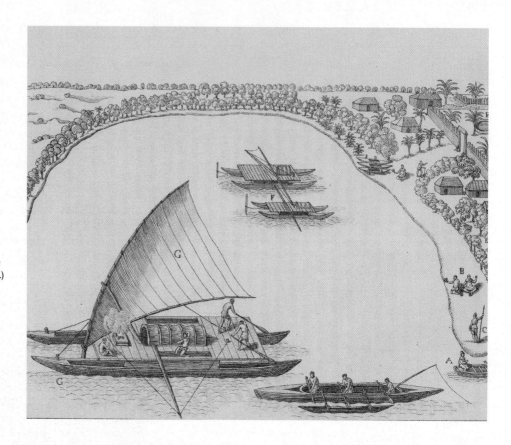

Environmental Transformation and Population Growth

bananas, coconuts, breadfruit, and various medicinal and fiber plants. The intrusion of these alien species and human manipulation of fragile island landscapes had large and long-lasting consequences for both the environment and its human inhabitants. In many places native bird, turtle, and sea mammal species were hunted to extinction, and **deforestation**, the cutting down of forests, sharply reduced the islands' natural resources.

Most of the tropical food plants transported by colonizers readily thrived in the Pacific Islands. Settlers practiced horticulture (the cultivation of fruits and vegetables), planting orchards of coconuts and bananas around their villages while cutting down rain forests to make room for root and tuber crops that required little care. As in Iceland's early history (see Chapter 9), explosive population growth typically followed initial settlement on uninhabited islands. Settlers had a compelling reason—fear of extinction—to have enough children to attain populations large enough to maintain their societies. Population densities on many islands reached 250 persons per square mile. Ecological constraints, however, ultimately curbed unrestricted population growth.

Micronesia's low-lying atolls—rings of coral surrounding a central lagoon—presented the most challenging environments. Exposed to destruction by typhoons and tsunamis, lacking fresh water other than rainfall, with just sand and crushed coral for soil, atolls offered only slender footholds for human colonists. Because cultivating taro and breadfruit was impossible on many coral atolls, coconut trees were essential to human survival. In addition to depending on coconuts for food, atoll dwellers used coconut leaves for textile fiber and for construction material. Lacking ceramics and metals, the atoll peoples fashioned utensils and tools from coconuts, seashells, and fish bones.

On many islands, population pressure began to strain resources after 1100. Where possible, islanders applied more laborious agricultural methods, building irrigation canals and terraced or walled garden plots. In the Marquesas, swelling population growth increased competition and warfare. More fortified villages were built, and the authority of warrior chiefs rose. Settlement became concentrated in the island interiors, which afforded

deforestation The cutting down of forests, usually to clear land for farming and human settlement.

not only protection from sea raiders but lands more suitable for intensive cultivation. A similar pattern of intensified agriculture and warfare in response to population pressure appeared in Fiji. The growing diversity of local ceramic styles in Fiji also suggests a greater demarcation of ethnic groups and political boundaries. Here, too, constant warfare shifted the basis of chiefship from priestly duties to military leadership.

The most striking example of the fragility of island ecosystems and the risk of demographic catastrophe is Easter Island. When Polynesian voyagers originally settled Easter Island sometime after 600 C.E., the island was well endowed with fertile soils and abundant forests. These rich resources supported a population that at its peak numbered ten thousand people. Easter Island's famous stone monuments—thirty-ton sculptures believed to be images of ancestors who were transformed into gods—were carved and installed on more than two hundred temple platforms across the island between 1100 and 1500. But the clearing of forests for agriculture depleted fuel and construction resources, and erosion and exposure to wind and surf ruined soil fertility. After 1500, the island was plunged into incessant raiding and warfare, accompanied by ritual cannibalism. Construction of stone monuments halted. As the once plentiful flora and fauna of Easter Island were decimated, its human population dwindled to a mere several hundred persons subsisting mainly on fishing, the Pacific Ocean's most reliable resource.

Increased Competition and Warfare

Easter Island

COUNTERPOINT
Social Complexity in Bougainville

Bougainville (bow-gahn-VEEL), one of the chain of islands stretching in a long arc southeastward from New Guinea, typifies the phenomenon of **ethnogenesis**, the formation of separate ethnic groups from common ancestors. In contrast to the underlying social and cultural unity of many of the societies studied in this chapter, the long-settled islands of Melanesia display extraordinary social and cultural diversity. The complexity of the Melanesian world presents an important challenge for any theory of the evolution of human societies. Here the progress of history fostered not closer interaction and cross-cultural borrowing but rather more acute social differences and strong ethnic boundaries.

FOCUS

Why did the historical development of the Melanesian island of Bougainville depart so sharply from that of contemporaneous societies in the Americas and the Pacific?

Bougainville's Diverse Peoples

Situated slightly below the equator, Bougainville has a tropical climate with virtually no seasonal variation, enabling the island's farmers to cultivate food crops, mainly taro, year-round. Yet with four active volcanoes, Bougainville is one of the most geologically unstable places on earth. Volcanic eruptions have periodically covered major portions of the island with ash and forced the inhabitants to relocate, at least temporarily. The island, roughly the size of Puerto Rico, is sparsely populated even today. The mountainous interior remains virtually uninhabited. Settlements are concentrated along streams on the relatively flat terrain of the northern coast and in the southern interior.

Twenty different languages are spoken on Bougainville today. Scholars classify twelve of these languages as Austronesian (AW-stroh-NEE-zhuhn), the language group of the seafarers who settled in the islands of Southeast Asia and the Pacific during the Lapita colonization. Linguists broadly define the rest as Papuan (PAH-poo-en), the languages spoken by the ancient inhabitants of New Guinea, although their relationship to the other Papuan languages is uncertain. Four of Bougainville's languages are so idiosyncratic that the associations among them confound linguists.

Linguistic and Cultural Diversity

ethnogenesis The formation of separate ethnic groups from common ancestors.

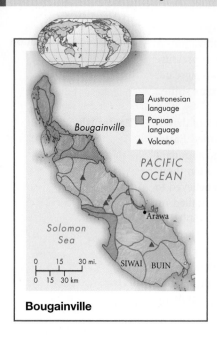

Bougainville

Beyond the striking language differences, Bougainville's inhabitants also vary so much in stature, body type, and biological chemistry that Bougainville islanders rank among the most genetically diverse populations on the planet. Cultural variation is similarly striking. Although pottery manufacture on Bougainville dates back to the pre-Lapita era, some groups apparently have never made pottery and rarely sought ceramic wares from those who did.

What accounts for such remarkable diversity within the confines of this one island? One popular theory is that the kind of tropical agriculture practiced in Bougainville is relatively rich and reliable, and so the islanders have not had to build trading networks or other kinds of connections between communities to meet their needs. Traditions of matrilineal descent and local **endogamy**—marriage within the group—reinforced this pattern of isolated village life. The social isolation of individual villages also tended to raise language barriers over time. With two exceptions, the geographical range of the languages spoken on Bougainville does not exceed fifteen miles in diameter. Further, as modern biological research shows, small populations are more likely to experience large genetic fluctuations from one generation to the next, which fosters more, not less, genetic diversity. Not surprisingly, genetic variation among Bougainville's modern populations correlates strongly with language groups.

The Historical Roots of Social Difference

The Siwai and the Buin: A Case Study

Yet the diversity of Bougainville's languages did not result from a long period of isolation. The island probably experienced a number of separate immigrations both before and after the Lapita era. The island's Austronesian speakers did not simply all arrive together at the time of the Lapita migrations. There is clear evidence that some coastal regions were resettled by Austronesian speakers after volcanic eruptions displaced the previous inhabitants.

Further, it is not possible to make neat distinctions between the cultures of "native" Papuan speakers and "immigrant" Austronesian speakers. The Siwai (sih-why), a Papuan-speaking community in southern Bougainville, is noted in anthropological theory as a model **big man society**. According to the American anthropologist Marshall Sahlins, so-called big man societies are characterized by an egalitarian social structure and strong communal identity based on sharing and reciprocal exchange. The role of the big man is to redistribute wealth among members of the community to ensure the well-being of all, but the big man does not hold a position above the rest of society. Sahlins has contrasted Melanesian big man societies with the sharply stratified social hierarchy of Polynesian chiefdoms, in which a hereditary elite of chiefs monopolized political power and the control of economic resources. Near the Siwai in southern Bougainville, however, is another Papuan-speaking group, the Buin (boo-een), whose society developed the high degree of stratification and inherited rank and privilege typical of Polynesian chiefdoms.

Environmental adaptation does not explain the different social structures of the Siwai and the Buin: the two groups occupy virtually identical habitats, practice similar forms of irrigated taro agriculture, and speak closely related languages. Despite their similar livelihoods, the Siwai and Buin embraced different notions of prestige and status. For example, the Buin regarded pottery making as women's work, whereas the Siwai, uniquely among Melanesian societies, reserve pottery making exclusively for men. Scholars have explained this peculiar feature of Siwai culture as a consequence of the unusually cloistered life of Siwai women. According to this theory, knowledge of pottery making was acquired by men, who, unlike women, could travel outside the village, and it became a mark of their superior status.

This contrast underscores one important difference between the Buin and their Siwai neighbors. The Buin had access to the coast and, unlike the Siwai, interacted with peoples in neighboring islands. They learned their techniques of pottery making from Austronesian-speaking inhabitants of the nearby Shetland Islands in around 1000. Indeed, immigrants

endogamy Marriage within a defined group, such as a village or a kinship network.

big man society In modern anthropological theory, an egalitarian society in which a chosen leader, the "big man," supervises the distribution of the community's collective wealth and resources.

from the Shetlands probably arrived in southern Bougainville at that time and may have been absorbed into Buin society.

Yet differences in contact with the outside world cannot fully explain the variations in social practices among Bougainville societies. Some scholars have suggested that in the past, a more pronounced social hierarchy was common in Melanesian societies. In their view, the egalitarian big man societies for which Melanesia became the model were not ancient or primitive forms of social organization; rather, they resulted from the profound changes set in motion by contact with Europeans, including population losses from disease. At the very least, we can no longer attribute the complex human ecology of Melanesia in general, and of Bougainville in particular, to the former historical interpretation of unchanging island cultures cut off from the march of history by the encircling ocean.

Conclusion

During the period 300 to 1200, distinctive regional cultures coalesced in many parts of the Americas and the Pacific Islands. As in Latin Christendom and East Asia, the spread and intensification of agriculture, expanding networks of trade and cultural exchange, and the founding of cities and states led to the formation of common civilizations.

This period marked the classical age in Mesoamerica and the Andean region. There, the development of urban societies and states generated lasting traditions concerning knowledge, livelihoods, and social organization. Rulers such as the Maya Holy Lord Eighteen Rabbit built monumental cities and conducted elaborate public rituals to display their supreme power and bind their subjects to their will.

Permanent towns and long-distance networks of exchange also developed in North America. The spread of prestige goods and ritual art in the eastern woodlands and the southwestern deserts also indicates active cross-cultural borrowing in these regions, at least among elites.

The rapid peopling of the islands of Remote Oceania between 600 and 1000 gave this vast region a common cultural identity as Polynesia. Similar political and social structures and forms of livelihood took root across Polynesia, even though many island populations, such as those of the Hawaiian archipelago and Easter Island, lost contact with the outside world.

Striking, too, are patterns of regional diversity. Different types of social order evolved as new crops and technologies diffused and were adopted, people adjusted social and political institutions and forms of livelihood to new or transformed habitats, and notions of prestige, status, and authority changed. In all of these regions—even among the small village societies of Bougainville, which mostly shunned contact and interaction with their neighbors—social identities and community boundaries changed constantly. Ethnogenesis was a dynamic, continuous, and open-ended process.

By the year 1200, many of these societies were suffering from economic decline and political fragmentation. Scholars have attributed the collapse of the Maya city-state network in the ninth century, the disintegration of the Tiwanaku state in around 1000, and the abandonment of Chaco Canyon and Cahokia in the twelfth and thirteenth centuries primarily to ecological causes: either some climatic catastrophe, or the inability of the existing agricultural technologies and political systems to provide for their growing populations. The collapse of these societies reminds us of the fragility of their agricultural systems, still limited to Stone Age technologies, and their vulnerability to long-term ecological and climatic changes. As we shall see in the next chapter, advances in agricultural and industrial technology and the development of new economic institutions in Eurasia during the eleventh to thirteenth centuries laid the foundations for more sustained economic and demographic growth.

RESOURCES FOR RESEARCH

General Works

Our knowledge of the history of all the societies in this chapter except the Maya depends on research in fields such as archaeology and linguistics rather than written sources. The essays in Quilter and Miller use broad comparative and interdisciplinary analysis to survey the Americas as a whole in the era before the arrival of Europeans. Diamond's provocative analysis of human responses to ecological crises and the collapse of social systems includes case studies of Easter Island, the southwestern deserts of North America, and the Maya.

Diamond, Jared. *Collapse: How Societies Choose to Fail or Succeed.* 2004.

Quilter, Jeffrey, and Mary Miller, eds. *A Pre-Columbian World.* 2006.

Renfrew, Colin, and Steven Shennan, eds. *Peer Polity Interaction and Socio-Political Change.* 1986.

The Classical Age of Mesoamerica and Its Aftermath

The scholarship on the Maya is especially rich. Drew provides an excellent overview of both Maya civilization and the development of scholarship on the Maya. Carrasco's study of the Feathered Serpent is a pioneering investigation of the common cultural heritage of Mesoamerica as a whole.

Carrasco, David. *Quetzalcoatl and the Irony of Empire: Myth and Prophecies in the Aztec Tradition,* rev. ed. 2000.

Drew, David. *The Lost Chronicles of the Maya Kings.* 1999.

Pasztory, Esther. *Teotihuacan: An Experiment in Living.* 1997.

Schele, Linda, and Peter Mathews. *The Code of Kings: The Language of Seven Sacred Maya Temples and Tombs.* 1998.

Sharer, Robert J. *Daily Life in Maya Civilization,* 2d ed. 2009.

City and State Building in the Andean Region

Recent studies have sought to trace the social and political evolution of precolonial Andean societies through comparative studies of archaeological remains. Kolata's study remains the most thorough examination of Tiwanaku's archaeological record. Janusek proposes new models for understanding the formation of social identity and political power in the Andean region in a very accessible fashion.

Janusek, John Wayne. *Ancient Tiwanaku.* 2008.

Janusek, John Wayne. *Identity and Power in the Ancient Andes: Tiwanaku Cities Through Time.* 2004.

Kolata, Alan. *The Tiwanaku: Portrait of an Andean Civilization.* 1993.

Stanish, Charles. *Ancient Titicaca: The Evolution of Complex Society in Southern Peru and Northern Bolivia.* 2003.

von Hagen, Adriana, and Craig Morris. *The Cities of the Ancient Andes.* 1998.

Agrarian Societies in North America

Reconstruction of the history of North American societies during this period relies especially heavily on the fruits of archaeological research. Fagan's skill at weaving up-to-date coverage of new archaeological evidence into a compelling narrative is displayed in both his textbook survey of North American societies and his Chaco Canyon volume.

Emerson, Thomas E. *Cahokia and the Archaeology of Power.* 1997.

Fagan, Brian. *Ancient North America: The Archaeology of a Continent,* rev. ed. 2005.

Fagan, Brian. *Chaco Canyon: Archaeologists Explore the Lives of an Ancient Society.* 2005.

Milner, George R. *The Moundbuilders: Ancient Peoples of Eastern North America.* 2005.

Pauketat, Timothy R. *Ancient Cahokia and the Mississippians.* 2004.

Habitat and Adaptation in the Pacific Islands

Kirch's 2000 book provides the most comprehensive survey of settlement and social development in the Pacific Islands, and the essays in Howe focus on voyaging and exploration. Challenging the idea of universal stages of social evolution, Earle marshals evidence from case studies of Denmark, Hawaii, and the Andes to distinguish the sources of power in chiefdom societies.

Earle, Timothy. *How Chiefs Come to Power: The Political Economy in Prehistory.* 1997.

Howe, K. R., ed. *Vaka Moana, Voyages of the Ancestors: The Discovery and Settlement of the Pacific.* 2007.

Kirch, Patrick V. *The Evolution of the Polynesian Chiefdoms.* 1984.

Kirch, Patrick V. *On the Road of the Winds: An Archaeological History of the Pacific Islands Before European Contact.* 2000.

Terrell, John. *Prehistory in the Pacific Islands: A Study of Variation in Language, Customs, and Human Biology.* 1986.

COUNTERPOINT: Social Complexity in Bougainville

Since the 1930s anthropologists have considered Melanesia, and Bougainville in particular, as a laboratory for the study of social evolution. The classic works by Sahlins and Service drew on extensive cross-cultural comparisons to develop highly influential models of the emergence of complex social organization and political hierarchy in human societies.

Sahlins, Marshall. *Social Stratification in Polynesia.* 1958.

Service, Robert. *Origins of the State and Civilization: The Process of Cultural Evolution.* 1975.

Spriggs, Matthew. *The Island Melanesians.* 1997.

▶ **For additional primary sources from this period,** see *Sources of Crossroads and Cultures.*

▶ **For Web sites, images, and documents related to topics in this chapter,** see Make History at bedfordstmartins.com/smith.

The major global development in this chapter ▶ The formation of distinctive regional cultures in the Americas and the Pacific Islands between 300 and 1200.

IMPORTANT EVENTS

c. 150–300	Building of the city of Teotihuacán in the Valley of Mexico
c. 250–900	Mesoamerica's classical age
c. 500	First permanent settlements in Chaco Canyon
c. 500–1000	Andean state of Tiwanaku
c. 550–650	Fall and destruction of Teotihuacán
c. 600–1000	Polynesian settlement of Pacific Islands
c. 700	Moche city of Pampa Grande destroyed
c. 700–900	Heyday of the Andean state of Wari
c. 800–900	Collapse of the Maya city-states
c. 850–1150	Building of the large pueblos in Chaco Canyon
c. 900	Rise of the Chimú state centered at Chan Chan
c. 950–1150	Toltec state's reign as the dominant power in the Valley of Mexico
c. 1050	Consolidation of Cahokia's dominance in the lower Mississippi Valley region
c. 1100–1500	Construction of Easter Island's stone monuments
c. 1150	Abandonment of the pueblos in Chaco Canyon
c. 1250–1300	Collapse and abandonment of Cahokia

KEY TERMS

ayllu (p. 353)
big man society (p. 368)
chiefdom (p. 343)
ch'ulel (p. 347)
city-state (p. 343)
deforestation (p. 366)
endogamy (p. 368)
ethnogenesis (p. 367)
fealty (p. 365)

Holy Lord (p. 347)
human ecology (p. 363)
kiva (p. 357)
Mississippian emergence (p. 359)
obsidian (p. 344)
prestige good (p. 344)
pueblo (p. 357)
Tollan (p. 344)

CHAPTER OVERVIEW QUESTIONS

1. How did these societies, equipped with only Stone Age technology, develop the institutions and patterns of exchange to tame often hostile environments and build complex civilizations?

2. How did differences in environment foster or discourage exchanges among adjacent regions?

3. What were the sources of political power in the societies discussed in this chapter, and how were they similar or dissimilar?

4. How did differences in urban design reflect distinctive forms of political and social organization?

SECTION FOCUS QUESTIONS

1. What common beliefs and social and political patterns did the various local societies of Mesoamerica's classical age share?

2. How did environmental settings and natural resources shape livelihoods, social organization, and state building in the Andean region?

3. How did the introduction of Mesoamerican crops transform North American peoples?

4. In what ways did the habitats and resources of the Pacific Islands promote both cultural unity and cultural diversity?

5. Why did the historical development of Bougainville depart so sharply from that of contemporaneous societies in the Americas and the Pacific?

MAKING CONNECTIONS

1. Why were the human populations of the regions covered in this chapter more vulnerable to ecological changes than the settled societies of Eurasia?

2. How did the political and social organization of North American chiefdoms compare with those of the Maya city-states?

3. Although North America's eastern woodlands farmers began to cultivate the same food crops as Mesoamerican peoples during the Mississippian emergence, their societies developed in different ways. What might explain these variations?

AT A CROSSROADS ▶

Arabs and Persians
dominated the Indian
Ocean trade routes, but
by the eleventh century
Indian and Malay mariners
also plied Asian seas from
Africa to China. This
thirteenth-century
illustration depicts a
dhow, the most common
type of Indian Ocean
sailing vessel, on a voyage
from East Africa to Basra,
the great port linking
Mesopotamia to the
Persian Gulf. Indian Ocean
trade vastly expanded
cultural as well as
economic exchange:
although the passengers
are Arabs, the crew
appears to be Indian.
(Bibliothèque Nationale, Paris,
France/Bildarchiv Preussischer
Kulturbesitz/Art Resource, NY.)

The Rise of Commerce in Afro-Eurasia

900–1300

Early in the twelfth century, the Jewish merchant Allan bin Hassun wrote home from Aden, in Yemen on the coast of the Arabian Sea, upon his return from India. Allan had been sent to Yemen by his father-in-law, a prominent Cairo cloth merchant, to sell the purple-dyed cloth that was the father-in-law's specialty. But the cloth had proved unprofitable, so Allan persuaded his reluctant father-in-law to supply him with coral and perfume for a trading venture to India. The journey to India and back had been long and dangerous, and Allan's return had been delayed repeatedly by local uprisings, storms, and accidents.

Upon finally reaching Aden, Allan reported, "I sold the iron for a good price, 20 gold dinars a *bahar* [one bahar equaled 300 pounds]. I had with me 72 bahars and 50 separate pieces, 30 *mann* [one mann equaled 2 pounds] of spices, and 40 mann of cloves. After customs I had obtained 1500 dinars and a lot in other currencies." Allan had intended to return to Cairo, but the high prices that pepper fetched in Aden instead spurred him to immediately set out for India again.

Only fragments of Allan's correspondence survive today, and we do not know how he fared during his return voyage to India. But however successful he was as a businessman, Allan's long sojourns took their toll on his family. In a letter his wife sent to Allan in North

Agricultural Innovation and Diffusion

FOCUS Which groups took the most active role in adopting new agricultural technologies in the different regions of Eurasia during the centuries from 900 to 1300?

Industrial Growth and the Money Economy

FOCUS How did the composition and organization of the industrial workforce change in different parts of Eurasia during this period?

Merchants and Trade Networks in Afro-Eurasia

FOCUS How did the commercial revival of 900 to 1300 reorient international trade routes across Afro-Eurasia?

COUNTERPOINT: Production, Tribute, and Trade in the Hawaiian Islands

FOCUS How did the sources of wealth and power in the Hawaiian Islands differ from those of market economies elsewhere in the world?

BACKSTORY

The collapse of the Han Empire in China and the Western Roman Empire ended a prolonged era of growth in agriculture and trade in the agrarian heartlands of Eurasia (see Chapters 6 and 7). The steppe nomad invasions devastated many cities in China, India, and the Roman Empire's former territories. Political disunity hindered efforts to revive agriculture and commerce. Yet the rise of steppe empires such as that of the Turks also fostered trade and cultural exchange across the caravan routes of Central Asia.

In the seventh century, the formation of a vast Islamic empire and the reestablishment of a unified empire in China by the Sui and Tang dynasties created stable political and social foundations for economic recovery (see Chapters 9 and 10). Latin Christendom remained divided into many kingdoms and city-states, and here the reinvigoration of trade and industry came later. The expanding Islamic world also began to reach across the seas and deserts to bring parts of sub-Saharan Africa into its orbit.

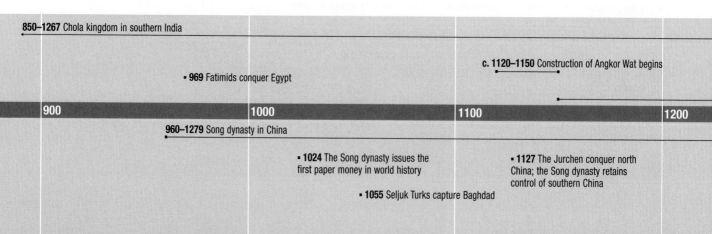

Africa, she bitterly chided him for his absence: "We are in great distress, owing to bad health and loneliness." Caring for their sick infant had forced her to sell furniture and rent out the upper story of their house to pay for doctors and medicines. Lamenting that her father was abroad on business at the same time, the wife urged her husband, "By God, do not tarry any longer . . . we remain like orphans without a man."

Allan's last surviving letter, written when he was an old man about to embark on another expedition to India, warned his adult sons not to abandon their families as he had done. He advised his sons, merchants themselves, to form a partnership that would spread the burdens of travel among them, and admonished them to take good care of their families and one another. His letter conveyed heartfelt regrets about the personal costs of his life as a merchant: "Had I known how much I would be longing after you, I would not have undertaken this voyage altogether."[1]

Merchants such as Allan bin Hassun faced formidable challenges: slow and frail modes of transportation, unfamiliar and sometimes dishonest clients and competitors, and the constant threat of bandits, pirates, and greedy rulers. To overcome these obstacles they devised new business organizations and practices. Allan, an Arabic-speaking Jew from Cairo who roamed westward to Spain and eastward to India, epitomized this cosmopolitan merchant class.

In Allan bin Hassun's day, a sustained economic expansion was spreading across Eurasia and Africa. Favorable climatic conditions, improved agricultural efficiency and output, increases in population and growth of cities, and new patterns of consumption led to rapid expansion of the money economy, culminating in a veritable commercial revolution. Long-distance merchants such as Allan opened new trade routes that connected Europe and the Mediterranean with the Islamic lands and the Indian Ocean. Vigorous commercial growth in China stimulated an unprecedented flowering of maritime trade between East Asia and the Indian Ocean world. The thirst for gold brought parts of sub-Saharan Africa into these trade networks as well. In all of these places, commercial wealth reshaped social and political power.

MAPPING THE WORLD

Commercial Crossroads in Afro-Eurasia, c. 900–1300

After 900, the maritime routes across the Mediterranean Sea and the Indian Ocean eclipsed the overland Silk Road as the great avenues of Eurasian trade. The shift in trade patterns led to the rise of new centers of international trade: Venice became the gateway to Europe, Cairo replaced Baghdad as the commercial capital of the Islamic world, and Nagapattinam, the chief port of the Chola kingdom, flourished as the main crossroads of the Indian Ocean.

ROUTES ▼

— Old Silk Road

— Other land trade route

— Maritime trade route

→ Voyages of
Allan bin Hassun, c. 1115

1250–1517 Mamluk dynasty in Egypt

c. 1150–1300 Heyday of the Champagne fairs

| 1300 | 1400 | 1500 |

1323–1325 Pilgrimage to Mecca of Musa Mansa, ruler of Mali

1258 The Italian city-states of Florence and Genoa mint the first gold coins issued in Latin Christendom

c. 1400–1450 Great Zimbabwe in southern Africa reaches peak of prosperity

1230–1255 Reign of Sunjata, founder of the Mali Empire in West Africa

c. 1200–1400 Formation of first chiefdoms in the Hawaiian Islands

Although the pace and dynamics of economic change varied from region to region, the underlying trends were remarkably consistent. Similarly, in the fourteenth century this surge in economic prosperity suddenly ended across all of Eurasia, from Spain to China. This cycle of economic growth and decline was powered by the progressive integration of local economies into regional and cross-cultural networks of exchange. Parts of the world, however, were still cut off from this web of economic connections. In relatively isolated places such as the Hawaiian Islands, more intensive exploitation of economic resources also had important social and political consequences, but with strikingly different results.

OVERVIEW
QUESTIONS

The major global development in this chapter: The sustained economic expansion that spread across Afro-Eurasia from 900 to 1300.

As you read, consider:

1. How did agricultural changes contribute to commercial and industrial growth?

2. What technological breakthroughs increased productivity most significantly?

3. What social institutions and economic innovations did merchants devise to overcome the risks and dangers of long-distance trade?

4. In what ways did the profits of commerce translate into social and economic power?

5. Above all, who benefited most from these economic changes?

Agricultural Innovation and Diffusion

> **FOCUS**
>
> Which groups took the most active role in adopting new agricultural technologies in the different regions of Eurasia during the centuries from 900 to 1300?

Commercial growth, the most robust feature of economic change during these centuries, was rooted in an increasingly productive agrarian base. The invention, adaptation, and diffusion of new farming techniques raised yields and encouraged investment in agriculture and specialization of production. Rulers, landowners, and peasants all contributed innovations and more intense agricultural production. As urban demand for foodstuffs and industrial raw materials increased, it became more rewarding to produce goods for sale than for household consumption. Increased agricultural production transformed patterns of rural life and community, and changed the relationship between peasants working the land and the lords and states that commanded their loyalty and labor.

Retrenchment and Renewal in Europe and Byzantium

serf A peasant who was legally bound to the land and who owed goods, labor, and service to the lord who owned the land.

The third-century collapse of the unified Roman Empire disrupted economic life in the cities, but it had little direct impact on work and livelihoods in the countryside. In subsequent centuries great lords and peasant smallholders alike concentrated on growing food for their own consumption. Even in the tenth and eleventh centuries, when political stability had restored some measure of economic prosperity in the Byzantine Empire and Latin Europe, self-sufficiency was the goal. Kekaumenos, an eleventh-century Byzantine official, instructed his sons that proper household management meant minimizing expenses, diversifying assets, and avoiding dependence on the market. His first priority was to ensure that the family had "an abundance of wheat, wine, and everything else, seed and livestock, edible and movable." In addition, Kekaumenos advised, "Make for yourself things that are 'self-working'—mills, workshops, gardens, and other things as will give you an annual return whether it be in rent or crop."[2] Vineyards, olives, and fruit trees would yield steady income year after year with the least amount of effort or expenditure. The greatest danger was debt, and the worst evil was to lose one's property to moneylenders.

Great landowners were the main agents of agricultural development and innovation in Europe. Although the population of Europe rose in the tenth and eleventh centuries, labor remained scarce. After the death of Charlemagne in 814, the imperial authority of the Frankish kings declined, and power was largely privatized. The warrior nobility and monastic establishments founded manorial estates that reduced the rural population to the condition of **serfs**, who were bound to the soil they tilled as well as to their masters' will. The spurt of castle-building that swept across western Europe beginning in the late tenth century remade the landscape. Lords gathered their serfs into compact villages and subjected them to their laws as well as the rules of parish priests. Although free smallholder farmers were probably still the majority, they too sought the protection of local lords.

As lordship came to be defined in terms of control over specific territories and populations, the nobility took greater interest in increasing their revenue. Landowners began to invest in enterprises such as watermills, vineyards, and orchards that required large initial outlays of capital but would yield steady long-term returns. In addition to owing their lords numerous dues and services, serfs were obliged to grind their grain at their master's mill, bake their bread in their master's ovens, and borrow money from their master.

Manorial lords also introduced other new technologies, such as the wheeled moldboard plow. Pulled by horses rather than oxen, this device was better than the light Mediterranean-style plow at breaking up northern Europe's heavy, clayey soils. Monasteries and manorial lords also promoted grape cultivation and wine making. Still, some fundamental aspects of European agriculture continued unchanged in both the Latin west and the Byzantine east. Wheat and barley remained the dominant crops. Farmers combined livestock-raising with cereal cultivation, providing more protein in European diets. The large amount of land needed to pasture animals kept population densities relatively low, however.

Agricultural innovation had less impact in the Byzantine Empire than in western Europe. For example, waterwheels were conspicuously absent, perhaps because Byzantine peasants, unlike European serfs, were not compelled to use the mills of the great landowners, who thus had less incentive to invest in expensive machinery. The recovery of Byzantium's political fortunes in the tenth and eleventh centuries led to renewed economic growth. Cultivation of olives, grapes, and figs expanded throughout the Mediterranean

Manorial Lords and Serfs

A Managerial Landlord

In this illustration from a fifteenth-century French handbook on farming, a landowner personally supervises the agricultural work on his estate. The laborers are engaged in various tasks, including plowing, sowing, and harvesting. The team of horses is pulling a wheeled moldboard plow, which allowed farmers to till the heavy soils of northern Europe more efficiently. (HIP/Art Resource, NY.)

lands. In Anatolia (modern Turkey), however, the scarcity of labor prompted landowners to replace agriculture with stock-raising—a trend that accelerated when the Seljuk (SEL-juk) Turks, nomadic Muslim warriors from Central Asia, conquered most of Anatolia in the late eleventh century.

Agricultural Transformation in the Islamic World

Emergence of Landed Estates

The Arab conquerors of Syria, Iraq, and Iran initially were confined to towns, and thus had little immediate impact on the already well-developed agricultural systems in these regions. Undeveloped areas were another matter, however. The new rulers awarded wilderness lands to Arab governors to reduce the fiscal burdens of the caliphate's far-flung empire. The governors were expected to convert the wastelands to agriculture and use the revenues to defray the costs of public administration. In the ninth and tenth centuries, as the caliphate began to lose its grip over the provinces, local governors turned to slave armies to maintain control. They allocated landed estates, *iqta* (ihk-ta), to military commanders for the upkeep of these slave forces. Under the rule of the Seljuk Turks, first in Iran and subsequently in the central Muslim lands, most of the land was held as iqta estates to support the slave armies.

New Crops and Farming Practices

Islamic agriculture was transformed by new crops and farming practices. The burgeoning trade with Asia (discussed later in this chapter) introduced into Islamic domains a host of new crops—including rice, cotton, sugar cane, sorghum, and citrus fruits—from the lands surrounding the Indian Ocean. Cultivating these tropical imports as summer crops in the arid Middle East and North Africa required more elaborate irrigation systems. Thus, the spread of Asian crops in Syria, Egypt, and Spain was accompanied by irrigation technologies originally developed in India and Iran.

By 1200, Asian tropical crops had been domesticated throughout the Islamic world, from Iran to Spain (see Map 12.1, page 380). In addition to providing a more diverse diet and better nutrition, the new imports spurred industrial production and trade. New processing industries such as cotton textile manufacture and sugar refining emerged, primarily in Egypt and Syria.

Surprisingly, Europeans adopted few of the new crops and farming practices that were spreading throughout the Islamic world. One exception was hard wheat (durum), a variety developed in North Africa in about 500 to 600. Muslims introduced hard wheat, used to make pasta and couscous (and now pizza crust), to Spain and Italy. The earliest mention of pasta making in Italy dates from the thirteenth century, but it is unclear whether this was an Italian novelty or a Muslim export.

In northern Europe, climate prevented cultivation of most warm-weather crops. Yet prevailing habits and food preferences also figured significantly in Europeans' lack of interest in Muslim innovations, as the experience of Spain shows. Rice, citrus fruits, and sugar cane were widely grown in Muslim-ruled Spain, whose rulers also invested heavily in irrigation projects. But in the wake of the Christian reconquest of Spain in the thirteenth and fourteenth centuries (discussed in Chapter 14), the new landowners converted the wheat and cotton fields to pasture for sheep and allowed the irrigated rice fields to revert to swamps.

Retreat to Pastoral Livelihoods

The Seljuk conquests disrupted the agrarian basis of the Islamic world's economic prosperity. As nomadic warriors, the Seljuks were ill suited to maintaining the fragile ecology of intensive irrigated farming in these arid regions. Moreover, unlike in the manorial order of Western Europe, possession of an iqta estate gave the owner no political or legal powers over the peasants who worked it. Further, the estates could not be sold, leased, or passed on to one's heirs. Lacking ownership of the land and control over the peasants' labor, estate holders had little incentive to try to improve the efficiency of agriculture. Economic regression was most severe in Iraq and Anatolia. Neglect of irrigation systems and heavy taxation prompted massive peasant flight, leading to depopulation and a retreat from farming to pastoralism.

iqta In the Islamic world, grants of land made to governors and military officers, the revenues of which were used to pay for administrative expenses and soldiers' salaries.

Rice Economies in Monsoon Asia

Between 700 and 1200, an agricultural revolution also transformed economic life and livelihoods throughout monsoon Asia. Earlier Asian farmers had mainly grown dry land cereals such as wheat and millet. Beginning in the eighth century, however, Asian agriculture shifted to irrigated rice as the main staple food. The high efficiency and yields of irrigated rice agriculture, which can feed six times as many people per acre as wheat, generated substantial surpluses and fostered rapid population growth.

Nowhere was the scale of this agricultural transformation greater than in China. The An Lushan rebellion in the mid-eighth century had devastated the north China plain, the traditional Chinese heartland (see Chapter 10). Refugees fleeing the war-torn north resettled in the south, especially in the well-watered plains of the Yangzi River Valley. Massive investment of labor and capital in dikes, canals, and irrigation channels made it possible to control the annual Yangzi floods and reclaim land in the Yangzi Delta. Man-made canals, along with the abundant natural waterways of southern China, also encouraged mobility and trade. Southern products such as tea, sugar, porcelain, and later cotton led to new industries and new patterns of consumption. The unprecedented growth of cities and towns widened the circulation of goods and made it possible to acquire great fortunes through landowning and commerce. Yet the imperial state, which gained renewed strength under the Song dynasty (960–1279), strictly limited the social and legal powers exercised by the landed elite. In contrast to other parts of Eurasia during this era, in China small property owners drove agricultural expansion and economic growth.

Water conservation, irrigation technologies such as pedal-powered water pumps, and the construction of terraced fields along hillsides dramatically increased the amount of land under rice cultivation. The introduction of faster-ripening, drought-resistant rice varieties from Southeast Asia allowed Chinese farmers to develop a double-cropping rotation. Fields were planted with rice during the summer, and then reused to cultivate winter crops such as wheat, barley, and soybeans. Yangzi Delta farmers also planted mulberry trees, whose leaves provided fodder for silkworms, on the embankments dividing the rice paddies.

Growing exchanges between town and countryside also altered dietary and consumption habits. The brisk market activity in the Yangzi Delta countryside deeply impressed one thirteenth-century visitor from another province. He observed that peasants coming to town to sell rice returned home "arms laden with incense, candles, paper money offerings for the ancestors, cooking oil, salt, soy sauce, vinegar, flour, noodles, pepper, ginger, and medicines."[3] The introduction of irrigated rice cultivation thus had consequences well beyond the production of more food for rural families. The surplus food made possible by rice cultivation helped create new connections between rural and urban peoples, changing both city and country life in the process.

In mainland Southeast Asia, wet rice cultivation became common probably in the first centuries C.E., and it had spread to Java by the eighth century. Fish and coconuts (a source of fruit, sugar, oil, and wine) also were important staple foods in tropical agriculture. Dried or fermented fish could be stored for lengthy periods, and coconut trees typically yielded fruit four times a year. Tuber crops such as taro and yams provided alternative sources of subsistence.

Women Making Pasta

The Chinese made noodles from millet flour as early as 3000 B.C.E., but pasta was introduced to Europe from the Islamic world much later. A twelfth-century Muslim geography mentions that *itriya*—long, thin noodles like those being made by the women in this fourteenth-century Italian illustration—was manufactured in Sicily and exported throughout Muslim and Christian lands around the Mediterranean. (Alinari/Art Resource, NY.)

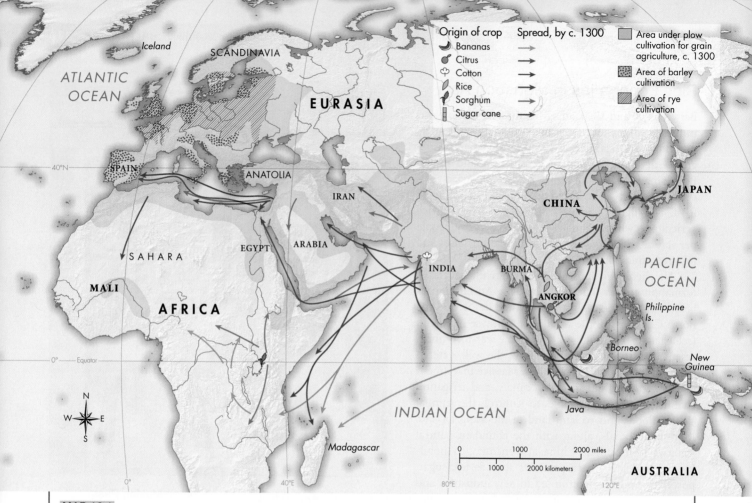

Principal Crops of Afro-Eurasia, c. 1300

The commercial prosperity of this era rested on the population growth made possible by
the rising productivity of agriculture. New staple crops expanded the frontiers of agriculture: irrigated rice in Southeast Asia, rye and barley in northern Europe, and bananas in
tropical Africa. Techniques of sugar and cotton production developed in India spread west
to the Middle East and east to China.

Rise of Powerful Monarchies in Southeast Asia

The development of irrigated rice agriculture from the eighth century onward laid the
economic foundations for the rise of powerful monarchies, most notably Angkor in Cambodia. In contrast to Chinese traditions, the Khmer kings of Angkor never created a centralized bureaucratic state. Instead, they extended their overlordship by recruiting local
landowning elites as allies. The Angkor kings established networks of royal temples supported by ample land endowments. In addition to revenue from landholdings, royal and
aristocratic patrons gave temples donations of rice, cattle, goats, coconut palms, fruit trees,
betel nuts, and clothing. The temples became storehouses of goods shared with the whole
community. Java and Burma had similar patterns of intensive rice cultivation, organized
by allocating land and labor rights to temple networks. Hence, in Angkor, Java, and
Burma, temples acted as local crossroads, functioning as hubs for the collection and distribution of resources and as points of connection between rural communities and the king.

In keeping with Indian political traditions, the Angkor monarchs portrayed themselves as servants of the gods and custodians of their temples. The kings ceded neither sacred authority nor temple administration to an independent priesthood, however. Even
without a centralized bureaucracy, the Angkor kings retained control over temples and the
land and wealth attached to them. The revenues that flowed to Angkor from the temple
network financed massive construction projects, including irrigation works and new temple complexes. The power and wealth of Angkor reached its peak during the twelfth cen-

Annual Cycle of Rice Cultivation

Highly productive rice agriculture fueled Song China's dramatic economic growth. Irrigated rice fields could feed six times as many people per acre as dry-land crops such as wheat or maize. This twelfth-century painting depicts the annual cycle of rice farming in the Yangzi Delta (clockwise from top): sowing, irrigation with pedal-powered water pumps, harvesting, threshing, husking, and storing the husked grain in a granary. (The Palace Museum, Beijing/ChinaStock.)

tury, when Angkor Wat was built. The world's largest religious monument, it was originally covered in gold leaf. Designed to represent the world in miniature, it served both as a shrine dedicated to the Hindu god Vishnu and as a royal mausoleum.

In Japan, too, land reclamation efforts organized by aristocratic and religious estates fostered the spread of rice cultivation. Because most large landowners lived in the capital at Kyoto, actual cultivation of the land was divided among tenant farmers and serflike laborers working under the direction of a village headman. The estate economy remained highly localized and self-sufficient until the early fourteenth century, when double-cropping (combining, as in China, a winter harvest of wheat or soybeans with the summer rice crop) and other technical improvements raised rural incomes. Peasants began to sell their surplus produce at rural markets. Although traders still conducted most exchange through barter, imported Chinese coins began to appear in local markets as well.

Estate-Based Economy in Japan

Favorable climatic trends also contributed to agricultural expansion across Eurasia. After 900 warmer temperatures set in, lengthening growing seasons and boosting yields. With rising agricultural productivity, farmers could feed more people, leading to population expansion and the growth of cities. Increasing commercial ties between the countryside and the towns brought more people into the market economy: rural inhabitants obtained more of their daily necessities from markets and fairs, while urban merchants and artisans developed new products to satisfy the mounting consumer demand.

Industrial Growth and the Money Economy

Economic growth during these centuries was driven by rising agricultural productivity, population increases, and the expansion of markets, rather than revolutionary changes in industrial organization and technology. A world in which labor was cheap and often unfree offered little incentive for investing in labor saving technology. Although no "industrial revolution" occurred, important strides in technological progress stimulated expansion of manufacturing and transport. In both technical innovation and scale of output, textiles,

FOCUS

How did the composition and organization of the industrial workforce change in different parts of Eurasia during this period?

metallurgy, and shipbuilding were the leading industries. As the volume of transactions increased, so did the demand for money and credit. Money became the lifeblood of urban society and an increasingly important measure of social status.

Technological Change and Industrial Enterprise

Human and animal power continued to serve as the main sources of energy in both agriculture and industry. However, water and windmills, first used in Europe in Roman times, proliferated rapidly from the tenth to the thirteenth centuries. People used mills primarily to grind grain, but they also adapted milling techniques to industrial purposes such as crushing ore, manufacturing woolen cloth, and pressing oil seeds.

Increased Iron Production

The production of iron expanded in Europe during these centuries, though no significant technological breakthrough occurred until blast furnace technology using water-driven bellows emerged in Germany sometime after 1300. In China, innovations such as piston-driven blast furnaces and the use of coke (refined coal) as fuel made vigorous growth in iron and steel output possible. In the eleventh century China produced perhaps as much as 125,000 tons of iron per year, more than twice the entire output of Europe. The loss of China's chief iron mines after the Jurchen conquest of the north in 1127 severely slowed iron production, however, and even led to regression to more primitive iron-making techniques.

Advances in Shipbuilding and Navigation

Probably the farthest-reaching technological advances during this era came in shipbuilding and navigation. Arab seafarers had conquered the monsoon winds of the Indian Ocean by rigging their ships (known as *dhows*) with lateen sails, which allowed them to sail against the wind. By the thirteenth century, Arabian ships were equipped with stern-post rudders that greatly enhanced their maneuverability. Because of the dhow's relatively flimsy hull, though, its range was limited to the placid waters of the Indian Ocean (see At a Crossroads, page 372).

The Chinese were slow to develop seagoing vessels, for reasons we will consider in Chapter 15. But by the twelfth century, Chinese merchants were sailing to Korea, Japan, and Southeast Asia in "Fuzhou ships," which featured deep keels, stern-post rudders, nailed planking, and waterproofed bulkheads. The magnetic compass had been known in China since ancient times, but the earliest mention of its use as a navigational aid at sea refers to Arab and Persian vessels in the Indian Ocean in the eleventh century.

Important innovations in seafaring and navigation came somewhat later in Europe. The traditional Mediterranean galley, powered by oars, was designed for war rather than commerce, and had little space for cargo. Beginning in the late thirteenth century, the Venetians developed more capacious galleys specifically designed as cargo vessels. In addition, a new kind of sailing ship known as the "cog" was introduced from northern Europe in the early fourteenth century. Equipped with square-sail rigging and stern-post rudders, the cogs could be built on a much larger scale, yet they required only one-fifth the crew needed to man a galley.

Equally important to the expansion of European maritime trade were innovations in navigation. The nautical compass came into use in the Mediterranean in around 1270. At around the same time, European navigators began to compile sea charts known as "portolans" that enabled them to plot courses between any two points. The combination of compass, portolans, and the astrolabe—introduced to Europe via Muslim Spain—vastly broadened the horizons of European seafarers. Mediterranean mariners began to venture beyond the Straits of Gibraltar into the Atlantic Ocean. A Genoese ship made the first voyage from Italy to Flanders in 1277, the initial step in the reorientation of European trade away from the Mediterranean and toward the Atlantic.

Expansion of Textile Manufacture

In addition to metallurgy and shipbuilding, textile manufacture—the most important industrial enterprise in every premodern society—was also transformed by technological innovation. Egypt, renowned for its linen and cotton fabrics, continued to produce high-quality cloth that was sold across the Islamic world and in Europe as well. Egyptian cloth-making techniques were copied in many other Muslim societies. Knowledge of silk manufacture, brought to Iran from China by the seventh century, was later passed on to Syria and Byzantium. Woolen cloth manufacture was the largest industry in Europe. The expansion of textile weaving sparked the rise of industrial towns in Flanders (modern Belgium), while Italian cities such as Milan and Florence specialized in dyeing and finishing cloth.

Innovations such as spinning wheels, treadle-operated looms, and water mills sharply increased productivity at virtually every step in textile manufacturing. The new technologies also encouraged a more distinct division of labor. As textile manufacture shifted from a household or manorial activity to an urban, market-oriented industry, skilled tasks such as weaving and dyeing became the exclusive preserve of male artisans. Women were relegated to the low-skilled and laborious task of spinning yarn.

In the twelfth century the Chinese silk industry underwent momentous changes. Previously, silk production had been almost exclusively a northern industry, carried out in state-run workshops or by rural women working at home. However, in 1127 the Jurchen Jin kingdom in Manchuria seized north China, forcing the Song court to take refuge at a new capital at Hangzhou (hahng-jo) in the Yangzi Delta. Subsequently China's silk industry shifted permanently to the Yangzi Delta, where the humid climate was more conducive to raising silkworms (see Map 12.2, page 394). New machinery such as the silk spinning reel and the treadle-operated loom greatly increased the output of silk yarn and cloth.

Like woolen manufacture in Europe, silk production in China steadily ceased to be a cottage industry and moved into urban industrial workshops. Instead of weaving cloth themselves, peasant households increasingly specialized in producing raw silk and yarn for sale to weaving shops. Although state-run silk factories continued to employ some women, private workshops hired exclusively male weavers and artisans.

Indeed, as the role of the market in the household economy grew, men began to monopolize the more skilled and better-paid occupations throughout Eurasia. In European cities especially, women found their entry barred to occupations that had formerly been open to them. Moreover, for urban women throughout Eurasia, public participation in social and economic activities became a mark of lower-class status.

Cultural preconceptions about the physical, emotional, and moral weaknesses of women aroused anxieties about their vulnerability in the public realm. The Muslim philosopher and

Exclusion of Women from the Workforce

Chinese Silk Weaving

Growing demand for luxury silks with fancy weaves stimulated technological innovations in the Chinese silk industry. This thirteenth-century scroll painting shows various stages of silk production, including sorting cocoons, extracting the silk filaments (right background), and winding yarn on a silk reeling machine (center foreground). At left a female weaver operates a treadle-powered loom. Peasant women could not afford such expensive equipment, however; most stopped weaving and concentrated on raising silkworms and producing raw silk.
(Attributed to Liang Kai (Chinese). Sericulture (The Process of Making Silk), early 13th Century. Handscroll, ink and color on silk. 27.3x93.5 cm. The Cleveland Museum of Art. John L. Severance Collection 1977.5.)

jurist Ibn Hazm (994–1064) warned that men preyed on women working outside the home: "Women plying a trade or profession, which gives them ready access to people, are popular with lovers [men looking for sexual partners]—the lady broker, the coiffeuses, the professional mourner, the singer, the soothsayer, the school mistress, the errand girl, the spinner, the weaver, and the like."[4] At the same time, the segregation of women in Muslim societies conferred high status on women doctors and midwives, which were considered necessary and honorable professions. Muslim women's control over their dowries enabled them to invest in moneylending, real estate, and other commercial activities.

Hazm's list of occupations that exposed women to public scrutiny provides a glimpse of women's jobs in his home city, Córdoba in Muslim Spain. Household surveys conducted in Paris in around 1300 show that female taxpayers were represented in more than a hundred trades at all levels of income. Many worked as independent artisans, although nearly three-quarters were employed as servants, in preparing and selling food, and in the textile and clothing industries. But the urban economy of Paris was relatively open. Elsewhere, merchant and artisan guilds (see page 388) almost always excluded women. By the fifteenth century, independent wage-earning women had virtually disappeared from European cities, even in Paris. The majority of women who earned wages were domestic servants. Married women typically worked at family businesses—as innkeepers, butchers, bakers, and clothiers—serving as helpers to their husbands.

Expanding Circulation of Money

Before 1000, most parts of Eurasia suffered from acute shortages of money. The use of money in Latin Christendom sharply contracted after the demise of the Roman Empire. Local rulers began to issue their own coins, but their circulation was limited. With gold scarce, the Frankish kings minted silver coins known as pennies. Kings and princes across Europe also frequently granted coinage privileges to various nobles and clerical authorities, and a great profusion of currencies resulted. Silver pennies were still relatively high in value, though, and their use was largely restricted to the nobility and merchants. The great majority of European peasants paid their lords in goods and services rather than money.

Byzantine Monetary System

Europeans used silver pennies for tax payments and local commerce, but they conducted international trade using the gold coins issued by the Byzantine emperors. The gold *nomisma* (nom-IHS-mah) coin, the cornerstone of Byzantine monetary and fiscal systems, ruled supreme throughout the Mediterranean world from Justinian's time until the end of the eleventh century. The Byzantine state collected taxes in gold coins, which it spent on official salaries, public works, foreign subsidies, the ecclesiastic establishment, and above all its standing army. Payment of soldiers' salaries in gold coin ensured their wide dispersal throughout the empire. Byzantium's prominence as the main trading partner of Italy's mercantile cities established the nomisma as the monetary standard in Italy as well.

Islamic Monetary System

The Umayyad caliph Abd al-Malik's currency reforms in the 690s had established the silver *dirham* (DEER-im) as the monetary standard for the Islamic world (see Seeing the Past: Imitation and Innovation in Islamic Coinage). The ease with which merchants circulated throughout the Islamic world is demonstrated by a hoard of nine hundred dirhams buried in Oman in around 840, which included coins issued by fifty-nine different mints from Morocco to Central Asia. Most of the coins found in Viking hoards scattered across the Baltic region, Scandinavia, and the British Isles are also Muslim silver dirhams.

The Islamic world suffered from shortages of gold until, as we will see, the rise of trans-Saharan trade in the ninth century. North African rulers reaped enormous profits from minting this gold into coins known as *dinars*. The Arab geographer Ibn Hawqal reported that the king of Sijilmasa (sih-jil-MAS-suh), in southern Morocco, obtained annual revenues of 400,000 gold dinars, equivalent to 1.9 tons of gold, from commercial tolls and his mint.

European Monetary System

The revival of gold coinage in Italy in the mid-thirteenth century, first by Florence and Genoa in 1258 and later by Venice, confirms Italian merchants' growing supremacy over Mediterranean trade. The dominance of Venice and Genoa in trade with Byzantium enabled the Italian city-states to supply their mints with gold imported from Constantinople. Italian merchants also obtained an increasing portion of the African gold crossing the Sahara. The Venetian gold ducat, introduced in 1284, soon established itself as the new monetary standard of Mediterranean commerce. Although gold coins filled the purses of nobles and great merchants throughout Europe, artisans continued to receive their wages in silver coin, and so-called black money (silver debased with lead and other cheap metals that gave it a black color) was widely used for everyday purchases and almsgiving.

Chinese Monetary System

The Chinese Empire developed an entirely different monetary system based on low-value bronze coins rather than precious metals. Shortages of bronze coins had forced the Tang government to collect taxes in grain, bolts of cloth, and labor services, with only a few commercial duties paid in coin. In the early eleventh century the Song dynasty launched an ambitious policy of monetary expansion. By the 1020s, the output of Song mints already far surpassed that of earlier dynasties, and it soared to nearly 6 billion coins per year (requiring ninety-six hundred tons of copper) in the 1070s. Yet even this level of coinage failed to satisfy the combined needs of the state and the private market. Beginning in the early eleventh century, the Song government introduced paper money to expand the money supply and facilitate the movement of money across long distances.

Credit and the Invention of Paper Money

Despite the influx of African gold, shortages of gold and silver coin persisted in the Mediterranean world. These shortages, coupled with the high risk and inconvenience of shipping coin over long distances, encouraged the development of credit and the use of substitutes for metallic currency, including bank money, deposit certificates, and bills of exchange. The growing sophistication of business skills and commercial practices during this period was the product of pragmatic solutions to the problems of long-distance trade.

Genoese Bankers
The Christian church's ban on usury clashed with the financial needs of Europe's rising merchant class. In his *Treatise on the Seven Vices* (c. 1320), an Italian nobleman chose to portray the sin of greed with an illustration of the counting house of a Genoese banker. Genoa's bankers were pioneers in the development of bills of exchange and interest-bearing deposit accounts. (© 2011 The British Library Add. 27695, f.8.)

Imitation and Innovation in Islamic Coinage

Since their invention in the sixth century B.C.E., metallic coins have served a variety of purposes. The first goal of Eurasian rulers who issued the coins was to facilitate trade, but coins were also used to pay taxes, and in many cultures coins played an important role in religious ritual and offerings to the gods. Coins also possessed symbolic significance. The stamp or design on a coin became synonymous with the authority of the ruler or state that minted it. Coins thus became vehicles for expressing sovereign power and political and religious beliefs.

During its rapid expansion in the seventh and eighth centuries C.E., the Islamic realm spread over two distinct monetary zones: the Mediterranean region, where Byzantine gold coins prevailed as the international monetary standard, and the former Sasanid Empire in Iran and Mesopotamia, where Sasanid silver coins known as *drachm* dominated. At first Muslim rulers imitated the design, weight, and metallic content of Byzantine and Sasanid coins. Thus the first Muslim coins minted in Iran (known as *dirham*, an Arabic rendering of *drachm*) continued to display a bust of the Sasanid king on one side and a fire altar, the centerpiece of the Zoroastrian religion, on the reverse; the words "In the name of God" in Arabic were added along the edge. In 661 the first Umayyad caliph, Mu'awiya, issued a new coin that retained the imagery of the Sasanid king's bust and the fire altar, but a Persian inscription identified the ruler as Mu'awiya.

Similarly, the first Umayyad gold coins (dinars) portrayed the caliphs in the style of Byzantine emperors (A), but they removed the cross that Byzantine coins prominently displayed atop the tiered platform (B). Moreover, the legend encircling the image of the caliph defiantly proclaims that "Muhammad is the Prophet of God whom He sent with guidance and the religion of truth that he may make it victorious over every other religion" (Qur'an IX: 33).

A   **B**

(© The Trustees of the British Museum/Art Resource, NY.)

Provoked by this religious broadside, in 692 the Byzantine emperor Justinian II radically changed the design of Byzantine coins. He replaced the emperor's bust with an image of Jesus Christ and made the Christian cross even more obvious.

Overcoming Bans Against Usury

In Muslim and Christian societies, merchants had to overcome strong religious objections to profiting from commercial enterprise, especially the prohibitions against **usury**, the practice of charging interest on debts. The Qur'an, which took shape within the commercial world of Mecca, devotes much attention to codifying ethical principles for merchants. The Qur'an firmly forbids usury, but later Islamic jurists devised means of permitting buying and selling on credit as well as investments aimed at earning a profit. Christian merchants evaded similar prohibitions against usury by drawing up contracts that disguised interest payments as fees or fines. In cases such as loans for overseas trading expeditions, where the borrower was obligated to repay the loan only if the ship and its cargo returned safely, clerical authorities allowed lenders to collect interest as compensation for the high risk.

The global connections created by long-distance trade required institutional support, mechanisms to facilitate the exchanges of goods and wealth between peoples from distant parts of the world. Thus, every major trading city had moneychangers to handle the diverse assortment of coins in use. Rudimentary banks that acted primarily as safe deposits but also transferred funds to distant cities were operating in China and the Islamic world by the ninth century and appeared in Genoa and Venice by the early twelfth century.

Long-distance merchants also benefited from new forms of credit such as the **bill of exchange**. The bill of exchange was a written promise to pay or repay a specified sum of money at a future time, which enabled a merchant to deposit money with a bank in one place and collect payment from the bank's agent in another place. Bills of exchange were

usury The practice of charging interest on loans, forbidden under Christian and Muslim legal codes.

bill of exchange A paper note that allowed the bearer to receive money in one place and repay the debt in another currency at another place at a later date.

In response, the caliph Abd al-Malik introduced a change in 696, one that would establish the style for Islamic coins for centuries to come. Abd al-Malik removed all images, including the depiction of the ruler, and replaced them with quotations from the Qur'an (C, D).

C   **D**

(© The Trustees of the British Museum/Art Resource, NY.)

The main face of the coin shown here (C) bears the Islamic declaration of faith (*shahada*): "There is no god but God; there is no partner with him." In addition to other quotations from the Qur'an, such coins often state the name of the caliph or provincial governor who issued them. This change reflected Muslim clerics' growing concern that the images of rulers on coins violated the Muslim prohibition against idolatry.

Later Muslim rulers modified this basic model to reflect their political or doctrinal independence. The Fatimid rulers in Egypt, for example, issued coins with legends testifying to their Shi'a affiliation. Thanks to their control over the trans-Saharan gold trade, the Fatimids and the Almoravid dynasty in Morocco began to issue gold dinars in such

great quantities that they displaced the Byzantine coin as the international monetary standard of the Mediterranean. Some Christian rulers in Iberia and Italy issued their own copies of Islamic dinars. The gold coin struck by King Alfonso VIII (r. 1158–1214) of Castile imitated the style of the Almoravid dinar, but replaced the shahada with professions of Christian faith (still written in Arabic) and the image of a cross (E, F).

E   **F**

(Courtesy of the American Numismatic Society.)

EXAMINING THE EVIDENCE

1. Why did Muslim rulers at first retain the images of Byzantine and Sasanid rulers on their own coins?

2. How did Muslim and Christian rulers differ in expressing their religious commitments and values through the images on their coins?

used in the Islamic world by the tenth century, when we hear of a Moroccan merchant using one to remit a payment of 42,000 gold dinars to a client in a Saharan oasis town. In Europe, traders at the Champagne fairs, which, as we will see, began in the twelfth century, conducted most of their business on the basis of credit. But not until the fourteenth century, about three hundred years later than financiers in Baghdad and Cairo, did European bankers begin to issue bills of exchange that were payable on demand.

Development of Credit

The flood of African gold into the Fatimid capital of Cairo in the tenth and eleventh centuries made that city the first great international financial center. The Arab geographer Al-Muqaddasi, writing in about 985, boasted that Cairo "has superseded Baghdad and is the glory of Islam, and is the marketplace for all mankind."[5] Muslim, Jewish, and Christian merchants in Cairo did business with each other and frequently cooperated in business deals, money transfers, and information sharing. The Cairo Exchange acted as a clearinghouse for moneychanging and the settlement of debts for merchants from Morocco to Persia. The guiding principle of trade was to keep one's capital constantly at work. "Do not let idle with you one dirham of our partnership, but buy whatever God puts into your mind and send it on with the very first ship sailing," wrote a Spanish merchant in Lebanon to his partner in Cairo.[6]

Cairo, a Commercial Crossroads

In China, too, merchants used letters of credit to transfer funds to distant regions. In the late tenth century, private merchants in western China began to issue their own bills of exchange. In 1024 the Song government replaced these private bills with its own official

Invention of Paper Money in China

ones, creating the world's first paper money. By the thirteenth century paper money had become the basic currency of China's fiscal administration, and it was widely used in private trade as well. At the same time merchants carried great quantities of Chinese bronze coin overseas to Japan, where by 1300 nearly all Japanese paid their rent and taxes and conducted business using imported Chinese coin.

The flow of money across borders and oceans testified to the widening circulation of goods. Few villagers would ever see a gold coin. Yet the demand for gold, luxury goods, and industrial raw materials drew many peasants—however unwittingly—into networks of long-distance trade.

Merchants and Trade Networks in Afro-Eurasia

FOCUS

How did the commercial revival of 900 to 1300 reorient international trade routes across Afro-Eurasia?

During the period 900 to 1300, major trading centers across Eurasia and Africa came to be linked in a series of regional and international networks of exchange and production. To be sure, the great majority of rural inhabitants remained largely disengaged from the commercial life of the cities and toiled strictly to feed their families and fulfill their obligations to their lords. Yet if the channels of commerce remained narrow, they were far more extensive than ever before, reaching from China to Europe and from southern Africa to the Mediterranean.

Much of this trade consisted of luxury goods such as spices, silk, and gold intended for a select few—rulers, nobles, and urban elites. Yet bulk products such as grain, timber, and metal ores also became important commodities in maritime trade, and processed goods such as textiles, wine, vegetable oils, sugar, and paper became staple articles of consumption among the urban middle classes. Although the movement of goods would seem sluggish and sporadic to modern eyes, the volume of trade and its size relative to other forms of wealth grew enormously. Genoa's maritime trade in 1293 was three times greater than the entire revenue of the kingdom of France.

Merchant Partnerships and Long-Distance Trade

Long-distance merchants venturing far from their homelands had to overcome the hazards of travel across dangerous seas and alien lands; cultural barriers created by different languages, religions, and laws; and the practical problems of negotiating with strangers. The expansion of trade required new forms of association and partnership and reliable techniques for communication, payment, credit, and accounting. Notable advances in all of these spheres of trade and finance were made during the "commercial revolution" of the twelfth and thirteenth centuries.

Guild System

Not all innovations in commercial institutions promoted open access to trade. The **guild** system that took root in European towns during this period reflected the corporate character of urban government and merchant society. Guilds were granted extensive authority to regulate crafts and commerce, restrict entry to a trade, and dictate a wide array of regulations ranging from product specifications to the number of apprentices a master might employ. In the name of guaranteeing a "just" price and goods of uniform quality, the guild system also stifled competition and technical innovation. In China and the Islamic world, by contrast, guilds were formed chiefly to supply goods and services to the government, and they had no authority to regulate and control trade. Muslim rulers appointed market inspectors to supervise commerce and craftsmen. These officials upheld Islamic law, adjudicated disputes, and collected taxes and fees.

guild An association of merchants or artisans organized according to the kind of work they performed.

Merchants who engaged in international trade usually operated as individuals, carrying with them their entire stock of goods and capital, although they often traveled in caravans and convoys for protection against bandits and pirates. As in the case of the Jewish trader Allan bin Hassun, whose story opened this chapter, a family firm might dispatch its members to foreign markets, sometimes permanently, to serve as agents. But as the volume of trade grew, more sophisticated forms of merchant organization emerged.

Commercial Partnerships

Islamic legal treatises devoted much attention to commercial partnerships. Muslim law permitted limited investment partnerships in which one partner supplied most of the capital, the other traveled to distant markets and conducted their business, and the two shared the profits equally. Apparently caravan traders of the Arabian deserts first developed such cooperative agreements in pre-Islamic times. Italian merchants later imitated this type of partnership in what became known as the *commenda* (coh-MEHN-dah) (see Reading the Past: The Commenda Partnership Among Venetian Merchants). Artisans such as bakers, tailors, silversmiths, and pharmacists as well as entrepreneurs in industrial enterprises such as weaving, metalworking, wine making, and sugar refining also formed investment partnerships. Chinese merchants likewise created joint trading ventures in the form of limited partnerships for both domestic and international trade.

READING THE PAST

The Commenda Partnership Among Venetian Merchants

New institutions and business practices to raise capital for conducting long-distance trade facilitated the expansion of Mediterranean trade in the eleventh century. One new practice was the *commenda*, a form of partnership in which one partner provides investment capital and the other partner acts as business agent. Byzantine and Jewish merchants in the Mediterranean developed similar partnerships, but the precise model for the commenda was the Muslim *qirad* contract, which appeared in Islamic law codes by the eighth century. The following commenda contract drawn up in Venice is the earliest known example from Latin Christendom.

In the year . . . 1073, in the month of August . . . I, Giovanni Lissado of Luprio, together with my heirs, have received in partnership from you, Sevasto Orefice, son of Ser Trudimondo, and from your heirs, the amount of £200 [Venetian]. And I myself have invested £100 in it. And with this capital we have acquired two shares in the ship of which Gosmiro da Molino is captain. And I am under obligation to bring all of this with me on a commercial voyage to Thebes [in Greece] in the ship in which the aforesaid Molino sails as captain. Indeed, by this agreement and understanding of ours I promise to put to work this entire sum and to strive the best way I can. Then, if the capital is preserved, we are to divide whatever profit the Lord may grant us from it by exact halves, without fraud and evil device. And whatever I can gain with those goods from any source,

I am under obligation to invest all of it in the partnership. And if all these goods are lost because of the sea or of people [pirates], and this is proved—may this be averted—neither party ought to ask any of them from the other. If, however, some of them remain, in proportion as we invested so shall we share. Let this partnership exist between us so long as our wills are fully agreed.

But if I do not observe everything just as is stated above, I together with my heirs then promise to give and to return to you and your heirs everything in the double, both capital and profit, out of my land and my house or out of anything that I am known to have in this world. [signed by Lissado, two witnesses, the ship captain, and the clergyman who acted as notary]

Source: Robert S. Lopez and Irving W. Raymond, eds., *Medieval Trade in the Mediterranean World: Illustrative Documents* (Cambridge, U.K.: Cambridge University Press, 1955), 176–177.

EXAMINING THE EVIDENCE

1. What did these Italian merchants regard as the greatest risks in investing in maritime trade?

2. In what ways was the commenda partnership different from modern business organizations such as corporations?

Joint Stock Companies

The commenda partnerships were the forerunners of permanent **joint stock companies**, which were first founded in Italian cities in the thirteenth century. These companies, in which investors pooled their capital for trading ventures, engaged in finance as well as trade and often maintained their own fleets and branch offices in foreign cities. The merchant banks of Florence and other cities of northern Italy gradually became involved in fund transfers, bills of exchange, and moneychanging. Bardi, the largest Florentine bank, had over three hundred agents stationed throughout Europe and the Mediterranean in 1340, and its capital resources were more than four times as large as the annual income of the English crown, one of its main customers. Apart from trade and banking, such firms provided insurance for maritime trading expeditions; insuring such expeditions became a common practice after 1350.

Karimi Merchant Associations

In the late twelfth century, merchants based in Egypt created a commercial association known as the *karimi* (KUH-ree-mee) to organize convoys for trading expeditions in the Indian Ocean. Cairo's karimi merchants became a powerful **cartel**—a commercial association whose members join forces to fix prices or limit competition—that squeezed small entrepreneurs out of the lucrative spice trade. The karimi merchants cooperated closely with the sultans of Egypt, especially under the Mamluk dynasty (1250–1517), generating substantial tax revenue for the state in exchange for their trade privileges. By 1300 Cairo's two-hundred-plus karimi merchants had become the chief middlemen in trade between Asia and Europe.

Merchants and Rulers

The sumptuous wealth and rising social stature of merchant groups such as the Italian bankers and Cairo's karimi inevitably altered relationships between government and commerce. Rulers who had formerly depended almost exclusively on revenue from the land increasingly sought to capture the scarcely imaginable profits of the money economy. In places as far removed as England and Japan, landowners and governments began to demand payments in money rather than agricultural products or labor services. In Europe the expanding availability of credit was an irresistible temptation to monarchs whose ambitions outgrew their resources. Italian bankers became the chief lenders to the papacy and to the kings and princes of Latin Christendom.

Merchant-Ruler Relations in Europe

The Italians took the lead in putting private capital to work in service to the state. Merchant communities became closely allied with political leaders in the Italian city-states, most notably in Venice. In the late twelfth century the Venetian government imposed a system of compulsory loans that required contributions from every citizen. In 1262, the city's magistrates consolidated all of these debts into a single account. Public debt proved to be more efficient than taxation for raising revenue quickly to cope with war and other emergencies. Investment in state debt provided the men, fleets, and arms that enabled Venice to become the great maritime power of the Mediterranean.

As mercantile interests came to dominate the Venetian state, the government took charge of the republic's overseas trade. The state directed commercial expeditions, dictated which merchants could participate, built the vessels at its publicly funded shipyard, and regulated the prices of exports as well as crucial imports such as grain and salt. Venice was fortunate in its ability to maintain civic solidarity even as its mercantile oligarchy tightened its grip on the state and its resources.

Economic regulation was a powerful unifying force elsewhere in Europe as well. For example, the merchant communities of the trading cities along the Baltic seacoast formed an alliance known as the Hanseatic League. The League acted as a cartel to preserve its members' monopoly on the export of furs, grain, metals, and timber from the Baltic region to western Europe.

Efforts to merge commercial and political power did not, however, always result in increased prosperity and political strength. In Genoa,

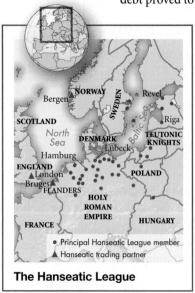

The Hanseatic League

antagonisms between the landed aristocracy and the city's rising merchant and financier families provoked frequent and sometimes bloody feuds that paralyzed the city's leadership. In the industrial cities of Flanders, fiscal policies and economic regulation that favored merchants over workers ultimately incited revolts that undermined Flanders' preeminence in the textile industry.

In most of the Islamic world, merchants—regardless of their religious commitments— enjoyed high status and close ties to the political authorities. The Fatimid government in Egypt largely entrusted its fiscal affairs to Coptic Christian officials, and Jewish merchant houses achieved prominence as personal bankers to Muslim rulers in Baghdad and Cairo. Private trade and banking were largely free of government interference during the Fatimid dynasty. But state intervention in commerce intensified under the Mamluk sultans, who came to power in Egypt after a palace coup in 1250.

Merchant-Ruler Relations in the Islamic World

The Mamluks' political and military strength rested on their slave armies, which were supported by revenues from iqta estates and commercial taxes. The karimi-controlled spice trade was an especially important source of income for the Mamluk state. Karimi merchants—most of whom were Jewish—also managed the fiscal administration of the Mamluk regime, helping to collect provincial revenues, pay military stipends, and administer state-run workshops and trade bureaus. Like European monarchs, the Mamluk sultans became heavily dependent on loans from private bankers to finance wars. And, again like their European counterparts, Mamluk sultans were always on the lookout for new sources of revenue. In the fifteenth century the Mamluk government took over many commercial enterprises, most notably the spice and slave trades and sugar refining, and operated them as state monopolies.

In China, the fiscal administration of the imperial state penetrated deeply into the commercial world. The revenues of the Song Empire far exceeded those of any other contemporary government. The state generated more than half of its cash revenue by imposing monopolies on the production of rice wine and key mineral resources such as salt, copper, and alum. Yet in the most dynamic commercial sectors—iron mining and metallurgy, silk textiles, and the emerging industries of south China such as tea, porcelain, paper, and sugar—private enterprise was the rule. The Song government mainly intervened in private commerce to prevent private cartels from interfering with the free flow of goods.

Merchant-Ruler Relations in China

The Song thus effectively stifled the formation of strong merchant organizations such as the European guilds. The state also assumed major responsibility for famine relief, stockpiling grain in anticipation of periodic harvest failures. Foreign trade was strictly regulated, and the export of strategic goods such as iron, bronze coin, and books was prohibited. Still, Chinese officials recognized the value of international trade as a source of revenue and of vital supplies such as warhorses, and they actively promoted both official trade with foreign governments and private overseas trading ventures.

Merchants in China did not enjoy the social prestige accorded to their Italian or Muslim counterparts. Confucianism viewed the pursuit of profit with contempt and relegated merchants to the margins of respectable society. Yet Confucian moralists expressed even greater hostility toward government interference in the economy than to private profit-seeking. Moreover, Confucian values applauded the prudent management of the household economy and the accumulation of wealth to provide for the welfare of one's descendants. As a minor twelfth-century official named Yuan Cai (you-ahn tsai) wrote in his *Family Instructions*, "Even if the profession of scholar is beyond your reach, you still can support your family through recourse to the arts and skills of medicine, Buddhist or Daoist ministry, husbandry, or commerce without bringing shame upon your ancestors."[7] Like his Byzantine counterpart Kekaumenos, Yuan Cai counseled his peers to be frugal in spending, to invest wisely in land, moneylending, and business ventures, to diversify their assets, and to never become dependent on the goodwill and honesty of those with whom one does business (see Reading the Past: A Chinese Official's Reflections on Managing Family Property).

joint stock company A business whose capital is held in transferable shares of stocks by its joint owners.

cartel A commercial association whose members join forces to fix prices or limit competition.

Despite their wealth, merchants led a precarious existence. Long-distance trade offered opportunities to make great profits, but the risks of failure were equally great. To lessen these risks, merchants built communities, negotiated alliances with ruling authori-

A Chinese Official's Reflections on Managing Family Property

In *Precepts for Social Life* (1179), Yuan Cai departed from the focus on personal ethics found in earlier Chinese writings on the family. A Chinese official living in a time of rapid economic change, Yuan concentrated on the practical problems of acquiring wealth and transmitting it to future generations. Yuan also adopted a more pragmatic attitude toward individual behavior in addressing the inevitable conflicts that arise within families. In the following selections, Yuan confronts the problem of disparities of wealth among relatives who live together as a joint family.

Wealth and liberality will not be uniform among brothers, sons, and nephews. The rich ones, only pursuing what's good for them, easily become proud. The poor ones, failing to strive for self-improvement, easily become envious. Discord then arises. If the richer ones from time to time would make gifts of their surplus without worrying about gratitude, and if the poorer ones would recognize that their position is a matter of fate and not expect charity, then there would be nothing for them to quarrel about. . . .

Some people actually start from poverty and are able to establish themselves and set up prosperous businesses without making use of any inherited family resources. Others, although there was a common family estate, did not make use of it, separately acquiring their individual wealth through their own efforts. In either case their patrilineal kinsmen will certainly try to get shares of what they have acquired. Lawsuits taken to the county and prefectural courts may drag on for decades until terminated by the bankruptcy of all parties concerned. . . .

When brothers, sons, and nephews live together, it sometimes happens that one of them has his own personal fortune. Worried about problems arising when the family divides the common property, he may convert his fortune to gold and silver and conceal it. This is perfectly foolish. For instance if he has one million cash [bronze coins] worth of gold and silver and used this money to buy productive property, in a year he would gain 100,000 cash; after ten years or so, he would have regained the one million cash and what would be divided among the family would be interest. Moreover, the one million cash could continue to earn interest. If it were invested in a pawnbroking business, in three years the interest would equal the capital. . . . What reason is there to store it in boxes rather than use it to earn interest for the profit of the whole family?

Source: Patricia Buckley Ebrey, *Family and Property in Sung China: Yuan Ts'ai's* Precepts for Social Life (Princeton, NJ: Princeton University Press, 1984), 197–200.

EXAMINING THE EVIDENCE

1. What did Yuan identify as the greatest threats to the preservation of the family's wealth and property?

2. What values did Yuan regard as crucial for gaining and maintaining wealth?

ties, and developed reliable methods of communication. Although some rulers coveted the profits of trade for themselves, and others treated merchants as pariahs, traders and rulers usually reached an accommodation that benefited both. The spread of new techniques and institutions for conducting trade strengthened the foundations of international commerce.

Maritime Traders in the Indian Ocean

The seventh century, when the Tang dynasty in China was at its height (see Chapter 10), marked the heyday of trade and travel along the Silk Road across Central Asia. As we have seen, however, overland commerce between India and China collapsed after the outbreak of the An Lushan rebellion in 755. By the time the Song dynasty was founded in 960, China's principal trade routes had shifted away from Central Asia to the maritime world (see Map 12.2).

Dominance of Muslim Merchants

Muslim merchants, both Arab and Persian, dominated Indian Ocean trade in the ninth century thanks to their superior shipbuilding and organizational skills. Travel across the Indian Ocean was governed by monsoon winds, which blew steadily from east to west in winter and from west to east in summer, making it impossible to complete a round trip between China and India in a single year. Initially, Muslim seafarers from Persian Gulf ports sailed all the way to China, taking two or three years to complete a round-trip voyage. A ninth-century Arab chronicler claimed that more than half of the two hundred thousand residents of Guangzhou (gwahng-joe) (Canton), southern China's principal port, were Arab, Persian, Christian, and Jewish traders, a testimony to the dense web of trading connections that had developed by this time.

By the tenth century, merchants more commonly divided the journey to China into shorter segments. By stopping at ports along the Strait of Melaka (Malacca), between Sumatra and the Malay peninsula, Muslim merchants could return to their home ports within a single year. The Srivijaya (sree-vih-JUH-yuh) merchant princes of Sumatra grew wealthy from their share of profits in this upsurge in trade between India and China.

In the eleventh century, however, new maritime powers arose to contest the dominance of Srivijaya and the Muslim merchants in Asian international commerce. The most assertive new entrant into the Indian Ocean trade was the Chola (chohz-ah) kingdom (907–1279), at the southeastern tip of the Indian peninsula. At first Chola nurtured cordial diplomatic and commercial relations with Srivijaya. The Chola port of Nagapattinam (Nah-gah-POT-tih-nahm) flourished as an international trading emporium under the patronage of both the Chola and Srivijaya rulers, who funded the construction of mosques, temples, and shrines for the city's expatriate merchant communities of Muslims, Jews, Christians, Parsis (Zoroastrian immigrants from Iran), and Chinese. Yet in 1025 Chola suddenly turned against Srivijaya, and its repeated attacks on Sumatran ports over the next fifty years fatally weakened the Srivijaya princes. But Chola's aggressiveness made many enemies, including the Sinhala kings of Sri Lanka, who stymied its attempt to succeed Srivijaya as the region's supreme maritime power.

Chola's Quest for Maritime Supremacy

Chola's foreign trade was controlled by powerful Tamil merchant guilds that mobilized convoys and founded trading settlements overseas. Tamil merchants carried cargoes of Indian pepper and cotton cloth and Sumatran ivory, camphor, and sandalwood to the southern Chinese ports of Guangzhou and Quanzhou (chwehn-joe). Numerous architectural and sculptural fragments from Hindu temples found in Quanzhou attest to the city's once-thriving Tamil merchant colony.

Tamil Merchants and the China Trade

Silk textiles had long been China's principal export commodity. After the tenth century, however, the growth of domestic silk industries in India and Iran dampened demand for Chinese imports. Although Chinese luxury fabrics such as brocades and satins still were highly prized, porcelain displaced silk as China's leading export. Maritime trade also transferred knowledge of sugar refining and cotton manufacture from India to China, leading to major new industries there.

During the twelfth century Chinese merchants began to mount their own overseas expeditions. Chinese commercial interests increasingly turned toward the Indonesian archipelago in search of fine spices such as clove and nutmeg (which grew only in the remote Moluccas, the so-called Spice Islands), and other exotic tropical products. Chinese merchants also imported substantial quantities of gold, timber, and sulfur (used in gunpowder and medicines) from Japan in exchange for silk, porcelain, and contraband bronze coin.

The advent of Muslim traders in Indian Ocean trade had stimulated commerce along the east coast of Africa as well. The Swahili peoples of the coasts of Tanzania and Kenya were descended from Bantu settlers who arrived in the region in around 500 C.E. The Swahili lived in coastal villages or on offshore islands, where they combined farming and fishing with small-scale trade. Beginning in the ninth century, Swahili merchants transformed the island towns of Shanga and Manda into major trading ports that functioned as regional crossroads, exporting ivory, hides, and quartz and other gems to the Islamic heartland in return for cotton, pottery, glass, and jewelry. When Swahili merchants ventured southward in search of ivory, they discovered an abundance of gold as well.

Swahili Merchants and East African Trading Cities

The reorientation of East African trade networks toward the export of gold had far-reaching political and economic repercussions. In the twelfth century, Mapungubwe

South African Gold Trade

International Commerce in Afro-Eurasia, c. 1150

New developments on opposite ends of Afro-Eurasia spurred the expansion of international trade. Song China became the world's most dynamic economy thanks to the dramatic growth of its silk, porcelain, iron, and shipbuilding industries. Muslim merchants pioneered trade routes across the Sahara Desert and along the eastern coast of Africa in pursuit of gold, ivory, copper, and other precious goods.

(Ma-POON-goo-bway), the first identifiable state in southern Africa, arose in the middle Limpopo River Valley, at the junction of the trade routes bringing ivory and copper from the south and gold from the north. The monsoon winds allowed Arab merchants to sail as far south as Kilwa, which eclipsed the older towns of Shanga and Manda as the preeminent trading center along the East African coast (see again Map 12.2). Control of the gold trade greatly enriched the Muslim sultans, possibly of Arabian origin, who ruled Kilwa. By the early fourteenth century the city boasted stone palaces, city walls, a Muslim law school, and a domed mosque constructed in the Indian style. South of Kilwa trade goods were relayed by local merchants from the interior and the Swahili colonies along the coast.

Rise and Fall of Great Zimbabwe

The mid-thirteenth century brought the rise of another powerful state, Great Zimbabwe, that would exert direct control over the main goldfields and copper mines in the interior. The capital of Great Zimbabwe consisted of a large complex of stone towers and enclosures housing a warrior elite and perhaps as many as eighteen thousand inhabitants. Similar but smaller stone enclosures (known as *zimbabwe*), built to shelter livestock as

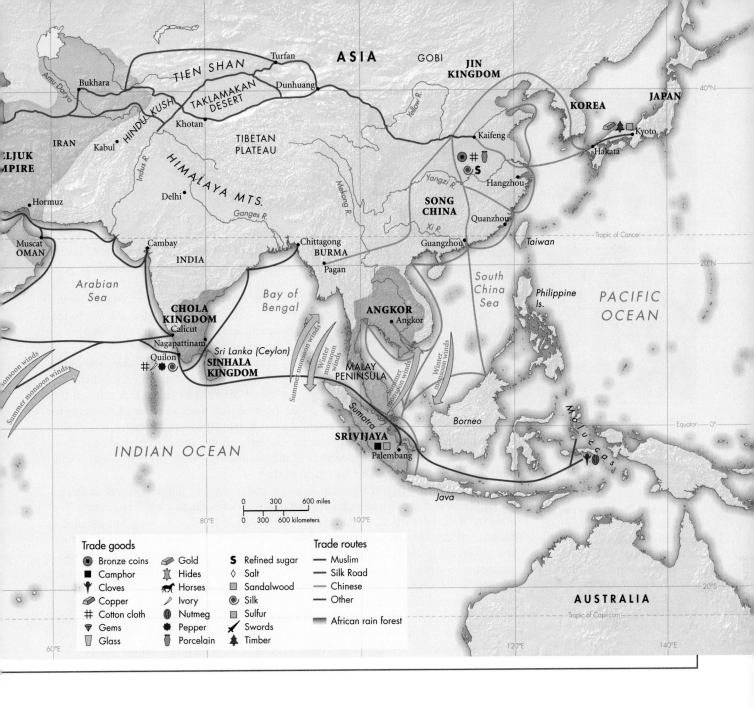

Trade goods

- ◉ Bronze coins
- ■ Camphor
- ⚑ Cloves
- ◳ Copper
- # Cotton cloth
- ▽ Gems
- ⬚ Glass
- ◈ Gold
- ⚒ Hides
- 🐎 Horses
- ✎ Ivory
- ◖ Nutmeg
- ✱ Pepper
- ⬙ Porcelain
- **S** Refined sugar
- ◇ Salt
- ◻ Sandalwood
- ◉ Silk
- ◻ Sulfur
- ⚔ Swords
- 🌲 Timber

Trade routes

- —— Muslim
- —— Silk Road
- —— Chinese
- —— Other
- ▨ African rain forest

well as protect their inhabitants, sprang up throughout the region. The abandonment of Mapungubwe at around the same time can probably be attributed to the diversion of commercial wealth to Great Zimbabwe. Traders prized gold for its value as an export commodity and conducted local exchange using cross-shaped copper currency. The rich array of copper goods in royal and elite burials across southern Africa confirms the importance of copper as the chief sign of wealth and status. Textiles made of raffia palm fronds, bark cloth, and cotton were also important trade items in the continent's interior.

Great Zimbabwe's dominance over the export trade could not be sustained indefinitely. In the fourteenth century the copper and ivory trade routes shifted to the Zambezi River Valley to the north. The empire fashioned by the rulers of Great Zimbabwe disintegrated in the early fifteenth century, and the capital city was abandoned by the 1450s. Although no single dominant state emerged, trade continued to flourish. The great volume of Chinese coins and porcelain shards that archaeologists have found at Great Zimbabwe and sites along the coast documents East Africa's extensive trade across the Indian Ocean.

Kilwa

Located on an island off the coast of Tanzania, Kilwa grew rich and powerful thanks to its dominance over the trade in African gold and ivory. The large quantities of Chinese pearls, porcelains, and coins unearthed at Kilwa attest to its prominence in Indian Ocean trade as well. In this German engraving from 1572, the city's domed mosques stand out among a dense cluster of multistory buildings made from stone and coral. (The National Library of Israel, Shapell Family Digitization Project and The Hebrew University of Jerusalem, Department of Geography—Historic Cities Research Project.)

Trans-Saharan Traders

The vast Sahara Desert separated most of the African continent from the Mediterranean world, but the thirst for gold breached this seemingly impenetrable barrier in the wake of the Muslim conquest of North Africa. The conversion of the Berbers to Islam and their incorporation into the far-flung Muslim trading world during the seventh century provided the catalyst for the rapid escalation of trans-Saharan trade. Reports of the fabulous gold treasure of *al-Sudan* ("country of the blacks"), the Sahel belt of grasslands spanning the southern rim of the Sahara from the Atlantic to the Indian Ocean, lured Berber and Arab merchants across the desert.

Trade across the western Sahara was negligible before the second century C.E., when Berber camel caravans began to trek through the desert, bringing food and animal products to remote salt and copper mines. Salt, essential for sustaining life in arid climates, was a valuable commodity, so precious that Saharan peoples used salt rather than gold as money. Gold from the mines at the headwaters of the Senegal and Niger rivers began to trickle northward across the Sahara by the fourth century.

Well before the rise of the trans-Saharan trade, growing interaction and exchange among the Sahel societies had begun to generate social differentiation and stratification. The majority of the population, the farmers and herders, remained free people not assigned a caste. In villages, however, communities began to specialize in manufacturing activities such as ironworking, pottery, leather making, and cotton weaving. Many in these occupational groups began to marry only among themselves. Occupational specialization, residential segregation, and endogamy—marriage within a closed group of families—fostered the formation of castes of skilled tradesmen.

By 400 C.E., clusters of specialized manufacturing villages in the inland delta of the Niger River coalesced into towns trading in iron wares, pottery, copper, salt, and leather goods as well as foodstuffs and livestock. Towns such as Jenne-jeno preserved the independent character of its various artisan communities. But in other Sahelian societies, powerful warrior elites dominated. Originating as clan leaders, these warrior chiefs appropriated ideas of caste status to define themselves as an exclusive and hereditary nobility. They also drew on traditions of sacred kingship originating in the eastern Sudan, which exalted the king as a divine figure and required him to live a cloistered private life, rarely visible to his subjects.

Gold Trade and Ghana

The earliest Muslim accounts of West Africa, dating from around 800, report that a great king—whose title, Ghana, came to be applied to both the ruler's capital and his state—monopolized the gold trade. Ghana's exact location remains uncertain, but its ruler, according to Muslim merchants, was "the wealthiest king on the face of the earth because of his treasures and stocks of gold."[8] The Muslim geographer al-Bakri described the capital of Ghana as consisting of two sizable towns, one in which the king and his court resided and a separate Muslim town that contained many clerics and scholars as well as merchants. Although the king was a pagan, al-Bakri deemed him to have led a "praiseworthy life on account of his love of justice and friendship for Muslims."[9]

Advance of Islam

At first the impact of Islam on the indigenous peoples was muted. Berber caravans halted at the desert's edge, because camels had little tolerance for the humidity and diseases of the savanna belt. Confined to segregated enclaves within the towns, Muslim merchants depended on the favor of local chiefs or the monarchs of Ghana. Yet local rulers found the lucrative profits of trade in gold and slaves irresistible, and the wealth and literacy of Muslim merchants made them valuable allies and advisers. Trade also yielded access to coveted goods such as salt, glass, horses, and swords (see again Map 12.2). The kings of Ghana and other trading cities converted to Islam by the early twelfth century, and to varying degrees required their subjects to embrace the new religion as well. At the same time Muslim commercial towns displaced many of the older trading centers such as Jenne-jeno, which were abandoned. Thus, the desire to engage in trade was a major stimulus for cultural exchange and adaptation in West Africa.

During the twelfth century Ghana's monopoly on the gold trade eroded, and its political power crumbled as well. In the thirteenth century a chieftain by the name of Sunjata (r. 1230–1255) forged alliances among his fellow Malinke to create a new empire known as Mali. Whereas Ghana probably exercised a loose sovereignty within the savanna region, Mali enforced its dominion over a much larger territory by assembling a large cavalry army equipped with horses and iron weapons purchased from Muslim traders. Unlike Ghana, Mali exercised direct control over the gold mines.

Rise of Mali

The kings of Mali combined African traditions of divine kingship with patronage of the Islamic faith. The Mali monarch Mansa Musa (MAHN-suh MOO-suh) (r. 1312–1337) caused a great sensation when he visited Cairo on his pilgrimage to Mecca in 1325. According to a contemporary observer, "Musa flooded Cairo with his benefactions, leaving no court emir nor holder of a royal office without a gift of a load of gold. . . . They exchanged gold until they depressed its value in Egypt and caused its price to fall."[10] The visit provided evidence of both the power and wealth of Mali and the increasing cultural connections between West Africa and the rest of the Muslim world.

Trade and industry flourished under Mali's umbrella of security. Muslim merchants formed family firms with networks of agents widely distributed among the oasis towns and trading posts of the Sahara. Known as *Juula* (meaning "trader" in Malinke), these Muslim merchants also extended their operations into the non-Muslim states of the rainforest belt and brought a variety of new goods, such as kola nuts, textiles, and brass and copper wares, into the Saharan trading world. Like other town-dwelling craftsmen and specialists, such as the blacksmiths and leatherworkers, the Juula became a distinct occupational caste and ethnic group whose members lived in separate residential quarters and married among themselves (see Lives and Livelihoods: The Mande Blacksmiths).

Mediterranean and European Traders

The contraction of commerce that followed the fall of the western Roman Empire persisted longer in Europe than did the economic downturn in Asia and the Islamic world. By the twelfth century, however, the rising productivity of agriculture and population growth in western Europe had greatly widened the horizons for trade. Lords encouraged the founding of towns by granting **burghers**—free citizens of towns—certain legal liberties as well as economic privileges such as tax exemptions, fixed rents, and trading rights. In England and Flanders a thriving woolen industry developed—the towns of Flanders, notably Bruges, Ghent, and Ypres, became highly specialized in weaving cloth using raw wool imported from Britain. Merchant guilds in both England and Flanders grew so powerful that they chose their own city councils and exercised considerable political autonomy. In northern Europe, repeating a dynamic we have seen before in other parts of the world, commercial expansion altered the political landscape (see Map 12.3, page 399).

Revival of Towns

The prosperity of the woolen industry made Flanders the wealthiest and most densely urbanized region in twelfth-century northern Europe, yet the Flemish towns were dwarfed by the great cities of Italy. Although social tensions often flared between the landed aristocracy and wealthy town-dwellers, the political fortunes of the Italian city-states remained firmly wedded to their mercantile interests. The city-states of Pisa, Genoa, and Venice aggressively pursued trade opportunities in the Mediterranean, often resorting to force to seize trade routes and ports from Muslim, Greek, and Jewish competitors. By the twelfth century Italian navies and merchant fleets dominated the Mediterranean, with Genoa paramount in the west and Venice the major power in the east.

Growing Power of the Italian City-States

burgher In Latin Christendom, a free citizen residing in a town who enjoyed certain legal privileges, including the right to participate in town governance.

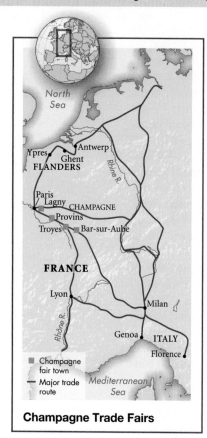

Champagne Trade Fairs

Economic revival in northern and western Europe breathed new life into the long-defunct Roman commercial network. In the county of Champagne, southeast of Paris, a number of towns located at the intersections of Roman roads had continued to serve as local markets and sites of periodic fairs. In the twelfth century the counts of Champagne offered their protection and relief from tolls to the growing number of merchants who traveled between the textile manufacturing towns of Flanders and Italy's commercial centers. They established an annual cycle of six two-month fairs that rotated among the towns. Champagne's location midway between Flanders and Italy enhanced its stature as the major crossroads of international commerce and finance in western Europe. Merchants adopted the coins and weights used at the fairs as international standards.

Champagne's heyday as a medieval version of a free-trade zone came to an end in the early fourteenth century. Political tensions between Champagne's counts and the French monarchy frequently interrupted the smooth flow of trade. The Champagne fairs were also victims of their own success: the innovations in business practices spawned by the Champagne fairs, such as transfers of goods and money via agents and bills of exchange, made actual attendance at the fairs unnecessary. Champagne would regain fame after the seventeenth century, when its famous sparkling wine was invented, but trade and finance shifted to the rising commercial cities of northern Europe such as Antwerp and London.

COUNTERPOINT
Production, Tribute, and Trade in the Hawaiian Islands

FOCUS

How did the sources of wealth and power in the Hawaiian Islands differ from those of market economies elsewhere in the world?

During the period of this chapter, rulers everywhere sought to regulate the exchange of goods to both preserve the existing social structure and enhance their own authority. In the temple- and estate-based economies of India, Southeast Asia, Japan, and western Europe, payments in goods and services prevailed over market exchange. These payments took the form of **tribute**, obligations social inferiors owed to their superiors; thus, by its very nature tribute reinforced the hierarchical structure of society. Yet in all of these societies markets played some role in meeting people's subsistence needs. Expansion of the market economy provided access to a wider range of goods and allowed entrepreneurs to acquire independent wealth. Both the circulation of goods and the new concentrations of commercial wealth threatened to subvert the existing social hierarchy.

In societies that lacked market exchange, such as the Hawaiian Islands, rulers maintained firmer control over wealth and social order. During the thirteenth and fourteenth centuries, when hierarchical chiefdoms first formed in Hawaii, investment in agricultural production remained modest. Intensive agricultural development took off after 1400, however, as chiefs consolidated their control over land and labor. The construction of irrigation systems further strengthened the chiefs' authority, allowing them to command more resources, mobilize more warriors, and expand their domains through conquest. Complex systems of tribute payment—from commoners to local chiefs and ultimately to island-wide monarchs—facilitated the formation of powerful states.

tribute Submission of wealth, labor, and sometimes items of symbolic value to a ruling authority.

Urban population, c. 1300
- ● Over 80,000
- ● 40,000–80,000
- ● 10,000–40,000
- · Under 10,000
- ▨ Area of high urban development

The Hanseatic League
- Danzig Major member
- Riga Minor member

MAP 12.3 **Europe, c. 1300**

Europe in 1300 boasted three cores of urban development: the mercantile city-states of northern Italy, the wool manufacturing towns of Flanders, and the former Muslim city-states of southern Spain, which still flourished as centers of trade and industry. Many independent cities in northern Europe banded together to form the Hanseatic League, a trade cartel that monopolized the export of furs, grain, metals, and timber from the Baltic region.

Settlement and Agriculture

Humans first arrived in the Hawaiian Islands during the great wave of Polynesian voyaging of the first millennium C.E. (see Chapter 11). The dating of the initial settlement of Hawaii is disputed, with scholarly opinion ranging from as early as 300 C.E. to as late as 800. The early colonists maintained contact with distant societies in the Marquesas (the most likely origin

The Mande Blacksmiths

Komo Mask

Among the Mande peoples of West Africa, komo associations governed many aspects of community life, such as the secret rites of passage that inducted young males into adulthood. The komo associations may date back to the period 700 to 1100, when blacksmiths first emerged as a powerful social caste. Blacksmiths, who worked with wood as well as metal, carved the animal masks used in komo religious rituals. (Barakat Gallery.)

In West Africa, ironworking was far more than a useful technology for manufacturing tools and weapons. It also became a fearsome instrument of symbolic power, especially among the Mande peoples inhabiting the Sahelian savanna between the Senegal and Niger river valleys. Mande society was divided into three principal groups: free persons (including both commoners and the warrior nobility); specialized professional castes (*nyamakala*) such as blacksmiths, leatherworkers, and storytelling bards; and slaves. This three-tiered structure had taken shape at least by the time of the Mali Empire in the thirteenth and fourteenth centuries. But the unique status of blacksmiths in Mande society clearly had more ancient origins.

The nyamakala possessed closely guarded knowledge of technical arts, and this knowledge was tinged with supernatural power. It gave them special abilities that set them apart from the rest of society. The nyamakala were considered alien peoples who married only with their own kind. The right to practice their craft was a hereditary monopoly.

An aura of mystery surrounded the blacksmiths in particular, whose work involved transforming rock into metal through the sublime power of fire. Ordinary people regarded them with a mixture of dread and awe. Similarly, the women of blacksmith clans had the exclusive right to make pottery. Like iron metallurgy, pottery making required mastery of the elemental force of fire.

Armed with secret knowledge and "magical" powers, blacksmiths occupied a central place in the religious life of the community. The right to perform circumcision, a solemn and dangerous ritual of passage to adulthood, was

Agriculture and Ecological Change

of the Hawaiians) and Society Islands. But long-distance voyaging ceased in around 1300. For the next five centuries, until the British explorer Captain Cook arrived in 1788, the Hawaiian archipelago remained a world unto itself.

The original settlers, probably numbering no more than a few hundred persons, introduced a wide range of new plants and animals, including pigs, dogs, and chickens, tuber crops (taro and yams), banana, coconut, and a variety of medicinal and fiber plants. Colonists soon hunted some native species to extinction, notably large birds such as geese and ibis, but the human impact on the islands' ecology remained modest until after 1100. Between 1100 and 1650, however, the human population grew rapidly, probably doubling every century. Agricultural exploitation intensified, radically transforming the natural environment. In the geologically older western islands, the inhabitants constructed irrigated taro fields fed by stone-lined canals on the valley floors and lower hillsides. But irrigation was not practicable on the large eastern islands of Hawaii and Maui because they were largely covered by lava flows. As a result agriculture in the eastern islands lagged behind that of the western islands.

entrusted to blacksmiths. Blacksmiths also manufactured ritual objects, such as the headdresses used in religious ceremonies. They were believed to have healing powers, too. Together with leatherworkers, they made amulets (charms) for protection against demonic attack.

The social distance that separated blacksmiths from the rest of Mande society enhanced their reputation for fairness. Blacksmiths commonly acted as mediators in disputes and marriage transactions. Mande peoples often swore oaths upon a blacksmith's anvil. Most important, only blacksmiths could hold leadership positions in *komo* associations, initiation societies composed mostly of young men and charged with protecting the community against human and supernatural enemies. The ritual masks used by komo associations in their religious ceremonies were carved by blacksmiths, whose occult powers imbued the masks with magical potency.

The caste status of blacksmith clans affirmed their extraordinary powers, but it simultaneously relegated them to the margins of society. In Mande origin myths, blacksmiths appear as a powerful force to be tamed and domesticated. The Mande epics trace the founding of the Mali Empire to an intrepid warrior hero, the hunter Sunjata (see page 397), who is said to have overthrown the "blacksmith king" Sumanguru (soo-mahn-guh-roo) in the mid-thirteenth century. Sumanguru is depicted as a brutal tyrant. Sunjata's triumph over Sumanguru enabled him to gain mastery of spiritual forces without being polluted and corrupted by them. In the new social order of the Mali Empire, the dangerous powers of the blacksmiths were contained by marginalizing them as an occupational caste that was excluded from warfare and rulership and forbidden to marry outside their group. Despite their crucial importance to economic and religious life, the caste identity of the blacksmiths branded them as inferior to freeborn persons in Mande society.

QUESTIONS TO CONSIDER

1. Why did Mande society regard blacksmiths as exceptional?

2. In what ways was the caste system of West African peoples such as the Mande different from the caste system in India discussed in Chapter 6?

3. Why did the rulers of Mali perceive the Mande blacksmiths as a threat?

For Further Information:
McIntosh, Roderick. *The Peoples of the Middle Niger: The Island of Gold.* Oxford, U.K.: Blackwell, 1998.
McNaughton, Patrick R. *The Mande Blacksmiths: Knowledge, Power, and Art in West Africa.* Bloomington, IN: Indiana University Press, 1988.

Population growth and the building of irrigation systems reached their peak in the fifteenth and sixteenth centuries. This was also the period when the *ahupua'a* (ah-HOO-poo-ah-hah) system of land management developed. The ahupua'a consisted of tracts of land running down from the central mountains to the sea, creating wedge-shaped segments that cut across different ecological zones. Each ahupua'a combined a wide range of resources, including forests, fields, fishponds, and marine vegetation and wildlife.

In other Polynesian societies, kinship groups possessed joint landownership rights, but in Hawaii the land belonged to powerful kings. These rulers claimed descent from the gods and sharply distinguished themselves from the rest of society. The kings distributed the ahupua'a under their control to subordinate chiefs in return for tribute

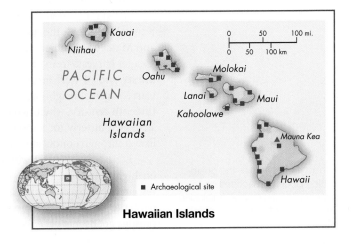

Hawaiian Islands

Hawaiian Landscape

The first European visitors to Hawaii were impressed by the intensive agriculture practiced by the Hawaiian islanders. This sketch of a Hawaiian village was drawn by a member of the expedition led by the British explorer George Vancouver, who landed at Hawaii in 1792. Cultivated fields lined with stone irrigation channels can be seen in the background. (Bishop Museum Library & Archives.)

and fealty, especially in times of war. Local chiefs in turn allocated rights to land, water, and fishing grounds to commoners, who were obliged to work on the personal lands of the chief and to pay tribute in produce. These rights were etched into the landscape by the construction of stone walls that lined fields, ponds, and canals.

Exchange and Social Hierarchy

Social Stratification

Strict rules of descent and inheritance determined social rank in Hawaiian society, and an elaborate system of **taboos** reinforced social stratification. Taboos also regulated gender differences and boundaries. Women were forbidden to eat many foods, including pork, bananas, and certain kinds of fish, and had to cook their food in separate ovens and eat apart from men. Chiefs proclaimed their exalted status through temple construction, ritual performances, and personal dress. Specialized craftsmen directly under the control of the chief class fashioned the elaborate feather cloaks, capes, and helmets worn by rulers that signified their divine status.

Omnipotent Kings

In the genealogical lore of Hawaii, the oldest royal lineages were in the densely populated islands of Kauai (kah-WAH-ee) and Oahu. The ruling elites of these islands drew their power and wealth from irrigated agriculture and focused their religious worship on Kane (KAH-nay), the god of flowing waters and fertility. On the larger islands of Hawaii and Maui, where chiefs and kings derived their power from military might rather than the meager harvests from dry-land farming, their devotion centered instead on Ku, the bloodthirsty god of war. From 1400 onward the local rulers in Hawaii and Maui incessantly warred against neighboring rivals. Temple-building on Maui escalated dramatically in the fifteenth century, when two regional chiefdoms formed on opposite ends of the island and struggled bitterly for supremacy. By 1650, single, island-wide kingdoms would be established through conquest on both Maui and Hawaii.

Long before contact with Europeans, then, Hawaiian rulers forged powerful states based on highly stratified systems of social ranking. Private property did not exist. All land and resources belonged to chiefs and kings, who were regarded as gods. In the absence of the kind of market networks that emerged in Eurasia and Africa, rulers could effectively monopolize the prestige goods that gave them exalted status. Through their monopoly of not only productive

taboo In Polynesia, the designation of certain actions or objects as sacred and forbidden to anyone not of royal or chiefly status.

resources but the exchange and use of goods, Hawaiian rulers gained full command over the wealth of their realm and the labor of their subjects. Taboos served above all to regulate consumption and to enforce the sharp social divide between rulers and commoners.

Conclusion

Beginning in the tenth century, agricultural growth and commercial integration generated a sustained economic expansion across much of Eurasia and Africa. A warmer global climate and the introduction of new crops increased agricultural productivity in both the ancient centers of civilization of the Mediterranean, India, and China and the newly developing areas of settlement such as northern and eastern Europe and mainland Southeast Asia. Larger and more stable food supplies nourished population growth in cities and the countryside alike.

The farthest-reaching transformations in economic life and livelihood were the expansion of trade networks and the growing sophistication of commercial practices. Cairo, Venice, Quanzhou, and other leading commercial cities served as the crossroads for enterprising merchants such as Allan bin Hassun; their trade ventures linked the Mediterranean and the Middle East to sub-Saharan Africa, the Indian Ocean, and China. The cosmopolitan merchant communities of these cities were the forefathers of this "commercial revolution" and the new forms of business organization and banking that it spawned. In contrast to places such as Hawaii, where wealth remained yoked to political power, the dynamic market economy threatened to subvert the existing social order. Commercial cities harbored new centers of education and intellectual inquiry, too, and these also posed challenges to established political and cultural authority, as we will see in the next chapter.

Dramatic as the changes in economic life were during these centuries, we should remember their limitations. Population growth eventually outpaced increases in productivity. The profits generated by commerce accrued mainly to merchants and their fellow investors—including religious establishments and landowning aristocrats—rather than producers. Hunger was a constant threat, and the poor had to survive on the last dregs of grain and chaff in the final months before the new harvest.

By 1300, the capacities of existing agricultural and commercial systems were reaching their limits. Under the intensifying strain of population growth, natural disasters, and political pressures, the commercial networks spanning Eurasia and Africa began to break down, ushering in an age of crisis and economic contraction that we will consider in Chapter 15.

NOTES

1. Quotations from S. D. Goitein, "Portrait of a Medieval India Trader: Three Letters from the Cairo Geniza," *Bulletin of the School of Oriental and African Studies,* 50, no. 3 (1987): 461; S. D. Goitein, *A Mediterranean Society: The Jewish Communities of the World as Portrayed in the Documents of the Cairo Geniza* (Berkeley: University of California Press, 1978–88), 3:194; 5:221.
2. Kekaumenos, *Strategikon,* quoted in Angeliki E. Laiou, "Economic Thought and Ideology," in Angeliki E. Laiou, ed., *The Economic History of Byzantium from the Seventh Through the Fifteenth Century* (Washington, DC: Dumbarton Oaks Research Library and Collection, 2002), 3:1127.
3. Quotation from Fang Hui (1227–1307), cited in Richard von Glahn, "Towns and Temples: Urban Growth and Decline in the Yangzi Delta, 1100–1400," in Paul Jakov Smith and Richard von Glahn, eds., *The Song Yuan-Ming Transition in Chinese History* (Cambridge, MA: Harvard University Council on East Asian Studies, 2004), 182.
4. Ibn Hazm, *The Ring of the Dove: A Treatise on the Art and Practice of Arab Love* (London: Luzac, 1953), 74.
5. Al-Muqaddasi, *The Best Divisions for Knowledge of the Regions,* trans. Basil Anthony Collins (Reading, U.K.: Garnet Publishing, 1994), 181.
6. Quoted in Goitein, *A Mediterranean Society,* 1:200.
7. Translation adapted from Yuan Ts'ai, *Family Instructions for the Yuan Clan,* quoted in Patricia Buckley Ebrey, *Family and Property in Sung China* (Princeton, NJ: Princeton University Press, 1984), 267.

8. Ibn Hawqal, *The Picture of the Earth*, translated in N. Levtzion and J. F. P. Hopkins, eds., *Corpus of Early Arabic Sources for West African History* (Cambridge, U.K.: Cambridge University Press, 1981), 49.

9. Al-Bakri, *Kitab al masalik wa-'l-mamalik*, translated in Levtzion and Hopkins, eds., *Corpus of Early Arabic Sources*, 79.

10. Al-Umari, "The Kingdom of Mali and What Appertains to It" (1338), cited in Levtzion and Hopkins, eds., *Corpus of Early Arabic Sources*, 270–271.

RESOURCES FOR RESEARCH

Agricultural Innovation and Diffusion

The diffusion of crops and the invention of new technologies gave impetus to major advances in agricultural productivity across Eurasia between 900 and 1300. Duby's classic work on the early medieval European economy remains unsurpassed, but Verhulst, who reviews the large historiography on this topic and the growing body of archaeological evidence, provides a valuable supplement for the early part of this period.

Bray, Francesca. *The Rice Economies: Technology and Development in Asian Societies*. 1986.

Chaudhuri, K. N. *Asia Before Europe: Economy and Civilization of the Indian Ocean from the Rise of Islam to 1750*. 1990.

Duby, Georges. *The Early Growth of the European Economy: Warriors and Peasants from the Seventh to the Twelfth Century*. 1974.

Verhulst, Adriaan. *The Carolingian Economy*. 2002.

Watson, A. M. *Agricultural Innovation in the Early Islamic World: The Diffusion of Crops and Farming Techniques, 700–1100*. 1983.

Industrial Growth and the Money Economy

Technological innovation was also a key stimulus to industrial growth, especially in China. Lopez was the pioneer in establishing the now widely accepted idea of a "commercial revolution" in medieval Europe. Herlihy and Bray are landmarks in the study of women, work, and the domestic economy.

Bray, Francesca. *Technology and Gender: Fabrics of Power in Late Imperial China*. 1997.

Epstein, Steven A. *An Economic and Social History of Later Medieval Europe, 1000–1500*. 2009.

Herlihy, David. *Opera Muliebria: Women and Work in Medieval Europe*. 1990.

Laiou, Angeliki E., and Cécile Morrison. *The Byzantine Economy*. 2007.

Lombard, Maurice. *The Golden Age of Islam* (rpt.). 2004.

Lopez, Robert S. *The Commercial Revolution of the Middle Ages, 950–1350*. 1976.

Merchants and Trade Networks in Afro-Eurasia

We have much more abundant documentary evidence of the increasingly far-flung activities of merchants than we have for those of farmers and industrialists. Abu-Lughod provides the most comprehensive synthesis of the development of cross-cultural exchange and commercial practices in this era. Favier and Constable both marshal impressive bodies of evidence on the merchant world of western Europe.

Abu-Lughod, Janet. *Before European Hegemony: The World System, A.D. 1250–1350*. 1989.

Constable, Olivia Remie. *Trade and Traders in Muslim Spain: The Commercial Realignment of the Iberian Peninsula, 900–1500*. 1994.

Coquery-Vidrovitch, Catherine. *The History of African Cities South of the Sahara: From the Origins to Colonization*. 2005.

Favier, Jean. *Gold and Spices: The Rise of Commerce in the Middle Ages*. 1998.

Sen, Tansen. *Buddhism, Diplomacy, and Trade: The Realignment of Sino-Indian Relations, 600–1400*. 2003.

COUNTERPOINT: Production, Tribute, and Trade in the Hawaiian Islands

Through painstaking archaeological research, the major developments in land use and economic life in the Pacific Islands before European contact are gradually becoming clear. Kirch is the foremost authority on the archaeology of the Hawaiian Islands and Polynesia generally. Earle's study of the different types of chiefdom societies emphasizes the crucial importance of economic power in the formation of Hawaiian chiefdoms.

Earle, Timothy. *How Chiefs Come to Power: The Political Economy in Prehistory*. 1997.

Kirch, Patrick V. *Feathered Gods and Fishhooks: An Introduction to Hawaiian Archaeology and Prehistory*. 1985.

Kirch, Patrick V., and Jean-Louis Rallu, eds. *The Growth and Collapse of Pacific Island Societies: Archaeological and Demographic Perspectives*. 2007.

▶ **For additional primary sources from this period**, see *Sources of Crossroads and Cultures*.

▶ **For Web sites, images, and documents related to topics in this chapter**, see Make History at bedfordstmartins.com/smith.

The major global development in this chapter ▶ The sustained economic expansion that spread across Afro-Eurasia from 900 to 1300.

IMPORTANT EVENTS

850–1267	Chola kingdom in southern India
960–1279	Song dynasty in China
969	Fatimids conquer Egypt
1024	The Song dynasty issues the first paper money in world history
1055	Seljuk Turks capture Baghdad
c. 1120–1150	Construction of Angkor Wat begins
1127	The Jurchen conquer north China; the Song dynasty retains control of southern China
c. 1150–1300	Heyday of the Champagne fairs
c. 1200–1400	Formation of first chiefdoms in the Hawaiian Islands
1230–1255	Reign of Sunjata, founder of the Mali Empire in West Africa
1250–1517	Mamluk dynasty in Egypt
1258	The Italian city-states of Florence and Genoa mint the first gold coins issued in Latin Christendom
1323–1325	Pilgrimage to Mecca of Musa Mansa, ruler of Mali
c. 1400–1450	Great Zimbabwe in southern Africa reaches peak of prosperity

KEY TERMS

bill of exchange (p. 386)
burgher (p. 397)
cartel (p. 390)
guild (p. 388)
iqta (p. 378)
joint stock company (p. 391)

serf (p. 376)
taboo (p. 402)
tribute (p. 398)
usury (p. 386)

CHAPTER OVERVIEW QUESTIONS

1. How did agricultural changes contribute to commercial and industrial growth?

2. What technological breakthroughs increased productivity most significantly?

3. What social institutions and economic innovations did merchants devise to overcome the risks and dangers of long-distance trade?

4. In what ways did the profits of commerce translate into social and economic power?

5. Above all, who benefited most from these economic changes?

SECTION FOCUS QUESTIONS

1. Which groups took the most active role in adopting new agricultural technologies in the different regions of Eurasia during the centuries from 900 to 1300?

2. How did the composition and organization of the industrial workforce change in different parts of Eurasia during this period?

3. How did the commercial revival of 900 to 1300 reorient trade routes across Afro-Eurasia?

4. How did the sources of wealth and power in the Hawaiian Islands differ from those of market economies elsewhere in the world?

MAKING CONNECTIONS

1. In what ways did the spread of new crops and farming technologies during this period have a different impact in the Islamic world and in Asia?

2. How had the principal east-west trade routes between Asia and the Mediterranean world changed since the time of the Han and Roman empires (see Chapters 6 and 7)?

3. To what extent did the Christian, Jewish, and Muslim merchant communities of the Mediterranean adopt similar forms of commercial organization and business practices during the "commercial revolution" of 900 to 1300? How can we explain the differences and similarities among these groups?

AT A CROSSROADS ▲

Schools in Latin Christendom organized the learning of ancient Greece and Rome into the seven liberal arts. The trivium (Latin for "three roads") of logic, rhetoric, and grammar endowed the student with eloquence; the quadrivium ("four roads") of arithmetic, geometry, astronomy, and music led to knowledge. This detail from a mural composed between 1365 and 1367 for a Franciscan chapel in Florence depicts the trivium (at right in first row) and the quadrivium (at left) in the persons of the ancient scholars credited with their invention; behind each scholar sits his muse, represented in female form. (Scala/Art Resource, NY.)

Centers of Learning and the Transmission of Culture

900–1300

I n her masterful novel of court life in Heian Japan, *The Tale of Genji*, Murasaki Shikibu (c. 973–1025) sought to defend the art of fiction and women as readers of fiction. Murasaki's hero, Genji, finds his adopted daughter copying a courtly romance novel and mocks women's passionate enthusiasm for such frivolous writings. Genji protests that "there is hardly a word of truth in all of these books, as you know perfectly well, but here you are utterly fascinated by such fables, taking them quite seriously and avidly copying every word." At the end of his speech, though, Genji reverses his original judgment. Romance novels, he concludes, may be fabricated, but they have the virtue of describing "this world exactly as it is."[1]

Many of Murasaki's contemporaries shared Genji's initial low opinion of the content of courtly romances, but they also rejected such works at least in part because they were written in vernacular Japanese—the language of everyday speech. In Lady Murasaki's day, classical Chinese was the language of politics and religion at the Heian court. Writing in the Japanese vernacular was considered at best a trifling skill, acceptable for letters and diaries but ill-suited to the creation of literature or art.

Lady Murasaki had been born into an aristocratic family of middling rank. She was a quick study as a child and, she tells us, far more proficient at Chinese than her brother.

BACKSTORY

As we saw in Chapters 9 and 10, from 400 to 1000 religious traditions consolidated in the main centers of civilization across Eurasia. Christianity prevailed in many parts of the former Roman Empire, but divisions deepened between the Greek church, which was closely allied with the Byzantine Empire, and the Latin church of Rome. Islam was fully established as the official religion across a vast territory extending from Spain to Persia. In India, the classical Brahmanic religion, recast in the form of Hinduism, steadily displaced Buddhism from the center of religious and intellectual life. In contrast, the Mahayana tradition of Buddhism enjoyed great popularity at all levels of society in East Asia. In China, however, Buddhist beliefs clashed with the long-cherished secular ideals of Confucian philosophy. In all of these regions, the study of scripture—and the written language of sacred texts—dominated schooling and learning.

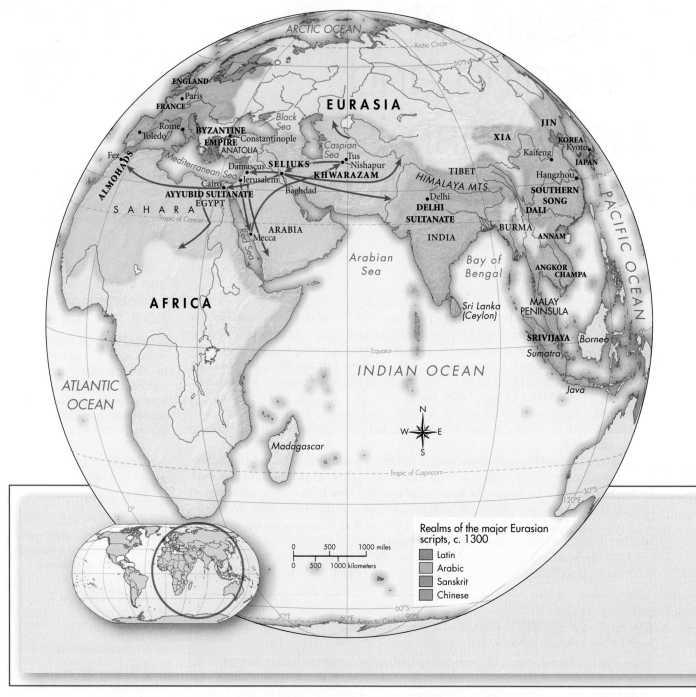

Realms of the major Eurasian scripts, c. 1300

- Latin
- Arabic
- Sanskrit
- Chinese

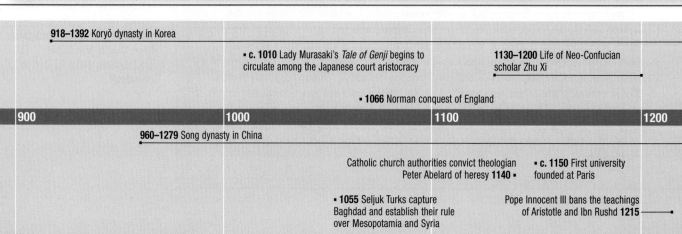

918–1392 Koryŏ dynasty in Korea

- **c. 1010** Lady Murasaki's *Tale of Genji* begins to circulate among the Japanese court aristocracy

1130–1200 Life of Neo-Confucian scholar Zhu Xi

- **1066** Norman conquest of England

900	1000	1100	1200

960–1279 Song dynasty in China

Catholic church authorities convict theologian Peter Abelard of heresy **1140** •

- **c. 1150** First university founded at Paris

- **1055** Seljuk Turks capture Baghdad and establish their rule over Mesopotamia and Syria

Pope Innocent III bans the teachings of Aristotle and Ibn Rushd **1215**

Knowledge of Chinese was considered unbecoming in a woman, however. Calligraphy (brush writing), poetry, and music were deemed appropriate subjects for female education. Like many women of her class, Murasaki was also fond of romance tales, which typically revolved around the lives, loves, and marriages of court women. Widowed in her twenties, Murasaki had already acquired some fame as a writer when she was summoned in around 1006 to serve as lady-in-waiting to the empress. During her years at the court Murasaki completed her *Tale of Genji*. Manuscript copies circulated widely among court women in Murasaki's lifetime and captivated a sizable male readership as well. From Murasaki's time forward, fiction and poetry written in the Japanese vernacular gained distinction as serious works of literature.

Yet Chinese remained the language of officials, scholars, and priests. The role of Chinese as the language of public discourse and political and religious authority throughout East Asia paralleled that of Latin in western Europe, of Arabic in the Islamic world, and of Sanskrit in South and Southeast Asia. Between the tenth and the fourteenth centuries these cosmopolitan languages—languages that transcended national boundaries—became deeply embedded in new educational institutions, and as a result their intellectual and aesthetic prestige grew. Although writing in vernacular languages gained new prominence as well, the goal was not to address a wider, nonelite audience. Rather, the emergence of vernacular literature was often closely tied to courtly culture, as in Murasaki's Japan. Authors writing in the vernacular still wrote for elite, learned readers.

Choosing to write in the vernacular was both a political and an artistic statement. The turn toward the vernacular was undoubtedly related to the ebbing authority of vast multinational empires and the rise of national and regional states. But the emergence of vernacular literary languages did not simply reflect existing national social and political identities; they were instrumental in inventing regional and national identities. Thus, both cosmopolitan and vernacular languages helped create new cultural connections, the former by facilitating the development of international cultural communities, and the latter by broadcasting the idea that nations were defined, in part, by the shared culture of their inhabitants.

MAPPING THE WORLD

The Major Written Languages of Eurasia, c. 1300

The use of a common written language fostered cultural unity within each of the four major regional societies of Eurasia. The spread of the four "classical" languages—Latin, Arabic, Sanskrit, and Chinese—resulted from their prominent role as the written word of religious scriptures. After 1000, a shift toward vernacular, or everyday, written languages occurred in all of these regions, but the classical languages retained their cultural authority, especially in religion and higher education.

ROUTES ▼

→ Spread of Sufi orders, 1150–1300

→ Travels of Abu Hamid al-Ghazali, 1091–1111

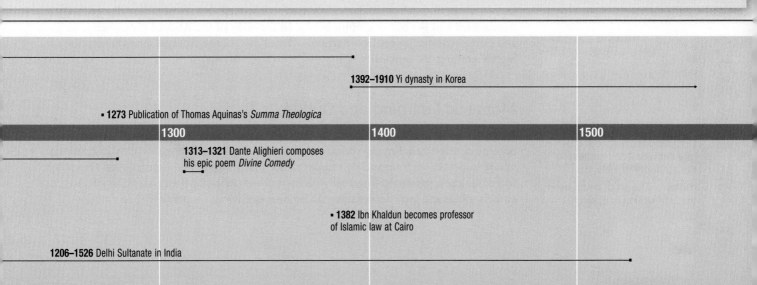

1392–1910 Yi dynasty in Korea

1273 Publication of Thomas Aquinas's *Summa Theologica*

1300   1400   1500

1313–1321 Dante Alighieri composes his epic poem *Divine Comedy*

1382 Ibn Khaldun becomes professor of Islamic law at Cairo

1206–1526 Delhi Sultanate in India

OVERVIEW
QUESTIONS

The major global development in this chapter: The expansion of learning and education across Eurasia from 900 to 1300 and its relationship to the rise of regional and national identities.

As you read, consider:

1. Did the spread of higher learning reinforce or undermine established political and religious authority?

2. How did educational institutions reshape social hierarchy and elite culture?

3. What were the different uses of cosmopolitan languages (which transcended national boundaries) and vernacular (everyday) languages, and to what degree did they broaden access to written knowledge?

4. How did the different technologies of writing affect the impact of the written word?

Church and Universities in Latin Christendom

FOCUS

What political, social, and religious forces led to the founding of the first European universities?

Between the tenth and the fourteenth centuries, Latin Christendom witnessed the emergence of a unified learned culture. The values and self-images of clergy and knights increasingly converged. For knights, chivalric virtue and dedication to defense of the Christian faith replaced the wanton lifestyle of the Germanic warriors. At the same time, the clergy became more militant in their promotion of orthodoxy, as reform-minded religious orders devoted themselves to spreading the faith and stamping out heresy.

Schooling created a common elite culture and a single educated class. The career of Peter Abelard (1079–1142) captures this transformation. Abelard's father, a French knight, engaged a tutor to educate young Peter in his future duties as a warrior and lord. Abelard later recalled that "I was so carried away by my love of learning that I renounced the glory of a soldier's life, made over my inheritance and rights of the elder son to my brothers, and withdrew from the court of Mars [war] in order to kneel at the feet of Minerva [learning]."[2] Abelard's intellectual daring ultimately provoked charges of heresy that led to his banishment and the burning of his books. In the wake of the Abelard controversy, kings and clerics wrestled for control of schools. Out of this contest emerged a new institution of higher learning, the university.

Monastic Learning and Culture

cathedral school In Latin Christendom, a school attached to a cathedral and subject to the authority of a bishop.

rhetoric The art of persuasion through writing or speech.

From the time of Charlemagne (r. 768–814), royal courts and Christian monasteries became closely allied. Royally sponsored monasteries grew into huge, wealthy institutions whose leaders came from society's upper ranks. Many monks and nuns entered the cloisters as children, presented (together with their inheritances) by their parents as gifts to the church. Kings and local nobles safeguarded monasteries and supervised their activities.

Devoted to the propagation of right religion and seeking educated men to staff their governments, Charlemagne and his successors promoted a revival of classical learning consistent with the established doctrines of Latin Christianity. Charlemagne summoned famous scholars to his court and gave them the tasks of reforming ecclesiastic practices and establishing an authoritative text of the Bible. Although he never realized his hope that schooling would be widely available, local bishops began to found **cathedral schools**—schools attached to a cathedral and subject to a bishop's authority—as a complement to monastic education.

Cathedral Schools

Elementary schools trained students to speak and read Latin. Advanced education in both monasteries and cathedral schools centered on the "liberal arts," particularly the Roman *trivium* (TREE-vee-um) (Latin for "three roads") of grammar, rhetoric, and logic. Roman educators had championed **rhetoric**—the art of persuasion through writing or speech—and especially oratorical skill as crucial to a career in government service. Monastic teachers likewise stressed the importance of rhetoric and oratory for monks and priests. Unlike the Romans, however, the clergy deemphasized logic; they sought to establish the primacy of revelation over philosophical reasoning. Similarly, the clergy separated the exact sciences of the Greeks—the *quadrivium* (kwo-DRIV-ee-uhm) ("four roads") of arithmetic, geometry, music, and astronomy—from the core curriculum of the trivium and treated these fields as specialized subjects for advanced study.

Emphasis on Liberal Arts

Bishops appointed "master scholars" to take charge of teaching at the cathedral schools. The masters in effect had a monopoly on teaching within their cities. Individuals who ventured to teach without official recognition as a master faced excommunication. The privileged status of these masters and their greater receptivity to logic and the quadrivium caused friction between cathedral schools and monasteries.

The revival of learning encouraged by Charlemagne and the Germanic kings led to a dramatic increase in book production, including theological works, biblical commentaries, encyclopedias, and saints' lives. The kings distributed manuscripts to monasteries, where scribes and artists made copies. By the eleventh century many religious texts were created as lavish works of art featuring copious illustration and expensive materials such

Boom in Book Production

Deluxe Illustrated Manuscript
Monastic communities in Latin Christendom created many beautifully illustrated copies of the Gospels, the accounts of the life of Christ. The first page of this *Gospel of Matthew*, produced at a German monastery in around 1120 to 1140, shows Saint Matthew writing with a quill pen and sharpening knife. On the next page the first line of the Gospel begins with a large letter *L* (the beginning of the word *liber*, "book"), nested among golden vines against a background resembling the luxurious Byzantine silks highly prized in Europe. (The J. Paul Getty Museum, Los Angeles, Ms. Ludwig II 3, fol.10, Decorated Incipit Page, ca.1120-1140, Temera colors, gold and silver on parchment, Leaf: 9 × 6½ in.)

Medical Professionals of Latin Christendom

Economic revival and urban growth in Europe after 1000 spurred major changes in the practice and study of medicine. The rising urban commercial and professional classes increasingly demanded academically trained physicians. The cathedral schools, and later the universities, added medicine as an advanced subject of study. The institutionalization of medicine as an academic discipline transformed learned doctors into a professional class that tightly regulated its membership, practices, and standards.

In around 1173, the Jewish traveler Benjamin of Tudela described Salerno, in southern Italy, as the home of "the principal medical university of Christendom." By *university* Benjamin meant an organized group of scholars, not a formal educational institution. By the tenth century Salerno had already achieved renown for its skilled doctors. Many hailed from the city's large Jewish and Greek communities and were familiar with Arabic and Byzantine medical traditions. Beginning in the eleventh century, Salerno's learned doctors produced many medical writings that profoundly influenced medical knowledge and training across Latin Christendom.

Among the notable scholars at Salerno was Constantine the African, a Muslim who arrived from North Africa, possibly as a drug merchant, in around 1070. Constantine converted to Christianity and entered the famed Montecassino monastery north of Salerno. His translations of Muslim, Jewish, and Greek works on medicine became the basis of medical instruction in European universities for centuries afterward.

Salerno's doctors also contributed important writings on gynecology and obstetrics. A local female healer named Trota became a famed authority on gynecology ("women's medicine"). A Salerno manuscript falsely attributed to Trota justified singling out women's illnesses as a separate branch of medicine:

Trota Expounds on the Nature of Women
The *Trotula*, a set of three treatises on gynecology and women's health, was probably composed in Salerno in the twelfth century. All three works were attributed to Trota, a healer acclaimed as an authority on female physiology, although only one is likely to have come from her hand. In this illustration from a fourteenth-century French encyclopedia on natural science, Trota sits before a large open book and instructs a clerk in "the secrets of nature." (Bibliothèque de Rennes Métropole, MS593, folio 532.)

Because women are of a weaker nature than men, so more than men they are afflicted, especially in childbirth. It is for this reason also that more frequently diseases abound in them than in men, especially around the organs assigned to the work of nature. And because only with shame and embarrassment do they confess the fragility of the condition of their diseases that occur around their secret parts, they do not dare reveal their distress to male physicians. Therefore,

as gold leaf. A strikingly different style of creating manuscripts, however, was developed by the Cistercians, a new religious order that spread like wildfire across Europe within fifty years of its founding in 1098 (see Chapter 14). The Cistercians rebelled against the opulent lifestyle of wealthy monastic communities and dedicated themselves to lives of simplicity and poverty. In keeping with its principles of frugality, the Cistercian order produced great numbers of religious texts without elaborate decoration. Cistercian clergy also abhorred the growing importance of reasoning and logic in the cathedral schools, instead emphasizing religious education based on memorization, contemplation, and spiritual faith. Thus, the expansion of learning created both new connections and new divisions in Europe's intellectual and cultural elite.

their misfortune, which ought to be pitied, and especially the sake of a certain woman, moved me to provide some remedy for their above-mentioned diseases.[1]

The author attributed women's infirmity to their physical constitution and the trauma of childbirth, but also noted that women were less likely to seek treatment from male doctors. Local authorities, however, typically prohibited women other than midwives from treating patients.

Despite its outpouring of medical treatises, Salerno had no formal institution for medical training until the thirteenth century. By that time the universities of Bologna and Paris had surpassed Salerno as centers of medical learning. Bologna, for example, revived the study of anatomy and surgery and introduced human dissection as part of the curriculum. At the universities, students studied medicine only after completing rigorous training in the liberal arts.

The growing professionalization of medicine nurtured a new self-image of the doctor. Guy de Chauliac, a surgeon trained at Paris in the fourteenth century, wrote:

I say that the doctor should be well mannered, bold in many ways, fearful of dangers, that he should abhor the false cures or practices. He should be affable to the sick, kindhearted to his colleagues, wise in his prognostications. He should be chaste, sober, compassionate, and merciful: he should not be covetous, grasping in money matters, and then he will receive a salary commensurate with his labors, the financial ability of his patients, the success of the treatment, and his own dignity.[2]

The emphasis on high ethical standards was crucial to the effort to elevate medicine's stature as an honorable occupation given the popular image of doctors and pharmacists as charlatans who, in the English poet Chaucer's mocking words, "each made money from the other's guile."[3]

This professional class of doctors steeped in rigorous study and guided by Christian compassion largely served the upper classes, however. Care of the poor and the rural populace was left to uneducated barber-surgeons, bonesetters, and faith healers.

---

1. Monica H. Green, ed. and trans., *The Trotula: An English Translation of the Medieval Compendium of Women's Medicine* (Philadelphia: University of Pennsylvania Press, 2002), 65.
2. Guy de Chauliac, "Inventarium sive chirurgia magna," quoted in Vern L. Bullough, *The Development of Medicine as a Profession: The Contribution of the Medieval University to Modern Medicine* (New York: Hafner Publishing, 1966), 93–94.
3. Geoffrey Chaucer, "Prologue," *The Canterbury Tales* (Harmondsworth, U.K.: Penguin), 30.

QUESTIONS TO CONSIDER

1. What kind of education and personal characteristics were considered necessary to become a professional physician?

2. Why did the public hold doctors in low regard? How did university education aim to improve that image?

For Further Information:

Bullough, Vern L. *The Development of Medicine as a Profession: The Contribution of the Medieval University to Modern Medicine.* New York: Hafner Publishing, 1966.
Siraisi, Nancy. *Medieval and Early Renaissance Medicine: An Introduction to Knowledge and Practice.* Chicago: University of Chicago Press, 1990.

The Rise of Universities

During the eleventh and twelfth centuries, demand for advanced education rose steadily. Eager young students traveled to distant cities to study with renowned masters. Unable to accommodate all of these students by themselves, masters began to hire staffs of specialized teachers who taught medicine, law, and theology in addition to the liberal arts. Certain schools acquired international reputations for excellence in particular specialties: Montpellier and Salerno in medicine, Bologna in law, Paris and Oxford in theology. These schools also applied higher learning to secular purposes. Montpellier and Salerno incorporated Greek and Arabic works into the study of medicine (see Lives and Livelihoods: Medical Professionals of Latin Christendom). At Bologna separate schools were established for civil and church law.

Increased Demand for Advanced Education

Influence of Greek and Muslim Learning

Christian conquests of Muslim territories in Spain and Sicily in the eleventh century reintroduced Greek learning to Latin Christendom via translations from Arabic. In 1085, King Alfonso VI (r. 1072–1109) of Castile captured Toledo, a city renowned as a center of learning where Muslims, Jews, and Christians freely intermingled. He made it his capital, and he and his successors preserved its multicultural heritage and spirit of religious toleration. In the twelfth century Toledo's Arabic-speaking Jewish and Christian scholars translated into Latin the works of Aristotle and other ancient Greek writers as well as philosophical, scientific, and medical writings by Muslim authors. Access to this vast body of knowledge had a profound impact on European intellectual circles. The commentaries on Aristotle by the Muslim philosopher Ibn Rushd (IB-uhn RUSHED) (1126–1198), known in Latin as Averröes (uh-VERR-oh-eez), sought to reconcile the paradoxes between faith and reason. They attracted keen interest from Christian theologians grappling with similar questions.

Ibn Rushd's insistence that faith is incomplete without rational understanding, for which he was persecuted and exiled, added new fuel to the intellectual controversies that flared up in Paris in the 1120s. Peter Abelard, who based his study of theology on the principle that "nothing can be believed unless it is first understood," attracted thousands of students to his lectures. Abelard's commitment to demonstrating the central tenets of Christian doctrine by applying reason and logical proof aroused heated controversy. Church authorities in 1140 found Abelard guilty of heresy and exiled him from Paris. He died a broken man two years later.

The First European Universities

The dispute over the primacy of reason or faith continued after Abelard's death. Paris's numerous masters organized themselves into guilds to defend their independence from the local bishop and from hostile religious orders such as the Cistercians, who had led the campaign against Abelard. The popes at Rome, eager to extend the reach of their own authority, placed Paris's schools of theology under their own supervision. In 1215 Pope Innocent III (1198–1216) formally recognized Paris's schools of higher learning as a **university**—a single corporation including masters and students from all the city's schools—under the direction of the pope's representative. Universities at Oxford and Bologna soon gained similar legal status.

In the end, though, chartering universities as independent corporations insulated them from clerical control. European monarchs, eager to enlist educated men in government service, became ardent patrons of established schools and provided endowments to create new ones. Consequently, during the thirteenth century more than thirty universities sprang up in western Europe (see Map 13.1). Royal patrons gave the universities leverage against local bishops and municipal councils. In some places, such as Oxford in England, the university became the dominant institution in local society, thanks to its substantial property holdings and control over both ecclesiastic and civil courts.

Among all the university towns, Paris emerged as the intellectual capital of Latin Christendom in the thirteenth century. Despite a papal ban on teaching Aristotle's works on natural science, the city swarmed with prominent teachers espousing Aristotle's ideas and methods. Even conservative scholars came to recognize the need to reconcile Christian doctrine with Greek philosophy. Thomas Aquinas (c. 1225–1274), a theologian at the University of Paris, incorporated Abelard's methods of logical argument into his great synthesis of Christian teachings, *Summa Theologica*. It stirred turbulent controversy, and much of it was banned until shortly before Aquinas's canonization as a saint in 1323. Academic freedom in the universities, to the extent that it existed, rested on an insecure balance among the competing interests of kings, bishops, and the papacy for control over the hearts and minds of their students.

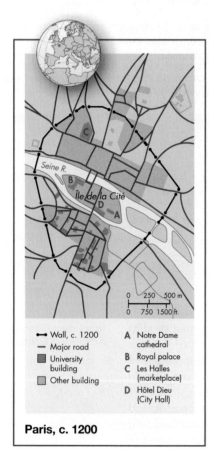

Wall, c. 1200
— Major road
■ University building
□ Other building

A Notre Dame cathedral
B Royal palace
C Les Halles (marketplace)
D Hôtel Dieu (City Hall)

Seine R.
Île de la Cité

0   250   500 m
0   750 1500 ft.

Paris, c. 1200

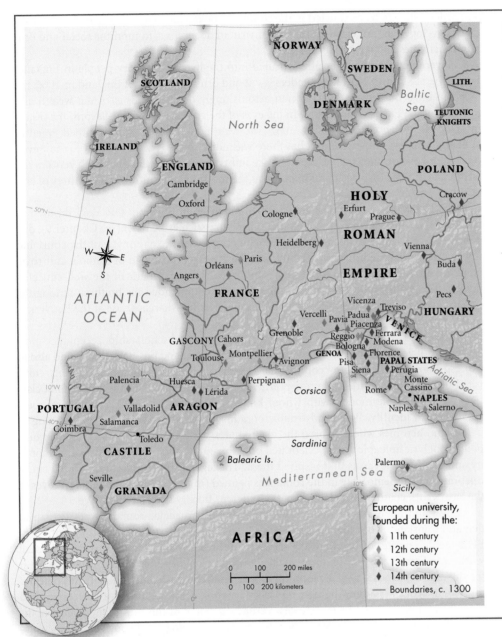

MAP 13.1

Founding of Universities in Latin Christendom, c. 1150–1400

By the twelfth century, universities eclipsed monasteries and cathedral schools as the most prestigious centers of learning in Latin Christendom. Universities were created by royal or municipal charters that affirmed their independence from clerical control. They attracted students from many lands and thus helped to forge a common elite culture across most of Europe.

Vernacular Language and Literature

The growing need for literacy was a driving force behind the expansion of schooling and the founding of universities in Latin Europe. The mental agility and practical knowledge obtained by mastering the liberal arts curriculum had wide applications in bureaucratic and ecclesiastic office, professional careers, and private business. Schooling based on literacy in Latin fostered a unified elite culture across western Europe, well beyond national boundaries. At the same time, however, the practical needs of government and business and changes in the self-image of the rising administrative and commercial classes encouraged writing in a **vernacular language**—the language of everyday speech.

Despite the dominance of Latin in formal education, commercial growth and political expansion demanded more practical forms of literacy. The everyday business of government—recording disputes and judicial settlements, collecting vital statistics, transmitting warrants

university In Latin Christendom, a single corporate body that included teachers and students from a range of different academic disciplines.

vernacular language The language of everyday speech, in contrast to a language that is mainly literary.

Practical Uses of Vernacular Writing

and orders—had to be conducted in the common spoken language. The growth of bureaucracy developed in tandem with the use of written documents to monitor social and economic activities and control resources.

Government most powerfully intruded into the lives of ordinary people in England. Following the French Norman invaders' swift and brutal conquest of England in 1066, the Norman king William I undertook an astonishingly detailed census of the wealth and property of the English population. In the eyes of the vanquished Anglo-Saxons, the resulting *Domesday Book*, completed in 1087, was a monument to the unrestrained greed of William, who "was not ashamed that there was not a single [parcel of land] . . . not even one ox, or cow, or pig which escaped notice in his survey."[3] By the thirteenth century the written record had displaced oral memory as the indispensable authority in matters of law, business, and government.

The Norman conquest also transformed language in England. Old English, used to compose the Anglo-Saxon law codes and epic poetry such as *Beowulf* (see Chapter 9), disappeared as a written language, while French became the spoken tongue of the court and upper-class society. Latin served as the standard written language of schools and royal government. Mastery of the three main languages became a mark of the well-educated person. The mathematician Roger Bacon (d. 1294) commended his brethren among the Oxford faculty for teaching in English, French, and Latin, whereas those at the University of Paris exclusively used Latin.

Vernacular Literary Traditions

Although Latin prevailed as the language of liturgy and scholarship, acceptance grew for the use of vernacular languages to manage government and business affairs, and also to express emotion. Enriched by commercial wealth and land revenues, court society cultivated new fashions in dress, literature, art, and music. Yet the Bible and the Roman classics offered few role models with whom kings and princes, let alone knights and merchants, could identify. Poets and troubadours instead used vernacular speech to sing of heroes and heroines who mirrored the ideals and aspirations of their audiences. An outpouring of lyric and epic poetry celebrated both the public and private virtues of the nobility and the chivalric ideals that inspired them. The legends of King Arthur and his circle, celebrated most memorably in the romances penned (in French) by Chrétien de Troyes in the late twelfth century, mingled themes of religious fidelity and romantic love.

Royal and noble patrons who eagerly devoured vernacular romances also began to demand translations of religious and classical texts. Scholars such as Nicole Oresme (or-EHZ-meh), a master of theology at Paris, welcomed the challenge of translating classical works into French as a way to improve the vernacular language and enable people to use it for the higher purposes of philosophical debate and religious contemplation. In the early fourteenth century, Dante Alighieri (DAHN-tay ah-lee-JIHR-ee) (1265–1321), composed his *Divine Comedy*, perhaps the greatest vernacular poem of this era, in the dialect of his native Florence. Dante's allegory entwined scholastic theology and courtly love poetry to plumb the mysteries of the Christian faith in vivid and captivating language. The influence of Dante was so great that modern Italian is essentially descended from the language of the *Divine Comedy*. Thus, even as the rise of universities promoted a common intellectual culture across Latin Christendom, the growth of vernacular languages led to the creation of distinctive national literary traditions.

Students and Scholars in Islamic Societies

FOCUS

To what extent did Sunni and Sufi schools foster a common cultural and religious identity among Muslims?

In contrast to Latin Christendom, in the Islamic world neither the caliphs nor dissenting movements such as Shi'ism sought to establish a clergy with sacred powers and formal religious authority. Instead, the task of teaching the faithful about matters of religion fell to the **ulama** (oo-leh-MAH), learned persons whose wisdom and holiness earned them the respect of their peers. But the ulama did not claim any special relationship to God.

The ulama remained immersed in the secular world because Islam disdained the celibacy and monastic withdrawal from society that were so central to Latin Christianity. Ulama could be found in all walks of life, from wealthy landowners and government officials to ascetic teachers and humble artisans and shopkeepers. Some ulama earned their living from official duties as judges, tax collectors, and caretakers of mosques. But many were merchants and shopkeepers; the profession of religious teacher was by no means incompatible with pursuit of personal gain.

During the heyday of Abbasid power in the eighth and ninth centuries (discussed in Chapter 9), educated professional men such as bureaucrats, physicians, and scribes—often trained in Persian or Greek traditions of learning—competed with theologians for intellectual leadership in the Islamic world. Following the decline of caliphal authority in the tenth century, religious scholars regained their privileged status. The ulama codified what became the Sunni orthodoxy by setting down formal interpretations of scriptural and legal doctrine, founding colleges, and monopolizing the judgeships that regulated both public and private conduct.

The Rise of Madrasas

Hadith and Shari'a

During the Umayyad and Abbasid caliphates, scriptural commentators sought to apply Muhammad's teachings to social life as well as religious conduct. Scholars compiled anthologies of the sayings and deeds of Muhammad, known as *hadith* (hah-DEETH), as guidelines for leading a proper Muslim life. The need to reconcile Islamic ethical principles with existing social customs and institutions resulted in the formation of a comprehensive body of Islamic law, known as *shari'a* (sha-REE-ah). Yet the formal pronouncements of hadith and shari'a did not resolve all matters of behavior and belief.

Varying Interpretations of Islamic Law

During the eighth and ninth centuries four major schools of legal interpretation emerged in different parts of the Islamic world to provide authoritative judgments on civil and religious affairs. These schools of law essentially agreed on important issues. Yet as in Latin Christendom, the tension between reason and revelation—between those who emphasized rational understanding of the divine and the free will of the individual and those who insisted on the incomprehensible nature of God and utter surrender to divine will—continued to stir heated debate. The more orthodox schools of law—Hanafi, Maliki, and Shafi'i—were receptive to the rationalist orientation, but the Hanbali tradition firmly rejected any authority other than the revealed truths of the Qur'an and the hadith.

Founding of Madrasas

These schools of law became institutionalized through the founding of *madrasas* (MAH-dras-uh), formal colleges for legal and theological studies. Commonly located in mosques, madrasas received financial support from leading public figures or the surrounding community. In addition, charitable foundations often subsidized teachers' salaries, student stipends, and living quarters and libraries. In the twelfth and thirteenth centuries, donations to construct madrasas became a favorite form of philanthropy.

Higher education was not confined to the madrasas. The world's oldest university, in the sense of an institution of higher education combining individual faculties for different subjects, is Al-Qarawiyyin, founded at Fez in Morocco in 859 by the daughter of a wealthy merchant. In 975, the Fatimid dynasty established Al-Azhar University, attached to the main mosque in their new capital at Cairo, as a Shi'a theological seminary. Al-Azhar grew into a large institution with faculties in theology, law, grammar, astronomy, philosophy, and logic. In the twelfth century, Saladin, after ousting the Fatimids (see Chapter 14), reorganized Al-Azhar as a center of Sunni learning, which it remains today.

Islamic education revolved around the master-disciple relationship. A madrasa was organized as a study circle consisting of a single master and his disciples. Most madrasas were affiliated with one of the four main schools of law, but students were mainly attracted by the master's reputation rather than school affiliation. "One does not acquire learning nor profit from it unless one holds in esteem knowledge and those who possess it," declared a thirteenth-century manual on education.[4] Several assistants might instruct students in subjects such as Qur'an recitation and Arabic grammar, but Islamic schools had

ulama Deeply learned teachers of Islamic scripture and law.

hadith Records of the sayings and deeds of the Prophet Muhammad.

shari'a The whole body of Islamic law—drawn from the Qur'an, the hadith, and traditions of legal interpretation—that governs social as well as religious life.

madrasa A school for education in Islamic religion and traditions of legal interpretation.

Firdaws Madrasa

The proliferation of madrasas beginning in the eleventh century strengthened the dominance of Sunni teachings in Islamic intellectual circles. Far from being cloistered enclaves of students and scholars, however, madrasas served as the centers of religious life for the whole community. Aleppo in Syria reportedly had forty-seven madrasas, the grandest of which was the Firdaws madrasa, built in 1235. (Photograph by K.A.C. Creswell, © The Creswell Photographic Archive, Ashmolean Museum of Art and Archaeology, University of Oxford.)

no fixed curriculum like the trivium and quadrivium of Latin Europe. Knowledge of hadith and shari'a law and insight into their application to social life were the foundations of higher education. Because learning the hadith was a pious act expected of all Muslims, schools and study circles were open to all believers, whether or not they were formally recognized as students. Although madrasas rarely admitted women as formal students, women often attended lectures and study groups. In twelfth-century Damascus, women took an especially active role as patrons of madrasas and as scholars and teachers as well.

Under the Seljuk sultans (1055–1258), who strictly enforced Sunni orthodoxy and persecuted Shi'a dissidents, the madrasas also became tools of political propaganda. The Seljuks lavishly patronized madrasas in Baghdad and other major cities (see Map 13.2). The Hanafi school became closely allied with the sultanate and largely dominated the judiciary. The Hanbalis, in contrast, rejected Seljuk patronage and refused to accept government positions. The Hanbalis' estrangement from the Seljuk government made them popular among the inhabitants of Baghdad who chafed under Seljuk rule. Charismatic Hanbali preachers frequently mustered common people's support for their partisan causes and led vigilante attacks on Shi'a "heretics" and immoral activities such as drinking alcohol and prostitution.

Role of the Ulama

Turkish military regimes such as the Seljuks in Mesopotamia and Syria, and later the Mamluks in Egypt, came to depend on the cooperation of the ulama and the schools of law to carry out many government tasks and to maintain social order. Yet the authority of the ulama was validated by their reputation for holiness and their personal standing in the community, not by bureaucratic or clerical office. Urban residents were considered adherents of the school of law that presided over the local mosque or madrasa and were subject to its authority. The common people often turned to the neighborhood ulama for counsel, protection, and settlement of disputes, rather than seeking recourse in the official law courts. Ulama were closely tied to their local communities, yet at the same time the ulama's membership in a school of law enrolled them in fraternities of scholars and students spanning the whole Muslim world.

The proliferation of madrasas between the tenth and thirteenth centuries promoted the unification of Sunni theology and law and blurred the boundaries between church and state. The Islamic madrasas, like the universities of Latin Christendom, helped to forge a common religious identity. But to a much greater degree than the Christian universities, the madrasas merged with the surrounding urban society and drew ordinary believers, including women, into their religious and educational activities.

Sufi Mysticism and Sunni Orthodoxy

In addition to the orthodox schools of law and the tradition of revelation expressed in hadith, an alternative tradition was **Sufism** (SOO-fiz-uhm)—a mystical form of Islam that emphasizes personal experience of the divine over obedience to scriptures and Islamic law. Sufis cultivated spiritual and psychological awareness through meditation, recitation, asceticism, and personal piety. Over the course of the ninth century Sufi masters elaborated comprehensive programs of spiritual progress that began with intensely emotional expressions of love of God and proceeded toward a final extinction of the self and mystical union with the divine. Some Sufis spurned the conventions of ordinary life, including the authority of the Qur'an and hadith, instead claiming to directly apprehend divine truth. This version of Sufism, deeply unsettling to political authorities, thrived in the distant regions of

Sufism A mystical form of Islam that emphasizes personal experience of the divine over obedience to the dictates of scripture and Islamic law.

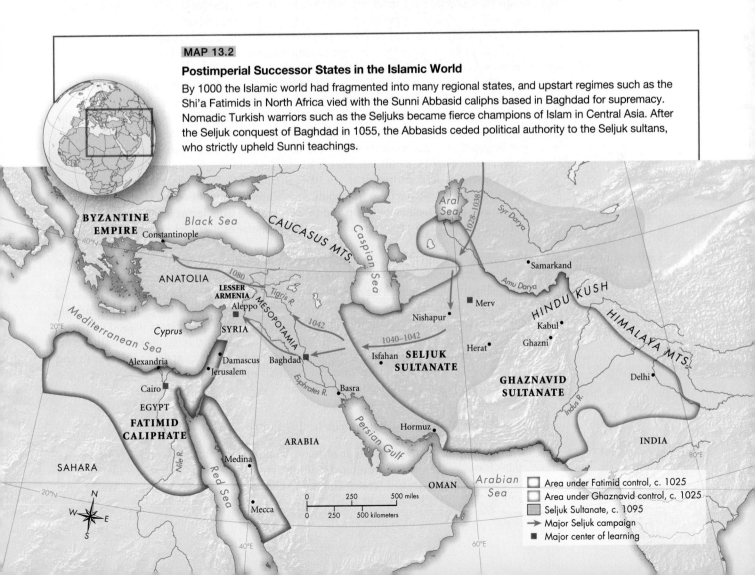

MAP 13.2

Postimperial Successor States in the Islamic World

By 1000 the Islamic world had fragmented into many regional states, and upstart regimes such as the Shi'a Fatimids in North Africa vied with the Sunni Abbasid caliphs based in Baghdad for supremacy. Nomadic Turkish warriors such as the Seljuks became fierce champions of Islam in Central Asia. After the Seljuk conquest of Baghdad in 1055, the Abbasids ceded political authority to the Seljuk sultans, who strictly upheld Sunni teachings.

Iran and Central Asia. A more sober-minded form of Sufism, endorsing practical virtue and conformity to Islamic law, flourished in Baghdad and the central Islamic lands.

Sufism's Broad Appeal

Originating as a quest for personal enlightenment, Sufism evolved into a broad social movement. Sufis, like the madrasas, reached out to the common faithful. In their public preaching and missionary work, Sufis addressed everyday ethical questions and advocated a life of practical morality and simplicity. The Sufi ethic of personal responsibility, tolerance and sympathy toward human failings, and moderation in enjoyment of worldly pleasures, had broad appeal among all social classes.

Revered as holy persons with a special relationship to God, Sufi masters acquired an aura of sainthood. Tombs of renowned Sufi masters became important pilgrimage sites that drew throngs of believers from near and far, helping forge a sense of community among like-minded devotees. Women played a more prominent role in Sufism than in other Islamic traditions. One of the earliest Sufi teachers, Rabi'a al-'Adawiyya (717–801), attracted many disciples, chiefly men, with her fierce asceticism and her insistence that God should be loved for God's own sake, not out of fear of punishment or desire for reward. In the words of her biographer, Rabi'a was "on fire with love and longing, enamored of the desire to approach her Lord," and men accepted her "as a second spotless Mary."[5]

By the eleventh century the Sufi masters' residences, known as *khanaqa* (CON-kah) had developed into lodges where religious teachers lived, taught their disciples, and provided accommodations for traveling Sufis. Relationships between master and disciple became more formalized, and Sufis expected each student to submit wholeheartedly to the master's instruction and guidance. In the early thirteenth century Sufis began to form brotherhoods that integrated groups of followers into far-flung religious orders. Bonds of Sufi brotherhood cut across national borders and parochial loyalties, restoring a measure of unity sorely lacking in the Islamic world since the Abbasid caliphate's decline. Muslim rulers warmly welcomed leading Sufi masters as spiritual counselors. Yet the khanaqas and the tombs of Sufi saints—centers of congregational devotion and religious instruction—remained the heart of the Sufi movement.

Ongoing tensions between reason and faith sharply divided the intellectual world of Islam. This dilemma was epitomized by the personal spiritual struggle of Abu Hamid al-Ghazali (AH-boo hah-MEED al-gahz-AHL-ee) (1058–1111), the greatest intellectual figure in Islam after Muhammad himself. Al-Ghazali was appointed to a senior professorship at Baghdad's leading madrasa in 1091, at the young age of thirty-three. Although he garnered great acclaim for his lectures on Islamic law and theology, al-Ghazali was beset by self-doubt and deep spiritual crisis. In 1095, al-Ghazali found himself "continuously tossed about between the attractions of worldly desires and the impulses toward eternal life" until "God caused my tongue to dry up and I was prevented from lecturing."[6] He then resigned his position and spent ten years as a wandering scholar exploring the mystical approach of Sufism.

Synthesis of Sunni and Sufi Teachings

In the end, al-Ghazali's immersion in Sufism restored his faith in Muslim beliefs and traditions. In the last years of his life, al-Ghazali returned to the academy and wrote a series of major philosophical treatises that reaffirmed the primacy of revelation over rational philosophy in matters of faith and morals. According to al-Ghazali, a proper Muslim life must be devoted to the purification of the soul and the direct experience of God that lay at the core of the Sufi quest. But he also insisted that the personal religious awakening of individuals must not violate the established principles of Islam set down in the Qur'an and the hadith. Al-Ghazali's ideas provided a synthesis of Sunni and Sufi teachings that would come to dominate Islamic intellectual circles.

Oral and Written Cultures in Islam

Primacy of Oral Traditions

As the teaching methods of the madrasas reveal, oral instruction took precedence over book learning in Islamic education. Tradition holds that the Qur'an was revealed orally to Muhammad, who was illiterate. The name *Qur'an* itself comes from the Arabic verb "to recite," and recitation of the Qur'an became as fundamental to elementary education as it was to religious devotion. Moreover, the authority of any instruction rested on the reputation of the teacher, which in turn was validated by chains of transmission down through generations of scholars. Sufism reinforced this emphasis on direct person-to-person oral instruction. The persistence of ambivalent attitudes toward written documents is also evident in the priority Islamic law gives to the oral testimony of trustworthy witnesses over documents that could be easily forged or altered. Nonetheless, by the eleventh century books were regarded as indispensable aids to memorization and study, though learning solely from books was dismissed as an inferior method of education (see Reading the Past: Ibn Khaldun on Study and Learning). This preference for oral communication would ensure that the connections between individuals formed by Islamic schooling would be direct and deeply personal.

Primacy of Arabic Language

As the sacred language of scripture, Arabic occupied an exalted place in Islamic literary culture. To fulfill one's religious duty one had to master the Qur'an in Arabic. Arabic

READING THE PAST

Ibn Khaldun on Study and Learning

Ibn Khaldun (ee-bin hal-DOON) (1332–1406), born in Tunis in North Africa, was one of the greatest Islamic historians and philosophers. Khaldun served various Muslim rulers in North Africa before devoting himself to study and teaching. He spent the last twenty-four years of his life in Cairo, where he completed his monumental *Universal History*.

In the prologue of his *Universal History* Khaldun discusses the proper methods of study and learning. Like other Muslim scholars, he valued oral instruction over mere book learning. A good scholar was expected to be well traveled, seeking insight from a variety of teachers. Citing Muhammad bin Abdallah (1077–1148), Khaldun urges that education begin with the study of Arabic and poetry.

Human beings obtain their knowledge and character qualities and all their opinions and virtues either through study, instruction, and lectures, or through imitation of a teacher and personal contact with him. The only difference here is that habits acquired through personal contact with a teacher are more strongly and firmly rooted. Thus, the greater the number of authoritative teachers, the more deeply rooted is the habit one acquires.

When a student has to rely on the study of books and written material and must understand scientific problems from the forms of written letters in books, he is confronted by the veil that separates handwriting and the form of the letter found in writing from the spoken words found in the imagination.

Judge Abdallah places instruction in Arabic and poetry ahead of all other sciences: "Poetry is the archive of the Arabs. . . . From there, the student should go on to arithmetic and study it assiduously, until he knows its basic norms. He should then go to the study of the Qur'an, because with his previous preparation it will be easy for him." He continues, "How thoughtless are our compatriots in teaching children the Qur'an when they are first starting out. They read things they do not understand. . . . He also forbids teaching two disciplines at the same time, save to the student with a good mind and sufficient energy."

Source: Ibn Khaldun, *The Muqaddimah: An Introduction to History*, trans. Franz Rosenthal (Princeton, NJ: Princeton University Press, 1967), 426, 431, 424.

EXAMINING THE EVIDENCE

1. Why did Ibn Khaldun value oral instruction over reading books?

2. To what extent was the curriculum proposed by Ibn Khaldun parallel to the study of the liberal arts found in the cathedral schools and universities of Latin Christendom?

Basra Library

Although Islamic scholars esteemed oral instruction by an outstanding teacher over book learning, libraries served as important places for intellectual exchange as well as repositories of knowledge. In this illustration to a story set in the Iraq seaport of Basra—a city renowned as a seat of scholarship—a group of well-dressed men listen to a lecture on Arabic poetry delivered by the figure at right. In the background, leather-bound books are stacked on their sides in separate cupboards. (Bibliothèque Nationale, Paris, France; Scala/White Images/Art Resource, NY.)

became the language of government from Iran to Spain. The Sunni orthodoxy endorsed by the Abbasid caliphs and the Seljuk sultans was also based on codification in Arabic of religious teachings and laws. Thus, the Arabic language came to occupy an important place in the developing Islamic identity.

Book collecting and the founding of libraries helped expand book learning in Islamic society. The size of Muslim libraries dwarfed the relatively small libraries of Latin Christendom. The most eminent Christian monasteries in France and Italy had libraries of about four hundred to seven hundred volumes, and an inventory of the University of Paris collections from 1338 lists about two thousand books. By contrast, the House of Knowledge, founded by an Abbasid official at Baghdad in 991, contained over ten thousand books. The Islamic prohibition against the worship of images discouraged the use of illustrations in books, but Arabic calligraphy became an extraordinarily expressive form of art (see Seeing the Past: A Revolution in Islamic Calligraphy).

The breakup of the Abbasid caliphate and the rise of regional states fractured the cultural and linguistic unity of the Islamic world. In the ninth century, Iranian authors began to write Persian in the Arabic script, inspiring new styles of poetry, romance, and historical writing. The poet Firdausi (fur-dow-SEE) (d. c. 1025), for example, drew from Sasanid chronicles and popular legends and ballads in composing his *Book of Kings*. This sprawling history of ancient monarchs and heroes has become the national epic of Iran. The Persian political heritage, in which monarchs wielded absolute authority over a steeply hierarchical society, had always clashed with the radical egalitarianism of Islam and the Arabs. But the reinvigorated Persian poetry of Firdausi and others found favor among the upstart Seljuk sultans.

Revival of Persian Literature

Court poets and artists drew from the rich trove of Persian literature—ranging from the fables of the sailor Sinbad to the celebrated love story of Warqa and Gulshah—to fashion new literary, artistic, and architectural styles that blended sacred and secular themes. The Seljuks absorbed many of these Persian literary motifs into a reinvented Turkish language and literature, which they carried with them into Mesopotamia and Anatolia. Persian and Turkish gradually joined Arabic as the classical languages of the Islamic world. Following the founding of the Muslim-ruled Delhi Sultanate in the early thirteenth century (discussed later in this chapter), Persian and Turkish literary cultures expanded into India.

In the absence of a formal church, the Islamic schools of law, madrasas, and Sufi khanaqa lodges transmitted religious knowledge among all social classes, broadening the reach of education to a wider spectrum of society than the schools and universities of Latin Christendom. The schools of law and madrasas helped to unify theology and law and to forge a distinct Sunni identity.

Nevertheless, regional and national identities were not completely subsumed by the overarching Islamic culture. Moreover, although most religious teachers harbored a deep

A Revolution in Islamic Calligraphy

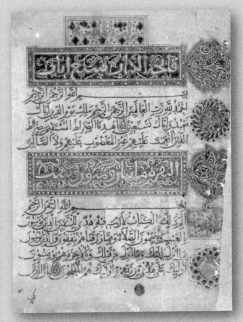

Early Kufic Script on Parchment (©The Trustees of the Chester Beatty Library, Dublin.)

Calligraphy of Ibn al-Bawwab (©The Trustees of the Chester Beatty Library, Dublin.)

During the early centuries of Islam, the sacredness of the Qur'an was reflected in the physical books themselves. Early manuscripts of the Qur'an, like this example, are invariably written in an Arabic script known as Kufic on parchment. The introduction of paper into the Islamic world from China in the late eighth century led to an explosion in the output of Qur'an manuscripts. Legal and administrative texts, poetry, and works on history, philosophy, geography, mathematics, medicine, and astronomy also began to appear in great numbers in the tenth century. At the same time professional copyists developed new cursive styles of script, easier to write as well as to read, that revolutionized the design and artistry of the Qur'an and other sacred texts.

A leading figure in this revolution in Islamic calligraphy, Ibn al-Bawwab (ih-bihn al-bu-wahb) (d. 1022), had worked as a house decorator before his elegant writing launched him into a career as a manuscript illustrator, calligrapher, and librarian. Only six specimens of Ibn al-Bawwab's calligraphy have survived, the most famous being a complete Qur'an in 286 folio sheets, one of which is shown here. The writing—a graceful and flowing script, with no trace of the ruling needed for parchment—is more compact than the Kufic script, but also more legible. Unlike Kufic, Ibn al-Bawwab's writing is composed in strokes of uniform thickness, with each letter equally proportioned. On this page, which contains the opening verses of the Qur'an, the first two chapter headings appear in large gold letters superimposed on decorative bands with dotted frames. By contrast,

the parchment Qur'an simply marks the end of chapters by inserting small decorative bands without text. Ibn al-Bawwab also indicated the beginning of each of the Qur'an's 114 chapters with large, colored roundels in the margin. The roundels are generally floral designs, such as the lotus in the bottom roundel shown here, but no two are exactly alike. Smaller roundels in the margins mark every tenth verse and passages after which prostrations should be performed.

This copy lacks a dedication, and scholars believe that it was made for sale rather than on commission from a mosque or other patron. Ibn al-Bawwab reportedly made sixty-four copies of the Qur'an in his lifetime.

EXAMINING THE EVIDENCE

1. How does the design of Ibn al-Bawwab's Qur'an make it easier to use for prayer than the parchment manuscript?

2. How does the style of decoration of Ibn al-Bawwab's Qur'an differ from that of the Latin Christian Gospel pages shown on page 411? What religious and aesthetic values might account for these differences?

suspicion of the "rational sciences" of the ancient Greeks, in the Islamic world—as in Latin Christendom—the tension between reason and revelation remained unresolved. The Sunni ulama were also troubled by the claims of Sufi masters to intuitive knowledge of the divine, and by the tendency of Sufis to blur the distinction between Islam and other religions. Nowhere was the Sufi deviation from orthodox Sunni traditions more pronounced than in India, where Sufism formed a bridge between the Islamic and Hindu religious cultures.

The Cosmopolitan and Vernacular Realms in India and Southeast Asia

FOCUS

What political and religious forces contributed to the development of a common culture across India and Southeast Asia and its subsequent fragmentation into regional cultures?

Between the fifth and the fifteenth centuries, India and Southeast Asia underwent two profound cultural transformations. In the first phase, from roughly 400 to 900, a new cultural and political synthesis emerged simultaneously across the entire region. Local rulers cultivated a common culture reflecting a new ideology of divine kingship. Sanskrit became a cosmopolitan language for expressing rulers' universal claims to secular as well as sacred authority. In the second phase, from 900 to 1400, rulers instead asserted sovereign authority based on the unique historical and cultural identity of their lands and peoples. The spread of diverse vernacular cultures fragmented the cosmopolitan unity of Sanskrit literary and political discourse. The growing differentiation of India and Southeast Asia into regional vernacular cultures after 900 received added impetus from the Turkish conquests and from the founding of the Delhi Sultanate in 1206.

The Cosmopolitan Realm of Sanskrit

Beginning in about the third century C.E., Sanskrit, the sacred language of the Vedic religious tradition, became for the first time a medium for literary and political expression as well. The emergence of Sanskrit in secular writings occurred virtually simultaneously in South and Southeast Asia. By the sixth century a common cosmopolitan culture expressed through Sanskrit texts had become fully entrenched in royal courts from Afghanistan to Java. The spread of Sanskrit was not a product of political unity or imperial colonization, however. Rather, it came to dominate literary and political discourse in the centuries after the demise of the Gupta Empire discussed in Chapter 6, when the Indian subcontinent was divided into numerous regional kingdoms (see Map 13.3).

Sanskrit and Political Ideology

Sanskrit's movement into the political arena did not originate with the Brahman priesthood. Instead, the impetus came from the Central Asian nomads, notably the Kushan, who, as we saw in Chapter 6, ruled over parts of Afghanistan, Pakistan, and northwestern India from the first century B.C.E. to the fourth century C.E. The Kushan kings patronized Buddhist theologians and poets who adopted Sanskrit both to record Buddhist scriptures and to commemorate their royal patrons' deeds in inscriptions and eulogies. Later, the Gupta monarchs used Sanskrit to voice their grand imperial ambitions. The Gupta state collapsed in the mid-fifth century, but subsequent rulers embraced its ideology of kingship centered on the ideal of the *chakravartin*, or universal monarch.

This conception of kingship connected political authority to the higher lordship of the gods, above all Shiva and Vishnu. Temples became not only centers of community life but also places for individual worship. Modest acts of devotion—offerings of food presented to a deity's image, vows and fasting, and pilgrimages to temples—complemented Brahmanic rituals. Thus the egalitarian ethic and more personal relationship to the divine espoused by Buddhism left a lasting legacy in the devotional cults dedicated to the Hindu gods.

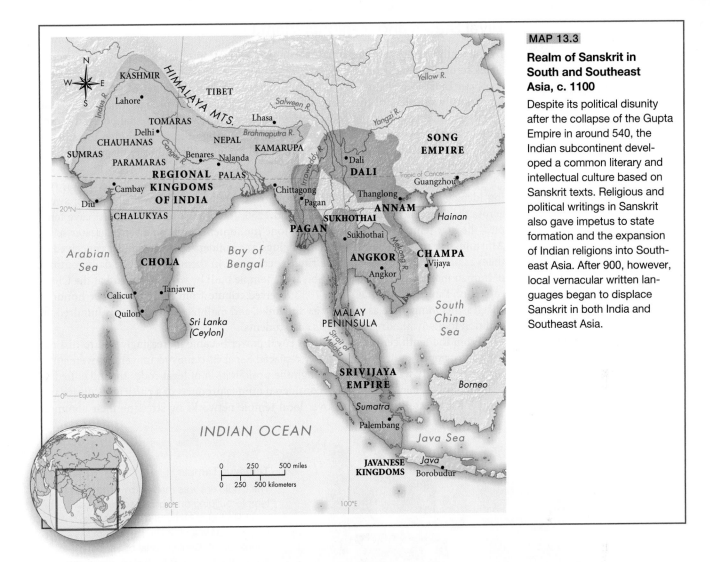

MAP 13.3

Realm of Sanskrit in South and Southeast Asia, c. 1100

Despite its political disunity after the collapse of the Gupta Empire in around 540, the Indian subcontinent developed a common literary and intellectual culture based on Sanskrit texts. Religious and political writings in Sanskrit also gave impetus to state formation and the expansion of Indian religions into Southeast Asia. After 900, however, local vernacular written languages began to displace Sanskrit in both India and Southeast Asia.

Brahmanic colleges attached to temples and Buddhist and Jain monasteries provided formal schooling. These colleges were open to anyone from the "twice-born" (that is, ritually pure) castes of Brahmans, warriors, and *Vaishya* (herders, farmers, and merchants). Beginning in the eighth century, hostels known as *mathas*, often devoted to the worship of a particular deity, became important as meeting places where students, scholars, and pilgrims gathered for religious discussion. Above all, royal courts served as the centers of intellectual life and literary production. The cultural realm of Sanskrit lacked a single paramount center such as the capitals of the Roman or Chinese empires, but through borrowing and imitation, political ideology and royal government assumed remarkably similar forms in many lands.

The predominance of Sanskrit was equally strong in the Angkor state in Cambodia and in the Javanese kingdoms. Public display of royal power and virtue through monumental architecture and Sanskrit inscriptions took forms in Angkor identical to those found in the Indian subcontinent. Although Khmer (kih-MAY) served as the language of everyday life, used to record matters such as land grants, tax obligations, and contracts, Sanskrit prevailed as the language of politics, poetry, and religion in Cambodia down to the seventeenth century.

Sanskrit's rise as a cosmopolitan language thus allowed local rulers and intellectual elites to draw on a universal system of values and ideas to establish their claims to authority. Royal mystique was expressed symbolically through courtly epics, royal genealogies, and inscriptions that depicted the ruler as a divinely ordained monarch.

Centers of Sanskrit Learning

Sanskrit Culture in Southeast Asia

Rival States and Regional Identity

By the tenth century, a long period of economic expansion produced a series of powerful states across the Sanskrit realm. Most prominent were Angkor in Cambodia and Chola in southern India (see again Map 13.3), but there were also a number of smaller regional kingdoms. The rulers of these states deemed themselves "great kings" (*maharajas*), the earthly representatives of the gods, particularly Shiva and Vishnu. Actual political power rested on the growing interdependence between the kings and the Brahman priesthood. At the same time, the kings sought to affirm and extend their authority through ostentatious patronage of gods and their temples.

Temple architecture most strikingly reveals the maharajas' (mah-huh-RAH-juh) ruling ideology. A wave of temple-building, most of it funded by royal donations, swept across the Sanskrit realm between 1000 and 1250. In contrast to the Buddhist cave temples, the new temples were freestanding stone monuments built on a vastly greater scale. Affirming the parallels between gods and kings, the builders of these temples conceived of them as palaces of the gods, but the rituals performed in them imitated the daily routines of human monarchs. Dedicated to Shiva, the temple built by royal command at the Chola capital of Tanjavur (tan-JOOR) in 1002 received tribute from more than three hundred villages, including some as far away as Sri Lanka, and maintained a staff of six hundred, in addition to many hundreds of priests and students.

Rising Regional Identity   From the tenth century onward, as royal power became increasingly tied to distinct territories, appeals to regional identity replaced Sanskrit claims to universal sovereignty. Regional identity was expressed through the proliferation of legal codes that, like the law codes of post-Roman Europe, were considered unique products of a particular culture and people. Kings asserted their rule over local temple networks by stressing their common

Tanjavur Temple

The Chola era was marked by a wave of temple-building on a grand scale across southern India. Many of these building projects, such as the Rajarajeshvara temple at the Chola capital of Tanjavur seen here, benefited from royal donations intended to underscore the connections between divine authority and kingship. But Hindu temples also attracted patronage from merchant and artisan guilds and obtained revenues from their landholdings, commercial activities, and contributions by village assemblies. (Bob Krist/CORBIS.)

identity with a distinct territory, people, and culture. Consequently the cosmopolitan cultural community based on Sanskrit writings no longer suited their political goals.

The displacement of Sanskrit by vernacular languages accompanied this political transformation. Between the tenth and fourteenth centuries, political boundaries increasingly aligned with linguistic borders. By the tenth century royal inscriptions began to use local vernacular languages rather than Sanskrit. The Chola kings, for example, promoted a Tamil cultural identity defined as "the region of the Tamil language" to further their expansionist political ambitions. Royal courts, the major centers of literary production, also championed a rewriting of the Sanskrit literary heritage in vernacular languages. The first vernacular versions of the *Mahabharata* epic (discussed in Chapter 6) appeared in the Kannada (kah-nah-DAH) language of southwestern India in the tenth century and in the Telugu (tehl-oo-JOO) and Old Javanese languages in the eleventh century. The poet Kamban composed his celebrated Tamil version of the *Ramayana* at the Chola court at the same time. These vernacular versions of the epics were not merely translations, but a rewriting of the classic works as part of local history rather than universal culture. Although Sanskrit remained the language of Brahmanic religion (and many sacred scriptures were never translated into vernacular languages), after 1400 Sanskrit all but disappeared from royal inscriptions, administrative documents, and courtly literature. The turn toward vernacular literary languages did not broaden the social horizons of literary culture, however. Vernacular literatures relied heavily on Sanskrit vocabulary and rhetoric and were intended for learned audiences, not the common people.

Displacement of Sanskrit by Vernacular Languages

Sufism and Society in the Delhi Sultanate

In the late twelfth century Muhammad Ghuri, the Muslim ruler of Afghanistan, invaded India and conquered the Ganges Valley. After Ghuri's death in 1206, a Turkish slave-general declared himself sultan at Delhi. Over the next three centuries a series of five dynasties ruled over the Delhi Sultanate (1206–1526) and imposed Muslim rule over much of India. By about 1330 the Delhi Sultanate reached its greatest territorial extent, encompassing most of the Indian peninsula.

The Delhi sultans cast themselves in the mold of Turko-Persian ideals of kingship, which affirmed the supremacy of the king over religious authorities. Nonetheless, like their Turkish predecessors, the Delhi sultans cultivated close relations with Sufi masters. Sufism affirmed the special role of the saint or holy man as an earthly representative of God, insisting that it was the blessing of a Sufi saint that conferred sovereign authority on monarchs. A leading Iranian Sufi proclaimed that God "made the Saints the governors of the universe . . . and through their spiritual influence [Muslims] gain victories over the unbelievers."[7] Implicitly recognizing the practical limits of their authority, the Delhi sultans sought to strengthen their control over their Indian territories by striking an alliance between the Turkish warrior aristocracy and the revered Sufi masters.

Initially the Delhi sultans staffed their government with Muslims, recruiting ulama and Sufis, mostly from Iran and Central Asia. The sultans also founded mosques and madrasas to propagate Islamic teachings, but the ulama and their schools had little impact on the native Hindu population. Instead, it was the missionary zeal of the Sufi orders that paved the way for Islam's spread in South Asia.

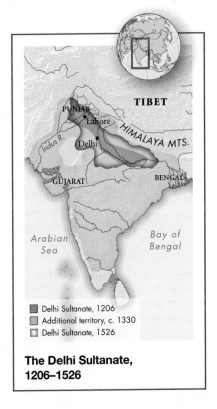

The Delhi Sultanate, 1206–1526

■ Delhi Sultanate, 1206
■ Additional territory, c. 1330
□ Delhi Sultanate, 1526

In the wake of Muslim conquests, the Sufi orders established khanaqa lodges in the countryside as well as in the cities, reaching more deeply into local society. United by total devotion and obedience to their master, the Sufi brotherhoods formed tightly knit networks whose authority paralleled that of the sultans, and in some respects surpassed it.

Sufi Influence in the Sultanate

Sufi masters presided over the khanaqas much like princes over their courts. For example, they welcomed local people seeking justice, dispute mediation, and miraculous cures. Learned dignitaries, both Muslim and Hindu, sought out Sufi masters for spiritual counsel and instruction. The monumental tombs of renowned saints became cultural and religious crossroads as they attracted steady streams of both Hindu and Muslim worshipers and pilgrims.

Sufis used vernacular language to address local audiences. In the Delhi region they adopted Hindi as a spoken language, and it was Sufis who developed Urdu, a literary version of Hindi, as the common written language among Muslims in South Asia. In the fifteenth century, as the political fortunes of the Delhi Sultanate waned, provincial Muslim regimes promoted the integration of Hindu and Muslim cultures and the use of vernacular literary languages. For example, the independent sultans of Bengal sponsored translations of the epics and other Sanskrit classics into Bengali, and they also patronized Bengali writers. A Chinese visitor to Bengal in the early fifteenth century reported that although some Muslims at the court understood Persian, Bengali was the language in universal use.

Sufi-Hindu Accommodation

Leading Sufis often sought spiritual accommodation between Islamic and Hindu beliefs and practices. In their quest for a more direct path to union with the divine, many Sufis were attracted to the ascetic practices, yoga techniques, and mystical knowledge of Hindu yogis. Similarly, Hindus assimilated the Sufi veneration of saints into their own religious lives without relinquishing their Hindu identity. Most important, the Sufi ethic of practical piety in daily life struck a responsive chord among Hindus. Sufis, like Brahmans, valued detachment from the world but not rejection of it. They married, raised families, and engaged in secular occupations. Nizam al-Din Awliya (1236–1325), an eminent Sufi master, ministered to the spiritual needs of Hindus as well as Muslims. His message—forgive your enemies, enjoy worldly pleasures in moderation, and fulfill your responsibilities to family and society—was closely aligned with the basic principles of Hindu social life. Thus, Sufism served as a bridge between the two dominant religious traditions of India.

Relations Between Muslim Leaders and Hindu Subjects

Although some sultans launched campaigns of persecution aimed at temples and icons of the Hindu gods, most tolerated the Hindu religion. Particularly in the fourteenth century, after the Delhi Sultanate extinguished its major Hindu rivals, the sultans adopted more lenient religious and social policies. They also made greater efforts to recruit Brahmans for government office. Sultans and regional governors even bestowed patronage on major Hindu shrines as gestures of magnanimity toward their non-Muslim subjects.

Despite this growing political accommodation, Muslim and Hindu elites preserved separate social and cultural identities. Both groups, for example, strictly forbade intermarriage across religious lines. Nonetheless, the flowering of regional cultures and inclusion of non-Muslim elites into government and courtly culture foreshadowed the synthesis of Islamic and Indian cultures later patronized by the Mughal Empire, which replaced the Delhi sultans as rulers of India in 1526 (see Chapter 19).

Learning, Schools, and Print Culture in East Asia

FOCUS

To what extent did intellectual and educational trends in Song China influence its East Asian neighbors?

Compared to the worlds of Christendom and Islam, in East Asia learning and scholarship were much more tightly yoked to the state and its institutions. Beginning with the Song dynasty (960–1279), the civil service examination system dominated Chinese political life and literary culture. At the same time the political and social rewards of examination success led to a proliferation of schools and broader access to education (see Map 13.4).

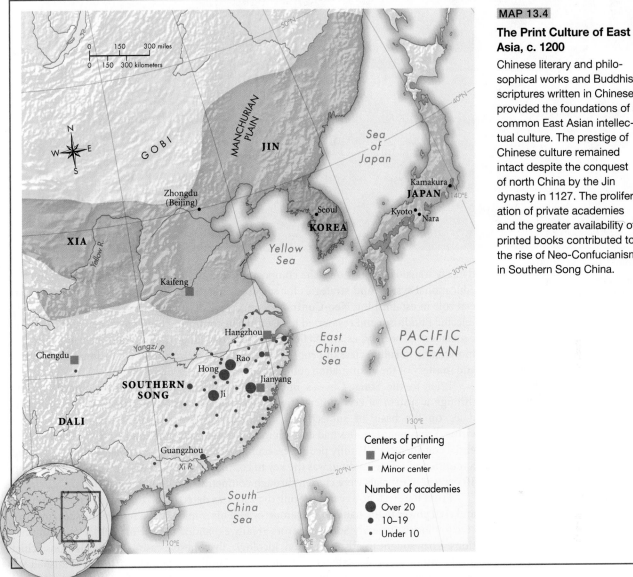

MAP 13.4

The Print Culture of East Asia, c. 1200

Chinese literary and philosophical works and Buddhist scriptures written in Chinese provided the foundations of a common East Asian intellectual culture. The prestige of Chinese culture remained intact despite the conquest of north China by the Jin dynasty in 1127. The proliferation of private academies and the greater availability of printed books contributed to the rise of Neo-Confucianism in Southern Song China.

The invention and spread of printing transformed written communication and intellectual life in China. Neither the state nor the Confucian-educated elite played a significant role in the invention and early development of printing. Yet throughout the Song dynasty, the period when Confucian education and examination success became the marks of elite status in China, the emerging culture of the educated classes dominated printing and publishing. Elsewhere in East Asia, however, the spread of printing and vernacular writing had a much more limited impact on government and social hierarchy. In Japan and Korea, literacy and education remained the preserve of the aristocratic elites and the Buddhist clergy.

Civil Service Examinations and Schooling in Song China

Chinese civil service examinations were a complex series of tests based on the Confucian classics, history, poetry, and other subjects. They served as the primary method for recruiting government officials from the eleventh century onward. Their use starting in the Song

Institution of Civil Service Exams

Examination Candidates

No institution exercised a more powerful influence on the culture and lifestyle of China's ruling class than the civil service examinations. Success in the examinations not only opened the path to a political career but also conferred prestige and privileges on the whole family. In this sixteenth-century painting, a crowd of men dressed in scholars' robes anxiously scan the lists of successful candidates posted outside the examination hall. (National Palace Museum, Taiwan, Republic of China.)

State Schools

Neo-Confucianism The revival of Confucian teachings beginning in the Song dynasty that firmly rejected Buddhist religion and reasserted the Confucian commitment to moral perfection and the betterment of society.

dynasty transformed not only the composition and character of the political elite, but the educational system and strategies for social success. The examinations also played a crucial role in establishing **Neo-Confucianism**, a revival of Confucian teachings that firmly rejected Buddhism and reasserted the Confucian commitment to moral perfection and the betterment of society, as an intellectual orthodoxy. Finally, the system helped produce a more uniform ruling class of people connected by their common educational experiences and mastery of the examination subject matter.

Prior to the Song, China's imperial governments recruited their officials mostly through a system of recommendations. Local magistrates nominated promising candidates on the basis of subjective criteria such as literary talent and reputation for virtue. Prominent families had enough influence to ensure that their sons received preferential consideration. Family pedigree, secured through wealth, marriage connections, and a tradition of office-holding, was the key to continued access to political office. Fewer than 10 percent of officials were chosen through competitive written examinations.

From the start, however, the Song dynasty was determined to centralize both military and civil power in the hands of the emperor and his ministers. To restore the supremacy of civil authority, the early Song emperors greatly expanded the use of civil service examinations. They sought to create a skilled, ideologically cohesive cadre of officials whose chief loyalty would be to the state rather than to their families. Competitive tests diminished the influence of family prestige in the selection of government officials. The impulse behind the civil service examinations was less democratic than autocratic, however: the final choice of successful candidates rested with the emperor.

By the mid-thirteenth century four hundred thousand men had taken the civil service examinations. Of this number, only eight hundred were selected for appointment to office. The enormous number of examination candidates reflected the crucial importance of government office to achieving social and political success. It also testified to the powerful influence of schooling in shaping the lives and outlook of the ruling class. The Song government set up hundreds of state-supported local schools, but budget shortfalls left many of them underfunded. For the most part, primary education was limited to those who could afford private tutors.

At every level of schooling, the curriculum mirrored the priorities of the civil service examinations. Although the central government constantly tinkered with the content of the examinations, in general the examinations emphasized mastery of the Confucian classics, various genres of poetry, and matters of public policy and statecraft. Over time the prominence of poetry diminished, and the application of classical knowledge to public policy and administrative problems grew in importance.

Critics of the civil service examinations complained that the impartiality of the evaluation procedures did not allow for proper assessment of the candidates' moral character. They advocated replacing the examinations with a system of appointment based on promotion through the state school system, in which student merit would be judged on the basis of personal qualities as well as formal knowledge. Other critics condemned the examination system and government schools for stifling intellectual inquiry. In their view, the narrow focus of the curriculum and the emphasis on rote knowledge over creative thinking produced petty-minded pedants rather than dynamic leaders.

Private Academies

These various criticisms spurred the founding of private academies. Moreover, many leading scholars rejected political careers altogether. This trend received a major boost from Zhu Xi (jew she) (1130–1200), the most influential Neo-Confucian scholar, who reordered the classical canon to revive humanistic learning and infuse education with moral purpose. Zhu mocked the sterile teaching of government schools, instead engaging his students (and critics) in wide-ranging philosophical discussions, often held under the auspices of private academies. Zhu Xi championed the private academy as the ideal environment for the pursuit of genuine moral knowledge. His teachings inspired the founding of at least 140 private academies during the twelfth and thirteenth centuries. Nevertheless, many students enrolled at private academies out of the self-serving conviction that studying with a renowned scholar would enhance their prospects for success in the examinations.

Influence of Zhu Xi's Neo-Confucianism

Ironically, later dynasties would adopt Zhu Xi's philosophical views and interpretations of the classics as the official orthodoxy of the civil service examinations. Consequently, his Neo-Confucian doctrines were more influential even than Thomas Aquinas's synthesis of Greek philosophy and Christian revelation, or al-Ghazali's contributions to Islamic theology.

For educated men, the power of the examination system was inescapable. Only a few rare individuals would ever pass through, as contemporaries put it, "the thorny gate of learning." Yet examination learning defined the intellectual and cultural values not only of officials, but of the educated public at large. In a poem, a Song emperor exhorted young men to apply themselves to study:

> To enrich your family, no need to buy good land;
> Books hold a thousand measures of grain.
> For an easy life, no need to build a mansion;
> In books are found houses of gold.
> When traveling, be not vexed at the absence of followers;
> In books, carriages and horses form a crowd.
> When marrying, be not vexed by lack of a good matchmaker;
> In books there are girls with faces of jade.
> A boy who wants to become somebody
> Devotes himself to the classics, faces the window, and reads.[9]

The average age of men who passed the highest level of the civil service examinations was thirty-one. Thus China's political leaders commonly underwent a long apprenticeship as students that lasted well into their adult life.

The Culture of Print in Song China

Invention of Printing

Just as papermaking originated in China (see Chapter 6), the Chinese invented the technology of printing, probably in the early eighth century. The Chinese had long used carved stone, bronze, and wood seals to make inked impressions on silk, and the process of using carved wooden blocks to print on paper probably derived from this practice.

The earliest known example of woodblock printing is a miniature Buddhist charm dating from the first half of the eighth century. Chinese inventors devised movable type by the mid-eleventh century, but this technology was not widely used. Chinese is a **logographic** language that uses symbols to represent whole words, not sounds. Given the large number of Chinese logographs in common use, printers found that carving entire pages of

logographic A system of writing that uses symbols to represent whole words, not sounds (as in the case of alphabetic writing systems).

Chinese Woodblock Printing

The religious merit earned for spreading Buddhist teachings appears to have been the motivating force behind the invention of printing in China. Nearly all early printed Chinese books are Buddhist scriptures and other religious works. This copy of the *Diamond Sutra*, a popular digest of Mahayana Buddhist teachings, bears the date 868, making it the oldest known dated example of block printing. (©2011 The British Library Or.8210.)

a book was less laborious than producing fonts that would require tens of thousands of individual pieces of type.

Mass Production of Books

By the ninth century printing had developed into a substantial industry in China. Printers produced a wide range of written materials, ranging from single-sheet almanacs to poetry anthologies and commentaries on the Confucian classics. But the most important use of print was to reproduce Buddhist scriptures and other religious texts. Buddhists regarded the dissemination of scriptures as an important act of piety that earned karmic merit for the sponsor. Mass production of religious texts and icons was very probably the original motivation behind the invention of printing.

Song Sponsorship

The founding of the Song dynasty marked the ascendancy of government-sponsored printing. Just as the Song took the lead in education to reinforce their rule, the Song government used printing to help disseminate official ideas and values. In the 970s the Song emperor ordered government workshops to print encyclopedias, dictionaries, literary anthologies, and official histories of all earlier dynasties, in addition to the Confucian classics. One of the government's largest printing projects was an official edition of the Buddhist canon, consisting of 1076 titles, published in 983. This project required the carving of 130,000 woodblocks and took twelve years to complete.

Before the twelfth century, the Song government dominated the world of publishing. The state printed collections of statutes, laws, and government procedures and works on medicine, astronomy, and natural history, as well as standard editions of classics, histories, and literary anthologies. Many of these works were sold through private booksellers or donated to government schools. In the twelfth century, however, private publishers, including schools as well as commercial firms, surpassed the Song government as the main source of printed books. Schools and academies had the intellectual and financial resources to publish fine-quality, scrupulously edited editions (see again Map 13.4).

Commercial firms usually issued cheaply printed texts that catered to market tastes, especially demand for a wide variety of aids to prepare students for the civil service exams. These works included classical commentaries by famous scholars, dictionaries, school primers, writing manuals, phrase books, collections of examination essays by the highest-ranked candidates, and—most notorious of all—so-called kerchief albums, crib sheets that candidates could fold like a kerchief and smuggle into the examination hall. Books largely for personal enjoyment, such as poetry and prose anthologies by famous authors and works of drama and fiction, also became staples of commercial publishing, along with medical and divination texts purveying practical knowledge.

Despite the advantages of printing as a means of mass reproduction, the technology of printing spread slowly. Elsewhere in East Asia, state and religious institutions monopolized printing. Although Muslims were aware of printing by the eleventh century, they felt deep reverence for the handwritten word and fiercely opposed mechanical reproduction of the sacred words of the Qur'an and other religious texts. No printing presses were established in the Islamic world before the eighteenth century. The printing press invented by the goldsmith Johannes Gutenberg in the German city of Mainz in the 1440s appears to have been a separate invention unrelated to Chinese printing technology.

Printing Outside China

Classical and Vernacular Traditions in East Asia

Just as Latin endured as the common literary language of Latin Christendom, the classical Chinese language unified East Asian intellectual life. Since the logographic forms of written Chinese could not be adapted to represent sounds in other languages, Korean and Japanese writers at first composed their works in classical Chinese. Even in China the written language had long been divorced from vernacular speech.

The earliest writings that use vernacular Chinese are all Buddhist works, especially translations of Indian texts but also sermons, hymns, and parables, written by monks in China to make the foreign religion more familiar and comprehensible to ordinary Chinese. Although works of popular entertainment such as drama and fiction begin to include colloquial speech during the Song period, classical Chinese prevailed as the dominant literary language of East Asia down to modern times.

China

In Korea, mastery of Chinese literary forms, especially poetry, became an essential mark of accomplishment among aristocrats. The advent of the Koryŏ (KAW-ree-oh) dynasty (918–1392), which brought the Korean peninsula under unified rule in 935, signaled the dominance of Confucianism in Korean political culture. The Koryŏ state preserved aristocratic rule, but it also instituted civil service examinations. Schooling and the examination system were highly centralized in the capital of Kaesong, and they were largely restricted to aristocratic families. From the mid-eleventh century, eminent officials and scholars encouraged the study of Confucian ideas at private academies. Although Buddhism continued to enjoy public and private patronage, study at a private academy became a badge of honor for sons of the aristocracy.

Korea

Confucian culture became even more deeply entrenched in the ruling class during the succeeding Yi dynasty (1392–1910). The Yi monarch Sejong (SAY-johng) (r. 1418–1450) took the initiative in creating a native writing system, known as *han'gul* (HAHN-goor), to enable his people to express themselves in their everyday tongue. But the Korean aristocracy, determined to preserve its monopoly over learning and social prestige, resisted the new writing system. As in Japan, it was women of aristocratic families who popularized the native script by using it extensively in their correspondence and poetry.

In Japan, too, Chinese was the learned, formal, written language of public life. Aristocratic men studied the Chinese classics, history, and law and composed Chinese poetry. By 850 the Japanese had developed a phonetic system for writing Japanese, but they rarely used it in public life. The Japanese kana script instead was relegated to the private world of letters and diaries; it became so closely associated with women writers that it was called "woman's hand." Women of the Heian aristocracy were expected to be well versed in poetry and composition, and this era witnessed a remarkable outpouring of great literature by women writing vernacular Japanese. In fact, women composed much of the memorable writing of this era. Men confined themselves to writing in Chinese, whereas gifted women of the Japanese aristocracy used the full resources of their native language to express themselves in the frank and evocative styles found in outstanding works such as the *Pillow Book* of Sei Shōnagon (SAY SHON-nah-gohn) and Lady Murasaki's *Tale of Genji*. Although the world immortalized by Murasaki was narrowly self-centered, she and her fellow women writers gave birth to Japanese as a written language, and in so doing gave Japanese literature its distinctive genius (see Reading the Past: Lady Murasaki on Her Peers Among Women Writers).

Japan

The heyday of women's literature in Japan had no parallel elsewhere in the premodern world, but it was short-lived. By 1200 the Japanese court had been reduced to political impotence, and a rising class of warrior lords seized political power (as we will see in Chapter 15). New cultural forms replaced both Chinese literary fashions and the courtly romances of the Heian era. Prose narratives chronicled not the love affairs of courtiers but the wars and political rivalries among warrior brotherhoods. Women often strode onto the political stage in the era of the shoguns, but they were no longer at the center of its literary culture.

To different degrees, the spread of vernacular writing broadened access to written knowledge throughout East Asia. In China, the classical language retained its preeminence as a literary language, but the early development of printing and public schools fostered a relatively high level of literacy. In Mesoamerica, by contrast, writing remained a jealously guarded prerogative of the ruling class.

READING THE PAST

Lady Murasaki on Her Peers Among Women Writers

In addition to her great novel *Tale of Genji*, Lady Murasaki composed a memoir, covering a brief period from 1008 to 1010, that reflects on events and personalities at the Heian court. Among its more personal elements are Murasaki's observations about other women writers of her day, such as Izumi Shikibu (EE-zoo-mee SHEE-kee-boo), who earned the scorn of many for the frankly amorous tone of her poems and her flamboyant love affairs, and Sei Shōnagon, the renowned author of the *Pillow Book*, a collection of writings on taste and culture. Murasaki's tart judgments reveal the intense rivalry for literary fame among women in the court's status-conscious circles.

Now someone who did carry on a fascinating correspondence was Izumi Shikibu. She does have a rather unsavory side to her character but she has a talent for tossing off letters with ease and seems to make the most banal statement sound special. Her poems are most interesting. Although her knowledge of the canon and her judgments of other people's poetry leave something to be desired, she can produce poems at will and always manages to include some clever phrase that catches the attention. Yet when it comes to criticizing or judging the works of others, well, she never really comes up to scratch—the sort of person who relies on a talent for extemporization, one feels. I cannot think of her as a poet of the highest rank.

Sei Shōnagon, for instance, was dreadfully conceited. She thought herself so clever and littered her writings with Chinese words; but if you examined them

closely, they left a great deal to be desired. Those who think of themselves as being superior to everyone else in this way will inevitably suffer and come to a bad end.[1]

Yet Murasaki is no less harsh in her self-appraisal:

Thus do I criticize others from various angles—but here is one who has survived this far without having achieved anything of note. . . . Pretty yet shy, shrinking from sight, unsociable, fond of old tales, conceited, so wrapped up in poetry that other people hardly exist, spitefully looking down on the whole world—such is the unpleasant opinion that people have of me.[2]

---

1. Ivan Morris, *The World of the Shining Prince: Court Life in Ancient Japan* (New York: Knopf, 1964), 251.
2. *The Diary of Lady Murasaki*, trans. Richard Bowring (London: Penguin, 1996), 53–54.

EXAMINING THE EVIDENCE

1. Although women writers such as Murasaki did not compose their major works in Chinese, they still held literary skill in Chinese in high regard. Why?

2. Why might Lady Murasaki have believed that a woman writer's talent was best expressed by poetry? (Consider the chapter narrative as well as this excerpt in formulating your response.)

COUNTERPOINT
Writing and Political Power in Mesoamerica

The Greeks coined the word *hieroglyph* (priestly or sacred script) for the Egyptian language, whose signs differed radically from their own alphabetic writing. In ancient societies such as Egypt, writing and reading were skills reserved for rulers, priests, and administrators. Writing was both a product and an instrument of political control. Because of their sacred character or strategic importance, written records were closely guarded secrets. Rulers denied ordinary people access to books and other forms of written knowledge.

This monopoly over the written word vanished in the major civilizations of Eurasia and Africa during the first millennium B.C.E. Subsequently the evangelical zeal of Buddhists, Christians, and Muslims encouraged the spread of literacy and written knowledge. The desire to propagate Buddhist scriptures appears to have been the catalyst for one of the most significant technological milestones of human history, the invention of printing. But in more isolated parts of the world, such as Mesoamerica, writing, like ritual, served to perpetuate the profound social gulf that separated the rulers from the common people.

FOCUS

How did the relationship between political power and knowledge of writing in Mesoamerica differ from that in the other civilizations studied in this chapter?

Mesoamerican Languages: Time, History, and Rulership

In Mesoamerica, written languages took the form of symbols with pictorial elements, much like the hieroglyphs of ancient Egypt. Mesoamerican texts also display many parallels with Egyptian writings. Writing was a product of the violent competition for leadership and political control. Most surviving texts are inscriptions on monuments that commemorate the great feats and divine majesty of rulers. Knowledge of astronomical time-keeping, divination and prophecy, and rituals intended to align human events with grand cycles of cosmic time were indispensable to political power.

The earliest writing in Mesoamerica was the Zapotec (sah-po-TEHK) script of the Monte Alban state in southern Mexico, which was in use at least as early as 400 B.C.E. The Zapotec language achieved its mature form in 300–700 C.E., the Monte Alban state's heyday. Unfortunately, the Zapotec language remains undecipherable: the ancient written language does not correspond to modern spoken Zapotec. Nonetheless, Zapotec inscriptions display many of the same themes found in later Mesoamerican literary traditions. For example, the earliest Zapotec monuments with writing depict slain enemies and captives, a common motif in Maya monuments. Like Maya texts, too, Zapotec inscriptions apparently focus on diplomacy and war.

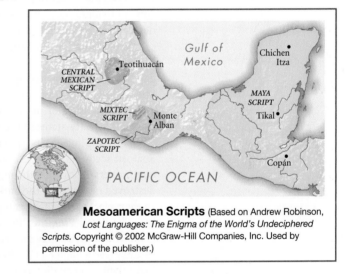

Mesoamerican Scripts (Based on Andrew Robinson, *Lost Languages: The Enigma of the World's Undeciphered Scripts.* Copyright © 2002 McGraw-Hill Companies, Inc. Used by permission of the publisher.)

Zapotec Script

Classic Maya Script

Maya rulers wielded the written word to consolidate their power, using it to display both divine approval of their reign and the fixed course of human history. Maya scribes used calendrical calculation to create genealogical histories organized around the crucial events and persons—birth, marriage, ancestors, offspring—in the lives of royal and noble persons. Maya inscriptions also commemorated the rulers' accomplishments by portraying them as reenacting the triumphs of ancient heroes (see Reading the Past: The Maya Hero Twins Vanquish the Lords of the Underworld, page 348). Creating new monuments gave rulers opportunities to rewrite history, but only within the framework of a set interpretation of the past that affirmed the social order of the present. The regular destruction of monuments

Maya Scribe

In the Maya classical age, the power of the pen often was mightier than that of the sword. Court scribes combined writing ability, artistic skill, and esoteric knowledge of such fields as calendrical science to create the monuments and artifacts that perpetuated the authority of Maya royalty. Scribes were also associated with divine figures, as in this painted vase from the period 600 to 900 C.E., which depicts a scribe in the guise of the maize god. (Photograph K1185 ©Justin Kerr.)

testifies to the power of the visible word in Mesoamerican societies. The Zapotecs at Monte Alban plastered over or reused old monuments in new construction. The Maya frequently defaced, sawed, buried, or relocated monuments of defeated enemies or disgraced persons.

In addition to stone inscriptions on monuments, temples, and dwellings, a handful of Maya bark-paper books have survived. Whereas stone monuments served as public propaganda, the bark-paper books contained the technical knowledge of astronomy, calendrical science, divination, and prophecy that governed the lives of the Maya elite.

The tradition of monument-building lapsed almost entirely after the demise of the classic Maya city-states in the ninth and tenth centuries. Yet the nobility preserved knowledge of the Maya script down to the Spanish conquests in the sixteenth century. Early Spanish accounts observed that although only noble Maya could read, they instructed the commoners in history through storytelling and song. Spanish missionaries deliberately destroyed nearly all of the bark-paper books, which they condemned as works of the devil. In their place the Spanish taught the Maya to write their language using the Roman alphabet. The *Popul Vuh*, the "Book of Council" that has served as a rich mine of information about Maya mythology and religion, was composed in Roman script in the mid-sixteenth century (see Chapter 11). After an alphabet was adopted, however, knowledge of the Maya hieroglyphic script died out.

The Legacy of Mesoamerican Languages

Although the classical Maya language became extinct, scholars today can decipher as much as 80 percent of surviving Maya texts. Linguists have found that the political institutions and cultural values embedded in the Maya literary legacy also appear, in altered form, in the later written records of the Mixtecs and Aztecs of central Mexico. All of these languages, as well as Zapotec, were part of a broader Mesoamerican tradition that used writing and calendrical science to create histories designed to enhance rulers' prestige and power. Although command of writing was restricted to a tiny elite, Mesoamerican rulers addressed the mass of the populace through public monuments, which were intended to convey a sense of the immobility of history and the permanence of the present-day social order. Here, as in many cultures, the sacred and imperishable character of writing, in contrast to the fleeting nature of ordinary speech, endowed the ruler's words with a powerful aura of truth.

Yet it was precisely because of such tight control that written languages like classic Maya became extinct once the social and political systems that created them disappeared. In the cosmopolitan civilizations of Eurasia, by contrast, rulers and religious authorities failed to maintain a monopoly over the power of the written word, especially when vernacular tongues displaced classical languages as the chief media of written communication.

Conclusion

The tenth to the fourteenth centuries witnessed a remarkable expansion of learning and schooling across Eurasia. This expansion of knowledge and education was fostered by the growing penetration of religious institutions and values in local society and by the creation of formal institutions of higher learning. The languages of sacred texts and religious instruction—Latin, Arabic, Sanskrit, and Chinese—achieved new prominence in higher education and intellectual discourse. The growing prestige of these cosmopolitan languages led them to be adopted in government and literary expression as well.

The deepening infusion of religious faith into traditions of learning thus produced more distinct and coherent cultural identities in each of the major civilizations of Eurasia. At the same time the friction between sacred and secular learning—between faith and reason—intensified. In Latin Christendom, struggles erupted among the Roman church, monarchs and city councils, and guilds of masters, each seeking to dictate the structure and content of university education. In the Islamic world, in the absence of a centralized religious authority or even an ordained clergy, individual ulama and madrasas aligned themselves with one of several separate traditions of Islamic law and theological study. Sufis proposed a radically different understanding of Islam. In China, a resurgent, secular Neo-Confucianism dominated public discourse through the state-run civil service examinations and schools, pushing Buddhism to the margins of intellectual life. In the Maya world, by contrast, the rulers' monopoly of the written word ensured their domination over all aspects of political, social, and religious life.

The unity of learned culture was increasingly undercut by the emergence of vernacular literary languages. Writing in the vernacular was stimulated by political fragmentation and rivalry, governments' desire to intrude more deeply into the everyday lives of their subjects, and the flowering of local and regional literary and artistic expression in an era of vigorous economic prosperity. By the tenth century the cosmopolitan Sanskrit culture had fragmented into a chain of regional literary cultures across South and Southeast Asia. In the eleventh century Japanese authors, notably elite women such as Lady Murasaki, fashioned a new national literary culture written in the Japanese vernacular. In much of the Islamic world, Arabic persevered as the dominant written and spoken language, but Persian and Turkish achieved new stature in religion, government, and literature. Despite this proliferation of vernacular literatures, however, the cultural and social gulf between the literate and the illiterate remained as wide as ever.

The intense struggles over the definition of religious truth and social values in the major regions of Eurasia during these centuries aggravated conflicts between different civilizations and ways of life. As we will see in the next chapter, the launch of the Crusades and the Mongol conquests inflamed the already smoldering tensions between Christians and Muslims and between nomadic and settled peoples.

NOTES

1. Lady Murasaki, *The Tale of Genji*, quoted in Ivan Morris, *The World of the Shining Prince: Court Life in Ancient Japan* (New York: Knopf, 1964), 308–309.
2. *The Letters of Abelard and Heloise*, trans. Betty Radice (Harmondsworth, U.K.: Penguin, 1974), 58.
3. *The Anglo-Saxon Chronicle*, trans. G. N. Garmonsway (London: J. M. Dent, 1954), 216.
4. Burhan ad-Din Az-Zarnuji, *Ta'lim al-Muta'allim-Tariq at-Ta'allum, Instruction of the Student: The Method of Learning*, trans. G. E. von Grunebaum and Theodora M. Abel (New York: King's Crown Press, 1947), 32.
5. Farid al-Din Attar, *Tadhkirat al-Awliya*, quoted in Margaret Smith, *Rabi'a the Mystic and Her Fellow Saints in Islam* (Cambridge, U.K.: Cambridge University Press, 1928), 3–4.

6. W. Montgomery Watt, *The Faith and Practice of al-Ghazali* (London: George Allen & Unwin, 1967), 57.

7. Ali Hujwiri, *The Kashf al-Mahjūb: The Oldest Persian Treatise on Sufism*, trans. Reynold A. Nicholson (rpt. ed.; London: Luzac & Co., 1976), 213.

8. *The Itinerary of Rabbi Benjamin of Tudela*, trans. A. Asher (New York: Hakesheth Publishing, n.d.), 43.

9. Quoted in Ichisada Miyazaki, *China's Examination Hell: The Civil Service Examinations of Imperial China* (New Haven, CT: Yale University Press, 1981), 17.

RESOURCES FOR RESEARCH

Church and Universities in Latin Christendom

Scholars regard the rediscovery of Greek philosophy and science via translations from Arabic and the rise of the universities as the catalysts for a "twelfth-century renaissance" in European intellectual life. Moore's examination of the emergence of a distinctive European ruling culture provides historical background for assessing the political and social influence of higher learning. Cobban's classic study highlights the distinctive characters of the major European universities.

Clanchy, M. T. *Abelard: A Medieval Life*. 1997.

Cobban, A. B. *The Medieval Universities: Their Development and Organization*. 1975.

Ferruolo, Steven. *The Origins of the University: The Schools of Paris and Their Critics, 1100–1215*. 1985.

Moore, R. I. *The First European Revolution, c. 970–1215*. 2000.

Pedersen, Olaf. *The First Universities: Studium Generale and the Origins of University Education in Europe*. 1997.

Students and Scholars in Islamic Societies

Much scholarship has been devoted to the educational and legal institutions that shaped Islamic intellectual and cultural life. In recent years, scholars such as Chamberlain and Ephrat have examined the role of knowledge and teaching in the social life of the ulama and urban society in general. Trimingham remains the basic work on the social history of Sufism.

Berkey, Jonathan. *The Transmission of Knowledge in Medieval Cairo: A Social History of Islamic Education*. 1992.

Chamberlain, Michael. *Knowledge and Social Practice in Medieval Damascus, 1190–1350*. 1994.

Ephrat, Daphna. *A Learned Society in a Period of Transition: The Sunni Ulama of Eleventh-Century Baghdad*. 1995.

Makdisi, George. *The Rise of Colleges: Institutions of Learning in Islam and the West*. 1981.

Trimingham, J. S. *The Sufi Orders in Islam*. 1971.

The Cosmopolitan and Vernacular Realms in India and Southeast Asia

After the demise of the Gupta Empire, India's intellectual and political culture initially remained unified, but the Muslim conquests fostered strong regional diversity in vernacular languages and literary cultures. Pollock's seminal work on "the Sanskrit cosmopolis" has dramatically enhanced our understanding of the relationship between language and political and cultural authority.

Asher, Catherine B., and Cynthia Talbot. *India Before Europe*. 2006.

Eaton, Richard M., ed. *India's Islamic Traditions, 711–1750*. 2003.

Pollock, Sheldon. *The Language of the Gods in the World of Men: Sanskrit, Culture, and Power in Premodern India*. 2006.

Talbot, Cynthia. *Precolonial India in Practice: Society, Religion, and Identity in Medieval Andhra*. 2001.

Wink, André. *Al-Hind: The Making of the Indo-Islamic World*, 2d ed. 1997.

Learning, Schools, and Print Culture in East Asia

Civil government by officials selected through competitive examinations shaped the distinctive political, social, and cultural traditions not only of China but of East Asia as a whole. Chaffee provides a succinct institutional history of the Song civil service examinations that focuses on the question of social mobility, while Miyazaki offers a lively social history spanning the late imperial era. Morris remains the most engaging introduction to the literary culture of Heian Japan.

Bol, Peter K. *Neo-Confucianism in History*. 2008.

Chafee, John. *Thorny Gates of Learning in Song China: A Social History of Examinations*, 2d ed. 1995.

Chia, Lucille. *Printing for Profit: The Commercial Publishers of Jianyang, Fujian (11th–17th Centuries)*. 2002.

Miyazaki, Ichisada. *China's Examination Hell: The Civil Service Examinations of Imperial China*. 1981.

Morris, Ivan. *The World of the Shining Prince: Court Life in Ancient Japan*. 1964.

COUNTERPOINT: Writing and Political Power in Mesoamerica

Scholars' painstaking efforts to decode the Maya language have now yielded impressive results. Schele and Mathews combine archaeology, art history, and linguistic analysis to retrieve the history and meaning of key Maya monuments. Tedlock's study provides translations of a wide range of Maya literary texts down to modern times.

Coe, Michael D. *Breaking the Maya Code*, rev. ed. 1999.

Marcus, Joyce. *Mesoamerican Writing Systems: Propaganda, Myth, and History in Four Ancient Civilizations*. 1992.

Schele, Linda, and Peter Mathews. *The Code of Kings: The Language of Seven Sacred Maya Temples and Tombs*. 1998.

Tedlock, Dennis. *2000 Years of Mayan Literature*. 2010.

▶ **For additional primary sources from this period**, see *Sources of Crossroads and Cultures*.

▶ **For Web sites, images, and documents related to topics in this chapter**, see Make History at bedfordstmartins.com/smith.

REVIEW

The major global development in this chapter ▶ The expansion of learning and education across Eurasia from 900 to 1300 and its relationship to the rise of regional and national identities.

IMPORTANT EVENTS

918–1392	Koryŏ dynasty in Korea
960–1279	Song dynasty in China
c. 1010	Lady Murasaki's *Tale of Genji* begins to circulate among the Japanese court aristocracy
1055	Seljuk Turks capture Baghdad and establish their rule over Mesopotamia and Syria
1066	Norman conquest of England
1130–1200	Life of Neo-Confucian scholar Zhu Xi
1140	Catholic church authorities convict theologian Peter Abelard of heresy
c. 1150	First university founded at Paris
1206–1526	Delhi Sultanate in India
1215	Pope Innocent III bans the teachings of Aristotle and Ibn Rushd
1273	Publication of Thomas Aquinas's *Summa Theologica*
c. 1313–1321	Dante Alighieri composes his epic poem *Divine Comedy*
1382	Ibn Khaldun becomes professor of Islamic law at Cairo
1392–1910	Yi dynasty in Korea

KEY TERMS

cathedral school (p. 410)
hadith (p. 417)
logographic (p. 431)
madrasa (p. 417)
Neo-Confucianism (p. 430)
rhetoric (p. 410)

shari'a (p. 417)
Sufism (p. 419)
ulama (p. 417)
university (p. 415)
vernacular language (p. 415)

CHAPTER OVERVIEW QUESTIONS

1. Did the spread of higher learning reinforce or undermine established political and religious authority?

2. How did educational institutions reshape social hierarchy and elite culture?

3. What were the different uses of cosmopolitan languages and vernacular languages, and to what degree did they broaden access to written knowledge?

4. How did the different technologies of writing affect the impact of the written word?

SECTION FOCUS QUESTIONS

1. What political, social, and religious forces led to the founding of the first European universities?

2. To what extent did Sunni and Sufi schools foster a common cultural and religious identity among Muslims?

3. What political and religious forces contributed to the development of a common culture across India and Southeast Asia and its subsequent fragmentation into regional cultures?

4. To what extent did intellectual and educational trends in Song China influence its East Asian neighbors?

5. How did the relationship between political power and knowledge of writing in Mesoamerica differ from that in the other cultures in this chapter?

MAKING CONNECTIONS

1. In what ways did the cathedral schools and universities of Latin Christendom modify the classical traditions of learning of ancient Greece and Rome?

2. How did the madrasas of the Islamic world differ from European universities in their curricula, their teachers, and their relationships with political and religious authorities?

3. How can we explain the failure of printing technology to spread from China to neighboring societies such as Japan, India, or the Islamic world until centuries later?

14

AT A CROSSROADS ▶

Qubilai, grandson of the great conqueror Chinggis, cemented his claim as Great Khan of all the Mongols only after winning a bloody struggle against one of his brothers. In his single-minded quest to make himself the first foreign emperor of China, Qubilai turned his back on the Mongols' steppe homeland. His success in conquering China came at the cost of undermining the unity of the Mongol Empire, which fragmented into four separate khanates. (The Art Archive.)

Crusaders, Mongols, and Eurasian Integration

1050–1350

"The empire can be won on horseback, but it cannot be ruled from horseback." Reciting this old Chinese proverb, Yelu Chucai, a Chinese-educated adviser, delivered a tart rebuke to the Mongol Great Khan Ogodei (ERG-uh-day). A council of Mongol princes had just chosen Ogodei (r. 1229–1241) to succeed his father, Chinggis (CHEEN-gihs). The Mongol armies had overrun much of the territory of the Jin kingdom that then ruled north China. Now the princes urged Ogodei to massacre the defeated population and turn their farmlands into pasture for the Mongol herds. But Yelu Chucai persuaded Ogodei that preserving China's agricultural way of life would generate far greater rewards.

Yelu Chucai had served as a Jin official until the Mongols captured him in 1215. Three years later Yelu accompanied Chinggis (Genghis was the Persian version of his name) on his campaigns in western Asia, serving the Mongol khan as scribe, astrologer, and confidential adviser. Upon gaining the confidence of Ogodei, Yelu in effect became chief minister of the Mongol Empire and began to construct a strong central government based on Chinese models. But Yelu made many enemies among the Mongol princes, who distrusted his promotion of Chinese ways. After initially approving Yelu's plans, Ogodei withdrew his support.

BACKSTORY

By the twelfth century, economic revival and commercial integration had begun to stimulate unprecedented cultural contact and exchange across Eurasia (see Chapters 12 and 13). But economic prosperity did not necessarily translate into political strength. The weakened Abbasid caliphs, already challenged by rival caliphates in Egypt and Spain, had become pawns of the Seljuk Turks, invaders from Central Asia. In China, the Song dynasty was also vulnerable to invasion by its northern neighbors. In 1127 Jurchen Jin invaders from Manchuria seized the northern half of the empire, forcing the Song court to flee to the south. Within Christendom, the division between the Latin West and the Byzantine East widened into outright hostility, and the Roman and Byzantine churches competed against each other to convert the pagan peoples of eastern Europe and Russia to Christianity.

The Crusades and the Imperial Papacy, 1050–1350

FOCUS In what ways did the Roman popes seek to expand their powers during the age of the Crusades?

The Making of Christian Europe, 1100–1350

FOCUS How did the efforts to establish Christianity in Spain and eastern Europe compare with the Crusaders' quest to recover Jerusalem?

The Mongol World-Empire, 1100–1368

FOCUS How did the organization of Mongol society and government change from the time of Chinggis Khan to that of his grandson Qubilai, the ruler of China?

The Mongol Khanates and the Islamic World, 1240–1350

FOCUS In what respects did the Turkish Islamic states of the Mamluks and Ottomans pursue policies similar to those of the Mongol regimes in Iran and Russia?

COUNTERPOINT: The "New Knighthood" of the Christian Military Orders

FOCUS In what ways did the self-image and mission of the Christian military orders resemble or differ from those of the papal and royal leaders of the Crusades?

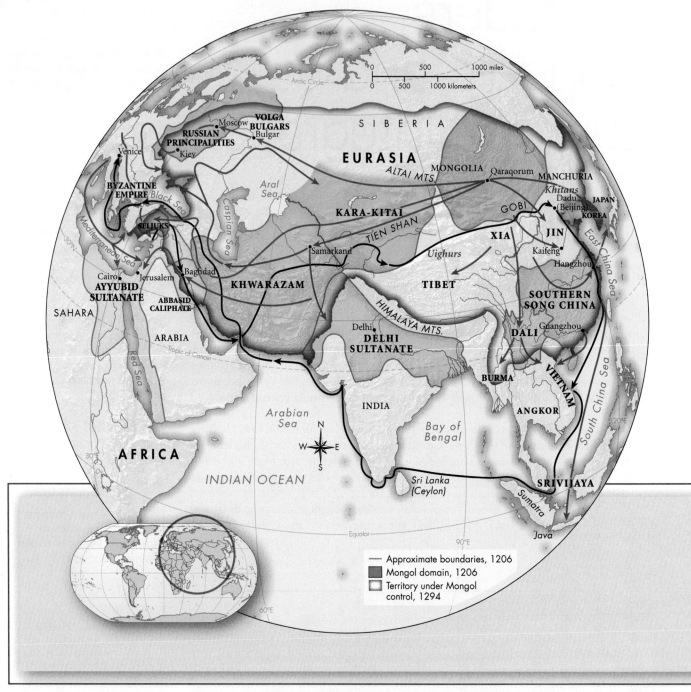

Legend:
— Approximate boundaries, 1206
■ Mongol domain, 1206
□ Territory under Mongol control, 1294

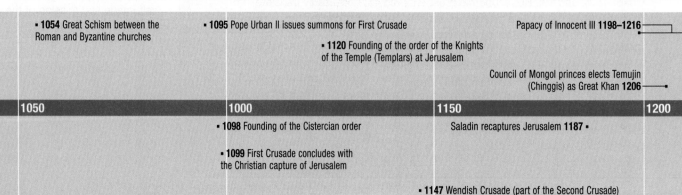

▪ **1054** Great Schism between the Roman and Byzantine churches

▪ **1095** Pope Urban II issues summons for First Crusade

Papacy of Innocent III **1198–1216**

▪ **1120** Founding of the order of the Knights of the Temple (Templars) at Jerusalem

Council of Mongol princes elects Temujin (Chinggis) as Great Khan **1206**

▪ **1098** Founding of the Cistercian order

Saladin recaptures Jerusalem **1187** ▪

▪ **1099** First Crusade concludes with the Christian capture of Jerusalem

▪ **1147** Wendish Crusade (part of the Second Crusade)

Following Ogodei's death in 1241 and Yelu Chucai's death two years later, Mongol leaders dismantled Yelu's efforts to remake the Mongol Empire in the likeness of China. Wracked by conflict among the sons and grandsons of Chinggis, the empire fragmented into a series of independent regional khanates. Two decades later, many features of Yelu's vision of bureaucratic government were adopted by Qubilai (KOO-bih-lie) Khan, who made himself emperor of China. But by then the unified Mongol Empire had ceased to exist.

The Mongol conquests dominate the history of Eurasia in the thirteenth century. From humble origins among the nomadic herders of Central Asia, the Mongols became world conquerors. They terrified settled peoples from Korea to Hungary, laid waste to dozens of cities, and toppled many rulers. Yet they also unified Eurasia in unprecedented ways. Merchants and missionaries, groups who received special favor from the Mongols, moved with ease from the Mediterranean to China. The Mongol Empire exerted a powerful influence on the histories of China, Russia, and the Islamic world.

A century before the Mongol armies swept across Eurasia, another clash of civilizations, the Crusades, had erupted—this one in the Mediterranean world. In this conflict, the tense hostility that had divided Christians and Muslims exploded into a succession of religious wars. Although the Crusaders ultimately failed to turn the Holy Land into a Christian stronghold, the Crusades marked a crucial moment in the definition of Europe as the realm of Latin Christendom. At the same time, centralization of administrative control and theological orthodoxy within the Latin church brought about a final rupture between Rome and the Christian churches of Byzantium and Asia. But the papacy's drive to create a united Latin Christendom under clerical leadership collapsed, and national monarchies enhanced their power throughout Europe.

For all of the destruction they caused, both the Mongol conquests and the Crusades expanded the horizons of cross-cultural contact and influence. Exotic goods whetted new appetites—elites in Europe and China alike craved the pepper grown in India. The Mongols introduced knowledge of gunpowder and cannon to the Islamic world, from whence it spread to Europe. Christian missionaries journeyed to the courts of the Mongol khans,

MAPPING THE WORLD

Eurasian Integration, c. 1050–1350

Although the Mongol conquests caused much devastation and loss of life, they also stimulated an unprecedented surge of people and goods across Eurasia. The Venetian Marco Polo, who after traveling overland to the court of Qubilai Khan returned to Italy via maritime routes through Southeast Asia and the Indian Ocean, exemplified this new mobility. The Crusades intensified religious and political tensions between Christians and Muslims, but also led to greater economic interaction between Europe and the Middle East.

ROUTES ▼

→ Mongol campaigns under Chinggis, 1206–1227

→ Later Mongol campaigns, 1229–1295

→ General routes of the Crusades, 1096–1291

→ Travels of Marco Polo, 1271–1295

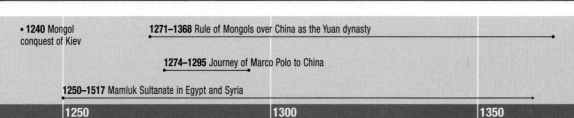

▪ **1240** Mongol conquest of Kiev

1271–1368 Rule of Mongols over China as the Yuan dynasty

1274–1295 Journey of Marco Polo to China

1250–1517 Mamluk Sultanate in Egypt and Syria

1250	1300	1350

▪ **1248** Christian armies capture the Almohad stronghold of Seville

▪ **1291** Mamluks recapture Acre, last Christian stronghold in Palestine

▪ **1258** Mongols sack Baghdad

1295–1304 Rule of Ghazan as Ilkhan; conversion of Ilkhan Mongols to Islam

seeking converts and allies in their holy war against Islam. The Mongols, rulers of the largest contiguous land empire in human history, built bridges that connected diverse civilizations rather than walls that divided them. But ultimately the contradictions between the political and cultural traditions of the nomadic Mongols and the settled lives of the peoples they conquered proved too great, and the Mongol empires collapsed. By 1400 Europe and Asia had once again grown distant from each other.

OVERVIEW
QUESTIONS

The major global development in this chapter: The Eurasian integration fostered by the clashes of culture known as the Crusades and the Mongol conquests.

As you read, consider:

1. In what ways did the growing economic and cultural unity of Latin Christendom promote the rise of powerful European national monarchies?

2. To what degree did the expansion of Latin Christendom remake eastern Europe in the image of western Europe?

3. In what ways did the Mongol conquests foster cultural and economic exchange across Eurasia?

4. How and why did the Mongol rulers of China, Iran, and Russia differ in their relationships with the settled societies they ruled?

The Crusades and the
Imperial Papacy 1050–1350

FOCUS

In what ways did the Roman popes seek to expand their powers during the age of the Crusades?

The **Crusades** are generally understood as an effort to reclaim control of the sacred sites of the Christian religion from Muslim rule. More broadly, the Crusades developed into an evangelical movement to Christianize the world. The summons to rescue Jerusalem from the "heathen" Muslims, announced at a church council in 1095, escalated to include campaigns to recover Islamic Spain; to impose orthodox Christianity on the pagan Celtic, Slavic, and Baltic peoples of Europe; and to eradicate heresy—doctrines contrary to the church's official teachings—from within Latin Christendom. The era of the Crusades also witnessed the temporary rise of an "imperial" papacy as administrative reforms within the church broadened the Roman popes' authority over secular affairs as well as the spiritual life of the Christian faithful. Both "Christendom" and "Europe" acquired more precise meaning: the lands of the Christian peoples subject to the spiritual commands of the Roman pope.

The Papal Monarchy

Crusades The series of military campaigns instigated by the Roman papacy with the goal of returning Jerusalem and other holy places in Palestine to Christian rule.

The transformation of Latin Christendom that led to the crusading movement began with initiatives to reform the church from within. In the eyes of both lay and clerical critics, abuses such as violations of celibacy and the sale of church offices had compromised the clergy's moral authority. The reformers also sought to renew the church's commitment to spread the teachings of Christ to all peoples of the world. Pope Gregory VII (r. 1073–1085) was the staunchest advocate of the primacy of the pope as the leader of all Christian peoples. Within the church, Gregory campaigned to improve the moral and educational caliber of the clergy by holding the priesthood to high standards of competence, and also—especially in matters of sexual behavior—to stringent standards of conduct. Gregory also demanded strict conformity to the standard religious services authorized by the church hierarchy and the use of Latin as the universal language of Christianity. Thus, under Gregory VII, the movements for clerical reform and centralization of authority within the church merged. As a result, clerical reform became a force for the religious and cultural unification of Europe.

Long before Gregory VII's papacy, the rivalry between the Roman and Byzantine churches had resulted in bitter division in the Christian world. The Roman pope's claim to supreme authority over all Christians rankled both the Byzantine emperor and the patriarch at Constantinople. Half-hearted efforts at reconciliation came to an end in 1054, when the Roman pope and the patriarch at Constantinople expelled each other from the church. This mutual excommunication initiated a formal break between the Latin and Orthodox churches that came to be known as the **Great Schism**. As the split between the Christian leadership widened, Rome and Constantinople openly competed for the allegiance of new converts in eastern Europe and Russia.

Great Schism of the Christian Churches

The leaders of the Orthodox church were not the only powerful figures who challenged the supremacy of the Roman popes. In their efforts to assert and consolidate their authority, the popes faced competition from within Europe as well as from without. Secular leaders in many parts of Europe had the right to make appointments to key church positions in their domains. In effect, this gave them control over church lands and officials. Pope Gregory demanded an end to such secular control, seeing it as a threat to the papacy's dominion over Latin Christendom. In a deliberately public disagreement with the Holy Roman Emperor Henry IV (r. 1056–1106) known as the **investiture controversy** (*investiture* refers to the appointment of church officials), Gregory challenged the emperor's authority to appoint bishops within his domains. The struggle for control of the church pitted the most powerful secular and sacred rulers of Christendom against each other. Gregory invalidated Henry's right to rule over his territories, provoking the emperor's enemies among the German princes to rise against him. Henry was forced to prostrate himself before the pope and beg forgiveness. Ultimately, a compromise gave kings and princes some say in appointments to major church offices in their territories but ceded leadership of the church to the papacy.

Investiture Controversy

Deprived of control over the church, the Holy Roman emperors lost their primary base of support. The German princes consolidated their power over their own domains, reducing the emperorship to a largely ceremonial office. The Roman papacy, in contrast, increasingly resembled a royal government, with its own law courts, fiscal officers, and clerical bureaucracy.

Although the assertion of papal authority was originally linked to the movement for clerical reform, ironically, papal success and the church's growing immersion in worldly affairs gave rise to a new round of calls for change within the church. The Cistercian order, founded in France in 1098, epitomized the renewed dedication to poverty, chastity, and evangelism among the Latin clergy. Within half a century the Cistercians had more than three hundred affiliated monasteries stretching from Spain to Sweden—even while refusing to admit female convents into their order. Although the Cistercians preserved the tradition that monks must confine themselves to their monastery for life, the order developed elaborate networks of communication to coordinate their activities. Passionate defenders of Roman orthodoxy, the Cistercians worked tirelessly to uproot what they perceived as the heresies of their fellow Christians. It was the Cistercians who secured the papal condemnation that ended the career of the Parisian theologian Peter Abelard in 1140 (discussed in Chapter 13).

Cistercian Religious Order

Great Schism The separation of the Latin Catholic and Greek Orthodox churches following the mutual excommunication by the Roman pope and the Byzantine patriarch in 1054.

investiture controversy Conflict between the pope and the Holy Roman emperor over who had the authority to appoint bishops and other church officials.

Crusaders Voyaging to Holy Land

Pope Urban's summons for a crusade to recapture Jerusalem was directed at knights and other men experienced in war. Nonetheless, people of all walks of life—including women and the urban poor—rallied to the Crusader cause. This Spanish illustration from 1283 shows the Crusaders embarking for the Holy Land aboard galleys powered chiefly by oars, the typical type of warship used in the Mediterranean Sea. (Biblioteca Monasterio del Escorial, Madrid/ Giraudon/Bridgeman Art Library.)

The Crusades 1095–1291

The First Crusade

Upon receiving an appeal from the Byzantine emperor for aid against the advancing armies of the Seljuk Turks in 1095, Pope Urban II (r. 1088–1099) called upon "the race of Franks [Latin Christians] . . . beloved and chosen by God" to "enter upon the road to the Holy Sepulcher; wrest that land from the wicked race, and subject it to yourselves."[1] Urban II's summons for a crusade to liberate Jerusalem drew inspiration from the reform movements within the church, and from a desire to transform the warrior rulers of Latin Christendom, constantly fighting among each other, into a united army of God. A papal dispensation granted to the Crusaders by Urban II transformed participation in the crusade into a form of penance, for which the Crusader would receive a full absolution of sins. This helped create enthusiasm for crusading among the knightly class, which saw the crusade as a means of erasing the heavy burden of sin that inevitably saddled men of war and violence.

The Crusader forces, more a collection of ragtag militias under the command of various minor nobles than a united army, suffered setbacks, yet achieved surprising success in capturing Jerusalem in 1099 (see Map 14.1). To some extent this success reflected the disunity prevailing in the Islamic world. The Seljuk sultans of Baghdad had ceded control of Palestine and Syria to the emirs of individual towns, who had failed to join forces for common defense. Yet the victors also lacked strong leadership and failed to follow up their initial success by establishing unified political and military institutions. Spurning the Byzantine emperor's claims to sovereignty, the Crusaders divided the conquered territories among themselves and installed a French duke as king of Jerusalem and defender of the Holy Land. Perhaps the greatest beneficiaries of the crusading movement were Venice and Genoa, whose merchants rushed to secure trading privileges in the Crusader kingdoms along the eastern shores of the Mediterranean. The capture of the Holy Land also prompted the founding of **military orders** that pledged themselves to the defense of the Holy Land (see Counterpoint: The "New Knighthood" of the Christian Military Orders). But in the long run, lack of coordination and unity of purpose among the leaders of

military order One of the new monastic orders, beginning with the Knights of the Temple founded in 1120, that combined the religious vocation of the priesthood with the military training of the warrior nobility.

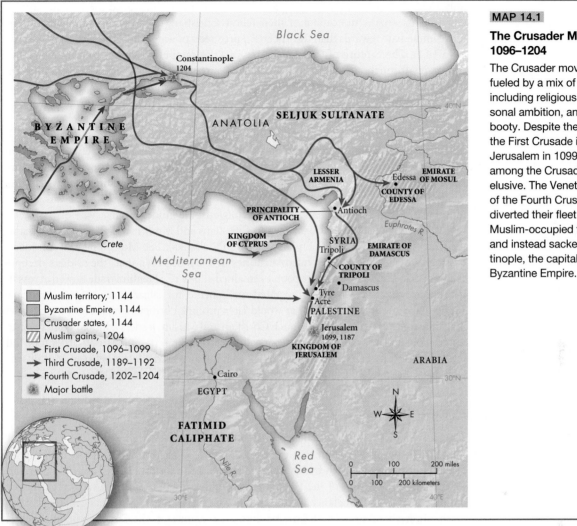

MAP 14.1

The Crusader Movement, 1096–1204

The Crusader movement was fueled by a mix of motives, including religious piety, personal ambition, and the lure of booty. Despite the success of the First Crusade in capturing Jerusalem in 1099, unity among the Crusaders proved elusive. The Venetian captains of the Fourth Crusade diverted their fleet away from Muslim-occupied territories and instead sacked Constantinople, the capital of the Byzantine Empire.

Crusader kingdoms, merchants, and military orders would doom Christian aspirations for permanent domination of the Holy Land.

At first Muslims did not understand the religious aspirations of the Crusaders and failed to rally against the Christian invaders. Nearly a century elapsed before a serious challenge arose to Christian rule over Jerusalem. In 1169 the Seljuk emir of Damascus dispatched one of his lieutenants, Saladin (c. 1137–1193), to Egypt to shore up defenses against a possible Christian attack. Saladin soon seized power from the much-weakened Fatimid caliphate and declared himself an independent sultan. He sought to muster support by declaring a holy war against the Christian occupiers of Jerusalem. In 1187 Saladin conquered Jerusalem and most of the Crusader principalities.

Saladin's Recapture of Jerusalem

This unexpected reversal prompted Christendom's leading monarchs—the kings of England and France and the Holy Roman emperor—to join together in what became known as the Third Crusade (1189–1192). Dissension among the Christian kings hobbled the military campaign, however, and the crusade ended with a truce under which the Christian armies withdrew in exchange for a Muslim pledge to allow Christian pilgrims access to holy sites.

Failure of the Later Crusades

Over the next century new crusades were repeatedly launched, with little success. Moreover, the original religious motivations of the Crusaders came to be overshadowed by political and economic objectives. The riches of Egypt beckoned but proved to be an elusive prize. The army mustered under the banner of the Fourth Crusade initially set sail for Egypt, only to be diverted to Constantinople. The Venetians, who financed the Fourth Crusade, decided that seizing the capital of their fellow Christian, the Byzantine emperor, offered more immediate rewards than the uncertain prospects of war against the Muslims (see again Map 14.1). The capture of Constantinople in 1204 catapulted Venice to dominance over commerce throughout the eastern Mediterranean and the Black Sea. The Byzantine emperor recovered his capital in 1260 thanks to the naval support of Genoa, Venice's perennial rival. After the Venetian seizure—with the pope's tacit approval—of Constantinople, the schism between the Roman Catholic and Greek Orthodox churches became irreparable.

The Crusades also intensified the cultural divide between Christians and Muslims. The militant rhetoric and propaganda of holy war rendered any lasting peace between Christians and Muslims inconceivable. Chronicles from both sides are filled with grotesque caricatures and misconceptions of each other's beliefs and customs. The proliferation of new *madrasas* and Sufi lodges following the Muslims' humiliating defeat in the First Crusade was part of a moral rearmament of the Islamic community against the infidel "Franks."

In reality, not all interactions between Christians and Muslims were hostile (see Reading the Past: A Muslim Courtier's Encounters with the Franks). The Muslim pilgrim Ibn Jubayr, passing through the Crusader-ruled territories in 1184, observed that "the soldiers occupied themselves in their war, while the people remained at peace."[2] Plentiful trade flowed across the battle lines, and the Crusaders acquired an appetite for sugar (previously unknown in Europe) and the spices of Asia that would later prompt Portuguese seafarers to seek a new maritime route to Asia. However much Christian and Muslim leaders admired their adversaries' religious zeal and courage in battle or valued each other as trading partners, they took little interest in each other's cultures or ideas. Indeed, the increased contact between Muslims and Christians that resulted from the Crusades only intensified religious and ethnic differences.

Papal Supremacy and the Christian People

Expansion of Papal Authority

The reorientation of the Crusades toward political aims originated within the papacy itself. Pope Innocent III (r. 1198–1216) tried to capitalize on the crusading spirit to strengthen papal authority both within the church and over secular society. The Crusaders had rallied together under the sign of the cross, the common symbol of all Christians regardless of national origins and allegiances. Innocent likewise invoked the Crusaders' language of universal brotherhood to redefine Christendom as an empire of "the Christian people" subject to the authority of the pope in both spiritual and worldly matters. Declaring himself "the vicar of Christ," Innocent insisted on his right to grant sovereign powers to Christian kings and princes. Legislation enacted at Innocent's instigation created a more centralized Christian church and deprived bishops of much of their independence. Civil matters such as marriage now fell under church jurisdiction. Innocent also established a judicial body, the **Inquisition**, to investigate and punish anyone who challenged the pope's supreme authority. The Inquisition expanded, with the eager support of lay monarchs, into a broad-based campaign directed against heretics and nonbelievers alike. Thus, it became, in many ways, an internal Crusade. In the view of European elites, just as military expeditions to the Holy Land would strengthen Christendom by bringing sacred sites outside of Europe under Christian control, the Inquisition would strengthen Christendom by eliminating religious diversity within Europe.

Persecution of Jews

Jewish communities in Christian Europe were early targets of Innocent's Inquisition. Many Christians regarded Jews as an alien race whose presence corrupted Christian society. Jews had suffered various kinds of legal discrimination since Roman times, but their persecution intensified from the eleventh century onward. Christian rulers prohibited Jews from owning land, forcing them to take up occupations as urban craftsmen and merchants. Jews were often vilified because of their prominence in trades such as moneylending, which tainted them with the stigma of usury. In many places Jews lacked legal protections and were subject to the arbitrary whims of kings and princes. Innocent's new orders, which compelled Jews to wear distinctive forms of dress such as special badges or hats, were intended to reinforce existing laws forbidding marriage between Christians and Jews.

Inquisition A system of courts and investigators set up by the Roman papacy in the early thirteenth century to identify and punish heretics.

A Muslim Courtier's Encounters with the Franks

Usamah ibn Mundiqh (1095–1188) was a Muslim courtier in the entourage of Mu'in ad-Din Unur, a general in command of Damascus. Usamah fought in numerous battles against the Crusaders, but he also frequently visited Christian-ruled Jerusalem on diplomatic business and had cordial relations with some Christians. He wrote his *Learning by Example*, a book of moral advice and instruction, as a gift to Saladin, who conquered Jerusalem four years later.

Among the Franks—God damn them!—no quality is more highly esteemed in a man than military prowess. The knights have a monopoly of the positions of honor and importance among them, and no one else has any prestige in their eyes. . . .

The Franks are without any vestige of a sense of honor and jealousy. If one of them goes along the street with his wife and meets a friend, this man will take the woman's hand and lead her aside to talk, while the husband stands by waiting until she has finished the conversation. . . .

I was present myself when one of them came up to the emir Mu'in ad-Din—God have mercy on him—in the Dome of the Rock and said to him: "Would you like to see God as a baby?" The emir said he would, and the fellow proceeded to show us a picture of Mary with the infant Messiah on her lap. "This," he said, "is God as a baby." Almighty God is greater than the infidels' concept of him! . . .

[Upon entering a Christian church I found] about ten old men, their bare heads as white as combed cotton. They were facing the east, and wore on their breasts staves ending in crossbars turned up like the rear of a saddle. They took their oath of this sign, and gave hospitality to those who needed it. The sight of their piety touched my heart, but at the same time it displeased and saddened me, for I had never seen such zeal and devotion among the Muslims. . . . One day, as Mu'in ad-Din and I were passing the Peacock House, he said to me, "I want to dismount and visit the Old Men.". . . [Inside] I saw about a hundred prayer-mats, and on each a Sufi, his face expressing peaceful serenity, and his body humble devotion. This was a reassuring sight, and I gave thanks to Almighty God that there were among the Muslims men of even more zealous devotion than those Christian priests. Before this I had never seen Sufis in their monastery, and was ignorant of the way they lived.

Source: Usamah ibn Mundiqh, *The Book of Learning by Example*, quoted in Francesco Gabrieli, ed., *Arab Historians of the Crusades* (Berkeley: University of California Press, 1969), 73, 77, 80, 84.

EXAMINING THE EVIDENCE

1. What virtues did Usamah admire in the Christians, and why?

2. Why did Usamah find the picture of Mary and the child Jesus offensive?

Franciscan and Dominican Religious Orders

Efforts to impose religious conformity on Latin Christendom received further impetus from the formation of new religious orders, most notably the Franciscans and the Dominicans. Like the Cistercians, these new orders dedicated themselves to the principles of poverty and evangelism. Unlike the Cistercians, who remained confined to their monasteries, Franciscan and Dominican friars traveled widely, preaching to the populace and depending on almsgiving for their livelihood. The new preaching orders sought to carry out the church's mission to regulate and reform the behavior of lay believers. The Dominicans assumed a conspicuous role in leading the Inquisition. The Franciscan and Dominican orders were also in the forefront of campaigns to convert the non-Christian peoples of eastern Europe.

End of the Crusades

During the thirteenth century the precarious position of the Christian outposts along the coast of Palestine and Syria became dire. The rise of a powerful Islamic state under the Mamluk dynasty in Egypt (discussed later in this chapter) after 1250 sealed the fate of the crusading movement. In 1291 the Mamluks captured Acre, the last Christian stronghold in Palestine. Dissension among the leaders of Christendom, especially between the pope and the French king, made it impossible to revive an international alliance to recapture the Holy Land.

The Making of Christian Europe 1100–1350

FOCUS

How did the efforts to establish Christianity in Spain and eastern Europe compare with the Crusaders' quest to recover Jerusalem?

Despite their ultimate failure, the Crusades had profound consequences for the course of European history. Among the most important was their role in consolidating the social and cultural identity of Latin Christendom. Even as the movement to retake the Holy Land from the Muslim occupiers foundered and sank, the crusading spirit provided the crucial momentum for Christendom to expand into northern and eastern Europe.

The crusading ideal also encouraged assimilation of the warrior class into the monastic culture of the Christian church. This merger produced the culture of **chivalry**—the knightly class's code of behavior, which stressed honor, piety, and devotion to one's ideals. The code of chivalry confirmed the moral as well as social superiority of the warrior nobility. Knights played at least as great a role as clerical evangelists in spreading Christian culture.

We can see the connection between the Crusades and the expansion of Latin Christendom in the use of the term "Franks," the term both Christian and Islamic chroniclers used to refer to the Crusaders. Along the frontiers of Latin Christendom, the term assumed a special meaning. "Frankish" knights were aggressive colonizers who combined ambitions for conquest with the missionary zeal of the Roman church. In the thirteenth and fourteenth centuries such kings and knights conquered and colonized territories from Spain in the west to the Baltic Sea in the east. Europe took form out of the processes of military conquest, migration, and cultural colonization that would later also characterize European expansion into the Americas.

The Reconquest of Spain 1085–1248

Under its Umayyad dynasty (756–1030), Muslim-ruled Spain had enjoyed relative religious peace. Although religious toleration was often compromised by sharp differences in social standing among Muslims, Jews, and Christians, the Umayyad rulers fostered a tradition of mutual accommodation. Yet the subjection of Christian peoples to Muslim rulers in Spain, as in Palestine and Syria, became increasingly intolerable to Christian rulers and church leaders alike. At the same time that he issued his summons for the First Crusade, Pope Urban II urged Christian rulers in northern Spain to take up arms against their Muslim neighbors. The *Reconquista* ("reconquest" of Spain) thus became joined to the crusading movement.

Muslim Rule in Spain

In its heyday the Umayyad caliphate in Spain was the most urbanized and commercially developed part of Europe. In the early eleventh century, however, the Umayyad caliphate disintegrated, and Muslim-ruled Spain splintered into dozens of feuding city-states. The conquest of Toledo, Spain's second-largest city, by King Alfonso of Castile in 1085 lifted Castile into a preeminent position among Spain's Christian kingdoms. The Muslim emirs turned to the Almoravid (al-moe-RAH-vid) rulers of North Africa for protection. The Almoravids, fervently devoted to the cause of holy war, halted the Christian advance but imposed their own authoritarian rule over the Muslim territories in Spain.

The Almohad (AHL-moh-had) dynasty, which supplanted the Almoravids in North Africa and Spain in 1148, was even more fiercely opposed to the Umayyad heritage of tolerance toward non-Muslims. Almohad policies, which included the expulsion of all Jews who refused to convert to Islam, were highly unpopular. Despite a major victory over Castile in 1195, the Almohads were unable to withstand intensified Christian efforts to "reconquer" Spain. Between 1236 and 1248 the major Muslim cities of Spain—Córdoba, Valencia, and finally Seville—fell to Castile and its allies, leaving Granada as the sole remaining Muslim state in Spain.

After capturing Toledo in 1085, the kings of Castile made the city their capital. Toledo was renowned as a cultural and intellectual crossroads and, despite the rhetoric of holy war, the Castilian kings preserved Toledo's multicultural character. Toledo's large

chivalry The code of behavior, stressing honor, piety, and devotion to one's ideals, of the knightly class of medieval Europe.

Arabic-speaking Christian and Jewish communities epitomized this spirit of religious pluralism. During the twelfth century, Toledo prospered as Europe's brightest intellectual center, a city in which Arabic and Jewish culture and learning flourished under Christian rule.

But Toledo's intellectual and religious tolerance steadily eroded as the Reconquista advanced. Christian monarchs expelled most of the Muslims from the cities and awarded Muslim lands and dwellings to Christian princes, bishops, and military orders. The religious toleration that the kings of Castile had extended to Muslim and Jewish minorities gradually dissipated. At first, the Christian kings allowed their Muslim subjects, known as Mudejars (mu-DAY-hahr), to own property, worship in mosques, and be judged by Islamic law before *qadi* jurists. After 1300, however, judicial autonomy eroded, and Mudejars accused of crimes against Christians were tried in Christian courts under Christian law. Christian rulers also converted the great mosques of Córdoba, Seville, and Toledo into Christian cathedrals.

The place of Jews also deteriorated in a European world that had come to define itself as the realm of "the Christian people." Attacks on Jews escalated dramatically with the onset of the Crusades. In the 1230s, when the Inquisition began a deliberate persecution of Jews, many fled from France, England, and Germany to seek sanctuary in Spain. Yet in Spain, too, Jews occupied an insecure position. In the fourteenth century, as in other parts of Latin Christendom, violence against Jews swept Spain. Anti-Jewish riots in Toledo in 1370, encouraged by the Castilian king, wiped out the city's Jewish population almost overnight. In 1391 wholesale massacres of Jews in Spain's major cities dealt a catastrophic blow to Jewish communities from which they never recovered. Rigid intolerance had replaced the vibrant multiculturalism of Umayyad Spain.

Reconquest of Spain, 1037–1275

Christianizing Eastern Europe 1150–1350

Wendish Crusade

In issuing a summons in 1145 for the Second Crusade to recover territories retaken by the Muslims, Pope Eugene III also invited the knights of Christendom to launch a crusade against the non-Christian populations of northern and eastern Europe—collectively referred to as the Wends. The pope acted at the instigation of his teacher Bernard of Clairvaux (d. 1153), the Cistercian abbot who had put Peter Abelard on trial for heresy. Bernard had urged Christian knights to take up arms against pagan peoples everywhere "until such a time as, by God's help, they shall be either converted or wiped out" (see Reading the Past: Bernard of Clairvaux's Summons to the Wendish Crusade).[3] In the three centuries following the Wendish Crusade of 1147, Latin Christendom steadily encroached upon the Baltic and Slavic lands. Latin Christendom incorporated northern and eastern Europe through a combination of conquest and colonization that transformed political, cultural, and economic life.

The fissure that split the Latin and Greek Christian churches also ran through eastern Europe. In the tenth and eleventh centuries, the rulers of Poland and Hungary had chosen to join the Roman church, but Christian converts in the Balkans such as the Serbs and Bulgars as well as the Rus princes had adopted the Greek Orthodoxy of Constantinople. In subsequent centuries, Latin and Greek clerics waged war against each other for the allegiance of the eastern European peoples along a frontier stretching from the Adriatic Sea to the Baltic Sea (see Map 14.2).

Freebooting nobles enthusiastically joined the Wendish Crusade and were the first to profit from its military successes. The lightly armed Wendish foot soldiers and cavalry were no match for the mounted Frankish knights, clad in heavy armor, and their superior siege weapons. Small groups of knights subjugated the Wendish peoples in piecemeal fashion, built stoutly fortified castles to control them, and recruited settlers from France

Bernard of Clairvaux's Summons to the Wendish Crusade

In March 1147, the Cistercian abbot Bernard of Clairvaux came to Frankfurt to promote what would become the Second Crusade. Few German knights expressed enthusiasm for a new crusade in the east, but they clamored to attack their pagan Slav and Balt neighbors in eastern Europe. Eager to capitalize on this fervor, Bernard secured the pope's permission to launch the part of the Second Crusade known as the Wendish Crusade. In this letter— addressed "to all Christians"—Bernard seeks to drum up recruits for the Wendish Crusade.

[Satan] has raised up evil seed, wicked pagan sons, whom, if I may say so, the might of Christendom has endured too long, shutting its eyes to those who with evil intent lie in wait, without crushing their poisoned heads under its heel. . . . Because the Lord has committed to our insignificance the preaching of this crusade, we make known to you that at a council of the king, bishops, and princes who had come together at Frankfurt, the might of Christians was armed against them, and that for the complete wiping out or, at any rate, the conversion of these peoples, they have put on the Cross, the sign of our salvation. And we by virtue of our authority promised them the same spiritual privileges as those enjoy who set out toward Jerusalem. Many

took the Cross on the spot, the rest we encouraged to do so, so that all Christians who have not yet taken the Cross for Jerusalem may know that they will obtain the same spiritual privileges by undertaking this expedition, if they do so according to the advice of the bishops and princes. We utterly forbid that for any reason whatsoever a truce should be made with these peoples, either for the sake of money or for the sake of tribute, until such a time as, by God's help, they shall be either converted or erased. . . . The uniform of this army, in clothes, in arms, and in all else, will be the same as the uniform of the other, for it is fortified with the same privileges.

Source: Bernard of Clairvaux, *Letters,* trans. Bruno Scott James (London: Burns, Oates, 1953), 466–468.

EXAMINING THE EVIDENCE

1. In Bernard's view, who is the real enemy of the Christian faithful?

2. How and why does Bernard link the Wendish Crusade to the original crusading goal of capturing Jerusalem?

Colonization and Conversion in Eastern Europe

and the Low Countries to clear the forests for cultivation. The colonists were accompanied by missionaries, led by the Cistercians, seeking to "civilize" the Slavs by converting them to Latin Christianity. Thus, from the start the goal of the Frankish conquerors was to remake the east in the image of Latin Christendom.

Many Slavic princes opted to embrace Latin Christianity and to open their lands to settlement by immigrants from the west. Conversion not only preserved the political independence of native rulers but offered material rewards: willing settlers knowledgeable about advanced farming techniques, more reliable revenues from the land, and a retinue of Christian clerics determined to impose discipline on their subjects using the long arm of church law. For their part, Christian missionaries believed that the salvation of the pagan peoples required changing their work habits as well as ministering to their souls. A poem penned by a Cistercian monk in the early fourteenth century depicted Poland at the time his predecessors first arrived there as backward and poverty-stricken:

The land lacked cultivators and lay under wood
And the Polish people were poor and idle,
Using wooden ploughs without iron to furrow the sandy soil,
Knowing only how to use two cows or oxen to plough.
There was no city or town in the whole land,
Only rural markets, fallow fields, and a chapel near the castle.

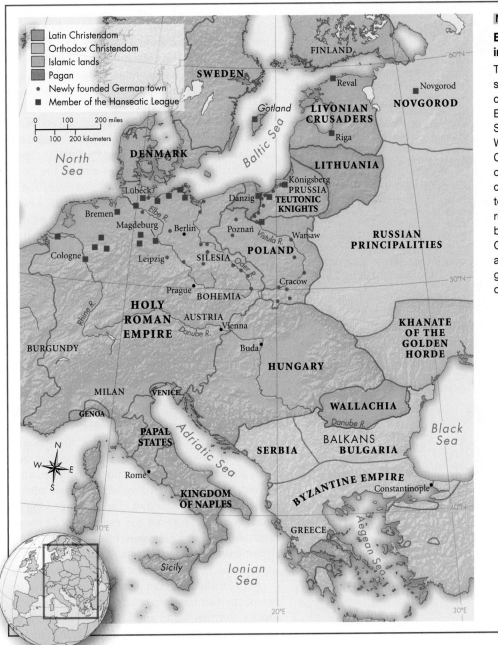

Expansion of Christianity in Eastern Europe, c. 1300

The Crusader movement spearheaded the expansion of Latin Christendom into Eastern Europe and the Baltic Sea region. In the wake of the Wendish Crusade of 1147, the Cistercians and other religious orders zealously pursued the conversion of pagan peoples to Latin Christianity. Local rulers encouraged settlement by immigrants from the German-speaking lands by allowing them to found self-governing towns under their own laws.

> Neither salt, nor iron, nor coinage, nor metal,
> Nor good clothes, nor even shoes
> Did that people have; they just grazed their flocks.
> These were the delights that the first monks found.[4]

Hence, remaking the east would require more than the religious conversion of its people. It would require the reordering of the region's society and economy. With this belief in mind, princes, bishops, and monks often took the lead in recruiting farmers and craftsmen from the west to settle newly opened territories in the east. To attract settlers, local lords usually exempted homesteaders from feudal obligations and the legal condition of serfdom. For example, a charter issued by the king of Hungary in 1247 to new settlers in a sparsely populated corner of his realm declared, "Let the men gathered there, of whatever

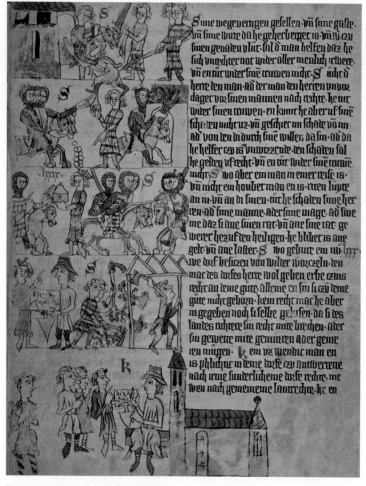

Peasants Receiving Land Title

New peasant settlers brought fresh labor and superior farming technology that transformed the landscape of eastern Europe. The legal and economic privileges granted to immigrants created conditions favorable for economic development. This illustration from the *Sachsenspiegel* (c. 1220), the first major law code written in German rather than Latin, shows homesteaders receiving titles of ownership to the lands they cleared for farming. (akg-images.)

status or language, live under one and the same liberty."[5] Perhaps as many as two hundred thousand immigrants, mostly from Germany and Flanders, had already settled east of the Elbe River by 1200.

Local princes, both conquerors and natives, also promoted the founding of cities. To attract merchants and artisans, princes granted city charters that guaranteed considerable political and economic autonomy. Lübeck, founded in 1159, dominated maritime trade in the Baltic Sea. By 1300, independent Christian trading colonies ringed the Baltic (see again Map 14.2). In 1358, a confederation of commercial cities formed the Hanseatic League discussed in Chapter 12. In addition to regulating trade among its more than one hundred members, the Hanseatic League provided a counterweight against rulers seeking to extort heavy customs duties from traders passing through their lands.

Throughout eastern Europe, cities and towns became oases of foreign colonists who differed sharply from the rural inhabitants in language and culture as well as wealth and status. For example, in 1257 a Polish duke reestablished Cracow, an ancient Polish fortress, as a center of international trade populated by German immigrants whom he recruited. The duke forbade Poles to reside in the town, which was governed by German municipal law.

This Germanization of eastern Europe provoked a backlash. In 1312, Cracow's German burghers backed a German contender for the crown of Poland, but they suffered violent reprisals when a native Pole, Wladyslaw Lokieteck, became king instead. Lokieteck ordered the execution of his enemies and expelled Germans from their mansions fronting the city's market square, turning the buildings over to Poles. Lokieteck also conducted a campaign to remove German priests and prohibited the use of the German language in municipal records. Once a German island amid a sea of Poles, Cracow now became a Polish city with a substantial German minority. It was precisely by embracing Christianity and making peace with the Roman pope and the new military order of the Teutonic Knights, however, that the Polish kings could establish themselves as independent monarchs within the expanding realm of Christendom.

Rise of National Monarchies

By 1350, Latin Christianity was firmly implanted in all parts of Europe except the Balkan peninsula. But the rise of strong national monarchies had thwarted the Roman popes' ambitions to create a unified Christendom under papal rule. The vigorous commercial expansion during this era discussed in Chapter 12 had swelled royal treasuries. Kings and princes increased their demands for tax revenue, extended the jurisdiction of royal courts, and convened assemblies (known as "parliaments") of leading nobles, clergy, and townsmen to rally support for their policies. Europe's patchwork of feudal domains and independent cities began to merge into unified national states, especially in England and France. The French philosopher Nicole Oresme (c. 1323–1382) expressed the spirit of his age when he rejected a "universal monarchy" as "neither just nor expedient."[6] Instead,

Oresme argued, practical necessity dictated that separate kingdoms, each with its own laws and customs, should exercise sovereign power over their own people.

Neither did the Muslims' success in repelling the Crusaders restore unity to the Islamic world. After enduring for sixty years, the Ayyubid dynasty founded by Saladin was overthrown in 1250 by Turkish slave soldiers. At that same time, the Islamic world faced a new challenge, the Mongol invasions, that would have a far more lasting impact on the development of Islamic societies than did the Crusades.

The Mongol World-Empire 1100–1368

The era of Mongol domination marked a watershed in world history. Although the Mongols drew on long-standing traditions of tribal confederation, warfare, and tribute extraction, the Mongol Empire was unprecedented in its scope and influence. Historians give much of the credit for the Mongols' swift military triumphs and political cohesion to the charismatic authority of the empire-builder Chinggis Khan. Later generations of Mongol rulers built upon Chinggis's legacy, seeking to adapt steppe traditions of rulership to the complex demands of governing agrarian societies.

FOCUS

How did the organization of Mongol society and government change from the time of Chinggis Khan to that of his grandson Qubilai, the ruler of China?

Despite the brutality and violence of the Mongol conquests, the Mongol Empire fostered far-reaching economic and cultural exchanges. The Mongols encouraged the free movement of merchants throughout their domains and embraced religious and intellectual diversity. Wherever they went the Mongols sought to impose their own political, social, and military institutions, but the Mongol conquerors of Iran and central Asia adopted the Islamic religion of their subjects. The Mongol courts also became flourishing centers of artistic, literary, and religious patronage. The Mongols transformed the world—and were themselves transformed by the peoples they subjugated.

Rise of the Mongols

In the several centuries before the rise of the Mongols, the dynamics of state formation in the Eurasian steppe underwent dramatic transformation. The Turkish and Uighur confederations had depended on control of the lucrative Silk Road trade routes and extraction of tribute from the settled empires of China and Iran (see Chapter 10). In the aftermath of the Tang dynasty in 907, the Khitans (kee-THANS) of eastern Mongolia annexed Chinese territories around modern Beijing and established a Chinese-style dynasty, Liao (lee-OW) (937–1125). The new dynasty was a hybrid state that incorporated elements of Chinese bureaucratic governance, including the taxation of settled farmers, while retaining the militarized tribal social structure and nomadic lifestyle of the steppe.

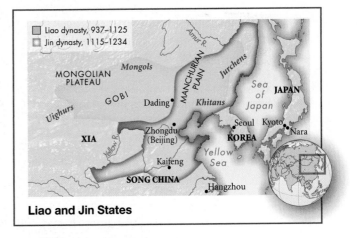

Liao and Jin States

In the 1120s the Jurchens, a seminomadic group from northern Manchuria, overran the Liao and the rest of northern China and founded their own state of Jin (1115–1234). The Jin state largely retained the dual administrative structure of the Liao. But in contrast to the Liao, the Jin conquerors were dwarfed by the enormous Chinese population under their rule. The Jin rulers struggled to preserve their cultural identity in the face of overwhelming pressures to assimilate to Chinese ways.

Temujin (teh-MU-jihn) (c. 1167–1227), the future Chinggis Khan, was born into one of the numerous tribes living in eastern Mongolia, on the margins of the Jin realm. Tribal affiliations were unstable, however, and at that time the "Mongol people" was not a clearly

Steppe Society

Mongol Women in the Household Economy and Public Life

The prominent roles of women in the social and economic life of the pastoral nomads of the Eurasian steppe contrasted starkly with women's reclusive place in most settled agrarian and urban societies. Under Chinggis Khan's permanently militarized society, nearly all adult men had to embark on lengthy campaigns of conquest far from home. The women left behind were compelled to shoulder even the most arduous tasks. Kinship and gender relations among the pastoral nomads also differed in many ways from the practices of settled societies. Mongol women remained subservient to their husbands, but royal and noble women participated vigorously in public life and political affairs.

European travelers to the Mongol domains expressed surprise at women's key roles in the pastoral economy. John of Plano Carpini, a papal envoy dispatched to the Mongol court in 1245, claimed that productive labor fell entirely to the Mongol women:

> The men do not make anything at all, with the exception of arrows, and they sometimes tend the flocks, but they hunt and practice archery. . . . Their women make everything, including leather garments, tunics, shoes, and everything made of leather. They also drive the carts and repair them. They load the camels, and in all tasks they are very swift and energetic. All the women wear breeches, and some of them shoot like the men.[1]

Marco Polo agreed that Mongol women "do all the work that is needed for their lords and family and themselves" while the men "trouble themselves with nothing at all but with hunting and with feats of battle and of war and with hawking [falconry]."[2]

Despite women's vital contributions to the family's economic welfare, however, Mongol society was based on a patrilineal system of inheritance in which men controlled property and wealth. Mongol women had no property of their own. Women who lacked the protection of a husband often found themselves abandoned and destitute. Such was

Mongol Empress Chabi

Mongol leaders often had multiple wives, each of whom took charge of her own household. Chabi, the second of Qubilai's four wives, became one of the most powerful figures at the Mongol court after Qubilai's election as Great Khan. Her ambition to become empress of China rather than merely the wife of a tribal chieftain was a driving force behind Qubilai's conquest of the Southern Song. (National Palace Museum, Taiwan, Republic of China.)

defined group. Family and clan were the basic units of Central Asian nomadic societies. Tribal allegiances grew out of political expediency, providing the means for mobilizing isolated groups for common purposes ranging from herding and migration to trade and war.

The pastoral livelihood of the steppe nomads was vulnerable to catastrophic disruptions, such as prolonged drought, severe winters, and animal diseases. Scarcity of resources often provoked violent conflict among neighboring tribes. Raiding to steal livestock, women, slaves, and grazing lands was common. The constant violence of the steppe produced permanently militarized societies. For most of the male population, warfare became a regular profession, and women took charge of tending herds and other activities usually reserved for men in the premodern world (see Lives and Livelihoods: Mongol Women in the Household Economy and Public Life).

the fate that befell Chinggis's mother, Hoelun, whose husband was murdered when Chinggis was nine years old. Deserted by her husband's kinfolk, Hoelun doggedly raised her sons on her own, at times forced to forage for roots and berries to survive.

Nonetheless, royal Mongol women were outspoken figures whose voices carried much weight in court deliberations. When Ogodei died in 1241, his widow ruled over the Mongol confederation for five years before ceding power to one of her sons. Qubilai's mother, Sorqaqtani-Beki, likewise played a decisive role in the history of the Mongol Empire. The pastoral nomads of the Eurasian steppe commonly protected widows by remarrying them to younger male relatives of their deceased husbands, and when Sorqaqtani-Beki's husband, Tolui, died in 1232, Ogodei offered to marry her to one of his sons. She firmly declined Ogodei's proposal and instead demanded a fiefdom to provide for her upkeep. Ogodei reluctantly granted her a fief of eighty thousand households in northern China, which Sorqaqtani-Beki insisted on governing herself. In keeping with the policies of Ogodei's minister Yelu Chucai, Sorqaqtani-Beki instituted a Chinese-style civil administration and engaged Chinese scholars to tutor her sons. Qubilai's upbringing thus turned his attention, and the direction of the Mongol Empire, away from the Mongols' steppe homeland and toward China.

Sorqaqtani-Beki proved to be a shrewd politician who earned wide admiration among Mongols and foreigners alike. She had converted to Nestorian Christianity, but promoted toleration of all of the major faiths of the subject peoples. The Ilkhan historian Rashid al-Din, a Muslim, wrote that "in the care and supervision of her sons and in the management of their affairs and those of the army and the people, Sorqaqtani-Beki laid a foundation that would have been beyond the capability of any crowned head."[3]

In 1251, her popularity and political agility paid off when she succeeded in elevating her son Mongke to the position of Great Khan, displacing the lineage of Ogodei. Sorqaqtani-Beki died the following year, but the supreme authority of the Great Khans remained with her sons, including Qubilai, the future emperor of China.

---

1. Christopher Dawson, ed., Mission to Asia: Narratives and Letters of the Franciscan Missionaries of Mongolia and China in the Thirteenth and Fourteenth Centuries (New York: Harper & Row, 1966), 18.
2. Marco Polo: The Description of the World, eds. A. C. Moule and Paul Pelliot (London: George Rutledge & Sons, 1938), 1:169.
3. Rashiduddin Fazullah's Jami'u't-tawarikh (Compendium of Chronicles): A History of the Mongols, trans. W. M. Thackston (Cambridge, MA: Harvard University, Department of Near Eastern Languages and Civilizations, 1999), Part II, 400–401.

QUESTIONS TO CONSIDER

1. How did the division of household work in pastoral societies such as the Mongols differ from that found among settled farming peoples?

2. How might the role of women in the Mongol household economy explain the power they wielded in tribal affairs?

For Further Information:
Lane, George. Daily Life in the Mongol Empire. Westwood, CT: Greenwood Press, 2006.
Rossabi, Morris. Khubilai Khan: His Life and Times. Berkeley: University of California Press, 1988.

The instability of steppe life worked against social stability, but it also created opportunities for new leadership. Personal charisma, political skills, and prowess in war counted far more than hereditary rights in determining chieftainship. We see this fluidity of Mongol society reflected in Temujin's rise to power. Orphaned at age nine and abandoned by his father's tribe, Temujin gained a following through his valor and success as a warrior. Building on this reputation, he proved extraordinarily adept at constructing alliances among chiefs and transforming tribal coalitions into disciplined military units. By 1206 Temujin had forged a confederation that unified most of the tribes of Mongolia, which recognized him as Chinggis (meaning "oceanic"), the **Great Khan**, the universal ruler of the steppe peoples.

Chinggis Khan

Great Khan "Lord of the steppe"; the Great Khan of the Mongols was chosen by a council of Mongol chiefs.

Creation and Division of the Mongol Empire 1206–1259

Maintaining unity among the fractious coalition of tribal leaders required a steady stream of booty in the form of gold, silk, slaves, and horses. Thus, once installed as Great Khan, Chinggis led his army in campaigns of plunder and conquest. Initially he set his eye on the riches of China and aimed at conquering the Jin kingdom. But in 1218, Chinggis's attention turned toward the west after the Turkish shah of Khwarazam (in Transoxiana) massacred a caravan of Muslim merchants traveling under the Mongol khan's protection. Enraged, Chinggis laid waste to Samarkand, the shah's capital, and other cities in Transoxiana and eastern Iran in what was perhaps the most violent of the Mongol campaigns. After deposing the Khwarazam shah, Chinggis returned to the east and renewed his campaign to conquer China.

By the time of Chinggis's death in 1227, Mongol conquests stretched from eastern Iran to Manchuria. Up to this point, the impact of the Mongol invasions had been almost wholly catastrophic. Solely interested in plunder, Chinggis had shown little taste for the daunting task of ruling the peoples he vanquished (see Map 14.3).

Chinggis's Successors

Throughout Central Asian history the death of a khan almost always provoked a violent succession crisis. But Chinggis's charisma sufficed to ensure an orderly transition of power. Before he died, Chinggis parceled out the Mongol territories among his four sons or their descendants, and he designated his third son Ogodei to succeed him as Great Khan.

The Mongol state under Chinggis Khan was a throwback to the Turkish-Uighur practice of allowing conquered peoples to maintain their own autonomy in exchange for tribute. Ogodei, in contrast, began to adopt features of the Liao-Jin system of dual administration under the direction of the Khitan statesman Yelu Chucai, whom we met at the start of this chapter. Creating an enduring imperial system required displacing tribal chiefs with more centralized political and military control. Thus Ogodei also established a permanent capital for the Mongol Empire at Qaraqorum.

Formation of Independent Mongol Khanates

Under Ogodei's leadership the Mongols steadily expanded their dominions westward into Russia, and they completed the conquest of the Jin. Mongol armies had invaded Hungary and Poland and were threatening to press deeper into Europe when Ogodei's death in 1241 halted their advance. After Ogodei's nephew Mongke was elected Great Khan in 1252, he radically altered Chinggis's original allocation of Mongol territories, assigning the richest lands, China and Iran, to his brothers Qubilai and Hulegu. Mongke's dispensation outraged the other descendants of Chinggis. By the end of his reign, the Mongol realm had broken into four independent and often hostile khanates (see again Map 14.3).

Qubilai Khan and the Yuan Empire in China 1260–1368

Conquest of China

The death of Mongke in 1259 sparked another succession crisis. After four years of bitter struggle Mongke's brother Qubilai secured his claim as Great Khan. Qubilai devoted his energies to completing the conquest of China. In 1271 he adopted the Chinese-style dynastic name Yuan and moved the Great Khan's capital from Mongolia to China, where he built a massive city, Dadu, at the former capital of Zhongdu (modern Beijing). Five years later, Mongol armies captured the Southern Song capital of Hangzhou, and by 1279 Chinese resistance to Mongol rule had ceased. The Yuan Empire (1271–1368) would last only about one hundred years, but for the first time all of China had fallen under foreign rule.

Qubilai was not content with the conquest of China. In 1281, he mustered a great armada, carrying forty-five thousand Mongol soldiers and their horses, for an invasion of Japan. Most of the Mongol fleet was destroyed by a typhoon, which the Japanese gratefully saluted as the *kamikaze*, the "divine wind" that defended them from the Mongol onslaught. The would-be invaders abandoned their effort to take over Japan. Qubilai's army captured the central plains of Burma in 1277, but attempts to conquer Vietnam and naval invasions of Java and Sumatra failed. After 1285, when one of his favorite sons died fighting in Vietnam, Qubilai halted his campaigns of conquest.

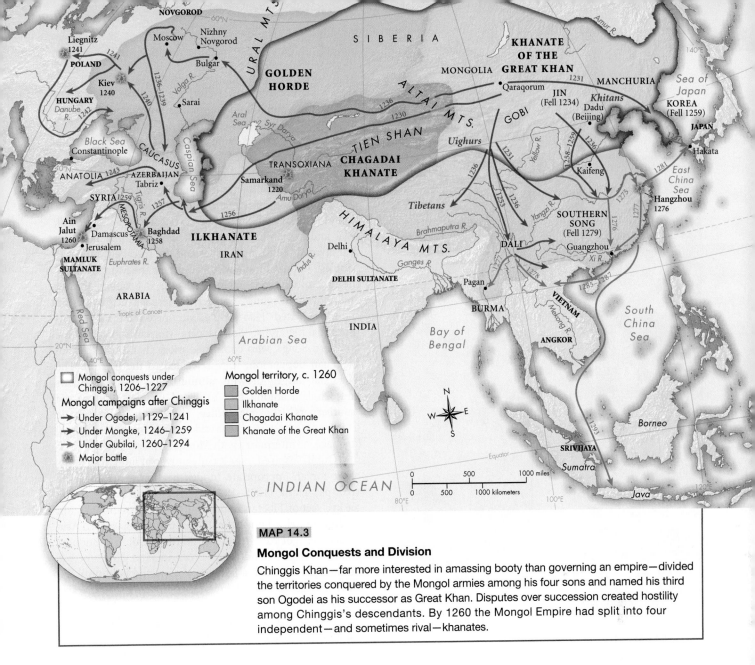

MAP 14.3

Mongol Conquests and Division

Chinggis Khan—far more interested in amassing booty than governing an empire—divided the territories conquered by the Mongol armies among his four sons and named his third son Ogodei as his successor as Great Khan. Disputes over succession created hostility among Chinggis's descendants. By 1260 the Mongol Empire had split into four independent—and sometimes rival—khanates.

Qubilai envisioned himself not merely as first among the Mongol princes but also as an exalted "Son of Heaven" in the style of the Chinese emperors. He surrounded himself with foreign advisers, including Muslims, Uighurs, and Chinese, and laid the foundations for permanent Mongol rule over China. Building on the precedents of the Liao and Jin states, Qubilai created a highly centralized administration designed to extract the maximum revenue from China's land, people, and commerce. The Venetian merchant Marco Polo (1254–1324), astonished at the splendor of the Great Khan's capital, proclaimed that Qubilai was "the most powerful man in people and in lands and in treasure that ever was in the world or that now is from the time of Adam our first father till this moment."[7]

Although Qubilai was a conscientious and diligent ruler, his successors gave little attention to the tasks of maintaining the infrastructure of the agrarian economy or protecting people's welfare. Instead, they relied on a system of **tax farming** that delegated tax collection privileges to private intermediaries, mostly Muslim merchants. Many of these tax farmers abused their authority and demanded exorbitant payments from an increasingly disgruntled agrarian population.

Qubilai as Chinese Emperor

tax farming The assignment of tax collection powers to private individuals or groups in exchange for fixed payments to the state.

Religious Tolerance

Mongol Passport

The Mongols established a comprehensive network of post stations to maintain communications with their far-flung armies. Only those with proper authorization, in the form of metal or wooden paiza tablets, were allowed use of the lodgings, supplies, and horses provided at these post stations. The Mongolian inscription on this silver paiza reads, "By the power of the Eternal Heaven, may the name of Mongke Khan be sacred. He who does not honor it shall perish and die." (© The State Hermitage Museum/photo by Vladimir Terebenin, Leonard Kheifets, Yuri Molodkovets.)

At the same time, however, the Mongols strongly encouraged commerce, and international trade flourished. The Mongols created a vast network of post stations and issued passports to merchants to ensure safe passage throughout the Mongol realm. The chief beneficiaries of expanding trans-Eurasian trade were the Uighur and Muslim merchants who acted as commercial agents for their Mongol patrons.

The Yuan Empire maintained the Central Asian tradition of a social structure based on tribal loyalties. Political, legal, and economic privileges rested on an ethnic hierarchy that favored the Mongol tribes and the so-called "affiliated peoples"—non-Chinese who had served the Mongols since the time of Chinggis, including Turks, Tibetans, Persians, and above all Uighurs. Former Chinese subjects of the Jin state, designated "Han people," occupied the third rung of this social hierarchy. "Southerners" (former subjects of the Southern Song), who composed more than 80 percent of the Yuan population, were relegated to the bottom. The Yuan state largely drew its administrators from merchants and scholars among the "affiliated peoples" and barred "southerners" from high office. The Mongols also forbade Chinese to possess firearms, ride horses, learn the Mongol language, or intermarry with Mongols.

Qubilai aspired to be a truly universal monarch. In his quest for an appropriate model, he turned to Phags-pa (pak-pa) Lama (1235–1280), the spiritual leader of the Saskya sect of Tibetan Buddhism. As a transnational faith, Buddhism helped unite the diverse peoples of eastern Asia under Mongol rule. At the same time, Qubilai's support enabled Phags-pa and the Saskya Lamas to gain supreme authority over Tibet, a position they would hold until the rival lineage of Dalai Lamas displaced them in the sixteenth century.

Even as Qubilai declared Phags-pa the head of the Buddhist church, the Mongols accorded full tolerance to all religions. Muslim, Jewish, and Nestorian Christian communities flourished in China under Mongol rule. John of Montecorvino, a Franciscan missionary dispatched by the pope, arrived at the Yuan capital in 1294. John erected a church near the khan's palace, translated the New Testament into Chinese and Uighur, and by his own estimate attracted six thousand converts—mostly non-Chinese—to Christianity. Pleased with John's reports of the progress of his missionary work, in 1308 the pope consecrated him as the first Latin bishop of Beijing.

Under Qubilai's leadership the Mongol Empire in China departed from the practices of the early steppe empires, which relied on plunder and extraction of tribute from settled societies. Instead the Yuan state, like its Liao and Jin predecessors, developed institutions for imposing direct rule on its Chinese subjects, even if it did not penetrate local society to the extent that native Chinese empires had. At the same time, the Mongols in China turned their backs on their steppe homeland. By 1300 the Yuan emperors were raised exclusively within the confines of the capital at Dadu and had largely severed their connections with the independent Mongol khanates in central and western Asia.

The Mongol Khanates and the Islamic World 1240–1350

In 1253 the Great Khan Mongke assigned his brother Hulegu (HE-luh-gee) responsibility for completing the Mongol conquest of Iran and Mesopotamia. In 1258 Baghdad fell to Hulegu's army, and the last Abbasid caliph was reportedly wrapped in a carpet and trampled to death, to avoid spilling royal blood on the ground. In their hunger for booty, the Mongol victors utterly destroyed the city of Baghdad, the official capital of Islam. By Hulegu's own estimate, two hundred thousand people perished. Survivors of the Mongol conquest fled to Cairo, where the Mamluk (MAM-luke) sultanate, a regime of military slave origins, had overthrown the dynasty of Saladin and was consolidating its power over Egypt and Syria. The Mamluks became the new political leaders of the Islamic world, rallying their fellow Muslims to the cause of holy war against the Mongol onslaught.

The conquest of Baghdad was the last great campaign conducted jointly by the Mongol princes. As we have seen, by the time of Qubilai's succession in 1263 as Great Khan, rivalry among Chinggis's heirs had fractured the Mongol Empire into four independent khanates: the Golden Horde along the frontiers of Russia; the Chagadai (shah-gah-TY) khanate in Central Asia; the Ilkhanate based in Iran; and the khanate of the Great Khan in China (see again Map 14.3).

FOCUS

In what respects did the Turkish Islamic states of the Mamluks and Ottomans pursue policies similar to those of the Mongol regimes in Iran and Russia?

Mongol Rule in Iran and Mesopotamia

After conquering Iran and Mesopotamia, Hulegu's army suffered a decisive defeat at the hands of the Mamluks in Palestine in 1260 and withdrew. At around this time Hulegu adopted the Turkish title of *Ilkhan* ("subordinate khan"), implying submission to his brother Qubilai, the Great Khan. Hulegu and his successors as Ilkhan (il-con) also made diplomatic overtures to the Christian monarchs of Europe with the goal of forming an alliance against their common enemy, the Mamluks. In 1287 the Ilkhanate sent Rabban Sauma, a Nestorian Christian monk from China, as an envoy to the courts of England, France, and the Roman pope to enlist their aid against the Mamluks, to no avail.

The Ilkhans ruled over their domains from a series of seasonal capitals in Azerbaijan, a region in the northwestern corner of Iran where good pastureland was plentiful. Unlike Qubilai in China, the Ilkhans did not build a fixed, monumental capital in the style of their subjects. Instead they followed the nomadic practice of moving their camps in rhythm with the seasonal migrations of their herds. The Mongol conquests of Iran and Mesopotamia had caused immense environmental and economic harm. Abandonment of farmlands and the deterioration of irrigation systems

Mongol Siege of Baghdad

The Mongol conquest of Baghdad in 1258 ended the caliphate, the main political institution of the Islamic world since the death of Muhammad. In this illustration of the siege of Baghdad, a group of Mongols at lower right beat a flat drum; the archers and soldiers are all in Persian dress. At upper left the last Abbasid caliph makes a futile attempt to escape by boat. (Bildarchiv Preussischer Kulturbesitz/ Art Resource.)

sharply curtailed agricultural production. Much land was turned over to pasture or reverted to desert.

As in China, Mongols composed a tiny minority of the Ilkhanate's population. Even in the Ilkhan armies, Turks far outnumbered Mongols. Like the Yuan state, the Ilkhanate initially recruited its administrative personnel from foreigners and members of minority groups. Christian communities, notably the Nestorians and Armenians, had been quick to side with the Mongol invaders against their Muslim overlords. Christians hoped that their connections to the Ilkhan court—Hulegu's queen was a Christian, and a number of Christians rose to high positions in the Ilkhanate government—might win official endorsement of their religion. Instead, the Mongols in Iran increasingly turned toward the faith of the Muslim majority. The proselytizing efforts of Sufi sheikhs attracted many converts, especially among the Mongol and Turkish horsemen who were the backbone of the Ilkhanate's military strength. Muslim advisers became influential in the ruling circles of the Ilkhanate as well.

By the late thirteenth century, escalating religious tensions and the familiar pattern of violent succession disputes among the Mongol leaders threatened to tear apart the Ilkhan state. The ascension of Ghazan (haz-ZAHN) (r. 1295–1304) as Ilkhan revived the Ilkhanate and marked a decisive turning point in Mongol rule in Iran.

Ghazan's Reforms   A convert to Islam, Ghazan took pains to show his devotion to the faith of the great majority of his subjects. Ghazan reduced Christians and Jews to subordinate status and banished Buddhist monks from the Ilkhan realm. He also placed the Ilkhanate government on sounder footing by reforming the fiscal system, investing greater resources in agriculture, instituting a new currency system, and reducing taxes. Ghazan broke with the practice of seasonal migration and constructed a permanent capital at Tabriz appointed with palaces, mosques, Sufi lodges, a grand mausoleum for himself, and baths and caravanserais to accommodate traveling merchants. Tabriz quickly developed into a major center of international trade and artistic production.

Rashid al-Din (ra-SHEED al-DEEN) (1247–1318), a Jewish doctor who converted to Islam, served as chief minister and architect of Ghazan's program of reform. Rashid al-Din also carefully embellished Ghazan's image as ruler, forging a new ideology of sovereignty that portrayed Ghazan as a devout Muslim, a Persian philosopher-king, and a second Alexander the Great. Ghazan ceased to refer to himself as Ilkhan, a title that implied subordination to the rulers of Yuan China, and adopted the Turkish and Persian royal titles sultan and *shah*. Under Rashid al-Din's direction, court scholars compiled the *Compendium of Chronicles*, a history of the world that glorified the Mongol rulers as rightful heirs to the legacies of the Persian kings and the Abbasid caliphate.

Patronage of Arts and Letters   The Ilkhans became great patrons of arts and letters. Rashid al-Din boasted that "in these days when, thank God, all corners of the earth are under our rule and that of Chinggis Khan's illustrious family, philosophers, astronomers, scholars, and historians of all religions and nations—Cathay and Machin (North and South China), India and Kashmir, Tibetans, Uighurs, and other nations of Turks, Arabs, and Franks—are gathered in droves at our glorious court."[8] Manuscript painting, luxury silks, architectural decoration, metalworking, and ceramics all reflected the impact of new aesthetic ideas and motifs, with Chinese influences especially prominent. Prolific production of luxury editions of the Qur'an and lavish decoration of mosques, shrines, and tombs also attest to the vitality of the religious art promoted by the Muslim Ilkhans.

Under Rashid al-Din's stewardship, the ideological basis of the Ilkhanate shifted away from descent from Chinggis Khan and toward the role of royal protector of the Islamic faith. Nonetheless, diplomatic ties and cultural and economic exchanges with China became even closer. In the early fourteenth century, a renewal of cordial relations among the leaders of the four Mongol khanates eased the passage of caravans and travelers across the Silk Road. Conversion to Islam did not alienate their fellow Mongols, but neither did it repair the breach with the Mamluk regime.

Sultan, Poet, and Courtiers
The Mongol elite of the Ilkhanate quickly became ardent patrons of Islam after Ghazan's conversion in 1295. In addition to building religious monuments and establishing charitable foundations, Mongol leaders commissioned numerous lavishly illustrated manuscripts attesting to their Muslim faith. In this illustration from a poetry anthology copied in 1315, a poet holding a scroll recites poetry before a seated Mongol ruler surrounded by his courtiers. (©2011 The British Library I.O. Islamic 132.)

End of the Ilkhanate

Ghazan's reforms failed to ensure the long-term stability of the Ilkhanate regime, however. Ghazan's attempt to recast the Ilkhanate as a monarchy in the tradition of the Islamic caliphate ran into strong opposition among Mongol leaders accustomed to tribal independence and shared sovereignty. The reign of Ghazan's nephew Abu Said (r. 1316–1335) was wracked by factional conflicts that sapped the Ilkhan leadership and cost Rashid al-Din his life. After Abu Said died without an heir in 1335, the Ilkhanate's authority steadily disintegrated. In 1353 members of a messianic Shi'a sect murdered the last Ilkhan.

The Golden Horde and the Rise of Muscovy

Founding of the Golden Horde

The Golden Horde in Central Asia and Russia proved more durable than the Ilkhanate. In 1237 a Mongol army led by Chinggis's grandson Batu conquered the Volga River Valley and sacked the main cities of the Bulgars and the Rus princes, including the fortified outpost of Moscow. In 1240 Kiev succumbed to a Mongol siege, and the Mongol armies quickly pushed westward into Poland and Hungary, prompting the Roman pope to declare a crusade against this new menace. But feuding among the Mongol princes after the death of Ogodei in 1241 halted the Mongol advance into Europe. Instead, Batu created an independent Mongol realm known as the **Golden Horde**, with its capital at Sarai in the lower Volga River Valley (see again Map 14.3).

Batu's successor, Berke (r. 1257–1267), was the first of the Mongol khans to convert to Islam. A fierce rivalry erupted between Berke and the Ilkhan Hulegu for control over the Caucasus region. Berke allied with the Mamluks against the Ilkhanate and opposed the election of Hulegu's brother Qubilai as Great Khan. Political and commercial competition with the Ilkhanate also prompted the khans of the Golden Horde to seek close ties with Genoese merchant colonies around the shores of the Black Sea and with the Byzantine emperors.

Indirect Rule in Russia

In the Rus lands, as in Iran, the Mongols instituted a form of indirect governance that relied on local rulers as intermediaries. The Mongols required that the Rus princes conduct censuses, raise taxes to support the Mongol army, maintain post stations, and personally appear at the khan's court at Sarai to offer tribute. The Golden Horde and the Ilkhanate both adopted the Persian-Turkish institution of *iqta*, land grants awarded to military officers to feed and supply the soldiers under their command. The administrative structure of the Golden Horde and its system of military estates were subsequently adopted by the expanding Muscovy state in the fifteenth century.

Rus's Commercial Growth and Religious Independence

As elsewhere in the Mongol realms, the khans of the Golden Horde strongly encouraged commerce, and their favorable policies toward merchants increased the volume of trade passing through Rus lands. The Rus princes and the Christian church benefited enormously from the profits of commerce. Moscow flourished as the capital of the fur trade. As a result of this commercial prosperity, the first Grand Prince of Muscovy, Ivan I (r. 1328–1340), nicknamed "Moneybags" by his subjects, was able to build the stone churches that became the heart of the Kremlin, the seat of future Russian governments. New commercial towns were founded, most importantly Nizhny Novgorod (1358), populated by German and Scandinavian merchants from the Baltic region. The wealth accumulated by the Orthodox Christian clerics and the protection they enjoyed under the traditional Mongol respect for religious institutions strengthened the church's position in Rus society and fostered greater independence from the Byzantine patriarch.

The Golden Horde and the Mongol Heritage

Despite its commercial expansion, Rus was marginal to the khanate, which focused its attention instead on controlling the steppe pasturelands and trade routes. In contrast to the Yuan dynasty and the Ilkhanate, the Golden Horde retained its connections to the steppe and the culture of pastoral nomadism. Nor did conversion to Islam bring about substantial changes in the Golden Horde culture comparable to those that occurred in the Ilkhanate. Berke's conversion to Islam arose from personal conviction and was not accompanied by a mandate to adopt the new faith. Not until the 1310s did the Golden Horde adopt Islam as its official religion. Although conversion to Islam pulled the Mongols of the Golden Horde more firmly into the cultural world of their Turkish subjects (and away from that of Christian Rus), it did not lead them to abandon their pastoral way of life.

Retrenchment in the Islamic World: The Mamluk and Ottoman States

The fall and destruction of Baghdad in 1258 delivered a devastating blow to the Islamic world—even greater than the shock that reverberated across Latin Christendom when Jerusalem fell to Saladin in 1187. The sack of Baghdad and the execution of the Abbasid caliph left the Islamic confederacy leaderless and disorganized. Out of this political crisis emerged two new dynastic regimes, the Mamluks in Egypt and the Ottomans in Anatolia (modern Turkey). Together, these two dynasties restored order to the Islamic lands of the eastern Mediterranean and halted further Mongol advances (see Map 14.4). Both the Mamluks and the Ottomans were warrior states, but they owed their political longevity to their ability to adapt to the requirements of governing large settled populations. The Mamluk Sultanate ruled from 1250 to 1517, nearly three times as long as the Yuan dynasty. The Ottoman Empire would prove to be one of the most enduring in world history, stretching from its origins in the late thirteenth century to final eclipse in 1923, following World War I.

Rise of the Mamluk Sultanate

In 1250 the Mamluks, a regiment of Turkish slave soldiers, overthrew the Ayyubid dynasty in Egypt and chose one of their officers as sultan. The Mamluk regime gained enormous stature among Muslims when it repelled the Mongol incursions into Syria in 1260. Its prestige was further burnished after it expelled the last of the Crusader states from Palestine in 1291.

The Mamluk elite consisted solely of foreigners, predominantly Turks, who had been purchased as slaves and raised in Egypt for service in the Mamluk army or administrative corps. Sons of Mamluk soldiers were excluded from government and military service, which therefore had to be replenished in each generation by fresh slave imports from the steppe. The Mamluk soldiers and administrators were bound to the state by personal allegiance to their officers and the sultan. Except from 1299 to 1382, when a form of hereditary succession prevailed, the sultans were chosen by the officer corps.

The Mamluk regime devoted itself to promoting the Islamic faith and strengthening state wealth and power. Although barred from the overland caravan trade by the Ilkhans, Mamluk Egypt sat astride the maritime routes connecting the Mediterranean to the Indian Ocean. Revenues from the burgeoning commerce with Asia, driven especially by Europeans' growing appetite for spices such as pepper and ginger, swelled the coffers of the Mamluk treasury. To offset the Ilkhanate's partnership with Byzantium and the Genoese merchants, the Mamluk regime cultivated close commercial and political ties with Venice—evidence that the Mamluks, like the Ilkhans, were willing to set aside intense religious differences with their Christian allies to further their own political and commercial interests.

Relations with the Ilkhanate thawed, however, after Ghazan's conversion to Islam. In 1322 the Mamluks concluded a commercial treaty with the Ilkhans that ensured free movement of slave caravans from the Black Sea through Ilkhan territories to Egypt. Although the Ilkhan regime would unravel during the next several decades, the Mamluk state now enjoyed peace and prosperity.

Despite the stability of the Mamluk regime, membership in the ruling class was insecure. Not only were sons of the slave-soldiers excluded from military and government service, but family fortunes were often vulnerable to confiscation amid the factional conflicts that beset the Mamluk court. Sultans and other affluent notables sought to

Stability Under Mamluk Rule

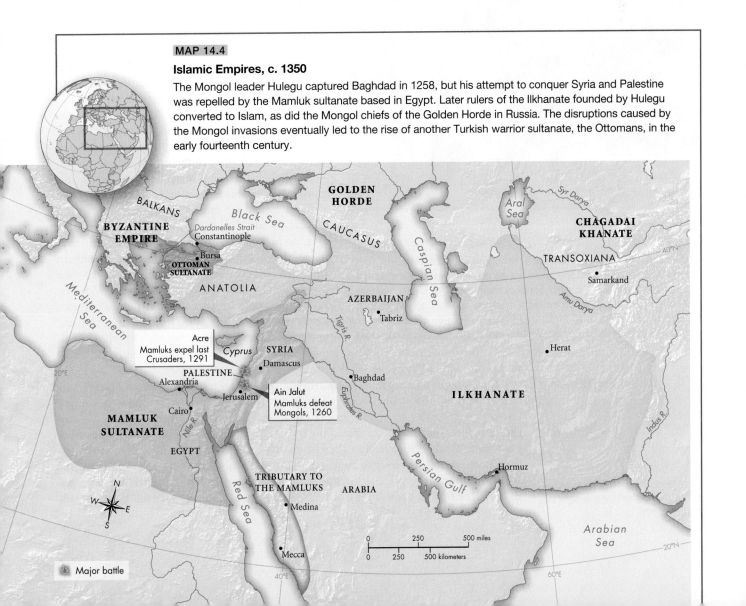

MAP 14.4

Islamic Empires, c. 1350

The Mongol leader Hulegu captured Baghdad in 1258, but his attempt to conquer Syria and Palestine was repelled by the Mamluk sultanate based in Egypt. Later rulers of the Ilkhanate founded by Hulegu converted to Islam, as did the Mongol chiefs of the Golden Horde in Russia. The disruptions caused by the Mongol invasions eventually led to the rise of another Turkish warrior sultanate, the Ottomans, in the early fourteenth century.

Qala'un Complex in Cairo

Since the Mamluk leaders could not pass on their status and privileges to their sons, they turned to creating monuments and charitable foundations—whose property could not be confiscated by the state—that remained under the control of family members. The Mamluk sultan Qala'un (r. 1280–1290) incorporated a madrasa and a hospital into the ornate mausoleum he built for himself (center). A similar complex built by Qala'un's son stands in the right foreground. (akg-images/Gerard Degeorge.)

preserve control of their wealth by establishing charitable trusts that were exempt from such seizures. The founding patrons often used the resources of these trusts to build large ceremonial complexes that housed a variety of religious and charitable institutions, including mosques, madrasas, elementary schools, hospitals, and Sufi hospices, as well as their own tombs.

Another Islamic warrior state, one that would ultimately contest the Mamluks' leadership within the Islamic world, emerged in Anatolia. The Ottomans traced their origins to Osman (d. 1324), who arose as the leader of an expanding confederation of nomadic warriors in the late thirteenth century. In Osman's day, Anatolia was the frontier between the Byzantine Empire and the Ilkhanate (see again Map 14.4). There, tribes of Muslim herders competed with Christian farmers and pagan nomads for lands and followers. Like other nomadic confederations, the Ottoman alliance was based on political expediency rather than permanent ethnic allegiances, and Osman's first invasions targeted neighboring Turks. Then, in 1302, after bad weather decimated their herds, Osman's warriors turned against the Byzantine towns of Anatolia. Osman's victories over the Byzantines prompted the surrender of much of the population of western Anatolia, Christians and Muslims alike. Osman's son and successor Orkhan (r. 1324–1362) led the Ottoman army in conquests of the major cities of Anatolia and made Bursa, a prosperous center of silk manufacture, his capital in 1331.

Although the tribal society of the Turkish nomads was a flexible institution in which loyalty and service counted far more than lineage and faith, it was poorly suited to the needs of governing a large agrarian population. Osman granted pasturelands to his followers, but he also cultivated the support of Christian farmers and town folk and protected their property rights. The stable revenue base provided by agriculture could support a greater number of warriors than the booty obtained from raiding. Thus the Ottoman rulers sought to restore the wheat fields and olive orchards that had flourished in the fertile valleys of Anatolia before the Seljuk invasions in the eleventh century.

Rise of the Ottomans

Early on Orkhan began to transform himself from a tribal chief into a Muslim sultan at the head of a strongly centralized state. The rapid growth of Ottoman military power was propelled by the incorporation into the army's ranks of bands of Muslim holy warriors—**gazi**, who combined the qualities of frontier bandits and religious zealots. Under Orkhan's leadership the Ottoman army also underwent a metamorphosis from horse-riding archers into large infantry units capable of sophisticated siege tactics. In 1354, Ottoman forces crossed the Dardanelles to seize Byzantine territories in the Balkans, the first step toward the conquest of Constantinople and the fall of the Byzantine Empire in 1453.

gazi "Holy warriors"; in Islam, fighters who declare war against nonbelievers.

COUNTERPOINT
The "New Knighthood" of the Christian Military Orders

Following the success of the First Crusade, a new church institution was formed: the military orders, religious orders that combined the vocations of monk and warrior. Inspired by new international monastic orders dedicated to the spread of the Christian faith, such as the Cistercians, these armed monks redefined both the monastic calling and the ideals of knighthood.

FOCUS

In what ways did the self-image and mission of the Christian military orders resemble or differ from those of the papal and royal leaders of the Crusades?

Their movement began with the Knights of the Temple, an order founded in 1120 to protect Christian pilgrims and merchants; it was named after their headquarters near the site of the ancient Temple of Solomon in Jerusalem. Subsequently, the Templars (as they were commonly known) and other military orders spearheaded the militant Christian expansionism that resulted in the "reconquest" of Spain and the conversion of much of eastern Europe to Latin Christianity. Yet in the end Christian monarchs and the papacy turned against the military orders, annihilating the Templars and sharply restricting other military orders' activities. The ideal of an international brotherhood united in faith and in arms—the Crusader ideal—was swept away by the rising tide of national monarchies.

The Templar Model and the Crusading Movement

The Templar knights were expected to maintain equal fidelity to both the code of chivalry and monastic rules. Like the Cistercians, the Templars took vows of poverty, chastity, and obedience. The Cistercian abbot Bernard of Clairvaux praised what he called the "new knighthood" of the Templars for its steadfast commitment to combating both the evil within—the temptations of the devil—and the external enemy, the Muslims.

The Templars and Their Followers

Critics of the military orders voiced misgivings about their unseemly combination of religious devotion with armed violence. Nonetheless, donations to the orders, strongly encouraged by the church, led to rapid expansion of their ranks. Within thirty years the Templars had taken proprietorship of scores of estates and castles throughout western Europe and in the Crusader states. The outpouring of patronage for the Templar order encouraged imitation. Two new military orders based on the Templar model, the Hospitallers and the Teutonic Knights, were formed to tend to the poor and infirm among the pilgrims to the Holy Land. In the late twelfth century a number of military orders also sprang up in Spain to aid the cause of the "reconquest."

Members of the military orders committed themselves to lifelong service. Strict rules imbued the military orders with the discipline and solidarity that other Crusaders lacked. The knights' brave defense of the Christian enclaves against the Muslim counterattack led by Saladin earned them high regard from the enemy as well as from their fellow Christians. After vanquishing Christian armies, Saladin ordered the immediate beheading of captured Templars and Hospitallers, whom he regarded as the backbone of the Christian defenders.

Destruction of the Templars

Despite Jerusalem's fall to Saladin in 1187, the military orders continued to attract new recruits and donations. Pope Innocent III staunchly supported the military orders, which he regarded as crucial allies in his campaign to create an imperial papacy. But the Mamluks' final expulsion of Latin Christians from Acre in 1291 deprived the military orders of their reason for existence. Moreover, the Templars had powerful enemies, especially the French king Philip IV (r. 1285–1314), who resented their autonomy and coveted their wealth. With the cowardly consent of a weak pope, Philip launched a campaign of persecution against the order. The officers of the Inquisition found the Templars guilty of heresy. Hundreds of knights were burned at the stake, and in 1312 the pope disbanded the Templar order.

The Teutonic Knights and Christian Expansion in Eastern Europe

In contrast to the Templars, the Teutonic military order gained renewed life after the failure of the Crusades. In the late 1220s a Polish duke recruited members of the Teutonic order (so called because nearly all its members were German) to carry out a crusade against his rivals among the pagan lords of Prussia. Anticipating sharing in the spoils of victory, German princes and knights rushed to join the new crusading enterprise in their own backyard. The popes claimed sovereign authority over Prussia and delegated the Teutonic order to rule the region on their behalf. In 1309 the Teutonic Knights relocated to Prussia and focused exclusively on building up their own territorial state in the Baltic region.

After 1370, when the Teutonic Knights defeated the pagan princes of Lithuania, new commercial towns affiliated with the Hanseatic League arose and the Baltic region was rapidly colonized. Town charters gave urban burghers considerable independence but reserved sovereign rights to the order, which possessed large rural estates and received annual tribute from town dwellers.

Domains of the Teutonic Knights, 1309–1410

Marienburg Castle

After withdrawing from the Mediterranean, the Teutonic Knights found a new mission: spearheading the Christian advance among the pagan peoples of eastern Europe. From 1309 the order's leaders took up residence at a grand new headquarters at Marienburg on the Vistula River (now Malbork, Poland). The state created by the Teutonic order in the Baltic Sea region was considered a model of bureaucratic efficiency. (Photolibrary.)

Unschooled in Latin, the Teutonic order promoted Christianity through books, libraries, and schools in the German vernacular. The law codes adopted by the German overlords reminded the natives of their subordinate status by imposing various forms of legal discrimination. For example, the fine for killing a German was twice that for killing a native Prussian. Ethnic tensions were also evident in the rule that when drinking together, the Germans required the Prussians to drink first, for fear of poisoning.

When economic conditions worsened in the waning years of the fourteenth century, local landowners began to challenge the order's autocratic rule. The marriage of the Lithuanian king and the Polish queen in 1386 prompted Lithuanians to convert to Christianity, removing the last justification for the Teutonic order's holy war against paganism. During the fifteenth century the Prussian towns and rural lords gained independence from the order's rule. By the early sixteenth century the order had ceased to function as a sovereign state.

End of the Teutonic State

The Teutonic order was thus a victim of its own success. Once the order completed its mission of implanting Christianity through conquest, colonization, and conversion of pagans, the Knights no longer had a cause to serve. The military orders had represented the ideal of a universal Christian brotherhood championed by the Roman popes. Yet the dramatic expansion of Christendom to all corners of Europe between the twelfth and the fifteenth centuries had fostered national rivalry rather than political unity. With the failure of the Crusades and the demise of the military orders, the papacy's ambitions to rule over a united Christian people likewise perished.

Demise of the Crusader Ideal

Conclusion

The initial waves of the Mongol invasions spread fear and destruction across Eurasia, and the political and cultural repercussions of the Mongol conquests would resound for centuries. Adapting their own traditions to vastly different local settings, the Mongols reshaped the societies and cultures of Iran, Russia, and China as well as Central Asia. The Mongol legacy of steppe empires spanning the pastoral and settled worlds would inspire later empire-builders from Timur to the Mughals and the Manchus.

The Mongol incursions most profoundly affected the Islamic states and societies of Iran and Mesopotamia and the Rus lands. Many areas never recovered from the disruption of irrigated agriculture and reverted to pasture for stock raising, and in some cases even to barren desert. The Mongol invasions also erased the last of the Seljuk emirates, clearing the ground for the rise of new Turkish sultanates, the Mamluks and the Ottomans.

Like the Ilkhans in Iran, the Mongols of the Golden Horde converted to Islam, although their Rus subjects remained Christians. The rising Muscovy state would retain Mongol military and political institutions in building its own Russian empire. In China, by contrast, the Mongol legacy proved fleeting. Ignoring Yelu Chucai's warning that "the empire cannot be ruled on horseback," the Mongols failed to adapt their style of rule to the requirements of a large agrarian empire. The Yuan regime in China had badly deteriorated by the 1330s and collapsed into civil war and rebellion in the 1350s. As we will see in the next chapter, the founder of the Ming Empire (1368–1644) in China would seek to eliminate all traces of Mongol influence.

The Mongols brought the worlds of pastoral nomads and settled urban and agrarian peoples into collision, but a different kind of clash of civilizations had been triggered by the Crusades. Although the Crusaders failed to achieve their goal of restoring Christian rule over Jerusalem, the crusading movement expanded the borders of Latin Christendom by advancing the "reconquest" in Spain and by converting the Wendish peoples of eastern Europe.

The crusading movement and institutions such as the Christian military orders played a crucial role in the formation of Europe as the realm of "the Christian people" obedient to the Roman papacy. But the growing power of national monarchies frustrated the popes' efforts to establish supreme rule over secular as well as spiritual affairs. The unity imposed by the Mongol conquests also was short-lived. Although the creation of the Mongol Empire made possible an unprecedented movement of people, goods, and ideas throughout Eurasia, such cross-cultural exchanges vanished almost completely after the collapse of the Ilkhan and Yuan states in the mid-fourteenth century. By then, as the next chapter will reveal, both Europe and the Islamic lands had plunged into a new era of crisis following the devastating catastrophe of the Black Death.

NOTES

1. *The Deeds of the Franks and the Other Pilgrims to Jerusalem*, cited in James Harvey Robinson, ed., *Readings in European History* (Boston: Ginn & Co., 1904), 1:312.
2. Ibn Jubayr, "Relation de voyages," *Voyageurs arabes: Ibn Fadlan, Ibn Jubayr, Ibn Battuta et un auteur anonyme*, trans. Paul Charles-Dominique (Paris: Éditions Gallimard, 1995), 310.
3. Bernard of Clairvaux, *Letters*, trans. Bruno Scott James (London: Burns, Oates, 1953), 467.
4. Cited in Robert Bartlett, *The Making of Europe: Conquest, Colonization and Cultural Change, 950–1350* (Princeton, NJ: Princeton University Press, 1993), 154.
5. Cited in Bartlett, *The Making of Europe*, 132.
6. Nicole Oresme, "Le Livre de Politiques d'Aristotle," *Transactions of the American Philosophical Society*, new series, vol. 60, part 6 (1970), 292.
7. *Marco Polo: The Description of the World*, eds. A. C. Moule and Paul Pelliot (London: George Routledge & Sons, 1938), 1:192.
8. *Rashiduddin Fazullah's* Jami'u't-tawarikh (Compendium of Chronicles): *A History of the Mongols*, trans. W. M. Thackston (Cambridge, MA: Harvard University, Department of Near Eastern Languages and Civilizations, 1998), Part I, 6.

RESOURCES FOR RESEARCH

The Crusades and the Imperial Papacy, 1050–1350

The story of the Crusades has almost always been told from European and Christian perspectives. Hillenbrand's survey of Muslim attitudes helps to correct this bias. In his short, provocative study Tyerman challenges the conventional historiography and questions whether the Crusades constituted a coherent movement.

(Crusades: Introduction): http://www.theorb.net/encyclop/religion/crusades/crusade_intro.html.

France, John. *The Crusades and the Expansion of Catholic Christendom, 1000–1714*. 2005.

*Gabrieli, Francesco, ed. *Arab Historians of the Crusades*. 1969.

Hillenbrand, Carole. *The Crusades: Islamic Perspectives*. 2000.

Madden, Thomas F. *A Concise History of the Crusades*. 1999.

Tyerman, Christopher. *The Invention of the Crusades*. 1998.

The Making of Christian Europe, 1100–1350

Recent scholarship considers this the formative period for the emergence of a distinct European political and cultural identity. In Bartlett's view, this European identity was closely interwined with Latin Christendom's expansion and colonization of eastern and northern Europe and Spain. Nirenberg's pathbreaking work analyzes the culture of violence that led to persecution of Jews and other minorities.

Bartlett, Robert. *The Making of Europe: Conquest, Colonization, and Cultural Change, 950–1350*. 1993.

Christiansen, Eric. *The Northern Crusades: The Baltic and the Catholic Frontier, 1100–1525*, 2d ed. 1997.

Nirenberg, David. *Communities of Violence: Persecution of Minorities in the Middle Ages*. 1996.

Reilly, Bernard F. *The Medieval Spains*. 1993.

Reynolds, Susan. *Kingdoms and Communities in Western Europe, 900–1300*. 1984.

The Mongol World-Empire, 1100–1368

Despite the wealth of books on the Mongols, there is no comprehensive study of the Mongol Empire in its entirety. Lane and Morgan, both Islamic specialists, concentrate primarily on the Mongol domains in the west. Most treatments of the Mongols focus on the lives and deeds of the great khans, but Lane details many features of Mongol social life and customs.

Biran, Michal. *Chinggis Khan*. 2007.

Lane, George. *Daily Life in the Mongol Empire*. 2006.

Larner, John. *Marco Polo and the Discovery of the World.* 1999.

Morgan, David. *The Mongols.* 2d ed. 2007.

*Polo, Marco. *The Travels of Marco Polo.* 1958.

The Mongol Khanates and the Islamic World, 1240–1350

Revisionist scholars, while acknowledging the destructive effects of the Mongol conquests in Russia and Iran, have emphasized the transformative influences of Mongol rule as well. Lane rejects depictions of Ilkhan rule in Iran as a "dark age" and instead sees this period as one of cultural renaissance.

Allsen, Thomas. *Culture and Conquest in Mongol Eurasia.* 2001.

Kafadar, Cemal. *Between Two Worlds: The Construction of the Ottoman State.* 1995.

Lane, George. *Early Mongol Rule in Thirteenth-Century Iran: A Persian Renaissance.* 2003.

Morgan, David. *Medieval Persia, 1040–1797.* 1988.

Ostrowski, Donald. *Muscovy and the Mongols: Cross-Cultural Influences on the Steppe Frontier, 1304–1589.* 1998.

COUNTERPOINT: The "New Knighthood" of the Christian Military Orders

The history of the military orders is full of drama and controversy, and modern scholars have struggled to separate fact from fiction. Barber has written the definitive scholarly study of the Templar order, and the same can be said of Riley-Smith's work on the Hospitallers.

Barber, Malcolm. *The New Knighthood: A History of the Order of the Temple.* 1994.

(Military Orders: A Guide to On-line Resources): http://www
.theorb.net/encyclop/religion/monastic/milindex.html .

Nicholson, Helen. *Templars, Hospitallers and Teutonic Knights: Images of the Military Orders, 1128–1291.* 1993.

Riley-Smith, Jonathan. *Hospitallers: The History of the Order of St. John.* 1987.

* Primary source.

▶ **For additional primary sources from this period,** see *Sources of Crossroads and Cultures.*

▶ **For Web sites, images, and documents related to topics in this chapter,** see Make History at bedfordstmartins.com/smith.

The major global development in this chapter ▶ The Eurasian integration
fostered by the clashes of culture known as the Crusades and the Mongol conquests.

IMPORTANT EVENTS

1054	Great Schism between the Roman and Byzantine churches
1095	Pope Urban II issues summons for First Crusade
1098	Founding of the Cistercian order
1099	First Crusade concludes with the Christian capture of Jerusalem
1120	Founding of the order of the Knights of the Temple (Templars) at Jerusalem
1147	Wendish Crusade (part of the Second Crusade)
1187	Saladin recaptures Jerusalem
1198–1216	Papacy of Innocent III
1206	Council of Mongol princes elects Temujin (Chinggis) as Great Khan
1240	Mongol conquest of Kiev
1248	Christian armies capture the Almohad stronghold of Seville
1250–1517	Mamluk Sultanate in Egypt and Syria
1258	Mongols sack Baghdad
1271–1368	Rule of Mongols over China as the Yuan dynasty
1274–1295	Journey of Marco Polo to China
1291	Mamluks recapture Acre, last Christian stronghold in Palestine
1295–1304	Rule of Ghazan as Ilkhan; conversion of Ilkhan Mongols to Islam

KEY TERMS

chivalry (p. 450)   Inquisition (p. 448)
Crusades (p. 444)   investiture controversy
gazi (p. 466)   (p. 445)
Great Khan (p. 457)   military order (p. 446)
Great Schism (p. 445)   tax farming (p. 459)

CHAPTER OVERVIEW QUESTIONS

1. In what ways did the growing economic and cultural unity of Latin Christendom promote the rise of powerful European national monarchies?

2. To what degree did the expansion of Latin Christendom remake eastern Europe in the image of western Europe?

3. In what ways did the Mongol conquests foster cultural and economic exchange across Eurasia?

4. How and why did the Mongol rulers of China, Iran, and Russia differ in their relationships with the settled societies they ruled?

SECTION FOCUS QUESTIONS

1. In what ways did the Roman popes seek to expand their powers during the age of the Crusades?

2. How did the efforts to establish Christianity in Spain and eastern Europe compare with the Crusaders' quest to recover Jerusalem?

3. How did the organization of Mongol society and government change from the time of Chinggis Khan to that of his grandson Qubilai, the ruler of China?

4. In what respects did the Turkish Islamic states of the Mamluks and Ottomans pursue policies similar to those of the Mongol regimes in Iran and Russia?

5. In what ways did the self-image and mission of the Christian military orders resemble or differ from those of the papal and royal leaders of the Crusades?

MAKING CONNECTIONS

1. How did the relationship between the Roman popes and the Christian monarchs of western Europe change from the reign of Charlemagne (see Chapter 9) to the papacy of Innocent III?

2. In what ways did the Crusades contribute to the definition of Europe as the realm of Latin Christendom?

3. To what extent were the policies of the Mongols similar to those of earlier Central Asian nomad empires such as the Khazars and the Turks (see Chapter 10)?

15

AT A CROSSROADS ▶

The fall of Constantinople
to the Ottoman Turks in
1453 marked the end of
the Byzantine Empire and
heralded the coming age
of gunpowder weapons.
The Ottoman forces under
Sultan Mehmed II
breached the massive
walls of Constantinople
using massive cannons
known as *bombards*. The
Turkish cannons appear
in the center of this book
illustration of the siege of
Constantinople, published
in France in 1455. (The Art
Archive/Bibliothèque Nationale
Paris.)

Collapse and Revival in Afro-Eurasia

1300–1450

In August 1452, as the armies of the Ottoman sultan Mehmed II encircled Constantinople, the Byzantine emperor Constantine XI received a visit from a fellow Christian, a Hungarian engineer named Urban. Urban had applied metallurgical skills acquired at Hungary's rich iron and copper mines to the manufacture of large cannons known as *bombards*. He came to the Byzantine capital to offer his services to repel the Ottoman assault. But although Urban was a Christian, he was a businessman, too. When Constantine could not meet his price, Urban quickly left for the sultan's camp. Facing the famed triple walls of Constantinople, Mehmed promised to quadruple the salary Urban requested and to provide any materials and manpower the engineer needed.

Seven months later, in April 1453, Ottoman soldiers moved Urban's huge bronze bombards—with barrels twenty-six feet long, capable of throwing eight-hundred-pound shot—into place beneath the walls of Constantinople. Although these cumbersome cannons could fire only seven rounds a day, they battered the walls of Constantinople, which had long been considered impenetrable. After six weeks of siege the Turks breached the walls and swarmed into the city. The vastly outnumbered defenders, Emperor Constantine among them, fought to the death.

Urban's willingness to put business before religious loyalty helped tip the balance of power in the Mediterranean. During the siege, the Genoese merchant community at Constantinople—along with their archrivals, the Venetians—maintained strict neutrality. Although the Italian merchants, like Urban, were prepared to do business with Mehmed II, within a decade the Venetians and Ottomans were at war. Venice could not produce

BACKSTORY

In the fourteenth century, a number of developments threatened the connections among the societies of the Afro-Eurasian world. The collapse of the Mongol empires in China and Iran in the mid-1300s disrupted caravan traffic across Central Asia, diverting the flow of trade and travel to maritime routes across the Indian Ocean. Although the two centuries of religious wars known as the Crusades ended in 1291, they had hardened hostility between Christians and Muslims. As the power of the Christian Byzantine Empire contracted, Muslim Turkish sultanates—the Mamluk regime in Egypt and the rising Ottoman dynasty in Anatolia (modern Turkey)—gained control of the eastern Mediterranean region. Yet the Crusades and direct contact with the Mongols had also whetted European appetites for luxury and exotic goods from the Islamic world and Asia. Thus, despite challenges and obstacles, the Mediterranean remained a lively crossroads of commerce and cross-cultural exchange.

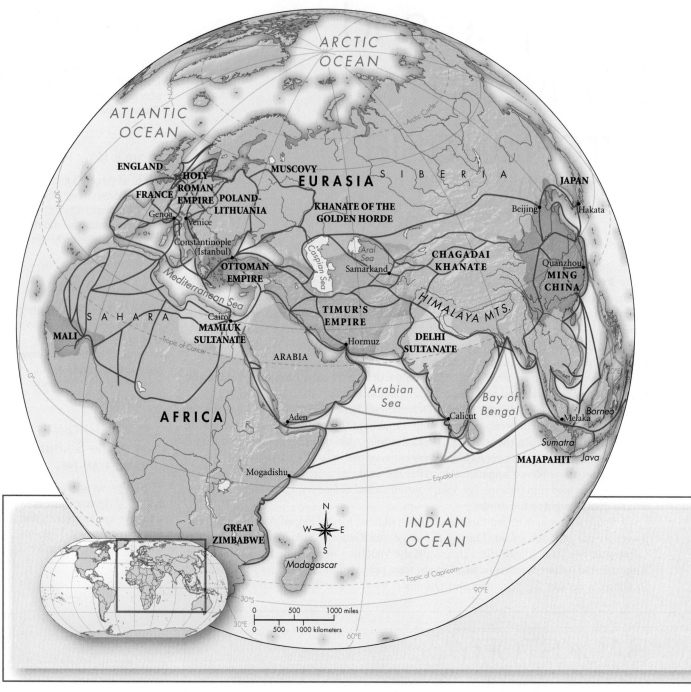

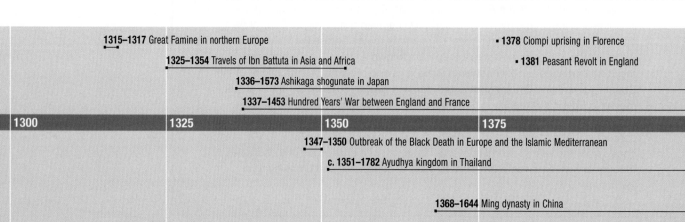

1315–1317 Great Famine in northern Europe

1325–1354 Travels of Ibn Battuta in Asia and Africa

1336–1573 Ashikaga shogunate in Japan

1337–1453 Hundred Years' War between England and France

▪ 1378 Ciompi uprising in Florence

▪ 1381 Peasant Revolt in England

1300	1325	1350	1375

1347–1350 Outbreak of the Black Death in Europe and the Islamic Mediterranean

c. 1351–1782 Ayudhya kingdom in Thailand

1368–1644 Ming dynasty in China

enough cannons to match the heavily armed Ottoman army and navy, which expelled the Venetians from the Black Sea in 1475. Although Venetian merchants still flocked to Constantinople, which Mehmed renamed Istanbul, to obtain spices, silks, and other Asian goods, the Ottomans held the upper hand and could dictate the terms of trade.

The fall of Constantinople to the Ottomans marks a turning point in world history. After perpetuating ancient Rome's heritage and glory for a thousand years, the Byzantine Empire came to an end. Islam continued to advance; in the fourteenth and fifteenth centuries, it expanded most dramatically in Africa and Asia. Italian merchants and bankers lost their dominance in the eastern Mediterranean and turned westward toward the Atlantic Ocean in search of new commercial opportunities. And this shift in commercial power and focus was not the only profound change that followed the Ottoman capture of Constantinople. The bombards cast by the Hungarian engineer for the Ottoman sultan heralded a military revolution that would decisively alter the balance of power among states and transform the nature of the state itself.

The new global patterns that emerged after Constantinople changed hands had their roots in calamities of the fourteenth century. The Ottoman triumph came just as Europe was beginning to recover from the previous century's catastrophic outbreak of plague known as the Black Death. The demographic and psychological shocks of epidemic disease had severely tested Europe's political and economic institutions—indeed, even its Christian faith.

The Black Death also devastated the Islamic world. Economic depression struck hard in Egypt, Syria, and Mesopotamia, the heartland of Islam. However, Europe's economy recovered more quickly. One consequence of the plague was the slow demise of serfdom, which contributed to the growing political and economic power of European monarchs and the urban merchant classes. By 1500 European merchants, bankers, and artisans had surpassed their Muslim counterparts in innovation and efficiency.

In Asia, the fourteenth century witnessed the rise and fall of the last Mongol empire, that of Timur (also known as Tamerlane). The end of the Mongol era marked the passing of nomadic rule, the resurgence of agrarian bureaucratic states such as Ming China and

MAPPING THE WORLD
Afro-Eurasia in the Early Fifteenth Century

After the Mongol Empire disintegrated, trans-Eurasian trade shifted from the overland Silk Road to the maritime routes stretching from China to the Mediterranean. Muslim merchants crossed the Sahara Desert and the Indian Ocean in pursuit of African gold, Chinese porcelain, and Asian spices. Although Chinese fleets led by Admiral Zheng He journeyed as far as the coasts of Arabia and Africa, the Ming rulers prohibited private overseas trade.

ROUTES ▼

— Major trade route

— Silk Road

— Voyages of Zheng He

1392–1910 Yi dynasty in Korea

▪ **1405** Death of Timur; breakup of his empire into regional states in Iran and Central Asia

▪ **1453** Ottoman conquest of Constantinople marks fall of the Byzantine Empire

1400   **1425**   **1450**

1405–1433 Chinese admiral Zheng He's expeditions in Southeast Asia and the Indian Ocean

▪ **1421** Relocation of Ming capital from Nanjing to Beijing

1428–1788 Le dynasty in Vietnam

the Ottoman Empire, and the shift of trade from the overland Silk Road to maritime routes across the Indian Ocean. Commerce attained unprecedented importance in many Asian societies. The flow of goods across Eurasia and Africa created new concentrations of wealth, fostered new patterns of consumption, and reshaped culture. The European Renaissance, for example, although primarily understood as a rebirth of the classical culture of Greece and Rome, also drew inspiration from the wealth of goods that poured into Italy from the Islamic world and Asia. By contrast, Japan remained isolated from this global bazaar, and this isolation contributed to the birth of Japan's distinctive national culture. For most Afro-Eurasian societies, however, the maritime world increasingly became the principal crossroads of economic and cultural exchange.

OVERVIEW
QUESTIONS

The major global development in this chapter: Crisis and recovery in fourteenth- and fifteenth-century Afro-Eurasia.

As you read, consider:

1. In the century after the devastating outbreak of plague known as the Black Death, how and why did Europe's economic growth begin to surpass that of the Islamic world?

2. Did the economic revival across Eurasia after 1350 benefit the peasant populations of Europe, the Islamic world, and East Asia?

3. How did the process of conversion to Islam differ in Iran, the Ottoman Empire, West Africa, and Southeast Asia during this period?

4. What political and economic changes contributed to the rise of maritime commerce in Asia during the fourteenth and fifteenth centuries?

Fourteenth-Century Crisis and Renewal in Eurasia

FOCUS

How did the Black Death affect society, the economy, and culture in Latin Christendom and the Islamic world?

Black Death The catastrophic outbreak of plague that spread from the Black Sea to Europe, the Middle East, and North Africa in 1347–1350, killing a third or more of the population in afflicted areas.

pandemic An outbreak of epidemic disease that spreads across an entire region.

No event in the fourteenth century had such profound consequences as the **Black Death** of 1347–1350. The unprecedented loss of life that resulted from this **pandemic** abruptly halted the economic expansion that had spread throughout Europe and the Islamic heartland in the preceding three centuries. Although the population losses were as great in the Islamic world as in Latin Christendom, the effects on society, the economy, and ideas diverged in important ways.

Largely spared the ravages of the Black Death, following the collapse of the Mongol empires in the fourteenth century Asian societies and economies faced different challenges. Expanding maritime trade and the spread of gunpowder weapons gave settled empires a decisive edge over nomadic societies, an edge that they never again relinquished. The founder of the Ming dynasty (1368–1644) in China rejected the Mongol model of "universal empire" and strove to restore a purely Chinese culture and social order. The prestige, stability, and ruling ideology of the Ming state powerfully influenced neighbors such as Korea and Vietnam—but had far less effect on Japan.

The "Great Mortality": The Black Death of 1347–1350

On the eve of the Black Death, Europe's agrarian economy already was struggling under the strain of climatic change. Around 1300 the earth experienced a shift in climate. The warm temperatures that had prevailed over most of the globe for the previous thousand years gave way to a **Little Ice Age** of colder temperatures and shorter growing seasons; it would last for much of the fourteenth century. The expansion of agriculture that had occurred in the Northern Hemisphere during the preceding three centuries came to a halt. The Great Famine of 1315–1317, when severe winters and overly wet summers brought on successive years of crop failure, killed 10 percent of the population in northern Europe and the British Isles. Unlike famine, though, the Black Death pandemic struck the ruling classes as hard as the poor. Scholars estimate that the Black Death and subsequent recurrences of the pandemic killed approximately one-third of the population of Europe.

Although the catastrophic mortality (death rates) of the Black Death is beyond dispute, the causes of the pandemic remain mysterious. The Florentine poet Giovanni Boccaccio (1313–1375), an eyewitness to the "great mortality," described the appearance of apple-sized swellings, first in the groin and armpits, after which these "death-bearing plague boils" spread to "every part of the body, wherefrom the fashion of the contagion began to change into black or livid blotches . . . in some places large and sparse, and in others small and thick-sown." The spread of these swellings, Boccaccio warned, was "a very certain token of coming death."[1]

The prominence of these glandular swellings, or buboes, in eyewitness accounts has led modern scholars to attribute the Black Death to bubonic plague, which is transmitted by fleas to rats and by rats to humans. Yet the scale of mortality during the Black Death far exceeds levels expected in plague outbreaks. Moreover, in Egypt the Black Death struck in winter, when bubonic plague is usually dormant, and the chief symptom was spitting blood rather than developing buboes, suggesting an airborne form of the plague. The pandemic killed as many livestock, especially cattle, as it did humans. Although it is difficult to identify the Black Death with any single modern disease, there is no doubt that the populations of western Eurasia had no previous experience of the disease, and hence no immunity to it. Outbreaks of plague continued to recur every decade or two for the next century, and intermittently thereafter.

Boccaccio and other eyewitnesses claimed that the Black Death had originated in Central Asia and traveled along overland trade routes to the Black Sea. The first outbreak among Europeans occurred in 1347 at the Genoese port of Caffa, on the Crimean peninsula. At that time Caffa was under siege by Mongols of the Golden Horde. Legend relates that the Mongols used catapults to lob corpses of plague victims over the city walls. Whether or not the Mongols really used this innovative type of germ warfare, the Genoese fled, only to spread the plague to the seaports they visited throughout the Mediterranean. By the summer of 1350 the Black Death had devastated nearly all of Europe (see Map 15.1).

The historian William McNeill has suggested that the Black Death was a byproduct of the Mongol conquests. He hypothesized that Mongol horsemen carried the plague bacillus from the remote highland forests of Southeast Asia into Central Asia, and then west to the Black Sea and east to China. The impact of the plague on China remains uncertain, however. The Mongol dynasty of Kubilai (Qubilai) (KOO-bih-lie) Khan already was losing its hold on China in the 1330s, and by the late 1340s China was afflicted by widespread famine, banditry, and civil war. By the time the Ming dynasty took control in 1368, China's population had fallen substantially. Yet Chinese sources make no mention of the specific symptoms of the Black Death, and there is no evidence of pandemic in the densely populated areas of South and Southeast Asia.

The demographic collapse resulting from the Black Death was concentrated in Europe and the Islamic lands ringing the Mediterranean. In these regions population growth halted for over a century. England's population did not return to pre-plague levels for four hundred years.

Causes and Spread of the Black Death

Demographic Consequences

Little Ice Age Name applied by environmental historians to periods of prolonged cool weather in the temperate zones of the earth.

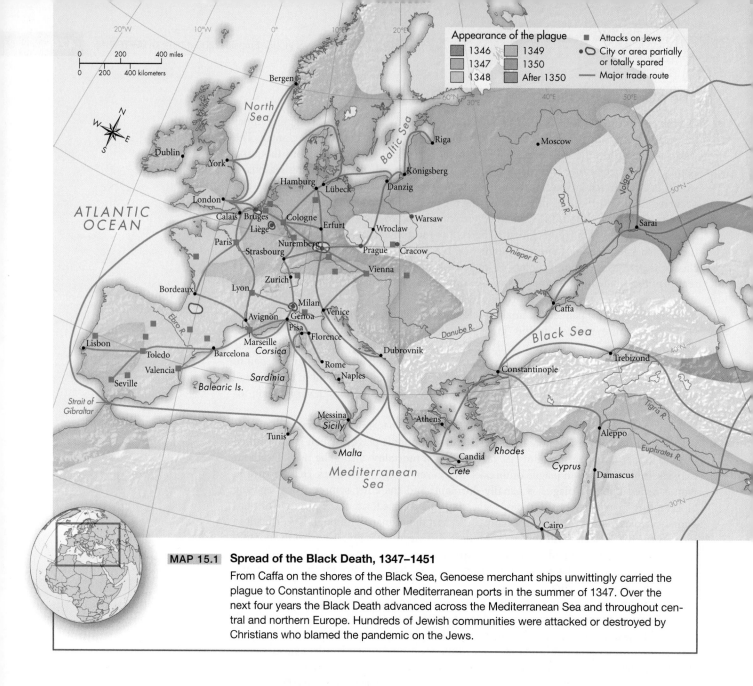

MAP 15.1 **Spread of the Black Death, 1347–1451**

From Caffa on the shores of the Black Sea, Genoese merchant ships unwittingly carried the plague to Constantinople and other Mediterranean ports in the summer of 1347. Over the next four years the Black Death advanced across the Mediterranean Sea and throughout central and northern Europe. Hundreds of Jewish communities were attacked or destroyed by Christians who blamed the pandemic on the Jews.

Population losses from the Black Death were equally devastating in the Islamic parts of the Mediterranean. Italian ships brought the plague to Alexandria in the autumn of 1347. The Egyptian historian al-Maqrizi (al-mak-REE-zee) recorded that twenty thousand people died each day in Cairo, then the most populous city in the world. Although this estimate surely is exaggerated, the plague probably did cause more than one hundred thousand deaths in Cairo alone. In the Islamic world, as in Europe, the loss of human lives and livestock seriously disrupted agriculture. While rural inhabitants flocked to the towns in search of food and work, urban residents sought refuge in the countryside from the contagion that festered in crowded cities.

Decline of the Mamluk Sultanate

The devastation of the plague dealt a serious blow to the agricultural economy of the Mamluk (MAM-luke) Sultanate, which ruled over Egypt and Syria. The scarcity of labor following the pandemic prompted a return to pastoral nomadism in many rural areas, and the urban working classes who survived benefited from rising wages. "The wages of skilled artisans, wage workers, porters, servants, stablemen, weavers, masons, construction workers, and the like have increased manyfold," wrote al-Maqrizi, who served as Cairo's market inspector from 1399 to 1405. But, he added, "of this class only a few remain, since most have died."[2]

The Mamluk Sultanate depended on agricultural wealth for its support, so population losses and declining agricultural production following the Black Death undermined the Mamluk government. A struggle for power broke out among rival factions. Bureaucratic mismanagement compounded the economic distress. Faced with decreasing revenues, the sultanate tried to squeeze more taxes from urban commerce and industry. But the creation of state monopolies in the spice trade and the sugar industry throttled private enterprise and undermined the commercial vitality of Cairo and Damascus. The impoverishment of the urban artisan and merchant classes further weakened the Mamluk regime, leading to its ultimate downfall at the hands of Ottoman conquerors in 1517. In the fall of the Mamluk Sultanate, we can see how the plague produced a chain of interconnected consequences. Population decline led to agricultural decline, which in turn produced economic problems, undermined political authority, and created the conditions for significant social, political, and military upheaval.

Although the horrific mortality caused by the Black Death afflicted Latin Christendom and the Islamic world in equal measure, their responses to the epidemic diverged in significant ways. Christians interpreted the plague as divine punishment for humanity's sins (see Reading the Past: A French Theologian's View of the Black Death). Acts of piety and atonement proliferated, most strikingly in the form of processions of flagellants (from *flagella*, a whip used by worshipers as a form of penance), whose self-mutilation was meant to imitate the sufferings of Christ. In many places Christians blamed vulnerable minorities—such as beggars, lepers, and especially Jews—for corrupting Christian society. Although the Roman Church, kings, and local leaders condemned attacks against Jews, their appeals often went unheeded. For example, the citizens of Strasbourg threw the municipal council out of office for trying to protect the city's Jewish population and then burned nine hundred Jews on the grounds of the Jewish cemetery. The macabre images of death and the corruption of the flesh in European painting and sculpture in the late fourteenth and fifteenth centuries vividly convey the anguish caused by the Black Death.

Christian Responses to the Black Death

Dance of Death

The scourge of the Black Death pandemic dramatically influenced attitudes toward death in Latin Christendom. Literary and artistic works such as this woodcut of skeletons dancing on an open grave vividly portrayed the fragility of life and the dangers of untimely death. For those unprepared to face divine judgment, the ravages of disease and death were only a prelude to the everlasting torments of hell. (akg-images/ Imagno.)

A French Theologian's View of the Black Death

This account of the Black Death comes from Jean de Venette (d. c. 1368), a monk and master of theology at the University of Paris who compiled, probably in the late 1350s, a chronicle of his own lifetime.

Some said that this pestilence was caused by infection of the air and waters. . . . As a result of this theory. . . . the Jews were suddenly and violently charged with infecting wells and water and corrupting the air. . . . In Germany and other parts of the world where Jews lived, they were massacred and slaughtered by Christians, and many thousands were burned everywhere, indiscriminately. . . . But in truth, such poisonings, granted that they actually were perpetrated, could not have caused so great a plague nor have infected so many people. There were other causes; for example, the will of God and the corrupt humors and evil inherent in air and earth. . . .

After the cessation of the epidemic, or plague, the men and women who survived married each other. There was . . . fertility beyond the ordinary. Pregnant women were seen on every side. . . . But woe is me! The world was not changed for the better but for the worse by this renewal of the population. For men were more avaricious and grasping than before, even though they had far greater possessions. They were more covetous and disturbed each other more frequently with suits, brawls, disputes, and pleas. Nor by the mortality

resulting from this terrible plague inflicted by God was peace between kings and lords established. On the contrary, the enemies of the king of France and of the Church were stronger and wickeder than before and stirred up wars on sea and on land. Greater evils than before pullulated everywhere in the world. And this factor was very remarkable. Although there was an abundance of all goods, yet everything was twice as dear, whether it were utensils, victuals, or merchandise, hired helpers or peasants and serfs, except for some hereditary domains which remained abundantly stocked with everything. Charity began to cool, and iniquity with ignorance and sin to abound, for few could be found in the good towns and castles who knew how or were willing to instruct children in the rudiments of grammar.

Source: Richard A. Newhall, ed., *The Chronicle of Jean de Venette* (New York: Columbia University Press, 1953), 50–51.

EXAMINING THE EVIDENCE

1. How did Venette's interpretation of the causes of the epidemic differ from those of his European contemporaries?

2. In Venette's view, what were the social and moral consequences of the Black Death?

Muslim Responses to the Black Death

Muslims did not share the Christian belief in "original sin," which deemed human beings inherently sinful, and so they did not see the plague as a divine punishment. Instead, they accepted it as an expression of God's will, and even a blessing for the faithful. The Muslim cleric Ibn al-Wardi (IB-unh al-wahr-dee), who succumbed to the disease in 1349, wrote that "this plague is for Muslims a martyrdom and a reward, and for the disbelievers a punishment and rebuke."[3] Most Muslim scholars and physicians rejected the theory that the pandemic was spread through contagion, counseling against abandoning stricken family members. The flagellants' focus on atonement for sin and the scapegoating of Jews seen in Christian Europe were wholly absent in the Islamic world.

Rebuilding Societies in Western Europe 1350–1492

Just as existing religious beliefs and practices shaped Muslim and Christian responses to the plague, underlying conditions influenced political and economic recovery in the two regions. Latin Christendom recovered more quickly than Islamic lands. In Europe, the death toll caused an acute labor shortage. Desperate to find tenants to cultivate their lands, the nobility had to offer generous concessions, such as release from labor services, that liberated the peasantry from the conditions of serfdom. The incomes of the nobility and the Church declined by half or more, and many castles and monasteries fell into ruin. The shortage of labor enabled both urban artisans and rural laborers to bargain for wage increases. Rising wages improved living standards for ordinary people, who began to consume more meat, cheese, and beer. At the same time, a smaller population reduced the demand for grain and manufactured goods such as woolen cloth. Many nobles, unable to find tenants, converted their agricultural land into pasture. Hundreds of villages were abandoned. In much of central Europe, cultivated land reverted back to forest. Thus, the plague redrew the economic map of Europe, shifting the economic balance of power.

Economic change brought with it economic conflict, and tensions between rich and poor triggered insurrections by rural peasants and the urban lower classes throughout western Europe. In the Italian city-states, the working classes of Florence, led by unemployed wool workers, revolted against the patricians (the wealthy families who controlled the city's government) in 1378. Their demand for a greater share of wealth and political rights alarmed the city's artisan guilds, which allied with the patricians to suppress what became known as the Ciompi revolt ("uprising by the little people"). While the revolt failed, it clearly demonstrated the awareness of Florence's working classes that the plague had undermined the status quo, creating an opportunity for economic and political change.

The efforts of elites to respond to the new economic environment could also lead to conflict. In England, King Richard II's attempt to shift the basis of taxation from landed wealth to a head tax on each subject incited the Peasant Revolt of 1381. Led by a radical preacher named John Ball, the rebels presented a petition to the king that went beyond repeal of the head tax to demand freedom from the tyranny of noble lords and the Christian Church:

> Henceforward, that no lord should have lordship but that there should be proportion between all people, saving only the lordship of the king; that the goods of the holy church ought not to be in the hands of men of religion, or parsons or vicars, or others of holy church, but these should have their sustenance easily and the rest of the goods be divided between the parishioners, . . . and that there should be no villeins [peasants subject to a lord's justice] in England or any serfdom or villeinage, but all are to be free and of one condition.[4]

In the end the English nobles mustered militias to suppress the uprising. This success could not, however, reverse the developments that had produced the uprising in the first place. High wages, falling rents, and the flight of tenants brought many estates to the brink of bankruptcy. Declining aristocratic families intermarried with successful entrepreneurs, who coveted the privileges of the titled nobility and sought to emulate their lifestyle. A new social order began to form, one based on private property and entrepreneurship rather than nobility and serfdom, but equally extreme in its imbalance of wealth and poverty.

Perhaps nowhere in Europe was this new social order more apparent than in Italy. In the Italian city-states, the widening gap between rich and poor was reflected in their governments, which increasingly benefited the wealthy. Over the course of the fifteenth century, the ideals and institutions of republican (representative) government on which the Italian city-states were founded steadily lost ground. A military despot wrested control of Milan in 1450. Venice's **oligarchy**—rule by an exclusive elite—strengthened its grip over the city's government and commerce. In Florence, beset by constant civil strife after the Ciompi uprising, the Medici family of bankers dominated the city's political affairs. Everywhere, financial power was increasingly aligned with political power.

In the wake of the Black Death, kings and princes suffered a drop in revenues as agricultural production fell. Yet in the long run, royal power grew at the expense of the nobility and the Church. In England and France, royal governments gained new sources of income and established bureaucracies of tax collectors and administrators to manage them. The rulers of these states transformed their growing financial power into military and political strength by raising standing armies of professional soldiers and investing in new military technology. The French monarchy, for instance, capitalized on rapid innovations in gunpowder weapons

Social Unrest and Rebellion

Rise of National States

oligarchy Rule by a small group of individuals or families.

to create a formidable army and to establish itself as the supreme power in continental Europe. Originally developed by the Mongols, these weapons had been introduced to Europe via the Islamic world by the middle of the fourteenth century.

Hundred Years' War

The progress of the Hundred Years' War (1337–1453) between England and France reflected the changing political landscape. On the eve of the Black Death pandemic, the war broke out over claims to territories in southwestern France and a dispute over succession to the French throne. In the early years of the conflict, the English side prevailed, thanks to the skill of its bowmen against mounted French knights. As the war dragged on, the English kings increasingly relied on mercenary armies, paid in plunder from the towns and castles they seized. By 1400, combat between knights conducted according to elaborate rules of chivalry had yielded to new forms of warfare. Cannons, siege weapons, and, later, firearms undermined both the nobility's preeminence in war and its sense of identity and purpose. An arms race between France and its rivals led to rapid improvements in weaponry, especially the development of lighter and more mobile cannons. Ultimately the French defeated the English, but the war transformed both sides. The length of the conflict, the propaganda from both sides, and the unified effort needed to prosecute the increasingly costly war all contributed to the evolution of royal governments and the emergence of a sense of national identity.

Consolidating State Power

To strengthen their control, the monarchs of states such as France, England, and Spain relied on new forms of direct taxation, as well as financing from bankers. The French monarchy levied new taxes on salt, land, and commercial transactions, wresting income from local lords and town governments. The kings of England and France promoted domestic industries such as textiles and metallurgy to enhance their national power. The marriage of Isabella of Castile and Ferdinand of Aragon in 1469 created a unified monarchy in Spain. This expansion of royal power in Spain depended heavily on loans from Genoese bankers, who also financed the maritime ventures of the Portuguese and Spanish monarchs into the Atlantic Ocean. Thus, in all three of these states, new economic conditions contributed to the growth of monarchical power (see Map 15.2).

Ultimately, consolidation of monarchical power in western Europe would create new global connections. In their efforts to consolidate power, Ferdinand and Isabella, like so many rulers in world history, demanded religious conformity. In 1492 they conquered Granada, the last Muslim foothold in Spain, and ordered all Jews and Muslims to convert to Christianity or face banishment. With the *Reconquista* (Spanish for "reconquest") of Spain complete, Ferdinand and Isabella turned their crusading energies toward exploration. That same year, they sponsored the first of Christopher Columbus's momentous transatlantic voyages in pursuit of the fabled riches of China.

Wheeled Cannon

The Hundred Years' War between England and France touched off an arms race that spurred major advances in the technology of warfare. Initially, gunsmiths concentrated on making massive siege cannons capable of firing shot weighing hundreds of pounds. By 1500, however, military commanders favored more mobile weapons, such as this wheeled cannon manufactured for the Holy Roman Emperor Maximilian I. (Erich Lessing/Art Resource.)

MAP 15.2

Europe and the Greater Mediterranean, 1453

The century following the Black Death witnessed the growth of royal power and territorial consolidation across Europe, most notably in England and France. But central Europe and Italy remained politically fragmented. The Ottoman conquest of Constantinople in 1453 extinguished the Byzantine Empire and sharpened the conflict between Christendom and the Islamic world in southeastern Europe.

Ming China and the New Order in East Asia 1368–1500

State building in East Asia, too, fostered the development of national states. The Yuan dynasty established in China by the Mongol khan Kubilai had foundered after his death in 1294. Kubilai's successors wrung as much tribute as they could from the Chinese population, but they neglected the infrastructure of roads, canals, and irrigation and flood-control dikes that the Chinese economy depended on. By the time the Mongol court at Dadu (modern Beijing) began to enlist the services of the Confucian-educated elite in the late 1330s, economic distress and social unrest already had taken a heavy toll. When peasant insurrections and civil wars broke out in the 1350s, the Mongol leaders abandoned China and retreated to their steppe homeland. After a protracted period of war and devastation, a Chinese general of peasant origin restored native rule, founding the Ming dynasty in 1368 (see Map 15.3).

MAP 15.3

The Ming Empire, 1449

After expelling the Mongols, the rulers of the Ming dynasty rebuilt the Great Wall to defend China from nomad invasions. Emperor Yongle moved the Ming capital from Nanjing to Beijing and launched expeditions commanded by his trusted aide Zheng He that voyaged throughout Southeast Asia and the Indian Ocean.

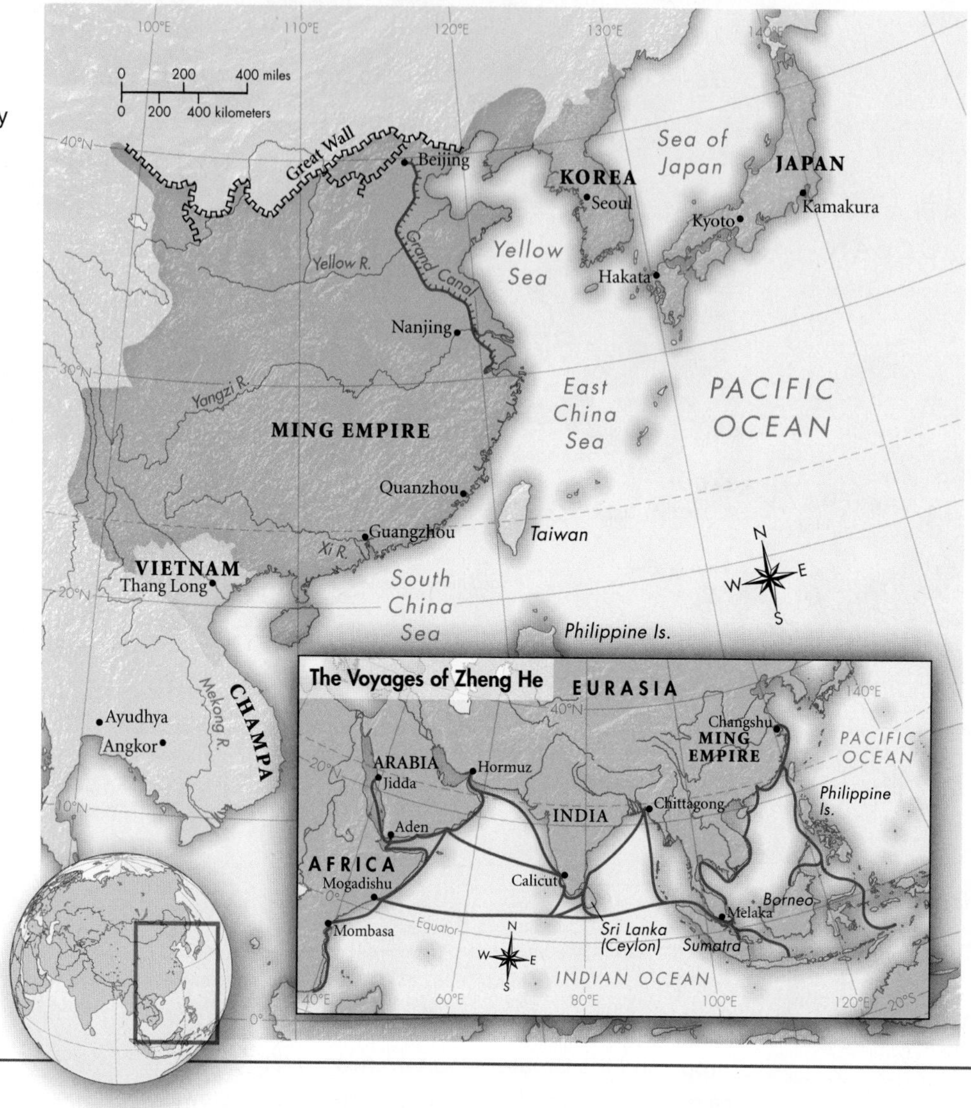

Ming Autocracy

The Ming founder, Zhu Yuanzhang (JOO yuwen-JAHNG) (r. 1368–1398)—better known by his imperial title, Hongwu (hoong-woo)—resurrected the basic Chinese institutions of civil government. But throughout his life Hongwu viewed the scholar-official class with suspicion. Born a peasant, Hongwu saw himself as a populist crusading against the snobbery and luxurious lifestyle of the rich and powerful. Once in command, he repeatedly purged high officials and exercised despotic control over his government. Hongwu reinstituted the civil service examinations system to select government officials, but he used the examinations and the state-run school system as tools of political indoctrination, establishing the teachings of twelfth-century Neo-Confucian philosopher Zhu Xi (JOO shee) as the standard for the civil service exams. Zhu shared the Neo-Confucian antipathy toward Buddhism as a foreign religion and sought to reassert the Confucian commitment to moral perfection and the betterment of society. **Neo-Confucianism** advocated a strict moral code and a patriarchal social hierarchy, and the Ming government supported it with the full force of imperial law. Thus, Hongwu drew on tradition and a belief in China's cultural superiority as he created a new state.

This strong sense of Chinese superiority can be seen in many of Hongwu's policies. Determined to eradicate any taint of Mongol customs, Hongwu rejected the Mongol model of a multiethnic empire and turned his back on the world of the steppe nomads. He located his

Neo-Confucianism The reformulation of Confucian doctrines to reassert a commitment to moral perfection and the betterment of society; dominated Chinese intellectual life and social thought from the twelfth to the twentieth centuries.

capital at Nanjing, on the south bank of the Yangzi River, far from the Mongol frontier. Foreign embassies were welcome at the Ming court, which offered trading privileges in return for tribute and allegiance to the Chinese emperor. But Hongwu distrusted merchants as much as he did intellectuals. In 1371 he forbade Chinese merchants from engaging in overseas commerce and placed foreign traders under close government scrutiny.

Hongwu's son, the Emperor Yongle (r. 1402–1424), reversed his father's efforts to sever China from the outside world. Instead, Yongle embraced the Mongol vision of world empire and rebuilt the former Mongol capital of Dadu, creating the modern city of Beijing. Throughout his reign Yongle campaigned to subdue the Mongol tribes along the northern frontier, but with little success. He also wanted to expand southward. In 1405 he launched a series of naval expeditions under Admiral Zheng He (JUNG-huh) that, as we will see, projected Chinese power deep into the Indian Ocean, and in 1407 he invaded and conquered Vietnam (see again Map 15.3). Nonetheless, Yongle's reign did not represent a complete break with that of Hongwu. Like his father, Yongle was an autocrat who promoted Neo-Confucian policies, even as he sought to reestablish some of the global connections Hongwu had tried to sever.

The impact of Hongwu's policies went far beyond the realms of court politics and international diplomacy. He envisioned his empire as a universe of self-sufficient and self-governing villages, where men worked in the fields and women remained at home. The Neo-Confucian ideology of Hongwu emphasized the patriarchal authority of the lineage, and his policies deprived women of many rights, including a share in inheritance. It outlawed the remarriage of widows. By the fourteenth century, many elite families practiced foot binding, which probably originated among courtesans and entertainers. From around age six the feet of young girls were tightly bound with bandages, deforming the bones and crippling them. The feet of adult women ideally were no more than three to four inches long; they were considered a mark of feminine beauty and a symbol of freedom from labor. Foot binding accompanied seclusion in the home as a sign of respectable womanhood.

Ming Patriarchal Society

Despite the strictures of patriarchal society, in the households of nonelite groups, women played an essential economic role. Women worked alongside men in rice cultivation and performed most tasks involved in textile manufacture. As national and international markets for Chinese silk expanded beginning in the twelfth century, male artisans in urban workshops took over skilled occupations such as silk weaving. But the spread of cotton, introduced from India in the thirteenth century, gave peasant women new economic opportunities. Most cotton was grown, ginned (removing the seeds), spun into yarn, and woven into cloth within a single household, principally by women. Confucian moralists esteemed spinning, weaving, and embroidery as "womanly work" that would promote industriousness and thrift; they became dismayed, however, when women displayed entrepreneurial skill in marketing their wares. Nevertheless, women did engage in commercial activities, suggesting that there were limits to the moralists' control of women's lives.

The Ming dynasty abandoned its designs for conquest and expansion after the death of Yongle in 1424. Yet the prestige, power, and philosophy of the Ming state continued to influence its neighbors, with the significant exception of Japan (see Counterpoint: Age of the Samurai in Japan, 1185–1450). Vietnam regained its independence from China in 1427, but under the long-lived Le dynasty (1428–1788), Vietnam retained Chinese-style bureaucratic government. The Le rulers oversaw the growth of an official class schooled in Neo-Confucianism and committed to forcing its cultural norms, kinship practices, and hostility to Buddhism on Vietnamese society as a whole. In Korea, the rulers of the new Yi dynasty (1392–1910) also embraced Neo-Confucian ideals of government. Under Yi rule the Confucian-educated elite acquired hereditary status with exclusive rights to political office. In both Vietnam and Korea, aristocratic rule and Buddhism's dominance over daily life yielded to a "Neo-Confucian revolution" modeled after Chinese political institutions and values.

Neo-Confucianism in Vietnam and Korea

Islam's New Frontiers

FOCUS

Why did Islam expand dramatically in the fourteenth and fifteenth centuries, and how did new Islamic societies differ from established ones?

In the fourteenth and fifteenth centuries, Islam continued to spread to new areas, including central and maritime Asia, sub-Saharan Africa, and southeastern Europe. In the past, Muslim rule had often preceded the popular adoption of Islamic religion and culture. Yet the advance of Islam in Africa and Asia came about not through conquest, but through slow diffusion via merchants and missionaries. The universalism and egalitarianism of Islam appealed to rising merchant classes in both West Africa and maritime Asia.

During this period, Islam expanded by adapting to older ruling cultures rather than seeking to eradicate them. Timur, the last of the great nomad conquerors, and his descendants ruled not as Mongol khans but as Islamic sultans. The culture of the Central Asian states, however, remained an eclectic mix of Mongol, Turkish, and Persian traditions, in contrast to the strict adherence to Muslim law and doctrine practiced under the Arab regimes of the Middle East and North Africa. This pattern of cultural adaptation and assimilation was even more evident in West Africa and Southeast Asia.

Islamic Spiritual Ferment in Central Asia 1350–1500

The spread of Sufism in Central Asia between 1350 and 1500 played a significant role in the process of cultural assimilation. **Sufism**—a mystical tradition that stressed self-mastery, practical virtues, and spiritual growth through personal experience of the divine—had already emerged by 1200 as a major expression of Islamic values and social identity. Sufism appeared in many variations and readily assimilated local cultures to its beliefs and practices. Sufi mystics acquired institutional strength through the communal solidarity of their brotherhoods spread across the whole realm of Islam. In contrast to the orthodox scholars and teachers known as *ulama*, who made little effort to convert nonbelievers, Sufi preachers were inspired by missionary zeal and welcomed non-Muslims to their lodges and sermons. This made them ideal instruments for the spread of Islam to new territories.

Timur One of Sufism's most important royal patrons was Timur (1336–1405), the last of the Mongol emperors. Born near the city of Samarkand (SAM-ar-kand) when the Mongol Ilkhanate in Iran was on the verge of collapse, Timur—himself a Turk—grew up among Mongols who practiced Islam. He rose to power in the 1370s by reuniting quarreling Mongol tribes in common pursuit of conquest. Although Timur lacked the dynastic pedigree enjoyed by Chinggis Khan's descendants, like Chinggis he held his empire together by the force of his personal charisma.

From the early 1380s, Timur's armies relentlessly pursued campaigns of conquest, sweeping westward across Iran into Mesopotamia and Russia and eastward into India. In 1400–1401 Timur seized and razed Aleppo and Damascus, the principal Mamluk cities in Syria. In 1402 he captured the Ottoman sultan in battle. Rather than trying to consolidate his rule in Syria and Anatolia (modern Turkey), however, Timur turned his attention eastward. He was preparing to march on China when he fell ill and died early in 1405. Although Timur's empire quickly fragmented, his triumphs would serve as an inspiration to later empire builders, such as the Mughals in India and the Manchus in China. Moreover, his support of Sufism would have a lasting impact, helping lay the foundation for a number of important Islamic religious movements in Central Asia.

The institutions of Timur's empire were largely modeled on the Ilkhan synthesis of Persian civil administration and Turkish-Mongol military organization. Like the Ilkhans and the Ottomans, Timur's policies favored settled farmers and urban populations over pastoral nomads, who were often displaced from their homelands. While Timur allowed local princes a degree of autonomy, he was determined to make Samarkand a grand imperial capital.

Sufism A tradition within Islam that emphasizes mystical knowledge and personal experience of the divine.

He forcibly relocated artists, craftsmen, scholars, and clerics from many regions and put them into service in Samarkand (see Reading the Past: A Spanish Ambassador's Description of Samarkand). The citadel and enormous bazaar built by Timur have long since perished, but surviving mosques, shrines, and tombs illuminate Timur's vision of Islamic kingship: all-powerful, urbane and cosmopolitan, and ostentatious in its display of public piety.

After Timur's death in 1405, his sons carved the empire into independent regional kingdoms. Like Timur, his successors sought to control religious life in royal capitals such as Herat and Samarkand by appointing elders (*shayks*) and judges (*qadis*) to administer justice, supervise schools and mosques, and police public morality. Yet Sufi brotherhoods and the veneration of Sufi saints exerted an especially strong influence over social life and religious practice in Central Asia. Timur had lavished special favor on Sufi teachers and had strategically placed the shrines of his family members next to the tombs of important Sufi leaders. The relics of Timur in Samarkand, along with the tombs of Sufi saints, attracted pilgrims from near and far.

Elsewhere in the Islamic world, a number of religious movements combined the veneration of Sufi saints and belief in miracles with unorthodox ideas derived from Shi'ism, the branch of Islam that maintains that only descendants of Muhammad's son-in-law Ali have a legitimate right to serve as caliph. Outside the major cities, Islamic leadership passed to Sufis and popular preachers. One of the most militant and influential of these radical Islamic sects was the Safavid (SAH-fah-vid) movement founded by a Sufi preacher, Safi al-Din (SAH-fee al-dean) (1252–1334). Like other visionary teachers, Safi preached the need for a purified Islam cleansed of worldly wealth, urban luxury, and moral laxity. His missionary movement struck a responsive chord among the pastoral Turk and Mongol tribes of Anatolia and Iran. The Safavids roused their followers to attack Christians in the Caucasus region, but they also challenged Muslim rulers such as the Ottomans and Timur's successors. At the end of the fifteenth century, a charismatic leader, Shah Isma'il (shah IS-mah-eel), combined Safavid religious fervor with Shi'a doctrines to found a **theocracy**—a state subject to religious authority. It would rule Iran for more than two centuries and shape modern Iran's distinctive Shi'a religious culture.

Timur Enthroned

We can glean some sense of Timur's self-image from the *Book of Victories*, a chronicle of Timur's campaigns commissioned by one of his descendants in the 1480s. This scene portrays the moment in 1370 when Timur declared himself successor to the Chagadai khans. (Rare Books and Manuscripts Department, The Sheridan Libraries, The Johns Hopkins University.)

Ottoman Expansion and the Fall of Constantinople 1354–1453

The spread of Islam in Central Asia would have profound consequences for the region. In the eyes of Europeans, however, the most significant—and alarming—advance was the Ottoman expansion into the Balkan territories of southeastern Europe. The Byzantine state was severely shaken by the Black Death, and in 1354 the Ottomans took advantage of this weakness to invade the Balkans. After a decisive victory in 1389, the Ottoman Empire annexed most of the Balkans except the region around Constantinople itself, reducing it to an isolated enclave.

The growing might of the Ottoman Empire stemmed from two military innovations: (1) the formation of the **janissary corps**, elite army units composed of slave soldiers, and (2) the use of massed musket fire and cannons, such as the bombards of Urban, the Hungarian engineer whom we met at the start of this chapter. In the late fourteenth century the Ottomans adopted the Mamluk practice of organizing slave armies that would be more reliably loyal to the sultan than the unruly *ghazi* ("holy warrior") bands that Osman

theocracy A state ruled by religious authorities.

janissary corps Slave soldiers who served as the principal armed forces of the Ottoman Empire beginning in the fifteenth century; also staffed much of the Ottoman state bureaucracy.

A Spanish Ambassador's Description of Samarkand

In September 1403, an embassy dispatched by King Henry III of Castile arrived at Samarkand in hopes of enlisting the support of Timur for a combined military campaign against the Ottomans. Seventy years old and in failing health, Timur lavishly entertained his visitors, but made no response to Henry's overtures. The leader of the Spanish delegation, Ruy Gonzalez de Clavijo, left Samarkand disappointed, but his report preserves our fullest account of Timur's capital in its heyday.

The city is rather larger than Seville, but lying outside Samarkand are great numbers of houses that form extensive suburbs. These lay spread on all hands, for indeed the township is surrounded by orchards and vineyards. . . . In between these orchards pass streets with open squares; these are all densely populated, and here all kinds of goods are on sale with breadstuffs and meat. . . .

Samarkand is rich not only in foodstuffs but also in manufactures, such as factories of silk. . . . Thus trade has always been fostered by Timur with the view of making his capital the noblest of cities; and during all his conquests . . . he carried off the best men to people Samarkand, bringing thither the master-craftsmen of all nations. Thus from Damascus he carried away with him all the weavers of that city, those who worked at the silk looms; further the bow-makers who produce those cross-bows which are so famous; likewise armorers; also the craftsmen in glass and porcelain, who are known to be the best in all the world. From Turkey he had brought their gunsmiths who make the arquebus. . . . So great therefore was the population now of all nationalities gathered together in Samarkand that of men with their families the number they said must amount to 150,000 souls . . . [including] Turks, Arabs, and Moors of diverse sects, with Greek, Armenian, Roman, Jacobite [Syrian], and Nestorian Christians, besides those folk who baptize with fire in the forehead [i.e., Hindus]. . . .

The markets of Samarkand further are amply stored with merchandise imported from distant and foreign countries. . . . The goods that are imported to Samarkand from Cathay indeed are of the richest and most precious of all those brought thither from foreign parts, for the craftsmen of Cathay are reputed to be the most skillful by far beyond those of any other nation.

Source: Ruy Gonzalez de Clavijo, *Embassy to Tamerlane, 1403–1406*, trans. Guy Le Strange (London: Routledge, 1928), 285–289.

EXAMINING THE EVIDENCE

1. What features of Timur's capital most impressed Gonzalez de Clavijo?

2. How does this account of Samarkand at its height compare with the chapter's description of Renaissance Florence?

(r. 1280–1324), the founder of the Ottoman state, had gathered as the core of his army. At first, prisoners and volunteers made up the janissary corps. Starting in 1395, however, the Ottomans imposed a form of conscription known as *devshirme* (dev-SHEER-may) on the Christian peoples of the Balkans to supplement Turkish recruits. Adolescent boys conscripted through the devshirme were taken from their families, raised as Muslims, and educated at palace schools for service in the sultan's civil administration as well as the army. The Mamluks purchased slaves from Central Asia, but the Ottomans obtained a cheaper and more abundant supply from within their empire. At the same time, they created a government and military wholly beholden to the sultan. Janissaries were forbidden to marry and forfeited their property to the sultan upon their death.

Practical concerns dictated Ottoman policies toward Christian communities. Where Christians were the majority of the population, the Ottomans could be quite tolerant. Apart from the notorious devshirme slave

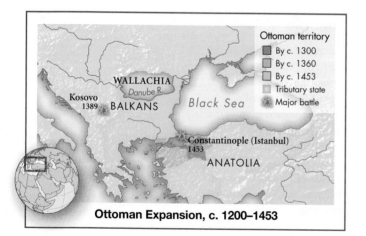

Ottoman Expansion, c. 1200–1453

levy, the Ottoman impositions were less burdensome than the dues the Balkan peoples had owed the Byzantine emperor. The Ottomans allowed Balkan Christians freedom to practice their religion, and they protected the Greek Orthodox Church, which they considered indispensable to maintaining social order. In Anatolia and other places where Christians were a minority, however, the Ottomans took a much harder line, seeing such minorities as a potential threat to the Ottoman order. Muslim governors stripped Christian bishops of their authority, seized church properties and revenues, and curbed public worship. By 1500 Christian society in Anatolia had nearly vanished; most Christians had converted to Islam.

Like the Ming emperors of China, Ottoman rulers favored the creation of a stable peasant society that would serve as a reliable source of revenue. A married peasant with a plot of land that could be worked by two oxen became the basic unit of Ottoman society. The state controlled nearly all cultivated land, but peasant families enjoyed permanent rights to farm the land they occupied. The government sold the rights to collect land taxes (a practice known as tax farming) to merchants and other wealthy individuals, including non-Muslims such as Greeks and Jews. The practice of tax farming guaranteed revenues for the state, but it distanced Ottoman officials from their subjects.

Despite their own nomadic origins, the Ottomans regarded nomadic tribes, like religious minorities, as a threat to stability. Many nomads were forcibly deported and settled in the Balkans and western Anatolia, where they combined farming with stock raising. Due to heavy taxes imposed on animal herds, nomads had to earn additional income through transport, lumbering, and felt and carpet manufacture. The push toward such activities created by harsh Ottoman policies was matched by the pull of global trade connections. Strong demand from European customers and the imperial capital of Istanbul (the name Mehmed II gave to Constantinople) stimulated carpet weaving by both peasants and herders.

The patriarchal family, in which the wife is subject to her husband's control, was a pillar of Ottoman law, just as it was in Ming China. Although the Ottoman state barred women from owning cultivated land, it did not infringe on women's rights to a share of family inheritance, as prescribed in the Qur'an. Thus, although men usually controlled property in the form of land and houses, women acquired wealth in the form of money, furnishings, clothes, and jewelry. Women invested in commercial ventures, tax farming, and moneylending. Because women were secluded in the home and veiled in public—long-established requirements to maintain family honor and status in the central Islamic lands—women used servants and trusted clients to help them conduct their business activities.

The final defeat of the Byzantine Empire by Ottoman armies in 1453 shocked the Christian world. Mehmed II's capture of Constantinople also completed a radical transformation of the Ottoman enterprise. The Ottoman sultans no longer saw themselves as roving ghazi warriors, but as monarchs with absolute authority over a multinational empire at the crossroads of Europe and Asia: "ruler of the two seas and the two continents," as the inscription over Mehmed's palace gate proclaimed. A proudly Islamic regime, the Ottoman sultanate aspired to become the centerpiece of a broad cosmopolitan civilization spanning Europe, Asia, and Africa.

Commerce and Culture in Islamic West Africa

West African trading empires and the merchants they supported had long served as the vanguard of Islam in sub-Saharan Africa. The Mali Empire's adoption of Islam as its official religion in the late thirteenth century encouraged conversion to Islam throughout the West African savanna. Under Mali's protection, Muslim merchant clans expanded their activities throughout the towns of the savanna and the oasis trading posts of the Sahara. Islam continued to prosper despite the collapse of Mali's political dominion in the mid-fourteenth century.

Timbuktu Manuscript

Timbuktu became the hub of Islamic culture and intellectual life in the western Sahara. Scholars and students at Timbuktu assembled impressive libraries of Arabic texts, such as this twelfth-century Qur'an. Written mostly on paper imported from Europe, Timbuktu's manuscripts were preserved in family collections after the city's leading scholars were deported to North Africa by Moroccan invaders in 1591. (Candace Feit.)

Muslim Merchants and Scholars

The towns of Jenne and Timbuktu, founded along the Niger River by Muslim merchants in the thirteenth century, emerged as the new crossroads of trans-Saharan trade. Jenne benefited from its access to the gold mines and rain forest products of coastal West Africa. Timbuktu's commercial prosperity rose as trade grew between West Africa and Mamluk Egypt. Islamic intellectual culture thrived among the merchant families of Timbuktu, Jenne, and other towns.

As elsewhere in the Islamic world, West African trader families readily combined religious scholarship with mercantile pursuits. Thus, in West Africa, trade and Islamic culture went hand in hand. In fact, West Africa saw the development of a profitable trade *in* Islamic culture. Since the eleventh century, disciples of renowned scholars had migrated across the Sahara and founded schools and libraries. The Moroccan Muslim scholar and traveler Ibn Battuta (IB-uhn ba-TOO-tuh), who visited Mali in 1352–1353, voiced approval of the people's "eagerness to memorize the great Qur'an: they place fetters on their children if they fail to memorize it and they are not released until they do so."[5] Books on Islamic law, theology, Sufi mysticism, medicine, and Arabic grammar and literature were staple commodities of trans-Saharan trade. The Muslim diplomat Hasan al-Wazzan (hah-SAHN al-wah-zan), whose *Description of Africa* (published in Italian in 1550) became a best-seller in Europe, wrote that in Timbuktu "the learned are greatly revered. Also, many book manuscripts coming from the Berber [North African] lands are sold. More profits are realized from sales of books than any other merchandise."[6]

Muslim Clerics and Native Religious Leaders

Muslim clerics wielded considerable influence in the towns. Clerics presided over worship and festival life and governed social behavior by applying Muslim law and cultural traditions. Yet away from the towns the majority of the population remained attached to ancestral beliefs in nature spirits, especially the spirits of rivers and thunder. Healer priests, clan chiefs, and other ritual experts shared responsibility for making offerings to the spirits, providing protection from evil demons and sorcerers, and honoring the dead. Much to the chagrin of purists such as Ibn Battuta, West African rulers maintained their authority in rural areas by combining Muslim practices with indigenous rituals and traditions. Islam in West Africa was largely urban, and West African rulers knew that their control of the countryside depended on religious accommodation.

trade diaspora A network of merchants from the same city or country who live permanently in foreign lands and cooperate with one another to pursue trading opportunities.

Advance of Islam in Maritime Southeast Asia

Muslim Arab merchants had dominated maritime commerce in the Indian Ocean and Southeast Asia since the seventh century. Not until the thirteenth century, however, did Islam begin to gain converts in Malaysia and the Indonesian archipelago. By 1400 Arab and Gujarati traders and Sufi teachers had spread Islam throughout maritime Asia. The dispersion of Muslim merchants took the form of a **trade diaspora**, a network of merchant settlements dispersed across foreign lands but united by common origins, religion, and language, as well as by business dealings.

Political and economic motives strongly influenced official adoption of Islam. In the first half of the fourteenth century, the Majapahit (mah-jah-PAH-hit) kingdom (1292–1528), a bastion of Hindu religion, conquered most of Java and the neighboring islands of Bali and Madura and forced many local rulers in the Indonesian archipelago to submit tribute. In response, many of these rulers adopted Islam as an act of resistance to dominance by the Majapahit kings. By 1428 the Muslim city-states of Java's north coast, buoyed by the profits of trade with China, secured their independence from Majapahit. Majapahit's dominion over the agricultural hinterland of Java lasted until 1528, when a coalition of Muslim princes forced the royal family to flee to Bali, which remains today the sole preserve of Hinduism in Southeast Asia.

Cosmopolitan port cities, with their diverse merchant communities, were natural sites for religious innovation. The spread of Islam beyond Southeast Asia's port cities, however, was slow and uneven. Javanese tradition attributes the Islamization of the island to a series of preachers, beginning with Malik Ibrahim (mah-leek EE-bra-heem) (d. 1419), a Gujarati spice trader of Persian ancestry. Because merchants and Sufi teachers played a far greater role than orthodox ulama in the spread of Islam in Southeast Asia, relatively open forms of Islam flourished. The Arab shipmaster Ibn Majid (IB-uhn maj-jid), writing in 1462, bemoaned the corruption of Islamic marriage and dietary laws among the Muslims of Melaka (mah-LAK-eh): "They have no culture at all. The infidel marries Muslim women while the Muslim takes pagans to wife. . . . The Muslim eats dogs for meat, for there are no food laws. They drink wine in the markets and do not treat divorce as a religious act.[7] Enforcement of Islamic law often was suspended where it conflicted with local custom. Southeast Asia never adopted some features of Middle Eastern culture often associated with Islam, such as the veiling of women.

Local pre-Islamic religious traditions persisted in Sumatra and Java long after the people accepted Islam. The most visible signs of conversion to Islam were giving up the worship of idols and the consumption of pork and adopting the practice of male circumcision. In addition, the elaborate feasting and grave goods, slave sacrifice, and widow sacrifice (*sati*) that normally accompanied the burials of chiefs and kings largely disappeared. Yet Southeast Asian Muslims continued to honor the dead with prayers and offerings adapted to the forms of Islamic rituals. Malays and Javanese readily adopted veneration of Sufi saints and habitually prayed for assistance from the spirits of deceased holy men. Muslim restrictions on women's secular and religious activities met with spirited resistance from Southeast Asian women, who were accustomed to active participation in public life. Even more than in West Africa, Islam in Southeast Asia prospered not by destroying existing traditions, but by assimilating them.

In regions such as West Africa and Southeast Asia, then, Islam diffused through the activities of merchants, teachers, and settlers rather than through conquest. The spread of Islam in Africa and Asia also followed the rhythms of international trade. While Europe recovered slowly from the Black Death, thriving commerce across the Indian Ocean forged new economic links among Asia, Africa, and the Mediterranean world.

Politics of Conversion

Religious Diversity

The Global Bazaar

Dynastic changes, war, and the Black Death roiled the international economy in the fourteenth century. Yet even before the end of the century, trade and economic growth were reviving in many areas. The maritime world of the Indian Ocean, largely spared both pandemic and war, displayed unprecedented commercial dynamism. Pepper and cotton textiles from India, porcelain and silk from China, spices and

FOCUS

How did the pattern of international trade change during the fourteenth and fifteenth centuries, and how did these changes affect consumption and fashion tastes?

other exotic goods from Southeast Asia, and gold, ivory, and copper from southern Africa circulated through a network of trading ports that spanned the Indian Ocean, Southeast Asia, and China. These trading centers attracted merchants and artisans from many lands, and the colorful variety of languages, dress, foods, and music that filled their streets gave them the air of a global bazaar.

The crises of the fourteenth century severely disrupted the European economy, but by 1450 Italy regained its place as the center within Latin Christendom of finance, industry, and trade. Previously, European craftsmen had produced only crude imitations of Islamic luxury wares. By the early fifteenth century, however, mimicry had blossomed into innovation, and Italian production of luxury goods surpassed Islamic competitors' in both quantity and quality. Wealth poured into Italy, where it found new outlets in a culture of conspicuous consumption. In contrast, the Islamic heartlands of the Middle East never recaptured their former momentum. In sum, the crises of the fourteenth century did not destroy the shared economy and commerce of the Afro-Eurasian world, but they did reshape them in profound and long-lasting ways (see Map 15.4).

Economic Prosperity and Maritime Trade in Asia 1350–1450

In Kubilai Khan's day, hostility among the Mongol khanates disrupted Central Asian caravan trade. Thus when the Venetian traveler Marco Polo returned home in 1292, he traveled by ship rather than retracing the overland route, known as the Silk Road, that had brought him to China two decades before. Polo's experience was a sign of things to come. After 1300 maritime commerce largely replaced inland trade over the ancient Silk Road. Asian merchants from India to China would seize the opportunities presented by the new emphasis on maritime commerce.

India: Cotton and Pepper

In India, improvements in spinning wheels and looms, and above all the invention of block printing of fabrics in the fourteenth century, led to a revolution in cotton textile manufacture. Using block printing (carved wooden blocks covered with dye), Indian weavers produced colorful and intricately designed fabrics—later known in Europe as chintz, from the Hindi *chint* ("many-colored")—that were far cheaper than luxury textiles such as silk or velvet. Gujarat in the northwest and the Tamil lands in southeastern India became centers of cotton manufacture and trade. Although cotton cultivation and weaving spread to Burma, Thailand, and China, Indian fabrics dominated Eurasian markets (see Lives and Livelihoods: Urban Weavers in India).

Along with textiles, India was famous for its pepper, for which Europeans had acquired a taste during the age of the Crusades. Muslim merchants from Gujarat controlled both cotton and pepper exports from the cities of Calicut and Quilon (KEE-lon). By 1500 Gujarati merchants had created a far-flung trade network across the Indian Ocean from Zanzibar to Java. Gujarati *sharafs* (from the Persian word for "moneylender") and Tamil *chettis* ("traders") acted as bankers for merchants and rulers alike in nearly every Indian Ocean port.

China: Silk and Porcelain

China's ocean-going commerce also flourished in the fourteenth century. The thriving trade between India and China deeply impressed Ibn Battuta, who found thirteen large Chinese vessels, or *junks*, anchored at Calicut when he arrived there in 1341. These junks, Battuta tells us, carried a complement of a thousand men and contained "four decks with rooms, cabins, and saloons for merchants; a cabin has chambers and a lavatory, and can be locked by its occupant, who takes along with him slave girls and wives."[8]

Silk had long dominated China's export trade, but by the eleventh century domestic silk-weaving was flourishing in Iran, the Byzantine Empire, and India. Because Iranian and Byzantine silk manufacturers were better positioned to respond to changing fashions in the Islamic world and Europe, China primarily exported raw silk rather than finished fabrics. At the same time, China retained its preeminent place in world trade by exporting porcelain, which became known as "chinaware."

Much admired for their whiteness and translucency, Chinese ceramics already had become an important item of Asian maritime trade in the tenth century. Bulky and fragile,

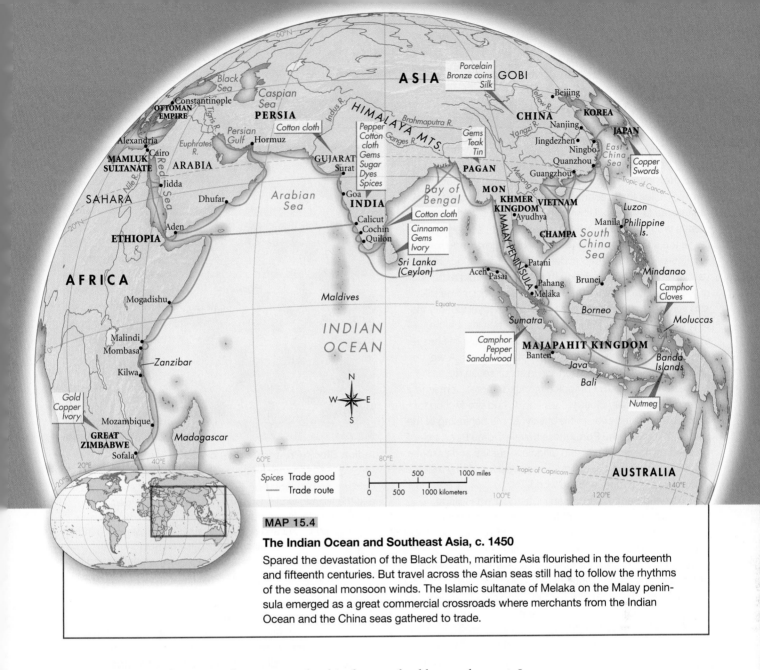

MAP 15.4

The Indian Ocean and Southeast Asia, c. 1450

Spared the devastation of the Black Death, maritime Asia flourished in the fourteenth and fifteenth centuries. But travel across the Asian seas still had to follow the rhythms of the seasonal monsoon winds. The Islamic sultanate of Melaka on the Malay peninsula emerged as a great commercial crossroads where merchants from the Indian Ocean and the China seas gathered to trade.

ceramic wares were better suited to transport by ship than overland by camel or cart. In the thirteenth century, artisans at Jingdezhen (JING-deh-JUHN) in southern China perfected the techniques for making true porcelains, which transform into glass the glaze and pigments, as well as the body of the piece. Porcelain wares, which were harder and whiter than previous types of ceramics, could be made into thin yet strong vessels. Although the Chinese preferred monochromatic (single-colored) porcelains that imitated the colors and texture of jade, consumers in the Islamic world prized intricate designs executed with the metallic pigments used by glassmakers. Muslim merchants introduced the cobalt blue pigment (which Chinese potters called "Mohammedan blue") used to create blue-and-white decorated porcelains. By 1400, Jingdezhen had become the largest manufacturing city in the world, housing more than one thousand kilns with some seventy thousand craftsmen engaged in several dozen specialized tasks. Thus, technological innovation and the demands of the international marketplace shaped both the production and decoration of Chinese ceramics.

The most avid consumers of Chinese porcelains were in the Islamic world, reflecting the global nature of the Chinese ceramics industry. Muslims used Chinese porcelains both as eating and drinking vessels and to decorate mosques, tombs, and other holy places. Imports of Chinese porcelain devastated local ceramic manufacturing in many parts of maritime Asia,

Urban Weavers in India

Industry and commerce in India, especially in textiles, grew rapidly beginning in the fourteenth century. Specialized craftsmen in towns and regional groups of merchants formed guilds that became the nuclei of new occupational castes, *jati* (JAH-tee). Ultimately these new occupational castes would join with other forces in Indian society to challenge the social inequality rooted in orthodox Hindu religion.

It was growth in market demand and technological innovations such as block printing that drove the rapid expansion of India's textile industries. Luxury fabrics such as fine silks and velvet remained largely the province of royal workshops or private patronage. Mass production of textiles, on the other hand, was oriented toward the manufacture of cheaper cotton fabrics, especially colorful chintz garments. A weaver could make a woman's cotton *sari* in six or seven days, whereas a luxury garment took a month or more. Domestic demand for ordinary cloth grew steadily, and production for export accelerated even more briskly. At the beginning of the sixteenth century, the Portuguese traveler Tomé Pires, impressed by the craftsmanship of Indian muslins and calicoes (named after the port of Calicut), observed that "they make enough of these to furnish the world."[1]

Weaving became an urban industry. It was village women who cleaned most of the cotton and spun it into yarn; they could easily combine this simple if laborious work with other domestic chores. But peasants did not weave the yarn into cloth, except for their own use. Instead, weaving, bleaching, and dyeing cloth were skilled tasks performed by professional urban craftsmen, or in some cases by artisans living in separate weavers' settlements in the countryside.

Like other trades in India, weaving was a hereditary occupation that conferred a distinct *jati* caste status and identity. Families of weavers belonged to one of a number of regional guilds with branches in different towns, and members married within their guilds. Unlike European guilds, Indian guilds did not have exclusive monopolies over their trades. A single town could include a number of different weaving guilds, which could become fierce economic and social rivals.

Indian Block-Printed Textile, c. 1500
Block-printed textiles with elaborate designs were in great demand both in India and throughout Southeast Asia, Africa, and the Islamic world. Craftsmen carved intricate designs on wooden blocks (a separate block for each color), which were then dipped in dye and repeatedly stamped on bleached fabric until the entire cloth was covered. This cotton fabric with geese, lotus flower, and rosette designs was manufactured in Gujarat in western India. (Ashmolean Museum, University of Oxford/ Bridgeman Art Library.)

Increased affluence brought further social and economic differentiation to the ranks of weavers. Although guild leaders negotiated orders from merchants and princes, artisans could freely sell their own wares through urban shops and country fairs. The most successful weavers became merchants and brokers, buying more looms and hiring others to work under their supervision. By the fourteenth century some weavers had begun to add the honorific title *chetti* (merchant) to their names.

Southeast Asia: Spices and Rain Forest Products

from the Philippines to East Africa. Chinese porcelains became potent prestige goods among the tribal societies of the Philippines and Indonesia, who attributed magical powers to them.

In mainland Southeast Asia, the shift in political power from the inland rice-growing regions toward coastal port cities reflected the new prominence of maritime trade in the region's economic life. Burma exported cotton to China as early as 1400 and became an important source of metals, gems, and teak for shipbuilding. The profits of maritime commerce fueled the emergence of Ayudhya (a-YOOD-he-ya) in Thailand as the dominant power in mainland Southeast Asia in the late fourteenth century. By 1400 Ayudhya was challenging Majapahit for control of the Southeast Asian trade routes between India and China.

The rising prosperity of weavers whetted their aspirations for social recognition. Amid the whirl and congestion of city life, it was far more difficult than in villages to enforce the laws governing caste purity and segregation. As a fourteenth-century poet wrote about the crowded streets of his hometown of Jaunpur in the Ganges Valley, in the city "one person's caste-mark gets stamped on another's forehead, and a brahman's holy thread will be found hanging around an untouchable's neck."[2] Brahmans objected to this erosion of caste boundaries, to little avail. Weaver guilds became influential patrons of temples and often served as trustees and accountants in charge of managing temple endowments and revenues.

In a few cases the growing economic independence of weavers and like-minded artisans prompted complete rejection of the caste hierarchy. Sufi preachers and *bhakti* (BAHK-tee)—devotional movements devoted to patron gods and goddesses—encouraged the disregard of caste distinctions in favor of a universal brotherhood of devout believers. The fifteenth-century bhakti preacher Kabir, who was strongly influenced by Sufi teachings, epitomized the new social radicalism coursing through the urban artisan classes. A weaver himself, Kabir joined the dignity of manual labor to the purity of spiritual devotion, spurning the social pretension and superficial piety of the brahmans ("pandits") and Muslim clerics ("mullahs"):

> I abandoned kin and caste, I weave my threads at ease
>
> I quarrel with no one, I abandoned the pandits and mullahs,
>
> I wear what I have woven; forgetful of myself, I come close to God.[3]

In Kabir's mind, genuine piety was rooted in honest toil, devotion to family, and abstinence from sensual pleasure.

By the seventeenth century, such ideas had coalesced into a separatist religious movement, Sikhism, centered on a trinity of labor, charity, and spiritual devotion. The Sikhs, who gained a following principally among traders and artisans in the northwestern Punjab region, drew an even more explicit connection between commerce and piety. In the words of a hymn included in a sixteenth-century anthology of Sikh sacred writings:

> The true Guru [teacher] is the merchant;
>
> The devotees are his peddlers.
>
> The capital stock is the Lord's Name, and
>
> To enshrine the truth is to keep His account.[4]

Sikh communities spurned the distinction between pure and impure occupations. In their eyes, holiness was to be found in honest toil and personal piety, not ascetic practices, book learning, or religious rituals.

1. Tomé Pires, *The Suma Oriental of Tomé Pires*, ed. and trans. Armando Cortes (London: Hakluyt Society, 1944), 1:53.
2. Vidyapati Thakur, *Kirtilata*, quoted in Eugenia Vanina, *Urban Crafts and Craftsmen in Medieval India (Thirteenth–Eighteenth Centuries)* (New Delhi: Munshiram Manoharlal, 2004), 443.
3. Quoted in Vanina, *Urban Crafts and Craftsmen*, 149.
4. *Sri Guru Granth Sahib*, trans. Gophal Singh (Delhi: Gur Das Kapur & Sons, 1960), 2:427.

QUESTIONS TO CONSIDER

1. In what ways did the organization of textile production reinforce or challenge the prevailing social norms of Hindu society?

2. In what ways did religious ideas and movements reflect the new sense of dignity among prosperous Indian merchants and craftsmen?

For Further Information:

Ramaswamy, Vijaya. *Textiles and Weavers in Medieval South India*. Delhi: Oxford University Press, 1985.

Vanina, Eugenia. *Urban Crafts and Craftsmen in Medieval India (Thirteenth–Eighteenth Centuries)*. New Delhi: Munshiram Manoharlal, 2004.

Thus, China influenced patterns of international trade not only as a producer, as with ceramics, but as a market for exported goods large enough to shape production elsewhere in the world. China was the principal market for the international trade in pepper, and it was Chinese demand that drove the rapid expansion of pepper cultivation in Southeast Asia, in particular Sumatra, during the fifteenth century. In return for exports of pepper, sandalwood, tin and other metals, fine spices, and exotic products of the tropical rain forests, Southeast Asia imported cotton cloth from India and silks, porcelain, and bronze coins from China. In the wake of this trade boom, Indian and Chinese merchant communities sprouted across maritime Southeast Asia. The trade diasporas of Gujarati Muslims and Chinese from Guangzhou

(Canton) and Quanzhou (CHYWAN-joe) created networks of cultural as well as economic influence, ultimately altering the balance of political power as well (see again Map 15.4).

China's Overseas Overture: The Voyages of Zheng He 1405–1433

The growth of South Asian maritime trade attracted the attention of the Chinese government, and in the early fifteenth century, the Ming dynasty in China took a more active role in maritime Southeast Asia, becoming a rival for political and economic supremacy. From the 1390s Malay princes in Sumatra appealed to the Ming court for protection against the demands of the Majapahit kings. In 1405 the Ming emperor Yongle decided to intervene by sending a naval expedition to halt the expansionist aggression of Majapahit and Ayudhya and to assert Chinese authority over the maritime realm.

Zheng He's Mission

Yongle entrusted the fleet to the command of a young military officer named Zheng He (1371–1433). Zheng was born into a Muslim family who had served the Mongol rulers of the Yuan dynasty. In 1383, Zheng He, then age twelve, was conscripted into the eunuch corps (castrated males employed as guardians of the imperial household) and placed in the retinue of the prince who would become Emperor Yongle. Zheng assisted the prince in the overthrow of his nephew that brought Yongle to the throne in 1402, and became his most trusted confidant.

Renaissance A period of intense intellectual and artistic creativity in Europe, beginning in Italy in the fourteenth century as a revival of the classical civilization of ancient Greece and Rome.

humanism The study of the humanities (rhetoric, poetry, history, and moral philosophy), based on the works of ancient Greek and Roman writers, that provided the intellectual foundations for the Renaissance.

For his mission to Southeast Asia, Yongle equipped Zheng He with a vast armada, a fleet of sixty-three ships manned by nearly twenty-eight thousand sailors, soldiers, and officials. Zheng's seven-masted flagship, more than four hundred feet long, was a marvel of Chinese nautical engineering. His fleet later became known as the "treasure ships" because of the cargoes of exotic goods and tribute they brought back from Southeast Asia, India, Arabia, and Africa. But Zheng's primary mission was political, not economic. Yongle, as we have seen, had a vision of world empire, in part borrowed from the Mongols, in which a multitude of princes would pay homage to Ming sovereignty. The constant flow of foreign embassies, the display of exotic tribute, and the emperor's pivotal role as arbitrator of disputes among lesser rulers were crucial to his sense of imperial dignity.

Departing in November of 1405, Zheng's fleet sailed first to Java in a show of force designed to intimidate Majapahit. He then traveled to Sumatra and Melaka and across the Indian Ocean to Ceylon and Calicut. No sooner had Zheng He returned to China in the autumn of 1407 than Yongle dispatched him on another voyage. Yongle had recently launched his invasion of Vietnam, and the purpose of the second voyage was to curtail Ayudhya's aggression and establish a Chinese presence at strategic ports such as Melaka along the Straits of Sumatra. Altogether Yongle commissioned six expeditions under Zheng He's command. During the fourth and subsequent voyages, Zheng He sailed beyond India to Arabia and down the east coast of Africa.

The projection of Chinese power over the sea-lanes of maritime Asia led to far-reaching economic and political changes. The close relations Zheng He forged with rulers of port cities strengthened their political independence and promoted their commercial growth. Under the umbrella of Chinese protection, Melaka flourished as the great cross-roads of Asian maritime trade.

The Last of the Treasure Fleets

The high cost of building and equipping the treasure ships depleted the Ming treasury, however, and after Yongle's death in 1424, Confucian ministers at the Ming court prevailed on his young successor to halt the naval expeditions. In 1430, Yongle's successor nonetheless overcame bureaucratic opposition and dispatched Zheng He on yet another voyage, his seventh. After traveling once again to Africa, Zheng died during his return home. With the passing of the renowned admiral, enthusiasm for the expeditions evaporated. Moreover, the Ming court faced a new threat: a resurgent Mongol confederation in the north. In 1449 a foolish young Ming emperor led a military campaign against the Mongols, only to be taken captive. The Ming court obtained the emperor's release by paying a huge ransom, but its strategic priorities had been completely transformed. Turning its back on the sea, the Ming state devoted its energies and revenues to rebuilding the Great Wall, much of which had crumbled to dust, as a defense against further Mongol attacks. The Great Wall that survives today was largely constructed by the Ming dynasty.

The shift in Chinese policy did not mean the end of Chinese involvement in maritime trade. Chinese merchants continued to pursue trading opportunities in defiance of the imperial ban on private overseas commerce. Even though Muslim merchants dominated Asian maritime commerce, Chinese merchant colonies dotted the coasts of Southeast Asia. Melaka's rulers converted to Islam but welcomed merchants from every corner of Asia. The population probably reached one hundred thousand before Melaka was sacked by the Portuguese in 1511. The Portuguese, like the Chinese before them, were drawn to Southeast Asian waters by the tremendous wealth created by maritime trade. Spurred by the growing European appetite for Asian spices, the violent intrusion of the Portuguese would transform the dynamics of maritime trade throughout Asia.

Commerce and Culture in the Renaissance

European expansion in the late fourteenth and early fifteenth centuries was preceded and influenced by a period of dramatic cultural change. The century after the outbreak of the Black Death marked the beginning of a sweeping transformation in European culture known as the **Renaissance**. In its narrow sense *Renaissance* (French for "rebirth") refers to the revival of ancient Greek and Roman philosophy, art, and literature that originated in fourteenth-century Italy. Scholars rediscovered classical learning and began to emulate the language and ideas of Greek and Roman philosophers and poets; these individuals became known as humanists, students of the liberal arts or humanities. The new intellectual movement of **humanism** combined classical learning with Christian piety and dedication to civic responsibilities.

At the same time the Renaissance inaugurated dramatic changes in the self-image and lifestyle of the wealthy. The new habits of luxurious living and magnificent display diverged sharply from the Christian ethic of frugality. Innovations in material culture and aesthetic values reflected crucial changes in the Italian economy and its relationship to the international trading world of the Mediterranean and beyond. These transformations in turn led to a reorientation of Europe away from Asia and toward the Atlantic world.

Italy's Economic Transformation

The Black Death had hit the Italian city-states especially hard. Some contemporary observers claimed that the pandemic had radically reshaped the social order. Although artisan guilds became a powerful force in urban government for a time in Florence, Siena, and other cities, over the long term the patrician elite of wealthy merchants and landowners reasserted their oligarchic control. The rich became richer, and status and power were increasingly measured in visible signs of wealth.

Still, the economies of the Italian city-states underwent fundamental transformation. Diminishing profits from trade with the Islamic world prompted many Italian merchants to abandon commerce in favor of banking. Squeezed out of the eastern Mediterranean by the Turks and Venetians, Genoa turned its attention westward. Genoese bankers became financiers to the kings of Spain and Portugal and supplied the funds for their initial forays into the Atlantic in search of new routes to African gold and Asian spices. European monarchs' growing reliance on professional armies, naval fleets, and gunpowder weapons also stimulated demand for banking services, forcing them to borrow money to meet the rising costs of war.

Italy became the primary producer of luxury goods for Europe, displacing the Islamic world and Asia. Before 1400, Islamic craftsmanship had far surpassed that of Latin Christendom. The upper classes of Europe paid handsome sums to obtain silk and linen fabrics, ceramics, rugs, glass, metalwork, and jewelry imported from the Mamluk Empire. "The most beautiful things in the world are found in Damascus," wrote Simone Sigoli, a Florentine who visited the city in 1386. "Such rich and noble and delicate works of every kind that if you had money in the bone of your leg, without fail you would break it to buy these things. . . . Really, all Christendom could be supplied for a year with the merchandise of Damascus."[9] But the Black Death, Timur's invasions, and Mamluk mismanagement devastated industry and commerce in Egypt and Syria. According to a census of workshops in Alexandria recorded in 1434, the number of looms operating in the city had fallen to eight hundred, compared with fourteen thousand in 1395.

Seizing the opportunity these developments created, Italian entrepreneurs first imitated and then improved on Islamic techniques and designs for making silk, tin-glazed ceramics known as *maiolica* (my-OH-lee-kah), glass, and brassware. By 1450 these Italian products had become competitive with or eclipsed imports from Egypt and Syria. Italian firms captured the major share of the international market for luxury textiles and other finished goods, and the Islamic lands were reduced to being suppliers of raw materials such as silk, cotton, and dyestuffs.

A Culture of Consumption

Along with Italy's ascent in finance and manufacturing came a decisive shift in attitudes toward money and its use. The older Christian ethics of frugality and disdain for worldly gain gave way to prodigal spending and consumption. This new inclination for acquisition and display cannot be attributed simply to the spread of secular humanism. Indeed, much of this torrent of spending was lavished on religious art and artifacts, and the Roman papacy stood out as perhaps the most spendthrift of all. Displaying personal wealth and possessions affirmed social status and power. Civic pride and political rivalry fueled public spending to build and decorate churches and cathedrals. Rich townsmen transformed private homes into palaces, and artisans fashioned ordinary articles of everyday life—from rugs and furniture to dishes, books, and candlesticks—into works of art. Public piety blurred together with personal vanity. Spending money on religious monuments, wrote the fifteenth-century Florentine merchant Giovanni Rucellai (ROO-chel-lie) in his diary, gave him "the greatest satisfaction and the greatest pleasure, because it serves the glory of God, the honor of Florence, and my own memory."[10]

"Magnificence" became the watchword of the Renaissance. Wealthy merchants and members of the clergy portrayed themselves as patrons of culture and learning. Their private townhouses became new settings for refined social intercourse and conspicuous display. Magnificence implied the liberal spending and accumulation of possessions that advertised a person's virtue, taste, and place in society. "The magnificence of a building," the architect Leon Battista Alberti (1404–1472) declared, "should be adapted to the dignity of its owner."[11] Worldly goods gave tangible expression to spiritual refinement. The paintings of Madonnas and saints that graced Renaissance mansions were much more than objects of devotion: they were statements of cultural and social values. Thus, as with Islam in West Africa, changes in commerce and culture were closely linked. New commercial wealth created an expanded market for art, which was in turn shaped by the values associated with commerce.

Again, as with Islam in West Africa, the intellectual ferment of the Renaissance was nurtured in an urban environment. Humanist scholars shunned the warrior culture of the old nobility while celebrating the civic roles and duties of townsmen, merchants, and clerics. Despite their admiration of classical civilization, the humanists did not reject Christianity. Rather, they sought to reconcile Christian faith and doctrines with classical learning. By making knowledge of Latin and Greek, history, poetry, and philosophy the mark of an educated person, the humanists transformed education and established models of schooling that would endure down to modern times.

Nowhere was the revolutionary impact of the Renaissance felt more deeply than in visual arts such as painting, sculpture, and architecture. Artists of the Renaissance exuded supreme confidence in the ability of human ingenuity to equal or even surpass the works of nature. The new outlook was exemplified by the development of the techniques of perspective, which artists used to convey a realistic, three-dimensional quality to physical forms, most notably the human body. Human invention also was capable of improving on nature by creating order and harmony through architecture and urban planning. Alberti advocated replacing the winding narrow streets and haphazard construction of medieval towns with planned cities organized around straight boulevards, open squares, and monumental buildings whose balanced proportions corresponded to a geometrically unified design.

Above all, the Renaissance transformed the idea of the artist. No longer mere manual tradesmen, artists now were seen as possessing a special kind of genius that enabled them to express a higher understanding of beauty. In the eyes of contemporaries, no one exemplified this quality of genius more than Leonardo da Vinci (1452–1519), who won renown as a painter, architect, sculptor, engineer, mathematician, and inventor. Leonardo's father, a Florentine lawyer, apprenticed him to a local painter at age eighteen. Leonardo spent much of his career as a civil and military engineer in the employ of the Duke of Milan, and developed ideas for flying machines, tanks, robots, and solar power that far exceeded the engineering capabilities of his time. Leonardo sought to apply his knowledge of natural science to painting, which he regarded as the most sublime art (see Seeing the Past: Leonardo da Vinci's *Virgin of the Rocks*).

The flowering of artistic creativity in the Renaissance was rooted in the rich soil of Italy's commercial wealth and nourished by the flow of goods from the Islamic world and Asia. International trade also invigorated industrial and craft production across maritime Asia and gave birth there to new patterns of material culture and consumption. In Japan, however, growing isolation from these cross-cultural interactions fostered the emergence of a national culture distinct from the Chinese traditions that dominated the rest of East Asia.

COUNTERPOINT

Age of the Samurai in Japan 1185–1450

In Japan as in Europe, the term *Middle Ages* brings to mind an age of warriors, a stratified society governed by bonds of loyalty between lords and vassals. In Japan, however, the militarization of the ruling class intensified during the fourteenth and fifteenth centuries, a time when the warrior nobility of Europe was crumbling. Paradoxically, the rise of the **samurai** (sah-moo-rye) ("those who serve") warriors as masters of their own estates was accompanied by the increasing independence of peasant communities.

In contrast to the regions explored earlier in this chapter, Japan became more isolated from the wider world during this era. Commercial and cultural exchanges with China reached a peak in the thirteenth century, but after the failed Mongol invasion of Japan in 1281, ties with continental Asia became increasingly frayed. Thus, many Japanese see this era as the period in which Japan's unique national identity—expressed most distinctly in the ethic of *bushidō* (boo-shee-doe), the "Way of the Warrior"—took its definitive form. Samurai warriors became the

FOCUS

How and why did the historical development of Japan in the fourteenth and fifteenth centuries differ from that of mainland Eurasia?

samurai Literally, "those who serve"; the hereditary warriors who dominated Japanese society and culture from the twelfth to the nineteenth centuries.

Leonardo da Vinci's *Virgin of the Rocks*

Virgin of the Rocks, c. 1483–1486
(Erich Lessing/Art Resource.)

Leonardo's Botanical Studies with Star-of-Bethlehem, Grasses, Crowfoot, Wood Anemone, and Another Genus,
c. 1500–1506 (The Royal Collection © 2011 Her Majesty Queen Elizabeth II/Bridgeman Art Library.)

the menacing darkness of the cavern; desire to see if there was any marvelous thing within."[1]

Fantastic as the scene might seem, Leonardo's meticulous renderings of rocks and plants were based on close observation of nature. The Star of Bethlehem flowers at the lower left of the painting, symbolizing purity and atonement, also appear in the nearly contemporaneous botanical drawing shown here. Geologists have praised Leonardo's highly realistic sandstone rock formations and his precise placement of plants where they would most likely take root.

Masterpieces such as the *Virgin of the Rocks* display Leonardo's careful study of human anatomy, natural landscapes, and botany. Although he admired the perfection of nature, Leonardo also celebrated the human mind's rational and aesthetic capacities, declaring that "we by our arts may be called the grandsons of God."[2]

While living in Milan in the early 1480s, Leonardo accepted a commission to paint an altarpiece for the chapel of Milan's Confraternity of the Immaculate Conception, a branch of the Franciscan order. Leonardo's relationship with the friars proved to be stormy. His first version of the painting (now in the Louvre), reproduced here, apparently displeased his patrons and was sold to another party. Only after a fifteen-year-long dispute over the price did Leonardo finally deliver a modified version in 1508.

In portraying the legendary encounter between the child Jesus and the equally young John the Baptist during the flight to Egypt, Leonardo replaced the traditional desert setting with a landscape filled with rocks, plants, and water. Leonardo's dark grotto creates an aura of mystery and foreboding, from which the figures of Mary, Jesus, John, and the angel Uriel emerge as if in a vision. A few years before, Leonardo had written about "coming to the entrance of a great cavern, in front of which I stood for some time, stupefied and uncomprehending. . . . Suddenly two things arose in me, fear and desire: fear of

1. Arundel ms. (British Library), p. 115 recto, cited in Martin Kemp, *Leonardo da Vinci: The Marvelous Works of Nature and Man* (Oxford: Oxford University Press, 2006), 78.
2. John Paul Richter, ed., *The Notebooks of Leonardo da Vinci* (rpt. of 1883 ed.; New York: Dover, 1970), Book IX, 328 (para. 654).

EXAMINING THE EVIDENCE

1. How does Leonardo express the connection between John (at left) and Jesus through position, gesture, and their relationships with the figures of Mary and the angel Uriel?

2. The friars who commissioned the painting sought to celebrate the sanctity and purity of their patron, the Virgin Mary. Does this painting achieve that effect?

patrons of new forms of cultural expression whose character differed markedly from the Chinese traditions cherished by the old Japanese nobility. A culture based on warriors, rather than Confucian scholars, created a different path for the development of Japanese society.

"The Low Overturning the High"

During the Kamakura period (1185–1333), the power of the **shogun**, or military ruler, of eastern Japan was roughly in balance with that of the imperial court and nobility at Kyoto in the west. Warriors dominated both the shogun's capital at Kamakura (near modern Tokyo) and provincial governorships, but most of the land remained in the possession of the imperial family, the nobility, and religious institutions based in Kyoto. The shoguns appointed low-ranking samurai among their retainers to serve as military stewards on local estates, with responsibility for keeping the peace.

After the collapse of the Kamakura government in 1333, Japan was wracked by civil wars. In 1336 a new dynasty of shoguns, the Ashikaga (ah-shee-KAH-gah), came to power in Kyoto. Unlike the Kamakura shoguns, the Ashikaga aspired to become national rulers. Yet not until 1392 did the Ashikaga shogunate gain uncontested political supremacy, and even then it exercised only limited control over the provinces and local samurai.

In the Kamakura period, the samurai had been vassals subordinated to warrior clans to whom they owed allegiance and service. But wartime disorder and Ashikaga rule eroded the privileges and power of the noble and monastic landowners. Most of their estates fell into the hands of local samurai families, who formed alliances known as *ikki* ("single resolve") to preserve order. The *ikki* brotherhoods signed pacts pledging common arbitration of disputes, joint management of local shrines and festivals, and mutual aid against outside aggressors.

Just as samurai were turning themselves into landowners, peasants banded together in village associations to resist demands for rents and labor service from their new samurai overlords. These village associations began to assert a right to self-government, claiming legal powers formerly held by the noble estate owners.

Like the *ikki* leagues, villages and districts created their own autonomous governments. Their charters expressed resistance to outside control while requiring strict conformity to the collective will of the community. As one village council declared, "Treachery, malicious gossip, or criminal acts against the village association will be punished by excommunication from the estate."[12] Outraged lords bewailed this reversal of the social hierarchy, "the low overturning the high," but found themselves powerless to check the growing independence of peasant communities.

The political strength of the peasants reflected their rising economic fortunes. Japan's agrarian economy improved substantially with the expansion of irrigated rice farming. The village displaced the manorial estate as the basic institution of rural society. Rural traders, mostly drawn from the affluent peasantry, formed merchant guilds and obtained commercial privileges from local authorities. Japan in the fifteenth century had little involvement in foreign trade, and there were few cities apart from the metropolis of Kyoto, which had swelled to 150,000 inhabitants by midcentury. Yet the prosperity of the agrarian economy generated considerable growth in artisan crafts and trade in local goods.

The New Warrior Order

After the founding of the Ashikaga shogunate, provincial samurai swarmed the streets of Kyoto seeking the new rulers' patronage. Their reckless conduct prompted the shoguns to issue regulations forbidding samurai to possess silver swords, wear fine silk clothing, gamble, stage tea-drinking competitions, and consort with loose women—to little effect. In this world of "the low overturning the high," warriors enjoyed newfound wealth while much of the old nobility was reduced to abject poverty.

Rise of the Samurai

Japan, 1185–1392

shogun The military commander who effectively exercised supreme political and military authority over Japan during the Kamakura (1185–1333), Ashikaga (1338–1573), and Tokugawa (1603–1868) shogunates.

Night Attack on the Sanjo Palace

The Heiji Revolt of 1159 marked a key turning point in the shift from aristocratic to warrior rule in Japan. This scene from a thirteenth-century scroll painting depicts the samurai rebels storming the imperial palace and taking the emperor hostage. Although the leaders of the insurrection were captured and executed, the revolt plunged Japan into civil wars that ended only when the Kamakura shogun seized power in 1185. (Werner Forman/Art Resource.)

Cultural and Social Life of the Samurai

While derided by courtiers as uneducated and boorish, the shoguns and samurai became patrons of artists and cultural life. The breakdown of the traditional social hierarchy allowed greater intermingling among people from diverse backgrounds. By the early fifteenth century the outlandish antics of the capital's samurai had been tempered by a new sense of elegance and refinement. The social and cultural worlds of the warriors and courtiers merged, producing new forms of social behavior and artistic expression.

In the early years of the Ashikaga shogunate, the capital remained infatuated with Chinese culture. As the fourteenth century wore on, however, this fascination with China was eclipsed by new fashions drawn from both the court nobility and Kyoto's lively world of popular entertainments. Accomplishment in poetry and graceful language and manners, hallmarks of the courtier class, became part of samurai self-identity as well. A new mood of simplicity and restraint took hold, infused with the ascetic ethics of Zen Buddhism, which stressed introspective meditation as the path to enlightenment.

The sensibility of the Ashikaga age was visible in new kinds of artistic display and performance, including poetry recitation, flower arrangement, and the complex rituals of the tea ceremony. A new style of theater known as *nō* reflected this fusion of courtly refinement, Zen religious sentiments, and samurai cultural tastes. The lyrical language and stylized dances of *nō* performances portrayed samurai as men of feeling rather than ferocious warriors. Thus, the rise of warrior culture in Japan did not mean an end to sophistication and refinement. It did, however, involve a strong focus on cultural elements that were seen as distinctly Japanese.

In at least one area, developments in Japan mirrored those in other parts of the world. The warriors' dominance over Ashikaga society and culture led to a decisive shift toward patriarchal authority. Women lost rights of inheritance as warrior houses consolidated landholdings in the hands of one son who would continue the family line. Marriage and sexual conduct were subject to stricter regulation. The libertine sexual mores of the Japanese aristocracy depicted in Lady Murasaki's *Tale of Genji* (c. 1010) gave way to a new emphasis on female chastity as an index of social order. The profuse output of novels, memoirs, and diaries written by court women also came to an end by 1350. Aristocratic women continued to hold positions of responsibility at court, but their literary talents were devoted to keeping official records rather than expressing their personal thoughts.

By 1400, then, the samurai had achieved political mastery in both the capital and the countryside and had eclipsed the old nobility as arbiters of cultural values. This warrior culture, which combined martial prowess with austere aesthetic tastes, stood in sharp contrast to the veneration of Confucian learning by the Chinese literati and the classical ideals and ostentatious consumption prized by the urban elite of Renaissance Italy.

Conclusion

The fourteenth century was an age of crisis across Eurasia and Africa. The population losses resulting from the Black Death devastated Christian and Muslim societies and economies. In the long run Latin Christendom fared well: the institution of serfdom largely disappeared from western Europe; new entrepreneurial energies were released; and the Italian city-states recovered their commercial vigor and stimulated economic revival in northern Europe. However, the once-great Byzantine Empire succumbed to the expanding Ottoman Empire and, under fire by Urban's cannon, came to an end in 1453. Although the Ottoman conquest of the Balkan peninsula threatened Latin Christendom, the central Islamic lands, from Egypt to Mesopotamia, never regained their former economic vitality. Still, the Muslim faith continued to spread, winning new converts in Africa, Central Asia, and Southeast Asia.

The fourteenth century also witnessed the collapse of the Mongol empires in China and Iran, followed by the rise and fall of the last of the Mongol empires, that of Timur. In China, the Ming dynasty spurned the Mongol vision of a multinational empire, instead returning to an imperial order based on an agrarian economy, bureaucratic rule, and Neo-Confucian values. New dynastic leaders in Korea and Vietnam imitated the Ming model, but in Japan the rising samurai warrior class forged a radically different set of social institutions and cultural values.

The Black Death redirected the course of European state-making. Monarchs strengthened their authority, aided by advances in military technology, mercenary armies, and fresh sources of revenue. The intensifying competition among national states would become one of the main motives for overseas exploration and expansion in the Atlantic world. At the same time, the great transformation in culture, lifestyles, and values known as the Renaissance sprang from the ruin of the Black Death. But the Renaissance was not purely an intellectual and artistic phenomenon. Its cultural innovations were linked to crucial changes in the Italian economy and the international trading world of the Mediterranean and beyond.

Asia was largely spared the ravages of the Black Death pandemic. Maritime Asia, from China to the east coast of Africa, enjoyed a robust boom in trade during the fifteenth century, in contrast to the sluggish economic recovery in much of Europe and the Islamic world. The intrusion of the Portuguese into the Indian Ocean in 1498 would upset the balance of political and economic power throughout Asian waters and dramatically alter Asia's place in what became the first truly global economy. But the arrival of the Europeans would have far more catastrophic effects on the societies of the Americas, which were unprepared for the political and economic challenges—and especially the onslaught of epidemic disease—that followed Columbus's landing in the Caribbean islands in 1492.

NOTES

1. Giovanni Boccaccio, *The Decameron* (New York: Modern Library, 1931), 8–9.
2. Quoted in Adel Allouche, *Mamluk Economics: A Study and Translation of Al-Maqrizi's* Ighathah (Salt Lake City: University of Utah Press, 1994), 75–76 (translation slightly modified).
3. Quoted in Michael W. Dols, "Ibn al-Wardi's *Risalah al-naba' 'an al'waba*': A Translation of a Major Source for the History of the Black Death in the Middle East," in *Near Eastern Numismatics, Iconography, Epigraphy and History: Studies in Honor of George C. Miles*, ed. Dickran K. Kouymjian (Beirut, Lebanon: American University of Beirut, 1974), 454.
4. *Anonimalle Chronicle*, in *The Peasants' Revolt of 1381*, ed. R. B. Dobson (London: Macmillan, 1970), 164–165.
5. Ibn Battuta, "The Sultan of Mali," in *Corpus of Early Arabic Sources for West African History*, trans. J. F. P. Hopkins, ed. N. Levtzion and J. F. P. Hopkins (Cambridge, U.K.: Cambridge University Press, 1981), 296.
6. Leo Africanus, *History and Description of Africa*, trans. John Poy (London: Hakluyt Society, 1896), 3:825.
7. Shihab al-Din Ahmad ibn Majid, "Al'Mal'aqiya," in *A Study of the Arabic Texts Containing Material of South-East Asia*, ed. and trans. G. R. Tibbetts (Leiden, Netherlands: Brill, 1979), 206.

8. Ibn Battuta, *Travels in Asia and Africa, 1325–1354*, trans. H. A. R. Gibb (London: Routledge & Kegan Paul, 1929), 235.

9. Simone Sigoli, "Pilgrimage of Simone Sigoli to the Holy Land," in *Visit to the Holy Places of Egypt, Sinai, Palestine and Syria in 1384 by Frescobaldi, Gucci, and Sigoli*, trans. Theophilus Bellorini and Eugene Hoade (Jerusalem: Franciscan Press, 1948), 182.

10. Quoted in Lisa Jardine, *Worldly Goods: A New History of the Renaissance* (New York: Doubleday, 1996), 126.

11. Quoted in Richard A. Goldthwaite, *Wealth and the Demand for Art in Italy, 1300–1600* (Baltimore: Johns Hopkins University Press, 1993), 220.

12. Declaration of Oshima and Okitsushima shrine association, dated 1298, quoted in Pierre François Souyri, *The World Turned Upside Down: Medieval Japanese Society* (New York: Columbia University Press, 2001), 136.

RESOURCES FOR RESEARCH

Fourteenth-Century Crisis and Renewal in Eurasia

William McNeill's landmark work drew attention to the profound impact of epidemic diseases on world history. The exact cause of the Black Death remains a subject of debate, as the works of Cantor and Herlihy show, but few dispute that the pandemic had lasting consequences for European history. The influence of the Black Death in the Islamic world is less well studied, but Borsch's recent study seeks to explain why the economic depression it caused lasted longer in Egypt than in Europe.

Borsch, Stuart J. *The Black Death in Egypt and England: A Comparative Study.* 2005.

British History in Depth: The Black Death. http://www.bbc.co.uk/history/british/middle_ages/black_01.shtml

Brook, Timothy. *The Confusions of Pleasure: Commerce and Culture in Ming China.* 1998.

Cantor, Norman. *In the Wake of the Plague: The Black Death and the World It Made.* 2001.

Herlihy, David. *The Black Death and the Transformation of the West.* 1997.

McNeill, William H. *Plagues and Peoples.* 1976.

Islam's New Frontiers

The study of Islam in Africa has advanced rapidly in recent years. Robinson serves as a good overview; the essays in Levtzion and Pouwells provide comprehensive regional coverage. Imber provides the best introduction to the early history of the Ottoman Empire.

Dunn, Ross E. *The Adventures of Ibn Battuta: A Muslim Traveler of the 14th Century.* 1989.

Imber, Colin. *The Ottoman Empire, 1300–1650: The Structure of Power,* 2d ed. 2009.

Levtzion, Nehemia, and Randall L. Pouwells, eds. *The History of Islam in Africa.* 2000.

Manz, Beatrice Forbes. *The Rise and Rule of Tamerlane.* 1989.

Robinson, David. *Muslim Societies in African History.* 2004.

The Global Bazaar

New scholarship has erased the older image of this period as "the Dark Ages." The original understanding of the Renaissance as an intellectual and artistic movement centered in Italy has been broadened to include transformative changes in trade, industry, material culture, and lifestyles. Similarly, accounts of voyages of Zheng He—lucidly described by Levathes—have opened a window on the vigorous cultural and economic interchange across Asia; Reid examines this topic in greater detail.

Burke, Peter. *The European Renaissance: Centres and Peripheries.* 1998.

Finlay, Robert. *The Pilgrim Art: Cultures of Porcelain in World History.* 2010.

Goldthwaite, Richard A. *Wealth and the Demand for Art in Italy, 1300–1600.* 1993.

Jardine, Lisa. *Worldly Goods: A New History of the Renaissance.* 1996.

Levathes, Louise. *When China Ruled the Seas: The Treasure Fleet of the Dragon Throne, 1405–1433.* 1994.

Reid, Anthony. *Southeast Asia in the Age of Commerce, 1350–1750.* Vol. 1, *The Land Below the Winds*; Vol. 2, *Expansion and Crisis.* 1989, 1993.

COUNTERPOINT: Age of the Samurai in Japan, 1185–1450

Recent years have seen a wave of revisionist scholarship on medieval Japan. Souyri's work stands out for its finely detailed depiction of social diversity. *Tale of the Heike,* an account of the struggle between warlords that led to the founding of the Kamakura shogunate, provides a sharp contrast to earlier courtly literature such as Lady Murasaki's *Tale of Genji.*

Adolphson, Mikael S. *The Gates of Power: Monks, Courtiers, and Warriors in Premodern Japan.* 2000.

Mass, Jeffrey P., ed. *The Origins of Japan's Medieval World: Courtiers, Clerics, Warriors, and Peasants in the Fourteenth Century.* 1997.

McCullough, Helen Craig, trans. *Tale of the Heike.* 1988.

Souyri, Pierre-François. *The World Turned Upside Down: Medieval Japanese Society.* 2001.

Wakita, Haruko. *Women in Medieval Japan: Motherhood, Household Economy, and Sexuality.* 2006.

▶ **For additional primary sources from this period,** see *Sources of Crossroads and Cultures.*

▶ **For Web sites, images, and documents related to topics in this chapter,** see Make History at bedfordstmartins.com/smith.

The major global development in this chapter ▶ Crisis and recovery
in fourteenth- and fifteenth-century Afro-Eurasia.

IMPORTANT EVENTS

1315–1317	Great Famine in northern Europe
1325–1354	Travels of Ibn Battuta in Asia and Africa
1336–1573	Ashikaga shogunate in Japan
1337–1453	Hundred Years' War between England and France
1347–1350	Outbreak of the Black Death in Europe and the Islamic Mediterranean
c. 1351–1782	Ayudhya kingdom in Thailand
1368–1644	Ming dynasty in China
1378	Ciompi uprising in Florence
1381	Peasant Revolt in England
1392–1910	Yi dynasty in Korea
1405	Death of Timur; breakup of his empire into regional states in Iran and Central Asia
1405–1433	Chinese admiral Zheng He's expeditions in Southeast Asia and the Indian Ocean
1421	Relocation of Ming capital from Nanjing to Beijing
1428–1788	Le dynasty in Vietnam
1453	Ottoman conquest of Constantinople marks fall of the Byzantine Empire

KEY TERMS

Black Death (p. 478)   pandemic (p. 478)
humanism (p. 498)   Renaissance (p. 498)
janissary corps (p. 489)   samurai (p. 501)
Little Ice Age (p. 479)   shogun (p. 503)
Neo-Confucianism   Sufism (p. 488)
  (p. 486)   theocracy (p. 489)
oligarchy (p. 483)   trade diaspora (p. 492)

CHAPTER OVERVIEW QUESTIONS

1. How and why did Europe's economic growth begin to surpass that of the Islamic world in the century after the Black Death?

2. Did the economic revival across Eurasia after 1350 benefit the peasant populations of Europe, the Islamic world, and East Asia?

3. How did the process of conversion to Islam differ in Iran, the Ottoman Empire, West Africa, and Southeast Asia during this period?

4. What political and economic changes contributed to the rise of maritime commerce in Asia during the fourteenth and fifteenth centuries?

SECTION FOCUS QUESTIONS

1. How did the Black Death affect society, the economy, and culture in Latin Christendom and the Islamic world?

2. Why did Islam expand dramatically in the fourteenth and fifteenth centuries, and how did new Islamic societies differ from established ones?

3. What were the principal sources of growth in international trade during the fourteenth and fifteenth centuries, and how did this trade affect patterns of consumption and fashion tastes?

4. How and why did the historical development of Japan in the fourteenth and fifteenth centuries differ from that of mainland Eurasia?

MAKING CONNECTIONS

1. What social, economic, and technological changes strengthened the power of European monarchs during the century after the Black Death?

2. How and why did the major routes and commodities of trans-Eurasian trade change after the collapse of the Mongol empires in Central Asia?

3. In what ways did the motives for conversion to Islam differ in Central Asia, sub-Saharan Africa, and the Indian Ocean during this era?

4. In this period, why did the power and status of the samurai warriors in Japan rise while those of the warrior nobility in Europe declined?

PART 3

The Early Modern World

1450–1750

CH 16

MAJOR GLOBAL CHANGES occurred between 1450 and 1750, as regional societies gave way to multiethnic empires, and horse-borne raiders gave way to cannon and long-distance sailing craft. Historians call this era "early modern" because it was marked by a general shift toward centralized, bureaucratic, monetized, and technologically sophisticated states. Yet nearly all of these "modern" states also clung to divine kingship and other remnants of the previous age, and most sought to revive and propagate older religious or philosophical traditions. Some states embraced mutual tolerance, but many others fought bitterly over matters of faith.

One of the most striking breaks with the past was the creation of new linkages between distant regions, most notably the Americas and the rest of the world. Early globalization accelerated changes in everything from demography to commerce to technology, allowing populations to grow and many individuals to get rich. Yet globalization also enabled the spread of disease, and some technical innovations increased the scale and deadliness of warfare; early modernity did not promise longer and better lives for everyone. The shift to modernity was not a uniquely Western phenomenon either, although western Europeans were key players in its spread, usually as traders, missionaries, or conquerors.

CH 17

Beginning in around 1450, Iberians—the people of Spain and Portugal—used new ships and guns to venture into the Atlantic, where they competed in overseas colonization, trade, and conquest. They set out to claim new territories for their monarchs and to spread their Roman Catholic faith. They did both at the expense of many millions of native peoples, first in Africa and the East Atlantic and then throughout the Americas and beyond. Wherever they went, Iberians moved quickly from plunder to the creation of settled colonies, creating a new trading sphere that historians call the "Atlantic world." Other Europeans soon followed in the Iberians' wake, but the silver of Spanish America became the world's money.

Modernity affected Africa most deeply via the slave trade. The older flow of captive workers to the Muslim Middle East and Indian Ocean basin continued well into early modern times, but it was soon overshadowed by a more urgent European demand in the Atlantic. This desire for slaves to staff distant plantations and mines fueled

CH 18

existing antagonisms within Africa even as it spawned new ones, each generating captives and refugees to be traded abroad for select commodities, including firearms, textiles, and metal ware. Europeans did not penetrate, much less conquer, sub-Saharan Africa at this time, however, in part due to their general lack of resistance to tropical disease.

In the vast Indian Ocean basin a freer model of interaction and integration developed. Islamic merchants had come to dominate these seas by 1450, not through imperial means but rather by establishing trading networks from East Africa to Southeast Asia. Luxury products from the African interior were traded abroad for spices, cloth, porcelain, and other compact valuables. Ships also carried bulk commodities and religious pilgrims. After 1500, European interlopers discovered that in such a thriving, diverse, and politically decentralized region, they would have to compete fiercely for space. This they did, first by establishing coastal trading forts, then by moving inland.

On the Eurasian mainland, with the aid of modern firearms, powerful Ottoman, Russian, Safavid, and Mughal leaders turned from regional consolidation to massive imperial expansion by the sixteenth century. Each combined religious fervor with considerable political ambitions, but several of these states, notably the Ottomans and Mughals, embraced religious diversity. Collecting tributes in cash and establishing the appropriate bureaucracies to collect them were shared objectives. Unlike the Safavids and Mughals, the Ottomans sought to extend their empire overseas, taking on Venice and the Habsburgs in the Mediterranean and the Portuguese in the Indian Ocean. Russia would venture abroad under Peter the Great.

Europe remained mostly embroiled in religious and political conflict. The religious schism known as the Protestant Reformation touched off over a century of bloody war after 1500, and doctrinal disputes would carry on well into modern times. Warfare itself was transformed from knightly contests and town sieges to mass infantry mobilization and bombardment of strategic fortresses. These models would be exported, along with armed sailing ships. Europe's political fractures enabled the rise of market economies as well, with more states sponsoring overseas colonizing ventures

CH 19

CH 20

over time to augment their share of business. New forms of government emerged, and also a marked tendency to question ancient authorities. From this came a revolution in science, emphasizing physical observation and secular reasoning, and at the end of the early modern period, a new intellectual movement known as the Enlightenment.

In East Asia, by contrast, introversion rather than foreign engagement was the rule in early modern times. Although both China and Japan had strong seafaring traditions by 1450, state policies from the fifteenth to sixteenth centuries gradually discouraged external affairs. Despite official isolation, both regions proved to be extraordinarily dynamic. Political consolidation and population growth were matched with a general shift from tributary to money economies. In the Chinese Ming and Qing empires this led to a massive rise in demand for silver, stimulating global circulation of this mostly American-produced metal. Porcelain and silk, much of it produced by poor women working in the household, were sent abroad in exchange. With the patronage of newly wealthy merchants and bureaucrats, the arts flourished on a scale not seen before.

By 1700, the American colonies were not the neo-Europes their first colonizers had envisioned. Centuries of ethnic and cultural mixture, forced labor regimes, frontier expansion, and export-oriented economies all led to the formation of distinct societies. Native populations were recovering in some areas, and African and African-descended populations had grown to dominate whole regions. Europeans continued to migrate to the colonies in search of new livelihoods, but most soon adopted the nativist attitudes of earlier colonizers. In much of the Americas, the different outlooks of European colonizers and colonists would prove irreconcilable by the end of the early modern era.

CH 21

	1400	1500
Americas	1325–1521 Aztec Empire · 1430–1532 Inca Empire · Columbus reaches the Americas 1492 · Portuguese reach Brazil 1500 ·	Spanish conquest of Aztecs 1519–1521 · Discovery of silver at Potosí 1545 · Spanish conquest of Inca 1532–1536
Europe	1462–1505 Ivan III unites Russia · Christian reconquest of Spain completed 1492 · 1473–1543 Copernicus	· 1517 Luther confronts Catholic Church, sparking the Protestant Reformation
Middle East	· 1453 Ottoman conquest of Constantinople	Ottoman conquest of Egypt 1517 · Battle of Lepanto 1571 · 1520–1566 Reign of Suleiman the Magnificent
Africa	First sub-Saharan Africans captured and taken to Portugal 1441 · · 1450 Height of kingdom of Benin · 1464–1492 Reign of Songhai emperor Sunni Ali	1506–1543 Reign of Afonso I of Kongo
Asia and Oceania	1405–1433 Voyages of Ming admiral Zheng He · 1421 Relocation of Ming capital to Beijing · 1428–1788 Vietnamese Le dynasty	· 1498 Vasco da Gama reaches India · Portuguese establish fort in Ceylon 1517

Despite these profound transformations, many people remained largely unaffected by the currents of early modernity. Though not densely populated, most of North and South America, Polynesia, Oceania, central and southern Africa, and highland Asia remained beyond the zone of sustained contact with foreigners. New commodities and biological transfers were only beginning to be felt in many of these places at the end of the early modern period. As a result of their long isolation, inhabitants of these regions would be among the most drastically affected by modernity's next wave.

CH 22

1600		1700		1800

- **1625** Dutch settle New Amsterdam; English establish colony on Barbados
- **1607** English establish colony at Jamestown, Virginia
- **1608** French establish colony at Quebec City
- **1763** Rio de Janeiro becomes capital of Brazil
- **1695–1800** Brazil's "gold rush"

- **1588** English defeat Spanish Armada
- **1618–1648** Thirty Years' War
- **1643–1715** Reign of Louis XIV
- **1600** English East India Company founded
- **1642–1727** Newton
- **1688** England's Glorious Revolution
- **1712–1714** War of the Spanish Succession
- **1712** Peter the Great founds St. Petersburg
- **1700–1800** The Enlightenment

- **1600–1629** Peak of Safavid Empire
- Last Ottoman siege at Vienna defeated **1683**
- **1736–1747** Nadir Shah reunites Iran
- **1722** Fall of Safavid Empire

- **1591** Moroccan raiders conquer Songhai Empire
- **1624–1663** Reign of Queen Nzinga in Ndongo
- **1638–1641** Dutch seize São Jorge da Mina and Luanda
- **1680s** Rise of kingdom of Asante
- **1720s** Rise of kingdom of Dahomey
- **1750–1800** Height of Atlantic slave trade

- **1602–1867** Tokugawa Shogunate
- **1644** Manchu invasion of Beijing; Ming Empire replaced by Qing
- **1500–1763** Mughal Empire
- **1736–1799** Reign of Qing emperor Qianlong
- **1751** Qing annexation of Tibet

AT A CROSSROADS ▲

Perched on a granite ridge high above Peru's Urubamba River, the Inca site of Machu Picchu continues to draw thousands of visitors each year. First thought to be the lost city of Vilcabamba, then a convent for Inca nuns, Machu Picchu is now believed to have been a mid-fifteenth-century palace built for the Inca emperor and his mummy cult. It was probably more a religious site than a place of rest and recreation. (The Art Archive/Gianni Dagli Orti.)

Empires and Alternatives in the Americas

1430–1530

In 1995, American archaeologist Johan Reinhard and his assistants discovered a tomb atop Mount Ampato, a peak overlooking the Peruvian city of Arequipa. Inside were the naturally mummified remains of a fourteen-year-old girl placed there some five hundred years earlier. Material and written evidence suggests she was an *aclla* (AHK-yah), or "chosen woman," selected by Inca priests from among hundreds of regional headmen's daughters. Most aclla girls became priestesses in temples and palaces dedicated to the Inca emperor or the imperial sun cult. Others became the emperor's concubines or wives. Only the most select, like the girl discovered on Mount Ampato, were chosen for the "debt-payment" sacrifice, or *capacocha* (kah-pah-KOH-chah), said to be the greatest honor of all.

According to testimonies collected soon after the Spanish conquest of the Incas in 1532 (discussed in the next chapter), the capacocha sacrifice was a rare and deeply significant event preceded by numerous rituals. First, the victim, chosen for her (and rarely, his) physical perfection, trekked to Cuzco, the Inca capital, to be feasted and blessed. The child's father brought gifts and sacred objects from his province and in turn received fine textiles from the emperor. Following an ancient Andean tradition, reciprocal ties between ruler and ruled were reinforced through such acts of ritualized gift exchange, feasting, and finally, sacrifice. The girl, too, received fine alpaca and cotton skirts and shawls, along with tiny gold and silver votive objects, a necklace of shell beads, and tufts of tropical bird feathers. These items adorned her in her tomb, reached after a long journey on foot from Cuzco.

As suggested by later discoveries in Chile and Argentina, at tomb-side the aclla girl was probably given a beaker filled with beer brewed from maize. In a pouch she carried coca leaves. The sacred coca, chewed throughout the Andes, helped fend off the headaches

BACKSTORY

By the fifteenth century, the Americas had witnessed the rise and fall of numerous empires and kingdoms, including the classic Maya of Mesoamerica, the wealthy Sicán kingdom of Peru's desert coast, and the Cahokia mound builders of the Mississippi Basin. Just as these cultures faded, there emerged two new imperial states that borrowed heavily from their predecessors. The empires treated in this chapter, the Aztec and Inca, were the largest states ever to develop in the Americas, yet they were not all-powerful. About half of all native Americans, among them the diverse peoples of North America's eastern woodlands, lived outside their realms.

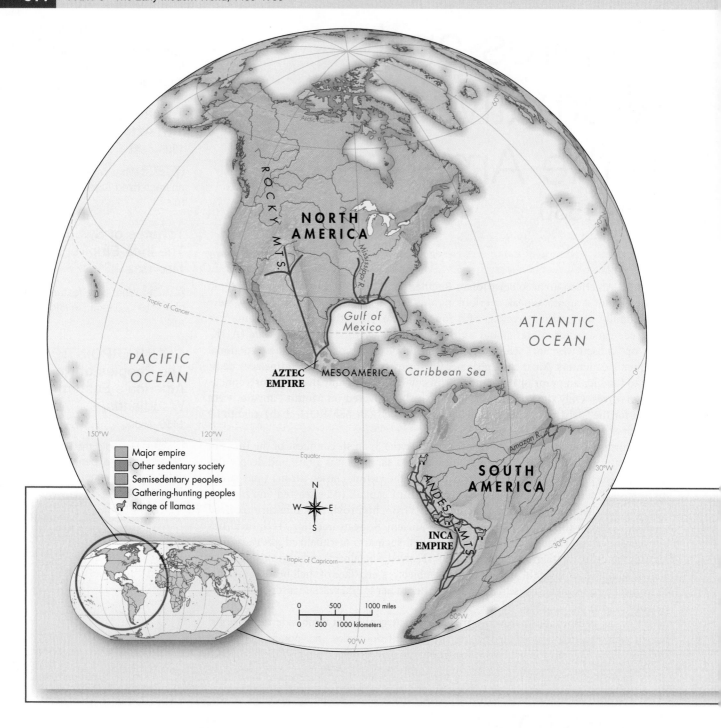

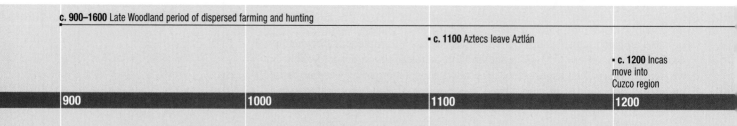

c. 900–1600 Late Woodland period of dispersed farming and hunting

▪ **c. 1100** Aztecs leave Aztlán

▪ **c. 1200** Incas move into Cuzco region

| 900 | 1000 | 1100 | 1200 |

and nausea brought on by oxygen starvation at high altitude, whereas the maize beer induced sleepiness. Barely conscious of her surroundings, the girl was lowered into her grass-lined grave, and, according to the forensic anthropologists who examined her skull, struck dead with a club. Other Inca sacrificial victims appear to have been buried alive and left to freeze to death, as described in postconquest accounts.

Why did the Incas sacrifice children, and why in these ways? By combining material, written, and oral evidence, scholars are beginning to solve the riddle of the Inca mountain mummies. From what is now known, it appears that death, fertility, reciprocity, and imperial links to sacred landscapes were all features of the capacocha sacrifice. Although macabre practices such as this may challenge our ability to empathize with the leaders, if not the common folk, of this distant culture, with each new fact we learn about the child mummies, the closer we get to understanding the Inca Empire and its ruling cosmology.

The Incas and their subjects shared the belief that death occurred as a process rather than in an instant, and that proper death led to an elevated state of consciousness. In this altered state a person could communicate with deities directly, and in a sense join them. If the remains of such a person were carefully preserved and honored, they could act as an oracle, a conduit to the sacred realms above and below the earth. Mountains, as sources of springs and rivers, and sometimes fertilizing volcanic ash, held particular spiritual significance.

In part, it was this complex of beliefs about landscape, death, and the afterlife that led the Incas to mummify and otherwise preserve respected ancestors, including their emperors, and to bury chosen young people atop mountains that marked the edges, or heights, of empire. Physically perfect noble children such as the girl found on Mount Ampato were thus selected for the role of communicants with the spirit world. Their sacrifice unified the dead, the living, and the sacred mountains, and also bound together a far-flung empire that was in many ways as fragile as life itself.[1]

MAPPING THE WORLD

The Western Hemisphere, c. 1500

Native Americans inhabited the entire Western Hemisphere from the Arctic Circle to the tip of South America. Their societies varied tremendously in density and political sophistication, largely as a result of adaptation to different natural environments. Empires were found only in the tropical highlands of Mesoamerica and the Andes, but large chiefdoms based on farming could be found in eastern Canada, the bigger Caribbean islands, and the lower Amazon Basin. Gatherer-hunters were the most widespread of all native American cultures, and despite their relatively small numbers they proved most resistant to conquest by settled neighbors.

ROUTES ▼

— Inca road
— Other trade route

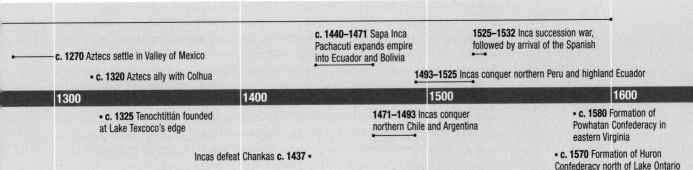

c. 1270 Aztecs settle in Valley of Mexico

c. 1320 Aztecs ally with Colhua

c. 1440–1471 Sapa Inca Pachacuti expands empire into Ecuador and Bolivia

1525–1532 Inca succession war, followed by arrival of the Spanish

1493–1525 Incas conquer northern Peru and highland Ecuador

1300   **1400**   **1500**   **1600**

c. 1325 Tenochtitlán founded at Lake Texcoco's edge

1471–1493 Incas conquer northern Chile and Argentina

c. 1580 Formation of Powhatan Confederacy in eastern Virginia

Incas defeat Chankas c. 1437

c. 1570 Formation of Huron Confederacy north of Lake Ontario

Great famine in Valley of Mexico 1450–1451

1487–1502 Aztecs dedicate Coatepec (Templo Mayor) and expand sacrificial wars

c. 1570 Formation of Iroquois League south of Lake Ontario

1502–1519 Reign of Moctezuma II, conquered by Spanish

But this fragility was not evident to the people gathered at the capacocha sacrifice. By about 1480, more than half of all native Americans were subjects of two great empires, the Aztec in Mexico and Central America and the Inca in South America. In part by drawing on ancient religious and political traditions, both empires excelled at subduing neighboring chiefdoms through a mix of violence, forced relocation, religious indoctrination, and marriage alliances. Both empires demanded allegiance in the form of tribute. Both the Aztecs and Incas were greatly feared by their many millions of subjects. Perhaps surprisingly, these last great native American states would prove far more vulnerable to European invaders than their nonimperial neighbors, most of whom were gatherer-hunters and semisedentary villagers. Those who relied least on farming had the best chance of getting away.

OVERVIEW
QUESTIONS

The major global development in this chapter: The diversity of societies and states in the Americas prior to European invasion.

As you read, consider:

1. In what ways was cultural diversity in the Americas related to environmental diversity?

2. Why was it in Mesoamerica and the Andes that large empires emerged in around 1450?

3. What key ideas or practices extended beyond the limits of the great empires?

Many Native Americas

FOCUS

What factors account for the diversity of native American cultures?

Scholars once claimed that the Western Hemisphere was sparsely settled prior to the arrival of Europeans in 1492, but we now know that by the end of the fifteenth century the overall population of the Americas had reached some 60 million or more. Vast open spaces remained, but in places the landscape was more intensively cultivated and thickly populated than western Europe (see Map 16.1). Fewer records for nonimperial groups survive than for empire builders such as the Incas and Aztecs, but by combining archaeological, artistic, anthropological, linguistic, and historical approaches, scholars have shed much new light on these less-studied cultures. Outside imperial boundaries, coastal and riverside populations were densest. This was true in the Caribbean, the Amazon and Mississippi river basins, the Pacific Northwest, parts of North America's eastern seaboard, and the upper Río de la Plata district of southeastern South America.

Population Density

Environmental and Cultural Diversity

Ecological diversity gave rise in part to political and cultural diversity. America's native peoples, or Amerindians, lived scattered throughout two vast and ecologically diverse continents. They also inhabited a variety of tropical, temperate, and icy environments that proved more or less suitable to settled agriculture. Some were members of wandering, egalitarian gatherer-hunter bands; others were subjects of rigidly stratified imperial states. In between were many alternatives: traveling bands of pilgrims led by prophets, as in Brazil and southeastern North America; chiefdoms based on fishing,

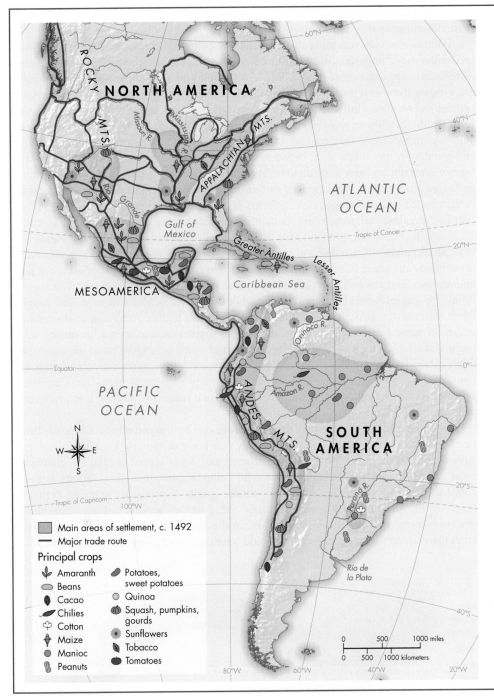

MAP 16.1

Main Settlement Areas in the Americas, c. 1492

Most native Americans settled in regions that supported intensive agriculture. In Mesoamerica and greater North America, maize, beans, and squash were key crops. Andean peoples also grew these crops, but they relied more on potatoes and related tubers, supplemented by quinoa. People throughout the tropical Americas grew cotton, and tobacco was even more widespread. The trade routes shown here linked peoples from very different cultures, mostly to exchange rare items such as shells, precious stones, gold dust, and bird feathers, but seeds for new crops also followed these paths.

whaling, or farming, as in the Pacific Northwest and Greater Antilles; large confederacies of chiefdoms as in highland Colombia and northeastern North America; commercially vibrant and independent city-states as in the Maya heartland of Central America. Others, such as the peoples of coastal Ecuador and the Lesser Antilles, had mastered the sea, routinely ferrying goods and ideas from one continent to the other, and throughout the Caribbean islands. Gold working and maize farming were among the many technologies that traversed American waters. Long-distance overland traders were equally important, carrying copper and tropical feathers from Central America to North America's desert Southwest in exchange for turquoise or, in South America, trekking between distant jungle, mountain, and coast settlements to trade gold and precious stones for seashells, animal pelts, and salt.

Political diversity was more than matched by cultural diversity. The Aztecs and Incas spread the use of imperial dialects within their empires, but elsewhere hundreds of distinct Amerindian languages could be heard. Modes of dress and adornment were even more varied, ranging from total nudity and a few tattoos to highly elaborate ceremonial dress. Arctic peoples had no choice but to bundle up, yet even their style choices distinguished one group from another. In imperial societies strict rules of dress and decorum separated elites from commoners, women from men, and juniors from seniors. Lip and ear piercing, tooth filing, and molding of the infant skull between slats of wood were but a few of the many ways human appearances were reconfigured. Architecture was just as varied, as were ceramics and other arts. In short, the Americas' extraordinary range of climates and natural resources both reflected and encouraged diverse forms of material and linguistic expression. Perhaps only in the realm of religion, where shamanism persisted, was a unifying thread to be found.

Shamanism

Not a formal ideology or doctrine but rather a broadly similar set of beliefs and practices, **shamanism** consisted of a given tribe's or chiefdom's reliance on healer-visionaries for spiritual guidance. In imperial societies shamans constituted a priestly class. Both male and female, shamans had functions ranging from fortuneteller to physician, with women often acting as midwives (see Lives and Livelihoods: The Aztec Midwife, page 528). Judging from material remains and eyewitness accounts, most native American shamans were males. In some Amerindian cultures the role of shaman was inherited; in others, select juniors announced their vocation following a vision quest, or lengthy ritual seclusion. This often entailed a solo journey to a forest or desert region, prolonged physical suffering, and controlled use of hallucinogenic substances. In many respects Amerindian shamanism reflected its Central Asian origins, and in other ways it resembled shamanistic practices in sub-Saharan Africa.

Often labeled "witch-doctors" or "false prophets" by unsympathetic Christian Europeans, shamans maintained and developed a vast body of esoteric knowledge that they passed along to juniors in initiations and other rituals. Some served as village or clan historians and myth-keepers. Most used powerful hallucinogens, including various forms of concentrated tobacco, to communicate with the spirits of predatory animals. Perhaps a legacy of the ancient era of great mammals and a sign of general human vulnerability, predators were venerated almost everywhere in the Americas. Animal spirits were regarded as the shaman's alter ego or protector, and were consulted prior to important occasions

Canadian War Club

This stone war club with a fish motif was excavated from a native American tomb in coastal British Columbia, Canada, and is thought to date from around 1200 to 1400 C.E. Such items at first suggest a people at war, but this club was probably intended only for ceremonial use. Other clubs from the same tomb share its overt sexual symbolism. Modern Tsimshian inhabitants of the region, who still rely on salmon, describe the exchange of stone clubs in their foundation myths. (National Museum of the American Indian, Smithsonian Institution. Catalog number: 5/5059. Photo by Katherine Fogden.)

shamanism Widespread system of religious belief and healing originating in Central Asia.

such as royal marriages, births, and declarations of war. Shamans also mastered herbal remedies for virtually all forms of illness, including emotional disorders. These rubs, washes, and infusions were sometimes highly effective, as shown by modern pharmacological studies. Shamans nearly always administered them along with complex chants and rituals aimed at expelling evil spirits. Shamans, therefore, combined the roles of physician and religious leader, using their knowledge and power to heal both body and spirit.

Range of Livelihoods

The many varieties of social organization and cultural practice found in the early modern Americas reflect both creative interactions with specific environments and the visions of individual political and religious leaders. Some Amerindian gatherer-hunters lived in swamplands and desert areas where subsistence agriculture was impossible using available technologies. Often such gathering-hunting peoples traded with—or plundered—their farming neighbors. Yet even farming peoples, as their ceramic and textile decorations attest, did not forget their past as hunters. As in other parts of the world, big-game hunting in the early modern Americas was an esteemed, even sacred activity among urban elites, marked by elaborate taboos and rituals.

Just as hunting remained important to farmers, agriculture could be found among some of the Americas' least politically complex societies, again characterized by elaborate rituals and taboos. According to many early modern observers, women controlled most agricultural tasks and spaces, periodically making offerings and singing to spirits associated with human fertility. Staple foods included maize, potatoes, and manioc, a lowland tropical tuber that could be ground into flour and preserved. Agricultural rituals were central in most cultures, and at the heart of every imperial state. With the ebb and flow of empires, many groups shifted from one mode of subsistence to another, from planting to gathering-hunting and back again. Some, such as the Kwakiutl (KWAH-kyu-til) of the Pacific Northwest, were surrounded by such abundant marine and forest resources that they never turned to farming.

Kwakiutl Culture Area, c. 1500

Natural abundance combined with sophisticated fishing and storage systems allowed the Kwakiutl to build a settled culture of the type normally associated with agricultural peoples. Thus, the ecological diversity of the Americas helped give rise to an equally diverse array of native American cultures, many of which blurred the line between settled and nomadic lifestyles.

Tributes of Blood:
The Aztec Empire 1325–1521

Mesoamerica, comprised of modern southern Mexico, Guatemala, Belize, El Salvador, and western Honduras, was a land of city-states after about 800 C.E. Following the decline of ancient cultural forebears such as Teotihuacán (tay-oh-tee-wah-KAHN) in the Mexican highlands and the classic Maya in the greater Guatemalan lowlands, few urban powers, with the possible exception of the Toltecs, managed to dominate more than a few neighbors at a time.

FOCUS

What core features characterized Aztec life and rule?

This would change with the arrival in the Valley of Mexico of a band of former gatherer-hunters from a mysterious northwestern desert region they called Aztlán (ost-LAWN), or "place of cranes." As newcomers these "Aztecs," who later called themselves Mexica (meh-SHE-cah, hence "Mexico"), would suffer a number of humiliations at the hands of powerful city-dwellers centered on Lake Texcoco, now overlain by Mexico City. The Aztecs were at first regarded as coarse barbarians, but as with many conquering outsiders, in time they would have their revenge (see Map 16.2).

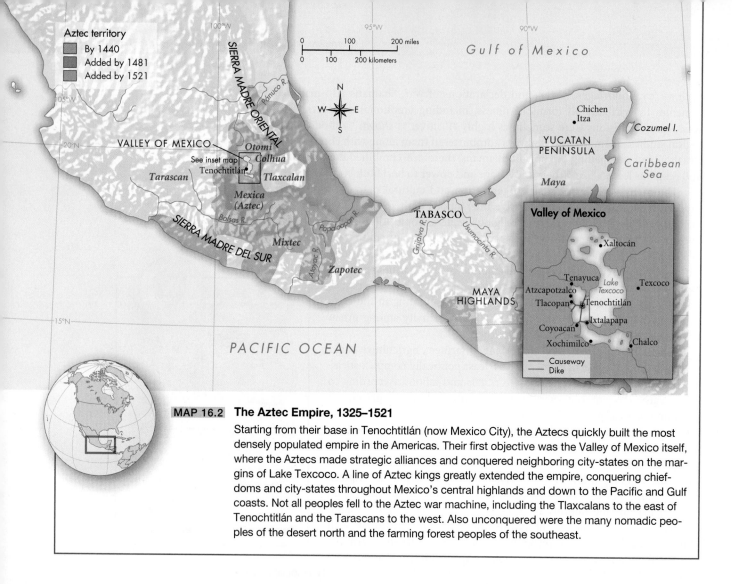

MAP 16.2 The Aztec Empire, 1325–1521

Starting from their base in Tenochtitlán (now Mexico City), the Aztecs quickly built the most densely populated empire in the Americas. Their first objective was the Valley of Mexico itself, where the Aztecs made strategic alliances and conquered neighboring city-states on the margins of Lake Texcoco. A line of Aztec kings greatly extended the empire, conquering chiefdoms and city-states throughout Mexico's central highlands and down to the Pacific and Gulf coasts. Not all peoples fell to the Aztec war machine, including the Tlaxcalans to the east of Tenochtitlán and the Tarascans to the west. Also unconquered were the many nomadic peoples of the desert north and the farming forest peoples of the southeast.

Humble Origins, Imperial Ambitions

Unlike the classic Maya of preceding centuries, the Aztecs did not develop a phonetic writing system. They did, however, preserve key aspects of their history in a mix of oral and symbolic, usually painted or carved, forms. Aztec elders developed and maintained a series of chronicles of the kind historians call master narratives, or state-sponsored versions of the past meant to glorify certain individuals or policies. These narratives related foundation myths, genealogies, tales of conquest, and other important remembrances. Though biased, fragmentary, and otherwise imperfect, many Aztec oral narratives were preserved by dozens of young native scribes writing in Nahuatl (NAH-watt), the Aztec language, soon after the Spanish Conquest of 1519–1521 (discussed in the next chapter).

Historical Documentation   Why is it that the Spanish victors promoted rather than suppressed these narratives of Aztec glory? In one of history's many ironic twists, Spanish priests arriving in Mexico in the 1520s taught a number of noble Aztec and other Mesoamerican youths to adapt the Latin alphabet and Spanish phonetics to various local languages, most importantly Nahuatl. The Spanish hoped that stories of Aztec rule and religion, once collected and examined, would be swiftly discredited and replaced with Western, Christian versions. Not only did this quick conversion not happen as planned, but an unintended consequence of the information-gathering campaign was to create a vast and diverse body of Mesoamerican literature written in native languages.

Despite the agony of the immediate postconquest years, the Aztecs were a quick study in the production of written historical documents. Indeed, most of what we know of Aztec history relies heavily on these hybrid and often enigmatic sixteenth-century sources (see Seeing the Past: An Aztec Map of Tenochtitlán). Aside from interviews with the elders,

An Aztec Map of Tenochtitlán

Tenochtitlán, from the *Codex Mendoza* (The Granger Collection, New York.)

contains an illustrated history of Aztec conquests, crimes and punishments, and even a map of Tenochtitlán, the Aztec capital. This symbol-filled map is reproduced here.

According to legend, the Aztec capital came into existence when an eagle landed on a cactus in the middle of Lake Texcoco. This image, now part of the Mexican national flag, is at the center of the map. Beneath the cactus is a picture of a stone carving of a cactus fruit, a common Aztec symbol for the human heart, emblem of sacrifice. Beneath this is a third symbol labeled afterwards by a Spanish scribe "Tenochtitlán."

The city, or rather its symbol, marks the meeting of four horizontal, spatial quarters as well as a vertical axis linking the sky, earth, and watery underworld. In each quarter are various Aztec nobles, only one of whom, Tenochtli (labeled "Tenuch" on the map), is seated on a reed mat, the Aztec symbol of supreme authority. He was the Aztecs' first emperor; the name "Tenochtli" means "stone cactus fruit."

The lower panel depicts the Aztec conquests of their neighbors in Colhuacan and Tenayuca. Framing the entire map are symbols for dates, part of an ancient Mesoamerican system of time keeping and prophesying retained by the Aztecs. Finally, barely legible in the upper left-hand corner is the somewhat jarring signature of André Thevet, a French priest and royal cosmographer who briefly possessed the *Codex Mendoza* in the late sixteenth century.

Named for Mexico's first Spanish viceroy, the *Codex Mendoza* was painted by Aztec artists about a dozen years after the Spanish Conquest of 1519–1521. It was commissioned by the viceroy as a gift for the Holy Roman emperor and king of Spain, Charles V. After circulating among the courts of Europe, the *Codex Mendoza* landed in the Bodleian Library in Oxford, England, where it remains. Much of the document consists of tribute lists, but it also

EXAMINING THE EVIDENCE

1. What does this map reveal about the Aztec worldview?

2. How might this document have been read by a common Aztec subject?

several painted books, or codices, marked with precise dates, names, and other symbols, survive, along with much archaeological and artistic evidence. In combining these sources with Spanish eyewitness accounts of the conquest era, historians have assembled a substantial record of Aztec life and rule.

Aztec Origins

According to most accounts, the Aztecs arrived in the Valley of Mexico sometime in the thirteenth century, but it was not until the early fourteenth that they established a permanent home. The most fertile sites in the valley were already occupied by farmers who had no interest in making room for newcomers, but the Aztecs were not dissuaded; they had a reputation for being tough and resourceful. Heeding an omen in the form of an eagle perched on a cactus growing on a tiny island near the southwest edge of Lake Texcoco, the refugees settled there in 1325. Reclaiming land from the shallow lakebed, they founded a city called Tenochtitlán (teh-noach-teet-LAWN), or "cactus fruit place." Linked to shore by three large causeways, the city soon boasted imposing stone palaces and temple-pyramids.

The Aztecs quickly transformed Tenochtitlán into a formidable capital. By 1500 it was home to some two hundred thousand people, ranking alongside Nanjing and Paris among the world's five or six most populous cities at the time. At first the Aztecs developed their city by trading military services and lake products such as reeds and fish for building materials, including stone, lime, and timber from the surrounding hillsides. They then formed marriage alliances with regional ethnic groups such as the Colhua, and by 1430 initiated the process of imperial expansion.

Intermarriage with the Colhua, who traced their ancestry to the mighty Toltec warriors, lent the lowly Aztecs a new, elite cachet. At some point the Aztecs tied their religious cult, focused on the war god Huitzilopochtli (weetsy-low-POACH-tlee), or "hummingbird-on-the-left" to cults dedicated to more widely known deities, such as Tlaloc, a powerful water god. Also known to the distant Maya, the fearsome Tlaloc resembled a goggle-wearing crocodile, and was usually surrounded by shells and other marine symbols. A huge, multilayered pyramid faced with carved stone and filled with rubble, now referred to by archaeologists as the Templo Mayor, or "Great Temple," but called by the Aztecs Coatepec, or "Serpent Mountain," became the centerpiece of Tenochtitlán. At its top, some twenty stories above the valley floor, sat twin temple enclosures, one dedicated to Huitzilopochtli, the other to Tlaloc. Like many imperial structures, Coatepec was built to awe and intimidate. In the words of one native poet:

Causeway	A	Great Temple
Major road	B	Ritual center
Major canal	C	Palace
Aqueduct	D	Assembly hall

Lake Texcoco and Tenochtitlán, c. 1500

> Proud of itself
> Is the City of Mexico-Tenochtitlán
> Here no one fears to die in war
> This is our glory
>
> This is Your Command
> Oh Giver of Life
> Have this in mind, oh princes
> Who could conquer Tenochtitlán?
> Who could shake the foundation of heaven?[2] *

As these words suggest, the Aztecs saw themselves as both stagehands and actors in a grand-scale cosmic drama centered on their great capital city.

---

* Miguel Leon-Portilla. *Pre-Columbian Literatures of Mexico*, by and Leon-Portilla, translated from the Spanish by Grace Lobanov. Copyright © 1969 by The University of Oklahoma Press. Used by permission of the publisher.

Enlarging and Supplying the Capital

Land Reclamation

With Tenochtitlán surrounded by water, subsistence and living space became serious concerns amid imperial expansion. Fortunately for the Aztecs, Lake Texcoco was shallow enough to allow an ingenious form of land reclamation called *chinampa* (chee-NAHM-pah). Still visible in a few Mexico City neighborhoods today, **chinampas** were long, narrow terraces built by hand from dredged mud, reeds, and rocks, bordered by interwoven sticks and live trees. Chinampa construction also created rows of deep canals, which served as waterways, or suburban "canoe roads." Because the Aztecs lacked iron or bronze metallurgy, wheeled vehicles, and draft animals, construction of large-scale agricultural works such as chinampas and massive temple-pyramids such as Coatepec absorbed the labors of many thousands of workers. Their construction, therefore, is a testimony to the Aztecs' ability to command and organize large amounts of labor.

Over time, Tenochtitlán's canals accumulated algae, water lilies, and silt. Workers periodically dredged and composted this organic material to fertilize maize, bean, and tomato plantings on the newly formed island-terraces. Established chinampa lands encompassing several square miles were eventually used for building residences, in part to help ease urban crowding. Always hoping not to anger Tlaloc, the fickle water god, by the mid-fifteenth century the Aztecs countered problems such as chronic flooding and high salt content at their end of the lake with dikes and other complex, labor-intensive public works.

Long-Distance Trade

Earlier, in the fourteenth century, an adjacent "twin" city called Tlatelolco (tlah-teh-LOLE-coe) had emerged alongside Tenochtitlán. Tlatelolco served as the Aztec marketplace. Foods, textiles, and goods from throughout Mesoamerica and beyond were exchanged here. Highly prized cocoa beans from the hot lowlands served as currency in some exchanges, and more exotic products, such as turquoise and the iridescent tail feathers of the quetzal bird, arrived from as far away as northern New Mexico and southern Guatemala, respectively. Though linked by trade, these distant regions fell well outside the Aztec domain. No matter how far they traveled, all products were transported along well-trod footpaths on the backs of human carriers. Only when they arrived on the shores of Lake Texcoco could trade goods be shuttled from place to place in canoes. Tlatelolco served as crossroads for all regional trade, with long-distance merchants, or *pochteca* (poach-TEH-cah), occupying an entire precinct. For the Aztecs, Tenochtitlán was the center of the political and spiritual universe. Tlatelolco was the center of Aztec commerce, connecting the peoples of the Valley of Mexico to diverse societies scattered across the Americas.

From City-State to Empire

Genuine Aztec imperial expansion began only in around 1430, less than a century before the arrival of Europeans. An auspicious alliance between Tenochtitlán and the neighboring city-states of Texcoco and Tlacopan led to victory against a third, Atzcapotzalco (otts-cah-poat-SAUL-coh). Tensions with Atzcapotzalco extended back over a century to the Aztecs' first arrival in the region, and these early slights were not forgotten. Whether motivated by revenge or something else, the Aztecs used the momentum of this victory to overtake their allies and lay the foundations of a regional, tributary empire. Within a generation they controlled the entire Valley of Mexico, exacting tribute from several million people representing many distinct cultures. The Nahuatl language helped link state to subjects, although many newly conquered and allied groups continued to speak local languages. These persistent forms of ethnic identification, coupled with staggering tribute demands, would eventually help bring about the end of Aztec rule.

Holy Terror: Aztec Rule, Religion, and Warfare

A series of six male rulers, or *tlatoque* (tlah-TOE-kay, singular *tlatoani*), presided over Aztec expansion. When a ruler died, his successor was chosen by a secret council of elders from among a handful of eligible candidates. Aztec kingship was sacred in that each tlatoani traced his lineage back to the legendary Toltec warrior-sages. For this, the incorporation of the Colhua lineage had been essential. In keeping with this Toltec legacy, the Aztec

chinampa A terrace for farming and house building constructed in the shallows of Mexico's Lake Texcoco by the Aztecs and their neighbors.

The Coyolxauhqui Stone

Coyolxauhqui Stone (The Art Archive/Museo del Templo Mayor Mexico/Gianni Dagli Orti.)

Like many imperial peoples, the Aztecs sought to memorialize their deities in stone. The Aztec war god Huitzilopochtli was central, but as in other traditions, so were his mother and other female relatives. Huitzilopochtli's mother was Coatlicue (kwat-lih-KWAY), "Serpent Skirt," a fearsome and not obviously maternal figure. Huitzilopochtli's birth was said to be miraculous; Coatlicue had been inseminated by downy feathers while sweeping a temple, a ruse of the trickster-creator god Tezcatlipoca (tess-caught-lee-POH-cah), "Smoking Mirror."

A daughter, Coyolxauhqui (coe-yole-SHAU-key), "She Who is Adorned with Copper Bells," was so outraged at her mother's suspicious pregnancy that she incited her four hundred siblings to attempt matricide. Coatlicue was frightened at the prospect, but her unborn child, Huitzilopochtli, spoke from the womb to calm her. Upon the arrival of the angry children, dressed for war and led by Coyolxauhqui, Huitzilopochtli burst out of his mother's womb fully grown. He quickly prepared for battle and confronted his sister, whom he dismembered with a fire serpent. Huitzilopochtli went on to rout his other siblings, running them down like a proper Aztec warrior, stripping and sacrificing each without mercy.

The circular stone shown here, discovered by electrical workers near Mexico City's cathedral in 1979, depicts Coyolxauhqui dismembered on the ground. Some ten feet across, this stone apparently sat at the base of the Aztec Templo Mayor. Sacrificed warriors from all over the Aztec Empire probably got a good look at it before climbing the temple stairs to their deaths. Although shown in defeat, Coyolxauhqui is the ideal woman warrior, her serpent belt buckled with a human skull. Earth Monster knee- and elbow-pads, as well as heel-cups, add to her fearsome appearance, as do serpent ties on her severed arms and legs. An elaborate headdress and huge, Toltec-style ear-spools top off the battlefield ensemble.

EXAMINING THE EVIDENCE

1. How does the Coyolxauhqui stone reflect women's roles in Aztec society?

2. What does the stone suggest about death in Aztec thought?

Empire was characterized by three core features: human sacrifice, warfare, and tribute. All were linked to Aztec and broader Mesoamerican notions of cosmic order, specifically the fundamental human duty to feed the gods.

Sacrifice   Like most Mesoamerican peoples, the Aztecs traced not only their own but all human origins to sacrifices made by a wide range of deities. In most origin stories male and female gods threw themselves into fires, drew their own blood, and killed and dismembered one another, all for the good of humankind. These forms of sacrifice were considered essential to the process of releasing and renewing the generative powers that drove the cosmos (see Seeing the Past: The Coyolxauhqui Stone).

According to Aztec belief, humans were expected to show gratitude by following the example of their creators in an almost daily ritual cycle. Much of the sacred calendar had been inherited from older Mesoamerican cultures, but the Aztecs added many new holidays to celebrate their own special role in cosmic history. The Aztecs' focus on sacrifice also appears to have derived from their acute sense that secular and spiritual forces were

Aztec Human Sacrifice

This image dates from just after the Spanish Conquest of Mexico, but it was part of a codex about Aztec religious practices and symbols. Here a priest is removing the beating heart of a captive with a flint knife as an assistant holds his feet. The captive's bloody heart, in the form of a cactus fruit, ascends, presumably to the gods (see the same icon in Seeing the Past: An Aztec Map of Tenochtitlán, page 521). At the base of the sacrificial pyramid lies an earlier victim, apparently being taken away by noble Aztec men and women responsible for the handling of the corpse. (Scala/Art Resource, NY.)

inseparable and interdependent. Affairs of state were affairs of heaven, and vice versa. Tenochtitlán was thought to be the foundation of heaven, its enormous temple-pyramids the center of human-divine affairs. Aztec priests and astrologers believed that the universe, already in its fifth incarnation after only three thousand years, was inherently unstable, always on the verge of chaos and collapse. Only human intervention in the form of sustained sacrificial ritual could stave off apocalypse.

As an antidote, or at least a brake against impending doom, the gods had given humans the "gift" of warfare. Human captives, preferably able-bodied, energetic young men, were to be hunted and killed so that the release of their blood and spirits might satisfy the gods. Warrior sacrifice was so important to the Aztecs that they believed it kept the sun in motion. Thus the act of human sacrifice, which involved removing the hearts of live victims using a flint knife, was in part a reenactment of several creator gods' own acts of self-sacrifice.

Devout Aztec subjects, rather like the classic Maya before them, also took part in nonlethal cosmic regeneration rituals in the form of personal bloodletting, or **autosacrifice**. According to a number of eyewitness sources, extremities and genitals were bled using thorns and stone blades, with public exhibition of suffering as important as blood loss. Blood offerings were absorbed by thin sheets of reed paper, which were burnt before an

autosacrifice The Mesoamerican practice of personal bloodletting as a means of paying debts to the gods.

altar. These bloodlettings, like captive sacrifices, emphasized the frailty of the individual, the pain of life, and most of all indebtedness to the gods. Autosacrifice was, in short, a physical expression of the empathy and subordination humans were to feel before their creators. Human blood fueled not only the Aztec realm, but the cosmos.

Warfare

Given these sacrificial obligations, Aztec warfare was aimed not at the annihilation, but rather at live capture of enemies. This is not to say that "stone age" weapons technology was an impediment to determined killers: two-handed broadswords with razor-sharp obsidian blades could slice feather-clad warriors to ribbons, and ceramic projectiles could be hurled from slings with deadly accuracy. Spears, lances, clubs, and other weapons were equally menacing. Still, according to most sources, Aztec combat was ideally a stylized and theatrical affair similar to royal jousts in contemporary Eurasia, with specific individuals paired for contest.

In the field, Aztec warriors were noted for their fury, a trait borrowed from their patron deity, Huitzilopochtli. Chronic enemies such as the Tlaxcalans of east-central Mexico, and the Tarascans to the west, apparently learned to match the ferocious Aztec style. Despite their proximity to Tenochtitlán, they remained unconquered when Europeans arrived. Some enemies, such as the nearby Otomí, were eventually overwhelmed, then incorporated into Aztec warrior ranks.

All Mesoamerican warriors considered death on the battlefield the highest honor. But live capture was the Aztecs' main goal, and most victims were marched naked and bound to the capital to be sacrificed. Although charged with religious meaning, Aztec warrior sacrifices were also intended to horrify enemies; visiting diplomats were made to watch them, according to sources. Aztec imperial expansion depended in part on religious terror, or the ability to appear chosen by the gods for victory.

Tribute

In addition to sacrificial victims, the Aztecs demanded **tribute** of conquered peoples, a common imperial practice worldwide. In addition to periodic labor drafts for temple building and other public works, tribute lists included useful things such as food, textiles, and craft goods, crucial subsidies for the empire's large priestly and warrior classes. Redistribution of certain tribute items to favored subjects of lower status, a tactic also practiced by the Incas, further helped cement loyalties. Other tribute items were purely symbolic. Some new subjects were made to collect filth and inedible insects, for example, just to prove their unworthiness before the Aztec sovereign. As an empire that favored humiliation over co-optation and promotion of new subjects, the Aztecs faced an ever-deepening reservoir of resentment.

Daily Life Under the Aztecs

Class Hierarchy

Aztec society was highly stratified, and class divisions firm. As in most imperial societies, Mexica nobles regarded commoners, particularly farming folk, as uncouth and generally beneath contempt. In between were imperial bureaucrats, priests, district chiefs, scribes, merchants, and artisans. Although elites at several levels showed off the fruits of their subordinates' labors in lavish displays, most Aztec art seems to have been destined not for wealthy people's homes but rather for temples, tombs, and religious shrines. Despite heavy emphasis on religious ceremonies, the Aztecs also maintained a multitiered civil justice system. In many instances, and quite unlike most of the world's imperial cultures, including the Incas, Aztec nobles received harsher punishments than commoners for similar misdeeds.

Class hierarchy was further reinforced by a host of detailed dress and speech codes, along with many other social rules and rituals. The tlatoani, for example, could not be touched or even looked in the face by any but his closest relatives, consorts, and servants. Even ranking nobles were supposed to lie face down on the ground and put dirt in their mouths before him. Nobles guarded their own rank with vigilance, going so far as to develop a restricted form of speech. Chances for social advancement were severely limited, but some men, all of whom were expected to serve in the military for a period, gained status on the battlefield.

At the base of the social pyramid were peasants and slaves. Some peasants were ethnic Aztecs, but the vast majority belonged to city-states and clans that had been conquered after 1430. In either case, peasants' lives mostly revolved around producing food for subsistence

tribute Taxes paid to a state or empire, usually in the form of farm produce or artisan manufactures but sometimes also human labor or even human bodies.

and providing overlords with tribute goods and occasional labor. Slavery usually took the form of crisis-driven self-indenture; it was not an inherited social status. Chattel slavery existed, in which slaves were treated as property and traded in the marketplace, but slavery remained unimportant to the overall Aztec economy.

Merchants, particularly the mobile pochteca, responsible for long-distance trade, occupied an unusual position. Although the pochteca sometimes accumulated great wealth, they remained resident aliens much like other ethnic merchant communities operating in the contemporary Mediterranean and Indian Ocean basins. They had no homeland, but made a good living supplying elites with exotic goods, including slaves. Yet even among merchants there seems to have been little interest in capital accumulation in the form of money, land, or saleable goods. There is no evidence of complex credit instruments, industrial-style production, or real estate exchange of the sort associated with early merchant capitalism in other parts of the world at this time. The Aztec state remained at root tributary, the movement of goods mostly a reflection of power relations underpinned by force. Merchants, far from influencing politics, remained ethnic outsiders. Thus, both the Aztec economy and social structure reinforced the insularity of Aztec elites. The inflexible Aztec society could not incorporate outsiders, and economic exchange, even long-distance trade, did little to add new ideas and beliefs to Aztec culture.

The life of an Aztec woman was difficult even by early modern standards. Along with water transport and other heavy household chores, maize grinding and tortilla making became the core responsibilities of most women in the Valley of Mexico, and indeed throughout Mesoamerica. Without animal- or water-driven grain mills, food preparation was an arduous, time-consuming task, particularly for the poor. Only noblewomen enjoyed broad exemption from this and other forms of manual work.

Women's Roles

Sources suggest that some women achieved shaman status, performing minor priestly roles and working as surgeons and herbalists. Midwifery was also a fairly high-status, female occupation (see Lives and Livelihoods: The Aztec Midwife). These were exceptions; women's lives were mostly hard under Aztec rule. Scholars disagree, however, as to whether male political and religious leaders viewed women's substantial duties and contributions as complementary or subordinate. Surviving texts do emphasize feminine mastery of the domestic sphere and its social value. However, this emphasis may simply reflect male desire to limit the sphere of women's actions, since female reproductive capacity was also highly valued as an aid to the empire's perpetual war effort.

Indeed, Aztec society was so militarized that giving birth was referred to as "taking a captive." This comparison reflects the generalized Aztec preoccupation with pleasing their gods: women were as much soldiers as men in the ongoing war to sustain human life. Women's roles in society were mostly domestic rather than public, but the home was a deeply sacred space. Caring for it was equivalent to caring for a temple. Sweeping was a genuine ritual, for example, albeit one with hygienic benefits. Hearth tending, maize grinding, spinning, and weaving were also highly ritualized tasks, each accompanied by chants and offerings. Insufficient attention to any of these daily rituals put families and entire lineages at risk.

Children's Lives

Aztec children, too, lived a scripted existence, their futures predicted at birth by astrologers. Names were derived from birthdates, and in a way amounted to a public badge of fate. According to a variety of testimonies taken just after the Spanish Conquest, Aztec society at all levels emphasized duty and good comportment rather than rights and individual freedom. Parents were admonished to police their children's behavior and to help mold all youths into useful citizens. Girls and boys at every social level were assigned tasks considered appropriate for their sex well before adolescence. By age fourteen, children of both sexes were fully engaged in adult work. One break from the constant chores was instruction between ages twelve and fifteen in singing and playing instruments, such as drums and flutes, for cyclical religious festivals. Girls married at about age fifteen, and boys nearer twenty, a pattern roughly in accordance with most parts of the world at the time. Elder Aztec women usually served as matchmakers, and wedding ceremonies tended to be elaborate, multiday affairs. Some noblemen expanded their prestige by retaining numerous wives and siring dozens of children.

The Aztec Midwife

Aztec Midwife

Women were expected to be tough in Aztec culture, which described giving birth as "taking a captive." But as in war, medical attention was often required, so a trained class of professional midwives stood by to administer aid. This image accompanies a description in Nahuatl, the Aztec language, of the midwife's duties written soon after the Spanish Conquest. (Firenze, Biblioteca Medicea Laurenziana, Ms. Med. Palat. 219, c. 132v.)

In Aztec culture, childbirth was a sacred and ritualized affair. Always life-threatening for mother and child, giving birth and being born were both explicitly compared to the battlefield experience. Aside from potential medical complications, the Aztecs considered the timing of a child's birth critical in determining his or her future. This tricky blend of physical and spiritual concerns gave rise to the respected and highly skilled livelihood of midwife. It is not entirely clear how midwives were chosen, but their work and sayings are well described in early postconquest records, particularly the illustrated books of Aztec lore and history collectively known as the *Florentine Codex*. The following passage, translated directly from sixteenth-century Nahuatl, is one such description. Note how the midwife blends physical tasks, such as supplying herbs and swaddling clothes, with shamanistic cries and speeches.

And the midwife inquired about the fate of the baby who was born.

When the pregnant one already became aware of [pains in] her womb, when it was said that her time of death had arrived, when she wanted to give birth already, they quickly bathed her, washed her hair with soap, washed her, adorned her well. And then they arranged, they swept the house where the little woman was to suffer, where she was to perform her duty, to do her work, to give birth.

If she were a noblewoman or wealthy, she had two or three midwives. They remained by her side, awaiting her word. And when the woman became really disturbed internally, they quickly put her in a sweat bath [a kind of sauna]. And to hasten the birth of the baby, they gave the pregnant woman cooked *ciuapatli* [literally, "woman medicine"] herb to drink.

And if she suffered much, they gave her ground opossum tail to drink, and then the baby was quickly born. [The midwife] already had all that was needed for the baby, the little rags with which the baby was received.

And when the baby had arrived on earth, the midwife shouted; she gave war cries, which meant the woman had fought a good battle, had become a brave warrior, had taken a captive, had captured a baby.

Then the midwife spoke to it. If it was a boy, she said to it: "You have come out on earth, my youngest one, my boy, my young man." If it was a girl, she said to it: "My young woman, my youngest one, noblewoman, you have suffered, you are exhausted.". . . [and to either:] "You have come to arrive on earth, where your relatives, your kin suffer fatigue and exhaustion; where it is hot, where it is cold, and where the wind blows; where there is thirst, hunger, sadness, despair, exhaustion, fatigue, pain. . . ."

And then the midwife cut the umbilical cord. . . .

Source: Selection from the *Florentine Codex* in Matthew Restall, Lisa Sousa, and Kevin Terraciano, eds., *Mesoamerican Voices: Native-Language Writings from Colonial Mexico, Oaxaca, Yucatan, and Guatemala* (New York: Cambridge University Press, 2005), 216–217.

QUESTIONS TO CONSIDER

1. Why was midwifery so crucial to the Aztecs?
2. How were boys and girls addressed by the midwife, and why?

For Further Information:

Carrasco, Davíd, and Scott Sessions. *Daily Life of the Aztecs, People of the Sun and Earth*, 2d ed. Indianapolis, IN: Hackett Publishing, 2008.

Clendinnen, Inga. *Aztecs: An Interpretation*. New York: Cambridge University Press, 1994.

At around harvest time in September, Aztec subjects of all classes ate maize, beans, and squash lightly seasoned with salt and ground chili peppers. During other times of the year, and outside the chinampa zone, food could be scarce, forcing the poor to consume roasted insects, grubs, and lake scum. Certain items, such as frothed cocoa, were reserved for elites. Stored maize was used to make tortillas year-round, but two poor harvests in a row, a frequent occurrence in densely populated highland Mexico, could reduce rations considerably.

Food and Scarcity

In addition to periodic droughts, Aztec subjects coped with frosts, plagues of locusts, volcanic eruptions, earthquakes, and floods. Given such ecological uncertainty, warfare was reserved for the agricultural off-season, when hands were not needed for planting, weeding, or harvesting. In the absence of large domesticated animals and advanced metallurgy, agricultural tasks throughout Mesoamerica demanded virtual armies of field laborers equipped only with fire-hardened digging sticks and obsidian or flint knives.

Animal protein was scarce in highland Mexico, especially in urban areas where hunting opportunities were limited and few domestic animals were kept. Still, the people of Tenochtitlán raised significant numbers of turkeys and plump, hairless dogs (the prized Xolo breed of today). Even humble beans, when combined with maize, could constitute a complete protein, and indigenous grains such as amaranth were also highly nutritious. Famines still occurred, however, and one in the early 1450s led to mass migration out of the Valley of Mexico. Thousands sold themselves into slavery to avoid starvation.

The Limits of Holy Terror

As the Aztec Empire expanded in the later fifteenth century, sacrificial debts grew to be a consuming passion among pious elites. Calendars filled with sacrificial rites, and warfare was ever more geared toward satisfying what must have seemed a ballooning cosmic budget.

By 1500 the Aztec state had reached its height, and some scholars have argued that it had even begun to decline. Incessant captive wars and related tribute demands had reached their limits, and old enemies such as the Tlaxcalans and Tarascans remained belligerent. New conquests were blocked by difficult terrain, declining tributes, and resistant locals. With available technologies, there was no place else for this inherently expansive empire to grow, and even with complex water works in place, agricultural productivity barely kept the people fed. Under the harsh leadership of Moctezuma II ("Angry Lord the Younger") (r. 1502–1520), the future did not look promising. Although there is no evidence to suggest the Aztec Empire was on the verge of collapse when several hundred bearded, sunburnt strangers of Spanish descent appeared on Mexico's Gulf Coast shores in 1519, points of vulnerability abounded.

Underlying Weaknesses

Tributes of Sweat: The Inca Empire 1430–1532

At about the same time as the Aztec expansion in southernmost North America, another great empire emerged in the central Andean highlands of South America. There appears to have been no significant contact between them. Like the Aztecs, the Incas burst out of their highland homeland in the 1430s to conquer numerous neighboring cultures and huge swaths of territory. They demanded tribute in goods and labor, along with allegiance to an imperial religion. Also like the Aztecs, the Incas based their expansion on a centuries-long inheritance of technological, religious, and political traditions.

> **FOCUS**
> What core features characterized Inca life and rule?

Despite enormous geographical, technological, and cultural barriers, by 1500 the Incas ruled one of the world's most extensive, ecologically varied, and rugged land empires, stretching nearly three thousand miles along both sides of the towering Andean mountain range from just north of the equator to central Chile. Like most empires ancient and modern, extensive holdings proved to be a mixed blessing (see Map 16.3, page 531).

From Potato Farmers to Empire Builders

Inca Origins

Thanks to abundant archaeological evidence and early postconquest interviews and narratives, much is known about the rise and fall of the Inca state. Still, like the early Ottoman, Russian, and other contemporary empires, numerous mysteries remain. As in those cases, legends and sagas of the formative period in particular require careful and skeptical analysis. The Inca case is somewhat complicated by the fact that their complex knotted-string records, or *khipus* (also *quipus*, KEY-poohs), have yet to be deciphered.

Scholars agree that the Incas emerged from among a dozen or so regional ethnic groups or allied clans living in the highlands of south-central Peru between 1000 and 1400 C.E. Living as scattered and more-or-less egalitarian potato and maize farmers, the Incas started out as one of many similar groups of Andean mountaineers. Throughout the Andes, clan groupings settled in and around fertile valleys and alongside lakes between eighty-five hundred and thirteen thousand feet above sea level. Though often graced with clear mountain springs and fertile soils, these highland areas were subject to periodic frosts and droughts, despite their location within the tropics. Even more than in the Aztec realm, altitude (elevation above sea level), not latitude (distance north or south of the equator), was key.

Environment and Exchange

Anthropologist John Murra once described Inca land use as a "**vertical archipelago**," a stair-step system of interdependent environmental "islands." Kin groups occupying the altitudes best suited to potato and maize farming established outlying settlements in cold uplands, where thousands of llamas and alpacas—the Americas' only large domestic animals—were herded, and also in hot lowlands, where cotton, peanuts, chilis, and the stimulant coca were grown. People, animals, and goods traveled constantly between highland and lowland ecological zones using well-maintained and often stone-paved trails and hanging bridges, yet the incredibly rugged nature of the terrain (plus the stubborn nature of llamas) made use of wheeled vehicles impractical.

vertical archipelago Andean system of planting crops and grazing animals at different altitudes.

Clans with highland ties and even some states of considerable size inhabited Peru's long desert coast. Here, urban civilization was nearly as old as that of ancient Egypt. Andean coast dwellers engaged in large-scale irrigated agriculture, deep-sea fishing, and long-distance trade. Trading families outfitted large balsawood rafts with cotton sails and plied the Pacific as far as Guatemala. Inland trade links stretched over the Andes and deep into the Amazon rain forest. Stopping at pilgrimage sites along the way, coast-dwelling traders exchanged salt, seashells, beads, and copper hatchets for exotic feathers, gold dust, and pelts. The Incas would move rapidly to exploit all of these diverse Andean regions and their interconnections, replacing old exchange systems and religious shrines with their own. Around 1200 C.E. they established a base near Cuzco (KOOS-coh), deep in the highlands of Peru not far from the headwaters of the Amazon, and soon after 1400 they began their remarkable drive toward empire.

The Great Apparatus: Inca Expansion and Religion

Cuzco, located in a narrow valley at a breathtaking altitude of over two miles above sea level, served as the Incas' political base and religious center. Like the Aztecs, the Incas saw their capital as the hub of the universe, calling it the "navel of the world." An array of dirt paths and stone-paved roads radiated out in all directions and tied hundreds of subsidiary shrines to the cosmically-ordained center. Much like the Aztecs' Tenochtitlán, Cuzco served as both the preeminent religious pilgrimage site and the empire's administrative capital. Compared with the Aztec capital, however, the city was modest in size, perhaps home to at most fifty thousand. Still, Cuzco had the advantage of being stoutly built

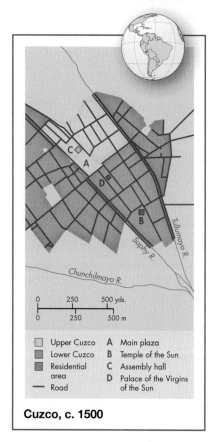

0   250   500 yds.
0   250   500 m

☐ Upper Cuzco   A Main plaza
▨ Lower Cuzco   B Temple of the Sun
▨ Residential   C Assembly hall
   area   D Palace of the Virgins
— Road   of the Sun

Cuzco, c. 1500

of hewn stone. Whereas most of Tenochtitlán's temples and palaces were dismantled in the centuries following the Spanish Conquest, Cuzco's colossal stone foundations still stand.

For obscure reasons, the Incas in the early fifteenth century began conquering their neighbors. In time each emperor, or Sapa ("Unique") Inca, would seek to add more territory to the realm, called Tawantinsuyu (tuh-wahn-tin-SUE-you), or, "The Four Quarters Together." The Sapa Inca was thought to be descended from the sun and was thus regarded as the natural lord and sustainer of all humanity. To worship the sun was to worship the Inca, and vice versa. Devotion to lesser mountain and ancestor deities persisted, however, absorbed over time by the Incas in a way reminiscent of the Roman Empire's assimilation of regional deities and shrines. This religious inclusiveness helped the empire spread quickly even as the royal cult of the sun was inserted into everyday life. In a similar way, *runasimi*, later mislabeled "Quechua" (KETCH-wah) by the Spanish, became the Incas' official language even as local languages continued to be spoken.

Inca expansion was so rapid that the empire reached its greatest extent within a mere four generations of its founding. In semilegendary times, Wiracocha Inca (r. 1400–1438) was said to have led an army of followers to defeat an invading ethnic group called the Chankas near Cuzco. According to several royal sagas, this victory spurred Wiracocha to improve the defensive position of his people further by annexing the fertile territories of other neighbors. Defense turned to offense, and thus was primed the engine of Inca expansion.

Wiracocha's successor, Pachacuti Inca Yupanki (r. 1438–1471), was far more ambitious, so much so that he is widely regarded as the true founder of the Inca Empire. Substantial archaeological evidence backs this claim. Pachacuti (literally "Cataclysm") took over much of what is today Peru, including many coastal oases and the powerful Chimú kingdom. Along the way, Pachacuti perfected the core strategy of Inca warfare: amassing and mobilizing such overwhelming numbers of troops and backup forces that actual fighting was usually unnecessary.

Thousands of peasants were conscripted to bear arms, build roads, and carry grain. Others herded llamas, strung bridges, and cut building stone. With each new advance, huge masonry forts and temples were constructed in the imperial style, leaving an indelible Inca stamp on the landscape still visible today from Ecuador to Argentina. Even opponents such as the desert-dwelling Chimú, who had their aqueducts cut off to boot, simply capitulated in the face of the Inca juggernaut. Just after the Spanish Conquest, Pachacuti was remembered by female descendants:

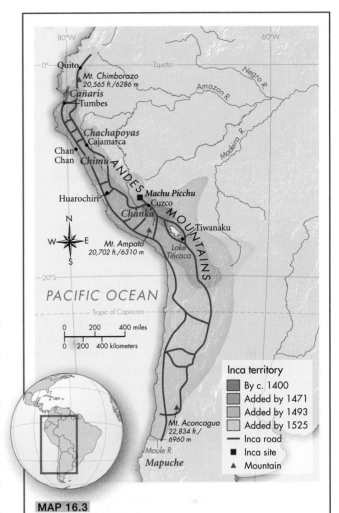

MAP 16.3

The Inca Empire, 1325–1521

Starting from their base in Cuzco, high in the Andes, the Incas built the most extensive empire in the Americas, and the second most populous after that of the Aztecs. They linked it by a road system that rivaled that of the ancient Romans. Inca expansion was extremely rapid as each ruler competed with his predecessor to extend tributary control. Some groups, such as the Cañaris and Chachapoyas, resisted Inca domination for many years, and the Mapuche of Chile were never conquered.

Imperial Expansion

> As [Pachacuti] Inca Yupanki remained in his city and town of Cuzco, seeing that he was lord and that he had subjugated the towns and provinces, he was very pleased. He had subjugated more and obtained much more importance than any of his ancestors. He saw the great apparatus that he had so that whenever he wanted to he could subjugate and put under his control anything else he wanted.[3]

These early colonial remembrances underscore the Sapa Inca's tremendous power. Pachacuti could at any time deploy the "great apparatus" of empire as his personal conquest machine.

Pachacuti's successors continued in the same vein, extending conquests southward deep into what are today Chile and Argentina, and also eastward down the slope of the Andes and into the upper Amazon Basin. It is from this last region, the quarter the Incas called Antisuyu (auntie-SUE-you), that we derive the word *Andes*. On the northern frontier, the Incas fought a series of bitter wars with Ecuadorian ethnic groups to extend Inca rule into the southernmost part of present-day Colombia (see again Map 16.3). Here the imperial Inca conquest machine met its match: instead of capitulating, awestruck by the Inca, many Ecuadorian and Colombian highlanders fought to the death.

According to most sources, Inca advances into new territory were couched in the rhetoric of diplomacy. Local headmen were told they had two options: (1) to retain power by accepting Inca sovereignty and all the tributary obligations that went with it, or (2) to defy the Inca and face annihilation. Most headmen went along, particularly once word of the Incas' battlefield prowess spread. Those who did not were either killed in battle or exiled, along with their subject populations, to remote corners of the empire. Several of these exile colonies are still identifiable today in southern Ecuador and northern Bolivia.

The Incas seem to have been most interested in dominating productive peoples and their lands, although they also succeeded to some extent in spreading their imperial solar cult. Whatever their motives, like the Aztecs they defined political domination in simple, easily understood terms: tribute payment. Conquered subjects showed submission by rendering significant portions of their surplus production—and also labor—to the emperor and his subordinates. Tribute payment was a grudgingly accepted humiliation throughout the Andes, one that many hoped to shake off at the first opportunity.

Inca Religion

Scholars argue that to understand Inca religion one must set aside familiar distinctions between sacred and secular and between life and death. As the chapter-opening description of child sacrifice suggests, a continuum of life was assumed throughout the Andes, despite permanent loss of consciousness, and spirit and body were deemed inseparable. Likewise, features in the landscape, ranging from mountain springs and peaks to ordinary boulders, were almost always thought to house or emit spiritual energy (see Reading the Past: An Andean Creation Story). Even practical human-made landforms, such as irrigation canals, walls, and terraces, were commonly described as "alive." These sacred places, **wakas** (or *huacas*), received sacrifices of food, drink, and textiles from their human caretakers in exchange for good harvests, herd growth, and other bounties. In addition, most Andeans venerated images and amulets carved from wood, shell, stone, metal, and bone.

Andeans also venerated the human corpse. As long as something tangible remained of one's deceased relatives or ancestors, they were not regarded as entirely dead. It was generally thought wise to keep them around. Of course it helped that the central Andes' dry highland and coastal climates were ideal for mummification: preservation often required little more than removal of internal organs. In wetter areas, the dead were sometimes smoked over a slow fire, a process that led some outsiders to suspect cannibalism. In fact, it would have been fairly common in Inca times to encounter a neighbor's "freeze-dried" or smoked grandparents hanging from the rafters, still regarded as very much involved in household affairs. Andeans sometimes carried ancestor mummies to feasts and pilgrimages as well. Thus, Inca society included both past and present generations.

The Incas harnessed these and other core features of Andean society at its most ancient, yet like the Aztecs they put a unique stamp on the vast and diverse region they came to dominate. Though warlike, the Incas rarely sacrificed captive warriors, a ritual archaeologists now know was practiced among ancient coastal Peruvians. As for cannibalism, it was something the Incas associated with barbaric forest dwellers. Inca stone architecture, though clearly borrowing from older forms such as those of Tiwanaku, a temple complex in modern Bolivia, is still identifiable thanks to the frequent use of trapezoidal (flared) doors, windows, and niches (see the illustration of Machu Picchu in At a

waka A sacred place or thing in Andean culture.

READING THE PAST

An Andean Creation Story

The small Peruvian town of Huarochirí (wahr-oh-chee-REE), located in the high Andes east of Lima, was the target of a Spanish anti-idolatry campaign at the end of the sixteenth century. The Spanish conquest of the Incas, which began in 1532 (see Chapter 17), had little effect on the everyday life of Andean peasants, and many clung tenaciously to their religious beliefs. In Huarochirí, Spanish attempts to root out these beliefs and replace them with Western, Christian ones produced written testimonies from village elders in phonetically rendered Quechua, the most commonly spoken language in the Inca Empire. Like the Aztec codices, the resulting documents—aimed at eradicating the beliefs they describe—have unwittingly provided modern researchers with a rare window on a lost mental world. The passage here, translated directly from Quechua to English, relates an Andean myth that newly arrived or converted Christians considered a variation on the biblical story of Noah and the Great Flood. In the Christian story, God, angered by the wickedness of man, resolves to send a flood to destroy the earth. He spares only Noah, whom he instructs to build an ark in which Noah, his family, and a pair of every animal were saved from the Great Flood.

> In ancient times, this world wanted to come to an end. A llama buck, aware that the ocean was about to overflow, was behaving like somebody who's deep in sadness. Even though its owner let it rest in a patch of excellent pasture, it cried and said, "In, in," and wouldn't eat. The llama's owner got really angry, and he threw a cob from some maize he had just eaten at the llama. "Eat, dog! This is some fine grass I'm letting you rest in!" he said. Then that llama began speaking like a human being. "You simpleton, whatever could you be thinking about? Soon, in five days, the ocean will overflow. It's a certainty. And the whole world will come to an end," it said. The man got good and scared. "What's going to happen to us? Where can we go to save

ourselves?" he said. The llama replied, "Let's go to Villca Coto mountain. There we'll be saved. Take along five days' food for yourself." So the man went out from there in a great hurry, and himself carried both the llama buck and its load. When they arrived at Villca Coto mountain, all sorts of animals had already filled it up: pumas, foxes, guanacos [wild relatives of the llama], condors, all kinds of animals in great numbers. And as soon as that man had arrived there, the ocean overflowed. They stayed there huddling tightly together. The waters covered all those mountains and it was only Villca Coto mountain, or rather its very peak, that was not covered by the water. Water soaked the fox's tail. That's how it turned black. Five days later, the waters descended and began to dry up. The drying waters caused the ocean to retreat all the way down again and exterminate all the people. Afterward, that man began to multiply once more. That's the reason there are people until today.

[The scribe who recorded this tale, an Andean converted by Spanish missionaries, then adds this comment:] "Regarding this story, we Christians believe it refers to the time of the Flood. But they [i.e., non-Christian Andeans] believe it was Villca Coto mountain that saved them."

Source: Excerpt from *The Huarochirí Manuscript: A Testament of Ancient and Colonial Andean Religion*, trans. and ed. Frank Salomon and George L. Urioste (Austin: University of Texas Press, 1991), 51–52.

EXAMINING THE EVIDENCE

1. What do the similarities and differences between the Andean and Judeo-Christian flood stories suggest?
2. What do the differences between them reveal?

For Further Information:
Spalding, Karen. *Huarochirí: An Andean Society Under Inca and Spanish Rule.* Stanford: Stanford University Press, 1988.
Urton, Gary. *Inca Myths.* Austin: University of Texas Press, 1999.

Crossroads, page 512). It is worth noting, however, that the cult of the sun, which the Incas transformed and elevated to something new and imperial, proved far less durable than local religious traditions once the empire fell. Despite the Incas' rhetoric of diplomacy, most Andeans appear to have associated their rule with tyranny. Like the Aztecs, they failed to inspire loyalty in their subjects, who saw Inca government as a set of institutions designed to exploit, rather than protect, the peoples of the empire.

Inca Mummy

The Incas did not sacrifice humans as often as the Aztecs did, but headmen in newly conquered regions were sometimes required to give up young sons or daughters for live burial on high mountains. The victims, including this adolescent girl found in a shallow tomb atop 20,000-foot Mount Lullaillaco in the Argentine Andes, died of exposure after the long climb, but the Incas believed them to remain semiconscious and in communication with the spirit world. The girl seen here wears fine camelid-fiber garments bound by a *chumbi* (traditional Andean belt) and silver *topos* (shawl pins). She is also adorned with a shell necklace and other amulets, and her hair is pleated as described in early postconquest accounts. Such sacrifices were known as *capacocha*, or "debt payment." (AP Photo/Natacha Pisarenko.)

Daily Life Under the Incas

Inca society, like Aztec society, was highly stratified, with few means of upward mobility. Along with class gradations tied to occupation, the Incas maintained a variety of divisions and ranks according to sex, age, and ethnic or regional origin. Everyday life thus varied tremendously among the Inca's millions of subjects, although the vast peasant majority probably had much in common with farming folk the world over. Seasonal work stints for the empire were a burden for men, whereas women labored constantly to maintain households, raise children, and care for elderly kin. Unlike that of the Aztec, the Inca legal system, in common with most such systems in early modern times, appears to have been more harshly punitive against commoners than nobles. Exemplary elite behavior was expected, but not so rigidly enforced.

At the pinnacle of society was the Sapa Inca himself, the "son of the Sun." As in most imperial cultures, the emperor's alleged divinity extended to matters of war; he was believed to be the greatest warrior in the world. As a sign of unworthiness, everyone who came before him was obliged to bear a symbolic burden, such as a load of cloth or large water vessel. Only the Inca's female companions had intimate, daily contact with him. Although the ideal royal couple according to Inca mythology was a sibling pair, it was in fact dozens of wives and concubines who assured that there would be numerous potential heirs. Unlike monarchs in Europe and parts of Africa, the imperial household did not practice primogeniture, or the automatic inheritance of an estate or title by the eldest son. Neither did they leave succession to a group of elders, the method preferred by the Aztecs. Violent succession struggles predictably ensued. Though barred from the role of Inca themselves, ambitious noblewomen came to exercise considerable behind-the-scenes power over imperial succession.

Just beneath the Inca imperial line was an assortment of Cuzco-based nobles, readily identifiable by their huge ear-spools and finely woven tunics. Rather like their Aztec counterparts, they spoke a dialect of the royal language forbidden among commoners. Among this elite class were

Class Hierarchy   decorated generals and hereditary lords of prominent and ancient clans. Often drawn from these and slightly lower noble ranks was a substantial class of priests and astrologers, charged with maintaining a vast array of temples and shrines.

Many noble women and girls deemed physically perfect, like the sacrificial victim described at the start of this chapter, were also selected for religious seclusion, somewhat like nuns in contemporary Western societies. Seclusion was not always permanent, because some of these women were groomed for marriage to the Inca. Still more noblewomen, mostly wives and widows, were charged with maintaining the urban households and country estates of the Incas, dead and alive.

Next came a class of bureaucrats, regional military leaders, and provincial headmen. Bureaucrats kept track of tribute obligations, communal work schedules, and land appropriations. Following conquest, up to two-thirds of productive land was set aside in the name of the ruling Inca and the cult of the sun. Bureaucrats negotiated with headmen as to which lands these would be, and how and when their subjects would be put to work on behalf of their new rulers. If negotiations failed, the military was called in for a show of force. Lower-ranking Inca military men, like bureaucrats, often faced service at the most hostile fringes of empire. They had little beyond the weak hold of local power to look forward to. As a result, in sharp distinction with the Aztecs, death in battle was not regarded as a glorious sacrifice among the Incas, but rather as yet another humiliation. Furthermore, many officers were themselves provincial in origin and thus had little hope of promotion to friendlier districts closer to the imperial core.

The Inca and his substantial retinue employed and received tribute from numerous artisans, mostly conquered provincials. Such specialists included architects, khipu-keepers, civil engineers, metalworkers, stonecutters, weavers, potters, wood-carvers, and many others. Unlike the Aztecs, the Incas did not tolerate free traders, instead choosing to manage the distribution of goods and services as a means of exercising state power. Partly as a result, chattel, or market-oriented, slavery appears not to have existed under the Incas, although some conquered young men and women spared from death or exile were absorbed into the labor force as personal servants. Most Inca subjects and tribute payers were peasants belonging to kin groups whose lives revolved around agriculture and rotational labor obligations. For them, the rigors of everyday life far outweighed the extra demands of Inca rule. Only in the case of recently conquered groups, or those caught in the midst of a regional rebellion or succession conflict, was this not true. Even then, subsistence remained the average Andean's most pressing concern; battlefields were abandoned at planting and harvest times.

Andean artisans living under Inca rule produced remarkable textiles, metalwork, and pottery, but the empire's most visible achievements were in the fields of architecture and civil engineering. The Incas' extensive road systems, irrigation works, and monumental temples were unmatched by any ancient American society. No one

Inca Road

Stretching nearly 10,000 miles across mountains, plains, deserts, and rain forests, the Inca Royal Road held one of the world's most rugged and extensive empires together. Using braided fiber bridges to span chasms and establishing inns and forts along the road, the Incas handily moved troops, supplies, and information—in the form of khipu records and messages—across vast distances. The Royal Road had the unintentional consequence of aiding penetration of the empire by Spanish conquistadors on horseback. (akg-images/ Aurélia Frey.)

Material Achievements

else moved or carved such large stones or ruled such a vast stretch of terrain. Linking coast, highlands, and jungle, the Incas' roads covered nearly ten thousand miles. Draft workers and soldiers paved them with stones whenever possible, and many sections were hewn into near-vertical mountainsides by hand. Grass weavers spanned breathtaking gorges with hanging bridges strong enough to sustain trains of pack llamas for years at a time. These engineering marvels enabled the Incas to communicate and move troops and supplies across great distances with amazing speed, yet they also served the important religious function of facilitating pilgrimages and royal processions. Massive irrigation works and stone foundations, though highly practical, were similarly charged with religious power. Thus, the Inca infrastructure not only played an important practical role in imperial government, but it also expressed the Incas' belief in the connection between their own rule and the cosmic order.

The Incas appropriated and spread ancient Andean metalworking techniques, which were much older and thus far more developed than those of Mesoamerica. On the brink of a genuine Bronze Age by 1500, Inca metallurgy ranged from fine decorative work in specially prepared alloys to toolmaking for the masses. As in many parts of the early modern world, the forging of metals was as much a religious as an artistic exercise in the Andes, and metals themselves were regarded as semidivine. Gold was associated with the sun in Inca cosmology, and by extension with the Sapa Inca and his solar cult. Silver was associated with the moon and with several mother goddesses and Inca queens and princesses. Copper and bronze, considered less divine than gold and silver, were put to more practical uses.

Another ancient Andean tradition inherited by the Incas was weaving. Weaving in fact predates even ceramics in the Andes. Inca textiles, made mostly from native Peruvian cotton and alpaca fibers, were of extraordinary quality, and cloth became in essence the coin of the realm. Cooperative regional lords were rewarded by the Incas with substantial gifts of blankets and ponchos, which they could then redistribute among their subjects. Unlike some earlier coastal traditions, Inca design features favored geometric forms over representations of humans, animals, or deities. Fiber from the vicuña, a wild relative of the llama, was reserved for tunics and other garments worn only by the Sapa Inca. Softer than cashmere, it was the gold standard of Andean textile components. Some women became master weavers, but throughout most of the Inca Empire men wove fibers spun into thread by women, a gendered task division later reinforced by the Spanish.

With such an emphasis on textiles, it may come as no surprise that the Incas maintained a record-keeping system using knotted strings. Something like the Chinese abacus, or accounting device, in its most basic form, the **khipu** enabled bureaucrats and others to keep track of tributes, troop movements, ritual cycles, and other important matters. Like bronze metallurgy, the khipu predates the Inca Empire, but was most developed by Inca specialists. Although the extent of its capabilities as a means of data management remains a subject of intense debate, the khipu was sufficiently effective to remain in use for several centuries under Spanish rule, long after alphabetic writing was introduced.

Social Relations

Other ancient Andean traditions appropriated and spread by the Incas include reciprocity, the expectation of equal exchange and returned favors, complementary gender roles, and a tendency to view all social relations through the lens of kinship. Villagers, for example, depended on one another for aid in constructing homes, maintaining irrigation works, and tilling and harvesting fields. Whereas they chafed at service to the Inca ruler, they regarded rotational group work and communal care for disadvantaged neighbors not as burdens, but rather—after the work was done—as excuses for drinking parties and other festivities. Even in such a reciprocal environment, stresses and strains accumulated. In some villages, aggression was periodically vented during ritual fights between clan divisions.

Throughout the Andes, women occupied a distinct sphere from that of men, but not a subordinate one. For example, sources suggest that although the majority of Andeans living under Inca rule were patrilineal, or male-centered, in their succession preferences, power frequently landed in the hands of sisters and daughters of headmen. Literate Inca descendants described a world in which both sexes participated equally in complementary agricultural tasks, and also in contests against neighboring clans. Women exempted from rotational labor duties handled local exchanges of food and craft goods. Whether or not they were allowed to accumulate property as a result of these exchanges remains unknown.

Women's fertility was respected, but never equated with warfare, as in Aztec society. Interestingly, Andean childbirth was almost regarded as a nonevent, and rarely involved midwives. The Andean creator god, Wiracocha (weer-ah-COACH-ah), somewhat similar to the Aztecs' Tlaloc, had both male and female aspects. As in many traditional societies, Andean social hierarchy was described in terms of age and proximity of kin relation. "Mother" and "father," for example, were terms used to describe both gods and the most prominent earthly individuals (including one's parents). Next in line were numerous aunts, uncles, cousins, and so on down the family tree. Almost any respected elder was referred to as "uncle" or "aunt."

As in most early modern societies, parents treated Inca children much like miniature adults, and dressed them accordingly. Parents educated children by defining roles and duties early, using routine chores deemed appropriate to one's sex and status as the primary means of education. Girls and boys also participated in community and even state-level

khipu Knotted cotton or alpaca fiber strings used by the Incas and other Andeans to record tributes, troop numbers, and possibly narratives of events.

work projects. The expectation of all children was not to change society but to reproduce and maintain it through balanced relations with deities and neighbors. Contact with the Inca himself was an extremely remote possibility for most children living in the empire. A rare exception was capacocha sacrificial victims, such as the headman's daughter described at the opening of this chapter.

Just as maize was native to highland Mesoamerica and served as the base for urban development, the potato was the indigenous staple of the central Andes. A hearty, high-yield tuber with many varieties, the potato could be roasted, stewed, or naturally freeze-dried and stored for long periods. Control of preserved food surpluses was a hallmark of enduring imperial states, in large part because marching armies needed to eat. Maize could also be dried or toasted for storage and snacking, but among Andeans it was generally reserved for beer making. Along with maize, many lowland dwellers subsisted on manioc, peanuts, beans, and chili peppers.

Unique in the Americas, though common in much of Eurasia and Africa, Andean pastoralism played a critical role in Inca expansion. Andean domesticated animals included the llama, alpaca, and guinea pig. Llamas, in addition to carrying light loads, were sometimes eaten, and alpacas provided warm cloth fiber, much appreciated in the cold highlands. Slaughter of domestic animals, including fertilizer-producing guinea pigs, usually accompanied ritual occasions such as weddings or harvest festivals. Although like most early modern elites, the Inca and other nobles preferred to dine on freshly hunted deer, wild pig, and other meats. The average Andean diet was overwhelmingly vegetarian. Nevertheless, a common component of Inca trail food was *charqui* (hence "jerky"), bits of dried and salted llama flesh. Apparently for cultural rather than practical reasons, llamas and alpacas were never milked. Like many other peoples, Andeans restricted consumption of and even contact with certain animal fluids and body parts.

Khipu

The Incas did not invent the knotted-string record-keeping method known as khipu, but they used it extensively as they rapidly built their vast empire. Khipu masters braided and knotted cords of different colors and thicknesses in many combinations. Some khipus were kept as stored records and others sent as messages carried across the Andes by relay runners. (The Art Archive/Archaeological Museum Lima/Gianni Dagli Orti.)

Food and Subsistence

The high Inca heartland, though fertile, was prone to periodic droughts and frosts. The warmer coast was susceptible to catastrophic floods related to the so-called El Niño phenomenon, or periodic fluctuation in the eastern Pacific Ocean's surface temperature and resulting onshore moisture flow. Only by developing food storage techniques and exploiting numerous microenvironments were the Incas and their subjects able to weather such events. Added to these cyclical catastrophes were volcanic eruptions, earthquakes, mudslides, tsunamis, and plagues of locusts. Still, the overall record suggests that subsistence under the Incas, thanks to the "vertical archipelago," was much less precarious than under the Aztecs.

The Great Apparatus Breaks Down

In its simplest form Inca expansion derived from a blend of religious and secular impulses. As in Aztec Mexico, religious demands seem to have grown more and more urgent, possibly even destabilizing the empire by the time of the last Sapa Inca. As emperors died, their mummy cults required permanent and extravagant maintenance. In a context where the dead were not separate from the living, such obligations could not be shirked. The most eminent of mummies in effect tied up huge tracts of land. Logically, if vainly, successive emperors strove to make sure their mummy cults would be provided for in equal or better fashion. Each hoped his legacy might outshine that of his predecessor. Given the extraordinary precedent set by Pachacuti Inca, some scholars have argued that excessive mummy veneration effectively undermined the Inca Empire.

Despite this potentially unsustainable drive to conquer new territories, it was the Incas' notable organizational and diplomatic skills that held their enormous, geographically fractured empire together until the arrival of the Spanish in 1532. The Incas' ability to control the distribution of numerous commodities over great distances, to maintain communications and transport despite the absence of written texts and wheeled vehicles, to erect temples and centralize religious observation, and finally, to monopolize violence, all marked them as an imperial people.

As with the Aztecs, however, rapid growth by means of competitive violence sowed seeds of discontent. On the eve of the Spanish arrival both empires appear to have been on the verge of contraction rather than expansion, with rebellion at court and in the provinces the order of the day. The Incas had never done well against Amazonian and other lowland forest peoples, and some such enemies kept up chronic raiding activities. Highlanders such as the Cañaris of Ecuador and the Chachapoyas of northern Peru had cost the Incas dearly in their conquest, only just completed in 1525 after more than thirty years. Like the Tlaxcalans of Mexico, both of these recently conquered groups would ally with Spanish invaders in hopes of establishing their independence once and for all.

The Inca state was highly demanding of its subjects, and enemy frontiers abounded. Yet it seems the Incas' worst enemies were ultimately themselves. A nonviolent means of royal succession had never been established. This was good for the empire in that capable rather than simply hereditary rulers could emerge one after another, but bad in that the position of Sapa Inca was always up for grabs. In calmer times, defense against outside challengers would not have been much trouble, but the Spanish had the good fortune to arrive in the midst of a civil war between two rivals to the throne, Huascar and Atawallpa (also "Atahualpa"). By 1532 Atawallpa defeated his half-brother in a series of epic battles, only to fall prey to a small number of foreign interlopers.

COUNTERPOINT
The Peoples of North America's Eastern Woodlands 1450–1530

FOCUS

How did the Eastern Woodlanders' experience differ from life under the Aztecs and Incas?

By 1450 a great variety of native peoples, several million in all, inhabited North America's eastern woodlands. East of the Great Plains, dense forests provided raw materials for shelter, cooking, and transportation, as well as habitat for game. Trees also yielded nuts and other edible byproducts, and served as fertilizer for crops when burned. The great mound-building cultures of the Mississippi Basin had mostly faded by this time, their inhabitants having returned to less urban, more egalitarian ways of life. Villages headed by elected chiefs, not empires headed by divine kings, were the most common form of political organization (see Map 16.4).

Most of what we know about the diverse native inhabitants of eastern North America in early modern times derives from European documents from the contact period (1492–1750), plus archaeological studies. Although far less is known about them than about the Aztecs or Incas, the evidence suggests that Eastern Woodlands peoples faced significant changes in both their politics and everyday lives at the dawn of the early modern period, just before Europeans arrived to transform the region in other ways. Climate change may have been one important factor spurring conflict and consolidation.

Eastern Woodlands peoples were like the Aztecs in at least one sense. Most were maize farmers who engaged in seasonal warfare followed by captive sacrifice. According to archaeological evidence, both maize planting and warrior sacrifice spread into the region from Mesoamerica around the time of the Toltecs (800–1100 C.E.). The century prior to European contact appears to have been marked by rapid population growth, increased warfare, and political reorganization. Multisettlement ethnic alliances or leagues, such as the Iroquois Five Nations of upstate New York and the Powhatan Confederacy of Tidewater, Virginia, were relatively new to the landscape. Some confederacies were formed for

Population Growth and Political Organization

MAP 16.4

Native Peoples of North America, c. 1500

To the north of Mesoamerica, hundreds of native American groups, most of them organized as chiefdoms, flourished in a wide array of climate zones, from the coldest Arctic wilderness to the hottest subtropical deserts. Populations were highest where maize and other crops could be grown, as in the Mississippi Valley, Great Lakes, and eastern woodlands regions. Dense, sedentary populations also developed in the Pacific Northwest, where peoples such as the Kwakiutl lived almost entirely from gathering, hunting, and fishing. Nomadic hunters lived throughout the Great Plains, the Rocky Mountains, the Sierra Nevada, and the desert Southwest. Conflict between sedentary farmers and nomadic hunters was common, and some groups formed alliances to defend themselves against these and other attackers.

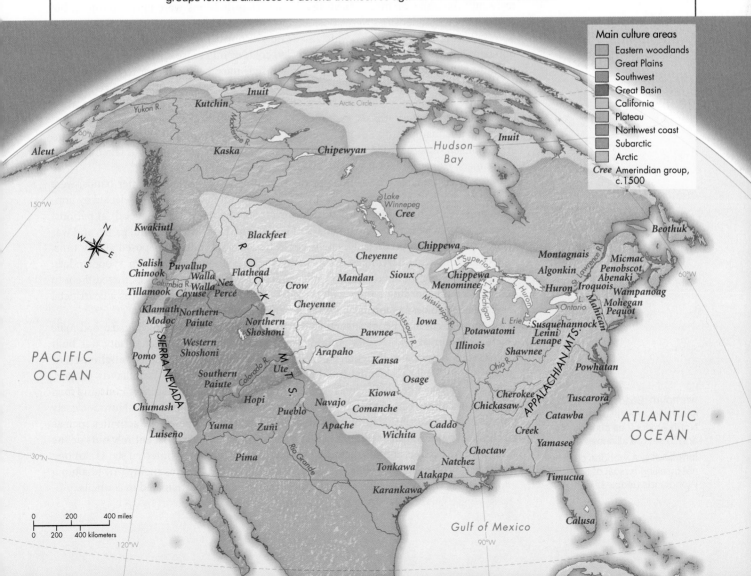

Huron Wampum Belt

For many Eastern Woodlands peoples such as the Huron, seashells like the New England quahog (a variety of clam) were sacred trade goods. Shell beads, generically called *wampum* after the arrival of Europeans, were woven into ceremonial belts whose geometrical designs and color schemes represented clans and sometimes treaties between larger groups. The linked-hands motif in this belt suggests a treaty or covenant. (National Museum of the American Indian, Smithsonian Institution. Catalog number: 1/2132. Photo by Katherine Fogden.)

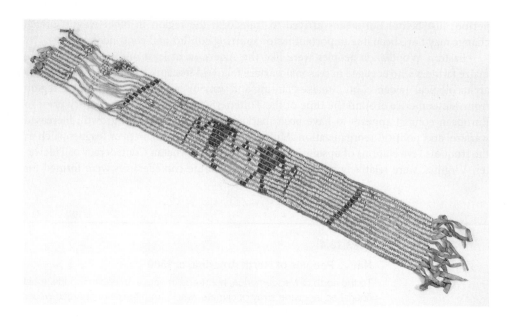

Matrilineal Society

wampum Beads made of seashells; used in eastern North America as currency and to secure alliances.

longhouse A wooden communal dwelling typical of Eastern Woodlands peoples.

temporary defensive or offensive purposes, and others were primarily religious. Village populations sometimes exceeded two thousand inhabitants, and confederacies counted up to twenty thousand or more. As in the Andes, clan divisions were fairly common, but overall population densities were considerably lower.

Gathering-hunting groups, which made up a minority of the total Eastern Woodlands population, tended to occupy large but rocky, cold, or otherwise challenging landscapes. Notably, thanks to their varied diet, these nonsedentary peoples seem to have suffered fewer vitamin and mineral deficiencies than settled maize eaters. Even maize farmers, however, were generally taller than their European (or Mesoamerican) contemporaries. Throughout the eastern forests, including the vast Great Lakes region, metallurgy was limited to simple manipulation of native copper. Raw copper, found in abundance in northern Michigan, was regarded as a sacred substance and was associated with chiefly power. Beads made from polished seashells, or **wampum**, were similarly prized.

Nearly all Eastern Woodlands groups, including small gatherer-hunter bands, were headed by chiefs. These men were usually exceptional warriors or shamans elected by popular agreement. Chiefs retained power, however, only by redistributing goods at periodic ceremonies; generosity was the hallmark of leadership. Since surplus food, game, and war booty were far from predictable, chiefs could be unceremoniously deposed at any time. Few chiefdoms were hereditary. As in many societies, individual Eastern Woodlanders, particularly young men, yearned for independence even as circumstances forced them to cooperate and subordinate their wills to others. If the chief's generosity was a centripetal force, egalitarian desires formed a powerful centrifugal one.

Some agricultural peoples, such as the Huron of central Ontario, Canada, had male chiefs or headmen but were organized matrilineally. This meant that society was built around clans of mothers, daughters, and sisters. Matrilineal clans occupied **longhouses**, or wooden multifamily residential buildings, typical of most Eastern Woodlands peoples. Elder women consulted with chiefs regularly, and all women played a part in urging men to war. Agriculture was regarded as a strictly female preserve among the Huron, closely linked to human fertility. Huron men were relegated to risky, perennial activities such as hunting, warfare, and tree felling. Their sphere of influence lay almost entirely outside the village. Men's exploits abroad, including adolescent vision quests, conferred status. Among all Eastern Woodlanders, public speech making, or rhetoric, was as highly prized among adult men as martial expertise. Only the most esteemed men participated in councils.

Children's lives were generally unenviable among North America's Eastern Woodlanders (keeping in mind that this was true of childhood throughout the early modern world). Thanks to a multitude of vermin and pathogens, generally poor nutrition, smoky residences, and manifold hazards of war and accident, relatively few children survived to adulthood. Partly for these reasons, Eastern Woodlands cultures discouraged severe discipline for children, instead allowing them much freedom.

Children's Lives

Playtime ended early for surviving girls and boys, however, as each was schooled before puberty in the arts and responsibilities deemed appropriate for their sex. Girls learned to farm and cook, boys to hunt and make war. Soon after puberty young people began to "try out" mates until a suitable match was found. This preference for trial marriage over forced arrangements was found in the Andes and other parts of the Americas as well. Though this and the seemingly casual practice of divorce among Eastern Woodlanders were considered scandalous by early modern European standards, stable monogamy prevailed.

Warfare was endemic throughout the Eastern Woodlands in the summer season, when subsistence itself was less of a battle. In form, these wars resembled blood feuds, or vengeance cycles. According to European witnesses, wars among the Iroquois, Mahicans, and others were spawned by some long-forgotten crime, such as the rape or murder of a clan member. As such, they did not constitute struggles over land or other natural resources, which were relatively abundant, but rather male contests intended to prove courage and preserve honor.

Warfare

Warfare closely resembled hunting in that successful warriors gained status for their ability to ambush and capture their equivalents from the opposite camp. These unlucky individuals were then brought to the captor's longhouse for what can only be described as an excruciating ordeal, nearly always followed by slaughter and ritual consumption. (Female and child captives, by contrast, were "adopted" as replacements for lost kin.) The religious significance of captive sacrifice among Eastern Woodlands peoples has been less clearly explained than that of the Aztecs and other Mesoamericans, but it seems to have been tied to subsistence anxieties.

Religious thought among Eastern Woodlands peoples varied, but there were commonalities. Beyond the realm of everyday life was a complex spirit world. Matrilineal societies such as the Huron traced their origins to a somewhat malevolent female spirit whose grandsons were responsible for various technical innovations and practices considered essential to civilized human life. The sky itself was often more important than the sun or moon in Eastern Woodlands mythologies, and climatic events were associated with enormous bird spirits, such as the thunderbird.

Religion

Like Andean peoples, many Eastern Woodlanders believed that material things such as boulders, islands, and personal charms contained life essences, or "souls." Traders and warriors, in particular, took time to please spirits and "recharge" protective amulets with offerings and incantations. Periodic feasts were also imbued with spiritual energy, but were unlike those of the Aztecs or Incas in that none was held on a specified date. As in many nonurban societies, religious life was an everyday affair, not an institutionalized one. Instead of priesthoods, liturgies, and temples, most Eastern Woodlands peoples relied on elders and shamans to maintain traditions and remind juniors of core beliefs.

Dreams and visions were carefully analyzed for clues to personal and group destinies. Dreams were also analyzed for evidence of witchcraft, or malevolent spell casting, within the group. Stingy or secretive individuals were sometimes suspected of this practice, often associated with jealousy, greed, and other socially unacceptable impulses. As in many semisedentary cultures worldwide, malicious witchcraft was blamed for virtually all sickness and death.

Unlike many other native American groups, most Eastern Woodlanders did not regard death as a positive transition. They believed that souls lived on indefinitely and migrated to a new home, usually a recognizable ethnic village located in the western distance. Even dogs' souls migrated, as did those of wild animals. The problem with this later existence was that it was unsatisfying. Dead souls were said to haunt the living, complaining of hunger and other insatiable desires. The Huron sought to keep their dead ancestors together and send them off well through elaborate burial rituals, but it was understood that ultimately little could be done for them.

Conclusion

By the time Europeans entered the Caribbean Sea in 1492, the two continents and many islands that make up the Americas were home to over 60 million people. Throughout the Western Hemisphere, native American life was vibrant and complex, divided by language, customs, and sometimes geographical barriers, but also linked by religion, trade, and war. Cities, pilgrimage sites, mountain passes, and waterways served as crossroads for the exchange of goods and ideas, often between widely dispersed peoples. Another uniting factor was the underlying religious tradition of shamanism.

The many resources available in the highland tropics of Mesoamerica and the Andes Mountains promoted settled agriculture, urbanization, and eventually empire building. Drawing on the traditions of ancestors, imperial peoples such as the Aztecs and Incas built formidable capitals, road systems, and irrigation works. As the Inca capacocha and Aztec warrior sacrifices suggest, these empires were driven to expand at least as much by religious beliefs as by material desires. In part as a result of religious demands, both empires were in crisis by the first decades of the sixteenth century, when Europeans possessing steel-edged weapons, firearms, and other technological advantages first encountered them. Other native peoples, such as the Huron, Iroquois, and Powhatan of North America's eastern woodlands, built chiefdoms and confederacies rather than empires, and to some degree these looser structures would prove more resilient in the face of European invasion.

NOTES

1. For the archaeologist's own account of these discoveries, see Johan Reinhard, *The Ice Maiden: Inca Mummies, Mountain Gods, and Sacred Sites in the Andes* (Washington, DC: National Geographic, 2005).
2. Miguel León-Portilla, *Pre-Columbian Literatures of Mexico* (Norman: University of Oklahoma Press, 1969), 87.
3. Juan de Betanzos, *Narrative of the Incas*, c. 1557, trans. Roland Hamilton and Dana Buchanan (Austin: University of Texas Press, 1996), 92.

RESOURCES FOR RESEARCH

Many Native Americas

Native American history has long been interdisciplinary, combining archaeology, anthropology, history, linguistics, geography, and other disciplines. Here is a small sample of works on the last centuries before European arrival plus several venerable encyclopedias.

Conrad, Geoffrey, and Arthur Demarest. *Religion and Empire.* 1984.

Denevan, William, ed. *The Native Population of the Americas in 1492,* 2d ed. 1992.

National Museum of the American Indian, Washington, DC: http://www.nmai.si.edu/.

Steward, Julian, ed. *The Handbook of South American Indians,* 7 vols. 1946–1959.

Sturtevant, William E., ed. *The Handbook of North American Indians,* 20 vols. 1978–2008.

Trigger, Bruce, ed. *The Cambridge History of the Native Peoples of the Americas,* 3 vols. 1999.

Tributes of Blood: The Aztec Empire, 1325–1521

Scholarship on the Aztecs has exploded in recent years. The following small sample includes new works that synthesize the perspectives of history, anthropology, and comparative religions.

Carrasco, Davíd. *City of Sacrifice: The Aztec Empire and the Role of Violence in Civilization*. 1999.

Carrasco, Davíd, and Scott Sessions. *Daily Life of the Aztecs, People of the Sun and Earth*, 2d ed. 2008.

Clendinnen, Inga. *Aztecs, an Interpretation*. 1994.

For more on Mexico City's Templo Mayor, see: http://archaeology.asu.edu/tm/index2.htm.

Hassig, Ross. *Aztec Warfare: Imperial Expansion and Political Control*, 2d ed. 2006.

Townsend, Richard F. *The Aztecs*, rev. ed. 2000.

Tributes of Sweat: The Inca Empire, 1430–1532

As with the Aztecs, studies of the Incas have proliferated in recent years. Exciting work has taken place in many fields, including archaeology, linguistics, history, and anthropology.

D'Altroy, Terrence. *The Incas*. 2002.

McEwan, Gordon F. *The Incas: New Perspectives*. 2006.

On khipus, see also Prof. Urton's Web site: http://khipukamayuq .fas.harvard.edu.

Urton, Gary. *Signs of the Inka Khipu: Binary Coding in the Andean Knotted-String Records*. 2004.

Von Hagen, Adriana, and Craig Morris. *The Cities of the Ancient Andes*. 1998.

COUNTERPOINT: The Peoples of North America's Eastern Woodlands, 1450–1530

The history of North America's Eastern Woodlands peoples was pioneered by Canadian and U.S.-based anthropologists and historians. It has continued to grow and broaden in scope. Indigenous voices are best heard in James Axtell's documentary history.

The American Indian Studies Research Institute, University of Indiana, Bloomington. http://www.indiana.edu/%7Eaisri/ index.shtml.

Axtell, James. *Natives and Newcomers: The Cultural Origins of North America*. 2001.

Axtell, James, ed. *The Indian Peoples of Eastern North America: A Documentary History of the Sexes*. 1981.

Richter, Daniel. *The Ordeal of the Longhouse: The Peoples of the Iroquois League in the Era of European Colonization*. 1992.

Trigger, Bruce. *The Children of Aataentsic: A History of the Huron People to 1660*, 2d ed. 1987.

▶ **For additional primary sources from this period**, see *Sources of Crossroads and Cultures.*

▶ **For Web sites, images, and documents related to topics in this chapter**, see Make History at bedfordstmartins.com/smith.

The major global development in this chapter ▶ The diversity of societies and states in the Americas prior to European invasion.

IMPORTANT EVENTS

c. 900–1600	Late Woodland period of dispersed farming and hunting
c. 1100	Aztecs leave Aztlán
c. 1200	Incas move into Cuzco region
c. 1270	Aztecs settle in Valley of Mexico
c. 1320	Aztecs ally with Colhua
c. 1325	Tenochtitlán founded at Lake Texcoco's edge
c. 1437	Incas defeat Chankas
c. 1440–1471	Sapa Inca Pachacuti expands empire into Ecuador and Bolivia
1450–1451	Great famine in Valley of Mexico
1471–1493	Incas conquer northern Chile and Argentina
1487–1502	Aztecs dedicate Coatepec (Templo Mayor) and expand sacrificial wars
1493–1525	Incas conquer northern Peru and highland Ecuador
1502–1519	Reign of Moctezuma II, conquered by Spanish
1525–1532	Inca succession war, followed by arrival of the Spanish
c. 1570	Formation of Huron Confederacy north of Lake Ontario and of Iroquois League south of Lake Ontario
c. 1580	Formation of Powhatan Confederacy in eastern Virginia

KEY TERMS

autosacrifice (p. 525)
chinampa (p. 523)
khipu (p. 536)
longhouse (p. 540)
shamanism (p. 518)

tribute (p. 526)
vertical archipelago (p. 530)
waka (p. 532)
wampum (p. 540)

CHAPTER OVERVIEW QUESTIONS

1. In what ways was cultural diversity in the Americas related to environmental diversity?

2. Why was it in Mesoamerica and the Andes that large empires emerged in around 1450?

3. What key ideas or practices extended beyond the limits of the great empires?

SECTION FOCUS QUESTIONS

1. What factors account for the diversity of native American cultures?

2. What core features characterized Aztec life and rule?

3. What core features characterized Inca life and rule?

4. How did the Eastern Woodlanders' experience differ from life under the Aztecs and Incas?

MAKING CONNECTIONS

1. Compare the Aztec and Inca empires with the Ming (see Chapter 15). What features did they share? What features set them apart?

2. How did Aztec and Inca sacrificial rituals differ, and why?

3. What were the main causes of warfare among native American peoples prior to the arrival of Europeans?

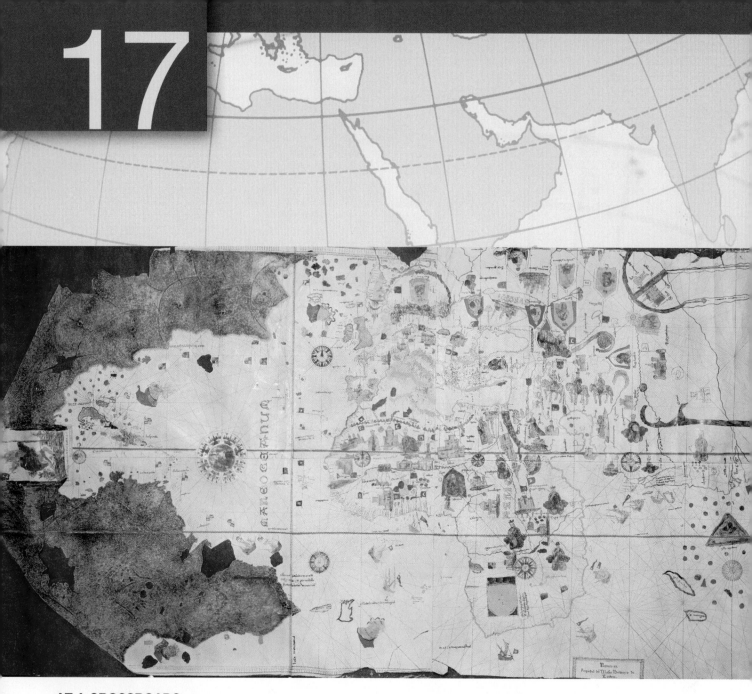

17

AT A CROSSROADS ▲

Painted on calfskins, portolan ("port finder") charts were used by mariners in the Mediterranean and North Atlantic beginning in the late fourteenth century. In addition to ports, the charts showed coasts and islands and corresponded, at least theoretically, to compass bearings. Like medieval manuscript illuminators, chart-makers occasionally filled blank or unknown spaces with renditions of ships, sea monsters, and freakish foreigners. After Christopher Columbus's momentous transatlantic voyage in 1492, portolan charts began to depict new European discoveries in the Americas with great accuracy. This 1500 map by Juan de la Cosa, who sailed with Columbus, is the earliest such chart. (Museo Naval, Madrid/Bridgeman Art Library.)

The Fall of Native American Empires and the Rise of an Atlantic World

1450–1600

The woman the Aztecs called Malintzin (mah-LEEN-tseen) was only a young girl when she was traded away by her parents around 1510. Malintzin was sent to serve a noble family living in what is today the state of Tabasco, on the Gulf coast of Mexico. She herself was of noble birth, a native speaker of the Aztec language, Nahuatl (NAH-watt). Malintzin's new masters were Chontal Maya speakers, and soon she learned this language, quite different from her own.

Throughout Malintzin's servitude in Tabasco, stories circulated there and in the neighboring Yucatan peninsula of bearded strangers. One day in the year 1519 eleven large vessels filled with these strangers arrived in Tabasco. The Tabascans assembled an attack when one party came ashore in a rowboat, but they were quickly defeated. In exchange for

BACKSTORY

By the mid-1400s, some 60 million people inhabited the Americas, about half of them subjects of the Aztec and Inca empires (see Chapter 16). These empires relied on far-flung tribute networks and drew from diverse cultural traditions even as they spread their own religious practices and imperial languages. Outside the Aztec and Inca realms, smaller states and chiefdoms occupied much of the hemisphere. Conflict between groups, whether in Peru, Brazil, Mexico, or eastern North America, was frequent.

The inhabitants of western Eurasia and North Africa were slowly recovering from the Black Death of 1347–1350 (see Chapter 15). Weakened nobilities and rebounding populations stimulated trade, political consolidation, and the adoption of new technologies for war and transport. The long-distance trade in luxury goods such as silk and spices also recovered, but by the early 1400s the rise of the Ottoman Empire in the eastern Mediterranean intensified competition and limited western European access to overland routes such as the Silk Road. The Asian luxury trade drained Europe of precious metals, prompting enterprising Italians and the seafaring Portuguese and Spanish of the Iberian peninsula to seek gold in Africa, to plant slave-staffed sugar colonies in the islands of the Mediterranean and eastern Atlantic, and to search for sea routes to Asia. In so doing they would link distant continents and initiate the development of a new Atlantic world.

Guns, Sails, and Compasses: Europeans Venture Abroad

FOCUS Why and how did Europeans begin to cross unknown seas in the fifteenth century?

New Crossroads, First Encounters: The European Voyages of Discovery, 1492–1521

FOCUS What were the main sources of conflict between Europeans and native Americans in the first decades after contact?

Spanish Conquests in the Americas, 1519–1600

FOCUS What factors enabled the Spanish to conquer the Aztec and Inca empires?

A New Empire in the Americas: New Spain and Peru, 1535–1600

FOCUS Why was the discovery of silver in Spanish America so important in the course of world history?

Brazil by Accident: The Portuguese in the Americas, 1500–1600

FOCUS How and why did early Portuguese Brazil develop differently from Spanish America?

COUNTERPOINT: The Mapuche of Chile: Native America's Indomitable State

FOCUS How did the Mapuche of Chile manage to resist European conquest?

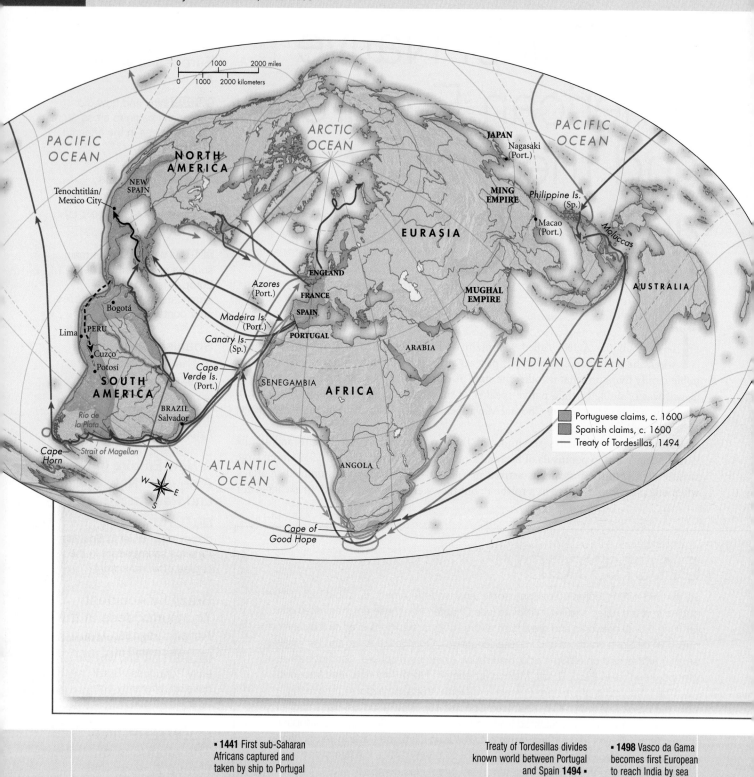

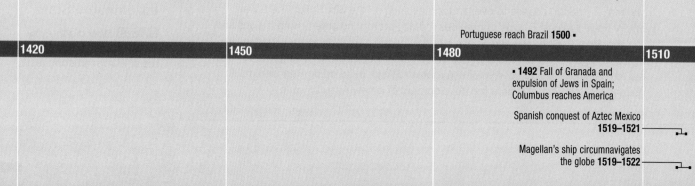

- **1441** First sub-Saharan Africans captured and taken by ship to Portugal

Treaty of Tordesillas divides known world between Portugal and Spain **1494** ·

- **1498** Vasco da Gama becomes first European to reach India by sea

Portuguese reach Brazil **1500** ·

| 1420 | 1450 | 1480 | 1510 |

- **1492** Fall of Granada and expulsion of Jews in Spain; Columbus reaches America

Spanish conquest of Aztec Mexico **1519–1521**

Magellan's ship circumnavigates the globe **1519–1522**

peace, they offered the strangers gold and feather work, and also several servant girls, among them Malintzin. When asked through an interpreter where the gold had come from, the Tabascans said "Mexico."

The strangers' interpreter was a bearded Spanish castaway called Jerónimo de Aguilar. He had lived several years in the Yucatan, but had now been ransomed by his countrymen. Aguilar soon discovered that Malintzin knew the language of Aztec Mexico. Their strangers' leader, Hernando Cortés, took a special interest in her for this reason, but as several of the strangers would later write, he also considered her the most beautiful and intelligent of the group of young female captives.

Twice given away now, and less certain than ever of her future, Malintzin joined the bearded foreigners in their cramped, floating homes. Heading west in the direction of the Aztec heartland, they reached a tiny island within sight of the mainland. Here Cortés ordered a party ashore to make contact with local villagers and, through them, to initiate a conversation with a group of traveling Aztec representatives. Only Nahuatl was spoken.

Suddenly the bilingual Malintzin was thrust into a mediating role of global significance. She passed along in Nahuatl the words the Spanish castaway gave her in Chontal Mayan. Then she did the reverse when the Aztec ambassadors replied. Aguilar made sense of the Mayan replies in the strangers' language for Cortés, who was already planning a risky march to take over the Aztec capital. Malintzin soon learned Castilian Spanish,

MAPPING THE WORLD
European Exploration and Conquest, c. 1450–1600

Combining a variety of shipbuilding and navigating technologies in innovative ways, and arming themselves with powerful new guns, western Europeans set out in search of spices, gold, and slaves. Some also sought Christian allies and converts. Merchants shared knowledge and pooled capital in Portugal's capital of Lisbon, the first seat of truly global maritime exploration. Soon after the Portuguese came the Spanish, among them settlers, traders, missionaries, and—most famously—conquistadors. These toppled the great American empires of the Aztecs and Incas within a generation of Columbus's landing in the Caribbean. The French, Dutch, and English followed the Iberian lead, but had little to show for their efforts before 1600.

ROUTES ▼

European exploration

→ Portuguese, 1487–1500
→ Spanish, 1492–1522
→ English, 1497–1580
→ French, 1534–1536
→ Dutch, 1596

Spanish conquistadors

→ Hernando Cortés, 1519–1521
--▸ Francisco Pizarro, 1531–1533

1532–1536 Spanish conquest of Inca Peru

- **1549** Portuguese establish royal capital of Salvador; first Jesuits arrive in Brazil

- **1572** Mita labor draft and mercury amalgamation formalized in Potosí

- **1555** French establish colony in Brazil's Guanabara Bay

1540

- **1545** Discovery of silver deposits at Potosí

1570

1570–1571 Inquisition established in Lima and Mexico City

1600

- **1592** Potosí reaches peak production

- **1564** Discovery of mercury mines in Huancavelica, Peru

- **1567** Portuguese drive French from Brazil

- **1599** Great Mapuche uprising in Chile

rendering Aguilar unnecessary. From here until the end of the conquest campaigns in 1521, Malintzin served as Cortés's key to Aztec Mexico.

In the midst of conquest Malintzin bore Cortés a son, but she ultimately married another Spaniard and lived with the respect given to European ladies in the first years of colonial rule. Malintzin joined a host of other former Aztec subjects who helped the foreigners build Mexico City from the rubble of the former Aztec capital of Tenochtitlán, and eventually a vast Christian kingdom called New Spain.

In modern Mexican mythology Malintzin, or Malinche (mah-LEEN-cheh), as she is commonly known, is regarded as a traitor, a collaborator, even a harlot. Recent scholars have shown these characterizations to be both anachronistic and unfair. Malintzin was not seen as a traitor in her own day, even by the Aztecs. In their paintings of the conquest, Nahuatl-speaking artists working shortly after the arrival of the Spanish often placed Malintzin at the center, poised and confident, speech scrolls emanating from her mouth. For a culture that called its kings *tlatoque*, or "speakers," this was significant.

But why was it mostly southern Europeans who were sailing across the Atlantic in Malintzin's and Cortés's time? In part it was because residents of the old European crossroads of Iberia (the peninsula occupied by Spain and Portugal), including colonies of Italian merchants, had begun charting the eastern Atlantic at least a century before. Also, in finishing what they called the *Reconquista* (Reconquest) of their homeland, Christian Iberians were driven to outflank the growing Ottoman Empire in North Africa and to revive the global crusade against Islam. Over time, a mix of commercial, political, and religious motives inspired the merchants and monarchs of Portugal and Spain, Europe's southwestern-most kingdoms, to develop the technologies needed to navigate open seas, exploring first the west coast of Africa and then crossing the vast Atlantic itself. Flush with capital, Italian bankers helped fund these enterprises (as we saw in Chapter 15).

The Iberian encounter with the Americas that resulted from all of these factors was an accident of monumental significance. In quest of legendary Asian riches, Columbus and his successors landed instead in the vast and populous but previously isolated regions they called the New World. It was new to them, of course, but hardly so to its roughly 60 million native American inhabitants. Cultural misunderstandings, political divisions among indigenous peoples, and European firearms aided conquest and settlement, but germs made the difference in a way not seen anywhere in Africa or Asia. Only certain Pacific Islanders proved as vulnerable.

Among the manifold effects of European expansion across the Atlantic was a biological exchange of profound importance for all humanity. Dubbed by historian Alfred Crosby "the Columbian Exchange," this was the first major biological relinking of the earth since the continents had drifted apart in prehuman times. Although the Columbian Exchange brought many deadly diseases to the Americas, it also brought new animals for transport, plowing, and consumption. Among the many effects of this global exchange was rapid population growth in parts of the world where American crops such as potatoes and maize took root. As a result of European expansion to the west, the Atlantic became a global crossroads, the center of a new pattern of exchange that would have consequences for the entire world.

Finally, we should not make the mistake of assuming that Europeans met little or no significant resistance in the Americas. As we shall see in the Counterpoint that concludes this chapter, one group of native Americans who successfully fought off European conquest, in part by adopting the horse and turning it against their oppressors, were the Mapuche of Chile.

OVERVIEW
QUESTIONS

The major global development in this chapter: European expansion across the Atlantic and its profound consequences for societies and cultures worldwide.

As you read, consider:

1. What were the main biological and environmental consequences of European expansion into the Atlantic after 1492?

2. What roles did misunderstanding and chance play in the conquests of the Aztecs and Incas?

3. How did Eurasian demand for silver and sugar help bring about the creation of a linked Atlantic world?

Guns, Sails, and Compasses: Europeans Venture Abroad

Since late medieval times, Nordic and southern European mariners had been venturing farther and farther out to sea, testing seasonal winds and following currents as they founded new colonies and connected markets to regions of supply. Sailors and navigators shared information, but as in

FOCUS

Why and how did Europeans begin to cross unknown seas in the fifteenth century?

the Mediterranean, colonizing distant lands was a competitive, religiously charged, and violent process, one that also entailed fusing technologies from around the world. In the fifteenth century tiny Portugal emerged as the world's first truly global maritime empire. Neighboring Spain followed, spurred on by Christopher Columbus and a crusading spirit.

Motives for Exploration

Early modern Europeans had many reasons for engaging in overseas ventures, but most shared a common interest in accumulating wealth, gaining power against their rivals, and spreading Christianity. Commerce was a core motive for expansion, as European merchants found themselves starved for gold and silver, which they needed to purchase Asian spices, silks, gems, and other luxuries. With the exception of Mediterranean coral and, increasingly, guns, Europe produced little to offer in exchange for eastern luxuries. In part because of Europe's relative poverty, ambitious monarchs and princes adopted violent means to extend their dominions overseas and to increase their tax and tribute incomes. Finally, Europe's many Christian missionaries hoped to spread their religion throughout the globe. These motives would shape the early encounters between Europeans and the peoples of the Americas, as well as the subsequent hybrid societies that would emerge in the conquered lands.

"Gold is most excellent," wrote Christopher Columbus in a letter to the king and queen of Spain. "Gold constitutes treasure, and anyone who has it can do whatever he likes in the world."[1] Columbus, a native of the Italian city-state of Genoa, knew what he was talking about. Genoese merchants had long traded for gold in North Africa, where Muslim traders who crossed the Sahara from West Africa brought it to exchange for a variety of goods. African gold lubricated Mediterranean and European trade, but population growth, commercial expansion, and intensifying competition among Christian and Islamic states

Gold and Spices

strained supplies. It was thus the well-placed Portuguese, who established a North African foothold in Morocco in 1415, who first sought direct access to African gold.

Italian merchants made some of their greatest profits on spices, which were used as both medicines and flavoring agents. Since most spices came from the farthest tropical margins of Asia, they rose considerably in value as they passed through the hands of mostly Islamic middlemen in the Indian Ocean and eastern Mediterranean. Indian pepper and Indonesian nutmeg were but a few of the many desired drugs and condiments that Portuguese and other European merchants hoped to purchase more cheaply by sailing directly to the source. This entailed either circumnavigating Africa or finding a western passage to the Pacific.

Slaves and Sugar

Throughout the Mediterranean basin, slaves were prized as field laborers and household servants, and demand for them grew with the expansion of commercial agriculture and the rise of wealthy merchant families. Prices also rose as source regions near the Black Sea were cut off after 1453 by the Ottomans. As the word *slave* suggests, most captives came initially from the Slavic regions of eastern Europe. Others were prisoners of war taken in battles and pirate raids. In part to meet growing Christian European demand, increasing numbers of sub-Saharan Africans were transported to North African ports by caravan. As with gold, southern European merchants engaged in this trade were quick to seek captives by sailing directly to West Africa.

Sugar, yet another exotic commodity in high and growing demand in Europe, required large investments in land, labor, and machinery. Produced mostly by enslaved workers on eastern Atlantic islands such as Portuguese Madeira by the mid-fifteenth century, cane sugar, in medieval times considered a spice or drug, increasingly became a common commodity in Europe as both a sweetener and preservative. As sugar took the place of honey in Old World cuisines, few consumers pondered its growing connection to overseas enslavement. In time, European demand for sugar would lead to the establishment of the Atlantic slave trade and the forced migration of millions of Africans to the Americas.

Technologies of Exploration

Firearms Manufacture

As they set sail for new horizons, Europeans employed innovations in three technological spheres: gun making, shipbuilding, and navigation. First was firearms manufacture. Gunpowder, a Chinese invention, had been known since at least the ninth century C.E. Chinese artisans experimented with rockets and bombs, but it was late medieval and early modern Europeans who developed gunpowder and gun making to their greatest destructive effect.

Europeans had also borrowed and improved on ancient Chinese papermaking and movable type technologies, and by 1500 they published treatises detailing the casting and operation of bronze and iron cannon. Soon, crude handguns and later muskets transformed field warfare, first in Europe, then worldwide. As gun and powder technologies improved and fighters acquired shooting and reloading skills, contingents of musketeers replaced archers, crossbowmen, and other foot soldiers.

Shipbuilding and Navigation

The second key technological leap was in ship construction. Although numerous small, swift-sailing vessels traversed the Mediterranean in late medieval times, long-distance carriers were cumbersome and even dangerous when overloaded. The Roman-style galley, used mostly in the Mediterranean, was a long and narrow fighting vessel propelled by captive oarsmen with occasional help from sails. Galleys functioned effectively where seas were calm, distances short, and prisoners plentiful. Galleys also worked well to defend against pirates and for massive showdowns, but they were almost useless for carrying cargo.

The galley proved unreliable for the rougher waters and longer voyages common in the North Atlantic. Here, in the old trading ports and fishing villages of Portugal, Spain, western France, the Netherlands, and England, shipwrights combined more rigid North Sea hull designs and square sail rigs with some of the defensive features of the galley, such as the high aft-castle, or fortified cabin built on the rear deck. They also borrowed and incorporated the galley's triangular or lateen sails, which in turn had been adapted from the Arabian *dhows* of the Indian Ocean.

The resulting hybrid vessel combinations, which included the caravel form used by ocean-crossing mariners such as Columbus, proved greater than the sum of their parts. Although slow and unwieldy by modern standards, these late-fifteenth-century European ships were the world's most durable, swift-sailing, and maneuverable means of heavy transport to date. Later modified into galleons, frigates, and clippers, they would serve as the basic models for virtually all European carriers and warships until the advent of steam technology in the early nineteenth century.

European innovations in navigational technology also propelled overseas expansion. Learned cosmographers believed the world to be more or less spherical by Columbus's time, but finding one's way from port to port beyond sight of land was still a source of worry. One aid in this dilemma was the magnetic compass, like gunpowder and printing a fairly ancient Chinese invention developed in a novel way by Europeans. We know from travelers' accounts that sailors in the Indian Ocean also used compasses in medieval and early modern times, but rarely in combination with sea charts, which contained detailed compass bearings and harbor descriptions. The combination of charts and compasses soon changed European navigators' perceptions of what had formerly been trackless seas.

Another borrowed instrument, apparently Arabic in origin, was the astrolabe. A calculator of latitude (one's location north or south of the equator), it proved even more critical for long-distance maritime travel than the compass. Precise knowledge of latitude was essential for early modern sailors in particular since longitude, a more complicated east-west calculation, was little known until the invention of seaworthy clocks in the mid-eighteenth century.

Thus armed with an impressive ensemble of borrowed and modified tools, weapons, and sailing vessels, Europeans were well poised to venture out into unknown or unfamiliar worlds. Add the recent development of the printing press, and they were also able to publicize their journeys in new if not altogether honest ways.

Portuguese Ship

The Portuguese were the first Europeans to develop ocean-going ships for extended, return voyages. Initially they combined rigid hull designs from the Atlantic with maneuverable triangular sails of Arabic origin to build caravels, but these small vessels had limited cargo space and were vulnerable to attack. This evocative image from a contemporary manuscript shows Vasco da Gama's flagship, the *St. Gabriel*, on its way to India in 1497–1498 with every stitch of canvas out. For such long trips the Portuguese chose to sacrifice the maneuverability of the caravel in favor of maximizing sail surface and relying on trade winds. The resulting ships, which could carry up to 1200 tons of cargo and were built like floating fortresses, are known as "carracks." Portugal's national symbol until recent times, the red cross of the Order of Christ identified such ships as Portuguese. (The Art Archive/Science Academy Lisbon/Gianni Dagli Orti.)

Portugal Takes the Lead

Historians have long wondered why tiny Portugal, one of Europe's least populated and developed kingdoms, led the way in overseas expansion. A closer look at key factors helps solve this puzzle. First, the kingdom of Portugal was an ancient maritime crossroads straddling two vibrant commercial spheres, the Mediterranean and northeast Atlantic. Coastal shipping had grown efficient in late medieval times while overland transport between northern and southern Europe remained slow, costly, and prone to banditry. Well before 1400, long-distance merchants from as far away as Venice and Stockholm put in at Lisbon,

Overseas Incentives

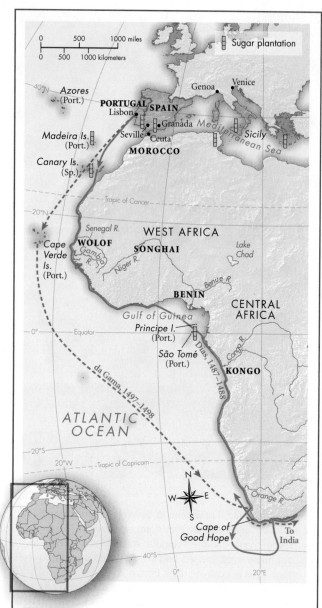

MAP 17.1

The East Atlantic, c. 1500

The Portuguese were the first Europeans to seek a sea route to Asia, and they did so by making their way south along the Atlantic coast of Africa. The diseases of tropical Africa limited Portuguese colonization to a few fortified enclaves, but they established lucrative settlement colonies in the eastern Atlantic island chains of the Azores, Madeiras, and Cape Verdes, along with the wet tropical island of São Tomé in the Gulf of Guinea. By 1500 the Portuguese had discovered that the fastest way to round the tip of Africa was to follow the prevailing winds and currents that swept to the west of the African coast before turning southeast.

the Portuguese capital, to break up their long journeys. Commercial competition was fostered by Portugal's kings, and along with money and exotic goods, important shipbuilding and sailing knowledge was exchanged. Capital, in the form of money, ships, and goods, also accumulated in the hands of powerful merchant clans, many of them foreign.

Other factors besides accumulating capital and foreign merchants pushed the Portuguese abroad. By the 1430s, fishermen regularly ventured far out into the Atlantic in pursuit of better catches. Moreover, arable land in Portugal grew scarce as populations grew and large estates expanded, rendering overseas colonization ever more attractive. Also, religious and strategic concerns drove Portuguese nobles to capture the Islamic port city of Ceuta (SYOO-tah), on Morocco's Mediterranean coast, in 1415. Crusade-like ventures such as this continued to overlap with commercial ones throughout early modern times. Thus, the push of limited resources at home and the pull of opportunities abroad stimulated Portuguese expansion.

With support from ambitious nobles such as Prince Henry "the Navigator" (1394–1460), Portuguese and foreign investors pooled capital accumulated in shipping and moneylending and invested it in a variety of new technologies to create a far-flung network of settlement colonies and *feitorias* (fay-toe-REE-ahs), or fortified trading posts. Some invested in overseas plantations in the eastern Atlantic and Mediterranean, others in the gold and slave trades of West Africa (see Map 17.1).

Gaining confidence with each new experience, Portuguese merchants and sailors learned to navigate the complex currents and prevailing winds of the West African coast. By 1430 they had come upon the Azores and Madeiras, uninhabited island chains in the eastern Atlantic. With incentives from the Crown and some Italian merchant investment, Portuguese settlers immediately colonized and farmed these islands. The Canaries, farther south, were somewhat different. Inhabited by dozens of bands and chiefdoms descended from pre-Islamic Moroccan immigrants, these rugged volcanic islands posed distinct political and moral challenges. "They go about naked without any clothes," wrote one Portuguese chronicler, "and have little shame at it; for they make a mockery of clothes, saying they are but sacks in which men put themselves."[2]

What was to be done? Should the inhabitants of the Canary Islands be conquered and their lands taken over by Europeans, and if so, by what right, and by whom? The presence of indigenous Canarians in fact spurred competition among a variety of European adventurers. Among them were Spanish missionaries and militant French and Portuguese nobles, but Spanish nobles under Isabella and Ferdinand, Columbus's future sponsors, ultimately won title to the islands. The Guanches (HWAN-chehs), as the Europeans called the largest group of native inhabitants, lost to the point of annihilation. A few survivors were enslaved and made to work on sugar plantations. In many ways, the Canarian experience foretold Iberian, and more generally European, actions in the Americas. When they stood in the way of European ambitions, the interests of indigenous peoples counted for little or nothing.

Always in search of gold, which the eastern Atlantic islands lacked, and spurred on by Prince Henry, the Portuguese in 1444 reached the mouth of the Senegal River. On the Senegal, the Portuguese traded Arabian warhorses for gold dust with representatives of the Muslim Wolof kingdoms. They also traded, and on a few occasions raided, for slaves. The victims of these 1440s raids and exchanges were the first Africans to be shipped en masse across Atlantic waters. Most ended up in the households and artisan workshops of Lisbon.

Portuguese reconnaissance in the eastern Gulf of Guinea in the 1480s led to contacts with the kingdom of Benin and also to settlement of the offshore islands of Príncipe and São Tomé. Some captives from Benin were forced to plant and refine sugar on São Tomé. The slave-staffed tropical sugar plantation, which would define the economy and culture of colonial Brazil and much of the Caribbean basin from the fifteenth to nineteenth centuries, found a prototype here off the coast of central Africa in the years just before Columbus's famous voyages. Iberians developed similar plantations in the Canaries and Madeira.

By 1488, Bartolomeu Dias rounded Africa's Cape of Good Hope, and ten years later, Vasco da Gama became the first European to reach India by sea. Given the momentum, cumulative knowledge, and overall success of the Portuguese enterprise, it is understandable that when in the early 1480s Christopher Columbus proposed to open a westward route to "the Indies," the Portuguese king, on the advice of his cosmographers, declined. Columbus's calculations were in doubt, as was the need for an alternative of any kind. Once in the Indian Ocean, the Portuguese used their sturdy ships and superior firepower to terrifying effect, taking more than a dozen key ports from their mostly Muslim inhabitants by 1510. The emphasis on capturing ports reflected Portuguese ambitions. They sought to dominate the existing maritime Asian trade, not to establish a colonial land empire. Thus, as we shall see, Portuguese and Spanish expansion would take very different forms.

Origins of the Atlantic Slave Trade

Push to Asia

New Crossroads, First Encounters: The European Voyages of Discovery 1492–1521

Portugal's Spanish neighbors had long been interested in overseas expansion as well, although by Columbus's time they lagged far behind. Spanish sailors and shipbuilders were as competent as those of Portugal, and some nobles and merchant families were tied to the early African trade. What would quickly distinguish Spain's overseas enterprises from Portugal's, however, was a stronger tendency to acquire large landmasses by force, colonize them with large numbers of settlers, and force Catholicism on all inhabitants. To some extent this pattern of expansion derived from the centuries-long Christian Reconquest of the Iberian peninsula that ended with the defeat of the Muslim caliphate of Granada in January 1492. As if fated, it was at Ferdinand and Isabella's royal military encampment, Santa Fe de Granada, that Columbus received his license to sail across the Ocean Sea, the name then given to the Atlantic.

> **FOCUS**
>
> What were the main sources of conflict between Europeans and native Americans in the first decades after contact?

Christopher Columbus in a New World

Christopher Columbus, born in the Italian city of Genoa in 1451, was just one of many ambitious merchants who came of age in the dynamic, profit-seeking East Atlantic world centered on Lisbon. Columbus married Felipa de Perestrelo, a Portuguese noblewoman, but did not settle down. Instead, he spent most of his time sailing on Portuguese merchant vessels bound for West Africa, England, and even Iceland. He soon became obsessed with a scheme to sail west to China and Japan, which he had read about in the already two-hundred-year-old account of the Venetian merchant Marco Polo. In around 1485 Columbus left for Spain,

feitoria A Portuguese overseas trading post, usually fortified.

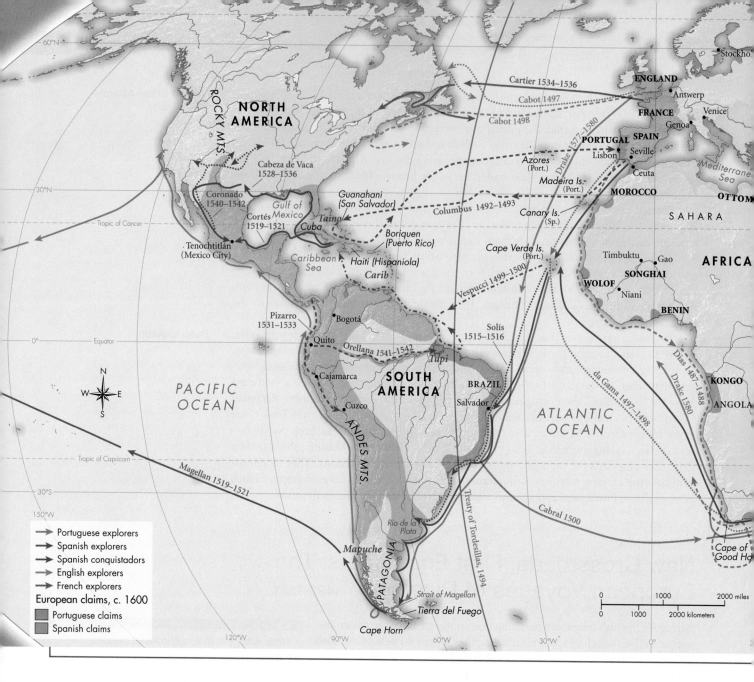

where he eventually won the sponsorship of Isabella and Ferdinand. By 1492 he was off to cross the Atlantic in search of the successors of Qubilai Khan, China's famed thirteenth-century Mongol ruler. "I set out for Your Highnesses' Canary Islands," he wrote to Ferdinand and Isabella in his ship's log, "in order to begin my journey from there and sail until I should arrive in the Indies, there to deliver Your Highnesses' embassy to those princes."[3]

On October 12, 1492, barely a month after leaving his last stopover point in the Canary Islands, Christopher Columbus and his mostly Spanish crew made contact with the native Taino (tah-EE-no) inhabitants of Guanahani, one of the smaller Bahama Islands. Unable to communicate with them, Columbus imagined himself somewhere near Japan, or at least "east of India." He christened the island San Salvador, or "Holy Savior," as a religious gesture of thanks, and called the native Bahamians and all other indigenous peoples he subsequently encountered "Indians" (see Map 17.2).

Remarking in his journal that the "Indians" he met in the Bahamas were tall, well built, scantily clad, and ignorant of iron weapons, Columbus proposed that they would make excellent slaves. The Indians reminded him of the native Canary Islanders whom the

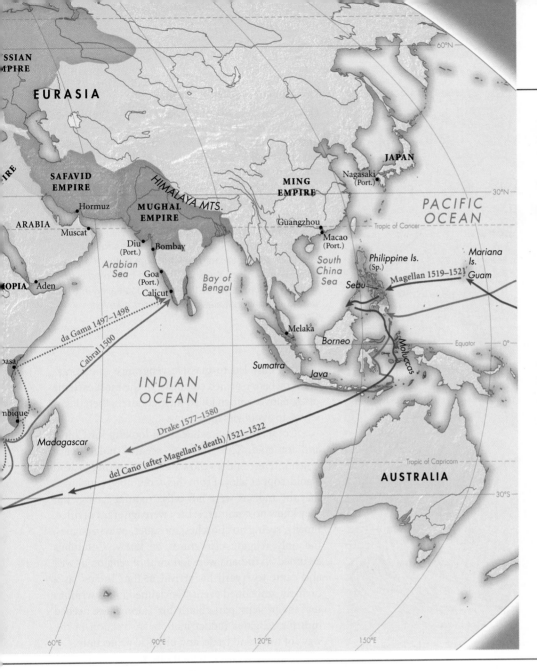

MAP 17.2

European Voyages of Discovery, c. 1420–1600

In a remarkably short time, the Portuguese and Spanish went from exploring the eastern Atlantic to circumnavigating the globe. Christopher Columbus's first Spanish-sponsored voyage across the Atlantic in 1492 and Vasco da Gama's Portuguese-sponsored trip to India in 1497–1498 heightened the competition, and by 1519 Ferdinand Magellan, a Portuguese navigator sailing for the Spanish, set out to circle the globe by rounding South America and crossing the Pacific. Magellan was killed in the Philippines, but some of his crew survived to return to Spain in 1522. It was not until the 1577–1580 voyage of the English privateer Francis Drake, led by a kidnapped Portuguese pilot, that another European circumnavigated the globe.

Spanish and Portuguese had conquered and enslaved. True to his word, Columbus eventually shipped some five hundred Caribbean natives to the markets of Seville.

After the first landfall in the Bahamas, Columbus sailed southwest to Cuba, then east to the large island known locally as Haiti. He renamed it "Española" ("Hispaniola," "Little Spain" in English) and began looking for a town site to settle in the name of his queen. In the course of this and three subsequent voyages, Christopher Columbus claimed and named everything and everyone that came into his view for his royal Spanish sponsors. In his logbook, Columbus constantly reiterated his hopes of finding gold, spices, and news of "the Great Khan." He died in 1506, still believing he was near China.

For the diverse American peoples who met Columbus and his crewmembers, the heavily clothed and armed foreigners provoked mixed feelings. They brought some useful goods, including hatchets and sewing needles, but when their incessant demands for food, gold, and sexual companionship were not met, they turned violent, torturing, raping, and murdering native islanders at will. No one, least of all Columbus, seemed willing to punish the newcomers or rein them in. Before long, some frustrated Taino hosts returned the violence in kind,

Exploring the Caribbean

Early Native American–Spanish Relations

Columbus Meets Native Americans

On October 12, 1492, the Italian navigator Christopher Columbus reached the Bahama Islands, and soon afterward Haiti, which he renamed "Española," partly pictured here. The native Taino welcomed Columbus, hoping to recruit him as an ally against fierce neighbors the admiral dubbed "Caribs," and later, "cannibals." News of these meetings soon spread throughout Europe, and very early images such as this one accompanying a portion of one of Columbus's published letters show how difficult it was for European artists to imagine what was to them a truly "New World." Even the ship is drawn from medieval tradition, since we know that Columbus sailed in what were then the most sleek and modern caravels. (Corbis.)

but this only led to massive vengeance raids organized by better-armed colonists. In the most extreme cases, native women killed their children, then themselves, to avoid violation.

Columbus, meanwhile, kept looking for China, and for gold. The "Indians" seemed not to have much interest in the yellow metal, preferring instead a gold-copper alloy. From this, Columbus concluded that the Indians were not only "natural slaves," but they knew no commerce; they were ignorant of price. Finally, seeing no churches, mosques, or synagogues, the only religious structures he knew, Columbus assumed all Indians were ignorant of religion as well and came to regard his arrival in the "Indies" as a divinely sanctioned event. He claimed in his writings that the Indians, particularly his Taino allies, needed him for religious indoctrination, instruction in the ways of work and trade, and physical protection.

Protection was essential due to the presence of "evil" Indians, as Columbus described them, chronic enemies of the Taino. The word *Caribbean* derives from Carib, or *caribe*, apparently an ethnic term. Groups of so-called Caribs did in fact inhabit the smaller islands to the east and south of Borinquen, the large island renamed Puerto Rico, or "Rich Port," by the Spanish. Although culturally similar to the Taino, these Caribs were said to have a particularly bad habit: they ate human flesh.

"Man-eating" natives were in some ways a predictable New World wonder, the sort of marvel medieval travelers had often described for sensation-hungry readers. Columbus happily played along. It appears he blended the Latin *canis* (dog) and local ethnic name *caribe* to produce a new word: *canibal*, or "cannibal." *Carib* and *cannibal* soon became interchangeable terms in the lexicon of Spanish conquest, and the image of the cannibal stuck fast in the European imagination. Indeed, almost as quickly as news of the Indies reached Europe, printers rushed to illustrate the alleged atrocities of the Caribbean "dog-people."

Given the circumstantial nature of the evidence, historians and anthropologists remain divided as to whether the so-called Caribs practiced cannibalism. What mattered for Columbus and his followers was that their allies, the "good Indians," said they did. With such a legal pretext (the eating of human flesh being regarded as a clear violation of natural law in the Western tradition), the newcomers could claim to be serving a necessary

Dog-Faced Cannibals

European readers of chivalry tales and travel accounts expected the American "New World" to yield fantastic and horrible creatures. Early news from the Caribbean and Brazil suggested the existence of humans with doglike, omnivorous appetites, seeming to confirm the alleged observations of Marco Polo and other medieval travelers. In this 1527 woodcut, a German artist fused Weimaraner-like dogs' heads with naked German butchers, one with a raised steel cleaver, to represent native Americans. Since this image predates the Spanish conquest of the Incas by five years, the horned llama-like animal at lower left is of special interest. (Courtesy of the John Carter Brown Library at Brown University.)

police role. By this argument, the Spanish alone could adequately "protect" and "punish"—that is, take over Western-style functions of government in the "New World." Thus, drawing on a variety of assumptions and preconceptions, Europeans imposed their own interpretations on the social and cultural patterns of New World peoples, interpretations that justified European domination.

Spanish sovereignty in the Americas was soon defined against the backdrop of Portugal's older overseas claims. With the pope's backing, in 1494 the Spanish and Portuguese split the world into two zones of influence. According to the terms of the Treaty of Tordesillas, the Spanish were to rule everyone living 370 leagues (roughly 1110 miles) or more west of the Canaries; all inhabitants beyond this line were now subjects of the crown of Spain according to European law. Africa, Asia, and eventually Brazil, which was not known to Europeans until 1500, fell to the Portuguese.

Why was the Roman Catholic pope involved in an agreement of this kind? First, fifteenth-century Europeans regarded his authority as above that of secular rulers. More important, however, was the matter of spreading the Christian gospel, a job Columbus himself embraced. Iberian monarchs, all pious Catholics at this time, promised to sponsor the conversion of everyone their subjects encountered abroad and also to continue the medieval fight against "infidels." Commerce may have supplied the initial and most powerful motive for overseas expansion, but a drive for religious and cultural hegemony soon came to play an important part in European colonization.

Treaty of Tordesillas

From Independence to Servitude: The Encomienda System

Although missionaries were present in the Caribbean from the 1490s, early Spanish colonization of this vast island region amounted mostly to a mad dash for gold and slaves. Early Spanish settlers had little interest in working the land themselves, preferring instead to live from the rents and labor provided by native American slaves and tribute payers. As news of massive abuse and alarming death rates among the Taino and captive Caribs reached Spain, Queen Isabella demanded an end to Amerindian slavery. After 1503 only violent rebels and alleged cannibals were to be enslaved.

**Compromise on Native
American Slavery**

Would the Taino then be free in exchange for accepting Catholicism and Spanish protection against the Caribs? No, in large part because their labor was thought necessary to mine gold, which Spain's monarchs desperately wanted. Compromise came in the form of the *encomienda* system. Native villages headed by chieftains were entrusted to leading Spanish citizens in a manner resembling medieval European feudalism: village farming folk were to offer labor and surplus produce to their "lord" in exchange for military protection. Chiefs served as middlemen, exempted from tribute and manual work. The Spanish *encomenderos* who received these fiefdoms were self-styled men-at-arms, and from their ranks would come the conquerors of the mainland.

Indians deemed good and faithful subjects of Crown and Church paid tributes to their encomendero, or "trustee," as he was called, in farm products, textiles, and other local goods, twice a year. Adult men were also required to lend their labor to the encomendero from time to time, helping him clear farmland, round up livestock, and construct buildings. For his part, the encomendero was to protect his tributaries from outside attack and ensure their conversion to Christianity. However reciprocal in theory, the encomienda system was in fact used mostly to round up workers for the gold mines. It looked like slavery to the few Spanish critics who denounced it, and even more so to the many thousands of native peoples who suffered under it.

**Bartolomé de Las Casas's
Defense of Native
American Rights**

"And on the Day of Judgment it shall all be more clear," thundered Bartolomé de Las Casas in a sermon-like tract, "when God has His vengeance for such heinous and abominable insults as are done in the Indies by those who bear the name of Christians."[4] Las Casas was a Hispaniola encomendero's son turned Dominican priest who emerged as the leading defender of native American rights in early modern times. Some historians have argued that he represented another, more humanitarian side of the Spanish character in the otherwise violently acquisitive era of Columbus and his successors. Through constant pleading at court, and in widely publicized university debates and publications, Las Casas helped to suppress the indigenous slave trade and sharply restrict the encomienda system by the early 1540s. For the Tainos who first met Columbus, the reforms came too late. By 1510 there were only a few hundred encomienda subjects where a decade before there had been hundreds of thousands. By almost any measure, the Columbian era in the Caribbean was a disaster.

Columbus's Successors

Columbus's accomplishments as a navigator spawned dozens of like-minded expeditions (see again Map 17.2). These included the four voyages of Amerigo Vespucci (1497–1504), a Florentine merchant for whom the continents of the Western Hemisphere would later be named. Vespucci gained most fame as an early publicist of the new lands and peoples that southern Europeans were rapidly encountering throughout the American tropics. Vespucci came to realize that the Americas were not part of Asia. This did not, however, prevent him from embracing other European preconceptions. In relating his voyages to Brazil to Medici rulers in Florence, Vespucci calmly described the roasting and eating of human flesh among the local inhabitants. His reports only added to the European fixation on native American cannibalism.

Early Global Reconnaissance

Other voyages of reconnaissance included those of Juan de Solís and Ferdinand Magellan. Both were seasoned Portuguese explorers sailing in the service of Spain, and both, like Columbus, sought a westward route to Asia. Solís sailed up the Río de la Plata estuary near modern Buenos Aires in 1516, but was captured and killed in a skirmish with local inhabitants. Magellan learned details of the Argentine coast and its currents and winds from survivors of the Solís expedition, then organized a much more ambitious voyage to the Moluccas, or Maluku, in what is today Indonesia. The epic journey that followed, arguably one of the boldest ever undertaken, was recorded by yet another Italian, the Venetian Antonio de Pigafetta.

encomienda A feudal-style grant of a native American village to a conquistador or other Spaniard.

Columbian Exchange Historian Alfred Crosby's term for the movement of American plants, animals, and germs to the rest of the world and vice versa.

Of the five ships that left Spain in 1519, two were wrecked before Magellan reached the treacherous straits at the southern tip of South America that still bear his name. When food ran short, crewmembers shot, salted, and ate penguins and sea lions. Encounters with the native inhabitants of Tierra del Fuego and the neighboring mainland were mostly brief and hostile, reminiscent of Columbus's early encounters. Always the good publicist,

Pigafetta described exchanges and conflicts with primitive giants, giving rise to the legend of Patagonia, or "the land of Big Foot."

Once in the Pacific, Magellan set a northwesterly course that eventually led to Guam, in the Mariana Islands east of the Philippines. The four-month ocean crossing had left much of the crew suffering from malnutrition, and many others died from the effects of scurvy, a debilitating disease caused by lack of vitamin C. Magellan then sailed to the Philippine island of Sebu, where he became embroiled in a dispute between local chieftains. Alarmed to find Muslim merchants active in the region, Magellan sought to create an alliance with new converts to Christianity through a show of force. Instead, he and forty crew-members were killed. Only one vessel managed to escape and return to Spain in 1522 by following the new Portuguese sailing route through the Indian and Atlantic oceans. For the first time in recorded history, the world had been circumnavigated (see again Map 17.2).

Meanwhile, in the Caribbean, Spanish colonists became rapidly disillusioned with the fabled "West Indies" of Columbus. Unhappiest of all were newly arrived immigrants from the Iberian peninsula, desperate young men with dreams of gold and a more promising future in a new world. Such men, and most immigrants were men in the early years, fanned out across the Caribbean in search of new sources of wealth, both human and metallic. Most failed, and many died, but some eventually found what they sought: fabled continental empires rich beyond belief.

The Columbian Exchange

In a landmark 1972 book, historian Alfred Crosby argued that the most significant consequences of 1492 were not political or even commercial, but biological.[5] What Crosby called the **Columbian Exchange** referred to the massive interoceanic transfer of animals (including humans), plants, and diseases that followed in Columbus's wake. Many of these transfers, such as the introduction of rats and smallpox to the Americas, were unintentional. Yet all had profound consequences.

Maize

Perhaps the most globally transformative native American crop (vying with the potato), maize was first domesticated in highland Mexico some 7000 years ago. This 1542 German depiction is the most accurate to survive from the first decades after maize was introduced to Europe. Similar varieties soon transformed global dietary patterns, particularly in sub-Saharan Africa. Some cultures adopted maize only as livestock feed. (*De Historia Stirpium*, 1542, Leonhard Fuchs, Typ 565.42.409(B), Houghton Library, Harvard University.)

Since European explorers circled the globe shortly after Columbus's time, this process of biological exchange was almost from the start a worldwide phenomenon. Indigenous cuisines, farming practices, and transportation modes were changed, sometimes for the better. Northern European populations, for example, grew rapidly following the introduction of Andean potatoes, which thrived in cool, wet climates. South and Southeast Asian cuisines were forever changed after the introduction of American capsicum peppers and peanuts, which flourished in the Old World tropics.

But European cattle, sheep, pigs, goats, horses, and other large domestic mammals also rapidly altered landscapes, sometimes with catastrophic consequences. In the worst case, the highlands of central Mexico were quickly denuded and reduced to deserts following the introduction of sheep in the sixteenth century. Lacking predators, and having access to vast new pastures, their populations exploded. Similar processes of environmental transformation were later repeated in Australia, New Zealand, Argentina, and the western United States.

Biological and Environmental Transformations

**Epidemic Diseases
and Population Loss**

As in the case of ship borne rats, many unwanted exchanges took place in the first phases of global interaction. Worst among these were diseases, mostly caused by viruses, bacteria, and blood parasites, introduced to previously unexposed hosts. Since Africa and Eurasia had long been linked by waves of trade, warfare, migration, and pilgrimage, the repeated spread of diseases such as smallpox, measles, and mumps had allowed people over time to develop immunity against these and other pathogens. As seen in Chapter 15, pandemics of plague could be devastating in Africa and Eurasia, but never to the extent that they would be in long-isolated regions overseas. The peoples of the Americas, Australia, and Polynesia proved tragically vulnerable in this regard; they suffered what was probably the worst demographic collapse in history.

In the early modern Americas poor hygiene and medical care, chronic warfare, forced labor, and malnutrition all accompanied European conquest, rendering new disease agents more destructive. Documentary evidence suggests that throughout the Americas and Pacific Islands, indigenous populations declined by almost 90 percent within a century. Recovery and acquired immunity came slowly. With the introduction of malaria, yellow fever, and other mosquito-borne blood parasites—as deadly for Europeans as anyone else—America's lowland tropics did not recover their precontact populations until the introduction of insect-killing pesticides following World War II. On the plus side, world food exchanges spurred rapid population growth in Europe, Africa, and Asia, and contributed to the rebound of the Americas. Overall, the spread of American food crops boosted world population significantly before the end of early modern times. The peoples of the Americas, however, paid a steep price for these new and more productive connections between the world's societies.

Spanish Conquests in the Americas   1519–1600

FOCUS

What factors enabled the Spanish to conquer the Aztec and Inca empires?

Two men disappointed by their prospects in the Caribbean islands were Hernando Cortés and Francisco Pizarro. Cortés gained fame by the 1520s as conqueror of the Aztecs, and Pizarro after 1532 as conqueror of the Incas. Their extraordinary actions on the American mainland gave rise to the almost mythical Spanish-American livelihood of **conquistador**, or conqueror. Like Columbus, neither man acted alone, but both altered the course of global history. Also like Columbus, these two famous conquistadors, though made hugely rich by their exploits, both ended their lives unappreciated and disgraced. The sword of conquest was double-edged.

The Fall of Aztec Mexico

As we saw in Chapter 16, the people known as Aztecs called themselves Mexica (meh-SHEE-cah). By the time Spaniards arrived on Central America's Atlantic shores in the late 1510s, the Mexica ruled much of Mesoamerica, often by terror. The empire centered on the fertile highlands surrounding modern Mexico City, but extended south to the Pacific coast and east into Guatemala. Cortés would soon discover, however, that the Aztec Empire was vulnerable.

The Road to Tenochtitlán

A brash and ambitious leader, Hernando Cortés left his base in southern Cuba after a dispute with his sponsor, the governor. In Yucatan, as we have seen, he found an extraordinarily valuable translator in the person of Malintzin. By September of 1519 Cortés set out for the interior from the new town of Veracruz on Mexico's Gulf coast. With him were Malintzin and several hundred horses and well-armed men. The Spanish also brought with them fierce mastiffs, huge dogs bred for war. After a series of attacks on both Aztec allies and enemies, the Spanish and several thousand new allies entered Tenochtitlán in November 1519 as guests of the emperor, Moteuczoma, or "Moctezuma," II.

conquistador Spanish for "conqueror," a new livelihood in the Americas after Columbus.

Shortly after being welcomed and treated to a feast by the curious and gracious Moctezuma, Cortés and his followers managed to capture and imprison the unsuspecting emperor. Fearful for their ruler's life, the Aztec people, now leaderless, faced great uncertainty. Not afraid to use terror in his own way, Cortés ordered that anyone who opposed the Spanish and their allies would be publicly cut to pieces and fed to the dogs. Treachery, terror, and seizure of indigenous leaders were in fact stock tactics developed by Spanish conquistadors in the course of their decades of Caribbean slave raiding. These tactics proved even more effective against mainland imperial peoples who depended on divine kings. Attached to their subsistence plots, settled farmers had nowhere to run.

There followed almost eight months of looting and destruction, accompanied by a mix of open battles and informal skirmishes. Some former Aztec subjects supported the Spanish, most significantly the Tlaxcalans, but others resisted violently. Soon unfamiliar diseases such as smallpox and influenza swept through Tenochtitlán and the entire Valley of Mexico, decimating a vast and densely populated region already facing food shortages. Ironically, the people who would give the world maize, tomatoes, chocolate, vanilla, and a thousand other life-sustaining and pleasurable foods were now receiving only the most deadly ingredients of the Columbian Exchange: viruses and bacteria. Cortés ordered that images of the Virgin Mary be placed atop Aztec temples to assert the power of the invaders' Christian deities.

Cortés's Invasion of the Aztec Empire, 1519–1521

While Cortés went to negotiate with soldiers sent by Cuba's governor to arrest him in early 1520, the Spaniards left behind in Tenochtitlán provoked a siege by massacring Aztec nobles. Rushing to the city with Cuban recruits whom he had just won over, Cortés reached his comrades only to be trapped by the Aztec warriors. The desperate Spaniards brought out the captive emperor, Moctezuma, in hopes of calming tempers, but he was killed in a hail of stones. The besieged Spanish tried to flee Tenochtitlán, but there was no sneaking out of a city linked to the mainland by only three narrow causeways. Cortés and a handful of conquistadors escaped at the head of the pack, but many other Spaniards, about half the total number, fell into Aztec hands. One Spanish soldier recalled: "As we marched along we were followed by the Mexicans who hurled arrows and darts at us and stones from their slings, and the way in which they surrounded us and continually attacked us was terrifying."[6] According to Aztec accounts, when the city's male warriors fell dead or exhausted, women warriors took over, attacking the foreign enemy with equal vigor (see Reading the Past: Tlatelolcan Elders Recall the Conquest of Mexico). Despite the ravages of disease and the loss of their emperor, the Aztecs were still capable of dishing out terror in kind.

Cortés and his bedraggled Spanish forces eventually regrouped with aid from the Tlaxcalans, their staunchest allies, but it was over a year before Tenochtitlán and its twin city of Tlatelolco fell. Cut off from the mainland, the Aztecs faced starvation, then attack by land and water. Cortés ordered thirteen small, European-style sailing vessels built on the shores of Lake Texcoco, and armed with cannon these helped pound remaining Aztec warrior contingents in canoes. By August 1521 Cortés and his men and allies had forced the Aztecs to retreat to Tlatelolco. Soon, both cities were occupied and pillaged. Yet the Aztec capital proved hard to hold. Angry at the lack of valuable plunder, the Spanish responded to persistent urban rebels by razing virtually all residential buildings.

Soon after, a successor emperor to Moctezuma was captured and killed, after having been tortured for allegedly hiding booty. Dissatisfied conquistadors then fanned out across Mesoamerica in search of riches and empires. The self-promoting Cortés traveled to Spain in hopes of consolidating his gains, but found little support from the emperor Charles V. The material and political conquest of the Aztec center had not

Spanish Setbacks

Final Victory

Tlatelolcan Elders Recall the Conquest of Mexico

In what would become New Spain, or colonial Mexico, Spanish missionaries quickly introduced European-style writing systems. Indigenous scribes picked them up within a few decades of the conquest, rendering Nahuatl, Maya, and other local languages in a Latinate script with Spanish phonetics. Formal documents, including histories and sermons, were produced in this manner, but also interviews, myths, genealogies, criminal testimonies, and a host of everyday transactions. The following excerpt is a direct English translation of a Nahuatl document from about 1540 relating the conquest of both Tenochtitlán and its "twin city," Tlatelolco. The Tlatelolcan elders relating the story to junior scribes apparently witnessed and participated in the events in question.

And when they reached Yacocolco here, Spaniards were captured on the Tlilhuacan [tleel-WALK-on] road, as well as all the people from the various altepetl [allied city-states]. Two thousand died there, and the Tlatelolcans were exclusively responsible for it. At this time we Tlatelolcans set up skull racks; skull racks were in three places. One was in the temple courtyard at Tlillan, where the heads of our [present] lords [the Spaniards] were strung; the second was in Yacocolco,

where the heads of our lords [the Spaniards] were strung, along with the heads of two horses; the third place was in Çacatla, facing the Cihuateocalli (see-wah-tayoh-CAH-yee) [Woman-Temple]. It was the exclusive accomplishment of the Tlatelolcans. After this they drove us from there and reached the marketplace. That was when the great Tlatelolcan warriors were entirely vanquished. With that the fighting stopped once and for all. That was when the Tlatelolcan women all let loose, fighting, striking people, taking captives. They put on warriors' devices, all raising their skirts so that they could give pursuit.

Source: James Lockhart, ed. and trans. *We People Here: Nahuatl Accounts of the Conquest of Mexico* (Berkeley: University of California Press, 1993), 265–267.

EXAMINING THE EVIDENCE

1. What does this document tell us about Aztec political identity during the conquest?

2. What does it tell us about military culture and gender roles?

been easy, and at the fringes conquest was far from over. Far more difficult would be the winning of the hearts and minds of millions of former Aztec subjects now anxious to assert their own agendas. This would be the long story of colonial Mexico, a "New Spain" so unlike its Iberian namesake.

The Fall of Inca Peru

When Francisco Pizarro left the small Spanish settlement of Panama City in 1522 in search of "Pirú," a mythical chieftain, he had no idea that events high in the Andes Mountains to the south would conspire to favor his dream of repeating the success of Cortés. But as with Cortés and his many companions and aides, an empire—even with guns, germs, and steel on one's side—could not be toppled overnight.

In fact it took a decade of coastal reconnaissance and humiliating failure before Pizarro at last marched into what is today the Republic of Peru. In the meantime he had acquired Quechua translators immersed for several years in Castilian Spanish; a small army of men with horses, armor, and state-of-the-art weapons; and a license from Charles V. By late 1532, when Pizarro's forces began their inland march across a coastal desert reminiscent of southern Spain, Peru at last seemed ripe for the taking.

Tawantinsuyu (tuah-wahn-tin-SUE-you), as the Incas called their empire, was in deep crisis in 1532. A five-year battle over succession had recently ended with Atawallpa (also Atahualpa) emerging the winner. According to several eyewitness accounts, when

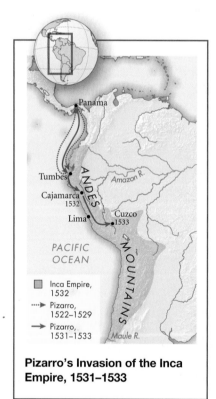

Pizarro's Invasion of the Inca Empire, 1531–1533

Pizarro Meets Atawallpa

Throughout colonial times native and European artists depicted the day in 1532 when Inca emperor Atawallpa met Francisco Pizarro. This is the first known image of the Peruvian encounter, a woodcut accompanying an eyewitness account published in Seville, Spain, in 1534. It depicts Atawallpa on a litter holding up what is probably the prayer book given him by the priest Vicente de Valverde, also pictured. Pizarro stands back with his fellow Spaniards, armed but not poised to attack. In the distance is a European-style castle presumably meant to stand for an Inca city. Notably absent is the native Andean interpreter whom we know only by his Christian name, "Little Philip." (Courtesy of the John Carter Brown Library at Brown University.)

Pizarro and his 168 men climbed into the Andes to meet Atawallpa in the sacred city of Cajamarca, the new Sapa Inca was flush with victory. Atawallpa did not feel vulnerable, and in fact intended, rather like Moctezuma in Mexico, to draft the strangely bearded and well-armed foreigners into his service. Though their horses, firearms, and steel swords were cause for wonder, the Inca did not mistake the Spanish for gods.

According to survivor testimonies, in November 1532 Pizarro and his men captured Atawallpa in a surprise attack reminiscent of Cortés's seizure of Moctezuma. Humiliated, Atawallpa was held hostage for nearly a year as his subjects scrambled to gather up gold and silver to free him. The Incas possessed far more gold and silver than the Aztecs, and the hoard of metals offered to free their leader, whom most Andeans regarded as a divine being, was staggering. Suddenly Pizarro and his followers were rich beyond their wildest dreams.

Thus "Peru" became instantly synonymous with great wealth among Europeans, an association that would soon be reinforced by the discovery of immensely rich silver mines. Despite the ransom, however, Atawallpa was killed on Pizarro's orders in 1533. The treachery was complete, and by 1534 Tawantinsuyu was in Spanish hands.

The Conquest: Myths and Realities

How did a small number of Spanish men manage to topple two of the world's most populous and extensive empires in a relatively short time? Some biologists and anthropologists have claimed that these great, isolated indigenous empires faced inevitable defeat because they lacked iron, sufficient protein, draft animals, wheeled vehicles, writing, acquired immunity to numerous pathogens, and other advantages. Historians have long puzzled over this riddle, too, but more with an eye on human actors and the timing of events.

For their part, the conquistadors and their Spanish contemporaries regarded these victories as the will of their Christian God. Spain's enemies—and internal critics such as Las Casas—emphasized the conquistadors' "sins" of treachery, cruelty, lust, and greed. By the nineteenth century, historians less interested in judging the Spanish focused on the leadership abilities of individuals. They emphasized the intelligence and tenacity of Cortés and Pizarro, and the apparent weakness and indecisiveness of their adversaries, Moctezuma and Atawallpa. This emphasis on "great men" was aided by the conquistadors' own insistence that they were mistaken for gods everywhere they went.

Malintzin and the Meeting Between Moctezuma and Cortés

This image, taken from the early postconquest document known as the *Florentine Codex*, was drawn and colored by an indigenous Mexican artist who had been exposed to European prints and paintings while being schooled by Spanish friars. In it, Malintzin translates the words between Aztec emperor Moctezuma and Hernando Cortés at their momentous first meeting.

Malintzin Interprets for Cortés and Moctezuma
(The Granger Collection, New York.)

EXAMINING THE EVIDENCE

1. How does this drawing reflect the indigenous artist's instruction by Spanish friars?

2. To what extent is it a reflection of Malintzin's perceived importance in the conquest of Mexico?

Factors of Conquest

Recently, historians have focused on other causal factors. These include the importance of indigenous allies and interpreters; the conquistadors' accumulated experience as "Indian fighters" in the Caribbean; internal imperial politics and the timing of Spanish arrival; indigenous adaptation to Spanish fighting methods; contrasting goals of warfare; and of course, the introduction of novel weapons, animals, and diseases. Most historians agree that the conquests resulted from the convergence of these many variables—a number of them, such as the appearance of Malintzin the able translator, completely unpredictable (see Seeing the Past: Malintzin and the Meeting Between Moctezuma and Cortés).

A final point worth emphasizing is that indigenous peoples were not overawed by Spanish horses and technology, nor did they view the newcomers as gods. As this quote from a Spanish soldier who participated in the conquest of Mexico suggests, Aztec warriors adapted rapidly to the threat of cannon and armored opponents on horseback:

> One day an Indian I saw in combat with a mounted horseman struck the horse in the chest, cutting through to the inside and killing the horse on the spot. On the same day I saw another Indian give a horse a sword thrust in the neck that laid the horse dead at his feet. . . . Among them are extraordinary brave men who face death with absolute determination.[7]

The evidence from Inca Peru barely differs. After the capture of Atawallpa in 1532, Andean warriors quickly learned to avoid open field engagements where they might be run down by mounted Spaniards, preferring instead to ambush their enemies as they crossed rivers and traveled through narrow canyons. Simple stones and slingshots proved a surprising match for guns and steel-edged weapons in these conditions. Rebellions and raids continued for decades in the Mexican and Peruvian backcountry, but the rapid Spanish conquest of the Aztec and Inca imperial cores was sealed by those empires' own former subjects; although they did not know what was in store for them, most were anxious for something different.

A New Empire in the Americas: New Spain and Peru 1535–1600

Within a few generations of conquest, Spanish settlers penetrated deep into the Americas, transforming the world's largest overseas land empire into the world's greatest source of precious metals. Spain's monarchs in turn used this mineral bounty to pursue their religious and territorial ambitions in Europe and beyond. Merchants used it to link the world economy in unprecedented ways. But for the millions of native Americans subjected to Spanish rule, life would revolve around negotiating a measure of freedom within an imperial system at least as taxing as those of the Aztecs and Incas.

FOCUS

Why was the discovery of silver in Spanish America so important in the course of world history?

American Silver and the Global Economy

In 1545 an indigenous prospector came across silver outcrops on a high, red mountain in what is today south-central Bolivia. The Cerro Rico, or "Rich Hill," of Potosí (poh-toe-SEE), as it was soon known, turned out to be the most concentrated silver deposit ever discovered (see Map 17.3). Indeed, no other silver strike approached the extraordinary wealth of Potosí until modern times. This and related silver discoveries in early Spanish America radically transformed not only life in the colonies, but the global economy. As we will see in subsequent chapters, in regions as distant as China and South Asia, American silver affected people's livelihoods in profound and unexpected ways. Even before Potosí, silver mines had been discovered in highland Mexico in around 1530, and many new finds followed. Mexican districts such as Zacatecas (zah-cah-TAY-cus) and Guanajuato (hwan-uh-WAH-toe) were expanding rapidly by the 1550s and would continue to drive Mexico's economy well into the modern period.

Refining Innovations

Although the Spanish quickly adopted efficient Old World techniques of tunneling and refining, the silver boom also spurred important technical innovations. Chief among these was the use of mercury to separate silver from crushed ore. Amalgamation, as this process is known, was practiced in antiquity, but it was Bartolomé de Medina, a merchant working in the Mexican mines of Pachuca in the mid-1550s, who developed and patented a low-energy, large-scale refining process suitable for New World environments. Medina's invention revolutionized Spanish-American silver mining even as it spread one of the world's most persistent toxins, mercury.

Amalgamation was implemented in Potosí on a large scale after 1572 as part of a crown initiative to stimulate production. Although Spain itself produced substantial mercury, New World sources had been avidly sought since Potosí's discovery. Before long, the mine owners' dreams came true; in the Peruvian highlands southeast of Lima, the mercury mines of Huancavelica (wan-kah-bell-EE-cah) were discovered in 1564. Thus the Spanish paired Andean mercury with Andean silver, touching off an enormous boom in production. Potosí yielded tens of millions of ounces of silver annually by the 1580s. It was enough to pave the main streets of the town with silver bricks during religious processions.

Environmental Hazards

Even with abundant mercury, silver production remained costly. Unlike gold panning, underground mining required massive capital inputs, especially in labor and technology. Water-powered silver-processing mills, first developed in Germany, were among the most complex machines in use in early modern times. Mercury remained expensive despite a crown monopoly meant to assure availability. Less often calculated, although well known even in the sixteenth century, were the environmental and health costs of mercury pollution. Soils, rivers, and refinery workers' clothing were saturated with mercury, leading to a range of neurological disorders and birth defects. "Trembling like someone with mercury poisoning" became a common colonial metaphor for fright, akin to "shaking like a leaf."

More costly than mercury and machines combined was labor. Mining was hard and deadly work, attracting few volunteers. African and African-descended slaves supplemented

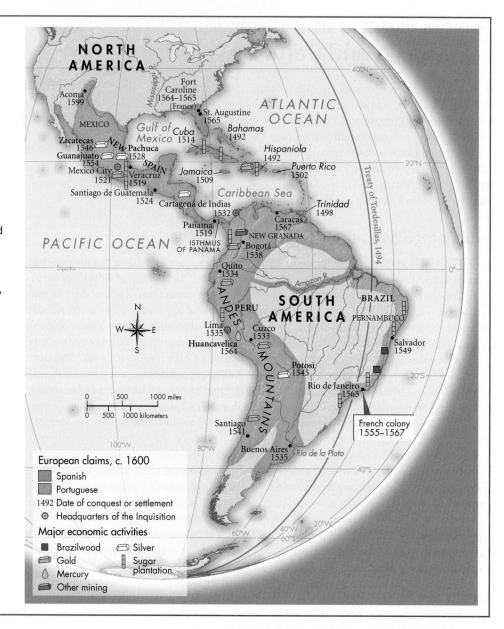

MAP 17.3

European Claims in the Americas, c. 1600

Beginning in the 1510s, the Spanish used bases in Cuba and on the Isthmus of Panama to launch the conquests of the Aztec and Inca empires. In search of similar empires, Spanish explorers drove deep into the interiors of North and South America; by the 1540s they had penetrated the U.S. Southwest and South America's Río de la Plata basin, and made their way down the Amazon. Other conquests in Central America, northwest Mexico, and New Granada led to the creation of a vast Spanish-American Empire, under the twin capitals of Mexico City and Lima. Portuguese Brazil, by contrast, consisted only of a few small settlements along the Atlantic coast, but by 1600 it was the world leader in sugar production, increasingly dependent on the labor of enslaved Africans.

European claims, c. 1600

■ Spanish
■ Portuguese
1492 Date of conquest or settlement
⊕ Headquarters of the Inquisition

Major economic activities

■ Brazilwood   ◻ Silver
◻ Gold   ▮ Sugar plantation
◊ Mercury
◻ Other mining

The Mine Draft

the workforce from an early date in boomtowns such as Zacatecas and Potosí, but Spanish-American silver mines came to rely mostly on native American draft and wageworkers. The draft, or ***mita*** (MEE-tah) as it was called in the Andes, entailed a year of service in Potosí, Huancavelica, or some other mining center, followed by six years of work in one's own home region, usually in subsistence farming or herding. In Mexico the Spanish implemented a similar system called ***repartimiento*** (reh-par-tee-MYEN-toe).

Drafted indigenous laborers received a small wage and rations during their work stints, but given the danger of these jobs and the high cost of living in mining towns, the mita and repartimiento proved hugely disruptive of indigenous lifeways. Many considered draft work a death sentence. The miners of Huancavelica, in particular, faced lifelong degenerative illnesses caused by mercury poisoning. Others were killed by cave-ins and falls. Furthermore, indigenous women and children forced to occupy Spanish-American mining towns suffered from contaminated food, air, and water supplies. Exposure to heavy metals, a hazard usually associated with modern industrialization, was probably worst for native American draftees and African slaves engaged in refining tasks. Here in

mita A Spanish revival of the Inca draft labor system.

repartimiento An allotment of indigenous laborers in colonial Mexico, similar to the Andean mita.

The Rich Mountain of Potosí

This c. 1603 image of Potosí's famous Cerro Rico shows not only the legendary red mountain with its silver veins but also workers, most of them native Andeans, refining silver by mercury amalgamation, and antlike llamas carrying ore down the mountain. The ore-crushing mill in the foreground is powered by a stream of water supplied by canals coming down from artificial reservoirs built high in a neighboring mountain range. (The Hispanic Society of America Museum and Library, New York.)

the mills mercury was routinely vaporized, and large quantities of lead, arsenic, and other heavy metals were smelted along with silver. Such was the human cost of making money.

Potosí boomed in the first years of the mita, reaching peak production in 1592, but heightened demand for mine laborers in this remote and unhealthy site only worsened an already dramatic indigenous demographic collapse. Most eligible workers who remained in the region quickly learned to avoid the most dangerous tasks, and many sold whatever they could to pay a cash fee for exemption. Mine owners were increasingly forced to pay wages to stay in business.

American Silver and Everyday Life

The silver bonanza of the sixteenth century altered livelihoods worldwide. In the Spanish colonies, everything from ranch work to church building was connected in one way or another to the flow of silver. The armies of dependent miners living in towns such as Potosí and Zacatecas spurred merchants and landowners to expand their inventories, crops, and livestock herds. Mule-drivers, weavers, tanners, and countless other specialists came to rely on the continued productivity of the mines for their sustenance. In town centers, indigenous and mixed-heritage market women took advantage of crown-mandated tax exemptions to carve out a lucrative space as well. But along with this new orientation of the colonial economy toward silver production came an intensification of conversion efforts on the part of Spanish missionaries. Worldwide, Spanish-American silver funded a massive expansion of the Catholic Church.

Whereas most indigenous peoples adapted quickly to Spanish legal and civic traditions and even tolerated the oppressive obligations of mine work, most resisted total conversion to Catholicism. Confident in the universality of their religion, European missionaries expected indigenous populations to accept Christianity as the one true faith. When they did not, the process of cultural exchange shifted from conversion to coercion. After a brief period of optimism, in which a small number of newly arrived European priests met and mingled with tens of thousands of indigenous subjects, violence erupted. Within a few decades of military conquest, the Catholic Church was commonly using prosecution, public humiliation, and even torture and execution throughout Spanish America.

Challenges of Religious Conversion

Native Americans were not the only victims of religious intolerance. Offices of the **Inquisition**, a branch of the Catholic Church dedicated to enforcing orthodox beliefs and practices, were established in Mexico City and Lima in 1570 and Cartagena in 1610. Their purpose was to punish alleged deviants and heretics among the Spanish settlers, including a number of secretly practicing Jews and a few Muslims. In the indigenous majority (soon exempted from prosecution by the Inquisition due to their newness to the faith), complete conversion was limited by long-held, core religious beliefs. Most native American converts rejected monotheism, belief in a single, supreme god. Instead, they adopted the Christian God, his holy intermediaries, and saints on their own terms, as new additions to an already crowded pantheon. There were other misunderstandings. Thousands of native converts were baptized, only to return the next day to request that this new and pleasant ceremony be performed again. Catholic missionary priests became pessimistic and often angry with their seemingly stubborn parishioners. Conversion, unlike military conquest, was a slow process that depended on more than missionary zeal. It also required missionaries to achieve a better understanding of would-be converts.

It was only after some priests learned to speak indigenous languages fluently that Europeans began to fathom, and in some cases transform, native cosmologies. One way around the obstacle of conflicting core beliefs was to ignore elders and focus conversion efforts on native youths, particularly boys. Upon maturity, they would presumably serve as exemplary believers, leaders in the new faith. Many such boys were removed from their parents' custody, taught to read and write, and ordered to collect and collate essential myths and sagas. These stories were then rewritten by European priests to match Christian history and beliefs.

Yet even as the missionaries succeeded with some native men, they failed miserably with women. Indigenous women, despite repeated sexual assaults by conquistadors, merchants, overseers, and even priests, carried on with their lives, teaching their children the old ways and also pressing for social recognition and advancement within the new social order. Some, like Malintzin, refashioned themselves as something in between Spanish and indigenous, often bearing **mestizo** (meh-STEE-soh) or mixed-heritage children. But the extraordinary persistence of indigenous American languages, religious practices, food ways, and dress through modern times is due mostly to humble indigenous women, unsung keepers of the hearth. Despite the determination of Spanish priests and conquistadors to remake the Americas to serve European interests and ambitions, indigenous culture would continue to play a powerful role in colonial society.

Brazil by Accident: The Portuguese in the Americas 1500–1600

FOCUS

How and why did early Portuguese Brazil develop differently from Spanish America?

Despite some notable similarities with their Spanish neighbors north and south, the Portuguese followed a distinct path in colonizing Brazil. The general trend in the century after contact in 1500 was from benign neglect and small-scale trade with indigenous coast-dwellers toward a more formal royal presence and settled plantation agriculture, mostly concentrated along the northeast coast. By 1600, Brazil was the world's largest sugar producer. It also became the prime destination for sub-Saharan African slaves. A key stimulus for this tectonic shift in colonial policy and economy was French encroachment between 1503 and 1567. The arrival of French traders and religious refugees in Brazil forced the Portuguese to briefly take their eyes off India.

Native Encounters and Foreign Competitors

Inquisition A branch of the Catholic Church established to enforce orthodoxy.

mestizo A person of mixed European and native American ancestry.

It was on the way to India in early 1500 that the Portuguese captain Pedro Alvares Cabral and his large fleet were blown westward from Cape Verde, in West Africa. Toward the end of April the fleet unexpectedly sighted land, which the captain dubbed the "Island of the True Cross." The landmass was later found not to be an island, but rather a mountainous stretch of the continent of South America. Columbus and the Spanish were at this time only

First Encounter in Brazil: Cabral's Report to King Manoel of Portugal

On May 1, 1500, Pedro Alvares Cabral's scribe, Pero Vaz de Caminha, recorded the first known meeting between Europeans and Tupi-speaking tribespeople in a letter to the king. Unlike the Tainos who met Columbus, the indigenous peoples who met Cabral and his crew had no gold—perhaps luckily. Unimpressed, the foreigners dispatched a small vessel home to Lisbon to report on their "discovery," and the great fleet sailed on to India.

In appearance they are dark, somewhat reddish, with good faces and good noses, well shaped. They go naked, without any covering; neither do they pay more attention to concealing or exposing their shame than they do to showing their faces, and in this respect they are very innocent. Both [captives taken from a canoe to see Cabral] had their lower lips bored and in them were placed pieces of white bone, the length of a handbreadth, and the thickness of a cotton spindle and as sharp as an awl [pointed tool] at the end. . . . Their hair is smooth, and they were shorn, with the hair cut higher than above a comb of good size, and shaved to above the ears. And one of them was wearing below the opening, from temple to temple towards the back, a sort of wig of yellow birds' feathers . . . very thick and very tight, and it covered the back of the head and the ears. This was glued to his hair, feather by feather, with a material as soft as wax, but it was not wax. Thus the headdress was very round and very close and very equal, so that it was not necessary to remove it when they washed. . . .

One of them saw . . . some white rosary beads; he made a motion that they should give them to him, and he played much with them, and put them around his neck; and then he took them off and wrapped them around his arm. He made a sign towards the land and then to the beads and to the collar of the captain, as if to say that they would give gold for that. We interpreted this so, because we wished to, but if he meant that he would take the beads and also the collar, we did not wish to understand because we did not intend to give it to him. And afterwards he returned the beads to the one who gave them to him. . . .

There were also among them four or five young women just as naked, who were not displeasing to the eye, among whom was one with her thigh from the knee to the hip and buttock all painted with black paint and all the rest in her own color; another had both knees and calves and ankles so painted, and her privy parts so nude and exposed with such innocence that there was not there any shame.

Source: William Brooks Greenlee, trans., *The Voyage of Pedro Alvares Cabral to Brazil and India* (Nendeln/Lichtenstein: Kraus Reprint Limited, 1967, reproduced by permission of the Hakluyt Society, 1938), 10–21.

EXAMINING THE EVIDENCE

1. Why might Cabral's scribe have been so keen to describe the physical features, piercings, and personal adornments of Tupi men and women in such detail in a letter to the king of Portugal?

2. What does the passage concerning the captain's collar reveal about European and indigenous attitudes and communication?

beginning to touch upon its northern shores, and had no sense of its size. The huge portion of the continent claimed by Portugal would later be called Brazil (see again Map 17.3).

Brazil was of little interest to Portugal for some time despite the fact that it fell within the domain delineated by the 1494 Treaty of Tordesillas, signed with Spain and sanctioned by the pope (see Reading the Past: First Encounter in Brazil: Cabral's Report to King Manoel of Portugal). Without gold or some other lucrative export, there seemed to be little point in colonizing this distant land. Brazil's one obvious resource, and what earned it its name, was brazilwood, a tree with a deep-red, pithy heart. Portuguese traders, soon followed by French competitors, set up posts all along Brazil's vast coast to barter with indigenous Tupi speakers for precut, red-hearted logs.

Cut and carried to shore by indigenous men, brazilwood was then shipped to Europe, where dye was extracted and sold at profit. Native Brazilians willingly participated in this trade because it brought them tangible benefits: metal hatchets, knives, sewing needles, and other utilitarian items, along with beads, mirrors, bells, and other personal and ritual adornments. For some, it also brought military alliances against traditional enemies. In several places Portuguese *degredados*, or criminal castaways, survived their tropical exile and married into eminent indigenous families, becoming translators and commercial middlemen.

Early Dyewood Trade

This use of criminal exiles to spearhead colonization was quite different from Spanish practices in the Americas.

Portuguese Response to French Competition

French competition for control of Brazil and its dyewood pressed the Portuguese to assert their claims more forcefully. A fleet of warships was sent from Lisbon in 1532 to protect Portuguese traders and to punish French interlopers. Land claims were to be organized differently, too. After 1534 Brazil was carved into fifteen proprietary colonies, granted by King Manoel to courtiers ranging from noble warriors to scholars. Brazil's proprietary governors were told to encourage permanent settlement by farmers and artisans from their home districts. This was similar to Spanish plans in the early Caribbean, but the models the king had in mind were Madeira and the Azores, Portugal's earlier experiments with overseas settlement colonies. Brazil's new proprietors were also expected to organize the defense of their holdings against French and indigenous enemies. The closest the Spanish ever came to such private colonization schemes was Charles V's grant of parts of Venezuela to German banking families in the 1530s and 1540s, all of which failed.

With few exceptions, the Brazilian proprietary colonies also failed; the French were still a menace, and native Brazilians, not Portuguese colonists, had the run of the land. In 1549 the Crown tried another strategy: Salvador, a defensible hamlet located at the tip of the wide Bay of All Saints in northeastern Brazil, was made the royal capital and seat of a governor general. Jesuit missionaries, only a half dozen of them at first, also arrived. They soon fanned out across Brazil to convert tens of thousands of native, Tupi-speaking allies to Roman Catholicism. From here forward, enemies of the Crown or faith, indigenous and otherwise, would be given no quarter.

French Retreat from Brazil

The French did not easily give up on their Brazilian enterprise, and in fact redoubled their efforts at midcentury. In 1555 they established a new colony in Guanabara Bay, near modern Rio de Janeiro (see again Map 17.3). The colony's leader proved incapable of sorting out disputes between Catholics like himself and numerous Protestant refugees, or Huguenots. Divided by religion, like France itself at the time (as we will see in Chapter 20), the French colony was doomed. The Portuguese drove out Catholics and Protestants alike by 1567. As for indigenous enemies, including the allies of the French, Portuguese wars and slaving expeditions would continue throughout colonial times.

Bitter Sugar: Slavery and the Plantation Complex in the Early Atlantic World 1530–1600

A search for precious metals and gems came up short soon after the royal capital of Salvador was established in 1549, but the Portuguese found other ways beyond brazilwood to profit from a tropical colony. On Brazil's northeast coast, sugar cane was planted along the banks of several rivers as early as the 1530s. By 1570, Brazil was the world's number-one sugar producer, a position it still holds. Cane sugar was Brazil's answer to Spanish-American silver. It was an exotic cash crop with a growing market abroad. Europeans, in particular, could not get enough of it. First indigenous, then African, slaves were made to do the bulk of the burdensome work required to produce sugar (see Lives and Livelihoods: Atlantic Sugar Producers).

Dependence on Enslaved Africans

Sugar growers in the region surrounding Salvador competed vigorously with their counterparts in Pernambuco, one of the few surviving proprietary colonies to the north. Each region vied for the greater share of total output, with Pernambuco usually ahead. Native Brazilian slaves were exploited in large numbers in both regions, but well before 1600 Portuguese planters turned to Africa for still more enslaved laborers. Indigenous workers died in large numbers from disease and abuse, as happened in the early Spanish Caribbean, and were also prone to run away to the interior. As will be seen in greater detail in the next chapter, the Portuguese had the advantage of established market ties with dozens of western African chiefdoms and states from Senegambia to Angola. More even than the Spanish, they sought to replace indigenous cane cutters with enslaved Africans.

Though more resistant to Old World diseases than their native American co-workers, Africans died in alarming numbers in the early cane fields of Brazil. Many were literally worked to death. Instead of moderating workloads, improving nutrition and medical care, and encouraging family formation, Portuguese masters opted to exhaust the labor power of their slaves, the vast majority of them young men. The reason was as logical as it was cold-hearted: having direct access to more and more captives at relatively low cost in western Africa, sugar planters "used up" laborers much like mine owners did mita workers in Peru. Even when female slaves were introduced and families formed, high child mortality rates discouraged reproduction. Brazil would subsequently become so dependent on Africa for labor that by the time the slave trade ended in the nineteenth century over 40 percent of all slaves transported across the Atlantic had landed in this single destination.

COUNTERPOINT
The Mapuche of Chile: Native America's Indomitable State

The climate of southern Chile, a land of rugged coasts and dense forests, is wet and cool. Gently rolling hills are interspersed with picturesque lakes, rivers, and volcanoes. Near the coast is a temperate rain forest comparable to parts of the Pacific Northwest of the United States and Canada. Fish and

FOCUS

How did the Mapuche of Chile manage to resist European conquest?

wildlife are abundant and varied. Towering araucaria pines yield nuts rich in fat and protein, and vitamin-packed wild berries abound in the thickets. This is the homeland of the Mapuche (mah-POOH-cheh), or Araucanians (a term derived from the Bay of Arauca), one of the Americas' most resilient native cultures. Across nearly five centuries, they successfully resisted attempted conquests by the Incas, the Spanish, and the Chilean nation-state.

Today, more than five hundred years after Columbus, the Mapuche, half a million strong, are still proclaiming their independence. It was only in the 1880s that Chilean armed forces managed to partially subdue the Mapuche using modern weapons and threats of annihilation, a process similar to that used against native peoples of western North America and the Argentine *pampas*, or plains, in the same era. But what of colonial times, the era of the conquistadors? There was substantial gold in the Mapuche heartland, yet the Spanish failed to conquer them despite knowing this since the time of Pizarro. Why?

A Culture of Warfare

The historical record suggests that successful Mapuche resistance owed much to entrenched cultural patterns. As poets, ex-captives, and Mapuche commentators themselves have noted since the sixteenth century, this was a fiercely independent people raised to fight. The Mapuche reared boys for a life of warfare, apparently before as well as after Spanish arrival in the region. Girls were raised to produce and store the food surpluses needed for the war effort. Despite their access to horses, iron and steel-edged weapons, and firearms, the Spanish fared little better than the Incas against the native Chileans.

There were early successes, however. The first conquistadors in Chile, headed by Pedro de Valdivia, in fact managed to reduce a large number of Mapuche to encomienda servitude by 1550. Rich gold deposits were subsequently discovered, and Mapuche men were forced to

The Mapuche of Chile, c. 1550

Atlantic Sugar Producers

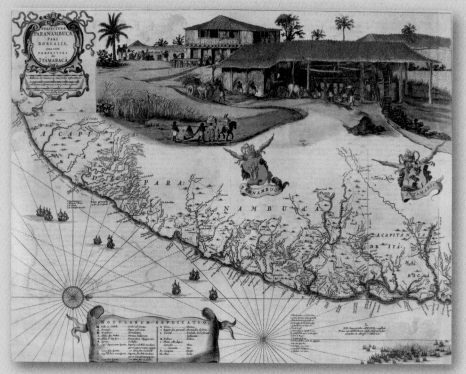

Sugar Plantations

Enslaved sugar-makers worked not only in fields but also in powerful mills and refining furnaces. Men, women, and children were all involved. This Dutch 1662 image of Pernambuco, Brazil, depicts enslaved sugar refinery and transport workers during the intense harvest period when the mills ran all night. The Dutch controlled Pernambuco and its sugar plantations from 1630 to 1654. (Courtesy of the John Carter Brown Library at Brown University.)

Found in countless foods and beverages, and now a major global source of biofuels, cane sugar was once a rare commodity. Introduced to the Mediterranean by Muslim traders and colonists in the eighth or ninth century C.E., sugar was at first a medicine and high-status condiment. Its source, sugar cane, a tall, thick grass, was eventually planted in Egypt, Sicily, Cyprus, and southern Iberia, and by at least the fourteenth century was processed not only by Muslims but also by Christian landowners in southern Spain and Portugal. Though later associated exclusively with slavery, sugar making in this era was done by a mixed free and enslaved labor force. Before long, women joined men in both cane fields and processing plants.

Sugar cane is so tough that considerable energy is required to extract maximum juice. Efficient presses were thus a technical hurdle for commercial producers. Like silver refining, sugar making required technical expertise and a complex sequence of chemical processes that allowed for few errors. In the Mediterranean basin, cane millers borrowed from long-established techniques of wine grape and olive pressing. Specialists were required to design and build ever larger and more powerful machines, which were among the most complex mechanical apparatus known at the time.

Animals such as oxen were often used for power, but waterwheels were preferred for their greater efficiency. In the

work them. Once it became clear that the Spanish were only after gold and captive laborers, the Mapuche resisted violently. To drive their point home, they captured, killed, and ate portions of Valdivia's corpse in a great public ceremony. Mapuche cannibalism was plainly intended to terrorize the enemy.

Uprisings Against the Spanish

What followed was a general uprising lasting from 1553 to 1557. Raids on Spanish settlements continued until 1598, when the Mapuche captured and ate yet another governor, Martín García de Loyola, a close relative of the founder of the Catholic Jesuit order, Ignatius Loyola (see Chapter 20). This incident was followed by a mass uprising in 1599, in

generally dry and sometimes frost-prone Mediterranean basin, access to warm, well-watered plains and consistently flowing millstreams was severely limited. Bounded by ecological and capital constraints, mill ownership remained a dream of most sugar producers. This soon proved equally true in the Atlantic islands and Brazil. For their part, mill workers, particularly the women and sometimes children who fed canes through the rollers, faced loss of limbs and sometimes death. "And in these Mills (during the season of making Sugar) they work both day and night," wrote English visitor Richard Flecknoe in 1654, "the work of immediately applying the canes to the Mill being so perilous [that] if through drowsiness or heedlessness a finger's end be but engaged between the posts, their whole body inevitably follows."[1] Rendering the precious juice into white crystal sugar was also difficult and labor intensive. Workers had to boil the juice in huge copper vats, then reduce it in a series of smaller vats into a concentrated syrup they poured into molds to crystallize. Women were usually in charge of whitening the resulting brown sugar loaves with wet clay and removing them from the molds and packing them for shipment. European consumers considered white sugar purer than brown, "purged" of imperfections. Each phase of the process required skill and close monitoring, and fires had to be stoked throughout the night. Sugar making thus produced a number of task-specific livelihoods, such as purger (purifier), mold-maker, and crating supervisor. Given its complexity, high capital investment, and careful attention to timing, sugar making has been described as an early modern precursor of industrial, or factory, production. However labeled, sugar work was monotonous and occasionally deadly.

On the consumer end of sugar making, first Muslim and then Jewish and Christian chefs made the most of the new sweetener, inventing a wide variety of candies, pastries, and preserves. Thus was born the livelihood of confectioner, or candy-maker. When American cacao took Europe by storm in the 1600s, the specialty of chocolatier emerged.

Europeans' taste for sugar grew slowly at first, but by 1600, sugar was an ordinary ingredient in many foods. Sugar's association with slavery also gradually increased. Numerous slaves labored in the early cane fields and mills of the eastern Atlantic islands of Madeira and the Canaries, but the pattern replicated in the Americas—predominantly African slaves manning large plantations—appeared first on the Portuguese island of São Tomé, off equatorial West Africa. By 1550, the so-called plantation complex was established in the Spanish Caribbean and Brazil. In the Americas, as in the Canaries, with the decimation of local cultures indigenous slavery gave way to African slavery.

---

1. E. Bradford Burns, ed., *A Documentary History of Brazil* (New York: Alfred A. Knopf, 1966), 82.

QUESTIONS TO CONSIDER

1. How did the rise of Atlantic sugar affect the global economy?
2. How did it transform livelihoods?

For Further Information:
Mintz, Sidney W. *Sweetness and Power*. New York: Viking, 1985.
Schwartz, Stuart B., ed. *Tropical Babylons: Sugar and the Making of the Atlantic World, 1450–1680*. Chapel Hill: University of North Carolina Press, 2004.

which established rebels united with Mapuches who had been subjected to Spanish rule. It was a resounding success. No Spanish town remained south of the Biobío River after 1600, and Spanish attempts to reconquer the Mapuche and occupy their lands failed throughout the colonial period.

What factors besides a culture of warfare allowed the Mapuche to succeed when so many other native American cultures fell to European invaders? As in North America's Great Plains, the inadvertent introduction of horses by the Spanish greatly enhanced Mapuche warrior mobility. Steel and iron guns, knives, and swords were also captured and quickly adopted. Further, the Mapuche "Columbian Exchange" included Old World foods and animals such as wheat, apples, chickens, and pigs, markedly increasing their subsistence base.

Mapuche Man and Woman

The Mapuche peoples of Chile proved as resistant to the Spanish as they had been to the Incas. Hostilities began in 1549, and by 1599 Mapuche warriors had destroyed all inland Spanish settlements south of the Biobío River. This image, painted by a Spanish priest who fled the Mapuche in 1600, depicts a Mapuche woman with her spinning equipment and trademark horned hairstyle. To the left is the great Mapuche leader Lautaro, who led the first uprisings. As is evident, the Mapuche adopted Spanish-style helmets and body armor, which they fashioned from the raw hides of introduced cattle. Like the Plains peoples of North America, the Mapuche also adopted the horse to great effect. (Courtesy of the University of Oviedo Library, Spain.)

Despite their new mounts and access to new weapons, Chile's native warriors did not alter their overall style of warfare. Rather than face the better-armed Spanish on the open field, as these European-trained fighters would have liked, the Mapuche preferred night attacks, long-distance raiding, captive-taking, and other tactics later termed *guerrilla*, or "little war," by the Spanish. Very long native-style bamboo lances remained the weapon of choice, not to be replaced by cumbersome and inaccurate handguns or dueling rapiers, and Mapuche men continued to fight barefoot. Alliances were another key to success. The great uprising of 1599 linked culturally related neighbors in a confederacy that the Spanish termed "the Indomitable State."

As a result of sustained Mapuche resistance, southern Chile became a permanent frontier of Spanish South America, a region of defensive rather than offensive operations. The Mapuche, though still frequently at war with their European neighbors, had proved the fact of their independence. Throughout the Spanish world, they became legendary. Only in the late nineteenth century was a tenuous peace established with the Chilean government and reservations created. Like many treaties between nation-states and indigenous peoples, this peace brought not integration but marginalization and poverty. As a result, the Mapuche are still fighting.

Conclusion

The first wave of European overseas expansion in the Atlantic was transformative in many ways, and would not be repeated in Africa, Asia, or Oceania for several centuries. Hundreds of isolated cultures were brought into contact with one another, often for the first time. Agents of the Columbian Exchange, European farmers and ranchers migrated to new landscapes, which they and their plants, livestock, and germs quickly transformed. Millions of sub-Saharan Africans, most of them captive laborers, joined a fast-emerging Atlantic, and soon globally integrated, world.

Spearheading this transformation were the uniquely positioned and highly motivated Portuguese, armed and outfitted to undertake risky voyages of reconnaissance and chart new routes to commercial gain abroad. By the 1440s they were trading for gold and slaves in sub-Saharan Africa, and by the 1540s they had reached Japan. Although most interested in commerce, the Portuguese also carried with them a militant Christianity that they promoted with some success alongside their expanding global network of trading posts. In Brazil they took another tack, establishing hundreds of slave-staffed sugar plantations.

Early modern Spaniards sought the same gold, spices, sugar, and slaves that motivated their Portuguese neighbors, but after encountering the Americas, they turned away from trading posts in favor of territorial conquest. Those they defeated were forced to extract wealth and accept conversion to the Catholic faith. Ironic as it may seem, it was imperial peoples such as the Aztecs and Incas who proved most vulnerable to the Spanish onslaught, and more especially to foreign disease. Mobile, scattered cultures such as the Mapuche of Chile proved far more resistant. Even at the margins, however, violent conquest and the beginnings of the Atlantic slave trade transformed livelihoods for millions. Some individuals swept up in the early phases of colonial encounter and the Columbian Exchange, such as young Malintzin, found advantages and even a means to social gain. Countless others found themselves reduced to servitude in an emerging social order defined by race as much as by wealth or ancestry. This new order forged in the Americas would soon affect much of western Africa.

NOTES

1. Christopher Columbus, *The Four Voyages*, trans. J. M. Cohen (New York: Penguin, 1969), 300.
2. Gomes Eannes de Azurara, quoted in John H. Parry and Robert G. Keith, *New Iberian World: A Documentary History of the Discovery of Latin America to the Seventeenth Century* (New York: Times Books, 1984), 1:256.
3. Geoffrey Symcox and Blair Sullivan, *Christopher Columbus and the Enterprise of the Indies: A Brief History with Documents* (Boston: Bedford/St. Martin's, 2004).
4. Bartolomé de las Casas, *An Account, Much Abbreviated, of the Destruction of the Indies*, ed. Franklin Knight, trans. Andrew Hurley (Indianapolis: Hackett, 2003), 61.
5. Alfred Crosby, *The Columbian Exchange: Biological and Cultural Consequences of 1492*, 2d ed. (Westport, CT: Praeger, 2003).
6. Bernal Díaz del Castillo, *The History of the Conquest of New Spain*, ed. Davíd Carrasco, trans. A. P. Maudslay (Albuquerque: University of New Mexico Press, 2008), 230.
7. Quoted in Ross Hassig, *Aztec Warfare: Imperial Expansion and Political Control* (Norman: University of Oklahoma Press, 1992), 124.

RESOURCES FOR RESEARCH

General Works

There are several fine general surveys of early Latin America, but the following are exceptional for their helpful models and explanations of key colonial institutions such as the encomienda and early plantation complex, plus the tricky business of analyzing writings and images from the early postconquest era.

Brown University, John Carter Brown Library Archive of Early American Images. http://www.brown.edu/Facilities/John_Carter_Brown_Library/pages/ea_hmpg.html.

Library of Congress, Exploring the Early Americas. http://www.loc.gov/exhibits/earlyamericas/.

Lockhart, James, and Stuart B. Schwartz. *Early Latin America*. 1983.

Schwartz, Stuart B., ed. *Implicit Understandings: Observing, Reporting, and Reflecting on the Encounters Between Europeans and Other Peoples in the Early Modern Era*. 1994.

University of Texas, Latin American Network Information Center. http://www.info.lanic.utexas.edu/la/region/history.

Guns, Sails, and Compasses: Europeans Venture Abroad

The topic of early Iberian overseas expansion has drawn scholarly attention for many years, and several of the following works, though relatively old, are still considered classics.

Fernández Armesto, Felipe. *Before Columbus: Exploration and Colonization from the Mediterranean to the Atlantic, 1229–1492*. 1987.

Newitt, Malyn. *A History of Portuguese Overseas Expansion, 1400–1668*. 2005.

Parry, J. H. *The Age of Reconnaissance*. 1963.

Phillips, William D., and Carla Rahn Phillips. *The Worlds of Christopher Columbus*. 1992.

Symcox, Geoffrey, and Blair Sullivan. *Christopher Columbus and the Enterprise of the Indies: A Brief History with Documents*. 2004.

New Crossroads, First Encounters: The European Voyages of Discovery, 1492–1521

The literature on the Columbian Exchange and environmental transformations has grown in recent years, with special emphasis on the role of disease as a major factor distinguishing European success in the Americas from their less penetrating early experiences in Africa and Asia.

Alchon, Suzanne Austin. *A Pest in the Land: New World Epidemics in a Global Perspective*. 2003.

Cook, Noble David. *Born to Die: Disease and New World Conquest, 1492–1650*. 1998.

Crosby, Alfred. *The Columbian Exchange: Biological and Cultural Consequences of 1492*, 2d ed. 2003.

Emmer, Pieter C., ed. *General History of the Caribbean*. Vol. 2. *New Societies: The Caribbean in the Long Sixteenth Century*. 1997.

Melville, Elinor. *A Plague of Sheep: Environmental Consequences of the Conquest of Mexico*. 1994.

Spanish Conquests in the Americas, 1519–1600

Recent scholarship on the Spanish conquests has evolved to emphasize the many factors, such as the help of thousands of indigenous allies, that enabled relatively small numbers of Europeans to bring down two of the world's most populous empires.

Powers, Karen V. *Women in the Crucible of Conquest: The Gendered Genesis of Spanish American Society, 1500–1600*. 2005.

Restall, Matthew. *Seven Myths of the Spanish Conquest*. 2003.

Schwartz, Stuart B., ed. *Victors and Vanquished: Spanish and Nahua Views of the Conquest of Mexico*. 2000.

Townsend, Camilla. *Malintzin's Choice: An Indian Woman in the Conquest of Mexico*. 2006.

Wood, Stephanie. *Transcending Conquest: Nahua Views of Spanish Colonial Mexico*. 2003.

A New Empire in the Americas: New Spain and Peru, 1535–1600

Good regional and topical studies of colonial Spanish America abound. The following have been selected to highlight the themes of this chapter. Bakewell's treatment of early mining, trade, and administration is superlative.

Bakewell, Peter. *A History of Latin America to 1825*, 3d ed. 2009.

Clendinnen, Inga. *Ambivalent Conquests: Maya and Spaniard in Yucatan, 1517–1570*, 2d ed. 2003.

Gibson, Charles. *The Aztecs Under Spanish Rule*. 1964.

Mangan, Jane E. *Trading Roles: Gender, Ethnicity, and the Urban Economy in Colonial Potosí*. 2005.

Brazil by Accident: The Portuguese in the Americas, 1500–1600

The early history of Brazil is becoming a more popular topic, mostly focusing on European-indigenous relations.

Bethell, Leslie, ed. *Colonial Brazil*. 1986.

Hemming, John. *Red Gold: The Conquest of the Brazilian Indians, 1500–1760*. 1978.

Léry, Jean de. *History of a Voyage to the Land of Brazil*. Translated by Janet Whatley. 1990.

Metcalf, Alida. *Go-Betweens in the History of Brazil, 1500–1600*. 2005.

Schwartz, Stuart B. *Sugar Plantations and the Formation of Brazilian Society*. 1985.

COUNTERPOINT: The Mapuche of Chile: Native America's Indomitable State

Few studies of the colonial Mapuche have been published in English. The following are three important exceptions.

Dillehay, Tom. *Monuments, Empires, and Resistance: The Araucanian Polity and Ritual Narratives*. 2007.

Jones, Kristine. "Warfare, Reorganization and Redaptation at the Margins of Spanish Rule: The Southern Margin (1573–1882)." In *The Cambridge History of the Native Peoples of the Americas*, vol. 3, pt. 2, 138–187. Edited by Stuart B. Schwartz and Frank Salomon. 1999.

Padden, Robert C. "Cultural Adaptation and Militant Autonomy Among the Araucanians of Chile." In *The Indian in Latin American History: Resistance, Resilience, and Acculturation*, rev. ed. 71–91. Edited by John Kicza. 2000.

▶ **For additional primary sources from this period**, see *Sources of Crossroads and Cultures.*

▶ **For Web sites, images, and documents related to topics in this chapter**, see Make History at bedfordstmartins.com/smith.

The major global development in this chapter ▶ European expansion
across the Atlantic and its profound consequences for societies and cultures worldwide.

IMPORTANT EVENTS

1441	First sub-Saharan Africans captured and taken by ship to Portugal
1492	Fall of Granada and expulsion of Jews in Spain; Columbus reaches America
1494	Treaty of Tordesillas divides known world between Portugal and Spain
1498	Vasco da Gama becomes first European to reach India by sea
1500	Portuguese reach Brazil
1519–1521	Spanish conquest of Aztec Mexico
1519–1522	Magellan's ship circumnavigates the globe
1532–1536	Spanish conquest of Inca Peru
1545	Discovery of silver deposits at Potosí
1549	Portuguese establish royal capital of Salvador; first Jesuits arrive in Brazil
1555	French establish colony in Brazil's Guanabara Bay
1564	Discovery of mercury mines in Huancavelica, Peru
1567	Portuguese drive French from Brazil
1570–1571	Inquisition established in Lima and Mexico City
1572	Mita labor draft and mercury amalgamation formalized in Potosí
1592	Potosí reaches peak production
1599	Great Mapuche uprising in Chile

KEY TERMS

Columbian Exchange (p. 560)
conquistador (p. 562)
encomienda (p. 560)
feitoria (p. 555)

Inquisition (p. 570)
mestizo (p. 570)
mita (p. 568)
repartimiento (p. 568)

CHAPTER OVERVIEW QUESTIONS

1. What were the main biological and environmental consequences of European expansion into the Atlantic after 1492?
2. What roles did misunderstanding and chance play in the conquests of the Aztecs and Incas?
3. How did Eurasian demand for silver and sugar help bring about the creation of a linked Atlantic world?

SECTION FOCUS QUESTIONS

1. Why and how did Europeans begin to cross unknown seas in the fifteenth century?
2. What were the main sources of conflict between Europeans and native Americans in the first decades after contact?
3. What factors enabled the Spanish to conquer the Aztec and Inca empires?
4. Why was the discovery of silver in Spanish America so important in the course of world history?
5. How and why did early Portuguese Brazil develop differently from Spanish America?
6. How did the Mapuche of Chile manage to resist European conquest?

MAKING CONNECTIONS

1. How did Spanish and Portuguese imperial aims differ from those of the Incas and Aztecs (see Chapter 16)?
2. How would you compare the Spanish conquest of Mexico with the Ottoman conquest of Constantinople discussed in Chapter 15?
3. What role did European consumers play in the rise of the American plantation complex?
4. How did global demand for silver affect the lives of ordinary people in the Spanish colonies?

18

AT A CROSSROADS ▶

This dramatic brass plaque depicts the oba, or king, of Benin in a royal procession, probably in the sixteenth century. He is seated sidesaddle on a seemingly overburdened horse, probably imported and sold to him by Portuguese traders. The larger attendants to each side shade the monarch while the smaller ones hold his staff and other regal paraphernalia. Above, as if walking behind, are two armed guards. (Image copyright © The Metropolitan Museum of Art/Art Resource, NY.)

Western Africa in the Era of the Atlantic Slave Trade

1450–1800

I n 1594 a youth of about seventeen was captured in a village raid in the interior of western Africa. The Portuguese, who controlled the Atlantic port of Luanda, where the young captive was taken, called this vast region Angola, a corruption of the Kimbundu term for "blacksmith." The young man was now a nameless body to be branded, examined like a beast, and sold; he was also, in the words of his captors, "a black." In Luanda, the captive was housed in a stifling barracks with many others, perhaps including some who spoke his language and probably even a few who came from his village. Most, however, were strangers whose words, looks, hairstyles, and "country marks," or ritual scars, were unfamiliar.

Eventually, men dressed in black robes appeared among the captives. These odd-looking men were Roman Catholic priests, members of the Jesuit order. They had only recently established a missionary base in Luanda. In grave tones and mostly unintelligible

BACKSTORY

Prior to 1450, the lives of most western Africans focused on hoe agriculture, supplementary herding and hunting, and in some places mining and metallurgy. Chiefdoms were the dominant political form throughout the region, from the southern fringes of Morocco to the interior of Angola, although several expansive kingdoms rose and fell along the Niger and Volta rivers, notably Old Ghana, which thrived from about 300 to 1000, and most recently, as the early modern period dawned, Mali, which flourished from about 1200 to 1400.

Trade in many commodities extended over vast distances, often monopolized by extended families or ethnic groups. Muslim traders were dominant along the southern margins of the Sahara Desert after about 1000 C.E. Some western African merchants traded slaves across the Sahara to the Mediterranean basin, and others raided vulnerable villages for captives, some of whom were sent as far away as the Red Sea and Indian Ocean. Islam predominated by 1450 along many trade routes into the savanna, or grasslands, but most western Africans retained local religious beliefs, usually combining ancestor veneration with healing and divination practices similar to native American shamanism (see Chapter 16).

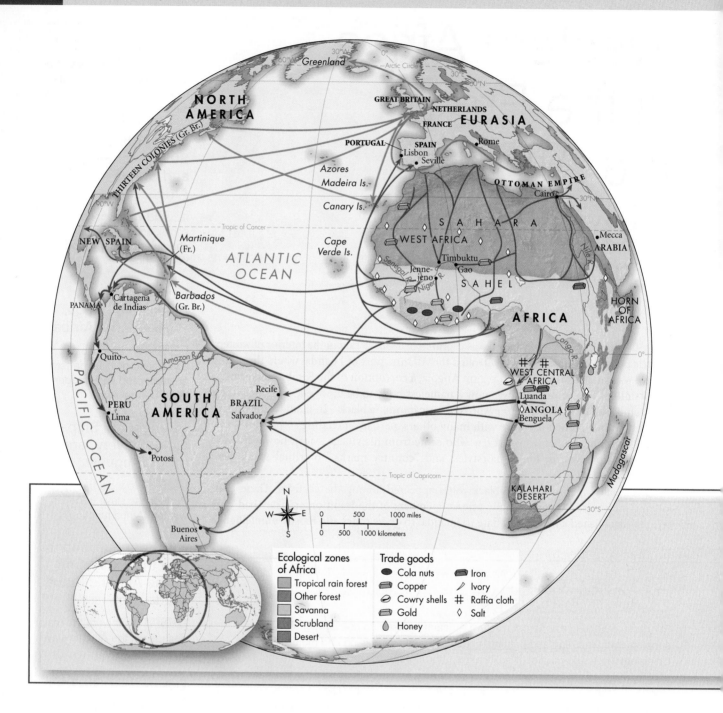

Ecological zones of Africa
- Tropical rain forest
- Other forest
- Savanna
- Scrubland
- Desert

Trade goods
- Cola nuts
- Copper
- Cowry shells
- Gold
- Honey
- Iron
- Ivory
- Raffia cloth
- Salt

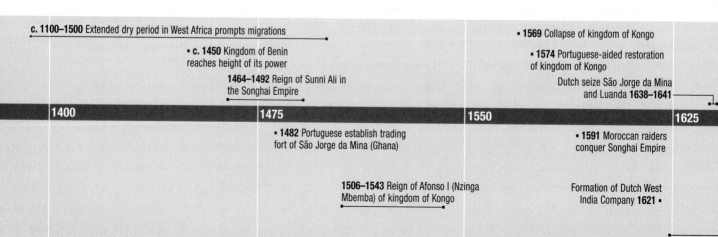

c. 1100–1500 Extended dry period in West Africa prompts migrations

c. 1450 Kingdom of Benin reaches height of its power

1464–1492 Reign of Sunni Ali in the Songhai Empire

1569 Collapse of kingdom of Kongo

1574 Portuguese-aided restoration of kingdom of Kongo

Dutch seize São Jorge da Mina and Luanda **1638–1641**

| 1400 | 1475 | 1550 | 1625 |

1482 Portuguese establish trading fort of São Jorge da Mina (Ghana)

1591 Moroccan raiders conquer Songhai Empire

1506–1543 Reign of Afonso I (Nzinga Mbemba) of kingdom of Kongo

Formation of Dutch West India Company **1621**

words, they spoke to the captives. The young man must have listened with puzzlement. At last, after several weeks, each captive was sprinkled with water and made to accept a lump of salt on the tongue. After this conversion ritual, names were assigned. The young man was now called "Domingo," "Sunday" in Portuguese. Once in the Americas, Spanish scribes recorded his name as "Domingo Angola, black slave." His sale records are the only evidence we have of his existence.

Domingo was one of the lucky ones. He survived barracks life in Luanda and then the grueling two-month voyage, or "middle passage," from Luanda to Cartagena de Indias, a bustling port on the Caribbean coast of present-day Colombia. More than one in five died during these ordeals. After stumbling out of the sickening hold of the slave ship and into the bright Caribbean sun, Domingo Angola would have been washed, oiled, examined for signs of contagious illness, and fed a simple meal of maize gruel and tough, salted beef. Both foods were new to him, and they would form the core of his diet for the rest of his enslaved life in Spanish South America.

After being transported by ship to Panama, Domingo was sold to a merchant on his way to Quito, the former northern Inca capital high in the Andes Mountains of Ecuador. There, according to notary records for the year 1595, he was sold yet again, this time to two merchants planning a multiyear sales trip to the distant silver-mining town of Potosí, several thousand miles to the south. In all, Domingo spent almost another year of hard and dangerous tropical travel. Documents listing travel costs say he fell ill while waiting for a ship on the Pacific coast and had to be treated. In Potosí, Domingo was sold yet again, and probably not for the last time. He had not yet turned nineteen.[1]

Meanwhile, back in Angola, a terrifying story arose about men and women such as Domingo who had been captured and taken away across the sea. People began to imagine that they were being captured to feed a distant race of cannibals. These "people eaters," red in color, lived somewhere beyond the sunset, it was said, on the far side of an

MAPPING THE WORLD

Africa and the Atlantic, c. 1450–1800

The vast and ecologically diverse continent of Africa had long been linked together by trade in salt, copper, iron, cola nuts, and other commodities. It had also been connected since ancient times to the Mediterranean and the Indian Ocean maritime worlds. Goods traded beyond Africa consisted mostly of gold and ivory, but there was also substantial traffic in human captives. After 1450 the Portuguese extended this pattern into the growing Atlantic world, establishing fortified trading posts all along Africa's west coast.

ROUTES ▼

→ Slave and trade route, c. 1450–1800

→ Voyage of Domingo Angola, c. 1594–1597

→ Voyages of Olaudah Equiano, c. 1755–1797

- **1672** Formation of English Royal African Company

1750–1800 Atlantic slave trade reaches highest volume

| 1700 | 1775 | 1850 |

- **1807** British declare Atlantic slave trade illegal

1624–1663 Reign of Queen Nzinga in the Ndongo kingdom of Angola

enormous lake, and there they butchered ordinary Angolans. Human blood was their wine, brains their cheese, and roasted and ground long-bones their gunpowder. The red people—the sunburnt Portuguese—were slavish devotees of Mwene Puto, God of the Dead. How else to explain the massive, ceaseless traffic in souls, what Angolans called the "way of death"?[2]

Domingo's long journey from western Africa to highland South America was not unusual, and in fact he would have met many other Angolans arriving in Potosí via Brazil and Buenos Aires. Victims of the Atlantic slave trade in this period were constantly on the move, some sailing from Africa as far as India, the Molucca Islands in the East Indies, and even Japan. This trend of slave mobility diminished somewhat with the rise of plantation agriculture in the seventeenth and eighteenth centuries, but Africans continued to work on sailing ships and in port cities all over the world. On land or at sea, massive disruption and shuffling of ethnic groups was typical of the Atlantic slave trade and what historians call the **African diaspora**, or "great scattering" of sub-Saharan African peoples. As we will see in the next chapter, millions of slaves were sent across the Indian Ocean from East Africa as well, a phenomenon predating the Atlantic trade but in the end not as voluminous. This chapter focuses on western or "Atlantic" Africa, a vast portion of the continent that geographers normally split into two parts: West and West Central Africa (see Mapping the World, page 583).

Although slavery and slave trading were established practices in western Africa prior to the arrival of Europeans, both institutions and their effects changed dramatically as a result of the surge in European demand for African slaves that coincided with European colonization of the Americas. Beginning in the late sixteenth century, new patterns of behavior emerged. African warriors and mercenaries focused more and more on attacking and kidnapping their neighbors in order to trade them to foreign slavers for weapons, stimulants, and luxury goods; coastal farmers abandoned arable lands vulnerable to raiders; formerly protective traditions and customs were called into question; and Islam and Christianity made new inroads. We now know that even cultures inhabiting zones far inland from the Atlantic coast, such as the Batwa, or Pygmies, of the Congo rain forest, were affected by reverberations of the slave trade. They were driven deeper into the forest as other internal migrants, forced to move under pressure from slavers, expanded their farms and pasturelands. There, as we will see in the Counterpoint to this chapter, the Pygmies forged a lifestyle far different from that of their settled neighbors.

African diaspora The global dispersal, mostly through the Atlantic slave trade, of African peoples.

OVERVIEW
QUESTIONS

The major global development in this chapter: The rise of the Atlantic slave trade and its impact on early modern African peoples and cultures.

As you read, consider:

1. How did ecological diversity in western Africa relate to cultural developments?

2. What tied western Africa to other parts of the world prior to the arrival of Europeans along Atlantic shores?

3. How did the Atlantic slave trade arise, and how was it sustained?

Many Western Africas

It has been estimated that the African continent, comprising a little over 20 percent of the earth's landmass, was home to 100 million people at the time of Columbus's famous 1492 transatlantic voyage. About 50 million people inhabited West and West Central Africa, what we refer to here as "western Africa." Western Africa thus had a population comparable to that of all the Americas at that time. It contained several dozen aspiring tributary states in various stages of expansion and contraction, along with a vast number of permanent agricultural and mobile, warrior-headed chiefdoms. There were also wide-ranging pastoral or herding groups, trading peoples, fishing folk, and scattered bands of desert and rain forest gatherer-hunters. The array of livelihoods was wide, yet the vast majority of western Africans lived as hoe agriculturalists, primarily cultivators of rice, sorghum, millet, and cotton (see Map 18.1).

FOCUS

What range of livelihoods, cultural practices, and political arrangements typified western Africa in early modern times?

Cultural Diversity

Religious ideas and practices varied as much as livelihoods, but most Africans south of the Sahara, like many peoples the world over, placed great emphasis on fertility. Fertility rituals were an integral aspect of everyday life; some entailed animal sacrifice, and others, rarely, human sacrifice. Also as in many other early modern societies, discord, illness, and material hardship were often thought to be the products of witchcraft. The capacity to identify and punish witches helped define power in many societies.

Islam, introduced by long-distance traders and warriors after the seventh century C.E., became dominant in the dry *sahel* (from the Arabic for "shore") and savanna, or grassland, regions just south of the Sahara, and along the rim of the Indian Ocean. Christian and Jewish communities were limited to tiny pockets in the northeastern Horn and along the Maghreb, or Mediterranean coast. Over two thousand languages were spoken on the continent, most of them derived from four major roots. All told, Africa's cultural and linguistic diversity easily exceeded that of Europe in the era of Columbus.

Even where Islam predominated, local notions of the spirit world survived. Most western Africans believed in a distant creator deity, sometimes equated with Allah, and everyday ritual tended to emphasize communication with ancestor spirits, who helped placate a host of other, potentially malevolent forces. As in many ancient cosmologies, animal and plant spirits were considered especially potent.

Places were also sacred. Rather like Andean *wakas*, western African **génies** (JEHN-ees) could be features in the landscape: boulders, springs, rivers, lakes, and groves. Trees were especially revered among peoples living along the southern margins of the savanna, and villagers built alongside patches of old-growth forest. Through periodic animal sacrifice, western Africans sought the patronage of local tree spirits, since they were literally most rooted in the land.

Environmental Challenges

Western Africa fell entirely within the lowland tropics and was thus subject to a number of endemic diseases and pests. The deadly falciparum variety of malaria and other serious mosquito-borne fevers attacked humans in the hot lowlands, and the wide range of the tsetse fly, carrier of the fatal trypanosomiasis virus, limited livestock grazing and horse breeding. As in modern times, droughts could be severe and prolonged in some densely populated regions, spurring mass migration and warfare. Western Africans nevertheless adapted to these and other environmental challenges, in the case of malaria developing at least some immunity against the disease.

Animal Husbandry and Metalsmithing

In the arid north where Islam predominated, beasts of burden included camels, donkeys, and horses. Cattle were also kept in the interior highlands and far south, where they were safe from tsetse flies. Arabian warhorses were greatly prized, and were widely traded among kingdoms and chiefdoms along the southern margins of the Sahara. They were most valued where fly-borne disease made breeding impossible. Other domestic animals included goats, swine, guinea fowl, sheep, and dogs. In general, animal **husbandry**, as in greater Eurasia, was far more developed in western Africa than in the Americas. There were also more large wild mammals in sub-Saharan Africa than in any other part of the world, and these featured prominently in regional cosmologies.

génie A sacred site or feature in the West African landscape.

husbandry Human intervention in the breeding of animals.

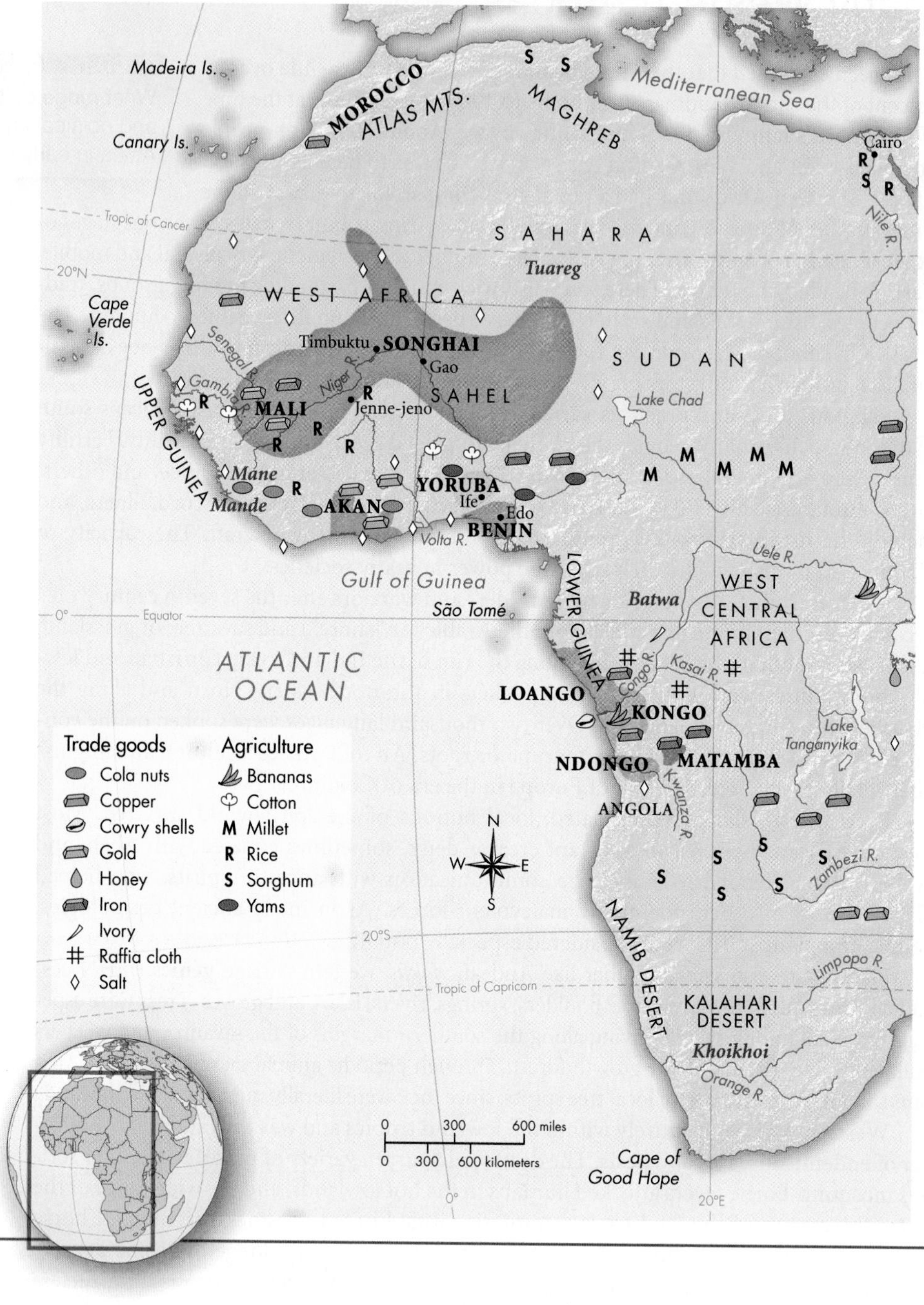

MAP 18.1

Western Africa, c. 1500

The huge regions of West and West Central Africa were of key importance to early modern global history as sources of both luxury commodities and enslaved immigrants. But western Africa was also marked by substantial internal dynamism. The Songhai Empire on the middle Niger rose to prominence about the time of Columbus. Large kingdoms and city-states also flourished on the Volta and lower Niger rivers and near the mouth of the Congo (Zaire). Rain forests and deserts were home to gatherer-hunters such as the Batwa (Pygmies) and Khoikhoi. Since tropical diseases severely limited the raising of large livestock, most western Africans used iron hand tools to plant and harvest millet, sorghum, rice, bananas, and, after trade with the Americas, maize and manioc.

Trade goods	Agriculture
Cola nuts	Bananas
Copper	Cotton
Cowry shells	**M** Millet
Gold	**R** Rice
Honey	**S** Sorghum
Iron	Yams
Ivory	
Raffia cloth	
Salt	

Mining and metalsmithing technologies were also highly developed and widely dispersed. Throughout West and West Central Africa, copper and copper-alloy metallurgical techniques had grown complex by 1500. Goldsmithing was also advanced, though less widespread. This was in part because African gold was being increasingly drawn away into commercial trade networks extending to the Mediterranean Sea and Indian Ocean. To a large extent, western Eurasia's "bullion famine" spurred early European expansion into Africa.

Since ancient times, Africans had been great producers and consumers of iron. Whether in Mali or Angola, African ironmongers were not simply artisans but also shamanlike figures and even **paramount chiefs**—heads of numerous village clans. In fact, throughout sub-Saharan Africa, metalwork was a closely guarded and mystical pro-

paramount chief A chief who presided over several headmen and controlled a large area.

cess similar to alchemy (the transmutation of base metals into gold) in contemporary Europe, the Middle East, and China. African metalsmiths produced great quantities of tools, ornaments, and lasting works of art. They made the iron hoes most people tended crops with, and sometimes they traded in bulk over vast distances.

Africa's internal trade was linked to craft specialization, but mostly it served to redistribute basic commodities. Those who mined or collected salt, for example, usually bartered it for other necessities such as cloth. Highly prized in the vast West African interior, where springs and deposits were extremely scarce, Saharan salt was an essential dietary supplement. Similarly, manufactured goods such as agricultural tools were widely traded for food, textiles, and livestock, but bits of gold, copper, and iron also served as currency. Among the most important trade goods were cola nuts, the sharing of which cemented social relations in much of West Africa, particularly among elites.

Copper and bronze bracelets were prized by some of western Africa's coastal peoples, and eventually they were standardized into currency that the Portuguese called *manillas* (mah-KNEE-lahs). In some areas seashells such as the cowry, brought all the way from the Maldive Islands off the west coast of India, functioned in the same way. The desire for brightly colored cotton textiles from India fueled Africa's west coast demand for shell and copper-bronze currency, which in time would also contribute to the expansion of the Atlantic slave trade. Africa's east coast, meanwhile, remained integrated into the vast and mostly separate Indian Ocean trade circuit through the monsoon-seasonal export of ivory, gold, and to a lesser extent, human captives, as we will see in Chapter 19.

African societies linked by trade were sometimes also bound by political ties. A shared desire to both expand household units and improve security led many Africans to form short- and long-term confederations and conglomerates. Like the Iroquois and Powhatan confederacies of eastern North America (discussed in Chapter 16), some of these alliances had a religious core, but just as often such collaborative actions were spurred by ecological stresses such as droughts. In this politically fluid context, ethnic and other forms of identity often blended and blurred as groups merged and partially or wholly adopted each other's languages, cosmologies, farming techniques, and modes of dress and adornment.

Nevertheless, as in the Americas, intergroup conflict was hardly unusual in western Africa prior to the arrival of Europeans. Expansionist, tributary empires such as Mali and Songhai grew independently of outside forces, and both managed to make lifelong regional and internal enemies. The motives of African warfare varied, but they frequently had to do with the control of resources, and especially people, sometimes as slaves put to work on agricultural estates. As in other parts of the early modern world, European trading and political meddling on Africa's Atlantic coast would spawn or exacerbate major new conflicts that would reverberate deep within the continent. Full-blown imperialism would come much later, with the development of new technologies and antimalarial drugs, but it would benefit in part from this earlier political disruption.

A Young Woman from West Africa

Since at least medieval times, West African women surprised outside visitors with their independence, visibility, and political influence, in both Islamic and non-Islamic societies. This drawing by an English artist during a slave-trading voyage to West Africa in around 1775 depicts a young woman with elaborately braided hair, pearl earrings, and a choker strung with coral or large stones. It is possible that she is a member of an elite family given these proudly displayed ornaments, but we do not know. The portrait reveals neither her identity nor her destiny, though it is clear that she made a strong impression on the foreign artist. (National Maritime Museum, London/The Image Works.)

Trade, Politics, and Warfare

West Africa's Gold Miners

Implements of the Gold Trade

West Africa was long legendary for its gold, which was first traded across the Sahara and later to Europeans arriving along the Atlantic coast. In the Akan region of present-day Ghana, gold dust circulated as currency, with portions measured by merchants in a hanging balance against tiny, fancifully designed brass weights. Gold dust was stored in brass boxes and dished out with decorated brass spoons. Smaller exchanges employed cowry shells, brought to Atlantic Africa from the Maldive Islands in the Indian Ocean. (Aldo Tutino/Art Resource, NY.)

Until 1650, gold was a more valuable West African export than slaves, and it remained highly significant for many years afterward. The mines and their workers, some of whom were enslaved, were controlled by local kings, whose agents traded the gold to long-distance merchants with ties to Europeans on the coast. Gold diggings were concentrated along the upper reaches of the Senegal, Niger, and Volta rivers, mostly in and around streams flowing down from eroded mountain ranges. Sources describing West African gold mining in early modern times are rare, but anecdotal descriptions combined with somewhat later eyewitness accounts suggest that women did many of the most strenuous tasks. The Scottish traveler Mungo Park described nonenslaved West African women miners among the Mande of the upper Niger in the 1790s as follows:

> About the beginning of December, when the harvest is over, and the streams and torrents have greatly subsided, the Mansa, or chief of the town, appoints a day to begin *sanoo koo*, "gold washing"; and the women are sure to have themselves in readiness by the time appointed. . . . On the morning of their departure, a bullock is killed for the first day's

Landlords and Strangers: Peoples and States in West Africa

FOCUS

What economic, social, and political patterns characterized early modern West Africa?

According to mostly archaeological and some textual references, West Africans in the period following 700 C.E. faced several radical new developments. Two major catalysts for change were the introduction and spread of Islam after the eighth century and a long dry period lasting from roughly 1100 to 1500 C.E. At least one historian has characterized human relations in this era in terms of "landlords" and "strangers," a reference to the tendency toward small and scattered agricultural communities offering safe passage and hospitality to a variety of travelers and craft specialists.[3] In return, these "strangers"—traders, blacksmiths, tanners, bards, and clerics—offered goods and services. The model "landlord" was an esteemed personage or even group of elders capable of ensuring the security and prosperity of a wide range of dependents and affiliates, usually conceived of as members of an extended family.

entertainment, and a number of prayers and charms are used to ensure success; for a failure on that day is thought a bad omen. . . . The washing of the sands of the streams is by far the easiest way of obtaining the gold dust, but in most places the sands have been so narrowly searched before that unless the stream takes some new course, the gold is found but in small quantities. While some of the party are busied in washing the sands, others employ themselves farther up the torrent, where the rapidity of the stream has carried away all the clay, sand, etc., and left nothing but small pebbles. The search among these is a very troublesome task. I have seen women who have had the skin worn off the tops of their fingers in this employment. Sometimes, however, they are rewarded by finding pieces [nuggets] of gold, which they call *sanoo birro*, "gold stones," that amply repay them for their trouble. A woman and her daughter, inhabitants of Kamalia, found in one day two pieces of this kind.

Mande men, according to Park, participated in excavating deep pits in gold-bearing hills "in the height of the dry season," producing clay and other sediments "for the women to wash; for though the pit is dug by the men, the gold is always washed by the women, who are accustomed from their infancy to a similar operation, in separating the husks of corn from the meal." To be efficient, panning required intense concentration and careful eye-hand coordination, and use of several pans to collect concentrates. This skill was appreciated, as Park explains: "Some women, by long practice, become so well acquainted with the nature of the sand, and the mode of washing it, that they will collect gold where others cannot find a single particle." Gold dust was then stored in quills (the hollow shafts of bird feathers) plugged with cotton, says Park, "and the washers are fond of displaying a number of these quills in their hair."

Source: Mungo Park, *Travels in the Interior Districts of Africa*, ed. and introduced by Kate Ferguson Masters (Durham, NC: Duke University Press, 2000), 264–267.

> ### QUESTIONS TO CONSIDER
>
> 1. Why was West African gold mining seasonal?
>
> 2. How were tasks divided between men and women, and why?
>
> 3. Was gold washing demeaning labor, or could it be a source of pride?

For Further Information:
Philip D. Curtin. *Economic Change in Precolonial Africa: Senegambia in the Era of the Slave Trade*. Madison: University of Wisconsin Press, 1975.

Empire Builders and Traders

The late medieval dry period also witnessed the rise of mounted warriors: the stranger as conqueror and captive-taker. On the banks of the middle and upper Niger River rose the expansionist kingdoms of Mali and Songhai, both linked to the Mediterranean world via the caravan terminus of Timbuktu (see again Map 18.1). Both empires were headed by devout, locally born Muslim rulers. One, Mansa Musa (*mansa* meaning "conqueror") of Mali, made the pilgrimage to Mecca in 1325. Musa spent so much gold during a stop in Cairo that his visit became legend.

It was gold, concentrated near the headwaters of the Senegal, Niger, and Volta rivers, that put sub-Saharan Africa on the minds—and maps—of European and Middle Eastern traders and monarchs. Most West African mines were worked by farming peoples forced to pay tribute in gold dust unearthed in the fallow (inactive) season (see Lives and Livelihoods: West Africa's Gold Miners). As in North America, India, and many other parts of the world at this time, warfare was also limited by the seasonal demands of subsistence agriculture. Yet land was a less-prized commodity than labor in West Africa. Prestige derived not from own-

Politics of the Gold Trade

ership of farmland or mines but from control over productive people, some of whom—and in places like Songhai, many of whom—were enslaved. Captive-taking was thus integral to warfare at all political levels, from the smallest chiefdom to the largest empire. Like the seasonal production of gold, the seasonal production of slaves, who for centuries had been sent north across the Sahara to Mediterranean markets and east to those of the Red Sea and Indian Ocean, would vastly expand once Europeans arrived on Atlantic shores.

With the exception, as we will see, of the Songhai Empire, West African politics in this period was mostly confederated. Dozens of paramount chiefs or regional kings relied on a host of more-or-less-loyal tributaries and enslaved laborers for their power, wealth, and sustenance. In general, as in much of Southeast Asia (see Chapter 19), early modern West Africa witnessed the periodic rise of charismatic and aggressive rulers, with few bureaucrats and judges. Rulers typically extended their authority by offering to protect vulnerable agricultural groups from raiders. Some coastal rice growers in Upper Guinea drifted in and out of these kinds of regional alliances, depending on political and environmental conditions. Alliances did not always spare them from disaster. Still, as actors in the Columbian Exchange, enslaved rice farmers from this region transferred techniques and perhaps grains to the plantations of North and South America.

From Western Sudan to Lower Guinea, town-sized units predominated, many of them walled or otherwise fortified. Archaeologists are still discovering traces of these extensive enclosures, some of which housed thousands of inhabitants. As in medieval Europe, even when they shared a language, walled cities in neighboring territories could be fiercely competitive. These were not tribal units but rather highly stratified and populous urban enclaves.

Songhai Empire

Dating to the first centuries C.E., West Africa was also home to sizable kingdoms. Old Ghana flourished from about 300 to 1000 C.E., followed by Mali, which thrived from about 1200 to 1400. From about the time of Columbus, the Songhai Empire, centered at Gao, rose to prominence under Sunni Ali (r. 1464–1492). Similar to the mansas of Mali, Sunni Ali was a conqueror, employing mounted lancers and huge squads of boatmen to great and terrifying effect. Sunni Ali's successor, Muhammad Touré, extended Songhai's rule even farther. At his zenith Touré, who took the title *askiya* (AH-skee-yah), or hereditary lord, and later *caliph*, or supreme lord, controlled a huge portion of West Africa (see again Map 18.1). Ultimately, like many Eurasian contemporaries, he was limited more by sheer logistics and distance than armed resistance.

The wealth and power of Songhai derived from the merchant crossroads cities of the middle Niger: Jenne, Gao, and Timbuktu (see Reading the Past: Al-Sa'di on Jenne and Its History). Here gold from the western mines of the upper Niger and Senegal, salt from the Sahara, and forest products from the south such as cola nuts and raffia palm fiber were exchanged, along with a host of other commodities. Slaves, many of them taken in Songhai's wars of expansion, were also traded to distant buyers in North and East Africa. Stately Timbuktu, meanwhile, retained its reputation as a major market for books and a center of Islamic teachings.

Touré's successors were less aggressive than he, and as Songhai's power waned in the later sixteenth century, the empire fell victim to mounted raiders from distant Morocco. With alarming audacity, and greatly aided by their state-of-the-art firearms and swift mounts, the Moroccans (among them hundreds of exiled Spanish Muslims, or Moriscos) captured the cities of Gao and Timbuktu in 1591. As their victory texts attest, these foreign conquistadors took home stunning quantities of gold and a number of slaves. Yet unlike their Spanish and Portuguese contemporaries in the Americas, they failed to hold on to their new conquest. The mighty Sahara proved a more formidable barrier to colonial governance than the Atlantic Ocean. After the fall of Songhai there emerged a fractured dynasty of Moroccan princes, the Sa'dis, who were in turn crushed by new, local waves of warfare in the late seventeenth and early eighteenth centuries. Most fell victim to the Sahara's best-known nomads, the Tuareg (TWAH-regh).

Sculptors and Priest-Kings

Farther south, near the mouth of the Niger River, was the rain forest kingdom of Benin, with its capital at Edo. Under King Ewuare (EH-woo-AH-reh) (r. c. 1450–1480), Benin

Al-Sa'di on Jenne and Its History

The historian known as Al-Sa'di (1594–c. 1656) was an imam, or religious scholar, descended from the Moroccan Sa'dis who invaded and toppled the Songhai Empire on the middle Niger River in 1591. He lived in the cities of Timbuktu and Jenne, and he appears to have learned most of what he knew about the region's past from a mix of written Arabic sources and local oral historians who spoke the Songhai language. The following passage, from about 1655, is translated from Al-Sa'di's Arabic history of the middle Niger region from medieval times to his own.

Jenne is a large, well-favored and blessed city, characterized by prosperity, good fortune, and compassion. God bestowed these things upon that land as innate characteristics. It is the nature of Jenne's inhabitants to be kind, charitable, and solicitous for one another. However, when it comes to matters of daily life, competitiveness is very much a part of their character, to such an extent that if anyone attains a higher status, the rest uniformly hate him, though without making this apparent or letting it show. Only if there occurs some change of fortune—from which God protect us—will each of them display his hatred in word and deed.

Jenne is one of the great markets of the Muslims. Those who deal in salt from the mine of Taghaza meet there with those who deal in gold from the mine of Bitu. These two blessed mines have no equal in the entire world. People discovered their great blessing through going to them for business, amassing such wealth as only God—Sublime is He—could assess. This blessed city of Jenne is why caravans come to Timbuktu from all quarters—north, south, east, and west. Jenne is situated to the south and west of Timbuktu beyond the two rivers [the Niger and Bani]. When the [Bani] river is in flood, Jenne becomes an island, but when the flood abates, the water is far from it. It begins to be surrounded by water in August, and in February the water recedes again. . . .

With the exception of Sunni Ali [of Songhai], no ruler had ever defeated the people of Jenne since the town was founded. According to what its people tell, Sunni Ali besieged them for seven years, seven months, and seven days, finally subduing them and ruling over them. His army was encamped at Joboro [original site of Jenne, south of the city] and they would attack the people of Jenne daily until the flood encircled the city. Then he would retire with his army to a place called Nibkat Sunni ("the hillock of Sunni"), so named because he stayed there. His army would remain there and keep watch until the waters receded and then would return to Joboro to fight. I was told by Sultan Abd Allah son of Sultan Abu Bakr that this went on for seven years. Then famine struck and the people of Jenne grew weak. Despite that, they contrived to appear still strong, so that Sunni Ali had no idea what condition they were really in. Weary of the siege at last, he decided to return to Songhai. Then one of the Sultan of Jenne's senior army commanders, said to be the grandfather of Unsa Mani Surya Muhammad, sent word to Sunni Ali and revealed the secret, and told him not to return home until he saw how things would turn out. So Sunni Ali exercised patience and became even more eager [to take Jenne].

Then the sultan took counsel with his commanders and the senior men of his army. He proposed that they should surrender to Sunni Ali, and they agreed. . . . So the Sultan of Jenne and his senior army commanders rode forth to meet Sunni Ali, and when he got close to him he dismounted and walked towards him on foot. Sunni Ali welcomed him and received him with honor. When he saw that the sultan was only a young man, he took hold of him and seated him beside him on his rug and said, "Have we been fighting with a boy all this time?" Then his courtiers told him that the young man's father had died during the siege, and that he had succeeded him as sultan. This is what lies behind the custom of the Sultan of Songhai sitting together with the Sultan of Jenne on a single rug until this day.

Source: John O. Hunwick, ed. and trans., *Timbuktu and the Songhay Empire: Al-Sadi's Tarikh al-sudan Down to 1613 and Other Contemporary Documents* (Leiden, the Netherlands: Brill, 1999), 13–21.

EXAMINING THE EVIDENCE

1. How does Al-Sa'di characterize the city and people of Jenne?

2. Why is the city's location on the Niger River important?

3. How does Al-Sa'di characterize the Songhai Empire founder Sunni Ali's conquest of Jenne?

Art of the Slave Trade: A Benin Bronze Plaque

Copper and bronze metallurgy were advanced arts in western Africa long before the arrival of Europeans. Metal sculpture, in the form of lifelike busts, historical plaques, and complex representations of deities, was most developed in western Nigeria and the kingdom of Benin. Realistic representations of elite men and women appear to have served a commemorative function, as did relief-sculpted plaques depicting kings, chiefs, and warlords in full regalia. Beginning in the 1500s, sculptors in Benin and neighboring lands began to depict Portuguese slave traders and missionaries, bearded men with helmets, heavy robes, and trade goods, including primitive muskets. This plaque depicts Portuguese slavers with a cargo of manillas, the bronze bracelets that served as currency in the slave trade until the mid-nineteenth century.

EXAMINING THE EVIDENCE

1. How were Portuguese newcomers incorporated into this traditional Benin art form?

2. How might this bronze representation of foreigners and their trade goods have been a commentary on the slave trade?

Plaque of Portuguese Traders with Manillas
(Gift of Mr. and Mrs. Klaus G. Perls, 1991 (1991.17.13).
The Metropolitan Museum of Art, New York, NY/Art
Resource, NY.)

reached the height of its power in the mid-fifteenth century, subjecting dozens of neighboring towns and chiefdoms to tributary status. Benin grew wealthy in part by exporting cloth made by women working on domestic looms in tributary villages. This trade expanded substantially with the arrival of Portuguese coastal traders around 1500, revitalizing Benin's power. Some of the most accomplished sculptors in African history worked under King Ewuare and his successors, producing a stunning array of cast brass portraits of Benin royalty, prominent warriors, and even newly arrived Europeans. This was but one of the many specialized livelihoods afforded by urban living (see Seeing the Past: Art of the Slave Trade: A Benin Bronze Plaque).

Yoruba City-States

Just west of Benin were a number of city-states ruled by ethnic Yoruba clans. At their core was the city of Ife (EE-feh), founded in around 1000 C.E. Ife metalsmiths and sculptors were as accomplished as those of Benin, and their large cast works, especially in copper, have been hailed as inimitable. As in the precontact Americas, Yoruba political leaders, called *obas*, performed a mix of political and religious duties. Most of these priest-kings were men, but a significant number were women. One of the obas' main functions was to negotiate with an array of ancestor deities thought to govern key aspects of everyday life. Some slaves later taken from this region to the Americas appear to have adapted these ideas to Christian monotheism, masking multiple ancestor worship behind the Roman Catholic cult of saints.

Akan City-States

oba A priest-king or queen of the Yoruba culture (modern southern Nigeria).

Urban life also matured along the banks of the lower Volta River, in what is today Ghana, at the beginning of early modern times. Here Akan peoples had formed city-states, mostly by controlling regional gold mines and trading networks. The Akan initially focused on transporting gold and cola nuts to the drier north, where these commodities found a ready market among the imperial societies of the middle Niger. With the arrival of Europeans on the Atlantic coast in the late fifteenth century, however, many Akan traders turned their attention toward the south. Throughout early modern times, women held great power in Akan polities, and matrilineal inheritance was the recognized standard. Matrilineal societies were relatively rare in West Africa, but other exceptions included the nomadic Tuareg. Even in patrilineal empires such as Mali and Songhai, women could wield considerable power, especially in matters of succession.

Land of the Blacksmith Kings: West Central Africa

Human interaction in West Central Africa, called by some historians "land of the blacksmith kings," was in part defined by long-term control of copper and iron deposits. As in West Africa, however, the vast majority of people were engaged in subsistence agriculture, limited to hoe tilling because the tsetse fly eliminated livestock capable of pulling plows. For this reason, few people other than gatherer-hunters such as the Pygmies inhabited the most prominent geographical feature of the region, Africa's great equatorial forest (see again Mapping the World, page 583). Most preferred to farm the surrounding savanna and fish along the Atlantic coast and major riverbanks.

> **FOCUS**
>
> What economic, social, and political patterns characterized early modern West Central Africa?

The Congo (Zaire) River basin and estuary, second only to the Amazon in terms of forest cover and volume of freshwater catchment, were of central importance to human history in West Central Africa. Although patterns of belief and material culture varied, most people spoke derivations of Western Bantu, an ancestral root language. Islam was known in some areas but remained marginal in influence. Most inhabitants of West Central Africa lived in matrilineal or patrilineal kin-based villages, a small minority of them subordinate to paramount chiefs or small kings. In all, the region was marked by a cultural coherence similar to that of Mesoamerica (discussed in Chapter 16).

Farmers and Traders

Farmers

The hoe-agriculturalists who formed the vast majority of West Central Africans grew mostly millet and sorghum, complemented by yams and bananas in certain areas. Bananas, a crop introduced to the region some time before 1000 C.E., enabled farmers to exploit the forest's edge more effectively and devote more energy to textile making and other activities. Some forested areas were too wet for staple crops but still offered game, medicinal plants, and other products. Pygmy forest dwellers, for example, traded honey, ivory, and wild animal skins to their farming neighbors for iron points and food items. Tsetse flies and other pests limited the development of animal husbandry in West Central Africa, except in the drier south. In the vast plains of southern Angola, livestock survived, but rains were highly uncertain.

Wherever they lived, West Central Africans, like Europeans and Asians, embraced a host of native American crops in the centuries following Columbus's voyages. Maize became a staple throughout Central Africa, along with cassava (manioc), peanuts, chili peppers, beans, squash, and tobacco. Peanuts, probably introduced by the Portuguese from Brazil soon after 1500, were locally called *nguba* (NGOO-bah), from which the American term "goober peas" derives.

Traders

As the introduction of American crops demonstrates, West Central Africa may have had less direct ties to global trade than coastal West Africa, but it was still part of the system. Likewise, the internal African trade networks were of great importance to West Central African life. As in West Africa, salt was traded over great distances, along with food products, textiles, metal goods, and other items. Raffia palm fiber was used to manufacture a supple and durable cloth, and coastal lagoons were exploited for cowry shells for trade.

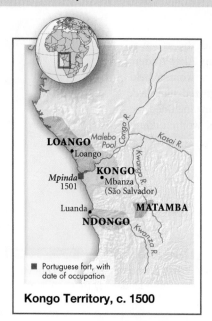

Kongo Territory, c. 1500

Throughout the region political power came to be associated with control of these sorts of trade goods and also of routes of access to the interior. For example, in around 1300 two kingdoms arose above and below the Malebo Pool alongside the Congo River. This was the first major cataract, and hence portage site, for all traders moving between the coast and interior. The kings of Loango, living above the falls but also controlling access to the Atlantic coast, taxed trade and also drew legitimacy from their role as caretakers of an ancient religious shrine. Below the falls and to the south, in Kongo—a kingdom misnamed by the Portuguese after the title of its warlords, the **manikongos** (mah-nee-CONE-goes)—leaders came to power in part by monopolizing copper deposits. The kings of Kongo also controlled access to cowry shells, the region's main currency.

Smiths and Kings

As in West Africa, power also derived from the mystique surrounding metallurgy. The introduction of ironworking to the region sometime early in the Common Era had made the majority of farmers dependent on smiths for hoes, blades, and other implements. Making the most of this reliance, some blacksmiths became kings. By 1500, Kongo commanded an area stretching inland from the right bank of the Congo River south and east some 185 miles, absorbing numerous villages, slaves, and tributaries along the way. A few small kingdoms existed to the north and east, often with copper deposits serving as their lifeblood. These kingdoms eventually challenged Kongo directly, in part because they were subjected to Kongo slave-raiding. In what is today Angola, just north of the Kwanza River, there emerged in the sixteenth century the Ndongo (NDOAN-go) kingdom. Just northeast of Ndongo lay the Matamba kingdom. Initially tributaries of Kongo, the people of Matamba shifted their relations in favor of Ndongo as Portuguese influence there grew in the sixteenth century. By 1600, the Portuguese held forts deep in Ndongo country, using them to procure slaves from farther inland.

Less is known about the peoples of the more isolated and forested middle Congo basin, but archaeologists have recently shown that large chiefdoms were being consolidated there as early as the thirteenth century, and they lasted into early modern times. Here, innovations in sword manufacture seem to have enabled some paramount chiefs to monopolize trade along Congo River tributaries. Like elites everywhere, these chiefs considered themselves the spiritual kin of various predatory lords of the animal kingdom, in this case the leopard and eagle.

We know less about women's livelihoods than men's, but it appears that in early modern West Central Africa, as in many preindustrial societies, women tended to work mostly at domestic tasks such as child rearing, food preparation, and other aspects of household management. Men were frequently engaged in hunting, herding, trade, and warfare, so women's responsibilities often extended to agriculture. In many places, women planted yams in hard soils by slicing through the crust with machetes made by village men. Almost everywhere, women tended the food crops and men cleared forest.

Women formed the foundation of West Central African society in terms of both subsistence and reproduction. Yet

Mbundu Blacksmiths

This late-seventeenth-century watercolor depicts a Mbundu blacksmith and assistant at work. As the assistant operates the typical African bellows with rods attached to airbags, the master smith hammers a crescent-shaped iron blade on an anvil. Other blades, including what may be a sickle or hoe, lie on the ground to the left of the anvil. In the background a curious audience looks on. (Illumination by Padre Giovanni Antonio Cavazzi da Montecuccolo (died 1692) from the Manoscritti Araldi; reproduction courtesy of Michele Araldi.)

women did still more. Evidence for the early modern period is slim, but it appears that while men controlled metal smelting and smithing, women both managed and worked in mining crews. Some were probably enslaved, but others were likely associated with ethnic groups famed for their expertise in these tasks. Even children were employed in mines, particularly salt and copper mines. Experienced West and West Central African miners, including women and children, were probably among the first slaves sent by the Portuguese to work the gold mines of the Spanish Caribbean. Many later found their skills in demand in Colombia, Mexico, Peru, and Brazil.

Strangers in Ships: Gold, Slavery, and the Portuguese

As we saw in Chapter 17, the Portuguese arrived in western Africa soon after 1400 in search of gold and a sea route to India. For well over a century they were the only significant European presence in the region. During that time, a number of Portuguese explorers, merchants, missionaries, and even criminal castaways established a string of *feitorias*, or fortified trading posts, and offshore island settlements. There were no great marches to the interior, no conquests of existing empires. Instead, the Portuguese focused their efforts on extracting Africa's famed wealth in gold, ivory, and slaves through intermediaries. In a pattern that would be continued in Asia, the Portuguese sought to dominate maritime trade.

> **FOCUS**
>
> How did the early Portuguese slave trade in western Africa function?

From Voyages of Reconnaissance to Trading Forts 1415–1650

On the wide Gambia River the Portuguese sailed far inland, seeking the famed gold of Mali, at this time an empire in decline but still powerful in the interior (see again Map 18.1). The warring states of the region were happy to trade gold for horses, which were far more valuable than the crude European guns available at this time. Chronic conflicts yielded a surplus of captives. With explicit backing from the pope, Portuguese merchants did not hesitate to accept African slaves as payment. Once in Portuguese hands, each healthy young male was reduced to an accounting unit, or *peça* (PEH-sah) literally "piece." Women, children, the disabled, and the elderly were discounted in terms of fractions of a peça.

African enslavement of fellow Africans was widespread long before the arrival of Europeans, and the daily experience of slavery in most African households, farms, or mines was no doubt unpleasant. What differed with the arrival of the Portuguese in the fifteenth century was a new insistence on innate African inferiority—in a word, racism—and with it a closing of traditional avenues of reentry into free society, if not for oneself, then for one's children, such as faithful service, or in Islamic societies, religious conversion. The Portuguese followed the pope's decree that enslaved sub-Saharan Africans be converted to Catholicism, but they also adopted an unstated policy that regarded black Africans as "slaves by nature." To sidestep the paradox of African spiritual equality and alleged "beastly" inferiority, the Portuguese claimed that they sold only captives taken in "just war." Many such slaves were sold, like young Domingo Angola, to the Spanish, who took the Portuguese sellers at their word (see Reading the Past: Alonso de Sandoval, "General Points Relating to Slavery").

Iberian demand for African slaves remained limited prior to American colonization. Word of goldfields in the African interior encouraged the Portuguese to continue their dogged search for the yellow metal. By 1471 caravels reached West Africa's so-called Gold Coast, and in 1482 the Portuguese established a feitoria in present-day Ghana. Built by

Racism as Justification for Slavery

manikongo A "blacksmith" king of Kongo.

peça Portuguese for "piece," used to describe enslaved Africans as units of labor.

Alonso de Sandoval, "General Points Relating to Slavery"

Alonso de Sandoval (1577–c. 1650) was a Jesuit priest born in Seville, Spain, and raised in Lima, Peru. He spent most of his adult life administering sacraments to enslaved Africans arriving at the Caribbean port city of Cartagena de Indias, in present-day Colombia. In 1627 he published a book entitled *On Restoring Ethiopian Salvation*. In it, he focused on cultural aspects of sub-Saharan African societies as he understood them, with the aim of preaching to Africans more effectively, but he also discussed the Atlantic slave trade and its justifications.

The debate among scholars on how to justify the arduous and difficult business of slavery has perplexed me for a long time. I could have given up on explaining it and just ignored it in this book. However, I am determined to discuss it, although I will leave the final justification of slavery to legal and ecclesiastical authorities. . . . I will only mention here what I have learned after many years of working in this ministry. The readers can formulate their own ideas on the justice of this issue. . . .

A short story helps me explain how to morally justify black slavery. I was once consulted by a captain who owned slave ships that had made many voyages to these places. He had enriched himself through the slave trade, and his conscience was burdened with concern over how these slaves had fallen into his hands. His concern is not surprising, because he also told me that one of their kings imprisoned anyone who angered him in order to sell them as slaves to the Spaniards. So in this region, people are enslaved if they anger the king. . . .

There is a more standard way in which slaves are traded and later shipped in fleets of ships to the Indies. Near Luanda are some black merchants called pombeiros worth a thousand pesos. They travel inland eighty leagues [c. 250 miles], bringing porters with them to carry trade goods. They meet in great markets where merchants gather together to sell slaves. These merchants travel 200 or 300 leagues [c. 650–1000 miles] to sell blacks from many different kingdoms to various merchants or pombeiros. The pombeiros buy the slaves and transport them to the coast. They must report to their masters how many died on the road. They do this by bringing back the hands of the dead, a stinking, horrific sight. . . .

I have spent a great deal of time discussing this subject because slaves are captured in many different ways, and this disturbs the slave traders' consciences. One slave trader freely told me that he felt guilty about how the slaves he had bought in Guinea had come to be enslaved. Another slave trader, who had bought 300 slaves on foot, expressed the same concerns, adding that half the wars fought between blacks would not take place if the Spanish [or more likely, Portuguese] did not go there to buy slaves. . . . The evidence, along with the moral justifications argued by scholars, is the best we can do to carefully address this irredeemable situation and the very difficult business of the slave trade.

Source: Alonso de Sandoval, *Treatise on Slavery*, ed. and trans. Nicole Von Germeten (Indianapolis, IN: Hackett Publishers, 2008), 50–55.

EXAMINING THE EVIDENCE

1. Who was Alonso de Sandoval, and why did he write this passage?

2. How does Sandoval try to justify African enslavement?

3. Are Africans themselves involved in this discussion?

Early Portuguese Slave Trade

enslaved Africans, São Jorge da Mina, or "St. George of the mine," served for over a century as Portugal's major West African gold and slaving fort.

After 1500, as slave markets in Spanish America and Brazil emerged, new trading posts were established in choice spots all along the West African coast. It so happened that invasions of Mande and Mane (MAH-nay) peoples into modern Guinea, Liberia, Sierra Leone, and Ivory Coast in the fifteenth and sixteenth centuries produced yet more streams of captives through the seventeenth century (see Map 18.2). As in the first years after their arrival, the Portuguese continued to trade copper, iron, textiles, horses, and guns (now much more advanced) for gold, ivory, and a local spice called malaguetta pepper, but by the early 1500s the shift toward slave trading was evident. The coexistence of rising

The Early Atlantic Slave Trade, c. 1450–1650

The first enslaved Africans transported by ship in Atlantic waters arrived in Portugal in 1441. The Portuguese won a monopoly on African coastal trade from the pope, and until 1500, they shipped most enslaved African captives to the eastern Atlantic islands, where plantations were booming by the 1450s. Soon after 1500, Portuguese slave traders took captives first to the Spanish Caribbean (West Indies), then to the mainland colonies of New Spain and Peru. Claimed by the Portuguese in 1500, Brazil was initially a minor destination for enslaved Africans, but this changed by about 1570, when the colony's sugar production ballooned. Another early Atlantic route took slaves south to Buenos Aires, where they were marched overland to the rich city of Potosí. Death rates on the ships and on overland marches were always high in this traffic in human lives.

demand for slaves in the Americas and increased supply in Africa as the result of warfare made the dramatic growth of the Atlantic slave trade all but inevitable.

Throughout western Africa the Portuguese both extracted and transported wealth. They frequently ferried luxury goods such as cola nuts and textiles, as well as slaves, between existing African trade zones. As we will see, a similar pattern would emerge when the Portuguese reached India, and later China, Japan, and the Spice Islands. Virtually everywhere the Portuguese docked their lumbering but well-armed ships, Africans found that they benefited as much from access to the foreigners' shipping, which was relatively secure and efficient, as from their goods. As a result, many competing coastal lords made the most of these new trade ties, often to the detriment of more isolated and vulnerable neighbors.

At times commerce with the Portuguese, which increasingly turned to the import of bronze and copper bracelets, or manillas, as currency, would upend a region's balance of power, touching off a series of interior conflicts. Some such conflicts were ignited by Portuguese convicts, who survived abandonment along the coast to establish marriage alliances with local chiefdoms. As seen in Chapter 17 in the case of Brazil, this was in fact the Portuguese plan, to drop expendable subjects like seeds along the world's coasts. Some took root, learned local languages, and built trading posts. In several West African coastal enclaves, mulatto or "Eurafrican" communities developed. These mixed communities were nominally Catholic, but much cultural blending occurred. Some scholars now refer to these new intermediaries of global exchange as "Atlantic creoles."

New Markets in the Niger Delta

After 1510, the Portuguese moved eastward. Here among the Niger delta's vast tidal flats and mangroves, Ijaw (EE-jaw) boatmen were initially willing to trade an adult male captive for fewer than a dozen copper manillas. Rates of exchange moderated with competition and a steadier flow of goods, but overall, Portuguese demand for slaves remained relatively low and was met by other captive-producing zones. What historians call the "Nigerian diaspora" mostly developed later in this densely populated region, in the seventeenth and eighteenth centuries. By then rival Dutch and English slavers had begun operating posts to the west and east of the Niger delta (see Map 18.4, page 602). After 1650 this region was known simply as the Slave Coast.

Portuguese Strategy in the Kingdom of Kongo

Portuguese interest in Atlantic Africa shifted southeastward after 1500, based in part on alliances with the kingdom of Kongo. Within West Central Africa generally, ongoing cycles of trade, war, and drought profoundly influenced relationships with outsiders. Once again, local nobles forced the Portuguese to operate according to local systems of influence and local rules. Still, whereas Portuguese slavers were to be largely displaced by the French, English, and Dutch in West and even northern West Central Africa by 1650, in the southern portion of the continent they held on for much longer. As a result, the fortunes of Kongo and Angola became ever more intimately entwined with those of Brazil, Portugal's vast colony on the other side of the Atlantic. Historians now speak of a functionally separate South Atlantic slave trade circuit.

Missionary Efforts

Portuguese religious initiatives in Africa had long been split between armed conflict with Muslim kingdoms in the far north, epitomized by the 1415 conquest of Ceuta in Morocco (see Chapter 17), and more peaceful, although scattered and inconsistent, missionary efforts in the south. Portuguese missionaries, like merchants, tended not to survive long in the tropical interior, where malaria and other diseases took a heavy toll. Thus scores of Franciscans, Jesuits, and others died denouncing the persistent **fetishism** (roughly, "idolatry") of their local hosts.

Quite unlike their Spanish contemporaries in the Americas, the Portuguese made barely a dent in African religious traditions, despite centuries of contact. This was not for lack of trying—the Portuguese worked much harder at conversion than did later-arriving northern Europeans—but rather due to a mix of hardening Portuguese racism and sub-Saharan Africa's punishing disease regime. Falciparum malaria, in particular, severely restricted the movements of European missionaries, who also faced language barriers and other cultural obstacles. The obvious solution was to train African priests, and for a time this option was pursued and even sponsored by the Portuguese royal family.

In the early sixteenth century, African priests were trained in Lisbon, in the university city of Coimbra, and even in Rome. African seminaries also were established, notably in the Cape Verde Islands and the island of São Tomé, located off the western coast in the Gulf of Guinea. Despite promising beginnings, however, these endeavors met with sharp opposition from an increasingly racist and self-righteous Portuguese clergy. A similar process had taken place in Spanish America, where ambitious plans for training and ordaining a native American clergy were scrapped within a few generations of contact. Emerging colonial racial hierarchies, indelibly linked to status, trumped the universal ideal of spiritual equality. An African clergy could also prove subversive of the slave trade and other such commercial projects. Already in decline before 1600, most of the local African seminaries languished in the seventeenth and early eighteenth centuries. Only with the Enlightenment-inspired reforms of the later eighteenth century (discussed in Chapter 23) were African novices again encouraged to become priests beyond the secular, or parish, level, and only after the abolition of slavery did their numbers become significant. Thus, although the Atlantic slave trade would result in the forced migration of millions of Africans and the creation of new hybrid cultural communities in the Americas, in Africa itself the racial basis of the trade inhibited cultural merger and exchange.

Portuguese Soldier

Here a Benin artist depicts a Portuguese soldier in what appears to be light armor and a crested metal helmet typical of the later sixteenth century. Portuguese soldiers like this one aided several African allies, including the Christian kings of Kongo, as they fought for regional supremacy and engaged in the growing slave trade. (Snark/Art Resource, NY.)

This did not mean that Christianity had no impact on early modern Atlantic Africa. Rather, it meant that its presence was less deeply felt than might otherwise have been the case. Aside from the offshore islands, only in Kongo and Angola did Christianity play a critical historical role. Beginning in the 1480s, the Portuguese applied their usual blend of trade, military alliances, and religious proselytizing to carve out a niche in West Central Africa. By 1491 they had managed to convert much of the Kongo aristocracy to Roman Catholicism. Key among the converts was the paramount chief's son, Nzinga Mbemba, who later ruled as Afonso I (r. 1506–1543).

Afonso's conversion was apparently genuine. He learned to read, studied theology tirelessly, and renamed Mbanza, the capital city, São Salvador ("Holy Savior"). One of his sons became a priest in Lisbon and returned to Kongo following consecration in Rome. He was one of the earliest exemplars of western African indigenous clergy.

Ultimately, however, Christianity, like copper, tended to be monopolized by Kongo's elites; the peasant and craft worker majority was virtually ignored. Most Kongolese commoners recognized deities called **kitomi** (key-TOE-mee), each looked after by a local (non-Catholic) priest. Meanwhile, Portuguese military aid buttressed Kongo politically while fueling the slave trade.

Here, as elsewhere in Africa, the slave trade, though it offered considerable gains, also exacerbated existing dangers and conflicts and almost always created new ones. King Afonso wrote to the king of Portugal in 1526, complaining that "every day the merchants carry away our people, sons of our soil and sons of our nobles and vassals, and our relatives, whom thieves and people of bad conscience kidnap and sell to obtain the coveted things and trade goods of that [Portuguese] Kingdom."[4] Even in its earliest days, the slave trade in West Central Africa was taking on a life of its own.

As a result of Kongo's slaving-based alliance with the Portuguese, King Afonso's successors faced growing opposition from every direction. The kingdom of Kongo finally collapsed in 1569. São Salvador was sacked, and its Christian nobles were humiliated and sold into slavery in the interior. Lisbon responded to the fall of its staunchest African ally with troops, in this case six hundred Portuguese harquebusiers (the precursor of musketeers). With this violent intervention, the monarchy was effectively restored in 1574. In exchange, Kongo traders called *pombeiros* (pohm-BEH-rohs) supplied their Portuguese saviors with a steady stream of slaves. The process of propping up regimes in exchange for captives was to continue throughout the long history of the slave trade.

Kongo-Portuguese Slaving Alliance

Portuguese Strategy in Angola

A second pillar of Portuguese strategy in West Central Africa entailed establishing a permanent military colony in Angola, home of the young man named Domingo whose story began this chapter. Beginning with the port city of Luanda, this new colony was to become one of the largest and longest-lived clearinghouses for the Atlantic slave trade (see Map 18.3). It was perhaps here more than anywhere else in Africa that the Portuguese, aided again by droughts and other factors, managed to radically alter local livelihoods.

According to Portuguese documents and climatological evidence, the major stimulus to the early Angolan slave trade was a severe and prolonged drought affecting the interior in the 1590s. The drought uprooted numerous groups of villagers already weakened by slave-raiding, and these luckless refugees in turn were preyed upon by still more parasitic and aggressive warrior-bandits calling themselves Imbangala. The Imbangala, organized around secret military societies, soon became slaving allies of the Portuguese. These were probably Domingo Angola's captors.

Employing terrifying tactics, including human sacrifice and—allegedly—cannibalism, Imbangala raiders eventually threatened to snuff out the Ndongo kingdom. That Ndongo survived at all, in fact, depended on the creativity and wile of a powerful woman, Queen Nzinga (r. 1624–1663). Following the maxim "if you can't beat 'em, join 'em," Queen Nzinga sought to thwart the Imbangala by allying with their sometime business partners, the Portuguese. In Luanda she was baptized "Dona Ana," or "Queen Ann."

fetishism The derogatory term used by Europeans to describe western African use of religious objects.

kitomi Deities attended by Kongo priests prior to the arrival of Christian Europeans.

pombeiro A slave-trade middleman in the West Central African interior.

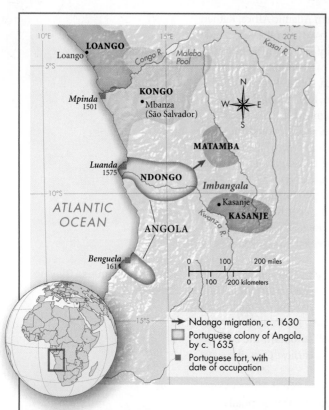

MAP 18.3 **West Central Africa, c. 1500–1635**

No African region was more affected by European interlopers in early modern times than West Central Africa, the Atlantic world's main source of enslaved captives, nearly all of them shipped abroad by the Portuguese. At first, Portuguese missionaries and diplomats vied for the favor of the kings of Kongo. Before long, however, the Portuguese shifted their interest south to Luanda, a base built almost exclusively for slave trading. Peoples of the interior suffered periodic slave raids as the Portuguese extended their networks south to Benguela. Some refugees migrated eastward, only to encounter new enemies—most of them allies of the Portuguese.

Adopting the example of the kings of Kongo, Queen Nzinga promised to supply slaves to her new friends. She soon discovered that the Portuguese had little authority over the Imbangala, however. Their warriors continued to attack the Ndongo, who were forced to move to a new homeland, in deserted Matamba. From this newer, more secure base Queen Nzinga built her own aggressive slaving and trading state. When the Dutch occupied Luanda in the 1640s, the queen adapted, trading slaves to them in exchange for political immunity for her followers. Before her death at the age of eighty-one, Queen Nzinga reestablished ties with the Portuguese, who again controlled the coast in the 1650s.

To the south and west, meanwhile, Imbangala warriors began to intermingle with various peoples, eventually establishing the kingdom of Kasanje (see again Map 18.3). After 1630, Kasanje merchant-warriors operated alternately as slavers and middlemen, taking or trading for captives from the east. Farther south, other warriors began to interact with Portuguese settlers around the Atlantic port of Benguela. By the later seventeenth century Benguela rivaled Luanda as the key conduit for the South Atlantic slave trade.

By this time, Portuguese trade in Africa focused almost entirely on slaves. Overall, West Central Africa, mostly Kongo and Angola, supplied over 5 million, or nearly half of the about 12 million recorded slaves sent to the Americas between 1519 and 1867. The victims were overwhelmingly peasants, poor millet and sorghum farmers struggling to eke out a living in a largely drought-prone and war-torn region. Very occasionally, as in the case of Kongo, the enslaved included nobles and prominent warriors. At least two-thirds of all African captives sent across the Atlantic were men, a significant number of them boys. Some historians have argued that growing demand for young men abroad and the African desire to be rid of these potentially vengeful captives proved mutually reinforcing. Into the vortex were thrust young men such as Domingo Angola, who was sent all the way to the Andean boomtown of Potosí.

Due to Portuguese entrenchment on the West Central African coast and a fairly formalized system of enslavement, a majority of Angolan and Kongolese slaves reached the Americas as baptized Catholics more or less fluent in Kimbundu or Kikongo, the common languages of the coast, and sometimes even Portuguese. Ethnic differences existed, but on the whole slaves given the monikers "Kongo" and "Angola," like Domingo, had more in common than any comparable group of Africans taken to the Americas.

Northern Europeans and the Expansion of the Atlantic Slave Trade 1600–1800

FOCUS

What were the major changes in the Atlantic slave trade after 1600?

Other Europeans had vied for a share of the Portuguese Atlantic slave trade since the mid-sixteenth century, among them famous figures such as the English corsair Francis Drake, but it was only after 1600 that competition grew significantly. First the French, then the English, Dutch, Danish,

and other northern Europeans forcibly displaced Portuguese traders all along the western shores of Africa. Others set up competing posts nearby. By 1650, the Portuguese were struggling to maintain a significant presence even in West Central Africa. They began to supplement western African slaves with captives transshipped from their outposts in the Indian Ocean, primarily Mozambique and Madagascar. As a result, slaves arriving in Brazil in the seventeenth century were of increasingly diverse ethnic origins (see Map 18.4).

Since it was both profitable and logistically complex, the slave trade was among the most thoroughly documented commercial activities of early modern times. Beginning after 1650, we can cross-check multiple documents for numbers of slaves boarded, origin place-names, and age or sex groupings. These sources, a bland accounting of mass death and suffering, suggest that the volume of the trade grew slowly, expanding gradually after 1650 and very rapidly only after 1750. The British, despite profiting greatly from the slave trade in western Africa through the 1790s, when volume peaked, suddenly reversed policy under pressure from abolitionists in 1807. After 1808, the British Navy actively suppressed the Atlantic slave trade until it was formally abolished by international treaty in 1850. Despite these measures, contraband slaving continued, mostly between Angola and Brazil. In terms of numbers of lives, families, and communities destroyed, the Atlantic slave trade was primarily a modern phenomenon with deep early modern roots.

The Rise and Fall of Monopoly Trading Companies

Following the example of the Spanish and Portuguese, northern European participation in the Atlantic slave trade grew in tandem with colonization efforts in the Americas. Tobacco-producing Caribbean islands such as Barbados and Martinique and mainland North American regions such as Virginia and the Carolinas were initially staffed with indentured, or contracted, European servants and only a small number of African slaves. As sugar cultivation increased in the Caribbean after 1650 and tobacco took off in Virginia,

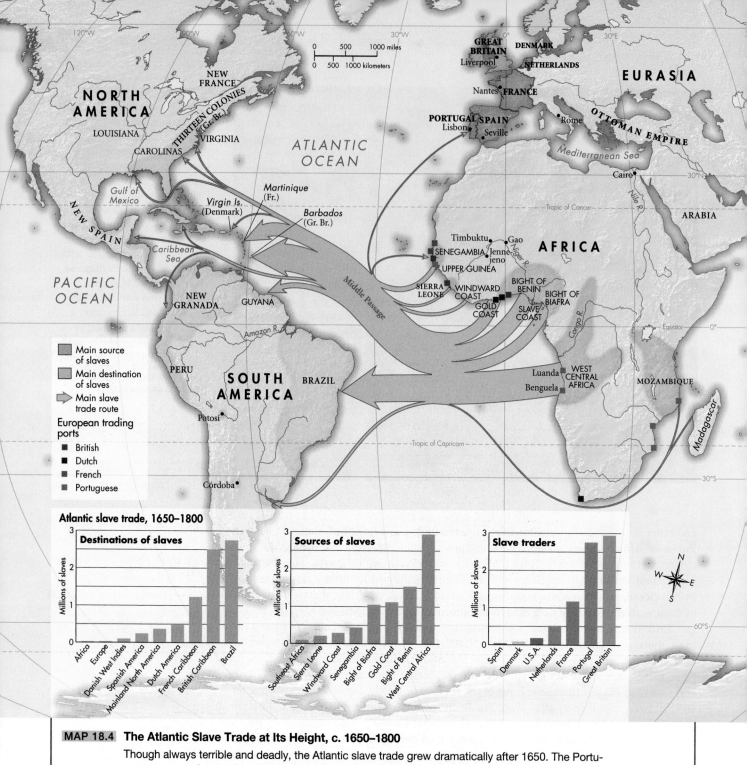

MAP 18.4 The Atlantic Slave Trade at Its Height, c. 1650–1800

Though always terrible and deadly, the Atlantic slave trade grew dramatically after 1650. The Portuguese were no longer the only slave traders, and demand was no longer limited to Spanish America and Brazil. New slaving nations included the Netherlands, England, France, and Denmark, all of which had colonies in the Caribbean and on the North American mainland that relied on plantation agriculture. The regions from which enslaved Africans came also shifted during this long period. West Central Africa remained a major source region, but the Upper Guinea Coast was increasingly overshadowed by the so-called Slave Coast located between the Bight of Benin and the Bight of Biafra.

however, planters shifted overwhelmingly to African slavery. This had been their wish, as their documents attest, and a declining supply of poor European contract laborers, particularly after 1700, accelerated the trend.

Origins of American Racism

For historians of the North Atlantic, this transition from indentured servitude to African slavery has raised a host of questions about the origins of American racism. In sum, can modern notions of racial difference be traced to early modern American slavery and the Atlantic slave trade? Some prominent scholars of English and French colonialism have argued that racist ideologies grew mostly *after* this shift from European to African labor. Before that, they argue, "white" and "black" workers were treated by masters and overseers with equal cruelty. In Virginia and Barbados during the early to mid-1600s, for instance, black and white indentured servants labored alongside each other, experiencing equal exploitation and limited legal protection in the brief years before racial slavery was codified by law. Scholars working in a broader historical context, however—one that takes into account Spanish, Portuguese, Dutch, and Italian experiences in the Atlantic, Mediterranean, and beyond—have been less convinced by this assertion. They argue that while racist notions hardened with the expansion of slavery in the Caribbean and North America after 1650—and grew harder still following the Scientific Revolution with its emphasis on biological classification—European views of sub-Saharan Africans had virtually never been positive. Put another way, racism was more a cause of slavery than a result.

Although numerous challengers were gathering force by 1600, Portuguese slavers remained the most significant suppliers to early English and French planters in the Americas. As we have seen, the Portuguese had a distinct advantage in that over several centuries they had established the financial instruments and supply networks necessary to run such a complex and risky business. To compete, northern Europeans were forced to establish state-subsidized monopoly trading companies. The highly belligerent Dutch West India Company was founded in 1621 to attack Spanish and Portuguese colonial outposts and take over Iberian commercial interests in the Atlantic. Several slaving forts in western Africa were eventually seized. São Jorge da Mina fell in 1638, and Luanda, Angola, in 1641. Although these colonial outposts were returned in subsequent decades, the era of Portuguese dominance was over.

The French, whose early overseas activities had been stunted by the religious wars described in Chapter 20, finally organized a monopoly trading company in 1664 to supply their growing Caribbean market. The English, fresh from their own civil conflicts, followed suit by forming the Royal African Company in 1672. By 1700, the French and English were fighting bitterly to supply not only their own colonial holdings but also the highly lucrative Spanish-American market. Dutch slavers also competed, supplying nearly one hundred thousand slaves to the Spanish up to the 1730s. After 1650, Spanish-Americans were not

Formation of Northern European Trading Companies

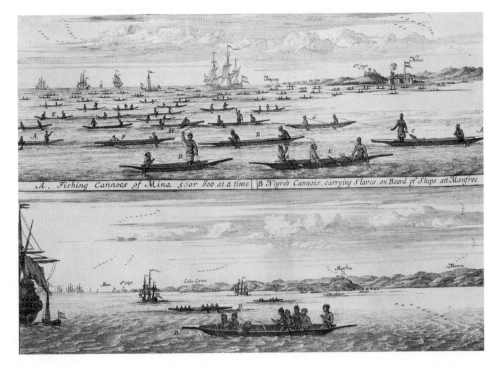

A. *Fishing Cannoes of Mina 5 or 600 at a time* | B *Negro's Cannoes, carrying Slaves, on Board of Ships att Manfroe*

Filling the Slave Ships
The upper half of this 1732 engraving by Dutch artist Johannes Kip shows West African fishermen in canoes off the coast of present-day Ghana, with the old Portuguese fortress of São Jorge da Mina in the distance. The lower half shows slaves being ferried to a Dutch ship in a somewhat longer canoe, with a string of other European slave-trading forts in the distance. Slave ships often cruised African coasts for several months, acquiring a diverse range of captives before crossing the Atlantic. (Beinecke Rare Book and Manuscript Library, Yale University.)

buying as many slaves as in the first century after conquest, but unlike other colonists they paid for them with gold and silver. Danish slavers also entered the competition by the 1670s, when they established several Caribbean sugar plantations in the Virgin Islands.

The company model did not last. By 1725, if not before, most of the northern European monopoly companies had been dismantled. Stuck with costly forts, salaried officers, and state-mandated contract obligations, they proved to be too inflexible and inefficient to survive in a world of limited information and shifting supply and demand. Thus the French, English, and Dutch resorted to a system more like that long practiced by the Portuguese, in which small numbers of private merchants, often related to one another by marriage if not blood, pooled capital to finance individual voyages. Like their Mediterranean predecessors in Venice, Genoa, and elsewhere, the trade in slaves was but one of many overlapping ventures for most of these investors. Their profits, usually averaging 10 percent or so, were reinvested in land, light industry, and numerous other endeavors. In time, investors inhabiting bustling slave ports such as Liverpool, England, and Nantes, France, had little to do with the actual organization of slaving voyages. Nonetheless, the profits slavery produced would flow through these ports into Europe, fueling the continent's economic growth and development.

How the Mature Slave Trade Functioned

The slave trade proved most lucrative when European investors cut every possible corner. Profit margins consistently trumped humanitarian concerns. By the late seventeenth century, ships were packed tightly, food and water rationed sparingly, and crews kept as small as possible. Unlike other shipping ventures at this time, the value of the captives held as cargo far exceeded the costs of ship and crew on typical slaving voyages. In part this was a reflection of the considerable risks involved.

European Risk and Profit   Risks and uncertainties abounded in the slave trade. Despite a growing number of more or less friendly European forts scattered along Africa's vast Atlantic coast, slavers were mostly on their own when it came to collecting captives. In short, the system was much more open and African-dominated than has generally been acknowledged. Ships spent an average of three months cruising coastal towns and estuaries in search of African middlemen willing to trade captives for commodities. By the late seventeenth century, competition was on the rise, affecting supply and thus price. Violence, mostly in the form of slave uprisings and hostile attacks by fellow Europeans, was a constant concern.

European ship captains in charge of this dangerous and drawn-out leg of the trip hoped to receive at the other end a bounty of 2 to 5 percent on all surviving slaves. Somewhat like modern human traffickers, they were in fact betting their lives on a relatively small fortune. As we saw with regard to Portuguese missionaries, western Africa was notoriously unhealthy for "unseasoned" Europeans, due mostly to endemic falciparum malaria, and according to the documentary record, as many as one in ten ship captains died before leaving the African coast for the Americas. Few who survived repeated the trip. Ships' doctors had scant remedies on hand even for common ailments such as dysentery, which also afflicted slaves and crewmembers to a great extent. When not ill themselves, doctors inspected slaves before embarkation, hoping to head off premature death or the spread of disease aboard ship and thereby to protect the investment.

African Gains and Losses   On the African consumer side, few northern European products were attractive enough to stimulate trade. More than anything, Africans wanted colorful cotton fabrics from India to supplement their own usually indigo-dyed or plain products. Thus the Dutch, French, English, and others followed the Portuguese example yet again by importing huge quantities of cotton cloth from South Asia, cowry shells from the Indian Ocean, and iron, brass, and copper from parts of Europe, particularly Spain and Sweden. European traders struggled to meet the particular and often shifting demands of each slaving region's inhabitants. Cloth was the most sought-after trade item throughout the period of the slave trade, constituting at least two-thirds of imports carried by British slavers between the 1690s and 1808. Other tastes were introduced by Europeans. By 1700, American plantation commodities such as rum and tobacco were being exchanged for slaves in significant quantities. Thus, the Atlantic slave trade was a global concern, drawing in people and goods from around the world.

It is clear from many contemporary sources that chiefs and kings throughout western Africa greatly augmented their prestige by accumulating and redistributing the commodities they procured through the slave trade. The captives they sent abroad were not their kin, and western Africans appear to have had no sense of the overall magnitude of this commerce in human bodies. There were few internal brakes on captive-taking besides the diminishing pool of victims and shifting political ambitions; the African desire to hold dependents to boost prestige and provide domestic labor meshed with European demands. Along these lines, whereas female war captives might be absorbed into elite households, men and boys were generally considered dangerous elements and happily gotten rid of. It so happened that European planters and mine owners in the colonies valued men over women by a significant margin. Thus, however immoral and disruptive of African life it appears in retrospect, the slave trade probably seemed at the time to be mutually beneficial for European buyers and African sellers. Only the slaves themselves felt otherwise.

The Middle Passage

It is difficult to imagine the suffering endured by the more than 12 million African captives forced to cross the Atlantic Ocean in early modern times. The ordeal itself has come to be known as the **Middle Passage** (see again Map 18.4). As noted at the opening of this chapter, some West Central Africans imagined the slavers' ships to be floating slaughterhouses crossing a great lake or river to satisfy white cannibals inhabiting a distant, sterile land. Portuguese sailors unambiguously dubbed them "death ships" or "floating tombs." Perhaps troubled by this sense of damnation, Portuguese priests in Luanda, Benguela, and elsewhere baptized as many slaves as they could before departure. Portuguese ships were virtually all named for Catholic saints.

Slave Conditions and Mortality

Northern Europeans, increasingly in charge of the slave trade after 1650, took a more dispassionate approach. Slaves, as far as they were concerned, were a sort of highly valued livestock requiring efficient but impersonal handling. Put another way, the care and feeding of slaves were treated as pragmatic matters of health, not faith. Rations were the subsistence minimum of maize, rice, or millet gruel, with a bit of fish or dried meat added from time to time. Men, women, and children were assigned separate quarters. Women were given a cotton cloth for a wrap, whereas men were often kept naked, both to save money and to discourage rebellion by adding to their already abject humiliation. Exercise was required on deck in the form of dancing to drums during daylight hours. Like cattle, slaves were showered with seawater before the nighttime lockdown. The hold, ventilated on most ships after initial experiences with mass suffocation and heatstroke, was periodically splashed with vinegar.

Despite these measures, slave mortality on the one- to three-month voyage across the Atlantic was high. On average, between 10 and 20 percent of slaves did not survive the cramped conditions, physical abuse, and generally unsanitary environment aboard ship. This high mortality rate is all the more alarming in that these slaves had been selected for their relative good health in the first place, leaving countless other captives behind to perish in makeshift barracks, dungeons, and coastal agricultural plots. Many more died soon after landing in the Americas, often from dysentery and other intestinal ailments. Some who were emotionally overwhelmed committed suicide along the way by hurling themselves into the ocean or strangling themselves in their chains. A few enraged men managed to kill a crewmember or even a captain before being summarily executed. Slaves from different regions had trouble communicating. Thus successful slave mutinies, in which women as well as men participated, were rare but not unknown.

The general conditions of the Middle Passage worsened over time. In the name of increased efficiency, the situation belowdecks went from crowded to crammed between the seventeenth and eighteenth centuries. On average, crews of 30 to 40 common

Middle Passage The Atlantic crossing made by slaves taken from Africa to the Americas.

Olaudah Equiano

Olaudah Equiano, whose slave name was Gustavus Vassa, became a celebrity critic of the Atlantic slave trade in the late eighteenth century after writing a memoir of his experiences as a slave and free man of color in Africa, North America, the Caribbean, and Europe. The book, published in 1789, offered a rare victim's perspective on the Atlantic slave trade and the daily humiliations and punishments suffered by slaves in the Americas. (British Library, London/© British Library Board. All Rights Reserved/Bridgeman Art Library.)

sailors oversaw 200 to 300 slaves in around 1700, whereas the same number oversaw 300 to 400 slaves after 1750. These are only averages; even in the 1620s, some ships carried 600 or more slaves.

Although some Iberian clergymen protested the horrors of this crossing as early as the sixteenth century, it took the extraordinary eighteenth-century deterioration of conditions aboard slave ships to awaken the conscience of participating nations. In England, most importantly, African survivors of the Middle Passage such as Olaudah Equiano (c. 1745–1797) were called to testify before Parliament by the late eighteenth century. "Permit me, with the greatest deference and respect," Equiano began his 1789 autobiography, "to lay at your feet the following genuine Narrative, the chief design of which is to excite in your august assemblies a sense of compassion for the miseries which the Slave-Trade has entailed on my unfortunate countrymen."[5] Such testimonies, backed by the impassioned pleas of prominent Quakers and other religious figures, were finally heard. Abolition of the Atlantic slave trade, first enforced by the British in 1808, would come much more easily than abolition of slavery itself.

Volume of the Slave Trade

It is important to note that the trans-Saharan and East African slave trades preceded the Atlantic one discussed here, and that these trades continued apace throughout early modern times. In fact, the volume of the Atlantic trade appears only to have eclipsed these other avenues to foreign captivity after 1600. That said, the Atlantic slave trade ultimately constituted the greatest forced migration in early modern world history. Compared with the roughly 2 million mostly free European migrants who made their way to all parts of the Americas between the voyage of Columbus in 1492 and the British abolition of the slave trade in 1808, the number of enslaved Africans to cross the Atlantic and survive is astounding—between 10 and 12 million.

Also astounding is the fact that the vast majority of these Africans arrived in the last half century of the slave trade, that is, after 1750. Up until 1650 a total of approximately 710,000 slaves had been taken to American markets, most of them to Spanish America (262,700). Brazil was the next largest destination, absorbing about a quarter of a million slaves to that date. São Tomé, the sugar island in the Gulf of Guinea, and Europe (mostly Iberia) absorbed about 95,000 and 112,000 slaves, respectively. Madeira and the Canaries imported about 25,000 African slaves, and the English and French West Indies, 21,000 and 2500, respectively. The average annual volume for the period up to 1650 was approximately 7500 slaves per year.

Eighteenth-Century Explosion

The second (1650–1750) and third (1750–1850) stages of the Atlantic slave trade witnessed enormous, historically transformative growth. By 1675, nearly 15,000 slaves were being carried to the colonies annually, and by 1700 nearly 30,000. The total volume of the trade between 1700 and 1750 was double that of the previous fifty years, bringing some 2.5 million slaves to the Americas. The trade nearly doubled yet again between 1750 and 1800, when some 4 million Africans were transported. By this time the effect of the Atlantic slave trade on western African societies was considerable. The trade was increasingly restricted by British naval interdiction after 1808, but slavers still managed to move some 3 million slaves, mostly to Brazil, and to a lesser extent Cuba and the United States, by 1850. Northern U.S. shipbuilders were key suppliers to Brazilian slavers to the very end.

It appears that in the first three centuries of the Atlantic slave trade most African captives came from the coastal hinterland. This changed only after about 1750, when colonial demand began to outstrip local sources of supply. Thereafter, slaves were brought to the coast from increasingly distant interior regions. In West Africa this amounted to something of an inversion of the caravan trading routes fanning out from the Niger River basin, but in West Central Africa entirely new trails and trade circuits were formed. Also, whereas war captives and drought refugees had been the main victims in the past, now random kidnapping and slave-raiding became widespread.

COUNTERPOINT
The Pygmies of Central Africa

As in the Americas, certain forest, desert, and other margin-dwelling peoples of Africa appear to have remained largely immune to the effects of European conquest, colonization, and trade throughout early modern times. But such seeming immunity is difficult to gauge, especially since we now know some margin-dwelling groups once thought to be naturally isolated were in fact refugees from conquest and slaving wars. Many were driven from the more accessible regions where they had once hunted or otherwise exploited nature to survive. Distinct cultures such as the Batwa (BAH-twah), a major Pygmy group of the great Congo rain forest, and the Khoikhoi (COY-coy) and other tribespeople of southern Africa's Kalahari Desert, were until only recently thought to have been unaffected by outsiders before the nineteenth century. Recent scholarship, and most surviving gatherer-hunters themselves, suggest otherwise.

> **FOCUS**
>
> How did the Pygmies' rain forest world differ from the better-known environment of savannas and farms?

Life in the Congo Rain Forest

Still, for the Pygmies, as for many of the world's tropical forest peoples, life has long been distinct from that of settled agriculturalists. Even now, Pygmies live by exploiting the natural forest around them, unaided by manufactured goods. These forests, marked by rugged terrain and washed by superabundant rains, make agriculture and herding impossible. Short of cutting down huge swaths of trees, which in this region often leads to massive soil erosion, neither can be practiced. This is not to say space is limited. Indeed, the Congo River basin is home to the world's second-largest rain forest, after that of the Amazon in South America; it is vast. As in the Amazon, most forest animals are modest in size, with the important exception of the African elephant, which early modern Pygmies occasionally hunted for food and tusks.

Until recent times, most Pygmies were gatherer-hunters. Their superior tracking abilities, limited material possessions, and knowledge of useful forest products such as leaves for dwellings and natural toxins for bow hunting allowed them to retreat in times of external threats such as war. Herding and farming Bantu-speaking and Sudanic neighbors were at a disadvantage in Pygmy country, which

Pygmies of the Congo Rain Forest

Modern-day Pygmies
Here Baka Pygmies of Cameroon and the Central African Republic hunt in the Congo rain forest using nets, sticks, and vines. The woman also carries a machete for butchering the catch and a basket for the meat. Pygmy hunters arrange nets fashioned from vines in forest enclosures to catch small antelope and other game lured or scared into the trap by chants and songs. (Martin Harvey/Peter Arnold/ Photolibrary.)

seems to have prevented Pygmy militarization or formation of defensive confederacies. The Congo rain forest is also attractive in that it is much less affected by malarial mosquitoes than the surrounding farmland. In recent times only a few Pygmy groups, such as the much-studied Mbuti (M-BOOH-tee), have remained separate enough from neighboring farmers and herders to retain their famously short stature and other distinct characteristics. The Pygmies' highly distinctive singing style and instrumentation, most of it Mbuti, has become renowned with the rise of world music recording and distribution.

Everyday Pygmy life has been examined in most detail by anthropologists, many of whom have emphasized differences between Pygmy and neighboring Bantu rituals. Whereas Bantu speakers have venerated dead ancestors in a way that has deeply affected their long-term settlement patterns, warfare, and kin groupings, the Pygmies have long preferred to "let go" of their dead—to move on, as it were. Similarly, whereas Bantu coming-of-age rituals such as circumcision have tended to be elaborate and essential to social reproduction, Pygmies have traditionally marked few distinct phases in life. Most important, the Pygmies have venerated the forest itself as a life-giving spirit, whereas outsiders have treated it as a threatening space and potential source of evil. Has it always been so?

Legendary since ancient Egyptian times for their small, reedlike bodies, simple lifestyles, good-natured humor, and melodious music, the Pygmies have long been held up as the perfect counterpoint to urban civilization and its discontents. It is only recently that the Pygmies and other nonsedentary peoples like them have been treated historically, as makers rather than "nonactors" or victims of history. The absence of written records produced by the Pygmies themselves has made this task difficult, but anthropologists, historians, linguists, and archaeologists working together have made considerable headway.

Pygmy-Bantu Relations

It seems that some time after 1500, the introduction of iron tools and banana cultivation to the central African interior began to alter settlement patterns and overall demography. This change placed Pygmies and Bantu neighbors in closer proximity, as more and more forest was cut for planting and Bantu moved into Pygmy territory. Bantu speakers, some of them refugees from areas attacked by slavers or afflicted by drought, appear to have displaced some Pygmy groups and to have intermarried with others. They seem to have adopted a variety of Pygmy religious beliefs, although Bantu languages mostly displaced original Pygmy ones. Also after 1500, American crops such as peanuts and manioc began to alter sedentary life at the forest's edge, leading to still more interaction, not all of it peaceful, between the Pygmies and their neighbors. Pygmies adopted American capsicum peppers as an everyday spice.

Were the Pygmies driven from the rain forest's edge into its heart as a result of the slave trade? Perhaps in some places, yes, but the evidence is clearer for increased interaction with Bantu migrants. Early effects of globalization on Pygmy life are more easily tracked in terms of foods adopted as a result of the Columbian Exchange. Despite these exchanges and conflicts, the Pygmies have managed to retain a distinct identity that is as intertwined with the rhythms of the forest as it is with the rhythms of settled agriculture.

Although the story of the Pygmies' survival is not as dramatic as that of the Mapuche of Chile (see Chapter 17), their culture's richness and resilience serve as testaments to their peoples' imagination, will, and ingenuity. Their extraordinary adaptation to the rain forest—probably in part a result of early modern historical stresses, which pushed them farther into the forest—reminds us of a shared human tendency to make the most of a given ecological setting, but also that the distinction between civilized and "primitive" lifestyles is a false one, or at least socially constructed.

Conclusion

Western African societies grew and changed according to the rhythms of planting, harvest, trade, and war, and these rhythms continued to define everyday life in early modern times. Droughts, diseases, and pests made subsistence more challenging in sub-Saharan Africa than in most parts of the world, yet people adapted and formed chiefdoms, kingdoms, and empires, often underpinned, at least symbolically, by the control of iron and other metals. Iron tools helped farmers clear forest and till hard soils.

Islam influenced African society and politics across a broad belt south of the Sahara and along the shores of the Indian Ocean, but even this powerful religious tradition was to a degree absorbed by local cultures. Most African states and chiefdoms were not influenced by outside religious influences—or by the conquistadors who wished to impose them—until the late nineteenth century. It was malaria, a disease against which many sub-Saharan Africans had at least some acquired immunity, that proved to be the continent's best defense.

But Africa possessed commodities demanded by outsiders, and despite their failure to penetrate the interior in early modern times, it was these outsiders, first among them the seaborne Portuguese, who set the early modern phase of African history in motion. The Portuguese came looking for gold in the mid-fifteenth century, and once they discovered the dangers of malaria, they stuck to the coast and offshore islands to trade through intermediaries, including coastal chiefs and kings. First they traded for gold, but very soon for war captives. In return, the Portuguese brought horses, cloth, wine, metal goods, and guns. Local chiefs became powerful by allying with the newcomers, and they expanded their trading and raiding ventures deep into the continental interior. Thus began a symbiotic relationship, copied and expanded by the English, Dutch, French, and other northern Europeans, that swelled over four centuries to supply the Americas with some 12 million enslaved African laborers, the largest forced migration in world history. Among these millions of captives, most of whose names we shall never know, was young Domingo Angola, a West Central African teenager caught up in a widening global web of trade, conquest, and religious conversion.

NOTES

1. The story of Domingo Angola is reconstructed from notary documents found in the Ecuadorian National Archive in Quito (Archivo Nacional del Ecuador, Protocolos notariales 1:19 FGD, 1-x-1601, ff. 647–746, and 1:6 DLM, 5-x-1595, f. 287v.) and various studies of the early slave trade, especially Linda Heywood and John Thornton, *Central Africans, Atlantic Creoles, and the Foundation of the Americas, 1585–1660* (New York: Cambridge University Press, 2007). On the Jesuits in Luanda and their involvement in the slave trade at this time, see Dauril Alden, *The Making of an Enterprise: The Society of Jesus in Portugal, Its Empire, and Beyond, 1540–1750* (Stanford, CA: Stanford University Press, 1996), 544–546.

2. Joseph Miller, *Way of Death: Merchant Capitalism and the Angolan Slave Trade, 1730–1830* (Madison: University of Wisconsin Press, 1988), 4–5.

3. George E. Brooks, *Landlords and Strangers: Ecology, Society, and Trade in Western Africa, 1000–1630* (Boulder, CO: Westview Press, 1994).

4. This and other letters are published in António Brásio, ed., *Monumenta Missionaria Africana*, vol. 1, *África Ocidental (1471–1531)* (Lisbon: Agência Geral do Ultramar, 1952), 470–471. (Special thanks to José Curto of York University, Canada, for pointing out this reference.)

5. Olaudah Equiano, *The Interesting Narrative of the Life of Olaudah Equiano, Written by Himself*, 2d ed., introduction by Robert J. Allison (Boston: Bedford/St. Martin's, 2007), 7.

RESOURCES FOR RESEARCH

Many Western Africas

General surveys of precolonial Africa have proliferated in recent years, many incorporating a new range of findings from archaeology, climate studies, and linguistics. The Collins and Burns text is exceptional.

Bisson, Michael, S. Terry Childs, Philip de Barros, and Augustin Holl. *Ancient African Metallurgy: The Socio-cultural Context.* 2000.

Collins, Robert O., and James M. Burns. *A History of Sub-Saharan Africa.* 2007.

Connah, Graham. *African Civilizations: An Archeological Perspective*, 2d ed. 2001.

Ehret, Christopher. *The Civilizations of Africa: A History to 1800.* 2002.

McCann, James C. *Maize and Grace: Africa's Encounter with a New World Crop, 1500–2000.* 2005.

Northrup, David. *Africa's Discovery of Europe, 1450–1850.* 2002.

Webb, James L. A., Jr. *Humanity's Burden: A Global History of Malaria.* 2009.

Landlords and Strangers: Peoples and States in West Africa

Works on West Africa in the early modern period have begun to link internal developments to external factors such as the slave trade and the rise of global markets in a variety of innovative ways, including a focus on metals such as gold, copper, and bronze and crops such as rice, peanuts, and oil palm.

Brooks, George E. *Eurafricans in Western Africa: Commerce, Social Status, Gender, and Religious Observance from the Sixteenth to the Eighteenth Century.* 2003.

Brooks, George E. *Landlords and Strangers: Ecology, Society, and Trade in Western Africa, 1000–1630.* 1994.

Charney, Judith A. *Black Rice: The African Origins of Rice Cultivation in the Americas.* 2001.

Herbert, Eugenia. *Iron, Gender, and Power: Rituals of Transformation in African Societies.* 1993.

Herbert, Eugenia. *Red Gold of Africa: Copper in Precolonial History and Culture.* 1984.

Wright, Donald R. *The World and a Very Small Place in Africa: A History of Globalization in Niumi, The Gambia*, 2d ed. 2004.

Land of the Blacksmith Kings: West Central Africa

Works on early modern West Central Africa have become more detailed and transatlantic in nature in recent years, thanks in part to a host of newly discovered (or newly appreciated) sources in Portuguese, Spanish, and Italian.

Heywood, Linda M., and John Thornton. *Central Africans, Atlantic Creoles, and the Foundation of the Americas, 1585–1660.* 2007.

Hilton, Anne. *The Kingdom of Kongo.* 1985.

Sweet, James H. *Recreating Africa: Culture, Kinship, and Religion in the African-Portuguese World, 1441–1770.* 2003.

Vansina, Jan. *Paths in the Rainforest.* 1990.

Strangers in Ships: Gold, Slavery, and the Portuguese

Literature about the Atlantic slave trade is vast and fast growing. The following is only a small selection of helpful introductory works on the Portuguese era of the slave trade.

Barry, Boubacar. *Senegambia and the Atlantic Slave Trade.* 1998.

Blackburn, Robin. *The Making of New World Slavery from the Baroque to the Modern, 1492–1800.* 1997.

Hawthorne, Walter. *From Africa to Brazil: Culture, Identity, and an Atlantic Slave Trade, 1600–1830.* 2010.

Miller, Joseph. *Way of Death: Merchant Capitalism and the Atlantic Slave Trade, 1780–1830.* 1988.

Thomas, Hugh. *The Slave Trade: The Story of the Atlantic Slave Trade, 1440–1870.* 1997.

Northern Europeans and the Expansion of the Atlantic Slave Trade, 1600–1800

Among the burgeoning literature on the later stages of the Atlantic slave trade are these helpful works. Eltis and Klein offer clear overviews that draw in part from recently constructed databases.

Eltis, David. *The Rise of African Slavery in the Americas.* 2001.

Equiano, Olaudah. *The Interesting Narrative of the Life of Olaudah Equiano, Written by Himself*, 2d ed. Introduction by Robert J. Allison. 2007.

Handler, Jerome S., and Michael L. Tuite Jr. *The Atlantic Slave Trade and Slave Life in the Americas: A Visual Record* (University of Virginia/Virginia Foundation for the Humanities). http://hitchcock.itc.virginia.edu/Slavery/index.php.

Klein, Herbert. *The Atlantic Slave Trade.* 1999.

Law, Robin C. *The Slave Coast of West Africa, 1550–1750: The Impact of the Atlantic Slave Trade on an African Society.* 1990.

COUNTERPOINT: The Pygmies of Central Africa

The Mbuti Pygmy culture has been described in most detail by the anthropologist Colin Turnbull, and his works remain essential. Klieman offers a more historical look at Pygmy relations with Bantu neighbors over the long term.

Klieman, Kairn. *"The Pygmies Were Our Compass": Bantu and Batwa in the History of West Central Africa, Early Times to c. 1900 C.E.* 2003.

Turnbull, Colin. *The Forest People.* 1968.

Turnbull, Colin. *The Mbuti Pygmies: Change and Adaptation.* 1983.

Turnbull, Colin, Francis Chapman, and Michelle Kisliuk. *Mbuti Pygmies of the Ituri Rainforest.* Sound recording. 1992.

▶ **For additional primary sources from this period,** see *Sources of Crossroads and Cultures.*

▶ **For Web sites, images, and documents related to topics in this chapter,** see Make History at bedfordstmartins.com/smith.

The major global development in this chapter ▶ The rise of the Atlantic slave trade and its impact on early modern African peoples and cultures.

IMPORTANT EVENTS

c. 1100–1500	Extended dry period in West Africa prompts migrations
c. 1450	Kingdom of Benin reaches height of its power
1464–1492	Reign of Sunni Ali in the Songhai Empire
1482	Portuguese establish trading fort of São Jorge da Mina (Ghana)
1506–1543	Reign of Afonso I (Nzinga Mbemba) of kingdom of Kongo
1569	Collapse of kingdom of Kongo
1574	Portuguese-aided restoration of kingdom of Kongo
1591	Moroccan raiders conquer Songhai Empire
1621	Formation of Dutch West India Company
1624–1663	Reign of Queen Nzinga in the Ndongo kingdom of Angola
1638–1641	Dutch seize São Jorge da Mina and Luanda
1672	Formation of English Royal African Company
1750–1800	Atlantic slave trade reaches highest volume
1807	British declare Atlantic slave trade illegal

KEY TERMS

African diaspora (p. 584)
fetishism (p. 599)
génie (p. 585)
husbandry (p. 585)
kitomi (p. 599)
manikongo (p. 595)

Middle Passage (p. 605)
oba (p. 592)
paramount chief (p. 586)
peça (p. 595)
pombeiro (p. 599)

CHAPTER OVERVIEW QUESTIONS

1. How did ecological diversity in western Africa relate to cultural developments?

2. What tied western Africa to other parts of the world prior to the arrival of Europeans along Atlantic shores?

3. How did the Atlantic slave trade arise, and how was it sustained?

SECTION FOCUS QUESTIONS

1. What range of livelihoods, cultural practices, and political arrangements typified western Africa in early modern times?

2. What economic, social, and political patterns characterized early modern West Africa?

3. What economic, social, and political patterns characterized early modern West Central Africa?

4. How did the early Portuguese slave trade in western Africa function?

5. What were the major changes in the Atlantic slave trade after 1600?

6. How did the Pygmies' rain forest world differ from the better-known environment of savannas and farms?

MAKING CONNECTIONS

1. How does the Moroccan conquest of Songhai compare with the Spanish conquest of the Aztecs (see Chapter 17)?

2. How did gender roles differ between the kingdoms of West Africa and those of North America's Eastern Woodlands (see Chapter 16)?

3. How did the Portuguese experience in Africa differ from events in Brazil (see Chapter 17)?

4. How did growing European competition for enslaved Africans alter the nature of enslavement and trade in Africa itself?

611

19

AT A CROSSROADS ▶

In this exquisite miniature painting from the 1590s, the Mughal emperor Akbar receives the Persian ambassador Sayyid Beg in 1562. The painting is an illustration commissioned for Akbar's official court history, the *Akbarnama*, and thus would have been seen and approved by the emperor himself. The meeting is emblematic of the generally amiable relationship between the Mughals and their Safavid neighbors in Iran. (Victoria & Albert Museum, London/Art Resource, NY.)

Trade and Empire in the Indian Ocean and South Asia

1450–1750

Born to Persian immigrants in the Afghan city of Kandahar, Princess Mihr un-nisa (meer oon-NEE-sah), known to history as Nur Jahan, or "Light of the World," married the Mughal emperor Jahangir (jah-hahn-GEER) in 1611, at the age of thirty-four. As the emperor increasingly turned his attention to science and the arts, as well as to his addictions to wine and opium, Nur Jahan increasingly assumed the ruler's duties throughout the last decade of her husband's life, which ended in 1627. She had coins struck in her name, and most importantly, she made certain that a daughter from an earlier marriage and her brother's daughter both wed likely heirs to the Mughal throne.

As her husband withdrew from worldly affairs, Nur Jahan actively engaged them. After a visit from the English ambassador in 1613, she developed a keen interest in European manufactures, especially quality textiles. She established domestic industries in cloth manufacture and jewelry making and developed an export trade in indigo dye. Indigo from her farms was shipped to Portuguese and English trading forts along India's west coast, then sent to Lisbon, London, Antwerp, and beyond.

In 1614, Nur Jahan arranged for her niece, Arjumand Banu Begum (AHR-joo-mond bah-noo BEH-goom), to marry Jahangir's favorite son, Prince Khurram, known after he became emperor as Shah Jahan. Arjumand Banu Begum, who took the title Mumtaz Mahal,

BACKSTORY

For centuries before the rise of the Atlantic system (see Chapter 17), the vast Indian Ocean basin thrived as a religious and commercial crossroads. Powered by the annual monsoon wind cycle, traders, mainly Muslim, developed a flourishing commerce over thousands of miles in such luxury goods as spices, gems, and precious metals. The network included the trading enclaves of East Africa and Arabia and the many ports of South and Southeast Asia. Ideas, religious traditions—notably Islam—and pilgrimages moved along the same routes. Throughout the Indian Ocean basin, there was also a trade in enslaved laborers, mostly war captives, including many non-Africans, but this trade grew mostly after the rise of plantation agriculture in the later eighteenth century. The vast majority of the region's many millions of inhabitants were peasant farmers, many of them dependent on wet-rice agriculture.

At the dawn of the early modern period, Hindu kingdoms still flourished in southern India and parts of island Southeast Asia, but these were on the wane. By contrast, some Muslim kingdoms began an expansive phase. After 1500, a key factor in changes throughout the Indian Ocean basin was the introduction of gunpowder weapons from Europe.

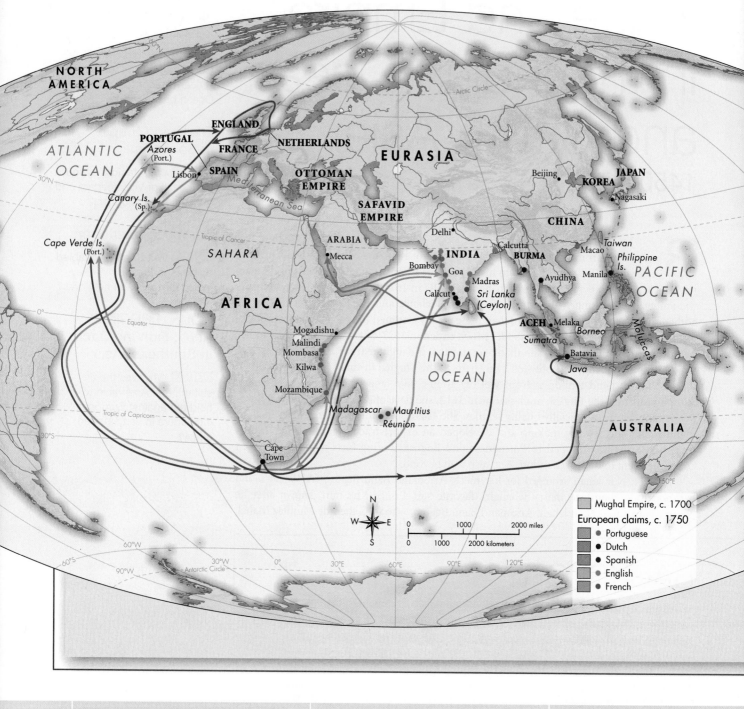

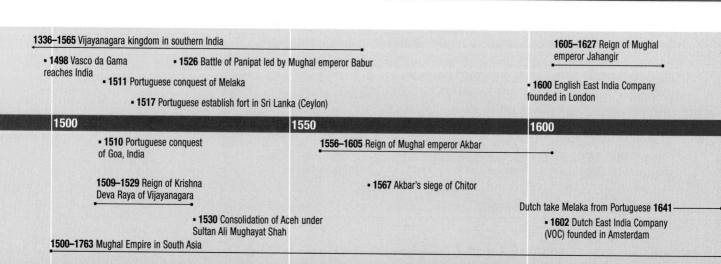

1336–1565 Vijayanagara kingdom in southern India

1498 Vasco da Gama reaches India

1526 Battle of Panipat led by Mughal emperor Babur

1511 Portuguese conquest of Melaka

1517 Portuguese establish fort in Sri Lanka (Ceylon)

1605–1627 Reign of Mughal emperor Jahangir

1600 English East India Company founded in London

1500

1550

1600

1510 Portuguese conquest of Goa, India

1509–1529 Reign of Krishna Deva Raya of Vijayanagara

1556–1605 Reign of Mughal emperor Akbar

1567 Akbar's siege of Chitor

1530 Consolidation of Aceh under Sultan Ali Mughayat Shah

1500–1763 Mughal Empire in South Asia

Dutch take Melaka from Portuguese **1641**

1602 Dutch East India Company (VOC) founded in Amsterdam

died in 1631 while bearing her fourteenth child for her emperor husband. Heartbroken, Shah Jahan went into mourning for two full years. He commissioned the construction of an extraordinary mausoleum for his beloved Mumtaz in the sacred city of Agra. This graceful structure of white marble, among the architectural wonders of the world, is known as the Taj Mahal.

Nur Jahan attended court with her head and breasts covered only by wisps of gauze. She rode horses proudly in public without her husband. Such conduct was not considered inappropriate for a woman of her status in her time. Like other South Asian noblewomen, Nur Jahan expressed her rank through public piety, commissioning a number of religious buildings, including her father's and her husband's mausoleums, as well as many elaborate gardens, several of which survive. She continued to play an active and sometimes controversial role in politics until her death in 1644, occasionally supporting rivals of Shah Jahan.

For most of the early modern period the lands surrounding the Indian Ocean remained in the hands of powerful local rulers, as exemplified by Nur Jahan. As in western Africa, but in stark contrast to much of the Americas, it took European interlopers several centuries to gain the lasting footholds that enabled the widespread imperial takeover after 1800 (discussed in Chapter 26). Again like western Africans and unlike the native peoples of the Americas, the inhabitants of the greater Indian Ocean basin had acquired over time at least some immunity to European microbes, so their resistance was not hobbled by waves of deadly disease.

Trade on the Indian Ocean during the age of sail followed the **monsoons**, semiannual alternating dry and humid winds generated by the seasonal heating and cooling of air masses above the vast Asian continent. To exploit these reliable winds, Arab sailors developed swift, triangular-rigged vessels. Southeast Asians introduced much larger square-riggers influenced by Chinese shipbuilding techniques, and by 1500 the Portuguese arrived from the North Atlantic in well-armed, sturdy vessels rigged with both square and triangular sails and capable of years-long voyages through heavy seas. It was the wide array of luxury trade goods, along with religious pilgrimage sites such as Mecca and Benares, that made this area a vibrant saltwater crossroads.

monsoon A wind system that influences large climatic regions such as the Indian Ocean basin and reverses direction seasonally.

MAPPING THE WORLD
The Indian Ocean and South Asia, 1450–1750

Harnessing the power of monsoon winds, Arab and Asian sailors traversed the Indian Ocean and Arabian Sea for centuries before the Portuguese arrived in the 1490s, in search of pepper and other commodities. In subsequent years, competing Eurasian interlopers, including the Ottomans, conquered key ports from East Africa to Southeast Asia in an attempt to control both exports to Europe and interregional trade. The Ottomans retreated after the mid-sixteenth century, but many Muslims continued to sail to the Arabian peninsula to make the pilgrimage to Mecca and to engage in trade.

ROUTES ▼

→ Portuguese *Carreira da India* (Voyage to India)
→ Dutch trade route
→ Major pilgrimage route

1641–1699 Sultanate of Women in Aceh

1764 British East India Company controls Bengal

1700 **1750** **1800**

1658 Dutch drive Portuguese from Ceylon

1701 William Kidd hanged in London for piracy

1739 Persian raiders under Nadir Shah sack Delhi

The Indian Ocean basin, which some historians and linguists have termed the Afrasian Sea, was defined by interlinked maritime and overland networks. Despite repeated attempts, no state ever totally controlled the great basin's exchange of goods, people, and ideas. Religious diversity and relative political independence were the rule. Even Islam, the most widespread religion, was not practiced in exactly the same way in any two places. Muslims from East Africa, Arabia, Persia, and South, Southeast, and East Asia all maintained distinct identities despite a shared religion, distant mercantile connections, and even long-term residence and intermarriage in foreign ports.

India, with its huge, mostly Hindu population, lay at the center of the Afrasian Sea trading system. The black pepper of Malabar, on the southwest coast, was world-famous, as were the diamonds of Golconda, in the southern interior. But it was India's cotton fabrics, linking countless farmers, artisans, and brokers, that brought in most foreign exchange. As in the Mediterranean and Atlantic trading systems, gold from sub-Saharan Africa and later silver from the Americas were the essential lubricants of trade. Nur Jahan minted rupees in American silver and African gold.

The Portuguese reached India in 1498. They had three key goals: to monopolize the spice trade to Europe, to tax or take over key shipping lanes, and to fight the expansion of Islam and spread Christianity instead. With the brief exception of the Ottomans in the first half of the sixteenth century, no land-based empire in the region attempted to stop them. Persia's Safavids and South Asia's Mughals might have done so, but they preferred to play off the later-arriving English, French, and Dutch against the Portuguese—and against one another. Given these empires' overwhelming strength on land, this strategy made sense, but as in Africa, leaving sea power to the Europeans proved a fateful decision.

The arrival of the Portuguese coincided with the rise of the Islamic Mughal Empire in India beginning about 1500. Though a land empire much like China under the Ming (see Chapter 15), the Mughal state was thoroughly connected to the outside world. Wealthy and well armed, the Mughals seemed invincible to many neighbors and outsiders. Certainly European conquest was unthinkable in the seventeenth century, the era of Nur Jahan. Her life exemplifies both the colorful court life typical of Eurasia's so-called gunpowder empires, as well as the outward gaze and self-consciousness these states' rulers exhibited.

The term "gunpowder empire" was coined by historian Marshall Hodgson to help explain the rise of the Mughal, Safavid, Ottoman, and other states whose rapid expansion after 1500 was enabled by Western-style cannons, muskets, and other firearms.[1] Historians also apply the term to the Safavid and Ottoman states and the Spanish, Portuguese, and other European kingdoms that took their new and powerful weaponry abroad in the name of commerce and Christianity. Unlike their ocean-going European adversaries, however, the great land empires of Central and South Asia were motivated by neither trade nor religion; their goal in expanding was to extract tributes from neighboring populations.

Despite the rise and fall of gunpowder empires on land and at sea, historical records suggest that most inhabitants of the greater Indian Ocean carried on much as they had before. There were certain changes, however. Especially in cash-crop-producing regions, such as Ceylon (Sri Lanka) off India's south coast and Aceh in Indonesia, demands on ordinary laborers and on productive lands sharply increased. Religious change took place, too. Although Islamic land empires such as that of the Mughals advanced, Islam grew most notably in politically fractured Southeast Asia. As in western Africa and unlike in the Americas, very few people in this vast region adopted Christianity.

For a time, South Asia held competing Europeans at bay in spite of their advanced gun-making and shipbuilding technologies. Starting in the seventeenth century, however, the European powers began to exploit the region's open seas and political divisions to advance land-based conquest and colonization. As they had done in the Americas, Europeans divided the Indian Ocean's shores, waterways, and islands into rigidly controlled colonial plantations and monopoly trading zones. Local lords were co-opted or, if resistant, deposed. In the end, the relative peace, prosperity, and cultural diversity that had once blocked foreign control helped facilitate it.

OVERVIEW
QUESTIONS

The major global development in this chapter: The Indian Ocean trading network and the impact of European intrusion on maritime and mainland South Asia.

As you read, consider:

1. What environmental, religious, and political factors enabled trading enclaves to flourish in the Indian Ocean basin?

2. How did the rise and fall of India's land empires reflect larger regional trends?

3. How did Europeans insert themselves into the Indian Ocean trading network, and what changes did they bring about?

Trading Cities and Inland Networks: East Africa

The history of early modern East Africa is best understood in terms of linkages among the numerous Indian Ocean traders from as far away as China and the cities and peoples of the African interior. Brokering Africa's ties to Asia were merchant families and local princes clustered along a string of port towns and cities stretching from Ethiopia in the northeast to Mozambique in the southeast.

FOCUS

How did Swahili Coast traders link the East African interior to the Indian Ocean basin?

By 1500, it was mainly Muslims who lived in these thriving East African trading ports. Some were descendants of early Persian, Arabian, and South Asian overseas traders and missionaries, but the vast majority were native Africans, mostly Bantu speakers. Swahili, still commonly spoken in much of this region, is a Bantu language laced with Arabic terms. In early modern times, scribes recorded transactions in Swahili using Arabic script. Thus, the society and culture of East African trading ports blended African and Asian elements, reflecting the economic connections between the two regions.

Portuguese and Ottoman traders arrived in these ports around 1500, but neither managed to control more than a few of them at a time. Dutch, French, and English merchants arrived in the seventeenth century, but they, too, failed to monopolize East African trade. Offshore, the French established a minor presence on the huge island of Madagascar and then on much smaller Réunion, a future plantation colony, but neither island had been vital to the ancient monsoon trading circuit. As free from each other as they were from outsiders, the hundred-odd ports of East Africa's Swahili Coast remained largely independent until the imperial scramble of the late nineteenth century (discussed in Chapter 26).

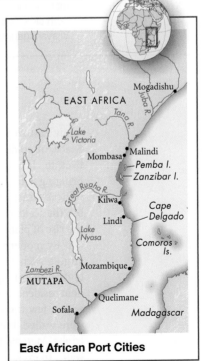

East African Port Cities

Port Towns and Beginnings

By the early modern period, the East African coast had served as a regional crossroads for more than a thousand years. Archaeologists have recently determined that Muslim trader-missionaries had reached

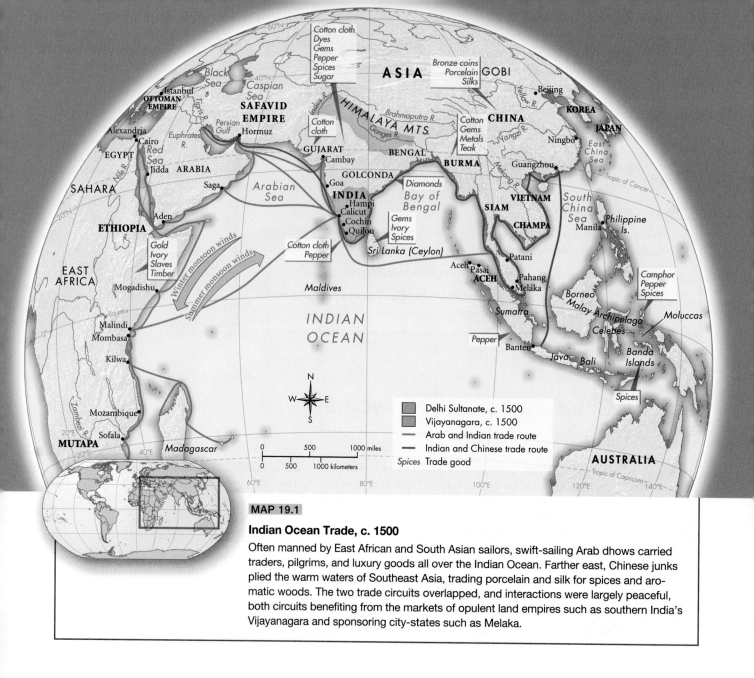

MAP 19.1

Indian Ocean Trade, c. 1500

Often manned by East African and South Asian sailors, swift-sailing Arab dhows carried traders, pilgrims, and luxury goods all over the Indian Ocean. Farther east, Chinese junks plied the warm waters of Southeast Asia, trading porcelain and silk for spices and aromatic woods. The two trade circuits overlapped, and interactions were largely peaceful, both circuits benefiting from the markets of opulent land empires such as southern India's Vijayanagara and sponsoring city-states such as Melaka.

many East African port towns by the eighth century C.E., soon after the founding of Islam. Seaborne trade in ivory, gold, ceramics, and other items was even older, however, dating back to classical antiquity. Early modern East African traders continued this commerce, bringing luxury goods from Central, South, and even East Asia to the coast in exchange for Africa's treasured raw materials. Traders also exchanged slaves for luxuries on occasion, but the scale of the Indian Ocean slave trade seems to have remained relatively small until the rise of plantations in the nineteenth century.

By modern urban standards, most East African trading ports were small towns. The largest, such as Kilwa, Sofala, Malindi, and Mombasa, had no more than 10,000 inhabitants at their height. Most towns were much smaller, home to only several hundred permanent residents. Quelimane (keh-lee-MAH-neh) and Mogadishu fell somewhere in between, with a few thousand inhabitants. Nearly all of the region's cities and many of the towns were walled, but only the most opulent had mosques of stone or coral block rather than adobe. Merchants, resident and foreign, occupied house blocks clustered within each city's walls. In exchange for tributes, local princes protected merchant families, negotiating with sometimes hostile inland chiefdoms for trade goods and subsistence items.

Indian Ocean Connections

East African traders exported elephant tusks and gold in exchange for South Asian cloth, much of it from Cambay in the Gujarat region of northwest India (see Map 19.1). They also imported Persian and even Chinese ceramics, along with spices, tobacco (after 1500), and a host of other items. African ivory was especially prized throughout Asia for its soft texture, and African gold, mostly from the southern interior, was always in high demand as currency. In much of India, women brought dowries of gold when they married, displaying it in the form of fine jewelry. As we have seen in previous chapters, African gold was an essential world currency prior to European expansion into the Americas.

Most goods were carried in **dhows** (dowz), swift, single-decked ships with triangular sails and about two hundred tons' capacity. Traders used smaller vessels and dugout canoes to navigate rivers such as the great Zambezi and to ferry goods through the treacherous coral reefs that lay between East Africa's towns.

Despite the extraordinary value of most Indian Ocean trade goods, shippers traveled only lightly armed. Although piracy had long been known, and was even expected in waters such as India's Malabar Coast, violent theft at sea seems to have become a serious threat to Indian Ocean commerce only after the arrival of the Portuguese, who sought to establish and defend their trading monopolies through brute force. Their actions in turn encouraged contraband trade and the fencing of stolen goods.

Chinese maritime visits to East Africa, though memorable, were few and far between. As we saw in Chapter 15, the famous Ming admiral Zheng He arrived first in Malindi in the late 1410s, and then at Mogadishu in the early 1430s. Zheng He's vessels were enormous, more than double the size of the largest Portuguese ships to arrive about a century later. In addition to the standard gold and ivory, the Ming admiral filled his ample holds with local items, including a veritable zoo for the Chinese emperor. There is no evidence of attempts to conquer or to establish trading posts or colonies, and afterward Chinese goods came to East Africa

dhow A small sailing vessel with triangular rigs used in monsoon trade to East Africa.

Exchanger of Cambay

In this early-sixteenth-century watercolor, apparently by a self-taught Portuguese artist, a merchant in Cambay, on India's northwest coast, collects and changes gold, silver, and other coins of many mint marks and denominations. A tiny balance hangs behind him on one side, and a strongbox seems to float in midair on the other. To the right, people of many faiths, clothing styles, and colors come to seek his services. At least two are women bearing gold coins. (Ms 1889 at the Biblioteca Casanatense, Rome.)

again only through Southeast Asian intermediaries, often Muslim Malays. The Chinese retreat from the Indian Ocean left a void that early modern European interlopers were happy to fill.

Links to the Interior

Less often described than East Africa's ties to overseas merchants were its links to the African interior. The extent of each port's productive hinterlands or subsistence grounds was generally small, but coastal towns and cities did not simply face outward, as once believed. Almost all Swahili town-dwellers relied on nearby agricultural plots for their day-to-day survival, and many engaged in regular exchanges with independent cattle herders. Many Swahili elites owned slaves purchased from the interior, who produced food for both their masters and themselves. The African products in greatest demand overseas, however, came from the more densely populated southern interior.

Products from the Interior   This was most true of gold dust, traded northward from the mouth of the Zambezi River (see again Map 19.1). Its main sources were the many goldfields of the Mutapa kingdom (formerly Great Zimbabwe), located on the Zimbabwe Plateau. Here, as in parts of contemporary West Africa, men and women panned for gold in the agricultural off-season. A few mines went underground. The historical record is spotty, but it appears that an annual average of at least a ton of gold entered the Indian Ocean trade circuit during the sixteenth century.

Ivory was a different sort of product; collecting it required the hunting and slaughter of wild animals. Although modern demand for ivory has led to the extinction of elephants in parts of Africa, it appears that most of the tusks fed into the early modern Indian Ocean circuit were a byproduct of subsistence hunting. Hunters only went out seasonally, and without firearms. Bringing down an adult elephant with spears and longbows was an extremely dangerous business, and the compensation was not attractive enough to make it a livelihood. Aside from the dangers of ivory procurement, interior peoples such as the Shona speakers of the Mutapa kingdom were not easily pressured into market exchanges of any kind. With no particular need for Asian products, they carried ivory and gold to the seaports at their leisure.

An important export from the north Swahili Coast was lumber, specifically mangrove hardwoods for residential construction in desert regions of Arabia and the Red Sea. The exact ecological consequences of this enterprise have yet to be determined, but like the trade in tusks and gold, it appears not to have exhausted the resource. Extractive industries in the early modern period usually damaged the environment only in relation to their scale.

Arrival of the Portuguese   By 1500 trade was thriving throughout East Africa and its partners in the Indian Ocean basin. The arrival of the Portuguese at about that time would disrupt that valuable balance. With nothing to offer the well-off merchants of East Africa, India, and the Arabian Sea region, the Portuguese turned to force. Using their guns, stout vessels, and Mediterranean fort-building techniques, they sought to profit from the Indian Ocean trade by impeding it—that is, by enforcing monopolies on certain items and taking over vital ports. Ultimately this worked better in India than elsewhere, but the Portuguese tried desperately to gain control of East African trade, and even to penetrate the continent's southeast interior in search of Mutapa's fabled gold. Although they failed to conquer the Mutapa state, the Portuguese traded with its rulers and gained control of gold exports. As they had done in western Africa, in East Africa the Portuguese concentrated most of their energies on capturing and fortifying posts, or *feitorias*, which they established at Mozambique, Sofala, and Mombasa. The Dutch and English would soon follow.

Trade and Empire in South Asia

FOCUS

What factors account for the fall of
Vijayanagara and the rise of the Mughals?

As in East Africa, despite competition and occasional violence, dozens of independent trading enclaves in South Asia prospered in early modern times. Many coastal cities and their surrounding hinterlands were subject to Muslim sultans or Hindu princes, most of whom drew their sustenance from the merchants they protected. Trading populations were larger than those of East

Africa and more diverse. Religious minorities included Jains, Jews, Parsis (Zoroastrians), and Christians. Among the region's most densely packed commercial crossroads, India's port cities maintained close ties to the subcontinent's rich and well-interconnected interior, at this time home to two major empires. One was in ascendance, the Muslim Mughal Empire in the north, and the other in decline, the Hindu kingdom of Vijayanagara (vizh-ah-ya-na-GAR-ah) in the south (see again Map 19.1).

Vijayanagara's Rise and Fall 1336–1565

Vijayanagara grew into an empire around 1500, only to disintegrate due to internal factionalism and external, mostly northern Muslim (although not Mughal) attacks. Because of its swift demise and the near-total loss of its written records, Vijayanagara remains one of the most enigmatic empires of the early modern period. With Muslim kingdoms dominating much of the subcontinent by the time the Portuguese arrived offshore around 1500, Hindu Vijayanagara appears to have been something of an anachronism. Like the contemporary Aztec and Inca empires of the Americas, Vijayanagara was neither a gunpowder empire nor an early modern, bureaucratic state. Its material record constitutes a major but still limited source for historians. Massive stone temple structures and lively artistic works hint at great opulence and power, but the nature of daily life for commoners remains obscure, although it has been reconstructed in part by archaeological work and from the observations of early European visitors.

Literally, "city of triumph," the kingdom of Vijayanagara was said to have been founded by two brothers in 1336. They chose the town site of Hampi, deep in the southern interior, to revive a purist version of the Hindu state. According to legend, the brothers had been captured in northern frontier wars and forced to convert to Islam in Delhi, but once back in their homeland they renounced that faith and sought the advice of Hindu Brahmans.

Hampi
This is an aerial view of part of Hampi, ancient capital of the Hindu kingdom of Vijayanagara in south-central India. The main temple rises in the smoky distance, marking the end of a long ceremonial promenade fronted by stone structures. The Tungabhadra River winds alongside, and all around are hills strewn with granite boulders, giving the city a primeval, almost timeless feel. Hampi fell to northern invaders in 1565. (Colin McPherson/Corbis.)

Hundreds of temples were quickly built along the Tungabadhra River gorge to venerate the state's patron deity, Virupaksha (vee-rooh-PAHK-shah), among others. Thus, the kingdom's identity was explicitly Hindu. By 1370, the empire covered most of southern India, with the exception of Malabar in the far southwest.

Divine Kingship

Whereas Muslim and Christian rulers were generally regarded as pragmatic "warriors of the faith," Hindu rulers were often seen as divine kings. Their most important duties involved performing the sacred rituals believed to sustain their kingdoms. Whether in Vijayanagara or in distant Bali in Southeast Asia, Hindu kingship relied on theatricality and symbolism quite removed from the everyday concerns of imperial administration. Early modern Hindu kings did participate in warfare and other serious matters, but their lives were mostly scripted by traditional sacred texts. Their societies believed that they would ensure prosperity in peacetime and victory in war by properly enacting their roles, which bordered on the priestly.

Life in Vijayanagara cycled between a peaceful period, when the king resided in the capital and carried out rituals, and a campaign season, when the king and his retinue traveled the empire battling with neighboring states and principalities. Like so much under Hindu rule, even victory on the field was scripted, and the warring season itself served as a reenactment of legendary battles. Each campaign started with a great festival reaffirming the king's divinity. Although he was renowned for his piety, it was his martial prowess that most set him apart from mere mortals. He was the exemplar of the **Kshatriya** (K-SHAH-tree-yah) or warrior **caste**, not the technically higher-ranking **Brahman** or priestly caste.

Krishna Deva Raya

Celebratory temple inscriptions record the names and deeds of many monarchs, but thanks to the records of foreign visitors the Vijayanagara king we know most about was Krishna Deva Raya (r. 1509–1529). Portuguese merchants and ambassadors traveled to his capital and court on several occasions, and all were stunned by the monarch's wealth and pomp. At his height, Krishna Deva Raya controlled most of India south of the Krishna River. Most of India's famed diamonds were mined nearby, providing a significant source of state revenue. But it was the constant flow of tribute from the *rajas*, the subject princes, that built his "city of triumph." Imperial demand drove the rajas to trade their products for Indian Ocean luxuries such as African gold and ivory. The king sat upon a diamond-studded throne, and two hundred subject princes attended him constantly at court. Each wore a gold ankle bracelet to indicate his willingness to die on the king's behalf.

Krishna Deva Raya welcomed the Portuguese following their 1510 conquest of Muslim-held Goa (GO-ah), a port on India's west coast that would become the keystone of Portugal's overseas empire. His armies required warhorses in the tens of thousands, and an arrangement with the Portuguese would give him easier access to horses from Arabia and Iraq. As they had done in western Africa, the Portuguese happily served as horse-traders to conquering non-Christian kings in exchange for access to key trade goods. Krishna Deva Raya used the imported mounts to extend Vijayanagara's borders north and south, and the Portuguese sent home some of the largest diamonds yet seen in Europe.

Imperial Organization

Vijayanagara shared some features with the roughly contemporaneous Aztec and Inca states—it was a tributary empire built on a combination of military force and religious charisma. Subject princes were required to maintain substantial armies and give surpluses to their king at periodic festivals; material display reaffirmed the king's divinity. Proper subordination of the rajas was equally important. Krishna Deva Raya was said to require so much gold from certain rajas that they were forced to sponsor pirates to generate revenue. Most tribute, however, came from the sale of farm products, cloth, and diamonds.

Above the rajas, Krishna Deva Raya appointed district administrators called *nayaks*. These were usually trusted relatives, and each oversaw a number of lesser kingdoms. The whole system was intended to both replicate and feed the center, with each raja and nayak sponsoring temple construction and revenue-generating projects of various sorts. Large-scale irrigation works improved agricultural yields, and at bridge crossings and city gates, officials taxed goods transported by ox-cart, donkey, and other means. The demands of the city and empire inevitably placed great pressure on southern India's forests and wetlands, and increased diamond mining sped deforestation and erosion of riverbanks. As in most

Kshatriya A member of the warrior caste in Hindu societies.

caste A hereditary social class separated from others in Hindu societies.

Brahman A member of the priestly caste in Hindu societies.

instances of imperial expansion, environmental consequences quickly became evident but were not, as far as we know, a major cause of decline.

Dependent as it was on trade, the expansion of Vijayanagara required a policy of religious tolerance similar to that later practiced by the Mughals. Jain merchants and minor princes were particularly important subjects since they helped link Vijayanagara to the world beyond India. Brahmanic or priestly law largely restricted Hindu trade to the land, whereas Jains could freely go abroad. Muslim coastal merchants were also allowed into the imperial fold, especially because they had far greater access than the Jains to luxury imports and warhorses. They had their own residential quarter in the city of Hampi. The early Portuguese policy in India was to exploit niches in this pre-existing trade system—not to conquer Vijayanagara, but simply to drive out competing Muslim merchants.

Though connected to the outside world mainly through the luxury goods trade, the empire's economy was based on large-scale rice cultivation. While kings and Brahmans reenacted the lives of the gods, the vast majority of Vijayanagara's subjects toiled their lives away as rice farmers. Around 1522 the Portuguese visitor Domingos Paes (see Reading the Past: Portuguese Report of a Vijayanagara Festival) described work on a huge, stone-reinforced reservoir: "In the tank I saw so many people at work that there must have been fifteen or twenty thousand men, looking like ants, so that you could not see the ground on which they walked."[2]

Vijayanagara's irrigated rice fed its people, but it was also a key export product. Special varieties were shipped as far abroad as Hormuz, on the Persian Gulf, and Aden, at the mouth of the Red Sea. More common rice varieties, along with sugar and some spices, provisioned the merchants of many Indian Ocean ports, including those of East Africa and Gujarat. It was through the sale of rice abroad that many subject princes obtained African gold for their king, with annual payments said to be in the thousands of pounds each by the time of Krishna Deva Raya. Hence, like luxury goods, rice was not only a key component in the trade relationships connecting the kingdom to the outside world; it also connected Vijayanagara's elites to each other, helping to define their political and social relationships.

Following Krishna Deva Raya's death in 1529, Vijayanagara fell victim first to internal succession rivalries, and then to Muslim aggressors. In 1565, under King Ramaraja, a coalition of formerly subject sultans defeated the royal army. Hampi, the capital city, was sacked, plundered, and abandoned; it was an overgrown ruin by 1568. Remnant Hindu principalities survived for a time in the southeast but eventually fell to the expansionist Mughals. By the seventeenth century only a few Hindu states remained around the fringes of South Asia, including remote Nepal. The Hindu principalities of Malabar, meanwhile, fell increasingly into the hands of Europeans and Muslim Gujarati merchants. Still, the memory of Vijayanagara's greatness and wealth lived on, to be revived much later by Hindu nationalists.

Rice Cultivation and Export

The Power of the Mughals

Another empire was expanding rapidly in India's north as Vijayanagara crumbled in the south. Beginning around 1500, under a Timurid (from Timur, the famed fourteenth-century Central Asian ruler discussed in Chapter 15) Muslim warlord named Babur (the "Tiger," r. 1500–1530), the Mughal Empire emerged as the most powerful, wealthy, and populous state yet seen in South Asia. By the time of Nur Jahan in the early 1600s, the Mughals (literally "Mongols," the great fourteenth-century emperors from whom the Mughals descended) had over 120 million subjects, a population comparable only to that of Ming China. Accumulating wealth from plunder and tribute and employing newly introduced gunpowder weapons and swift warhorses to terrifying effect, the Mughals subdued dozens of Hindu and Muslim principalities as they pushed relentlessly southward (see Map 19.2). Like many early modern empire builders, the Mughals were outsiders who adapted to local cultural traditions to establish and maintain legitimacy. In terms of Indian Ocean commerce, their rapid rise drove up demand for luxury imports, and, as in the case

READING THE PAST

Portuguese Report of a Vijayanagara Festival

The Portuguese merchant Domingos Paes (PAH-ish) visited Vijayanagara in 1520 with a larger diplomatic and commercial mission sent from Goa, the Portuguese trading post on India's southwest coast. Paes's report of the capital of Hampi and King Krishna Deva Raya's court, apparently written for the Portuguese court's official chronicler back in Lisbon, is among the richest to survive. Below, Paes describes part of a multiday festival that served to glorify the king and reaffirm the hierarchy of the state, and also to reenact cosmic battles.

> At three o'clock in the afternoon everyone comes to the palace. They do not admit everyone at once . . . but there go inside only the wrestlers and dancing-women, and the elephants, which go with their trappings and decorations, those that sit on them being armed with shields and javelins, and wearing quilted tunics. As soon as these are inside they range themselves around the arena, each one in his or her place. . . . Many other people are then at the entrance gate opposite to the building, namely Brahmins, and the sons of the king's favorites, and their relations; all these noble youths who serve before the king. The officers of the household go about keeping order amongst all the people, and keep each one in his or her own place. . . .
>
> The king sits dressed in white clothes all covered with [embroidery of] golden roses and wearing his jewels—he wears a quantity of these white garments, and I always saw him so dressed—and around him stand his pages with his betel [to chew], and his sword, and the other things which are his insignia of state. . . . As soon as the king is seated, the captains who waited outside make their entrance, each one by himself, attended by his chief people. . . . As soon as the nobles have finished entering, the captains of the troops approach with shields and spears, and afterwards the captains of archers. . . . As soon as these soldiers have all taken their places the women begin to dance. . . . Who can fitly describe to you the great riches these women carry on their persons?—collars of gold with so many diamonds and rubies and pearls, bracelets also on their arms and upper arms, girdles below, and of necessity anklets on their feet. . . .
>
> Then the wrestlers begin their play. Their wrestling does not seem like ours, but there are blows [given], so severe as to break teeth, and put out eyes, and disfigure faces, so much so that here and there men are carried off speechless by their friends; they give one another fine falls, too. They have their captains and judges who are there to put each one on equal footing in the field, and also to award the honors to him who wins.

Source: Robert Sewell, *A Forgotten Empire (Vijayanagara): A Contribution to the History of India* (London: Sonnenschein, 1900), 268–271.

EXAMINING THE EVIDENCE

1. What does the selection suggest regarding social hierarchy and prescribed gender roles in Vijayanagara?

2. How does the divine kingship described here compare with that of the Incas (see Chapter 16)?

of Nur Jahan, some high-ranking Mughal nobles invested directly in exports of items such as indigo and gems.

Religious Toleration

Despite rule by Muslim overlords, most South Asians remained Hindus in early modern times, but those who converted to Islam enjoyed some benefits. Initially, conversion to Islam brought exemption from certain taxes, but these exemptions were suspended in the late sixteenth century under Emperor Akbar. As we will see, during and after his reign, lasting fusions between Hinduism and Islam emerged in various parts of the subcontinent.

Expanded Trade

Like its religion, South Asia's dynamic and highly productive economy was little changed after conquest. Under Mughal rule, South Asia's legendary textiles, grains, spices, gems, and many other products continued to find buyers worldwide. Truly new markets for Indian goods emerged in the Americas and parts of sub-Saharan Africa, supplied by Portuguese and other European shippers. Lacking commodities Indians wanted, European traders paid for South Asia's goods in hard cash. As a result India, like China, enjoyed a consistently favorable balance of trade throughout early modern times. Along with funding armies, this wealth from abroad fueled construction, especially of religious buildings. With royal sponsorship like that of Nur Jahan, many of India's most famous architectural gems, such as the Taj Mahal and Red Fort, were built along the Ganges River plain.

True to the Timurid heritage it shared with its Safavid Persian and Ottoman Turkish neighbors (discussed in the next chapter), Mughal rule in India was marked by both extraordinary court opulence and near-constant power struggles and rebellions. As in many other empires not constrained by rules of primogeniture, factionalism and succession crises eventually led to Mughal decline. Soon after 1700, this decline in central authority left Mughal India vulnerable to European as well as Persian imperial designs. Persian raiders sacked the capital of Delhi in 1739, and by 1763 the English East India Company won rights to tax former Mughal subjects in the vast province of Bengal, effectively exercising sovereignty in the Indian interior. Despite these top-level reversals of fortune, life for the bulk of South Asia's millions of poor farmers and artisans scarcely changed.

Gunpowder Weapons and Imperial Consolidation 1500–1763

The emperor, or "Mughal," Babur spent most of his life defeating Afghan warlords. Horses and archers were still critical in these early victories, as was Babur's charismatic leadership, but by the 1510s some of the emperor's most important forces were using matchlock guns in battle. By the 1526 Battle of Panipat, outside Delhi, Babur's armies had perfected the use of cannons (see again Map 19.2). As Babur recalled nonchalantly in his memoir, the *Baburnama*: "Mustafa the artilleryman fired some good shots from the mortars mounted on carts to the left of the center [flank]." Some 16,000 men were said to have died in this battle, and Babur celebrated by plundering the great city of Agra. In 1527, although hugely outnumbered by a Hindu Rajput alliance of some 80,000 cavalry and 500 armored war elephants, Babur and his army won handily. "From the center [flank of troops commanded by] our dear eldest son, Muhammad Humayun, Mustafa Rumi brought forward the caissons, and with matchlocks and mortars broke not only the ranks of the infidel but their hearts as well."[3] Gunpowder weapons continued to prove decisive as Babur and his successors drove south.

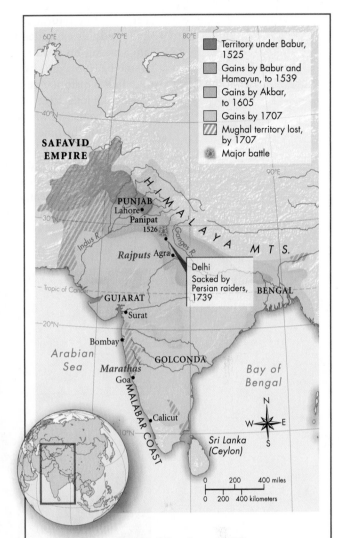

MAP 19.2 **The Mughal Empire, c. 1700**

Descendants of mounted Central Asian raiders, the Mughals expanded their control over the Indian subcontinent from the northwest after 1500. They did so with devastating, gunpowder-backed force followed by ethnic and religious accommodation. The majority of Mughal subjects did not practice the conquerors' Islamic faith, and some historians have even argued that India conquered the Mughals rather than the other way around. By 1700, the empire was approaching its greatest extent, after which rebellions and invasions began to force it to contract.

Humayun, as Babur's son was known, took over the emerging Mughal Empire at his father's death in 1530, but he suffered setbacks. In 1535, he employed Ottoman military engineers and Portuguese gunners to attack the kingdom of Gujarat, a major textile exporter facing the Arabian Sea, but sources say his crippling addiction to opium cost valuable time and led to a forced withdrawal of troops. In the course of this ill-fated adventure, an Afghan warlord rose from the ashes to reconquer almost everything Babur had won in the north. Humayun went into exile in Safavid

Persia, but he returned to India aided by gun-toting Safavid forces. By 1555, Humayun had used this expanded firepower to regain his father's conquests, only to die in 1556 after hitting his head on the stairs of his library. Councilors decided the next Mughal would be Humayun's twelve-year-old son, Akbar.

Akbar the Great

India's historic role as an interfaith and intercultural crossroads was only heightened during the long reign of Akbar (literally "the Great," r. 1556–1605). Though founded by Timurid horsemen who regarded themselves as warriors of the Islamic faith in the Sunni tradition, by the time of Akbar a quick succession of marriages had linked Shi'ite Safavid and Hindu royalty to the central Mughal line. For over a century Persian remained the language of the court, and relations with the Safavids were friendly. Most notable, however, was the steady "Indianization" of the Mughal emperors themselves. The wealth and diversity of the subcontinent, not to mention the beauty and charm of Hindu Rajput princesses, absorbed them. Akbar was no exception; his son Jahangir, the next emperor, was born to a Hindu princess.

Taj Mahal

The Mughal emperor Shah Jahan (r. 1627–1658) commissioned this spectacular mausoleum, the Taj Mahal, in memory of his wife, Mumtaz Mahal. The structure includes Persian elements, in part because many Persian artisans worked in the Mughal court. But its quality of near-ethereal lightness, rising from the delicately carved white marble and long reflecting pool, marks it as Indian and Mughal. (Marco Pavan/Grand Tour/Corbis.)

This process of absorption was greatly accelerated by Akbar's eclectic personality. Fascinated with everything from yogic asceticism to the fire worship of India's Parsi, or Zoroastrian, minority, by the 1570s Akbar began formulating his own hybrid religion. It was a variety of emperor worship forced mostly upon high-ranking subjects. Somewhat like the early modern Inca and Japanese royal cults that tied the ruling house to the sun, Akbar's cult emphasized his own divine solar radiance. Staunch Muslim advisers rebelled against this seeming heresy in 1579, but Akbar successfully repressed them. In the end, Akbar's faith won few lasting converts—and left visiting Jesuit missionaries scratching their heads—yet its mere existence demonstrated an enduring Mughal tendency toward accommodation of religious difference.

Despite his eclecticism and toleration, Akbar clung to core Timurid cultural traditions, such as moving his court and all its attendant wealth and servants from one grand campsite to another. He was said to travel with no fewer than 100,000 attendants. He also never gave up his attachment to gunpowder warfare. Recalcitrant regional lords such as the Rajput Hindu prince Udai Singh defied Akbar's authority in the 1560s, only to suffer the young emperor's wrath. A protracted 1567 siege of the fortified city of Chitor ended with the deaths of some 25,000 defenders and their families. Akbar himself shot the commander of the city's defenses dead with a musket, and his massive siege cannons, plus the planting of explosive mines, brought down its formidable stone walls. A similar siege in 1569 employed even larger guns, hauled into position by elephants and teams of oxen. Few princes challenged Akbar's authority after these devastating demonstrations of Mughal firepower.

By the end of Akbar's reign, the Mughal Empire stretched from Afghanistan in the northwest to Bengal in the east, and south to about the latitude of Bombay (today Mumbai; see again Map 19.2). Emperor Jahangir (r. 1605–1627) was far less ambitious than his father Akbar, and as we saw in the opening paragraphs to this chapter, his addictions and interests led him to hand power to his favored wife, Nur Jahan, an effective administrator and business woman but not a conqueror. Jahangir's reign was nevertheless culturally significant. A devoted patron of the arts and an amateur poet, Jahangir took Mughal court splendor to new heights (see Seeing the Past: Reflections of the Divine in a Mughal Emerald). His illustrated memoir, the *Jahangirnama*, is a remarkably candid description of life at the top of one of the early modern world's most populous and wealthy empires.

Akbar's Successors

New conquests under Shah Jahan (r. 1628–1658) and Aurangzeb (aw-WRONG-zeb) (r. 1658–1707) carried the empire south almost to the tip of the subcontinent. These rulers had made few innovations in gunpowder warfare; as in the days of Babur, religion was as important a factor in imperial expansion as technology. Shah Jahan was an observant but tolerant Muslim, whereas Aurangzeb was a true holy warrior who called for a return to orthodoxy and elimination of unauthorized practices. Aurangzeb's religious fervor was a major force in the last phase of Mughal expansion.

The emperor's main foe was Prince Shivaji (c. 1640–1680), leader of the Hindu Marathas of India's far southwest. Aurangzeb employed European gunners, whose state-of-the-art weapons and high-quality gunpowder helped him capture several of Shivaji's forts, but he mostly relied on muskets, cannons, and other weapons designed and cast in India. Many large swivel guns were mounted on camels, a useful adaptation. For his part, Shivaji was never able to field more than a few hundred musketeers, relying instead on swift mounts and guerrilla raids. Despite a major offensive sent by Aurangzeb after Shivaji's death, the Marathas bounced back within a few decades and won recognition of their homeland.

Only with the accession of Aurangzeb's successor, Muhammad (r. 1720–1739), did Mughal stagnation and contraction set in. Rebellions by overtaxed peasants and nobles alike sapped the empire's overstretched bureaucratic and defensive resources, and Muhammad's guns proved increasingly outmoded. Europeans were by this time shifting to lighter and more mobile artillery, but the Mughals were casting larger and ever-more-unwieldy cannons. A cannon said to be capable of shooting 100-pound balls, dubbed "Fort Opener," was so heavy it had to be pulled by four elephants and thousands of oxen. Most of the time, it remained stuck in the mud between siege targets. Muhammad Shah

Jahangir Being Helped to Bed

This Mughal miniature from about 1635 shows the emperor Jahangir being put to bed by the ladies of his court after celebrating a Hindu new year's eve festival called Holi. As one of the illustrations in Jahangir's own memoir, the *Jahangirnama*, this image matches well with the emperor's self-description as a regular user of alcohol and other intoxicating substances. Though his interests were not as eclectic as those of his father, Akbar, Jahangir was tolerant of religious diversity. (© The Trustees of the Chester Beatty Library, Dublin.)

finally lost Delhi and the great Mughal treasury to Iran's Nadir Shah, successor to the Safavids, in 1739. The empire fell into disarray until the reign of Shah Alam II, who took the throne in 1759, only to fall under British influence in 1763. He ruled as a puppet of English East India Company until 1806.

Typical of early modern empire builders, the Mughals shifted between peaceful pragmatism and deadly force. They made a variety of alliances with subject peoples, offering them a share of power and the right to carry on established livelihoods. When not engaged in wars of expansion, emperors such as Akbar and Shah Jahan spent considerable time

Reflections of the Divine in a Mughal Emerald

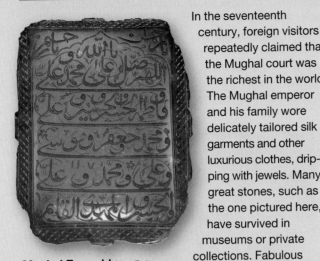

Mughal Emerald (Van Pelt Photography.)

In the seventeenth century, foreign visitors repeatedly claimed that the Mughal court was the richest in the world. The Mughal emperor and his family wore delicately tailored silk garments and other luxurious clothes, dripping with jewels. Many great stones, such as the one pictured here, have survived in museums or private collections. Fabulous gemstones weighing hundreds of carats were routinely exchanged and given as gifts to important visitors, loyal subjects, and favored heirs.

India's early modern rulers had direct access to precious metals, diamonds, rubies, and pearls, but emeralds—especially prized because green was the color of Islam—were hard to come by. Old mines in Egypt had long since played out, and sources in Afghanistan and Pakistan remained unknown, or at least untapped.

Emeralds were found, however, in faraway New Granada, the Spanish-American colony now roughly comprised by the Republic of Colombia. Beginning in the late sixteenth century, Spanish mine owners traded emeralds dug from the high Andes to Spanish and Portuguese merchants with ties to Goa, Portugal's most important trading post in India. From there, merchants traded the stones inland to intermediaries and even to the Mughal emperor himself. Once in the hands of the renowned artisans of the world's most opulent court, raw Colombian emeralds were faceted, tumbled, and carved for incorporation into a wide variety of royal jewels. Some were carefully inscribed with Arabic verses from the Qur'an or special prayers. The one pictured here contains a Shi'a prayer praising the Twelve Imams. It was meant to be sewn into a ritual garment, prayer-side in, as a protective amulet.

EXAMINING THE EVIDENCE

1. How does this precious object reflect patterns of early modern globalization?

2. Why would the royal owner commission a religious object of such magnificence?

---

mediating disputes, expanding palace structures, and organizing tribute collection. Elite tax-collectors and administrators called *zamindars* (SAW-mean-dars) lived off their shares of peasant and artisan tribute, ruling like chiefs over zones called *parganas*, similar to the Ottoman *timars* (discussed in the next chapter). Somewhat medieval in structure, this sort of decentralized rule bred corruption, which in turn led to waves of modernizing reform.

As in the similarly populous and cash-hungry empire of Ming China, Mughal tax reform moved in the direction of a centralized money economy (India's rulers had long enjoyed the privilege of minting gold, silver, and copper coins), stimulating both rural and urban markets. By Akbar's time, most taxes were paid in cash. Meanwhile, European merchants, ever anxious for Indian commodities such as pepper, diamonds, and cotton textiles, reluctantly supplied their South Asian counterparts with precious metals. As in China, this boost to the Mughal money supply was critical, since India had few precious metals mines of its own. The influx of cash, mostly Spanish-American silver pesos, continued even after the 1739 Persian sack of Delhi, but it was arguably a mixed blessing. As in contemporary China, and indeed in Spain itself, the heightened commercial activity and massive influx of bullion did not beget modern industrialization in India. Instead, it bred increased state belligerence and court grandeur. In a sense, the old "Mongolian" notions of governance were simply magnified, financed in a new, more efficient way. Even gunpowder weapons became little more than objects of show.

Tax Reform and Its Effects

Everyday Life in the Mughal Empire

Continuance of the Caste System

Despite its Islamic core and general policy of religious toleration, Mughal India remained sharply divided by status, or caste, as well as other types of social distinctions. India's caste divisions, like the so-called estates of Europe (nobility, clergy, and commoners), were thought to be derived from a divine order, or hierarchy, and could scarcely be challenged. Women's lives were circumscribed, if not oppressed, in virtually all but regal and wealthy merchant circles. The Hindu practice of **sati**, in which widows committed suicide by throwing themselves onto their husbands' funeral pyres, continued under Islamic rule,

sati The ancient Indian practice of ritual suicide by widows.

Building a Palace

This Mughal miniature from the 1590s is quite unusual in depicting ordinary working folk, along with a pair of animal helpers. Men of several colors, ages, and states of dress engage in heavy labor, transporting and lifting stones, beams, and mortar; splitting planks; setting stones; and plastering domes. Several women are sifting sand or preparing mortar, and at center-right are two well-dressed men who appear to be architects or inspectors. Two similar inspectors appear in the upper right, and only in the upper left corner do we glimpse the elite palace inhabitants, seemingly oblivious to the goings-on below. (Victoria & Albert Museum, London/Art Resource, NY.)

although there is much debate about its frequency. Akbar opposed the practice, but he did not ban it. Polygamy, sanctioned by Islam and embraced by Akbar and other rulers, was practiced by any man who could afford to support what amounted to multiple households.

Lower-caste folk, meanwhile, suffered regardless of gender. Men, women, and children were equally banished to a humiliated, slavelike existence in many areas, urban and rural. Worst off were the so-called Untouchables, who were relegated to disposing of human waste, animal carcasses, and other jobs requiring the handling of filth. Like those in many other parts of the early modern world, Mughal elites defined their own dignity most clearly by denying it to those around them—all the while displaying their innate goodness and superiority through ritualized, ostentatious acts of charity. After Akbar, the Mughal emperors had themselves publicly and lavishly weighed on their solar and lunar birthdays against piles of gold and silver coins, which they then distributed to the poor. Similar charitable practices were copied down to the lowest levels of society.

As in much of the early modern world, the vast majority of Mughal subjects were sub- **Farmers** sistence farmers, many of them tied to large landlords through tributary and other customary obligations. The Mughal state thrived mostly by inserting itself into existing tributary structures, not by reordering local economies. Problems arose when Mughal rulers raised tax quotas sharply, or when droughts, floods, and other natural disasters upset the cycle of agricultural production. Unlike the Ming and Qing Chinese, or even the Spanish in Mexico, the Mughals devoted very little of their tremendous wealth to dams, aqueducts, and other massive public works projects. What was new, or modern, was that paper-pushing bureaucrats recorded farmers' tax assessments.

Even in good times, most South Asians lived on only a small daily ration of rice or millet, seasoned with ginger or cumin and—lightly—salt, an expensive state-monopoly item. Some fruits, such as mangoes, were seasonally available, but protein sources were limited. Even in times of bounty, religious dietary restrictions kept most people thin. After centuries of deforestation, people used animal dung as cooking fuel. Intensive agriculture using animal-drawn plows and irrigation works was widespread, but mass famines occurred with notable frequency. The Columbian Exchange was marginally helpful. After about 1600, American maize and tobacco were commonly planted, along with the capsicum peppers that came to spice up many South Asian dishes. Maize spurred population growth in some parts of India, whereas tobacco probably shortened some people's lives. Most tobacco was produced as a cash crop for elite consumption.

India's cities grew rapidly in Mughal times, in part due to stress-induced migration. **Urban Artisans** Nine urban centers—among them Agra, Delhi, and Lahore—exceeded 200,000 inhabitants before 1700. After Akbar's rule, the shift to tax collection in cash was a major stimulus to urban growth and dynamism. Even smaller towns bustled with commercial activity as the economy became more thoroughly monetized, and all urban centers formed nuclei of artisan production.

A number of South Asian coastal and riverside cities and nearby hinterlands produced cotton and silk textiles in massive quantities. They usually followed the putting-out, or piecework, system, in which merchants "put out" raw materials to artisans working from home. As in China and northern Europe, women formed the backbone of this industry, not so much in weaving but rather in the physically harder tasks of fiber cleaning and spinning. Other, mostly male artisans specialized in woodworking, leather making, blacksmithing, and gem cutting. Perhaps the most visible artisanal legacy from Mughal times was in architecture. Highly skilled stonemasons produced Akbar's majestic Red Fort and Shah Jahan's inimitable Taj Mahal, both in the early Mughal capital of Agra.

Some men found employment in the shipyards of Surat, Calicut, and the Bay of Bengal, and others set sail with their seasonal cargoes of export goods and pilgrims. Gujarati Muslim merchants were dominant in the Arabian Sea even after the arrival of Europeans, but Hindus, Jains, and members of other faiths also participated. Unlike the Ottomans, the Mughals never developed a navy, despite their control of maritime

Gujarat since Akbar's conquest of the region in 1572 (see again Map 19.2). On land, by contrast, the empire's vast military apparatus absorbed many thousands of men. Frontier wars with fellow Muslims and southern Hindus were nearly constant. Christian Europeans were mostly seen as tangential commercial allies, technical advisers, and arms suppliers.

The Sikh Challenge

In the northwestern Punjab region an internal challenge of lasting significance emerged, this time mounted by leaders of a relatively new religious sect, Sikhism. Sikhism was something of a hybrid between Islam and Hinduism, but it tended more toward the latter and thus found deeper support among Hindu princes than among Islamic ones. Merchants and artisans were particularly attracted to the faith's recognition of hard work and abstinence (as we saw in Chapter 15). Peasant and artisan followers of Guru Gobind Singh (1666–1708) rebelled in 1710, and their plundering raids reached Delhi. The rebellion was violently quashed by Shah Farrukhsiyar (far-ROOK-see-yar) (r. 1713–1720) in 1715, but sporadic raids and uprisings continued until the end of the eighteenth century, when the Sikhs at last established a separate state.

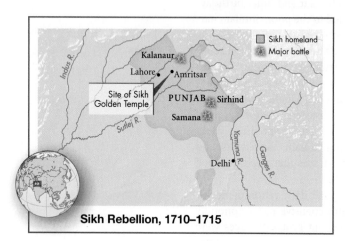

Sikh Rebellion, 1710–1715

In sum, the mighty Mughals ruled over the richest and most populous of Eurasia's early modern Islamic empires, and theirs remained by far the most culturally diverse. Mounted warriors used guns to crush or intimidate neighbors in new and terrifying ways, quickly absorbing huge swaths of terrain and millions of subject peoples. Yet generally, the resulting rule was neither intolerant nor authoritarian. As long as they paid cash tributes, regions could preserve their religious diversity and a degree of local autonomy. Problems arose with imperial overstretch, succession crises, and excessive taxation. Rebels, particularly non-Muslim ones, increasingly shook imperial foundations. More subtle but ultimately more serious were the inroads made by European commercial agents, in particular those of Britain's East India Company. These men, from Connecticut-born clerk Elihu Yale to Governor-general Robert Clive, formed the spearhead of a new imperialism.

European Interlopers

FOCUS

What factors enabled Europeans to take over key Indian Ocean trade networks?

Direct trade for Indian luxuries had been a dream of Europeans since the days of Marco Polo. Unfortunately, as the Portuguese explorer Vasco da Gama and his followers quickly discovered, Europeans had little that appealed to South Asians. With the exception of certain types of guns and clocks, the Portuguese had no products that could not be had in some form already, often more cheaply, and guns would soon be copied. Like Portugal, India was an ancient crossroads, but it was far larger and richer, and vastly more productive. Complex trade circuits had long linked India's rich interior and bustling ports to the wider world. In such a crowded marketplace, only silver and gold found universal acceptance because they functioned as money. Frustrated, the Portuguese turned to piracy, financing their first voyages by plunder rather than trade.

Portuguese Conquistadors 1500–1600

As would prove true in China, only precious metals opened India's doors of trade to newcomers. Even with powerful guns and swift ships on their side, the vastly outnumbered Portuguese had no choice but to part with their hard-won African gold and Spanish-American silver. Taking a somewhat different track than in western Africa, the Portuguese inserted themselves into Indian Ocean trade circuits with an uncompromising mix of belligerence and silver money. They were fortunate in that silver soon arrived in quantity through Portugal's growing Atlantic trade with the Spanish, particularly after 1550. Profits made in the slave trade were routinely reinvested in spices and other goods from India. Meanwhile, the security of all exchanges was guaranteed with brute force, and in some places, such as Goa in India and Melaka in Malaysia, outright conquest.

Genuine Portuguese conquests in Asia were few but significant. Crown-sponsored conquistadors focused on strategic sites for their fortified trading posts, mostly traditional mercantile crossroads and shipping straits not effectively monopolized or defended by local princes. These *feitorías* resembled those already established along the western coast of Africa, but most proved far more expensive and difficult to maintain. The Indian Ocean's sea traffic was already huge, by comparison, and competition was fierce.

The Portuguese grand plan, one that was never realized, was to monopolize all trade in the Indian Ocean by extracting tolls and tariffs from local traders of various ethnicities and political allegiances. For a time they sold shipping licenses to Gujarati Muslim and other long-distance shippers. If traders failed to produce such licenses when passing through Portuguese-controlled ports, their goods were confiscated. On top of this, they had to pay duties.

Within a half-century of da Gama's 1498 voyage to India the Portuguese controlled access to the Persian Gulf, Red Sea, South China Sea, and Atlantic Ocean, along with many major coastal trading enclaves, from Mombasa on the coast of Kenya to Macao on China's Pearl River delta (see Map 19.3). Being so few in a region of millions, the Portuguese strategy was pragmatic. By tapping existing trade networks and setting up feitorías, they could efficiently collect spices and textiles, along with what were essentially extortion payments. Friends would be given silver, enemies lead. The method worked as long as the Portuguese faced no competition from other belligerent sea powers and remained unified and consistent in their use of violence.

Despite some early Ottoman attacks, seaborne trade competitors would not arrive until about 1600, but given the distance to Lisbon, it immediately proved impossible to enforce Portuguese unity and consistency in dealing with Indian Ocean merchants and princes. Ironically, it was "friendly" local merchants, rajas, and sultans—Arab, Hindu, and otherwise—who benefited most from Portuguese sponsorship and protection. As in western Africa, for several centuries the Portuguese unwittingly did as much to facilitate local aspirations as to realize their own. What they grandly called the "State of India," *Estado da Índia*, gradually proved more "Indian" than Portuguese, though for a short time it was highly profitable to the Crown.

Portugal's grand religious project was similarly absorbed. In 1498 Vasco da Gama expressed confidence in the spread of Roman Catholicism to East Africa: "On Easter day the Moors [Muslims] we had taken captive told us that in the town of Malindi [a Swahili port on the coast of Kenya] there were four vessels belonging to Christians from India, and if we should like to convey them there they would give us Christian pilots, and everything else we might need, including meats, water, wood, and other things."[4] Da Gama wrongly took this to mean that there was a pre-existing Christian base or network in the region upon which the Catholic Portuguese could build. Ultimately, Portuguese efforts to convert the many peoples of the Indian Ocean basin failed even more miserably than in Atlantic Africa, though not for lack of trying. Francis Xavier, an early Jesuit missionary (see Chapter 20), worked tirelessly and died an optimist. Whereas he focused on converting the region's countless slaves and lower-caste people, others sought to bend the will of monarchs such as Akbar, hoping they would set an example. Small Christian communities formed at Goa and other strongholds, but everywhere they went, Portuguese missionaries faced literally millions of hostile Muslims and perhaps equal or greater numbers of uninterested Hindus, Buddhists, Confucianists, Jains, Parsis, Sikhs, Jews, and others. In short, Christianity, at least in the form presented by the Portuguese, did not appeal to the vast majority of people inhabiting the Indian Ocean basin. As we will see in Chapter 21, only in

Portuguese Advances

**Failed Efforts
at Religious Conversion**

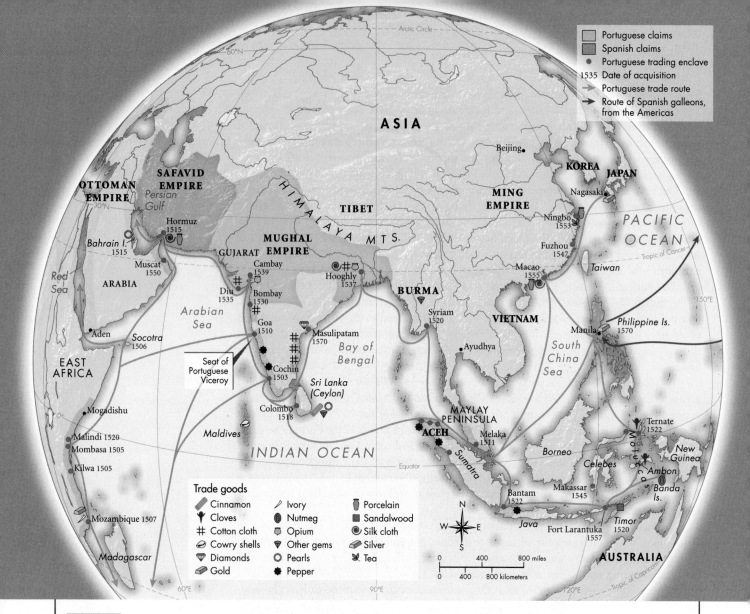

MAP 19.3

Portugal's Seaborne Empire, c. 1600

With their castle-like sailing vessels and potent gunpowder weapons, the Portuguese inserted themselves violently into the greater Indian Ocean basin beginning in 1498. From their stronghold in Goa, they monopolized regional and export trade in luxury goods, either by shipping these items themselves or by forcing others to purchase licenses. After 1580, the Portuguese were under Spanish rule, which linked the lucrative East and South Asia trade routes to New World silver arriving in the Philippines.

Japan, the Philippines, East Timor, and other select areas, mostly in the western Pacific, did early modern Catholic missionaries appear to strike a chord.

The "India Voyage"
Despite the failure of Christian missionary efforts, trade was brisk, at least for a time. The so-called *carreira da India* (cah-HEY-rah dah EENDJ-yah), or India voyage, became legendary in Portuguese culture, and for good reason. Even on successful trips, death rates on this annual sail between Lisbon and Goa were high due to poor onboard sanitation, prolonged vitamin C deprivation, questionable medical therapies such as bloodletting, and other health challenges typical of the era. Also, although early modern navigators were arguably more adept than medieval ones, shipwrecks were not uncommon on the India voyage. Unlike local dhows, sixteenth- and seventeenth-century Portuguese vessels were huge, round-hulled, and built for cargo rather than speed or maneuverability, and foundered due to overloading. The coral reefs of southeast Africa became a notorious graveyard of the carreira.

By the later sixteenth century, Portuguese monopolies on East Indian spices and sea-lanes had weakened considerably. With so much wealth at stake and so few enforcers on hand, corruption and contraband flourished. Spices were, after all, the drugs of their day, more valuable by weight than gold. Shipwrecks and piracy became more frequent throughout Portugal's ocean empire, as did competition from new, better-armed Europeans—Protestants, to boot. As Luiz Vaz de Camões (cah-MOYSH), veteran of many adventures in the East Indies, composed the triumphant poem that would become Portugal's national epic, *The Lusíads*, Portugal was actually on the eve of losing not only its heirless king but also its hard-won trading monopolies in the Indian Ocean. It was the Spanish under Philip II who would offer the first humiliation. Shortly after, Spain's sworn enemies, the Dutch, would deal the Portuguese a series of crushing blows.

Weakening of Portuguese Power

The Dutch and English East India Companies 1600–1750

As Portuguese fortunes declined and Mughal expansion continued toward the turn of the seventeenth century, South Asia's overseas trade underwent notable reorganization. This shift involved many players, including the familiar Gujarati merchants, the increasingly powerful Ottomans, Persia's expanding Safavids, and others. But ultimately it was Dutch and English newcomers, and to a lesser extent the French, who would have the greatest long-term impact. All formed powerful **trading companies** in the seventeenth and eighteenth centuries, each backed by state-of-the-art cannons and first-rate sailing ships.

Despite these important changes, it would be highly misleading to project the later imperial holdings of these foreigners back onto the seventeenth and early eighteenth centuries. Only the Dutch came close to establishing a genuine "Indian Ocean Empire" during early modern times. Meanwhile, East Africans, South and Southeast Asians, and other native peoples of the Indian Ocean continued to act independently, in their own interests. It was the sudden, unexpected collapse of the Mughals and other gunpowder-fueled Asian states in the later eighteenth century that allowed Europeans to conquer large landmasses and to plant colonies of the sort long since established in the Americas.

The Dutch East India Company, known by its Dutch acronym VOC, was founded in 1602. The company's aim was to use ships, arms, and Spanish-American silver to displace the Portuguese as Europe's principal suppliers of spices and other exotic Asian goods. Though not officially a state enterprise, the Dutch East India Company counted many ranking statesmen among its principal investors, and its actions abroad were as belligerent as those of any imperial army or navy. In the course of almost two centuries, the VOC extended Dutch influence from South Africa to Japan. Its most lasting achievement was the conquest of Java, base for the vast and diverse Dutch colony of Indonesia.

Dutch VOC

Although they never drove the Portuguese from their overseas capital at Goa, the mostly Protestant Dutch displaced their Catholic rivals nearly everywhere else. Their greatest early successes were in southern India and Java, followed by Sri Lanka (Ceylon), Bengal, Melaka, and Japan (see Map 19.4). In Southeast Asia their standard procedure was to follow conquest with enslavement and eventually plantation agriculture of the sort established by the Spanish and Portuguese in the Americas. They also imposed this sequence on Ceylon (see Lives and Livelihoods: Cinnamon Harvesters in Ceylon).

The monopolistic mentality of contemporary Europe is what drove Dutch aggression: profits were ensured not by open competition but by absolute control over the flow of commodities and the money to pay for them. Faced with competition from both regional authorities such as the Mughals and fellow foreign interlopers such as the English and Portuguese, the VOC concentrated on monopolizing spices. After seizing the pepper-growing region of southern Sumatra, the VOC turned to the riskier business of establishing plantations to grow coffee and other tropical cash crops. Like the Portuguese before them, the Dutch devoted at least as much cargo space to interregional trade as to exports. Thus clever local traders and many thousands of Chinese merchants benefited from the Dutch determination to monopolize trade.

trading companies Private corporations licensed by early modern European states to monopolize Asian and other overseas trades.

Cinnamon Harvesters in Ceylon

Harvesting Cinnamon

This engraving, based on a simpler one from 1672, depicts cinnamon harvesters in Ceylon (Sri Lanka). The Portuguese were the first Europeans to attempt to monopolize the global export of this spice, but local kings were difficult to conquer and control. Only in the later seventeenth century did the Dutch manage to establish plantation-type production, with the final product, the now familiar cinnamon sticks, monopolized by the Dutch East India Company. (The Granger Collection, New York.)

Long before the arrival of Europeans in 1506, the island of Sri Lanka, or Ceylon (its colonial name), was world-renowned for its cinnamon exports. As far away as Persia this wet tropical island off India's southeast tip, largely under control of competing Buddhist kings, was famous for its sapphires, rubies, pearls, and domesticated elephants (see again Map 19.3). Like India's pepper and Southeast Asia's cloves, mace, and nutmeg, Ceylonese cinnamon fetched extraordinary prices throughout Eurasia and parts of Africa, where it was used as a condiment, preservative, and even medicine. As late as 1685 a Portuguese observer noted: "Every year a great number of vessels arrive from Persia, Arabia, the Red Sea, the Malabar Coast [of India], China, Bengal, and Europe to fetch cinnamon." Attempts to transplant the spice elsewhere, including Brazil, consistently failed, and early conquistador claims of finding cinnamon in Ecuador's eastern jungles proved false. As part of the Columbian Exchange,

Ceylonese cinnamon became a necessary ingredient in hot chocolate, a beverage developed in colonial Mexico that soon took Europe by storm.

The spice grew wild in forests belonging to the kingdom of Kandy, in Ceylon's southwest highlands. In 1517, the Portuguese struck a deal with the king of Kandy that allowed them to use and fortify the port of Colombo to monopolize cinnamon exports in exchange for cloth, metalware, and military assistance against rivals. The Portuguese did not engage directly in cinnamon production, but rather traded for it with the king and certain nobles. The king and his nobles in turn collected cinnamon as a tribute item produced on feudal-type estates called *para-wenia*. A special caste of male workers known as *chalias* was specifically responsible for planting, harvesting, slicing, drying, and packaging Ceylon's most prized crop. The chalias were not enslaved, but rather served as dependents of the king and various noblemen and military officers in exchange for the right to use land for subsistence farming in the off-season, plus rations of rice and occasionally a cash wage.

Cinnamon is derived from the shaved and dried inner bark of the small *Cinamomum verum* tree, a variety of laurel. Although the spice can be harvested wild, Ceylon's chalias pruned, transplanted, and even grew the trees from seed to maximize output and improve quality. With southwest Ceylon's white sand soils and reliable monsoon rains, the crop flourished year after year. Cinnamon is best when taken from young saplings three to five years old, no more than ten feet high, and about the thickness of a walking stick. Due to Ceylon's latitude, two harvests were possible, one concentrated in May-June and another in November-December. At harvest time the chalias cut ripe cinnamon trees with hatchets and then removed the bark. Daily collection quotas were set by the king and other holders of parawenia estates.

Next came peeling, the key process and the one for which the chalias were best known. As a seventeenth-century Portuguese writer described them: "These cinnamon peelers carry in their girdle a small hooked knife as a mark of their occupation." Working in pairs, one chalia made two lengthwise incisions on the ripe sticks using his hooked knife and carefully removed the resulting half-cylindrical strips of bark. His companion then used other tools to separate a gray outer bark from the thin, cream-colored inner bark. Leaving even a tiny amount of the outer bark on the inner bark made the cinnamon inedibly bitter. The inner bark was then left to dry, curling, thickening, and turning brown as it oxidized. The chalias then packaged the resulting "cinnamon sticks" in cloth-covered bundles weighing about 100 lbs. These were given to overlords; the king of Kandy alone was said to demand over 500 tons each year. Cinnamon was often bundled with black pepper for long sea voyages to help draw out moisture.

We have no documents written by the chalias to give us a sense of their views, but we do know that a leader of a 1609 rebellion against the Portuguese was a member of this caste and the son of a cinnamon cutter. Tapping into local discontent, the Dutch East India Company (VOC) displaced the Portuguese in 1658 after making an alliance with the king of Kandy. Once established on the island, the Dutch shifted to direct planting and harvesting, using enslaved laborers and totally monopolizing trade in cinnamon to maximize profits. The king was reduced to the status of client. Work on cinnamon plantations was not as difficult a livelihood as gem mining or pearl diving, but Dutch work demands were rigorous and punishments harsh for even light offenses. Dissatisfaction with the VOC administrators ran deep. The British took over Ceylon in 1796 following the collapse of the VOC, but their management of the cinnamon economy was not as careful or exacting, and both price and quality fell. Ceylon's export sector would be revived after 1800 with the introduction of American tropical crops adapted by British botanists: cinchona (quinine), cacao, and rubber.

QUESTIONS TO CONSIDER

1. How was cinnamon grown, harvested, and prepared for export?

2. How did cinnamon harvesting fit into traditional, pre-colonial landholding and labor systems?

3. How did Dutch rule change the lives and livelihoods of cinnamon harvesters? Of Sri Lanka (Ceylon) in general?

For Further Information:

Valentijn, François. *Description of Ceylon,* ed. Sinnappah Arasaratnam. London: Hakluyt Society, 1978 [orig. publ. 1720].
Winius, George D. *The Fatal History of Portuguese Ceylon: Transition to Dutch Rule*. New York: Cambridge University Press, 1971.

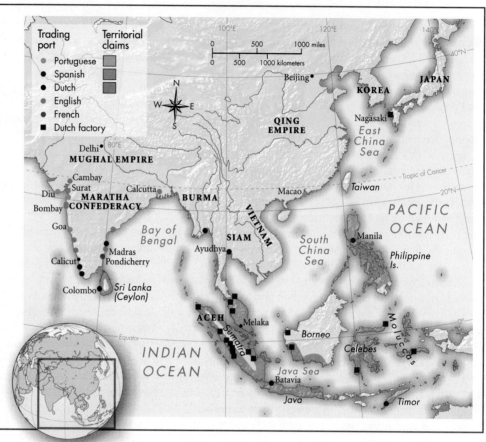

MAP 19.4

Dutch and English Colonies in South and Southeast Asia, to 1750

Although the Portuguese remained active in the Indian Ocean basin and South China Sea until the twentieth century, after 1600 the Dutch and English had largely displaced them. The East India Companies of these two countries sought to conquer and defend key trading enclaves, both against each other and against the later-arriving French. Outside the Spanish Philippines, only the Dutch managed to establish a significant land empire before 1750. In the hands of the company, or VOC, Dutch holdings grew to encompass most of Indonesia. The English and French would follow suit in South and Southeast Asia in subsequent decades.

The VOC, like other Indian Ocean traders, relied on a steady supply of Spanish-American silver to lubricate commerce. Between 1600 and 1648, when these rival empires were at war, some silver was plundered from the Spanish in the Caribbean by Dutch pirates, but most was extracted through trade, both official and contraband. Recent research has revealed the importance of illegal Dutch slave traders in Buenos Aires after a major peace agreement was signed with Spain in 1648. The silver of Potosí in this case bypassed Europe entirely to go to Dutch trading posts in India, Southeast Asia, and China. Mexican silver, meanwhile, flowed out of Dutch Caribbean ports such as Curaçao, through Amsterdam, and into the holds of outbound company ships. Trade in Manila extracted still more Spanish silver. Though ever more divided in its political loyalties, the world was becoming ever more unified in its monetary system.

English East India Company

Compared with the VOC, the English East India Company (EIC), founded two years earlier in 1600, had more modest aims and much less capital. Nevertheless, it used brute force and a royal charter to displace the Portuguese in several strategic ports, especially around the Arabian peninsula and on the coasts of India. Given England's civil wars and other internal problems in the seventeenth century (discussed in the next chapter), progress was slow and uneven. Only in the late seventeenth century did English traders in India begin to amass considerable fortunes, mostly by exporting spices, gems, and cloth from their modest fortresses at Surat, Bombay, Madras, and Calcutta (see again Map 19.4). Like the VOC, however, the EIC grew increasingly powerful over time, eventually taking on a blatantly imperial role.

Two very different individuals from the turn of the eighteenth century illustrate the slow but steady ascent of the English East India Company. Elihu Yale, a native New Englander whose book collection was used to establish a college in Connecticut in his name, rose from the position of Company clerk to serve for over a dozen years as the

Dutch Headquarters in Bengal

This painting from 1665 depicts the Dutch East India Company (VOC) trading fort at Hugly, on the banks of the Ganges River branch of the same name in the Indian province of Bengal. As they did elsewhere along the rim of the rich and populous Indian Ocean basin, the Dutch sought to establish exclusive control over specific commodities, usually after driving out the Portuguese. In Bengal, the main export items were fine cotton print fabrics, which, along with a variety of products already circulating in the region, they traded mostly for Spanish-American silver. The VOC would eventually be displaced by the English East India Company. (Courtesy of Rijksmuseum, Amsterdam, The Netherlands.)

governor of the East India Company's fort at Madras. He quickly learned to exploit his post to export cloth, pepper, saltpeter, opium, and diamonds. Upon his return to England in 1699, Yale was the contemporary equivalent of a multimillionaire. Although he never visited New Haven, his philanthropic capital, skimmed from East India Company profits, was piously invested in colonial higher education.

At about the same time, England's Admiralty, under pressure from EIC investors, commissioned a Scottish-born but New York City–based privateer named William Kidd to search for English pirates interfering with Company-protected trade in the Indian Ocean, especially in the Red Sea. Instead, Kidd foolishly attacked and plundered a Mughal-sponsored merchantman off the southwest coast of India. Now a pirate himself, Kidd fled to Madagascar in the stolen vessel, then across the Atlantic to the Caribbean. Eventually, Kidd tried to contact his wife in New York, but he was captured and sent in chains to Boston, then London. At the urging of East India Company officials, whose friendship with Emperor Aurangzeb had been severely strained by the renegade pirate hunter's actions, Kidd was hanged in 1701. The company's interests in distant seas were, it seems, increasingly the government's.

COUNTERPOINT
Aceh: Fighting Back in Southeast Asia

FOCUS

Why was the tiny sultanate of Aceh able to hold out against European interlopers in early modern times?

The province and city of Aceh (AH-cheh), at the northwest tip of the island of Sumatra in Indonesia, was transformed but not conquered in early modern times. Like many trading enclaves linked by the Indian Ocean's predictable monsoon winds, Aceh was a Muslim sultanate that lived by exchanging the produce of its interior, in this case black pepper, for the many commodities supplied by other, distant kingdoms. Aceh's rulers participated directly in trade, dictating its terms and enjoying many of its benefits. Yet unlike most such enclaves, which fell like dominoes to European interlopers, Aceh held out. For a variety of reasons, but perhaps most importantly a newfound religious fervor, the Acehnese defeated a long string of would-be conquistadors.

The Differing Fortunes of Aceh and Melaka

Aceh's rulers were probably related to those of the less fortunate Malay trading city of Melaka. Melaka was a former fishing village with a fine natural harbor and highly strategic location on the east end of the narrow Melaka Strait. It was said to have been founded by a Hindu prince who converted to Islam in around 1420. Melaka's rulers forged deft, profitable alliances to regions as far away as China, but ties to the interior were weak, drawing predators. Melaka was attacked repeatedly by Javanese sultans, and in the end it fell to Portuguese cannons in 1511. Although Melakan forces had guns of their own and fought valiantly against the Europeans, when the tide turned they found themselves without a backcountry into which guerrilla warriors might flee and reorganize. The Dutch followed in 1641, displacing the Portuguese.

Unlike Melaka, Aceh's influence reached deep into the interior and across hundreds of miles of coast. After defeating Portuguese invaders in 1518, Aceh emerged as one of the most assertive seaborne Islamic states in the entire Indian Ocean, tapping military aid from the distant Ottomans and shipping considerable quantities of pepper to the Mediterranean via the Red Sea. But Aceh's repeated efforts to conquer Portuguese-controlled Melaka failed, and by the late seventeenth century the kingdom declined as both a political and commercial force. Still, it was not until the late nineteenth century that the Dutch reduced Aceh to colonial status.

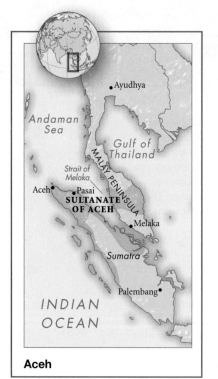

Aceh

Aceh, "the Veranda of Mecca"

Aceh's early modern history has been gleaned from a variety of outside sources, and also local, sometimes official, chronicles, including epic poems written in Malay and Acehnese in the sixteenth and seventeenth centuries to celebrate the deeds of its sultans. Although poets tended to exaggerate the greatness of their patrons and to conflate or compress events, the epics express Acehnese Islamic pride, mostly as the region's bulwark against the militant Christian Portuguese. Ottoman, Portuguese, Dutch, and English sources note that Aceh was a great meeting place for Southeast Asian pilgrims on their way to Mecca, and it came to be known as *Serambi Mekkah*, the Veranda of Mecca.

Islamic Identity

Despite its intensely Islamic identity, Acehnese culture respected female independence. Women controlled and inherited nearly all property, from houses to rice fields, and at marriage men moved to their wives' households. Men in fact spent much of their time

Dutch Merchants Learn How to Act in Aceh

In this passage, originally composed in the Malay language just after 1600, a Dutch merchant in Aceh created a dialogue between an imaginary European visitor, "Daud," and a local informant, "Ibrahim." The sample exchange was meant to instruct future Dutch visitors. Should they come to Aceh for business, they would know something of the cultural intricacies of local exchange, and also how to ask about them. This passage describes the formal reception of a Gujarati merchant from western India by the local raja. Every detail of court etiquette was critical. To make mistakes in the course of observing and participating in these rituals, particularly when one had little knowledge of local languages, was to risk permanent expulsion, and in some cases death.

Daud: Who is it coming on this great elephant, who has such a crowd of people behind him?

Ibrahim: It is the Shahbandar with the Penghulu kerkun [secretary].

Daud: I also see some foreign traders sitting up there. Who are they?

Ibrahim: That is a Gujarati *nakhoda* [merchant], who has just come with his ship, and whom they are going to take to salute the raja.

Daud: What does it mean, that elephant caparisoned in red cloth, with those people in front of it playing on tambourines, trumpets, and flutes?

Ibrahim: The elephant you see and the man sitting in a palanquin [curtained couch] upon it, means that a letter is being brought from their raja to our lord. . . .

Daud: Who is seated up there?

Ibrahim: It is one of the sultan's *orangkaya* [courtier], that he has chosen for that.

Daud: And what is all that for?

Ibrahim: To honor the raja whose letter it is.

Daud: And what is that I see, so many men and slaves, each bringing a painted cloth in his hands?

Ibrahim: These are the presents which the nakhoda will offer to the king.

Daud: Is that the tariff he must pay for his goods, or must he pay another tariff?

Ibrahim: No, the tariff is extra, seven percent.

Daud: What honor will the raja give them in return?

Ibrahim: Indeed, when they enter the raja's palace, they will be given great honor.

Daud: What happens there?

Ibrahim: There they eat and drink, all sorts of food and fruits are brought, they play, dance, with all sorts of entertainments, they play on the trumpet, flute, clarinet, and *rebab,* and then the king asks for a garment of our local style to be brought, which he gives to the nakhoda.

Source: Frederick de Houtman, 1603, quoted in of Anthony Reid, *Southeast Asia in the Age of Commerce* (New Haven: Yale University Press, 1993), 2: 237–238. Credit: Anthony Reid. *Southeast Asia in the Age of Commerce*, Volume 2. Yale University Press, 1993. Copyright © Yale University Press, 1993. Used by permission of the publisher.

EXAMINING THE EVIDENCE

1. What does this dialogue suggest about the balance of power in Aceh?

2. What does it reveal about the interplay of rulership and trade?

away on business or engaged in religious study, leaving women in charge of most aspects of everyday life. Pre-Islamic kin structures governed daily affairs, while *ulama*, or religious scholars, oversaw matters of business and state. Criminal cases reveal that local custom could override Islamic prescriptions, especially when it came to capital punishment. The result was a somewhat mild, woman-friendly Southeast Asian blend of secular and religious life reminiscent of West Africa.

Aceh was immediately recognized as a powerful state by northern European visitors in the early seventeenth century. The first Dutch envoys were jailed from 1599 to 1601 for

Trade and Diplomacy

mishandling court etiquette (see Reading the Past: Dutch Merchants Learn How to Act in Aceh), but soon after, English visitors representing Queen Elizabeth I and the newly chartered East India Company made a better impression. Of particular interest to the Acehnese shah was Dutch and English hostility to Portugal, which also sent ambassadors. Playing competing Europeans off one another soon became an absorbing and sometimes profitable game. And the Europeans were by no means alone—sizable trading and diplomatic missions arrived in Aceh from eastern and western India, Burma, and Siam. Sultan Iskandar Muda used English and Dutch traders to drive the Gujaratis out of the pepper trade in the 1610s, only to force the Europeans out of it in the 1620s. He continued to ship pepper to Red Sea intermediaries, but steadily lost market share to both English and Dutch merchants, who turned to other Southeast Asian sources.

Sultanate of Women

Aceh's decline has been traditionally associated with the rise of female sultans in the seventeenth century, much as occurred in the Ottoman Empire at about the same time (as we will see in Chapter 20). Sultana Taj al-Alam Safiyat al-Din Shah ruled from 1641 to 1675. She was the daughter of the renowned conqueror and deft handler of foreign envoys, Iskandar Muda Shah (r. 1607–1636), but her politics focused mostly on domestic affairs, in part because Aceh was in a period of restructuring after her father's failed 1629 attack on Portuguese Melaka. Like her counterparts in Istanbul and Agra, Safiyat al-Din was a great patron of artists and scholars. Under her sponsorship, Acehnese displaced Malay as the language of state and the arts.

Safiyat al-Din was succeeded by three more sultanas, the last of whom, Kamalat Shah, was deposed following a 1699 decree, or **fatwa**, from Mecca declaring women unfit to serve as sultans. Careful reading of sources suggests that female sultans were not the cause of Aceh's declining power in the region, but rather a symptom of a general shift toward the Malay style of divine kingship. Even in decline, Aceh held out throughout early modern times and beyond against European attempts to subject it to colonial rule.

Conclusion

Thanks to reliable monsoon winds, the vast Indian Ocean basin had long been interconnected by ties of trade and religion, and this general pattern continued throughout early modern times. The region's countless farmers depended as they had for millennia on the monsoon rains.

Change came, however, with the rise of gunpowder-fueled empires both on land and at sea. Beginning about 1500, seaborne Europeans forcibly took over key ports and began taxing the trade of others, while Islamic warriors on horseback blasted resistant sultans and rajas into tribute-paying submission in South and Southwest Asia. Smaller sultanates and kingdoms also adopted gunpowder weapons after 1500, both to defend themselves against invaders and to attack weaker neighbors. Although such armed conflict could be deadly or at least disrupt everyday life, for most ordinary people in the long run it meant a rise in tribute demands, and in some places a turn to forced cultivation of export products such as cinnamon or pepper.

Despite the advances of increasingly belligerent Islamic and Christian empires throughout the Indian Ocean, most inhabitants, including India's 100 million-plus Mughal subjects, did not convert. Religious tolerance had long been the rule in this culturally complex region, and although the Portuguese were driven by an almost crusading fervor to spread Catholicism, in the end they were forced to deal with Hindus, Buddhists, Jews, and Muslims to make a profit. Later Europeans, most of them Protestants, scarcely bothered to proselytize prior to modern times, choosing instead to offer themselves as religiously neutral intermediaries, unlike the intolerant Portuguese.

fatwa A decree issued by Islamic religious officials.

The Mughals, like the kings of Vijayanagara before them, followed a tradition of divinely aloof religious tolerance, although conversion to the state faith had its benefits, particularly in trade. Emperor Akbar went so far as to create his own hybrid cult, although it never took root, and in the provinces Sikhism emerged as an alternative to Hinduism or Islam. As with Christianity, Islamic practices varied greatly throughout this vast region, and these differences were visible in customs of female mobility, dress, and access to positions of power. Nur Jahan represented a temporary period of Mughal openness to feminine power and public expression, and Aceh's Sultanate of the Women represented another in Southeast Asia.

Europeans sought to adapt to local cultures of trade when using force was impractical. For most of the early modern period, they had no choice, at least outside their tiny, fortressed towns. Only with the decline of great land empires such as that of the Mughals in the eighteenth century did this begin to change. Though it happened much more slowly than in contemporary Latin America or western Africa, by the end of the early modern period European imperial designs had begun to alter established lifeways throughout the Indian Ocean region. Expansion into the interior, first by overseas trading companies such as the English East India Company and the Dutch VOC, would grow in the nineteenth century into full-blown imperialism. Only a few outliers, such as the Muslim revivalist sultanate of Aceh, managed to hold out, and even their time would come.

NOTES

1. Marshall Hodgson, *The Venture of Islam*, 2 vols. (Chicago: University of Chicago Press, 1974), 2: 34.
2. Robert Sewell, *A Forgotten Empire (Vijayanagar): A Contribution to the History of India* (London: Sonnenschein, 1900), 245.
3. Thackston Wheeler, ed. and trans., *The Baburnama: Memoirs of Babur, Prince and Emperor* (Washington, D.C.: Smithsonian Institution, 1996), 326, 384.
4. Vasco da Gama, *The Diary of His Travels Through African Waters, 1497–1499*, ed. and trans. Eric Axelson (Somerset, U.K.: Stephan Phillips, 1998), 45.

RESOURCES FOR RESEARCH

General Works

The Indian Ocean has recently become a unit of study on par with the Atlantic and Mediterranean, but synthetic interpretations are still few. For the early modern period, Barendse's synthesis is essential.

Barendse, R. J. *The Arabian Seas: The Indian Ocean World of the Seventeenth Century.* 2002.

Risso, Patricia. *Merchants and Faith: Muslim Commerce and Culture in the Indian Ocean.* 1995.

The Sultan Qaboos Cultural Center at Washington D.C.'s Middle East Cultural Center maintains a superb site on the Indian Ocean in world history at http://www.indianoceanhistory.org/.

The University of Wisconsin's Center for South Asia maintains a Web site with links to texts, timelines, maps, and other materials relevant to the study of South Asia and the Indian Ocean. http://www.southasia.wisc.edu/resources.html.

Trading Cities and Inland Networks: East Africa

The following authors are among the leading specialists writing on early modern East Africa, including in their work both African and Portuguese perspectives.

Newitt, Malyn. *A History of Portuguese Overseas Expansion, 1400–1668.* 2005.

Pearson, Michael N. *Port Cities and Intruders: The Swahili Coast, India, and Portugal in the Early Modern Era.* 1998.

Trade and Empire in South Asia

The literature on maritime India is vast and growing, but the following works offer a good sense of both the questions being pursued and the types of sources available. Whereas works on Vijayanagara are few, and based mostly on art and archaeology, document-based studies on Mughal India have multiplied more rapidly than for any of the other gunpowder empires.

Dale, Stephen. *Indian Merchants and Eurasian Trade, 1600–1750*. 1994.

Mukhia, Harbans. *The Mughals of India*. 2004.

Pearson, Michael N. *The Portuguese in India* (The New Cambridge History of India, Part 1, vol. 1). 1987.

Schimmel, Annemarie. *The Empire of the Mughals: History, Art, and Culture*. Translated by Corinne Attwood. 2004.

Stein, Burton. *Vijayanagara*. 2005.

European Interlopers

The literature on Europe's "East India Companies" and related enterprises is voluminous, but recent work has attempted to go beyond a focus on business and bureaucracy to fathom cross-cultural meanings.

Boyajian, James C. *Portuguese Trade in Asia Under the Habsburgs, 1580–1640*. 1993.

Chaudhury, Sushil, and Michel Morineau, eds. *Merchants, Companies, and Trade: Europe and Asia in the Early Modern Era*. 1999.

Gaastra, Femme S. *The Dutch East India Company: Expansion and Decline*. 2003.

Keay, John. *The Honourable Company: A History of the East India Company*. 1993.

Ritchie, Robert C. *Captain Kidd and the War Against the Pirates*. 1986.

COUNTERPOINT: Aceh: Fighting Back in Southeast Asia

Work on the early modern history of island Southeast Asia has ballooned in recent years. The following authors treat Aceh in this wider context.

Lockard, Craig. *Southeast Asia in World History*. 2009.

Reid, Anthony. *Southeast Asia in the Age of Commerce*. 2 vols. 1988.

Reid, Anthony, ed. *Southeast Asia in the Early Modern Era: Trade, Power, and Belief*. 1993.

Reid, Anthony, ed. *Verandah of Violence: The Background to the Aceh Problem*. 2006.

▶ **For additional primary sources from this period**, see *Sources of Crossroads and Cultures*.

▶ **For Web sites, images, and documents related to topics in this chapter**, see Make History at bedfordstmartins.com/smith.

The major global development in this chapter ▶ The Indian Ocean trading
network and the impact of European intrusion on maritime and mainland South Asia.

IMPORTANT EVENTS

1336–1565	Vijayanagara kingdom in southern India
1498	Vasco da Gama reaches India
1500–1763	Mughal Empire in South Asia
1509–1529	Reign of Krishna Deva Raya of Vijayanagara
1510	Portuguese conquest of Goa, India
1511	Portuguese conquest of Melaka
1517	Portuguese establish fort in Sri Lanka (Ceylon)
1526	Battle of Panipat led by Mughal emperor Babur
1530	Consolidation of Aceh under Sultan Ali Mughayat Shah
1556–1605	Reign of Mughal emperor Akbar
1567	Akbar's siege of Chitor
1600	English East India Company founded in London
1602	Dutch East India Company (VOC) founded in Amsterdam
1605–1627	Reign of Mughal emperor Jahangir
1641	Dutch take Melaka from Portuguese
1641–1699	Sultanate of Women in Aceh
1658	Dutch drive Portuguese from Ceylon
1701	William Kidd hanged in London for piracy
1739	Persian raiders under Nadir Shah sack Delhi
1764	English East India Company controls Bengal

KEY TERMS

Brahman (p. 622)
caste (p. 622)
dhow (p. 619)
fatwa (p. 642)
Kshatriya (p. 622)

monsoon (p. 615)
sati (p. 630)
trading companies (p. 635)

CHAPTER OVERVIEW QUESTIONS

1. What environmental, religious, and political factors enabled trading enclaves to flourish in the Indian Ocean basin?

2. How did the rise and fall of India's land empires reflect larger regional trends?

3. How did Europeans insert themselves into the Indian Ocean trading network, and what changes did they bring about?

SECTION FOCUS QUESTIONS

1. How did Swahili Coast traders link the East African interior to the Indian Ocean basin?

2. What factors account for the fall of Vijayanagara and the rise of the Mughals?

3. What factors enabled Europeans to take over key Indian Ocean trade networks?

4. Why was the tiny sultanate of Aceh able to hold out against European interlopers in early modern times?

MAKING CONNECTIONS

1. In what ways did Indian Ocean trade differ from the contemporary Atlantic slave trade (see Chapter 18)? What role did Africa play in each?

2. How did traditional kingdoms such as Vijayanagara differ from those of the Americas prior to the Spanish conquest (see Chapter 16)?

20

AT A CROSSROADS ▶

Court artists painted this 1588 Ottoman miniature to illustrate Suleiman the Magnificent's 1526 victory over Christian forces at the Battle of Mohacs, which left Hungary without a monarch and divided between the Habsburg and Ottoman empires. Traditional cavalry forces face off in the left foreground, but most prominent is the sultan himself in the upper right, on a white horse just behind a line of large Ottoman cannon. (Topkapi Palace Museum, Istanbul/ Giraudon/Bridgeman Art Library.)

Consolidation and Conflict in Europe and the Greater Mediterranean

1450–1750

In 1590, forty-three-year-old Miguel de Cervantes Saavedra, an office clerk working in the Spanish city of Seville, applied for a colonial service job in South America. Such assignments usually went to applicants with nobler connections than Cervantes enjoyed, but perhaps he hoped his military service would count in his favor. Cervantes had been wounded in a major naval conflict, the Battle of Lepanto, in 1571, fighting against the mighty Ottomans. He also suffered five years of captivity in Algiers as the prisoner of North Africa's Barbary pirates. Despite all of this, he was turned down.

Before taking up his desk job in Seville, Cervantes had tried his hand at writing, publishing a modestly successful novel in 1585. Spain at this time was a literary leader in Europe. The novels, plays, and poems of Spain's "Golden Century" drew on medieval models, but they were both enriched and transformed by the changes resulting from overseas colonization and religious upheavals. Playwrights and poets rewrote the conquests of the Aztecs and Incas as tragedies, and one writer, "El Inca" Garcilaso de la Vega, son of a Spanish conquistador and an Inca princess, thrilled his Spanish readers with tales of a

The Power of the Ottoman Empire, 1453–1750

FOCUS What factors explain the rise of the vast Ottoman Empire and its centuries-long endurance?

Europe Divided, 1500–1650

FOCUS What sparked division in Europe after 1500, and why did this trend persist?

European Innovations in Science and Government, 1550–1750

FOCUS What factors enabled European scientific and political innovations in the early modern period?

COUNTERPOINT: The Barbary Pirates

FOCUS Why were the Barbary pirates of North Africa able to thrive from 1500 to 1800 despite Ottoman and European overseas expansion?

BACKSTORY

Europe and the greater Mediterranean basin gradually recovered from the devastating Black Death of 1347–1350 (see Chapter 15), but the inhabitants of this geographically divided region faced many challenges at the start of the early modern period. Christian Europeans grew increasingly intolerant of religious diversity. In the most extreme case, Iberian Muslims and Jews were forced to convert to Catholicism or leave the peninsula after 1492, prompting a great diaspora, or scattering, largely into Morocco and Ottoman lands, but also into Italy, France, and northern Europe. Resource-poor and avid for Asian trade goods and precious metals, western Europeans raced to develop new technologies of war and long-distance transport to compete with one another as well as with non-Europeans abroad. In contrast, the Muslim Ottomans of the eastern Mediterranean had been expanding their tributary land empire since the fourteenth century. By the later fifteenth century they would take to the sea to extend their conquests into the Mediterranean and the Indian Ocean.

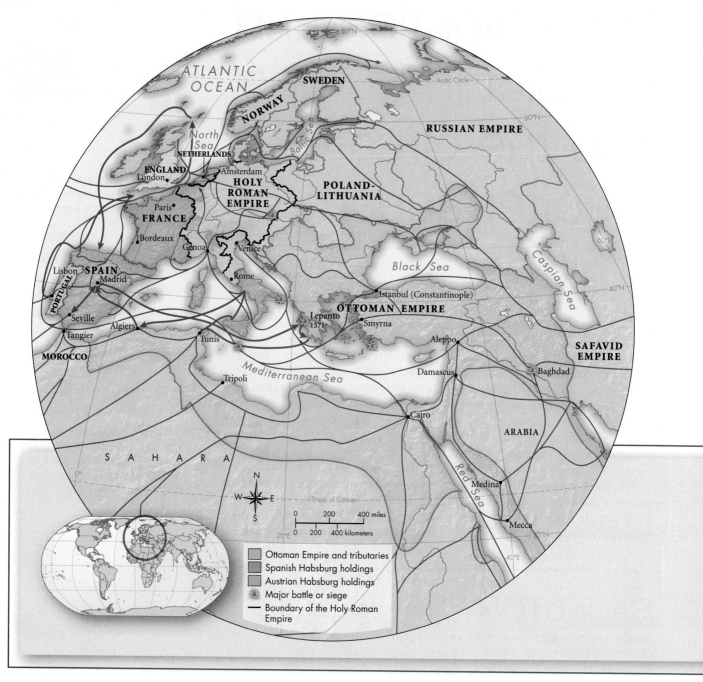

Ottoman Empire and tributaries

Spanish Habsburg holdings

Austrian Habsburg holdings

Major battle or siege

Boundary of the Holy Roman Empire

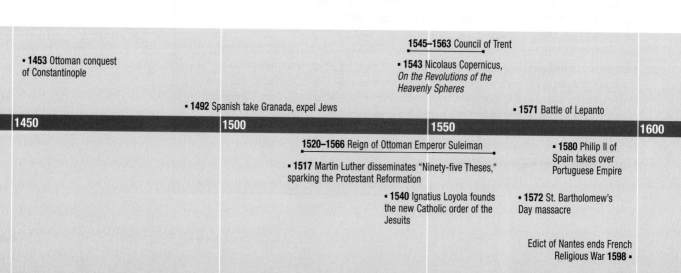

1545–1563 Council of Trent

1453 Ottoman conquest of Constantinople

1543 Nicolaus Copernicus, *On the Revolutions of the Heavenly Spheres*

1492 Spanish take Granada, expel Jews

1571 Battle of Lepanto

| 1450 | 1500 | 1550 | 1600 |

1520–1566 Reign of Ottoman Emperor Suleiman

1580 Philip II of Spain takes over Portuguese Empire

1517 Martin Luther disseminates "Ninety-five Theses," sparking the Protestant Reformation

1540 Ignatius Loyola founds the new Catholic order of the Jesuits

1572 St. Bartholomew's Day massacre

Edict of Nantes ends French Religious War **1598**

vanished Inca paradise. He based his best-selling *Royal Commentaries of the Incas*, composed in the Spanish countryside, on stories told by his mother in Cuzco.

Cervantes never crossed the Atlantic, but he found plenty to inspire him in the vibrant crossroads city of Seville, Spain's largest city with over one hundred thousand inhabitants. Yet as Cervantes' 1605 masterpiece, *Don Quixote*, revealed, it was the author's experiences as a prisoner in Algiers that most prepared him to bridge cultures and upend literary conventions. Although regarded as the quintessential Spanish novel—set in the Spanish countryside, with poor Catholic villagers as its central characters—*Don Quixote* includes long passages describing the many peoples, especially forced converts to Christianity from Islam and renegade Christians living in North Africa, who routinely crossed borders and seas, risking their lives to find love or maintain family fortunes. Cervantes died in 1616, in the midst of a brief truce between Spain and its greatest rival of the day, the emerging Dutch Republic. "El Inca" Garcilaso died the same year.

Europe and the greater Mediterranean in the age of Cervantes was, like the Indian Ocean basin, home to diverse peoples who had long been linked by deep and multifaceted connections. Yet it was increasingly divided by political, religious, and ethnic conflict. Christians fought Jews and Muslims, and, in the movements known as the Protestant and Catholic reformations, one another. Emerging national identities based on language and shared religion began to harden, even as local and regional trade increased. Christian Europe viewed Ottoman expansion with alarm, and fear of growing Muslim power contributed to rising tension and conflict between Christians and Muslims. Piracy flourished from the Atlantic to the Indian Ocean, and war raged from the Low Countries to the Balkans, eventually engulfing nearly all of Europe by 1618. In the course of the Thirty Years' War that followed, Catholics and Protestants, led by ambitious princes, slaughtered each other by the tens of thousands. Economic woes compounded the chaos, exacerbated by a sudden drop in silver revenues from

MAPPING THE WORLD

Europe and the Greater Mediterranean, c. 1600

The Mediterranean was an ancient global crossroads, and its role in connecting Africa, Asia, and Europe only intensified during early modern times. After 1450, African gold and Spanish-American silver lubricated trade, but they also financed warfare, notably an increasingly bitter rivalry between the Ottoman and Habsburg empires. The period also witnessed the rise of the so-called Barbary pirates, based mostly in Algiers, Tunis, and Tripoli, who offered only a tenuous allegiance to the Ottomans against their Christian foes. Mediterranean trade, sea routes to the Indian Ocean, and overland routes to East Asia were all increasingly tied to Europe's North Atlantic trade. As trade grew, conflict became ever more intense.

ROUTES ▼

— Major trade route

→ Voyages of Miguel de Cervantes Saavedra, c. 1571–1609

→ Route of the Spanish Armada, 1588

1618–1648 Thirty Years' War

1642–1646 English Civil War

1687 Isaac Newton, *Principia Mathematica*

1688 Glorious Revolution in England

1650　　　**1700**　　　**1750**

1643–1715 Reign of Louis XIV of France

1640 Portugal wins independence from Spain

1683 Ottomans defeated in Vienna by Polish-Austrian alliance

1701–1714 War of the Spanish Succession

the mines of Spanish America. Prolonged cold weather led to a cycle of failed harvests. Amid growing anxiety, large-scale rebellions broke out from Scotland to the Persian frontier.

Out of this prolonged period of religious, political, and economic instability, which some historians have labeled the "seventeenth-century crisis," came profound and eventually world-changing innovations in science, government, and the economy. The combination of growing religious skepticism, deep interest in the physical world sparked by overseas discoveries, and new optical technologies led a small cluster of European intellectuals to turn to scientific inquiry, initiating what later would be hailed as a "scientific revolution." Political innovations included absolutism and constitutionalism, two novel approaches to monarchy. Whatever their political form, nearly all of Europe's competing states engaged in overseas expansion, using the Atlantic as a gateway to the wider world. With the support of their governments, merchants and investors in western Europe launched new efforts to challenge the long-established global claims of the Spanish and Portuguese.

Christian Europe's overseas expansion was driven in part by the rise of its powerful Sunni Muslim neighbor, the Ottoman Empire. The Ottoman state, which by 1550 straddled Europe, the Middle East, North Africa, Arabia, and parts of Central Asia, was strategically located between three vast and ancient maritime trade zones. To the west lay the Mediterranean, Atlantic, and all of Europe; to the east and north, the Silk Road and Black Sea region; and to the south, East Africa, Arabia, and the vast Indian Ocean basin. Along with such major commercial crossroads as Istanbul (formerly Constantinople), Aleppo, and Cairo, the Ottomans controlled key religious pilgrimage sites, including Mecca and Jerusalem. No early modern European state approached the Ottomans' size, military might, or cultural and religious diversity, and no contemporary Islamic empire, not even the mighty Mughals, did as much to offset rising Christian European sea power. The Ottomans were arguably the most versatile of the early modern "gunpowder empires."

OVERVIEW
QUESTIONS

The major global development in this chapter: Early modern Europe's increasing competition and division in the face of Ottoman expansion.

As you read, consider:

1. To what degree was religious diversity embraced or rejected in early modern Europe and the greater Mediterranean, and why?

2. How did Christian Europe's gunpowder-fueled empires compare with that of the Ottomans?

3. What accounts for the rise of science and capitalism in early modern western Europe?

The Power of the Ottoman Empire   1453–1750

FOCUS

What factors explain the rise of the vast Ottoman Empire and its centuries-long endurance?

Founded by mounted Turkic warriors in the early fourteenth century, the Ottoman Empire grew rapidly after its stunning 1453 capture of the Byzantine capital, Constantinople (see Chapter 15). As in Mughal India, gunpowder weapons introduced by Christian Europeans sped the Ottomans' rise and helped them spread their dominions deep into Europe as well as the Middle East and North Africa. The Ottomans also took to the sea, challenging the Venetians, Habsburgs, and other contenders in the Mediterranean, as well as the Portuguese in the Indian Ocean. But it was arguably clever governance, minimal trade restrictions, and religious tolerance, not gunpowder weapons or naval proficiency, that permitted this most durable of Islamic empires to survive until the early twentieth century.

Tools of Empire

As we saw in Chapter 15, Mehmed II's conquest in 1453 of Constantinople not only shocked the Christian world but also marked a dramatic shift in the Ottoman enterprise. The sultans no longer viewed themselves as the roving holy warriors of Osman's day. Instead, they took on the identity of Islamic rulers with supreme authority over a multinational empire at the crossroads of Europe and Asia.

Devshirme System

Like other expansive realms, the Ottoman state faced the challenge of governing its frontier regions. To maintain control over the provinces, the Ottomans drew on the janissary corps, elite infantry and bureaucrats who owed direct allegiance to the sultan. Within a century of the capture of Constantinople, the janissaries were recruited nearly exclusively through the *devshirme* (dev-SHEER-may), the conscription of Christian youths from eastern Europe. Chosen for their good looks and fine physiques, these boys were converted to Islam and sent to farms to learn Turkish and to build up their bodies. The most promising were sent to Istanbul to learn Ottoman military, religious, and administrative techniques. Trained in Ottoman ways, educated in the use of advanced weaponry, and shorn of all family connections, the young men recruited through the devshirme were thus prepared to serve as janissaries wholly beholden to the sultan and dedicated to his service. In later years the janissaries would directly challenge the sultan's power, but for much of the early modern era, these crack soldiers and able administrators extended and supported Ottoman rule. A few rose to the rank of Grand Vizier (roughly, "Prime Minister").

Timar System

The *timar* system of land grants given in compensation for military service was another key means through which the Ottomans managed the provinces while ensuring that armed forces remained powerful. It was similar to Mughal India's *parganas* and Spanish America's *encomiendas* in that all three imperial systems were put in place to reward frontier warriors while preventing them from becoming independent aristocrats. Sultans snatched timars and gave them to others when their holders failed to serve in ongoing wars, an incentive to keep fighting. Even in times of stability, the timars were referred to as "the fruits of war." Timar-holders slowly turned new territories into provinces. Able administrators were rewarded with governorships. Although the timar and devshirme systems changed over time, it was these early innovations in frontier governance and military recruitment that stabilized and buttressed Ottoman rule in the face of succession crises, regional rebellions, natural disasters, and other shocks.

Expansion and Consolidation

Mehmed II's 1453 capture of Constantinople earned him the nickname "Conqueror." By 1464, Mehmed had added Athens, Serbia, and Bosnia to the Ottoman domain, and by 1475, the Golden Horde khanate of the Crimean peninsula was paying tribute to the Ottomans (see Map 20.1). In the Mediterranean, powerful Venice was put on notice that its days of dominance were coming to an end, and the Genoese were driven from their trading posts in the Black Sea. In 1480 the Ottomans attacked Otranto, in southern Italy, and in 1488 they struck Malta, a key Mediterranean island between Sicily and North Africa. At the imperial center, Constantinople, now named Istanbul, became a reflection of Mehmed's power, and also his piety. The city's horizon was soon dotted with hundreds of domes and minarets. With over one hundred thousand

devshirme The Ottomans' conscription of Christian male youths from eastern Europe to serve in the military or administration.

timar A land grant given in compensation for military service by the Ottoman sultan to a soldier.

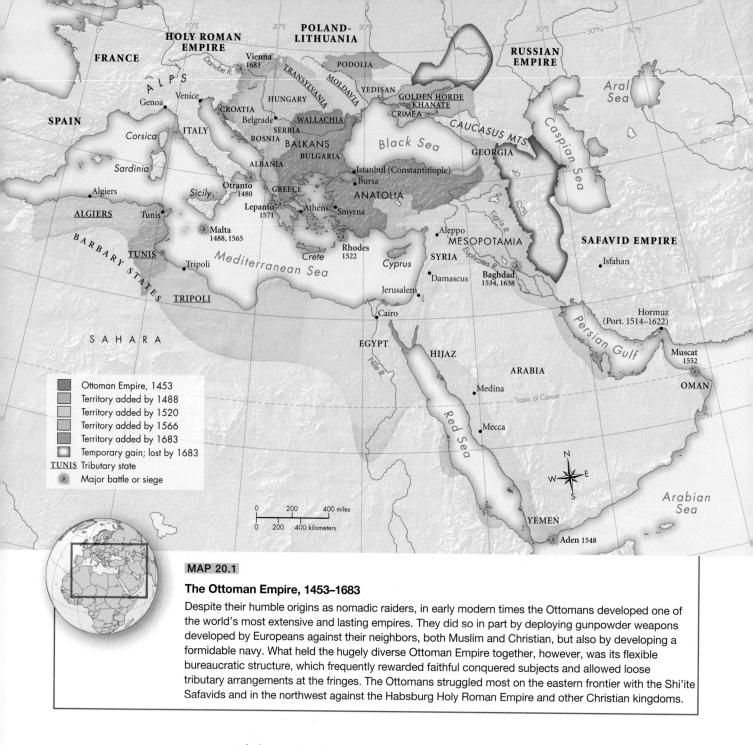

MAP 20.1

The Ottoman Empire, 1453–1683

Despite their humble origins as nomadic raiders, in early modern times the Ottomans developed one of the world's most extensive and lasting empires. They did so in part by deploying gunpowder weapons developed by Europeans against their neighbors, both Muslim and Christian, but also by developing a formidable navy. What held the hugely diverse Ottoman Empire together, however, was its flexible bureaucratic structure, which frequently rewarded faithful conquered subjects and allowed loose tributary arrangements at the fringes. The Ottomans struggled most on the eastern frontier with the Shi'ite Safavids and in the northwest against the Habsburg Holy Roman Empire and other Christian kingdoms.

inhabitants by the time of the sultan's death in 1481, Istanbul was one of the largest capitals in Eurasia.

The Ottomans turned newly obtained European artillery and highly trained janissary fighters on Islamic neighbors such as the Safavids and Mamluks in Syria and Egypt. Under Selim I (r. 1512–1520), called "the Grim," both were overwhelmed, although the Safavids would continue to challenge Ottoman power. Ottoman influence now touched the shores of the Indian Ocean, where Selim and the Ottomans challenged Portuguese expansion. The Muslim holy cities of Medina and Mecca became Ottoman protectorates, a boon for the state's religious reputation. Ottoman control of the Arabian peninsula would not be challenged until the end of the eighteenth century by the Wahhabi Saudis (discussed in Chapter 23).

Reign of Suleiman the Magnificent

Christian Europe again felt the sting of Ottoman artillery under Selim's successor, Suleiman (soo-lay-MAHN) (r. 1520–1566), called "the Magnificent." Suleiman ended

Istanbul's Skyline

When the former Constantinople became the capital of the Ottoman Empire, its rulers and court patrons soon transformed its architecture and overall skyline. The domes in the foreground make up part of the formerly Christian basilica Hagia Sophia, which was transformed into a mosque after 1453. In the distance rises Istanbul's imposing Blue Mosque, built between 1609 and 1616 for Sultan Ahmed I. (Photo by Ketan Gajria.)

the first year of his reign with the capture of two more symbolic prizes, Belgrade and Rhodes. The former feat gave Suleiman near-total control of eastern Europe, and the latter gave him effective rule over the eastern Mediterranean. In the western Mediterranean, the sultan supported Muslim pirates such as the Barbarossa brothers of Algiers, who targeted Europeans and held thousands of Christian captives for ransom (see Counterpoint: The Barbary Pirates). In 1565 the Ottomans laid siege to Malta. Though ultimately unsuccessful, this huge expedition provided yet another display of "the Great Turk's" naval capacity.

As the siege of Malta and other gunpowder-fueled seaborne offensives attested, Suleiman was determined to challenge the Habsburg Holy Roman Empire, as was his successor, Selim II (r. 1566–1574). But the Ottomans were dealt a terrible blow in 1571 when Habsburg forces sponsored by Spain's Catholic king Philip II (r. 1556–1598) overpowered Selim's navy at the Battle of Lepanto off the Greek coast (see again Map 20.1). Some six thousand janissaries armed with matchlock handguns faced off against over twenty thousand similarly armed European recruits and missionaries, among them the future author of *Don Quixote*. The Christians prevailed and commemorated their victory against the "infidels" in artwork ranging from painting to tapestry.

Although the Battle of Lepanto marked the beginning of a general decline in Ottoman sea supremacy, Selim II's will was far from broken. His forces managed to capture Tunis and Cyprus, and the navy was quickly rebuilt. A poet praised the sultan's vision:

> If it were not for the body of Sultan Selim,
> This generous king, this source of happiness
> The enemy would have occupied
> The country from one end to the other
> God would not have helped us.
> Neither would he have granted us conquest.[1]

Conflict with the Catholic Habsburgs

Battle with the Habsburgs reached a crescendo with the 1683 siege of Vienna. Ottoman gun technology had kept pace with that of western Europe, and some observers claimed that Ottoman muskets in fact had better range and accuracy than those used by Vienna's defenders. Heavy siege artillery was not employed here on the scale regularly practiced in Persia and Mesopotamia, however, and this may have proved a fatal mistake. Ottoman attempts to mine and blow up Vienna's walls failed just as tens of thousands of allies led by the Polish king arrived to save the day for the Habsburgs. At least fifteen thousand Ottoman troops were killed. Never again would the Ottomans pose a serious threat to Christian Europe.

Conflict with the Shi'ite Safavids

To the east, war with Persia occupied the sultans' attention throughout the sixteenth century. Since 1500, Safavid shahs had incited rebellions against Ottoman rule in outlying provinces, denouncing its Sunni leadership as corrupt and illegitimate. The Ottomans responded by violently persecuting both rebels and many innocents caught in between. Under Suleiman, campaigns against the Safavids in the 1530s and 1540s were mostly successful thanks to new guns, but territorial advances proved difficult to sustain. As one Ottoman eyewitness put it in the 1550s, "The territories called Persia are much less fertile than our country; and further, it is the custom of the inhabitants, when their land is invaded, to lay waste and burn everything, and so force the enemy to retire through lack of food."[2] The Safavids were just far enough away to prove unconquerable, leaving intermediate cities such as Baghdad as the key battlegrounds (see Reading the Past: Weapons of Mass Destruction: Ottomans vs. Persians in Baghdad).

Beginning in the late 1570s, Murad III took advantage of Safavid political instability to expand Ottoman influence beyond the frontier established by Suleiman. By the time a peace was arranged in 1590, the Ottomans controlled Mesopotamia and had established a firm presence in the Caucasus region. Still, the empire was rocked in the decades around 1600 by price inflation caused by a massive influx of Spanish-American silver, which flowed into the empire from Europe in exchange for Ottoman silks and spices. Ottoman attempts to fix prices of basic commodities and reduce the silver content of their coins only worsened the problem, and troops facing food shortages and poor pay rioted.

Some historians have argued that the Ottoman Empire was in decline following the reign of Suleiman the Magnificent, even though expansion continued into the seventeenth century, beginning with a long struggle for Hungary (1593–1606). Like Habsburg Spain, also said to be in decline in this era despite its vast size and wealth, Ottoman efforts to conquer new lands increasingly ended in stalemate, with military expenses far exceeding the value of the territory gained. The crushing weight of rising costs forced sultans and viziers to make humiliating concessions. Among the worst of these were losses to the Safavids that amounted to a total reversal of Murad III's gains. Frontier setbacks were not always evident from the center. Istanbul, with some four hundred thousand inhabitants by this time, was by far Eurasia's largest and most opulent city.

Sultanate of the Women

Murad IV (r. 1623–1640) managed to recapture Baghdad and several other eastern losses, but a crippling succession crisis ensued. Only after 1648 was the matter settled, with seven-year-old Mehmed IV (r. 1648–1687) on the throne. A child emperor required interim rule by regency, and in this case Mehmed's mother, Turhan, took control after fighting off challenges from other powerful women at court whose sons claimed a right to the throne. As a result of this direct feminine management of the Ottoman Empire, analogous to that of much tinier Aceh in these years (see Chapter 19), the period of Turhan's regency has been called "the Sultanate of the Women."

Indeed, as the Ottoman realm consolidated, court women became a powerful political force, despite their strict seclusion from society. First, the politics of succession dictated close control over the sultan's sexual life. Women came to dominate this key arena as early as the mid-sixteenth century. It was not seductive young wives and concubines who counted most, but rather elder women, particularly the Queen Mother. Second, much like

Weapons of Mass Destruction: Ottomans vs. Persians in Baghdad

In 1722 an Afghan army invaded the Safavid Empire from the east, seized the capital of Isfahan, and repulsed an Ottoman invasion from the west. The ambitious Afghan warlord Nadir Shah took over. Until his murder in 1747 Nadir attacked virtually all of Persia's neighbors, including the Mughals, but spent most of his energies fighting the Ottomans. Below is an excerpt from a chronicle of Nadir's campaigns written in around 1733 by an Armenian participant, Abraham of Erevan.

After laying siege to the city [Baghdad] for forty-eight days, Nadir received the twenty-five cannons that he had left behind in Zohab. They began to place the cannons and to fire on the city. Both sides exchanged cannon fire. Since the Ottoman cannons were larger than Nadir's, they were capable of hurtling larger cannon balls. One particular cannon, the largest, could hurl a cannon ball filled with approximately forty *okhas* [about one hundred pounds] of gunpowder. Although Nadir's forces were not concentrated in one area, such a cannon ball was fired from the fort. It exploded in the middle of the camp and killed one hundred troops. Seeing such casualties, Nadir moved the front further back. After that, the Ottoman cannon balls could not harm his troops, but neither could his cannon balls reach Baghdad. Thus they faced each other for fifty-five days without firing their artillery. The Ottomans then fired the large cannon once again, but the explosion damaged a wall of the fortifications and destroyed many houses, after which the Turks did not use it again. After fifty-five days of siege, the Ottomans, fully armed, made a sudden sortie with the intention of attacking the Persians. . . . The Pasha, however, remained in the city and did not permit the citizens to leave either, for half of them were Persians and he suspected that they would join the troops of Nadir.

The minute Nadir saw that the Ottomans had attacked him, he moved his troops forward without his cannons. The Ottomans, who had brought ten loaded cannons with them, began to fire on the Persian forces. Nadir then divided his troops into four groups so that he would not subject his entire army to the cannon fire. Having used their guns, the Ottomans could not reload their cannons fast enough, and while they were busy reloading, the Persians fell upon them from four sides and stopped the enemy from using its firepower. The two armies clashed and began to slaughter each other with swords and muskets for some seven hours. Eight thousand Ottomans and six thousand Persians perished. The Ottoman army suffered a defeat and fled back into the fortress and did not venture out again.

Source: Abraham of Erevan, *History of the Wars (1721–1738)*, ed. and trans. George A. Bournoutian (Costa Mesa, CA: Mazda Publishers, 1999), 77–78.

EXAMINING THE EVIDENCE

1. What role did cities such as Baghdad play in the battles between the Ottomans and Persians?

2. How do battles such as this one reveal the advantages and drawbacks of heavy guns?

Nur Jahan in Mughal India, powerful Ottoman women were important patrons of the arts and of pious works, and they figured prominently in royal rituals and mosque and hospital construction. The sultan was the ultimate patriarch, but it was his larger family that constituted the model of Ottoman society. Documents reveal that the royal harem, source of much lurid speculation by Europeans, was in fact a kind of sacred, familial space, more haven than prison.

Daily Life in the Ottoman Empire

Social Structure

As in most early modern states, the vast majority of Ottoman subjects lived in the countryside and were peasants and herders. Urban society, by contrast, was hierarchical, divided by occupation. Beneath the Osman royal family was the *askeri* (AS-keh-ree), or "military" class, which was exempt from taxes and dependent on the sultan for their well-being. In addition to military leaders, the askeri included bureaucrats and *ulama*, religious scholars versed in Arabic and canon law. Whereas the Safavids considered religious authorities superior to the shahs, the Ottoman sultans only took the advice of their chief ulama—a distinction that persists today in Shi'ite and Sunni states. Beneath the askeri was a much broader class of taxpayers called *reaya* (RAH-ya), or "the flock." The reaya included everyone from common laborers and artisans to traders and merchants. Thanks to a long-established Ottoman tradition of meritocracy and inclusion, provincial members of the lower classes could make considerable gains in status through education or military service.

In the countryside, peasant farmers' and pastoralists' lives revolved around cycles of planting and harvest, seasonal movement of animal herds, and the rhythms of commerce and religious observance. Some men were drafted into military service, leaving women to manage households, herds, and farms. Women in both rural and urban contexts also engaged in export crafts such as silk weaving, carpet making, and ceramic manufacture. Thus, although few country folk of either gender experienced urban life for more than a few days in a lifetime, rural life in the Ottoman Empire was shaped by the larger forces of international trade and the demands of the Ottoman military.

More mobile by far were merchants, whose livelihood was considered highly respectable. The merchants of trading crossroads such as Aleppo, Damascus, Smyrna, and Cairo profited handsomely from their access to Asian and African luxuries. Ottoman taxes on trade were relatively low, and the empire rarely resorted to the burdensome wartime demands made by European states on their often less-well-regarded merchant communities. On the flip side, the Ottoman state invested little in trading infrastructure beyond maintenance of **caravanserais**, or travelers'

Istanbul Street Scene

This rare sixteenth-century Ottoman street scene depicts men and women exchanging a variety of goods near the famous bazaar of Istanbul, formerly Constantinople. A proud merchant holds up a bouquet of flowers, and another weighs what may be almonds. Two women with different head coverings bring what appear to be ducks and bread for sale, while a woman in the left foreground seems to be making a cash purchase from a merchant balancing a basket of fruit or flowers on his head. The exchanges take place right next to the Column of Constantine, a relic of Roman rule under the city's namesake emperor. (The Art Archive/Museo Correr Venice/Alfredo Dagli Orti.)

lodges located along otherwise desolate trade routes. Like the Inca roadside inns taken over by the Spanish after conquest in 1532, these structures also served a military purpose.

Women's Experience

Recent research has revealed that ordinary women under Ottoman rule, much like court women, enjoyed more power than previously thought. Women had rights to their own property and investments, fully protected by shari'a, or Islamic law, before, during, and after marriage. This was, however, a rigidly patriarchal society. Women were expected to marry, and when they did they had few legal rights in relation to their husbands, who were permitted multiple wives and could divorce them at any time. Although women were treated as inferiors under Ottoman rule, it is worth noting that they had greater access to divorce than women in most early modern European societies.

caravanserai A roadside inn for merchants on the Silk Road and other overland trade routes.

The religious diversity of their subjects led the Ottomans to compromise in matters of gender. Islamic judges, or *qadis*, occasionally intervened in Christian married life, for example. Some Christian women won divorce by converting to Islam, as happened in the following case from Cyprus, decided in 1609: "Husna, daughter of Murad, Armenian wife, says before her husband Mergeri, son of Kuluk, Armenian: 'He always treats me cruelly. I do not want him.' He denies that. But now Husna becomes honored with Islam. After she takes the name Ayisha, her husband is invited to Islam, but he does not accept, so Ayisha's separation is ordered."[3] Although such conversions could be insincere, it is certain that religious diversity and legal oversight under Ottoman rule increased the range of options for female victims of domestic oppression.

Although devoutly Muslim at its core, the Ottoman state, with some 40 million subjects by the mid-seventeenth century, was at least as tolerant of religious diversity as the Islamic Mughal Empire, with policies similarly dictated by a practical desire to gain the cooperation of its diverse subjects. Religious tolerance and coexistence were most tested in frontier districts such as Cyprus and the Balkans. A description of Belgrade from 1660 illustrates just how diverse a frontier city could be: "On the banks of the river Sava there are three Gypsy neighborhoods, and on the banks of the Danube there are three neighborhoods of Greek unbelievers [i.e., Christians], as well as Serbs and Bulgarians also living in three neighborhoods. Right by the fortress is a neighborhood of Jews, those belonging to the seven communities known as the Karaim Jews. There is also a neighborhood of Armenian unbelievers. . . . All the rest are Muslim neighborhoods, so that families of the followers of Muhammad possess all the best, the most spacious and the airiest parts, located on the high or middle ground of the city."[4] Converts to Islam gained tax benefits (plus residential preferences, apparently), but punitive measures to force subjects to convert to the state religion were never used.

Religious Tolerance

Many Jews in the Ottoman Empire maintained their religious independence permanently. Some Jewish communities were centuries old and had local roots, but many more came as *Sephardim*, refugees from Iberian expulsions in the late fifteenth and early sixteenth centuries. Sephardic physicians, merchants, and tax collectors were a common sight in the capital city of Istanbul, and by the later sixteenth century many Ottoman towns had full-fledged Jewish communities. Members of the prominent Jewish Mendes family served as merchants, bankers, and advisers to the sultan in the sixteenth and seventeenth centuries.

In large part because of its incorporative nature and flexible structures, the Ottoman state proved one of the most durable in world history. Gunpowder weapons, though always important, were most critical in the early phases of expansion. Individual rulers varied widely in terms of aptitude and ambition, but the state itself remained quite stable. Fierce allegiance to Sunni Islam and control of its key shrines lent the Ottomans religious clout, yet their system of governance did not persecute Jews, Christians, or others who followed the state's rules regarding non-Muslims. Shi'ite Muslims faced more difficulties, by contrast, and this religious schism fueled a lasting rivalry with neighboring Persia.

**Ottoman Rule:
A Summing Up**

Finally, in the realm of commerce, powerful merchants and trade guilds could be found in several Ottoman cities, notably Aleppo, but overseas ventures and entrepreneurial activities remained limited, at most sizable family businesses (see Lives and Livelihoods: Ottoman Coffeehouse Owners and Patrons). The state placed minimal restrictions on trade and provided some infrastructure in the form of caravanserais, but there was no policy equivalent to Iberian support of overseas commerce in the form of trading forts and convoys. In this regard the Ottoman Empire was profoundly different from the rising "merchant empires" of western Europe, where an increasingly global and highly competitive mercantile capitalism hitched state interests directly to those of bankers and merchants.

Ottoman Coffeehouse Owners and Patrons

Ottoman Coffeehouse

This late-sixteenth-century miniature depicts a packed Ottoman coffeehouse. The patrons and serving staff all appear to be male, but they represent many classes and age groups, and possibly several religious traditions. In the upper middle, elite men with large turbans are conversing; a worker prepares a tray of cups in a small room to their right. In the lower middle, one man appears to be speaking as others turn their attention to a backgammon game under way near his feet. When rebellions or other political troubles brewed, coffeehouses were a source of concern for Ottoman authorities.

An institution of modern life in much of the world today, the coffeehouse, or café, originated on the southern fringes of the Ottoman Empire in around 1450. The coffee bean, harvested from a small tree that scientists would later call *Coffea arabica*, had long been roasted, ground, and brewed in the Ethiopian and Somalian highlands of East Africa. At some point, coffee was transplanted to the highlands of Yemen, at the southern tip of the Arabian peninsula (see again Map 20.1). Here members of Sufi Muslim brotherhoods adopted coffee drinking to aid them in their all-night meditations and chants. Merchants sailing north on the Red Sea carried the new habit-forming beverage to Cairo and Constantinople. From there it spread quickly throughout the entire Mediterranean commercial world. By the late seventeenth century, there were coffeehouses in all the major cities of western Europe. By the early eighteenth century, coffee itself was planted in the tropical Americas.

Despite coffee's sobering effects, many *imams*, or religious scholars, were initially skeptical of its propriety. The

Europe Divided 1500–1650

FOCUS

What sparked division in Europe after 1500, and why did this trend persist?

Europe in the age of Ottoman ascendancy was diverse, fractured, and dynamic. By 1500, commerce and literacy were on the rise, populations were growing, and armies of craftsmen were perfecting technologies of warfare, manufacture, and navigation. Savvy publishers capitalized on demand for fiction long before Cervantes, but they also made available new thoughts on religion and science as well as new translations of classical works. Thus, the growth of literacy helped unsettle old notions of time, space, and human potential. A less visible transformation was taking place in the countryside, where traditional, reciprocal relationships tying peasants to feudal lords were increasingly replaced with commercial ones. Most notable in western Europe, especially in England, this shift entailed a rise in renting, sharecropping, and wage work, a proliferation of market-oriented farms owned by urban elites, and the privatization of lands formerly enjoyed as common community resources. Peasants displaced by this early capitalist restructuring of the countryside increasingly filled Europe's cities. Some went overseas to try their luck in the colonies.

word coffee apparently derives from *qahwa*, one of several Arabic terms for wine. Imams used this word since the beverage altered consciousness in a noticeable, if not necessarily debilitating, way. Eventually, coffee was decreed an acceptable drink in accordance with scripture, and was widely consumed during fasts such as Ramadan. Both men and women were allowed to drink coffee, but several *fatwas*, or religious prohibitions, were issued against female coffee vendors in the early sixteenth century. As a result, both the public sale and public consumption of coffee became male preserves in the Ottoman Empire.

Coffee's troubles were far from over. If coffee itself was declared wholesome, the places where it was commonly consumed were not. Coffeehouses, sometimes run by non-Muslims, proliferated in major market cities such as Cairo by the early 1500s, drawing hoards of lower-class traders, artisans, and even slaves. Unable to suppress the café even at the core of their empire, Ottoman religious leaders simply denounced them as places of iniquity, dens of sinners. Female musicians played and danced scandalously in some, conservative clerics argued, while other cafés promoted homosexual prostitution. Some coffeehouses served as well-known hangouts for opium and hashish addicts, further tainting their reputation. Then came the vice of tobacco smoking, introduced from the Americas by European merchants in the early seventeenth century.

As later proved true in Europe, there were other reasons to fear the coffeehouse. Ottoman officials suspected the cafés as hotbeds of insurrection and treason. Still, they proved impossible to suppress, and coffee vendors quickly sprang back into action when the authorities closed them down. The Ottomans finally relented, deciding that the coffeehouse was an ideal place to gauge popular reactions to state policy and planting spies. In an era before restaurants, and in a religious climate hostile to alcohol and hence taverns, the coffeehouse met a variety of social needs. It was first a place where traveling merchants far from the comforts of home could exchange information, buy their associates a few rounds of satisfying coffee, and perhaps relax with a game of backgammon and a water-cooled smoke. For men of the working class, the coffeehouse became a place of rest and collegiality, and occasionally of political ferment.

QUESTIONS TO CONSIDER

1. How did Islamic clerics' attitude toward coffee change? What factors might account for this shift?

2. How and why did the Ottoman state come to accept the coffeehouse as a social institution?

For Further Information:
Hattox, Ralph. *Coffee and Coffee Houses: The Origins of a Social Beverage in the Medieval Near East*. Seattle: University of Washington Press, 1985.
Schivelbusch, Wolfgang. *Tastes of Paradise: A Social History of Spices, Stimulants, and Intoxicants*. Translated by David Jacobson. New York: Vintage, 1993.

Everyday Life in Early Modern Europe

Historians estimate that Europe in 1492 had a population of about 70 million, or slightly more than the population of the Americas just prior to Columbus's arrival. By 1550, Europe counted some 85 million inhabitants, and it was still growing rapidly. This population increase was mostly due to reduced mortality rather than increased births. Unlike larger Ming China and Mughal India, Europe's high growth rate was not sustained. A series of epidemics and climatic events beginning in around 1600, coupled with the effects of the Thirty Years' War (1618–1648) and numerous other conflicts, led to population stagnancy and even decline. Europe's population in 1630 was below 80 million, and would not reach 100 million until just before 1700.

The Columbian Exchange was largely responsible for the sixteenth-century population increase. In both city and countryside, American crops radically altered European diets after 1500. Maize, potatoes, tomatoes, capsicum peppers, and many other foods reordered both peasant and elite tastes and needs. In some cases this sped population growth, and in others it simply spiced up an otherwise bland diet. Potatoes came to be associated with Ireland and

Changing Patterns of Consumption

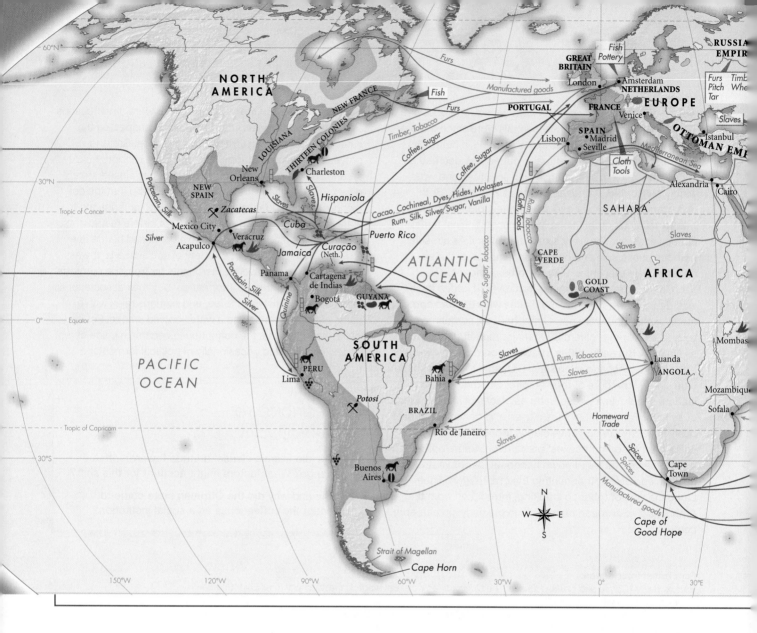

paprika with Hungary and Spain, but these and other American foods were widely embraced and helped spur an increasingly sophisticated consumer culture. American-grown sugar, tobacco, and later chocolate, vanilla, and coffee also figured prominently in Europe's taste revolution, as did Asian-grown tea and a host of exotic spices. European consumers also demanded new drugs such as opium and quinine bark, and merchants who trafficked in these and other tropical goods often made enormous profits. Thus, Europe's new connection with the Americas had a profound impact on its population, culture, and economy (see Map 20.2).

Environmental Transformations

The rise of commercial farming and peasant displacement, as well as overseas expansion, transformed ecosystems. Throughout Europe, more and more forest was cleared. Some princes passed decrees to limit deforestation, usually to preserve hunting grounds rather than for the good of the forest itself, but peasants still entered reserves in search of fuel and timber. Laws against such common use did little to relieve the stress, turning environmental problems into social ones. Shipbuilders, metalsmiths, and construction workers consumed forest as well, and wars and fires destroyed still more. By 1500, many Mediterranean cities, and even some northern European ones, relied on imported wood, sometimes looking as far afield as the Americas for new supplies. Not all environmental transformations were negative, however. The Dutch improved transportation by building canals and reclaimed land for agriculture from the sea by erecting dikes and filling wetlands.

Life Expectancy and Marriage Patterns

More people than ever crowded into European cities. Naples, London, and Paris were each home to more than two hundred thousand inhabitants by 1600. Nearly a dozen other

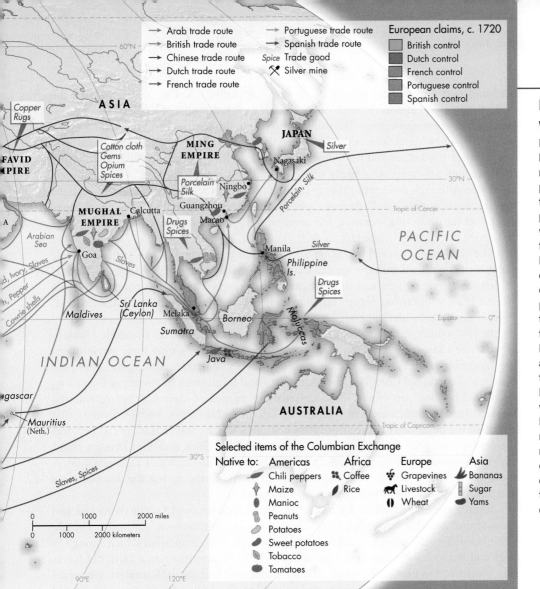

MAP 20.2

World Trade, c. 1720

Europeans progressively revolutionized global trade through maritime expansion and competition. Overland trade continued apace, but it was European seaborne merchants who were most responsible for bringing exotic goods to Europe, Africa, and the Americas, and for transporting tropical plantation products and precious metals to the rest of the world. The Atlantic slave trade was just one sector of Europe's increasingly global and deeply interconnected trading sphere. A byproduct of European maritime expansion was the so-called Columbian Exchange, the introduction of new foods, animals, and microbes to regions never exposed to them before. The effects were by turns devastating and phenomenally successful.

cities in Iberia, the Netherlands, and Italy were close behind, with populations over one hundred thousand. Still, the vast majority of Europeans remained in the countryside. Life for most, including the nobility, was short. A lucky few survived into their eighties and even nineties in both urban and rural settings, but high infant mortality yielded overall life expectancies of only eighteen to thirty-six years.

Most early modern Europeans did not rush to marry, nor were they compelled to enter arranged marriages, as in some Asian societies. Women were between twenty and twenty-five, on average, when they married. Men married slightly later, between twenty-three and twenty-seven, in part due to itinerant work and military obligations. Relatively few children were born out of wedlock, at least according to surviving church records, but many were conceived before marriage. Most partners could expect to be widowed within twenty years, in which time half a couple's offspring would probably also have died. Moreover, one in ten women died in childbirth. In Europe, as in much of the world at this time, the prospect of death was never far away.

Protestant and Catholic Reformations

Like Islam, Christianity had long been subject to disagreements and schisms. Yet the critiques of Roman Catholicism presented by several sixteenth-century northern European theologians marked the deepest split thus far. Catholic reformers beginning with the German monk Martin Luther argued that the church had so deviated from early Christian teachings that only radical reform could save the institution. For such reformers, the evident corruption and worldliness of the church were symptoms of a much deeper problem. In their view, the church had drifted into profound doctrinal and theological error. Inspired by a newfound faith in the individual that had its roots in Renaissance humanism (see Chapter 15), Luther and his followers emphasized the individual's ability to interpret scripture and communicate directly with God, without the intercession of priestly intermediaries. Although their opposition to Church teachings was theological, its implications were profoundly political. Outraged Catholic officials branded Luther and his followers Protestant (or protesting) heretics, and much of Europe fell into a century of bloody conflict fueled by religious hatred (see Map 20.3).

The Protestant Challenge

The challenge mounted by Luther amplified old complaints. Many ordinary people had grown dissatisfied with the Roman Catholic Church, particularly in northern Europe. Widespread abuse of benefices, or parish territories, reached a breaking point in the years around 1500, with far too many church officeholders concerned only with the financial rewards associated with their positions.

In 1517 Luther circulated "Ninety-five Theses"—propositions for academic debate—in which he charged that church policy encouraged priests to ignore their parishioners, keep concubines, and concentrate on money-grubbing. Worse, according to Luther, the church had corrupted Christian teachings on sin and forgiveness by inventing Purgatory, a spiritual holding pen where the deceased were purged of their sins before entering Heaven. Luther denounced the widespread sale of **indulgences**, written receipts that promised the payer early release from Purgatory, as a fraud. Heaven, Luther claimed, was the destination of the faithful, not the wealthy or gullible. Such teachings struck a chord among oppressed German peasants, many of whom took up arms in a 1525 rebellion. A social conservative, Luther withheld support from the uprising, but the revolutionary potential of Protestant Christianity was now revealed.

Church fathers balked at the notion of reform and ordered Luther defrocked and excommunicated. He responded by breaking away to form his own "Lutheran" church. Critiques similar to Luther's issued from the pens of the Swiss Protestant Ulrich Zwingli in 1523 and France's John Calvin in 1537. By the 1550s, Protestantism in a variety of forms was widespread in northern Europe, and its democratic and antiauthoritarian undercurrents soon yielded radical and unexpected political results. Still, most Europeans remained Catholic, revealing a deep, conservative countercurrent. That countercurrent soon resurfaced with a vengeance, although Catholicism, too, would be transformed.

Anglican Protestant Church

Another major schism occurred in 1534 when England's King Henry VIII declared his nation Protestant. Although Henry broke with the church for personal and political reasons rather than theological ones (the king wanted a divorce that the pope refused to grant), Anglican Protestantism was quickly embraced as the new state religion. Critics were silenced by Henry's execution of England's most prominent Catholic intellectual, Sir Thomas More, author of *Utopia* (1517). As in central and northern Europe, however, this early, mostly peaceful break hardly marked the end of Catholicism in England.

Founding of the Jesuit Order

The Catholic Church's leaders responded to Protestantism first with stunned disbelief, then vengeful anger. Some among the outraged Catholic majority launched strong but peaceful assaults. In Spain, for example, a Basque soldier calling himself Ignatius of Loyola became a priest and in 1534 founded a new religious order. Approved by the pope in 1540, the Society of Jesus, or Jesuits, soon became the Catholic Church's greatest educators and wealthiest property managers. More importantly for global history, they set out as missionaries to head off Protestant initiatives overseas. Within a few decades of Loyola's founding of the order there were Jesuit preachers in places as far-flung as Brazil, West Africa, Ceylon, and Japan (see Seeing the Past: Gift Clocks for the Emperors of China). Others stuck closer to home and won back converts in central Europe on the eve of the Thirty Years' War.

indulgence In early modern Europe, a note sold by the Catholic Church to speed a soul's exit from Purgatory.

In the face of the Protestant challenge, some high officials within the church called for self-examination, and even the pope ultimately agreed that it was time for the church to

MAP 20.3 **Protestant and Catholic Reformations in Europe**

In the midst of early overseas expansion, a great schism among Christians emerged in Europe. What Protestants called the Reformation was a fundamental questioning of Roman Catholic doctrine and practice. The dispute quickly produced violence and led some kingdoms, such as England, to break entirely from papal authority. France dissolved into civil war pitting Catholics against Protestants, and Spain and Portugal used their Inquisitions to persecute Protestants as heretics. A Catholic Reformation sought to reform and strengthen the church, but conflict continued to bubble up, leading soon after 1600 to the disastrous Thirty Years' War, the most deadly for civilians yet experienced in world history.

Witches persecuted throughout northern Europe, c. 1520–1720

Nantes
Edict of Nantes 1598

Birthplace of Ignatius Loyola, founder of Jesuit Order, 1540

Trent
Council of Trent 1545–1563

PORTUGAL
(Spanish, 1580–1690)

Portuguese Inquisition, from 1497

Spanish Inquisition prosecutes witches, Protestants, and suspected Jews, from 1478

Europe After the Thirty Years' War, 1648

Predominant religion, c. 1560
- Lutheran
- Anglican
- Calvinist
- Calvinist influenced
- Roman Catholic
- Mixed Protestant-Catholic
- Site of St. Bartholomew's Day massacre, 1572

- Spanish Habsburg lands
- Austrian Habsburg lands
- Other German states
- Swedish lands
- Ottoman Empire
- Boundary of the Holy Roman Empire

Gift Clocks for the Emperors of China

Courting the Qing: European Gift Clocks in the Forbidden City (The Palace Museum, Beijing/ChinaStock.)

dynasty, the great Westerner Li Madou [Matteo Ricci] presented a self-sounding bell, a mysterious and unknown art. The great bell sounds the hours, at midday, one sound."

The Chinese were relatively uninterested in Western notions of timekeeping in itself because they had their own means and units of measurement. Instead, the Chinese admired the clocks for their intricate mechanical construction and welcomed them as "high-tech" status symbols. The Jesuits were for many years allowed special access to Beijing's Forbidden City primarily as clock repairmen. Their efforts to link clockwork to godliness in a Western Christian sense failed, but they did eventually spawn royal workshops capable of producing elaborate if not particularly accurate timepieces by the early eighteenth century. Under Qing rule, the Royal Office of Clock Manufacture opened in 1723. By this time, advances in English clock- and watchmaking coincided with increased British interest in China, leading to a new wave of gift timepieces meant to win favor at court. Those shown here are on display today in the Forbidden City, the Ming and Qing imperial palace in Beijing that now houses the Palace Museum. Gifts from a range of Western ambassadors, they reveal European states' centuries-long effort to curry favor with the powerful Chinese Empire.

Source: Catherine Pagani, *Eastern Magnificence and Western Ingenuity: Clocks of Late Imperial China* (Ann Arbor: University of Michigan Press, 2001).

With the exception of raw silver, China had little need of products introduced by Europeans hoping to trade for silk, porcelain, and eventually, tea. This presented a great problem for merchants short of silver, but it also challenged early modern European missionaries. The first Jesuits arrived in China in the 1550s, barely a decade after the pope's formal recognition of their order. They spent their first years trying to win poor converts inhabiting the cities along the South China Sea, but by the 1580s some Jesuit priests, such as the Italian Matteo Ricci, began working their way toward Beijing. Given China's huge population, it made sense to try to convert those at the top of the social order in hopes that they would mandate the conversion of their many millions of subjects. Chinese officials, courtiers, and princes were not easily swayed even by the most sophisticated philosophical arguments, but they were almost universally fascinated by advances in Western science and technology.

Aware of this, Ricci developed a special program of "Christian science," attempting to link Western cartography, optics, metallurgy, and clockmaking to notions of divine order. He carried a European clock to Beijing in hopes of wowing the emperor in 1601, and it proved a big hit. A Chinese chronicle from 1603 records the event as follows: "In the twenty-eighth year of the reign of Wanli of the Ming

EXAMINING THE EVIDENCE

1. Why did Western missionaries such as Ricci think that introducing European clocks to China would aid conversion efforts?

2. How did Chinese appreciation of these clocks reflect cultural differences between them and Europeans?

clarify its mission. The Council of Trent (1545–1563) yielded a new charter for the Roman Catholic Church. Far from offering compromises, however, Trent reaffirmed the Catholic Church's conservatism. Purgatory and indulgences were not eliminated, nor was priestly celibacy. Sacraments such as marriage were reinforced and sexual behavior more circumscribed than ever before. The church also policed ideas and banned books. Cervantes was fortunate to have only one sentence of *Don Quixote* removed. In some places, such as the staunchly Catholic Iberian world, the Holy Office of the Inquisition acted as enforcer of the new precepts, rooting out and punishing alleged deviance. Historians have shown that ordinary Catholics could be skeptical of the church's dogmatic claims, but much of what we know about these freethinkers comes from their Inquisition trial records.

Council of Trent

In the wake of Trent, France's Catholics began persecuting Huguenots, as Calvinist Protestants were known in France, in earnest. This culminated in the Saint Bartholomew's Day massacre of 1572, in which tens of thousands of Huguenots were slaughtered and their bodies mutilated (see again Map 20.3). Just back from America, horrified Huguenot Jean de Léry wrote how "civilized" French Christians had proved themselves far more barbaric than Brazil's Tupinamba cannibals, who at least killed one another according to rigid honor codes. Hostilities ended only in 1598 when the French king Henry IV signed the Edict of Nantes granting Protestants freedom to practice their religion. It helped that Henry IV was a former Protestant, but the Huguenots' troubles were not over.

French Wars of Religion

Imperial Spain and Its Challenges

With religiously and politically fractured kingdoms and duchies the rule in early modern Europe, unified Spain proved to be the exception. Largely financed by the wealth of their numerous overseas colonies, Spain's Catholic Habsburg monarchs sought to consolidate their gains in Europe, and more importantly, to challenge the much larger and more powerful Ottoman Empire to the east. As we have seen, the fight against the "Great Turk," to use the language of the day, forever altered the lives of veterans such as Miguel de Cervantes.

Philip II came to the throne of Spain in 1556, when his father, Holy Roman Emperor Charles V (r. 1516–1556), abdicated. The title of "Emperor" passed to Ferdinand, Charles's brother, but Philip inherited extensive holdings of his own. Taken together, his kingdoms were much larger and richer than his uncle's. Indeed, by 1598, the year of his death, Philip II ruled the world's first empire "upon which the sun never set." The distant Philippines were claimed and named for him in 1565. Still, governing a far-flung and culturally diverse empire brought more burden than pleasure. A forceful but pious monarch, Spain's so-called Prudent King would die doubting his own salvation.

Reign of Philip II

One of Philip's first concerns, inherited from his father, was centralization in the core kingdoms. Castile and Aragon had been nominally united with the marriage of Isabella and Ferdinand in 1469, but local nobles and semiautonomous cities such as Barcelona continued to challenge royal authority. Charles's attempts to assert his will had sparked rebellions in the 1520s, and regional resentments in Iberia itself continued to fester throughout the period of overseas expansion. Philip responded in part by turning Madrid, formerly a dusty medieval crossroads in central Castile, into a world-class capital and Spain's unequivocal center. The capital's building boom was funded in large part by American treasure. Palaces, churches, monasteries, and residential structures proliferated, often blending traditional Castilian and northern European architectural styles. Envious neighbors joked that the Spanish had discovered a magic formula for turning silver into stone.

Thanks to New World treasure, Spain had become Europe's most formidable state by the second half of the sixteenth century. Among other successes, Philip's forces had beaten, as we have seen, the Ottoman navy at Lepanto in 1571. Philip's biggest setback was the revolt of the Netherlands, a politically and religiously divided region inherited from his father. The so-called Dutch Revolt, which began in 1566, taxed Iberian resources severely before its end in 1648. This was a war the Spanish lost, despite enormous effort.

Annexation of Portugal

Two other key events in Philip II's reign were the assumption of the Portuguese throne in 1580 and the 1588 attempt to invade England by sea. Both events had global significance. Portugal's King Sebastian died without an heir in 1578, and the subsequent succession crisis ended only when Philip, whose mother was Isabella of Portugal, stepped in to take the crown. Legitimate or not, Philip's move required an armed invasion, and the Portuguese always regarded Spanish rule, which lasted from 1580 until 1640, as unlawful and oppressive. In global terms, Spanish-Portuguese union meant that one monarch now ruled a substantial portion of Europe, much of the Americas, and dozens of far-flung Asian and African ports, islands, and sea routes. No European challenger was even close.

Philip knew this, and he assumed his good fortune was a reflection of divine will. Like many powerful individuals at their peak, Philip overstretched his mandate. Irritated by English harassment of the Spanish in the Americas and by English aid to the Dutch rebels, and motivated first and foremost by a determination to bring England back into the Catholic fold, Philip decided to launch a full-scale invasion of the British Isles. Such an undertaking would require the concentration of an enormous amount of military resources, and as at Lepanto, the stakes were correspondingly huge.

The Spanish Armada

Route of the Spanish Armada, 1588

The Spanish **Armada** of 1588, the largest and most expensive naval force assembled up to that time, appears in retrospect to have been an ill-considered enterprise. Means of communication were few and slow, and most Spanish sailors were poorly equipped for foul weather. Neither side regarded the invasion as foolish at the time, however, and ultimately it was defeated due to a host of factors, only some of them within Spanish control. The Spanish stockpiled supplies for years, and even Cervantes took part, as a clerk charged with cataloguing stores of olive oil and other foods. When it came time to fight, English defenders such as the famous pirate Francis Drake, aided by numerous Dutch allies, were critical; they knew the English Channel and understood Spanish tactics and technology. English guns were also powerful, carefully placed, and well manned. Aiding this defense were harsh weather, contrary winds, poorly mounted cannon, and numerous other complications. Spanish luck went from bad to worse.

Ships not sunk by English and Dutch artillery were battered by waves and drawn off course by fierce gusts. The great Spanish fleet scattered, and the remaining vessels were forced to sail north around Scotland to avoid capture. Here in the cold North Atlantic, Spanish sailors died by the hundreds of hunger and exposure. Some survivors were captured off the coast of Ireland. The English, hardly the sea power they would later become, were jubilant. Subjects of the fiercely Protestant Elizabeth I had proved that mighty Philip and his great armada were not invincible after all.

Spain's misfortunes only compounded in the wake of the armada disaster, and although the world's most extensive empire was hardly crumbling, Philip II's successors faced a potent new competitor in the form of the breakaway Dutch Republic. The Dutch projected their power overseas beginning in the 1590s, and by 1640 the Dutch East and West India companies took over many of the key trading posts held by the joint Spanish-Portuguese Empire from the Caribbean islands to Japan. Beginning in 1630, the West India Company occupied northeastern Brazil, calling this vast territory New Holland. What the Dutch did not know was that at precisely this time the main sources of Spanish wealth, the great silver mines of Potosí in present-day Bolivia, were petering out. Much of the world was deeply affected. Declining silver revenues combined with other chance factors sparked what has become known as "the seventeenth-century crisis" (see Figure 20.1).

armada A fleet of warships; usually used in reference to the Spanish naval fleet defeated by England in 1588.

Defeat of the Spanish Armada

Gunpowder weapons are very much on display in this dramatic 1601 painting by Dutch marine artist Hendrik Cornelisz Vroom of the 1588 Anglo-Dutch defeat of the Spanish Armada in the English Channel. High winds, shown by the stretched sail canvas, helped English and Dutch forces to outmaneuver and trap Spanish ships, which they blasted with their superior cannon. Several large vessels went down, and all on board drowned. Surviving Spanish ships sailed north around Scotland, where many crewmembers died of exposure. Others were captured in Ireland. It was one of the greatest naval defeats of early modern times. (Scala/White Images/Art Resource, NY.)

The Seventeenth-Century Crisis

Few topics have generated as much debate among historians as the seventeenth-century crisis, a complex series of events and trends that affected much of Europe and the Mediterranean basin from about 1600 to 1660. Some scholars have even claimed that no general crisis occurred, only a cluster of unrelated catastrophes. In any case, Europe's post-1660 rebound and push toward global maritime dominance seems remarkable. How did one of the world's most politically divided, religiously intolerant, and economically fractured regions give rise, in a relatively short time, to secular models of government, rational scientific inquiry, and financial capitalism, all hallmarks of modernity?

Historians focus on different causes, depending on their interpretive bent. Political and military historians focus on the "modern" horrors and early nationalism of the Thirty Years' War and related conflicts. Here, unlike in Asia and North Africa, gunpowder led to the dissolution rather than consolidation of empires. Economic historians focus on the shifting influx of American silver and its effects on food and other commodity prices. Some argue that inflated prices and economic depression had both negative and positive effects, sparking riots while prompting technical and financial innovations. Still other historians, informed by modern scientific techniques, focus on climate, analyzing ice cores and tree rings, along with traditional historical sources, to document the extent of the so-called Little Ice Age, which, as we will see, enveloped Europe from about 1550 to 1700. In the end it is hard to say which of these factors was most responsible for either the widespread turmoil or the swift turnaround that followed, but most historians agree that something transformative had occurred.

In the midst of a twelve-year truce between the Spanish and Dutch, the Thirty Years' War (1618–1648) broke out in

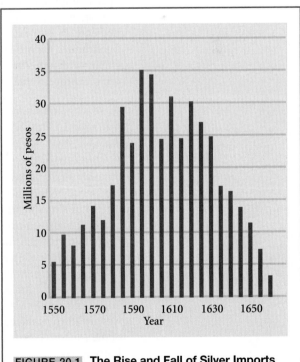

FIGURE 20.1 **The Rise and Fall of Silver Imports to Spain, 1550–1660**

The Thirty Years' War

Dutch artist Jan Maertszen de Jonghe graphically depicts the horrors of the battlefield in this 1634 rendering of the 1627 Battle of Dirschau, near Gdansk, Poland. The battle pitted Swedish king Gustav II, whose slain body appears in the foreground, against Polish-Lithuanian forces led by General Stanislaw Koniecpolski, shown here astride a chestnut horse. Soldiers and horses lie dead or wounded in this picture, but later in the Thirty Years' War, it was civilian casualties that reached levels not seen before in Europe. The Battle of Dirschau was one of several bloody encounters leading to stalemate in 1629, and this painting emphasizes the war's chaos and destruction more than its heroism. (akg-images.)

The Thirty Years' War

central Europe. This complex conflict pitted Christian factions against one another in a civil and international war that radically reshaped Europe's borders. The Thirty Years' War was devastating for civilians. Caught in the crossfire, they were forced to support occupying troops, only to be massacred for doing so when the tide turned and the other side's troops moved in.

In essence, the Thirty Years' War was over the internal politics of the Holy Roman Empire in central Europe (see again Map 20.3). This was really only a loose confederacy—since the days of Emperor Charles V, substantial autonomy had been ceded to an increasing number of Lutheran and Calvinist principalities and duchies. Inhabitants of these Protestant enclaves rightly feared a more assertive Catholic emperor. Emperor Ferdinand II was such a person, an ambitious, Jesuit-educated militant. When it became clear that Ferdinand might re-Catholicize central Europe, the various enemies of the Habsburgs sent aid, then joined the fray.

Before the war ground to a close, a variety of German and Bohemian princes, the kings of Denmark, Poland, and Sweden, plus the English, French, Dutch, and finally the Spanish had all been drawn into the conflict. Contemporary engravings and paintings from its last phase depict the full range of human cruelty, a blatant reminder, like the Saint Bartholomew's Day massacre, that Europeans were as capable of savagery as America's famous warrior cultures. At war's end at least a third of the population of Germany had died, and the region's infrastructure lay in ruins. From population decline to decreased agricultural production, the war was a manifestation of the seventeenth-century crisis.

Silver and Depression

It was also enormously costly in terms of money, the supply of which was shifting. Economic historians have found that throughout Europe prices rose even as demand fell. In one interpretation, an overabundance of silver in the late sixteenth century drove prices up, after which a sequence of plagues, droughts, wars, and other disasters killed off both consumers and suppliers of basic goods throughout Europe, leading to depression. A sustained drop in silver income beginning in around 1600 made hard money scarce when it was already overvalued, forcing many people to resort to barter. Thus, the fabulous wealth of the Americas proved both a blessing and a curse, shifting the global balance of power in Europe's favor at the same time that it led to dangerous and destructive economic volatility.

The Dutch Exception

Hard times for the masses could be good for some, and it appears that the Dutch fared rather well, particularly in comparison with the Spanish and Portuguese. The Netherlands' unique mix of financial capitalism, religious toleration, and overseas conquest seemed to

An Exiled European Muslim Visits the Netherlands

After an Ottoman-supported rebellion in Andalusia from 1569 to 1571, Spain's remaining forced converts to Christianity from Islam, or Moriscos, faced increasing persecution. Many fled to Morocco, Algeria, and other Muslim havens in North Africa, especially during a last wave of expulsions ordered by Philip III from 1609 to 1614. Among the refugees was Ahmad Ibn Qasim al-Hajari, born with the Spanish surname Bejarano in around 1569 in a village in Extremadura, not far from the birthplaces of Francisco Pizarro and Hernando Cortés. Al-Hajari went on to become a major spokesman for the Morisco community in exile, and he wrote and traveled widely. His best-known work, composed and circulated in both Arabic and Spanish, is called *The Supporter of Religion Against the Infidel* (c. 1637). In this passage, al-Hajari describes his visit to the Netherlands.

About the Netherlands: You should know that I set out for that country deliberately, although it lies farther from our own country than France. But a man should seek protection from others or from himself, and after I had experienced the way French sailors were treating Muslims, I said: I will not return to my country in one of those ships, but I will go to the country of the Netherlanders, because they do not harm Muslims but treat them well. . . .

After I reached the City of Amsterdam, I marveled at the beauty of its architecture and the style of its buildings, its cleanness and the great number of its inhabitants. Its population was almost like that of the City of Paris in France. There is no city in the world with so many ships as it has! One says that the total number of its ships, including the smaller and the bigger ones, is six thousand. As for the houses, each of these is painted and decorated with marvelous colors from top to bottom. Not one resembles another in the art of its painting. All the streets are made of paved stones. . . .

One should know that the Netherlands consists of seventeen islands, all of which used to belong to the Sultan of al-Andalus [the king of Spain]. At a certain time, a man appeared in those lands who was held as a great scholar by them, called Luther, as well as another scholar called Calvin. Each of them wrote his view of the corruption and deviation from the religion of our lord Jesus and the Gospel that had come about in the religion of the Christians. They said the popes in Rome misled the people by worshiping idols and by the additions they introduced into the faith by forbidding priests and monks to marry, and many other things. All the people of the Netherlands . . . embraced this doctrine and they rose up against their sultan until today. The people of the Sultanate of the English also follow this doctrine. There are also many of them in France. Their scholars warn them against the popes and the worshiping of idols. They tell them they should not hate Muslims because they are the Sword of God on His earth against the worshipers of idols.

Source: Ahmad Ibn Qasim al-Hajari, *The Supporter of Religion Against the Infidel,* ed. and trans. P. S. Van Koningsveld, Q. al-Samarrai, and G. A. Wiegers (Madrid: Consejo Superior de Investigaciones Científicas, 1997), 194–195.

EXAMINING THE EVIDENCE

1. What aspects of the Netherlands most impress al-Hajari?

2. How clear is al-Hajari's understanding of the Protestant Reformation?

---

offset many of the difficulties faced by other states (see Reading the Past: An Exiled European Muslim Visits the Netherlands). The Dutch East India Company's spice-island takeovers in Southeast Asia were critical, as seen in Chapter 19, but Dutch pirates, many sponsored by the West India Company, were also busy capturing Spanish silver fleets in the Caribbean.

Historians have long suggested that the climatic change known as the Little Ice Age may have spurred rebellion and even war during the seventeenth century, but only recently have enough data been assembled to generate a fairly clear picture of the century's weather cycles. It now appears that four of the five coldest summers ever recorded in the Northern Hemisphere occurred in the seventeenth century, and that global volcanic activity was probably a major contributing factor to the cooldown. Global cooling shortened growing seasons just as Europeans were pushing into more marginal and thus vulnerable agricultural lands. In alpine valleys, for example, peasants and herders were driven from their highland homes by advancing glaciers. Unprecedented droughts ravaged traditionally wet regions such as Scotland in the 1630s and 1640s, sparking violent uprisings in the midst of an already unstable political climate.

Little Ice Age

The Little Ice Age affected regions far beyond European borders. The worst drought in five hundred years was recorded on the Yangzi River between 1641 and 1644, probably contributing to the 1644 fall of the Ming dynasty in China (discussed in Chapter 21). Ottoman territories were also hit: Egypt's Nile River fell to its lowest recorded levels between 1640 and 1643. Troops on the Persian frontier rebelled when their pay in silver coin proved insufficient to buy food.

Increased Persecutions

Within Europe, the seventeenth-century crisis took on more sinister social dimensions with the rise of witchcraft trials and Inquisition prosecutions. In Protestant Europe, thousands of women were executed for alleged acts of sorcery, and in Catholic Spain and its colonies an unprecedented number of Jews were killed by order of the Inquisition between 1637 and 1649. It is difficult to know why these repressive outbursts occurred in the midst of war, famine, and other problems, but the tendency to scapegoat vulnerable persons in uncertain times has been documented elsewhere. More positive outcomes of the seventeenth-century crisis included scientific discoveries and novel political ideas that eventually took on global importance.

European Innovations in Science and Government 1550–1750

FOCUS

What factors enabled European scientific and political innovations in the early modern period?

In the aftermath of the religious wars of the sixteenth and early seventeenth centuries, a new wave of political consolidation took place in northern and central Europe in the form of absolutist and constitutionalist monarchies. Many of these states, like their Spanish, Portuguese, and Dutch predecessors, took their expansionist energies overseas. Global expansion, as these earlier players had learned, entailed great risks and huge defense costs. In addition to building professional navies, states created licensing agencies and sponsored monopoly trading companies. Financial innovations included stock markets and double-entry accounting, essential ingredients of modern capitalism. Also emerging from the divided world of Europe was a new development aided by the printing press and other technologies: the "scientific revolution." Although restricted for many years to a small number of theorists and experimenters who shared their work in Latin treatises, Europe's embrace of science was to prove globally significant.

The Scientific Revolution

The rise of modern Western science is often described, rather like the Protestant Reformation, as a heroic struggle against a hidebound Catholic tradition. Certainly church patriarchs clung to traditional ideas when challenged by the new science. Still, it was very often Catholic-educated priests and seminarians, along with the odd basement alchemist, who broke the mold in early modern times. Even the Protestants' access to scientific books owed everything to the labors of countless Catholic monks who over centuries had transcribed, translated, and sometimes composed key treatises. They were in turn indebted to numerous medieval Islamic scholars based in cities such as Baghdad and Córdoba. Finally, in early modern times, the printing press and a general interest in technical improvements helped give thousands access to knowledge.

As with the "seventeenth-century crisis," historians have long debated whether or not Europe experienced a genuine "scientific revolution" in the early modern era. Skeptics argue that the key innovations of the period were too restricted to educated elites and court patrons to justify the term *revolution*. In contrast, proponents describe an unprecedented shift in worldview that resonated beyond the small circle of known "scientific rebels."

Call it what we may, European intellectuals after about 1550 increasingly expressed skepticism about received wisdom and began to employ mathematical formulas and empirical (observable) data in an effort to discover the rules by which nature operated. Inductive and deductive reasoning were guiding principles in their efforts. Inductive reasoning—deriving general principles from particular facts and empirical evidence—was most clearly articulated by the English statesman and writer Sir Francis Bacon. Its complement, deductive reasoning—the process of reasoning from a self-evident general principle to a specific fact—was the contri-

geocentrism The ancient belief that the earth is the center of the universe.

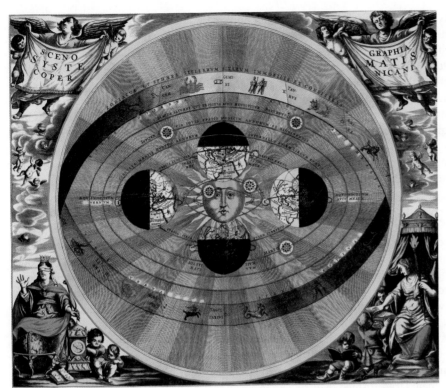

The Copernican Universe
The earth still appears quite large in relation to other planets in this 1660 rendering of a heliocentric, or sun-centered, cosmos, but the breakthrough initiated by Nicolaus Copernicus in 1543 is fully evident. Copernicus did not know that planets such as earth traced elliptical rather than perfectly circular orbits, but this was a minor error compared to the older view of a geocentric universe claimed since the days of the great ancient Greek philosopher Aristotle. (akg-images/historic-maps.)

bution of French thinker and mathematician René Descartes. One result of this new search for universal rules was a developing understanding of the way things worked, including the cosmos. Since this was akin to describing "Heaven" in a secular way, many churchmen bristled.

The first breakthroughs were made by a Polish monk, Nicolaus Copernicus. Copernicus was the first to systematically question the ancient Ptolemaic model of the cosmos, which was geocentric, or earth-centered. Copernicus's collected observations of solar, lunar, and planetary movements did not support **geocentrism**, suggesting instead that the stars and planets, including the earth, revolved around a fixed sun. Fearing ridicule, Copernicus did not publish his *On the Revolutions of the Heavenly Spheres* until 1543, the year of his death. Following Copernicus, the Danish astronomer Tycho Brahe compiled a wealth of "eyeball" data relating to planetary and stellar movements. This data was precise enough to help the German Johannes Kepler work out an elegant if not yet persuasive heliocentric, or sun-centered, model in which the planets circled the sun in elliptical orbits.

Many of Europe's most probing minds were open to the truth of **heliocentrism**, and some went on to risk not only reputations but lives to advance the project of wedding mathematics to observed phenomena. In works such as *The Advancement of Learning* (1605), Sir Francis Bacon attacked reliance on ancient writers and ardently supported the scientific method based on inductive reasoning and empirical experimentation. Bacon had his critics, but he was shielded from persecution by the Protestant English state, which he served as lord chancellor. By contrast, the Italian scientist Galileo Galilei is best remembered for his insistence, against an unforgiving Catholic Church, that nature was governed by mathematical laws. Although the Inquisition placed Galileo under house arrest, his use of new, high-grade telescopes to observe the moons of Jupiter furthered the cause of heliocentrism and challenged reliance on received wisdom.

Ultimately, minor deviations between Kepler's model and careful empirical observation were worked out in large part by the English scientist Isaac Newton. The elliptical planetary orbits discovered by Kepler, Newton argued through word and formula in *Principia Mathematica* (*Mathematical Principles*, 1687), resulted from the laws of motion, including the principle of gravity, which explained the forces that controlled the movement not only of

Early Breakthroughs

Newton's Synthesis

heliocentrism The early modern discovery that the sun is the center of our solar system.

planets but of objects on earth. The whole universe was brought together in one majestic system. Whereas Copernicus had feared publishing his findings in his lifetime, Newton faced a much more receptive audience. His synthesis would prevail until the twentieth century.

Advance of the New Science Beyond Europe

Other educated Europeans were testing boundaries in distant corners of the world. In the last years of the sixteenth century the Italian Jesuit Matteo Ricci stunned the Ming court with his vast knowledge of mechanics and mathematics. The Spanish-American metallurgist and parish priest Alvaro Alonso Barba went further, challenging received wisdom through experimentation in his 1627 treatise, *The Art of Metals*. Here in the remote silver mines of Potosí, high in the mountains of what is today Bolivia, Barba was sufficiently informed to comment on Galileo's observations of the moons of Jupiter as outlined in his 1610 publication, *Sidereus Nuncius* (*The Starry Messenger*).

The Emergence of Capitalism

Another great puzzle of early modern Europe regards the emergence of **capitalism**—an economic system in which private individuals or groups make their goods and services available on a free market and seek to take advantage of market conditions to profit from their activities. In developing a capitalist economic system, Europe diverged from the rest of the world, especially after 1650. To be sure, the desire to accumulate wealth and realize profits was by no means new. Ever since the introduction of agriculture and the production of surplus crops, some individuals and groups had accumulated great wealth. As we saw in Chapter 15, merchants in the fifteenth-century "global bazaar" avidly pursued profits from overseas trade. During early modern times, however, European merchants and entrepreneurs transformed their society in a way that none of their predecessors had.

Role of Trading Companies

Historians and economists remain divided as to how capitalism came about, as well as where it started. Most agree, however, that there were two overlapping stages: first commercial, and later industrial. Large trading companies such as the English East India Company and its Dutch competitor, the VOC, were especially important institutions in the commercial stage of capitalism. They spread the risks attached to expensive business enterprises and also took advantage of extensive communications and transportation networks. The trading companies organized commercial ventures on a larger scale than ever before in world history. They were supported by an array of businesses and services. Banks, for example, appeared in all the major commercial cities of Europe to safeguard funds and to grant loans to launch new ventures. Insurance companies mitigated financial losses from risky undertakings. Stock exchanges provided markets where investors could buy and sell shares in the trading companies, and they dealt in other commodities as well. Thus, innovative financial institutions and services created new connections among Europeans that facilitated expansion into global markets.

Rise of Wageworkers and the Bourgeoisie

In the countryside, meanwhile, innovations in mechanization and transport led to gains in productivity that exceeded population growth, especially in northwestern Europe. The arrival of potatoes and other New World crops boosted yields and filled peasant bellies. American sugar was increasingly used to preserve fruits through the long winter. Better food security enabled some peasants to sell their surplus labor for cash wages. Wages made peasants small-scale consumers, a new kind of market participant.

More dependable food supplies came with a social cost, however, most immediately felt by English peasants. Only landowners with secure titles to their property could take advantage of the new crops to practice commercial farming. Rich landowners therefore "enclosed" the land—that is, consolidated their holdings—and got Parliament to give them title to the common lands that in the past had been open to all. Land enclosure turned tenant farmers and sharecroppers into landless farm laborers. Many moved to the cities to seek work.

Cities became increasingly home to merchants, or burghers, as well as to wageworkers. The burghers, or **bourgeoisie**, grew to compete with the old nobility, particularly in England, the Netherlands, and parts of France, Germany, and Italy, as consumers of luxury goods. Especially after 1660 their economic power was boosting their political power.

capitalism In early modern Europe, a new way of conducting business by pooling money, goods, and labor to make a profit.

bourgeoisie In early modern Europe, a new class of burghers, or urban-dwelling merchants.

Europe's manufacturing sector was also deeply transformed. Beginning in the late Middle Ages, rising demand for textiles led to expanded production of woolen and linen fabrics. The major growth of the cloth industries took place in northern Europe beginning in the sixteenth century, when Spanish-American silver flowed through Spain to France, England, and Holland, despite ongoing conflicts. Asians did not much care for Europe's products, but colonists did. Millions of bolts of Dutch and French linens, as well as English woolens, were sent across the Atlantic, and even the Pacific, to Spanish and Portuguese colonies. Global interdependence grew ever tighter through the circulation of fabrics and silver. Europe's textile manufacturers begged Amsterdam and London merchants for Spanish-American dyes, along with Brazilian and Central American dyewood. Profits from growing international trade in textiles were then reinvested in more land for flax growing, larger weaving shops, and wages for increasing numbers of specialized workers. With the application of scientific principles and ever more innovative mechanical apparatus by the early eighteenth century, the stage was set for the emergence of industrial capitalism in England (discussed in Chapter 24).

England's commercial leadership in the eighteenth century had its origins in the mercantilism of the seventeenth century. European **mercantilism** was a system of economic regulations aimed at increasing the power of the state. It rested on the general premise that a nation's power and wealth were determined by its supply of precious metals, which were to be acquired by increasing exports (paid for with gold) and reducing imports to achieve domestic self-sufficiency. What distinguished English mercantilism was the notion that government economic regulations could and should serve the private interests of individuals and groups as well as the public needs of the state. For example, the Navigation Acts of the seventeenth century required that English goods be transported in English ships and restricted colonial exports to raw materials, enriching English merchants and manufacturers as well as the Crown.

Cornering the Atlantic slave trade and Indian Ocean cloth trade were England's two key overseas commercial objectives in the eighteenth century, and profits from both fueled industrial growth at home. As we will see in Chapter 22, English settlers amassed huge plantations in the Caribbean and North American mainland, based primarily on the labor of enslaved Africans, the profits from which they mostly sent home. English inroads in the Indian Ocean trade circuit, meanwhile, grew to eclipse all other European competitors. Capital that had been accumulated in the slave trade, Atlantic plantation complex, and East India monopolies was soon invested in industrial production in several English cities. Goods thus manufactured were subsequently forced on buyers in captive overseas markets, such as the North American colonies, enabling still greater capital accumulation in the imperial center. State power was exercised at every step, from the seizure of native American lands to the sale of African bodies, harsh reminders that the rise of industrial capitalism in England was not a magical or even a natural process, but rather the result of concerted applications of force in many parts of the world.

New Political Models: Absolutism and Constitutionalism

Europe in the wake of the Thirty Years' War witnessed the rise of two new state forms: absolutism and constitutionalism. Worn out by the costs of conflict, the Habsburg Empire fell into decline. A number of challengers sought to fill the void, including the commercially savvy Dutch, but it was the French under the Bourbon king Louis XIV who emerged pre-eminent. Not far behind, however, were the English, who despite a midcentury civil war moved to consolidate control over the British Isles and many overseas possessions by the early eighteenth century. As the great imperial rivals of the time, Britain and France developed distinct systems of governance later copied and modified by others. The monarchs of England found themselves sharply restricted by elected parliaments, whereas those of France sought absolute authority and claimed quasi-divinity. Despite their differing models of rule, the British and French managed to create the largest, most heavily armed, and widest-ranging navies yet seen in world history.

Although Spain's Philip II and other Habsburgs had acted in autocratic and grandiose ways since the mid-sixteenth century, no European monarch matched the heady blend of

Role of Textile Manufacture

Capitalism and Politics

mercantilism A system of economic regulations aimed at increasing the power of the state.

Absolutism in France

state drama and personal charisma of France's Louis XIV (r. 1643–1715). The "Sun-King," as he came to be known, personified the absolutist ruler who shared power with no one. Louis XIV spent much of his long reign centralizing state authority in order to make France a global contender. Though successful in the short run, Louis's form of **absolutism**— propped up in large part by rising taxes and a general contempt for the common masses— sowed the seeds of its own destruction.

Louis XIV came to the throne as a five-year-old, and his mother, Anne of Austria, and her Italian-born adviser and rumored lover, Cardinal Mazarin, ruled in his name. Under the regency, resistance quickly emerged in the form of the *Fronde*, a five-year period of instability from 1648 to 1653 that grew from a regional tax revolt into a potential civil war. Critics coined the term *Fronde*, French for a child's slingshot, to signify that the revolts were mere child's play. In fact, they posed an unprecedented threat to the Crown. Historians of the seventeenth-century crisis have often linked the uprisings to climate change, agricultural stresses, and price fluctuations. Whatever the Fronde's causes, nobles and district courts, or *parlements* (PARLE-mohn), asserted their power against the regency. In the end, the revolt was put down, and when Mazarin died in 1661, Louis XIV assumed total control. He would not forget the Fronde, drawing from it the lesson that the independent power of the French aristocracy must be eliminated and that all power and authority in France must derive from the king.

Like many other monarchs faced with entrenched power structures, Louis XIV spent the next several decades co-opting nobles and potential religious opponents through a mix of patronage and punishment. His rule was authoritarian, and like that of his Spanish Habsburg precursor, Philip II, intolerant of religious difference. After persecuting non-conformist Catholics in the 1660s, Louis exiled the country's remaining Huguenots, French Protestants whose protection had been guaranteed by Henry IV in the Edict of Nantes of 1598. Absolutism was extended to the press as well, with pro-state propaganda and harsh censorship of criticism the order of the day.

The French absolutist state also relied on loyal crown officers, called *intendants* (ON-tohn-don), whose authority superseded that of local parlements and nobles. These officials governed districts, or departments, in the king's name, administering justice, collecting taxes, and organizing defense. Loyal bureaucrats also included high-ranking commoners such as Jean-Baptiste Colbert, Louis's minister of finance. As a trusted favorite, Colbert also oversaw naval and overseas trade affairs, taking a close interest in French expansion in the Caribbean and North America. As the Ottomans had already shown, rewarding merit-worthy commoners with high office was as much a part of early modern government as containing the aspirations of high nobles. Building an overseas empire greatly expanded the scope of patronage politics.

Court Culture and State Power

More than any other early European monarch, Louis XIV arranged court life to serve as a sort of state theater. As in Inca Peru or Ming China, the ruler was allegedly divine, and physical proximity to him was regarded as both desirable and dangerous. A constant stream of propaganda in the form of poems, processions, statues, and medals celebrated the greatness of the monarch. "The state?" Louis asked rhetorically. "It is I."

To house his bulging court, which included growing numbers of fawning and reluctantly drafted nobles, Louis XIV ordered thousands of artisans and laborers to construct a palace befitting his magnificence. Built between 1662 and 1685, Versailles, just outside Paris, was to exceed the ambitious dimensions of Philip II's Escorial. Though hardly the pleasure dome outsiders and common folk imagined it to be, and far less opulent than the palace of Louis's near contemporary, Mughal emperor Shah Jahan, Versailles set a new model for European court grandeur. It was also a physical embodiment of Louis's political ideology. Versailles was a central point from which, at least in theory, all political power and authority flowed.

absolutism A political theory holding that all power should be vested in one ruler; also such a system of government.

constitutionalism An early modern system of government based on a written charter defining a power-sharing arrangement between a monarch and representative bodies, or parliaments.

Tax increases helped to cover the costs of building and maintaining Versailles. The point of raising taxes during Louis XIV's rule was not simply to underwrite court opulence, however. More costly by far were the armed forces. Naval construction grew tremendously under Colbert's direction, but the professionalization and reorganization of land forces was even more extensive. By 1700 France, a country of some 20 million people, could field three hundred thousand soldiers. This was more than ten times the number of soldiers in England, a country with about half of France's total population.

Palace of Versailles

In this 1668 aerial view of Versailles, painter Pierre Patel seeks to encompass the full grandeur and orderliness of French king Louis XIV's famous palace and retreat. Begun in 1661, Versailles instantly became a symbol of absolutist power, a virtual city unto itself. Many early modern rulers ordered the construction or expansion of similarly opulent structures, such as the Ottomans' Topkapi Palace in Istanbul and the Mughals' Red Fort complex in Delhi. (akg-images.)

Louis used his army and navy primarily to confront his powerful Habsburg neighbors to the east and south, although his aggression upset many others, including the English, Swedes, and Dutch. First were incursions into the Spanish Netherlands in the 1660s and 1670s, then into Germany in the 1680s and 1690s. Both conflicts ended with only minor gains for France, but Louis was feared enough to be dubbed the "Christian Turk." Meanwhile, the Crown sponsored French trading companies that vied with their Dutch and English counterparts to penetrate the markets of Africa, the Middle East, India, and Southeast Asia.

Most important in global terms was the War of the Spanish Succession (1701–1714). This long, bloody, and complex conflict proved disastrous for the French because most of Europe allied against them, fearing the consequences of French control over Spanish territories. It ended with England the ultimate victor and France forced to cede exclusive trading privileges with Spanish America (see Map 20.4). Military service, meanwhile, became a standard feature of life for French commoners, along with high taxes and periodic food shortages. Absolutism was good for centralizing authority, but not, as it would turn out, for keeping the peace.

The turmoil of seventeenth-century Europe resulted in both absolute monarchy and a lasting alternative form of government. **Constitutionalism** requires rulers to share power with representative bodies, or parliaments. In England, birthplace of constitutionalism, taxation was always at issue, but so were other matters such as religious freedom and class representation.

Constitutions were charters guaranteeing subjects certain rights, but which subjects and what rights? For a time, it was mostly elites whose economic and religious interests won out. Indeed, far from being democratically elected representatives of the popular classes, members of the constitutionalist parliament—whether in England, Holland, or Poland—were generally landlords and merchants. Some were prominent clergymen. None were artisans or peasants.

English constitutionalism did not emerge peacefully. Instead, when in 1641 King Charles I (r. 1625–1649) attempted to play absolutist monarch before England's centuries-old Parliament of wealthy property owners, he met a resistance so violent it cost him his life. Charles's timing, as historians of the seventeenth-century crisis have pointed out, could not have been worse: thousands were starving after a sequence of failed harvests. In what was surely among the most startling if not revolutionary acts of the early modern period, subjects decided that if the king was judged to be acting out-of-bounds, he should go.

England's showdown with the king had a long backstory. Charles had distrusted Parliament from the start of his rule and refused to call it into session throughout the 1630s.

Wars of Expansion

Constitutionalism in England

English Civil War

MAP 20.4

War of the Spanish Succession, 1701–1714

Unlike the Thirty Years' War of the previous century, the War of the Spanish Succession was openly understood to be a global power contest rather than a conflict over religious faith. With the Ottomans, Iberians, and even the Dutch in decline, the main contestants were Great Britain and France. Great Britain and its allies won the war, but in the Treaty of Utrecht they allowed the French prince to take the throne as Philip V in exchange for a monopoly on the slave trade to Spanish America and other concessions, such as the strategic Mediterranean post of Gibraltar and the island of Minorca.

Holdings at the outset of war, 1701
- French Bourbon lands
- Spanish Bourbon lands
- Austrian Habsburg lands
- Great Britain
- Prussian lands
- Savoy

Territorial gains after the Treaty of Utrecht, 1713
- To the Austrian Empire
- To Great Britain
- To Savoy
- Main areas of fighting
- Boundary of the Holy Roman Empire, 1713

Unconventional taxes and religious edicts eroded the king's support in England and provoked a rebellion in Scotland. Parliament was called in 1640 to meet this last crisis, but representatives surprised the monarch by demanding sweeping reforms. Many Protestants felt that the king supported Catholicism, the religion of his French wife, and the most radical among them, the Puritans, pushed hardest for checks on royal power. Charles reacted with force, touching off the English Civil War of 1642 to 1646.

After intense fighting, the Puritan faction under Oliver Cromwell emerged victorious. Cromwell and his Puritan supporters took over Parliament and brought Charles to trial. The king was convicted of tyranny and executed by beheading in 1649.

The Cromwell Dictatorship and Restoration

Cromwell, who styled himself "Lord Protector," proved instead to be a military dictator. Dissenters were killed or oppressed, and Cromwellian forces subjugated Scotland and Ireland with terror and mass displacement. Overseas conflicts with the Dutch and French resulted in few victories and expanded taxes. When Cromwell died in 1658, few English subjects mourned his passing. Instead, the reaction was a sweeping revival of Anglicanism and restoration of the monarchy in 1660.

The Glorious Revolution

King and Parliament, however, soon resumed their conflicts. After coming to power in 1685, James II ran afoul of Parliament with his absolutist tendencies and apparent desire to impose his and his wife's Catholicism on English subjects. In 1688 Parliament deposed James, an act that proved far less bloody than the removal of Charles I, and invited James's Protestant daughter Mary (r. 1689–1694) and her Dutch husband, William of Orange (r. 1689–1702), to assume the throne. The event was called the Glorious Revolution since it entailed the monarchs' signing an agreement to share power with Parliament. A genuine constitutional system, much copied worldwide in later years, was now in place.

COUNTERPOINT
The Barbary Pirates

To the vast land empire of the Ottomans and the fractured states of Europe, Africa's north coast, or Maghreb, offers a dual counterpoint. The early modern Maghreb consisted of sea-hugging city-states and tribal enclaves stretching from Morocco to present-day Libya. Although fiercely Islamic and sympathetic to the Ottoman cause against the Habsburgs and

FOCUS

Why were the Barbary pirates of North Africa able to thrive from 1500 to 1800 despite Ottoman and European overseas expansion?

their allies, no Maghribi city ever fell completely under the sway of the Ottoman Empire. Instead, the greatest threats to this centerless region's autonomy came from Christian Europe, whose merchants had long traveled to Africa in pursuit of slaves and gold. Energized by its gunpowder-fueled 1492 conquest of Granada, Spain invaded North Africa with fury, but struggled mightily and at great cost to hold onto a few rocky outposts. Subsequent European interlopers fared little better.

Reign of the Sea Bandits

After 1500, sea banditry flourished along what Europeans called the Berber, or Barbary, Coast. Early pirate leaders of great renown included Oruç and Hayreddin Barbarossa, Greek brothers from the island of Lesbos who settled in Algiers and ruled it from 1516 to 1546. The Barbarossa (Italian for "red beard") brothers were already famous for their bold raids on the coast of Italy. They briefly combined forces with neighboring Tunis to launch large-scale attacks and share out booty, but regional jealousies prevailed and the cities again competed. The raiders focused on capturing merchant vessels at sea, but what made the Barbarossas household names were their increasingly audacious land attacks and kidnappings. Hayreddin later strengthened ties to the Ottomans, but he remained independent of the sultan's orders.

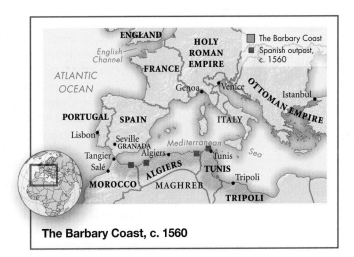

The Barbary Coast, c. 1560

As Ottoman sea power declined after 1580 and Atlantic shipping ballooned, other pirate bases sprang up along the west coast of Morocco. Key after 1600 was the tiny city of Salé (sah-LAY), whose pirate attacks on Spanish and Portuguese shipping were financed and sometimes manned by exiled Iberian Jews and Muslims. Some such foreign-born pirates were deeply involved in European court intrigues, acting as double agents and seeking support for pretenders to the Spanish-held Portuguese throne. Others were simply outlaws hoping to get rich at the expense of their former tormentors. Aside from these vengeful European "renegades," as they were called, a number of Morocco's own seafaring Berber tribes engaged in piracy and extortion as an extension of their culture. Countless young men came of age beneath the pirate flag.

By the time Miguel de Cervantes was held captive in Algiers in the late 1570s, Maghribi hostage trafficking and extortion rackets formed the core of a sophisticated business. The pirates used swift sailing vessels and state-of-the-art European guns to steal money and merchandise, but mostly they kidnapped Christian Europeans, preferably men and

Ransoming Christians

Piracy in the early modern Mediterranean entailed many daring captures at sea, along with several audacious ones on land. Unlike in the Americas, where piracy also thrived at this time, the Barbary pirates of Africa's north coast specialized in kidnapping and extortion. The ransom of Christian captives held in cities such as Algiers and Tunis was organized by Catholic religious orders, who collected sums from as far away as Spanish America to free men and women whose relatives in Spain, Italy, France, and elsewhere could produce no ransom. This seventeenth-century European engraving depicts Catholic priests heroically carrying ransom money, while Christian prisoners appear as cruelly mistreated victims cowering behind their Muslim captors. (The Art Archive.)

women of high status. Some hostages were mistreated and forced to do hard labor, but as Cervantes describes in *Don Quixote*, most were allowed to send letters to friends and relatives on the other side of the Mediterranean in hopes that they would raise sufficient ransom money. Barbary Coast extortion also consisted of selling safe passage to European shippers—that is, promising *not* to kidnap them or steal their merchandise in exchange for money, arms, and shipbuilding materials.

Unable to engage in the expensive conquest enterprises tried by the Spanish and Portuguese, northern European merchants, who were more answerable to shareholders than to kings after about 1600, struck deals with various sultans and tribal leaders in the Maghreb in exchange for safe passage. Maghribi leaders mostly welcomed these Protestant newcomers, because they had access to advanced weapons and shared their hatred of Catholic Iberians. Still, failure to pay for protection led to harsh reprisals. Some pirates raided as far away as the English Channel in the early 1600s, and before long thousands of northern Europeans languished, like the Spaniard Cervantes before them, in the jails of Algiers, Tunis, and Tripoli. In time, England, France, and the Netherlands funded permanent embassies in these and other competing city-states, but their primary purpose was to gather information and keep allied Muslim princes happy, not to seek the release of unlucky Christian subjects. After 1660, the English became a permanent presence in the Moroccan city of Tangier, a strategic base won from the Portuguese through royal marriage.

The Barbary Wars

Although internal divisions and poor leadership among Maghribi sovereigns became more evident over time, it was sustained rivalry among the Europeans that prevented any coordinated attack on the Barbary pirates until the early nineteenth century. Only then, when merchants from the fledgling United States reacted angrily to demands for protection money, did the Barbary pirates see a reversal in fortune. Outraged by what the merchants considered hypocrisy in an era of loudly proclaimed free trade, they proposed a new approach to the Mediterranean's piracy problem. In a pet project of President Thomas Jefferson, the United States won the support of traditional European powers, most significantly the French, to bomb the Barbary pirates into submission. The so-called Barbary Wars' unexpected result was near-total French takeover of North Africa, which ended only in the 1960s.

Conclusion

Fueled by gunpowder, silver, and religious fervor, Europe and the Mediterranean basin exploded after 1500 as the world's most belligerent region, but it was also the most commercially dynamic. Relative resource poverty had long compelled Europeans to trade with one another, but regional identities, exacerbated by religious differences, had led them to fight as often as they cooperated. This trend only continued in the late sixteenth century, when nationalist loyalties were hardened by the Protestant Reformation and its aftermath.

By contrast, in these years the Sunni Muslim Ottomans built a vast land empire encompassing eastern Europe, Southwest Asia, Egypt, and much of Arabia. They did so with force, but also by cleverly integrating new subjects into the ranks of government and the armed forces. Ottoman pragmatism also included a policy of religious tolerance. The Ottoman world became a haven for many of Europe's persecuted Jews, and conquered Christians were not forced to convert to Islam. Chronic wars with the Habsburgs and Safavids provided many opportunities for social advancement, but they also absorbed a huge portion of state resources, eventually bogging the empire down.

A battered Europe emerged from its seventeenth-century crisis to begin a new phase of national division. The century between 1650 and 1750 was no less bloody than the one before, but it marked the beginnings of three globally significant trends: a new science based on direct observation and experimentation, an increasingly capitalist economy, and increasingly centralized, national government. All of this sounds quite modern, but western Europe's competing kingdoms still saw the quest for wealth and power as a zero-sum game, in which gain by one side meant loss by the others, driving them to seek monopolies over resources and lay claim to ever more distant lands and peoples. To a degree, Europeans saw the world through the same mercantilist lens as the Portuguese of previous centuries, but the languages of science and rational economics, rather than religion, were increasingly used to justify conquest of traditional societies. Soon after, in the first years of the nineteenth century, it was a new language, that of free trade, rather than religious animosity that drove the fledgling United States and its European allies to attack the Barbary Coast pirates. Former Barbary captive Miguel de Cervantes of Spain could hardly have known what lay ahead for Europe and the greater Mediterranean, but his vision of a newly interconnected world continued to inspire his imagination. In the opening to the second part of *Don Quixote*, published in 1615, Cervantes jokingly claimed that he had received a letter from the Chinese emperor inviting him to establish a Spanish school at court for which his "world-famous" novel would be the main text. Cervantes claimed that he had declined the offer only because he was ill and could not afford the trip.

NOTES

1. Celalzade, Mustafa, *Selim-name* [In praise of Selim] (eds. Ahmet Uđur, Mustafa Huhadar), Ankara 1990; as it appears in Halil Berktay and Bogdan Murgescu, *The Ottoman Empire* (Thessaloniki: CDRSEE, 2005), 53.

2. Habsburg ambassador Ghiselin de Busbecq, quoted in Gérard Chaliand, ed., *The Art of War in World History from Antiquity to the Nuclear Age* (Berkeley: University of California Press, 1994), 457.

3. Jennings, Ronald C., *Christians and Muslims in Ottoman Cyprus and the Mediterranean World, 1571-1640*, New York – London 1993; as it appears in Halil Berktay and Bogdan Murgescu, *The Ottoman Empire* (Thessaloniki: CDRSEE, 2005), 116.

4. Evlija Celebi, Putopis. *Odlomci o jugoslovenskim zemljama* [Travel-records. Fragments about Yugoslav Countries], Sarajevo 1996; as it appears in Halil Berktay and Bogdan Murgescu, *The Ottoman Empire* (Thessaloniki: CDRSEE, 2005), 82.

RESOURCES FOR RESEARCH

General Works

Few historians have attempted to treat early modern Europe and the wider Mediterranean in a global context, but the following books are some of the best general syntheses in the field. Braudel remains the grand inspiration. Crosby challenges us to see what was special about growing European interest in numbers and calculation, which owed much to Islamic precedent.

Braudel, Fernand. *The Mediterranean and the Mediterranean World in the Age of Philip II.* 2 vols. Translated by Sian Reynolds. 1996.

Crosby, Alfred W. *The Measure of Reality: Quantification and Western Society, 1250–1600.* 1997.

Elliott, John H. *Spain, Europe, and the Wider World, 1500–1800.* 2009.

Elliott, John H. *Europe Divided, 1556–1598,* 2d ed. 2000.

Kamen, Henry. *Early Modern European Society.* 2000.

The Power of the Ottoman Empire, 1453–1750

Ottoman history is a vibrant field, and new work continues to link the empire to both West and East. A recent wave of regional studies of Ottoman Egypt and Syria joins better-known work on Ottoman eastern Europe and Anatolia. Giancarlo Casale's book takes the Ottomans overseas.

Casale, Giancarlo. *The Ottoman Age of Exploration.* 2010.

Goffman, Daniel. *The Ottomans and Early Modern Europe.* 2002.

Kafadar, Cemal. *Between Two Worlds: The Construction of the Ottoman State.* 1995.

Mansel, Philip. *Constantinople: City of the World's Desire, 1453–1924.* 1996.

Pierce, Leslie. *The Imperial Harem: Women and Sovereignty in the Ottoman Empire.* 1993.

Europe Divided, 1500–1650

Histories of the "seventeenth-century crisis" have come back into vogue in recent years, and now stress global linkages in trade, climate, and other spheres. Other authors, such as Davis and Schwartz, have expanded the study of women's self-fashioning and the popular religious toleration that existed despite harsh decrees from above.

Cunningham, Andrew, and Ole Peter Grell. *The Four Horsemen of the Apocalypse: Religion, War, Famine and Death in Reformation Europe.* 2000.

Davis, Natalie Zemon. *Women on the Margins: Three Seventeenth-Century Lives.* 1995.

"Introduction." AHR Forum: The General Crisis of the Seventeenth Century Revisited. *The American Historical Review* 113, no. 4 (October 2008): 1029–1030. http://www.jstor.org/stable/10.1086/ahr.113.4.1029.

Parker, Geoffrey. *Europe in Crisis, 1598–1648,* 2d ed. 2001.

Schwartz, Stuart B. *All Can Be Saved: Religious Tolerance and Salvation in the Iberian Atlantic World.* 2008.

Sturdy, David J. *Fractured Europe, 1600–1721.* 2002.

European Innovations in Science and Government, 1550–1750

Historians of science continue to debate the meaning and timing of the so-called Scientific Revolution, but when seen in a global context, the changes initiated in sixteenth-century Europe appear starkly important. Economic historians are even less in agreement with regard to the origins of modern capitalism, but the topic remains huge, and as treated by Chaudury, Pomeranz, and others, it has become more globally integrated.

Beik, William. *Louis XIV and Absolutism: A Brief Study with Documents.* 2000.

Chaudury, Sushil, and Michel Morineau, eds. *Merchants, Companies, and Trade: Europe and Asia in the Early Modern Era.* 1999.

Edwards, Philip. *The Making of the Modern English State, 1460–1660.* 2001.

Henry, John. *The Scientific Revolution and the Origins of Modern Science,* 2d ed. New York: Palgrave, 2002.

Pomeranz, Kenneth. *The Great Divergence: China, Europe, and the Making of the Modern World Economy.* 2000.

Smith, Pamela H., and Paula Findlen, eds. *Merchants and Marvels: Commerce, Science, and Art in Early Modern Europe.* 2002.

Smyth, Jim. *The Making of the United Kingdom, 1660–1800.* 2001.

COUNTERPOINT: The Barbary Pirates

The Barbary pirates have been a source of many legends, but serious historical research has also been undertaken. Braudel's classic study of the Mediterranean, cited above under General Works, includes considerable information on the sixteenth-century pirates, whereas Heers and Wolf provide more scope and detail.

Heers, Jacques. *The Barbary Corsairs.* 2003.

Pennell, C. R. *Bandits at Sea: A Pirates Reader.* 2001.

Vitkus, Daniel J., and Nabil Matar, eds. *Piracy, Slavery, and Redemption: Barbary Captivity Narratives from Early Modern England.* 2001.

Wolf, John B. *The Barbary Coast: Algeria Under the Turks.* 1979.

▶ **For additional primary sources from this period,** see *Sources of Crossroads and Cultures.*

▶ **For Web sites, images, and documents related to topics in this chapter,** see Make History at bedfordstmartins.com/smith.

The major global development in this chapter ▶ Early modern Europe's increasing competition and division in the face of Ottoman expansion.

IMPORTANT EVENTS

1453	Ottoman conquest of Constantinople
1492	Spanish take Granada, expel Jews
1517	Martin Luther disseminates "Ninety-five Theses," sparking the Protestant Reformation
1520–1566	Reign of Ottoman emperor Suleiman
1540	Ignatius Loyola founds the new Catholic order of the Jesuits
1543	Nicolaus Copernicus, *On the Revolutions of the Heavenly Spheres*
1545–1563	Council of Trent
1571	Battle of Lepanto
1572	St. Bartholomew's Day massacre
1580	Philip II of Spain takes over Portuguese Empire
1598	Edict of Nantes ends French Religious War
1618–1648	Thirty Years' War
1640	Portugal wins independence from Spain
1642–1646	English Civil War
1643–1715	Reign of Louis XIV of France
1683	Ottomans defeated in Vienna by Polish-Austrian alliance
1687	Isaac Newton, *Principia Mathematica*
1688	Glorious Revolution in England
1701–1714	War of the Spanish Succession

KEY TERMS

absolutism (p. 674)
armada (p. 666)
bourgeoisie (p. 672)
capitalism (p. 672)
caravanserai (p. 656)
constitutionalism (p.674)

devshirme (p. 651)
geocentrism (p. 670)
heliocentrism (p. 671)
indulgence (p. 662)
mercantilism (p. 673)
timar (p. 651)

CHAPTER OVERVIEW QUESTIONS

1. To what degree was religious diversity embraced or rejected in early modern Europe and the greater Mediterranean, and why?

2. How did Christian Europe's gunpowder-fueled empires compare with that of the Ottomans?

3. What accounts for the rise of science and capitalism in early modern western Europe?

SECTION FOCUS QUESTIONS

1. What factors explain the rise of the vast Ottoman Empire and its centuries-long endurance?

2. What sparked division in Europe after 1500, and why did this trend persist?

3. What factors enabled European scientific and political innovations in the early modern period?

4. Why were the Barbary pirates of North Africa able to thrive from 1500 to 1800 despite Ottoman and European overseas expansion?

MAKING CONNECTIONS

1. How did battles for control of the Mediterranean compare with those for control of Indian Ocean trade (see Chapter 19)?

2. How globally important was the Protestant Reformation?

3. In what ways were the Barbary pirates similar to the Atlantic slave traders (see Chapter 18)? How were they different?

21

AT A CROSSROADS ▶

This life-size portrait from Beijing's Palace Museum depicts China's Emperor Qianlong (1711–1799) at a grand old age. The use of perspective—the illusion of three-dimensional space—reflects the influence of European Jesuit artists who resided at court after the early seventeenth century, but the emperor's pose reflects a Chinese taste for a more statuelike representation of imperial power. His elaborate silk garments and pearl-encrusted headgear and necklace suggest the wealth of the Qing treasury, which despite massive expenditures and waste, boasted a huge surplus in silver for much of the emperor's reign. (The Palace Museum, Beijing/©Hu Weibiao/ChinaStock.)

Expansion and Isolation in Asia

1450–1750

Wang Yangming (1472–1529) had trouble on his hands. As governor of the south western Chinese province of Jiangxi, he was expected to collect taxes and keep the peace for his Ming overlords. Wang had risen through the ranks of the civil service through a mix of intelligence, connections, and raw ambition. Now he was faced with a rebellious prince, Zhu Chen-hao, and his loyal followers. Acting as general, Wang successfully attacked the rebels with every weapon at hand, including novel bronze cannon probably copied from the Portuguese. More important than the suppression of the rebellion was the aftermath. Wang chose not to terrorize the populace and destroy the land as his predecessors might have, but instead moved quickly to rebuild, pardoning many rebels and winning their loyalty to the Ming emperor.

Wang Yangming's effective governorship won praise, but he was far better known as a philosopher. Wang was among the most renowned **Neo-Confucianists** of early modern China. As described in Chapter 15, the broad philosophical movement known as Neo-Confucianism was a revival of an ancient tradition. The fifth-century B.C.E. Chinese philosopher Kongzi (Latinized as "Confucius") envisioned the ideal earthly society as a mirror of divine harmony. Although he prescribed ritual ancestor worship, Confucius

---

BACKSTORY

By the fifteenth century, Russia, a largely agrarian society straddling Eurasia, had shaken off Mongol rule and was beginning to expand from its base in Moscow. Russian expansion would eventually lead to conflict with China, which by the fifteenth century was by far the world's most populous state. Self-sufficient, widely literate, and technically sophisticated, China vied with Europe for supremacy in both practical and theoretical sciences. As we saw in Chapter 15, the Ming dynasty had also become a global power capable of mounting long-distance sea voyages, yet by the 1430s its rulers had chosen to withdraw and focus on consolidating internal affairs. By contrast, Japan was deeply fractured in the fifteenth century, its many districts and several islands subject to feuding warlords. Korea, though less densely populated than either of its neighbors east or west, was relatively unified under the Yi dynasty, which came to power in the late fourteenth century. In mainland Southeast Asia, several Buddhist kingdoms were by this time undergoing a major reconfiguration. Neo-Confucianism was on the rise in Vietnam. The Philippine Islands, meanwhile, remained politically and ethnically diverse, in part due to their complex geography.

Straddling Eurasia: Rise of the Russian Empire, 1462–1725

FOCUS What prompted Russian territorial expansion?

China from Ming to Qing Rule, 1500–1800

FOCUS How did the shift to a silver cash economy transform Chinese government and society?

Japan in Transition, 1540–1750

FOCUS How did self-isolation affect Japan?

Korea, a Land in Between, 1392–1750

FOCUS How did life for common folk in early modern Korea differ from life in China or Japan?

Consolidation in Mainland Southeast Asia, 1500–1750

FOCUS What trends did mainland Southeast Asia share with China, Korea, Japan, and Russia?

COUNTERPOINT: "Spiritual Conquest" in the Philippines

FOCUS In contrast to the general trend of political consolidation in early modern Asia, why did the Philippines fall to a European colonizing power?

Neo-Confucianism The revival of Confucius's ancient philosophy stressing agrarian life, harmony between ruler and ruled, and respect for elders and ancestors.

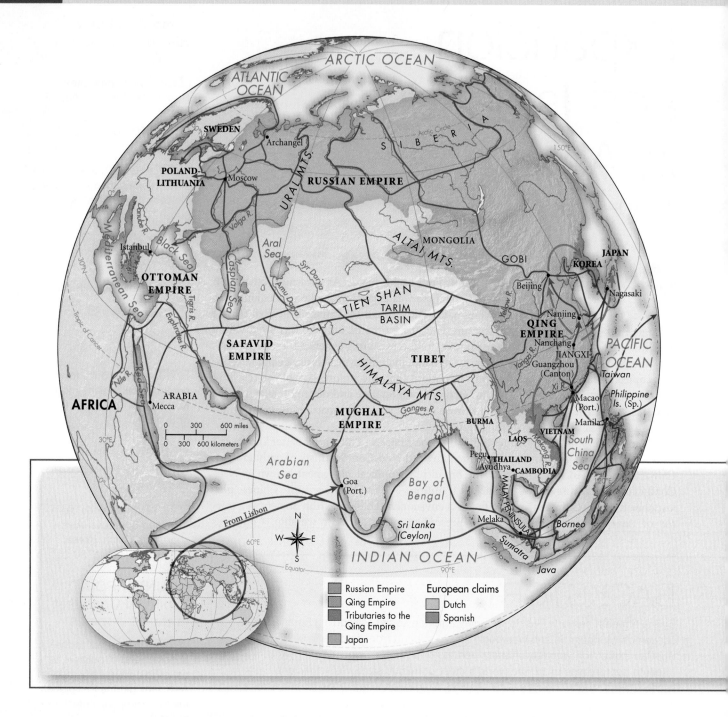

Russian Empire
Qing Empire
Tributaries to the Qing Empire
Japan

European claims
Dutch
Spanish

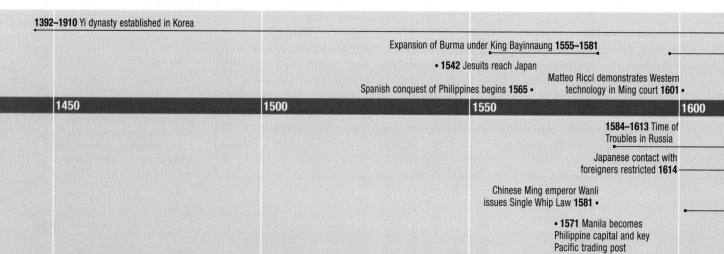

1392–1910 Yi dynasty established in Korea

Expansion of Burma under King Bayinnaung **1555–1581**

▪ **1542** Jesuits reach Japan

Spanish conquest of Philippines begins **1565** ▪

Matteo Ricci demonstrates Western technology in Ming court **1601** ▪

| 1450 | 1500 | 1550 | 1600 |

1584–1613 Time of Troubles in Russia

Japanese contact with foreigners restricted **1614**

Chinese Ming emperor Wanli issues Single Whip Law **1581** ▪

▪ **1571** Manila becomes Philippine capital and key Pacific trading post

developed a system of ethics rather than a formal religion. Education and scientific experimentation were highly valued, but so was submission to elders and other social superiors. Ideal Chinese citizens had duties rather than rights. Some of Confucius's core ideas were further developed by his fourth-century B.C.E. successor, Mengzi, or Mencius, whose commentaries inspired Wang Yangming.

As his response to the rebels in Jiangxi suggested, Wang was as much a man of action as he was a scholar. In fact, Wang saw no clear distinction between his military and intellectual lives, arguing that only by doing could one learn, and that action was in fact inseparable from learning. In addition to challenging older notions that privileged scholarly reflection in matters of policy, Wang argued that individuals possessed an innate sense of right and wrong, something akin to the Western notion of conscience. Some scholars have argued that at least one result of the wide diffusion of Wang's teachings was a heightened sense among Chinese elites of the worthiness of the individual as a historical actor.

Neo-Confucianists sought to restore order to societies they felt had descended into chaos and decadence. For Wang, putting Ming society back on track required forceful action. Other Neo-Confucianists argued in favor of more passive reflection, but Wang's ideas seemed to strike the right chord in early sixteenth-century China, and were widely promoted by educators, first in China and later in Korea and Vietnam. Japan borrowed more selectively from Neo-Confucianism. When blended with the underlying Buddhist beliefs already deeply rooted in all these regions, Neo-Confucianism emerged as a largely uncontroversial religion of state. A foundation for many legal as well as moral principles, it helped hold together millions of ethnically diverse and socially divided people. In other parts of Asia, however, religion fueled division and conflict. The Philippines were a battleground between recent converts to Islam and Roman Catholicism. Russia, meanwhile, was defining itself as a revived Byzantium, expanding frontiers across Asia in the name of Orthodox Christianity. Muslims and other non-Christians were treated as enemies of faith and state.

MAPPING THE WORLD

Eurasian Trade and Empires, c. 1700

With the decline of the Mongols, Central Asia returned to its former role as a trading crossroads, mostly for silk, gems, furs, and other high-value commodities, yet it also became a meeting ground for two new, expansive empires: Russia under the Romanovs and China under the Qing, or Manchu, dynasty. Despite their focus on land expansion, both empires sought trade ties with the outside world by sea, mostly to win foreign exchange in the form of silver. More isolated areas in the region included Korea and Japan, both of which experienced political consolidation influenced by the spread of Chinese Neo-Confucianist principles. Similar processes appeared in Vietnam, whereas most of mainland Southeast Asia remained under expansionist Buddhist kings.

ROUTES ▼

— Fur trade route

— Other trade route

➡ Spread of Neo-Confucianism

➡ Travels of Matteo Ricci, 1582–1598

1597–1630s Persecution of Japanese Christians

▪ **1644** Manchu invasion of Beijing; Ming dynasty replaced by Qing

| 1650 | 1700 | 1750 |

1627, 1636 Manchu invasions of Korea

1661–1722 Qing expansion under Emperor Kangxi

▪ **1751** Qing annexation of Tibet

1602–1867 Tokugawa Shogunate in Japan

1689–1725 Russian imperial expansion under Tsar Peter the Great

Over the course of early modern times, Asian monarchs varied between absolutist-style rulers, as in Ming and Qing China and in Russia, and more symbolic figureheads, as in Tokugawa Japan. Korea's Yi (yee) dynasty kings fell somewhere in between, as did some of the kings of mainland Southeast Asia. Ordinary people, as in most of the Middle East and Europe, had little chance to contact or communicate with their rulers, dealing only with royal intermediaries or provincial authorities. The vast majority of Asians worked at subsistence farming and paid tribute in cash or foodstuffs to landlords or royal administrators. Men were usually more mobile than women in that they were more likely to be caught up in public works or military drafts. Childhood—everywhere difficult to survive—was mostly an apprenticeship to adult labor.

Despite this continuity in everyday life, the early modern period was a time of sweeping change across Asia, sometimes sparked by the provocations of foreigners, but mostly resulting from long-range, internal developments. The overall trend was toward political consolidation under powerful dynasties. These centralizing governments sought to suppress internal dissent, encourage religious unity, and expand territorial holdings at the expense of weaker neighbors, often using new military technologies to achieve this end. Dependence on outsiders was for the most part limited to strategic items such as guns and hard currency. Whole new classes of bureaucrats and merchants flourished, and with them came wider literacy in vernacular languages, support of the arts, and conspicuous consumption. Despite some punishing episodes of war, rebellion, and natural disaster, the early modern period in East Asia was arguably more peaceful than in most of Europe, the Middle East, or Africa. It was an era of steady population growth, commercial expansion, political consolidation, and cultural florescence.

OVERVIEW
QUESTIONS

The major global development in this chapter: The general trend toward political and cultural consolidation in early modern Asia.

As you read, consider:

1. What factors led to imperial consolidation in Russia and China? Who were the new rulers, and what were the sources of their legitimacy?

2. Why was isolation more common in these empires than overseas engagement, and what were some of the benefits and drawbacks of isolation?

3. In what ways did early modern Asians transform their environments, and why?

Straddling Eurasia: Rise of the Russian Empire 1462–1725

FOCUS
What prompted Russian territorial expansion?

Whereas the emerging nation-states of western Europe expanded largely through overseas conquests, early modern Russia followed a land-based path of expansion and consolidation more like that of the Ottomans and other so-called gunpowder empires to the south and east. Beginning in 1462, Moscow-based princes combined new weapons technology with bureaucratic innovations to expand their holdings. By the time Tsar Peter the Great died in 1725, the Russian Empire encompassed a huge swath of northern Asia, stretching from the Baltic to the Pacific (see Map 21.1).

Russian imperialism was basically conservative, with Russian Orthodoxy, the state religion, serving as a kind of nationalist "glue" throughout early modern times. Religious and cultural unity, plus a tendency toward isolation, inhibited efforts at social and agricultural reform. Although Peter the Great would end his reign by copying elements of western European governance and science, Russia remained an essentially tributary, agricultural regime until the nineteenth century. Military reforms such as those embraced by the Ottomans were Peter's most modern legacy. Although a modest merchant class had long existed in cities such as Moscow and Novgorod, the majority of Russians remained **serfs**, bound peasants with little more freedom than slaves.

Consolidation in Muscovite Russia

After the fall of Constantinople in 1453, some Russian Christians prophesied that the principality of Muscovy was to be the new Byzantium, and Moscow the "third Rome." The

serf A dependent agricultural laborer attached to a property and treated much like a slave.

MAP 21.1 **Rise of Russia, 1462–1725**

Beginning with the consolidation of Muscovy in the mid-fifteenth century, Russia grew steadily to become one of the world's largest—albeit least densely populated—land empires. By the time of Peter the Great's death in 1725, the Russian Empire encompassed much of northern Eurasia and included key ports in the Atlantic, Arctic, and Pacific oceans, with links to the Mediterranean via the Black Sea and to Persia via the Caspian Sea. Alongside military and commercial endeavors, the Russians spread their Orthodox Christian faith as far as northwest North America.

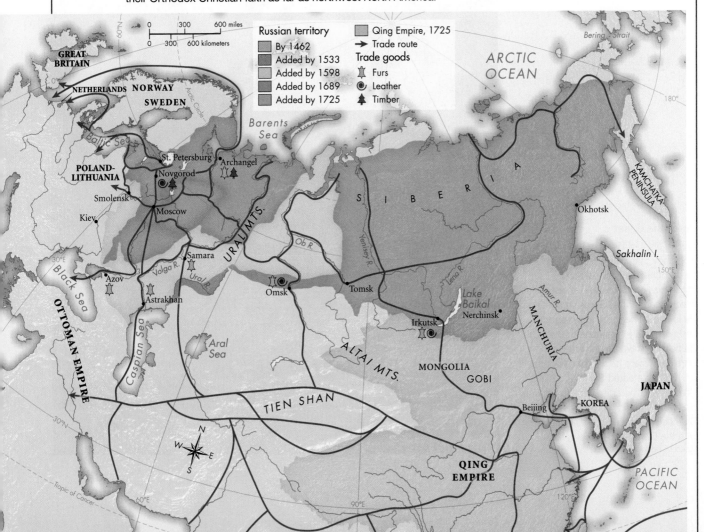

**Rise and Expansion
of Muscovy**

Russian Orthodox Church was fiercely anti-Catholic and frequently energized by apocalyptic visionaries. These visionaries inspired a succession of grand princes who ruled Moscow following the Black Death, and each seemed more determined than the last to expand both Muscovy and the Orthodox Church's domain. As the early modern period progressed, the Ottomans and their allies came to pose the greatest threat to Russia in the south, and the Poles, Lithuanians, and Swedes periodically threatened in the west. The eastern Tatars, though in decline after Timur (see Chapter 15), were also a chronic menace.

Russia took shape under Moscow's grand prince, Ivan III (r. 1462–1505), nicknamed "the Great." Under Ivan the Great, the Muscovites expanded northward, tying landlocked Muscovy to the commercially vibrant Baltic Sea region. By the later sixteenth century, Russian monarchs began to allow English, Dutch, and other non-Catholic northwest European merchants to settle and trade in the capital. Like other Europeans, these merchants sought to circumvent the Ottomans and Middle Eastern intermediaries in the quest for East and South Asian fabrics and spices. As a result of alliances with foreign merchants, Muscovite rulers gained access to artillery, muskets, and other Western gunpowder technologies in exchange for furs and Asian textiles. These new weapons in turn fueled Russian imperial expansion, mostly across the steppes to the east and south (see again Map 21.1).

Peter the Great

Truly a giant of Russian history, the Romanov tsar Peter the Great spent much of his adult life trying to modernize and expand his vast realm, which spanned the Eurasian continent. He is shown here, tall in the saddle and supremely confident, at the 1709 Battle of Poltava (in present-day Ukraine), where he and his modernized army defeated Sweden's King Charles XII. The artist depicts Peter as blessed by an angel, whereas King Charles was forced to seek refuge with the Ottomans. (Tretyakov Gallery, Moscow/Bridgeman Art Library.)

Russia's next great ruler, and first tsar (literally, "Caesar"), was Ivan IV (r. 1533–1584), "the Terrible." Although remembered mostly for bizarre and violent behavior in his later years, Ivan IV was for the most part an effective monarch. In addition to conquering cities in the distant territories of the Golden Horde in the 1550s and acquiring lucrative fur-producing territories in Siberia, Ivan IV also reformed the Muscovite bureaucracy, judiciary, and treasury in a manner befitting a growing empire. The church, always at the heart of Russian politics, was also reorganized and partly subordinated to the state.

Ivan earned his nickname beginning in the 1560s when he established a personal fiefdom called the *oprichnina* (oh-preech-NEE-nah), which, like the Ottoman *timar* and *devshirme* systems, was in part intended to break the power of nobles and replace them with dependent state servants. This abrupt political shuffling crippled vital commercial cities such as Novgorod, however, and generally threw the empire into disarray. Meanwhile, wars begun in 1558 with Poland and Sweden went badly for Ivan's outgunned and undertrained forces. Things went no better on the southern front, and in 1571 Moscow fell to the eastern Tatars. Increasingly psychologically unstable during the last decade of his life, Ivan died of a stroke in 1584. Thanks in part to Ivan's personal disintegration, which included his killing of the heir apparent, Russia descended into chaos after Ivan's death. Historians have designated the subsequent three decades Russia's "Time of Troubles."

The Time of Troubles (1584–1613) was punctuated by succession crises, but it was also an era of famine, disease, military defeat, and social unrest, akin to Europe's "seventeenth-century crisis." Taking advantage of the dynastic chaos, the king of Poland and Lithuania tried to place his son on the Russian throne. The prospect of a Catholic ruler sparked Russia's first massive peasant rebellion, which ended with the humiliating occupation of Moscow by Polish forces. In 1613 an army of nobles, townspeople, and peasants drove out the intruders and put on the throne a nobleman, Michael Romanov (r. 1613–1645), founder of Russia's last royal line.

Time of Troubles

The Romanovs' New Frontiers

Under Romanov leadership, the seventeenth century saw the rebuilding and expansion of Muscovy and the slow but steady return to empire. Starting at 7 million in 1600, Russia's population roughly doubled by 1700. Impressive as this growth was, all of Russia's inhabitants could have fit into a small corner of China. Further, they looked more to leadership from the church, which had regained the authority it lost under Ivan the Terrible, than from the crown.

By the time of Peter the Great (r. 1689–1725), the Russian tsar faced a powerful and insubordinate church. Peter responded by prosecuting wandering preachers as enemies of the state. But what made Peter "great" was not his harsh dealings with the church but his relentless push to make Russia a competitor on par with France and other emerging western European nation-states. To this end, he kept stoking the fires of expansion-driven war, importing arms and military experts, building a navy, and professionalizing the armed forces. The Imperial Russian Army soon became not only a major force against the strongest of European and Central Asian challengers, but also a gargantuan consumer of state revenue.

Peter, a man of formidable size and boundless energy, is often remembered for his attempts to Westernize Russia, to purge it of what he regarded as backward, mostly Asian characteristics. Boyars, or nobles, were ordered to shave their beards and change their dress, and all courtiers were required to learn French. A new capital, St. Petersburg, was built on the Baltic shore in the French style, complete with a summer palace inspired by Louis XIV's Versailles. Not

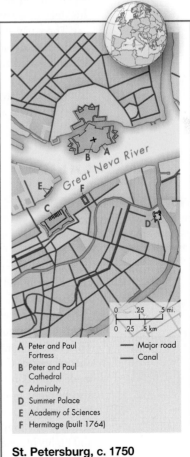

A Peter and Paul
   Fortress
B Peter and Paul
   Cathedral
C Admiralty
D Summer Palace
E Academy of Sciences
F Hermitage (built 1764)

— Major road
— Canal

St. Petersburg, c. 1750

everything Asian was bad, however. On southern expansion, Peter had this to say: "Approach as close to Constantinople and India as possible. He who rules there will be the real ruler of the world."[1]

Russian expansion across Asia was not only a military process. The growth of the fur trade reverberated ever more deeply through the many complex ecosystems of Siberia, and settling the great steppes of the south and east entailed wrenching social change and a wholesale transformation of the landscape. As frontier forts and agricultural colonization advanced, indigenous nomads were massacred, driven out, incorporated into trade or tributary networks, or forced to convert to Christianity. Well-watered riverbanks were tilled and planted in traditional fashion, and prairie grasslands became pasturage for large herds of domestic livestock. The steppe frontier was to some extent a haven for fugitives, too, including a number of runaway serfs, and it also proved to be a source of rebel leaders. The government was always playing catch-up, trying to bring order to the unruly fringe.

Foreign merchants, meanwhile, came to Russia not only from the west, but from the south and east. In addition to small colonies of northern Europeans, Moscow was home to thriving communities of Middle Eastern, Central Asian, South Asian, and Armenian merchants by the seventeenth century. As in most other mercantilist systems, however, the government granted foreign merchants only limited access to Russian urban markets and even less to interior supply regions. Thus Russian merchants continued to dominate both internal and long-distance trade, despite limited access to credit and precious metals. Mostly based in Moscow, they used distant ports such as Archangel, on the White Sea, to trade leather and other goods with the English and Dutch (see again Mapping the World, page 685). Furs were traded westward to eastern and central Europe, and also southward to the Ottoman and Persian empires. By the time of Peter the Great, England had become dependent on Russian timber, which it paid for with gold (coming mostly from Brazil by this time, as we will see in the next chapter).

The early modern Russian Empire, in sum, drew from a blend of religious self-confidence, demographic growth, commercial links, and the personal ambitions of its Moscow-based tsars. More gunpowder empire than modern state in many regards, Russia nevertheless grew to encompass more terrain than any other Eurasian state in its time, despite its relatively sparse population. The continued subjugation of the serf majority, however, would spark a new wave of rebellions before the end of the eighteenth century.

China from Ming to Qing Rule 1500–1800

FOCUS

How did the shift to a silver cash economy transform Chinese government and society?

By 1500, thanks to several millennia of intensive agriculture and a tradition of vast and innovative public works projects, China was home to at least 110 million people, almost twice as many as Europe. Moreover, China under the Ming dynasty (1368–1644) was virtually self-sufficient. Rice and other foodstuffs, along with livestock and manufactured goods, were transported and redistributed throughout the empire by way of a complex system of canals, roads, and fortified posts that had been constructed by drafted peasant laborers over the centuries.

Only silver was in short supply as Ming rulers shifted China's economy from copper or bronze currency and simple barter to silver money exchanges, especially after 1550. This shift to commercialization and a "hard money" economy necessitated links to the outside world. China's surplus of silk, a versatile fiber in demand abroad since antiquity, made exports not only possible, but highly profitable. Fine porcelain and lacquer wares also brought in considerable foreign exchange, and tea would later be added to the list. Western ideas and technologies arrived with Christian missionaries in the mid-sixteenth century, but they barely influenced Chinese culture. China, a technologically advanced and highly literate society, wanted only silver from the West, and, for a time, it managed to define its terms of connection and exchange with the outside world.

The final century of Ming rule, from about 1540 to 1644, witnessed a commercial revival and overall improvement in standards of living. It also saw the return of mounted enemies in the north, the Manchu. And, despite the general prosperity, there were no perfect guarantees against the famine and disease that plagued previous centuries due to the density of China's population and the primitive state of its medical care. Bureaucratic structures, though efficient by contemporary world standards, were inadequate to the task of mass relief. Peasant families could at best hope for community cooperation in hard times.

Late Ming Imperial Demands and Private Trade

The most important emperor of late Ming times was Wanli (r. 1573–1620). Wanli was a creature of the imperial palace and notoriously out of touch with his subjects, yet one of his policies had global implications. Previous emperors had enacted similar decrees on a small scale, but it was Wanli who ordered many of China's taxes collected in silver rather than in the form of labor service, rice, or other trade goods. The shift to hard currency eased price standardization across the empire. This was the "Single Whip Law" of 1581, so named since it bundled various taxes into one stinging payment.

Single Whip Law and the Shift to Hard Currency

Given China's immense population, approaching 200 million by this time, demand for silver soared. Portuguese merchants moved quickly to import Japanese silver acquired in exchange for guns, silk, and other items, but soon Chinese merchants all but eclipsed them. These merchants moored their ships in Nagasaki Bay alongside the Portuguese and later Dutch, but many more set up shop in Manila, the Philippine capital, where they exchanged silk, porcelain, and other goods for Spanish-American silver that had arrived from Mexico (see Map 21.3, page 709). Thanks to Wanli, a vibrant Chinese commercial colony emerged in Manila virtually overnight. Large numbers of Chinese merchants also settled in Thailand, Malaysia, and Java, where they offset the growing commercial power of Europeans.

Demand for Silver and the Manila Trade

Despite the great distances and risks involved, the Manila trade was particularly profitable for both Spanish and Chinese merchants. The annual transpacific voyages of the *naos de la China*, or "Manila galleons," that left Acapulco, Mexico, each year loaded with the silver of Potosí (Bolivia), Zacatecas (Mexico), and other American mining centers, continued unabated through the early nineteenth century. Like the arrival of the Atlantic silver fleet in Spain each fall, the safe arrival of the galleons in Manila was a longed-for and celebrated event in all quarters. Still more Spanish-American silver reached China from the West, traveling through Europe, the Middle East, and the Indian Ocean basin to ports such as Macao and Guangzhou (Canton). Since China, compared with contemporary Europe or India, valued silver at a relatively higher rate than gold, substantial profit could be made in almost any exchange. Put another way, the historically close relationship between favorable exchange rates and export profitability was quickly exploited by merchants on both sides of the exchange divide.

How China's economy managed to absorb millions of ounces of silver annually over the course of decades without dramatic price inflation or some other notable effect remains a matter of much scholarly debate. One outlet was government spending, for by the early seventeenth century Ming rulers became more like their western European contemporaries in outfitting costly armies. Defense against Manchu and other northern raiders as well as disgruntled peasants grew increasingly expensive, but in the end proved ineffectual. Were fluctuations in silver income to blame for Ming decline?

Echoing historians of the seventeenth-century crisis in Europe, scholars long claimed that a dip in silver revenues after about 1630 rendered the state unable to defend itself. More recent research, however, suggests no such dip occurred; silver kept pouring in through the 1640s. Other factors must have trumped the Ming state's budget issues. Meanwhile, private merchants who supplied the military with food, weapons, and other necessities clearly benefited from China's new, silver-based economy, as did those who exported silk to Manila and other overseas bazaars. Only in the nineteenth century would China's vast silver holdings begin to flow outward in exchange for opium and other imports brought by European traders.

Demand for Chinese Exports

China's new commercial links to the outside world stimulated the economy in several ways, especially in the coastal regions around Nanjing and Canton. Men continued to work in intensive rice agriculture since taxes in the form of raw commodities were still required despite rapid monetization of the overall economy. Women, however, were increasingly drawn into the production of silk thread and finished textiles for export. After silk, China's most admired product was its porcelain, known as "chinaware" in the West (see Seeing the Past: Blue-on-White: Ming Export Porcelain).

As in parts of northwest Europe described in the last chapter, Chinese textile making grew more efficient in response to export demands, but without the mechanization, standardization, and wage labor usually associated with modern industry. By the early sixteenth century not only finished fabrics were traded widely in China, but also their components, raw fiber and thread. Even mulberry leaves, which were fed to silkworms to produce thread, were traded on the open market. Only labor was not yet commodified in

SEEING THE PAST

Blue-on-White: Ming Export Porcelain

Ming Blue-on-White Export Porcelain (Paul Freeman/Bridgeman Art Library.)

Before industrialization, China's artisans produced a vast range of consumer goods, from ordinary metal nails to fine silk textiles. After silk, China was most renowned for its porcelain, a special variety of clay pottery fired to the point that it was transformed into glass. The center of this artisanal industry was (and remains) Jingdezhen (JING-deh-juhn) in southern China. The combination of properly mixed clay and high heat made it possible for artisans, mostly men, to fashion durable vessels, plates, and other items

of extraordinary thinness. Over many centuries, Chinese painters and calligraphers developed a range of styles and techniques for decorating porcelain, including the application of cobalt blue pigments that emerged from the kiln in stark contrast to the white base. The Ming developed this "blue-on-white" porcelain specifically for export, first, as we saw in Chapter 15, to the Muslim world and later to regions throughout the globe. The example shown here from about 1600 features Li Tieguai, a legendary Chinese religious figure, but many blue-on-white porcelain products were decorated with Western and other foreign images, including monograms and pictures of the Virgin Mary.

Porcelain making continued throughout the Qing period, as well, but with a shift toward individual artistic virtuosity rather than mass, anonymous production.

EXAMINING THE EVIDENCE

1. How did Ming craftsmen adapt their blue-on-white porcelain to match the tastes of foreign buyers?

2. Compare this Ming plate of around 1600 with the example on page 796 of "Wedgwood blue" china created in industrializing Britain around two centuries later. What aesthetic and physical qualities were the British manufacturers seeking to duplicate, and why?

the modern "hourly" or salaried sense. Unlike in neighboring Korea, chattel slavery, or full ownership of workers' bodies, was extremely rare in China, although penal labor—forced work by prisoners—was exploited in many public projects.

The explosive demand for export textiles that resulted from overseas expansion and American conquest had profound consequences for Chinese women. Women did most spinning and weaving in their own households in the form of piecework. This yielded essential income for the household but also added significantly to an already burdensome workload. Although being paid by the piece or task kept female workers at the mercy of male merchants, this new demand brought Chinese women, much like their Dutch and Irish contemporaries in the linen industry, fully into the global commercial economy. The products of their labors were consumed at the far edges of the world (see Lives and Livelihoods: Silk Weavers in China, page 696).

Manchu Expansion and the Rise of the Qing Empire

Some of the same environmental shocks that exacerbated the seventeenth-century crisis in Europe struck China in the last years of Ming rule. Droughts were particularly severe in the north from 1641 to 1644, but other factors also contributed to Ming decline. Court intrigues, often prompted by increasingly powerful eunuchs (castrated court officials), weakened Ming rulership just as China's economy grew in size and complexity. Manchu raids, meanwhile, became a severe threat and, consequently, a drain on resources as early as the 1620s. The Manchu were also on the march in Korea, which they reduced to tributary status in 1637. By 1642 the raiders reached Shandong province, but it was a local rebel, Li Zicheng, who ushered in the Manchu capture of Beijing in 1644. As the capital fell to Li, both the Ming emperor and his wife committed suicide rather than face the humiliation of captivity. To rid the capital of the rebels, a Ming official sought Manchu aid. The Manchus took advantage of the moment and occupied the capital. Calling themselves the Qing, or "Pure," dynasty, the Manchus quickly adapted to the role of ruling minority (see Map 21.2).

Qing Governance

The transition to Qing rule after 1644 proved surprisingly smooth, and most Chinese subjects' lives were barely changed. Although the new Qing emperors maintained a distinct ethnic identity and often dealt harshly with dissenters, they tended to improve on rather than revolutionize established patterns of Chinese governance. As a result, the empire rebounded with remarkable speed. Under Qing rule, Western gunpowder technology was so fully embraced that it enabled the rapid conquest of much of Mongolia, Tibet, and the Amur River basin (claimed by Russia) by the 1750s. Tributaries from these distant provinces trekked to Beijing to pay homage to the "pure" emperor.

Qing Expansion

The ascendancy of the Qing dynasty (1644–1911) was cemented with the accession of Emperor Kangxi (kang-shee) in 1661. By the end of his rule in 1722, China was for the first time in centuries an expansionist empire, with westward expansion by land China's principal aim. Mongolia, annexed in 1697, was a critical base for this project, and a buffer against Peter the Great's Russia. Even the traditionally defiant south began to give in, and by 1700 much of mainland Southeast Asia, including Burma, Thailand, Cambodia, and Vietnam, paid tribute to the Qing emperor in exchange for political autonomy. Kangxi's successors sought to follow his example. By 1751 Tibet and Nepal fell to the Qing. Chinese colonists, some of them hungry and homeless after floods and other disasters, were encouraged to move west with tax breaks, homesteads, and other incentives.

Most outlying regions were ruled indirectly, and some, like Korea, remained virtually autonomous, but by the 1750s, under the long-lived emperor Qianlong (chee-YEN-loong), China seemed to be reaching the limits of its bureaucratic and military capabilities. Victory in massive wars against southern Siberian peoples demonstrated Qing military might, but trouble was brewing, and not just at the fringes. Rebellions were now common throughout the realm. Subjects in the core districts grew increasingly restless, and guerrilla warfare and massacres of ethnic Chinese colonists became constant features of frontier life. Qianlong clung to power until 1796, and despite ballooning war costs, the emperor's reign

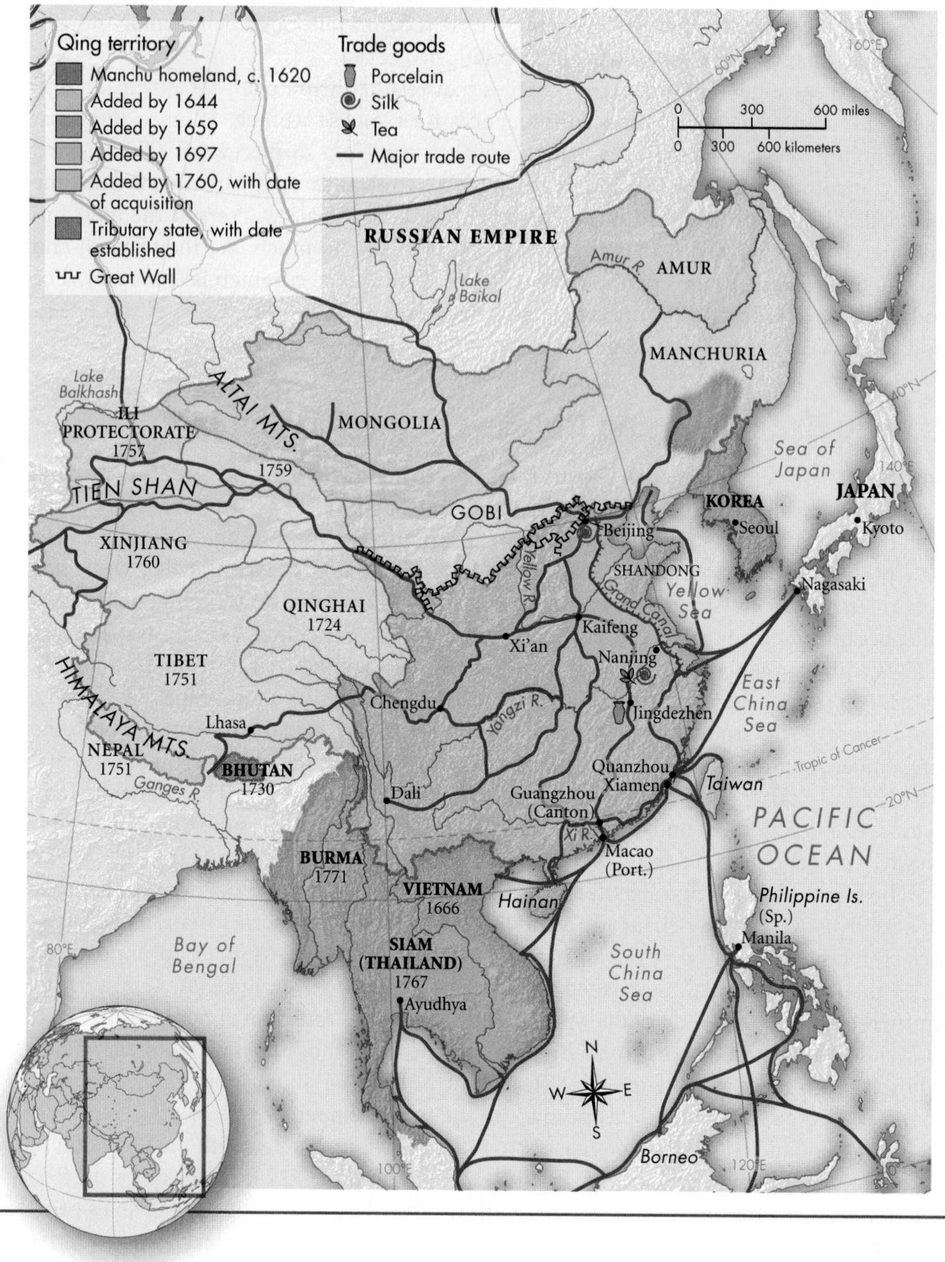

Qing territory
Manchu homeland, c. 1620
Added by 1644
Added by 1659
Added by 1697
Added by 1760, with date of acquisition
Tributary state, with date established
Great Wall
Trade goods
Porcelain
Silk
Tea
Major trade route
0 300 600 miles
0 300 600 kilometers
RUSSIAN EMPIRE
Amur R.
AMUR
Lake Baikal
MANCHURIA
Lake Balkhash
ALTAI MTS.
MONGOLIA
ILI PROTECTORATE 1757
1759
TIEN SHAN
GOBI
Sea of Japan
KOREA
Seoul
JAPAN
Kyoto
Beijing
Nagasaki
XINJIANG 1760
SHANDONG
Yellow R.
Grand Canal
Yellow Sea
QINGHAI 1724
Kaifeng
Xi'an
Nanjing
TIBET 1751
HIMALAYA MTS.
Chengdu
Yangzi R.
Jingdezhen
East China Sea
Lhasa
NEPAL 1751
BHUTAN 1730
Ganges R.
Dali
Quanzhou
Xiamen
Taiwan
Tropic of Cancer
Guangzhou (Canton)
Xi R.
PACIFIC OCEAN
Macao (Port.)
BURMA 1771
VIETNAM 1666
Hainan
Philippine Is. (Sp.)
Manila
Bay of Bengal
SIAM (THAILAND) 1767
Ayudhya
South China Sea
Borneo
N
S
E
W
60°N
40°N
20°N
160°E
140°E
120°E
100°E
80°E

MAP 21.2

The Qing Dynasty, 1644–1799

The Qing were mounted outsiders who developed a vast Asian empire, first by toppling the Ming dynasty to their south in 1644, then by annexing interior regions one by one through the eighteenth century. Taiwan was the only significant offshore conquest, but overseas trade with Japan and Southeast Asia, particularly the Spanish Philippine port of Manila, was critical to China's economy. Although conquered interior regions such as Tibet and Mongolia were extensive, most Qing subjects lived in the former Ming core, home to the world's largest concentration of people.

had boasted some of the biggest treasury surpluses in early modern history. The silver of the Americas had funded Qing expansion.

Environmental Transformations

Historians have only recently begun to examine how China's environment was changed by the general expansion of trade and population in the Ming and Qing eras. The disasters most remarked upon by contemporaries were floods, but their relationship to human rather than divine action was rarely explored except by a few alert public works officials. Deforestation, though not in itself a cause of floods, often exacerbated them. As peasants cleared more and more land for planting and cut forests for firewood and building materials, effective rainfall catchment areas were greatly diminished. Monsoon rains thus swept away more and more exposed soil, creating massive erosion upstream and devastating river sedimentation downstream. The problem became so widespread that Chinese territorial expansion and colonization in Qing times were in part aimed at resettling peasants displaced by environmental catastrophes in the heartland. In early modern times China was arguably the most human-molded landscape in the world in proportion to its population, and subsistence requirements absorbed an extraordinary amount of energy even before the rise of the Ming.

Everyday Life in Ming and Qing China

Ming intellectuals made note of China's broad shift to commercialism as early as the sixteenth century, and most found it annoying. As in many traditional societies (except Islamic ones), merchants and traders were something of a suspect class, esteemed only slightly above actors and musicians. Chinese society as defined by Confucius emphasized production over exchange, the countryside over the city, and continuity over change or mobility. The ideal was a linked grouping of agriculturally self-sufficient provincial units overseen by patriarchal figures. These units were to be connected not by trade, but by a merit-based governing hierarchy headed by a divine monarch.

Within this model, even peasant households were supposed to achieve self-sufficiency, relying on the market only in times of duress. Men were supposed to farm and women were supposed to spin and weave, both remaining in their home villages and producing only for their own consumption. Surpluses, a divine gift to the pious and industrious, were not to be sold but rather yielded up to the emperor at periodic intervals to express fealty and submission. Bureaucrats and scholars, who lived from these surpluses, kept track of them on paper.

Struggles of the Common Folk

Such was the ideal Neo-Confucian society. As we have seen, however, times of duress proved frequent in early modern China: droughts, floods, plagues, and even pirates took their toll. Peasants, as usual, suffered most, especially those driven to frontier lands by continued population growth. These stresses, along with increasing state demands for cash payment of taxes, compelled many individuals and families to migrate and sell their labor to whoever

Chinese Beggars
Although most early modern Chinese artists depicted idealized things of beauty, such as rugged landscapes and fanciful creatures in flight, some turned their attention to ordinary people. This c. 1500 Ming image depicts two wandering beggars, one apparently talking to himself as he walks and the other brandishing a serpent, presumably his helper at winning alms from curious or terrified passersby. The image offers a rare glimpse at an impoverished yet colorful Chinese subculture not often mentioned in historical documents. (The Granger Collection, New York.)

Silk Weavers in China

Chinese Silk Weaving

This rare detail from a Ming ceramic vase shows a group of Chinese women weaving silk on a complex loom. Chinese silk manufacture employed many thousands of women as well as men, doing everything from tending the mulberry bushes that produced the silkworms' food to finishing elaborate brocades and tapestries for export to the wider world, often in exchange for Spanish-American silver. Both highly technical and vast in scale, Chinese silk production was unmatched in early modern times. (Giraudon/ Bridgeman Art Library.)

Silk production, or sericulture, dates back several thousand years in China, but export volume grew most dramatically in early modern times, beginning with the late Ming. It was stimulated in particular by the massive influx of Spanish-American silver after China shifted to a silver-based economy in 1581. Most Chinese silk producers were concentrated in the southeast, especially along the lower Yangzi River (see again Map 21.2). Imperial factories were established under the Ming in Nanjing and Beijing, but most work was spread among peasants who worked at home at specific tasks assigned by private merchants. The merchants paid peasants for their mulberry leaves, cocoons, spun fiber, and finished fabrics.

Silk fiber is spun from the cocoons of the silkworm, produced by the worms' digestion of large quantities of

could pay. There is strong evidence that couples of even middling status practiced various forms of birth control to avoid the financial pressure of additional children.

The Newly Wealthy

Meanwhile, landlords and merchants accumulated increasing amounts of cash through market exchange. They were buying low and selling high, moving goods and getting rich. The social inequity resulting from this process was in part what bothered Chinese traditionalist intellectuals. What struck them as worse, however, since it had profound ethical and hence philosophical implications, was the market economy's tendency to reward nonproductive and even outright dishonest behavior. It was the appearance of the uppity rich, not the miserably poor, that most bothered the educated old guard.

The Flourishing of Art and Culture

As in Golden Age Spain, the arts and literature thrived in China during an era of political decline. This seeming paradox was due in part to the patronage of merchants who had made fortunes in the economic upswing, but it was also a function of the surplus of unemployed, literate civil servants. More and more smart people, in short, were angling for work and recognition. The end of the Ming was an era of increased literacy and mass distribution of books as well, and ideas and scientific knowledge were disseminated more widely than ever before. Novels and plays were also hugely popular. The play *The Lute*, published in 1610, included woodblock prints of scenes, for readers not able to see a live performance. Some writers devoted themselves to adventure travel in the interior, describing rugged landscapes and wild rivers for curious urban readers.

mulberry leaves. The worms are fragile creatures suscepti-ble to diseases and in need of constant supervision and feeding. Since they were tended in environments suscepti-ble to drastic temperature changes, the worms' welfare was a constant source of worry. This codependent relationship between humans and insects was perhaps matched only by that of beekeeping for honey collection or cochineal dye production in Mexico (cochineal bugs thrive on prickly pear cacti).

Rather like the linen industry in early modern Holland and Ireland, silk production in Ming and Qing China was extremely labor-intensive and largely dependent on women. Care of silkworms added to a host of domestic and agricul-tural tasks, and spinning, which had to be finished rapidly before the cocoons rotted, often lasted late into the night. Many households stopped interacting with neighbors entirely until silk season had passed, so intense and deli-cate was the work. Silk for export had to be reeled twice to guarantee consistent fineness. Still, silk making was attrac-tive to peasants since it allowed them to enter the market economy at greater advantage than with food products, which were heavy and susceptible to spoilage or consump-tion by rodents and other vermin. Because the industry itself was not taxed, many peasants planted mulberry bushes and tended cocoons to meet the emperor's silver cash tax demands.

Commercial producers eventually developed large reel-ing machines operated by men, but in early modern times most reeling was done by women on small hand-turned devices. Some peasants also wove textiles, but often not those who produced the raw fiber. With time, like European linen manufacture, Chinese silk production became a highly capitalized industry.

QUESTIONS TO CONSIDER

1. From its origins as an ancient Chinese art, how did silk manufacture change in early modern times?

2. Consider the Lives and Livelihoods essays in Chapters 17 and 18. How did silk weaving differ from sugar making in the Americas and gold mining in Africa?

For Further Information:

Shih, Min-hsiung. *The Silk Industry in Ch'ing China*. Translated by E-tu Zen Sun. 1976.

Vainker, S. J. *Chinese Silk: A Cultural History*. 2004.

In the years around 1600, foreign visitors, notably the Italian Jesuit Matteo Ricci in 1601, impressed the Chinese court with their knowledge of mathematics, alchemy, optics, and mechanics, though not with their religion. When he was not fixing European clocks brought as gifts for the emperor (see page 664), Ricci devoted his time to translating Confucius for a Western audience and composing religious tracts in court Chinese. As in Mughal India, Jesuit visitors at court had some influence on painting styles, particularly royal portraiture. Some artists also adopted European techniques of representing depth and perspective. The Jesuit presence at court and in the trading port of Macao remained important through the Qing era, even though the number of Chinese converts to Christianity remained very small in rela-tion to China's population. They were never expelled from China, as happened in Japan.

Japan in Transition 1540–1750

Located in the temperate latitudes of the North Pacific Ocean, Japan was shut off from the rest of the world for most of the early modern period. A brief opening in the feuding sixteenth century allowed foreign ideas and technologies to flow in and permitted a large but ineffectual invasion of Korea. Soon after 1600, however, Japan's leaders enforced seclusion from the outside world and, like their neighbors in China, concentrated their efforts on consolidating power. Japan would not be reopened for over two centuries.

FOCUS

How did self-isolation affect Japan?

Most inhabitants of the three major islands, Honshu, Kyushu, and Shikoku, were peasants, nearly all of them subjects of regional lords, called **daimyo**. Above Japan's rice-farming peasant majority was a class of warriors called **samurai**, some of them mercenaries and others permanent employees of powerful daimyo. Above the daimyo a small group of generals, including the top-ranking **shogun**, jockeyed to become Japan's supreme ruler. By 1600 the royal family had been reduced to ceremonial figureheads. In the peace that came with closure, Japan's population expanded steadily and the arts flourished.

Rise of the Tokugawa Shogunate and the Unification of Japan

As we saw in Chapter 15, following what is often described in Japanese history as a golden age of imperial unity and courtly life in the eleventh and twelfth centuries there ensued a breakdown of central authority and a rise in competing military factions. This politically chaotic period, heyday of the samurai warriors, lasted several centuries. The daimyo sometimes succeeded in bringing a measure of order to their domains, but no one daimyo family could establish predominance over others.

At the end of the sixteenth century several generals sought to quell civil war and to unify Japan. One such general, Toyotomi Hideyoshi (1535–1598), not only conquered his rivals but, with the Kyoto emperor's permission, assumed the role of top shogun. After Hideyoshi died, Tokugawa Ieyasu (1542–1616), a powerful military leader, seized control. Assuming the title of shogun in 1603, he declared that thereafter rulership was hereditary. The Tokugawa (TOH-koo-GAH-wah) Shogunate would endure until 1867.

With the uncompromising Tokugawa shoguns in charge of Japan's core districts, regional lords and military men found themselves forced to accept allegiance to the emerging unified state or face its growing might. The vast majority chose submission, and a long period of peace ensued. Peasant rebellions occurred from time to time, sometimes led by disgruntled samurai, but the state's adoption of Neo-Confucian ideals similar to those embraced in contemporary China and Korea stressed duty and hierarchy over rights and individual freedom. No elaborate, Neo-Confucianist civil service exam system was developed to match those of the mainland, but most Japanese accepted the benefits of peace and worked within their assigned roles.

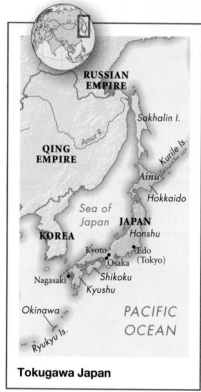

Tokugawa Japan

Containment of Foreigners

Hideyoshi's rule had been notable for tolerating Iberian Christian missionaries and launching two massive invasions of Korea in 1593 and 1597, part of a more ambitious project aimed at conquering China. Ieyasu reversed course, banning missionaries and making peace with Korea. Contact with foreigners, particularly Europeans—called **nanban**, or "southern barbarians," a reference to their arrival from southern seas—was restricted after 1614 to the tiny offshore island of Deshima near the city of Nagasaki, in westernmost Kyushu. Foreign families were not permitted to reside on Japanese soil, and by the 1630s all remaining Catholic priests and bachelor merchants had been expelled with the exception of one Dutch merchant. A representative of the Dutch East India Company, or VOC, he was strictly forbidden to discuss religion. The Dutch thus gained access, albeit limited, to the Japanese market, and the Tokugawa shoguns gained access to select information from the West, especially that regarding advances in science and technology. The much more numerous Chinese residents in Nagasaki, most of them silver-hungry merchants, were treated with similar suspicion. Scholars dispute the importance of Christianity in driving the early Tokugawa shoguns toward a policy of seclusion, but it clearly played a role. It was not the foreignness of the nanbans' religion that worried the shoguns, but rather its believers' insistence that it was the one true religion. Japan had long been a land of religious diversity, with a variety of foreign and local sects coexisting more or less peacefully. One

daimyo A regional lord in feudal and early modern Japan.

samurai The hereditary warriors who dominated Japanese society and culture from the twelfth to the nineteenth centuries.

shogun The supreme military commander in Japan, who also took political control.

nanban A Japanese term for "southern barbarians," or Europeans; also applies to hybrid European-Japanese artistic style.

could follow imported Confucian ethical principles, for example, as promoted by the Tokugawa state, yet also be a devout Buddhist. Taoist ideas and rituals were also embraced to a greater or lesser degree by most Japanese. Beyond this, one was expected to venerate nature spirits according to ancient Shinto traditions.

What was most unattractive about Christianity from the Tokugawa shogun's point of view was its intolerance of these or any other belief systems. Strictly monotheistic, focused on eternal salvation rather than everyday behavior, and fully understood only by foreign specialists, Christianity was branded subversive. Thus Roman Catholicism was harshly persecuted. The first executions of priests and followers began in 1597 and continued, with some breaks, to the end of the 1630s, when a major Christian-led rebellion was suppressed. Then, the shoguns ordered unrepentant priests and converts publicly beheaded, boiled, or crucified. The only remnants of Catholicism to survive this violent purge were scattered names of priests and saints, most of them venerated in older Japanese fashion by isolated peasants and fishing folk (see Reading the Past: Selections from the Hidden Christians' Sacred Book).

Harsh as it was, the shoguns considered their repression of Christianity a political rather than religious action. Stories of Spain's lightning-fast conquests in the distant Americas and nearby Philippines had long circulated in Japan, and Dutch and English contacts were quick to inform the Japanese of alleged Spanish cruelties. Portugal's similarly violent actions in India, Africa, and Southeast Asia were also well known, suggesting to Japan's new rulers that Catholic missionaries, particularly Iberians, were probably a spearhead for imperial designs. Several indiscreet Spanish visitors suggested as much in the 1590s, confirming Japanese fears.

There was an economic basis for seclusion as well. Japanese exports of silver surged in about 1600 in response to China's shift to a silver cash economy, then declined precipitously. A mining crisis in southwest Honshu in the 1630s forced the shoguns to keep as much silver as possible within the country to avert a currency shortage. This further isolated Japan from outside contact. With silver in short supply, the Dutch exported Japan's other metals, gold and copper, but connections to China and other outsiders gradually diminished. Japan, in short, had little need for the outside world. Even matchlock handguns, which had been successfully copied from early European imports, were abandoned soon after 1600 in favor of more traditional swords. Gunpowder was relegated to fireworks.

Following Christian suppression in the 1630s, the shoguns established firm control of the interior by forcing subordinate lords to maintain households in the new capital of Edo (modern Tokyo). Wives and children lived in the city and its growing suburbs as virtual hostages, and the daimyo themselves had to rotate in and out of the capital at least every other year. A new version of court life was one result of this shifting center, and with it grew both a vibrant capital city and a complex road and inn system lacing the rugged topography of Japan together. With Edo's primacy firmly established, Osaka became a major marketplace, producing its own class of newly rich merchants, and Kyoto thrived as a major cultural center.

Some Tokugawa subjects carried on trade with the Ryukyu Islands to the southwest, but only in the north was there anything like imperial expansion after the failed invasions of Korea in the 1590s. Japanese merchants had long traded rice for gold dust and rare seafoods with the Ainu of Hokkaido. The Ainu (EYE-new), who sported tattoos and whose men wore long beards, descended from Siberians from the north and probably also Austronesian islanders from the south. The Japanese considered them barbarians, and the Ainu considered the Japanese treacherous. By 1650 Japanese trading families had colonized portions of southernmost Hokkaido, but increasing pressures on the Ainu sparked rebellion. The Tokugawa state was reluctant to spend the necessary money to invade and fortify Hokkaido, but it did claim the island as Japanese territory. Only when the Russians threatened in the late eighteenth century to annex Ainu-inhabited islands farther north did the Japanese cement their claims and back them with force. Ainu culture was violently suppressed, but survives to the present day.

Suppression of Christianity

Withdrawal from Global Connections

Edo, the New Tokugawa Capital

Conquest of the Ainu

Selections from the Hidden Christians' Sacred Book

As seen in the last chapter with regard to Judaism and Islam in early modern Iberia, oppressed religions have survived in secret for centuries. Sometimes theologies endured with little change thanks to a preserved text or a sequence of tradition-keepers with good memories; in other cases only traces of old ritual behaviors persisted. In regions where a complex religious tradition had only recently been introduced before being harshly persecuted, considerable blending of local and imported ideas and forms was usually still in process. This yielded yet a third result, a kind of stunted blend. Thus Christianity's brief appearance in Japan produced an unusual underground religious tradition that was in general more Japanese than Christian. Compare the version of Genesis below to the standard Western text.

> In the beginning Deusu [Dios] was worshiped as Lord of Heaven and Earth, and Parent of humankind and all creation. Deusu has two hundred ranks and forty-two forms, and divided the light that was originally one, and made the Sun Heaven, and twelve other heavens. The names of these heavens are Benbo or Hell, Manbo, Oribeten, Shidai, Godai, Pappa, Oroha, Konsutanchi, Hora, Koroteru, and a hundred thousand Paraiso [Paradise] and Gokuraku.
>
> Deusu then created the sun, the moon, and the stars, and called into being tens of thousands of anjo [angels] just by thinking of them. One of them, Jusuheru [Lucifer], the head of seven anjo, has a hundred ranks and thirty-two forms. Deusu is the one who made all things: earth, water, fire, wind, salt, oil, and put in his own flesh and bones. Without pause Deusu worked on the Shikuda, Terusha, Kuwaruta, Kinta, Sesuta, and Sabata [all days of the week, mostly from Portuguese]. Then on the seventh day Deusu blew breath into this being and named him Domeigosu-no-Adan [Adam], who possessed thirty-three forms. So this is the usual number of forms for a human being.
>
> For this reason the seventh day of one cycle is observed as a feast day.
>
> Deusu then made a woman and called her Domeigosu-no-Ewa [Eve], had the man and woman marry, and gave them the realm called Koroteru. There they bore a son and a daughter, Chikoro and Tanho, and went every day to Paraiso to worship Deusu.

Source: Christal Whelan, ed. and trans., *The Beginning of Heaven and Earth: The Sacred Book of Japan's Hidden Christians* (Honolulu: University of Hawai'i Press, 1996) (portions of an early nineteenth-century Tokugawa-era Kakure Kirishitan, or "Hidden Christian," manuscript).

EXAMINING THE EVIDENCE

1. What elements of Christian teachings survive in this origin tale of the world?

2. What elements of the story are distinctly Japanese?

Everyday Life and Culture in Tokugawa Japan

Agricultural Expansion

Japan's population grew from about 10 million in 1600 to nearly 30 million in 1700, when it stabilized. This rapid growth was made possible in part by relative peace, but expansion and integration of the rice economy contributed as well. Rice's high yields encouraged creation of even the smallest irrigated fields, and some daimyo proved to be skillful marketers of their tributaries' main product. Most rice was sold in cities and to elites, while peasants ate a healthier diet of mixed grains, vegetables, and soy products. Urban-rural reciprocity was key, and processed human excrement collected in cities and villages was the main fertilizer. As surprising as it may seem, Japan's complex system of waste collection and recycling was easily the most hygienic and efficient in the world. Whole guilds were dedicated to the collection and marketing of what in the West was regarded as dangerous filth. The water supply of Edo, with over half a million people by the eighteenth century, was cleaner and more reliable than that of London. Thus, this system improved the health of the Japanese population as it created connections between urban and rural Japanese.

New strains of rice introduced from Southeast Asia also allowed farmers to extend cultivation into previously unproductive areas. By contrast, American crops such as maize and peanuts were not embraced in Japan as they were in China. Only sweet potatoes were appreciated, and they saved millions of lives during times of famine. As in China, however, Japanese agricultural expansion and diversification had profound ecological consequences. Leaders immediately recognized that deforestation intensified floods, and they responded to this problem with striking efficiency, organizing armies of workers to replant many depleted woodlands by the eighteenth century.

Transportation infrastructure was everywhere improved, from roads and bridges to ports and canals. Shoguns kept daimyos in check after 1615 by permitting only one castle in each domain, and sharply limiting improvement or expansion, but peace encouraged other forms of private construction. Like agriculture, the construction boom soon took a toll on Japan's forests, as did increased shipbuilding and other transport-related industries. Vulnerability to earthquakes gave rise to building codes and design innovations. A German-born employee of the Dutch VOC, Engelbert Kaempfer, described this Edo scene in 1691: "Today, one hour before noon, in bright and calm weather, a terrible earthquake shook the house with a loud sound. . . . This earthquake taught me that the country's laws limiting the height of buildings are based on necessity. It is also necessary that buildings be constructed of light wood, partitions, boards, and wood chips and then, below the timbers, be topped with a heavy pole, which with its weight pushes together the whole construction so that it does not collapse during an earthquake."[2] Hence, in agriculture, infrastructure, and construction, the leaders of Tokugawa Japan demonstrated the power of centralized government, controlling Japan's growth and development and shaping the connections between their subjects.

Improvements in Infrastructure

Although the majority of Tokugawa subjects remained peasants, a genuine leisure class also emerged, mostly concentrated in Kyoto. Merchants imported raw silk from China, which Japanese artisans processed and wove. Other imports included sandalwood, sugar, and spices from Southeast Asia. Consumption of fine fabrics and other products by the wealthy greatly expanded the artisan sector, but did not spark industrialization. There was simply not a large enough wage-earning consumer class in Japan to sustain industrial production. Instead, the trend was toward increasingly high-quality "boutique" goods such as samurai swords and ceremonial kimonos, rather than mass-produced consumer goods.

Rise of a Leisure Class and Expansion of the Artisan Sector

The period did, however, see the emergence of a precursor to modern Japanese industrialization. Like elites, peasants had to be clothed, if less opulently. What they wore most were locally produced cotton garments. Both the demand and supply of these textiles were new developments historically. Most traditional peasant clothing prior to the sixteenth century had been made from hemp fiber, and only through trade with Korea and China had cotton come to figure in Japan's economy. Initially, cotton was in demand among sixteenth-century samurai warriors, who used it for clothing, lining for armor, and fuses for matchlock handguns. Fishing folk also consumed cotton sailcloth. Trade restrictions in the Tokugawa era stimulated internal production of cotton textiles to such a degree that it reached near-industrial levels by the eighteenth century.

Growth of Cotton Textile Production

Japanese commoners got by on a diet of just under two thousand calories a day according to population historians, mostly consisting of grain porridges. They consumed very little meat and no milk or cheese, and away from coastal areas where seafood and fish could be harvested, most protein came from beans and soy products such as tofu. A huge variety of fruits, vegetables, herbs, grasses, fungi, insects, and larvae were roasted or pickled for consumption in winter or in lean times. Tobacco, an American crop, grew increasingly popular under Tokugawa rule. It was smoked by men and women of all social classes in tiny clay pipes, serving a social function much like the sharing of tea. When tea was too expensive, as it often was, common folk drank boiled water, which was at least safe. In all, the peasant diet in Tokugawa Japan, though short of protein, was at least as nourishing as that of western Europe at the same time.

Commoners' Diet

Both elite and ordinary Japanese folk lived according to a blend of agricultural and ritual calendars. In the simplest sense, time was measured according to lunar months and solar years, but there were numerous overlapping astrological and imperial cycles measured by Buddhist monks, who tolled bells to remind villagers and urbanites alike of ritual obligations. Western-style clocks, though known, were not adopted.

The Japanese Calendar

Kyoto Festival

This c. 1750 painting of a festival in Kyoto, Japan, depicts not only the daimyo, or local lord, and his ox-drawn cart and procession of armed samurai, but also daily goings-on about town. Many people seem to be engaged in conversation indoors, although they are quite visible thanks to open screens, allowing them to view the procession. Near the top of the panel, women and children walk leisurely toward what appears to be a recitation, possibly given by a samurai, and accompanied by a drummer. The use of patterned gold clouds to fill in empty spaces was a standard convention of early modern Japanese art, and here it adds a foglike layer to the painting's depth. (The Granger Collection, New York.)

Women's Lives   Women of every class faced obstacles to freedom in Japan's male-dominated and often misogynist society. Most were expected to marry at an early age and spend the majority of their lives serving their husbands, children, and in-laws. Still, as in other traditional societies, there were significant openings for female self-expression and even access to power in Tokugawa Japan. At court, noblewomen exercised considerable influence over succession and the everyday maintenance of proper decorum, and in the peasant sphere women managed household affairs, particularly when men were away on military duty or business. Widows could become quite powerful, especially those managing the affairs of dead merchant husbands.

Emergence of a National Culture

With the growth of cities and rise of a leisure class, Japanese literature and painting flourished, along with flower arranging, stylized and puppet theater, board games, and music. The writer Ihara Saikaku (EH-hah-rah sigh-kah-KOO) grew immensely popular at the end of the seventeenth century with his tales contrasting elite and working-class life. Saikaku idealized homosexual relations between senior and junior samurai, and also those among actors and their patrons, mostly wealthy townsmen. In "The Great Mirror of Male Love," Saikaku described most of these relationships as temporary, consensual, and often purchased. More than a hint of misogyny pervades the writings of Saikaku, but that sentiment is less evident in his "Life of an Amorous Woman" and other stories relating the adventures of courtesans and female prostitutes. In short, homosexuality, bisexuality, and prostitution were not only accepted but institutionalized in Tokugawa society.

In Edo, Kyoto, and especially the rice-trading city of Osaka, entertainments were many and varied. Daimyo and samurai landlords came to Osaka to exchange their rice tributes for money, which they then spent locally or in Edo, where they had to pay obeisance to the emperor. The frequent visits by regional elites to these two cities helped make them economic and cultural crossroads for Japan as a whole. Many samurai moved to these cities permanently as their rural estates diminished in size across generations. Social tension arose as the old warrior class tried to adapt to the cooperative requirements of urban life, but fortunately, there was much to distract them. Some worked for little compensation as teachers or policemen, but the wealthier samurai found time for the theater, musical concerts, and poetry readings. **Sumo** wrestling matches were popular even among non-samurai urbanites, as were board games, the tea ceremony, calligraphy, bonsai cultivation, and garden landscaping. More costly pursuits such as gambling, drinking, and sexual diversions were restricted to the so-called Licensed Quarters of the major cities. In general these activities were not considered "vices" as long as they did not prevent individuals from performing their civil duties.

Early modern European visitors, especially Catholic priests, found the general Japanese tolerance of prostitution, female impersonation, and homosexuality shocking, but they made little effort to understand Japanese cultural attitudes about sex and shame. Prostitution often was degrading to women and in some places approached the level of sex slavery. Still, there were groups of female escorts such as the geisha whom outsiders mistook for prostitutes. The **geisha** were indentured servants who made their living as private entertainers to the wealthiest merchants and landowners visiting or inhabiting cities. Geisha dress, makeup, and general comportment were all highly ritualized and distinctive. Although the geisha had control over their adult sexual lives, their first coital experience, or "deflowering," was sold to the highest bidder. Many young male prostitutes also acted as female impersonators in kabuki theater.

Kabuki was a popular form of theater that first appeared in Kyoto in 1603 as a way to advertise a number of female prostitutes. Subsequent shows caused such violence among potential customers that the Tokugawa government allowed only men to perform. As these female impersonators became associated with male prostitution, the state established official theaters that punished actors and patrons who engaged in sexual relations. By the eighteenth century, kabuki performances had become so "sanitized" that they included moralizing Neo-Confucian speeches. Even so, playwrights such as Chikamatsu Monzaemon (1653–1724) managed to retain ribald humor amid lessons in correct behavior. At the other end of the spectrum was the somber and ancient tradition of Noh theater, associated with Buddhist tales and Shinto shrines.

Poetry flourished as never before during the era of seclusion, and poets such as the itinerant and prolific Matsuo Bashō (1644–1684) were widely read. Here is a sample of his work:

> On my way through Nagoya, where crazy Chikusai is said to have practiced quackery and poetry, I wrote:
>
> With a bit of madness in me,
> Which is poetry,
> I plod along like Chikusai
> Among the wails of the wind.

Urban Sophistication

sumo A Japanese professional wrestler known for his heft.

geisha A professional female entertainer in Tokugawa Japan.

kabuki A popular Japanese theater known for bawdy humor and female impersonation.

Kabuki Theater

Something of a counterpoint to Neo-Confucian ideals of self-control and social order was Tokugawa Japan's ribald kabuki theater tradition, which became wildly popular in major cities after 1600. Kabuki actors were initially prostitutes, first young women and then young men, but objections from the samurai led by 1670 to the creation of a class of older men licensed to act in drag. In this c. 1680 screen painting by Hishikawa Moronobu, actors, costume designers, makeup artists, washerwomen, and stagehands all appear to be absorbed in their own little worlds. The painting seems to confirm early modern Japan's inward gaze and seemingly total cultural and material self-sufficiency. (The Granger Collection, New York.)

Sleeping on a grass pillow
I hear now and then
The nocturnal bark of a dog
In the passing rain.[3]

Despite isolation, Japan was among the most literate societies in the world in early modern times. By 1700 there were some fifteen hundred publishers active between Edo, Kyoto, and Osaka, publishing at least 7300 titles. Books on everything from tobacco farming to how young brides could find marital bliss were sold or rented in both city and countryside. Early forms of comic books were circulating by the eighteenth century, with the greatest sellers resembling what today would be classed as pulp fiction. Most books continued to be published on woodblock presses despite the fact that movable type was known from both mainland Asian and European sources—another example of the fact that early modern Japan, like China, had little need of the West.

Korea, a Land in Between 1392–1750

The Korean peninsula falls between China and Japan, with the Yellow Sea to the west and the Sea of Japan to the east. In 1392 Korea came to be ruled by the Yi (or Choson) dynasty, which remained in power until 1910. Though unified since the late seventh century, the Korean peninsula developed its distinctive culture primarily during Yi times, partly in response to Chinese and Japanese invasions. Korea had long been influenced by China, and had likewise served as a conduit linking the Asian mainland to Japan. The guiding principles of the early Choson state were drawn from the work of Confucius, as in contemporary China and Japan, and grafted onto a society that mostly practiced Buddhism, yet another imported tradition. Still, Koreans regarded themselves as a distinct and autonomous people, unified by a language and culture.

FOCUS

How did life for common folk in early modern Korea differ from life in China or Japan?

Capital and Countryside

It was under the first Yi ruler that Seoul, then known as Hanyang, became Korea's undisputed capital. Following Chinese principles of geomancy, or auspicious site selection, the Choson capital, backed by mountains and spread along the Han River plains, was considered blessed. Successive rulers drafted nearby peasants to expand the city and add to its grandeur. By 1450 Hanyang was home not only to substantial royal palaces but also bureaucratic buildings, markets, and schools.

The Choson state was not secular, but its leaders did move quickly to reduce the political and economic power of Buddhist temples and monasteries. Temple lands were widely confiscated and distributed to loyal officials. A kind of Neo-Confucian constitution was drafted in the first years of Yi rule advocating more radical state takeover and redistribution of land to peasants, but nobles balked and for the most part tenant farming persisted. Early modern Korea's government mirrored neighboring China's in some ways, but a significant difference was the prominence of a noble class, the **yangban**. Ancient ruling clans dominated the highest ranks of the bureaucracy, which consisted of a broad range of councils and regional governorships. A uniquely Korean institution known as the Samsa, a kind of academic oversight committee, had power even over the king himself, acting as a type of moral police force. Official historians, also drawn from the educated noble class, were allowed to write what they observed, keeping their work secret from the king. The Korean state did follow the Chinese model of civil service examinations, however, and through the hardest of these a few rare individuals of medium rank gained access to positions of power. The pressure was so great that some enterprising students hid tightly rolled crib-notes in their nostrils. Military service proved unpopular, partly because it was associated with slavery, and enrollment in school won exemption.

CHINA

KOREA

Sea of Japan

Hanyang (Seoul)

Yellow Sea

Korea Strait **JAPAN**

→ Japanese invasions, 1592, 1597
→ Manchu invasions, 1627, 1637

Choson Korea

Korea still needed a defense apparatus, though, and the early Yi rulers responded directly. The nobles' private forces were consolidated into a national, standing army by the mid-fifteenth century, and a complex system of ranks and divisions was instituted. Professional military men took exams, and peasants soon faced periodic draft service in frontier outposts. The Jurchen and other horse warriors threatened Korea's northern provinces from time to time, but many chieftains were successfully co-opted by the Choson state in the fifteenth century. Another defense strategy was to settle the northern frontier with land-hungry peasants from the south.

Foreign Challenges

yangban The noble class in early modern Korea.

Social Order in Early Modern Korea

Korean life under the Yi dynasty was marked by sharp class divisions, with a large portion of the poorer country folk living as slaves. This eighteenth-century painting on silk shows a notable individual on promenade, elaborately dressed, shaded, and otherwise attended, as more humble figures kneel in submission in the foreground. The broad-brimmed black hats and flowing garments were typical of high-ranking Koreans. Although Korean artists also depicted humble workers with some dignity, the Neo-Confucian ideal of a rigid social order comes through most strongly here. (The Art Archive/Musée Guimet Paris/Gianni Dagli Orti.)

After these early initiatives, defense became less of a concern, and the general devaluing of military service, which some Neo-Confucian reformers tried to address through incentives and fund-raising schemes, left Korea vulnerable by the time the Japanese invaded the peninsula in 1593 and 1597. Despite their massive forces and lightning speed, the Japanese under Shogun Hideyoshi were soon driven out with aid from Ming China. The Manchus were not so easily subdued, however. They invaded Korea in 1627 and 1636, reducing it to tributary status by 1637. Still, Korea managed to retain considerable autonomy.

Korea exported ginseng, furs, and a few other items to China in exchange for silk and porcelain, but its overseas trade was generally small, and only a few Korean merchants ventured beyond Japan or the nearby Ryukyu Islands, especially Okinawa. Aside from a general lack of high-value exports, which also dampened European interest, Korean merchants in the south faced constant threats from mostly Japanese pirates, the same ones who menaced China and its merchants from the thirteenth to seventeenth centuries. The Choson government attempted to suppress the pirates through both force and diplomacy, but Japan's fractured political system and occasional sponsorship of the pirates had the same hindering effect on Korean overseas trade felt in coastal China.

Everyday Life in Choson Korea

Despite rugged terrain, most Koreans under Yi rule were rice farmers. Wet-field rice cultivation expanded dramatically in the south beginning in the fifteenth century thanks to government initiatives and adaptation of Chinese techniques. Southern populations grew accordingly. Population estimates are debated, but it appears that Korea grew from about 5 million inhabitants in 1450 to some 10 million by 1600. In colder and drier parts of the peninsula, especially in the far north, peasants relied on millet and barley. As in Japan, these healthy grains were widely disdained as hardship rations in early modern times. Soybeans were later planted, adding a new source of protein. Koreans also exploited seacoasts and rivers for mollusks and fish, and some raised pigs and other livestock. Vegetables such as cabbage were pickled for winter consumption, spiced by the eighteenth century with capsicum peppers introduced from the Americas.

Gender Roles and Religious Beliefs

Ordinary folk probably did not obsess over genealogies and proper marriage matches to the extent that the noble class, or yangban, did, but their mating customs could still be rigid. Some marriages were arranged, occasionally between young children. Women appear to have lost a great deal of their former autonomy thanks to the rise of Neo-Confucianism, and widows were even presented with a knife with which to kill themselves should they be sexually violated or otherwise dishonored. According to some sources,

Korean women more often used their suicide knives to kill attackers. Female entertainers, or **kisaeng**—like their Japanese counterparts, the geisha—were sometimes able to accumulate capital and achieve literary fame.

Teachers in Choson Korea took on the moral advisory role played by priests or imams in early modern Christian or Islamic societies, and in the seventeenth century Neo-Confucian scholars, following the lead of China's Wang Yangming, attempted to reform Korean society and government wholesale. Education in general was highly valued, and literacy widespread (see Reading the Past: Scenes from the Daily Life of a Korean Queen). It was in the Choson era that Korean students became outspoken critics of the state, launching a number of mass protests in the late seventeenth and early eighteenth centuries. Despite the ruling class's attachment to Neo-Confucian philosophy and suppression of Buddhist monasteries, popular religious ideas persisted, especially in the countryside. Alongside some rooted Buddhist beliefs, mountain deities and sacred stones or trees continued to be venerated on a regular basis, much as in western Africa and the Andes Mountains of South America, and shamanism was widely practiced for divination and healing. Many of the best-known healing shamans were women.

kisaeng A geisha-like female entertainer in early modern Korea.

READING THE PAST

Scenes from the Daily Life of a Korean Queen

The following selection is taken from the diary of Lady Hong (1735–1815), a queen during Korea's Yi dynasty. Unlike most male authors of the time, who wrote in Chinese (in part to show off their education, much as many European men at this time wrote in Latin rather than their own vernaculars), Lady Hong wrote in the Korean script. She also devoted great attention to the details of everyday life, including close observations of individual emotions. After stating that she began to write her memoirs at the urging of a nephew, Lady Hong describes her birth and early upbringing:

I was born during the reign of King Yongjo, at noon on 6 August 1735, at my mother's family's home in Kop'yong-dong, Pangsongbang. One night, before I was born, my father had dreamed of a black dragon coiled around the rafters of my mother's room, but the birth of a daughter did not seem to fit the portent of his dream. . . .

My paternal grandfather, Lord Chong-hon, came to look at me, and took an immediate fancy to me, declaring, "Although it is a girl, this is no ordinary child!" As I grew up, he became so fond of me that he was reluctant to let me leave his lap. He would say jokingly, "This girl is quite a little lady already, so she is sure to grow up quickly!". . .

The womenfolk of our family were all connected with the most respected clans of the day. My mother came from the Yi family—an upright clan. My father's eldest sister was married to a famous magistrate; while

his second sister was a daughter-in-law of Prince Ch'ong-nung; and his youngest sister was a daughter-in-law of the minister of the board of civil office. Despite these connections, they were not haughty or extravagant, as is so often the case. When the family gathered together on festival days, my mother always treated the elder members with respect, and greeted the younger ones with a kind smile and an affectionate word. Father's second brother's wife was likewise virtuous, and her esteem for my mother was exceeded only by that for her mother-in-law. She was an outstanding woman—noble-minded and well educated. She was very fond of me; taught me my Korean alphabet and instructed me in a wide range of subjects. I loved her like a mother and indeed my mother used to say I had grown too close to her.

Source: Lady Hong, *Memoirs of a Korean Queen,* ed. and trans. Choe-Wall Yangh-hi (London: KPI, 1985), 1–4, 49.

EXAMINING THE EVIDENCE

1. In what ways do these passages reveal Neo-Confucian values?

2. What do these passages tell us about gender roles in a Neo-Confucian court society?

Slavery   Choson Korea appears unique among early modern states in that it was both ethnically homogeneous and heavily reliant on slave labor. Korea's enslaved population, perhaps as much as 30 percent of the total by 1550, appears to have emerged as a result of several factors: debt peonage (self-sale due to famine or debt) and penal servitude (punishment for crimes, including rebellion). Debt peonage and penal servitude were not unusual in the early modern world, and both could be found in neighboring China. What made slavery different in Korea was that the legal status of the enslaved, once proclaimed, was likely to be inherited for many generations. Self-purchase was extremely difficult, and slave owners clung to their chattels tenaciously. Korea's rigid social structure, far more hierarchical than neighboring China's or Japan's, only reinforced the notion of perpetual bondage. Moralists criticized slavery as early as the seventeenth century, but it was not until forced contact with outsiders after 1876 that the institution died out. Korea's last slaves were freed only in 1894.

Consolidation in Mainland Southeast Asia 1500–1750

FOCUS

What trends did mainland Southeast Asia share with China, Korea, Japan, and Russia?

Mainland Southeast Asia, encompassing the modern nations of Burma (Myanmar), Thailand, Cambodia, Laos, and Vietnam, followed a path more like that of China than of the Southeast Asian islands discussed in Chapter 19. Overall trends on the mainland included political consolidation, mostly by Buddhist kings; growth of large, tribute-paying populations due to intensive wet rice cultivation; and a shift toward planting of cash crops such as sugar for export. Unlike the more politically fractured islands of Indonesia and the Philippines, which fell increasingly into the hands of European interlopers (see Counterpoint: "Spiritual Conquest" in the Philippines), mainland Southeast Asia in early modern times experienced gunpowder-fueled, dynastic state-building.

Political Consolidation

The mainland Southeast Asian kingdoms in place by 1700 formed the basis for the nation-states of today. As happened in Muscovite Russia, access to European guns enabled some emerging dynasties, such as those of southern Burma, to expand and even briefly conquer their neighbors in the sixteenth and seventeenth centuries. Another catalyst for change was the rapid growth of global maritime trade, evident since the early fifteenth century (see Map 21.3). Overseas commerce transformed not only traditional maritime hubs such as Melaka and Aceh, as seen in Chapter 19, but also Pegu in Burma, Ayudhya (or Ayutthaya) in Thailand, and Lovek (near modern Phnom Penh) in Cambodia. The Buddhist kings who dominated these cities used trade revenues to expand and enhance their realms by attracting scholars, building libraries and monasteries, and constructing temples and images of the Buddha. The most confident saw themselves as incarnations of the Buddhist ideal of the universal king. Funded in part by growing trade, a massive bronze Buddha and supporting temple complex were built in the city of Luang Prabang, in Laos, beginning in 1512. A solid gold Buddha was also commissioned. Religious monuments on this scale, as seen in Europe, the Middle East, and even Spanish America, are a lasting reminder of early modern devotion and wealth.

The Example of Burma   A notable example of mainland Southeast Asian state-building driven by commercial wealth and access to European gunpowder weapons arose in southern Burma beginning in the 1530s. Portuguese mercenaries aided a regional king's takeover of the commercial city of Pegu, and a new, Pegu-based Buddhist dynasty with imperial ambitions soon emerged. Under King Bayinnaung (r. 1551–1581) the Burmese expanded into neighboring Thailand and Laos, conquering the prosperous capital of Ayudhya in 1569 and Vientiane, on the

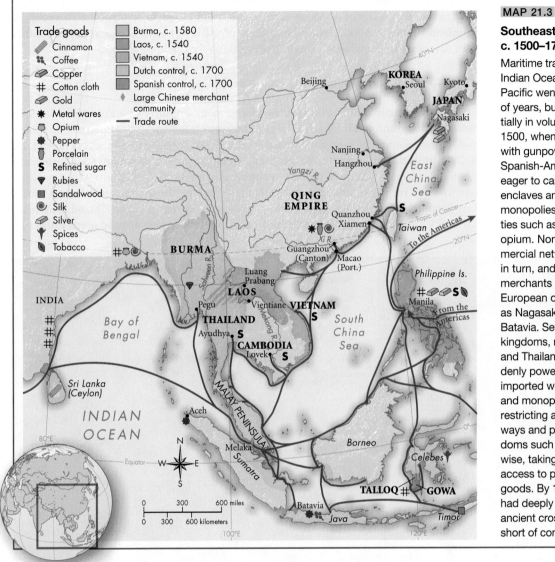

MAP 21.3

Southeast Asian Trade, c. 1500–1700

Maritime trade between the Indian Ocean and the western Pacific went back thousands of years, but it grew exponentially in volume and value after 1500, when Europeans arrived with gunpowder weapons and Spanish-American silver, eager to carve out trading enclaves and establish monopolies on key commodities such as pepper and opium. Non-European commercial networks expanded in turn, and many Chinese merchants set up shop in European outposts such as Nagasaki, Manila, and Batavia. Several mainland kingdoms, notably Burma and Thailand, became suddenly powerful by adopting imported weapons technology and monopolizing exports or restricting access to waterways and ports. Island kingdoms such as Aceh did likewise, taking advantage of their access to pepper and other goods. By 1700, Europeans had deeply affected this ancient crossroads, yet fell far short of controlling it.

upper Mekong River, in 1574. After building numerous pagodas, or ceremonial towers, in his new conquests, admirers referred to Bayinnaung as the "Victor of Ten Directions." He preferred the title "King of Kings."

Vietnam followed a different path, largely as a result of Chinese influence. Even before Ming expansion southward in the fourteenth and early fifteenth centuries, Neo-Confucian principles of law and governance had been adopted by Vietnamese royalty under the Le dynasty (1428–1788). Yet like Korea, whose nobility had also embraced the kinds of reformist ideas promoted by Wang Yangming, the Chinese veneer in Vietnam barely masked a vibrant regional culture whose sense of distinct identity was never in question. China brokered power-sharing arrangements between the northern and southern halves of Vietnam in the 1520s, but new, competitive dynasties, led by the Trinh and Nguyen clans, were already in the making. Their battles for control lasted until the late seventeenth century and hindered Vietnamese consolidation despite the region's shared language and culture.

Mainland Southeast Asia resembled China more than neighboring islands in another sense: high overall population. This was largely the result of wet-rice agriculture and acquired immunity to a range of lowland tropical maladies. Massive water-control projects reminiscent of those in China and Japan allowed Vietnam's feuding clans to field tens of

Vietnam's Different Path

thousands of troops by 1700. Rice-rich Burma was even more populous, capable of fielding hundreds of thousands of troops as early as 1650. Unlike China, most of the kingdoms of mainland Southeast Asia continued to collect tribute in the form of rice and goods rather than silver throughout the early modern period.

Commercial Trends

Exports   Exports from mainland Southeast Asia were not monopolized by Europeans in early modern times, and in fact many commodities found their principal markets in China and Japan. Sugar cane originated in Southeast Asia, but refined sugar found no market until the late seventeenth century, when growers in Vietnam, Cambodia, and Thailand adopted Chinese milling technology and began to export their product northward. Only Taiwan competed with these regions for the Japanese "sweet" market. That most addictive of Columbian exchange crops, tobacco, introduced from Mexico via Manila, joined betel leaves (traditionally wrapped around areca nuts) as a

Buddha from Luang Prabang

This enormous gilt bronze Buddha was cast in the early sixteenth century in the former royal capital of Laos, Luang Prabang, where it is still at the center of an active temple. For several centuries the temple also housed a solid gold Buddha, which is now in the nearby palace museum. The remarkably well-preserved city and temples of Luang Prabang evoke the heyday of the Buddhist kings of mainland Southeast Asia, when new gunpowder weapons and access to more distant foreign markets stoked expansionist urges. (Yoshio Tomii Photo Studio/Aflo FotoAgency/Photolibrary.)

popular stimulant throughout the region by the seventeenth century. Other drugs had more profound consequences. The Dutch were the first to push the sale of opium from India in the 1680s (initially as a tobacco additive), and it soon created a class of addicts among Southeast Asia's many Chinese merchants and others willing to pay any amount of silver cash for it.

Imports to mainland Southeast Asia consisted primarily of cloth from India, an old "monsoon circuit" trade good that fostered resident communities of merchants, most of them Muslims, from as far away as Gujarat, in the Arabian Sea. Chinese merchants brought cloth from home, too, along with metal wares, porcelain, and a wide range of goods acquired through interregional trade. On the whole, the Chinese were by far more competitive and successful middlemen in mainland Southeast Asia than Europeans in early modern times, a fact that led to much resentment.

Imports

Interregional and interethnic commerce and urbanization enabled many Southeast Asian women to engage in trade as well, and whether they were Islamic, Buddhist, or otherwise observant, this pattern fit well with the general regional tendency toward female independence noted in Chapter 19. The wives and concubines of prominent long-distance merchants not only carried on important business transactions on land, they traveled with their husbands and lovers at sea. Some Southeast Asian women served as fully autonomous intermediaries for European merchants, most famously Soet Pegu, a Burmese woman who lived in the Thai capital of Ayudhya. She was the principal broker for the Dutch in Thailand (then known as Siam) for many years beginning in the 1640s.

Women's Commercial Pursuits

The global financial crisis of the seventeenth century, coupled with a number of regional wars, epidemics, and droughts, left mainland Southeast Asia in a weakened state. Burma contracted considerably, as did neighboring Siam. Laos survived as a separate kingdom only due to its isolation from these two neighbors, and it became even more inward-looking. Cambodia was similarly introverted under Khmer rule, and Vietnam suffered an even more severe decline. Mainland Southeast Asia submitted to paying tribute to China's Qing emperors in the course of the eighteenth century. In spite of the trend toward contraction, however, the region remained nearly impervious to European designs.

Economic Contraction

COUNTERPOINT
"Spiritual Conquest" in the Philippines

The Philippine Islands are a large volcanic chain in the warm tropical waters of the western Pacific (see Map 21.4). Like most Southeast Asian islands, the Philippines were settled by Austronesian mariners who left southern China and Taiwan some three thousand years ago. With the exception of a few small Islamic sultanates in the southern islands, the Philippines at the dawn of early modern times had no dynastic rulers or overarching religious or ethical traditions to unify its population. Over one hundred languages were spoken throughout the archipelago, and material culture differed radically from one river valley or island to the next.

> **FOCUS**
>
> In contrast to the general trend of political consolidation in early modern Asia, why did the Philippines fall to a European colonizing power?

Kin-based political units rarely exceeded two thousand members, and most were mutually hostile, sometimes murderously so. The islands' total population was relatively high, probably between 1 and 2 million in 1500, and acquired immunity to Old World diseases appears to have been relatively robust, certainly superior to that of Europeans who came later. As in most of Southeast Asia, women in the Philippines were relatively powerful and autonomous in politics, business, and domestic affairs. Both slavery and long-distance trade were established, though not deeply entrenched institutions, and a writing system using bamboo slats, now lost, was more or less common.

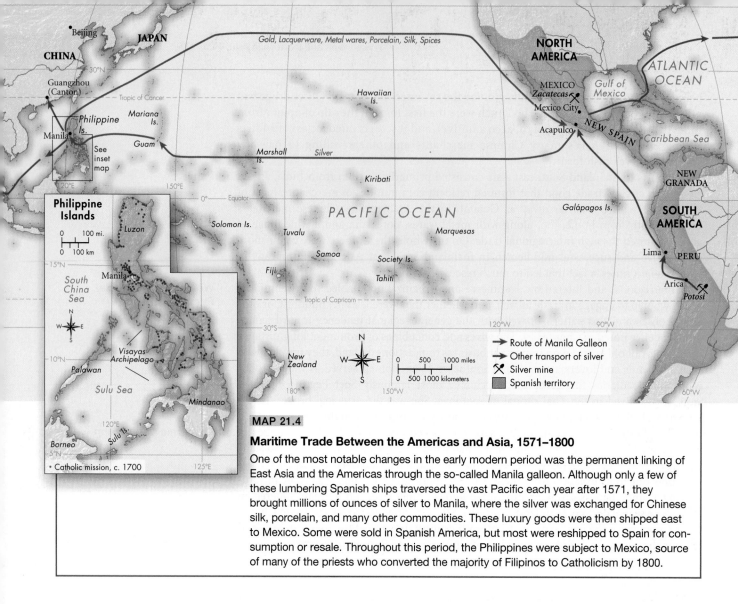

MAP 21.4

Maritime Trade Between the Americas and Asia, 1571–1800

One of the most notable changes in the early modern period was the permanent linking of East Asia and the Americas through the so-called Manila galleon. Although only a few of these lumbering Spanish ships traversed the vast Pacific each year after 1571, they brought millions of ounces of silver to Manila, where the silver was exchanged for Chinese silk, porcelain, and many other commodities. These luxury goods were then shipped east to Mexico. Some were sold in Spanish America, but most were reshipped to Spain for consumption or resale. Throughout this period, the Philippines were subject to Mexico, source of many of the priests who converted the majority of Filipinos to Catholicism by 1800.

Filipino traders sailing large outrigger vessels maintained contact with the East and Southeast Asian mainland, as well as with southern Japan, and Chinese merchants had long operated small trading posts in the Philippines, including one at Manila on the northern island of Luzon. Filipino exports included future plantation crops such as sugar and cotton, along with a bit of gold panned from mountain streams. Imports included metal goods, porcelain, spices, and a wide range of textiles. Most Filipinos mixed farming with fishing and the raising of small livestock, mostly pigs and chickens.

Arrival of the Spanish

Conquistadors

Filipino life was suddenly and forever altered when Spanish conquistadors arrived in 1565, following up on the claims of Ferdinand Magellan, who was killed on the islands in 1521. By 1571 the Spanish had made Manila their capital city: a base for trade with China and a springboard for regional conquest. Shipyards were established at nearby Cavite to outfit the great galleons sent annually to Mexico (see again Map 21.4). Conquest was not easy in such a divided region, but these same divisions prevented a unified effort to repulse the Spanish. European invaders managed to gradually dominate many regions of the Philippines by making alliances with local chieftains in exchange for gifts and favors. Where local headmen resisted, obedient substitutes were found and placed in power.

Early Spanish colonists feverishly searched for gold, pearls, and other exportable local commodities, but their hopes fizzled before the end of the sixteenth century. There was ultimately little to collect in the way of marketable tribute, and the small enclave around

An Elite Filipino Couple

When the Spanish established their Philippine capital at Manila in 1571, they began to deal regularly with local nobles as well as visiting Chinese merchants. This rare image from about 1600 shows a Filipino husband and wife with the local label of Tagalog. Although Filipinos spoke many languages and practiced many distinct religions, the Tagalog language was the one chosen by Spanish priests for evangelization. Alongside Spanish, it became the islands' official language. The couple shown here displays dress and grooming similar to those of Malay elites living throughout Southeast Asia. The man holds the hilt of a kris dagger, a key symbol of high status, while his demure wife stands draped in the finest Chinese silk. (Courtesy, The Lilly Library, Indiana University, Bloomington, Indiana.)

Manila became, rather like a contemporary Portuguese outpost, the exclusive preserve of Spanish merchants, soldiers, and missionaries. A few bureaucrats eventually followed, linking Manila to its official capital in faraway Mexico City.

Outside Manila's Spanish core there grew a substantial Chinese merchant community, and many of its residents eventually converted to Catholicism and intermarried with local Filipino elites. In the end it was Catholic priests arriving on the annual ships from Mexico who proved responsible for what has come to be known as the "spiritual conquest" of the Philippines. As a result of lax crown oversight, the absence of precious minerals or other high-value exports, and general Filipino receptiveness to Roman Catholicism, before the end of early modern times a fairly small number of highly energetic priests managed to transform much of the archipelago into a veritable theocracy (a state ruled by religious authority), amassing huge amounts of territory and much political power in the process.

Missionaries

Missionaries from several Catholic orders learned to preach in Tagalog, the language of the greater Manila area, as well as a few other regional languages. Lack of standardized languages and writing systems complicated missionary efforts in some places, as did the racist refusal to train an indigenous clergy, yet the absence of a regionwide state religion or code of ethics similar to Buddhism or Confucianism probably eased acceptance of Catholicism's universalist claims. Indigenous deities and interpretations of Catholicism nevertheless persisted, usually manifested through the cult of the saints and in hybrid practices described by priests as witchcraft. In time, scores of Spanish and Mexican missionaries established hundreds of rural churches and frontier missions, most of them concentrated in the northern islands but some stretching south through the Visayas archipelago and into northern Mindanao.

The Limits of "Spiritual Conquest"

The Muslim South Southern Mindanao and the Sulu Islands remained staunchly Muslim, however, and hence enemy territory in the Spanish view. Periodic battles pitted self-styled crusading Spaniards against the so-called Moors of this region, and some missionaries related harrowing stories of martyrdom and captivity among "pirate infidels" reminiscent of accounts from North Africa's Barbary Coast (discussed in Chapter 20). Indeed, hundreds of letters to Spain's kings and to the pope describe these mostly fruitless struggles.

Other threats to Christian hegemony came from bands of headhunters inhabiting the mountainous interior of Luzon and smaller islands. According to surviving documents, the ritual practice of headhunting, known in many parts of island Southeast Asia, was fairly widespread when the Spanish arrived, and it was periodically revived in some areas into modern times. Despite all these challenges to Spain's unarmed "Christian soldiers," the Philippines emerged from early modern times deeply transformed, in some ways more like Latin America than any other part of Asia. It would ironically be Filipino youths such as José Rizal, trained by the Jesuit and Franciscan successors of these early missionaries, who would lead the struggle to end Spanish colonialism at the last years of the nineteenth century.

Conclusion

China, Japan, Korea, and mainland Southeast Asia were home to a large portion of the world's peoples in early modern times. Russia was, by contrast, vast but thinly populated. In all cases, however, the most notable trend in northern and eastern Asia was toward internal political consolidation. The Philippines, though relatively populous, proved to be an exception, falling with relative ease into the hands of Spanish invaders. Outside Orthodox Russia and the Buddhist regions of Southeast Asia, Neo-Confucian principles of agrarian order and paternalistic harmony guided imperial consolidation. Despite some shocks in the seventeenth century, steady population growth and relative peace in China, Japan, and Korea only seemed to reinforce Confucius's ideal notions of educated self-sufficiency and limited need for foreign trade. Dynasty building and territorial expansion took on more charismatic and even prophetic religious tones in Orthodox Russia and Buddhist Southeast Asia.

Internal changes, however, particularly in China, did have profound effects on the rest of the world, and some regional political trends were accelerated by foreign imports such as gunpowder weapons. Wang Yangming, whose story began this chapter, was just one of many new imperial officials to use these deadly tools of power. Western weapons also aided Burmese and later Qing overland expansion in a way reminiscent of the Islamic "gunpowder empires" discussed in Chapters 19 and 20. Global trade also proved highly susceptible to East Asia's centralizing early modern policies. China's shift to a silver-based currency in the sixteenth century radically reordered world trade patterns. Suddenly, the Americas, Europe, and many Asian neighbors found themselves revolving in an increasingly tight, China-centered orbit. Virtually overnight, the village of Manila was transformed into one of the world's most vibrant trading crossroads. Manila was also an outlying colony, as will be seen in the next chapter, of an increasingly autonomous Spanish America. It was only in the nineteenth century that many parts of East and Southeast Asia began to experience the types of outside domination long experienced by these early established colonies.

NOTES

1. Peter the Great, quoted in Gérard Chaliand, ed., *The Art of War in World History from Antiquity to the Nuclear Age* (Berkeley: University of California Press, 1995), 578.
2. Engelbert Kaempfer, *Kaempfer's Japan: Tokugawa Culture Observed*, ed. and trans. Beatrice M. Bodart-Bailey (Honolulu: University of Hawai'i Press, 1999), 356.
3. Bashō, "The Records of a Weather-exposed Skeleton" (c. 1685), ed. and trans. Nobuyuki Yuasa, *The Narrow Road to the Deep North and Other Sketches* (London: Penguin, 1966).

RESOURCES FOR RESEARCH

General Works

Few works survey the many cultures treated as a cluster in this chapter, but some recent comparative studies have challenged established national categories of analysis. Liebermann and other contributors to the following volume try to relink Europe and Asia in early modern times.

Liebermann, Victor, ed. *Beyond Binary Histories: Re-imagining Eurasia to c. 1830.* 1999.

Straddling Eurasia: Rise of the Russian Empire, 1462–1725

The emphasis in early modern Russian history has largely moved away from court intrigues and suffering serfs toward broader processes of expansion into frontiers, environmental impacts, and cultural interaction. Other current scholarship focuses on the importance of the Orthodox Church. In economic history, classic works on the fur trade are still frequently cited.

For a broad-ranging Web site introduced by veteran Russian historian James H. Billington (author of *The Icon and the Axe: An Interpretive History of Russian Culture*, 1966), see http://www.pbs.org/weta/faceofrussia/intro.html.

Engel, Barbara A. *Women in Russia, 1700–2000.* 2004.

Kivelson, Valerie, and Robert H. Greene, eds. *Orthodox Russia: Belief and Practice Under the Tsars.* 2003.

LeDonne, John P. *The Grand Strategy of the Russian Empire, 1650–1831.* 2004.

Poe, Marshall T. *The Russian Moment in World History.* 2003.

Sunderland, Willard. *Taming the Wild Field: Colonization and Empire on the Russian Steppe.* 2004.

China from Ming to Qing Rule, 1500–1800

The literature on Ming and Qing China is vast. The following selections highlight both key internal developments and global interactions. Environmental history has experienced a recent boom.

Brook, Timothy. *The Confusions of Pleasure: Commerce and Culture in Ming China.* 1998.

Clunas, Craig. *Empire of Great Brightness: Visual and Material Cultures of Ming China, 1368–1644.* 2007.

Princeton University professor Benjamin Elman maintains a comprehensive Web site for Chinese history and culture: http://www.princeton.edu/~classbib.

Elvin, Mark. *The Retreat of the Elephants: An Environmental History of China.* 2004.

Mungello, D. E. *The Great Encounter of China and the West, 1500–1800,* 2d ed. 2005.

Struve, Lynn A., ed. *The Qing Formation in World-Historical Time.* 2004.

Von Glahn, Richard. *Fountain of Fortune: Money and Monetary Policy in China, 1000–1700.* 1996.

Japan in Transition, 1540–1750

The literature on Tokugawa Japan is extensive, and increasingly diverse. Some of the most exciting recent work treats cultural trends and environmental impacts.

Elison, George, and Bardwell L. Smith, eds. *Warlords, Artists, and Commoners: Japan in the Sixteenth Century.* 1981.

Fitzhugh, William W., and Chisato O. Dubreuil, eds. *Ainu: Spirit of a Northern People.* 1999.

Nakane, Chie, and Shinzaburō Ōishi, eds. *Tokugawa Japan: The Social and Economic Antecedents of Modern Japan.* Translated by Conrad Totman. 1990.

Perez, Louis G. *Daily Life in Early Modern Japan.* 2002.

The Public Broadcasting Service maintains a Web site with many Edo period images and links at http://www.pbs.org/empires/japan/.

Totman, Conrad. *The Lumber Industry in Early Modern Japan.* 1995.

Korea, a Land in Between, 1392–1750

Very few English-language histories of Korea give much attention to the early modern period. Seth is an exception.

Seth, Michael J. *A Concise History of Korea: From the Neolithic Period Through the Nineteenth Century.* 2006.

Consolidation in Mainland Southeast Asia, 1500–1750

Histories of mainland Southeast Asia are only beginning to break the old nationalist paradigm and take into account broad regional trends. Liebermann, a specialist on Burma, nicely complements Reid, whose work has mostly been on the islands.

Liebermann, Victor. *Strange Parallels: Southeast Asia in Global Context, c. 800–1830.* 2 vols. 2003–2004.

Northern Illinois University maintains a Southeast Asian digital library at http://sea.lib.niu.edu.

Reid, Anthony, ed. *Sojourners and Settlers: Histories of Southeast Asia and the Chinese.* 2001.

Tarling, Nicolas, ed. *The Cambridge History of Southeast Asia.* Vol. 1., *From Early Times to c. 1800.* 1992.

COUNTERPOINT: "Spiritual Conquest" in the Philippines

The colonial history of the Philippines still requires more scholarly examination, though many primary sources, such as that of Antonio de Morga, have been published in English translation. Phelan's account of early missionary endeavors remains a useful introduction.

Brewer, Carolyn. *Shamanism, Catholicism, and Gender Relations in the Colonial Philippines, 1521–1685.* 2004.

*de Morga, Antonio. *Sucesos de las Islas Filipinas.* Translated and edited by J. S. Cummins. 1971.

Majul, Cesar A. *Muslims in the Philippines.* 1973.

Phelan, John L. *The Hispanization of the Philippines: Spanish Aims and Filipino Responses, 1565–1700.* 1959.

Rafael, Vicente. *Contracting Colonialism: Translation and Christian Conversion in Tagalog Society Under Early Spanish Rule,* 2d ed. 1993.

*Primary source.

▶ **For additional primary sources from this period,** see *Sources of Crossroads and Cultures.*

▶ **For Web sites, images, and documents related to topics in this chapter,** see Make History at bedfordstmartins.com/smith.

The major global development in this chapter ▶ The general trend toward political and cultural consolidation in early modern Asia.

IMPORTANT EVENTS

1392–1910	Yi dynasty established in Korea
1542	Jesuits reach Japan
1555–1581	Expansion of Burma under King Bayinnaung
1565	Spanish conquest of Philippines begins
1571	Manila becomes Philippine capital and key Pacific trading post
1581	Chinese Ming emperor Wanli issues Single Whip Law
1584–1613	Time of Troubles in Russia
1597–1630s	Persecution of Japanese Christians
1601	Matteo Ricci demonstrates Western technology in Ming court
1602–1867	Tokugawa Shogunate in Japan
1614	Japanese contact with foreigners restricted
1627, 1636	Manchu invasions of Korea
1644	Manchu invasion of Beijing; Ming dynasty replaced by Qing
1661–1722	Qing expansion under Emperor Kangxi
1689–1725	Russian imperial expansion under Tsar Peter the Great
1751	Qing annexation of Tibet

KEY TERMS

daimyo (p. 698) **samurai** (p. 698)
geisha (p. 703) **serf** (p. 687)
kabuki (p. 703) **shogun** (p. 698)
kisaeng (p. 707) **sumo** (p. 703)
nanban (p. 698) **yangban** (p. 705)
Neo-Confucianism
    (p. 683)

CHAPTER OVERVIEW QUESTIONS

1. What factors led to imperial consolidation in Russia and China? Who were the new rulers, and what were the sources of their legitimacy?

2. Why was isolation more common in these empires than overseas engagement, and what were some of the benefits and drawbacks of isolation?

3. In what ways did early modern Asians transform their environments, and why?

SECTION FOCUS QUESTIONS

1. What prompted Russian territorial expansion?

2. How did the shift to a silver cash economy transform Chinese government and society?

3. How did self-isolation affect Japan?

4. How did life for common folk in early modern Korea differ from life in China or Japan?

5. What trends did mainland Southeast Asia share with China, Korea, Japan, and Russia?

6. In contrast to the general trend of political consolidation in early modern Asia, why did the Philippines fall to a European colonizing power?

MAKING CONNECTIONS

1. How did imperial Russia's rise compare with that of the Ottomans or Habsburgs (see Chapter 20)?

2. How did China under the Ming and Qing compare with the other most populous early modern empire, Mughal India (see Chapter 19)?

3. How did Iberian missionaries' efforts in the Philippines compare with those in western Africa (see Chapter 18)?

AT A CROSSROADS ▲

Scenes of everyday life in eighteenth-century Brazil are extremely rare, but fortunately an Italian military engineer known in Portuguese as Carlos Julião chose to depict enslaved and free people of color in Salvador da Bahia, Rio de Janeiro, and the diamond diggings of northern Minas Gerais during several tours of duty. This image of a free woman of color in the diamond town of Tejuco, home of Chica da Silva (whose story opens this chapter), suggests that she is attracting the romantic attention of a bespectacled Portuguese immigrant. Both are clothed with a mix of fine Asian and European fabrics, testament to the wealth of the diamond diggings. Opulence, violence, and the constant mixing of peoples were core features of life on Brazil's colonial mining frontier. (Acervo da Fundação Biblioteca Nacional, Rio de Janeiro, Brazil.)

Transforming New Worlds: The American Colonies Mature

1600–1750

B orn of an enslaved African mother and a Portuguese father in a small diamond-mining camp deep in the highlands of Brazil, the legendary Chica da Silva, "the slave who became queen," has long fired the imagination. In 1753, when Chica was about twenty, she was purchased by João Fernandes de Oliveira, who had come from Portugal to oversee diamond mines granted by the Crown to his father. Before long, Chica became the overseer's mistress and the talk of Tejuco, capital of the diamond district. Freed on Christmas Day, 1753, less than a year after being purchased, Chica established a household of her own, in the most opulent style. In time, she would bear Fernandes de Oliveira thirteen children. Her lover lavished upon Chica and her children gifts, fine clothing, a large townhouse, and country estates. Together, the couple owned hundreds of slaves. When Chica went down the street with her bright silk gowns and retinue of servants, people made way.

BACKSTORY

As we saw in Chapter 17, the Americas were transformed in early modern times, emerging as a global crossroads whose products, including silver, sugar, and tobacco, would change the world. The wealth of the Americas would be extracted at incalculable cost. By the early seventeenth century millions of native Americans had died from the effects of conquest, overwork, and epidemic disease. As a result, the Spanish and Portuguese enslaved West and West Central Africans and brought them to work the plantations and mines. Livestock imported from Europe roamed far and wide in the Americas, transforming the landscape and displacing native species.

Despite increasing challenges from northern Europeans, the Spanish remained dominant in the Americas through the early 1600s, and they retained control of all known sources of mineral wealth. Their colonies became increasingly mixed racially, and the people were ranked along a steep social hierarchy, but everyone was officially Catholic. In the early seventeenth century, Portuguese Brazil was a coast-hugging sugar colony dependent on the labor of enslaved Amerindians and Africans. Its European settler population was still a tiny minority, for whom most of Brazil was an unknown, untamed frontier. Although the great empires of the Aztecs and Incas had long since fallen, much of North and South America remained native territory.

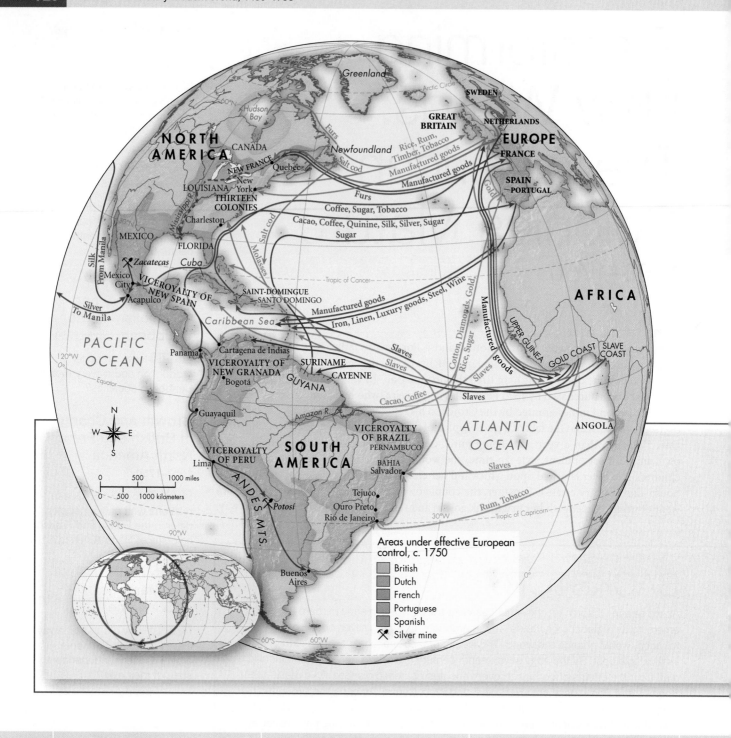

Areas under effective European control, c. 1750
- British
- Dutch
- French
- Portuguese
- Spanish
- Silver mine

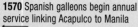

1570 Spanish galleons begin annual service linking Acapulco to Manila

▪ **1630** Dutch capture northeast Brazil

▪ **1654** Portuguese drive Dutch from Brazil; some colonists move to Suriname

▪ **1618** Dutch establish colony of New Netherland on upper Hudson River

▪ **1655** English seize Jamaica from the Spanish

1600   **1625**   **1650**   **1675**

▪ **1607** English establish colony at Jamestown, Virginia

▪ **1625** Dutch settle New Amsterdam on Manhattan Island; English establish colony on Barbados

Bacon's Rebellion in Virginia **1676** ▪

Henry Morgan's buccaneers sack Panama City **1671** ▪

▪ **1608** French establish colony at Quebec City

▪ **1664** English take New Amsterdam from Dutch, rename it New York

Visitors from Portugal were scandalized that an illegitimate "half-breed" woman could flaunt such extravagance. Indeed, numerous laws forbade such public display by persons of "free-colored" status. In Brazil's diamond and gold districts, however, such laws seemed made to be broken. After her death, storytellers surmised that Chica da Silva used cruelty and promiscuity to advance her wealth and status. According to the legends they constructed, Chica da Silva was a kind of Brazilian archetype: the sexually insatiable and power-hungry *mulata* (mulatto). In the popular imagination, the exceptional woman of color could make good only by seducing and manipulating her white oppressor.

However, the Brazilian historian Júnia Furtado has challenged this view of Chica. First, Furtado asks, how could a woman who bore thirteen children in fifteen years have been a seductress? Second, Chica was hardly unique: of 510 family residences in Tejuco, 197 were headed by free women of color, several of them recent slaves like Chica. Moreover, records show that Chica da Silva did attend to some matters of propriety: she did her best to educate her children and used much of her fortune to build churches, fund religious brotherhoods, organize church processions, and pay for baptisms, burials, and weddings, including those of her slaves. She was in these ways a typical elite "Portuguese" woman who happened to live in an atypical, racially mixed, mining frontier world.

The story of Chica da Silva highlights several features of colonial life in the Americas. First, these colonies were often born of the exploitation of slaves in the production of raw wealth for export. Second, the proximity of peoples of different colors, or "races," in these colonies led to racial mingling, a subject still marked by considerable taboo. For some, the

MAPPING THE WORLD

New World Colonies, c. 1750

Arguably the most profoundly transformed world region in the early modern period, the Americas soon came to be linked not only to western Europe, but also to Atlantic Africa and East Asia. Native American populations declined drastically due to disease and conquest. Their numbers began to rebound after 1650, however, and in Spanish America they served as the major producers of silver, dyes, hides, and other commodities exported to the rest of the world. Africa's role was also critical. The number of enslaved Africans forcibly brought to the Americas by 1750 far exceeded the number of Europeans who migrated voluntarily, and it was they and their descendants who produced the bulk of the world's sugar, cacao, tobacco, and eventually coffee. Colonial American life entailed more than forced labor and primary resource extraction, but both, like the Christianity introduced by missionaries and colonists, remained core features of the region long after colonialism ended.

ROUTES ▼

→ British trade route
→ Dutch trade route
→ French trade route
→ Portuguese trade route
→ Spanish trade route
⇢ Travels of Robert de la Salle, 1679–1682
→ Travels of Pehr Kalm, 1749

1695–1800 Discovery in Brazilian interior of gold and diamonds inaugurates Brazil's "gold rush"

▪ **1720** Brazil elevated to status of viceroyalty

| 1700 | 1725 | 1750 |

▪ **1694** Great Brazilian maroon community of Palmares destroyed

Rio de Janeiro elevated to status of capital of Brazil **1763** ▪

1701–1714 War of the Spanish Succession

emergence of new populations of mixed heritage upset notions of racial purity, ethnicity, hierarchy, and propriety. For others, breeding across color lines was a natural but not uncomplicated consequence of proximity. Although the abuses of colonialism can hardly be overstated, the life of Chica da Silva embodies the complexities and contradictions of colonial life in the Americas.

Beginning with the arrival of Columbus in the Caribbean in 1492 and Pedro Álvares Cabral on the coast of Brazil in 1500, waves of European conquerors, missionaries, and colonists, along with a host of alien plants, animals, and pathogens, swept across the Western Hemisphere. By 1750 few indigenous Americans remained unaffected. Even in the vast unconquered areas of the Amazon Basin and the Great Plains of North America, where native American refugee populations had been pushed by European encroachment, European-introduced diseases, animals, and trade goods steadily transformed everyday life. In some places native peoples were joined by runaway African slaves.

Despite its slower start, Portuguese Brazil came to resemble Spanish Mexico and Peru. Busy with their far-flung African and Asian colonies and trading posts, at first the Portuguese maintained only coastal plantations in Brazil. This situation began to change after 1695 when gold and diamonds were discovered in the interior. Along the northeast coast, the Portuguese created the first of several "neo-Africas" in the Americas, uprooting and enslaving hundreds of thousands of West and West Central Africans to plant, harvest, and refine sugar and other cash crops. The Atlantic slave trade and the plantation economy, both defining features of the Caribbean and of British North America after 1700, started in earnest in the Brazilian districts of Pernambuco and Bahia, where the Americas are nearest to Africa.

Desire for empire attracted the French, Dutch, and English to first prey on Spanish and Portuguese ships and ports, and then to establish American colonies of their own. They also searched desperately for a passage to China in hopes of outflanking the Spanish and Portuguese. Piracy and privateering, or state-sponsored piracy, proved to be serious problems for Iberian colonists and merchants until the end of early modern times, and both practices helped generate the initial capital and official interest needed to establish rival colonies. Despite some poor planning and occasional violent ejections, entrepreneurs and planters from northern European countries eventually developed thriving settlements. In time, Caribbean island and mainland colonies such as Barbados and Virginia came to compete with Spanish and Portuguese colonies in the export of sugar and tobacco.

Like the Spanish and the Portuguese, Dutch, French, and English planters in the Caribbean and eastern seaboard colonies of North America employed African slaves from an early date. Amerindian slavery was also practiced, despite proud claims by colonists that they treated native Americans more fairly than the Spanish and Portuguese had. Unlike their Iberian-American counterparts, however, northern European masters relied more heavily on indentured servants, poor women and men from their own countries who contracted terms of servitude in exchange for passage to the Americas, plus room and board. However, most terms of **indenture** were short, usually three years, and before long their masters reinvested the capital accumulated from their labors in African slavery.

In the far north, yet another model emerged. Here the French, Dutch, and English competed with a variety of indigenous groups for access to furs, timber, agricultural land, fish, and other natural resources. These European colonists, like their counterparts in the tropics, kept Amerindian and a few African slaves, but they did not rely wholly on them for subsistence or export products. Swedes, Germans, and Danes also entered into the competition for colonies in some regions, though less forcefully. To the chagrin of all northern Europeans, gold and silver were nowhere to be found in the regions not occupied by the Spanish and Portuguese. A water passage to China's fabled silk and porcelain was similarly elusive. The colonists would have to make do with less glamorous exports, such as salted cod and timber.

indenture A labor system in which Europeans contracted for several years of unpaid labor in exchange for free passage across the Atlantic and housing.

The World That Silver Made: Spanish America 1570–1750

FOCUS

How did mineral wealth steer the development of Spanish America?

As we saw in Chapter 17, following the discovery of precious metals in the early sixteenth century, the Spanish moved quickly to reconnoiter their claims while also building cities, widening roads, and fortifying ports. Their two great bases were Lima and Mexico City, each home to tens of thousands of Spaniards, Indians, Africans, mixed people of color, and even some Asians, mostly Filipinos, by the end of the sixteenth century. Although much territory remained in indigenous hands, the Spanish established themselves as far afield as northern New Mexico and southern Chile. A complex imperial bureaucracy functioned all over the colonies by 1570, and various arms of the Catholic Church were firmly in place, occupying stone buildings as imposing as many in Europe. Armed fleets hauled tons of gold and silver to Europe and Asia each year, returning with a wide array of luxury consumer goods, including Chinese silk and Dutch linen. The plundering of pirates could make only a small dent in this rich commerce in both Atlantic and Pacific waters (see Map 22.1).

Gold and silver also financed the purchase of slaves, and soon men, women, and children of African descent were found throughout Spanish America. Young Domingo Angola, whose story opened Chapter 18, was one of many such uprooted Africans. Captive Africans served on galleons in the Pacific, and some visited China, Japan, the Spice Islands, and the Philippines. Major port cities such as Lima and Cartagena de Indias counted black majorities soon after 1600, and highland mining boomtowns such as Zacatecas and Potosí had large African and African-descended populations throughout early modern times.

Perhaps the most significant trend in this long period, however, was the decline of the indigenous population. Ranking among the worst population collapses in world history, this decline was largely a result of sudden exposure to new diseases from Europe and Africa, against which native Americans had built up no natural immunities during thousands of years of isolation. From a total of some 40 million in 1500, the number of native Americans living within the sphere of Spanish dominance fell to less than 5 million by 1600. Labor conditions, displacement, and physical abuse greatly accelerated indigenous population decline in the early years. Although some recovery was evident by the mid-eighteenth century, native populations in the former Inca and Aztec realms never returned to precontact levels.

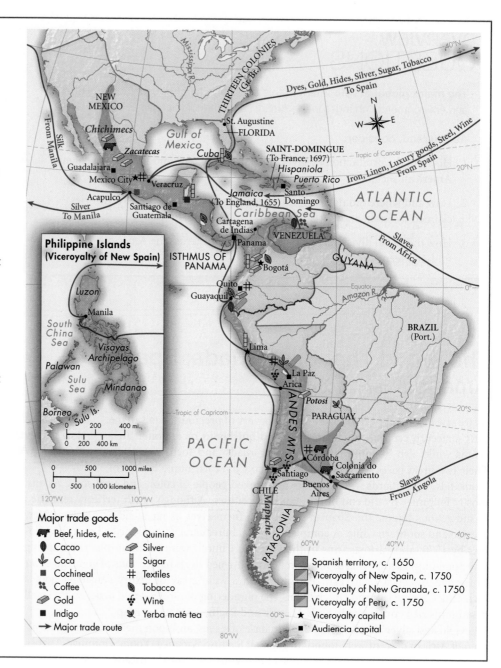

MAP 22.1

Spanish America, 1580–1750

In early modern times Spain was the most significant power in the Americas. Although Dutch, English, and French competitors gained ground in North America and the Caribbean after 1600, and the Portuguese finally moved to expand Brazil after 1700, during this period Spanish America, divided into three viceroyalties by 1750, remained the richest and most densely populated region in the Western Hemisphere by far. The mines of Potosí and Zacatecas alone supplied the bulk of the world's silver, and internal demand for cacao, sugar, and hides, among many other commodities, kept the colonies humming and interconnected. Meanwhile, the distant Philippines, governed from Mexico City, served as both a trade node with East Asia and a base for missionary expansion.

Governing and Profiting from the Colonies

Control Through Bureaucracy

To maintain control and authority over its ambitious settlers, the Spanish crown quickly spun a complex web of overlapping institutions for colonial governance. Some institutions, such as the high appeals court, or **audiencia**, were based on Spanish models; others were American innovations or hybrids. The process of bureaucratization was surprisingly rapid, in part thanks to Spain's growing ranks of university-trained lawyers. These lawyers often clashed with the conquistadors and their offspring, but by 1570 most government institutions were in place.

Spanish culture had long centered on towns and cities, and hundreds of new ones were founded throughout the Americas, some displacing pre-Columbian settlements. Santo Domingo, Mexico City, Lima, Bogotá, and Buenos Aires became capitals of vast districts,

audiencia The high appeals court in Spanish America.

Mexico City's Plaza Mayor

Mexico City's *plaza mayor*, or great square, painted here in 1695, served as the city's main marketplace, exposition grounds, and social crucible. In addition to ceremonial processions and religious devotions, the square was the site of public executions and *autos-da fé*, punishments of those convicted by the Inquisition. It was a place to see and be seen. In this anonymous painting one gets a sense of the size and grandeur of New Spain's capital at its height, although nature's wrath is on the horizon in the form of Popocatépetl, a huge, active volcano, spewing ash ominously into the darkened sky. (Corsham Court, Wiltshire/Bridgeman Art Library.)

but even small provincial towns exerted power over the surrounding countryside. As in Spain, town councils were the basic unit of governance throughout Spanish America.

Legally, the colonies were divided between a "republic of Indians," complete with separate legal codes, and a "republic of Spaniards." This divided system was created not out of fears of racial mixing, which occurred constantly regardless of the Crown's desires, but rather to shelter and thus more efficiently exploit Spanish America's indigenous population. In short, it was in the government's best interest to keep the number of officially registered "Indians" high, since only they were subject to tribute payment and labor drafts. Much like Russian peasants in the same period, native Americans under Spanish rule were legally bound to assigned villages. Officially recognized indigenous headmen were required to collect tributes from their subjects twice a year and to organize labor pools.

Spanish colonies were divided into provinces headed by crown-appointed governors or magistrates. Clusters of these provinces made up audiencia jurisdictions, or regions subject to the authority of a royal court of appeals. Audiencia judges were nearly all Spanish-born lawyers hoping to climb the ranks of colonial bureaucracy and one day return to Spain. Few subjects' legal appeals went beyond these courts, and indigenous groups quickly learned to use the audiencias to their advantage in disputes with Spanish landlords and mine owners.

Above the audiencias were two viceroyalties: New Spain and Peru. New Spain, with its capital at Mexico City, covered Spanish North America, Central America, the Caribbean islands, Venezuela, and the Philippine Islands across the Pacific. The Viceroyalty of Peru, which was subdivided in the eighteenth century, covered all of Spanish South America with the exception of Venezuela, but included the Isthmus of Panama (see again Map 22.1). Spain's king thus appointed only two viceroys for all of his overseas holdings. Both reported to the king and to a court council in Spain, the Council of the Indies. Consequently, at least in theory, all colonial officials were part of a political hierarchy headed by the Crown, the ultimate source of power and decision making.

Spain's transatlantic mail service was slow, and the transpacific one even slower, but both were surprisingly reliable once the annual fleet system was in place after the mid-sixteenth century. Word of trouble in the colonies—or new mineral finds—always reached the king, and his decrees and tax demands always made the return trip. Thanks to this complex bureaucracy and regular transportation system, Spain's many distant colonies felt connected to the motherland.

The first Spanish settlers in the Americas were few in number compared to the vast native populations. Still, these early settlers were an ambitious lot, and they quickly fanned out over an enormous area in search of gold, silver, and other commodities. Conquistadors gained land and encomiendas, or grants of the compelled labor and tribute of native Americans. Foreshadowing African slavery, the encomienda system allowed Spaniards to accumulate capital and gain access to credit without having to pay wages. The system persisted in frontier areas until the mid-eighteenth century, subsidizing development of cattle ranches, wheat farms, fruit orchards, and vineyards. The Spanish crown, meanwhile, also claimed its share of New World income.

Even without the encomienda, all men identified in census records as "Indian," with the exception of chiefs and nobles, were required to pay tribute to the Crown biannually as a reminder of their conquered status. By 1600, tribute had to be paid in cash, a requirement that forced native peoples to produce marketable goods or sell their labor. Tributes and taxes in raw commodities such as grains or textiles were no longer accepted; everyone had to participate in the market economy. Indigenous women and children were increasingly drawn into the workforce to help produce cash. In many cities, including Potosí, single indigenous women, exempt from tribute obligations and also exempt from the Spanish sales tax, became relatively

Spanish "Piece of Eight"

Most Spanish-American silver flowed out into the wider world in the form of large, brick-sized bars, but the Spanish also minted millions of coins throughout early modern times, both in the colonies and in Spain. This crudely struck *peso de a ocho*, or "piece of eight," was minted in the famous silver mining city of Potosí in 1688, during the reign of the last Habsburg king, Charles II. In addition to the coin maker's initials, "VR," the piece of eight bears symbols of Spain's overseas empire, including the Pillars of Hercules (the Strait of Gibraltar) and the great waves of the "Ocean Sea," or Atlantic. "Plus Ultra," or "Further Beyond," the motto of Spain's first Habsburg king and Holy Roman Emperor Charles V, became the motto of empire as well. The Spanish piece of eight served for several centuries as the standard world currency. (Hoberman Collection/Corbis.)

An Iraqi Traveler's Impressions of Potosí

The following selection was originally written in Arabic by an Iraqi Christian, Elias al-Musili, who traveled throughout Spanish America between 1675 and 1680 hoping to raise money for his church, which was located in Ottoman territory but sponsored by Rome. Al-Musili was among the very few foreigners permitted to visit Spain's colonies in the early modern era due to persistent crown fears of subversion and spying, and he was the only Middle Eastern Arabic speaker of whom we have record. He was given alms throughout the Andes, particularly by native Americans, for preaching in the ancient Aramaic language. He left Potosí with several mule-loads of silver.

A Visit to the Mint and Silver Mine

One day I went to the place where they minted dinars, piastres ["pieces of eight"], halves, and quarters. In this mint house there are forty black slaves and twelve Spaniards working. We saw the piles of coins, like hillocks on one side, the halves on another, and half-quarters still on another, heaped on the floor and being trampled underfoot like dirt that has no value.

On one side of this town is the mountain containing the mine[s]. It is known throughout the world on account of its excessive wealth; countless treasures have been extracted from all four sides of it for 140 years. They had fenced it off, dug it up, and reached the very bottom of it to extract the silver. They had prepared wooden props for it, to make sure the mountain did not cave in. From the outside it looks whole, but on the inside it is empty. Up to 700 Indians work inside to cut out stone for men who had already bought the rights from the king. Every miner has assigned a certain number of Indians to work his share of the mine. There is a royal decree ordering every village to offer a number of Indian men to mine. According to the law one out of five men is to be assigned to such a task.

Describing the Extraction of Silver

There are 37 mills used for grinding silver-bearing stones day and night, except for Sundays and holidays. After grinding it finely, they take it in quantities of fifty qintârs [about 5000 lbs.] and form separate piles with it. They add water to each . . . then add mercury to it according to need. They then stir it with shovels several times; and should it require more mercury, they add it up until perfected. If it is cold by nature, they add copper until it warms up. If it is warm by nature, they add lead until it cools. How can they tell whether it is warm or cool? They scoop up samples in a clay utensil and wash it with water until the dirt disappears and the mixture of silver and mercury remains. The sample is then smeared by finger on a piece of the aforementioned clay pot. If it crumbles, it is considered hot; if it sticks, it is considered cold. When perfect, or well tempered, it adheres to the clay and shines. Next they put it in a large basin with water flowing over it and stir it all the while with finesse. Silver and mercury settle on the bottom and dirt is carried off by the water. After thus completing the "washing" of this mixture, the overflow of water is cut off and the basin cleaned. The mixture of silver and mercury is taken out and put in gunnysacks hung from trees, under which are placed containers lined with cattle skin. Mercury flows out of the sacks into these containers underneath and only silver remains in them, like loaves of sugar.

Source: Cesar E. Farah, ed. and trans., *An Arab's Journey to Colonial Spanish America: The Travels of Elias al-Mûsili in the Seventeenth Century* (Syracuse, NY: Syracuse University Press, 2003).

EXAMINING THE EVIDENCE

1. What aspects of silver production seem to have most amazed al-Musili?

2. How does he portray workers in Potosí's mint, mines, and refineries?

wealthy, and soon ran afoul of town authorities for wearing silk garments and other adornments deemed inappropriate for their class.

Along with indigenous tributes, sales taxes, and customs duties, the Spanish crown and its many bureaucrats relied on mining taxes in the form of silver, the so-called *quinto real*, or "royal fifth," of the silver mined. The Crown also rented out the mercury monopoly, which was crucial in processing silver. However, by 1600 corruption was common, and crown control of mining and silver exports became weak. Mine owners and merchants found increasingly clever ways to avoid tax collectors. By the 1640s a vibrant contraband trade was flourishing, especially around Buenos Aires and along Caribbean shores, where newly arrived slaves and luxury merchandise were traded for silver ingots and "pieces of eight," all tax-free.

Despite a growing culture of corruption and tax evasion, some mine owners managed to follow the rules and still do very well for themselves. One who stood out was Antonio López de Quiroga, who used his profits from selling silver to the mint in Potosí to buy up abandoned mines, hire the most skilled workers available, and employ innovations such as black-powder blasting (see Reading the Past: An Iraqi Traveler's Impressions of Potosí). By the 1670s, López de Quiroga was the local equivalent of a billionaire, a major benefactor of churches, and even a sponsor of lowland conquest expeditions in the upper Amazon. Similar stories were repeated in the mining frontiers of northern Mexico.

Commodities Beyond Silver

Although the mining economy was most critical in stimulating the expansion of frontiers, much else was happening in Spanish America. Venezuela, for example, developed a vibrant economy based on the production of raw chocolate beans, or cacao. These were first destined for Mexico, a huge Spanish-American market, and subsequently for Europe, once the taste for chocolate developed there in the later seventeenth century. Partly due to Venezuela's location along the slave route to New Granada (present-day Colombia) and Mexico, in the cacao groves surrounding the regional capital of Caracas, African laborers soon displaced native Americans held in encomienda. Coffee was introduced from Arabia in the early eighteenth century and soon became another major export.

There were other ways to make money in Spanish America without entering the global export market. In Paraguay a tea called *yerba maté* was collected in the forest by native Guaraní speakers, many of whom lived on and around Jesuit missions. The tea was then carried by mule throughout the Andes, where it was consumed by all classes. This habit, unlike chocolate drinking, was not picked up in Europe. Huge cattle ranches developed in the hinterland of Buenos Aires and in north-central Mexico. Beef, tallow, and hides were consumed in great quantities in mining towns such as Potosí and Zacatecas. In seventeenth-century Mexico what historians call a "mining-ranching complex" developed, tying distant regions together across expanses of desert. Elites invested profits from mining in trade, and vice versa. By 1600, cheap cotton and woolen textiles were produced in quantity in both Mexico and the northern Andes, enough to nearly satisfy the substantial working-class market.

Spanish America's Unique Economy

Spanish America was unusual among early modern overseas colonies in that its economy was both export-oriented and self-sufficient from an early stage. Only luxury goods such as fine textiles and iron and steel items were not produced locally. Why a local iron industry did not develop might seem strange since iron deposits were available, but the short answer is silver. Spanish-American merchants simply had so much silver to export that they struggled to find enough imports to balance the trade. Spanish authorities later outlawed local iron production to protect merchant interests.

After textiles, which included vast quantities of Chinese silks and South Asian chintzes and calicoes along with a wide range of European cloths, common iron goods such as horseshoes were among the main items consumed. The Basques of northern Spain had long produced iron and steel products, and some artisan clans in cities such as Bilbao became wealthy by sending their wares to the colonies. Wine was another favorite import from Spain, mostly produced in the hinterland of Seville, but even this was being produced in large quantities on the coasts of Peru and Chile by the 1580s.

The net effect of silver exports on such a grand scale from both Mexico and the Andes was a colonial economy that was both internally interdependent in terms of food, common cloth, hides, and other basic items and dependent on the outside world for luxury products. As with iron, the Crown actively discouraged industrialization of the textile sector, but scientific innovations in mining and metallurgy—anything to increase the flow of silver—were rewarded with patents. Thus, the colonial system increased the density of economic connections within the Americas at the same time as it forged new connections between the Americas and the larger world.

As we saw in Chapter 20, Spain's Habsburg monarchs and ministers envisioned the colonial economy as a closed mercantile system, intended to benefit the mother country through taxation while enabling subjects of varying status to seek and consolidate wealth (although not to gain crown-challenging titles of nobility). No foreigners were supposed to trade with the American colonies except through approved monopoly holders based in Seville. These monopolists also controlled (theoretically) all trade through Acapulco to Manila and back. Although this closed-system ideal was realized to a surprising degree given the great distances, cultural divides, and other obstacles involved, it soon fell prey to individual wiles and corrupt cartels as Spain itself fell into decline under a succession of weak kings after Philip II (r. 1556–1598). Only after 1700, with the rise of the Bourbon dynasty, did the Crown manage to reassert itself forcefully in colonial economic affairs. As we will see in the next chapter, widespread rebellion would follow.

Everyday Life in Spanish America

As the colonies matured, Spain's increasingly diverse American subjects found new possibilities for social and material improvement, but they also faced many bureaucratic and natural constraints. Life spans in colonial Spanish America were similar to those of contemporary Europe for elites, but as we have seen, they were considerably shorter for people of indigenous and African descent. Epidemics, particularly of smallpox, hit everyone from time to time. Slaves, draft workers, and mixed-race criminals sent to fight the Mapuche in Chile or the Chichimecs of northern Mexico were often described in identification documents as having smallpox scars on their faces. Infant mortality was very high at all levels of society.

Many of the regions settled by the Spanish were prone to earthquakes and volcanic eruptions, which led many to regard natural disasters as judgments of God. When in 1661 a volcano dumped several feet of ash on Quito, now the capital of Ecuador, Catholic priests ordered that an image of the Virgin Mary be paraded through the streets until the eruption ceased. Such religiosity was manifest in many aspects of colonial Spanish-American society, including art and literature, and it helped shape local norms of gender and race relations. In fact, Catholicism came to serve as a common cultural touchstone, connecting the members of an ethnically and culturally diverse society.

Unlike parts of English, French, and Dutch America, as we will see, Spanish America was never intended as a refuge for religious dissenters. From the beginning the region was a Roman Catholic domain. Even recent converts to Christianity were not allowed to emigrate for fear of allowing Judaism or Islam into the colonies. Spain's Romas, or gypsies, were likewise banned due to their alleged fondness for fortunetelling and witchcraft. Still, some recent converts and Romas, along with miscellaneous "unorthodox" foreigners from Portugal, France, Italy, Germany, the Low Countries, and even Greece, managed to sneak aboard Indies-bound ships leaving Seville. In the colonies, the beginning of the Inquisition after 1570, plus waves of anti-idolatry campaigns after 1560, soon led to widespread persecution of nonconformists.

How did the mass of subject peoples, most of them indigenous peasants and enslaved Africans, respond to these demands for spiritual conformity? Faced with constant threats and punishments from priests and officials, along with the sometimes persuasive efforts of missionaries, the vast majority of native and African-descended subjects at least nominally accepted Catholicism. What soon emerged, however, was a complex fusion of Catholic practices with a more secretive, underground world of non-Christian cults, shamanistic healing practices, and witchcraft. Scholars have learned much about these alternative religious spheres in recent years from Inquisition and anti-idolatry records, and some have sought to trace their roots to parts of Africa and elsewhere.

According to Christian scripture, all human beings were redeemable in the creator's eyes, regardless of sex, age, status, color, or birthplace. Thus, many church leaders believed that non-Western habits such as nudity and even cannibalism could be reformed

Gentlemen of Esmeraldas

Andrés Sánchez Gallque, *Gentlemen of Esmeraldas* (The Art Archive/American Museum Madrid.)

In 1599 Andrés Sánchez Gallque, an indigenous artist from Quito, the former Inca capital located high in the Andes, painted a group portrait of three men who had climbed up from the Pacific coast province of Esmeraldas to sign a treaty with the colonial government. The three men, Don Francisco de Arobe and his two sons, Pedro and Domingo, were maroons, descendants of escaped slaves who swam ashore following a shipwreck in the 1540s. They were in Quito to sign a treaty agreeing not to ally with pirates. The Spanish honorific title "Don" was used for all three men since they were recognized as indigenous chiefs. As it happened, Don Francisco de Arobe was the son of an African man and a native woman from Nicaragua. Other Esmeraldas maroons had intermarried with local indigenous inhabitants.

In exchange for agreeing to defend the coast against intruders, the Arobes were sent to a professional tailor in Quito and given a wide variety of luxury textiles, including ponchos and capes made from Chinese silk brought to Acapulco by the Manila galleon, then south to Quito via Panama. The maroon leaders also received linen ruff collars from Holland and iron spearheads, probably from the Basque region of northern Spain. Their own adornments included shell necklaces and gold facial jewelry typical of South America's northwest Pacific coast. The painting was sent to Philip III in Madrid as a memento of peace. It is now housed in Spain's Museo de América.

Source: Kris Lane, *Quito 1599: City and Colony in Transition* (Albuquerque: University of New Mexico Press, 2002.)

EXAMINING THE EVIDENCE

1. **What might these men's wide array of adornments symbolize?**

2. **What image does Sánchez Gallque seem to wish to convey to the king of Spain?**

and did not justify permanent discrimination. It was on such grounds that Spanish priests such as Bartolomé de las Casas had argued so successfully against Amerindian slavery (see Chapter 17).

Condoning Slavery

By contrast, African slavery was hardly debated by Spanish priests and theologians. Some church leaders even sought to justify it. Settlers, particularly those in need of workers, were inclined to view both native Americans and Africans as inferior and uneducable; such racist views suited their interests. For its part, the Spanish crown sought protection of subject Amerindians not so much for reasons of faith, but because natives were a source of state revenue and paid their tributes in silver. Slaves, being outside the tributary economy, were left mostly to their own devices, although Spanish law contained some protections, certainly more than those developed by later colonists such as the Dutch, French, and English. It was assumed, often wrongly, that rational masters would be loath to harm their chattels.

By the seventeenth century, Spanish America was molded by a variety of religious, economic, and political forces. But it was only biology—some would say the law of human attraction—that could subvert the system. To start, a surplus of male European settlers, including farmers, artisans, and merchants, in the early years quickly led to *mestizaje* (mess-tee-ZAH-hey), Spanish for "mixture," and a significant mixed-heritage population. In some places it was indigenous women, ranging in status from servants such as Malintzin to Aztec and Inca princesses, who gave birth to a new generation of *mestizos*, as mixed-blood offspring were called. In other cases it was enslaved or free women of African descent who bore **mulatto** children to Spanish colonizers. There were many examples resembling Brazil's Chica da Silva throughout Spanish America, though none so rich or famous. Indigenous women also had children by African men, free and enslaved, and countless other "mixtures" occurred in the course of three centuries of colonial rule. The Mexican nation-state would later celebrate mestizaje as something dynamic and new, a "cosmic race."

To attribute all this to the power of physical attraction would be an oversimplification. Some relationships across color lines were forced and criminal, others merely fleeting, and still others were permanent and even church-sanctioned. Though some bureaucrats and bishops might have wished it so, neither state nor church outlawed interracial marriage in colonial Spanish America. Only marriage across huge status gaps, as, say, between a nobleman and a slave, was forbidden. By 1750 Spanish-American society was so "mixed" at virtually all social levels that the term *casta*, or "caste," formerly applied by the Portuguese in India, was adopted to categorize the bewildering range of socioracial types. Hundreds of paintings depict the various unions and offspring comprising Spanish America's so-called *sistema de castas*, or "system of castes" (see Seeing the Past: *Gentlemen of Esmeraldas*).

The experiences of women in colonial Spanish America varied more by social class than color. In time, immigrants born in Spain looked down upon even the whitest **creole**, or locally born Spaniard. Under the influence of age-old superstitions about sub-Saharan Africa, Europeans believed that life in the tropics was inherently debilitating, even for aristocratic Christians from northern Spain. Still, most creole women in Spanish America brushed off such suggestions of inferiority and made the most of their situations.

Peruvian Blacksmiths

Although all iron and steel were imported by privileged wholesalers to the Spanish-American colonies, it was local blacksmiths who fashioned these raw materials into horseshoes, hinges, nails, tools, and many other items. In this mid-eighteenth-century watercolor from the Pacific-coast city of Trujillo, Peru, a man and woman work together to forge tools. By this time, nearly all artisans were of indigenous, African, or mixed background, since hand labor was generally disdained by those claiming to be of pure European stock. This pair appears to be of mestizo, or mixed Spanish and indigenous, heritage. (Iberfoto/The Image Works.)

Racial Mixing

mestizaje Spanish for "mixture," referring to racial blending of any type.

mestizo Spanish for "mixed," or offspring of Europeans and native Americans.

mulatto Offspring of Europeans and Africans.

creole A European born in the Americas and his or her descendants.

Late marriage by men left many Spanish-American women widowed at a relatively young age. This gave some women a boost in terms of economic security and independence. Despite a generally stifling patriarchal culture, Spanish inheritance law, similar to Islamic law from which it borrowed, was relatively generous to women. The wives of merchants, in particular, frequently found themselves in charge of substantial enterprises and estates, with much freedom to administer them. More significantly, widows wielded extraordinary influence over their children's marriage choices. When children married well, estates could be combined and expanded over time, cementing a family's fortunes in the face of uncertainties and disruption. Such was the story of the family of Simón Bolívar, whose story opens the next chapter. Among his ancestors, it was women who made many of the most important choices.

Although elite women were concerned with maintaining wealth and improving the status of their offspring, poor women had other worries. Virtually all poor women were engaged in market-oriented activity at some level, even if they lived in the countryside. Weaving, spinning, and pottery-making were often female tasks. Urban women of poor to middling status were usually either servants or vendors, with some working alongside artisan husbands as cobblers, tanners, tailors, cigar-rollers, and even blacksmiths. Along with their burdensome duties as wet nurses, cooks, and cleaners, female domestic servants and slaves were also hired out, handing over the wages to their masters. Despite harsh conditions, access to markets meant access to cash, and even some socially marginalized urban women accumulated small fortunes or purchased freedom for their children.

In a different category altogether were Catholic nuns. Most were of elite parentage, but some were of humble background, including women born out of wedlock. Every Spanish-American city of note had at least one convent, and often half a dozen or more. Inside lived not only the nuns themselves, but their female servants and slaves. Lima, for example, in 1630 counted over 1366 nuns served by 899 female African slaves out of a total city population of about forty thousand. Convents also served as shelters for widows and women facing hardships, and as reformatories for those accused of prostitution and minor crime. Though confining, Spanish-American nunneries occasionally nurtured female intellectuals and mystics of great renown, such as St. Rose of Lima (1586–1617) and Juana Inés de la Cruz (1651–1595). Famous for her biting wit, de la Cruz even took on the misogynist ways of Mexican society in verse:

> Who would have the greatest blame
> In an errant love affair,
> She who falls to him who begs
> Or he who plays the beggar?
>
> Or who should be more guilty
> Though each is evil-doing,
> She who sins for pay,
> Or he who pays for sinning?[1]

Gold, Diamonds, and the Transformation of Brazil 1695–1800

FOCUS

How was Brazil transformed by the mining boom of the eighteenth century?

Beginning in around 1695, the coastal, sugar-based export economy of Portuguese Brazil began to change, sparked by the discovery of gold and diamonds in Brazil's south-central highlands. What followed was the greatest bonanza in world history prior to California's gold rush. The consequences were profound and lasting. First, over half a million Portuguese immigrants flowed into Brazil between 1700 and 1800. Second, the African slave trade was expanded,

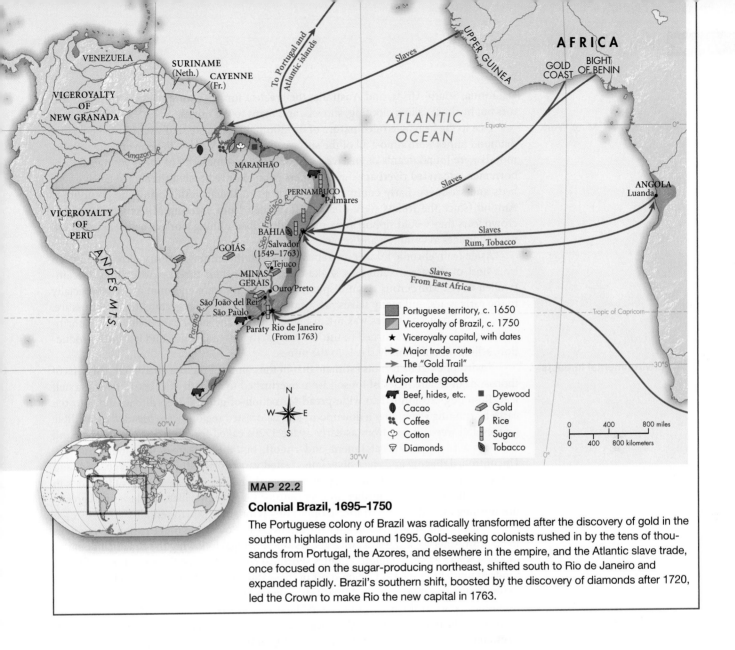

MAP 22.2

Colonial Brazil, 1695–1750

The Portuguese colony of Brazil was radically transformed after the discovery of gold in the southern highlands in around 1695. Gold-seeking colonists rushed in by the tens of thousands from Portugal, the Azores, and elsewhere in the empire, and the Atlantic slave trade, once focused on the sugar-producing northeast, shifted south to Rio de Janeiro and expanded rapidly. Brazil's southern shift, boosted by the discovery of diamonds after 1720, led the Crown to make Rio the new capital in 1763.

particularly in the hinterland of Angola. Third, the Portuguese crown elevated Brazil to the status of viceroyalty in 1720. Finally, Brazil's center of political and economic gravity shifted southward, away from the sugar zone of the northeast. Rio de Janeiro became Brazil's new capital in 1763 (see Map 22.2). On a global scale, Brazilian gold's importance briefly rivaled that of Spanish-American silver, flowing through Lisbon and into allied England, helping to finance the early stages of the Industrial Revolution.

Boom Times for Colonial Brazil

In the mid-1690s, while searching for indigenous slaves, a mulatto aide traveling with Brazilian backwoodsmen and slave hunters discovered gold in the rugged highlands northeast of São Paulo. By 1800 Brazil had exported between 2.5 and 4.5 million pounds of gold, and several million carats of raw diamonds. Up to this time diamonds had come almost entirely from India, and gold from West Africa and Spanish America. Soon after 1700, a district capital was set up in the town of Ouro Preto (OR-ooh PREH-too), or "Black Gold," and the region was dubbed Minas Gerais (MEAN-us jheh-HICE), or "General Mines." Prospectors and slaves flowed into Minas Gerais in droves, among them Chica da Silva's African mother and Portuguese father. Hordes of itinerant and wholesale merchants came close on their heels. As would happen in the later gold rush frontiers of

California, South Africa, and Australia, the greatest fortunes were made not by prospectors but by those selling clothing, shovels, and maps to the mines.

Mine Work

Due to the heavily eroded nature of its mountain ranges, Brazil's substantial gold and diamond mines were almost all of the surface, or "placer," variety. Wherever gold and diamonds were found, teams of enslaved workers, the vast majority of them young African-born men, excavated riverbanks while others panned or redirected streams to get at gravel beds and sandbars. Early commentators such as an Italian Jesuit using the pseudonym Antonil (since the Jesuits were officially forbidden from entering Minas Gerais, due to crown fears they would siphon away profits) described mining work as hellishly hard, and food shortages as common and severe.

Aside from chronic hunger and abuse, slaves in the mining country were endangered by a host of diseases, venomous snakes, and the constant threat of drowning in rain-swollen rivers. Murderous claim disputes and uprisings were common as well, especially in the early years, and many slaves ran away simply to avoid being caught in the crossfire. Slave mortality in the mines was much higher than in the sugar cane fields of the northeast. Some slave owners turned to the less risky activities of farming and livestock production, selling off only unruly slaves to the mines.

Environmental Impacts

Environmental historians estimate that in the course of the Brazilian gold rush tens of thousands of square miles of topsoil were overturned to a depth of at least one and a half feet. Resulting erosion led to widespread formation of gullies, deep ditches cut into the earth by running water after a downpour, and deforested regions were invaded by inedible grasses and weeds. Laws from as early as the 1720s called for preservation of forest and bush to control rainfall catchment and runoff, but these decrees were not observed. Uncontrolled digging and river diversion created vast badlands, areas of barren, arid land visible to the present day. Deforestation to support farming and the raising of livestock to feed the miners went even further, forever transforming the Brazilian highlands and greatly diminishing the Atlantic coast forest, only a tiny remnant of which remains.

Expansion of Portuguese Emigration and Atlantic Slave Trade

As happened in Spain soon after the discovery of Potosí and other major silver mines in Spanish America, a wave of emigration swept Portugal following the Brazilian bonanza of 1695. Never a very populous country, Portugal could ill afford the loss of tens of thousands of residents, especially when most of those leaving were young, able-bodied men. So many Portuguese men came to Minas Gerais in the first years after 1700 that a minor war broke out between them and the creole "Paulistas," or residents of São Paulo, who had discovered the mines. Crown authorities sided with the newcomers, and eventually sought to establish order in the backcountry by sending in troops.

The Atlantic slave trade expanded dramatically in response to the discovery of gold and diamonds in the Brazilian interior. Brazil's proximity to Africa and Portugal's long involvement in the slave trade led to a development quite distinct from the silver mines of Spanish America. In Mexico and Peru, most mine work was carried out by indigenous draft and later mestizo or mulatto wageworkers. By contrast, in the goldfields of Brazil, whose indigenous populations had been decimated by disease and slave raiding by 1700, African slavery quickly became the only form of labor employed. By 1800, there were nearly a million slaves in Minas Gerais. The few women to enter Minas Gerais in the early years of the rush were also primarily enslaved Africans, and they were in such high demand that most became the prized concubines of Portuguese men. Some were rented out as prostitutes in exchange for gold dust and diamonds. One such woman gave birth to Chica da Silva. Thus, the discovery of gold and diamonds in Brazil drew millions of migrants, some voluntary but many more forced, to the Americas. The cultural heritages these migrants brought with them have shaped Brazilian society to this day.

Royal Control and Its Limits

The Portuguese crown took an immediate interest in the Brazilian gold rush, establishing a taxation and monopoly trade system similar to that developed by the Spanish in Mexico and Peru. Gold taxes, the same "royal fifth" demanded by the Spanish crown, were collected at official sites in Ouro Preto and other towns, and all trade was directed along royal, stone-paved roads complete with official stations where mule-loads were inspected and taxed. The "gold trail" initially terminated in the tiny coastal town of Paraty, on Brazil's lush South Atlantic coast just beyond the Tropic of Capricorn, but soon it led to Rio de Janeiro, (see again Map 22.2). Rio became Brazil's largest city, and was elevated to the status of capital of the viceroyalty in 1763.

As in Spanish America, royal control over mining districts was more easily imagined than realized, and smuggling, particularly of diamonds, soon became a huge problem. Official control centered on the town of Tejuco (today's Diamantina) and was headed by royal contractors from Portugal, such as Chica da Silva's common-law husband, João Fernandes de Oliveira. Although the diamond mines were closely monitored and slaves were subjected to physical inspections, there were always ways of hiding and secretly trading stones. As an incentive to be honest and work hard, slaves were promised instant freedom if they found diamonds above a very large size, but few were so lucky.

Much more often, enslaved diamond miners set aside a few stones from time to time to trade to corrupt bureaucrats and merchants for cash. Slaves in the gold mines did the same. Wealth thus accumulated was then used to purchase the workers' freedom or the freedom of their children. One of the ironies of the Brazilian gold and diamond mines was that although the work itself was more dangerous than that of the cane fields and sugar mills of the northeast, the odds of obtaining freedom were considerably higher. Knowing that enslaved Africans outnumbered them by a huge margin here in the mountainous backlands, Portuguese masters and crown officials accepted a measure of secret trade and self-purchase.

Everyday Life in Golden-Age Brazil

With slavery such a central feature of Brazil's colonial economy, it is no surprise that this core institution deeply influenced society. Its influence would only increase over time. At first indigenous and then African cultural elements fused with Portuguese imports to create a new, hybrid culture. Only certain elites proved resistant to this hybridization, doing their best to mimic metropolitan styles and ideas. Some members of this elite class, such as the Portuguese diamond contractor João Fernandes de Oliveira, embraced "Afro-Brazil" in a more literal sense, by forming families of mixed ancestry. Other Brazilians practiced Catholicism while seeking the aid of numerous folk healers, clairvoyants, and other officially illegal religious figures, many of them of African ancestry.

As in Spanish America, a pressing matter for Portuguese authorities was the presence of Judaism and people of Jewish ancestry. In Brazil's early years some New Christians, or forced converts, had been allowed to immigrate. By the 1590s, some of these settlers were discovered to be secretly practicing Judaic rituals. Infrequent visits by the Inquisition, which never set up a permanent tribunal in Brazil, uncovered evidence of "heresy," or at least

Brazilian Diamond Diggers

Images of colonial mineworkers in the Americas are rare. Fortunately, the Italian military engineer Carlos Julião sought to depict the labors of Brazil's enslaved and mostly African-born diamond workers in Minas Gerais in the eighteenth century, precisely when Chica da Silva was the richest woman in the district and her common-law husband was possibly the wealthiest man in Portugal. The workers here are searching through diamond-bearing gravel under close surveillance (although the first overseer appears to be napping). When slaves found a diamond, they were to stand up and hold the stone above their heads before handing it to the overseer for safekeeping. Despite these and other controls, many slaves managed to hide diamonds in their mouths, ears, hair, and elsewhere, trading them later for food, clothing, alcohol, or cash. (The Art Archive/Biblioteca National do Rio de Janiero Brazil/Dagli Orti.)

unorthodox religious practices (such as kosher food preparation), but few were prosecuted. Brazil's Jewish community became more evident when several New Christians joined the Dutch during their occupation from 1630 to 1654 of Pernambuco in northeast Brazil. Under the Dutch, Brazil's Jews were allowed to build a synagogue and practice their religion openly. When the Portuguese regained control of the northeast in 1654, several New Christian planter families relocated to Dutch Suriname, where they set up slave-staffed plantations (see Counterpoint: The Maroons of Suriname). The Inquisition also persecuted secret Jews in Minas Gerais in the early eighteenth century, in part to confiscate their valuable estates and stocks of merchandise.

Afro-Brazilian Religion

The Portuguese Inquisition in Brazil also prosecuted Afro-Brazilian religious practitioners. None were burned, but many were publicly shamed, exiled, or sentenced to galley service. Usually denounced as "fetishists," devil-worshipers, and witches, these people maintained a wide variety of West and West Central African religious traditions, usually blended with some degree of Catholicism and native American shamanism. Often, Catholic saints were used to mask male and female West African deities, as later happened in Cuba and Saint-Domingue (Haiti). In other cases, religious brotherhoods combined West Central African spirit possession with Catholic Christianity. These brotherhoods, often devoted to black saints such as St. Benedict the Moor and St. Efigenia, were common throughout Brazil, but were especially powerful in Minas Gerais, where the missionary orders were banned for fiscal reasons. Orthodox black Catholics also enlivened their ceremonies, especially funerals and patron saints' days, with rhythmic music and dance.

Maroon Communities

Even before the discovery of gold, Brazil hosted the largest communities of **maroons** in the Western Hemisphere. By 1650 the maroon (from the Spanish term *cimarrón*, meaning "runaway") community of Palmares, really a confederation of a dozen fugitive villages, was home to some ten thousand or more ex-slaves and their descendants. Despite numerous military campaigns organized by planters in coordination with slave hunters, Palmares was only broken up in the 1690s and finally destroyed in 1694. With the development of Minas Gerais, dozens of new maroon villages popped up in the gold-rich backcountry. Several of their descendant communities have been formally recognized by the Brazilian government in recent years.

Artistic Legacies

As in Spanish America, it was in the cities most affected by the great mining boom—and later by sugar wealth—that Brazilian material culture grew most opulent. Churches modeled after European ones, such as those in Salvador in the northeast and Rio de Janeiro in the south, testify to the piety of both elites and poor religious brotherhoods. Even more stunning and original are the many churches and chapels of Minas Gerais, stretching from lonely Tejuco to São João del Rei (see again Map 22.2). A significant number of these extraordinary structures were designed, built, and decorated by slaves and their descendants. In Tejuco, several were commissioned by Chica da Silva, whose house still stands.

As the case of Chica da Silva illustrates, people of mixed heritage rose to prominent positions in Brazil, particularly in frontier districts. Arguably the colony's greatest artistic genius was the sculptor and architect Francisco Lisboa, like Chica the child of an enslaved African mother and free Portuguese father. Popularly known as Aleijadinho, or "Little Cripple" (due to leprosy), Lisboa was among the most original architects and sculptors of his era, carving fantastic soapstone façades with chisels strapped to the stumps of his hands.

Brazil's gold rush sputtered out around 1800, but by this time the northeastern sugar industry was undergoing a revival, along with tobacco, rice, cotton, and other cash crops. For the first time, Portuguese officials encouraged diversification and experimentation. The vast Amazon Basin was now being explored as a potential source of minerals, cacao, medicinal barks, and other export commodities. Coffee, which would later become Brazil's prime export, was also experimentally planted in various tropical climate zones, starting in the north. In export agriculture, Brazil's greatest competitors were in the Caribbean.

maroon In the seventeenth and eighteenth centuries, a runaway slave and his or her descendants.

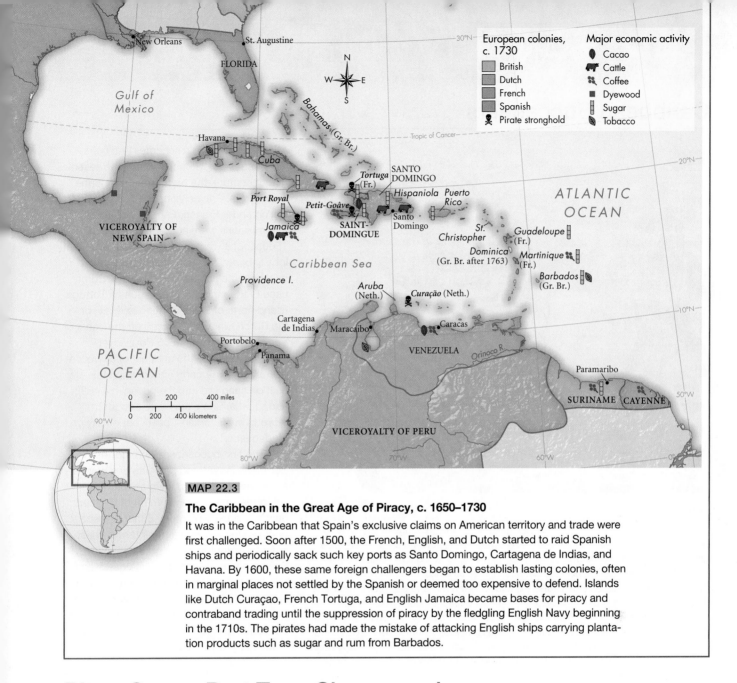

MAP 22.3

The Caribbean in the Great Age of Piracy, c. 1650–1730

It was in the Caribbean that Spain's exclusive claims on American territory and trade were first challenged. Soon after 1500, the French, English, and Dutch started to raid Spanish ships and periodically sack such key ports as Santo Domingo, Cartagena de Indias, and Havana. By 1600, these same foreign challengers began to establish lasting colonies, often in marginal places not settled by the Spanish or deemed too expensive to defend. Islands like Dutch Curaçao, French Tortuga, and English Jamaica became bases for piracy and contraband trading until the suppression of piracy by the fledgling English Navy beginning in the 1710s. The pirates had made the mistake of attacking English ships carrying plantation products such as sugar and rum from Barbados.

Bitter Sugar, Part Two: Slavery and Colonialism in the Caribbean 1625–1750

When the Dutch captured Pernambuco in 1630, they were most interested in sugar. How had the Portuguese managed to produce so much of it so cheaply? What the Dutch discovered was northeast Brazil's peculiar blend of loamy tropical soils, high-technology mills, and slave labor. By the time the Dutch abandoned Brazil in 1654, they had learned all they needed to know about the sugar business.

FOCUS

How did sugar production and slavery mold Caribbean societies?

English and French visitors had also taken careful notes as they displaced the Spanish in various parts of the Caribbean, such as Jamaica and western Hispaniola (later known as Saint-Domingue, then Haiti). These techniques of sugar manufacture were closely copied, and from the mid-seventeenth century onward the story of the Caribbean was but the story of sugar and slavery, continued. After Brazil, this diverse island region was the largest destination for enslaved Africans brought across the Atlantic—over one-third of the total (see Map 22.3).

Caribbean Buccaneers

"Black Bart"

The great age of maritime commerce also gave rise to the great age of piracy, an activity that peaked between 1660 and 1730. Most pirates preyed on Spanish ships and towns, since these were imagined to be rich in silver and gold, but as Spain's competitors gained footholds in the Caribbean, coastal Africa, and parts of the American mainland after 1600, pirates expanded their reach and captured whatever they could, including slave ships belonging to their outraged countrymen. Among the most successful pirates was Bartholomew "Black Bart" Roberts, shown here near the African port of Whydah, where he captured and ransomed a number of English slave ships. Roberts was killed in 1722 in an engagement with the English Royal Navy near present-day Gabon. There followed a new and long-lasting era of policing the sea. (National Maritime Museum, London/The Image Works.)

Atlantic colonization schemes and wars gave rise to a new social type in the seventeenth century: the **buccaneer**, or Caribbean pirate. Privately financed sea raiders sailing under French, English, or Dutch commissions were active from the early 1500s, but it was only in the mid-1600s that locally based sea bandits acting on their own became an endemic problem. Some used French trading posts such as Tortuga Island north of Saint-Domingue (Haiti) or the Dutch island of Curaçao off the coast of Venezuela, but after 1655 Port Royal, Jamaica, became the greatest of all buccaneer bases. The party ended when this city built on sand slid into the ocean in a 1692 earthquake. Some survivors sought to regroup in the Indian Ocean, especially on Madagascar.

The first buccaneers were northern European indentured servants and war veterans, many of whom were sent to the Caribbean sugar islands to meet the labor needs of greedy planters. Either by escape or by having served out their terms, these indentures took to living off the land in Saint-Domingue, shooting wild cattle and roasting their meat on crude barbecues, or *boucans*. Known by 1650 as *boucaniers* in French, and buccaneers in English, the hunters began to organize raids on straggling merchant vessels in dugout canoes. Their guerrilla tactics and expert marksmanship

Pirates and Planters

Development in the Caribbean was slow and not very methodical. Throughout the sixteenth century, French, English, and Dutch traders and raiders challenged Spanish monopolies, particularly on the mainland. Pirates and privateers preyed on slow-moving ships and lightly defended port towns. One of the most famous privateers was Sir Francis Drake, who in the late 1570s plundered one Spanish port after another. He also dabbled in the contraband slave trade, but the grateful English crown looked the other way to award him a knighthood. Only in around 1600 did these interlopers begin to establish permanent colonies. The Dutch focused on Guyana (later Suriname) and several small islands, such as Curaçao and St. Christopher. The English followed on Providence Island off the coast of modern Nicaragua. The French focused on western Hispaniola and Tortuga, a small island just offshore to the north. All these efforts combined experimental plantations, usually to grow tobacco or sugar, with contraband trade and piracy (see Lives and Livelihoods: Caribbean Buccaneers).

buccaneer A Caribbean-based pirate of the seventeenth century.

made them difficult to counter. Some, such as the Welshman Henry Morgan, made deals to share booty with colonial governors in exchange for legal protection, and later joined the colonial service. Others, such as François L'Ollonais, were unattached terrors of the Spanish Main. L'Ollonais was said to have carved the heart from a living victim and taken a bite. Piracy was about booty, not terror, however, and Spanish ships and towns, since they often contained silver and other portable treasures, were the main objects of buccaneer desire.

Once a raid was carried off, the pirates rendezvoused in the bars and brothels of Port Royal, whose markets thrived from the influx of stolen goods and money. When the buccaneers began to attack English, French, and Dutch ships with the same ferocity formerly reserved for Spanish ones in the late 1660s, the hunters became the hunted. Antipiracy laws from as early as the 1670s led to arrests and hangings, and by 1680 many buccaneers had fled to the Pacific and Indian oceans. A group of pirates who set out from the Virginia coast in the early 1680s returned to the Chesapeake with treasure stolen along the coast of Peru, only to land in jail and have their booty confiscated by royal officials. A portion of their loot was used to found the College of William and Mary in 1693.

At about the same time, a new pirate base was created on the island of Madagascar, which no Europeans had successfully colonized. From here buccaneers sailed north to stalk Muslim vessels traveling from India to the Arabian peninsula. The capture of several rich prizes by Henry Avery and other famous pirates in the 1690s led the English to send pirate hunters, among them the former buccaneer William Kidd. Kidd reverted to piratical activity off the coast of India; he was eventually arrested and jailed in New England before being sent to London for execution in 1701. After a break during the War of the Spanish Succession (1701–1714), which absorbed many buccaneers as privateers and even navy men, the war on Caribbean piracy returned in force, prosecuted mostly by the English Admiralty.

In the midst of England's war on piracy emerged some of the greatest figures of the era, among them Bartholomew Roberts. "Black Bart," as he was sometimes known, was one of the first pirates to prey on Portuguese ships carrying gold and diamonds to Europe from Brazil. When killed by English pirate hunters off the coast of Gabon in 1722, he was wearing a diamond-studded gold cross taken near Rio. By about 1725 the last wave of Anglo-American pirates, including the only known female pirate duo of Ann Bonny and Mary Read, was squelched.

QUESTIONS TO CONSIDER

1. What factors made buccaneer society possible in the seventeenth-century Caribbean?

2. What trends led to the sudden demise of the buccaneers' livelihood?

For Further Information:
Earle, Peter. *The Pirate Wars*. Boston: St. Martin's Griffin, 2006.

Spanish retaliation was fierce at first, but declined along with the empire's fortunes after 1648. The deepening seventeenth-century crisis rendered defense expenditures prohibitive. A massive English attack on Santo Domingo was successfully repulsed in 1655, but Jamaica was seized. Lacking minerals or a substantial native population, the Spanish had barely settled the island. Within a decade Port Royal, opposite Kingston Harbor on Jamaica's south coast, was a major base for contraband traders and buccaneers, among them Henry Morgan. Morgan and his followers sacked Panama City in 1671. The French followed a similar path on Martinique, Guadeloupe, and Saint-Domingue. Pirates of various nationalities meanwhile plagued the Spanish just as planters built a slave-staffed sugar economy farther inland. Some pirates, such as Henry Morgan, invested their plunder in their own Jamaican plantations, eventually gaining noble titles and general respectability.

Seizing Spanish Bases

The English colony of Barbados was a surprising success. A small and virtually uninhabited island at the easternmost edge of the Caribbean, Barbados had been of no interest

Developing Colonies

to the Spanish and Portuguese. The first English settlers came to plant tobacco in around 1625, and for a time the island's fortunes rested on production and export of this addictive drug. In time, capital accumulated from tobacco, along with advice and capital lent by Dutch refugees from Brazil, led the colony's planters to shift to sugar. Indentured servitude rapidly gave way to African slavery, and with slavery came rebellions. Even so, by the 1680s Barbados was a major world exporter of high-quality sugar, a position it held through the eighteenth century. Barbados showed that the Brazilian plantation model could transform even the smallest tropical island into a veritable gold mine.

With the expansion of slavery and sugar-growing on other Caribbean islands and parts of the mainland (especially Dutch Suriname), non-Iberian colonists began to surpass their predecessors in overall exports. In the course of the eighteenth century, the English, Dutch, and French embraced slavery on a scale and with an intensity not seen in Spanish America or Brazil. Slave codes grew increasingly harsh, and punishments cruel. There was virtually no interest expressed in protecting slaves' families or dignity, much less their souls. By 1750 the planters of Jamaica routinely tortured, raped, and otherwise terrorized enslaved Africans. They themselves admitted it, and wrote that such harsh measures were necessary to quell rebellion while maximizing production. Visitors to eighteenth-century Suriname described public executions as run-of-the-mill events, and those who visited Saint-Domingue wrote of sugar production on a vast, industrial scale. Slaves were consumed like so much timber.

The Rise of Caribbean Slave Societies

Whereas Brazilian planters used cheaper, enslaved native American workers as a bridge to mass African slavery, French, Dutch, and English planters in the Caribbean used indentured European servants. Throughout the seventeenth century thousands of poor servants and convicts staffed tobacco and sugar plantations alongside growing numbers of Africans and their descendants. If they survived the harsh conditions of the tropics, these servants could expect freedom within three to seven years. Many did not live to see that day, but the profits accumulated during these few years enabled plantation owners to purchase a permanently enslaved workforce. Scholars remain divided as to whether indentured Europeans were treated as badly as enslaved Africans.

Island Culture   By the early eighteenth century, Caribbean plantation society had begun to achieve the opulent material culture and African-influenced diversity found in Brazil's mining districts. Great houses in the European style dotted many islands, and slave communities grew into neo-African villages. Churches in these often Protestant lands were far more modest than in Catholic Brazil, however, and of several denominations. African religious traditions flourished, often with little influence from the colonizers' faiths. In Jamaica and Saint-Domingue, the constant influx of African-born slaves, coupled with general disdain for slaves' spiritual lives among planters, priests, and missionaries, led to the formation of new, hybrid religious traditions, called Obeah and Vodoun (or Voodoo), respectively.

A great difference that did exist between Brazil and the Caribbean sugar colonies lay in the realms of racial mixture and shared religious traditions. European men routinely kept African and mulatto mistresses, as in Minas Gerais and other parts of Brazil, but they were usually loath to recognize their children, much less educate them in Europe and incorporate them into high society. Treated as a dirty secret and even a petty crime, racial mixture soon gave rise to sharply graded color categories quite distinct from Spanish America's fluid sistema de castas. As for religion, Europeans showed nothing but contempt for "Obeah men" and "Voodoo priestesses," treating them as frauds and quacks. Partly as a result, some of these new religious leaders, male and female, played key roles in slave uprisings.

Maroons and Slaves   As in Brazil, *marronage* or slave flight was common throughout the Caribbean. Refuges for long-term runaways proved scarce on smaller, low-lying islands such as Barbados and Curaçao, but larger and more rugged islands such as Jamaica, Dominica, and Saint Domingue abounded with possibilities for safe haven. Here in rugged highlands such as Jamaica's Blue

Mountains, maroons were so successful they were able to negotiate treaties with planters and colonial officials by the early eighteenth century. Jamaican maroon leaders such as Nanny and Cudjoe were folk heroes to the enslaved and a constant thorn in the side of the British.

Sugar production as practiced by northern Europeans in the eighteenth century provided significant capital gains and, like Brazilian gold, probably helped to spark England's industrialization. Yet slavery of such horrific cruelty and scale also sowed the seeds of its own destruction. Slave traders responded to ratcheting Caribbean demand by packing their ships ever more tightly, turning slaving itself into an increasingly predatory exercise in more and more regions of West and West Central Africa. Some slaves were brought from as far away as the Indian Ocean island of Madagascar. By the late eighteenth century, white abolitionists at last began to join the long-ignored chorus of African and African-American voices against this enormous crime against humanity in the name of profit. For the first time, English tea drinkers thought twice before sweetening their brew.

Growth and Change in British and French North America 1607–1750

European colonization of the eastern seaboard of North America followed a different path than that of Spanish America or Brazil. There were, however, similarities: plantations developed, missionaries preached, people bred or married across color lines, and in places slave labor came to dominate. But overall, nontropical, Atlantic North America was characterized by a slow advance of European settler families practicing subsistence agriculture, livestock-raising, fishing, and commerce according to Old World norms. Eastern North America, both French and English, was to become, in the words of historian Alfred Crosby, a "neo-Europe" (see Map 22.4). Indigenous peoples, unlike in Spanish and Portuguese America where they had been absorbed and forcibly converted, were mostly driven from their lands or annihilated.

> **FOCUS**
>
> How did European relations with native peoples differ in the British and French colonies of North America?

Experiments in Commercial Colonialism

French, Dutch, and English colonization of eastern North America took root in the first decades of the seventeenth century. English Jamestown was founded on Virginia's Powhatan River (renamed "James" after the king) in 1607 and French Quebec, on Canada's St. Lawrence, in 1608. Henry Hudson, for a time an employee of the Dutch East India Company, began reconnoitering the river that took his name in 1609. Once it was clear that the Hudson River did not lead to the Pacific Ocean, a Dutch fur-trading post was established in 1618. As early as 1605 French Huguenots (or Protestant refugees) had also begun farming the coast of Maine and Nova Scotia, which they called Acadia.

Mariners such as Hudson continued searching in vain for a **northwest passage** to China. Others probed the soils of Newfoundland for signs of gold or silver. The survival of the earliest colonies in the tiny, fortified enclaves of "New France," "New Netherland," and "Virginia" depended on alliances with indigenous inhabitants. At the same time, all three European competitors were preoccupied with each other's designs on the region, a source of lasting conflict. Moreover, everyone worried about the Spanish, who had violently driven the French from Florida and the Dutch from Venezuela.

New France, first governed by Samuel de Champlain, marked France's renewed effort to colonize the Americas. Jacques Cartier and other mariners had explored the St. Lawrence Basin shortly after Columbus's time, and French colonists had planted forts in Florida and Brazil before being expelled by the Spanish and Portuguese in the 1560s. Only after France itself returned to calm, after the religious wars of 1562 to 1598 (discussed in Chapter 20), was a permanent colony deemed feasible. In North America, serious conflicts with the English

New France

northwest passage Searched-for sea route to Asia via North America.

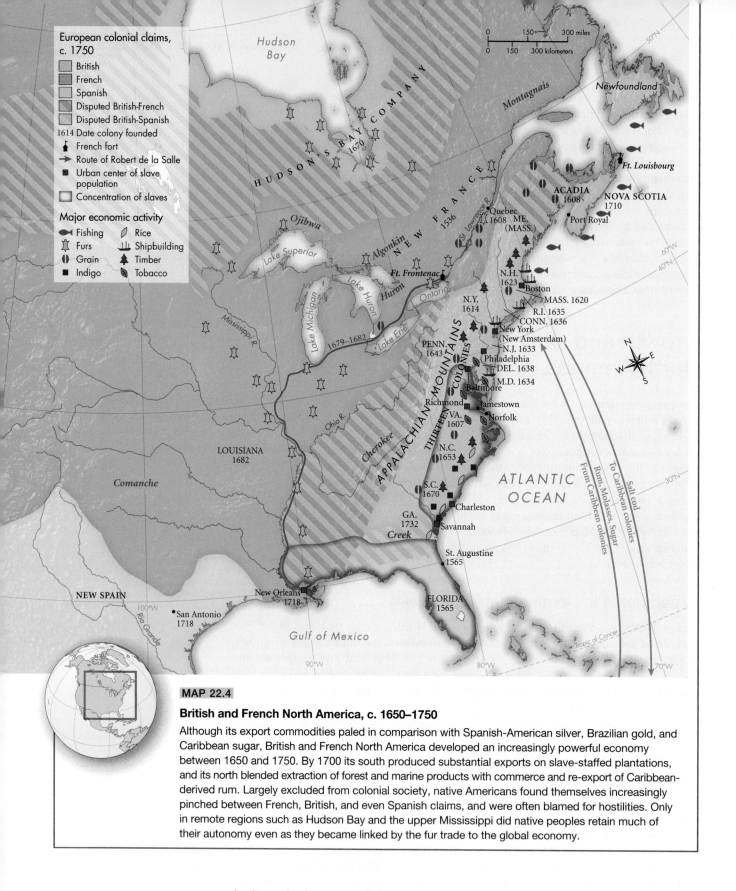

MAP 22.4

British and French North America, c. 1650–1750

Although its export commodities paled in comparison with Spanish-American silver, Brazilian gold, and Caribbean sugar, British and French North America developed an increasingly powerful economy between 1650 and 1750. By 1700 its south produced substantial exports on slave-staffed plantations, and its north blended extraction of forest and marine products with commerce and re-export of Caribbean-derived rum. Largely excluded from colonial society, native Americans found themselves increasingly pinched between French, British, and even Spanish claims, and were often blamed for hostilities. Only in remote regions such as Hudson Bay and the upper Mississippi did native peoples retain much of their autonomy even as they became linked by the fur trade to the global economy.

broke out by the 1610s and 1620s; they were resolved by treaty in 1632. Quebec would subsequently survive for over a century as a fortified trading post funded by absentee investors. Military alliances with indigenous groups such as the Montagnais and Huron proved critical throughout New France's history.

Unlike the Spanish and Portuguese, French, English, and Dutch colonizers created **joint-stock companies** that attracted numerous investors in the mother country and took on a financial and even political life of their own. Amsterdam's stock market was by far Europe's most vibrant, and the Dutch VOC was considered the shining model of such enterprises, because it successfully combined commercial, military, and diplomatic functions to turn a private profit from colonialism.

New France managed to survive through many a long winter only by tapping into the long chain of indigenous and *métis*, or mixed-heritage, fur traders and trappers extending deep into the Great Lakes and beyond. The beaver pelts they brought from the interior were processed for the European hat market. Only these men in canoes, the famed *coureurs de bois* ("runners of the woods," as the independent fur traders were known), and a few Jesuits went much beyond the fort. Settlers concentrated mostly in the St. Lawrence Valley, eking out a living in subsistence agriculture supplemented by fishing and hunting.

The early government of Jamestown, Virginia, funded like New France by a group of absentee investors, blended business and military models. This proved to be a bad idea. Despite investment and high hopes, the Virginia Company experiment failed disastrously, and it was nearly abandoned after only a few years. Men such as John Smith, though in some ways capable leaders, could not keep restless fellow settlers from antagonizing local indigenous groups, many of which belonged to a confederacy headed by the chieftain Powhatan. The settler-soldiers refused to farm, and theft of indigenous food stores led to reprisals, spawning decades-long cycles of vengeance. Tsenacommocah (sen-uh-COMB-uh-cuh), as Powhatan's subjects called the Chesapeake Bay region, was not easily conquered, and indigenous attacks in the 1620s nearly wiped out the first English settlers' plantations.

Eventually, English settlers got the upper hand and began to make money from tobacco exports. Although enslaved Africans arrived as early as 1619, initially indentured English servants were the primary source of labor. Soil exhaustion was rapid, causing the tobacco frontier to sweep inland toward the Appalachian Mountains and southward into North Carolina. Soaring demand for land to cultivate tobacco prompted Indian attacks and culminated in a settler rebellion led by Nathaniel Bacon in 1676. Bacon and some five hundred followers ran Virginia's governor out of Jamestown for allegedly dealing too kindly with the Powhatan and other native groups. Although colonial authorities rejected Bacon's calls to uproot the Indians, English policy turned sharply toward "removal." As Indians were forced westward, indentured servitude and small plots gave way to African slavery and large plantations.

The stony region dubbed New England, initially settled by religious dissenters called "Puritans," followed a distinct trajectory. Soon after arriving more or less by accident in Plymouth, Massachusetts, in 1620 the first "pilgrims," as they called themselves, faced the problem of establishing a working relationship with indigenous peoples in a land of limited agricultural and commercial potential. The colony, farther north than initially planned, was sponsored by the Virginia Company, but in 1629 a new corporation, the Massachusetts Bay Company, was chartered by prominent Puritans in England. Elder churchmen latched onto the ample rights of self-governance entailed by this charter, and Boston emerged as capital of the deeply religious Massachusetts Bay colony. As in cold New France, survival was a challenge. Servants suffered most in the first hard years; indigenous peoples were largely ignored.

Religious and labor discipline led to some success for early New Englanders, but both also bred division. Dissenters fled southward to found Rhode Island and Connecticut; others were punished internally. Expansion of subsistence farms throughout the region yielded surplus wheat and other grains in time, and cod fishing in the Newfoundland Banks

Chesapeake Bay, c. 1650–1700

Areas settled and under tobacco cultivation
■ By 1650
■ By 1700

Jamestown

New England

joint-stock company A colonial commercial venture with a royal charter and private shareholders.

métis French for "mixed," or offspring of Europeans and native Americans.

Champlain Fires on the Iroquois

Violent European encounters with native Americans continued long after the arrival of Christopher Columbus in the Caribbean in 1492. Soon after Columbus, French navigators explored Canada's St. Lawrence estuary, partly in hopes of finding a northwest passage to the Pacific Ocean and to Asia. Yet it was only in the early seventeenth century that the French established a lasting colony based in Quebec City. This image shows French commander Samuel Champlain firing on Iroquois warriors in 1613 near what is today Fort Ticonderoga, New York. The engraving puts European technology in stark relief as Champlain (aided by two armed men in the trees above) confronts a mass of naked warriors flowing out of their stockade. Champlain's armor renders him immune to enemy arrows, which mostly sail overhead. According to an accompanying report of the engagement, a single shot by Champlain felled two of the most feared Iroquois warriors. (Bettmann/Corbis.)

grew ever more important, as did whaling. Colonial authorities signed treaties with compliant indigenous neighbors; those who resisted faced enslavement or death. The Puritans were not pacifists, and like Samuel de Champlain and John Smith, they knew how to use firearms to terrorizing effect. They also had no qualms about enslaving war captives. As in Virginia, missionary efforts were few, perhaps in part because of emerging English notions of individual religious freedom, but also because of racism. The general pattern of European-indigenous relations in New England, as it would eventually be throughout British North America, was total displacement.

New Commercial Ventures   Newfoundland and Nova Scotia were chartered for commercial reasons in the 1620s, the latter disputed with the French for over a century. Proprietary colonies soon followed to the south of New England. Court favorites were given vast tracts of American lands in exchange for promises to defend and develop them as havens for settlers and for the export of raw materials to benefit the mother country. These proprietary colonies later yielded states such as Pennsylvania, Delaware, and Maryland. In 1664, the English captured Dutch

Pilgrims Set Sail on the *Mayflower*

In this iconic seventeenth-century woodcut, a trio of English separatists leaves the temporary refuge of Leiden, a major Dutch university town, to sail to North America on the *Mayflower*. The Pilgrims, as they came to be known, hoped to found a colony in Virginia territory, but after landing by accident on the coast of Massachusetts in 1620, they chose to stay. (Private Collection/ Bridgeman Art Library.)

New Amsterdam, a fur-trading post established in 1625 and increasingly a site of contraband trade; they renamed it New York. By 1700, England dominated eastern North America from Newfoundland to the Carolinas. Religiously diverse, British North America lacked an overarching structure of governance. In this the English differed from the bureaucratic and centralizing Spanish.

Southeastern Plantations

By the early eighteenth century, Virginia, Maryland, the Carolinas, and England's other mid-Atlantic and southern colonies were home to huge, export-oriented plantations. Planters focused first on tobacco, then rice, indigo, and other cash crops. More like the Caribbean and parts of Iberian America than New France or New England, the mid-Atlantic and southeast colonies grew quickly into slave-based societies. The region's trade was dominated by port towns such as Norfolk, Baltimore, and Charleston, their vast hinterlands dotted with great plantation houses and substantial, almost townlike slave quarters. Pockets of indigenous resistance could still be found in the eighteenth century, but native groups wishing to remain independent were increasingly forced westward beyond the Appalachian Mountains.

Northeastern Commerce

The northeast seaboard colonies, including the thriving port of New York, followed a different, less export-oriented path, although mercantile connections to the Caribbean and other primary goods-producing regions were strong. Rum distilling and re-export became a major New England industry, alongside shipbuilding and fishing. All of these businesses connected northeastern British America to the Atlantic slave trade, and bulk items such as salt cod soon became central to the diet of enslaved Africans in Jamaica. Perhaps most significant compared with Spanish and Portuguese America was the great freedom to trade with foreigners that English colonists generally enjoyed. This was not legal, but as Chapter 23 will show, England failed to enforce its colonial trading policies until after 1750. When it finally did so, it provoked violent rebellion.

Everyday Life in the Northern Colonies

Given the long winters and relative isolation of the St. Lawrence River Basin, life for early French Canadians was both difficult and lonely. Food stores were a major concern, and settlers long relied on a blend of native generosity and annual supply ships from France. Thousands of colonists were sent to develop the land, along with soldiers to guard against English or Indian attacks. The result was the militarization of the backcountry, displacing and massacring native groups in a way reminiscent of England's uncompromising "removal" policy.

Jesuit Missionaries

Jesuit missionaries, meanwhile, set out to convert these embattled, indigenous inhabitants to Roman Catholicism. The priests, relatively few in number, concentrated on large semisedentary groups such as the Huron, Algonkin, and Ojibwa, among others. Sometimes the missionaries learned local languages, made friends with prominent chieftains or their sons, and found success. At other times, their failures ended in their deaths, memorialized by their brethren as religious martyrdom. French Jesuits did not give up on North American Indians, in any case, and eventually worked their way from the Great Lakes down the Mississippi Basin. Military explorers followed, including the nobleman Robert de la Salle, who in 1682 claimed the lower Mississippi, which he called Louisiana, for King Louis XIV (see again Map 22.4).

Frontier Society

Life in the American backcountry claimed by France was in many ways dominated by native peoples, a frontier arrangement historian Richard White has labeled "the middle ground." Here at the edge of imperial control indigenous Americans, métis fur traders, and European missionaries, soldiers, and homesteaders all found themselves interdependent, none claiming a monopoly. Not everyone found this arrangement to their liking, least of all crown representatives, but on the frontier the social divisions of race, religion, gender, and culture were blurred or overlooked (see Reading the Past: A Swedish Traveler's Description of Quebec). Put another way, "the middle ground" was the most egalitarian space in the early modern Americas. Like Chica da Silva's fluid world in backcountry Brazil, the possibilities could be astonishing, at least in the eyes of outsiders.

Limited Racial Relations

Unlike in Spanish or Portuguese America, sexual relations across color lines were relatively rare in British North America, except in frontier outposts. In part, this was a result of demography: European men and women migrated to the eastern seaboard in close to equal numbers over time, and indigenous peoples were relatively few and were rarely incorporated into settler society. When racial mixture occurred, it was most commonly the result of illicit relations between white men and enslaved women of African descent. Such relations, which according to surviving documents were more often forced than consensual or long-term, were most common in the plantation districts of the Chesapeake and Carolina Low Country. Still, some mixed-race children were born in northern cities such as New York and Boston, where considerable numbers of slaves and free people of color could be found in close proximity to whites. Throughout the British colonies, blatantly racist "antimiscegenation" laws dating to the seventeenth century also discouraged black-white unions, because these were thought to undermine the social hierarchy. Racial codes and covenants were most rigidly enforced in regions highly dependent on African slavery, namely the mid-Atlantic and southeast. Still, as Virginia planter and future U.S. president Thomas Jefferson's long-term, child-producing relationship with his slave, Sally Hemings, demonstrates, human urges and affinities could override even the strictest social taboos and legal codes.

Slave Culture and Resistance

Slavery existed in New France, but on a small scale. A few Africans could be found in growing towns such as Montreal, but most slaves were indigenous war captives used for household labor. In early New England, enslaved Africans and a few indigenous slaves served in similar roles, and also in artisan workshops and on board ships. Thousands of enslaved Africans lived and worked in the bustling shops and port facilities of New York City by the early eighteenth century, and many more lived and worked on farms in rural Pennsylvania. Slave rebellions were relatively rare in these regions, although the slaves of New York were highly outspoken and sometimes alarmed city authorities. Slave resistance mostly consisted of work stoppages, tool breaking, truancy, and other "passive" means. Faced with racist exclusion, small black religious communities, mostly of the Anglican, Methodist, and Baptist denominations, eventually formed.

Even more distinct slave cultures emerged in regions where Africans predominated, from Maryland to Georgia. Here plantation life took on some of the features of the English Caribbean, with large numbers of enslaved Africans and their descendants concentrated in prisonlike barracks within view of great plantation houses. As archaeologists

A Swedish Traveler's Description of Quebec

Pehr ("Peter") Kalm was a Swedish naturalist who visited Canada in around 1749. In the following passages, translated from the Swedish in the 1770s, Kalm describes the inhabitants of the Christian Huron village of Lorette, just outside the capital of French Canada, Quebec City.

August the 12. This afternoon I and my servant went out of town, to stay in the country for a couple of days that I might have more leisure to examine the plants that grow in the woods here, and the state of the country. In order to proceed the better, the governor-general had sent for an Indian from Lorette to show us the way, and teach us what use they make of the spontaneous plants hereabouts. This Indian was an Englishman by birth, taken by the Indians thirty years ago, when he was a boy, and adopted by them, according to their custom, instead of a relation of theirs killed by the enemy. Since that time he constantly stayed with them, became a Roman Catholic and married an Indian woman: he dresses like an Indian, speaks English and French, and many of the Indian languages. In the wars between the French and English, in this country [a reference to chronic conflicts preceding the Seven Years' War], the French Indians have made many prisoners of both sexes in the English plantations [i.e., farms], adopted them afterwards, and they married with people of the Indian nations. From hence the Indian blood in Canada is much mixed with European blood, and a great part of the Indians now living owe their origin to Europe. It is likewise remarkable that a great part of the people they had taken during the war and incorporated with their nations, especially the young people, did not choose to return to their native country, though their parents and nearest relations came to them and endeavored to persuade them to it, and though it was in their power to do it. The licentious life led by the Indians pleased them better than that of their European relations; they dressed like the Indians and regulated all their affairs in their way. It is therefore difficult to distinguish them except by their color, which is somewhat whiter than that of the Indians. There are likewise examples of some Frenchmen going amongst the Indians and following their way of life. There is on the contrary scarce one instance of an Indian's adopting the European customs.

Source: Peter Kalm, *Travels into North America*, trans. John Reinold Forster (Barre, MA: Imprint Society, 1972) 3:184.

EXAMINING THE EVIDENCE

1. How does Kalm assess the "cultural divide" and racial mixture in French Canada?

2. What made Indian customs preferable to European ones in this region, according to Kalm?

and historians are increasingly discovering, enslaved Africans had a thriving religious and material world of their own, one that contrasted sharply to the tidy, well-heeled world of the English planter families who claimed lordship over them. African religious practices, while muted by comparison with those of the Caribbean or Brazil, were widely known and respected among the enslaved population. Secret shamanistic and medicinal practices were also common. Whites appear to have known virtually nothing about the slaves' hidden culture.

Violent rebellions and mass marronage along the Atlantic seaboard were rare in comparison with the Caribbean or even Brazil. There were simply far more whites who could be mustered to put down an uprising in Virginia or North Carolina than in Jamaica or Barbados, where slaves outnumbered white settlers by huge margins. Geography limited marronage as well. The mountains were distant and inhabited by Indians. During winter, maroons could be more easily tracked by hunters due to diminished forest cover, and they were hard-pressed to find food in the wild. Some slaves ran away to cities, and even to Spanish Florida, but it was nearly impossible to form lasting maroon communities. Unlike Spanish and Portuguese America, slaves' legal access to freedom through self-purchase or emancipation was severely limited, as was access to the religion of the planters. Only in places such as South Carolina were concentrations of recently arrived Africans great enough to create the kinds of "neo-Africas" found in much of Brazil and the Caribbean. Thus, while societies throughout the Americas included a mixture of Europeans, Africans, and indigenous Americans, the relationships among these groups and the hybrid cultures that emerged varied from region to region, depending on local conditions and the goals and beliefs of the colonizers in question.

COUNTERPOINT
The Maroons of Suriname

FOCUS

How did the runaway slaves of Dutch Suriname create a lasting independent state of their own?

In defiance of slavery on plantations and in mines, fugitive Africans and their descendants established free, or "maroon," communities throughout the Americas. Slaves ran away as soon as they could from brutal conditions in Hispaniola, Puerto Rico, Cuba, and Panama. Others fled into the hills east and southwest of Mexico City. Still others found refuge in backcountry Venezuela, Colombia, Ecuador, Peru, and Bolivia. Slaves in Portuguese Brazil did likewise, forming in the hills of Alagoas, a small province of northeastern Brazil, the largest maroon confederacy in history: the Quilombo (key-LOAM-boh) of Palmares. Similar maroon settlements emerged in English Jamaica, as well as French Saint-Domingue, Guadeloupe, and Martinique. But it was in the small colony of Dutch Suriname on South America's northern coast that African and African-American fugitives established the Americas' most resilient and distinctive maroon culture.

From Persecution to Freedom

Dutch and Portuguese Jewish planters ejected from Brazil after 1654 brought enslaved Africans to Suriname to grow and process sugar cane. By the 1660s, dozens of plantations dotted the banks of the Saramaka, Suriname, and Marowijne rivers. Faced not only with intensive, uncompensated labor in the hot sun but also with physical and psychological torture, many of the enslaved escaped upriver into dense forests once inhabited by Carib and Arawakan-speaking indigenous peoples. Sheltered by cataracts, rapids, and winding tributaries, dozens and then hundreds of runaways settled beyond the reach of planters and colonial authorities. If captured, the maroons, male and female, faced dismemberment and public execution, tactics of terror meant to dissuade those on the plantations from fleeing.

By 1700 Suriname's maroons had formed several independent chiefdoms, each augmenting its numbers through periodic raids on the plantations downriver. Women were especially prized. Within a few decades the maroons numbered in the thousands. Taking advantage of the rugged geography of the Suriname interior and adapting to its challenging environment, the maroons carved out a "neo-Africa" in the backlands. After numerous failed expeditions to capture and re-enslave the maroons, plantation owners sought peace in the 1740s, only to return with even larger and better-armed expeditions after 1750. The maroons remained resolute and eventually won freedom from the Dutch government, which sent them arms and other trade goods to keep peace. As early as the late eighteenth

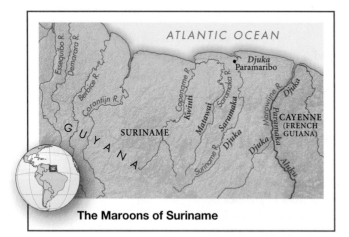

The Maroons of Suriname

century a few maroon groups allowed small numbers of Christian missionaries to visit them, but the missionaries won few converts and most of them soon died of malaria and other tropical diseases.

Suriname's Distinctive Maroon Culture

Six major maroon groups, the Saramaka, Djuka, Aluku, Paramaka, Matawai, and Kwinti, continue to live in Suriname and neighboring French Guiana, and many retain, thanks to vibrant oral traditions, substantial memories of the period of slavery and the punishing wars the planters prosecuted against them. Some maroon descendants began writing histories of these events as early as the 1880s. Others have moved in the decades following Suriname's independence from the Dutch in 1975 to the coastal capital of Paramaribo or even to Dutch cities such as Amsterdam and Leiden. Maroon culture nevertheless remains very much alive.

Maroon culture in Suriname, built around matrilineal villages, was so striking to early outside visitors that they assumed its rituals and complex artistic traditions to be direct transfers from some part of western Africa. The distinctive architecture, decorative patterns, textile traditions, and musical styles all hark back to Africa. Anthropologists looked for specific links in African art, language, and religion, but found no single traceable root—only broad associations and isolated words. Anthropologists Richard and Sally Price have argued that Suriname's distinctive maroon culture was something new, a product of resistance to colonialism. By combining archival and anthropological research they have shown how strands of western African thought and practice converged with the contingencies of fugitive life at the margins of a European-dominated plantation society. To survive, runaway Africans and their descendants learned to select the best local forest products such as wood for canoes and thatch for roofs, then planted known, imported crops such as bananas and plantains, as well as local ones like maize. Through raids and treaties they obtained cooking pots, textiles, and other manufactured goods, all of which they combined, then decorated, to create a new and distinctive material culture.

Descendants of the original maroon elders have preserved and passed along memories of the long-past horrors and escape from slavery, as in the following passage, recited by the Saramakan leader Lántifáya and recorded by Richard Price in 1978:

Maroon of Suriname

As slavery expanded throughout the Caribbean and many parts of the mainland Americas after 1650, so too did slave flight and the formation of "maroon," or runaway, communities. Although scattered throughout the tropics as well as the swamplands of the U.S. southeast, the largest and best-armed maroon communities in the Americas emerged in the backlands of Dutch Suriname, on the north coast of South America. Here escaped slaves armed themselves by raiding coastal plantations. Their raids sparked reprisals, which included full-blown wars by the later eighteenth century. A soldier in these wars, John Gabriel Stedman, wrote a sympathetic account of the struggles of slaves and maroons in Suriname that became evidence used by the emerging abolitionist cause in England. Engraver Francesco Bartolozzi followed Stedman's descriptions to depict this maroon warrior on the march, stolen gun in hand and death—or slain enemies—literally at his feet. (British Library/The Image Works.)

> In slavery, there was hardly anything to eat. It was at the place called Providence Plantation. They whipped you till your ass was burning. Then they would give you a bit of plain rice in a calabash [bowl made from the fruit of a tropical American tree]. (That's what we've heard.) And the gods told them that this is no way for human beings to live. They would help them. Let each person go where he could. So they ran.[2]

Conclusion

The colonial Americas underwent the deepest alterations of the world's regions in early modern times, environmentally and socially. Mining of precious metals for export to Europe and Asia drove the Spanish and Portuguese deep into the interior, transforming vast landscapes and giving rise to a wide range of new social and economic relations. Autonomous indigenous groups, followed later by enslaved Africans, were driven farther inland as they searched for refuge. Punishing forms of labor persisted at the old Aztec and Inca core through the eighteenth century, but indigenous populations began to recover from postconquest disease shocks. In the lawless mining frontier of Brazil, as in backcountry New France, racial mixing proved a pragmatic response to demographic realities, challenging notions of propriety and permissiveness.

More rigidly racist social orders developed in the French, Dutch, and English Caribbean and along the eastern seaboard of North America. That a successful and publicly recognized woman of color such as Chica da Silva could have emerged in such a place as Jamaica or Virginia is almost impossible to imagine. The intense religiosity of the seventeenth and early eighteenth centuries, manifested in both Spanish-American Catholicism and English Puritanism, faded only slowly and left a long-lasting legacy. American dependence on slavery and other forms of forced labor would also die a lingering death. In these and other key ways, the Americas and their European motherlands grew steadily and irreconcilably apart.

NOTES

1. Sor Juana Inés de la Cruz, quoted in Irving Leonard, *Baroque Times in Old Mexico: Seventeenth-century Persons, Places, and Practices* (Ann Arbor: University of Michigan Press, 1959), 189.
2. Saramakan elder Lántifáya, quoted in Richard Price, *First-Time: The Historical Vision of an Afro-American People* (Baltimore, MD: Johns Hopkins University Press, 1983), 71.

RESOURCES FOR RESEARCH

General Works

General surveys of the early modern Americas remain to be written, but the following are examples of border-crossing works. Benjamin and Egerton et al. are pioneering textbooks in Atlantic history, incorporating Africa and western Europe as well as the Americas.

Alchon, Suzanne Austin. *A Pest in the Land: New World Epidemics in a Global Perspective.* 2003.

Benjamin, Thomas. *The Atlantic World: Europeans, Africans, Indians, and Their Shared History, 1400–1900.* 2009.

Egerton, Douglas R., Alison Games, Jane Landers, Kris Lane, and Donald Wright. *The Atlantic World.* 2007.

Library of Congress: Hispanic Reading Room. This Web site features a wealth of materials on early Spanish and Portuguese America: http://www.loc.gov/rr/hispanic/onlinecol.html.

Socolow, Susan. *The Women of Colonial Latin America.* 2000.

University of Pennsylvania Library: Cultural Readings: Colonization and Print in the Americas. A useful mix of printed and pictorial sources on the early Americas: http://www.library .upenn.edu/exhibits/rbm/kislak/index/cultural.html.

The World That Silver Made: Spanish America, 1580–1750

Thanks to many researchers, Spanish America is at last beginning to come into focus as a global region. The following is a sampling of key studies and solid overviews. Bakewell is especially good on the mining economy, as are Guy and Sheridan on frontiers.

Andrien, Kenneth. *Andean Worlds: Indigenous History, Culture, and Consciousness Under Spanish Rule, 1532–1825.* 2001.

Bakewell, Peter. *A History of Latin America to 1825,* 3d ed. 2010.

Guy, Donna, and Thomas Sheridan, eds. *Contested Ground: Comparative Frontiers on the Northern and Southern Edges of the Spanish Empire.* 1998.

Hoberman, Louisa Schell, and Susan Socolow, eds. *Cities and Society in Colonial Latin America.* 1986.

Hoberman, Louisa Schell, and Susan Socolow, eds. *The Countryside in Colonial Latin America.* 1996.

Gold, Diamonds, and the Transformation of Brazil, 1695–1800

The story of Golden-Age Brazil is still being researched, but several classic and new works in English, including Charles Boxer's fine overview and Júnia Furtado's new biography of Chica da Silva, offer a solid start. Dean's is an excellent environmental study.

Boxer, Charles R. *The Golden Age of Brazil: Growing Pains of a Colonial Society.* 1964.

Dean, Warren. *With Broadax and Firebrand: The Destruction of Brazilian Atlantic Forest.* 1995.

Furtado, Júnia F. *Chica da Silva.* 2008.

Higgins, Kathleen. *"Licentious Liberty" in a Colonial Gold Mining Region: Sabará, Minas Gerais, in the Eighteenth Century.* 1999.

Schwartz, Stuart B. *Slaves, Peasants, and Rebels: Reconsidering Brazilian Slavery.* 1992.

Bitter Sugar, Part Two: Slavery and Colonialism in the Caribbean, 1625–1750

Caribbean history is a fast-growing field. This area is only starting to be treated as a region rather than as clusters of islands with a shared language, or "proto-nations." Dunn's work on the English Caribbean is classic, the Schwartz collection offers a sweeping update, and Moya Pons is a superb overview.

Burnard, Trevor. *Mastery, Tyranny, and Desire: Thomas Thistlewood and His Slaves in the Anglo-Jamaican World.* 2004.

Common-Place. A Web journal with research links sponsored by the American Antiquarian Society: http://www.common-place.org/.

Dunn, Richard S. *Sugar and Slaves: The Rise of the Planter Class in the English West Indies, 1624–1713,* 2d ed. 2000.

Moya Pons, Frank. *The Caribbean: A History.* 2007.

Schwartz, Stuart B., ed. *Tropical Babylons: Sugar and the Making of the Atlantic World, 1450–1680.* 2005.

Growth and Change in British and French North America, 1607–1750

The literature on British and French North America is vast. What follows is only a small sample of classic and recent contributions.

Gleach, Frederic W. *Powhatan's World and Colonial Virginia: A Conflict of Cultures.* 1997.

Hall, David D. *Worlds of Wonder, Days of Judgment: Popular Religious Belief in Early New England.* 1990.

Karlsen, Carol F. *The Devil in the Shape of a Woman: Witchcraft in Colonial New England.* 1987.

Morgan, Philip D. *Slave Counterpoint: Black Culture in the Eighteenth-Century Chesapeake and Lowcountry.* 1998.

Society of Early Americanists. Web site with links to teaching resources and documents: http://www.societyofearlyamericanists.org/.

White, Richard. *The Middle Ground: Indians, Empires, and Republics in the Great Lakes Region, 1650–1815.* 1991.

COUNTERPOINT: The Maroons of Suriname

Scholarship on maroon societies is growing, but few have written more on the maroons of Suriname than anthropologists Richard and Sally Price.

Price, Richard. *Alabi's World.* 1990.

———. *First-Time: The Historical Vision of an Afro-American People.* 1983.

———, ed. *Maroon Societies: Rebel Slave Communities in the Americas,* 3d ed. 1996.

Price, Richard, and Sally Price. *Maroon Arts.* 2000.

▶ **For additional primary sources from this period,** see *Sources of Crossroads and Cultures*.

▶ **For Web sites, images, and documents related to topics in this chapter,** see Make History at bedfordstmartins.com/smith.

The major global development in this chapter ▶ The profound social, cultural, and environmental changes in the Americas under colonial rule.

IMPORTANT EVENTS

1570	Spanish galleons begin annual service linking Acapulco to Manila
1607	English establish colony at Jamestown, Virginia
1608	French establish colony at Quebec City
1618	Dutch establish colony of New Netherland on upper Hudson River
1625	Dutch settle New Amsterdam on Manhattan Island; English establish colony on Barbados
1630	Dutch capture northeast Brazil
1654	Portuguese drive Dutch from Brazil; some colonists move to Suriname
1655	English seize Jamaica from the Spanish
1664	English take New Amsterdam from Dutch, rename it New York
1671	Henry Morgan's buccaneers sack Panama City
1676	Bacon's Rebellion in Virginia
1694	Great Brazilian maroon community of Palmares destroyed
1695–1800	Discovery in Brazilian interior of gold and diamonds inaugurates Brazil's "gold rush"
1701–1714	War of the Spanish Succession
1720	Brazil elevated to status of viceroyalty
1763	Rio de Janeiro elevated to status of capital of Brazil

KEY TERMS

audiencia (p. 724)
buccaneer (p. 738)
creole (p. 731)
indenture (p. 722)
joint-stock company (p. 743)
maroon (p. 736)

mestizaje (p. 731)
mestizo (p. 731)
métis (p. 743)
mulatto (p. 731)
northwest passage (p. 741)

CHAPTER OVERVIEW QUESTIONS

1. How did the production of silver, gold, and other commodities shape colonial American societies?

2. How and where did northern Europeans insert themselves into territories claimed by Spain and Portugal?

3. How did racial divisions and mixtures compare across the Americas by the mid-eighteenth century?

SECTION FOCUS QUESTIONS

1. How did mineral wealth steer the development of Spanish America?

2. How was Brazil transformed by the mining boom of the eighteenth century?

3. How did sugar production and slavery mold Caribbean societies?

4. How did European relations with native peoples differ in the British and French colonies of North America?

5. How did the runaway slaves of Dutch Suriname create a lasting independent state of their own?

MAKING CONNECTIONS

1. How did Spanish America's imperial bureaucracy compare with those of the Ottomans and other "gunpowder empires" discussed in Chapters 19 to 21?

2. How did the labor systems of the American colonies compare with those of western Eurasia (see Chapter 20)? With those of Russian and East Asia (see Chapter 21)?

3. What role did religious diversity play in colonial American life compared with contemporary South and Southeast Asia (see Chapter 19)?

4. In what ways did economic developments in colonial Brazil differ from developments in Spanish America?

PART 4

The World
from 1750 to the Present

CH 23

MANY OF THE TRENDS of the early modern period continued after 1750. Global connections continued to intensify, and science and technology advanced at an ever-faster pace. As part of their growing competition for land, natural resources, and the control of populations, governments armed themselves with more destructive weaponry. As technology developed, the variety of livelihoods expanded across the globe, and many people enjoyed the opportunity to purchase an array of consumer products. The accelerating rate of change in technology, population growth, consumerism, and the introduction of new livelihoods and forms of government marks the shift from early modern times to what historians call the late modern era, the period from about 1750 to the present.

The great empires of the early modern period—the Qing, Mughal, Ottoman, and Spanish—faced challenges as the modern period opened. Many of these challenges arose from the inroads outsiders made on their rule, but these empires also faced problems within their borders, such as the enormous costs of military supremacy. Religious dissent, natural disasters, and the social changes that accompanied modernity also undermined their security. Newly wealthy or ambitious people and those wanting more modern forms of government contested the power of traditional rulers. The Qing, Mughal, Ottoman, and Spanish empires would all disappear in the late modern period.

CH 25

CH 24

Lives and livelihoods were transformed as mechanical power came to substitute for human power in the Industrial Revolution, which began in around 1750 in western Europe and spread throughout the globe. Newly created factory work moved production out of the home to mechanized workplaces, and a variety of other new occupations connected with the rise of industry developed, such as railroad builders, engineers, and conductors, and later, flight

CHAPTERS IN THIS PART ▼

CH 26

attendants and workers in airplane plants. With the proliferation of science and technology, entirely new service work, in reproductive technology and systems analysis, for example, continued to transform work life. Nonetheless, agriculture remained a primary form of work for the vast majority of people until well into the twentieth century. That livelihood, too, was affected by farm machinery, the development of chemical fertilizers, and ultimately what was called in the late twentieth century a "green revolution" based on seeds and plants designed to flourish in particular parts of the world.

Modern industry did not displace older ways of doing things all at once. Slavery in fact gave a crucial boost to industrial growth by providing raw materials and food for industrial workers. Although a declining labor system, slavery has remained a livelihood down to the present. Women in the workforce often held the worst jobs and were paid less than men even for equivalent tasks.

Emboldened by new wealth and industrial technology, a cluster of European states, eventually joined by Japan and the United States, built cohesive, effective governments with modern military capabilities and mass armies. During this period, most of them developed constitutional governments based on the rule of law and the explicit elaboration of the rights of citizens. Constitutional government and legal rights were often gained through revolutions or other dramatic changes in rulership, but these states were backed by unified citizens. As dignified citizens, rather than servile subjects of kings, many felt empowered to join the commercial and industrial innovation that was going on around them. Historians characterize such states as "nation-states." As they became stronger because of their citizen support, the rising nation-states sought to extend their power through what is known as the "new imperialism." Unlike the expansionists of the early modern period, new imperialists had the "tools of empire" to take over the institutions

CH 27

CH 28 →

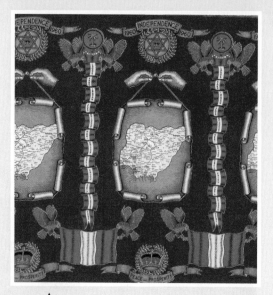

CH 29

and economies of other parts of the world more completely. Late modernity saw the imperial nations try to dominate Africa, Asia, and other parts of the world both economically and politically in the nineteenth century.

Imperial countries justified their rule by celebrating the modern ideas and institutions they would bring to the world's "backward" peoples. Local peoples both resisted and cooperated with the imperialists; some grew incredibly wealthy from trade, manufacturing, and governmental work. However, imperialism also brought devastation and death because of exploitation and outright violence. Imperialism nonetheless developed global networks of unprecedented density, as steamships, telegraphs, and other forms of communications technology circled the earth at a faster pace than ever before.

Competition and conflict among these imperial nations intensified, as did organized resistance to their rule. In the twentieth century the imperial powers waged two horrific wars—World Wars I and II—in the course of which tens of millions of people died. Eventually, colonial people took advantage of the war-weakened imperialists, winning their freedom and setting up independent states after World War II ended in 1945. The rest of the twentieth century down to the present has been a story of these nation-states expanding their capacities and livelihoods and asserting their place in the modern world.

Our most recent modern history is filled with the struggles involved in asserting this independence, first under the conditions of the Cold War between the Soviet Union and United States that followed World War II, and then during the period of U.S. dominance after

CH 30

	1750		1815	
Americas		1775–1781 North American Revolution U.S. Constitution formally adopted 1789 • 1791–1804 Haitian Revolution	1816–1825 Latin American revolutions of independence	U.S. Civil War 1861–1865 1846–1848 Mexican War
Europe	1750–1800 Spread of the Enlightenment beyond France • 1750 Industrialization begins in Great Britain	1789–1799 French Revolution Napoleon comes to power 1799 •	• 1815 Napoleon defeated at Waterloo; Congress of Vienna	1853–1856 Crimean War *Communist Manifesto* 1848 →
Middle East		• 1798 Napoleon invades Egypt • 1805 Muhammad Ali founds dynasty in Egypt		
Africa	Britain takes Cape Colony 1795 • Sokoto caliphate founded 1809 •		• 1821 Republic of Liberia founded	
Asia and Oceania	• 1765 English East India Company rule of Bengal begins 1769–1778 Captain Cook's exploration of Australia, New Zealand		Taiping Rebellion 1840s • 1839–1842 Opium War	

1989. Genocide, civil war, poverty, and an unprecedented migration of peoples globally have characterized human life in the past few decades. Terrorism, the pollution of the earth's atmosphere, and the spread of deadly diseases are also part of our most recent modernity.

Nonetheless, the world's peoples have simultaneously attempted to create new forms of world governance to eliminate the worst abuses of modern life. Writers and artists have innovatively explored modernity's difficulties. Historians and philosophers have also analyzed the consequences of growing military power on the one hand and life-enhancing developments such as medical breakthroughs and the communications revolution on the other. There is no alternative, many of these thinkers believe, to deliberate study of the past as the basis for informed decision-making in our world today.

CH 31

1880	1945	2010

- **1880–1940** Immigration from Europe surges
- Spanish-American War
- **1898** •
- **1910–1920** Mexican Revolution
- • **1917** United States enters World War I
- • **1929** U.S. stock market crash sparks the Great Depression
- *The Feminine Mystique* **1963** •
- **1945–1989** Cold War
- • **1969** U.S. astronauts land on moon
- NAFTA enacted **1994** •
- • **2001** Terrorists attack the United States
- **2007–2008** Global economic crisis unfolds

- **1861** Emancipation of the serfs in Russia
- **1880–1900** Impressionism flourishes
- **1891–1904** Construction of trans-Siberian railroad
- **1914–1918** World War I
- **1917–1918** Russian Revolution
- • **1930s** Welfare state begins in Sweden
- **1939–1945** World War II in Europe
- • **1952** Discovery of structure of DNA
- • **1967** EEC established
- • **1960** Introduction of birth-control pill
- • **1990s** New European nations emerge in wake of Soviet collapse

- **1869** Suez Canal completed
- Young Turks' uprising
- **1908** •
- • **1918** Breakup of Ottoman Empire
- **1922–1938** Mustafa Kemal modernizes Turkey
- • **1948** Founding of Israel
- Creation of OPEC **1960** •
- Yom Kippur War **1973** •
- **1980–1988** Iran-Iraq War
- **1978–1979** Revolution in Iran
- Start of Arab Spring uprisings **2010** •
- • **2003** United States invades Iraq

- **1867** End of Atlantic slave trade
- **1870–1914** New imperialism in Africa
- **1884–1885** Berlin Conference on Africa
- Ghana gains independence **1959** •
- • **1962** Algeria wins independence
- **1948–1989** Apartheid in South Africa
- Republic of South Sudan founded **2011** •

- **1868** Meiji Restoration
- **1870–1914** New imperialism in Asia
- **1894– 1895** Sino-Japanese War
- **1904–1905** Russo-Japanese War
- Gandhi's Salt March **1930** •
- **1937–1945** World War II in the Pacific
- • **1947** India and Pakistan win independence
- **1950–1953** Korean War
- **1966–1976** Cultural Revolution
- **1954–1975** Vietnam War
- • **1992** Beginning of socialist market economy in China

AT A CROSSROADS ▶

Simon Bolivar traveled the Atlantic world, gaining inspiration from the Enlightenment and revolutionary currents he felt firsthand in Spain, France, the United States, and the Caribbean. On his return to South America, he helped spearhead the movement for independence there. No democrat, Bolivar learned from hard experience that in an independent South America, the rich variety of slaves and other workers would need to be accommodated. (The Art Archive/Museo Historico Nacional Buenos Aires/Gianni Dagli Orti.)

Atlantic Revolutions and the World

1750–1830

S imon Bolivar (1783–1830) began life as the privileged son of a family that in the sixteenth century had settled in Caracas, a city in Spanish-controlled South America (now the capital of Venezuela). His early years were full of personal loss: his father died when he was three, his mother when he was five, and his grandfather, who cared for him after his mother's death, when he was six. Bolivar's extended family sent him to military school and then to Spain to study—typical training for prominent "creoles," as South Americans of European descent were called. Following the death of his young wife, he traveled to Paris to overcome his grief. There Bolivar's life changed: he saw the military hero Napoleon crown himself emperor in 1804 and witnessed crowds of patriotic French fill the streets of the capital with joy. "That moment, I tell you, made me think of the slavery of my country and of the glory that would come to the person who liberated it," he later wrote.[1] After a visit to the newly independent United States, Bolivar returned to his home in 1807, inspired by all he had seen, and determined to reform his homeland by freeing it from the oppressions of Spanish rule. He, too, took up arms, leading military campaigns, which along with popular uprisings eventually ousted Spain's government from much of Latin America. For his revolutionary leadership, contemporaries gave him the title "Liberator."

The creation of independent states in Latin America challenged centuries-old empires and was part of a powerful upheaval in the Atlantic world. North American colonists rebelled against Britain in 1776 and, with the help of the French and Spanish, successfully fought a war of independence, kindling other fires of liberty in the Atlantic world. The French rose up in 1789 against a monarchy that had bankrupted itself, ironically in part by giving military support to the American rebels. In 1791 a massive slave revolt erupted in the prosperous French sugar colony of Saint-Domingue, leading to the creation of the

The Promise of Enlightenment

FOCUS What were the major ideas of the Enlightenment and their impacts?

Revolution in North America

FOCUS What factors lay behind the war between North American colonists and Great Britain?

The French Revolution and the Napoleonic Empire

FOCUS What changes emerged from the French Revolution and Napoleon's reign?

Revolution Continued in the Western Hemisphere

FOCUS What were the motives and methods of revolutionaries in the Caribbean and Latin America?

COUNTERPOINT: Religious Revival in a Secular Age

FOCUS What trends in Enlightenment and revolutionary society did religious revival challenge?

BACKSTORY

Rising global trade and maturing slave systems brought wealth to merchants and landowners in many parts of the world during the seventeenth and eighteenth centuries. Emboldened by this newfound wealth, they joined bureaucrats and aristocrats in the struggle for more influence, not only in the great land-based empires such as the Qing, Mughal, and Ottoman states but also in some of the small states of Europe. These small European states had developed overseas empires, which after several centuries they hoped to exploit more efficiently. They had also built their military capability and gained administrative experience as they fought one another for greater global influence. Maintaining this influence was costly, however. Simultaneously the Scientific Revolution (see Chapter 20) and the beginnings of a movement to think more rationally about government were causing some critics in Europe to question the traditional political and social order.

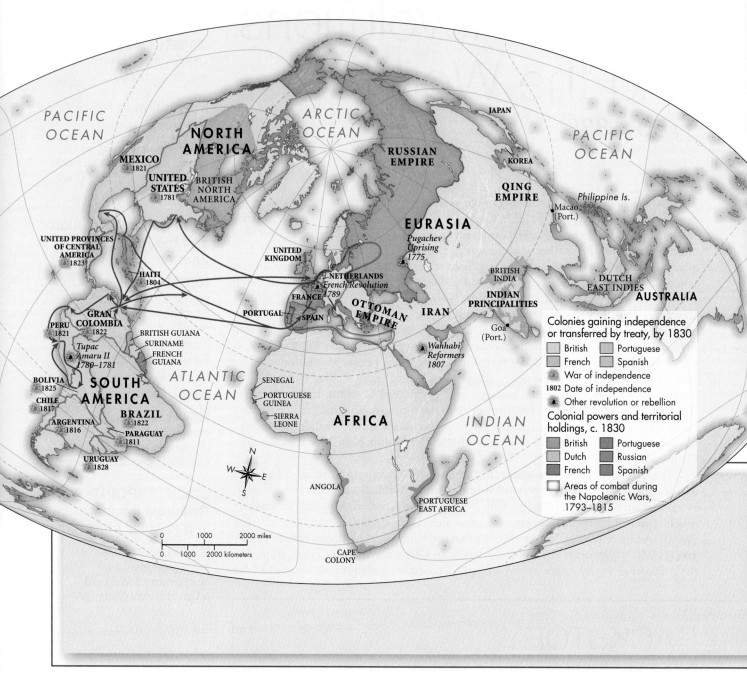

PACIFIC OCEAN

ARCTIC OCEAN

NORTH AMERICA

MEXICO
1821

UNITED STATES
1781

BRITISH NORTH AMERICA

RUSSIAN EMPIRE

JAPAN

KOREA

QING EMPIRE

PACIFIC OCEAN

Philippine Is.

Macao (Port.)

EURASIA

Pugachev Uprising 1775

UNITED PROVINCES OF CENTRAL AMERICA 1823

HAITI 1804

UNITED KINGDOM

NETHERLANDS
French Revolution 1789

FRANCE

PORTUGAL

SPAIN

OTTOMAN EMPIRE

IRAN

BRITISH INDIA

INDIAN PRINCIPALITIES

DUTCH EAST INDIES

AUSTRALIA

Goa (Port.)

PERU 1821

GRAN COLOMBIA 1822

Tupac Amaru II 1780–1781

BRITISH GUIANA
SURINAME
FRENCH GUIANA

ATLANTIC OCEAN

Wahhabi Reformers 1807

BOLIVIA 1825

CHILE 1817

ARGENTINA 1816

SOUTH AMERICA

BRAZIL 1822

PARAGUAY 1811

SENEGAL

PORTUGUESE GUINEA

SIERRA LEONE

AFRICA

INDIAN OCEAN

URUGUAY 1828

ANGOLA

CAPE COLONY

PORTUGUESE EAST AFRICA

N W E S

0   1000   2000 miles
0   1000   2000 kilometers

Colonies gaining independence or transferred by treaty, by 1830

British
French
Portuguese
Spanish

War of independence
1802 Date of independence
Other revolution or rebellion

Colonial powers and territorial holdings, c. 1830

British
Dutch
French
Portuguese
Russian
Spanish

Areas of combat during the Napoleonic Wars, 1793–1815

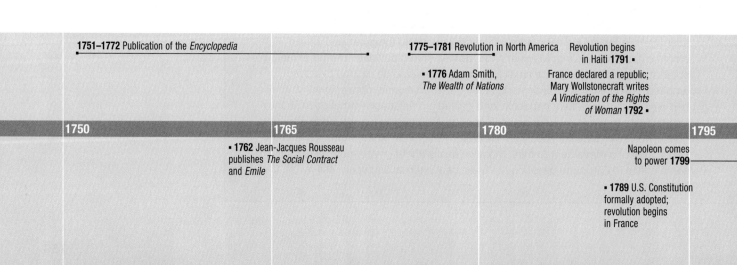

1751–1772 Publication of the *Encyclopedia*

1775–1781 Revolution in North America   Revolution begins in Haiti 1791

1776 Adam Smith, *The Wealth of Nations*

France declared a republic; Mary Wollstonecraft writes *A Vindication of the Rights of Woman* 1792

1750

1765

1762 Jean-Jacques Rousseau publishes *The Social Contract* and *Emile*

1780

1795

Napoleon comes to power 1799

1789 U.S. Constitution formally adopted; revolution begins in France

independent state of Haiti. The independence of Latin American states took longer to achieve, but it was globally inspirational. The English poet Lord Byron named his yacht *Bolivar* and in the 1820s went off to liberate Greece from the Ottomans.

These upheavals were connected with a transformation of thought and everyday life in the West called "the Enlightenment." Traders in Asia, Africa, and the Americas had brought ideas and goods to Europe. The arrival of new products such as sugar, coffee, and cotton textiles had freed many Europeans' lives from their former limits, and this new-found abundance led them to readjust their thinking. Wanting even greater wealth, they became discontented with the old order's regulation of trade and livelihoods. Both ordinary people and the upper classes proposed changing society, adding to the calls from Enlightenment thinkers whom the Scientific Revolution, the English Revolution, and global contact influenced to demand more rational government. Such ideas affected North American politicians, Caribbean activists, and creole reformers like Simon Bolivar, transforming them into revolutionaries. Thus, global trading connections played a key role both in creating the conditions that prompted the development of new ideas and in providing pathways for the spread of those ideas.

Indeed, the impulse for change extended far beyond the Atlantic world. In Ottoman-controlled Egypt, French revolutionary forces under the command of Napoleon Bonaparte invaded, claiming to bring new political ideas of liberty. A determined leader, Muhammad Ali, helped drive out the French and then promoted reform himself. As ideas of freedom took hold and as the increasingly ambitious Bonaparte decided to push into Russia, the old powers united to fight him. Long-established empires faced new, often grave challenges in this age of revolution and political change.

By 1830 the map of the world had changed, but that change came at a great cost. Alongside the birth of new nations and a growing belief in political reform, there had been widespread hardship and destruction. Soldiers died by the hundreds of thousands;

MAPPING THE WORLD
Wars and Revolutions in the Atlantic World, 1750–1830

Between 1775 and 1830 transplanted Europeans, their descendants, and their slaves and servants overwhelmed the Spanish, British, and French empires in the Western Hemisphere and created many independent nations. Europe and the Mediterranean also experienced revolutionary change as the ideas of just government and citizens' rights traveled the crossroads of the world and caused both transformation and turmoil.

ROUTES ▼

→ Voyages of Simon Bolivar, 1799–1816

→ Independence campaigns of Simon Bolivar, 1817–1825

- **1804** Haiti becomes independent from France
- **1822** Brazil becomes independent from Portugal
- **1815** Napoleon defeated at Waterloo; Congress of Vienna resettles the boundaries of European states

1810   **1825**   **1840**

- **1811** Simon Bolivar first takes up arms against Spain
- **1825** Bolivia becomes independent from Spain
- **1816** Argentina becomes independent from Spain
- **1817** Chile becomes independent from Spain
- **1821** Mexico and Peru become independent from Spain

civilians also perished because political and social change set them against one another. The breakdown of established kingdoms was the work of the warriors, the masses, and determined leaders, but this age of revolution crushed many. Napoleon Bonaparte was condemned to exile, and even so privileged a revolutionary as Bolivar died of utter exhaustion in 1830 just as the new nations of Latin America began their independent existence.

OVERVIEW
QUESTIONS

The major global development in this chapter: The Atlantic revolutions and their short- and long-term significance.

As you read, consider:

1. What role did the Scientific Revolution and expanding global contacts play in the cultural and social movement known as the Enlightenment?

2. Why did prosperous and poor people alike join revolutions in the Americas and in France?

3. Why were the Atlantic revolutions so influential, even to the present day?

The Promise of Enlightenment

FOCUS
What were the major ideas of the Enlightenment and their impacts?

Intense rethinking of society, politics, and the workings of the economy was under way in Europe in the eighteenth century, spurred by the Scientific Revolution's call for observation and rational thinking. Travelers' and missionaries' reports from the rest of the world provided ideas about alternative forms of government and social organization. Those reports added to the questioning—already under way in Europe—of beliefs in a uniform, God-given order in all states of the world. New global products such as brightly printed cottons, lacquered furniture, and porcelain raised the issue of where the European artisans learning to produce all these goods fit in a supposedly unchanging social structure. How the social and political order should change inspired lively conversation in salons and cafés as well as profound philosophical reflection in books and essays. Even monarchs began rethinking how the state should be run and their own role in government reform.

A New World of Ideas

Europeans in the eighteenth century had a great deal to think about. Science had challenged traditional views of nature and offered a new methodology for uncovering nature's laws. Changing techniques in agriculture and rising commerce led people to reflect on the meaning of greater abundance. Reports from around the world on foreign customs, ways of conducting government, and trade practices fueled intense discussion among Europeans. Moreover, participation in this intellectual ferment was not limited to the political and social elite. As literacy spread in Europe, ever more people were caught up in the debate over social, political, and economic change. These wide-ranging reconsiderations have come collectively to be called the Enlightenment.

contract government A political theory that views government as stemming from the people, who agree to surrender a measure of personal freedom in return for a government that guarantees protection of citizens' rights and property.

Some Enlightenment writers hammered away at the abuses of monarchies and proposed representative rule based on the consent of the governed that later became the foundation of many states. The will of a monarch is not the best basis for government, the English philosopher John Locke wrote late in the seventeenth century. Rather, he maintained, governments should be established rationally, by mutual consent of the governed. The idea of compact or **contract government** grew from Locke's philosophy that people were born free, equal, and rational, and that natural rights, including personal freedoms, were basic to all humans. In Locke's view, governments were formed when people made the rational choice to give up a measure of freedom and create institutions that could express the people's will, guarantee natural rights, and protect everyone's property. If a government failed to fulfill these purposes, it ceased to be legitimate and the people had the right to replace it. Locke's ideas had centered on the situation in England, where citizens and the Parliament had, over the course of the seventeenth century, twice ousted their king.

John Locke

In contrast to Locke, French writers Voltaire and Baron Louis Montesquieu criticized their own society's religious and political abuses by referring to the political situation elsewhere—in China and outside Europe. They conspicuously set their widely read writings in faraway lands or used wise foreigners as foils to show Europe's backwardness. A wealthy trained jurist, Montesquieu in *The Persian Letters* (1721) featured a Persian ruler visiting Europe and writing back home of the strange goings-on. The continent was full of magicians, Montesquieu's hero reports, such as those who could turn wine and wafers into flesh— a mocking reference to the Christian sacrament of communion. Voltaire, a successful author thrown several times into jail for insulting the authorities, portrayed worthy young men cruelly treated by their supposed betters, such as priests and kings, in his rollicking novels *Zadig* (1747) and *Candide* (1759). From a prosperous family, Voltaire asked for a society based on merit, not on aristocracy of birth: "There is nothing in Asia that resembles the European nobility: nowhere in the Orient does one find an order of citizens distinct from all the rest by their hereditary titles or by exemptions and privileges given them solely by their birth."[2] Voltaire did not have the story quite right, but other Enlightenment thinkers joined his call for reason, hard work, and opportunity in both economic life and politics.

Voltaire and Montesquieu

Swiss-born Jean-Jacques Rousseau took up the theme of freedom and opportunity in his many influential writings. In *The Social Contract* (1762) he claimed that "man is born free," but because of despotic government "he is everywhere in chains." Moving beyond the form of government to the process of shaping the modern citizen, Rousseau's bestselling novel *Emile* (1762) describes the ways in which a young boy is educated to develop many practical skills. Instead of learning through rote memory, as was common, Emile learns such skills as carpentry and medicine by actually working at them, and he spends much time outdoors, getting in touch with nature by living a simple life away from corrupt civilization. Like China's Kangxi monarch, whom Enlightenment thinkers held up as a model, Emile becomes a polymath, that is, someone with a knowledge of many subjects and numerous skills—in this case, artisanal and agricultural techniques that could earn him a livelihood. At the end of his apprenticeship in nature, Emile has become the responsible citizen who can fend for himself and regulate his movements according to natural laws, not despotically imposed ones.

Jean-Jacques Rousseau

Enlightenment thinkers also redesigned ideas about the economy. In 1776, Scottish philosopher Adam Smith published one of the most influential Enlightenment documents, *On the Wealth of Nations*. Citing China as an important example of how specialization of trades leads to prosperity, Smith proposed to free the economy from government monopolies and regulations. Merchants from South America to the Caribbean and Europe embraced the idea of freedom from mercantilist regulations that forced them to send goods exclusively through their national ports before trading them in other markets. This idea of **laissez faire** (French for "let alone") became part of the theory called **liberalism**, which endorsed economic and personal freedom guaranteed by the rule of law. Smith saw trade itself as benefiting an individual's character because it required cooperation with others in the process of exchanging goods. The virtues created by trade were more desirable

Adam Smith

laissez faire An economic doctrine that advocates freeing economies from government intervention and control.

liberalism A political ideology that emphasizes free trade, individual rights, and the rule of law to protect rights as the best means for promoting social and economic improvement.

than the military swaggering and roughness of aristocratic lives, and he continually stressed that alongside individualism there needed to be concern for the well-being of the community as a whole. Slavery, he argued, was inefficient and ought to be done away with. Still other Enlightenment writers said that a middle-class way of life promoted sensibility, love of family, thrift, and hard work—again, in stark contrast to the unfeeling, promiscuous, and spendthrift habits these reformers saw in the behavior of the nobility.

Spread of Enlightenment Thought

As we have seen, Enlightenment thinkers explicitly drew on the knowledge of the world beyond Europe that global economic connections had allowed them to acquire. Such connections also made it possible for Enlightenment ideas to spread around the world. Some Japanese thinkers and officials were so interested in new ideas that they began "Dutch Studies," referring to the body of European information brought in by Dutch traders. They wanted to learn about recent breakthroughs in practical subjects as well as scientific practices based on rational observation and deduction. Chinese scholars, though not directly influenced by Enlightenment thought, were reflecting on issues of good government and the capacities of the individual within the imperial system. In contrast, future nation builders in the North American colonies—Benjamin Franklin, John Adams, and Thomas Jefferson—were steeped in both the practical and political sides of the Enlightenment, running businesses, designing buildings, conducting scientific experiments, and writing political documents.

The Public Sphere

Enlightenment thought had an impact on all of Western society—high and low, male and female. Population growth in cities such as Paris strained traditional work patterns and neighborhoods, causing old social structures to weaken and new ideas to flourish. Another cause of change was the initiative of women of the wealthier classes, who conducted salons—that is, meetings in their homes devoted to discussing the most recent issues and publicizing the newest books and findings. German Jewish women, often kept at a distance from Christian society, made a name for themselves by forming such groups. Along with coffeehouses in European and colonial cities, modeled on those in the Ottoman Empire, salons created a **public sphere** in which people could meet outside court circles to talk about current affairs. Together with the new public libraries, reading groups, and a host of scientific clubs that dotted the Atlantic world, they built new community bonds and laid the groundwork for responsible citizenship. Instead of a monarchical government single-handedly determining public policy, ordinary people in Europe and its colonies, relying on knowledge gained from public discussion, could express their opinions on the course of events and thereby undermine government attempts at censorship and traditional ideas about society.

The ideals of the Enlightenment were well represented in the *Encyclopedia* (1751–1772) of France's Denis Diderot. The celebrated work highlighted the contributions of ordinary working people, particularly artisans, to the overall improvement of the human condition; it contained dozens of technical drawings of practical machinery that could advance prosperity. The *Encyclopedia* described the freedoms and rights nature endowed on *all* people, not just aristocrats or religious authorities. Like Rousseau, Diderot maintained that in a natural state all people were born free and equal. French writer Olympe de Gouges further proposed that there was no difference among people of different skin colors. "How are the Whites different from [the Black] race? . . . Why do blonds not claim superiority over brunettes?" she asked in her "Reflections on Negroes" (1788). "Like all the different types of animals, plants, and minerals that nature has produced, people's color also varies."[3] Essayists in the *Encyclopedia* added that women too were born free and endowed with natural rights.

Many of the working people of Europe's growing towns and cities responded enthusiastically to the ideas set forth by the leading philosophers of the Enlightenment, such as Voltaire and Rousseau. The French glassworker Jacques Ménétra, for example, acquired and also distributed these new antireligious and egalitarian ideas as he moved from city to town and village, installing glass windows. With some religious schooling and then an apprenticeship in his trade, Ménétra, like his fellow journeymen artisans, led this

public sphere A cultural and political environment that emerged during the Enlightenment, where members of society gathered to discuss issues of the day.

Eighteenth-Century English Drawing Room

When drinking their tea imported from Asia, middle- and upper-class Europeans aimed for elegance, inspired by Asian tea rituals. They used porcelain, whose production European manufacturers had recently figured out, and an array of new furnishings such as the tea table on display here. These English tea-takers are wearing sparkling white muslin, probably imported from India, which produced high-quality cloth that Europeans valued above cotton from anywhere else, including, as we will see in the next chapter, the new European industrial mills. (Private Collection/Bridgeman Art Library.)

kind of mobile life as a young man before establishing his own shop in Paris. During the course of his travels, he provided news of the Parisian thinkers to artisans along his route. In his autobiography—one of the few written by an ordinary European worker—he referred to Jean-Jacques Rousseau and gossiped about aristocrats. Young journeymen like Ménétra helped spread news of politics and current ideas before the coming of mass media, making the Enlightenment an affair not only of the well-born in salons but also of many average people.

Enlightenment and the Old Order

Despite its critique of monarchs, church officials, and the aristocracy, "Enlightenment" was a watchword of some of Europe's most powerful rulers. "Enlightened" rulers came to sense that more rational government could actually strengthen their regimes, for example by increasing governmental efficiency and increasing tax revenues. Thus, instead of touting his divine legacy, Prussian king Frederick the Great (r. 1740–1786) called a ruler someone who would "work efficiently for the good of the state" rather than "live in lazy luxury, enriching himself by the labor of the people."[4] A musician and poet, Frederick studied several languages, collected Chinese porcelain, and wrote librettos for operas, some of them about toleration. For him, Enlightenment made monarchs stronger. Spreading to Russia, the Enlightenment moved Catherine the Great (r. 1762–1796) to sponsor the writing of a dictionary of the Russian language, to correspond with learned thinkers such as Diderot, and to work to improve the education of girls. Additionally, Catherine's goal was to put a stop to aristocrats' "idle time spent in luxury and other vices corrupting to the morals," as she put it, and instead transform the nobility into active and informed administrators of her far-flung empire and its diverse peoples[5] (see Seeing the Past: Portrait of Catherine the Great).

The Spanish monarchy in the eighteenth century likewise instituted a series of policy changes called the Bourbon Reforms, so named because many of them aimed to make the monarchy—headed by the Bourbon dynasty—financially sound by taxing the colonies

Enlightened Rulers

SEEING THE PAST

Portrait of Catherine the Great

Catherine the Great as the Roman Goddess Minerva
(Hillwood Estate, Museum & Gardens; Photo by Ed Owen.)

Catherine the Great was a monarch of towering ability and ambition. Although her regime was known for smashing peasant uprisings, it also promoted the arts and knowledge. Even as her armies conquered some two hundred thousand square miles of territory and added it to the Russian Empire, Catherine commissioned the first dictionary of the Russian language and communicated with the greatest thinkers of the Enlightenment. While sponsoring education, she tried to reform her government to increase its power. In this regard, Enlightenment was not just about the fine arts but also about generally raising the economic and political profile of the monarchy through rationally devised policies.

Although Enlightenment thinkers often referred to the excellent customs and the rational policies of non-Western monarchs of their day—especially those in China—they also prized classical Greece and Rome for their democratic and republican forms of government. In this spirit of classical enthusiasm, monarchs were sometimes depicted as mythical figures, despite the often dark side to their regimes. For this image, a skilled Parisian craftsperson of the 1760s chose Minerva—Roman goddess of both war and wisdom—as the figure closest to the celebrated Catherine. The luxurious detail on this round box assures us that it was destined for an aristocratic palace, perhaps that of the monarch herself.

EXAMINING THE EVIDENCE

1. What does this depiction of the empress as Minerva tell you about the society over which Catherine ruled?

2. How does this image of leadership compare with others you have seen, including those of U.S. presidents? How do you account for the differences? For the similarities?

more efficiently. Following Enlightenment calls for rational and secular policies, Spain's rulers also attempted to limit the church's independence. Often opposing slavery and promoting better treatment of native peoples, the Jesuit order, for instance, had many followers in Spain's "New World" empire. Thus, the order was an alternate source of allegiance, and the monarchy outlawed it.

Leaders of the Spanish colonies adopted many Enlightenment ideas, including scientific farming and improvements in mining—both of them subjects dear to forward-looking thinkers who read publications such as the *Encyclopedia*. In Mexico, reformers saw the education of each woman as central to building responsible government. As one local journalist put it, under a mother's care the young citizen "grows, is nourished, and acquires his first notions of Good and Evil. [Therefore] women have even more reason to be enlightened than men."[6] In this view, motherhood was not a simple biological act but a livelihood critical to maintaining a strong national life.

Justification of Slavery   European prosperity depended on the productivity of slaves in the colonies, and wealthy slave owners used the Enlightenment fascination with nature to devise scientific explanations justifying the oppressive system. Though many Enlightenment thinkers such as Olympe de Gouges wanted equality for "noble savages," in slave owners' minds Africans were less than human and thus rightly subject to exploitation. Scientists captured Africans for study and came up with a list of their biological differences from whites and their similarities to animals, contributing to a sense of racial inferiority as a "scientific fact." Others justified race-based slavery in terms of character: blacks were, one British observer explained, "conceited, proud, indolent and very artful"—a rationale for harsh plantation discipline.[7] Thus, some strands of Enlightenment thought helped buyers and sellers of Africans and native Americans argue that slavery was useful and rational, especially because slaves could produce wealth and help society as a whole make progress.

Popular Revolts in an Age of Enlightenment

Pugachev Rebellion

Enlightened officials hoped to improve government at a time of popular uprising in many parts of the world. In Russia, people throughout society came to protest serfdom's irrationality and unfairness. One aristocrat believed that such unfairness "spread a plague in the hearts of the common people."[8] In 1773 the discontent of many serfs crystallized around Emel'ian Ivanovich Pugachev, once an officer in the Russian army, who claimed to be Peter III, the dead husband of Catherine. Tens of thousands of peasants, joined by rebellious workers, serf soldiers in Catherine's overworked armies, and Muslim minorities rose up, calling for the restoration of Pugachev, alias Peter, to the throne. Pugachev promised them great riches for their support. Serfs responded by plundering noble estates and killing aristocrats. They justified revolt in slogans and songs: "O woe to us slaves living for the masters. . . . how shameful and insulting / That another who is not worthy to be equal with us / Has so many of us in his power."[9] The rebellion was put down only with difficulty. Once Catherine's forces captured Pugachev, they cut off his arms and legs, then his head, and finally hacked his body to pieces—just punishment, nobles believed, for the crimes of this "monster" against the monarchy and upper classes.

Pugachev Uprising in Russia, 1773

Uprisings among the urban poor, farmworkers, and slaves also occurred in the Caribbean and other parts of the Western Hemisphere. Over the course of the eighteenth century the Latin American population grew rapidly and cities expanded. Rebels protested harsh conditions, which included their enslavement and only grew worse with Spain's demand for more revenue. Some native peoples envisioned the complete expulsion of the Spaniards or the overthrow of the wealthy creoles, who owned estates and plantations. Between 1780 and 1783, several different groups in Peru attempted to restore Inca power and end the increased burden of taxation under the Bourbon Reforms. The charismatic trader and wealthy landowner Tupac Amaru II (TOO-pack a-MAH-roo), an indigenous leader who took his name from the Inca leader of the late sixteenth century, led tens of thousands in the region of Tinta against corrupt local leadership and then against the administration of the region as a whole. Eventually captured by the authorities, Tupac Amaru II had his tongue cut out, was drawn and quartered by four horses, and was finally beheaded—after first watching the execution of most of his family. Rebellions continued nonetheless.

Latin American Uprisings

Revolution in North America

The Atlantic world was part of a global trading network. Thus, Europeans in North America, participating in global livelihoods as merchants, fishermen, and sailors, were exposed to ideas and goods from around the world. A Boston newspaper in the 1720s advertised the sale of Moroccan leather, Indian chintz and muslin fabrics, South American mahogany, and Asian tea. Sending out lumber, dried fish, tobacco, and furs, the British colonies grew prosperous and cosmopolitan, interesting themselves in all facets of the Enlightenment and commercial growth.

FOCUS

What factors lay behind the war between North American colonists and Great Britain?

Many enlightened North American colonists came to resent Britain's attempts to tax and rule them more efficiently, and people from various walks of life soon rebelled against what they saw as government contempt for their own rights as English people. Amid growing wealth and intellectual ferment, North American colonists along the Atlantic seaboard came to forge an independent nation—the future United States of America.

The British Empire and the Colonial Crisis 1764–1775

In the eighteenth century European states continued to wage increasingly costly wars for global trade and influence. Where governments were poorly run and taxes did not cover the huge military debt, as in the case of France, financial disaster loomed. The expense of the Seven Years' War of 1756–1763 was enormous as, for the first time in history, Europeans fought to gain influence in South Asia, the Philippines, the Caribbean, and North America. Ultimately beating both the French and the Spanish, Britain received all of French Canada and Florida at the end of the war (see Map 23.1). It hoped to boost colonial taxation to recoup its expenses and pay the costs of administering its empire.

Taxation Without Representation

In 1764 the British Parliament raised taxes on molasses with the Sugar Act, and in the following year it passed the Stamp Act, which taxed printed material and legal documents—all of them important to colonists' everyday lives. The Townshend Acts of 1767 put duties on other useful commodities, such as paper, glass, and paint, resulting in increasingly radical protests. Driven by England's own history of revolution and by the new political theories, some colonial activists insisted that if they were going to be taxed, they needed direct representation in the English Parliament, which they currently lacked. This argument followed Locke's theory of the social contract: a government where citizens were not represented had no right to take their property in taxes. With a literacy rate of 70 percent among men and 40 percent among women in the North American colonies—among the highest rates anywhere—new ideas about government and reports of British misdeeds spread rapidly, especially among townspeople.

The Birth of the United States 1775–1789

When yet another tax was placed on prized imported tea, a group of Bostonians, disguised as native Americans, dumped a load of tea into the harbor in December 1773. The British government responded to the "Boston Tea Party" by closing the seaport's thriving harbor, while colonial representatives gathered for an all-colony Continental Congress that resulted in a coordinated boycott of British goods.

U.S. Declaration of Independence

Tensions escalated. In April 1775 artisans and farmers in Lexington and Concord fought British troops sent to confiscate a stockpile of ammunition from rebellious colonists. On July 4, 1776, the Continental Congress issued its "Declaration of Independence," a short, dramatic document written largely by Thomas Jefferson that aimed—like the Enlightenment itself—to convert its readers to the side of reason in matters of government. The Declaration argued that the monarchy was tyrannical and had forfeited its right to rule. It went on to articulate an Enlightenment doctrine of rights—the famous rights of "life, liberty, and the pursuit of happiness." Some of the rebel colonists likened themselves to "slaves" lacking individual freedom, drawing a parallel—even though Declaration author Thomas Jefferson was himself a slave owner—with slave rebels across the Western world.

The War of Independence

The British sent a powerful army and navy to defeat the colonists. British forces burned coastal towns and occupied New York, Philadelphia, and other crucial centers of commerce and government. George Washington of Virginia headed the Continental Army. His forces suffered from lack of clothing, food, pay, and efficient recruiting. Yet the British deployed their larger armies in battle formation, whereas colonists were effective at guerrilla warfare, sniping at the invaders from behind trees and using bows and arrows if they lacked guns. Others joined in: colonial women fed armies in their vicinity, knitted and sewed clothing, and cared for the wounded. Critical help arrived from countries interested in blocking

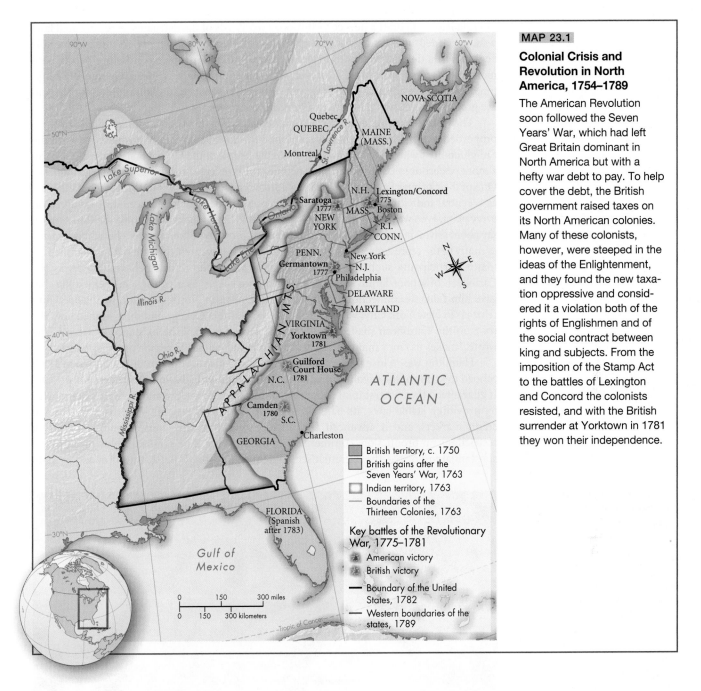

MAP 23.1

Colonial Crisis and Revolution in North America, 1754–1789

The American Revolution soon followed the Seven Years' War, which had left Great Britain dominant in North America but with a hefty war debt to pay. To help cover the debt, the British government raised taxes on its North American colonies. Many of these colonists, however, were steeped in the ideas of the Enlightenment, and they found the new taxation oppressive and considered it a violation both of the rights of Englishmen and of the social contract between king and subjects. From the imposition of the Stamp Act to the battles of Lexington and Concord the colonists resisted, and with the British surrender at Yorktown in 1781 they won their independence.

British expansionism, foremost among these France but also Spain and the Netherlands. Substantial assistance from the French under the Marquis de Lafayette ultimately brought the British down at Yorktown, where they surrendered their army in 1781 (see again Map 23.1).

Growing immigration had made the United States ethnically diverse well before its founding. Uprisings and disputes over trade and taxation followed the 1781 victory, showing that a strong **federation**, or union of states, was needed. The Articles of Confederation, drawn up in 1777 as a provisional constitution, however, proved weak because they gave the central government few powers. As the newly independent thirteen states pursued their own interests under the Articles of Confederation in the aftermath of the war, the "frail and tottering edifice [of the loosely aligned thirteen states] seems ready to fall upon our heads and crush us beneath its ruins," as Alexander Hamilton, Washington's trusted aide during the War of Independence, put it.[10] In 1787, a Constitutional Convention met

The U.S. Constitution

federation A union of equal and sovereign states rather than a thoroughly integrated nation.

in Philadelphia to draft a new constitution. Two-thirds of the delegates were educated lawyers, grounded intellectually in Enlightenment thought, but there were some of humble beginnings: a delegate from Connecticut had worked as a shoemaker before becoming a merchant, for example. Most, however, were men of property. Indeed, George Washington, who presided over the meeting, not only had a substantial plantation (like others in the group) but also was the owner of hundreds of slaves.

The Constitution reflected the broad understanding of just government shared by these propertied men. In it, the founders enshrined the contract theory of government from the Enlightenment with its opening words: "We the people of the United States in order to form a more perfect union." However, the document also reflected the authors' material interests. One of their primary motives in creating a strong government was to protect what they saw as a central individual right, the right to private property. The authors did not agree on every point, even when it came to private property. What, for example, should the Constitution say about slaves, individuals who were themselves property? Should slavery be acknowledged, as many of the representatives from the southern states wanted, or should it be abolished, as major participants such as Alexander Hamilton of New York believed? Born in the Caribbean of a poor family, Hamilton was a bookkeeper as a young teenager—a job that gave him valuable connections with merchant families in North America, who helped him relocate to New York City, where he attended Columbia College and then studied law. His roots in the Caribbean made him abhor the slave system. "The existence of slavery," he wrote, "makes us fancy many things that are founded neither in reason or experience."[11]

Hamilton was to lose this argument. The new Constitution, formally adopted in 1789, echoed the aims of the revolution and the rights of individuals—except slaves and women. It guaranteed the ownership of property and fostered commerce and the spirit of industry by providing stable laws. Its banking structure promised reliability in the international credit markets, and it advanced U.S. involvement with the global economy by lifting restrictions on production, commerce, and business life. The political rights given to the substantial minority—the enfranchised white men—by the U.S. Constitution and by state

Samuel Jennings, *Liberty Displaying the Arts and Sciences* (1792)

Enlightenment writers debated whether the ideals of liberty and equality should apply to everyone regardless of race, condition of servitude, and gender. This painting, commissioned early in U.S. history to urge the abolition of slavery, shows Liberty with the Cap of Liberty on a staff next to her; she is displaying Enlightenment accomplishments in the arts and sciences to freed slaves. Although in the United States and elsewhere Liberty was usually depicted as a woman, the principles of equal citizenship expressed in the Constitution and the Declaration of Independence did not apply to most women, African Americans, or native Americans. (The Library Company of Philadelphia.)

law inspired this burst of activity, innovation, and enterprise. To achieve the Constitution, the founders, as men of the Enlightenment, negotiated, made concessions, and came to hard-fought agreements. The U.S. Constitution thus became a monument to consensus politics and to the form of government called a **republic**. When the heated disputes were over and the Constitution finally framed, George Washington wrote to the Marquis de Lafayette in France that achieving the document was "little short of a miracle."

The French Revolution and the Napoleonic Empire

In 1780, on the eve of victory in its War of Independence, the fledgling United States had only about 2.7 million people, but its triumph had a powerful impact on the far larger population in Europe. "The [French] nation has been awakened by our revolution," Ambassador Thomas Jefferson wrote in 1788 to President George Washington, "they feel their strength, they are enlightened."[12] More directly, the cost of French participation in global warfare with Britain, including the North American War of Independence, hastened the collapse of the monarchy. France's taxation policy put the cost of warfare on the poor and exempted the wealthy from paying their share. In 1789, less than a decade after the victory at Yorktown, the French people took matters into their own hands, ultimately ousting the king and launching a republic. The French Revolution resonated far and wide, and under the French conqueror Napoleon Bonaparte, revolutionary principles advanced across Europe and beyond, even as Europe's monarchs struggled to halt the march of "liberty, equality, fraternity."

> **FOCUS**
>
> What changes emerged from the French Revolution and Napoleon's reign?

From Monarchy to Republic 1789–1792

Having borrowed recklessly (as had his predecessors) to pursue wars and princely living, the French monarch Louis XVI (r. 1774–1793) in 1787 met with a firm "no" when he asked for more loans from bankers and financial help from the aristocracy. The king was forced to summon the Estates General—a representative body that had not met since 1614—to the royal palace at Versailles to bail out the government. Members of the Estates General arrived at their meeting in May 1789, carrying lists of grievances from people of all occupations and walks of life, who had met in local gatherings across France to help representatives prepare for their momentous assembly.

There were several competing agendas at the meeting of the Estates General: those of the monarchy to repair its finances; those of the nobility to take power from the king; and those of the common people, who at the time were suffering from crop failures, heavy taxation, governmental restraints on trade, and a slowdown in business because of bad harvests. The meeting quickly broke down when representatives of the middle classes and common people left the general meeting. They were joined by sympathetic, reform-minded aristocrats and clergymen such as Abbé Sieyès, who asked what this mass of commoners meant to the kingdom. "Everything," he responded to his own question. "What has it been until now in the political order? Nothing."[13] These representatives declared themselves a National Assembly of "citizens" of France, not the lowly subjects of a king. The National Assembly included the lawyers and officials who had represented most of the people in 1789 as well as reform-minded deputies from the clergy and a substantial number of nobles.

Formation of the National Assembly

Soon much of France was overwhelmed by enthusiasm for this new government based on citizen consent. On July 14, 1789, crowds in Paris stormed the Bastille, a notorious prison where people could be incarcerated simply at the king's orders. The liberation of the Bastille by the people of Paris so symbolized the French Revolution that it became France's national holiday, just as the Declaration of Independence on July 4 eventually made that Independence Day in the United States.

Storming of the Bastille

republic A political system in which the interests of all citizens are represented in the government.

Declaration of the Rights of Man and of the Citizen

In its first years, the revolution was shaped by Enlightenment principles. Strong citizen protest also motivated the legislators of the National Assembly, who like U.S. revolutionary leaders were mostly from the propertied classes. With peasants rioting in the countryside against the unfair rule of aristocratic landowners, in August 1789 the nobility surrendered its privileges, such as its exemption from taxation. Later that month the National Assembly issued the "Declaration of the Rights of Man and of the Citizen," a stirring announcement of the basic rights possessed by each new citizen, including rights to free speech, to own property, and to be safe from arbitrary acts of the state. Soon, Olympe de Gouges would issue her own "Declaration of the Rights of Woman and the Female Citizen," declaring, "Woman is born free and lives equal to man in her rights."

Power to the People

In October 1789, the market women of Paris, protesting the soaring cost of food, marched to the palace of Versailles twelve miles away and captured the royal family, bringing it to live "with the people" in the city. In so doing, they showed that monarchs existed to serve the people—and that kings ignored this fact at their own peril. The government passed laws reducing the power of the clergy and abolishing the guild system and other institutions that would restrain trade. Suddenly people could pursue the jobs they wanted on their own terms outside guild restrictions. The liberal Enlightenment program of freedom for the person and for trade and property was now accomplished, pushed by enthusiastic demonstrations by newly empowered citizens.

These early acts of the French Revolution stirred the hearts and minds of many. Women petitioned for a range of rights, and for a time the power of the husband over his

Women's March to Versailles

Although the French Revolution began with the ceremonial meeting of the Estates General in May 1789, people from many walks of life soon became directly involved in the drive for fundamental change. That October, after the people of Paris had liberated the notorious Bastille prison, the market women of the city marched to the royal palace at Versailles. Joined by men who came from Paris to reinforce them, they captured the king and his family. This engraving shows the crowds escorting the monarch back to the city of Paris, where they could keep an eye on him. (The Art Archive/Marc Charmet.)

wife was eliminated. Across the English Channel, poet William Wordsworth captured the rush of youthful belief that through newly active citizens the world would be reborn: "Bliss was it in that dawn to be alive, / But to be young was very heaven!" The Declaration of the Rights of Man and of the Citizen inspired the addition of a Bill of Rights to the U.S. Constitution, which outlined the essential rights, such as freedom of speech, that the government could never overturn. English author Mary Wollstonecraft penned *A Vindication of the Rights of Man* (1790) in defense of the revolution.

Two years later Wollstonecraft wrote *A Vindication of the Rights of Woman*, a globally influential work that saw men's privileges over women as similar to the French aristocracy's privileges over the peasantry. Current laws in Britain made men into a privileged aristocracy that took women's property and wages on marriage, thus denying women their rights. Wollstonecraft knew all this from bitter experience. Born into a well-to-do family, her brother not only inherited most of the family estate but also confiscated his sisters' inheritances for himself. Destitute, they had to earn a living without having been trained to do so. Wollstonecraft first became a governess and then a journalist, whose classic works protested that the legal privileges of men allowed them to impoverish women.

Mary Wollstonecraft

War, Terror, and Resistance 1792–1799

As revolutionary fervor spread across national borders, the monarchs and nobility of Europe scrambled to survive. In the spring of 1792 the royal houses of Austria and Prussia declared war on France. Wartime brought to power the lawyer Maximilien Robespierre, leader in the popular Jacobin club, a political group that hoped to sweep away all institutions from the oppressive past. In the face of total defeat by Austria and Prussia and the counterrevolutionary efforts of Louis XVI, Robespierre and other politicians became convinced that it was time to do away with the monarchy, that the nation had to become a republic if the revolution were to survive. Patriotic holidays to replace religious ones, dishes with revolutionary slogans, an entirely new calendar, and new laws making the family more egalitarian turned the country upside down. Workshops were set up for the unemployed to earn a living by making war goods, and all citizens were urged to give their energy to help the war effort. In 1793 both King Louis XVI and Queen Marie Antoinette were executed by guillotine—an "enlightened" mode of execution because it killed swiftly and reduced suffering. France stood on the threshold of total transformation.

War Against France and Execution of the King

Claiming that there could be no rights in wartime, Robespierre and the newly created Committee of Public Safety stamped out free speech, squashed the various women's clubs that had sprung up to gain the rights of citizenship, and executed people such as Olympe de Gouges whom they judged to be traitors to the republic. This was the Terror, during which the government murdered people from all classes and livelihoods—from the highest to the lowest—because enemies of the republic, the government claimed, lurked on all rungs of the social ladder. To justify its actions, the Committee of Public Safety turned to Rousseau's idea of the **general will**. Rousseau's unique interpretation of the social contract maintained that once agreement among citizens had created a state, that state acted with a higher wisdom with which truly loyal citizens could not disagree, especially in wartime. The "general will" justified the Terror's mass executions and the suspension of individual rights and even free thought. The concept was one of the French Revolution's most powerful revolutionary legacies, enacted not only by totalitarian regimes in the twentieth century but even by democracies during times of stress.

The Terror

By 1794, largely because the war was turning in France's favor, moderate and propertied politicians were able to regain public support and overthrew Robespierre and the Committee of Public Safety. At the same time, France's revolutionary armies went on the offensive, taking the idea of rights, constitutions, and republicanism to countries such as Austria that had tried to stop the revolution. French pride, based on a belief in the superiority of a republican form of government and full, equal citizenship for men, blossomed,

general will The political concept that once agreement among citizens creates a state, that state is endowed with a higher wisdom about policies with which virtuous citizens could not disagree.

especially among citizen-soldiers who found upward mobility in the revolutionary army. No one took more advantage of this opportunity than a newly minted officer, the young Napoleon Bonaparte (1769–1821).

Napoleon's Reign 1799–1815

Napoleon's Rise to Power

Napoleon Bonaparte, born into a modest Corsican family, became commander in chief of the French revolutionary army in Italy at the age of twenty-seven. A student of Enlightenment thought and an avid reader of history throughout his life, Napoleon had the good fortune to enter the army just as its aristocratic officers were fleeing the revolution in France by moving to other countries. Rising to power through the ranks, he attempted the conquest of Egypt in 1798 but escaped the country as he began to lose the campaign. He returned to France months later, in 1799. There he used the uncertain political scene to establish himself first as co-consul and then, in 1804, as emperor. "As in Rome, it took a dictator to save the Republic,"[14] Napoleon said of the repression that followed his takeover. He reconciled France with the Catholic Church and even called back to his court some of the exiled aristocracy to help add grandeur to his regime.

The Napoleonic Code

Yet Napoleon solidified many revolutionary changes, notably those concerning citizenship and the right to private property, as outlined in the Code Napoleon (1803–1804), a new set of basic laws. The Code set rules for property, ending restrictions on sales of the nobility's land and establishing rules for assets such as bonds, stocks, and mortgages. The Code thus advanced prosperity by providing secure laws for commercial, industrial, and agricultural livelihoods; Napoleon's founding of national schools for teachers, engineers, and the military served this end too. In the realm of family law, however, the Code reversed gains made by women during the revolution by making the wages and other property of married women the legal property of their husbands, by forbidding them to appear as witnesses in court, and by not allowing them to be guardians of their own children. Financial impoverishment gave women no choices in life but to remain loyal wives—principles that Napoleon's triumphant armies spread through Europe and that encouraged imitators around the world. Instead of respecting the equality of women suggested by some Enlightenment thinkers, Napoleon enforced Rousseau's idea that women should raise the next generation of citizens but not be equal citizens themselves.

Napoleon's Military Campaigns

Maintaining his grip by keeping the nation at war and plundering other countries, Napoleon launched a series of successful wars against Spain, the German states, and Italy (see Map 23.2). Then, in 1812, he made a disastrous attempt to invade and conquer Russia. The Russian army, the Russian people, and deadly winter conditions combined to deal Napoleon a catastrophic defeat. After that, a coalition of German, Russian, Austrian, and British forces defeated Napoleon twice more, once in Paris in 1814 and then, in a victory that crushed Napoleon's forces, at Waterloo in 1815.

Congress of Vienna

At the Congress of Vienna (1814–1815), the coalition resettled the boundaries of European states. In doing so, many of Europe's rulers sought to overturn revolutionary and Napoleonic reforms to restore their old regimes. It was far too late to stamp out the principles of constitutional government and natural rights, however. Although monarchs (including France's) were restored to their thrones in 1815, there were now limitations on their powers. Moreover, Napoleon's military campaigns, which spread principles of rights and citizenship, ensured the continuation of these new values in people's minds and helped upset power arrangements around the world.

Muhammad Ali and the Revolutionary Spirit in Egypt

Despite Napoleon's ultimate defeat, the revolutionary legacy fomented reform activity for more rational government not only across Europe but also outside it. When the French revolutionary armies under Napoleon invaded Egypt in 1798, they faced the forces of the Ottoman Empire, whose administration, like that of other great land-based empires, was in decline. From time to time a modernizing sultan came to power hoping to enact reforms. The entrenched powers of the janissaries (elite troops) and ulamas (Muslim authorities), however, usually put a stop to such efforts. The similarly entrenched Mamluk (MAM-luke) military force that ran the Egyptian government increasingly alienated land-lords and other elites with its demands for more taxes.

Napoleon and Egypt

MAP 23.2 **Napoleonic Europe, 1796–1815**

Under Napoleon the military scene across Europe was tumultuous and bloody until 1815, when the allied forces of Austria, Prussia, Russia, and Great Britain finally defeated the French emperor's "Grand Army." French forces brought revolutionary ideas and aroused national feeling. Like many empires, Napoleon's suffered from overreach; after its defeat, the victors redrew the political map of Europe to ensure a balance of power across the continent.

Napoleon Celebrates the Birthday of Muhammad

Napoleon's invasion of Egypt simultaneously brutalized and tried to accommodate Egyptians. The French army ransacked homes and public buildings, but Napoleon himself made sympathetic gestures such as the celebration in 1799 of the birth of the Prophet Muhammad depicted here. Though they labeled the French as hypocrites, some Egyptians welcomed the books and scientific drawings Napoleon made available to them in the name of Enlightenment. (Private Collection/Roger-Viollet, Paris/ Bridgeman Art Library.)

To some among these elites, the Atlantic revolutions provided a wealth of ideas for reform. Napoleon entered the country not only accompanied by a huge team of doctors, artists, scientists, and other learned men, but also armed with proposals for more enlightened rule. Amid combined resistance from the Mamluks, Ottomans, and British, who aimed to stop the French, Napoleon and the French army departed Egypt. Nonetheless, they left behind rising interest in European ideas, political innovation, and technology. No one was a better student and imitator than Muhammad Ali, often called the founder of modern Egypt.

Muhammad Ali   An officer in the Ottoman forces, Muhammad Ali had worked his way up the military ranks during the anti-French campaign. Born in the Ottoman Balkans (present-day Albania), Muhammad Ali began his career as a merchant before the Ottoman army drafted him as part of the Albanian quota of young men owed to the Ottomans. Muhammad Ali's rise to power was based on military accomplishments, but also on the negotiating skills he learned as a merchant. As a politician he exchanged favors with ordinary people and persuaded wealthy traders and soldiers alike to support his ouster of the hated Mamluks.

Appointed viceroy in 1805, Muhammad Ali set out to modernize Egypt, hiring French and other European administrators, technicians, and military men to advise him. Illiterate until he was forty-seven, he had many works translated into Arabic, the translations being read to him as they progressed. One major work, a translation of Italian political theorist Machiavelli's *The Prince*, he cut short because the message was "commonplace," Muhammad Ali reportedly announced. "I see clearly that I have nothing to learn from Machiavelli. I know many more tricks than he knew."[15] He advanced economic specialization in the country, sponsoring the large-scale production of cotton by several hundred thousand slaves while discouraging agriculture that was not for the market. Centralization of government, founding of public schools, improvement of transportation, and tighter bureaucratic control of Islam rounded out Muhammad Ali's reforms. His death in 1849 left his dream to make Egypt fully independent of the Ottomans unfulfilled, but like Napoleon he proved successful in applying the rational programs of the age.

Revolution Continued in the Western Hemisphere

Such was the strength of late eighteenth-century global contacts that news of the French and American revolutions quickly spread to other parts of the Atlantic world. In the Western Hemisphere, revolutions broke out on the island of Hispaniola, motivating slave revolts elsewhere and arousing fear among whites. In Latin America, rebellion erupted not only among slaves and oppressed workers but also among middle- and upper-class creoles such as Simon Bolivar who wanted independence from Spain and Portugal. The Napoleonic Wars disturbed global trade, adding further to discontent and swelling the calls for political change. Soon concerted uprisings of peoples—rich, working-class, free peasants, and slaves—rose to fight for freedom in the Caribbean and across Latin America.

> **FOCUS**
>
> What were the motives and methods of revolutionaries in the Caribbean and Latin America?

Revolution in Haiti 1791–1804

News of the French Revolution spread to the Caribbean island of Hispaniola, where the sugar plantations and coffee farms enriched merchants, plantation owners, and sugar refiners—whites and free blacks alike. The western part of the island was the French colony of Saint-Domingue (san-doe-MANGH, modern Haiti). The eastern part of Hispaniola was Santo Domingo (modern Dominican Republic), a colony of Spain. Saint-Domingue was the wealthiest colony in the region, in part because the newly independent United States could now purchase sugar from French rather than British plantations, and it did so from Saint-Domingue. This thriving trade inspired investors and merchants in France to pour vast sums into expanding production there.

As we saw in Chapter 22, Caribbean slaves lived under inhumane conditions. The hot, humid climate made laborious work punishing and kept their life span short. Some committed suicide; women used plant medicines to induce abortions and prevent bearing children who would live in misery. Slaves also developed community bonds to sustain them. The spirit of community and resistance arose from the daily trade of vegetables grown by the slaves in their small garden plots, from the use of a common language made up of French and various African dialects, and from joint participation in Vodou—a religious tradition observed by slaves on the islands.

Solidarity and suffering made the Caribbean ripe for revolution. Slave uprisings took place regularly, and individual slaves escaped into the forests and hills to create new communities of independent people, as they did across the Hispanic world. Added to this, the Caribbean—like the entire Atlantic region—was a crossroads of ideas. Among those ideas were freedom and human rights, circulating not only among African and North American slaves but also among the several thousand free blacks and mulattos in Haiti, who constituted some 30 percent of the slave owners in the region. When their white counterparts passed legislation putting them at political and economic disadvantage despite their success as plantation owners and traders, these free blacks founded the Society for Friends of the Blacks in 1788 and used it to lobby enlightened politicians in Paris for equality. When the French Revolution broke out in 1789, their demands grew louder. "You must return to these oppressed citizens," a group of free blacks entreated the National Assembly in October 1789, "the rights that have been unjustly stripped from them." In the face of continuing white hostility, they became, as one free black put it in 1790, "more committed than ever to uphold [our rights] with the last drop of our blood."[16]

The slaves were roused by news of revolution too. Rumors that French revolutionaries had freed them spread among the slaves, and in 1791 an organized slave uprising erupted in Saint-Domingue (see Map 23.3). From a cluster of leaders, the free black Pierre-Dominique Toussaint Louverture (too-SAN loo-ver-CHURE) emerged as the most able military commander. The slave revolt moved from success to success, and an enthusiastic French official sent to calm the scene did quite the opposite of what the planters wanted: he issued

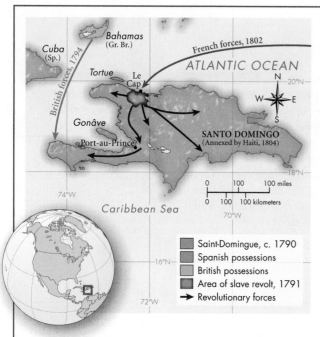

MAP 23.3   **Haitian Rebellion and Independence, 1791–1804**

The French colony of Saint-Domingue was a global crossroads for the sale of slaves and the sugar they produced. Commerce brought with it the flow of new ideas from around the world, whereas slavery produced not only grievances but solidarity. Even free blacks faced racism, and the Enlightenment ideas of human rights and dignity inspired them to protest. Soon after the French Revolution broke out in 1789, slaves in Saint-Domingue revolted and ultimately declared themselves the independent nation of Haiti.

Impact of the Napoleonic Wars

junta A ruling council.

a proclamation in 1793 granting slaves their freedom. In 1794, against the wishes of plantation owners and merchants—both black and white—the French revolutionary government formally declared that blacks had rights equal to those of whites. This news quickly passed across the Caribbean and Latin America, sparking further uprisings and rebellions against European rulers.

Conditions in Saint-Domingue evolved rapidly as Toussaint, himself a former slave and one grateful to France for its support of black equality, joined the French in driving back the British and Spanish, who hoped to conquer the French portion of the island for themselves. The black plantation owners refused to cooperate politically or economically with ex-slaves, and civil war broke out. In 1800 Toussaint defeated them too and issued a series of stiff reforms. Although slaves were free, they were to return to the sugar plantations, Toussaint legislated, and for their work they would receive a quarter of the profit from sugar production. The owners would receive another fourth, and the government would receive half.

By this time, however, Napoleon had come to power in France. Answering the appeal of Saint-Domingue plantation owners—who wanted far more profit than 25 percent—he determined to "pursue the rebels without mercy [and] flush them out," thereby regaining the upper hand in the colony.[17] The campaign led to the capture of Toussaint, who died in jail in 1803. With all blacks now uniting against any French takeover, however, the invading army suffered huge losses—some 50,000 of an army of 58,000—many of them from yellow fever. On January 1, 1804, the black generals who defeated the French proclaimed the independent republic of Haiti.

Revolutions in Latin America 1810–1830

The thirst for change gripped people in other empires. In Spain's Latin American empire discontent among artisans, agricultural workers, and slaves, along with rivalries among creoles and Spanish-born officials sent from the homeland, erupted under the pressures of the Napoleonic conquest of the Iberian peninsula in 1808. "It is now time to overthrow the [Spanish] yoke," a group of rebels in La Paz declared in 1809. "It is now time to declare the principle of liberty in these miserable colonies."[18] This spirit swept the Spanish lands, as the government back home in Europe crumbled.

When Napoleon invaded Spain and Portugal in 1807, he sent the ruling dynasties packing to give his own family control. With British help, the Portuguese monarch fled to Brazil in hopes of ruling the empire from the colonies, while in Spain the monarch was replaced by Napoleon's brother Joseph. Guerrilla warfare erupted against the French while Spanish activists also organized **juntas** (HUN-tahs), or ruling councils, around the country despite French rule. In 1808, a national junta unveiled a broad program for reform. In the Spanish colonies, political confusion set in as news of the junta's plan for a constitution-based government spread. Some creole leaders welcomed the planned constitution, but other creoles in business and agriculture sensed an opportunity not simply for constitutional reform but for ousting officials from Spain altogether. Like imperial rulers elsewhere, the Spanish kings had come to treat their colonies as cash cows, milking them dry to pay for a lavish way of life in Europe. In the disorder brought on by the Napoleonic invasions and the appearance of reform-minded leaders in Spain, colonial leaders saw an opportunity to end these heavy burdens.

The Napoleonic Wars opened up other avenues to economic and political change. Because Spain was allied with Britain in the wars against Napoleon, the people in the Spanish colonies had new contacts and new economic opportunities. Like Britain, Spain had formerly tried to prevent its colonies from manufacturing their own goods or trading directly with other countries. All goods were to be carried in Spanish vessels. Trade-minded local creoles resented these restrictions, as well as the privileged place of Spanish traders and the monopoly on good jobs enjoyed by Spanish aristocrats. The wars upset this state of affairs, throwing open ports to British vessels carrying both new ideas and exciting new products—both of them benefits of unrestricted trade. Mule drivers, parish priests, and market people also spread global news, alerting neighborhoods in distant towns to the possibility for change. Aspiring leaders saw a situation full of potential for new prosperity and freedom. Their struggles for independence would last until 1830 (see Map 23.4).

Reformers and rebels sprang into action throughout Latin America. In the lucrative colony of Mexico, Father Miguel Hidalgo, a Mexican priest trained in Enlightenment thought by the Jesuits and exiled by the Spanish to a rural parish because of his ideas, opened a campaign against colonial rule in 1810. His soldiers were his parishioners, most of them native Americans who worked as day laborers for the Spanish and creoles. The collapse of silver mining and the soaring prices of food made them desperate. Calling for the complete ouster of Spaniards, they wanted their jobs and their standard of living restored. Hidalgo's army swelled to some sixty thousand fighters, who hoped to get paid or fed as they fought. Drawn from the popular classes, the average fighter, in the opinion of the Mexican viceroy, was a "robber, assassin, and libertine."[19] Yet most of Hidalgo's followers were motivated by simple outrage at the poverty and oppression they faced—not by robbery or lust. They slaughtered entire contingents of Spaniards, creoles, and anyone else who stood in their path.

Father Hidalgo was captured and executed in 1811, but other armies appeared under the leadership of mulattos, mestizos (mixed-blood people of native American and European ancestry), and well-born creoles, who wanted the Spanish out and opportunity reborn. These armies—most notably that under the humbly born mestizo priest, Father José Maria Morelos—carried the uprising to the west of Mexico, using guerrilla tactics and living off the support of legions of women, who provisioned and tended the troops. The Spanish, however, were able to turn other native Americans, slaves, and mestizos against creole-led armies by pointing out that creoles owned the exploitative large farms. By 1815 the Spanish had put an end to this first stage of the Mexican drive for independence and had executed its leaders—adding to the hatred of colonialism that many felt.

Amid ongoing attacks from bandits and personal armies, new leadership emerged in Mexico, one that was more capable of victory. The key to its success lay in creoles' efforts to set aside their prejudices to unite with the native masses. Creoles adopted a nationalist sensibility, accepting the idea to distinguish *all* those inhabitants of Mexico born in the New World—the *Americanos*—from those born in Spain. Continued guerrilla fighting eroded the institutions of Spanish rule in Mexico, but the decisive move came when the creole leader Augustin de Iturbide (ee-tur-BEE-deh) allied his forces with Vicente Guerrero (goo-RER-eh), a leader of the popular armies, himself a mestizo and thus heir to the

Toussaint Louverture

In 1791, Toussaint Louverture, a freed slave and slave owner, joined a slave revolt that erupted in Saint-Domingue, the prosperous sugar colony of France in the Caribbean. Louverture, shown here in his general's uniform, possessed strong military skills and soon became the leader of the Haitian Revolution, writing the constitution of the fledgling nation and working to defeat the Spanish, British, and French, who in turn sought to take the former colony for themselves. Ironically, although he modeled his new nation on French ideals of freedom and citizenship, Louverture re-enslaved many Haitians. He died in a French prison in 1803. (Private Collection/Bridgeman Art Library.)

MAP 23.4

Revolutions in Latin America, 1810–1830

The Spanish government, influenced by Enlightenment ideas about rational government, attempted to streamline its rule and enhance colonial profitability. As revolution rolled across the Atlantic world, colonial subjects in Latin America were equally affected by Enlightenment ideas about liberty and the opportunities it would bring. Revolutions in Latin America were prolonged, however, and they were wide-ranging, bringing in people from many walks of life and ethnicities as well as soldiers from different parts of the world—all motivated by the potential for revolutionary transformation.

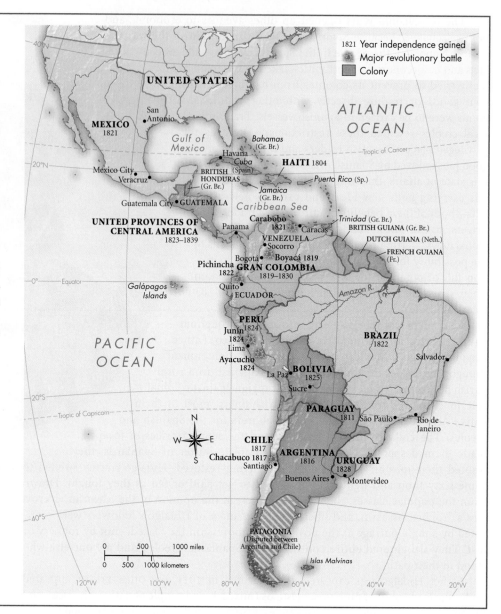

Independence for Mexico

Morelos legacy of native rights. Iturbide had once served the Spanish as an army officer, winning battles and collecting tribute for the government. As was so often the case, his creole birth blocked his advance in the Spanish colony, despite his record. Resentment of unearned Spanish privilege made him a natural ally of people who were also held back by what the Spanish saw as low birth—native American, black, mestizo, or mulatto. Iturbide's and Guerrero's forces reached an agreement for a constitutional monarchy independent of Spain. In 1821, the three hundredth anniversary of the Spanish conquest of Mexico, Iturbide entered Mexico City as Spanish rule disintegrated. Yet it was not this event but rather the start of Father Hidalgo's uprising of the common people on September 16, 1810 that came to mark Mexico's Day of Independence.

Across South America similar independent rebel armies sprang up, most of them controlled by a local strongman, or *caudillo* (kauh-DEE-yoh), who was able to raise armies from people of all classes and ethnicities. Such a caudillo was José Gervasio Artigas in Uruguay. Artigas was a rancher, cattle thief, and, by virtue of having his own army, a regional peacekeeper. While keeping peace locally, the *caudillos* had as many problems getting along with one another as they did enduring Spanish rule. One quality these creoles shared, however, was their contempt for native Americans, Africans, mulattos, and mestizos. Simon Bolivar mustered caudillo support to liberate Venezuela in 1811, but at the time he firmly believed that slavery could be maintained in the fight for national independence.

Nonetheless, with the Spanish monarch's return to power after the defeat of Napoleon in 1815, it became clear that creoles in Latin America needed to ally themselves with oppressed workers, agricultural laborers, and the *llaneros* (yah-NEH-rows), or local cowboys, of all races (see Lives and Livelihoods: The Cowboy Way of Life). Bolivar made himself one with the llaneros, demonstrating that his troops were militarily fit and daring riders; he called for the forging of a Gran Colombia—a united nation like the United States, composed of all the liberated lands. To create such a state, the foreign-born Spanish must be ousted for good. Increasing Spanish oppression and the appeal to all "Americans" did some good, enabling Bolivar, with the help of black troops, to take Bogotá, Caracas, and Quito by 1822. In the meantime Argentinean general José de San Martin was conquering Buenos Aires, western Argentina, and Chile, moving into Peru in 1818. His armies bogged down in Peru, however, leaving the final task of ousting the Spanish to Bolivar, whose armies finally took Lima in 1823 and upper Peru or Bolivia in 1825 (see again Map 23.4). Both San Martin and Bolivar had originally seen no conflict between their own freedom and the existence of slavery, but as the need for slave support became obvious, Bolivar declared it "madness that a revolution for liberty should try to maintain slavery."[20] To get the support of the vast number of slaves, many liberation leaders promised and awarded slave soldiers their emancipation, either immediately as a way of attracting fighters or after the wars as a reward for victory.

Independence for Peru

Brazil gained its independence from Portugal more tranquilly than the Spanish colonies did from Spain, and with little change in the social situation: slavery and the bureaucracy alike were left intact. The ruling family, safe in Brazil, was summoned back to Portugal at the end of the Napoleonic Wars, but the king left his son Pedro behind in the capital of Rio de Janeiro. Pedro proceeded to cooperate with business and other leaders and in 1822 declared Brazil independent of Portugal and made himself king. With the masses set

Independence for Brazil

Upper-Class Woman and Her Slaves in Eighteenth-Century Brazil
Many aristocrats and wealthy landowners in prerevolutionary South America followed European customs in such matters as display of class privileges. For instance, in Europe servants wore uniforms or livery, as do these slaves as they carry their upper-class mistress in a sedan chair and follow her on foot. Aristocratic status was often evident in the number of people accompanying a noble person, but these slaves also show the variety in slave livelihoods. (J. Bedmar/Iberfoto/The Image Works.)

The Cowboy Way of Life

Gauchos

Gauchos lived away from towns, cities, and settled ranches. Like cowboys, their North American counterparts, gauchos prided themselves on a range of skills with wild horses and other animals. In this nineteenth-century colored etching, a gaucho hurls a rope with a ball on its end to capture a rhea by entangling its legs in the rope. As South America developed commerce, manufacturing, and modern industry, the gaucho came to symbolize the independent spirit of the young nations. (akg-images.)

One of the most important livelihoods in the Western Hemisphere was that of cowboys or cattle hunters, who differed from the later settled ranchers for whom cowboys came to work. Called *gauchos* in Argentina, *llaneros* in Venezuela and Colombia, and *vaqueros* in Mexico, cowboys rode the prairies rounding up the wild horses and cattle that grazed there. They created their livelihood from scratch, for only after 1494 when Columbus first introduced cattle into the Caribbean did cattle spread across both North and South America. As the livestock multiplied, cowboys hunted down the wild animals and slaughtered them. Cowboys developed an entire range of skills, making lassos, for example, from horses' tails. But their most lucrative products were animal hides and byproducts such as leather and tallow for candle-making.

These herdsmen, similar to those on the Asian steppes, were usually nomadic, with their own customs and ways of life. Living as far as possible from cities and the centers of government, they aimed to keep their independence and to escape government regulation, which increased under the Bourbon Reforms. Cowboys in all areas usually refused to ride mares as an unmanly practice and generally prided themselves on maintaining the rough, masculine ways of frontiersmen. Enterprising landowners, however, set up vast ranches and challenged the claims of the gauchos, llaneros, and vaqueros, who saw wild horses as their own. Settled ranchers hired their own cattle tenders and then encouraged the government to see the independent cowboys as "cattle rustlers" and thieves.

Their independent way of life eventually led nation builders to mythologize gauchos, llaneros, and other cowboys as symbols of freedom for the nation as a whole. However, cowboys played a more direct role in both politics and nation building in the nineteenth century. Their experience with horses made them valuable fighters on both sides in the war for Latin American independence, and their survival skills helped them endure the rough conditions of battle.

QUESTIONS TO CONSIDER

1. For what reasons would some gauchos and llaneros ally themselves with upper-class creoles in the Latin American independence movements?

2. Why have cowboys become such icons in both North and South America?

For Further Information:

Loy, R. Philip. *Westerns and American Culture, 1930–1955*. 2001.
Oliven, Ruben George. *Tradition Matters: Modern Gaucho Identity in Brazil*. 1996.
Reding, Nick. *The Last Cowboys at the End of the World: The Last Gauchos of Patagonia*. 2001.
Slatta, Richard W. *Gauchos and the Vanishing Frontier*. 1983.

against Portuguese foreigners, there was widespread rejoicing at independence even without major social change. A frontier society like the United States, Brazil beckoned entrepreneurs, adventurers, and exiles from around the world as a land of opportunity.

Consequences of Independence

For the most part, however, the new Latin American countries had been so devastated by years of exploitation, misrule, banditry, and armed uprising that except in Brazil, economies lay in shambles. Instead of effecting social reform that would have encouraged economic initiative, most new governments worked to ensure creole dominance, often refusing the promised slave emancipation. In 1799 a Spanish bishop-elect had noted the "great conflict of interests and the hostility which invariably prevails between those who have nothing and those who have everything."[21] Independence did not transform this situation, and thus the popular forces that would have promoted innovation and increased activity at the grassroots did not materialize as effectively as in the newly independent United States.

New Ideologies and Revolutionary Legacies

The revolutions in the Americas and Europe achieved independence for some states but deliberately failed to bring full and free citizenship to slaves, women, and a range of indentured and oppressed peoples. Nonetheless, they left aspirations for the economic opportunity and personal freedom that define the term *liberalism*. Inspired by Enlightenment principles, revolutionaries sought to create centralized nation-states ruled under a constitution as opposed to monarchical governments given to arbitrary rulings by aristocrats and princes. In the early days of both the North American and French republics, this faith in a unified nation of like-minded peoples, which came to be known as **nationalism**, went hand in hand with liberalism. The idea was that the unified rule of law under a single nation, as embodied in the U.S. Constitution and the Declaration of the Rights of Man and of the Citizen, would guarantee constitutional rights and economic growth through free trade. Latin American leaders such as Bolivar had much less faith in all the people of the nation being ready for participation in government (see Reading the Past: Simon Bolivar on Latin American Independence).

The definition of nationalism became more complicated even as it was being born. For one thing, a host of opponents to the new governments of the United States and France believed that time-honored monarchical traditions were a better guarantee of a peaceful society than constitutions and republics. Such thought was called **conservatism**, and many prominent conservatives across Europe and the Americas argued the case for tradition, continuity, and gradual reform based on practical experience. Appalled by the violence and bloodshed of the French Revolution, Edmund Burke of England attacked Enlightenment ideas of a social contract, citizenship, and new fangled constitutions as destructive to the wisdom of the ages.

Like conservatism, **romanticism**—a philosophical and artistic movement that glorified nature, emotion, and the imagination—emerged partly in reaction to the Enlightenment's reliance on reason, especially after the violent excesses of the French Revolution. Closely related to early nationalism, romanticism was also a response to the political turmoil of the Napoleonic Wars. There thus grew up a romantic nationalism, especially in territories such as the German states. Romantic nationalists revered language and traditions as sources of a common feeling among peoples—for instance, among all the German peoples. "Perfect laws are the beautiful and free forms of the interior life of a nation," wrote one German jurist, criticizing reformers' desire to take the Napoleonic Code as a model for change. For him, the Napoleonic Code had not "come out of the life of the German nation."[22] Romantic nationalists took less pride in law codes, well-defined citizenship, and civic rights than in their ancient past and shared cultural experience.

To make the revolutionary legacy more complicated yet, Napoleon Bonaparte and Simon Bolivar ultimately became romantic heroes to rich and poor alike, even though they represented Enlightenment ideals of social mobility, consistent systems of laws, a rational approach to government, and economic modernizing. "My wife and I," said one distillery worker in southern France in 1822, "have the emperor in our guts."[23] The many poets,

nationalism A belief in the importance of one's nation, stemming from its unique laws, language, traditions, and history.

conservatism A political philosophy emphasizing the continuation of traditional institutions and opposition to sudden change in the established order.

romanticism A European philosophical and artistic movement of the late eighteenth and early nineteenth centuries that valued feeling over reason and glorified traditional customs, nature, and the imagination.

Simon Bolivar on Latin American Independence

Simon Bolivar was a heroic "Liberator" to some observers, an authoritarian creole to others. Some of these contradictory images come from Bolivar's own views of the situation in Latin America. This document is from Bolivar's "Letter from Jamaica," written in exile after his 1815 flight from Spanish forces. In it Bolivar expresses his thoughts about liberation from the Spanish and the possibilities for representative government thereafter.

The position of the inhabitants of the American hemisphere has for centuries been purely passive, its political role nonexistent. We are still at a level lower than slavery, and for that reason it is more difficult for us to raise ourselves to attain the enjoyment of freedom. . . . States are enslaved because of either the nature or the abuse of their constitutions; a people is therefore enslaved when the government by its essential nature or by its vices tramples on and usurps the rights of the citizens or subjects. . . .

As long as our countrymen do not acquire the political capacities and virtues that distinguish our brothers of the north, fully democratic systems, far from working to our advantage, will, I fear, bring about our downfall. Unfortunately, these traits, to the extent to which they are required, do not appear to be within our reach. On the contrary, we are dominated by the vices acquired during the rule of a nation like Spain, which has only distinguished itself in brutality, ambition, vindictiveness, and greed. . . .

South Americans have tried to create liberal, even perfect, institutions, doubtless out of that instinct which all men have to attain the greatest happiness possible, which necessarily follows in civil societies founded on the principles of justice, liberty, and equality. But can we maintain in proper balance the difficult charge of a republic? Is it conceivable that a newly liberated people can soar to the height of freedom, . . . without falling into an abyss? Such a marvel is inconceivable and never before seen.

Source: Carta de Jamaica, September 6, 1815, in *Escritos políticos*. Selección e introd., de Graciela Soriano (Madrid: Alianza Editorial, 1969). Translated by Donald R. Kelley.

EXAMINING THE EVIDENCE

1. How does Bolivar characterize Spanish rule?

2. How does he think this rule has affected his contemporaries' capacity for self-government?

3. What seem to be the political options left to Latin Americans once they have obtained their independence?

---

musicians, and artists influenced by romanticism earned their livelihoods not only by glorifying feelings instead of reason but by spreading the myth of Napoleon and Simon Bolivar as superhuman rulers who overcame horrific obstacles to become conquerors. These powerful, if conflicting, ideas—liberalism, nationalism, conservatism, and romanticism—resonated down through the next centuries, shaping both local and global politics.

COUNTERPOINT
Religious Revival in a Secular Age

FOCUS

What trends in Enlightenment and revolutionary society did religious revival challenge?

As we have seen in this chapter, in the challenge to long-established empires, some peoples declared their sovereignty and set up states in opposition to centuries-old forms of rulership. In the influential cases of France and the United States, the principle of a secular state—one tied to no particular religion—flourished, supported by the Enlightenment idea that reason rather than faith should determine social, political, and economic regulations. The French under Robespierre devised national festivals to substitute for religious holidays and even, at the height of revolutionary fervor, converted churches into "temples of reason." But secularism did not prevail everywhere, and movements arose that countered the weakening of religious belief or its supposedly empty ritual. In Europe and North America, great surges of religious fervor took hold of people's daily lives, and in the Arabian peninsula reformers sought to restore Muslims to the fundamental teachings of Islam.

Christianity's Great Awakening

The spirit of Christian revival first took shape in Prussia, where Lutherans had called for a renewal of faith in the late seventeenth century. As Protestant revival spread across the European continent, people joined new evangelical churches, most of them focused on sharpening the inward experience of faith. In the middle of the eighteenth century, a wave of revivals that historians term the "Great Awakening" took place throughout Britain and the North American colonies. Emotional orators such as the English preachers John Wesley and George Whitefield appeared at large rallies, rousing the faithful to break off from the sterile ritual of established churches and to join new communities of faith such as Methodism, the evangelical Protestant church founded by Wesley and characterized by active concern with social welfare and public morals. Some observers were appalled by the sight of worshipers literally weeping at the perils of damnation; in the words of one, the Great Awakening was "horrible beyond expression."[24] Nonetheless, in the middle colonies of British North America alone, some 550 new Protestant congregations were organized between 1740 and 1770.

The Great Awakening

Beginning in around 1800, the United States experienced a Second Great Awakening, where thousands at a time flocked to revival meetings. Describing the scene, one commentator wrote that "some of the people were singing, others praying, some praying for mercy," as they testified to their faith in the face of the growth of science, rationalism, and emotional coldness in the old churches. At the same time, African American slaves were also fervent believers, finding in religion evidence of their humanity (see Reading the Past: Phillis Wheatley, "On Being Brought from Africa to America"). Religion later provided arguments for an end to slavery and were part of a rising democratic impulse among people who together addressed their comments directly and emotionally to God. Despite the surge in religious enthusiasm, governments such as that of the United States declined to proclaim an official faith because of their people's religious diversity and because of Enlightenment thinkers' suspicion of churches as institutions.

New Churches and the State

Government and Religion Allied

In some instances, ties between government and religion became stronger, not weaker. In the Arabian peninsula an eighteenth-century religious reformer, Muhammad ibn Abd al-Wahhabi developed a strong alliance with Muhammad ibn Sa'ud, the head of a small market town. Ibn Abd al-Wahhabi called on Muslims to return to the tenets of Islam, most importantly the worship of the single god, Allah. He felt that Islam had been betrayed by an overemphasis on the Prophet Muhammad and other human saints. At the time, in fact, people worshiped local fortunetell-

Mecca and Wahhabism

Wahhabis fought for a purified Islamic faith, one that eliminated the common practice in the Middle East and elsewhere in the Muslim world of worshiping at religious shrines and the tombs of saints. They destroyed the tombs of the Prophet Muhammad's family but were stopped from overturning the tomb of the Prophet himself. Because the pilgrimage to Mecca was one of the five "pillars" of the faith, Mecca itself, depicted here, remained a center of religious devotion that grew in importance as Islam spread around the world. (Popular Traditions Museum, Damascus/Giraudon/Bridgeman Art Library.)

Phillis Wheatley, "On Being Brought from Africa to America"

Born in Senegal in 1853, Phillis Wheatley was seven when she was sold into slavery to a Boston family, who educated her along with their children. Wheatley published celebrated poetry while a slave, becoming a sensation in New England and even traveling to England in 1773. A voyager to three continents, Wheatley was a true child of the Atlantic world. This celebrated poem, written while she was a teenager, contains a host of ideas and images about slavery and her own condition. As you read, consider why this short verse might pose problems for some modern readers.

'Twas mercy brought me from my Pagan land,
Taught my benighted soul to understand
That there's a God, that there's a Saviour too:
Once I redemption neither sought now knew,

Some view our sable race with scornful eye,
"Their colour is a diabolic die."
Remember, Christians, Negroes, black as Cain,
May be refin'd, and join th' angelic train.

EXAMINING THE EVIDENCE

1. **In what ways does this poem reflect Enlightenment thought?**

2. **How does it relate to the Great Awakening?**

3. **Which ideas in the poem might present-day critics condemn? Which ideas might they praise?**

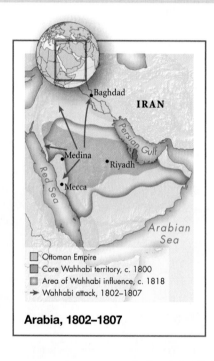

Arabia, 1802–1807

- Ottoman Empire
- Core Wahhabi territory, c. 1800
- Area of Wahhabi influence, c. 1818
- Wahhabi attack, 1802–1807

Wahhabi-Sa'ud Alliance

ers and healers as well as graves, rocks, and trees. One traveler found Arabs "so negligent of religion" that they were "generally considered infidels." This was certainly the opinion of ibn Abd al-Wahhabi and his followers, who declared these departures from the tenets of Islam to be paganism itself. He got help in his quest to return Arabs to the basic principles of Islam not only from his large and active following but from the house of Sa'ud—the town's leading family. Unity of worship would come with political unity, led in ibn Abd al-Wahhabi's mind by the Sa'uds. They would unite the various tribes under a purified Islamic practice, realizing al-Wahhabi's belief that "Arab" meant Muslim.

Muslims, if they are physically able, are instructed to make a pilgrimage to Mecca during their lifetime as one of their basic obligations. The Wahhabis, as the reformer's followers came to be called (at first, by their enemies), were determined to take control of Mecca for the Sa'uds and for their cause of Islamic fundamentalism. In 1802, making their first attempt, they destroyed all mosques dedicated to the worship of Muhammad. Being connected with the Sa'uds put real muscle to the Wahhabis' religious fervor, and in 1807 they finally wrenched the religious sites of Mecca and Medina from Ottoman control. Although the Ottomans would regain possession in 1840, the alliance between the Sa'uds and the Wahhabis remained, to become ever more powerful in the twentieth century as the discovery of oil in the region fortified the Sa'uds and the Wahhabis along with them.[25]

Conclusion

This period saw widespread challenges to centuries-old empires in the Americas, Europe, the Caribbean, West Asia, and Egypt. The most direct of these challenges came from the popular uprisings known as the Atlantic revolutions. In these revolutions, state power and rigid social structures impinged on people's lives by promoting high taxes and controlling commerce. Deepening poverty and frustrated ambition afflicted ordinary folk, whether in

France or in Peru, causing both riots and political activism. These economic conditions awakened some revolutionaries. Others were inspired to push for political reform by Enlightenment ideas about government based on individual rights and the rational rule of law rather than on inherited privilege and notions of a divine order. Simon Bolivar was one such secular-minded revolutionary and state-builder. Other political actors, such as the Sa'ud family of the Arabian peninsula, drew on religious fervor in their state-building, forming a counterpoint to the general trend.

Independence in the Western Hemisphere affected the entire world. As frontier societies, North American and Latin American countries served as magnets for European investment and for people searching for better livelihoods. Still, countless people of all classes and ethnicities who participated in the uprisings in the Atlantic world benefited not at all or in the most limited way. Slavery remained entrenched in some countries; women, free blacks, and other people of color were usually disqualified from participating in politics. As representative government developed, it too was uneven, especially in Latin America, where a creole elite dominated the new nations.

These political revolutions nonetheless formed a platform for further social and economic change, and we remember them for their powerful and enduring influence. In the short term, the revolutions created conditions for heightened manufacturing and eventually the Industrial Revolution. In the long term, they gave citizens confidence to use their freedom. "It is harder to release a nation from servitude than to enslave a free nation," Bolivar had written, and in this respect the age of revolutions nurtured aspirations and opened up opportunities.

NOTES

1. Luis Peru de Lacroix, *Diario de Cucuramanga* (Caracas: Comité ejecutivo del Bicentenario de Simon Bolivar, 1982), 67, quoted in Charles Minguet, ed., *Simon Bolivar: Unité impossible* (Paris: La Découverte, 1983), 13.
2. Voltaire, *Essai sur les moeurs*, 3:179.
3. Quoted in Hilda L. Smith and Berenice A. Carroll, eds., *Women's Political and Social Thought* (Bloomington: Indiana University Press, 2000), 133.
4. "Political Testament," in George I. Mosse et al., eds., *Europe in Review* (Chicago: Rand McNally and Co., 1957), 111–112.
5. Quoted in Richard Wortman, *Scenarios of Power: Myth and Ceremony in Russian Monarchy, From Peter the Great to the Death of Nicholas I* (Princeton, NJ: Princeton University Press, 1995), 130.
6. *Seminario Económico de México*, 1811, quoted in Silvia Marina Arrom, *The Women of Mexico City, 1790–1857* (Palo Alto, CA: Stanford University Press, 1985), 18.
7. Edward Long, quoted in Barbara Bush, *Slave Women in the Caribbean, 1650–1838* (London: Heinemann, 1990), 15, 51.
8. Quoted in Paul Dukes, ed. and trans., *Russia Under Catherine the Great: Select Documents on Government and Society* (Newtonville, MA: Priental Research Partners, 1978), 112.
9. Dukes, *Russia Under Catherine the Great*, 112, 115.
10. Alexander Hamilton, *Federalist Papers*, Number 15.
11. Letter to John Jay, March 14, 1779, http://www.c250.columbia.edu/c250_celebrates/remarkable_columbians/alexander_hamilton.html.
12. Quoted in Ron Chernow, *Alexander Hamilton* (New York: Penguin, 2004), 316.
13. Quoted in Lynn Hunt, *The French Revolution and Human Rights: A Brief Documentary History* (Boston: Bedford/St. Martins, 1996), 65.
14. Quoted in Annie Jourdain, *Napoléon: Héros, Imperator, Mécène* (Paris: Aubier, 1998), 34.
15. Quoted in Albert Hourani, *Arabic Thought in the Liberal Age, 1798–1939* (London: Oxford University Press, 1962), "Address to the National Assembly, to Our Lords the Representatives of the Nation," quoted in Laurent Dubois and John D. Garrigus, eds., *Slave Revolution in the Caribbean, 1789–1804: A Brief History with Documents* (Boston: Bedford/St. Martins, 2005), 69.
16. Quoted Dubois and Garrigus, *Slave Revolution*, 77.
17. "Notes [from Napoleon Bonaparte] to Serve as Instructions to Give to the Captain General Leclerc," quoted in Dubois and Garrigus, *Slave Revolution*, 176.
18. "Proclamation of 1809," quoted in Peter Bakewell, *A History of Latin America: Empires and Sequels, 1450–1930* (Oxford, U.K.: Blackwell, 1997), 362.
19. Juan Ruiz de Apodaca, quoted in Richard Boyer and Geoffrey Spurling, eds., *Colonial Lives: Documents on Latin American History, 1550–1850* (New York: Oxford University Press, 2000), 305.
20. Quoted in George Reid Andrews, *Afro-Latin America, 1800–2000* (New York: Oxford University Press, 2004), 57.

21. Quoted in John Lynch, "The Origins of Spanish American Independence," in *The Cambridge History of Latin America* (Cambridge, U.K.: Cambridge University Press, 1985), 3:32.

22. Quoted in Martyn Lyons, *Napoleon Bonaparte and the Legacy of the French Revolution* (London: Macmillan, 1994), 232.

23. Quoted in Lyons, *Napoleon Bonaparte*, v.

24. William Briggs, quoted in Phyllis Mack, *Heart Religion in the British Enlightenment: Gender and Emotion in Early Methodism* (New York: Cambridge University Press, 2008), 2.

25. John Esposito, *Islam, the Straight Path* (New York: Oxford University Press, 1991).

RESOURCES FOR RESEARCH

The Promise of Enlightenment

The Enlightenment had a global reach, sparking interest in South America and Japan as well as in Europe. Scientific curiosity among a range of people, as featured in Schiffer's book, led to ongoing experimentation.

Dalton, Susan. *Engendering the Republic of Letters: Reconnecting Public and Private Spheres.* 2003.

Gorbatov, Inna. *Catherine the Great and the French Philosophers of the Enlightenment: Montesquieu, Voltaire, Rousseau, Diderot and Grimm.* 2005.

Rowe, William T. *Saving the World: Chen Hongmou and Elite Consciousness in Eighteenth Century China.* 2001.

Schiffer, Michael B. *Drawing the Lightning Down: Benjamin Franklin and Electrical Technology in the Age of Enlightenment.* 2003.

Stein, Stanley J., and Barbara H. Stein. *Apogee of Empire: Spain and New Spain in the Age of Charles III, 1759–1789.* 2003.

Revolution in North America

The revolution in North America engaged the European powers, not only Britain but also France and Spain, as Elliott's masterful work shows. Linda Kerber highlights the many aspects of North American women's involvement as participants as well as symbols of liberty and rights.

Appleby, Joyce. *Inheriting the Revolution: The First Generation of Americans.* 2004.

Elliott, John H. *Empires of the Atlantic World: Britain and Spain in America, 1492–1830.* 2006.

Kerber, Linda. *Women of the Republic: Intellect and Ideology in the American Revolution.* 1986.

Middlekauff, Robert. *The Glorious Cause: The American Revolution, 1763–1789.* 2005.

Wood, Gordon S. *Revolutionary Characters: What Made the Founders Different?* 2006.

The French Revolution and the Napoleonic Empire

More than the American Revolution, this was the uprising heard round the world, and it has given rise to exciting studies of many kinds. The Web site at George Mason University has one of the most comprehensive online presentations of documents, images, and songs from the French Revolution.

French Revolution: http://chnm.gmu.edu/revolution/.

Hunt, Lynn. *Inventing Human Rights: A History.* 2007.

Marsot, Afaf Lutfi Al-Sayyid. *Egypt in the Reign of Muhammad Ali.* 1984.

Napoleonic Empire: http://www.bbc.co.uk/history/historic_figures/bonaparte_napoleon.shtml.

Shovlin, John. *The Political Economy of Virtue: Luxury, Patriotism, and the Origins of the French Revolution.* 2006.

Todd, Janet. *Mary Wollstonecraft: A Life.* 2000.

Revolution Continued in the Western Hemisphere

As revolution continued in the Atlantic world, the Caribbean and Latin America saw a wave of uprisings. Dubois movingly describes the causes and conduct of revolution in Haiti; the State University of New York/Albany maintains an excellent Web site on it.

Dubois, Laurent. *Avengers of the New World: The Story of the Haitian Revolution.* 2004.

Haitian revolution: http://www.albany.edu/~js3980/haitian-revolution.html.

Masur, Gerard. *Simón Bolívar.* 2006.

Morgan, Jennifer. *Laboring Women: Reproduction and Gender in New World Slavery.* 2004.

Van Young, Eric. *The Other Rebellion: Popular Violence, Ideology, and the Mexican Struggle for Independence, 1810–1821.* 2001.

COUNTERPOINT: Religious Revival in a Secular Age

The religious fervor that accompanied the age of reason is well chronicled in the works below.

Mack, Phyllis. *Heart Religion in the British Enlightenment: Gender and Emotion in Early Methodism.* 2008.

May, Cedrick. *Evangelism and Resistance in the Black Atlantic, 1760–1835.* 2008.

Qadhi, Abu Ammar Yasir. *A Critical Study of Shirk: Being a Translation and Commentary of Muhammad b. Abd al-Wahhab's Kashf al-Shubuhat.* 2002.

Vassiliev, Alexei. *A History of Saudi Arabia.* 1998.

▶ **For additional primary sources from this period,** see *Sources of Crossroads and Cultures.*

▶ **For Web sites, images, and documents related to topics in this chapter,** see Make History at bedfordstmartins.com/smith.

The major global development in this chapter ▶ The Atlantic revolutions
and their short- and long-term significance.

IMPORTANT
EVENTS

1751–1772	Publication of the *Encyclopedia*
1762	Jean-Jacques Rousseau publishes *The Social Contract* and *Emile*
1775–1781	Revolution in North America
1776	Adam Smith, *The Wealth of Nations*
1789	U.S. Constitution formally adopted; revolution begins in France
1791	Revolution begins in Haiti
1792	France declared a republic; Mary Wollstonecraft writes *A Vindication of the Rights of Woman*
1799	Napoleon comes to power
1804	Haiti becomes independent from France
1811	Simon Bolivar first takes up arms against Spain
1815	Napoleon defeated at Waterloo; Congress of Vienna resettles the boundaries of European states
1816	Argentina becomes independent from Spain
1817	Chile becomes independent from Spain
1821	Mexico and Peru become independent from Spain
1822	Brazil becomes independent from Portugal
1825	Bolivia becomes independent from Spain

KEY
TERMS

conservatism (p. 783)
contract government (p. 762)
federation (p. 769)
general will (p. 773)
junta (p. 778)

laissez faire (p. 763)
liberalism (p. 763)
nationalism (p. 783)
public sphere (p. 764)
republic (p. 771)
romanticism (p. 783)

CHAPTER OVERVIEW
QUESTIONS

1. What role did the Scientific Revolution and expanding global contacts play in the cultural and social movement known as the Enlightenment?

2. Why did prosperous and poor people alike join revolutions in the Americas and in France?

3. Why were the Atlantic revolutions so influential, even to the present day?

SECTION FOCUS
QUESTIONS

1. What were the major ideas of the Enlightenment and their impacts?

2. What factors lay behind the war between North American colonists and Great Britain?

3. What changes emerged from the French Revolution and Napoleon's reign?

4. What were the motives and methods of revolutionaries in the Caribbean and Latin America?

5. What trends in Enlightenment and revolutionary society did religious revival challenge?

MAKING
CONNECTIONS

1. What was the relationship between the Enlightenment and the political revolutions of the late eighteenth and early nineteenth centuries?

2. What are the common challenges that centuries-old empires faced during this period?

3. What makes Napoleon a significant historical figure?

4. Why was there so much bloodshed in the various efforts to achieve political and social change?

24

AT A CROSSROADS ▲

An artist from an elite samurai family, Kiyochika Kobayashi was so fascinated by technology and industry that in 1879 he placed a train front and center in this moonlit scene set in Takanawa Ushimachi, just outside of Tokyo. Earlier woodprints had portrayed the town as a slum called Oxtown with garbage strewn about its roads, but in this artist's eyes Takanawa Ushimachi became a prosperous, indeed alluring crossroads, thanks to the arrival of the railroad. Kiyochika changed the style of Japanese woodcuts by introducing into more traditional Japanese scenes such elements as clocks, cameras, electric lighting, and the massive cannons churned out by industry. (Santa Barbara Museum of Art, Gift of Dr. and Mrs. Roland A. Way.)

Industry and Everyday Life
1750–1900

As a seven-year-old in 1799, Robert Blincoe started working in a cotton mill outside the town of Nottingham, in central England. Robert was an orphan, and with others from his London orphanage he was sent to the mill. The idea was to have the orphans contribute to England's prosperity and learn the value of hard work, but it was not certain that Robert would even survive to adulthood. As his group of orphans reached the mill, he heard onlookers in the town mutter, "God help the poor wretches."[1] Robert soon found out why. He watched as his fellow child workers wasted away from the long hours and meager food, and he looked on in horror as the orphan Mary Richards was caught up in the machinery: he "heard the bones of her arms, legs, thighs, etc successively snap . . . her head appeared dashed to pieces, . . . her blood thrown about like water from a twirled mop."[2] Robert himself had to stand on a box to tend the machinery, but due to his small size he was less productive than the managers wanted, and he was constantly beaten. Robert's situation grew worse when his group was sent to another mill. The hours were even longer and the pace of work faster, and older workers tortured Robert, putting hot pitch into a blazing metal bowl and placing it on his head until his hair came off and his scalp was burned. Only when Robert reached age twenty-one, his entire body scarred for life from beatings, was he released from his grim "apprenticeship."

Robert Blincoe was a survivor of the Industrial Revolution—a change in the production of goods that substituted mechanical force for human energy. Beginning in Britain around 1750, European factories churned out machine-made products—first textiles and later manufactured items from sewing machines to automobiles—that came to replace

BACKSTORY

As we saw in Chapter 23, between 1750 and 1830 popular uprisings led to a revolutionary wave across the Atlantic world. Throwing off old political systems, revolutionaries also aimed to unchain their economies by eliminating stifling restrictions on manufacturing and commerce imposed by guilds and governments. Free global trade advanced further with the end of British control of the United States and Spanish control of much of Latin America. During the same period, slavery came under attack as an immoral institution that denied human beings equal rights and prevented a free labor force from developing. As Enlightenment ideas for good government flourished, reformers pushed to replace traditional aristocratic and monarchical privileges with rational codes of law. Free trade and free labor, promoted by enlightened laws and policies, helped bring dramatic changes to the global economy, most notably the unparalleled increase in productivity called the Industrial Revolution.

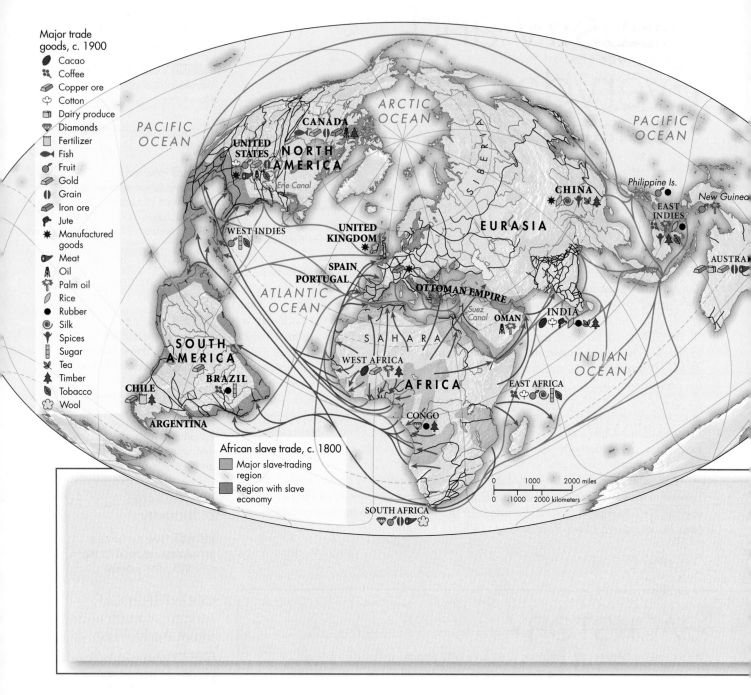

Major trade
goods, c. 1900

- 🫛 Cacao
- 🌰 Coffee
- ▱ Copper ore
- ♧ Cotton
- ☐ Dairy produce
- ◈ Diamonds
- ▯ Fertilizer
- 🐟 Fish
- 🍐 Fruit
- ▱ Gold
- ◖ Grain
- ▱ Iron ore
- 🎋 Jute
- ✳ Manufactured
   goods
- 🍖 Meat
- ▯ Oil
- 🌴 Palm oil
- ◖ Rice
- ● Rubber
- ◉ Silk
- ✲ Spices
- ▮ Sugar
- ✕ Tea
- 🌲 Timber
- 🍃 Tobacco
- ✿ Wool

African slave trade, c. 1800

◻ Major slave-trading
   region

◼ Region with slave
   economy

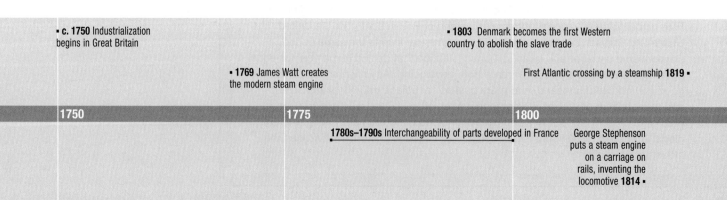

• **c. 1750** Industrialization
begins in Great Britain

• **1803** Denmark becomes the first Western
country to abolish the slave trade

• **1769** James Watt creates
the modern steam engine

First Atlantic crossing by a steamship **1819** •

1750   **1775**   **1800**

1780s–1790s Interchangeability of parts developed in France   George Stephenson
puts a steam engine
on a carriage on
rails, inventing the
locomotive **1814** •

higher-quality but more expensive artisanal goods. Agriculture continued to dominate the world economy, and farms such as those in Africa, worked largely by women, saw innovations in cultivation and irrigation techniques, as we will see in the Counterpoint to this chapter. In the twentieth century, industry would outstrip agriculture as the leading economic sector and the major source of employment in much of Europe and the United States, and eventually in other parts of the globe.

The Industrial Revolution transformed the livelihoods of tens of millions of people in the nineteenth century in a variety of ways. After his release, Robert Blincoe grabbed at opportunity, setting up a grocery store and even establishing a small factory of his own. The course of industrialization was thus ragged, offering both danger and advantage. Some were driven into factories where conditions were often dangerous and even criminal. Where countries industrialized, a working class arose to tend machines in the factories. These workers' lives were soon strikingly different from those of the artisans with whom they competed. The efficient new weaving machines gave jobs to some, but they impoverished artisans, such as the Indian and European handloom weavers who continued to follow traditional manufacturing methods. Industry also influenced agriculture around the world. Factories consumed more raw materials, and an increasing number of workers in cities no longer grew their own food, depending instead on distant farmers. With the global spread of industry, art, music, philosophy, and political thought echoed the transformation, as writers and painters described this new world in their art and theorists analyzed their new societies. Whether a region had comparatively few factories, as in India and South America, or a dense network of them, as in Britain, patterns of work and everyday life changed—and not always for the better, as Robert Blincoe's case shows.

MAPPING THE WORLD
The Spread of Industrialization

The world remained more agricultural than industrial in 1900. As the twentieth century opened, however, the Industrial Revolution that originated in eighteenth-century Britain was driving industry to ever higher peaks. Among its globally significant consequences was the decline of the slave trade and slavery itself, which had previously greatly increased the world's productivity.

ROUTES ▼

— Major sea trade route, c. 1775
→ African slave trade, to 1860
— Railroad, c. 1914

1839–1842 Opium War between China and Britain

▪ **1868** Meiji Restoration launches Japanese industrialization

▪ **1865** U.S. Civil War ends, rapid U.S. industrialization begins

▪ **1842** Treaty of Nanjing opens Chinese ports

1891–1904 Construction of trans-Siberian railroad

| 1825 | 1850 | 1875 | 1900 |

1840s–1864 Taiping Rebellion

▪ **1871** Germany gains resource-rich Alsace and Lorraine after defeating France

▪ **1848** *Communist Manifesto* published

1873–c. 1900 Deep global recession with uneven recovery

▪ **1853** U.S. ships enter Japanese ports

1890s Argentina's leading textile manufacturer produces 1.6 million yards of cloth annually

---

OVERVIEW
QUESTIONS

The major global development in this chapter: The Industrial Revolution and its impact on societies and cultures throughout the world.

As you read, consider:

1. In what ways did the Industrial Revolution change people's work lives and ideas?

2. How did the Industrial Revolution benefit people, and what problems did it create?

3. How and where did industrial production develop, and how did it affect society and politics?

The Industrial Revolution Begins   1750–1830

FOCUS

What were the main causes of the Industrial Revolution?

The **Industrial Revolution** unfolded first in Britain and western Europe, eventually tipping the balance of global power to favor the West. The coming of mechanization expanded productivity as never before. Many historians believe the only transformation as important was the rise of settled agriculture thousands of years earlier. The Industrial Revolution had global roots, occurring in the context of worldwide trade, economic inventiveness, and agricultural improvement. Although Britain led in industry, the economies of Qing (ching) China and India were larger until almost 1900, when Britain surpassed them in overall productivity. A burning question for historians is how, in a climate of worldwide industriousness, Britain came to the forefront of the great industrial transformation.

The Global Roots of Industrialization

Industriousness and Population Growth

The Industrial Revolution took place amid a surge in productive activity. Industriousness rose, as people worked longer hours and tinkered to find new ways to make goods, developing thousands of new inventions in the process. In Qing China from the mid-1650s to 1800, productivity increased along with population, which soared from 160 million people in 1700 to 350 million in 1800. The dynamic economy improved many people's lifestyles and life expectancy, and encouraged people to work harder to acquire the new products constantly entering the market. Chinese life expectancy increased to the range of 34 to 39 years, longer than almost anywhere else in the world, including western Europe, where in 1800 it was 30 in France and 35 in Britain.

Global Trade

Industrial Revolution A change in the production of goods that substituted mechanical power for human energy, beginning around 1750 in Britain and western Europe; it vastly increased the world's productivity.

The new global connections created by European expansion into the Americas and Asia contributed to both economic dynamism and population growth. Crops from the Western Hemisphere helped raise the standard of living where they were imported and grown, and awareness of such popular Chinese products as cotton textiles, porcelain, and lacquer ware spread through international trade. Silver flowed into China as Europeans purchased its highly desirable goods. As the nineteenth century opened, Qing China was the most prosperous country on earth.

Europe, in contrast, produced little that was attractive to foreign buyers, and in the seventeenth century warfare, epidemics, and famine reduced its population from 85 million

MAP 24.1 **Industrialization in Europe, c. 1900**

Beginning in the workshops of England's tinkerers, industrialization spread across western Europe to Germany and then to Russia. The presence of raw materials such as coal and iron ore sparked industrial development, but so did curiosity and inventiveness. Sweden, for example, lacks mineral resources, so its people harnessed water power to develop electricity. Industrialization would remain uneven into the twenty-first century, however, and this imbalance often led to deadly political conflict.

to 80 million. After 1700, however, Europe's population surged, more than doubling by 1800, thanks to global trade that introduced nutritious foods and other useful goods. Population growth put pressure on British energy resources, especially fuel and food. With their populations rising rapidly, both Britain and China faced the limits of artisanal productivity and natural resources. The Industrial Revolution allowed the British to be the first to surpass those limits (see Map 24.1).

Great Britain: A Culture of Experimentation

Why did the Industrial Revolution happen when it did, and why did it happen in Britain first? After all, many regions have the coal, iron deposits, and other resources that allowed the British to make and power the first modern machines. Moreover, bursts of economic innovation have occurred at many times and in many places.

It was not just resources, however, that propelled Britain to the industrial forefront. As we saw in Chapter 20, the Scientific Revolution had fostered both new reliance on direct observation and deep curiosity about the world. Before the rise of industry, the British and other Europeans traveled the globe, which exposed them to technological developments from other societies. From China, for example, they learned about such implements as seed drills and winnowing machines to process grain. Publications like the *Encyclopedia*, composed in France during the Enlightenment and widely read in Europe (see Chapter 23), included mechanical designs from around the world, making them available to a public increasingly eager to tinker and experiment. Global trade and exchange, the Scientific Revolution, and the Enlightenment thus formed the backdrop for the Industrial Revolution. The massive expansion in productivity was initially not about theoretical science, however, but about trial and error—which especially flourished in Britain.

Artisans and Tinkerers

British artisans produced some of the early machinery of the Industrial Revolution. Britain had a particularly well-developed culture of experimentation and, as its population grew, the country's curious and industrious craftspeople worked to supply the surging population, to meet the shortage in energy due to declining wood supplies, and to devise products that the world might want to buy. "The age," wrote critic Samuel Johnson, "is running mad after innovation."[3] From aristocrats to artisans, the British latched onto news of successful experiments both at home and abroad. They tinkered with air pumps, clocks, and telescopes. European craftspeople worked hard to copy the new goods imported from China, India, and other countries. From the sixteenth century on, for example, European consumers bought hundreds of thousands of foreign porcelain pieces, leading would-be manufacturers in the Netherlands, France, and the German states to try to figure out the process of porcelain production. They finally succeeded early in the 1700s. Despite inventive activity across Europe, it was England that soon pulled ahead (see Reading the Past: Industry Comes to the British Countryside).

One English innovator who stands out is Josiah Wedgwood (1730–1795), founder of the Wedgwood dishware firm that still exists. Wedgwood developed a range of new processes, colors, and designs, expanding his business and making it a model for large-scale production. He grew up in a family that produced rough, traditional kinds of pottery on a very small scale. As a poor, younger son with an inquisitive mind, he used his bent for experimentation to devise many different types of ceramics. Helped by his wife and by the personal wealth she invested in the company, Wedgwood kept meticulous records of his five thousand experiments with "china" (so called because Chinese porcelain set the standard for ceramic production). He traveled widely in Britain, his agents searched the world for the right grade of clay to compete with Asian products, and he copied Asian designs unashamedly. Hence, in Wedgwood, the distinctive British culture of artisanal experimentation came together with the materials and inspiration provided by new global connections; the result was industrial innovation.

Life was not always easy for Wedgwood: an accident on a business trip eventually required that his leg be amputated. This setback only made him more determined to succeed. Born into poverty, he became the acclaimed manufacturer of fine dishes for British monarchs and for Catherine the Great of Russia, and he died one of the wealthiest men in his country. Wedgwood's fortune and spirit of experimentation passed down to his grandson Charles Darwin, who proposed the theory of evolution.

Wedgwood China

Josiah Wedgwood, the eighteenth-century English potter-turned-industrialist who founded a company still prosperous today, worked day and night to figure out the ingredients, formulas, and processes necessary to make "china"—that is, inexpensive, heat-resistant dishware patterned after China's renowned but costly and fragile porcelain. Wedgwood copied designs from around the world to brighten his dishware, but he is best known for his "Wedgwood blue" products, which were directly inspired by China's famed blue-and-white patterns. In this 1810 example, Wedgwood designers had fashioned a product that could compete with Chinese manufactures in the global marketplace. (Cotehele House, Cornwall, UK/Bridgeman Art Library.)

World Trade and the Rise of Industry

Global shipping, developed over three centuries, became ever more central to industrial progress in the eighteenth and nineteenth centuries. As population rose in Europe and as England, France, and other European countries

Industry Comes to the British Countryside

Industrialization transformed the human landscape and natural environment. In this passage from a promotional brochure, George Perry, co-owner of an ironworks in Coalbrookdale, England, describes how industrialization had changed the town by 1758. Dozens of travelers through the British countryside made similar observations as they noted the rise of industry in the eighteenth and nineteenth centuries and its complicated effects.

In the year One Thousand Seven Hundred, the whole Village consisted of only One furnace, Five Dwelling Houses, and a Forge or two. About Forty years ago the present Iron-foundry was establish'd, and since that time its Trade and Buildings are so far increas'd that it contains at least Four Hundred and Fifty inhabitants, and finds employment for more than Five Hundred People, including all the several Occupations that are connected with the Works. . . .

THIS place affords a number of delightful prospects. . . . Some of the Hills are cover'd with Verdure [greenery], others overgrown with Wood, and some again are naked and barren. These, with a View of a fine fertile Country, Water'd by the Severn [River], all contribute to form as agreeable a Variety to the Eye, as can well be conceiv'd. The Beauty of the scene is in the meantime greatly increas'd by a new view of the Dale itself. Pillars of Flame and smoke rising to vast height,

large Reservoirs of Water, and a number of Engines in motion, never fail to raise the admiration of strangers, tho' it must be confess'd these things join'd to the murmuring of the Waterfalls, the noise of the Machines, and the roaring of the Furnaces, are apt to occasion a kind of Horror in those who happen to arrive in a dark Night. UPON the whole, there are perhaps few Places where rural prospects, and Scenes of hurry and Business are so happily united as at COALBROOKDALE.

Source: Prospectus for "A View of the Upperworks of Coalbrook Dale" (1758) by George Perry. Quoted in Sally and David Dugan, *The Day the World Took Off: The Roots of the Industrial Revolution* (London: Macmillan, 2000), 44.

EXAMINING THE EVIDENCE

1. What is Perry's opinion of the industrial world in which he lives?

2. How might other people have viewed the industrial landscape differently?

3. Compare Perry's observations of Coalbrookdale with the story of Robert Blincoe that opens this chapter. Which do you think more accurately describes the effects of industrialization, and why?

fought wars worldwide over trade, they needed more resources to supply people at home and far-flung armies and navies. To supply industry and feed the growing number of urban workers, global shipping brought grain from North America, wood from Canada and Russia, cotton from Egypt and the United States, and eventually meat from Australia. Imports and Europe's own produce fed urban workers. Foreign commodities such as tea, coffee, chocolate, and opium derivatives, which the lower classes were just coming to use in the nineteenth century, helped them endure the rigors of industry. Thus, dense global trade networks and raw materials produced by workers from around the world were critical to the Industrial Revolution.

Slaves produced many elements crucial to industrial success. Eleven million Africans captured on the continent were sold into slavery in the Americas, raising capital to invest in commerce and industry. The slaves themselves produced low-cost agricultural products such as sugar and rice that enriched global traders and provided critical components in Atlantic trade networks (see Counterpoint: African Women and Slave Agriculture). Cheaper foodstuffs cut the expenses of factory owners, who justified low wages by pointing out that working families' costs had decreased. To clothe their slaves, wealthy African and American owners bought inexpensive factory-made textiles pumped out by British machines. In the northern United States, slave ironworkers were put to work building the metallurgical business, and in the Western Hemisphere generally slaves' skills played a crucial role in producing copper and tin for factory use. They also worked to produce raw materials such as cotton. Had free labor alone been used in these processes, some historians believe, the higher cost of raw materials and food would have slowed development of global trade and the pace of experiments with factories and machines.

Slavery and Industry

The Technology of Industry

Mechanizing Textile Production

New technology was a final ingredient in the effort to meet the needs of a growing and increasingly interconnected population. In the eighteenth century, clever British inventors devised tools such as the flying shuttle (1733) to speed the weaving of textiles by individuals working at home. This, in turn, led to improvements in spinning to meet the increased demand for thread created by more efficient weavers. The spinning jenny, invented in about 1765 by craftsman James Hargreaves and named, it is said, after his wife or daughter, allowed an individual worker, using just the power of her hand, to spin not one bobbin of thread, but up to 120 at once. At about the same time, Richard Arkwright and partners invented the water frame, another kind of spinning machine that used water power. When hand-driven spinning machines could be linked to a central power source such as water, many could be placed in a single building. Thus, the world's first factories arose from the pressure to increase production of English cloth for the growing global market.

The Steam Engine Breakthrough

Still another, even more important breakthrough arose when steam engines were harnessed to both spinning and weaving machines. Steam engines could power a vast number of machines, which drew more people out of home textile production and into factories. Almost two thousand people worked in the British factories of Richard Arkwright alone. Although born in poverty, by the time of his death in 1792, Arkwright was a wealthy man who owned mills across England and Scotland. Industrial spies infiltrated these factories and sent their mechanical and organizational secrets to businessmen in Belgium, northern France, the United States, and elsewhere. The most dramatic innovation in European textiles was thus the adaptation of mechanized spinning and weaving machines to the mass production of cheap cotton, which in turn clothed a swelling global workforce.

The steam engine proved to be a pivotal piece of technology not just for textiles, but for the Industrial Revolution as a whole. It was used first in the gold and silver mining industry, then in textile production, and finally in driving trains and steamboats. The steam engine had been invented earlier in China, and was used there and elsewhere to pump water from mines. It was improved throughout the eighteenth century in Britain. In 1765, James Watt, a Scottish craftsman, figured out how to make the steam engine more practical, fuel-efficient, and powerful—"Cheap as well as good" was how he put it.[4] A slew of ideas for using and improving the engine followed, and in 1814, British engineer George Stephenson placed the machine in a carriage on rails, inventing the locomotive. The first steam-powered ship crossed the Atlantic soon after, in 1819.

Interchangeability of Parts

The **interchangeability of parts** was a final critical aspect of the Industrial Revolution. The many wars Europeans fought over global trade and influence in the eighteenth and early nineteenth centuries produced incredible demand for less expensive weapons and more of them. By 1790 French gunsmith Honoré Blanc, experimenting with tools and gauges, had produced guns with fully interchangeable parts. This lowered the cost per weapon and made repair possible for merchants and soldiers based in any part of the world. The goal was to "assure uniformity [of output], acceleration of work, and economy of price," as a government official in charge of weaponry put it in 1781.[5] By the early nineteenth century Blanc was producing 10,000 muskets a year. The idea of interchangeability in weaponry and machinery was crucial to the unfolding Industrial Revolution.

Industrialization After 1830

FOCUS

How did industrialization spread, and what steps did nations and manufacturers take to meet its challenges?

One striking feature of industrialization is its spread within countries, across regions, and around the world. Although threatened workers and fearful rulers have from time to time resisted industrialization, it has proved impossible to stop. Industrialization brings ongoing efficiencies, which have proven important to meet the needs of a growing global population. From its birth in England and western Europe, entrepreneurs across the continent advanced the industrial system, as did innovators in the United States. Japan did not

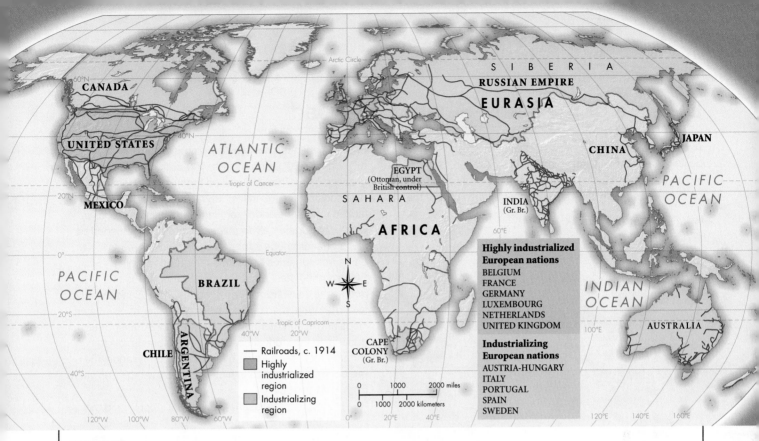

MAP 24.2

The Spread of Railroads, c. 1900

The spread of railroads throughout the world fostered industrialization because it required tracks, engines and railroad cars, and railway stations, which were increasingly made of iron, steel, and glass. Railroads generated economic growth beyond the building of trains and tracks, however. Entire cities grew up around railroad hubs, which attracted new migrants—not just hard-working builders but also professionals and service workers to fill the needs of the growing population. Railroads transported goods, turned handsome profits, promoted the fantasy world of tourism and travel, and almost immediately made warfare faster paced and more lethal.

industrialize until after 1870, but then it embraced technology enthusiastically. In many other countries, some enterprising individuals started factories, but full-scale industrialization across regions usually came later (see Map 24.2). Outside of Europe and the United States thorough industrialization generally did not develop until the twentieth century. Even though industry developed unevenly in different places, it affected the wider world by increasing demand for raw materials and creating new livelihoods.

Industrial Innovation Gathers Speed

By the end of the eighteenth century, entrepreneurs from the United States and across Europe joined British innovators, and the nineteenth century was one of widespread industrial, technological, and commercial innovation. Steam engines moved inexpensive manufactured goods on a growing network of railroads and shipping lanes, creating a host of new jobs outside of factory work (see Lives and Livelihoods: Builders of the Trans-Siberian Railroad). Around railroad hubs, for example, towns and cities filled with railroad and other workers who needed manufactured and agricultural goods. An increasing number of stores sold a soaring variety of products, ranging from the lowly cherry pitter to the reaping machine and bicycle, all of them proof of snowballing innovation in the nineteenth century.

Although independent craftsmen-tinkerers created the first machines, such as the spinning jenny and water frame, sophisticated engineers were more critical to later revolutionary technologies. In 1885 the German engineer Karl Benz devised a workable gasoline

interchangeability of parts
A late-eighteenth-century technological breakthrough in which machine and implement parts were standardized, allowing for mass production and easy repair.

799

Builders of the Trans-Siberian Railroad

Axes, saws, and wheelbarrows—these were the tools that built the greatest railway project ever undertaken. Stretching across Siberia from Moscow in the west to Vladivostok on the Sea of Japan (see again Map 24.2), the scale of the trans-Siberian railroad was enormous by any measure: miles laid (5700), earth moved (100 million cubic yards), rail installed (more than 100 million tons), and bridges and tunnels constructed (60 miles). Because this remote wilderness lacked roads, the endeavor was difficult and expensive. Except for lumber, all supplies needed to be transported. Cut stone for bridge supports and gravel for the railbed came from quarries sometimes hundreds of miles away. Ships carried steel parts for bridges thousands of miles across the seas, from Odessa on the Black Sea to Vladivostok. They were then moved inland. In winter horse-drawn sleds and in summer horse-drawn wagons transported material to the work sites. Cut through forests, blasted through rock, raised over rivers and swampy lands, the project was completed in nine sections over thirteen years from 1891 to 1904.

Convict Railroad Workers in Siberia, 1895

The tsarist government of Russia mobilized hundreds of thousands of workers to build the trans-Siberian railroad, the main line of which took thirteen years (1891–1904) to complete. Convicts provided essential manpower, and this image shows their housing and conditions of life. The labor entailed moving mountains of soil and rock and bringing in lumber and iron track, all without benefit of machinery and in the harsh Siberian climate. (Corbis.)

Hundreds of thousands of manual laborers did the work. At the height of its construction, the trans-Siberian employed as many as ninety thousand workers on each of its original nine sections. Many were recruited by contractors who scoured Russian cities and villages for hefty men. Prisoners and soldiers were forced to work on the project. Around the large work sites, the army and police stood guard to prevent disruption as the grueling, dangerous labor progressed. The government set up state liquor stores near work camps to appease laborers in their off-hours.

Doing the job quickly and cheaply was the government's top priority. Worker safety was of little concern, and casualties were many among the unskilled workforce. Cutting through forests to lay rail and dynamiting through hills to construct tunnels took thousands of lives. The anonymous dead lived on only in poetry:

The New Inventors: Engineers

engine, and six years later France's Armand Peugeot constructed the first automobile. Benz produced his first car two years later in 1893. After 1880, electricity became more available, providing power to light everything from private homes to government office buildings. The Eiffel Tower in Paris, constructed for the International Exhibit of 1889 and for decades the tallest structure in the world, was a monument to the age's engineering wizardry; visitors rode to its summit in electric elevators. In 1900 the tower's system of electric lights dazzled nighttime strollers.

Innovations in Machinery and Chemicals

To fuel this explosive growth, the leading industrial nations mined and produced massive quantities of coal, iron, and steel during the second half of the century. Output by the major European iron producers increased from 11 million to 23 million tons in the 1870s and 1880s alone. Steel output grew just as impressively in the same decades, from half a million to 11 million tons. Manufacturers used the metal to build more than 100,000 locomotives that pulled trains, transporting 2 billion people annually.

Historians sometimes contrast two periods of the Industrial Revolution. In the first, in the eighteenth and early nineteenth centuries, innovations in textile machinery

The way is straight, the embankment narrow,

Telegraph poles, rails, bridges,

And everywhere on both sides are Russian bones—. . .

Brothers! You remember our reward!

Fated to be strewn in the earth.[1]

The only apparent safety precaution was forbidding prisoners to work with explosives.

Other kinds of livelihoods developed around the railroad: its planning and design preoccupied Russia's ablest engineers, and the skilled aspects of its construction attracted stonemasons and other master builders from foreign lands. Financiers from around the world and producers of raw materials from as far away as the United States participated as well. Construction began in May 1891 when Nicholas, heir to the Russian throne, drove the first golden spike into the ground at Vladivostok.

Minister of Finance Sergei Witte maintained that the railroad would make Russia the dominant global market in the world: "The silk, tea, and fur trade for Europe, and the manufacturing and other trade for the Far East, will likely be concentrated in Moscow, which will become the hub of the world's transit movement," he predicted.[2] Long after the line's completion the trans-Siberian railroad provided good jobs for railway workers in Siberia. In settlements along the rail line, business thrived, and cities such as Novisibersk opened scores of new opportunities for service workers supporting railroad personnel.

The trans-Siberian railroad did indeed transform the livelihoods of the empire as a whole. The government sent some 5 million peasants from western Russia to Siberia between 1890 and 1914. The massive migration was intended to extend Russian power across the empire's vast expanse. The government designated millions of acres of land—populated at the time by the nomadic Asian foragers and herders—for Russian, Ukrainian, and Belorussian settlers. Russian bureaucrats hoped that as the peasants intermingled with indigenous peoples, the non-Russian ethnic groups would become "Russianized." They thus justified occupation on grounds similar to those the U.S. government used to justify white settlers' migration westward and takeover of American Indian lands. The completion of the longest railroad line in the world meant that hundreds of nomadic tribes lost hunting lands and pasturage that were the basis of their livelihoods, and the population of Siberia soared with the influx of farmers. Russia would never be the same.

---

1. Nicholai Nekrasov, quoted in J. N. Westwood, *A History of the Russian Railways* (London: George Allen and Unwin, 1964), 33.
2. Quoted in Stephen G. Marks, *Road to Power: The Trans-Siberian Railroad and the Colonization of Asian Russia, 1850–1917* (London: I. B. Tauris, 1991), 117.

QUESTIONS TO CONSIDER

1. What jobs were needed to construct the trans-Siberian railroad, and how were workers treated?

2. How did the railroad affect livelihoods other than those directly connected with its construction?

3. How would you balance the human costs of building the railroad with the human opportunities it created?

4. What changes did the trans-Siberian railroad bring to Russia?

powered by steam energy predominated. The second, in the later nineteenth century, concentrated on heavy industrial products and electrical and oil power. This was indeed the pattern in Britain, but as other areas industrialized, textile factories and blast furnaces were built simultaneously. Moreover, the number of small workshops grew faster than the number of factories, though factories dominated production. Although industrialization reduced household production in traditional crafts such as weaving, livelihoods pursued at home—called **outwork**—persisted in garment making, metalwork, and such "finishing trades" as metal polishing. In fact, factory production fostered "industriousness" more than ever, and factory, small workshop, and home enterprise have coexisted down to the present.

Industrial innovations in machinery and chemicals also transformed agriculture. Chemical fertilizers boosted crop yields, and reapers and threshers mechanized harvesting. In the 1870s, Sweden produced a cream separator, a first step toward mechanizing dairy farming. Wire fencing and barbed wire replaced more labor-intensive wooden fencing and stone walls, allowing large-scale cattle-raising. Refrigerated railroad cars and

outwork A method of manufacturing in which raw or semifinished materials are distributed to households where they are further processed or completed.

steamships, developed between the 1840s and 1870 in several countries, allowed fruits, vegetables, dairy products, and meat to be transported without spoiling, increasing the size and diversity of the urban food supply.

Challenge to British Dominance

Although Great Britain maintained its high industrial output throughout the second half of the 1800s and profited from a multitude of worldwide investments, other countries began to narrow Britain's industrial advantage. The United States industrialized rapidly after its Civil War (discussed in Chapter 25) ended in 1865, and Japan joined in after 1870. Argentina, Brazil, Chile, and Mexico gained industries at varying rates between 1870 and 1914, producing textiles, beer, soap, cigarettes, and an array of other products. In Argentina, the introduction of cigarette-rolling machinery allowed the National Tobacco Company's twenty-eight hundred workers to turn out four hundred thousand cigarettes per day by the end of the 1890s. In the same decade, its leading textile company produced 1.6 million yards of cloth annually. Industry—if not full-scale industrialization— circled the globe.

Germany   Two countries in particular began to surpass Britain in research, technical education, innovation, and growth rates: Germany and the United States. Germany's burst of industrial energy occurred after its states unified as a result of the Franco-Prussian War of 1870–1871 (discussed in Chapter 25). At this time, Germany took the French territories of Alsace and Lorraine with their textile industries, mineral deposits, and metallurgical factories. Investing heavily in research, German businesses began to mass-produce goods such as railroad stock and weapons, which other countries had pioneered in manufacturing. Germany also spent as much money on education as on its military in the 1870s and 1880s, producing highly skilled engineers and technical workers who made Germany's electrical and chemical engineering capabilities soar.

The United States   After its Civil War, the United States began to exploit its vast natural resources intensively, including coal, ores, gold, and oil. The value of U.S. industrial goods vaulted from $5 billion in 1880 to $13 billion in 1900. Whereas German accomplishments relied heavily on state promotion of industrial efforts, U.S. growth depended on innovative individuals, such as Andrew Carnegie in iron and steel and John D. Rockefeller in oil. As the nineteenth century came to a close, then, Britain struggled to keep ahead of its industrial competitors.

Industrialization in Japan

Foundation of Industriousness   Between 1750 and 1850 merchants, peasant producers, artisans, and even samurai warriors laid the foundation for Japan's industrialization. They engaged in brisk commerce, especially with the East and Southeast Asian mainland. Japan exported its sophisticated pottery—some 2 million pieces to Southeast Asia alone in the first decade of the nineteenth century—and it imported books, clocks, and small precision implements, especially from China. Internal trade increased too. Businessmen and farmers produced sake, silk, paper, and other commodities required by Japan's vast network of regional lords, the daimyo, and their retainers, the samurai. By law, the daimyo traveled from their own lands to the court at Edo for long periods every year, and they spent lavishly to support the travels of their large entourages. Japan's roads were clogged with traffic in people and goods (see Seeing the Past: Japan's Industrious Society).

The samurai of this era were what we might describe today as underemployed. After two centuries of peace under the Tokugawa Shogunate (see Chapter 21), there were many more samurai than the country needed for administration and defense. To occupy their time, some samurai studied the new findings in the botany, chemistry, and engineering coming from China and Europe. They experimented with electricity, created important devices such as thermometers that helped improve silkworm breeding, and awaited Dutch ships in the port of Nagasaki with their information from around the world. Craft-based innovation produced new kinds of seeds, new varieties of silkworms, and improvements

Japan's Industrious Society

Hiroshige, *Nihon-bashi*, from the series, *Fifty-three Stations on the Tokaido* (Road to Tokyo) (Brooklyn Museum/Corbis.)

Famed Japanese artist Ando Hiroshige (1797–1858) is best known for his prints of nature and for his several series about work life in early-nineteenth-century Japan. In these works, Hiroshige combined his great print-making skills with knowledge of Dutch and other Western art. The exchange went both ways, as Western artists borrowed from Hiroshige in return. Impressionists were especially drawn to his focus on daily life and his vibrant use of color. Later, Hiroshige's serial method and drawing technique influenced the creators of comic strips.

Hiroshige depicted the many livelihoods of Japan in some of his works. In particular he showed commercial life on the road to Edo (now Tokyo), the capital of Japan, before it industrialized. The road is clogged with busy people loaded with goods and supplies. Collectively, Hiroshige's drawings show a remarkably active commercial and productive life, demonstrating the prevailing view among historians today that many parts of the world enjoyed "industrious" economies in the seventeenth through the nineteenth centuries that laid the essential groundwork for full industrialization.

EXAMINING THE EVIDENCE

1. What attitude toward work comes through in this print?

2. How does it contrast with the attitude displayed in the document on pages 815 and 816 by Mexican women workers?

in their already highly technical looms. The inventive Japanese were more than ready to take advantage of Western machinery when the opportunity arose.

Merchants were also an economic force. As in Europe they supplied peasant families with looms and other machines for spinning and weaving at home. Under the Tokugawa regime, production was labor-intensive, and government encouraged these impressive levels of industriousness. Notable innovations took place in cotton and silk production and in manufacturing goods such as coins from precious metal, but output was limited. Japanese innovators aimed to replace this system with Western-style factory or mass production, beginning with textiles, guns, railroads, and steamships. It had become clear that, as one Japanese administrator wrote in 1868, "machinery is the basis of wealth."[6]

The final motive for change was concern about Western ships seeking access to Japanese ports and trade. Seeing outsiders as potential agents of social and political unrest, the Japanese had long restricted the flow of foreigners into the country. In the nineteenth century, however, they experienced for themselves the inroads they had seen Westerners make in China during the Opium War (discussed later in this chapter). In 1853 Commodore Matthew Perry steamed into Edo (now Tokyo) Bay and demanded diplomatic negotiations with the emperor. Some samurai urged resistance, but senior officials knew how defenseless the city would be against naval bombardment. The next year Perry signed an agreement on behalf of the United States under which Japan would open its ports on a regular basis.

Turn to Industry

Both individual Japanese and the government adjusted rapidly to the presence of these competitors. They were motivated in good part by the desire to learn the skills that would allow them to protect Japan through industrial prosperity and military strength. Inventors adapted European mechanical designs, using the country's wealth of skilled workers to make everything from steam engines to telegraph machines. The state sent delegations to Europe and the United States with the goal of "swiftly seizing upon the strengths of the Western industrial arts," as the minister of industry wrote in 1873.[7] By the early 1870s the reformed central government known as the Meiji Restoration (see Chapter 25) had overseen the laying of thousands of miles of railroad and telegraph lines, and by the early twentieth century the country had some 32,000 factories, many of them small; 5400 steam engines; and 2700 machines run by electricity. Although it is often said that Japan industrialized at state direction, a more accurate picture shows an effective mixture of state, local, and individual initiatives based on a foundation of industriousness. This combination eventually led to Japan's central role in the world economy.

Industrializing Japan, c. 1870–1900

Economic Crises and Solutions

Industry and the expansion of the global economy brought uneven prosperity to the world and seesawing booms and busts, especially in the second half of the nineteenth century. Because global trade bound industrialized western Europe to international markets, a recession—by today's definition, a period of negative economic growth lasting six months or longer—could simultaneously affect the economies of such diverse regions as Germany, Australia, South Africa, California, Argentina, Newfoundland, and the West Indies. At the time, economists, industrialists, and government officials did not clearly understand the workings of industrial and interconnected economies. When a stubborn recession struck in the 1870s and lasted in some places until the end of the century, they were stunned.

Late-Nineteenth-Century Recession

One reason for the recession of the 1870s was the skyrocketing start-up costs of new enterprises. Compared to steel and iron factories, the earliest textile mills had required little capital. After midcentury, industries became what modern economists call capital-intensive rather than labor-intensive: to grow, companies had to buy expensive machinery, not just hire more workers. This was especially true in developing countries such as those in Latin America, where the need to import machinery and hire foreign technicians added to costs.

Second, increased productivity in both agriculture and industry led to rapid price declines. Improved transportation allowed the expanding production of meat and grain in the United States, Australia, and Argentina to reach distant global markets rapidly, driving down prices. Wheat, for example, dropped to one-third its 1870 price by the 1890s. Consumers, however, did not always benefit from this persistent decrease in prices, or deflation, because employers slashed wages and unemployment rose during economic downturns. When this occurred, consumers just stopped purchasing manufactured goods.

Thus, a third major reason for the recession was underconsumption of manufactured products. Industrialists had made their fortunes by emphasizing production, not consumption. "Let the producers be many," went a Japanese saying, "and the consumers be few."[8] This attitude was disastrous because many goods were not sold, and the result was that prices for raw materials collapsed globally. People lost their land, jobs, and businesses, with consequences ranging from long stretches of unemployment to bankruptcy.

In response to these conditions, governments around the world took action to boost consumption and control markets and prices. New laws protected innovation through more secure patents and spurred development of the limited-liability corporation, which protected investors from personal responsibility, or liability, for a firm's debt. **Limited liability** greatly increased investor confidence in financing business ventures. As prices fell in the 1870s and 1880s, governments broke any commitments they had made to free trade. They imposed tariffs (taxes) on imported agricultural and manufactured goods to boost sales of domestic products. Latin American countries levied tariffs that were some five times those in Europe. Without this protection from cheap European goods, a Mexican official predicted, new industries would "be annihilated by foreign competition."[9]

Business people also took steps to end the economic turmoil. They advanced the development of **stock markets**, which financed the growth of industry by selling shares or part ownership in companies to individual shareholders. In an international economy linked by telegraph, telephone, railways, and steamships, the London Stock Exchange was a center of this financial activity. In 1882 it traded industrial shares worth £54 million, a value that surged to £443 million by 1900, dramatically increasing the capital individuals made available to industry. At the same time, firms in single industries banded together in **cartels** to control prices and competition. One German coal cartel founded in 1893 dominated more than 95 percent of coal production in Germany. Thus, business owners deliberately blocked open competition to ensure profitability and economic stability.

Another way to address the economic crisis was to add managerial expertise. In the late 1800s, industrialists began to hire others to run their increasingly complex day-to-day operations, which was a revolutionary change in business practices. A generation and more earlier, factory owners such as Richard Arkwright had been directly involved in every aspect of the business and often ran their firms through trial and error. Now, separate managers specializing in sales and distribution, finance, and purchasing made decisions. The rise of the manager was part of the emergence of a "white-collar" service sector of office workers, with managers (generally male) at the high end of the pay scale and secretaries, file clerks, and typists (increasingly female) at the low end. These office workers were essential to guide the flow of business information that managers needed to make profits. Banks needed tellers and clerks, just as railroads, insurance companies, and government-run telegraph and telephone companies needed armies of white-collar employees.

A final solution to the economic crisis was the development of consumer capitalism, sparked by the recognition that underconsumption of manufactured goods had directly led to the late-nineteenth-century recession. The principal institution for boosting consumption was the department store, which daring entrepreneurs founded after midcentury to promote sales of manufactured products. Department stores gathered an impressive variety of goods in one place, in imitation of the Middle Eastern bazaar and the large Asian merchant houses, and they eventually replaced many of the single-item stores to which people were accustomed. Buenos Aires alone had seven major department stores, among them Gath y Chaves (GOT e shah-VEZ), which by 1900 had grown to occupy a multistoried building of 13,000-plus square feet, and which tripled its space five years later. From the Mitsui family in Tokyo to the Bloomingdales in New York, entrepreneurs set up institutions for mass consumerism, and some, such as Harrods of London, established branches around the world.

Just as factories led workers to greater productivity, these modern palaces aimed to stimulate more consumer purchases. Luxury items like plush rugs and ornate draperies spilled over railings in glamorous disarray. Shoppers no longer bargained over prices; instead they reacted to sales, a new marketing technique that could incite a buying frenzy. Department stores also launched their own industrial ventures to meet consumer needs: Gath y Chaves began a line of ready-to-wear clothing, recognizing that busy urban workers no longer had time to make their own. Women explained their often lengthy trips to these stores as necessary to a healthy home and family life. Stores hired attractive salesgirls, another variety of service worker, to lure customers to buy. Shopping was not only an urban phenomenon: glossy mail-order catalogs from the Bon Marché in Paris and Sears, Roebuck in the United States arrived regularly in rural areas to help farmers buy the products

Governments and Businesses Respond

Rise of Managers and the "White-Collar" Service Sector

The Department Store

limited liability Legal protection for investors from personal responsibility for a firm's finances.

stock market A site for buying and selling financial interests, or stock, in businesses; examples include the London and Hong Kong stock exchanges.

cartel A group of independent business organizations in a single industry formed to control production and prices.

Gath y Chaves Department Store

The first department stores, such as this one in Buenos Aires, Argentina, were built to resemble palaces and present the possibility of luxury to everyone. Shoppers could walk on lush carpets, climb stately marble staircases, and purchase or imagine buying the items displayed from around the world. By assembling an array of goods once sold in individual small stores, the department store was revolutionary because it focused on increasing consumption rather than driving production, as industry had done. The first department stores were the direct ancestors of today's megastores and Internet shopping.

of industry. Thus, department stores were both commercial crossroads where urban shoppers could purchase a wide variety of manufactured goods from around the world and a means of connecting otherwise isolated rural consumers to the industrial marketplace.

The Industrial Revolution and the World

FOCUS

How did industrialization affect societies in China, South and West Asia, and Africa?

The Industrial Revolution transformed life in many parts of the world, even those with few factories of their own. Increased industrial development caused hardships for economies outside the West, eventually tipping trade balances and ultimately political power. The once-dominant economies of China, India, and the Ottoman Empire declined due to the Industrial Revolution, despite the real wealth that some local merchants, landowners, and entrepreneurs created for themselves. The Industrial Revolution allowed Western nations to pull ahead of these former world leaders.

Western nations used their powerful and increasingly reliable weaponry to open trade. Like Japan, other nations in the early nineteenth century were often unwilling to trade with Europe, which was widely seen as both uncivilized and a source of inferior goods. Even an English man, commenting on the high quality of a shawl from India, agreed, "I have never seen a European shawl I would use, even if it were given to me as a present."[10] This attitude, common not just in England but around the world, led Europeans and Americans alike to use threats of violence to open markets. Europe's immense industrial productivity demanded outlets for manufactured goods, its factories needed raw materials, and its growing population of industrial workers depended on foreign food and stimulants.

Reaction abroad to these demands and needs was mixed. Some governments, merchants, and producers around the world saw that there was money to be made from trading in Western products, setting up their own factories, and adopting technology. Others saw only danger to local artisanal economies and to the political status quo. In the long run, the rise of industry changed lives and livelihoods everywhere, not only because of the interconnected economic consequences of rising productivity, but because the industrialized West was willing to use violence to gain access to raw materials and to open new markets for manufactured goods.

The Slow Disintegration of Qing China

At the beginning of the industrial era, Qing China was the wealthiest and most productive country in the world, its prosperity built on the silver that flooded China in exchange for its cottons, porcelains, and other coveted items (see Map 24.3). Yet the Qing Empire was facing difficult problems, and the Industrial Revolution only compounded them. Revolutionary upheavals in North and South America and the Napoleonic Wars in France suddenly stopped the flow of silver and curtailed trade, eating away at the source of China's wealth and strangling job opportunities. On world markets, cheap industrial European goods competed with Chinese products, and social unrest erupted among the affected workers. Commercial rivalry soon turned to war.

Europeans had grown dependent on a variety of products from India and China, especially tea. The five chests of tea Europeans had purchased annually in the 1680s had soared to more than 23 million pounds by 1800. At the time this meant a severe trade imbalance for Europe, whose cheap but inferior textiles did not appeal to the Indians and Chinese.

By the 1820s, however, the British had found something the Chinese would buy—opium. Grown legally in British-controlled India, opium was smuggled into China, where its import and sale were illegal. So great was the demand for opium in China that even after buying tea the British merchants and smugglers turned a handsome profit. China's big payout in silver caused a drain on its economy, and Chinese officials worried that opium use was out of control. A Chinese government official charged with ending the illegal trade commanded the British to turn over all the opium they possessed; he burned what they surrendered. Determined to force opium on the Chinese, the British sent a fleet to China to keep the opium market open.

The Opium War

In the Opium War (1839–1842) that followed, Western firepower won decisive victories, and with the 1842 Treaty of Nanjing, China agreed to pay the British an indemnity (or fine), allow British diplomats access to the country, open five ports to trade, and reduce tariffs (see again Map 24.3). The treaty shifted power to Europeans, forcing the Chinese to deal with them as full trading partners and respected diplomats. The opium trade was legalized, making fortunes for British merchants and paving the way for other goods to enter China.

The Opium War made life difficult for Chinese workers. During the conflict, many lost their jobs as dockworkers, tea exporters, and commercial agents. A severe depression followed the war's end, and floods and famines between 1846 and 1848 compounded the hardships. In the late 1840s peasant religious leader Hong Xiuquan (hung she-o-chew-on) built a following among the underemployed and unemployed. Hong had failed to get the career he desperately wanted—a place in the prestigious Chinese civil service. He first tried to pass the nationwide civil service exam in 1836, and like others flunked this initial try. As Hong failed successive attempts to pass the exam, he fell feverishly ill and had religious visions that convinced him he was the brother of Jesus.

By 1850, his charismatic preaching of his version of Christianity had attracted some 20,000 disciples. Hong's social message promised a better future: he promoted work for all, equality of the sexes, and communal living, which appealed to hard-pressed ordinary people. It emphasized industriousness: "The diligent husbandman will be rewarded and the idle husbandman punished."[11] Like some of the Christian missionaries infiltrating China, Hong asked his followers to give up alcohol and opium and reject oppressive customs such as foot binding as first steps toward a more prosperous future. Hong's movement envisioned a perfect society—the Heavenly Kingdom of Peace, or Taiping Tianguo—and it began to move in vast armies across the country, ultimately gathering millions of adherents.

MAP 24.3

Qing China, 1830–1911

Qing officials knew that opium was dragging China's people into addiction, but the resulting Opium War with Britain to restrict the supply only made matters worse. Led by the British, Europeans forced open Chinese ports, destroyed historic Chinese cities, and helped create uprisings such as the Taiping Rebellion. While its officials debated how to protect the Qing Empire's mighty legacy of conquest and productivity, China maintained its vigorous trade in porcelain and other manufactured goods.

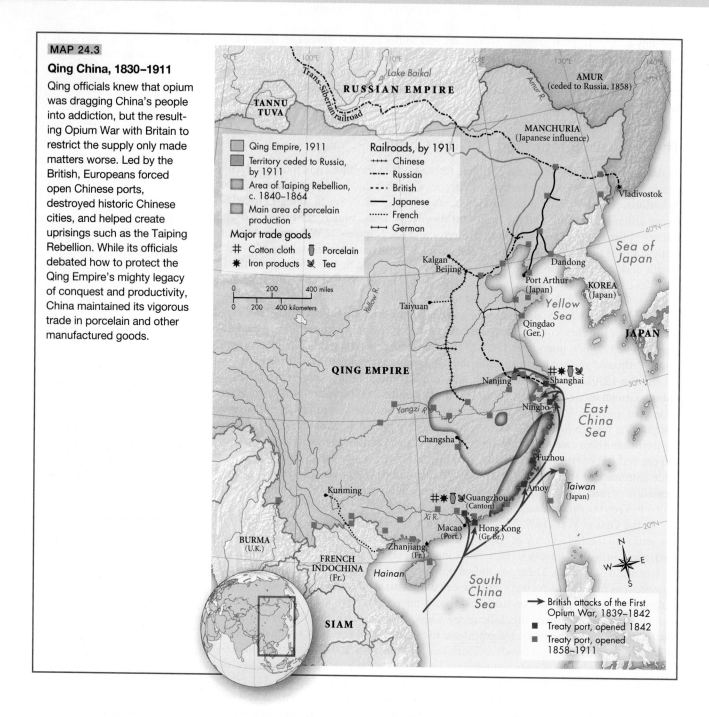

The Taiping Rebellion

To most Chinese, social discontent and economic distress were evidence that their rulers had lost "the Mandate of Heaven," their political legitimacy. The Taiping Rebellion accelerated the crisis of the Qing government, already weakened by the European economic and military assault. At this critical juncture, however, the movement's leaders began to quarrel among themselves and adopt a lavish lifestyle, which weakened the rebellion. The Hunan militia ultimately defeated the Taiping in 1864 under the leadership of the emperor's appointee, the scholar-official Zeng Guofan (zung gwoh-FAN). Hong himself died that year in the final siege of Nanjing.

The lesson learned by some intellectuals and officials—notably Zeng Guofan—was the value of Westernization, by which they meant modernizing the military, promoting technological education, and expanding industrialization. This led in the 1870s to the opening of mines and the development of textile industries, railroads, and the telegraph.

Weighing Opium in India
Opium grown in India went mostly to the Chinese market, though some found its way to Europe through Middle Eastern middlemen. Opium cured headaches, sleeplessness, and general aches and pains, but consumers in both Asia and Europe also welcomed the euphoric feeling of well-being the drug created. Many Chinese and European people became addicted, among them such famous Western artists as novelist Sir Walter Scott, poet Elizabeth Barrett Browning, and composer Hector Berlioz. British merchants and the British government, however, were concerned not with addiction but with sales, profits, and a favorable balance of payments. In the Opium Wars they crushed Chinese resistance with the help of their new steamships and industrially produced guns. (The Art Archive/Victoria and Albert Museum London/Eileen Tweedy.)

However, the Dowager Empress Cixi, who had seized power during the uprising, focused more on maintaining imperial control of the government than on Western-style modernization. It was unclear which impulse would triumph.

Competition in West and South Asia

Since early modern times, the Ottoman Empire in West Asia had profited from its extensive system of textile manufacture—one so far-reaching that Europeans, Africans, and Asians had long coveted its silks, dyes, fine cottons, and woven rugs. As Western industrial powers sent inferior but less expensive thread, yarn, and woven cloth to markets around the world, it changed the balance of trade. As prices dropped, artisans spinning and weaving at home suffered, working longer hours just to earn a living wage. Textile manufacturing had traditionally been done in the home during winter to provide income during the agricultural off-season. These artisanal ways persisted, but in the last third of the nineteenth century some carpet factories were established across the Ottoman lands. Young unmarried girls, who were less expensive to hire than men and worked for just three or four years (that is, long enough to earn a dowry to attract a husband), replaced lifelong artisans. The Industrial Revolution altered centuries-old work patterns and left many Ottoman subjects, in the words of a British traveler, "ragged beyond belief."[12]

Although the Industrial Revolution hurt craftworkers globally, it boosted the fortunes of other workers. After 1815, the ruler of Egypt, Muhammad Ali, set his subjects to mastering the industry's "strange machinery," and he eventually exempted workers in silk factories from service in the army.[13] Ottoman merchants prospered, as did owners of large estates who could send cotton and other agricultural products to markets around the world on railroads and steamships. New jobs opened up: in 1911 there were thirteen thousand railroad workers in the empire, and thousands more had helped construct the lines. In the Ottoman Empire, regional rulers such as Muhammad Ali who recognized the need for modern skills founded engineering schools and expanded technical education. The Industrial Revolution opened opportunities for some even as it made life more difficult for others.

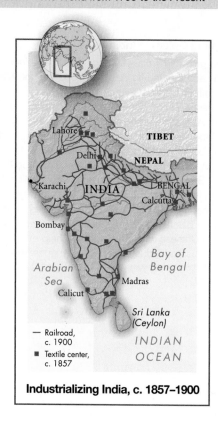

Industrializing India, c. 1857–1900

Railroad, c. 1900

Textile center, c. 1857

When Europe's cheap, lower-quality textiles flooded world markets, including those of the Indian subcontinent, the cut-rate competition hurt India's skilled spinners, weavers, and dyers. Furthermore, Britain taxed the textiles Indian craftsmen produced, tilting the economic playing field in favor of British goods. Even so, as in the Ottoman Empire, some in India's lively commercial economy adapted well. In Bengal between the 1830s and 1860s, entrepreneur Dwarkanath Tagore teamed up with British engineers and officials to found raw silk firms, coal mines, steamship companies, and an array of other businesses that made his family fabulously wealthy. The first textile factory started in Bombay in 1853, and by 1914 India had the fourth-largest textile industry and the fourth-longest railway system in the world. Some business people made fortunes. Yet the coming of industry hurt many of the region's independent artisans. The country did not industrialize enough to give them all factory jobs or business employment, and many returned to the countryside. As a result, India grew more rural as the West became more urban.

Besides textiles, India exported such manufactured goods as iron, steel, and jute, which contributed approximately 10 percent of the country's gross national product. Entrepreneurs such as Jamsetji Tata competed globally, founding a dynasty based first in textiles, then in iron and steel, and continuing in the twentieth century with airplanes and software. Yet the British presence was powerful. The East India Company and the British government filled their pockets by imposing high taxes and taking more than their share of the region's prosperity. Moreover, although the British improved the Indian infrastructure, building the rail system, for example, the benefits of such improvements were not spread evenly. By making it easier to extract and then sell agricultural goods on the world market, they favored large Indian landowners.

A New Course for Africa

Industrialization had long-term consequences for Africa as well. During the nineteenth century, the Atlantic slave trade declined quickly due to mounting protests against slavery and the growth of more profitable economic activities. As Denmark (1803) and Britain (1807) abolished the international slave trade, power in West Africa shifted away from the local rulers and traders who profited from it, and toward those who could provide raw materials to Western industry (see Map 24.4).

The Antislavery Movement

Since the Enlightenment, abolitionists had called for an end to the slave trade and to slavery itself. The antislavery message, often crafted by white religious leaders and blacks themselves, invoked Christian morality and the ideas of natural rights that had shaped the revolutions in the Atlantic world. In England, former slaves were eloquent participants in the antislavery movement, which expanded in the early nineteenth century to include international conferences. As the trade in humans was progressively outlawed, abolitionists worked to end slavery completely, a goal achieved in the Western Hemisphere in 1888 when Brazil became the last country in the Americas to outlaw it. Even after 1888, however, slavery continued in many parts of the world, including Africa and Asia.

The rationale for ending slavery also had an economic dimension, and many merchants, financiers, and workers supported the abolitionist movement. The price of slaves had risen during the eighteenth century, so the use of slaves became less profitable. Plantation owners, thinking that natural increase could supply them with slaves cheaply, tried to force slave women to have more children. Industrialists recognized that it was more profitable if Africans worked in Africa to produce raw materials such as palm oil and cotton. Factory workers supported abolition because they regarded slaves as cheap competition in the labor market. Free labor became a widely accepted ideology in industrial areas.

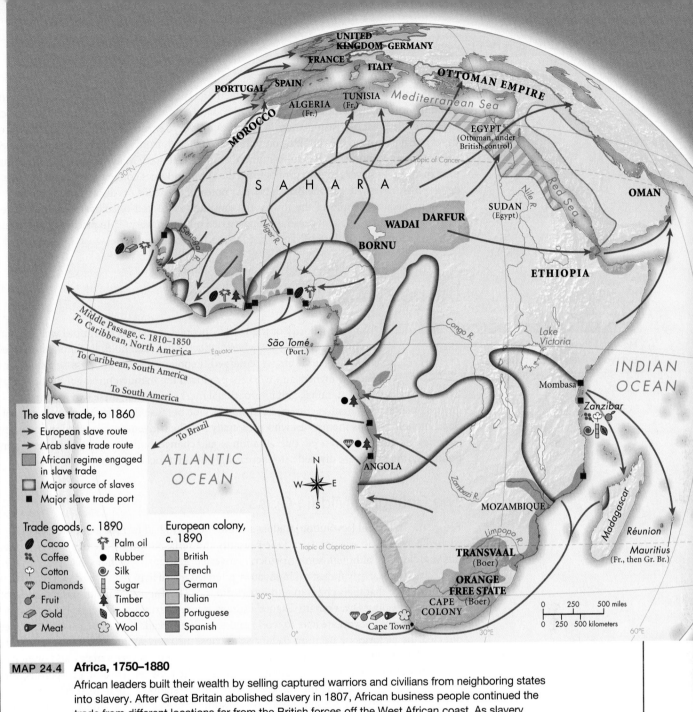

MAP 24.4 **Africa, 1750–1880**

African leaders built their wealth by selling captured warriors and civilians from neighboring states into slavery. After Great Britain abolished slavery in 1807, African business people continued the trade from different locations far from the British forces off the West African coast. As slavery further declined in the West, the Africans adapted once more, keeping their captives for themselves to provide raw materials for Western industrialists.

Expanding Slavery Within Africa

The decline of profits from the Atlantic slave trade threw some African elites into economic crisis. Many quickly adapted, simply moving the slave trade south to supply markets in Brazil and elsewhere. Slavers arriving in West African ports learned to load ships and depart in some 100 minutes to escape British surveillance. In the course of the nineteenth century, even as Europeans worked to abolish the trade, approximately 3.5 million slaves were taken from West Africa alone to sell in the Atlantic world. African rulers and business people used slaves to increase their efforts to provide raw materials for global manufacturing. They expanded slavery within Africa, waging war and kidnapping to capture slaves for their own use. For fear of enslavement, "One could not go to another town's sector of the market without being led by an armed elder," one Nigerian man recalled.[14]

Slaves in West Africa produced various materials for the textile industry: gum, redwood, and palm oil to lubricate machinery. The oil was also used to produce soap, which people in the West increasingly found essential to everyday life. Hundreds of thousands of slaves in Egypt worked the cotton fields. Other raw materials from Africa, such as gold, boosted the European economy; coffee, rubber, and diamonds followed. Many historians believe that the expansion of slavery to gain profits from these commodities condemned Africa to underdevelopment. West Africa, one British traveler noted in the 1830s, "is disorganized, and except in the immediate vicinity of the towns, the land lies waste and uncultivated, the wretched natives living under constant dread of being carried off into slavery."[15] In places both with and without factory labor, industrialization had far-reaching consequences.

Industry and Society

FOCUS

How did industrialization affect people's everyday lives and livelihoods?

The vast majority of the world's peoples remained rural until well into the twentieth century, but where industry did take hold, livelihoods changed and new social classes emerged. People were less and less self-sufficient. Factory owners and workers produced the manufactured goods that began to flood local, regional, national, and international markets. At first, these two growing social groups, workers and manufacturers, lived side by side because the first factory owners were often modest artisans themselves who personally put their inventions to work in their new factories. As industry advanced, this situation would change: both groups became important politically, but they were divided into increasingly distinct social classes.

The Changing Middle Class

Before the Industrial Revolution, traders around the world had formed a middle class, sandwiched between the aristocrats and the peasants and serfs. Now most factory owners joined this middle class, although some aristocrats invested in industry without losing their privileged class status. Early industrial innovators often led frugal lives full of hard work, and they tried to ensure that their children and others did too. The Tagore family in India thrived on hard work, leading Dwarkanath Tagore's son to refuse charity to a beggar-priest: "I shan't give you money. . . . you are able to work, and earn your bread."[16] While early businessmen directed the factories or went on distant sales trips, their wives often tended the accounts, dealt with subcontractors, supervised workers (especially if they were female), and organized shipments of finished goods. As factories grew and their owners became prosperous, they became society's leaders, rising far above the humble status of their workers. Leaders of industry built large houses and began to consume more goods, including luxuries. They removed their wives from factory supervision and from the working world, beginning what historians term a "cult of domesticity" for women that signaled a family's prosperity. These economic leaders have collectively been called the *bourgeoisie*, a French term for the middle-class groups at the center of the Industrial Revolution.

The Middle Class Promotes Progress

As we have seen, with the march of industry, scientists and engineers in research laboratories and universities replaced amateur tinkerers as industrial innovators. As part of the state's commitment to building national wealth, public monies often funded scientific research, which was increasingly expensive. The middle class grew to include those whose empirical and scientific knowledge benefited industrial society, and professionalization occurred in other fields as well. Doctors, lawyers, professors, and journalists—all of whom drew on the scientific method and objective analysis in their work—gained prestige as they served the wider population of industrial society.

Such prosperous men of the evolving middle class founded a range of societies and clubs to create solidarity and foster the exchange of knowledge. In Japan in 1876, the city fathers of Kanazawa opened an industrial museum to spread technical knowledge more widely among the public. Wealthy citizens around the world founded art, history, and science museums during these industrial years and worked to improve city life. "Reserve large areas for football, hockey, and parks," Indian industrialist Jamsetji Tata advised urban renovators. "Earmark areas for Hindu temples, Mohammedan mosques, and Christian churches."[17]

Well-to-do women banded together to provide baby clothes for newborn children and other goods to impoverished workers. Indian reformer Savithribai Phule, married at age nine, joined her husband in aiding the lowest-caste "Untouchables," despite mounting criticism and threats of violence against her. She founded schools for the girls of the Untouchable caste, claiming to feel "immeasurably happy" with her volunteer work. "Besides, it also demonstrates the horizons to which a human being can reach out," she wrote.[18] As industrialization and rapid urban growth disturbed centuries-old ways of life, these institutions, in the words of one English official, promoted "the protection of their [industrialists'] property" by reducing worker misery. Good works also helped to unite the middle classes in the face of challenges from those with "anti-social and revolutionary principles."[19]

The New Working Class

While the middle classes enjoyed increased comfort and prosperity, industrial workers led work lives governed by the machine, the factory whistle, and eventually the time clock of the office or department store. Initially, many industrial workers, whether in the United

An East Indian Middle-Class Family
Sometime in the late nineteenth century, this middle-class family donned their best clothes and sat for this formal portrait. The father may have worked for the British government or been an independent merchant or factory owner. Nevertheless, the British dominated the subcontinent politically, economically, and culturally. This family wore fashionable Western clothing, although some of the women adapted their outfits by adding elements of the traditional sari to their dress. (Dinodia Photos.)

States, Japan, Britain, or Argentina, were young, unmarried women whose families no longer needed them on farms, which now took fewer hands to run. Factories were magnets, offering steady wages and, often, supervised living quarters. Women and children were paid less than men, reducing labor costs, and this trend continued as industry spread. Despite the low pay, many women found factory work far preferable to domestic service as maids, where they were on call twenty-four hours a day. After her husband died in 1910, the Mexican widow Marcela Bernal del Viuda de Torres left her young sons to live with relatives and took her two daughters to Mexico City to find work for all three in its thriving factories. Marcela, like the underemployed around the world, sought opportunity. As she said when explaining the move to her daughters, "I'm sure not going to let you end up as maids."[20]

The worker's day was often long, grueling, and unsafe in the early days of industry, as Robert Blincoe witnessed firsthand. In 1844 England limited women's work to twelve hours per day, but in Japan men and women worked fourteen to seventeen hours a day even late in the century. They tended machines while they ate meals and usually had just half a day off per week. Machines lacked even minimal safety features, leading to amputated limbs, punctured eyes, torn-off scalps, and other crippling injuries. A Japanese observer described cotton workers in urban factories as "pale and exhausted with faces like invalids. . . . young girls with the lifeblood sucked out of them."[21]

Workers' health deteriorated in many cities, and critics said it was because the lower classes, as one British observer put it as early as 1795, lived "crowded in offensive, dark, damp and incommodious habitations, a too fertile source of disease."[22] The lure of industrial work swelled urban populations to the breaking point. There was not enough housing, and sanitary facilities were almost nonexistent. Europe's cities were usually surrounded by medieval walls, which limited their natural expansion, and humid factories nurtured disease. Wherever workers were crowded together, epidemics of deadly cholera

Working Conditions

might erupt, as happened, for example, in the camps housing thousands of Indian railroad builders. Deaths from tuberculosis and pneumonia soared. In its early days, industry's human costs were clear.

Fighting the Industrial Advance

Many people resisted the introduction of laborsaving machines into their towns and villages. Handloom weavers saw their livelihoods slipping away, and agricultural workers resented mechanization's threat to their livelihoods. Some handicraft workers—notably the Luddites (named after their leader, Ned Ludd), who attacked whole factories in northern England in 1812 and after—smashed the new machines, which they believed were putting them out of work. In the countryside, day laborers left menacing notes for those who introduced threshing machines, such as: "If providing you dont pull down your messhenes . . . we will burn down your barns and you in them this is the last notis."[23] The British government mobilized its armies to protect the new system from protesters. It executed and imprisoned many, and sent large numbers to populate Australia and New Zealand—which industrialized in turn.

Under the older values of city life, artisans mutually supported one another, but that system weakened. As rural folk migrated to cities in search of industrial jobs, workers were often strangers to one another. Between 1820 and 1840 the Russian government of Poland deemed that Lodz would become a textile center, for example, and thousands of migrant workers from the countryside and fledgling industrialists from several parts of Europe quickly moved there. Chinese migrated to the Caribbean to service the sugar industry, and South Asians took their commercial and other skills to East Africa. Single young people or widows migrating from the countryside lived beyond the reach of their families and old community networks. Prostitution soared, as did venereal disease and illegitimacy. Thus, as industrialization created dense networks of new economic connections throughout the world, it contributed to the breakdown of social connections in local communities.

Industrialization brought people's everyday lives into a mechanical orbit and changed the rhythms of earning a livelihood. No longer did sunrise and sunset determine the beginning and end of the workday. Now the clock, perfected in the early modern period to measure

Child Labor in Britain

Although the exploitation of children is still a feature of industrialization, the use of child labor by early industrialists was especially harsh, as the life of Robert Blincoe testifies and as this late-nineteenth-century illustration of children at work in the mines demonstrates. After these children were lowered side by side into claustrophobic conditions, they faced the rough job of physically hauling carts of coal out of the mines through narrow passageways. Like their adult counterparts, they suffered from coal dust and extremes of heat and cold. It is little wonder that even liberal British politicians of the time, who wanted no interference from government in business, agreed to governmental investigation and regulation of mining conditions. After parliamentary hearings on mine work, children's work and that of women who worked in and near the mines were regulated. (Photo: akg-images.)

even in seconds, set the hours for work of many kinds. Factory whistles signaled the start of the workday, while stopwatches timed the pace of work. The ongoing march of the machine, rather than the seasons, determined people's movements and organized their labor. Industrialists imposed heavy fines on anyone late by even a minute. With alcohol a prominent feature of life in a world where there was no safe water or milk supply, however, drunkenness sometimes undermined the strict discipline industrialists hoped to impose.

The Sexual Division of Labor

The Industrial Revolution ushered in major changes in the sexual division of labor. Industrialists and manufacturers followed the tradition of dividing work along gender lines; now, however, the division was generally arbitrary. In some factory towns the weavers were all men, and women performed some processes in finishing the woven cloth. In other places, women tended the looms, and men only repaired and maintained the machines. Women's work in factories, even though it might be identical to men's, was said to require less skill; it always received lower pay. Men dreaded the introduction of women into a factory, which could signal that the owner intended to save on wages by cutting men's jobs. Sometimes the wife or daughter in an artisanal family went to work in a factory because the husband's work as a shoemaker or handloom weaver no longer paid enough to support the household. In such cases the husband's independent identity as handloom weaver or shoemaker may have been a proud one, providing freedom from the oversight of a foreman and an industrialist. His wife, however, may have surrendered her freedom to earn the extra income that permitted him to maintain his.

Factory Workers

The vast majority of women, both unmarried and married, worked to support their families or themselves. Factory owners and supervisors often demanded sexual favors from women as the price of employment. The foreman supervising Adelheid Popp, a factory worker in late-nineteenth-century Germany, demanded kisses in exchange for higher wages. She quit the job, but others did not have such freedom. "Even the decent jobs, for example, those in banks," one Russian woman complained, "are rarely available unless one first grants favors to the director, the manager, or some other individual."[24] It was normal for supervisors to select one favorite woman, take her as a mistress, and then fire her once he tired of the relationship. Domestic service, which expanded with the rising prosperity of the middle class, was thought to be safer for young women, but many a housemaid fell victim to fathers and sons in middle-class families, who were regular harassers of working women. If these sexual relations became known, the women would be fired, and pregnant servants quickly lost their jobs. This is why Marcela de Torres feared for her daughters.

The new white-collar sector advanced the sexual division of labor. Cost-conscious employers looking for workers with mathematical, reading, and writing skills gladly offered jobs to women. Since respectable lower-middle-class women had few other employment options, businesses in the service sector paid women much less than men for the same work, as in factories. As women increasingly filled lower-level white collar jobs, all sectors of the industrial economy perpetuated the idea that women were simply worth less than men and should receive lower wages (see Reading the Past: Mexican Women on Strike).

White-Collar Workers

The Culture of Industry

Writers, artists, and ordinary people alike responded to the dramatic new sights and unexpected changes of industrialization. The railroad and expanded trade spread local customs, creating greater variety in everyday life and contributing to developing regional and national cultures. In Japan, for example, sashimi and sushi, once known in only a few fishing towns, became popular dishes across the nation. Better communication networks helped the spread of knowledge, and technological improvements helped knowledge flourish: gas lighting

FOCUS

How did writers and artists respond to the new industrial world?

Mexican Women on Strike

As industrialization progressed, factory workers increasingly responded to the harsh conditions of industrialization by organizing unions and banding together to strike. They directed their demands to factory owners and government officials, and they sought support from their fellow citizens. For instance, in 1881, women cigarette workers in Mexico City wrote a letter to a magazine for elite women in which they suggested that poverty might lead them to prostitution. At the same time, women cigar workers posted this placard around Mexico City to explain their strike against the factory owners.

Oppression by the Capitalist!

Until October 2, 1881, we used to make 2185 cigars for four reales [Mexican money], and now they have increased the number of cigars and lowered our salary. On October 3, 1881, through the mediation of El Congreso Obrero [The Congress of Workers], we agreed to make 2304 cigars for four reales. It is not possible for us to make more. We have to work from six in the morning until nine at night. . . . We don't have one hour left to take care of our domestic chores, and not a minute for education. The capitalists are suffocating us. In spite of such hard work, we still live in great poverty. What are our brother-workers going to do? What are the representatives of the Mexican press going to do? We need protection, protection for working women!

Source: Susie S. Porter, *Working Women in Mexico City: Public Discourses and Material Conditions, 1879–1931* (Tucson: University of Arizona Press, 2003), 80.

EXAMINING THE EVIDENCE

1. What major concerns do the women announce in this placard?

2. To what specific groups is the placard addressed? Why did the strikers single out these groups?

extended reading deep into the night, for example, and railroads exposed more travelers than ever to ideas far from home. The increased productivity associated with industrialization eventually led to more leisure time, and streams of workers entered cafés, dance halls, and parks to enjoy their new free time. Such changes in everyday life led to a torrent of artistic and literary reflections on the dramatic new industrial world.

In some, industry inspired optimism. For such thinkers, the rational calculation and technological progress that had produced industry raised the possibility that a perfect society could be created. A group of French and British thinkers, the "utopian socialists," spread this faith around the world. Their goal was to improve society as a whole, not just for the individual—hence the term **socialism**. They believed that rational planning would lead to social and political perfection—that is, to utopia—and to prove their point they often lived in communes where daily life could be as precisely organized as it was in the factory. The inefficient nuclear family became obsolete in their communes, where large numbers of people worked together to finish necessary tasks efficiently. At a time when many people still held monarchs and leisured aristocrats in the highest esteem, **utopian socialism** valued technicians and engineers as future rulers of nations.

Two middle-class German theorists—the lawyer and economist Karl Marx (1818–1883) and the wealthy industrialist Friedrich Engels (1820–1895)—had completely different ideas on how to best organize society. Although they shared the utopian socialists' appreciation of science, they saw the new industrial order as unjust and oppressive. In the 1840s they began to analyze the life of workers, publishing their results in Engels's *The Condition of the Working Class in England* (1844). In 1848 they published *The Communist Manifesto*, which became the bible of modern socialism. Marx elaborated on what he called "scientific socialism" in his most important work, *Das Kapital* (Capital), published between 1867 and 1894.

Marx held that the fundamental organization of any society derived from the relationships built into work, or what he called, simply, production. This idea, known as **materialism**, was that a society's structure was built on the class relationships that stemmed from production—such as those between serf and medieval lord, slave and master, or worker

Socialism and Marxism

socialism A social and political ideology dating from the early nineteenth century that stresses the need to maintain social harmony through communities based on cooperation rather than competition; in Marxist terms, a classless society of workers who collectively control the production of goods necessary for life.

utopian socialism A goal of certain French and British thinkers early in the nineteenth century, who envisioned the creation of a perfect society through cooperation and social planning.

materialism In Marxist terms, the idea that the organization of society derives from the organization of production.

and factory owner. Marx referred to these systems—feudalism, slavery, and **capitalism**, respectively—as modes of production. In the industrial era, people were in one of two classes: the workers, or **proletariat**, and the owners, or capitalists (also the **bourgeoisie**, in Marxist terms), who owned the means of production—the land, machines, factories, and other forms of wealth. Rejecting the eighteenth-century liberal focus on individual rights, he held that the cause of the inequality between classes such as the proletariat and the capitalists was the owners' control of the means of production. When capitalist control disappeared, as Marx was certain it would, a classless society of workers would arise.

Economic liberals such as Adam Smith thought the free market would ultimately produce balance and a harmony of interests among people in all classes of society. Marx, however, believed that the workers' economic oppression by their bosses inevitably caused conflict. He predicted that as workers became aware of their oppression they would unite in revolt against their capitalist exploiters. Their revolt—not reform or legislation—would be the mechanism for worldwide historical change. The proletariat would overthrow capitalism, and socialism would reign. The moment for revolt, Marx thought, was near. "The proletarians have nothing to lose but their chains. They have a world to win. WORKING MEN OF ALL COUNTRIES, UNITE!" So ends *The Communist Manifesto*.

Marx never precisely described the classless society, but he believed it would involve workers' control of production in large factories. In a socialist society, private ownership of the means of production would end. This in turn would end the need for a state, whose only function, Marx claimed, was to protect the propertied classes. Like many male intellectuals in Europe, Marx devoted little analysis to inequalities based on race and gender. He did conclude, however, that women's lives would automatically improve under socialism. The possibility of achieving socialism inspired workers around the world. As we will see in later chapters, Marxist ideas shaped both the Russian Revolution of 1917 and the Chinese Revolution of 1949.

Industry and the Arts

The new industrial world inspired artists as well as intellectuals. Some celebrated industry, welcoming the artistic influences from far-off places that it made possible. Japanese woodblocks showed trains racing through a countryside of blossoming cherries. Hiroshige's prints depicting roads teeming with industrious people influenced Western artists to turn from mythical topics and great historic scenes to the subject matter of ordinary working lives (see again Seeing the Past: Japan's Industrious Society). Deeply influenced by the color, line, and delicacy of Japanese art as well as by its focus on scenes of ordinary daily life, French painters such as Claude Monet pioneered the artistic style known as "impressionism," so called for the artists' effort to capture a single moment by focusing on how the ever-changing light and color transformed everyday sights. Industry contributed to the new style as factories produced products that allowed Western painters to use a wider, more intense spectrum of colors.

Other Western artists interpreted the Industrial Revolution differently, focusing instead on the grim working conditions brought about by wrenching change. One was Germany's Käthe Kollwitz, whose woodcuts realistically depict starving artisans. British author Charles Dickens wrote of the dark side of industrialization in popular novels that even reached a Japanese audience. Among them was *Oliver Twist* (1837–1839), which many scholars speculate was based in part on the life of Robert Blincoe. *Uncle Tom's Cabin* (1852), U.S. writer Harriet Beecher Stowe's shocking tale of slave life in the American South, influenced some in the Russian nobility to lobby for freeing the serfs.

Even musical forms showed the impact of the Industrial Revolution. Utopian socialists composed music celebrating the railroad and the sounds of industry. Concert halls, like factories, became bigger to accommodate the increasing urban population, and orchestras grew larger and included more instruments to produce a massive sound. Military bands marched through the widening streets of capital cities. Their increasing precision and noise matched that of the new machines and the precise movements of the industrial workers tending them.

capitalism An economic system in which the means of production—machines, factories, land, and other forms of wealth—are privately owned.

proletariat Under capitalism, those who work without owning the means of production.

bourgeoisie Originally a term meaning the urban middle class; Marx defined it as the owners of the means of production under capitalism.

Workers Going Home at the Lehrter Railroad Station, 1897

German artist Käthe Kollwitz came from a family of socially active reformers and was married to the doctor Karl Kollwitz, who worked among the poor. "My real motive for choosing my subjects almost exclusively from the life of the workers was that only such subjects gave me in a simple and unqualified way what I felt to be beautiful," she wrote. Kollwitz spent her entire artistic career depicting the struggles of ordinary men and women, as in this image of workers going home exhausted after a day of hard labor. Many in the upper classes, including the German Kaiser, disapproved of such sordid subjects, but they are now considered to be among the most important art of modern times. (Käthe Kollwitz, *Workers on the Way Home at the Lehrter Station* (NT 146) 1897–1899 Brush and watercolor with accents in white Käthe Kollwitz Museum Köln © 2011 Artists Rights Society (ARS), New York/ VG Bild-Kunst, Bonn.)

COUNTERPOINT
African Women and Slave Agriculture

FOCUS

What contributions did African women agricultural workers make to industrial development?

The story of the Industrial Revolution often centers on individual inventors and the laborsaving machinery they pioneered. But entire groups, many of them anonymous and uncelebrated, piloted advances critical to industrialization. A good example comes from Africa, which nineteenth-century Europeans and Americans often regarded as a continent full of unskilled people; they used this perspective to justify both their enslavement and discrimination against all people of color. Africans, however, were foremost among the collective innovators of their day.

Women and Farming in Africa

Many of these unnamed inventors were women, who have dominated African farming both as cultivators of their own land or as slaves on African plantations. Armies of male slaves kidnapped individuals or captured entire communities of neighboring peoples for regional leaders to sell or enslave in turn. Male slaves also served in urban commerce, working as artisans, porters, and traders. Women slaves largely did agricultural work to feed the slave armies and other male slaves. Some slave men hunted such prized commodities as elephant tusks, which were fashioned into piano keys, gun handles, combs, and other objects characteristic of middle-class lives around the world. Women slaves also served as domestic servants and concubines for African elites.

Women's agricultural labor supported African life. When they married, women received land to provide for themselves and their children. Free and slave women alike could themselves own slaves to increase their agricultural productivity. As farm workers, women served as a counterpoint to independent and free male farmers, peasants and large landowners alike. In Africa it was women, either as independent farmers or more usually

Nayemwezi Women Pounding Sorghum, 1864
As industrialization advanced around the world, women in Africa were central to its agricultural foundation, as this drawing shows. They planted, weeded, and harvested major crops such as sorghum, a grass whose kernels were pounded into flour and whose stalks were pressed to produce a sweet syrup. Sorghum is native to Africa, and there is evidence that slave women brought it, along with rice and other crops, to the North American colonies, and that these crops fed both industrial workers and local slaves. (Photo: akg-images.)

as slave laborers, who introduced new varieties of seeds, new tools for farming, and more productive farming techniques. Today it is estimated that African women grow some 80 percent of all agricultural produce on the continent.

On the west coast of Africa, although men participated in some aspects of rice farming, rice cultivation was known as "women's sweat." Women developed complex systems for cultivating the important rice crop, especially a variety called "red" rice. To control water supplies, they installed canals, sluices, and embankments, depending on whether they were capturing water from rain, tides, or floods. They reaped bountiful harvests through this manipulation of the environment.[25]

Rice Cultivation

Women Slaves in the North American South

Many landowners in South Carolina and Georgia prized West African slave women, considering them "choice cargo" because of their knowledge of rice cultivation. In fact, it was slaves from West Africa who established the "red" rice variety as a preferred crop on American plantations and provided the initial technological systems for growing it. This rice was so important to the U.S. South's developing commercial economy that Thomas Jefferson, for one, sought more information about it. Its main advantage, he learned, was that if cultivated according to African techniques of water management, it could be grown outside of swamps. The more usual practice of cultivating rice in standing water "sweeps off numbers of the inhabitants with pestilential fevers,"[26] according to Jefferson, so a growing system that eliminated the threat of disease was advantageous.

Jefferson, like some other American planters, never succeeded in cultivating red rice. The first African rice to be widely grown in North America was fragile, demanding special skills that planters, such as Jefferson, usually lacked. In contrast, West African women possessed an extensive knowledge of this and other forms of agriculture and passed this knowledge down through their families.

Slavers added these women to their cargo along with unhusked rice and many other plants and seeds. When they arrived in the United States, the technological knowledge to

Spread of Agricultural Technologies from Africa to the U.S. South

grow them moved from Africans to Europeans, not the other way around. In this regard West African women farmers form a counterpoint to the celebrated inventors of machines. Although they have been overlooked in history books, they created wealth for their owners, most of whom in the early days of rice cultivation were adventurers with little knowledge of how to grow these crops. Their story of the introduction of rice to North America, the perfection of seeds, and the complex technology of irrigation and processing that helped feed a growing workforce has seemed less heroic than that of an individual who invented one laborsaving machine.

Conclusion

The Industrial Revolution changed not only the world economy but the lives and livelihoods of tens of millions of people, from workers and manufacturers to the politicians trying to organize rapidly changing societies. By replacing simple machines operated by human energy with complex machines powered by steam engines, mechanization expanded productivity almost beyond measure. The results were both grim and liberating. Industrial laborers such as mill worker Robert Blincoe suffered abuse, and the flow of cheap goods from industrial countries drove down prices and threw artisans around the world into poverty. Slavery not only flourished but also allowed industry to advance. Unsung slave women spread rice cultivation to help feed the growing world population of workers. The new patterns of work in large factories transformed the rhythm of labor and the texture of urban life, and cities grew rapidly with the influx of migrants from the countryside and from other regions of the world. Political ideas and the arts also changed with the rise of industry and with the continuing global expansion of trade. Movements to end slavery and to create free workers succeeded in Europe and many parts of the Western Hemisphere.

Debate continues about whether industry was a force for good, but even opponents at the time saw that industrial life liberated people from the hardships and restrictions of rural life and gave them access to a wider array of inexpensive goods. Some theorists, such as Marx and Engels, believed that solidarity would grow among a global working class no longer isolated on individual farms, while artists depicted these new workers with paint and pen—occasionally romanticizing their productivity but more often presenting the poverty that accompanied industrialization. The middle and working classes that developed with industrialization led different lives even within the same industrial cities, but they often joined in a major global movement of the time—the development of the political form called the nation-state that increasingly shaped industrial society. As we will see in the next chapter, it was a form that spread around the world alongside industrialization and ushered in other conflicts and advances of the modern era.

NOTES

1. James R. Simmons Jr., ed., *Factory Lives: Four Nineteenth-Century Working-Class Autobiographies* (Peterborough, Ontario: Broadview, 2007), 110.

2. Ibid., 123.

3. Quoted in Brian Dolan, *Wedgwood: The First Tycoon* (New York: Viking, 2004), 54.

4. Quoted in Sally and David Dugan, *The Day the World Took Off: The Roots of the Industrial Revolution* (London: Macmillan, 2000), 54.

5. Quoted in Ken Alder, *Engineering the Revolution: Arms and Enlightenment in France, 1763–1815* (Princeton, NJ: Princeton University Press, 1997), 223.

6. Quoted in Tessa Morris-Suzuki, *The Technological Transformation of Japan from the Seventeenth to the Twenty-First Century* (Cambridge, U.K.: Cambridge University Press, 1994), 65.

7. Quoted in ibid., 73.

8. Quoted in T. R. Havens, "Early Modern Farm Ideology and Japanese Agriculture," in *Meiji Japan: Political, Economic and Social History*, ed. Peter Kornicki, 4 vols. (Routledge: New York, 1998), 1:235.

9. Quoted in Edward Beatty, *Institutions and Investment: The Political Basis of Industrialization in Mexico Before 1911* (Stanford: Stanford University Press, 2001), 59.

10. Thomas Munro, quoted in Romash Chunder Dutt, *The Economic History of India* (Delhi: Low Price, 1990 [orig. pub. 1902–1904]), 185–186.

11. "The Land System of the Heavenly Dynasty" (1853), quoted in *China: Readings in the History of China from the Opium War to the Present*, ed. J. Mason Gentzler (New York: Praeger, 1977), 56.

12. Quoted in Michael E. Meeker, *A Nation of Empire: The Ottoman Legacy of Turkish Modernity* (Berkeley: University of California Press, 2002), 103.

13. Afaf Lutfi Al-Sayyid Marsot, *Egypt in the Reign of Muhammad Ali* (Cambridge: Cambridge University Press, 1984), 169–171.

14. Quoted in Carolyn Brown, *"We Were All Slaves": African Miners, Culture, and Resistance at the Enugu Government Colliery* (Portsmouth, NH: Heinemann, 2003), 36.

15. Mr. Laird, quoted in Joseph Inicori, *Africans and the Industrial Revolution in England: A Study in International Trade and Economic Development* (New York: Cambridge University Press, 2002), 394.

16. Debendranath Tagore, quoted in Blair B. Kling, *Partner in Empire: Dwarkanath Tagore and the Age of Enterprise in Eastern India* (Berkeley: University of California Press, 1976), 184.

17. Quoted on the Tata Group Web site, http://www.tata.com/0_about_us/history/pioneers/quotable.htm.

18. Quoted in Susie Tharu and K. Lalita, eds., *Women Writing in India: 600 B.C. to the Early Twentieth Century*, 2 vols. (London: Pandora, 1991), 1:214.

19. Quoted in Caroline Arscott, "'Without Distinction of Party': The Polytechnic Exhibitions in Leeds, 1839–1945," in *The Culture of Capital: Art, Power, and the Nineteenth-Century Middle Class*, ed. Janet Wolff and John Seed (Manchester, U.K.: Manchester University Press, 1988), 145.

20. Quoted in Susie Porter, *Working Women in Mexico City: Public Discourse and Material Conditions, 1879–1931* (Tucson: University of Arizona Press, 2003), 3–4.

21. Quoted in E. Patricia Tsrumi, *Factory Girls: Women in the Thread Mills of Meiji Japan* (Princeton, NJ: Princeton University Press, 1990), 139.

22. Quoted in Ivy Pinchbeck, *Women Workers and the Industrial Revolution, 1750–1850* (London: Virago, 1981 [orig. pub. 1930]), 195.

23. Quoted in Eric Hobsbawm and George Rudé, *Captain Swing: A Social History of the Great English Agricultural Uprising of 1830* (New York: Norton, 1968), 208.

24. Quoted in Victoria E. Bonnell, *The Russian Worker: Life and Labor Under the Tsarist Regime* (Berkeley: University of California Press, 1983), 197.

25. Judith A. Carney, *Black Rice: The African Origins of Rice Cultivation in the Americas* (Cambridge, MA: Harvard University Press, 2001), 31.

26. Ibid., 147.

RESOURCES FOR RESEARCH

The Industrial Revolution Begins, 1750–1830

World history allows us to think differently about the Industrial Revolution, understanding it less as a radical departure and more as a burst of productivity and inventiveness taking place in many parts of the world. Bezis-Selfa's and Dolan's books depict the day-to-day toil of workers and manufacturers.

Bayly, C. A. *The Birth of the Modern World, 1780–1914: Global Connections and Comparisons.* 2004.

Bezis-Selfa, John. *Forging America: Ironworkers, Adventurers, and the Industrious Revolution.* 2004.

Clark, Gregory. *A Farewell to Alms: A Brief Economic History of the World.* 2007.

Dolan, Brian. *Wedgwood: The First Tycoon.* 2004.

Inikori, Joseph. *Africans and the Industrial Revolution in England: A Study in International Trade and Economic Development.* 2002.

Industrialization After 1830

Countries industrialized in different ways, though they often experienced similar problems. Morris-Suzuki and D'Costa show in exciting detail the road to industrialization in Japan and Argentina.

Beatty, Edward. *Institutions and Investment: The Political Basis of Industrialization in Mexico Before 1911.* 2001.

D'Costa, Anthony. *The Long March to Capitalism: Embourgeoisement, Internationalization, and Industrial Transformation in India.* 2005.

Morris-Suzuki, Tessa. *The Technological Transformation of Japan.* 1994.

Rappaport, Erica. *Shopping for Pleasure: Women in the Making of London's West End.* 2000.

Rocchi, Fernando. *Chimneys in the Desert: Industrialization in Argentina During the Export Boom Years.* 2006.

The Industrial Revolution and the World

Just as global innovation and trade provided much of the impetus for the Industrial Revolution, industrialists' efforts to sell their goods changed local and regional economies around the world. The books below describe the consequences for a variety of countries.

Bello, David Anthony. *Opium and the Limits of Empire: Drug Prohibition in the Chinese Interior, 1729–1850*. 2005.

Goswami, Manu. *Producing India: From Colonial Economy to National Space*. 2004.

Meeker, Michael E. *A Nation of Empire: The Ottoman Legacy of Turkish Modernity*. 2002.

Reilly, Thomas H. *The Taiping Heavenly Kingdom: Rebellion and the Blasphemy of Empire*. 2004.

Shepherd, Verene A. *A Maharani's Misery: Narratives of a Passage from India to the Caribbean*. 2002.

Industry and Society

The idea that a middle class arose during the Industrial Revolution is disputed, because world historians acknowledge that for centuries there had been merchants sandwiched between princes and peasants. At the same time, many believe that industrialist workers followed industrial rhythms and saw the world differently from their predecessors. For a real-life example of the opportunities seized by one striving industrialist, see the PBS Web site on Andrew Carnegie.

Banerjee, Swapna M. *Men, Women, and Domestics: Articulating Middle-Class Identity in Colonial Bengal*. 2004.

Igler, David. *Industrial Cowboys: Miller and Lux and the Transformation of the Far West, 1850–1920*. 2001.

Morgan, Kenneth. *The Birth of Industrial Britain: Social Change, 1750–1850*. 2004.

Porter, Susie. *Working Women in Mexico City: Public Discourses and Material Conditions, 1879–1931*. 2003.

Public Broadcasting Service. *American Experience*, "Andrew Carnegie." http://www.pbs.org/wgbh/amex/carnegie/.

The Culture of Industry

Those in the world of art and ideas responded to the sights and sounds of industry. The Metropolitan Museum of Art's Web site has many links to specific instances of cultural exchange during the nineteenth century, including the one listed on Japan's influence on the West during industrialization.

Callen, Anthea. *The Art of Impressionism: Painting Technique and the Making of Modernity*. 2000.

Izzard, Sebastian. *Hiroshige/Eisen: The Sixty-Nine Stations of the Kisokaido*. 2008.

Megill, Allan. *Karl Marx: The Burden of Reason*. 2002.

Metropolitan Museum of Art. *Timeline of Art History*, "Japonisme." http://www.metmuseum.org/toah/hd/jpon/hd_jpon.htm.

Peskin, Lawrence. *The Intellectual Origins of Early American Industry*. 2003.

COUNTERPOINT: African Women and Slave Agriculture

The unsung innovators of the past are in the process of being discovered. Carney looks at the West African women and men who brought rice cultivation, processing, and cooking to the U.S. South.

Carney, Judith A. *Black Rice: The African Origins of Rice Cultivation in the Americas*. 2001.

Carney, Judith A., and Richard N. Rosomoff. *In the Shadow of Slavery: Africa's Botanical Legacy in the Atlantic World*. 2009.

Hoerder, Dirk. *Cultures in Contact: World Migrations in the Second Millennium*. 2002.

▶ **For additional primary sources from this period,** see *Sources of Crossroads and Cultures.*

▶ **For Web sites, images, and documents related to topics in this chapter,** see Make History at bedfordstmartins.com/smith.

The major global development in this chapter ▶ The Industrial Revolution
and its impact on societies and cultures throughout the world.

IMPORTANT EVENTS

c. 1750	Industrialization begins in Great Britain
1769	James Watt creates the modern steam engine
1780s–1790s	Interchangeability of parts developed in France
1803	Denmark becomes the first Western country to abolish the slave trade
1814	George Stephenson puts a steam engine on a carriage on rails, inventing the locomotive
1819	First Atlantic crossing by a steamship
1839–1842	Opium War between China and Britain
1842	Treaty of Nanjing opens Chinese ports
1848	*Communist Manifesto* published
1853	U.S. ships enter Japanese ports
1840s–1864	Taiping Rebellion
1865	U.S. Civil War ends, rapid U.S. industrialization begins
1868	Meiji Restoration launches Japanese industrialization
1871	Germany gains resource-rich Alsace and Lorraine after defeating France
1873–c. 1900	Deep global recession with uneven recovery
1890s	Argentina's leading textile manufacturer produces 1.6 million yards of cloth annually
1891–1904	Construction of trans-Siberian railroad

CHAPTER OVERVIEW QUESTIONS

1. In what ways did the Industrial Revolution change people's work lives and ideas?
2. How did the Industrial Revolution benefit people, and what problems did it create?
3. How and where did industrial production develop, and how did it affect society and politics?

SECTION FOCUS QUESTIONS

1. What were the main causes of the Industrial Revolution?
2. How did industrialization spread, and what steps did nations and manufacturers take to meet its challenges?
3. How did industrialization affect societies in China, South and West Asia, and Africa?
4. How did industrialization affect people's everyday lives and livelihoods?
5. How did writers and artists respond to the new industrial world?
6. What contributions did African women agricultural workers make to industrial development?

MAKING CONNECTIONS

1. How did the Scientific Revolution (see Chapter 20) and the Enlightenment (see Chapter 23) contribute to industrialization?
2. How did industrialization in the United States and in Japan differ, and why?
3. What was the role of slavery in industrial development?
4. In what ways was the Industrial Revolution a world event?

KEY TERMS

bourgeoisie (p. 817)
capitalism (p. 817)
cartel (p. 805)
Industrial Revolution (p. 794)
interchangeability of parts (p. 799)
limited liability (p. 805)
materialism (p. 816)
outwork (p. 801)
proletariat (p. 817)
socialism (p. 816)
stock market (p. 805)
utopian socialism (p. 816)

25

AT A CROSSROADS ▲

The Meiji Restoration of 1868 was the foundation of Japanese nation building and industrialization. Its Charter Oath, the founding document of Japan's new regime, is shown here being read in the presence of the emperor. The Charter Oath established the rule of law over "evil customs" of the past and opened the door to freedom in livelihoods. It also called on the Japanese to scour the world for new findings and advances, making Japan a crossroads of nation building and economic development. (Art Resource, NY.)

The Rise of Modern Nation-States

1850–1900

In 1862 Matsuo Taseko, a prosperous Japanese peasant, packed a few possessions and, leaving her family behind, made her way to the capital at Kyoto. The trip was an unusual one for a woman to make on her own, and even more so because of its goal: to overthrow the country's civilian leadership. Taseko belonged to a group of conservative activists eager to restore the power of the Japanese emperor, who for centuries had played second fiddle to the Tokugawa shogun, or first minister. So subordinate was the emperor that he received just 5 percent of the government's revenues while the shogun took 25 percent. To those in Taseko's group, the shogun's position was a reversal of the natural order. In a proper world, decision-making and revenue should have been the other way around. "Despicable charlatans," she called the shogun's administration. Even worse to Taseko was the presence of foreigners in the country's port cities, notably the Americans and British, who had demanded in the 1850s that Japan open its harbors to global trade. Taseko wrote this poem about them:

> The superficial
> foreign barbarians
> pile up mountains
> of silver,
> but even I, who am not
> a brave warrior
> from the land of the rising sun,
> I do not want their money,
> I would rather be poor.[1]

BACKSTORY

As we saw in Chapter 24, throughout the nineteenth century Europe and the United States industrialized rapidly, if unevenly, allowing the West to catch up economically with India and China. Industrialization offered a host of advantages to the West. Both Europe and the United States excelled in producing weaponry, which made them especially successful in opening trade and gaining diplomatic power. Industrializing nations engaged in increasingly global commerce, enjoyed greater productivity, and developed dense networks of swift transportation. As the West's newly industrialized states extended their power around the world, industrialization also produced internal transformations. It gave rise to new social classes and new occupations, swelling the middle and working classes and giving both a stake in the growing prosperity of their nations. These groups had the awareness, and some of them the wealth, to challenge the political and social values of kings and the aristocracy, sometimes overthrowing existing political institutions entirely and at other times working to modify them.

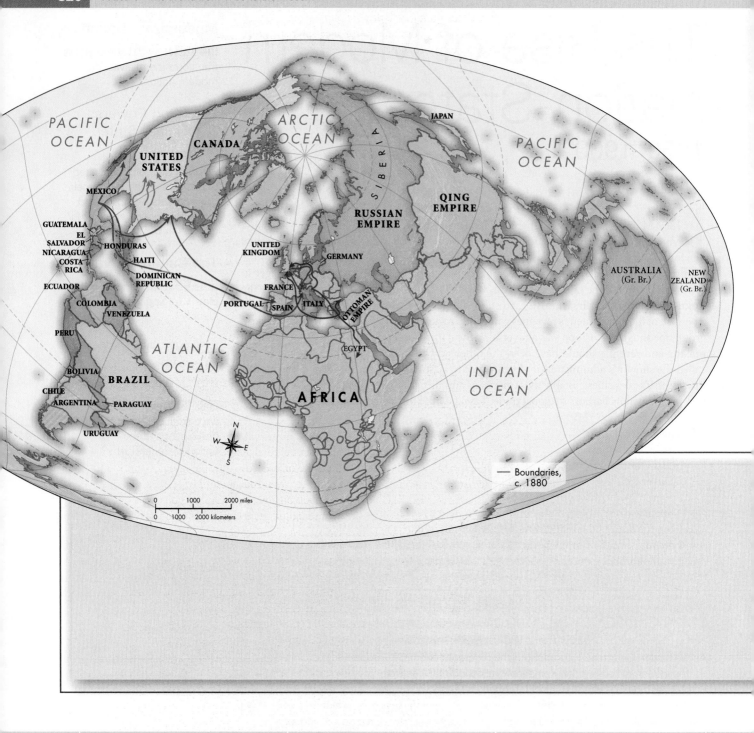

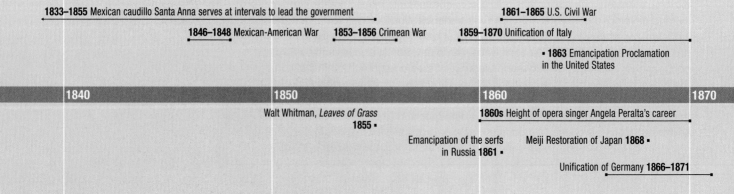

1833–1855 Mexican caudillo Santa Anna serves at intervals to lead the government

1861–1865 U.S. Civil War

1846–1848 Mexican-American War   **1853–1856** Crimean War

1859–1870 Unification of Italy

1863 Emancipation Proclamation in the United States

1840   **1850**   **1860**   **1870**

Walt Whitman, *Leaves of Grass* **1855**

1860s Height of opera singer Angela Peralta's career

Emancipation of the serfs in Russia **1861**   Meiji Restoration of Japan **1868**

Unification of Germany **1866–1871**

Beginning in 1862 members of Taseko's conservative group, aiming to free Japan from outside influences and to restore the emperor, took part in a virtual civil war with reformers who wanted trade, the latest technology, and a modern nation-state. Assassinations, riots, and street violence plagued the country, causing Taseko herself, who was sometimes seen as a spy by political opponents, to go into hiding in the spring of 1863 and eventually to return to her hometown. By 1868 the reformers had restored the emperor to his central position in a nation-building revolution that became known as the Meiji Restoration.

The Meiji Restoration was primarily the work of propertied individuals who wanted to update Japan's government and economy. It was part of a global nineteenth-century trend toward building strong states whose people felt bound together as part of a single political unity. In Latin America, leaders in Mexico, Argentina, and other states struggled to develop national institutions and to create connections between the central government and local elites. In Europe the nation-states of Germany and Italy unified amid economic ferment and calls for social and political reform. The United States fought a destructive civil war and killed and displaced native Americans to create a mighty nation-state stretching thousands of miles. Russia freed its serfs and reformed its legal and military systems—reforms designed to make it more competitive in a modernizing and global economic system.

Historians sometimes treat the rise of powerful nation-states and the sense of national identity among peoples as part of an inevitable process. However, it was not: as Italy and Germany were forming unified nations and Latin Americans were developing notions of modern citizenship, millions of individuals in the Austrian Empire, Africa, and Oceania, for example, held on to local identities based on village life or ethnic ties. Moreover, many

MAPPING THE WORLD

Nation-States, c. 1880

In many cases, but not all, industrial growth and revolutionary uprisings often led kingdoms to develop into nation-states. Around the world, nations reformed their administrative structures, created more effective armies, and encouraged national spirit. From Russia to Australia and across the Western Hemisphere, war and the seizure of native peoples' lands accompanied the rise of the nation-state.

ROUTES ▼

→ Forced migrations of Native Americans, 1832–1835

→ Travels of Florence Nightingale, 1820–1855

→ Travels of Camillo di Cavour, 1830–1838

→ Travels of Angela Peralta, 1862–1883

1880s Popular uprisings in Japan

▪ **1889** Brazilian emperor Pedro II abdicates and republic is installed

| 1880 | 1890 | 1900 |

▪ **1881** Young rebels assassinate Alexander II of Russia

▪ **1888** Emancipation of slaves in Brazil

1872–1876 Fukuzawa Yukichi, *Encouragement of Learning*

rulers had no interest in political and economic reforms, preferring to embrace tradition rather than change.

Other once-powerful states labored unsuccessfully to meet the challenges of global trade, rising population, and the growing industrial power of Europe. The Ottoman sultans found it difficult to modernize their administration of a complex empire; local governors such as the rulers of Egypt modernized cities, transportation, and other facilities on their own. China likewise failed to reform its governmental structures sufficiently to fight off the inroads made by the European powers, even though segments of its population were pushing for modern institutions and growing rich by dealing with the West.

Matsuo was a traditionalist—eager to restore the emperor to power and to rid Japan of outside influence. Although she was a peasant, she was well educated. Broader education also contributed to nation building as people circulated and debated political and philosophical writings, poetry, and other works. People came to be united not only by new institutions, but also by a common culture. However, modern nation-states also denied certain people within their borders full citizenship. Immigrants, women, and the conquered local peoples of Australia and the United States worked and paid taxes, for example, but they did not enjoy full equality and rights such as being able to vote. People hotly debated who did and did not belong to the nation, and Matsuo Taseko engaged in such debates, fighting for ideals that were centuries old. Even though she longed for an older way of doing things, she participated in the development of "the public"—that is, a wide arena of concerns and values that went beyond individual or family interests to create a shared national way of life. Thus, the era of nation building saw many forms of nation-states taking shape, all of them influenced by the public voices of many different people.

OVERVIEW
QUESTIONS

The major global development in this chapter: The causes and consequences of nation building in the nineteenth century.

As you read, consider:

1. Why did nation-states become so important to people in the nineteenth century?

2. What was the role of war in the rise of the nation-state?

3. What was the role of ordinary people in nation building?

4. Are nation-states still important today, and are there still outsiders inside nations?

Modernizing Nations

Politicians of this time and the citizens who backed them worked to bring varied peoples into cohesive nations and to develop more effective governments. This was an age of national growth and nation building when states industrialized and politicians changed the nature of government. To prosper in a more competitive and connected economic world, some even created entirely new entities, as occurred in Italy and Germany. Even where industry was slower to thrive, nation building occurred. People in the newly independent nations of Latin America began to develop a sense of themselves as citizens with common values. In Eurasia the mighty Russian Empire instituted dramatic reforms as part of a nationalizing effort after being decisively beaten in the Crimean War. What emerged from these efforts was a political and cultural form—the nation-state—that has shaped the course of modern world history, both for good and for ill.

"What Is a Nation?"

In an 1882 lecture, French writer Ernest Renan asked, "What is a nation?" The concept was a new one, and subject to debate. Nations came to be seen as political units in which citizens feel an allegiance to one another and are active in the government or state that represents them. Thus *nation-state* and *nation* are often treated as synonyms. A **nation** differs dramatically from a kingdom. A princely kingdom is the personal domain of a monarch, who sees people as subjects to be governed, not as active citizens with a political voice. Despite differences in their form, nations rely on the allegiance of a wide range of people within their geographic borders, who as citizens demand the rule of law and involvement in government. This active civic voice was essential to the rise of modern nations. Facing an enemy from without, people proudly protected the nation—that is, themselves and their community—as patriotic soldiers rather than military recruits forced to defend royal interests, as in a kingdom. Although women did not take up arms and lacked political rights, they too began to consider themselves active contributors to a nation's well-being, rearing young children to be virtuous citizens and volunteering their efforts in times of trouble.

In the nineteenth century and thereafter, politicians sought to mobilize whole populations to build powerful nation-states. Some waged external and civil wars in hopes of creating or maintaining national unity. The U.S. Civil War, for example, can be seen as a war for national unity waged by the North against the South. Other wars were fought to force outlying states to join a powerful military state permanently; this happened with Prussia, which formed the core of the new Germany. Historians have called the development of the nation-state a modernizing influence because the unity it created helped economic development spread over a wider territory. The nation-state also aided economic expansion by eliminating tariffs among cities and localities and by working to replace disruptive regional armies with a single fighting force operating to advance national, not local, power. Nation builders hoped to provide effective, centralized institutions—constitutions, bureaucracies, laws, and common military, education, and transportation systems. Theirs was a multifaceted undertaking in which centralizing authorities sought to challenge local identities and strengthen the connections and loyalties that bound populations together.

Latin American Nation Building

After the regions of South and Central America gained independence from Spain and Portugal early in the nineteenth century, they did not generally develop efficient or smoothly functioning democracies, but they did lay the groundwork for nation-states. Wars between states and civil wars between supporters of centralization and those wanting regional self-rule affected nation-building efforts. Although some people of individual nations were developing a sense of themselves as citizens, Latin American nation building was complex and often difficult (see Map 25.1).

Brazil's dominant ruler for more than five decades was the emperor Pedro II (r. 1831–1889)—a committed nation builder. "I have no rights; all I have is a power resulting from birth and chance," he claimed. "It is my duty to use it for the welfare, the progress, and the liberty of my people."[2] Pedro II tried to centralize government by gaining dominance over the wealthy landowning families and factions that controlled the countryside. As the capital of Rio de Janeiro prospered, Brazil fought a war against Paraguay

Brazil Takes the Lead

nation A sovereign political entity and defined territory of modern times representing a supposedly united people.

MAP 25.1

Latin America, c. 1900

The new nations of Latin America worked to create effective governments and engage citizens in the nation-building process. Like the new United States of America to the north, these nations often fought with their neighbors to expand boundaries and crushed native Americans to gain their lands. Simultaneously they created important institutions, such as systems of law, education, and culture, that would both enhance government power and advance citizens' capabilities.

Map legend:
1830 Year independence gained
Civil war or rebellion
Colony
Boundaries, 1900

(1864–1870), which built allegiance to the central government. A firm believer that nation building depended on legal equality and opportunity, Pedro surrounded himself with people of all races. He ended the slave trade in 1850, partly in response to the growing voice of people of color expressed through their newspapers and clubs. Brazil ended slavery altogether in 1888, and it also tried to eliminate hierarchies based on skin color and racial ancestry. In its openness to change, Brazil seemed to be ahead of all its neighbors. It produced one of the greatest Latin American writers, Joachim Machado de Assis (ma-KA-do day ah-SEES). Of African descent, Machado de Assis's masterful novels do not portray a rosy society of the sort that Pedro hoped for. They are full of satire, as Machado explores the worlds of the old moneyed classes, the new bureaucracies of the rising nation-state, and the outsider status of women—all shaped by the legacy of slavery.

Nation Versus Region

National cohesion quickly fell apart in Brazil. The emancipation of Brazil's slaves enraged plantation and mine owners in the countryside, who relied on cheap slave labor for their profits. Believers in small government, hierarchical social arrangements including slavery, and regional autonomy, they billed themselves as "federalists" and "liberals."

Brazilian Plantation Workers
Pedro II freed Brazil's slaves in 1888 as part of his nation-building efforts, believing that modern, unified nations needed to integrate all races into citizenship. Once regional leaders overthrew his monarchy, however, the weakened national authority could not protect newly freed workers from exploitation. The lack of protection for workers and the free hand given large landowners produced a huge disparity between the upper classes, who were virtually omnipotent, and impoverished ordinary people such as these workers on a manioc plantation in the 1890s. (The Art Archive/ Museu Nacional de Belas Artes Rio de Janeiro Brazil/Gianni Dagli Orti.)

In 1889 they overthrew Pedro's centralizing monarchy, returning power to provincial governments that they themselves controlled. Under the landlords' rule, movement toward a strong, tolerant nation-state seemed to go backward. As one newspaper complained in 1890 of the takeover, "In Brazil there are no more citizens; we are all slaves!"[3]

In fact, most of Latin America was shaped by the bold, powerful landowners in the countryside, who controlled the production of minerals, coffee, sugar, and other commodities sold on the global market. Such men believed that their wealth and power rested on the liberal, eighteenth-century belief in minimal government and the building of individual wealth. They felt that any policy or reform that challenged these principles should be resisted at all costs. In an age of nation building, their stance against strong centralized institutions went against the prevailing trend and kept individual states in turmoil. Almost every Latin American state experienced this contest between centralization and **federalism**.

Caudillos

Many wealthy landowners were themselves strongmen with their own armies, but there were also independent military leaders, *caudillos*, men at the head of unofficial bands of warriors who controlled the countryside by force. Caudillos ruled regions so far removed from the capital cities that they functioned as a law unto themselves. They gathered the support of peasants, workers, and the poor by offering protection in a turbulent countryside where the peasantry on large estates was intensely exploited.

Some caudillos stabilized the central government by acting as temporary dictators. General Antonio Lopez de Santa Anna was the quintessential caudillo. In Mexico, the period from the 1830s to 1855 is called the "Age of Santa Anna" because he wielded so much personal influence. In this period, conservatives favored the rule of large landowners, while the Catholic Church battled reformers who championed individual rights, foreign investment, and trade. During their disputes Santa Anna, who was called "Defender of the Homeland," was summoned some dozen times to head the government and stabilize the nation between 1833 and 1855. During this time of instability Mexico lost much of its territory to the United States in the Mexican-American War (1846–1848). Nonetheless, the

federalism A form of government in which power and administration are located in regions such as provinces and states rather than in a centralized administration.

caudillo remained an important figure in Latin American nation building, and at times even rescued nations from dissolution.

Although caudillos could mobilize masses of workers and peasants to political causes, gradually governments built state institutions such as national armies and military schools to train nationally oriented officers. Governments also took control of infrastructure such as railroads and ports along Latin America's extensive coastline. In the second half of the nineteenth century, state bureaucracies grew as the educated middle class came to fill government offices. Regional economic interests gave way to national economic interests; for instance, local tariffs exacted by the different regions of a nation gave way to tariffs collected at national borders.

A Sense of Citizenship

During the struggles to construct new, centralized governments, many people in individual Latin American countries developed a sense of belonging and citizenship that was crucial to nation building. José Gregorio Paz Soldán, a judge in Peru, had first supported slavery in the new republic but soon became an ardent supporter of liberty and equal treatment for all, commenting that "The Indians are no more savage or ferocious than other people who have been attracted to a social and civilized life."[4] Paz Soldán wanted solidarity among citizens of all classes. Employers, he urged, should give laborers "a salary and good treatment."[5] The Peruvian constitution of 1828 stated that "All citizens may be admitted to public employment, without any difference except that of their talents and virtues."[6] The qualifications for participating in the nation were in theory the same for everyone, uniting people of different ethnicities and classes instead of dividing them as the Spanish monarchy had done by giving preference to the Spanish-born.

Even in Cuba, where the Spanish crown still ruled, people came to believe in a common citizenship characteristic of an independent nation-state. Free blacks in Havana protested their exclusion from service in the militia because of their race, citing their commonality with other citizens. "Mulattoes and blacks, we are the ones who practice the mechanical arts to the highest degree of perfection, to the admiration and wonder of professors from other enlightened nations. We own property—houses that we live in with our families, workshops, and buildings to rent out to those who need them. We have farms and slaves in the same proportions as those other members of the people of Havana who possess such property."[7] The Spanish put down the protest, but they could not quell the sense of citizenship that gave rise to it.

After independence, cities in Latin American countries had thriving political clubs, mutual aid societies, newspapers and journals, and economic organizations that concerned themselves not only with the welfare of the community but with the nation as a whole. Although a nation might have a dictatorial ruler or a corrupt administration, commercial groups took part in public debate over building a strong national economy, and mutual aid societies focused on well-being in neighborhoods. "Clubs have enabled us to replace tyranny with liberty," was the opinion of one Mexican newspaper in 1855. "They have provided the government with a way to become acquainted with public opinion, and this is the reason we support them."[8] People became immersed in the public affairs of their nation as never before. Thus, the connections among citizens that were central to the nation-state were not solely the product of state policies imposed from the top down. They were also created from the bottom up by citizens themselves.

The Russian Empire's New Course

Other countries that seemed unlikely to embrace the institutions and values of modern nation-states were often transformed by events, such as peasant uprisings, inefficiencies, low productivity, and the revelation of internal problems from external defeat. The Russian Empire, for example, modernized its institutions when wartime defeat dramatically revealed the need for change. In the 1800s, Russia continued its centuries-old expansionism into Asia and the Middle East. Just as the British aimed for inroads in China, Tsar Nicholas I wanted to absorb much of the Ottoman Empire, which was fast becoming known as "the sick man of Europe" because of the disintegrating administration of its lands. As Russia grew more aggressive, war erupted in October 1853. The Crimean War (1853–1856) began as a conflict between the Russian and Ottoman empires but ended as a war with long-lasting consequences for Russia, much of Europe, and, indeed, for the world (see Map 25.2).

The war disrupted Europe's balance of power, as France and Great Britain, enemies for more than a century, united in declaring war on Russia to defend the Ottoman Empire's sovereignty. Their goal was to maintain power in the global economy by securing their full access to the eastern Mediterranean. British and French troops landed in the Crimea in September 1854 and waged a long siege of the Russian naval base at Sevastopol on the Black Sea. The war coincided with the continuing spread of the Industrial Revolution, which introduced powerful new technologies into warfare: the railroad, shell-firing cannon, breech-loading rifles, steam-powered ships, and the telegraph. With the telegraph and increased press coverage, the relationship of the home front to the battlefront changed. Home audiences received news from the Crimean front lines more rapidly and in more detail than ever before, intensifying national unity and thus nation building across Europe.

Despite the new weaponry, Sevastopol fell only after a year of savage and costly combat. Generals on both sides were incompetent, and governments failed to provide combatants with even minimal supplies, sanitation, and medical care. A million men died, more than two-thirds from disease and starvation. The casualties resulting from incompetence and poor sanitation showed that nations needed strong institutions. London reformer Florence Nightingale seized the moment to escape the confines of middle-class domesticity by organizing a battlefield nursing service to care for British troops. Through her tough-minded organization of nursing units, she pioneered nursing as a profession and also better sanitary conditions both in armies and in society in general. After the war, she contributed to nation building by publishing statistical studies showing that national effectiveness depended on public health and a scientifically prepared and centrally directed military.

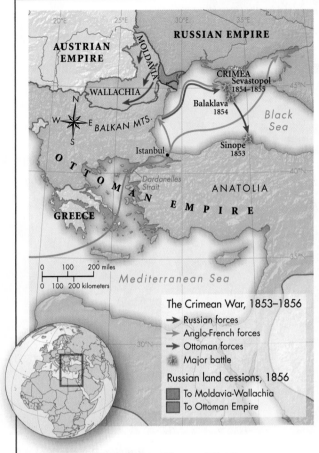

MAP 25.2 **The Crimean War and Postwar Settlement, 1853–1856**

The Crimean War has been called senseless, but it was rich in consequences. By splitting the conservative alliance between Austria and Russia that had effectively kept France and indeed all of Europe in check, it opened the way for ambitious politicians in Italy and Germany to unify their fragmented states into two strong nations. Additionally, its defeat caused Russia to free the serfs and institute significant reforms; the Ottoman Empire continued to attempt modern nation building as well.

The war exposed Russia's weakness and transformed the global balance of power. With casualties mounting, Tsar Alexander II (r. 1855–1881) asked for peace. As a result of the peace treaty of 1856, the Black Sea was declared neutral waters and Russia lost its claim to protect Christians in Ottoman lands. Austria's and Russia's grip on European affairs weakened, making way for the rise of new regional and global powers. The defeat forced the authoritarian Russian state to embark on a long-overdue renovation of the empire.

When Russia lost the Crimean War, the educated public, including some government officials, found the poor performance of serf-conscripted armies to be a disgrace. When a son was conscripted into the Russian army for the regular twenty-five-year term, parents held funerals because the army experience was so long and brutal and the chance of returning alive so slight. The system of serf labor was also seen as an intolerable liability for a country that needed economic and institutional modernization to be an effective nation-state on the world stage. The Russian economy had stagnated compared with western

Serfdom in Russia

Russian Peasants at a Soup Kitchen

Even after emancipation from serfdom in 1861 and other reforms that followed, Russian peasants were hard-pressed to earn a living. As a condition of emancipation, they were burdened with debt for farmland and could not migrate freely in search of greater opportunity. Tensions in the countryside grew, alleviated only by acts of charity and relief programs, such as the soup kitchen shown here. (©Sovfoto.)

Europe. Old-fashioned farming techniques led to worn-out soil and food shortages. For serfs, everyday life brought constant toil and obedience to flighty or cruel masters, who could marry them off at will or rent them out at great distances from home.

Challenges to serfdom had begun to grow during the decades before the Crimean War. Serf defiance ranged from malingering while at forced labor to small uprisings. Works of art such as novelist Ivan Turgenev's *A Hunter's Sketches* (1852) contributed to a spirit of reform with their sympathetic portrayals of serfs and frank depiction of brutal masters: "O Lord Jesus Christ!" one of his characters thunders. "Am I not free to use my slaves as I wish?"[9] But other inspiration came from serf artists and writers—the lucky ones among the serf population who were assigned artistic tasks such as piano tuning, fine cabinetry, or portrait painting on estates; some even became highly educated.

One of these was Alexander Nikitenko, born a serf in 1804. His father had been sent to sing in one of Russia's famous boys' choirs by his owner, a great landowner. Enraged at being returned to the estate still a serf, Nikitenko's father, who had learned to read while in the choir, made sure that his son received a good education. Alexander also fumed at the injustice of his serf condition, especially as he became known as one of the most learned young men in the land. In the late 1830s, a powerful Russian prince obtained Nikitenko's freedom, allowing him to become a high government official. Educated serfs such as Nikitenko were among the most bitter and vocal advocates of change (see Reading the Past: The Russian People Under Serfdom).

The Russian People Under Serfdom

Alexander Nikitenko gained his freedom from serfdom after proving himself a learned and conscientious teacher as well as an outstanding manager of households and general man of all work. Many serfs were accomplished; their achievements included painting and traveling in troupes of actors and singers, which brought Russians in contact with one another across vast spaces. Like Nikitenko, some of these serfs reached national eminence and came to be celebrated, but Nikitenko felt the degradation of serfdom long after he was free. These excerpts from his autobiography, first published in 1824, concern the early nineteenth century when he was between six and ten years old. They do not reflect the thinking of a child, however; Nikitenko observed serfdom for decades while honing this account of his life.

> The peasants suffered beneath the yoke of serfdom. If a master was wealthy and owned several thousand serfs, they suffered less oppression because most of them were tenant farmers. . . . On the other hand, small [landowners] literally sucked out the strength of unfortunates in their power. Neither time nor land was at their disposal. . . . In addition, sometimes there was inhuman treatment, and often cruelty was accompanied by debauchery. . . .
>
> People could be bought and sold wholesale or in small numbers, by families, or singly like bulls and sheep. . . . Tsar Alexander I, during the humanitarian phase of his reign, talked about improving the lot of his serf-subjects, but attempts to limit the [landowners'] power vanished without a trace. The nobility wanted to live in luxury befitting its station. . . .
>
> [E]veryone bore the burdens generated by the People's War [Napoleon's 1812 invasion] without complaint.

They supplied and equipped recruits at great personal expense. Yet I did not detect in their conversations a sign of deep interest in the events of the time. Evidently everyone was interested solely in their own affairs. The mention of Napoleon's name evoked awe rather than hate. The nonchalant attitude of our community toward the disaster hanging over Russia was startling. This may have been due in part to the distance of the theater of war. . . .

> But I think the main reason was apathy, characteristic of a people estranged from participation in society's affairs, as Russians were then. They were not accustomed to discussion [of] what went on around them and unconditionally obeyed the orders of the authorities.

Source: Alexander Nikitenko, *Up from Serfdom: My Childhood and Youth in Russia 1804–1824,* trans. Helen Saltz Jacobson (New Haven: Yale University Press, 2001), 54–56, 75.

EXAMINING THE EVIDENCE

1. How does Nikitenko characterize Russian serfs?

2. How did serfdom affect the Russian people and state more generally?

3. What was the mood of the Russian people as a nation facing the Napoleonic invasion of 1812? How might the emancipation of the serfs in 1861 have changed that mood?

Faced with Russia's dire situation, Alexander II proved more flexible than his predecessors in modernizing society. Better educated and more widely traveled, he ushered in what came to be known as the Great Reforms, granting Russians new rights from above as a way to ensure that violent action from below would not force change. The most dramatic reform was the emancipation of almost 50 million serfs beginning in 1861. Under the terms of emancipation, communities of former serfs, headed by male village elders, were given their personal freedom and grants of land. Each community, called a **mir** (mihr), was given full power to distribute this land among its members and to direct their own economic activity. Thus, although the serfs were free, the requirements of communal landowning and decision-making held back individuals with new ideas and those who wanted to find opportunity elsewhere. Nonetheless, millions surely received this news as former serf Alexander Nikitenko did: "with an inexpressible feeling of joy."[10] Ending serfdom and slavery was often the foundation for creating citizens and for nation building.

Emancipation of the Serfs

mir In Russia, the organization of land and former serfs following the emancipation of the serfs.

The state awarded peasant communities some 13 percent less land than they had tilled under serfdom, forced them to "redeem" or pay the government for this land in long-term loans, and in fact awarded the best land to the nobility. Although some landowners experimented with modern farming techniques, which made Russia the largest grain-exporting nation by 1900, the conditions of emancipation held Russian agriculture back. Nevertheless, idealistic reformers believed the emancipation of the serfs, whom the nobility once treated virtually as livestock, had produced miraculous results. As one writer put it, "The people are without any exaggeration transfigured from head to foot. . . . The look, the walk, the speech, everything is changed."

Other Nation-Building Reforms

The state also reformed local administration, the judiciary, and the military. The government set up *zemstvos* (ZEHMST-vohs), regional councils through which aristocrats could revive neglected public institutions for education, public health, and welfare. As aristocrats gained responsibility for local well-being, some became invested in Russia's health as a nation. Judicial reform in 1864 gave all Russians, even former serfs, access to modern civil courts, where ordinary people for the first time benefited from the principle of equality of all persons, regardless of social rank, under a unified set of laws. Military reform followed in 1874 when the government ended the twenty-five-year term of conscription, substituting a six-year term and devoting more attention to education, efficiency, and the humane treatment of recruits. These changes improved the fitness of Russian soldiers, helping them identify with the nation as a whole.

Limits of the Great Reforms

Alexander's reforms encouraged modernizers and gave many in the upper classes a more worldly outlook, but nation building also diminished the personal prerogatives of the nobility, leaving its authority generally weakened and sparking intergenerational rebellion. "An epidemic seemed to seize upon [noble] children . . . an epidemic of fleeing from the parental roof," one observer noted. Rejecting aristocratic values, youthful rebels from the upper class valued practical activity and sometimes identified with peasants and workers. Some formed communes, where they joined together in cooperative living to do humble manual labor. Others turned to higher education, especially the sciences, to gain modern knowledge. Rebellious daughters of the nobility flouted parental expectations by cropping their hair short, wearing black, and escaping from home through marriages in name only so they could study medicine and the sciences in European universities.

This repudiation of traditional society led Turgenev to label radical youth as *nihilists* (from the Latin for "nothing"), meaning people who lack belief in any values whatsoever. In fact, these individual rebellions showed a spirit of defiance percolating in Russian society that would soon fuel assassinations, including that of the reformer Alexander II in 1881, and ultimately produce the revolutions that would shape the world in the next century. For the time being, the tsarist regime only partially succeeded in developing the administrative, economic, and civic institutions that were strengthening nation-states elsewhere. The tsar and his inner circle held tightly to the reins of government, slowing the development of consensus politics and modern citizenship.

A Unified Italy and a United Germany

With the European powers divided over the Crimean War of 1853 to 1856, politicians in the German and Italian states took advantage of the opportunity to unify their respective countries. In 1848 workers, students, and professionals had revolted in many of the individual Italian and German states, hoping to reform and unify their countries. Despite their failure, the issue of unification simmered until two practical but visionary leaders took charge: Camillo di Cavour of the kingdom of Piedmont-Sardinia in the economically modernizing north of Italy, and Otto von Bismarck from the prosperous agrarian kingdom of Prussia. Both depended on modern railroads, strong armies, and power diplomacy to transform disunited states into coherent nations with a presence on the world stage.

Italy

The architect of the new Italy was Camillo di Cavour, prime minister of the kingdom of Piedmont-Sardinia from 1852 until his death in 1861. A rebel in his youth, the young

Cavour had conducted agricultural experiments on his aristocratic father's land. He organized steamship companies, played the stock market, and inhaled the fresh air of modernization during his travels to Paris and London. Cavour promoted economic development rather than democratic uprising as the means to achieve a united Italy. As prime minister, he helped develop a healthy Piedmontese economy, a modern army, and a liberal political climate to anchor Piedmont's drive to unite the Italian states.

To achieve this goal, however, Piedmont would have to confront Austria, which governed the provinces of Lombardy and Venetia and had a strong influence on most of the peninsula. Realizing that Austria was too powerful for Piedmont to take on by itself, Cavour first got a promise of help from France and then provoked the Austrians to invade northern Italy in April 1859. Nationalists seeking unity and political liberals seeking constitutions and modern institutions in Tuscany and other central Italian states joined the Piedmontese cause. Using the newly built Piedmontese railroad to move troops, the French and Piedmontese armies achieved rapid victories in the north. In May 1860, Giuseppe Garibaldi, an inspired guerrilla fighter and veteran of the revolutions of 1848, set sail from Genoa to liberate Sicily with a thousand red-shirted volunteers, many of them teenage boys and half from the urban working class, "splendid in the dress and cap of the student, and in the more humble dress of the bricklayer, the carpenter, and the [blacksmith]," as Garibaldi himself put it.[11]

Unification of Italy, 1859–1870

Kingdom of Piedmont-Sardinia before 1859

To Kingdom of Piedmont-Sardinia, 1859

To Kingdom of Piedmont-Sardinia, 1860

To Kingdom of Italy, 1866, 1870

Boundary of Kingdom of Italy after 1870

Across the Sicilian countryside peasant revolts against landlords and the corrupt government were under way in anticipation of ***Risorgimento***, the "rebirth" of a strong Italian state. Anger in the countryside was so violent against these oppressors that the farmers massacred opponents, leaving them to be "devoured by dogs . . . torn to pieces by their own brothers with a fury which would have horrified the hyenas."[12] Successfully mastering the scene in the south, Garibaldi threw his support to Piedmont-Sardinia's leadership. In 1861, the kingdom of Italy was proclaimed. Exhausted by a decade of overwork, Cavour soon died, but despite huge difficulties such as poverty in the south, many citizens of the new country took pride in the Italian nation and came to see themselves as one people.

A momentous act of nation building, for both Europe and the world, was the creation of a united Germany in 1871. The Prussian state brought an array of cities and kingdoms under its control within a single decade by using both the conservative military to wage war on behalf of unification and the liberal businessmen's enthusiasm for the profits to be gained from a single national market. The newly unified Germany prospered, continuing to consolidate its economic might as business people small and large enjoyed a bigger market to pursue profits. Its growing industrial and commercial wealth would make Germany the foremost power on the European continent by the end of the nineteenth century.

Germany

The architect of a unified Germany was Otto von Bismarck, the Prussian minister-president. Bismarck came from landed nobility on his father's side; his mother's family included high-ranking bureaucrats and middle-class intellectuals. As a university student, the young Bismarck had gambled and womanized; he was interested in only one course, on the economic foundations of politics. After failing in the civil service he worked to modernize operations on his family's estates while leading an otherwise rowdy life. His marriage to a pious Lutheran woman worked a transformation and gave him new purpose: to establish Prussia as a respected and dominant power.

In 1862, the king of Prussia appointed Bismarck prime minister in hopes that he would block the growing power of the liberals, who were the reformers and modernizers in the Prussian parliament, and instead build the army over their objections. Bismarck

zemstvo Regional council of the Russian nobility established after the emancipation of the serfs to deal with education and local welfare issues.

Risorgimento Italian for "rebirth," a nineteenth-century rallying cry for the unification of the Italian states.

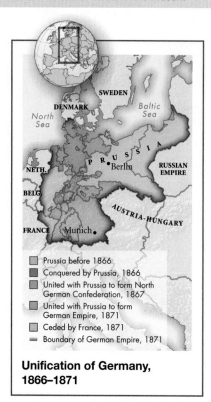

Unification of Germany, 1866–1871

Map legend:
- Prussia before 1866
- Conquered by Prussia, 1866
- United with Prussia to form North German Confederation, 1867
- United with Prussia to form German Empire, 1871
- Ceded by France, 1871
- Boundary of German Empire, 1871

indeed managed to ram through programs to build the army despite the opposition's belief in parliamentary control. His brand of nation building was based on *realpolitik*—a political strategy of hardheaded realism, armed might, and rapid industrial and commercial development. "Germany looks not to Prussia's liberalism, but to its power," he preached. "The great questions of the day will not be settled by speeches and majority decisions . . . but by iron and blood."

After his triumph over the parliament, Bismarck led Prussia into a series of victorious wars, against Denmark in 1864, against Austria in 1866, and, finally, against France in 1870. His victory over Austria-Hungary, which claimed to be the leader of the disunited German states, allowed Bismarck to create a North German Confederation led by Prussia. Prussia's swift victory over France persuaded all the German states to unify under Prussia's leadership. In January 1871, the king of Prussia was proclaimed the Kaiser, or emperor, of a new, imperial Germany.

Despite the growing wealth of liberal business people, the constitution of the newly unified empire ensured the continued political dominance of the aristocracy and monarchy. The Kaiser, who also remained Prussia's king, controlled the military and appointed Bismarck to the powerful position of chancellor for the Reich (empire). Bismarck balanced the right to vote, which the constitution granted to men, with an unequal electoral system in Prussia, which continued to be the dominant state within the German Empire. In the Prussian system, votes from the upper classes counted more than those from the lower. Bismarck's nation-building deals worked, allowing Germany, even more than Italy, to focus its national energy on industrial growth and power politics. Europe would never be the same.

Emerging Powers: The United States and Japan

FOCUS

How did the United States and Japan make their governments politically and economically powerful in the nineteenth century?

Two other newcomers, the United States and Japan, were also eager for global wealth and influence. These two states built national power in the nineteenth century and drastically reformed their societies and political structures to industrialize and to make their governments more focused and effective. By 1900 the United States and Japan were beginning to rival the great European powers as nation building promoted their economic strength and pumped ordinary people's ambitions.

Expansion and Consolidation of the United States

The United States went from a cluster of states hugging the eastern seaboard in the eighteenth century to a growing power in the nineteenth century. Like Germany and Italy, it did so through warfare. Confronted with the pressures of migration and the demands for raw materials, it fought Mexico and Indian peoples in order to seize their resources and land. It also engaged in a devastating civil war over issues arising from the brisk global trade in cotton, slaves, and—increasingly—industrial products. The series of wars the United States pursued in the nineteenth century expanded its territory and unified a rambunctious nation of adventurers, immigrants, farmers, ranchers, miners, entrepreneurs, and industrial innovators. Amid all this turmoil, the nation built up its common institutions, such as schools and transportation networks, and widened its global connections.

realpolitik A practical, toughminded approach to politics, wielded most famously by Otto von Bismarck in Germany.

U.S. settlers continued to push westward in the nineteenth century, seeking more land to profit from the global trade in raw materials, particularly cotton. They drove into Mexican territory in the continent's southwest, where struggles for control of both trade and territory resulted in sporadic warfare. Between 1846 and 1848 the United States first provoked and then won a war with Mexico over land in Mexico's north, and as a result almost doubled its territory, annexing Texas as well as large portions of California and the Southwest (see Map 25.3). Simultaneously, immigrants from around the world flocked to California and later to other places where gold was discovered. Americans came to see this western expansion as part of the nation's **Manifest Destiny**—that is, the belief that white Americans had a God-given right to control the entire continent no matter how many native Americans were killed or displaced.

Westward Expansion and Manifest Destiny

Manifest Destiny The nineteenth-century doctrine that the United States had the right and duty to expand throughout the North American continent.

MAP 25.3 **U.S. Civil War and Westward Expansion**

U.S. nation building advanced through the war with Mexico, the Civil War, and ongoing battles to take the land of native Americans. Calls for unity during wartime and appeals asserting the superiority of white Americans welded the country together both politically and culturally. These shared values helped the United States forge ahead economically, with innovation coming to justify U.S. claims to being more advanced than those whose property the expanding nation took.

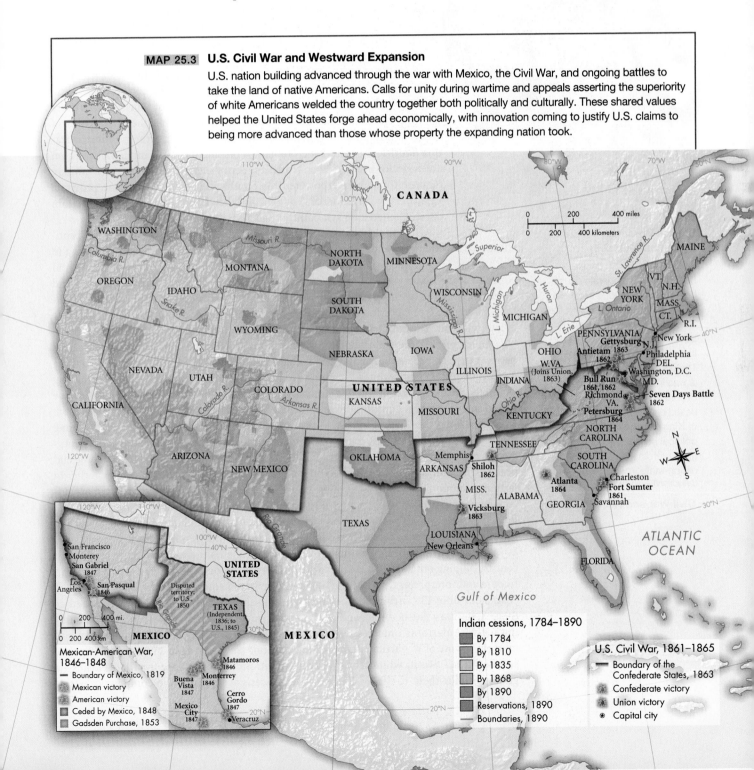

**English Porcelain Statue
of Abraham Lincoln**

Although the British generally backed the Confederate cause because they needed southern cotton for its textile industry, the Staffordshire porcelain company issued this statue on Abraham Lincoln's inauguration in 1861. The oddly regal garment Lincoln is wearing and the highly decorated horse he is riding were based on an earlier representation of King George III. Portrayals of political heroes such as Lincoln grew with the spread of the nation-state. (The Art Archive/Private Collection/Eileen Tweedy.)

Civil War and Reconstruction

Politicians and citizens alike argued over the status of the new western lands. The greatest quarrels came over the expansion of slavery to the new territories, and the main issue was livelihoods. Should the West be settled by free white farmers, or could southern plantation owners bring in their slaves, against whose unpaid labor white farmers could not compete? Like some Latin American nation builders, many saw equal legal status of citizens as essential to a thriving nation, but others disagreed so strongly that the country became polarized. In the North, where abolitionists had a strong organization to fight against slavery, the new Republican Party called for "free soil, free labor, free men." However, few Republicans backed the abolitionists' demand for an immediate end to slavery in the South. In the months following Republican Abraham Lincoln's election to the presidency in 1860, most of the southern slaveholding states seceded to form the Confederate States of America.

Under Lincoln's leadership the North fought the South in a civil war from 1861 to 1865 to uphold the union. Lincoln did not initially aim to abolish slavery, but in January 1863 his Emancipation Proclamation came into force as a wartime measure officially freeing all slaves in the Confederate States and turning the war into a fight not only for union but for the end of slavery—thus creating a pool of workers who were entirely free *and* connecting nation building to the liberal program of rights and opportunity. While the war dragged on, northern industrialization flourished: "Believe me," remarked one Pennsylvania industrialist, "I am not eager for peace."[13] The North's superior industrial strength and military might ultimately overpowered the South, and in April 1865 the prostrate Confederacy surrendered. For Lincoln, the victory was short-lived. Within days a Confederate sympathizer had assassinated the president.

During the postwar period known as Reconstruction (1865–1877), constitutional amendments ended slavery and granted the rights of citizenship and voting to black males. For a time under Reconstruction, the newly liberated slaves received land and education, and some served in government or moved up in the world of business and work. The way was open for continent-wide industrial expansion and commercial agriculture, based on a free labor force, common rights for citizens, and migration from virtually every continent. The country would soon become a thriving nation-state.

A final piece of the nation-building effort in the United States was crushing the various native American peoples by forcibly taking their North American homelands or killing them to open up resources for whites. "Manifest Destiny" became a strong post-Civil War rallying cry. In the 1820s the state of Georgia simply took the land of the Cherokees, a group of native Americans who had a constitution and practiced settled farming, forcing them to migrate westward along the "Trail of Tears"—so named because of the number of deaths along the way. Pushed from the east coast westward by European settlers in the seventeenth century, tens of thousands of North American Indians had moved onto the Great Plains by the end of the eighteenth century. Numerous other native Americans had settled there far earlier in farming communities. Many were horse traders and herders of an estimated 40 million buffalo, exchanging goods with communities in New Mexico to the south and the British and French to the north. "There was always fat meat, glad singing, and much dancing in our villages," one Crow woman remembered of her people's mid-nineteenth-century prosperity.[14]

All that was before Europeans moved onto the Plains themselves in the nineteenth century, wiping out the buffalo and spreading European diseases widely, through Indian traders and interpreters. The Mandan tribes numbered some 15,000 in 1750; a hundred years later only 138 survived. Hundreds of thousands of native Americans perished as the U.S. military finished the conquest, carrying out government orders to drive remaining native Americans onto reservations in Oklahoma and other states, where they had no right to vote or to participate in U.S. institutions (see again Map 25.3). As one Apache survivor described it, whites considered reservations "a good place for the Apaches—a good place for them to die."[15] For white Americans at the time, the conquest of native

Americans across the continent helped industry thrive, helped immigrants find new livelihoods, and helped the nation to unify.

Dramatic Change in Japan

When the United States forced the opening of Japan to foreigners in the 1850s, it disturbed the country's peace and, as the activism of Matsuo Taseko shows, threw Japan into political turmoil. Strange, unruly white men walked the streets of port cities, and Western emissaries made demands on the government. All the same, even some of Japan's provincial rulers sensed the excitement and opportunity. There was money to be made, local notables suspected, and they resented the Tokugawa shogun's control of trade with the foreigners and thus his monopoly on profits. More conservative leaders found the break with the tradition of relative isolation an affront to Japan's greatness, and they were willing to use violence to suppress Japanese contact with the outside world. For example, conservatives assassinated an official who accepted trade treaties with foreigners and murdered a scholar who used a Western saddle on his horse. Such traditionalists shared Matsuo Taseko's desire to drive the "barbarians" from Japan and return the Japanese people to their traditions.

The furor over political and economic life led to a dramatic realignment of power in Japan. Many of the provincial rulers adopted the goal of restoring the emperor Komei to the full dignity of his office. The emperor was their "jewel," and Japanese of almost all political positions now unified around him. By late 1867, support for the shogun's long-standing power had dwindled to virtually nothing, and he was forced to resign.

Sioux Women Line Up for Rations

Nation building allowed many citizens to prosper because of the rule of law and new rights and opportunities. For many others, however, nation building was a disaster. Whereas once the Sioux had prospered, by the 1890s they were confined to small sections of the continent that was their homeland. Native Americans were the last group given the vote in the United States, although romanticized portrayals of native Americans who aided the European colonists as well as tales of native American "savagery" became staples of U.S. nation-building lore. (Denver Public Library. Western History Collection, photo by C.G. Morledge, Call number X-31445.)

Meiji Restoration

The restoration of power to the emperor did not, however, bring with it a straightforward return to Japanese isolation as conservatives such as Matsuo Taseko had hoped. Although a series of shoguns had recognized the importance of relationships with the West, Emperor Komei had been against it. Conveniently for the modernizers, he fell ill and died as the shogunate collapsed, leaving the throne to his fifteen-year-old son, Mutsuhito (r. 1868–1912). The resulting new government revived the imperial house and gave priority to Westernization and the shogun's more open, global policies—largely to protect Japan from further inroads by foreigners. Having fought to gain influence, the victorious, reform-minded elites crafted an assembly of high-ranking men such as themselves to determine the laws, making imperial rule much less than absolute. The government announced the "Meiji Restoration"—*Meiji* means "enlightened rule"—as a combination of "Western science and Eastern values" offering both innovation and restoration. Thus, the revival of imperial power partly masked the reality of revolutionary change. Japan would be transformed by its new relationship with the West, but its leaders hoped that by embracing aspects of Westernization they could control that transformation, ensuring that the process would serve Japan's interests, and not those of the West (see Map 25.4).

The Meiji government stabilized itself through a series of necessary changes. A pressing issue was overturning the older decentralization of power embodied in the system of local lords, the daimyo, and their loyal retainers, the samurai. The government successfully centralized power by forcing the daimyo to surrender their political and economic control of the countryside and giving them large payments or positions in the new government instead. The tens of thousands of samurai, who became unemployed once their local lords had no need for them, were potentially troublesome members of the new social order—a good many of them had no skills at all, except roughhousing. The government bought them off with pensions and later with government bonds. The samurai's status further declined as some of the most prominent politicians toured the world to gain ideas for modernization and concluded that a centralized conscript army would be far more reliable than Japan's traditional, samurai-based forces. Whereas the samurai mostly relied on a code of individual heroism, a national, conscript army was a disciplined fighting mass trained to cooperate in the use of modern weaponry. As a result of these findings, Japan instituted universal military conscription. It simultaneously created a hereditary nobility, as in Europe, and limited the powers of elected representatives who might come from the people. These last changes, enshrined in the constitution of 1889, showed that despite centralization, the government would not be fully based on republican institutions or popular rule.

The first two decades of the Meiji Restoration were tumultuous. Discontent and disorder persisted, as people from many walks of life remade the economy. The first to revolt were the displaced samurai, followed by farmers such as Matsuo Taseko, merchants, and countless others who had fought to bring back the emperor and face down the "barbarian" challenge. Now the same people struggled for the recognition of what were called "People's Rights" within

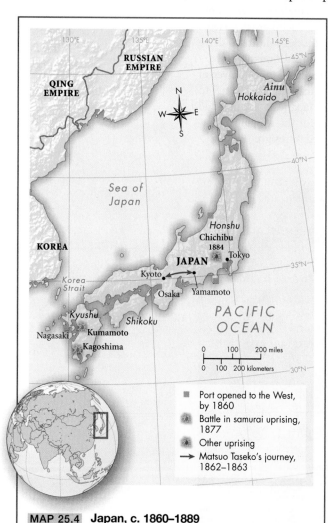

MAP 25.4 **Japan, c. 1860–1889**

Japan's rapid development of a more modern administration and economy cost many people their livelihoods, most notably the samurai. The changes the new government imposed during the Meiji Restoration of 1868 stirred uprisings and peasant revolts, particularly because Western nations appeared to be forcing Japan open with the goal of foreign domination.

the imperial system. They drafted constitutions of their own that laid out the fundamental powers of the people who, after all, were the building blocks of the nation. When their constitutions were ignored by the government during these first two decades of Meiji rule, they took up arms.

Social Unrest and Rebellion

Throughout the early Meiji period, people of the rural lower classes launched a series of rebellions. They found themselves squeezed by high taxes, intended to finance Japan's modernization and industrialization, and by a drop in agricultural prices that resulted from increased global competition. The new officials of the Meiji government, instead of respecting those on the land, seemed to inflict them with hardship even as cities were thriving. In Chichibu outside Tokyo, one resident expressed his despair: "The wind blows, / The rain falls, / Young men die. The groans of poverty / Flutter like flags in the wind."[16] In 1884, an army of eight thousand peasants in Chichibu began fighting for the people's rights, fully believing that they could force the central government to negotiate. In the Chichibu uprising, the armed populace talked about "deposing evil rulers" and "changing the mandate" as part of the program of ousting corrupt officials. Government forces smashed the uprising, imprisoning and executing many participants. Meiji officials attributed the uprising to criminals, but in fact this revolt, like others occurring across Japan, showed that successful nation building required more attention to the needs of the Japanese population as a whole. In the decades to come, Japan would continue on the difficult path to the creation of a modern nation-state.

The Culture of Nations

History, music, art, and other cultural works helped peoples forge national identities and built bonds across regions and localities. National cultures sometimes focused on reviving a country's literary past and celebrating long-dead authors' works. In other instances, people invented customs

FOCUS
What part did culture play in forging a national identity?

such as special dress or songs that over time came to be seen as "traditional." Still other peoples prized their nation's modernity, and citizens traveled miles to experience fast-paced new technology like the railroad or to see for themselves modern new structures such as the Eiffel Tower in Paris. Widely circulated books and newspapers for the masses also brought people together in national and even global unity. Cultural leaders such as composers, artists, editors, and even some university professors shaped the attitudes and experiences of a growing number of citizens, uniting them around shared knowledge and artistic achievement.

The Culture of Tradition

In the early days of the Meiji Restoration, Matsuo Taseko was invited to the home of a prince, where she heard a Western organ played. Taseko was appalled at the declining appreciation for Japan's own instruments and sent a poem to the princess. "In Japan / the koto cannot be quick / but I ask you not to listen gladly / to this barbarian harp / no matter how clever it is."[17] Taseko's nationalism was built on imitating the past and indeed protecting it from outside influences and from cultural mixture such as the playing of a Western instrument. She herself wrote hundreds of poems modeled on those from earlier centuries. In the culture of tradition, one followed not only the form but even the exact words of earlier poetry. As public schools developed, children across the nation recited poetic masterpieces from the past as a way to create and to participate in a national culture.

Forging National Unity

Leaders of monarchies, republics, and empires became symbols of national unity. Taseko carefully guarded gifts from the emperor to show to her closest friends and to pass down to her children and grandchildren as emblems of patriotism. Monarchs' and presidents' portraits appeared on dishware and on household walls and adorned public

The Korean Flag

The Korean Flag
(Tetra Images/Corbis.)

like lions, eagles, stars, and the sun were selected to portray a nation's strength and magnificence.

In the 1880s, as China, Russia, and Japan greedily eyed Korea for conquest, the kings of Korea adopted the more impressive title of emperor, and they also designed a flag. Its central figure represents the balance of yin and yang in the cosmos, while the four corners indicate the elements—fire, water, earth, and air—and the four seasons. After Japan had defeated both China and Russia (discussed in Chapter 26), it established a protectorate over Korea in 1905 and then annexed it in 1910, replacing the Korean flag with its own. On the defeat of Japan in World War II, the nineteenth-century flag became the standard of South Korea.

Flags existed in ancient times to distinguish regiments of an army, as was the case with Egyptian standards. Over the centuries, most flags continued to be standards for armies, but they also became important symbols of the nation. Designing a single flag around which citizens of an entire country could rally became a crucial part of the process of nation building. Colors were carefully chosen to represent virtues such as courage and purity, and figures

EXAMINING THE
EVIDENCE

1. What makes this flag or any flag distinctive to the nation?

2. Compare the Korean flag with the U.S. flag. What do the differences reveal about the political culture and national identity of each country?

spaces such as schools and office buildings, thus providing a unifying symbol. National flags were designed to serve a similar purpose (see Seeing the Past: The Korean Flag). Royal births were widely reported in the press, and in Britain, for example, officials carefully staged royal marriages, birthdays, and funerals as public ceremonies, which were not only viewed by the growing urban population but also commemorated with the new photographic technology. Nishimiya Hide, daughter of a samurai and lady-in-waiting to a member of the high Japanese nobility, found a way to use her knowledge of court traditions after the samurai and grand nobility had lost their leading role. She supported herself in part under the Meiji Restoration by teaching court ceremonies from an earlier time to members of the new elite.

Writing and teaching history became a popular way to legitimate nations (see Lives and Livelihoods: Historians of the Nation-State). The public latched onto the story of the rise of the nation-state from its origins as a princely kingdom to its current modern might. Historical pageantry was popular in the nineteenth century in the form of parades, theater, and the revival of rituals at shrines. Governments erected monuments in the capital and other cities to celebrate great moments in the nation's past; these suggested the nation's durability and antiquity, even though many nations were actually quite new. Official histories eventually integrated the story of native peoples to build pride in the nation's progress from barbarism to civilization. Governments built museums to house collections of national documents, coins, and other treasure, but also native artifacts such as baskets, arrowheads, and beadwork to illustrate the "primitive" condition before the nation took shape.

The reality of nation building was brutal, producing hundreds of thousands of casualties and entailing real suffering, but the stories of nation building told by artists and writers were often romantic and inspiring. From the late nineteenth century to the present, authors and artists have presented accounts of the birth of Latin American nations, the Meiji Restoration, and the U.S. Civil War as glamorous, heart-throbbing adventures. Towering heroes such as Simon Bolivar and their selfless officers and families were portrayed as sacrificing for a greater good—the nation. The idea of "founding fathers" erased the fact that people lived in the region before the nation-state appeared, and appeals to ancient gods and goddesses supported claims of a nation-state's eternal existence. Biographies of nation builders became popular reading from the nineteenth century on, which helped replace people's local identities with a shared national culture.

Romanticizing the Past

Westernization

The power of the nation-state fostered world trade, of both goods and ideas. Readers in East Asia and South America, for example, studied works by contemporary Western writers such as the Englishmen John Stuart Mill and Charles Darwin and the Russian novelist Fyodor Dostoevsky. The eighteenth-century French social and political theorist Jean-Jacques Rousseau was especially popular among reformers and modernizers for his ideas of the social contract and natural rights. Rapid steamships carried potential leaders from Asia, Africa, and South America to Europe for their education, and sometimes to the United States for firsthand observation of popular government and nation building. Japanese leaders were among those who identified military power as the foundation of Western success, and they visited Europe, especially Germany, and the United States to learn about new weaponry and modern military training techniques. Influences went in many directions: young Chinese people who wanted their nation to modernize studied in Japan, which was increasingly seen as strong and modern.

Back home, reformers popularized ideas from the West. Sometimes writers modified Western theories to suit the local situation. Japanese author and educator Fukuzawa Yukichi came from an impoverished samurai family but quickly achieved fame and fortune through his innovative reform message. Best-selling works such as *Encouragement of Learning* (1872–1876) made people aware of current thinking in the West. Fukuzawa maintained, like Rousseau, that the entire population created the state, agreeing to a social contract through a constitution, and that they entered this contract from a position of complete equality—a totally novel concept for the Japanese. Fukuzawa's theory differed from much of Western constitutional thought, however, when it maintained that once people had agreed to the formation of a state, they surrendered their right to criticize or protest. In this way, he recast Western liberal theory into a form that suited the Meiji Restoration, justifying reform but also fortifying an authoritarian, emperor-centered state.

Recasting Western Culture

Angela Peralta was a Mexican opera performer whose popularization of European operas helped build her country's national culture. Born in 1845, at a time when Mexicans were already wild about opera, she took audiences to new heights of rapture with her renditions of the most difficult European operas. Described as "angelic in voice and in name," Peralta sang across Europe and in Egypt. Her real triumphs, however, occurred in Mexico, where she traveled from city to city mobbed by fans—"an incomparable woman," they called her—and spreading her fame and the culture of opera. News of Peralta's comings and goings passed from city to village and back to other cities, uniting Mexicans culturally, as Santa Anna and other rulers were trying to do politically. By the time of her death from yellow fever at the age of thirty-seven, many a theater owner had become wealthy from her performances, and opera had received such a boost that Mexican composers began writing operas about Aztec princesses and other Mexican peoples, creating "national" traditions

Historians of the Nation-State

With the rise of the nation-state, the study of history became a profession in the nineteenth century. Historians—whether in Japan, Latin America, Europe, or North America—set out to collect the major documents that legitimated the rise of the unified nation-state. They concerned themselves above all with the story of institutional development, the formation of states and governments, and the expansion of imperial power. The tradition of official history writing went way back in China to the Han dynasty; in the eighteenth century, the Chinese emperors charged court historians with the job of celebrating their conquests to the west. Nineteenth-century nation builders appointed professional historians, trained in the study of the past, to posts in prestigious universities, where they were to research and write true, verifiable accounts of the national past.

The model of the new professional historian arose in Germany, and Leopold von Ranke and his followers became the most honored historians of their day, even in foreign lands. Merchants actually stood outside Ranke's classroom to sell his photograph to admiring students. Ranke was swept up by the enthusiasm for unity that gripped the German states. Nations drew individuals together, and he believed in a strong central government. He aimed in his investigation and verification of documents to provide an objective account of Germany's development over the centuries. Ranke had his disciples, such as Heinrich von Treitschke, who even as a supposedly dispassionate scholar lectured to his students about the genius of the German nation: "It is for us to stand together in manly discipline and self restraint, and to pass on the bulwark of our unity, the German kingdom, to our sons." These professional historians often advised rulers while they usually kept from their classrooms the same groups of people kept from citizenship—women and many people of color.

Source: Quoted in Andreas Dorpalen, *Heinrich von Treitschke* (New Haven, CT: Yale University Press, 1957), 156.

Leopold von Ranke

Historians wrote the story of a nation, giving it a solid foundation in facts and research. The most enduring figure in the professionalization of history is Leopold von Ranke, who took the writing of history out of the hands of amateurs and put it into those of university-trained scholars. Ranke wrote histories of Prussia and of Germany, basing his work on archival and documentary research and thus reinforcing the idea of the nation itself as true, reliable, and authoritative. (bpk, Berlin/ Nationalgalerie, Staatliche Museen, Berlin/Andres Kilger/Art Resource, NY.)

QUESTIONS TO CONSIDER

1. Why did nation-states promote history as a profession?

2. Compare this textbook with the description of Ranke's historical writing. What differences and similarities do you perceive, and what do these suggest about history as a field of study?

through a Western cultural form. Her tombstone reads: "She sang like no one has ever sung in this world."[18]

National Institutions

Institutional innovations helped consolidate and modernize the state. Citizens took pride in the modernization of their cities, especially capital cities such as Cairo, Tokyo, and Paris. Bureaucrats undertook efforts to improve sanitation, medicine, and other institutions to promote public health. Reformers recognized public education as a crucial ingredient of national development. A Japanese law of 1872, for example, mandated universal education so that in the modernized Meiji state there would be "no community with an illiterate family nor a family with an illiterate person."[19] Improved facilities, whether public transportation or cultural institutions such as opera houses, theaters, and museums, testified to a nation's power and greatness.

Ordinary persons in agrarian societies based on traditional rhythms of planting and harvest were often illiterate and untutored. The nation-state was based on citizen participation and required a more literate population with a common culture and common skills and ideals. China had long offered more widespread education than elsewhere because for centuries the positions of government officials had required literacy and extensive training. Nationally minded reformers sought not only to imitate the Chinese tradition of an educated officialdom but also to expand education more generally as the foundation of strong nations. Although he ruled an agrarian state, the emperor Pedro II of Brazil established a record number of schools as part of his commitment to nation building. When he came to power in 1831, the capital of Rio de Janeiro had 16 primary schools; when he abdicated in 1889, the number had climbed to 118. Schools built a sense of common purpose. "We must constantly strive to work diligently at our tasks," a third-grade Japanese textbook of 1892 instructed, "and, when an emergency arises, defend our nation."[20]

French emperor Napoleon I (r. 1803–1815) was among the first to see the importance of science, math, and engineering to national power, and he ordered the development of high-level technical schools to teach advanced skills such as engineering. Thereafter secondary and postsecondary education advanced across Europe and the United States. Universities added modern subjects such as science and math to the list of prestigious courses in the second half of the century, reshaping the curriculum to make it better serve the national interest in a competitive global environment.

Reformers bucked tradition when they opened public schools for girls and young women. Across the globe these activists touted the education of women as key to modernization, because ignorant or illiterate mothers would give children a poor start. By contrast, the educated mother, instructed in both national culture and practical skills, provided a living example of the cultured citizen and had the capacity to begin the educational process for preschool offspring (see Reading the Past: "Good Wives, Wise Mothers" Build Japan). Primary, secondary, and even university education for young women developed in the second half of the nineteenth century in most parts of the world. These changes were hotly contested, however; often, the education of women was seen as the final blow in the collapse of tradition.

Public Education

Another tactic of nation building was to foster a uniform culture and uniform beliefs. The Russian Empire, comprising more than a hundred ethnicities, sought to reduce the threat of future rebellion by forcing all its ethnic groups, from Poles to Afghans, to adopt the Russian language and culture and to worship in the Russian Orthodox church. When resistance to this "Russification" mounted, the government showed some leniency to encourage continued acceptance of the nation-state. Across Latin America, plantation owners had tolerated the many different religious practices that African slaves had brought with them because the differences, it was thought, would keep slaves divided and less likely to rebel.

Cultural Unity

With independence, however, nation builders in some countries tried to impose greater control over religious life, seeking to replace loyalty to religion with loyalty to

Angela Peralta

Mexican singer Angela Peralta was famed in her time for her range as a soprano and for the delicate beauty of her voice—"like the trill of a goldfinch," one critic noted in his diary. Peralta sang before kings and emperors and performed in the major opera houses of Europe. She toured Mexico itself, becoming an icon as she helped build a shared culture for its people. (Library of Congress Prints and Photographs DivisionLC-USZ62-132102.)

"Good Wives, Wise Mothers" Build Japan

In 1874 a group of reformers, many of them samurai, established a new Japanese journal, *Meiroku Zasshi*, to bring readers knowledge of Western philosophy, science, and customs—among them current attitudes toward women. Nakamura Masanao, of samurai background, brought to Japanese readers the new idea that mothers should actively raise their children as part of nation building. By 1900 the slogan "good wives, wise mothers" dominated the national ideology about women, making women's connection to children and love for their husbands part of patriotism.

Thus we must invariably have fine mothers if we want effectively to advance the people to the area of enlightenment and to alter their customs and conditions for the good. If the mothers are superb, they can have superb children, and Japan can become a splendid country in later generations. We can then have people trained in religious and moral education as well as in the sciences and arts whose intellects are advanced, whose minds are elevated, and whose conduct is high. . . .

Now to develop fine mothers, there is nothing better than to educate daughters. . . . It is then not excessive even to say that the foundations for [a man's] virtues of bravery, endurance, and perseverance of a later day were laid while he was still playing in his cradle and receiving his mother's milk. To fear harm from equal rights for men and women is no more than to fear that the uneducated woman will sit on her husband. This anxiety would not exist if women honored Divine Providence, respected noble sentiments, admired the arts, appreciated science, and helped their husbands, and if husbands and wives mutually loved and respected each other.

Aside from the matter of equal rights, the training of men and women should be equal and not of two types. If we desire to preserve an extremely high and extremely pure level among human beings as a whole, we should accord both men and women the same type of upbringing and enable them to progress equally. . . . A wife possessed of a feeling of deep love will bring her husband ease and happiness and encourage him to exert himself in enterprises useful to the country.

Source: *Meiroku Zasshi: Journal of the Japanese Enlightenment*, trans. and ed. William Reynolds Braisted (Cambridge, MA: Harvard University Press, 1976), 401–403.

EXAMINING THE EVIDENCE

1. What are the groups of people that Nakamura identifies?

2. How are they supposed to support the nation?

3. How do men and women compare in their standing in the nation?

the nation-state. Latin American officials made Carnival celebrations less African and more uniformly Spanish. In Germany in the 1870s, Otto von Bismarck sought to build cultural unity by striking out against Catholicism; he expelled the Jesuits, increased the government's power over the clergy, and introduced obligatory civil marriage. His *Kulturkampf*, or culture war, aimed to weaken allegiance to religion and to redirect it to the German nation. German Catholics and other citizens rebelled at this attack on freedom of religion, but overall Bismarck's achievements fostered a strong sense of German identity, especially because an excellent public school system served the cause of cultural uniformity.

Support of Multiculturalism   Some nations built their common ideology around multiculturalism, which allowed citizens to take pride in their diversity or regional strengths. In the United States, for instance, the poet Walt Whitman's *Leaves of Grass* (1855) celebrated the many types of ordinary people working across the country. African Americans developed powerful musical forms such as blues and jazz from the African tradition of the *griot* (or oral poet) and the sounds, rhythms, and tonalities of African and local music. Many Americans increasingly saw this music as part of American rather than African heritage. In Japan, even as a Shinto religion was declared to be the "traditional" Japanese faith, religious pluralism existed, and cultural leaders announced that this pluralism was part of the nation's cultural evolution. Although multiple religious and cultural traditions were allowed, they argued, the Japanese should nonetheless choose the highest form of religion and culture—which was none other than Shintoism—and Japanese forms of poetry such as the brief verses called haiku. Controversies over culture persisted over the course of nation building down to the present, but these debates can also bring people together around the search for consensus.

COUNTERPOINT
Outsiders Inside the Nation-State

Defining who was a true Brazilian, Russian, Japanese, or other citizen was an essential part of the process of nation building. Nation-states saw no contradiction between the ideal of universal membership and the exclusion of certain people from political participation and thus full citizenship.

> **FOCUS**
> Which groups were excluded from full participation in the nation-state, and why?

Sometimes these people—native Americans, for example—were those who had resisted nation building, often because it threatened their livelihoods, took their land, and devalued their beliefs. Other outsiders, notably women, often had helped in nation building from the start but were still excluded. Nation building created a body of "we's," insiders who felt their citizenship most keenly when they discriminated against a set of "they's," the outsiders.

People of Color

Native Peoples

From Japan to South America, nation-building efforts had a devastating effect on indigenous peoples. Settlers in South America, Australia, New Zealand, and Siberia treated native peoples—who had lived in the territory for centuries and even for millennia—as remnants of barbarism. "In point of fact," the *New York World* told its readers in 1874, "the country never belonged to the Indians in any other sense than it belonged to the wolves and bears, which white settlers shoot without mercy."[21] Indigenous civilization was dismissed, even when settlement usually depended on learning the skills and receiving aid in food and medicine from local peoples. Native peoples generally lived within national borders but without the rights of citizens. In the United States they were excluded from voting and full protection of the law until 1924, and in Peru Indians paid an extra tax, which constituted almost half of Peru's national income. The Australian and Canadian governments took native children from their families, sending them to live in white homes or in boarding schools to be "civilized." Russian officials simply moved settlers into the far reaches of Siberia and displaced reindeer herders in the name of strengthening the nation. As an article in one U.S. newspaper argued, settlers "are the people who develop a country; who carry a civilization with them."[22]

Ethnic and racial thinking justified exploitation in the name of civilized nation building, even though the people exploited were subject to the nation's laws and taxes. Japanese nation builders taught that the Ainu peoples on the country's outer islands were dirty and disheveled; their tattoos and physical features were judged as hideous. The caste systems of the Spanish Empire and of Brazil ranked people of pure European blood highest and those of native or African blood lowest; those of mixed blood fell in the middle. Whether it was the mother or father, a free or unfree parent, who had the darker skin could also alter one's status. In the long run, however, the hierarchy was simple: the darker the skin, the lower the person.

Former U.S. Slaves   In the United States the withdrawal of Union troops from the South in 1877 marked the end of Reconstruction and the withdrawal of the rights to citizenship given to black men in the Fourteenth Amendment to the Constitution. Southerners passed "Jim Crow" laws segregating blacks from whites in public places and effectively disenfranchising them with a variety of regulations. The Ku Klux Klan, a paramilitary group of white Southerners, terrorized blacks and lynched and mutilated black men, whom they falsely accused of raping white women. Unprotected by U.S. laws, blacks fought back in ways both brave and subtle. One woman took as her goal in life keeping her daughter from the common livelihood for African American girls and women of domestic service in a white family, "for [Southern men] consider the colored girl their special prey."[23] The exclusion of blacks and native Americans from rights became a unifying ideal for many white Americans.

Women

From Italy and Germany to the United States, and in the case of Matsuo Taseko, Japan, women joined the effort to create and preserve strong nation-states. "I am a U.S. soldier," wrote Clara Barton, nurse on a U.S. Civil War battlefield.[24] Women such as Barton were subject to the laws and taxes of the nation-state, but they too were denied rights of citizenship, including the right to vote, to own property, and to participate in public life. In countries as distant from one another as Japan and France, the government made it a crime for women to participate in political meetings under pain of arrest and imprisonment. Rape, other forms of physical abuse, and inequality of wages (and sometimes no wages at all) were seen as normal treatment for women.

Nonetheless, women became central to national myths of origin. In almost every modernizing country, the self-sacrifice of women to their nation or family was held up as a common model for citizenship. Just as women put aside their self-interest when being "good wives, wise mothers," as the new, nationalist Japanese slogan went, so women sacrificed their personal interests to strengthen the nation, even if this meant accepting beatings and the taxation and confiscation of their property by men and governments. Countries such as the United States, France, and Germany took mythical women—in these examples, Columbia, Marianne, and Germania—as their symbols on coins and other official artifacts even as they denied women the rights of citizenship.

Frederick Douglass

Frederick Douglass was an escaped slave, journalist, and civil rights pioneer of the nineteenth century. His goal was freedom for slaves and civil rights for all, and as such he became a hero to all outsiders down to the present day. As outsiders have been integrated, national histories make heroes of them to build a portrait of the nation as all-encompassing and based on mass participation of its citizenry. (National Portrait Gallery, Smithsonian Institution/Art Resource, NY.)

Begum Rokeya Sakhawat Hossain

Begum Rokeya Sakhawat Hossain was an outsider to political life, as women generally lived in seclusion from society. In 1905 this Muslim woman, born in present-day Bangladesh, wrote an unusual short story that described what a nation—"Ladyland," she called it—would be like if women ruled with their brains instead of men ruling with their muscle. Ladyland ran smoothly because the women harnessed high-tech solar power; men remained safely tucked away in seclusion the way women had once been.

The Struggle for Citizens' Rights

Throughout the nineteenth century, reformers asserted the rights of native peoples, former slaves, and women. Juan Manuel de Rosas, the powerful caudillo of Buenos Aires, Argentina, and its countryside, combated prejudices against people of Indian and African ancestry by incorporating them into his armies, promoting them to high ranks in the military, and giving them farms for their service. He built a loyal following, not through discrimination, but through nondiscrimination. In the United States, Frederick Douglass had been an abolitionist before the Civil War; after it he worked for the rights of freed black men. Ida B. Wells, U.S. newspaper woman and daughter of a former slave, campaigned in the late nineteenth century to end segregation of public facilities and, more forcefully and dangerously, to stop the lynching of black men. "I felt I owed it to myself and to my race to tell the whole truth now," Wells explained in her autobiography.[25] She received death threats and was forced to go into hiding. Across Latin America and the United States reformers worked, often for free, with native peoples, freed slaves, and poverty-stricken urban dwellers to build solidarity, provide education, and teach new work skills—all in the name of improving the nation by improving conditions within it.

Simultaneously, however, minorities such as African Americans in the United States and former slaves in the Caribbean began to see the source of their common nationality not as the Western Hemisphere, which to them was a place of captivity, but as Africa. By the end of the century **pan-Africanism**, an ideology that stresses the common bonds of all people of African descent, had taken root. Similarly, Jews, who were discriminated against in many parts of the world, also fought back with thoughts of building a nation of their own where they would have full rights. "Why should we be any less worthy than any other . . . people?" one Jewish leader asked. "What about our nation, our language, our land?" Jewish intellectuals began drawing upon Jewish folklore, language, customs, and history to establish a national identity parallel to that of other Europeans. By the late nineteenth century, a nationalist movement called **Zionism**, led by Hungarian-born writer Theodor Herzl, advocated the migration of Jews to their ancestral homeland of Palestine and the creation there of a Jewish nation-state.

Because rising nation-states refused women a whole series of rights, activists began lobbying for women's full citizenship. As the Chinese moved toward a program of national strengthening, activists denounced foot-binding and the lack of education for women. Activists often blamed men directly—"the basest of roughs," one German doctor called

pan-Africanism Originating in the late nineteenth century, an ideology that stresses the bonds of all people of African descent, both on the African continent and beyond.

Zionism A movement that began in the late nineteenth century among European Jews to form a Jewish state.

them.[26] In the United States the leading activists among a wide variety of mostly white women's organizations were Susan B. Anthony and Elizabeth Cady Stanton; black feminists included Sojourner Truth and Maria Cooper, who worked for the more complicated ends of both racial and gender equality. In 1903 the most militant of suffrage movements arose in England; there Emmeline Pankhurst and her daughters founded the Women's Social and Political Union in the belief that women would accomplish nothing unless they threatened men's property. In 1907, WSPU members staged parades in English cities, and in 1909 they began a campaign of violence, blowing up railroad stations, slashing works of art, and chaining themselves to the gates of Parliament.

When nationalist movements became strong in India, Egypt, the Middle East, and China, activist women focused on gaining rights and equality within an independent nation. Although these groups often looked to Western **suffragists** for some of their ideas, European suffragists were themselves inspired by non-Western women's less restrictive clothing, ownership of property, and recognized political roles. Latin American activists were also vocal, concerning themselves with education, the status of children, and the legal rights of women. Feminism thus became a global movement as women's writings, fictional and nonfictional, were translated across national boundaries and women from around the world met at international suffrage meetings. By 1904 feminist organizations from countries on almost all continents joined to form the International Woman Suffrage Alliance. International connections among feminist, African, and African American groups showed the ways in which national movements for citizenship took shape within a global context. The goal of most, however, was no longer to be an outsider to the nation by gaining full insider rights.

Conclusion

Regions throughout the world witnessed revolutionary change in the second half of the nineteenth century as leaders joined with ordinary people to create strong, centralized nation-states. Sometimes these striving nations, such as many in Latin America, simultaneously felt the strong, divisive forces of regionalism. The United States experienced a devastating civil war over competing political and economic systems that threatened to divide the country in two. In Russia, fear of revolution made that government change policies, liberating the serfs as a way to strengthen the state. But Russia remained an autocracy that failed to listen to the voice of the people—even the wealthy ones. This meant that fundamental flaws, unrecognized at the time, were woven into its nation-building efforts, which around the world were promoting access to education; urban improvements in sanitation, transport, and communications; and the development of public institutions such as museums and libraries.

Though it became increasingly central to nation building in the nineteenth century, nationalism ultimately became a destructive force. Critics add that the widespread discrimination against "outsiders" such as women and people of other races and ethnicities is unfortunately a characteristic of how nation-states create unity among those privileged to be its citizens. Nation building did not happen everywhere, nor did it proceed evenly. It did not eliminate monarchies and empires, although, as Matsuo Taseko witnessed, it changed them. Nation builders around the world recognized that, given the global web of trade, communications, and industrialization, the nation-state was an effective means of focusing political, economic, and military power, even becoming a tool for moving beyond the nation-state to create far-flung empires. Those who lacked the concentrated force of the nation-state were ripe for colonization rather than independence and prosperity.

suffragist An activist on behalf of the vote for women.

NOTES

1. Anne Walthall, *The Weak Body of a Useless Woman: Matsuo Taseko and the Meiji Restoration* (Chicago: University of Chicago Press, 1998), 98, 107.
2. Quoted in John Armstrong Crow, *The Epic of Latin America*, 4th ed. (Berkeley: University of California Press, 1992), 542.
3. Quoted in George Reid Andrews, *Afro-Latin America, 1800–2000* (New York: Oxford University Press, 2004), 113.
4. Quoted in Sarah C. Chambers, *From Subjects to Citizens: Honor, Gender, and Politics in Arequipa, Peru, 1780–1854* (University Park: Pennsylvania State University Press, 1999), 234–235.
5. Ibid.
6. Quoted in ibid., 184.
7. Quoted in Andrews, *Afro-Latin America*, 107, 181.
8. *El Republicano*, October 29, 1855, quoted in Carlos Froment, *Democracy in Latin America, 1760–1900: Civic Selfhood and Public Life in Mexico and Peru* (Chicago: University of Chicago Press, 2003), 155.
9. Quoted in Richard Stites, *Serfdom, Society, and the Arts in Imperial Russia: The Pleasure and the Power* (New Haven, CT: Yale University Press, 2005), 38.
10. "Alexander Nikitenko Responds to the Emancipation of the Serfs, 1861," http://artsci.shu.edu/reesp/documents/nikitenko.htm.
11. Quoted in Jasper Ridley, *Garibaldi* (London: St. Martins, 2001), 443.
12. Ibid., 448.
13. Quoted in James L. Roark et al., *The American Promise: A History of the United States*, 4th ed. (Boston: Bedford/St. Martins, 2009), 537.
14. Quoted in Frank Linderman, *Pretty-shield, Medicine Woman of the Crows* (Lincoln: University of Nebraska Press, 1972), 83.
15. Daklugie quoted in Colin G. Calloway, *First Peoples: A Documentary Survey of American Indian History*, 3d ed. (Boston: Bedford/St. Martins, 2008), 312.
16. Quoted in Mikiso Hane, *Peasants, Rebels, and Outcastes: The Underside of Modern Japan* (New York: Pantheon, 1982), 24.
17. Walthall, *The Weak Body of a Useless Woman*, 269.
18. Quoted in Ronald H. Dolkart, "Angela Peralta: A Mexican Diva," in Judith Ewell and William H. Beezley, eds., *The Human Tradition in Latin America: The Nineteenth Century* (Wilmington, DE: Scholarly Resources, 1989), 165, 167, 173.
19. Quoted in Irokawa Daikichi, *The Culture of the Meiji Period*, ed. and trans. Marius B. Jansen (Princeton, NJ: Princeton University Press, 1985), 56.
20. Quoted in Mikiso Hane, *Peasants, Rebels, and Outcastes*, 58.
21. Quoted in Richard Slotkin, *The Fatal Environment: The Myth of the Frontier in an Age of Industrialization* (Norman: University of Oklahoma Press, 1985), 339.
22. Ibid., 347.
23. "The Race Problem: An Autobiography: A Southern Colored Woman," *The Independent* 56 (1904): 586–589.
24. Quoted in Stephen Oates, *A Woman of Valor: Clara Barton and the Civil War* (New York: Free Press, 1994), 157–158.
25. Ida B. Wells, *Crusade for Justice: The Autobiography of Ida B. Wells*, ed. Alfreda M. Duster (Chicago: University of Chicago Press, 1970), 49.
26. Grete Meisel-Hess, *The Sexual Crisis*, trans. Eden and Cedar Paul (New York: The Critic and Guide Company, 1917), 6.

RESOURCES FOR RESEARCH

Modernizing Nations

Nations modernized and built their strength in different ways, but one common trend involved upgrading the education and general welfare of a wider segment of the population. Froment's book describes popular movements and official policies that worked toward that change.

Blackbourn, David. *Fontana History of Germany, 1780–1918: The Long Nineteenth Century*. 1997.

Froment, Carlos. *Democracy in Latin America, 1760–1900: Civic Selfhood and Public Life in Mexico and Peru*. 2003.

Mexican-American War, 1846–1848. Kera. PBS Online. www.pbs.org/kera/usmexicanwar/.

Meyer, Michael C., and William H. Beezley. *Oxford History of Mexico*. 2000.

*Nikitenko, Alexander. *Up from Serfdom: My Childhood and Youth in Russia, 1804–1824*. Translated by Helen Saltz Jacobson. 2001.

Emerging Powers: The United States and Japan

Two surprising newcomers on the nineteenth-century international stage were the United States and Japan, whose rise to prominence was full of struggle and bloodshed, as described in these works.

Faust, Drew Gilpin. *This Republic of Suffering: Death and the American Civil War.* 2008.

Foner, Eric. *The Fiery Trial: Abraham Lincoln and American Slavery.* 2010.

Keene, Donald. *Emperor of Japan: Meiji and His World, 1852–1912.* 2002.

Love, Eric T. L. *Race over Empire: Racism and U.S. Imperialism, 1865–1900.* 2005.

Walthall, Anne. *The Weak Body of a Useless Woman: Matsuo Taseko and the Meiji Restoration.* 1998.

The Culture of Nations

Culture was an integral part of creating a national identity. Stites's book shows how serf artists shaped not only the culture of the Russian Empire but its national politics.

Andrews, George Reid. *Afro-Latin America, 1800–2000.* 2004.

Huffman, James L. *Creating a Public: People and Press in Meiji Japan.* 1997.

Marchand, Suzanne, and David Lindenfeld, eds. *Germany at the Fin de Siècle: Culture, Politics, and Ideas.* 2004.

Stites, Richard. *Serfdom, Society, and the Arts in Imperial Russia: The Pleasure and the Power.* 2005.

Walthall, Anne, ed. *The Human Tradition in Modern Japan.* 2004.

COUNTERPOINT: Outsiders Inside the Nation-State

In an age when nations were defining themselves, outsiders to the nation were those who lived within its boundaries but were kept from full citizenship. The battles for full rights continue to this day, especially as citizenship becomes global rather than national.

Bay, Mia. *To Tell the Truth Freely: The Life of Ida B. Wells.* 2009.

Calloway, Colin G. *First Peoples: A Documentary Survey of American Indian Peoples.* 2011.

*Douglass, Frederick. *Narrative of the Life of Frederick Douglass, an American Slave, Written by Himself.* 1993.

Lowy, Dina. *The Japanese "New Woman": Images of Gender and Modernity.* 2007.

Lynch, John. *Argentine Caudillo: Juan Manuel de Rosas.* 2001.

* Primary source.

▶ **For additional primary sources from this period**, see *Sources of Crossroads and Cultures*.

▶ **For Web sites, images, and documents related to topics in this chapter**, see Make History at bedfordstmartins.com/smith.

The major global development in this chapter ▶ The causes and
consequences of nation building in the nineteenth century.

IMPORTANT EVENTS

1833–1855	Mexican caudillo Santa Anna serves at intervals to lead the government
1846–1848	Mexican-American War
1853–1856	Crimean War
1855	Walt Whitman, *Leaves of Grass*
1859–1870	Unification of Italy
1860s	Height of opera singer Angela Peralta's career
1861	Emancipation of the serfs in Russia
1861–1865	U.S. Civil War
1863	Emancipation Proclamation in the United States
1866–1871	Unification of Germany
1868	Meiji Restoration of Japan
1872–1876	Fukuzawa Yukichi, *Encouragement of Learning*
1880s	Popular uprisings in Japan
1881	Young rebels assassinate Alexander II of Russia
1888	Emancipation of slaves in Brazil
1889	Brazilian emperor Pedro II abdicates and republic is installed

KEY TERMS

federalism (p. 831)
Manifest Destiny (p. 839)
mir (p. 835)
nation (p. 829)
pan-Africanism (p. 851)

realpolitik (p. 838)
Risorgimento (p. 837)
suffragist (p. 852)
zemstvo (p. 837)
Zionism (p. 851)

CHAPTER OVERVIEW QUESTIONS

1. Why did nation-states become so important to people in the nineteenth century?
2. What was the role of war in the rise of the nation-state?
3. What was the role of ordinary people in nation building?
4. Are nation-states still important today, and are there still outsiders inside nations?

SECTION FOCUS QUESTIONS

1. How did some states transform themselves into modern nations?
2. How did the United States and Japan make their governments politically and economically powerful in the nineteenth century?
3. What part did culture play in forging a national identity?
4. What groups were excluded from full participation in the nation-state, and why?

MAKING CONNECTIONS

1. How did the spread of industrialization (see Chapter 24) affect the rise of modern nation-states?
2. What was the legacy of slavery in the new nations? Did it make a difference to nation building that some states—Germany and Italy, for example—did not have large numbers of slaves in their homelands?
3. Why did Russia fail to offer rights to citizens equal to those offered by Western nations?

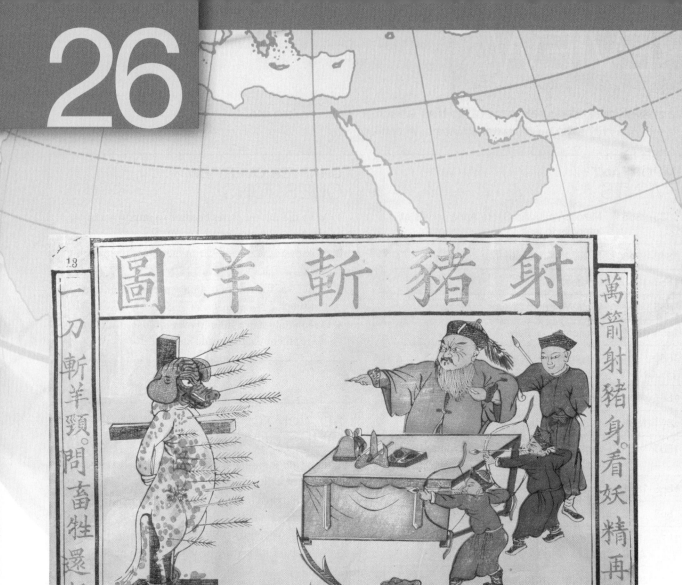

26

AT A CROSSROADS ▲

By 1900 China had become a crossroads of global ambitions. Japan, the United States, and the European powers had begun to exploit its markets and resources and in some cases to convert its population to Christianity. At the time, China was also a crossroads of famine and want, leading subjects of the Qing Empire to see their distress as the result of foreign inroads. The Chinese rebels known as the Boxers, illustrated here, were determined to "Kill the Pig"—that is, foreign missionaries, diplomats, and merchants. Armies from the foreign powers invaded China, suppressed the Boxers, rampaged across Chinese cities and farms, and further plundered the country's wealth. (Private Collection /Bridgeman Art Library.)

Imperial Order and Disorder

1850–1914

"Here come the foreign devils," a little boy shouted in 1900 in the northern Chinese city of Tianjin, "that's why we don't have any rain."[1] It was a time of intense drought in the region, and the Chinese were starving. Seedlings dried up in the fields, leaving peasants with time on their hands and with hunger killing both body and spirit. Many blamed the foreigners from Britain, Germany, Japan, and other parts of the world for these problems. On December 31, 1899, a British missionary, one of the many sent to convert the Chinese to Christianity, was assassinated in Shandong, an eastern province of China. By the summer of 1900, not only missionaries but also the German ambassador, European businessmen, and Chinese converts to Christianity by the thousands were being killed in antiforeign uprisings that came to be known as the Boxer Rebellion. The rebels believed that they were acting in self-defense, protecting their homeland from outsiders whose presence had brought the drought and the resulting hardship, devastation, and death.

Europeans had been fascinated by China for centuries. It had long been the most important power in the world with a tradition of excellence in philosophy, art, and literature; it was also the source of prized porcelain, silks, and cottons. In fact, it was the desire to gain a direct connection to the wealth and resources of Asia that had prompted early modern European expansion. The Japanese, too, had borrowed much from the Chinese, whose political and religious ideas played a key role in Japan's development. Nonetheless, in the nineteenth century the European powers, along with Japan and the expansionist United States, had come to see China—and most of the rest of the world—as areas to be dominated. Individual nation-states could increase their strength by gaining access to China's raw materials and cheap labor, and there was money to be made by seizing its taxes and financing development projects such as railroads. Britain, France, the Netherlands, Germany, Russia, Japan, and the United States all shared an impulse to control the wealth and, increasingly, even the governments of other regions of the world. In the second half

Building Empires

FOCUS What motivated the imperialists, and how did they impose their control over other nations?

Imperial Society

FOCUS How did imperialism change lives and livelihoods around the world?

Culture in an Imperial Age

FOCUS How did artists and writers respond to the age of empire?

Imperial Contests at the Dawn of the Twentieth Century

FOCUS What were the main issues in the contests over empire, and what were the results of these contests?

COUNTERPOINT: The West Copies from the World

FOCUS How did non-Western and colonized lands shape Western culture and society?

BACKSTORY

As we saw in Chapter 25, in the nineteenth century a number of states improved their governing institutions, expanded their bureaucracies, and attempted to build a shared sense of national identity in their often diverse populations. States also began to devote more attention to public education, seeing an educated population as a source of national strength. The drive to increase national power was a prime motive for commercial and military expansion, an outgrowth of state efforts to gain control of resources, markets, and strategic locations around the world. As states jostled with one another for power, their rivalries were increasingly played out in a competition for possessions outside of the nation-state's boundaries.

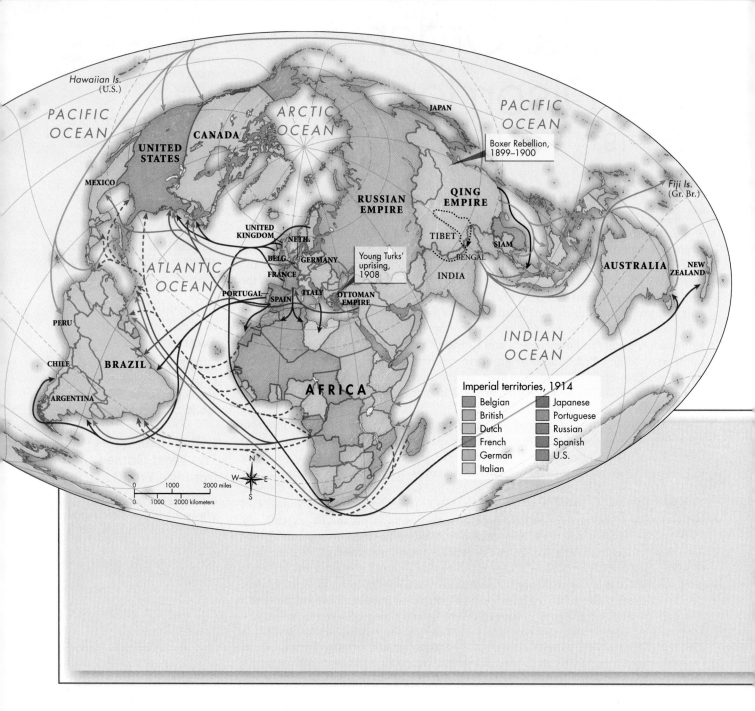

Imperial territories, 1914

- Belgian
- British
- Dutch
- French
- German
- Italian
- Japanese
- Portuguese
- Russian
- Spanish
- U.S.

Boxer Rebellion, 1899–1900

Young Turks' uprising, 1908

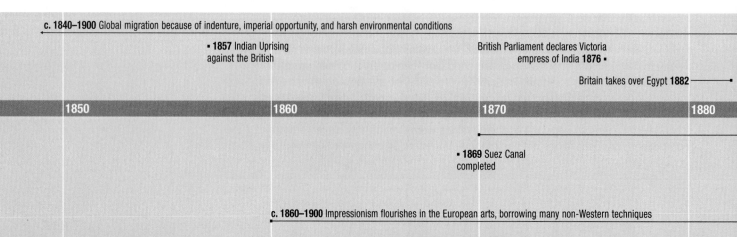

c. 1840–1900 Global migration because of indenture, imperial opportunity, and harsh environmental conditions

▪ **1857** Indian Uprising against the British

British Parliament declares Victoria empress of India **1876** ▪

Britain takes over Egypt **1882** ――――

| 1850 | 1860 | 1870 | 1880 |

▪ **1869** Suez Canal completed

c. 1860–1900 Impressionism flourishes in the European arts, borrowing many non-Western techniques

of the nineteenth century the word *imperialism* was used to describe this impulse toward global domination.

In the rush to dominate, these competing nations changed their tune, many claiming that they were bringing civilization and order to backward peoples of the world. Despite that promise, imperialism in China and elsewhere around the globe brought massive bloodshed and disorder, much of it inflicted by the imperialists themselves on those who would not bow to their rule. Empire builders in Asia, Africa, and the Mediterranean basin focused so exclusively on extracting wealth that they let the maintenance of traditional but crucial systems such as irrigation deteriorate because they did not yield immediate profit. The result was starvation and suffering. Imperialist inroads inspired heartfelt resistance, often increasing the bloodshed. Many in the colonies were inspired by some of the imperialists' accomplishments, including the creation of powerful nation-states and guarantees of liberal ideals such as self-determination and human rights. Even though such guarantees were hardly given to colonized peoples, the very existence of these ideals led many to fight for their freedom.

In the course of imperialism and the globalization of trade and finance that accompanied it, society and culture changed. Poets and artists reacted to the whirl of imperial activity around them, sometimes deploring the changes and at other times seizing on ideas from other cultures to spark their creativity. Tens of millions of people migrated either to find opportunity within empires or to escape the misery at home that imperialism brought. As they left their homes to take up livelihoods in other parts of the world, these migrants

MAPPING THE WORLD

The Spread of Imperialism, 1850–1914

The world's peoples interacted more in the late nineteenth century because of the spread of empire and increases in migration and travel. Behind this movement of peoples were the quest for opportunity and freedom, and also ambition and greed. Occasionally those driving imperialism had philanthropic and scientific motives, but imperialists often used naked violence to achieve their ends.

ROUTES ▼

Mass migrations, 1850–1910
- ┈➤ African slaves, c. 1800–1860
- ➝ Other European
- ➝ African, c. 1840–1910
- ➝ Indian
- ➝ Lebanese
- ➝ Chinese
- ➝ European Jewish

- ➝ Travels of Khaw Soo Cheang, c. 1820
- ┈➤ Travels of Nain Singh, 1873–1875

1884–1885 European nations carve up Africa at the Berlin Conference

1910 Japan annexes Korea

1894–1895 Sino-Japanese War

1900 Sigmund Freud, *The Interpretation of Dreams*

| 1890 | 1900 | 1910 |

c. 1870–1914 European powers, Japan, and the United States extend formal and informal control over Asia, Africa, and parts of Latin America

Spanish-American War **1898**

1899–1902 South African War

1908 Young Turks' uprising against the Ottoman Empire

1899–1900 Boxer Rebellion in China

1904–1905 Russo-Japanese War

created new communities, such as the Chinese in Singapore and San Francisco and the Lebanese in Rio de Janeiro and Montreal. Thus, imperialism brought wrenching change as well as new opportunity for peoples throughout the world while pulling societies, willingly or not, into ever-closer contact. The Boxer Rebellion against the "foreign devils" was but one expression of the complex enterprise of imperialism.

OVERVIEW
QUESTIONS

The major global development in this chapter: The accelerated competition among nineteenth-century nation-states for empire.

As you read, consider:

1. What are the arguments for and against imperialism?

2. How and why did some local peoples assist imperialists who took over their own countries?

3. Which were the major imperialist powers, and what made them so capable of conquest?

4. How did imperialism change the lives of people in the conquering countries and in the colonies?

Building Empires

FOCUS

What motivated the imperialists, and how did they impose their control over other nations?

The nineteenth century was an age of imperialism, a time when nations around the world built both formal and informal empires. The British government formally took over the governments of South Asian states, ending the East India Company's domination of the region through trade, taxation, and military might. It incorporated India into Britain politically and declared Queen Victoria empress. After midcentury, other nations instituted direct rule of areas once linked to them by trade alone. They sent soldiers and more settlers to distant lands and expanded their foreign office bureaucracies. Such takeovers—often called the "**new imperialism**" in contrast to the trader-based domination of preceding centuries—promoted both individual wealth and national power, albeit funded by ordinary taxpayers. The new imperialism was not, however, simply a story of violence inflicted by foreigners aiming for political and economic domination. Conquering nations provided social and cultural services such as schools to reflect the imperial power's values. In many instances local chieftains, merchants, and cultural leaders helped imperialists make their inroads abroad.

Imperialism: What Is It?

new imperialism The takeover in the second half of the nineteenth century of foreign lands by Western powers and Japan, which entailed political control as well as economic domination.

globalization A variety of behaviors and processes, such as trade, warfare, travel, and the spread of culture, that link the world's peoples.

Imperialism is associated with the domination that European powers, Japan, and the United States began to exercise over much of the rest of the world in the second half of the nineteenth century. The term is used to describe the ambitions, conquests, and power exercised over the trade, taxation, and governments of other states and their peoples—somewhat similar to the way in which the word **globalization** is used today to describe a variety of behaviors and processes that link the world's peoples. There had been empires throughout history, but the new imperialism of the nineteenth and twentieth centuries was both more and less than empire. The word connotes not just formally claimed territory, indirectly ruled lands, and economic domination, but even the strong desire to possess territory. Although modern imperialism motivated both governmental and private actions right through World War II, it was never a coherent system or a consistent set of practices. It also describes a control that was never complete and that colonized peoples constantly contested.

One important feature of modern imperialism was colonization, that is, the creation of settlements in foreign territories intended to dominate the land and its native peoples and to take its wealth. Colonization shaped the Roman Empire and others, including the later Spanish and Portuguese empires of the sixteenth century, and it remained a prominent part of the new imperialism. Colonization, it was believed, could secure distant territories at less expense than armies would require; it could train a foreign population in the imperial power's culture; in some cases, it could alleviate crowding in the mother country. **Colonialism** is the term for the system that dominated people in these ways.

Colonization and Colonialism

A second feature of imperialism was the range of motivations behind it. Some national leaders saw more extensive landholdings in and of themselves as a major ingredient of national strength; others saw the wealth that could be siphoned off to strengthen nations. Business leaders aimed to make money in underdeveloped areas by building harbors, railroads, and roads, while merchants wanted to increase commerce and thus profits through imperial networks. "Business" or "informal" imperialism based on foreign investment, commerce, and manufacturing could also exist without political rule. Britain, and later the United States, exerted considerable power over Latin American states through investments in and control of key industries. **Business imperialism** included economic domination of sugar, coffee, and other plantation agriculture in many parts of the world. Finally, many envisioned imperialism as an almost saintly undertaking. As one French economist put it in 1891, taking over countries would bring civilization to "barbarous and savage tribes, some enduring wars without end and destructive ways of life, others knowing nothing of the arts and having so few habits of work and invention that they have no way of knowing how to get riches from the land."[2]

Imperial Motivations

For the Spanish and Portuguese, who saw firsthand the immense accomplishment and wealth of American peoples, their own superiority rested on their Catholic faith. Increasingly, Christianity blended with racism to justify domination. In the second half of the nineteenth century, new "scientific" theories of race reinforced this sense of cultural superiority. The ideas of European scientists and doctors—especially those of Charles Darwin, the English naturalist who developed the theory of evolution—appealed to imperialists. Darwin himself, along with people later called Social Darwinists, explicitly stated that nonwhites, women, and members of the working class were less highly evolved than white men and therefore in need of domination. This inferiority was affirmed by a number of bogus measurements in the nineteenth century, such as the size of the cranium. Scientific racism was not confined to whites: the Japanese considered themselves far in advance of native peoples such as the Ainu who lived far from the capital, and of foreigners such as the Koreans.

Confident of their superiority, imperialists proposed that they would uplift and liberate the people they conquered from their own backwardness. Paradoxically, cultural pride prompted some "civilizers" such as missionaries to support the most brutal military measures to accomplish their goals. Thus, the building of schools and churches occurred alongside massacres of local people who would not turn over their property, animals, or houses. Forcing others to accept cultural values such as Christian belief was also part of imperialism.

Takeover in Asia

Great Britain, the era's mightiest colonial power, made a dramatic change of course by instituting governmental control of India while the Russians and British were also in constant struggle to rule Central Asia and the French and Dutch struggled with local peoples

colonialism The establishment of settler communities in areas ruled by foreign powers.

business imperialism The domination of foreign economies without military or political rule.

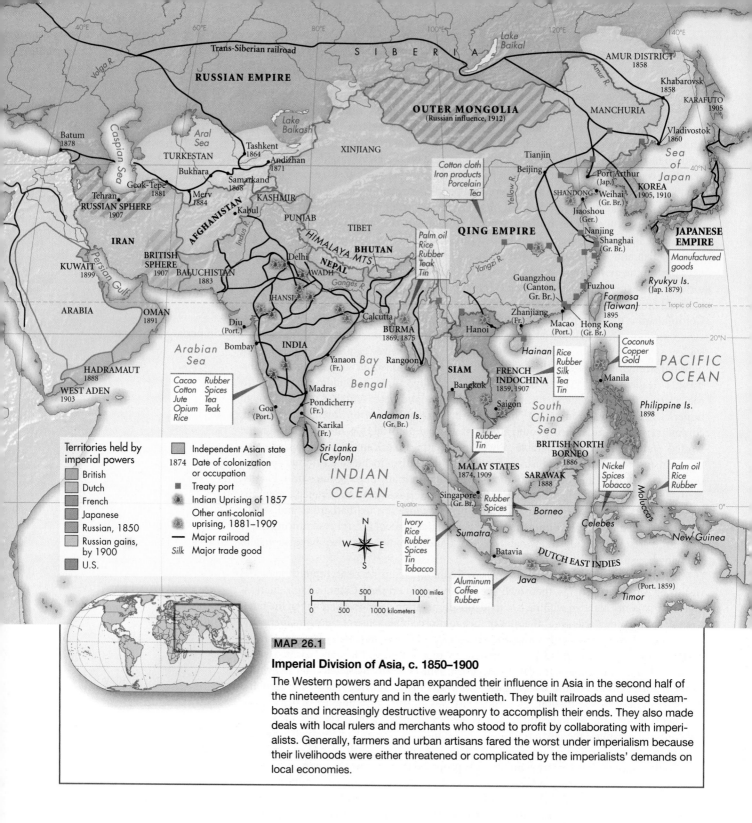

MAP 26.1

Imperial Division of Asia, c. 1850–1900

The Western powers and Japan expanded their influence in Asia in the second half of the nineteenth century and in the early twentieth. They built railroads and used steamboats and increasingly destructive weaponry to accomplish their ends. They also made deals with local rulers and merchants who stood to profit by collaborating with imperialists. Generally, farmers and urban artisans fared the worst under imperialism because their livelihoods were either threatened or complicated by the imperialists' demands on local economies.

for empire in Southeast Asia. The contest in Central Asia has been called the "Great Game," but that hardly conveys the destruction inflicted on local peoples and on the imperialists themselves—all in the name of advancing the nation by forging an empire (see Map 26.1).

The British in India

Since the eighteenth century and especially after the loss of Britain's thirteen North American colonies, the East India Company had expanded its reach to become the major tax collector for the Mughal emperor, princes, and other ruling officers on the subcontinent. The Company became the acting ruler of some of these Indian territories and later built railroads throughout the countryside to make commerce and revenue collecting more efficient. In 1856, wanting more revenue and control, the Company took over the wealthy northern kingdom of Awadh, contrary to formal treaties with the king about his sovereignty.

For Indians whose wealth and livelihoods derived from their connections with the Company, this event was of little importance. Outside of this small segment of the population, however, the takeover of Awadh fueled already rising anger over excessive taxation and the Company's increasingly high-handed ways. In 1857, Indian troops serving the Company, known as *sepoys*, heard rumors that the new Enfield rifles they were to use had cartridges greased with cow and pig fat, forbidden to Hindus (for whom cows are sacred) and Muslims (for whom pigs are unclean). The soldiers believed that they were deliberately being made impure and that the cartridges were part of a plot to convert them to Christianity. Spurred by the economic grievances of the peasant classes from which most of them sprang, the soldiers massacred their British officers and then conquered the Indian capital at Delhi, reinstating the emperor and declaring the independence of the Indian people.

Rebellions spread to the general populace, justified, so the emperor explained, by "the tyranny and oppression of the infidel and treacherous English." The Rani (Queen) Lakshmibai, widow of the ruler of the state of Jhansi in central India, led a separate military revolt when the East India Company tried to take over her lands, but she was only one among many to do so. The British had trouble motivating recruits to put down the uprisings. "All black men are one," said a newly recruited soldier, who vowed he would not fight the rebels.[3] Eventually British-led forces from other regions crushed the Indian Uprising of 1857, as this widespread revolt is now called. In the aftermath of the uprising, the British government substituted its control for that of the Company and in 1876 declared Queen Victoria the empress of India.

The British constructed India as a single colony formed from independent kingdoms and small princely territories, but in practice this apparent unity was partial at best. Many states remained semi-independent. Paradoxically, the British "unification" of India contributed to growing nationalist sentiment among Indian elites. It was in this context that, in 1885, wealthy and well-educated Indians created the Indian National Congress, an organization aiming to bring about reform, obtain rights and representation in the British government, and eventually gain independence.

British success in South Asia was part of a struggle for trade and empire that made entire continents a battlefield of competing interests and warring armies. In Central Asia, Russian and British armies blasted former centers of Silk Road trade into ruins and slaughtered Afghan resisters during decades of destructive conflict. After the fall of Kabul to British forces in 1842, a commander set his men loose on the city's population to avenge the killing of British soldiers and civilians by Afghani resisters. The Russian general who took the fortress of Geok-Tepe in modern Turkmenistan let his troops steal, rape, and butcher its inhabitants. He justified the sixteen thousand dead by saying, "The duration of peace is in direct proportion to the slaughter you inflict upon the enemy."[4] Publicly hanging only a few ringleaders of the rebellion, he explained, inspired further resistance to takeovers, whereas a reputation for massive killings would create fear—and thus obedience.

Imperial moves inspired countermoves. The British added to their holdings in Asia partly to block Russian and French expansion. Russia absorbed the small Muslim states of West and Central Asia, including Turkestan; some provinces of Afghanistan; and extending into the Ottoman Empire, Persia, northern India, and China, often encountering British competition but mostly fighting local peoples. Russia built the trans-Siberian railroad to help integrate Siberia—once considered a distant colony—into an expanding Russian Empire. Once completed, the new rail line helped transport settlers and soldiers into the region (see again Map 26.1).

From India the British military pushed to the east, moving into Burma in 1869 and taking the Malay peninsula in 1874. The presence of British troops guaranteed the order necessary to expand railroads for greater access to interior markets and more efficient

The British and Russians in Central Asia

extraction of raw materials—tin, oil, rice, teak, and rubber. The environmental consequences were severe as the British built factories and leased forests in the north of Burma to private companies that stripped them bare, "denuding the country," as one official put it, "to its great and lasting loss."[5] Famine and drought followed this ecological nightmare, weakening the local population and making it easier to annex Burma in 1875.

The French in Southeast Asia

In the 1860s the French were establishing their own control in Cochin China (modern southern Vietnam). Missionaries in the area, ambitious French naval officers stationed in Asia, native officials looking for work, and even some local peoples making profits from European trade urged the French government on. After sending in troops, France used favorable treaties (backed by the threat of military action) to create the Union of Indochina from the ancient states of Cambodia, Tonkin, Annam, and Cochin China in 1887 (the latter three constitute the modern nation of Vietnam). Rubber plantations and other money-making projects followed. Laos was added to Indochina in 1893.

Like the British in India, the French brought some Western innovations to the societies they conquered. Modern agricultural projects spurred rapid growth in the food supply. The French also improved sanitation and public health in Indochina. Such changes proved a mixed blessing, however, because they led to population growth that strained resources. Furthermore, French landowners and traders siphoned off the profits from economic development. The French also transformed cities such as Saigon by constructing tree-lined boulevards inspired by those in Paris. French literature, theater, and art were popular with colonial officials and upper-class Indochinese alike. Nonetheless, in the countryside ordinary Vietnamese saw things differently. As one peasant protested to the governor general in 1907, "the French are treating us like animals, looking at us like wood and stone."[6] Such treatment, combined with the exposure of native elites to Western ideas of "the rights of man," helped produce an Indochinese nationalist movement.

Europeans Scramble for Africa

North Africa

Imperialism often involved seizures of people's lands and goods after their military defeat. In Africa, however, the cruelty was notorious, as Europeans trained their sights on the continent in the second half of the nineteenth century. European conquest of the continent began with North Africa, and then moved on to sub-Saharan Africa with its rich supplies of raw materials such as palm oil, cotton, diamonds, cacao, and rubber (see Map 26.2, page 866). With its empire in India, Britain additionally hoped to keep the southern and eastern coasts of Africa secure for stopover ports on the route to Asia. While North Africa had commercial value, the Mediterranean as a whole was most important for its strategic location.

French emperor Napoleon III, remembering his uncle's campaign in Egypt, helped sponsor the building of the Suez Canal, which would connect the Mediterranean with the Red Sea and the Indian Ocean and thus dramatically shorten the route from Europe to Asia. The canal was completed in 1869, and beginning with Muhammad Ali, Egypt's enterprising rulers made Cairo into a bustling city, boosting commerce and manufacturing and attracting European capital investment. In an effort to further enhance the connections between Egypt's economy and the rest of the world, Egyptian businessmen and government officials supported the construction of thousands of miles of railroad track, the improvement of harbors, and the installation of telegraph systems. Many of these ventures were paid for with money borrowed from European lenders at far higher rates of interest than Europeans paid. Nonetheless, many Egyptian elites believed that such modernization projects were essential to their country's future and, therefore, that an Egyptian-European financial alliance was necessary, whatever its cost.

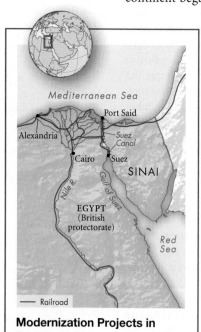

Modernization Projects in Egypt, c. 1910

Albert Rieger,
***Suez Canal* (1864)**

Workers from around the Mediterranean labored on the Suez Canal, which the French designed to connect the Mediterranean to the Red Sea and thus speed up commerce with Asia. The British saw the Suez Canal, completed in 1869, as important to protecting its Asian empire, and by 1882 they had taken over Egypt not only to control the canal but also to guarantee British financial investments in the canal and in other Egyptian modernization projects. The Suez Canal remains a major world crossroads to this day. (The Art Archive/Museo Civico Revoltella Trieste/Collection Dagli Orti.)

The alliance turned sour when Great Britain and France, eager to control business with Egypt, took over the Egyptian treasury with the excuse that they needed to guarantee loans that the Egyptian government found itself hard-pressed to repay. In 1882, after striking a deal with the French, the British invaded and essentially took control of the government, an act they claimed was necessary to put down those Egyptian nationalists who protested the seizure of the treasury. Soon Cairo had the air of "an English town," as one Egyptian local put it.[7] The English, in alliance with local entrepreneurs, shifted the Egyptian economy from a system based on multiple crops—a system that maintained the country's self-sufficiency—to one that emphasized the production of a few highly marketable crops, notably cotton and wheat, which were especially useful to the English. As the colonial powers and Egyptian elites grew rich, the bulk of the rural population, their livelihoods transformed, barely eked out an existence.

Meanwhile the French army, driving into the North African hinterland, occupied all of Algeria by 1870 and then neighboring Tunisia in 1881. As elsewhere, French rule in North Africa was aided by the attraction of local people to European trade and technology. Merchants and local leaders cooperated in building railroads, sought bank loans from the French, and sent their children to European-style schools. They became "evolved"—as the French called those who adopted European ways. Many local peoples, however, resisted French intrusions, attacking soldiers and settlers. Others died from European-spread diseases. By 1872, the native population in Algeria had declined by more than 20 percent from five years earlier.

In the 1880s, European governments raced to the African interior, both playing to local elites' self-interest and using military force to overwhelm resistance. The French, Belgians, Portuguese, Italians, and Germans jockeyed to dominate peoples, land, and resources—"the magnificent cake of Africa," as King Leopold II of Belgium (r. 1865–1909) put it. Driven by almost unparalleled greed, Leopold claimed the Congo region of central Africa, thereby initiating competition with France for that territory and inflicting on its peoples unspeakable acts of cruelty. German chancellor Otto von Bismarck established

Sub-Saharan Africa

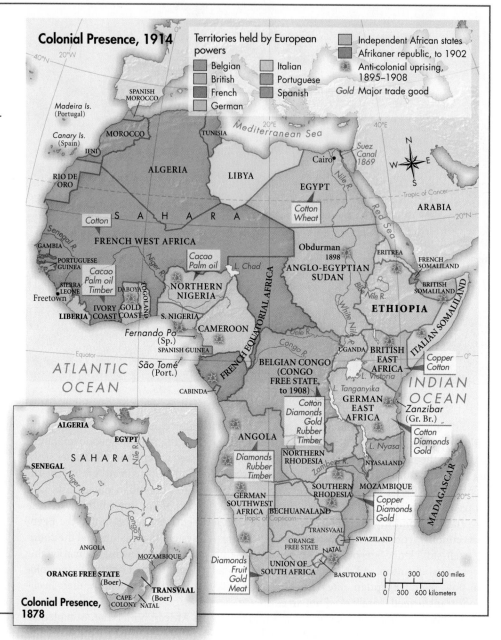

MAP 26.2

Imperial Division of Africa, c. 1880–1914

Though some Africans profited, most suffered from contacts with Europeans, which increased after the mid-nineteenth century, largely because the use of quinine cut down health risks for the invaders. Environmental factors also aided Europeans in their new pursuit of actual colonies on the continent. Where famine and drought failed to make Africans submit, the Europeans' outright brutality put down often stubborn resistance.

Colonial Presence, 1914

Territories held by European powers

- Belgian
- British
- French
- German
- Italian
- Portuguese
- Spanish
- Independent African states
- Afrikaner republic, to 1902
- Anti-colonial uprising, 1895–1908

Gold Major trade good

Colonial Presence, 1878

German control over Cameroon and a section of East Africa. Faced with stiff competition for African territory, the British spent millions of pounds attempting to take over the continent militarily "from Cairo to Cape Town," as the slogan went. The French cemented their hold on large portions of western Africa (see again Map 26.2).

Environmental disasters, regional tensions, and African rulers themselves scrambling for resources and territory helped the would-be conquerors. In 1882 the king of Daboya in northern Ghana explained his treaty with the British in these terms: "I want to keep off all my enemies and none to be able to stand before me."[8] The king expected guns and military backing from the British should it be necessary. The European powers put so much stake in the ability of local rulers to collect taxes and in the loyalty of African police and soldiers for maintaining order that during the 1890s, Germans in imperial Tanzania kept only one hundred military personnel to guard the entire territory.

Resistance in South Africa

The Zulu had maintained a powerful kingdom in southern Africa since early in the nineteenth century. Using excellent camouflage and stealthy movements, they consistently resisted the British, despite being outgunned. Finally, in the Anglo-Zulu War of 1879, they were defeated, and their king Cetshwayo was held and interrogated in an effort to prove he was a dictatorial savage and thus inferior to British rulers. Note that this painting makes it appear as if the British heroically fought dozens of Zulu individually. In fact, by the final battles the British were launching tens of thousands of African and European troops against the Zulu. (The Print Collector/HIP/The Image Works.)

Violent struggle occurred for control of southern Africa, where farmers of European descent and immigrant prospectors, rather than military personnel, battled the Xhosa (KOH-suh), Zulu, and other African peoples for the frontier regions of Transvaal, Natal, the Orange Free State, Rhodesia, and the Cape Colony. Although the Dutch were the first Europeans to settle the area permanently, the British had gained control by 1815. Thereafter descendants of the Dutch, called *Boers* (Dutch for "farmers"), were joined by British immigrants in their fight to seize farmland and mineral resources from natives. British businessman and politician Cecil Rhodes, sent to South Africa for his health at age seventeen, just as diamonds were being discovered, cornered the diamond market and claimed a huge amount of African territory with the help of official charters from the British government, all before he turned forty. Pushing hundreds of miles into the interior of southern Africa (a region soon to be named Rhodesia after him), Rhodes moved into gold mining too. His ambition for Britain and for himself was boundless: "I contend that we are the finest race in the world," he explained, "and that the more of the world we inhabit the better it is."

South Africa

The scramble for Africa intensified tensions among the imperial powers, leading to a conference of European nations in 1884. Statesmen from the fourteen nations represented at the Berlin Conference echoed Rhodes's racial pride; as representatives of a "superior"

The Berlin Conference

civilization, they considered themselves fully entitled to determine the fate of the African continent. To resolve territorial disputes, they decided that any nation that controlled a settlement along the African coast was also guaranteed the rights to the corresponding interior territory. This agreement led to the linear dissection of the continent, a process that ignored the actual territorial borders of some 70 percent of Africa's ethnic groups. In theory the meeting was supposed to reduce bloodshed and temper ambitions in Africa, but European leaders remained more committed than ever to expanding their power. Newspaper reports of daring conquests only stirred up citizens to demand more imperialist excitement.

Japan's Imperial Agenda

Japan escaped the "new" European imperialism by rapidly transforming into a modern industrial nation with its own imperial agenda. The Japanese, unlike China, endorsed technology and the quest for colonies. In contrast to Europe where there was often heated debate about imperial conquest, the Meiji regime insisted on unity: "All classes high and low shall unite in vigorously promoting the economy and welfare of the nation," ran one of its statements. By 1894, Japan had become powerful enough to force traders to accept its terms for commerce and diplomatic relations. Then, it went further.

The Sino-Japanese War   To expand its influence and resource base, the Meiji government entered the imperial fray by invading the Chinese island of Formosa (present-day Taiwan) in 1874. In 1876, Japan forced unequal trading treaties on China-dominated Korea. Further Japanese encroachments in Korea led to the 1894 Sino-Japanese War. Modern military technology carried Japan to a swift victory that left the once powerful Qing China humiliated and Japan the colonial overlord of Taiwan and Korea. The European powers, alarmed at Japanese expansion, forced it to relinquish many gains, a move that outraged Japanese nationalists. Tensions between Japan and Russia continued to escalate over the course of the 1890s. The extension of the trans-Siberian railroad through Manchuria and the arrival of millions of Russian settlers accelerated Russian expansion into East and South Asia. Russia sponsored anti-Japanese groups in Korea, making the Korean peninsula appear, as a Japanese military leader put it, like "a dagger thrust at the heart of Japan." As we will see, war soon erupted between the Russians and Japanese, showing the deadly potential for conflict among imperial rivals.

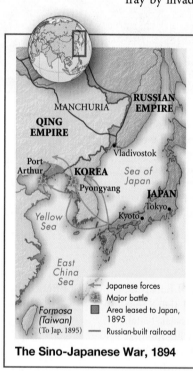

The Sino-Japanese War, 1894

Technology, Environment, and the Imperial Advantage

Industrial Technology   Imperialists were helped immeasurably by both industrial technology and a series of ecological disasters that weakened Asian and African societies. Powerful guns, railroads, steamships, and medicines greatly accelerated imperial conquest. The gunboats that forced the Chinese to open their borders to opium played the same role in forcing African ethnic groups to give up their rights and independence. Improvements to the breech-loading rifle and the development of the machine gun, or "repeater," between 1862 and 1880 dramatically increased firepower. "The whites did not seize their enemy as we do by the body, but thundered from afar," claimed one resister at the 1898 Battle of Obdurman in Sudan, where the British, losing fifty men, mowed down some twenty-five thousand Africans with machine guns (see again Map 26.2). "Death raged everywhere—like the death vomited forth from the tempest," as one African put it. Railroads sped troops and weapons to wherever there was resistance and thus cemented imperial domination.

Environmental Disaster   The ecological balance of power changed too. Whereas once the tropical climate had given Africans an advantage, quinine extracted from cinchona bark from the Andes protected Europeans from the deadly tropical disease malaria, which had once made Africa the "White Man's Grave." Disastrously for Africans and Asians, El Niño weather currents of the last quarter of the nineteenth century brought drought that resulted in deadly famine across a wide swath of both continents. Mysore, India, one official wrote, contained "none but the dead and the dying."[9] Desperate for food, the population began resorting to theft, eating the dead, and, if they had the energy, rioting against big landowners and tax collectors. It was amid environmental catastrophe that Europeans seized land and cattle and generally expanded their holdings. "Europeans," one African man observed at the time, "track famine like a sky full of vultures."[10] The Chinese Boxers could not have said it better.

Imperial Society

Imperialism brought closer connections among peoples far distant from one another, through trade, migration, and warfare. These interactions reshaped societies around the world—both for good and for ill. In the colonies, violence and disorder increased because of the imperialists' heavy taxation, theft of property, and intrusion on everyday life. Migration and the rapid spread of disease added to the burdens of colonial societies. However, imperialists were only able to dominate distant colonies and informally held areas such as China with the help of local people, many of whom profited from the economic opportunities such as new jobs and new technologies that imperial globalization offered. Thus, imperialism was full of paradox and contradiction.

> **FOCUS**
> How did imperialism change lives and livelihoods around the world?

Changing Conditions of Everyday Life

Citizens paid heavy taxes to maintain empires, which usually cost the country as a whole more than it gained. In trade, manufacturing, and international banking, however, individual business people reaped profits. For certain businesses, colonies provided crucial protected markets: late in the century, for instance, French colonies bought 65 percent of France's exports of soap and 41 percent of its metallurgical exports. People in port cities around the world had better jobs because of imperialism. Other segments of the population, however, simply paid the taxes to cover the costs of imperialism, without reward. Many had to leave home and family behind to seek jobs—whether in mines, on newly opened farmland, or in the factories springing up around the world. Imperial interactions changed local life for native peoples, often making it unhealthy and oppressive for many and bringing stupendous wealth to the few.

Networks of guides and translators were among those who dealt successfully with imperialists from Europe, Japan, and the United States, just as their ancestors centuries earlier had dealt with Mongols or Mughals. Nain Singh was the principal of a village school in the Himalayas, but the expanding British Empire transformed his life. Talented and knowledgeable about the vast, uncharted region that included Tibet, Nain Singh took a job with the British colonial service. There he learned to take measured steps of thirty-three inches in order to map terrain, to take the temperature of water so as to chart altitudes, and to speak many languages. After several years of training, Nain Singh attached himself to caravans, posing as a Buddhist pilgrim or a merchant. In fact, he was a British spy against Russia in the contest for control of Central Asia. In that capacity, he charted the forbidden region of Tibet and even spent time in the forbidden Tibetan capital, Lhasa, where he met the Dalai Lama. At great personal risk and sacrifice, intrepid local travelers such as Nain Singh acquired the geographic knowledge on which imperialists depended.

Local elites served the imperialists as soldiers and administrators in both India and Africa, and others helped ward off foreign competition. Khaw Soo Cheang left his home in China for Thailand in the 1820s, beginning his career as a fruit vendor but ending it as a

Working with and for the Imperialists

Nain Singh

Indian explorer Nain Singh worked for the British as a spy and a guide in Central Asia. His livelihood shows how imperialism created complicated relationships between the colonizers and the colonized. Tens of thousands of local Asians and Africans served in European armies, civil service jobs, and commercial and industrial ventures. For most local people, however, the relationship was far from equal, and many such employees testified to being treated with contempt and even physical violence. (TopFoto/The Image Works.)

magnate in the shipping and mining business. He also became an official of the Thai government and handed down his position to his five sons, who efficiently managed the southern states, collected taxes, and made important improvements to roads, mines, and public buildings. As Khaw's family initiatives flourished, Khaw's sons and daughters married into the wealthy world of regional shippers and other businessmen; the sons partnered with Europeans and Australians in their ventures, making the area profitable under Khaw control. A British official complained of the lack of opportunity in a region where, as he described it, a Khaw "has his finger in every pie"; in so doing the family had effectively immunized the region from full-scale intervention by outsiders.[11] There were many ways to work with imperialism.

Under imperialism a system of indirect rule often emerged, one that used local officials, chiefs, and princes to enforce imperial laws and keep order. In India, the best-known example, a few thousand British officials supervised close to half a million local civilian and military employees, who were paid far less than British employees would have been. Other powers adopted similar systems. Indirect rule reduced the cost of empire and invested local officials in the imperial project. As elsewhere, British civil servants attacked Indian cultural practices, such as female infanticide, child marriage, and *sati*, a widow's self-immolation on her husband's funeral pyre. Some in the upper classes of colonized countries were attracted to Japanese reforms and Western ideals—"the lofty tree of liberty," as one high Tunisian official praised them—and to notions of a scientifically ordered society.[12]

The vast majority of colonized peoples, however, were exploited. For example, to prevent superior Indian textiles from competing with British cloth, the government worked to close down Indian manufacturing centers and force artisans to become day laborers producing raw materials such as wheat and cotton. On land seized from peasants, imperialists and local business people set up plantations and opened mines in Africa and Asia. Once self-sufficient farmers became landless workers, either on their former lands or wherever labor was needed, not only in their home region but around the world, as cash agriculture became an instrument of imperial rule. A British governor of the Gold Coast in Africa put the matter succinctly in 1886: the British would "rule the country as if there were no inhabitants," as if local traditions of political and economic life did not exist. By confiscating land for tea, cotton, or rubber plantations, Europeans forced native peoples to work for them to earn a living. The agents of Leopold II of Belgium chopped off hands or simply shot Africans who did not provide their quota of rubber. "All of us wanted only one thing," reported a foreign worker in a Belgian Congo mine, "to terminate our contract and return to our country—we were so frightened by the number of people who died each day"[13] (see Reading the Past: Rubber Workers in the Congo). Subsistence agriculture based on growing a variety of crops and raising animals that supported families declined around the world, and communities were undermined as men left their homes to work in mines or on plantations to earn cash to pay imperial taxes.

Social Disorder

Imperialists brought not just economic but social disorder, upsetting established patterns of life. Even though some local people profited from the presence of outsiders, whom they often viewed as barbarians, other locals were victims of theft or physical abuse. While earlier merchants, administrators, and sailors had arrived without families and mingled with the local population, in the late nineteenth century governments began sending wives and children to accompany colonial officials, often clearing local people out of desirable urban neighborhoods to make room for European families. Women from Europe and the United States appeared in public in Western garb, which was unwelcome in Muslim regions where segregation of the sexes was a strong social norm. As men left their families

Rubber Workers in the Congo

In 1896 American manager Edgar Canisius began working for the Belgians in the Congo Free State, where rubber was harvested by forced labor. Canisius was thus part of the global workforce at the turn of the century, as were the inhabitants of Congo, who labored for a distant king— Leopold II of Belgium. After describing the atrocities the Belgians inflicted on Congolese whose harvest fell the slightest bit short of the quota, he noted the punishing work process itself. Canisius's report on his time in the Congo was published early in the twentieth century.

> The Congo native, when about to gather rubber, generally goes with his fellow villagers far into the jungle. Then, having formed a rough, shelterless camp, he begins his search for the creepers [rubber vines that wind themselves around other trees]. Having found one of sufficient size, he cuts with his knife a number of incisions in the bark, and, hanging a small earthenware pot below the vine, allows the sap to slowly trickle into it. Should the creeper have been already tapped, the man must climb into the supporting tree at more or less personal risk and make an incision in the vine high above the ground where the sap has not been exhausted. . . . Not infrequently the natives slumber on their lofty perches, and, falling to the ground, become victims of the white man's greed. Few Africans will imperil their lives in rubber-gathering unless under compulsion. . . .
>
> Each tribe has only a limited extent of forest which it can call its exclusive domain, and it consequently very frequently happens, when their own "bush" is worked out, that natives from one village penetrate the territory of the other in defiance of tribal usage. Such an invasion is naturally resented by their neighbors, who, equally pressed no doubt by circumstances and the white man, are themselves experiencing difficulty in making up the quota of rubber definitely fixed for each village, and a deficient production of which may entail dire punishment and even death. In consequence, disputes arise between villages which heretofore, perhaps for quite a long period, have been at peace; and then come wars, involving more or less loss of life, destruction and cannibalism. Natives, I may add, have often come to me with bitter laments over the disappearance of their brothers after accidents when rubber-gathering, or the attacks of leopards or hostile tribesmen.

Source: Edgar Canisius, "A Campaign Amongst Cannibals," in Captain Guy Burrows, *The Curse of Central Africa* (London: R. A. Everett and Co., 1903), 74–80, quoted in Robert O. Collins, ed., *Central and South African History*, vol. 3, *African History: Text and Readings.* (New York: Markus Wiener, 1990), 111–112.

EXAMINING THE EVIDENCE

1. What were the conditions of life for those gathering rubber in the Congo?

2. What were rubber gatherers' attitudes in the face of their task?

3. What were the consequences of rubber gathering for the individual, the community, and the region at large?

---

to work in mines, on urban docks, or on plantations, imperialists recruited local women into prostitution around these new workplaces.

Missionaries brought another kind of disorder, as the Boxer Rebellion demonstrated. European missionaries rushed to newly secured areas of Africa and Asia. A woman missionary working among the Tibetans reflected a common view when she remarked that the native peoples were "going down, down into hell, and there is no one but me . . . to witness for Jesus amongst them." In addition to their often unwanted arrival into native communities, missionaries fought among themselves, drawing locals into conflicts that sometimes led to military intervention and the expansion of imperial control. Women missionaries often found their new settings liberating as they left the domestic confines of their homelands for societies where they faced fewer restrictions. Their empowerment made some of them feel entitled to change local people's lives, and most earnestly hoped to improve daily life abroad. Christian missions attracted followers, upsetting local patterns of living.

Imperialists also disordered the traditional landscape, not only with large plantations in rural areas but also with administrative buildings, theaters, and schools, designed in styles of the so-called mother country (see Seeing the Past: Imperial Architecture in Saigon). Wide

Imperial Architecture in Saigon

An Imperial Cityscape: Saigon (ND/Roger-Viollet/The Image Works.)

Not only did imperialism take the wealth of foreign regions and the labor of their inhabitants, but the imperial powers also attempted to impose their own culture and values on subjected lands. One way of doing this was building monuments to imperial rulers and transforming cities according to Western ideas of proper urban architecture. The French filled the Vietnamese city of Saigon, for example, with the same wide boulevards found in Paris and with buildings such as cafés, private dwellings, and government offices that resembled those in Paris as well.

EXAMINING THE EVIDENCE

1. What does this photograph reveal about changing livelihoods in imperial Saigon?

2. Why would local residents welcome this grand hotel in the French style? Why would they object to it?

boulevards allowed passage of fine carriages—and also military parades that demonstrated the empire's power.

Everyday Resistance and Accommodation

Those in contact with imperialists practiced everyday resistance such as slowdowns at work or petty theft. Indian merchants used traditional tactics to block tax increases: they closed up shop and left town by the thousands. African merchants protested conditions around ports that seemed to favor imperial traders. In Freetown, Sierra Leone, local merchants found that the pathway to the customs house was constructed to block their goods from entering while providing the European merchants direct access for their wares. Their protests forced European officials to negotiate and ultimately change the port's arrangements. There was also accommodation: the British employed Sikhs in the colonial army because of their warrior skills and bravery in battle. But they wanted the Sikhs to control their hair, which they kept long for religious reasons. Sikh soldiers complied to keep their good jobs by adopting a turban as part of their uniform, making it a proud symbol of their separate identity. Missionaries also had to adapt when, as the price for attending church, local people wanted lessons in the colonial culture, languages, and practical skills such as Western science and math.

Although resistance sometimes led to compromise, it often prompted violent repression. In early-twentieth-century German East Africa, local people refused to pay taxes. "We do not owe you anything. We have no debt to you. If you as a stranger want to stay in this country, you will have to ask us."[14] In this case resistance was met with force: in 1907, the Germans massacred these East Africans, seizing their food supplies and leaving survivors to die of starvation. Highly organized resistance usually met with brutal mass repression, making subtle opposition a better choice.

Medicine, Science, and Well-Being in the Colonies

Imperialism changed the life of local people in myriad ways. It crucially affected health and well-being, which declined on some fronts and improved on others. Trains efficiently transported food crops away from the colonies, and equally efficiently transmitted diseases from railroad hub to railroad hub, often leaving local people both hungry and sick. Simultaneously, colonial agents introduced modern health and hygiene programs; the contradictory agendas of imperialists affected local life in complex and profound ways.

Spread of Famine and Disease

Famine, made worse by the policies of imperial powers, helped empire builders expand their holdings. During the El Niño conditions of the late nineteenth century, when weather disturbances in the tropical Pacific dried up farming lands in Asia, Africa, and parts of Brazil, acreage that was once green and productive turned brown and hard. Rivers and shallow wells dried up, making safe water and fresh food unavailable. When such conditions had occurred before, traditional rulers in India, China, and the Ottoman Empire had sent aid and cut taxes. Instead of relenting on taxes during this disaster, the Europeans redoubled their efforts to collect them, sending in tax collectors "whip in hand." As British officials announced in India: "The revenue must at all costs be gathered in."[15] Those who could not pay lost their lands, which were then given to wealthy local peoples or Europeans; colonial agents then shipped these newly landless people to plantations and mines, saving them from starvation by forcing them to work in semislavery. The plantation owners' profits in the Caribbean and elsewhere soared with the arrival of this virtually cost-free labor.

Similarly, government policies going back centuries had ensured that reservoirs and irrigation systems collected scarce water to save for droughts. The British in India, however, had no interest in such projects. Maintaining irrigation systems cost money, and the British were in India to make money. In the Qing Empire as well, with foreign powers in control of revenue collection as a result of the Opium War, taxes were no longer used for upkeep of the reservoirs, irrigation systems, or even waterways that might have transported aid to stricken regions. Imperialist neglect further devastated both agriculture and the environment.

Industrialization worsened the situation. As people in drought-stricken areas lost their ability to buy goods, including food, imperialists made fortunes, using trains to carry grain out of poor regions and store it until shortages led to rising prices and bigger profits. As trains moved back and forth among regions, they helped spread diseases to weakened people. Mortality rates soared as smallpox, influenza, typhus, cholera, and other lethal diseases worked their way through China, India, and other areas. Influential Europeans believed that no relief should be provided because any relaxation of laissez-faire principles would simply spoil recipients of aid. Lord Lytton, viceroy of India during the 1870s, spent handsomely for grand ceremonials celebrating the ascension of Britain's Queen Victoria to the imperial throne of India, yet he refused to send food to the starving, calling the cost of such aid harmful to the economy as a whole. According to Lytton, people who wanted to restore the water storage infrastructure were "irrigation quacks," and those proposing to give food to the starving were "humanitarian hysterics." When some citizens in the imperial countries became so ashamed at the photos of skeletal Indians and Chinese that they set up relief funds, colonial governors—most of them strict believers in laissez faire—diverted these funds to colonial wars in Afghanistan, South Africa, and elsewhere to expand imperialism.

Science and Hygiene

At the same time, the imperial powers aimed to transform local life with new public health programs, in large part to protect their own soldiers and officials. Governments set up scientific stations to study and adapt local plant life to serve imperial interests. Simultaneously, foreign doctors ordered that entire villages be burned to the ground when contagious diseases were found in a single household. Europeans also worked to increase hospital births in the colonies as a way to build the colonial workforce. (By contrast, the vast majority of European women still gave birth at home.) Hospitalization of expectant mothers undermined local customs and sociability and ruined the livelihoods of midwives and other healers. Sometimes changes that were not directly related to public health were explained in hygienic terms: the wide boulevards that destroyed neighborhoods and changed the face of cities opened infested areas to sunlight and cleaner conditions, for example. Local people created their own stories to accompany medical explanations. In African lore, the vampire, with its bloodsucking habit, reflected the natives' concern about colonial doctors who took blood. In other countries, such as China, those interested in change translated books on Western hygienic methods.

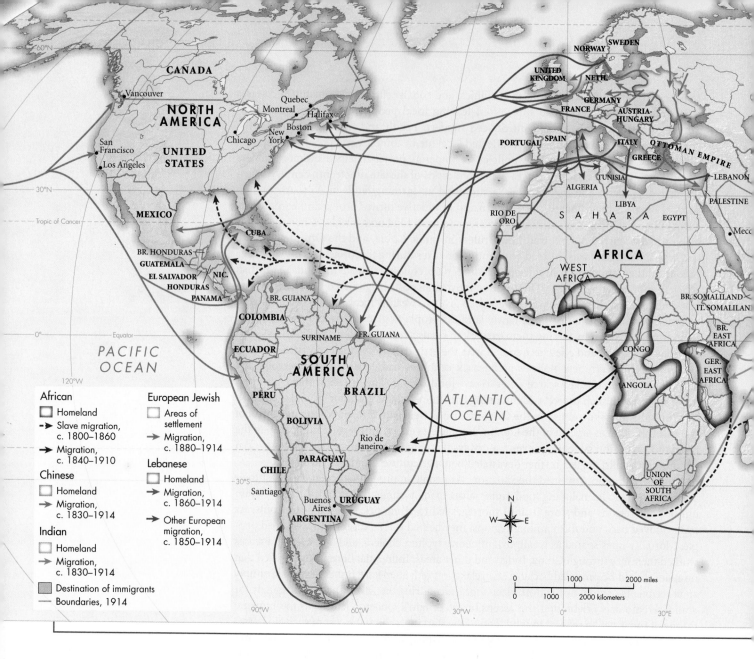

Migrants and Diasporas

The global expansion of industry and empire brought with it mass migration in the second half of the nineteenth century (see Map 26.3). In some cases, people moved because imperialists offered jobs outside their homelands. Others migrated simply because conditions at home were so bad: millions left the rural areas of Europe to escape persecution, crop failures, and eventually the hardship caused by global competition in agriculture. In Asia, Africa, and Latin America, people migrated regionally to cacao, rubber, coffee, and other plantations in response to the demands of imperialists that they pay new taxes and the lure of steady jobs.

Regional Migration   Both industrialization and imperialism affected the movement of people in search of livelihoods. Migrants left rural areas for industrialized cities, swelling their population to the bursting point. Migrants sometimes returned to the countryside at harvest time. Temporary migrants to the cities worked as masons, rickshaw drivers, or factory hands to supplement declining income from agriculture; in the winter, those remaining on the land turned to cottage industries producing a variety of goods, including bricks, pottery, lace, and locks. In Africa, dense networks of trade took Africans, Arabs, and Indians hundreds

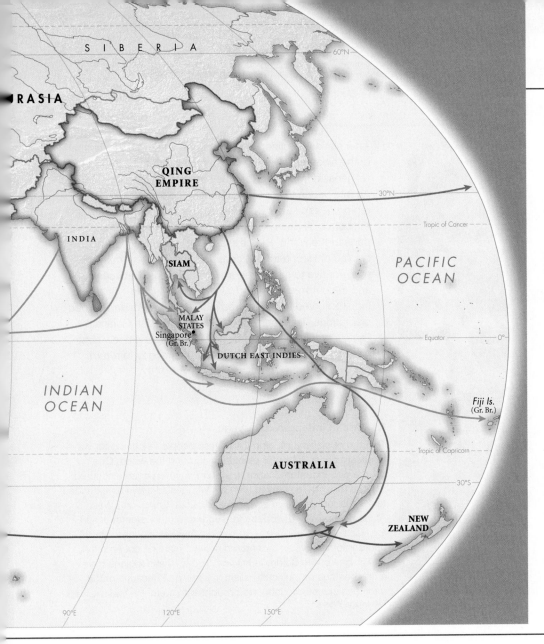

MAP 26.3

Global Migration, c. 1800–1910

People were on the move during these decades for many different reasons. Most were concerned with finding better livelihoods, or finding any livelihood. The formal ending of the slave trade and then slavery itself led underemployed people from Asia and Africa to migrate as indentured servants, which many saw as a new type of slavery. Europeans migrated from rural areas because the global trade in grain drove down prices for produce; others, however, hoped to escape religious and personal persecution on the continent while simultaneously finding new means of support.

and even thousands of miles in caravans packed with goods. These temporary migrations were often interrupted to pay tribute to traditional rulers—not necessarily to imperialists. Yet in the colonies regional migration was also coercive and tested family ties.

Europeans, Asians, and Africans alike followed a pattern of global migration, moving well beyond their national borders to countries where land was being taken from native peoples to give to white settlers, or where imperialism created new job opportunities (see Lives and Livelihoods: Indentured Laborers). In parts of Europe, China, and India, for example, the land simply could not produce enough to support rapidly expanding populations, especially when drought, agricultural diseases, and famine struck. Millions of rural Jews, especially from eastern Europe, left their villages for economic reasons to populate many regions of the world, but Russian Jews also fled in the face of vicious anti-Semitic **pogroms**. In the course of such state-approved riots, Russian mobs brutally attacked Jewish communities, destroying homes and businesses and even murdering some Jews. "People who saw such things never smiled anymore, no matter how long they lived," recalled one Russian Jewish woman who migrated to the United States in the early 1890s.

News of commercial, agricultural, and industrial opportunity, often from recruiting agents working for governments or businesses, determined destinations. Railroads and steamships

Global Migration

pogrom A systematic attack on Jews, as carried out, for example, in the late-nineteenth-century Russian Empire.

Indentured Laborers

After slavery declined in many countries during the first half of the nineteenth century, owners of plantations, mines, and refineries complained that they needed more workers. Agents began to scour the countryside of colonized regions—especially where there was famine and other economic distress—to find workers to transport to other parts of the world. By the system of indenture, workers were cajoled or forced to sign contracts that obliged them to work for five to seven years in distant lands. Between 1830 and the outbreak of World War I in 1914, some 1.5 million Indians served as indentured laborers on European-owned plantations. Transported to Mauritania, British Guiana, Fiji, Trinidad, Guadeloupe, and Natal, to name a few destinations, their goal was to earn enough money to return home with some kind of savings.

An African Indentured Servant

The end of slavery left global business people searching for ways to secure cheap labor for plantations around the world. One source was indentured labor, a system in which agents scoured regions for underemployed workers who would serve an extended term of labor, usually in a far-off land. India, China, and West Africa thus provided workers for sugar and other plantations in the Pacific and Caribbean—to name a few destinations. This photograph shows an indentured servant planting coconut trees on Fiji, one of the Solomon Islands. Today, these regions have a rich heritage of multiculturalism in large part because of the traditions indentured laborers brought with them. (Art Media/Heritage/The Image Works.)

made journeys across and out of Asia and Europe more affordable and faster, even though most workers traveled in steerage. Once established in their new countries, migrants frequently sent money back home, and thus remained part of the family economy. They might use the funds they earned to educate a younger brother or set up a daughter or son in a small business, thus contributing to advancement. Nationalists in eastern and central Europe bemoaned the loss of ethnic vigor as the young and active departed, but peasants everywhere welcomed the arrival of "magic" income from their overseas kin. The connection between migrants and their homelands was not, therefore, completely severed by their departure. In fact, migration helped create new connections among distant parts of the world.

Migration to another part of the world did, however, often mean the end to the old way of life for the migrants themselves. Working men and women immediately had to learn new languages and civic practices and to compete for jobs in growing cities where they formed the cheapest pool of labor, often working in factories or sweatshops. Most of the first Chinese and Indian migrants were men, but when women migrants arrived with their husbands, they stayed at home and tended to associate with others like themselves, preserving traditional ways in dress and housekeeping. Their children and husbands,

"A new form of slavery," a British aristocrat and opponent called the system of indentured servitude that European powers developed after ending the slave trade. Indentured laborers endured horrendous conditions cutting sugarcane, growing other cash crops, or working in mines. "I haven't had food for three days, my body is weak, my throat is parched," reported one worker in Fiji. Another worker in the Fiji cane fields said, "We were whipped for small mistakes. If you woke up late, i.e. later than three A.M., you got whipped. No matter whether there was rain or thunder you had to work . . . otherwise we were abused and beaten up." Even those whose working conditions were somewhat better found themselves without any basic cultural institutions: "There are no temples, no festivals, no idols, . . . no schools for our children, who receive no education of any kind," an Indian indentured worker in Guadeloupe wrote in 1884. "It seems to us that animals are better treated than us in this colony."

Indentured workers kept in touch with their home culture through missionaries from India itself, adopting the ancient texts of the *Ramayana*—a tale of exile and deliverance—as their spiritual sustenance. Some African indentured laborers traveled back and forth between the Caribbean and the West African coast, even serving as recruiters after one term on the plantations.

Many indentured laborers never returned to their homeland, however, constituting extensive diasporas far from Africa and South Asia. Nonetheless, they maintained many traditions: performing scenes from the *Ramayana*, for example, remains a joyous public celebration in Trinidad today. Indentured workers also transported African religions and rituals, which are still influential in binding descendants of these workers to the African continent.

Source: Quoted in Marina Carter and Khal Torabully, *Coolitude: An Anthology of the Indian Labour Diaspora* (London: Anthem Press, 2002), 90–91, 110.

QUESTIONS TO CONSIDER

1. How does the system of indentured servitude compare to slavery?

2. How did Africans and others help in the system of indentured labor, and why might they have cooperated?

3. What is the cultural legacy of indentured servitude?

For Further Information:

Carter, Marina, and Khal Torabully. *Coolitude: An Anthology of the Indian Labour Diaspora*. 2002.

Kale, Madhavi. *Fragments of Empire: Capital, Slavery, and Indian Indentured Labor Migration in the British Caribbean*. 1998.

forced to remake their lives in the schools and factories of their adopted land, were more likely to embrace the new and search out opportunity.

As migrants from extended families or the same region settled near one another, they formed ethnic **diasporas**, clusters of people who shared an ethnic identity. Continuing enslavement of Africans, Russians, and others created the harshest diasporas, but imperialism also encouraged diasporas born of opportunity. For example, the British persuaded skilled Chinese traders to settle in Singapore, and thousands of them migrated—usually without establishing permanent attachments—to build this commercial city virtually from scratch (see again Map 26.3). Other Chinese settled around the world, depending for their success on global networks to supply goods and thereby maintaining close ties to their ancestral roots. The same was true of the Lebanese diaspora to France, the United States, Argentina, and Brazil. Many of these migrants were Christians who wanted to make money in trade without having to deal with Ottoman restrictions on non-Muslims. Thus they moved to areas of opportunity, expecting to prosper and eventually to return home. In fact, historians estimate that in the early twentieth century as many as 40 percent of these Lebanese migrants found their way back—mostly to the area around Beirut—for at least a period, if not permanently.

Global Diasporas

diaspora The dispersal of a population, often resulting in large settlements in different parts of the world.

Migrants even proved influential in politics back home. The "Song of Revolution" of the turn of the century called on members of the Chinese diaspora to help overthrow the Manchu dynasty and reform the Qing Empire: "What use is the cumulation of silver cash? / Why not use it to eject the Manchus? / Ten thousand each from you isn't much / To buy cannons and guns and ship them inland."[16]

Culture in an Imperial Age

FOCUS

How did artists and writers respond to the age of empire?

The imperial age led to new ways of thought and changing norms around the world. Exposure to new environments inspired scientists and led to fresh discoveries. Ordinary people adjusted their ideas and habits to suit new city neighborhoods. Books and art from around the world inspired artists and writers as they produced works that reflected on life in the imperial age. Global contacts sparked debates over gender roles and interest in alternative ways of life. Accelerating cultural change produced what is called "modernism" in the arts—a style based on sometimes disturbing transformations in artistic expression. In fact, we may interpret spreading modernity in the realm of behavior and culture as part of globalization.

The Culture of Everyday Life

Migration from countryside to city in an age of empire meant that people transplanted rural habits and cultural life to urban settings. Bengali women who migrated to Calcutta to work as potters, basketmakers, dyers, and occasionally as factory workers, for example, celebrated their holidays in traditional ways, singing and dancing to stories of the gods and goddesses. They amused city folk with their country poetry at weddings and births, poetry that often featured tales of seduction, jealousy, and betrayal. Drug-smoking husbands and lovers who stole women's possessions were a favorite topic:

> My tears dry up in my eyes,
> I go around making merry. I'm writing in pain,
> Yet I act coy
> Swinging my hips.[17]

Such popular amusement outraged Calcutta's elites, who now preferred British middle-class norms for "civilized" female behavior. In their view, women who performed in public, such as actresses or singers, were prostitutes. Certain middle-class attitudes became standard among many Bengalis and elites in other parts of the world. As a result, the number of women performers in Calcutta declined drastically, from over seventeen thousand in the 1870s to three thousand in 1890.

In other places, local leaders were able to maintain cultural values and patterns of life. In West Africa, the French allowed Islam to flourish and used religious leaders to maintain the peace even as the region lost its economic and political independence. In turn, religious leaders preached the doctrine of accommodation to French rule. "Support the French government totally," the Sufi leader Malik Sy urged in the early twentieth century. "God has given special victory, grace, and favor to the French. He has chosen them to protect our persons and property."[18] In West Africa, France financed pilgrimages to Mecca for Muslim leaders and local officials and supported the building of mosques and the observance of Islamic law.

Urbanization and globalization remained powerful forces, breaking down traditional customs. The development of the mass media—particularly the newspaper—made millions of readers aware of other ways of doing things. Photography displayed the triumphs of technology for viewers around the world, making railroads appear even more modern by juxtaposing their images with photos of "savages," whether from the U.S. West or Oceania.

Indian Woman Dancing with Musicians

Indian women traditionally danced on many occasions and in both public and private celebrations. One popular dance was the pot dance, which revolved around the imagery of a full container whose contents must be protected: any spillage would symbolize the emptying of one's own or one's family's being. Many in the growing Indian middle class came to see these dancers, whose entire bodies were in motion, as overly sexual and bordering on barbaric. (The British Library/HIP/The Image Works.)

To build circulation, Western journalists puffed up the triumphs of "explorers" and roused readers' emotions with lurid stories of the global trade in women and girls. In celebrations of such holidays as "Empire Day" in Britain and in imperial ceremonies in South Asia and Africa, people around the world participated in an invented global culture that seemed to endorse empire. Monuments and portraits of conquerors and rulers were aimed at reshaping local loyalties into imperial ones.

Clothing traveled the world too. When French painter Paul Gauguin arrived in Tahiti late in the nineteenth century, he noted that local women had already adopted Western-style dresses with long sleeves and high necks. Chinese women had their portraits painted wearing perky Western straw hats adorned with feathers. Traditional patterns of thought and behavior loosened their hold on everyday life, especially in the world's teeming cities.

Art and Empire

The arts felt influences from empire. Japanese, Indian, Chinese, and Latin American artists adapted Western techniques that they learned of through training in Western art schools and the increasing availability of photographs. Simultaneously, writers across the globe read one another's works. Global celebrities such as Rabindranath Tagore emerged. Tagore, who won the Nobel Prize for literature in 1913, was educated in Bengal and in London, but backed by the enormous wealth of his grandfather, a financier, he was able to travel the world at leisure while composing poems, songs, short stories, and other works of prose. In his works, Tagore commented on the difficult lives of Bengali peasants while emphasizing Indian nationalism and education in Western knowledge. This ability to consider and often integrate different cultural traditions is called **cosmopolitanism**.

Similarly aware of world developments and foreign educated, Soseki Natsumi, called the greatest writer of the Meiji period, wove insights on local Japanese life as it modernized into his novels and journalism. Soseki's *Botchan* (*Little Master*, 1906) focused on a cranky youth—a "misfit" in the Meiji world—who had been educated in math and science and sent to the provinces to teach. He insults his colleagues, no one more than an art teacher who wears a French-style smock and floppy bow tie around his neck, affecting the attitude

cosmopolitanism The merging or acceptance of a variety of national and ethnic values and traditions.

The Durbar for Edward VII in Delhi, India

Lavish celebrations and rituals were invented to cement imperial relationships between rulers and ruled. Held at the very end of 1902 and into 1903, this durbar—a formal state reception given by Indian princes for a British sovereign—marked the ascension of Edward VII to the imperial throne and thus to rule over India. Maharajahs and other local dignitaries attended, riding elephants and wearing luxurious clothing and jewels, appearing to accept this foreign ruler. Such ceremonies masked the violence with which the British and other imperial powers attempted to rule and the ever-present resistance to these foreign invaders. (Getty Images.)

of a Western artist. Soseki railed against consumers of Western-style journalism, especially readers who gobbled up news of fires, murders, and accidents with the idea that they were now in touch with a Western kind of reality. In Soseki's view, this foreign habit actually cut them off from a deeper reality. At the same time, he transformed Japanese literature by probing the psychology of his characters as writers in the West did. The leading writers of Asia were thus engaged with styles and worldviews brought from afar by imperialism and globalization.

Western literature traveled the world, arousing both acclaim and controversy. The Norwegian playwright Henrik Ibsen's *A Doll's House* (1879), a drama about a woman who leaves a loveless marriage, riveted global audiences. It influenced many to think that their countries' modernization required changes in the situation of women. Inspired by the play, Japanese women started a feminist movement; some Chinese women campaigned to eliminate foot-binding. Similarly, women in Ottoman countries abandoned their veils in the belief that it would help free their countries if they looked more Western. Under the influence of imperialism and globalization, literature influenced rebellion against the West even as it promoted the adoption of Western values and cultural patterns.

Imperial Contests at the Dawn of the Twentieth Century

FOCUS

What were the main issues in the contests over empire, and what were the results of these contests?

Although cultural influences were shaping city life and traveling around the world, imperialism was increasingly chaotic and deadly at the start of the twentieth century. Large-scale rebellions by ordinary people fighting against imperial domination, such as the Boxer Rebellion, became more common. Competition among the imperial powers themselves was also heating up as their ambitions swelled. The United States and Japan pursued global empire more vigorously in these years, fighting successful wars against older empires. International politics became menacing and imperial nerves were on edge, especially as military spending grew amid competition for power.

Clashes for Imperial Control

After centuries of global expansion, imperial adventure soured for empires both old and new. Some of this trouble arose from newcomers to imperial competition, such as Japan and the United States, both of which took territory and expanded their markets at the turn of the century, defeating older rivals. Empires faced constant challenges to their survival: as empires were competing among themselves for influence, the colonized and otherwise oppressed people were fighting back with increasing vigor.

The South African War

The British experienced an unexpected setback to their imperial ambitions in 1896, when Cecil Rhodes, by then prime minister of the Cape Colony at Africa's southern tip, directed a raid on Johannesburg to stir up trouble between the Boers, descendants of early Dutch settlers, and the more recent immigrants from Britain who had come to southern Africa in search of gold. Rhodes hoped the raid would justify a British takeover of the Transvaal and the Orange Free State, which the Boers independently controlled. The Boers unexpectedly won, leading the British to wage the South African (or Boer) War directly against the Transvaal and the Orange Free State. As journalists reported on appalling bloodshed, rampant disease, and the unfit condition of the average British soldier, citizens back home were stunned. The British herded the Boers into a shocking and unfamiliar institution—the concentration camp, which became the graveyard of tens of thousands of women and children. Britain finally defeated the Boers in 1902 and annexed the area, but the cost of war in money, loss of life, and public morale was enormous.

Native Africans, who mostly had supported the British with the thought that they were more civilized and law-abiding than the Boers, were quickly disillusioned. Soon after the annexation, the government of South Africa passed a series of laws appropriating African-owned lands for whites, depriving Africans of free movement, and imposing an entire range of restrictions on their lives. It was the foundation for the policy of racial segregation and discrimination that would be called apartheid. "We expected deliverance," one local chieftain commented bitterly on postwar British policy, "whereas we have gone deeper into bond[age]."[19]

The Spanish-American War

At about the time the British were fighting the Boer War, Spain lost Cuba, Puerto Rico, and the Philippines to the United States, which defeated it in the Spanish-American War of 1898. As Spanish imperial power declined, the Spanish government tried to support itself by raising taxes to exorbitant levels on its remaining colonies. Meanwhile, the United States, a newcomer to imperialism overseas, had been killing native Americans and driving them from their lands since the seventeenth century. In addition it had asserted its diplomatic influence in the Western Hemisphere in the Monroe Doctrine (1823), purchased Alaska in 1867, and annexed Hawaii in 1898 at the urgings of missionaries and businessmen, who had set up plantations on the islands (see Reading the Past: The United States Overthrows the Hawaiian Queen).

Before the Spanish-American War, both Cuba and the Philippines had vigorous independence movements backed by all classes of people. Expansionist-minded Theodore Roosevelt, then assistant secretary of the navy, and the inflammatory daily press goaded the U.S. government to help the independence movements with armed force. However, after its swift victory over Spain the United States annexed Puerto Rico and Guam and bought the Philippines from its former ruler. In theory, Cuba remained independent, but U.S. businesses virtually controlled its sugar-exporting economy—a clear example of business imperialism. The lesson for the imperial powers was the unpredictability of empire. After that, the triumphant United States, encouraged by British poet Rudyard Kipling to "take up the white man's burden" by bringing the benefits of Western civilization to the Philippines, waged a bloody war against the Filipinos, who wanted independence, not simply a different imperial ruler. Reports of American brutality in the Philippines, where some twenty

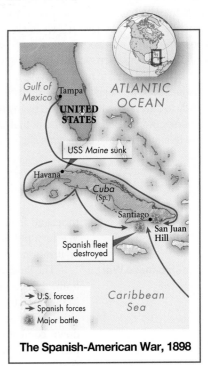

The Spanish-American War, 1898

The United States Overthrows the Hawaiian Queen

U.S. businessmen set themselves up in the Hawaiian Islands, establishing lucrative sugar plantations and other agricultural enterprises. With government support, they then worked to undermine the ruling monarchy, calling themselves the Committee of Safety. After imprisoning the Hawaiian queen under house arrest in 1893, they forced her to abdicate in a document that gave no indication of the trickery and violence behind their deeds. In this passage from her memoir of 1898, Queen Liliuokalani describes the threats that led to her abdication. The men she cites were members of the Committee.

For the first few days nothing occurred to disturb the quiet of my apartments save the tread of the sentry. On the fourth day I received a visit from Mr. Paul Neumann, who asked me if, in the event that it should be decided that all the principal parties to the revolt must pay for it with their lives, I was prepared to die? I replied to this in the affirmative, telling him I had no anxiety for myself, and felt no dread of death. He then told me that six others besides myself had been selected to be shot for treason, but that he would call again, and let me know further about our fate. . . .

About the 22d of January a paper was handed to me by Mr. Wilson, which, on examination, proved to be a purported act of abdication for me to sign. . . . For myself, I would have chosen death rather than to have signed it; but it was represented to me that by my signing this paper all the persons who had been arrested, all my people now in trouble by reason of their love and loyalty towards me, would be immediately released. Think of my position— sick, a lone woman in prison, scarcely knowing who was my friend, or who listened to my words only to betray me, without legal advice or friendly counsel, and the stream of blood ready to flow unless it was stayed by my pen.

My persecutors have stated, and at that time compelled me to state, that this paper was signed and acknowledged by me after consultation with my friends whose names appear at the foot of it as witnesses. Not the least opportunity was given to me to confer with anyone; but for the purpose of making it appear to the outside world that I was under the guidance of others, friends who had known me well in better days were brought into the place of my imprisonment, and stood around to see a signature affixed by me. . . . Then the following individuals witnessed my subscription of the signature which was demanded of me: William G. Irwin, H. A. Widemann, Samuel Parker, S. Kalua Kookano, Charles B. Wilson, and Paul Neumann. . . .

So far from the presence of these persons being evidence of a voluntary act on my part, was it not an assurance to me that they, too, knew that, unless I did the will of my jailers, what Mr. Neumann had threatened would be performed, and six prominent citizens immediately put to death. I so regarded it then, and I still believe that murder was the alternative. Be this as it may, it is certainly happier for me to reflect to-day that there is not a drop of the blood of my subjects, friends or foes, upon my soul.

Source: Liliuokalani, *Hawaii's Story by Hawaii's Queen* (Boston: Lothrop, Lee, and Shepard,1898), http://digital.library.upenn.edu/women/liliuokalani/hawaii/hawaii.html.

EXAMINING THE EVIDENCE

1. Why do you think that Queen Liliuokalani wrote this memoir?

2. What attitudes do you sense behind the actions of those who wanted to take over her lands and resources?

3. How does the queen portray herself in the face of these adversaries?

---

thousand freedom fighters and several hundred thousand civilians died, disillusioned the Western public, who liked to imagine native peoples joyously welcoming the bearers of civilization.

The Russo-Japanese War   The Japanese vigorously pursued empire, defeating China and then trouncing Russia— both of them Japan's rivals for influence in the Far East. Angered by Russian expansion in Manchuria, the Japanese attacked tsarist forces at Port Arthur in 1904 (see Map 26.4). Casualties were once again fearsome, as powerful new weaponry such as machine guns mowed down combatants on both sides. To the astonishment of the world, the Japanese completely destroyed the Russian fleet in the 1905 Battle of Tsushima Strait. The victory was the first by a non-European nation over a European great power in the modern age. As one

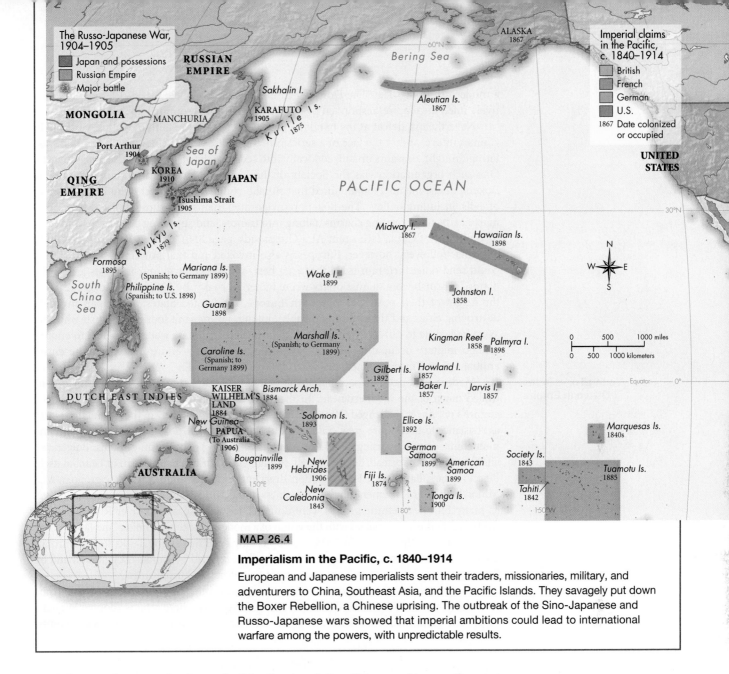

The Russo-Japanese War, 1904–1905

- Japan and possessions
- Russian Empire
- Major battle

Imperial claims in the Pacific, c. 1840–1914

- British
- French
- German
- U.S.

1867 Date colonized or occupied

MAP 26.4

Imperialism in the Pacific, c. 1840–1914

European and Japanese imperialists sent their traders, missionaries, military, and adventurers to China, Southeast Asia, and the Pacific Islands. They savagely put down the Boxer Rebellion, a Chinese uprising. The outbreak of the Sino-Japanese and Russo-Japanese wars showed that imperial ambitions could lead to international warfare among the powers, with unpredictable results.

English general ominously observed of the Russian defeat, "I have today seen the most stupendous spectacle it is possible for the mortal brain to conceive—Asia advancing, Europe falling back." Japan went on to annex Korea in 1910 and to eye other areas for colonization. Russia itself erupted in the Revolution of 1905, forcing the tsar to institute a weak form of parliament, the Duma. The double blow of military defeat by Japan and social revolution exposed Russia's internal weaknesses, especially the widespread discontent of ordinary people.

Growing Resistance to Foreign Domination

The Japanese military victory over two important dynasties—the Qing in China and the Romanov in Russia—reverberated around the world. People under foreign domination responded to Japan's victory with enthusiasm and hope, believing that if a small non-Western nation such as Japan could defeat a Western power, they too could defeat outside forces.

In China, students, elites, and ordinary people felt humiliated by the 1895 defeat by Japan and the forced economic concessions to Western powers that followed. Students demanded reform, presenting a memorandum asking for modern institutions such as an efficient tax system and national railroad, postal, and banking networks. The memo insisted that the government sponsor technology and commerce, the latter through creating

Boxers in China

a modern shipping fleet. The Dowager Empress Cixi (kee-shee) (1835–1908), who effectively ruled the empire, responded by having the reformers rounded up and executed.

Nevertheless, defeat at the hands of Japan had rocked the faith of ordinary people in China's future, and in the face of a series of natural disasters, including floods and devastating drought, peasants organized locally into secret societies to restore Chinese integrity. One such organization was the Society of the Righteous and Harmonious Fists, or the Boxers, whose members maintained that ritual boxing would protect them from a variety of evils, including bullets. The Boxers reinvigorated themselves through the discipline of martial arts, often reciting charms, falling into trances, and appealing to the gods and spirits on behalf of China (see again At a Crossroads, page 856). Facing these young Boxers and their followers, however, Europeans also invoked spiritual powers: "We know God could send relief thru rain if He thot [*sic*] best, and we know all our interests are in His hands," a British woman missionary wrote in her journal.[20] By 1900 as the Boxers reached the height of their power, troops from Europe, the United States, and Japan invaded, destroying cities and the countryside alike, killing, raping, and looting to crush what the West had come to call "the yellow peril." The defeated Chinese were compelled to endure foreign military occupation and to pay a huge indemnity—more than twice the entire annual national income. The Qing dynasty faced its downfall.

Young Turks in the Ottoman Empire

Modern nationalism was sapping the Ottoman Empire, which for centuries had controlled much of the Mediterranean. In the nineteenth century, rebellions in several of the empire's provinces challenged Ottoman rule, and more erupted early in the twentieth century as resistance to the empire grew. Sultan Abdul Hamid II (r. 1876–1909) tried to revitalize the multiethnic empire by using Islam to counteract the rising nationalism of Serbs, Bulgarians, and Macedonians. Instead, he unwittingly strengthened Turkish nationalism in Istanbul itself. Rejecting the sultan's pan-Islamic solution, dissident Turks, the dominant ethnic group in Asia Minor, built their movement on the uniqueness of the Turkish culture, history, and language, as many European ethnic groups were doing. The Japanese victory over Russia in 1905 electrified Turkish nationalists with the vision of a modern Turkey becoming "the Japan of the Middle East," as they put it. In 1908, a group calling itself the Young Turks took control of the government in Istanbul, which had been fatally weakened by nationalist agitation and by the empire's economic dependence on Western financiers and businessmen.

The Young Turks' triumph motivated other groups in the Middle East and the Balkans to demand an end to Ottoman domination in their regions. These groups adopted Western values and platforms, and some, such as the Egyptians, had strong contingents of feminist

Young Turks

The Young Turks formed a group committed to the modernization of the Ottoman Empire—one of the longest imperial reigns in history. By the early twentieth century, the Young Turks had grown impatient with declining Ottoman power and, trained in western European military strategies and tactics, sought a complete overhaul of Ottoman institutions, economy, and culture. Complete success would not come, however, until after World War I, when officers in the defeated Ottoman army beat back Allied and Greek attempts to take over Turkey. (Mary Evans/Grenville Collins/The Image Works.)

nationalists who mobilized women to become modern and work for independence. But the Young Turks, now in control of the Ottoman government and often aided by European powers with financial and political interests in the region, brutally tried to repress movements in Egypt, Syria, and the Balkans modeled after their own nationalist success.

Resistance to empire grew everywhere in the wake of the Japanese victory. In India, the fervently anti-British Hindu leader, B. G. Tilak, preached outright noncooperation. "We shall not give them assistance to collect revenue and keep peace. We shall not assist them in fighting beyond the frontiers or outside India with Indian blood and money." Tilak promoted Hindu customs, asserted the distinctiveness of Hindu values, and inspired violent rebellion in his followers. This brand of nationalism broke with that of the Indian National Congress, which was based on assimilating to British culture and promoting gradual change. Trying to repress Tilak, the British sponsored the Muslim League, a rival nationalist group, to divide Muslim nationalists from Hindus in the Congress.

Violence escalated, and inhabitants of the colonies—rulers and ruled alike—were often on edge. Imperial powers responded to growing resistance with harsh crackdowns. In German East Africa, colonial forces crushed native resistance in 1905 with a scorched-earth policy of destroying homes, livestock, and food, eventually killing more than one hundred thousand Africans there. Having set up police surveillance in colonies around the world, the French closed the University of Hanoi, executed Indochinese intellectuals, and deported thousands of suspected nationalists in an extreme attempt to maintain their grip on Indochina. A French general stationed there summed up the fears of many colonial rulers in the new century. "The gravest fact of our actual political situation in Indochina is not the recent trouble in Tonkin [or] the plots undertaken against us but in the muted but growing hatred that our subjects show toward us." Imperialists were right to worry.

Further Blows Against Empire

COUNTERPOINT
The West Copies from the World

In the late nineteenth century, Western political thought, technology, and science were increasingly triumphant around the world. At the same time, however, interest in non-Western religion, art, and literature was growing in the West. Thus, alongside the political and military rule of the imperialist powers, cultural exchange flourished.

FOCUS

How did non-Western and colonized lands shape Western culture and society?

Changes in the Arts

Art from around the world resonated in the imaginations of Western artists. The most striking changes came in the work of impressionist painters such as Claude Monet and Vincent Van Gogh. As Japanese woodcuts came on the European market, Monet painted water lilies, Japanese bridges, and trailing wisteria vines, all of them gracefully depicted and seeming to shimmer in the light. The concept of the fleetingness of situations came from a centuries-old Japanese concept—*mono no aware*, serenity before and sensitivity to the fleetingness of life. The color, line, and delicacy of Japanese art, which many impressionists collected, is also evident in the work of the American expatriate Mary Cassatt. Cassatt was known for her paintings of women and children, which were strongly influenced by similar Japanese prints that she owned. Van Gogh filled the backgrounds of portraits with copies of intensely colored Japanese prints, even imitating classic Japanese woodcuts.

With increased global contact, poetry, music, dance, and literature changed in Europe and the United States, never to return to their preimperialism forms. The translation of haiku poetry influenced Western poets to give up formal meter, simplify their verse, and surrender lofty subjects in favor of the everyday topics of Japanese rhyme. William Butler Yeats, in his attempts to create an authentic Irish literature, copied themes and images from Japanese Noh and

Vincent Van Gogh, *Flowering Plum Tree* (1887)

Western culture soaked up influences from afar, whether in the fine arts or in practices of everyday life. By the late nineteenth century, ordinary people drank chocolate, tea, and coffee and filled their gardens with non-native plants that had become naturalized to the West. Western artists' indebtedness to non-Western styles is epitomized in this painting by Dutch painter Vincent Van Gogh, who modeled this work on a print by Hiroshige (see page 803). The brief flowering of trees so dear to the Japanese represented the fleetingness of life, and impressionists built their entire style on capturing the rapid changes in light. (akg-images.)

kabuki plays and, rejecting the ornate classical patterns of English poetry, stripped his verses of all embellishment. Yeats was but one of many who followed this path. Composers such as Claude Debussy largely abandoned centuries of Western musical patterns to create modern music based on sounds from around the world that Europeans encountered during their travels or at world fairs. In the same way, choreographers studied steps and movements practiced around the world to develop modern dance, a new way of performing that rejected the formality of classical Western ballet.

Expansion of Ideas

Outside the arts, Viennese physician Sigmund Freud, trained as a neurologist, led the West in the study of the human mind. Freud practiced telepathy (communication through means other than the senses), hypnosis, and dream therapies—all developed from ideas and therapies used in Africa and Asia. Dreams, he explained in *The Interpretation of Dreams* (1900), reveal an unseen, repressed part of the personality—the "unconscious," where all sorts of desires are more or less hidden. His new science for the treatment of mental disturbances, called **psychoanalysis**, centered on the "talking cure," that is, discussing one's dreams to uncover the reasons for mental problems. Freud read anthropological literature about the practices of witch doctors and shamans, coming up with ideas for his "talking cure" and for understanding fetishes such as fixations on shoes, gloves, or other ordinary objects.

Other Western intellectuals studied Hinduism, Buddhism, African religions, and many other bodies of thought and culture to develop new ideas. For example, at the beginning of the twentieth century, discussions of sexuality in the West expanded beyond biblically defined boundaries. South Asian ideas about reincarnation inspired the thought that the physical indications of a person's sex were merely temporary because an eternal self without sex was reborn across time in differently sexed bodies. So-called homosexuality and transgendering were explained by this process. People began discussing sexuality as variable, using ideas that came from beyond the West and that continue to be influential to this day.

Lifestyles Transformed

In Europe and the United States, people began to live in efficiently designed single-family homes styled after the Indian bungalow; they had porches and verandas, and they often decorated their homes with palms, bamboo furniture, and textiles of Asian or African designs. European cookbooks carried recipes for curry and cakes made from an array of global products, such as sugar, chocolate, vanilla, and coconut. Women joined men in wearing slimmer, more informal clothing, much of it modeled on non-Western styles. Late in the nineteenth century, women adopted looser "reform clothing"—kimono-like garments or those modeled after Middle Eastern caftans—and they began following Asian and African women in not wearing corsets.

To get and stay in shape, Westerners, who had generally not thought in such terms, began to exercise more. Men kept fit by practicing martial arts, all of which came from outside Europe

psychoanalysis A psychiatric therapy developed by Sigmund Freud; some elements, such as dream interpretation, were influenced by Freud's knowledge of African and Asian practices.

and the United States. Even as national and international tensions were heating up and as the West thought itself superior in all things, Western military schools were using Sun Tzu's *The Art of War*, a Chinese classic from the sixth century B.C.E., in their courses on strategy. Despite the power of Western imperialism, ideas never followed a one-way street from West to East. Rather, imperialism was, among much else, a crossroads for ideas to travel in many directions.

Conclusion

The nineteenth century is called an age of imperialism because of the growing contest among Western nation-states to dominate the world's peoples politically and economically. New technology springing from ongoing industrialization helped people and ideas move more rapidly around the world, enabling the exercise of political and military power as well as cultural and economic exchange. Western technology gave its agents a real advantage in developing wealth globally and controlling the flow of resources. New forms of oppression such as indentured servitude developed; plantation agriculture increasingly replaced self-sufficient farming; and environmental catastrophes weakened societies and helped imperialism spread. Imperialism was complex. Some colonized peoples prospered by participating in the system and simultaneously developed goals such as national independence, based on the Western values of rights and freedom that were denied them.

Newly powerful countries vied with established ones for a share of world influence, fueling the "new" imperialism's explosive potential. Although global expansion led to increased wealth for some individuals and states, events such as China's Boxer Rebellion demonstrated that it brought violence and insecurity to most ordinary people and to governments. Imperial competition made the world more dangerous, as did the drive even within Europe to gain territory from the weakening Ottoman Empire. Thus, global and local battles raged during this period. Although it was meant to stabilize international politics, imperialism intensified distrust and insecurity among the powers. When global and local political ambitions met, as they did in the second decade of the twentieth century, catastrophic violence followed.

NOTES

1. Quoted in Paul A. Cohen, *History in Three Keys: The Boxers as Event, Experience, and Myth* (New York: Columbia University Press, 1997), 86–87.
2. Paul Leroy-Beaulieu, quoted in *Histoire de la colonisation française* (Paris: Fayard, 1991), 2:149.
3. Quoted in Rudrangshu Mukherjee, "The Sepoy Mutinies Revisited," in *War and Society in Colonial India, 1807–1945*, ed. Kaushik Roy (Delhi: Oxford University Press, 2006), 121.
4. General Skobelev, quoted in Peter Hopkirk, *The Great Game: The Struggle for Empire in Central Asia* (New York: Kodansha International, 1992), 407.
5. Quoted in Charles Lee Keeton, *King Thebaw and the Ecological Rape of Burma: The Political and Commercial Struggle Between British India and French Indo-China in Burma, 1878–1886* (Delhi, India: Manohar Book Service, 1974), 202.
6. Phan Chau Trinh, in Truong Buu Lam, *Colonialism Experienced: Vietnamese Writing on Colonialism, 1900–1931* (Ann Arbor: University of Michigan Press, 2000), 130.
7. William Morton Fullerton, *In Cairo*, quoted in Max Rodenbeck, *Cairo: The City Victorious* (New York: Knopf, 1999), 136.
8. Letter from the King of Daboya to Governor of the Gold Coast, 8 July 1892, quoted in A. Adu Boahen, *African Perspectives on Colonialism* (Baltimore, MD: Johns Hopkins University Press, 1987), 37.
9. Quoted in Mike Davis, *Late Victorian Holocausts: El Niño Famines and the Making of the Third World* (London: Verso, 2001), 46.
10. Davis, *Late Victorian Holocausts*, 139.
11. Quoted in Jennifer W. Cushman, *Family and State: The Formation of a Sino-Thai Tin-Mining Dynasty, 1797–1832* (Singapore: Oxford University Press, 1991), 62.
12. Khayr al-Din al-Tunisi, "The Surest Path to Knowledge Concerning the Condition of Countries," quoted in *Colonial Rule in Africa: Readings from Primary Sources*, ed. Bruce Fetter (Madison: University of Wisconsin Press, 1979), 57.
13. Quoted in Bruce Fetter, ed., *Colonial Rule in Africa*, 117.

14. Quoted in Robert O. Collins, ed., *Eastern African History*, vol. 2, *African History: Text and Readings* (New York: Markus Wiener Publishing, 1990), 124.

15. Quoted in Davis, *Late Victorian Holocausts*, 31, 57, 172.

16. "Song of Revolution," in Gungwu Wang, *Community and Nation: China, Southeast Asia and Australia* (St. Leonards, Australia: Allen and Unwin, 1992), 10.

17. Quoted in Sumanta Banerjee, "Women's Popular Culture in Nineteenth Century Bengal," in *Recasting Women: Essays in Indian Colonial History*, ed. Kumkum Sangari and Sudesh Vaid (New Brunswick, NJ: Rutgers University Press, 1990), 142.

18. Quoted in David Robinson, *Muslim Societies and French Colonial Authorities in Senegal and Mauritania, 1880–1920* (Athens: Ohio University Press, 2000), 204.

19. Chief Segale, quoted in Peter Warwick, *Black People and the South African War, 1899–1902* (Cambridge, U.K.: Cambridge University Press, 1983), 177.

20. Quoted in Cohen, *History in Three Keys*, 80.

RESOURCES FOR RESEARCH

Building Empires

There are many debates about the motivations for empire. Cain and Hopkins dispute the view that industrialists backed imperialism to provide them with markets, arguing instead that financial and other service providers were the major advocates of colonies. Steinmetz interestingly shows German imperialism as inconsistent, varying from one area to another, and he suggests that all colonies were similarly run, depending on the imperialists' evaluations of a particular region's culture.

Burbank, Jane, and Frederick Cooper. *Empires in World History: Power and the Politics of Difference.* 2010.

Cain, P. J., and A. G. Hopkins. *British Imperialism, 1688–2000.* 2002.

Feifer, George. *Breaking Open Japan: Commodore Perry, Lord Abe and the American Imperialism of 1853.* 2006.

Steinmetz, George. *The Devil's Handwriting: Precoloniality and the German Colonial State in Qingdao, Samoa, and Southwest Africa.* 2004.

Sunderland, Willard. *Taming the Wild Field: Colonization and Empire on the Russian Steppe.* 2004.

Imperial Society

Imperial powers showed their dominance through the exercise of military but also political and social power.

Armstrong, Charles K., et al., eds. *Korea at the Center: Dynamics of Regionalism in Northeast Asia.* 2006.

Carter, Marina, and Khal Torabully. *Coolitude: An Anthology of the Indian Labour Diaspora.* 2002.

Davis, Mike. *Late Victorian Holocausts: El Niño Famines and the Making of the Third World.* 2001.

Maugubane, Zine. *Bringing the Empire Home: Race, Class, and Gender in Britain and Colonial South Africa.* 2004.

Sahadeo, Jeff. *Russian Colonial Society in Tashkent, 1865–1923.* 2007.

Culture in an Imperial Age

The imperialists shaped colonial customs and attitudes, claiming to bring a superior civilization to their subjects.

Adas, Michael. *Dominance by Design: Technological Imperatives and America's Civilizing Mission.* 2006.

Berenson, Edward. *Heroes of Empire: Five Charismatic Men and the Conquest of Africa.* 2011.

Jansen, Marius B. *The Making of Modern Japan.* 2000.

Lowy, Dina. *The Japanese "New Woman": Images of Gender and Modernity.* 2007.

Robinson, David. *Muslim Societies and French Colonial Authorities in Senegal and Mauritania, 1880–1920.* 2000.

Imperial Contests at the Dawn of the Twentieth Century

The start of the twentieth century was a time of increasing global conflict. Several of the following authors describe the range of this conflict and the main issues in each example.

Cohen, Paul A. *History in Three Keys: The Boxers as Event, Experience, and Myth.* 1997.

Hobson, Rolf. *Imperialism at Sea: Naval Strategic Thought, the Ideology of Sea Power, and the Tirpitz Plan, 1875–1914.* 2002.

Parsons, Timothy. *The Rule of Empires: Those Who Built Them, Those Who Endured Them, and Why They Always Fall.* 2010.

Silbey, David J. *A War of Frontier and Empire: The Philippine-American War, 1899–1902.* 2007.

South African War. The Anglo-Boer War Museum maintains a helpful Web site. http://www.anglo-boer.co.za/.

Counterpoint: The West Copies from the World

As these works reveal, cultural exchange flourished alongside the rule of the imperialists.

Baas, Jacquelynn. *Smile of the Buddha: Eastern Philosophy and Western Art from Monet to Today.* 2005.

Brower, M. Brady. *Unruly Spirits: The Science of Psychic Phenomena in Modern France.* 2010.

Dixon, Joy. *Divine Feminine: Theosophy and Feminism in England.* 2001.

Treitel, Corinne. *A Science for the Soul: Occultism and the Genesis of the German Modern.* 2004.

▶ **For additional primary sources from this period,** see *Sources of Crossroads and Cultures.*

▶ **For Web sites, images, and documents related to topics in this chapter,** see Make History at bedfordstmartins.com/smith.

The major global development in this chapter ▶ The accelerated competition among nineteenth-century nation-states for empire.

IMPORTANT EVENTS

c. 1840–1910	Global migration because of indenture, imperial opportunity, and harsh environmental conditions
1857	Indian Uprising against the British
c. 1860–1900	Impressionism flourishes in the European arts, borrowing many non-Western techniques
1869	Suez Canal completed
c. 1870–1914	European powers, Japan, and the United States extend formal and informal control over Asia, Africa, and parts of Latin America
1876	British Parliament declares Victoria empress of India
1882	Britain takes over Egypt
1884–1885	European nations carve up Africa at the Berlin Conference
1894–1895	Sino-Japanese War
1898	Spanish-American War
1899–1900	Boxer Rebellion in China
1899–1902	South African War
1900	Sigmund Freud, *The Interpretation of Dreams*
1904–1905	Russo-Japanese War
1908	Young Turks' uprising against the Ottoman Empire
1910	Japan annexes Korea

KEY TERMS

business imperialism (p. 861)
colonialism (p. 861)
cosmopolitanism (p. 879)
diaspora (p. 877)
globalization (p. 860)
new imperialism (p. 860)
pogrom (p. 875)
psychoanalysis (p. 886)

CHAPTER OVERVIEW QUESTIONS

1. What are the arguments for and against imperialism?
2. How and why did some local peoples assist imperialists who took over their own countries?
3. Which were the major imperialist powers, and what made them so capable of conquest?
4. How did imperialism change the lives of people in the conquering countries and in the colonies?

SECTION FOCUS QUESTIONS

1. What motivated the imperialists, and how did they impose their control over other nations?
2. How did imperialism change lives and livelihoods around the world?
3. How did artists and writers respond to the age of empire?
4. What were the main issues in the contests over empire, and what were the results of these contests?
5. How did non-Western and colonized lands shape Western culture and society?

MAKING CONNECTIONS

1. How are the Industrial Revolution (see Chapter 24) and imperialism connected?
2. How are nation building (see Chapter 25) and imperialism connected?
3. In what ways might the globalization connected with imperialism undermine nation building?
4. Recall the empires discussed in Part 3. What were the key differences between empires in the early modern period and modern empires of the nineteenth century?

27

AT A CROSSROADS ▲

Diego Rivera spent most of the Mexican Revolution in Europe, where he learned a range of classical Western styles of painting. The bloodshed of the revolution and World War I and the coming of communism to Russia and elsewhere inspired him to become a communist and to take up the cause of oppressed native American peasants and workers on his return to Mexico. This mural, *Blood of the Revolutionary Martyrs Fertilizing the Earth* (1927), reflects the traditional Mexican idea that martyrdom makes the earth fertile. Rivera's strong belief in the value of workers and representations of this brutal era in human history make his art a crossroads of politics and cultural styles. The martyrs represented are peasant rebel leader Emiliano Zapata (right) and his follower Otilio Montano (left). (Schalkwijk/Art Resource, NY. /© 2011 Banco de México Diego Rivera Frida Kahlo Museums Trust, Mexico, D.F./ARS, NY.)

Wars, Revolutions, and the Birth of Mass Society

1910–1929

The rebel leader Emiliano Zapata was a dandy, wearing blinding white shirts and fitted black pants adorned with silver. Before 1910 he had worked the land of his part-Indian family in central Mexico, where small farmers such as Zapata struggled—usually unsuccessfully—to block the takeover of their traditional lands by big hacienda (plantation) owners producing sugar and other commodities for the global market. Zapata grew and sold watermelons, prospering by comparison with others in his village. A fighter against the takeover of local land, in 1910 he was galvanized by the call for revolution against the corrupt regime of Porfirio Diaz, a key ally of the big landowners. Gathering a peasant army, Zapata swept through central Mexico, motivating his followers with the slogan "It is better to die on your feet than live on your knees." During the long revolutionary struggle, Zapata became known as a shrewd, rational political leader, but he also provoked an emotional response: peasants who had never seen him boosted their spirits during the decade-long Mexican Revolution with cries of "Viva [Long Live] Zapata!"

By 1920, the Mexican Revolution had killed between 1 and 2 million people, some by rifles, machine guns, and bombs and others by disease, but it was just one of several lethal cataclysms in that decade. Between 1910 and 1920, tens of millions fought and died. In cities and villages, farms and battlefields around the world grew the grim sense that in this new century war would never end and that ordinary people would be endlessly called upon to support the slaughter. After Mexico, China erupted in revolution in 1911, throwing

BACKSTORY

The competition among Western powers heated up in the second half of the nineteenth century, fueled by the drive for overseas expansion known as imperialism (see Chapter 26). European nations used the economic and military advantages that resulted from industrialization to take direct and indirect control of territories in Asia, Africa, and Latin America. Newcomers Japan and the United States joined the race for empire, and many other states pursued policies intended to produce political centralization and national unification. Resistance to both new and old empires and to political elites mounted during these years, even as imperialism multiplied the connections among the world's peoples and intensified the pace of cultural and economic exchange. Both competition for power and resistance to existing power structures contributed to the violence that marked the early twentieth century. The application of industrial technology to warfare made conflicts between and within states more destructive than ever.

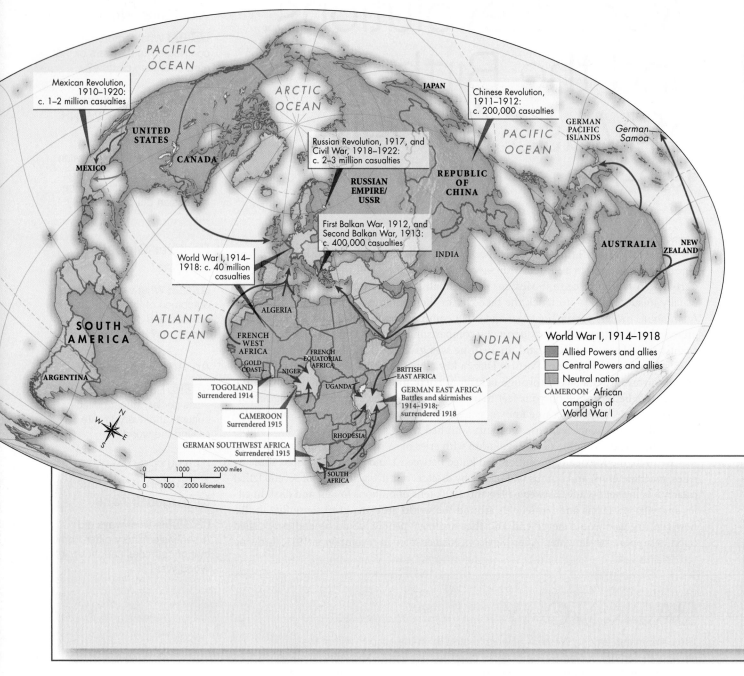

Mexican Revolution, 1910–1920: c. 1–2 million casualties

Chinese Revolution, 1911–1912: c. 200,000 casualties

Russian Revolution, 1917, and Civil War, 1918–1922: c. 2–3 million casualties

First Balkan War, 1912, and Second Balkan War, 1913: c. 400,000 casualties

World War I, 1914–1918: c. 40 million casualties

World War I, 1914–1918
- Allied Powers and allies
- Central Powers and allies
- Neutral nation

CAMEROON African campaign of World War I

TOGOLAND Surrendered 1914

CAMEROON Surrendered 1915

GERMAN SOUTHWEST AFRICA Surrendered 1915

GERMAN EAST AFRICA Battles and skirmishes 1914–1918; surrendered 1918

- **1910** Mexican Revolution begins

1911–1912 Revolutionaries overthrow Qing dynasty in China

Russian Revolution begins; United States enters World War I; Lenin returns to Russia **1917** ▪

▪ **1918** Bolsheviks take full control of Russian government; Treaty of Brest-Litovsk; armistice ends World War I

▪ **1912** First Balkan War

1910   **1915**   **1920**

▪ **1913** Second Balkan War

Treaties comprising Peace of Paris signed, including the Treaty of Versailles with Germany **1919–1920**

▪ **1914** World War I begins

Lenin introduces New Economic Policy in Russia **1921**

Germany forms Weimar Republic; May 4th movement in China **1919** ▪

off the Qing dynasty, and in 1912 and 1913 a host of Balkan peoples challenged the Ottoman and Austro-Hungarian empires. Their struggle led to World War I, which lasted from 1914 to 1918 and in turn spawned further wars and revolutions—most notably the Russian Revolution and the civil war that followed. The legacy of these conflicts shaped the rest of the century, and stories of soldiers' bravery—like that of Emiliano Zapata— filled the popular imagination through novels, films, and the new medium of radio.

These wars occurred on the crossroads of global trade and international politics. The Mexican Revolution, which was partly a struggle over U.S. control of the Mexican economy, led to American intervention, and even the peasant leader Emiliano Zapata corresponded with foreign leaders. The fall of the Qing left the future of a vast region in question and increased the interest of imperial powers in taking more of China's land and resources for themselves. World War I was a global war, fought not only on the European continent but in the Middle East, Africa, and the Pacific, as the powers pursued the goal of imperial expansion. All of these wars brought the masses into global politics, not only as soldiers but also as producers of the technology and supplies that soldiers needed. None of these wars, however, settled problems or restored social order as the combatants hoped. Instead, the Mexican Revolution destroyed the country's economy, while World War I produced political cataclysm, overturning the Russian, German, Ottoman, and Austro-Hungarian empires and changing the global balance of power. The Mexican Revolution, the fall of the Qing, World War I, and the Russian Revolution helped define early-twentieth-century history, and political uprisings continued into the 1920s, giving rise in turn to mass society.

Mass politics after the wars depended on mass culture, urbanization, and growing productivity, based on the postwar explosion of technology. Urban people from China to Argentina experienced the "Roaring Twenties," snapping up new consumer goods, drinking in the entertainment provided by films and radio, and relishing new personal freedoms. Modern communication technologies such as radio provided enjoyment, but they

MAPPING THE WORLD

Wars and Revolutions, 1910–1929

Wars and revolutions circled the globe in the early twentieth century. Areas where empire and imperial influence were at stake were especially hard hit, including a broad sweep of Eurasia. This era of local and global conflict brought dramatic political and other change, notably the fall of imperial dynasties, the exchange of colonial holdings and territory, and a stark toll in deaths from military campaigns, famine, and an influenza pandemic.

ROUTES ▼

→ Route of colonial and British Commonwealth troops in support of Allied Powers, 1914–1918

→ Route of U.S. forces during the Mexican Revolution, 1914–1916

→ Route of Pancho Villa, 1913–1916

• **1922** Civil war ends in Russia; Mussolini comes to power in Italy

1925   1930

• **1923** Founding of the independent republic of Turkey under Mustafa Kemal; formation of Union of Soviet Socialist Republics

1920s Mohandas Gandhi's nonviolent movement for India independence attracts millions; mass culture flourishes in film and publishing industries; growth of radio transmissions; technology increases global productivity

also spread political ideologies more widely than ever before. Some of these became the core of mass nationalist politics—some evil, like fascism, and some aimed at helping ordinary people, like the reform program of Emiliano Zapata.

OVERVIEW
QUESTIONS

The major global development in this chapter: The wars of the decade 1910 to 1920 and their role in the creation of mass culture and society.

As you read, consider:

1. Why did the Mexican Revolution, the Chinese Revolution, World War I, and the Russian Revolution cause so much change far from the battlefield?

2. How did these wars help produce mass culture and society?

3. What role did technology play in these developments?

Revolutions, Local Wars, and World War

FOCUS

What factors contributed to the wars of the early twentieth century?

The Mexican Revolution, the Chinese Revolution, and the Balkan wars opened one of the bloodiest decades in human history. The reasons for the violence were many and complex. Some fought to overthrow corrupt leaders, others to free their nations from outside threats, and still others to win the international competition for power and wealth. The conflicts of the early twentieth century did not always produce the social, economic, and political outcomes that had originally inspired individuals and nations to take up arms. Though some nations gained new territory, the fighting did not produce stability and order, but rather sowed the seeds for a new round of conflict and upheaval.

Revolutionaries and Warriors: Mexico, China, and the Balkans

The tensions created by imperialism and modern state-building were apparent in many parts of the world by 1910. In Mexico liberal reformers and peasant leaders, backed by local armies, attempted to reform a corrupt political order, while in China modernizers threw off the power of the Qing. In 1913 Balkan countries waged war against the weakening Ottoman Empire to claim more land and resources. When the victors fought against one another later that year, the chaos provoked further turmoil. In 1914, what some have called the Third Balkan War erupted, a regional conflict that sparked the global cataclysm of World War I.

The Mexican Revolution   In 1910, liberal Mexican reformers headed by the wealthy landowner Francisco Madero began a drive to force the dictator Porfirio Diaz from office. Diaz saw himself as a modernizer. During his forty years in power, Mexico had built some twelve thousand miles of railroads, and its mines yielded increasing amounts of lead, copper, and zinc. However, only a handful of wealthy families and foreign investors reaped the riches of Mexico's development. By encouraging the concentration of agricultural lands in the hands of a few, Diaz's policies had impoverished village people. By 1900, just 1 percent of the population held 85 percent of the land, much of it seized by the government for the wealthy. Compounding Mexican landlessness was the government's policy of granting huge tracts of this confiscated land for cattle-raising and mining to U.S. companies, which further hurt the prospects of ordinary citizens. Madero and his well-off friends were political reformers, seeking a more open political system and the rule of law, but peasants and workers, who were often paid in goods instead of cash, had survival on their minds.

Given this bleak situation, peasant armies arose to work for land reform—that is, for social, not just political, change—as conflict erupted on many fronts. Zapata described their situation and their goals: "Considering that for the great majority, villages and citizens of Mexico possess not even the land that they work and that they cannot ameliorate their condition in the slightest . . . because the land, the mountains, and the water are in the hands of a very small number, the following is decreed: one-third of all monopolies will be expropriated . . . and distributed to those villages and citizens who are now prevented from having their traditional rights to the land prevail."[1] In the north, butcher and landowner Pancho Villa headed another popular army that fought for the entire decade against U.S. citizens and others who were taking over local land and resources. Complicating the revolution was simple factional fighting for local and regional power.

The cause of the people was so strong, however, that in the end, long after the ouster of Diaz in 1911 and amid assassinations of leaders, including Zapata, the Mexican government announced land reform in its Constitution of 1917. The story of the hundreds of thousands of common warriors, many of them of Indian or mixed blood like Zapata, giving their lives for fundamental reform would inspire generations of Mexican writers and artists. The lasting cultural impact of this struggle is exemplified in the mural art of Diego Rivera, whose huge depictions of the Mexican Revolution were meant to show the masses their own past heroism and inspire them to remain committed to social justice.

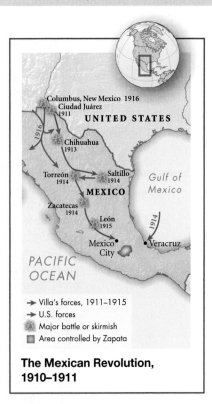

The Mexican Revolution, 1910–1911

As we saw in Chapter 26, the combination of Japan's lightning defeat of China in the Sino-Japanese War (1894) and the Boxer Rebellion (1899–1900) thoroughly discredited the Qing dynasty. These humiliating events ushered in a wave of reform, some of it sponsored by the Qing administration itself. Schools, urban planning, and women's rights all filled the agenda of reformers. Behind the flurry of change, modernizing businessmen, professionals, and intellectuals sensed that the Manchu dynasty was dangerously outdated and needed to be replaced by new rulers drawn from the Chinese people themselves. Influenced by Western ideas of evolution, reformers likened the Manchus, who descended from northern nomads, to undeveloped peoples of past times who "lived in dens and wore pelts."[2] In 1911 to 1912 a group of revolutionaries organized as the **Guomindang** (gwo-min-DAHNG), or Nationalist Party, overthrew the long-lived dynasty and declared China a republic. Their leader, the medical doctor Sun Yatsen (soon yot-SEN), who like many proponents of change had been educated outside of China, used a cluster of Western ideas in his slogan "nationalism, democracy, and socialism." However, he interpreted these ideas in the context of long-standing Chinese values. For example, whereas Marxist socialists called for an end to private property, Sun's socialism was based in such traditional charitable thinking as the view that all people should have enough food. Sun's Guomindang called for the revival of the Chinese belief in correct behavior between governors and the governed, economic and social reform in line with scientific theories, and the end of foreign domination over China.

Sun's stirring leadership helped set China on a modernizing course, but he was not a capable administrator and quickly resigned in favor of a powerful former Qing general, Yuan Shikai (yoo-ahn shee-KI). Yuan was no democrat, however, and in 1916 he broke with the Nationalists to declare the foundation of a new imperial dynasty. When regional generals rejected Yuan's imperial claims, formed their own armies, and began to act as warlords, the country descended into a decade of chaos.

The Chinese Revolution

Guomindang The Chinese nationalist party founded by Sun Yatsen that overthrew the Qing dynasty and fought to rule mainland China from 1911 to 1949.

Yet aspirations for a new way of life continued to grow, university life flourished, and literature became pointedly directed toward the need to modernize China. Reform-minded people were inspired by author Lu Xun, whose novella *The True Story of Ah Q* (1921–1922) presents what Lu called the typical Chinese, arrogant no matter how pathetic his station in life and full of useless maxims: "If a woman walks alone on the street, she must want to seduce bad men." Such backward thinking on Ah Q's part threatens his survival in modern times, just as China, in Lu's view, was held back by out-of-date ideas and the blindness of leaders who focused on China's glorious past and ignored the problems of its troubled present.

The Balkan Wars   In the Balkans politicians whipped up ethnic nationalism to challenge both Habsburg and Ottoman power. Greece, Serbia, Bulgaria, Romania, and Montenegro had recently emerged as autonomous states, almost all of them home to ethnically and religiously diverse populations. These small states sought strength as modern nations by taking Ottoman and Habsburg territory in which others from their own imagined majority ethnic group lived—a complicated desire, given the historic intermingling of ethnicities throughout the region. In the First Balkan War, in 1912, Serbia, Bulgaria, Greece, and Montenegro joined forces to break off Macedonia and Albania from the Ottomans. The victors divided up their booty, but they soon turned against one another. Serbia, Greece, and Montenegro contested Bulgarian gains in the Second Balkan War in 1913 and won a quick victory. In the peace treaty that followed the fighting, an alarmed Austria-Hungary managed to prevent Serbia from gaining parts of Albania, further inflaming Serb grievances toward the dual monarchy. Many Serbs dreamed of crushing Austria-Hungary with the help of their powerful Slavic ally Russia, a dream the Russian government did little to discourage. Thus, the nationalist aspirations of Slavic Serbs contributed to growing tensions between two great European powers, Austria-Hungary and Russia. Under these circumstances, events in the Balkans took on international importance.

Outbreak of World War I   The situation came to a head in June 1914 in the Habsburg-controlled Bosnian capital of Sarajevo when a Bosnian Serb, funded by the Serbian secret police, assassinated the heir to the Habsburg throne, Archduke Franz Ferdinand, and his wife Sophie. The young assassin hoped thereby to free his homeland from the Habsburgs and unite it with Serbia. According to its alliance with Germany, Austria-Hungary had the promise of full German support if it launched an offensive war to defeat the Serbians once and for all. So it issued a stern ultimatum: the Serbian government had just forty-eight hours in which to agree to demands that would amount to Austrian control of the Serbian state. When Serbia refused to meet one of these demands, Austria declared war on Serbia on July 28. Equipped with well-prepared war plans and armed to the teeth for war, the major European powers were eager to end the international tensions that existed among them over global, national, and even domestic issues. Thus, the origins of World War I lay in great-power interests in the Balkans, long-standing alliances and strategies for war among the powers, the buildup of military technologies, and a climate of rivalry for territory and influence. This so-called Third Balkan War proved to be more than any of the powers—or the world—bargained for.

Fighting World War I

World War I erupted in August 1914. On one side stood the Central Powers—Austria-Hungary and Germany—which had evolved from Bismarck's Triple Alliance of 1882 (see Chapter 25). On the other side were the Allies—France, Great Britain, and Russia—which had emerged as a bloc from an alliance between France and Great Britain that became the Triple Entente when Russia joined in 1907. In 1915, Italy, originally part of Bismarck's Triple Alliance, went over to the Entente (or Allies) in hopes of making postwar gains. As the fighting spread to the combatants' overseas colonies and non-European powers took sides, the war became a global conflict. Japan, eager to extend its empire into China, soon joined the Allies, while the Ottoman Empire united with the Central Powers against its traditional enemy, Russia (see Map 27.1, page 898). In time, the United States would enter the war as well, contributing to the Allied victory.

The antagonists hungered for the same power and prosperity that inspired imperialism. Germany hoped to acquire a far-flung empire by annexing Russian territory, parts of Belgium, France, and Luxembourg, and even Austria-Hungary. Austria-Hungary aimed to rebuild its power, which was under attack from the competing nationalist movements within its borders and by Serbs and other Slavs outside them. Russia wanted to reassert its great-power position as protector of the Slavs by adding all of Poland to the Russian Empire and by controlling other Slavic peoples. The French, too, craved territory, especially the return of Alsace and Lorraine, lost after the Franco-Prussian War of 1870 to 1871 (discussed in Chapter 25). The British sought to secure their world empire by defeating its competitors. The secret Treaty of London (1915) promised Italy territory in Africa, Anatolia (modern Turkey), and the Balkans in return for joining the Allies.

The Blueprint for War

In August 1914, armies had at their disposal machine guns and rifles, airplanes, battleships, submarines, and cars, railroads, and other motorized transport. Newer technologies such as chlorine gas, tanks, and bombs would develop between 1914 and 1918. Nonetheless, officers on both sides held to a nineteenth-century strategy, the "cult of the offensive," in which continuous spirited attacks and flashing sabers and bayonets would be decisive. The colonies of the European powers were to provide massive assistance to wage such offensives. Some 1 million Africans, another 2 million Indians, and more than a million members of the British Commonwealth countries, notably Canada, Australia, and New Zealand, served on the battlefronts, while the imperial powers conscripted uncounted numbers of colonists as forced laborers. In the face of massive firepower, the outdated "cult of the offensive" would cost millions of these lives.

The first months of the war crushed hopes of quick victory. All the major armies mobilized rapidly. The Germans were guided by a strategy devised by Alfred von Schlieffen, a former chief of the general staff. The Schlieffen Plan outlined a way to avoid a two-front war by concentrating on one foe at a time. It called for a rapid and concentrated blow to the west against France, accompanied by a light holding action to the east against France's ally, Russia. According to the plan, France would be defeated in six weeks, and only then would German forces be concentrated against Russia, which, the Germans believed, would mobilize slowly. The attack on France began in the summer of 1914 and proceeded through Belgium, but there it met unexpected and spirited resistance, slowing the German advance and allowing British and French troops to reach the northern front. In massive battles neither side could defeat the other, and casualties were in the millions. The unprecedented firepower of modern weaponry turned what was supposed to be an offensive war of movement into a stationary, defensive stalemate along a line of trenches that stretched from the North Sea through Belgium and northern France to Switzerland. Deep within trenches dug along this front, millions of soldiers lived in nightmarish shelters.

The Battlefronts, 1914–1916

Meanwhile, on the eastern front, the massive Russian army, some 12 million strong, mobilized more quickly than expected, driving into German territory by mid-August. The Russian generals believed that no matter how ill equipped their army was, no army could stand up to their massive numbers. Russian success was short-lived, however. The Germans crushed the tsar's army in East Prussia in the fall of 1914 and then turned south to Galicia. Victory against Russia emboldened the commanding generals to demand and get more troops for the eastern front. Nonetheless, by year's end Germany had failed to knock out the Russians and was bogged down in the very two-front war its military planners had taken such pains to avoid (see again Map 27.1).

War at sea proved equally indecisive. When the Allies blockaded ports to prevent supplies from reaching Germany and Austria-Hungary, the Germans responded with an intensive submarine, or U-boat ("underwater boat"), campaign against both Allied and neutral shipping. Despite U.S. deaths, President Woodrow Wilson maintained a policy of neutrality, and Germany, unwilling to provoke Wilson further, called off unrestricted submarine warfare—that is, attacks on neutral shipping. Throughout 1915 the British hoped to knock out the Ottomans and open ports to Russia by attacking at

MAP 27.1

World War I in Europe and the Middle East, 1914–1918

World War I transformed many parts of Europe and the Middle East into wastelands because of the increasingly devastating weaponry. Farmlands were put out of commission for years, and livestock near battlefields was decimated. On the western front the damage was mostly confined to northern France, but on the eastern front the destructive power was mobile as armies crossed some areas several times. An effective blockade added to the hunger that central and eastern Europeans suffered as the war came to an end in 1918.

the Dardanelles Strait. At Gallipoli, casualty rates for both sides of 50 to 60 percent only yielded stalemate. "A miserable time," one Irish soldier called Gallipoli, as his comrades from New Zealand, Australia, and elsewhere in the empire had their heads blown off and their limbs smashed to pulp. Horrific suffering in this single battle

The Dead of World War I
Even as the death toll mounted during World War I, politicians and crowned heads of state across Europe refused to give up the idea of victory. For most soldiers, this political decision meant ongoing suffering in the trenches and, for millions, hysteria, crippling wounds, or death. The bones of the unburied were collected from the battlefield as shown here in Verdun, for placement in ossuaries, at the war's end. (Bettmann/Corbis.)

strengthened Australia's and New Zealand's will to break with British leadership, which had led them into the tragedy.

Both sides refused a negotiated peace: "No peace before England is defeated and destroyed," Kaiser William II railed against his cousin, Britain's King George V. "Only amidst the ruins of London will I forgive Georgy." French leaders called for a "war to the death." General staffs on both sides continued to prepare fierce attacks: after heavy artillery pounded enemy trenches and gun emplacements, troops obeyed the order to go "over the top" by scrambling out of their trenches and into battle, usually to be mowed down by machine-gun fire from the tens of thousands of defenders in their own trenches. On the western front, casualties of one hundred thousand and more for a single campaign became commonplace. In 1916, in an effort to break French morale, the Germans launched massive assaults on the fortress at Verdun, firing as many as a million shells in a single day during the attack. Combined French and German losses totaled close to a million men, whose anonymous bones today fill a vast shrine at the site.

Had the military leaders thoroughly dominated the scene, historians judge, all armies would have been utterly demolished in nonstop offensives by the end of 1915. Yet ordinary soldiers in this war were not automatons, and in the face of what seemed to them suicidal orders, soldiers on both sides sometimes refused to engage in battle. Enemies facing each other across the trenches frequently ate their meals in peace, even though the trenches were within hand-grenade reach. Right up to the closing year of the war, soldiers fraternized with the "enemy," playing an occasional game of soccer, exchanging mementos, and entering into silent agreements not to fight. A British veteran of the trenches explained to a new recruit that the Germans "don't want to fight any more than we do, so there's a kind of understanding between us. Don't fire at us and we'll not fire at you." Male bonding aided survival: soldiers picked lice from one another's bodies and clothes and came to love one another, sometimes even passionately.

Troops from Asian and African colonies, taken like the European whites from their everyday lives, often had different experiences, especially because colonial soldiers were

The Soldiers' War

often put in the front ranks where the risks were greatest. Many suffered from the rigors of a totally unfamiliar climate and strange food, as well as from their encounter with Western war technology. Colonial troops' perspectives changed as they saw their "masters" completely undone and "uncivilized." For when fighting did break out, trenches became a veritable hell of shelling and sniping, flying body parts, rotting cadavers, and blinding gas. "I am greatly distressed in mind," one South Asian soldier wrote to his family, echoing the hopelessness that so many soldiers felt on seeing their comrades lose hands, feet, and entire limbs.[3] Colonizers and colonized could alike be reduced to hysteria through the sheer stress and violence of battle; others became cynical. "It might be me tomorrow," a young British soldier wrote his mother in 1916. "Who cares?"

Civilians at War: The Home Front

World War I quickly became a "**total war**," one in which all of the resources of each nation were harnessed to the war effort and lines between the home front and the battlefield were blurred. Civilians manufactured the machine guns, poisonous gases, bombs, airplanes, and eventually tanks that were the backbone of technological warfare. Increased and well-organized production of coffins, canes, wheelchairs, and artificial limbs was also a wartime necessity. Because their efforts were vital to military success, civilians were required to work overtime and sacrifice for victory. To supply the battlefront efficiently, governments took over the operation of the economy and suppressed dissent.

Politics Suspended   Initially, political parties in each combatant nation put aside their differences. For decades socialist parties had preached that "the worker has no country" and that nationalism was mere ideology meant to keep workers disunited and obedient to their employers. In August 1914, however, most socialists backed the war, trading worker solidarity for national unity in a time of crisis. Although many feminists were opposed to war, the British suffrage leader Emmeline Pankhurst was hardly alone in also becoming a militant nationalist. "What is the use of fighting for a vote if we have not got a country to vote in?" she asked. Others hoped that the spirit of nationalism could end prejudices. "In the German fatherland there are no longer any Christians and Jews, any believers and disbelievers, there are only Germans," one rabbi proudly announced. National leaders stressed ending political division in the name of victory: "I no longer recognize [political] parties," Kaiser William II declared on August 4, 1914. "I recognize only Germans." Governments mobilized the masses on the home front to endure long hours and food shortages with large doses of propaganda that promoted patriotism by demonizing the enemy (see Seeing the Past: Wartime Propaganda). New laws made it a crime to criticize official policies. For a time, it seemed as if old barriers would be broken down and new bonds formed among the citizens of each nation.

As the war dragged on, social and political tensions returned, and some individuals and groups began to lobby for peace. In 1915, activists in the international women's movement met in The Hague to call for an end to war. "We can no longer endure . . . brute force as the only solution of international disputes," declared Dutch physician Aletta Jacobs. Some socialists moved to neutral countries such as Switzerland to work for a negotiated peace settlement.

The Civilians' War   The requirements of total war upset the social and political order. In the early days of fighting many women lost their jobs when luxury shops, textile factories, and other non-military establishments closed. Wartime conditions, however, soon created new opportunities for women workers. As men left the workplace to join the fighting, women moved into a variety of high-paying jobs, including munitions production, metallurgy, and services like streetcar conducting and ambulance driving. Workingmen often protested that women, in the words of one metalworker, were "sending men to the slaughter" and robbing them of their role as breadwinner. Many people, including some women, objected to women's loss of femininity, as workers cut their hair short and wore utilitarian slacks and streamlined clothing. "The feminine in me decreased more and more, and I did not know

total war The vital involvement of civilians in the war industry, the blurring of home and battle fronts, and the use of industrial weaponry to destroy an enemy.

Wartime Propaganda

The French Are Using Monkeys: A German Magazine Cover
(Christel Gerstenberg/Corbis.)

Will Germany Take Over the World?: An Australian Poster
(K.J. Historical/Corbis.)

Propaganda agencies within governments on both sides in World War I touted the war as a patriotic mission to resist villainous enemies. They used both film and print to turn people who formerly saw themselves as neighbors into hate-filled enemies. British propagandists fabricated atrocities that the German "Huns" supposedly committed against Belgians, and German propaganda warned that French African troops would rape German women if Germany were defeated. Efforts were often clumsy: a British film, *The Battle of the Somme* (1916), so obviously sanitized the war's horrors that soldiers in the audience roared with laughter, though civilians found it riveting.

Brightly colored propaganda posters, representing the best lithographic technology, were pasted to walls and placed in windows. Government experts hired the best graphic artists to execute their carefully chosen themes. In the image on the left, German propagandists picked up on the widespread use of African soldiers in the French army to make their point, depicting the enemy in this magazine cover as monkeys. "The Ersatz Battalion—Senegal" speaks to the effectiveness of the

enemy. By contrast, an Australian artist drew the Allied poster on the right representing the German enemy with a frightening face and its hands dripping blood.

EXAMINING THE EVIDENCE

1. What accounts for these specific representations of the enemy?

2. How would the audience respond to each representation, and how would the images have aroused commitment to the war?

3. Alongside this type of caricature was sentimental wartime propaganda depicting brave soldiers, faithful wives, and children in need of their hardy fathers' and other male protection. Why was there such variety in propaganda, and which type of image would you judge to be most effective?

whether to be sad or glad about this," wrote one Russian nurse about putting on rough male clothing for the battlefield. Despite some alarm, a "new woman" with different clothing, a respectable job, and new responsibilities for supporting her family was emerging in great numbers from the war.

Rising social tensions revolved around issues of class as well as gender. Workers toiled longer hours eating less, while many in the upper classes bought abundant food and fashionable clothing on the black market (outside the official system of rationing). Governments allowed many businesses to keep raising prices and thus earn higher profits than ever, practices that caused the cost of living to surge and thus contributed to social strife. Shortages of staples such as bread, sugar, and meat caused hardships everywhere. A German roof-workers' association pleaded for relief: "We can no longer go on. Our children are starving." Civilians in occupied areas and in such colonies as German East Africa suffered oppressive conditions, facing harsh forced labor along with skyrocketing taxes and prices. Thus, even though political debate officially stopped during the war, the prolonged conflict created political grievances among people worldwide.

Revolution in Russia and the End of World War I

FOCUS

Why did the Russian Revolution take place, and what changes did it produce in Russian politics and daily life?

By 1917 the situation was becoming desperate for everyone—politicians, the military, and civilians. In February of that year, the German government, responding to public anger over mounting casualties, resumed unrestricted submarine warfare—a move that brought the United States into the war two months later, after German U-boats had sunk several American ships. Meanwhile, as prices soared, tenants across Europe conducted rent strikes, and factory hands and white-collar workers alike walked off the job. In the spring of 1917, French soldiers mutinied against further offensives, while in Russia, wartime protest turned into outright revolution.

Revolution in Russia

Of all the warring nations, Russia sustained the greatest number of casualties—7.5 million by 1917. Unlike other heads of state, Tsar Nicholas II failed to unify his government or his people. Nicholas was capable of making patriotic gestures, such as changing the German-sounding name of St. Petersburg to Petrograd, but he stubbornly insisted on conducting the war himself instead of using experienced and knowledgeable officials. "Is this stupidity or treason?" one member of the Russian Duma asked of the ineffective wartime effort. In March 1917, crowds of working women and civilians commemorating International Women's Day swarmed the streets of Petrograd and began looting shops for food. Other workers, furious at the government's inability to provide basic necessities, joined them. Many in the army defected, angered by the massive casualties caused by their substandard weapons. Nicholas abdicated that same month, bringing the three-hundred-year-old Romanov dynasty to an abrupt end.

The Provisional Government

Politicians from the old Duma formed a new ruling entity called the Provisional Government. At first hopes were high that under the Provisional Government, as one revolutionary poet put it, "our false, filthy, boring, hideous life should become a just, pure, merry, and beautiful life." However, the abdication of the tsar did not end internal conflict in Russia. Instead, the Russian Revolution unleashed social and political forces that had been building for decades. Spontaneously elected **soviets**—councils of workers and soldiers—campaigned to end favor of the wealthy and urged concern for workers and the poor. The peasantry, another force competing for power, began to seize aristocratic estates. Meanwhile, the Provisional Government seemed unwilling to end the war and unable to improve living conditions.

soviet A council of workers and soldiers elected to represent the people in the Russian revolutions of 1905 and 1917.

Lenin's False Identity Papers, 1917

Before the Russian Revolution began in 1917, Bolshevik leader V. I. Lenin had lived in forced exile, agitated among the Social Democrats in foreign lands, and preached loudly against World War I. During the Russian Revolution itself, he used many disguises and false identity papers such as the one shown here to escape notice by the Provisional Government, which he worked to bring down. By the autumn of 1917, the war was still going so badly for Russia and inflicted so much additional suffering that the Bolsheviks were able to take power. (Private Collection/The Stapleton Collection/Bridgeman Art Library.)

In April 1917, Vladimir Ilyich Lenin, leader of a faction of the Russian Socialist Party, returned from exile in Siberia, his safe rail transportation provided by the Germans, who hoped that Lenin might further weaken the Russian war effort. Son of a prominent provincial official, Lenin nonetheless lived his life as a revolutionary, beginning political activism while at university and then becoming a political organizer of Marxist and working-class groups across Europe. Among his principles was the belief that the Russian people needed to be led by an elite group of revolutionaries—not by the masses themselves. Those belonging to Lenin's faction were called **Bolsheviks**. On returning to Russia, Lenin quickly called on his countrymen to withdraw from World War 1, for the soviets to seize power on behalf of workers and poor peasants, and for all private land to be nationalized. The Bolsheviks challenged the Provisional Government with the slogans "All power to the soviets!" and "Peace, land, and bread!" In contrast, the Provisional Government—like governments across Europe—continued to seek popular support through battlefield victories, even as the Russian army continued to suffer staggering losses.

In November 1917, the Bolsheviks seized power in the name of the soviets. When in January 1918 elections for a constituent assembly failed to give the Bolsheviks a majority, the party took over the government by force. Observing Marxist doctrine, the Bolsheviks abolished private property, nationalizing factories in order to restore productivity. The new government asked Germany for peace and agreed to the Treaty of Brest-Litovsk (March 1918), which placed vast regions of the Russian Empire under German occupation (see again Map 27.1). Because the loss of millions of square miles put Petrograd at risk, the Bolsheviks relocated the capital to Moscow. To distinguish themselves from the socialists or Social Democrats who had voted for the disastrous war in 1914, the Bolsheviks formally adopted the name Communists, taken from Marx's writings. Lenin agreed to the huge loss of territory not only because he had promised to bring peace to Russia, but because he believed the rest of Europe would soon rebel and overthrow the capitalist order.

Opposition to Bolshevik policies swiftly formed and soon mushroomed into full-fledged civil war. The pro-Bolsheviks (or "Reds") faced an array of antirevolutionary forces

The Bolshevik Takeover

Bolshevik A faction of the Russian Socialist Party that advocated control of revolutionary activity by a disciplined group of the party elite instead of by the working class as a whole; renamed "Communist" by Lenin following the Russian Revolution.

Civil War

(the "Whites"). Among the Whites, the tsarist military leadership, composed of many aristocratic landlords, was joined by non-Russian-nationality groups eager to regain independence. Russia's former allies, notably the United States, Britain, France, and Japan, landed troops in the country, hoping to defeat the Bolsheviks. The Whites failed, however, because instead of conducting a united effort, the individual groups competed with one another: the pro-tsarist forces, for example, wanted a restored empire, whereas the nationality groups such as the Ukrainians and Lithuanians wanted freedom as individual nation-states.

In contrast, the Bolsheviks had a more unified leadership that essentially reshaped Marxism. Leon Trotsky, Bolshevik commissar of war, built a highly disciplined army by ending the democratic procedures, such as the election of officers, that had originally attracted soldiers to Bolshevism. The Cheka (secret police) set up detention camps for political opponents and often shot them without trial. The expansion of the Cheka, Red Army, and bureaucracy undermined the promise of Marxism that revolution would bring a "withering away" of the state.

Finally, the Bolsheviks organized revolutionary Marxism worldwide. In March 1919, they founded the **Comintern** (Communist International), a centrally run organization dedicated to preaching communism globally. By mid-1921, the Red Army had secured the Crimea, the Caucasus, and the Muslim borderlands in Central Asia, and in 1922 the Japanese withdrew from Siberia—the last of the foreign invaders to leave—ending the civil war. The Bolsheviks were now in charge of a state, the Union of Soviet Socialist Republics (USSR), as multiethnic as the former Russian Empire. In the meantime, civil war had brought Russia only unprecedented disease, hunger, and death. Nonetheless, people around the world saw in Soviet communism the promise of an improved life for the masses.

Ending the War: 1918

Although Russia was out of World War I by the spring of 1918, much of the rest of the world remained mired in the brutal conflict. Relying on Arab, African, and Indian troops, the British took Baghdad in 1917 as well as Palestine, Lebanon, and Syria from the Ottomans (see again Map 27.1). In sub-Saharan Africa, more than a million Kenyans and Tanzanians were conscripted by the Europeans to fight a vicious campaign for control of East Africa. African troops serving the imperial powers died by the thousands, as did the civilian population whose resources were confiscated and villages burned by competing powers. The Japanese seized German holdings in China to enlarge their influence on the mainland.

Allied Victory

In the spring of 1918 the Central Powers made one final attempt to smash through the Allied lines, but by then the British and French had started making limited but effective use of tanks that could withstand machine-gun fire. In the summer of 1918, the Allies, now fortified by U.S. troops, pushed back the Germans all along the western front and headed toward Germany. In an effort to shift the blame for defeat away from themselves, the German military leaders who had been running the country allowed a civilian government to form and ask for peace. After the war, the generals would claim that weak-willed civilians had dealt the military a "stab in the back," forcing Germany to surrender when victory was still possible. As the Central Powers collapsed on all fronts and mutinies and rebellions broke out across Germany, on November 11, 1918, delegates from the two sides signed an armistice ending the war.

Comintern An international organization of workers established by the Bolsheviks to spread communism worldwide.

Fourteen Points A proposal by U.S. president Woodrow Wilson for peace during World War I based on "settlement" rather than "victory" and on the self-determination of peoples.

In the course of four years, civilization had been sorely tested, if not shattered. Conservative figures put the battlefield toll at a minimum of 10 million dead and 30 million wounded, incapacitated, or eventually to die of their wounds. In every European combatant country, industrial and agricultural production had plummeted, and much of the reduced output had been put to military use. From 1918 to 1919, the weakened global population suffered an influenza epidemic that left as many as 100 million more dead. "They carried the dead people on mule-drawn carts without even being in boxes," one fighter in Pancho Villa's army reported of the flu in Mexico. "Many poor people left their small children as orphans . . . without father, without mother, without anything."[4] The influenza pandemic only added to the horrifying fact that total war had drained society of resources and population and had sown the seeds of future catastrophes.

Postwar Global Politics

Across Europe, civilians and returning soldiers rose in protest after the war. Even as peace talks began in 1919, the red flag of socialist revolution flew from the city hall in Glasgow, Scotland, while in cities of the collapsing Austro-Hungarian Empire, workers set up soviet-like councils to reshape politics. The conduct of the war—including forced labor—damaged Western claims to be more advanced than other parts of the world, causing a surging resistance to colonialism even as the victorious Allies took steps to secure and expand their empires. Such was the highly charged backdrop for peacemaking.

FOCUS

What were the major outcomes of the peacemaking process and postwar conditions?

The Paris Peace Conference 1919–1920

The Paris Peace Conference opened in January 1919 with the leaders of the United States, Great Britain, and France dominating the proceedings. Western leaders worried about communism spreading far beyond Russia's borders and about pressure from their angry citizens, who demanded revenge. France, for example, had lost 1.3 million people—almost an entire generation of young men, more than a million buildings, and thousands of miles of railroad lines and roads had been destroyed while the war was fought on French soil. The British slogan "Hang the Kaiser!" captured the public mood. Italian officials arrived on the scene demanding the territory promised to them in the 1915 Treaty of London. Meanwhile U.S. president Woodrow Wilson, head of the growing world power that had contributed to the Allied victory, had his own agenda. His **Fourteen Points**, the peace proposal on which the truce had been based, were steeped in the language of freedom and called for open diplomacy, an "open-minded" settlement of colonial issues, and the self-determination of peoples—meaning the right of national groups to have autonomy if they wanted it. Amid disagreements over the need to punish the Central Powers or to prevent too harsh or humiliating a peace, representatives from Middle Eastern states, Japan, and other deeply interested parties lobbied for fair treatment from the victorious powers. World War I had drawn in non-European peoples from around the world, and now, having fought in the war, they wanted a say in the peace.

Paris Peace Conference, 1918

Allied heads of state, diplomats, military personnel, and policy experts dominated the peace conference that opened in Paris in 1918. Also attending were a variety of other participants in the war seeking a just peace, national independence, or special acknowledgment of their ethnic or other interest group. Among these were leaders from the Middle East, who had rallied their own armed forces to fight for the Allies on the promise of postwar independence. Their small presence in this picture symbolizes the utter disregard for those promises in the Peace of Paris settlement. (The Art Archive/Domenica del Corriere/Collection Dagli Orti.)

MAP 27.2

The Peace of Paris in Central and Eastern Europe, 1920

Where mighty empires had once reigned over central and eastern Europe, new states appeared and new forms of government replaced dynastic rule. These small states were generally fragile due to their very novelty, postwar economic difficulties, and the need to modernize agriculture and to develop industrial capacity. Their citizens faced more powerful neighbors—Germany and the Soviet Union—whose aspirations to expand would soon menace the region's security.

Map legend:
— Boundaries of German, Russian, and Austro-Hungarian empires in 1914
New and reconstituted nations
Demilitarized or Allied occupation zone
— Boundaries of 1920

The Peace of Paris Treaties

After six months, the Allies produced the Peace of Paris (1919–1920), composed of a cluster of individual treaties. The treaties separated Austria from Hungary, reduced Hungary by almost two-thirds of its inhabitants and three-quarters of its territory, and broke up the Ottoman Empire. The Habsburg Empire was replaced by a group of small, internally divided, and relatively weak states: Czechoslovakia, Poland, and the Kingdom of the Serbs, Croats, and Slovenes, soon renamed Yugoslavia. Austria and Hungary were both left reeling at their loss of territory and resources (see Map 27.2).

The settlement with Germany, the Treaty of Versailles (named after the palace where the treaty was signed), was the centerpiece of the Peace of Paris. France recovered Alsace and Lorraine, and Germany was ordered to pay substantial reparations for civilian damage during the war—terms that would cripple the German economy. It was also directed to give up its colonies, reduce its army, stop manufacturing offensive weapons, and deliver a large amount of free coal each year to Belgium and France. The average German saw in the terms of the Treaty of Versailles an unmerited humiliation of "war guilt" that was compounded by Article 231 of the treaty, which assigned "responsibility" for the war to "the aggression of Germany and her allies." Germany, a powerful nation, was branded an outcast in the global community.

Besides redrawing the map of Europe, the diplomats created the **League of Nations**, an organization whose members had a joint responsibility for maintaining peace through negotiation—a principle called **collective security**, which was to replace the divisive secrecy of prewar power politics. In Woodrow Wilson's vision, the League would peacefully guide the world toward disarmament, arbitrate its members' disputes, and monitor labor conditions around the world. However, the U.S. Senate, in an embarrassing defeat for the president, both failed to ratify the peace settlement and refused to join the League. Moreover, both Germany and Russia initially were excluded from the League and were thus blocked from participating in international consensus-building with the forty-two founding member nations. The absence of these three major powers weakened the League as a global peacekeeper from the outset.

The end to imperialism was at the top of many non-Western representatives' agenda, but they were to be denied. The covenant, or charter, of the League of Nations organized the new administration of the surrendered colonies and territories of Germany and the Ottoman Empire through a system of mandates (see Map 27.3). The European powers

League of Nations

League of Nations The international organization set up following World War I to maintain peace by arbitrating disputes and promoting collective security.

collective security The system of international diplomacy, especially involving the peaceful resolution of disputes, established by the League of Nations.

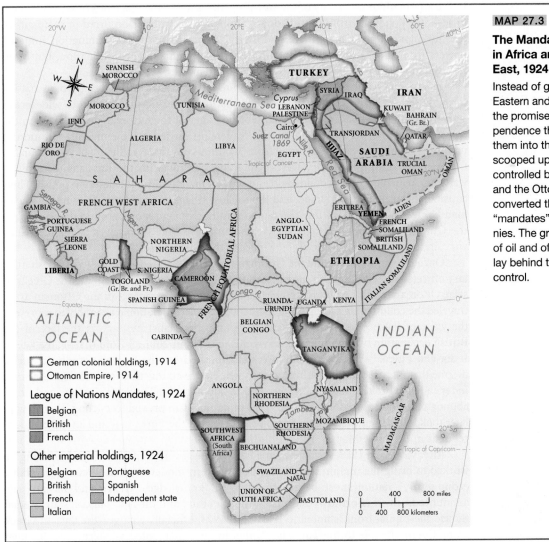

MAP 27.3

The Mandate System in Africa and the Middle East, 1924

Instead of granting Middle Eastern and African peoples the promised rights and independence that had brought them into the war, the Allies scooped up former territories controlled by the Germans and the Ottomans and converted them into "mandates"—in effect, colonies. The growing importance of oil and of other resources lay behind this seizure of control.

Mandate System

exercised political control over mandated territory, but some local leaders retained limited authority. The League covenant justified the **mandate system** as providing governance by "advanced nations" over territories "not yet able to stand by themselves under the strenuous conditions of the modern world."

Not surprisingly, the people of the new mandates were furious. Sharif Husayn ibn Ali had mobilized a substantial force to wage war against the Ottomans because of agreements with Britain for an independent Syria. His son Faisal was humiliated in Paris when it became clear that no such independence was forthcoming. On his return to the Middle East Faisal called on the crowds to "choose either to be slaves or masters of your own destiny."[5] Rebellions against France and Britain erupted in the Middle East, but they were put down. Outside of the Middle East, opponents of colonialism redoubled their organizational efforts in such movements as pan-Africanism, whose members now held regular international meetings with the goal of promoting solidarity among blacks everywhere and, eventually, a vast self-governing union of all African peoples. "Never again will the darker people of the world occupy just the place they had before," the African American leader W.E.B. Du Bois predicted in 1918. The postwar settlements, like the war itself, contributed to renewed activism among colonial peoples around the world.

Struggles for Reform and Independence

In the aftermath of war many of the world's peoples took advantage of Western weakness to seek independence from outside domination. These struggles occurred in remnants of the Ottoman Empire, China, India, and Africa. In the face of such determination, imperial powers from Japan to Britain not only resisted loosening their domination, but often resorted to violence to maintain and expand their empires.

Turkey Emerges from the Ottoman Empire

The Allied invasion of the Ottoman Empire caused chaos and suffering from Anatolia through Syria, Lebanon, and Egypt. Allied blockades during the war led to widespread starvation, and Allied agents provoked rebellion against the Ottoman grip to weaken the empire. From 1915 to 1916 the Ottoman leadership carried out the mass deportation of unknown numbers—estimates range from 300 thousand to 1.5 million—of Armenians in the empire, claiming that they were spying and plotting with the Russians to revolt in wartime. Armenians were rounded up and sent on marches into the desert to perish. Their considerable property was stolen, and their fellow villagers moved into abandoned Armenian homes. Witnesses based in the region sent horrifying reports around the world, but the Ottoman position was that "the Armenians have only themselves to blame." They were, in the words of one official, "a menace to the Turkish race."[6]

Once the war was over and the Ottoman Empire disbanded, determined Turkish military officers resisted the continuing presence of the Allies, who were inciting the Greeks to seize Ottoman lands. Led by General Mustafa Kemal, the remnants of the Ottoman army traveled the countryside calling for a democratically elected national assembly to represent the voice of the people. Kemal preached an anti-imperialist message in the face of the British occupation of Istanbul: "All we want is to save our country from sharing the fate of India and Egypt."[7] He and his followers also pushed for the primacy of ethnic Turks, despite the presence of many ethnic groups who had lived together for centuries. A war of independence broke out as the Allies tried to suppress the Turkish reformers and bring about a partition of Anatolia, but the spirit of nationalism proved too strong. Kemal, who later took the name Atatürk ("first among Turks"), led the Turks to found an independent republic in 1923 (see Map 27.4).

After victory in 1923, Kemal became head of the government. From the beginning he worked to bring the region into the orbit of Western modernity and to craft a capitalist economy. "A nation must be strong in spirit, knowledge, science and morals," he announced.[8] In an effort to Westernize Turkish culture and the new Turkish state, Kemal moved the capital from Istanbul to Ankara in 1923, officially changed the ancient Greek name *Constantinople* to the Turkish *Istanbul* in 1930, mandated Western dress for men

mandate system A system of regional control over former Ottoman lands awarded by the League of Nations' charter to the victors in World War I.

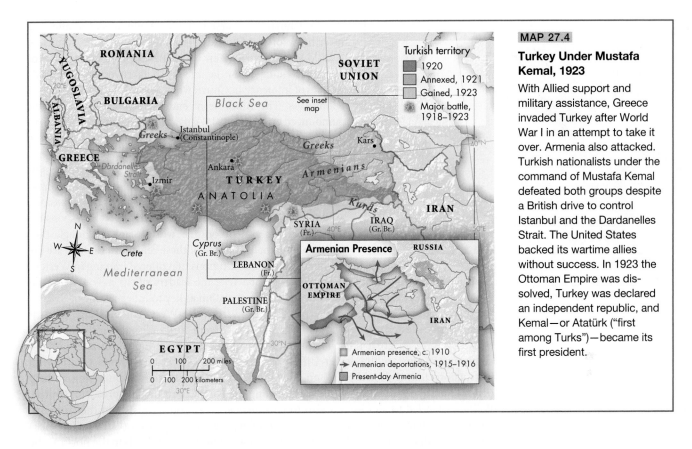

MAP 27.4

Turkey Under Mustafa Kemal, 1923

With Allied support and military assistance, Greece invaded Turkey after World War I in an attempt to take it over. Armenia also attacked. Turkish nationalists under the command of Mustafa Kemal defeated both groups despite a British drive to control Istanbul and the Dardanelles Strait. The United States backed its wartime allies without success. In 1923 the Ottoman Empire was dissolved, Turkey was declared an independent republic, and Kemal—or Atatürk ("first among Turks")—became its first president.

and women, introduced the Latin alphabet, and abolished polygamy. Ordinary people reacted to their world being turned topsy-turvy: "It's a Christian hat," a barber warned to a young soldier sporting a Western-style hat as part of his uniform. "If a Muslim puts such a shocking thing on his head the good God will surely punish him."[9] In 1936, women received the vote and were made eligible to serve in the parliament.

Reform in Turkey, 1923

Like many colonized countries and those seeking to free themselves from Western control, Turkey under Atatürk considered the condition of women an important element of modernization. Atatürk decreed that women and men alike should dress in Western clothes, receive a secular education, and switch from the Arabic to the Latin alphabet. There was much for the citizens of the new Turkey to learn and unlearn; women were at the center of this nation-building process, as we see in this image from a Turkish classroom. (Gamma-Keystone via Getty Images.)

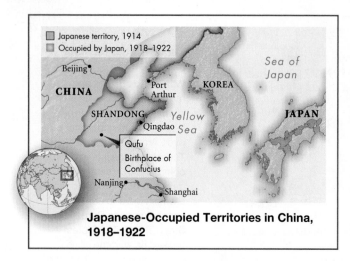

Japanese-Occupied Territories in China, 1918–1922

In China, the course of nation building stalled after the overthrow of the Qing dynasty in 1912, but the results of World War I gave it a new boost. People from many walks of life were outraged by Japan's 1915 takeover of Germany's sphere of influence in China, which included the birthplace of Confucius. The Allies' legal endorsement of that takeover, announced on May 4, 1919, galvanized student protest. Carrying signs that read, "China Belongs to the Chinese," they were joined by dockworkers, business people, and others from different walks of life. Among the middle and educated classes, the May 4th movement also targeted Chinese traditions— from Confucian values such as patriarchal control of women and the young to educational "backwardness"—as responsible for China's treatment on the world stage. Although they detested imperialism, some of these reformers came to see the value of Christian institutions that offered training in Western

China Seeks a Modern Government

languages, modern science, and political theory. Like the leaders of the new Turkey and Meiji Japan, they had come to see selective Westernization as key to independence.

Many other Chinese, however, turned away from the West. Students and workers declared that Western leaders at the Paris conference were "still selfish and militaristic and that they were all great liars," as one student put it.[10] Some adopted an alternative— communism—just as the Soviet Union sent aid to the Chinese Communist Party with instructions that it should help Sun Yatsen's nationalist party, the Guomindang, to help organize and politicize the people (see Reading the Past: Communism Spreads in China). Politicization led to strikes, but also to tensions between Communists and the Guomindang, which had been taken over by the military leader Jiang Jieshi (Chiang Kai-Shek) after the death of Sun in 1925. Jiang led his troops to put down warlords to the north as the beginning of reunification. As he took the cities of Nanjing and Shanghai, his followers murdered the Communists in hopes of stopping their influence for good. Jiang then turned to mobilizing his countrymen for modernization.

Ireland Demands Independence

War and its aftermath inspired other attempts at liberation from combatant countries. In Ireland, pro-independence activists attacked government buildings in Dublin on Easter Monday 1916, in an effort to gain Irish freedom from Britain. Ill-prepared, their Easter rebellion was easily defeated and many of them were executed. Demands for home rule only intensified, and in January 1919, republican leaders proclaimed Ireland's independence from Britain. Instead of granting it, the British government sent in the "Black and Tans," a volunteer army of demobilized soldiers—so called for the color of their uniforms. Terror reigned in Ireland, as both the pro-independence forces and the Black and Tans waged guerrilla warfare, taking hostages, blowing up buildings, and even shooting into crowds at soccer matches. By 1921 public outrage at the violence forced the British to negotiate a treaty. The Irish Free State was declared a self-governing dominion owing allegiance to the British crown. Northern Ireland, a group of six northern counties containing many Protestants, gained a separate status as a self-governing British territory with representation in the British Parliament. Partial independence and the rights of religious minorities remained contentious issues, producing violence for decades thereafter.

Ireland, 1921

Colonized peoples rose up after the war in virtually every empire. Those who had fought expected the rights that European politicians and military recruiters had solemnly promised in exchange for service. Instead, they met worsening conditions at home. "Is our reward to have our tax raised . . . and for our ownership of land to be called

Communism Spreads in China

Communism was one alternative for middle- and upper-class Chinese reformers angry that the Western powers had given part of their country to Japan at the Peace of Paris. In this passage, P'eng P'ai, son of a prosperous landowning family, recounts the creation in the early 1920s of the Hai-Feng Peasant Union in the early 1920s based on Communist ideas. P'eng P'ai himself had much to learn about building a mass movement. At first he searched out peasant activists while wearing a fancy, Western-style white suit and a white hat; most of the peasants fled. After changing his clothing to simpler attire, P'eng had greater success. The Peasant Union grew to more than twenty thousand out of a population of one hundred thousand and undertook a range of activities to protect peasant livelihoods. Below are some of the Union's activities.

> [W]e found that some peasants would try to get others' land to till, and landlords would increase rent and change tenants. So the Union drew up some regulations to prevent such incidents.
>
> 1. Unless permission is given by the member and by the Union, no one may encroach on a member's rented land.
> 2. Unless a member relinquishes his lease and the Union gives its permission, no one may rent the land already rented to a member of the Union. Violators are subject to severe punishment.
> 3. In case a landlord takes back his land from a member by means of increasing the rent, and as a result a member's livelihood is in danger, he may ask for help from the Union, which will either persuade nearby members to allow him to till part of their land, or will introduce him to another trade.
>
> After the regulations were publicized, there was no longer any competition for land among our members, and the landlords also were afraid to raise the rent of members of the Union. . . .
>
> Soon it was Chinese New Year of 1923. Dragon dancers and music troupes from all the villages came to celebrate, and the Union organized a New Year's Festival for all peasants in Hai-Feng. . . . More than six thousand members and three thousand non-members participated and the banners of each village's bands, dragon dancers, and music troupes danced in the open air. . . . The speakers . . . pointed out that before the proletarian revolution was realized, there could be no joyous New Year, for New Year's Day was a time for the exploiters to oppress us and to demand us to pay our debts. We were now united in our hardships, not in joy. However, this was an opportunity in which we might demonstrate our strength to our enemies and awaken the spirit of revolution in ourselves. We were prepared for a battle with our enemies. This was the reason why, on the one hand, we felt weighed down by our emotions, but on the other hand elated.
>
> On that day, we issued two thousand new membership cards, and received over four hundred dollars in dues.

Patricia Buckley Ebrey. Adapted with permission of Free Press, a division of Simon & Schuster, Inc., from *Chinese Civilization and Society: A Sourcebook* by Patricia Buckley Ebrey. Copyright © 1981 by The Free Press. All rights reserved.

Source: Patricia B. Ebrey, ed., *Chinese Civilization and Society: A Sourcebook* (New York: Free Press, 1981), 273, 276.

EXAMINING THE EVIDENCE

1. What types of activities did the Hai-Feng Peasant Union sponsor, and why did these activities prove effective?

2. What would lead peasants to fear the Union, and what would make them want to join it?

3. What insight into mass movements does this document provide?

into question?" one group of East Africans asked in 1921 (see Reading the Past: Léopold Sédar Senghor, "To the Senegalese Soldiers Who Died for France").[11]

Rebellions mostly met a brutal response. Fearful of losing India, British forces shot into crowds of protesters at Amritsar in 1919 and put down revolts in Egypt and Iran in the early 1920s. The Dutch jailed political leaders in Indonesia; the French punished Indochinese nationalists; and in 1929 the British crushed Ibo women's tax protest. Maintaining empires abroad was crucial to covering debts incurred during World War I, spurring colonial rule to become more brutal in the face of protest.

Protesting Colonization

Léopold Sédar Senghor, "To the Senegalese Soldiers Who Died for France"

Among the colonial troops in World War I were the Senegalese Sharpshooters, who fought on the side of their French imperial masters. Though the Senegalese riflemen served on the front lines, they received little credit from the French and were even forced to march around, rather than through, villages so that white citizens would not have to set eyes on black soldiers. They were immortalized in a poem by Léopold Sédar Senghor, who himself fought in the French colonial forces and who became the first president of an independent Senegal in 1960. Among the thousands of poems memorializing World War I, the one from which this excerpt was taken also served as Senegal's national anthem after liberation.

> They put flowers on tombs and warm the Unknown
>   Soldier.
> But you, my dark brothers, no one calls your names.
> . . .
> Listen to me, Senegalese soldiers, in the solitude of the
>   black ground
> And of death, in your deaf and blind solitude,
> More than I in my dark skin in the depths of the Province,
> Without even the warmth of your comrades lying close
>   to you,
> As in the trenches back then or the village palavers
>   [conversations] long ago,
> . . .
> We bring you, listen to us, we who spelled your names
> In the months of your deaths, we bring you,
> In these fearful days without memory,

The friendship of your age-mates.
> Ah! If I could one day sing in a voice glowing like embers,
> If I could praise the friendship of comrades as fervent
> And delicate as entrails, as strong as tendons.
> Listen to us, you Dead stretched out in water as far as
> The northern and eastern fields.
> Receive this red earth, under a summer sun this soil
> Reddened with the blood of white hosts
> Receive the salute of your black comrades,
> Senegalese soldiers
> WHO DIED FOR THE REPUBLIC!

Source: Léopold Sédar Senghor, *The Collected Poetry*, trans. Melvin Dixon (Charlottesville: University Press of Virginia, 1991), 46–47.

EXAMINING THE EVIDENCE

1. What emotions and values does Senghor express in this poem?

2. What views of World War I does the poem reveal?

3. Why do you think Senghor wrote this poem, and for whom?

4. Why would this poem about a specific group of people fighting on behalf of imperial powers become the national anthem of an independent country?

Postwar Imperial Expansion

Amid protest, imperialism reached its high tide in the 1920s and 1930s. Britain and France, enjoying control of Germany's African colonies and former Ottoman lands in the Middle East, were at the height of their global power. A new generation of adventurers headed for Middle Eastern and Indonesian oil fields, as the importance of oil increased along with the number of automobiles, airplanes, trucks, ships, and oil-heated homes. Investors from the United States and elsewhere grabbed land in the Caribbean and across Latin America, cornering markets in sugar, cocoa, and tropical fruit that were becoming a regular part of the Western diet. Competition for territory and business was alive and well.

The balance of power among the imperial nations was shifting, however. The most important change was Japan's growing competitiveness for markets, resources, and influence. During the war, Japanese output of industrial goods such as ships and metal grew some 40 percent because the Western powers outsourced their wartime needs for such products. As Japan took shipping, financial, and other business from Britain and France, its prosperity skyrocketed and officials touted its success as the key to an Asia free from Westerners. Ardently nationalist, the Japanese government was not yet strong enough to challenge Western powers militarily. Thus, although outraged at Wilson's abrupt rejection (with British backing) of a nondiscrimination clause in the charter of the League of Nations put forward by the Japanese, Japan cooperated in the Anglo-American-dominated peace, even agreeing both to restore Chinese possessions and to keep a ratio of English, American, and Japanese shipbuilding at 5:5:3 respectively. "Rolls Royce, Rolls Royce, Ford," a Japanese official commented bitterly.[12] This bitterness ultimately festered into war.

An Age of the Masses

War and revolutions demonstrated the centrality of the masses to modern life. With the collapse of autocratic governments from China to Germany, the sense of democratic potential based on mass participation grew. The condition of women came to symbolize the strength of the masses, which was reflected in the extension of the vote to many Western women during the 1920s. Modernizing the economy—a goal of many countries after the war—meant developing mass consumerism, while modern technology provided mass entertainment and news across the globe. By the end of the decade, a handful of political leaders were adopting new media to mobilize their citizenry.

> **FOCUS**
> How did the rise of mass society affect politics, culture, and everyday life around the world?

Mass Society

The development of mass society was a global phenomenon, fueled by the growing connections among economies. Urbanization surged in Asia, Latin America, Africa, and the United States as populations exploded and rural people migrated to cities in search of work. Global population, aided by the spread of medicine and improved sanitation, also soared. Tokyo had some 3.5 million inhabitants in 1920, New York 5.5 million, and Shanghai over 2 million. Calcutta's population quadrupled to 1.8 million from the late nineteenth century to 1920. City life was fast paced, brimming with trams, buses, and automobiles; in China rickshaws with cushioned wheels pulled by fast young men replaced the leisurely sedan chair as the conveyance of choice. Tall buildings lifted skylines, first in New York with its much-admired Chrysler and Empire State buildings, but soon in cities throughout the world. New urban cultural livelihoods arose, such as performing jazz and managing nightclubs. Across the globe class distinctions were blurred in the confusion of city life. Outside city centers, wealthy suburbs and exclusive beachside retreats flourished, such as that near the city of Bombay, India, started by the Tata family of industrialists (whom we met in Chapter 24). This mass society centered in cities depended on economic modernization—most notably, mass production and its byproduct, mass unionization.

Mass Production

Trade revived in the 1920s, and wartime innovations spurred new industries and created new jobs making cars, electrical products, and synthetic goods for peacetime use. The prewar pattern of mergers and cartels continued after 1918, giving rise to multinational food-processing firms such as Nestlé in Switzerland and global petroleum enterprises such as Royal Dutch Shell. Owners of these large manufacturing conglomerates wielded more financial and political power than entire small countries. By the late 1920s, many in Asia and Europe had survived the wild economic swings of the immediate postwar years to enjoy renewed economic growth.

Among economic leaders, the United States had become the trendsetter in modernization. Businessmen from around the world made pilgrimages to Henry Ford's Detroit assembly line, which by 1929 produced a Ford automobile every ten seconds. Ford claimed that this miracle of productivity resulted in a lower cost of living and increased purchasing power for workers, and indeed some 17 million cars were on U.S. streets by 1925. The new livelihood of scientific manager also played a part, as efficiency experts developed methods to streamline workers' tasks and motions for maximum productivity. Despite the rewards, many workers found the emphasis on efficiency inhumane, with restrictions on time and motion so severe that often they were allowed to use the bathroom only on a fixed schedule.

"When I left the factory, it followed me," wrote one French automobile worker. "In my dreams I was a machine."

Increased Unionization

As industry spread, the number of people in unions increased around the world, with both skilled and unskilled workers organizing to advance their collective interests. Sometimes the reasons for joining were basic: local workers on the French railroads in West Africa complained of "unsanitary food seasoned with dried fish and full of worms" and began unionizing.[13] White-collar workers and government clerks also had large, effective unions. Where male workers' jobs were threatened by laborsaving machinery, unions usually agreed with employers that women should receive lower wages, saving scarce high-paying jobs for men. Under these circumstances, women's participation in union activity was proportionally lower than men's.

Because they could mobilize masses of people, unions played a key role in politics, as they demonstrated when unionized workers in China struck against Britain's control of Hong Kong. "Down with imperialism!" was one of their cries, and they forced merchants to show that their goods did not originate in Britain.[14] India's ongoing industrialization during the war provided jobs, but in the postwar period some 125,000 Bombay textile workers were among those who struck to get their share of the profits. The British sent airplanes to attack strikers, first strafing civilians in 1920s India. As labor flexed its muscle around the world, union members blocked coups against Germany's newly elected democratic government, the Weimar Republic, and organized a general strike in Great Britain in the 1920s.

Changing Class Distinctions

Modernization and rising global productivity affected traditional social divisions. Advances in industrialization boosted the size of the modern middle class by expanding the need for managers and professionals and for skilled workers in new jobs. Often these opportunities reduced the influence of traditional elites and made society more complex in colonized areas such as India, where a modern working class and financial and industrialist classes grew alongside caste and religious divisions. Reformers such as those in China's May 4th movement pointed to the irrationality of traditional patterns of deference within families.

Class and racial prescriptions were also breaking down as a result of the war: men of all classes and ethnicities had served in distant trenches together and were even buried in common graves. As a result of the war, daughters around the world supported themselves in jobs, and their mothers did their own housework because people who once worked as servants could now earn more money in factories. A middle-class "look" became common around the world, promoted by global advertising that appealed to consumers with vivid images of sleek, modern styles.

The "New Woman"

One emblem of postwar modernity in most parts of the world was the "new woman," the "modern girl," or the "flapper," as she was called in the United States. In the 1920s many women around the world cut their hair, abandoned traditional clothes such as kimonos, smoked, had money of their own from working in the service sector, and went out unchaperoned, even dancing with men. Zhu Su'e, born in 1901 to a banking family in Changzhou, China, unbound her feet as a teenager and then left home in 1921 to study in Shanghai. She graduated from law school, married for love instead of having a traditional arranged marriage, and continued her career: "I understood that you must be able to earn money in order to be independent."[15] As an attorney, she often helped women in oppressive marriages, guiding them to become independent and educated. Attempts to impose "modern" standards were often rejected, however. When activists in the USSR urged Muslim women to remove their veils and change their way of life, fervent Muslims often attacked both the activists and the women who followed their advice.

Culture for the Masses

Wartime propaganda had aimed to unite classes, races, and countries against a common enemy. In the 1920s, phonographs, the radio, and film continued the development of mass or standardized culture. Print media, cheaper and more widely distributed to an increasingly literate global population, showed people what to buy and what to wear.

Mass media had the potential to create an informed citizenry, enhance democracy, and promote liberation in the colonies. Paradoxically, it also provided tools for dictatorship. Authoritarian rulers in the Soviet Union, Italy, Japan, and elsewhere were coming to see the advantage of mobilizing the masses through the control of information and culture.

By the 1920s, film flourished around the world, with Shanghai and Hong Kong joining the United States, Europe, and South Asia as important centers of production and regional distribution (see Lives and Livelihoods: The Film Industry). In India, where movie theaters had sprung up at the start of the century in Madras and Bombay, movies retelling the *Mahabharata* and history films on the story of the Taj Mahal developed Indians' sense of a common heritage. Bolshevik leaders underwrote the innovative work of director Sergei Eisenstein, whose films *Potemkin* (1925) and *Ten Days That Shook the World* (1927–1928) presented a Bolshevik view of history to Soviet and many international audiences, spreading standard Communist values. Films also showed the shared predicaments of ordinary people, helping to standardize behavior. Popular comedies of the 1920s and 1930s such as the Shanghai hits *Three Modern Women* (1933) and *New Woman* (1934) showed women viewers the ways of flappers.

Cinematic portrayals also played to postwar fantasies and fears, as threats to class and caste systems shaped movie plots from India to the United States. Impersonators, "gold diggers," and con artists abounded. The plight of gangsters appealed to veterans of revolutions and wars, who had seen that the modern world sometimes placed little value on life. English actor and producer Charlie Chaplin in *Little Tramp* (1914–1915) won international popularity as the defeated hero, the anonymous modern man, trying to keep his dignity in a mechanical world. Sporting events such as cricket, boxing, and martial arts were internationalized, and clips from matches were shown as newsreels before featured movies. As popular films and books crossed national borders, a cosmopolitan, global culture flourished.

Miss Brazil in Texas, 1929

Healthful sports and exercise, feats of daring, and a growing consumerism all signaled postwar revival in many parts of the world. In this photograph, Miss Brazil—an example of the new, modern woman with her trim clothing and cosmetically enhanced face—has traveled to the United States to participate in a beauty contest. International beauty contests introduced consumers around the world to global styles in fashion and self-presentation. (The Granger Collection, New York.)

Film and Radio

Radio was an even newer medium. Developed from the Italian inventor Guglielmo Marconi's wireless technology, radio broadcasts in the first half of the 1920s were heard by mass audiences in public halls (much like film theaters) and featured orchestras and song followed by audience discussion. The radio quickly became a relatively inexpensive consumer item, allowing public events to penetrate private homes. Specialized programming for men (such as sports reporting) and for women (such as advice on home management) soon followed. By the 1930s, politicians used radio to reach the masses wherever they might be—even alone at home.

Mass Marketing

The print media—newspapers and magazines—grew in popularity, and their advertising promoted mass consumption of modern conveniences such as electric clothes washers and irons. Mass marketing encouraged new personal habits, presenting mass-produced razors and deodorants as essential to modern hygiene. Politicians joined in as modernizers: Jiang Jieshi and Bolshevik leaders alike promoted toothpaste and toothbrushing as part of nationbuilding. "New woman" Rilda Marta of South Africa traveled to the United

The Film Industry

Butterfly Hu and Chinese Cinema

By the 1920s films were made and distributed throughout the world. *Twin Sisters* (1933), a product of Shanghai's bustling film industry, focused on the plight of twin sisters—raised apart with utterly different personalities—both played by the Chinese star Butterfly Hu. So easily could distant parts of the world now speak across cultural borders that the movie was a box office hit in China, Southeast Asia, Japan, and western Europe. (Still from "Zi Mei Hua" (Twin Sisters), directed by Zheng Zhengqiu.)

The development of the film industry worldwide from the late nineteenth century on led to the creation of dozens of new livelihoods. Although early films often were the work of a single author-director-cameraman, by the 1920s opportunities for new careers opened up as moviegoing became a mass phenomenon after World War I and as filmmaking itself came to involve many more jobs. Among the most notable new livelihoods were those of screenwriter, cameraman, art editor, and film financier, along with less-renowned jobs for stuntmen, animal trainers, baby actors, and in the United States especially,

States to learn about African American cosmetics and on her return advocated the subtle use of lipstick and rouge: "The key to Happiness and Success is a good appearance," she proclaimed. "You are often judged by how you look."[16] A multibillion-dollar global cosmetics industry sprang up almost overnight, and women from Tokyo to Buenos Aires bought their products to imitate the appearance of film celebrities.

Mobilizing the Masses

The 1920s saw the rise of politicians mobilizing the masses for their political causes. When the Bolsheviks encountered opposition to their rule, for example, they began massive propaganda efforts to bring communism to villages and cities, peasants and workers, and Muslims, Christians, and Jews alike. So successful were these efforts that people around the world came to believe that the USSR was an ideal state, a utopia. In the colonies and mandates, leaders like Mohandas Gandhi in India and groups such as the Muslim Brotherhood in Egypt mobilized the masses around spiritual teachings. In Italy, where postwar resentment simmered, Benito Mussolini first staged a coup and then consolidated his rule with mass propaganda.

Gandhi's Movement in India   From the beginning of the twentieth century, Indian leaders objected to British rule of their country and urged boycotts of British products. Indian activist Mohandas Gandhi (1869–1948) transformed this cause into a nonviolent mass movement that appealed to

film censors. The Chinese focus on martial arts in film increased the number of jobs for and prominence of these experts. Before the "talkies," films with sound, were invented in the 1930s, silent movies featured pianists who provided mood-setting music and soloists who entertained the audience during intermission. In Japan the work of the *benshi* was to explain throughout the film the action on the screen, sometimes even singing and dancing as part of the job.

From Southeast Asia to Central America, lavish cinema houses attracted hundreds of millions of weekly viewers, the majority of them women. The importance of the cinema house itself gave jobs to architects, construction workers, and even the elegant usher, who in some countries accompanied viewers to their seats in exchange for a tip. With India producing some fifteen hundred films of its own between 1912 and 1927, the need for all the accoutrements of film viewing provided a rich array of livelihoods.

In the 1920s the "star" system developed, turning performers from humble backgrounds in burlesque or comedy into national, even global, celebrities. In Japan's thriving film industry, almost all stars were men, who played both male and female roles as they had done in kabuki and Noh theater (discussed in Chapter 21). By contrast, in China, the highest-paid star was the actress Butterfly Hu, who made her film debut in 1925 and starred in the first "talkie," *Sing Song Red Peony*, in 1930. Butterfly Hu also filled the pages of the print media as she became a style setter in terms of fashion and grooming. Hu, like other stars, was promoted by professional publicists and hired agents and managers, still other new livelihoods. Media entrepreneurs earned a handsome living founding magazines and engaging Hu and others to sell products. New lines of work opened for journalists to provide gossip about film celebrities, biographies of directors, and reviews of films. Celebrity for a few men and women in the film industry spawned hundreds of new livelihoods across mass culture.

QUESTIONS TO CONSIDER

1. What skills did those working in the film industry need, and to what extent were they new?

2. What accounts for the popularity of cinema in these decades?

3. In what ways was film important to global culture and the world economy?

For Further Information:
Grieveson, Lee, and Peter Krämer, eds. *The Silent Cinema Reader*. 2004.
Sklar, Robert. *A World History of Film*. 2002.
Wada-Marciano, Mitsuyo. *Nippon Modern: Japanese Cinema of the 1920s and 1930s*. 2008.
Zhang, Yingjin. *Cinema and Urban Culture in Shanghai, 1922–1943*. 1999.

millions. Born of middle-class parents in a village on the west coast of India, Gandhi studied law in England and then began practice in the Indian community in South Africa. The racism he experienced there made him determined to liberate the Indian masses from British imperialism. When he returned to India permanently in 1915, he began a full-time drive for Hind Swaraj (HIHND swah-RAJ), or Indian Home Rule, to escape the violent, even genocidal values of Westerners engaged in world war. Using the media and making speeches, he challenged the view that Britain was "civilized" and thus worthy of respect. To Gandhi's way of thinking his fellow citizens had the story backward. South Asia had a very long tradition of civilization, he pointed out, while Britain and other Western countries, above all the United States, valued only one thing: material wealth. "Many problems can be solved," Gandhi wrote early in his career, "by remembering that money is their God."[17]

Gandhi envisioned a nonviolent return to an India of small self-sufficient communities in which people grew their own food and spun the cloth for their own clothes. Rejecting the modernization brought by factories and railroads, he dressed in a simple loincloth and shawl made from cloth he had woven himself. For Gandhi, the root cause of India's subjection was that Indian merchants had handed the country over to "Satanic" Western values and turned away from the Indian goals of contemplation and humility. He opposed scientific developments such as birth control and rejected the modern sensibility that wanted to eliminate the caste system.

Sheikh Hassan al-Banna, Founder of the Muslim Brotherhood

Sheikh Hassan al-Banna founded the Muslim Brotherhood in 1928 and worked to make it a mass movement that would revive the standing of Islam and Muslim culture in the world. Dismayed at the respect given Western culture and the power of the West's economy, al-Banna built his organization as a counterweight. His commitment to anti-colonialism and Islamic values made him an enemy of the West's allies in the Middle East; they had him assassinated in 1949. (AFP/Getty Images.)

New Economic Policy Lenin's compromise with capitalism that allowed peasants to sell their grain on the market and entrepreneurs to engage in trade and keep the profits.

fascism A political movement originating in postwar Italy under Mussolini that stressed the primacy of the state over the individual and the importance of violence and warfare in making nations strong.

In rejecting the West, Gandhi's resembled another potent organization for the empowerment of ordinary people—the Muslim Brotherhood, founded in Egypt in 1928. This organization called for a return to Islam along with a rejection of the secular, "modern" mindset. "Islam is the solution" was the Brotherhood's watchword as it sought to end British influence in the country. Like Gandhi's movement, the Muslim Brotherhood would grow in mass appeal.

In contrast, communism promised a shining future and a modern, technological culture. The reality was that workers' living conditions declined while Communist Party supervisors enjoyed a privileged life. In the early 1920s, workers, sailors, and peasant bands alike revolted against harsh Bolshevik policies toward ordinary people. The government had many of the rebels shot, but as production dropped to 13 percent of its prewar output, Lenin changed course. His **New Economic Policy** compromised with capitalism by allowing peasants to sell their grain freely and entrepreneurs to engage in trade and keep the profits. More food soon became available, and some peasants and merchants did indeed prosper.

Nonetheless, grassroots opposition drove the Bolsheviks to make communism not just a political ideology but a cultural reality that would guide the masses' daily lives and reshape their thoughts. Party leaders invaded the countryside to set up classes on a variety of political subjects, and volunteers pushed the importance of literacy—on the eve of World War I, less than half the people in the USSR could read. As commissar for public welfare, Aleksandra Kollontai promoted birth-control education, classes in "domestic science," and the establishment of day care for children of working parents. To advance literacy, she wrote simply worded novels about love and work in the new socialist state. The government tried to develop a mass proletarian culture through workers' universities, a workers' theater, and workers' publishing. For many, it worked: as one teacher and worker on a veterinary farm wrote in her diary, "I have discovered a new world for me in Marxism. I read with deep interest."[18]

Authoritarian rule came as well to Italy, though of a different nature from communism. Benito Mussolini (1883–1945) came to power as a mass hero. Since the late nineteenth century, some Europeans had come to blame their parliaments for economic ills. Thus many Italians were enthusiastic when Mussolini, a socialist journalist who had turned to the radical right, built a personal army called the "Black Shirts" of veterans and the unemployed and used it to overturn parliamentary government. In 1922, his supporters, known as Fascists, started a march on Rome, leading to Mussolini's appointment as prime minister. Although in theory he ruled with the consent of the masses, Mussolini consolidated his power by making criticism of the state a criminal offense, violently attacking opposition, and beating up striking workers. Yet the sight of hundreds of Black Shirts marching through the streets like disciplined soldiers signaled to many Italians that their country was ordered and modern.

Besides violence, Mussolini used mass propaganda and the media to promote traditional values and prejudices, though **fascism**, unlike communism, was never an organized set of principles, except for the principle that the state had supremacy over the people. Peasant men huddled around radios to hear him call for a "battle of wheat" to enhance farm productivity on behalf of the state. Peasant women worshiped him for appearing to value motherhood as a patriotic calling. In the cities the government built strikingly modern buildings and broad avenues for Fascist parades. Despite these signs of modernity, Mussolini introduced a "corporate" state that denied individual rights in favor of duty to the state, as in wartime. Decrees in 1926 outlawed independent labor unions, replacing them with state-controlled employer and worker groups, or corporations, that would settle grievances and determine conditions of work. Mussolini cut women's wages and banned women from the professions, confining them to menial and low-paying jobs. His popularity soared among war-torn men, making him a model for other militaristic leaders.

COUNTERPOINT
A Golden Age for Argentineans

World War I allowed some societies outside of Europe to flourish. Both Japan and Australia increased their trade during the war. Indian entrepreneurs, aided by nationalist boycotts of British goods early in the twentieth century, continued to build metallurgical and other factories, substituting their goods for those of the warring European powers. In the Western Hemisphere, as European, Mexican, and other leaders were marching their nations down the road to war, Argentineans were experiencing a "golden age" that offered a stark contrast to the suffering elsewhere.

> **FOCUS**
>
> In what ways did Argentina's history differ from that of countries caught up in World War I?

A Flourishing Economy and Society

Starting in the 1880s, immigrants flocked to Argentina. Between 1900 and the outbreak of World War I in 1914, hundreds of thousands of newcomers moved to the bustling commercial city of Buenos Aires and the surrounding area. Argentina offered a rich, exciting blend of livelihoods, as traders imported European goods and as ranchers supplied world markets with leather, meat, and agricultural products. Industry was also taking off in Argentina, adding a new, more prosperous type of worker to the laboring classes.

World War I broke Argentina's dependence on Britain's economy and turned its productivity inward, so that after the war the economy continued to grow even into the Great Depression of the 1930s (discussed in the next chapter). The landed elites controlled Argentina's politics for most of this time, although strikers and anarchists made vocal demands for change. Reform came in 1912 when President Roque Sáenz Peña, an outspoken advocate of honest government, ushered in universal and obligatory voting by secret ballot for all men. This led to the election in 1916 of Radical Civil Union leader Hipólito Yrigoyen, a candidate whose popularity with workers and the middle classes made for relatively stable politics. Instead of experiencing the surge of extremism seen in Russia and Italy, the Argentinean political scene remained relatively moderate during these years.

Argentina, c. 1920

But there was one glaring exception. In December of 1918, workers began a general strike, forcing the government to step in and negotiate in mid-January. Despite the successful end to the strike, the middle and upper classes, many of European heritage, began looking for scapegoats, encouraging vigilante groups to turn on Jews. From January 10 to 14, 1919, these groups attacked Jewish property and arrested Jews. This anti-Semitic frenzy, called the "tragic week," would repeat itself in the 1960s and 1970s in Argentina.

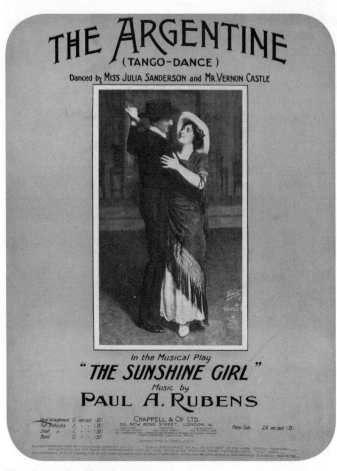

The Argentine Tango

The tango developed in the cafés frequented by the sailors, dockworkers, and sex workers of Argentina at the turn of the twentieth century. Starting in what was then considered low-life society, this creation of Argentina's golden age subsequently traveled to Europe, where it underwent some modification and then returned to the Americas as a newly respectable if somewhat daring dance. During the twentieth century many elements of popular culture, including films, jazz, and, more recently, video games and hip-hop music, followed complicated routes in their development, much like the tango. (Music Division, The New York Public Library for the Performing Arts, Astor, Lenox, and Tilden Foundations.)

Argentina's Cultural Riches

Argentina's overall climate of growth, prosperity, and immigration helped spark an outburst of cultural creativity. A rich working-class culture brought the world the tango, an erotic modern dance improvised from African, Spanish, and local music. Danced either by a man and woman or by two men together, the tango's sensuality shocked Argentina's polite society while it spread to dance halls and nightclubs around the world.

A participant in the 1920s cultural life of Buenos Aires was poet, essayist, and short story writer Jorge Luis Borges, one of the leading authors of the twentieth century. Determined to move beyond the fashionable literary modernism then shaping Latin America writing, Borges was fascinated both with questions of personal identity, including his own and his ancestors', and with the mysteries of learning, remembering, and forgetting. "Seek for the pleasure of seeking, not of finding," Borges wrote, and his whole life seemed more concerned with disorder than with order, as was suggested by his imagined "Chinese encyclopedia," which divided animals into categories from "belonging to the Emperor" to "that from a long way off look like flies." As he wrote,

> I think about things that might have been and never
>   were . . .
> The vast empire the Vikings declined to found.
> The globe without the wheel, or without the rose.
> John Donne's judgment of Shakespeare.
> The unicorn's other horn.
> The fabled Irish bird which alights in two places at
>   once.
> The child I never had.[19]

Borges's imagination laid the groundwork for "magical realism," the late-twentieth-century movement in Latin American fiction from Gabriel Garcia Marquez and Isabel Allende, among many others. Even as much of Latin America, including Argentina, came to feel economic stresses as the century advanced, the golden-age culture has remained powerful down to the present day.

Conclusion

Competition among nations and the clash of classes led to the loss of tens of millions of lives in the decade between 1910 and 1920. Major dynasties were destroyed and governments overthrown, the aristocratic classes collapsed, and millions more suffered starvation, disease, and permanent disability. The decade changed political institutions around the world, leading to demands for national liberation and for collective security such as that provided in the League of Nations. While dynasties fell, the centralization of power increased the scope of the nation-state. Internationally, the Peace of Paris that settled World War I rearranged the map of Europe and parts of the world beyond, dismantling the Habsburg and Ottoman empires into new, intentionally small states in eastern and central Europe—a settlement that, given the dense intermingling of ethnicities, religions, and languages in the area, failed to guarantee a peaceful future. Some political leaders, such as Emiliano Zapata in Mexico and Mustafa Kemal in Turkey, were inspired by Western ideals and models; others, such as Mohandas Gandhi in India, rejected them. In the midst of it all, the United States rose to the status of a world power.

Just as modern warfare had introduced mass armies, world war furthered the development of mass society and culture. It leveled social classes on the battlefield and in the graveyard and standardized beliefs and behaviors, first through wartime propaganda and then through postwar popular culture. Production techniques improved during wartime were turned in peacetime to churning out consumer goods and technological innovations such as air transport, cinema, and radio transmission for greater numbers of people. By the end of the 1920s, mass culture was a key ingredient in politicians' efforts to continue mobilizing the masses as they had in wartime. Among the leaders who saw cultural issues as central to reshaping society were Lenin, Gandhi, and Mussolini. The global economic collapse of 1929 would lead to further mobilization of the masses, this time to support cruel dictators and even genocide.

NOTES

1. Plan de Ayala, quoted in Manuel Plana, *Pancho Villa et la Révolution Mexicaine*, trans. Bruno Gaudenzi (Florence, Italy: Castermann, 1993), 28.
2. Wang Jingwei, quoted in Prasenjit Duara, *Rescuing History from the Nation: Questioning Narratives of Modern China* (Chicago: University of Chicago Press, 1995), 141.
3. Anonymous letter, 17 February 1915, in David Omissi, ed., *Indian Voices of the Great War: Soldiers' Letters, 1914–1918* (London: Macmillan, 1919), 38.
4. Quoted in Oscar J. Martinez, *Fragments of the Mexican Revolution: Personal Accounts from the Border* (Albuquerque: University of New Mexico Press, 1983), 52.
5. Quoted in Margaret Macmillan, *Paris 1919: Six Months That Changed the World* (New York: Random House, 2001), 403.
6. Quoted in Merrill Peterson, *"Starving Armenians": America and the Armenian Genocide, 1915–1930* (Charlottesville: University of Virginia Press, 2004), 48.
7. Quoted in Andrew Mango, *Atatürk: The Biography of the Founder of Modern Turkey* (Woodstock, NY: Overlook, 1999), 278.
8. Quoted in Mango, *Atatürk*, 219.
9. Irfan Organ, *Portrait of a Turkish Family* (London: Eland, 1993), 223.
10. Quoted in Macmillan, *Paris 1919*, 340.
11. Quoted in Geoffrey Hodges, "Military Labour in East Africa," in Melvin Eugene Page, ed., *Africa and the First World War* (New York: St. Martin's Press, 1987), 146.
12. Quoted in Sally Marks, *The Ebbing of European Ascendancy: An International History of the World, 1914–1945* (London: Arnold, 2002), 219.
13. Quoted in Babacar Fall, *Le travail force en Afrique occidentale française (1900–1946)* (Paris: Karthala, 1993), 181.
14. Quoted in Michael Tsin, *Nation, Governance, and Modernity in China: Canton, 1900–1927* (Palo Alto, CA: Stanford University Press, 1999), 151.
15. Quoted in Wang Zheng, *Women in the Chinese Enlightenment: Oral and Textual Histories* (Berkeley: University of California Press, 1999), 196.
16. Quoted in Lynn Thomas, "The Modern Girl and Racial Respectability in South Africa," *Journal of African History* 47 (2006): 3, 485.
17. Mohandas Gandhi, "Hind Swaraj," in *The Collected Works of Mahatma Gandhi* (Ahmedabad: Navjivan Trust, Government of India, Publications Division, 1963), 23.
18. Quoted in Jochen Hellbeck, *Revolution on My Mind: Writing a Diary Under Stalin* (Cambridge, MA: Harvard University Press, 2006), 146.
19. Jorge Luis Borges, "Things That Might Have Been," in *Selected Poems*, ed. Alexander Coleman (New York: Viking, 1999), 405.

RESOURCES FOR RESEARCH

Revolutions, Local Wars, and World War

The revolutionary and military enthusiasm of the second decade of the twentieth century was almost unprecedented in history, as nations and monarchies experienced bloodshed and political upheaval. The following selections provide either a broad picture of events or individual accounts of warfare.

Gordon, David B. *Sun Yatsen: Seeking a Newer China.* 2009.

Hart, Paul. *Bitter Harvest: The Social Transformation of Morelos, Mexico, and the Origins of the Zapatista Revolution, 1840–1910.* 2005.

Lear, John. *Workers, Neighbors, and Citizens: The Revolution in Mexico City.* 2001.

Morrow, John J. *The Great War: An Imperial History.* 2005.

Paice, Edward. *World War I: The African Front.* 2011.

Revolution in Russia and the End of World War I

The Russian Revolution was a cataclysmic event with worldwide repercussions throughout the twentieth century. Healy shows the suffering that occurred in Vienna, whereas Roshwald captures the ethnic chaos that existed in the wake of war and revolution.

Healy, Maureen. *Vienna and the Fall of the Habsburg Empire: Total War and Everyday Life in World War I.* 2004.

Holquist, Peter. *Making War, Forging Revolution: Russia's Continuum of Crisis, 1914–1921.* 2002.

Phillips, Howard, and David Killingray, eds. *The Spanish Influenza Epidemic of 1918–1919: New Perspectives.* 2003.

Reynolds, Michael A. *Shattering Empires: The Clash and Collapse of the Ottoman and Russian Empires, 1908–1918.* 2011.

Roshwald, Aviel. *Ethnic Nationalism and the Fall of Empires: Central Europe, Russia and the Middle East, 1914–1923.* 2001.

Postwar Global Politics

Politicians reworked the international order in the 1920s, with mixed results. One of the most striking leaders of this period is Mustafa Kemal (Atatürk), creator of modern Turkey. Mango's biography captures the difficulty of Atatürk's task, especially in the face of international opposition from the Western powers.

Callahan, Michael D. *A Sacred Trust: The League of Nations and Africa, 1929–1946.* 2005.

Macmillan, Margaret. *Paris 1919: Six Months That Changed the World.* 2001.

Manela, Erez. *The Wilsonian Moment: Self-Determination and the International Origins of Anti-Colonial Nationalism.* 2007.

Mango, Andrew. *Atatürk: The Biography of the Founder of Modern Turkey.* 1999.

Marks, Sally. *The Ebbing of European Ascendancy: An International History of the World, 1914–1945.* 2002.

An Age of the Masses

Radio, film, and print media expanded people's access to information and general culture during the 1920s and in so doing helped create mass society. Vaughan and Lewis's anthology shows the impact of the media on postrevolutionary Mexico.

Helstosky, Carol. *Garlic and Oil: The Politics of Food in Italy.* 2004.

Hu, Jubin. *Projecting a Nation: Chinese National Cinema Before 1949.* 2003.

Northrup, Douglas. *Veiled Empire: Gender and Power in Stalinist Central Asia.* 2004.

Vaughan, Mary Kay, and Stephen E. Lewis, eds. *The Eagle and the Virgin: Nation and Cultural Revolution in Mexico, 1920–1940.* 2006.

Weinbaum, Alys Eve, et al. *Modern Girl Around the World: Consumption, Modernity, and Globalization.* 2008.

COUNTERPOINT: A Golden Age for Argentineans

While much of the world suffered intense disruption during the early twentieth century, the period constituted a "golden age" in Argentina. The works below draw a picture of that multifaceted prosperity.

Rodriguez, Julia. *Civilizing Argentina: Science, Medicine, and the Modern State.* 2006.

Romero, Luis Alberto. *A History of Argentina in the Twentieth Century.* Translated by James P. Brennan. 2002.

Woodall, James. *Borges: A Life.* 1996.

▶ **For additional primary sources from this period,** see *Sources of Crossroads and Cultures.*

▶ **For Web sites, images, and documents related to topics in this chapter,** see Make History at bedfordstmartins.com/smith.

The major global development in this chapter ▶ The wars of the decade 1910 to 1920 and their role in the creation of mass culture and society.

IMPORTANT EVENTS

1910	Mexican Revolution begins
1911–1912	Revolutionaries overthrow Qing dynasty in China
1912	First Balkan War
1913	Second Balkan War
1914	World War I begins
1917	Russian Revolution begins; United States enters World War I; Lenin returns to Russia
1918	Bolsheviks take full control of Russian government; Treaty of Brest-Litovsk; armistice ends World War I
1919	Germany forms Weimar Republic; May 4th movement in China
1919–1920	Treaties comprising Peace of Paris signed, including the Treaty of Versailles with Germany
1920s	Mohandas Gandhi's nonviolent movement for India independence attracts millions; mass culture flourishes in film and publishing industries; growth of radio transmissions; technology increases global productivity
1921	Lenin introduces New Economic Policy in Russia
1922	Civil war ends in Russia; Mussolini comes to power in Italy
1923	Founding of the independent republic of Turkey under Mustafa Kemal; formation of Union of Soviet Socialist Republics

KEY TERMS

Bolshevik (p. 903)
collective security (p. 907)
Comintern (p. 904)
fascism (p. 918)
Fourteen Points (p. 904)
Guomindang (p. 895)
League of Nations (p. 907)
mandate system (p. 908)
New Economic Policy (p. 918)
soviet (p. 902)
total war (p. 900)

CHAPTER OVERVIEW QUESTIONS

1. Why did the Mexican Revolution, the Chinese Revolution, World War I, and the Russian Revolution cause so much change far from the battlefield?

2. How did these wars help produce mass culture and society?

3. What role did technology play in these developments?

SECTION FOCUS QUESTIONS

1. What factors contributed to the wars of the early twentieth century?

2. Why did the Russian Revolution take place, and what changes did it produce in Russian politics and daily life?

3. What were the major outcomes of the peacemaking process and postwar conditions?

4. How did the rise of mass society affect politics, culture, and everyday life around the world?

5. In what ways did Argentina's history differ from that of countries caught up in World War I?

MAKING CONNECTIONS

1. In what ways did conditions at the end of World War I differ from those expected at the outbreak of the war?

2. Consider the empires discussed in Chapter 26. How did they change in the 1920s, and why?

3. How did World War I affect work and livelihoods?

4. How did the mass political movements that emerged during and after the war differ from one another?

28

AT A CROSSROADS ▲

This photograph of a Nazi rally held in 1938 in Nuremberg reveals how young people, among others, admired Hitler and all that he stood for: quick fixes to a depressed economy and the promise of renewed global power. His rhetoric of hatred rallied Germans across the social order to envision a better future once their nation had been purified of enemies such as Jews, who were actually their neighbors and fellow Germans. Popular support for Hitler's violent bigotry has made historians aware that the history of Nazism is not just the story of one charismatic leader, but also of the masses whose devotion was the source of his power. (bpk, Berlin/Art Resource, NY.)

Global Catastrophe: The Great Depression and World War II

1929–1945

Eva Kantorowsky worked as a secretary and teacher of English in Shanghai during World War II. A cosmopolitan city, Shanghai attracted refugees from war-torn Europe from the 1930s on, especially those fleeing Adolf Hitler's brutal Nazi regime in Germany. Eva Kantorowsky was one of these, helped by her uncle's successful acquisition of three exit visas so that she, her mother, and her father—a rabbi in Berlin—could make their way across two continents to China in 1940. They left only after Eva's father had been repeatedly beaten by the Nazis. Their reluctance to leave Germany had another cause: Eva's uncle had neglected to get an exit visa for her brother Hans, who, the uncle mistakenly thought, had already left the country. After World War II ended in 1945, Eva's family received the crushing news that Hans had died in Auschwitz, murdered along with millions of fellow Jews as well as Slavs, Roma ("gypsies"), and other persecuted groups, in the genocide the Nazis hoped would purify their empire.

Eva Kantorowsky escaped this genocide—the Holocaust—and survived the most destructive war in world history. World War II, with a death toll of some one hundred

BACKSTORY

As we saw in Chapter 27, in 1918 World War I ended, and with it fell four major empires: the Ottoman, Russian, Austro-Hungarian, and German. The victorious Western powers took the colonies and other lands of the defeated German and Ottoman empires, expanding the "new imperialism" (see Chapter 26). Significant changes in the nature of government and in the relationship between governments and their peoples accompanied the new geopolitical order. In countries around the world, governments grew larger and more powerful, taking advantage of the new mass media to promote a uniform culture that stressed the central importance of patriotism and national identity. In the political and economic turmoil that followed the war, the same mass media contributed to the rise of stridently nationalist dictators. When a worldwide depression struck in the late 1920s, these dictators, backed by modern bureaucracies and military technology, grew more dangerous. Intent on expanding their nation's boundaries and empires, they posed a grave threat to world peace.

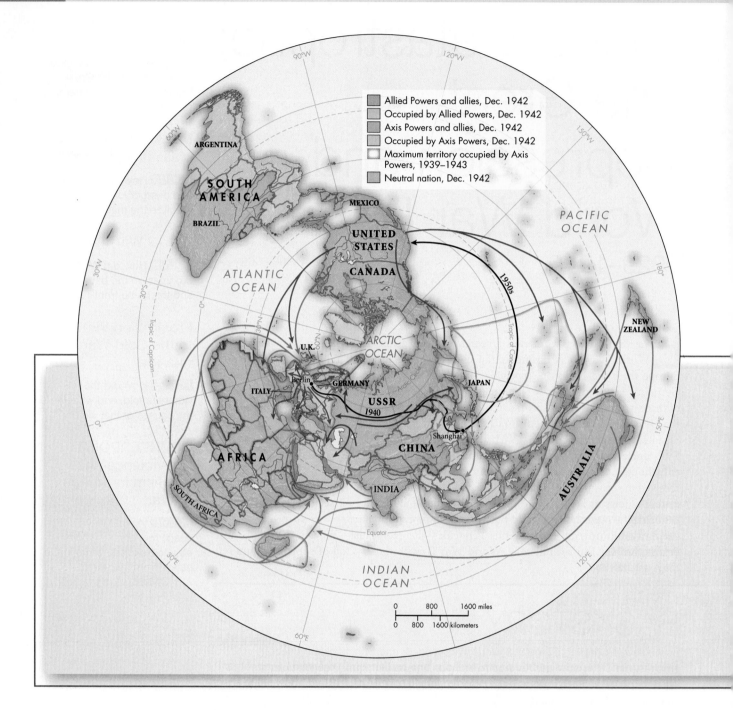

Allied Powers and allies, Dec. 1942
Occupied by Allied Powers, Dec. 1942
Axis Powers and allies, Dec. 1942
Occupied by Axis Powers, Dec. 1942
Maximum territory occupied by Axis Powers, 1939–1943
Neutral nation, Dec. 1942

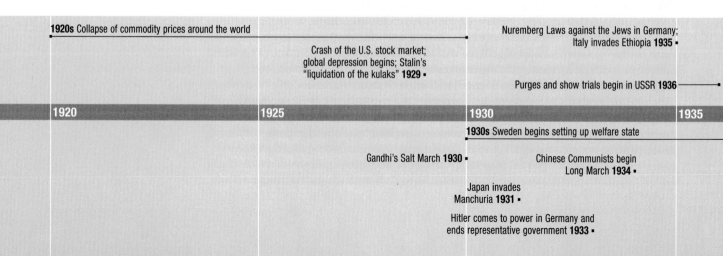

1920s Collapse of commodity prices around the world

Nuremberg Laws against the Jews in Germany; Italy invades Ethiopia **1935** ■

Crash of the U.S. stock market; global depression begins; Stalin's "liquidation of the kulaks" **1929** ■

Purges and show trials begin in USSR **1936**

| 1920 | 1925 | 1930 | 1935 |

1930s Sweden begins setting up welfare state

Gandhi's Salt March **1930** ■

Chinese Communists begin Long March **1934** ■

Japan invades Manchuria **1931** ■

Hitler comes to power in Germany and ends representative government **1933** ■

million people, capped off a decade of suffering that began with the Great Depression of the 1930s, a global economic catastrophe that was sparked by the crash of the U.S. stock market in 1929. The crash opened a tragic era in world history, a time when people around the world were connected by their shared experience of economic hardship, war, and genocide. The Great Depression intensified social protest throughout the world. In Japan, China, Italy, Germany, and across Latin America, strongmen took power and militarized the masses, promising that disciplined obedience would end their troubles. Adolf Hitler roused the German masses to pursue national greatness by scorning democracy and scapegoating "inferior" and "menacing" Jews such as the Kantorowsky family. Joseph Stalin believed that the Soviet Union's rapid industrialization was worth the lives of the millions of citizens who died remaking their nation in the 1930s. For militaristic authoritarian regimes around the world, human rights and democratic institutions were nothing more than obstacles to national greatness.

Elected leaders in established democracies reacted ineffectively to the depression and the militarism it spawned. The League of Nations, formed after World War I to preserve world peace, ignored Japan's aggression in China, Italy's in Ethiopia, and Germany's in Europe. Whether in China or central Europe, aggression followed aggression until Hitler's invasion of Poland in 1939 and Japan's bombing of Pearl Harbor in 1941 finally pushed the democracies to declare war. By the end of 1941, Great Britain, France, the Soviet

MAPPING THE WORLD
World War II, 1937–1945

The Great Depression spread economic hardship, which was compounded by the advance of militarism and empire. Japan's drive to expand its empire early in the 1930s was followed by Italy's campaigns for empire in Africa and the German takeover of central and eastern Europe. These aspiring powers used increasingly formidable weaponry, lightning speed, and massive attacks on civilians. The culmination was World War II, which broke out in 1937 in East Asia and 1939 in Europe, ending only in 1945. The Great Depression and World War II stand out in human history as an era of unprecedented suffering.

ROUTES ▼

Troop movements during World War II
Axis offensive, 1939–1942

→ German
→ Japanese

Allied counteroffensive to front lines, 1942–1945

→ British
→ British colonial and Commonwealth
→ Soviet
→ U.S.

→ Probable travels of Eva Kantorowsky, 1940–1950s

1937 Japan attacks China; World War II begins in Asia

1941–1945 Holocaust

1941 Germany invades USSR; Japan attacks Pearl Harbor; United States enters the war

1940

1945

1950

1945 Fall of Berlin and surrender of Germany; UN charter signed; United States drops atomic bombs; Japan surrenders

1939 Germany invades Poland; World War II begins in Europe

1943 USSR defeats Germany at Stalingrad

Union, and the United States were locked in combat with Germany, Italy, and Japan. The coalition that formed to stop Germany and its partners was an uneasy one, however, and by the end of the war the world's reigning military superpowers, the United States and the Soviet Union, regarded each other with deep distrust born of ideological differences. As hot war turned to cold war after 1945, tens of millions more became homeless refugees, among them Eva Kantorowsky. In this most destructive war in human history, however, she was among the lucky ones: global migration helped her survive. The dense network of economic and political connections that had made the Great Depression a global event and drawn the world into war also provided routes for some individuals to escape persecution and suffering in their home countries.

OVERVIEW
QUESTIONS

The major global development in this chapter: The causes and outcomes of the Great Depression and World War II.

As you read, consider:

1. How did ordinary people react to the Great Depression, and how did their reactions differ from country to country?

2. Why were dictators and antidemocratic leaders able to come to power in the 1930s, and how did all countries—autocratic and democratic alike—militarize the masses?

3. How are the Great Depression and World War II related historical events?

1929: The Great Depression Begins

FOCUS

What was the global impact of both the Great Depression and the attempts to overcome it?

A rapid decline in agricultural prices in the 1920s followed by the U.S. stock market crash of 1929 threw tens of millions out of work and wrecked the prospects of rural people worldwide. Economic depression spread from continent to continent as commerce and investment in industry declined, social life and gender roles were upset, and the birthrate plummeted. People everywhere, from farmers to industrial workers, saw their livelihoods destroyed. Despair turned to outrage, as many rose up in rebellion, embracing militaristic solutions to their nation's problems.

Economic Disaster Strikes

U.S. Stock Market Crash

In the 1920s, U.S. corporations and banks as well as millions of individual Americans invested their money (often borrowed) in the stock market, which seemed to churn out endless profits. Confident that stock prices would continue to rise, they used easy credit to buy shares in companies based on electric, automotive, and other new technologies. At the end of the decade, the Federal Reserve Bank—the nation's central bank, which controlled financial policy—tightened the availability of credit in an attempt to stabilize the market. To meet the new restrictions, brokers demanded that their clients immediately pay back the money they had borrowed to buy stock. As investors sold their stocks to raise cash and repay their loans, the wave of selling caused prices on the stock market to collapse. Between early October and mid-November 1929, the value of businesses listed on the U.S. stock market—and thus of people's investments through the stocks they owned in those businesses—dropped nearly two-thirds, from $87 billion to $30 billion. Individuals lost their money, and a breakdown of the economy as a whole followed.

The stock market crash helped spark the global economic collapse known as the **Great Depression**, because the United States, a leading international creditor, had financed the economic growth of the previous five years by lending money for business development around the world. Suddenly strapped themselves, U.S. financiers cut back drastically on loans and called in debts, weakening banks and industry at home and abroad. Creditors to newly created industries in India, for example, demanded repayment of loans and refused to finance further expansion. In Europe, the lack of credit and the decline in consumer buying caused businesses to close, workers to be laid off, and the European economy to slump. By 1933, almost 6 million German workers, or about one-third of the workforce, were unemployed, and many others were underemployed. The effects of the economic collapse were uneven, however: a few Latin American countries were able to expand domestic consumption enough at least partially to offset lost sales abroad.

In general, though, rural and urban folk alike suffered as tens of millions lost their livelihoods. For farmers, times had been tough for years. In the 1920s, technological innovation and a number of other factors combined to produce record crops and, consequently, falling farm prices. Canada, Australia, Argentina, and the United States had increased their production of wheat while World War I was raging in Europe; they did not cut back when the war ended and Europe became productive again. In the mid-1920s the price of wheat collapsed. Prices for other consumables, such as coffee and sugar, also tumbled, creating dire consequences in Africa, Asia, and some Latin American countries as large-scale farmers—either local magnates or white settlers—bought up the land of struggling small producers. Prices fell even for commodities such as rice, for which there was not a surplus, until by 1931 farmers were receiving 50 percent less for their crops than they had a few years earlier. As a result, rural consumption of manufactured goods dropped too. Thus, problems in agriculture were directly connected to industrial decline.

Government responses to the crisis made a bad situation worse. Great Britain went off the gold standard, which had the effect of depreciating its currency, thus making imports more expensive and cutting the sales of its trading partners. Other countries followed suit, blocking imports with high tariffs in hopes of sparking purchases of domestically produced goods. Measures such as cutting budgets were also part of accepted economic theory at the time, but reductions in spending only further undermined demand, leading to more business failures and higher unemployment. Governments in Latin America and eastern Europe often ignored the farmers' plight as they poured available funds into industrialization—a policy that increased tensions in rural society.

One solution for the imperial powers was to increase economic exploitation in the colonies. World War I and postwar investment had generated economic growth, a rising population, and explosive urbanization outside of Europe. Between 1920 and 1940, Calcutta ballooned from 1.8 million to 3.4 million residents and Saigon from 180,000 to 256,000, making them more attractive as markets and sources of tax revenue. Now the imperial powers demanded that colonial subjects pay higher taxes, no matter how desperate the local peoples' plight, to compensate for falling revenues back home. In the Belgian Congo, local farmers paid a per-person tax—called a poll or head tax—equivalent to one-sixth of their crops in the 1920s and one-fourth in the 1930s. Britain took its domestic economy off the gold standard, but it forced colonies such as India to pay taxes and other charges in gold. India's farmers stripped the subcontinent of its stores of gold to turn in every scrap of the precious metal, including women's jewelry, to meet British demands. During hard times, most imperial powers were able to shift at least some of their financial burden to their colonial subjects in Asia and Africa.

Global Economic Collapse

Government Response

Great Depression The economic crisis of the 1930s that began in agricultural regions through a severe drop in commodity prices in the 1920s and then, with the U.S. stock market crash of 1929, spread to industrial countries.

Promoting Business in the Great Depression

Winifred Tete-Ansa was an innovative businessman in Nigeria and the Gold Coast. He set up a cooperative so that Gold Coast cocoa growers could market their own products outside the imperial system. Then he established a bank to finance African-owned businesses such as trade in mahogany, palm oil, and other local commodities because European-owned banks would not. In 1930, at a time of economic depression and growing opposition to colonialism, Tete-Ansa explained to African Americans in this prospectus why he had started a bank to help finance African trade cooperatives. He urged these readers to contribute financially to his work.

> Picture a land one-eighth as large as the United States and with a population one-fifth as great, where the people grow three-fifths of the world's cocoa supply. . . .
>
> By the time this vast business has reached the ultimate consumer, over half a billion dollars have changed hands, and enormous profits have accrued to those of the white race who have furnished the necessary capital and directed the labor of thousands of the Negro race. A reasonable earning power on wealth of some five billion of dollars is thus developed, and the greater portion of these earnings go [sic] to the members of the white race. . . .
>
> Realize, if you will, the cities to be built and rebuilt, harbors to be developed, rivers to be harnessed, power to be developed and transmitted, railroads to be built, trains to be run, the cities to be lighted, water to be piped, sanitary arrangements to be installed and metals to be found and processed, the engines, motors, shafting, buildings necessary to turn the potential of raw products into highly saleable commodities at a higher price. . . .
>
> We of West Africa have taken the natural advantages of our country and have now fashioned them into a sphere of opportunity. On account of the vast area, the enormous number of our race habitant there and the sound foundation for progress that we have built, it now forms the most important sphere of opportunity for industrial success of the Negro and by the Negro; and a well-built, well-lubricated vehicle to carry on toward industrial emancipation.
>
> This vehicle needs capital to furnish it power to propel itself, and passengers to occupy its seats. We have provided the driver to direct it and the roads for it to travel. It is to be hoped that you, Negroes of America, will help furnish this power and the passengers for this journey to the Industrial Precedence of the Race.

Source: Winifred Tete-Ansa, *Africa at Work* (n.p., 1930), 78, 86–87.

EXAMINING THE EVIDENCE

1. What kind of global vision does Tete-Ansa present?

2. How would you describe his approach to colonialism?

3. How does he address the problem of livelihoods in hard times for Africans?

Social Effects of the Great Depression

The Great Depression caused enormous hardship for many, but its social and economic effects were complex and not entirely negative. Despite the economic crisis, modernization proceeded, whether in the form of building new roads in Africa or bringing electricity to the Soviet Union (see Reading the Past: Promoting Business in the Great Depression). Wealthy individual Chinese living abroad poured money into modernizing their homeland, investing in profitable development projects. Bordering English slums, one British observer in the mid-1930s noticed, were "filling stations and factories that look like exhibition buildings, giant cinemas and dance halls and cafés, bungalows with tiny garages, cocktail bars, Woolworth's [and] swimming pools." Municipal and national governments modernized sanitation, and running water, electricity, and sewage pipes were installed in many homes throughout the world for the first time. New factories manufactured synthetic fabrics, new electrical products such as stoves, and improved automobiles.

The Fortunate
Despite oft-repeated stories of thousands of ruined stockbrokers committing suicide, many in the upper classes prospered during the Great Depression. In Kenya, southern

Indochina, and elsewhere, large landowners evicted tenants who were unable to pay their rents and replaced them with cheaper day laborers. Moneylenders in India and Burma loaned peasants money to pay their rising taxes—due before the harvest. When agricultural prices fell early in the 1930s, some could not repay these loans, and moneylenders and large landowners alike took over the peasants' lands. Moreover, whereas rising tariffs, the turn to self-sufficiency, and the loss of foreign markets such as Britain hurt many international traders, merchants engaged in domestic trade managed to survive. Colombia, Brazil, Chile, Mexico, and Argentina actually showed either rising production or increased exports by 1932–1933. Throughout the Great Depression arms manufacturers made huge profits as nations such as Germany militarized. The majority of Europeans and Americans had jobs throughout the 1930s, and those with steady employment benefited from the drastic drop in consumer prices.

Even employed people, however, saw the millions of others around them struggling for a bare existence. In Cuba, where sugar prices collapsed, workers who did not lose their jobs were no longer paid, but simply fed a meal of "black or *caritas* beans, with their accompanying scum of weevils and worms . . . garbage that had no market," as one sugar worker described the food.[1] Because of the slump in agricultural prices, Japanese farmers were often reduced to eating tree bark, grass, and acorns and even gave up working: "Better to remain idle and eat less than work hard and eat more than can be earned," was the motto of some.[2] In towns with heavy industry, sometimes more than half the population was out of work. In a 1932 school assignment, a German youth wrote: "My father has been out of work for two-and-a-half years. He thinks that I'll never find a job." Under these conditions, a storm cloud of fear, resentment, and hopelessness settled over many parts of the globe.

The Destitute

Economic catastrophe strained social stability and upset gender relations. The collapse of prices for rice and raw silk made some Japanese peasants so desperate that they sold their daughters into prostitution. As taxes increased in Africa, men migrated to regions hundreds of miles from their families in search of better jobs, weakening family ties. In urban areas of Europe and the United States unemployed men stayed home all day, increasing the tension in small, overcrowded apartments. Men who stayed at home sometimes took over housekeeping chores, but others found this "women's work" emasculating. Women around the world could often find low-paying jobs doing laundry and other domestic service; some brewed and marketed beer and prepared foods from their homes. As many women became breadwinners, albeit for low wages, men could be seen standing on street corners begging—a reversal of gender expectations that fueled discontent.

Gender Relations

Rural men also faced the erosion of patriarchal authority, which was once central to overseeing farm labor and allocating property among heirs. Some lost their land entirely, and others had fewer children because of the economic slump. Mandatory education— and thus more years of required schooling—reduced family income and increased expenses for parents. Working-class children no longer earned wages to contribute to household income and were no longer available to help the family in other ways; instead they cost money while they went to school. Family-planning centers opened to help working people reduce family size in hard times. In a wide variety of ways, hard times disrupted the most fundamental human connections–the relationships among family members.

Protesting Poverty

The Great Depression produced rising protest by the unemployed. Often led by activists trained in the USSR, Communist parties flourished in the Chinese countryside, Indochina, the United States, Latin America, and across Europe, because they helped organize strikes and promised to end joblessness and exploitation. Mexican artist Diego Rivera captured the experiences of ordinary working people and the appeal of communism to them in huge murals he painted for public buildings. These massive paintings featured workers in factories and on farms, with portraits of Marx, Lenin, and Trotsky prominently intermingled with those of ordinary laborers. Union members in cities as distant as Shanghai, Detroit,

Diego Rivera, *Man at the Crossroads* (1934)

Communism and socialism appealed to workers both as ideologies and as political movements during the Great Depression, because they focused on ordinary people's needs. Mexican artist Diego Rivera had no love for the Soviet Union, yet he also considered communism to be an answer to the plight of native Americans and the oppressed around the world. In this mural, painted for Rockefeller Center in New York City but then torn down because of its image of Lenin, workers from many walks of life and ethnicities flock to the red flag and the message of Marx, Trotsky, and Lenin. (The Art Archive/Museo del Palacio de Bellas Artes Mexico/Dagli Orti.)

and Paris took to the streets to demand relief. In 1935, women textile workers in Medellin, Colombia, rose in angry protest about low wages and the insulting behavior of bosses. "Look, they'd go after the companies or whatever it was with rocks," said one woman of the strikers. "It was rough, it was bitter," she added.[3] Union leaders turned their wrath on big business. "Revolutions grow out of the depths of hunger," warned William Green, head of the American Federation of Labor, in 1931. For their part, governments and even factory owners responded with guns: police in Kobe, Japan, fought dockworkers, and government troops joined in crushing the demonstrators. U.S. automobile magnate Henry Ford turned his private police force on unemployed workers outside one of his plants, killing four of them and wounding far more. During the Great Depression, the masses had to defend their lives as well as their livelihoods.

Economic distress added to smoldering grievances in the colonies. As prices on commodities such as coffee, tin, and copper sank, colonial farmers withheld their produce from imperial wholesalers. Farmers in Ghana, for example, refused to sell cocoa in the 1930s. Discontent ran deep across the Middle East and Asia as well, fueled by the injustices of the World War I peace settlement, increasing colonial taxation, and hard economic times. General strikes rocked Palestine and India in 1936 and 1937, respectively. Their resolve fortified by bitter experiences, by the example of Japan's rising power, and by their own industrial development, colonial peoples roused themselves in an effort to overturn the imperial order.

Western-educated native leaders such as Ho Chi Minh, founder of the Indochinese Communist Party, led popular movements to contest their people's subjection. In 1930 the French government brutally crushed the peasant uprising Ho led. During the 1930s millions more working people came to follow Mohandas Gandhi, the charismatic leader of

Imperialist Response to Popular Uprisings

the Indian independence movement. The British jailed Gandhi repeatedly, stirred up Hindu-Muslim antagonism, and massacred protesters. Britain, France, and other European countries were quick to use their military might to put down colonial uprisings in an effort to preserve their empires. At the same time, however, they were slow to recognize a much greater threat to their well-being. As totalitarianism spread across Europe, the Western democracies responded with little more than words.

Militarizing the Masses in the 1930s

FOCUS

How did dictatorships and democracies attempt to mobilize the masses?

Representative government collapsed in many countries under the sheer weight of social and economic crisis. Japanese military men promoted overseas conquest as a solution to the depression, and even poor peasants donated funds to Japan's military cause. After 1929, Italy's Benito Mussolini, the Soviet Union's Joseph Stalin, and Germany's Adolf Hitler gained vast support for their regimes by mobilizing the masses in ways that had previously been attempted only in times of war. This common commitment to the use of political violence has led historians to apply the term **totalitarianism** to the Fascist, Communist, and Nazi regimes of the 1930s. The term refers to highly centralized systems of government that attempt to control society and ensure obedience through a single party and police terror. Many citizens admired Mussolini, Stalin, and Hitler for the discipline they brought to social and economic life, and overlooked the brutal side of totalitarian government. Unity and soldier-like obedience—not individual rights and open debate—were seen as keys to recovery.

To mobilize the masses, politicians also appealed to racist sentiment. "Superior" peoples were selfishly failing to flourish and breed, they charged, while growing numbers of "inferior" peoples were seeking to take their place. For the Japanese, the Chinese and Koreans were the "inferiors"; for Germans, Jews were the enemy and all others were inferiors. In the United States, some politicians built popular support by scapegoating Mexican Americans and other minorities. Targeting an enemy—whether fellow citizens of different faiths, colors, or ethnicities, or an entire country—enabled popular leaders to mobilize the masses to fight this internal or external enemy instead of building national unity around democratically solving economic problems.

The Rise of Stalinism

Joseph Stalin, who succeeded Lenin in 1929, led the astonishing transformation of the USSR in the 1930s from a predominantly agricultural society into a formidable industrial power. In 1929 Stalin ended Lenin's New Economic Policy, which (as we saw in Chapter 27) combined elements of Marxism and capitalism, and replaced it with the first of several **five-year plans** intended to mobilize Soviet citizens to industrialize the nation. Stalin's economic transformations reduced individual freedom and cost the lives of millions.

Stalin outlined a program for massive increases in the output of coal, iron ore, steel, and industrial goods over successive five-year periods. Without an end to economic backwardness, Stalin warned, "the advanced countries . . . will crush us." He thus established **central economic planning**, a policy of government direction of the economy, as used in World War I and increasingly favored by economists and industrialists around the world. Between 1929 and 1940, the number of Soviet workers in industry, construction, and transport grew from 4.6 million to 12.6 million, and production soared. Stalin's first five-year plan helped make the USSR a leading industrial nation, and one that was ultimately able to withstand the test of world war.

Central planning created a new elite class of bureaucrats and industrial officials, who dominated Soviet workers, forcing them to leave the countryside to work in state-run factories. While Communist officials enjoyed benefits such as country homes and luxurious vacations, untrained workers from the countryside were herded into barracklike dwellings or tents and endured dangerous factory conditions. Still, many believed in the promise of communism and took pride in learning new skills: "We mastered this profession—completely new to us—with great pleasure," a female lathe operator recalled. They tolerated intense suffering because, as one worker put it, "Man himself is being rebuilt." Nonetheless, new workers often lacked the technical education necessary to achieve the goals prescribed by the five-year plan, and official lying about productivity became a regular practice.

The Soviet government also drastically changed conditions on the land. Faced with peasants' refusal simply to turn over their grain to the government, Stalin called for the "liquidation of the kulaks" (koo-LAHKS). The word *kulak*, which literally means "fist," was first an insulting Soviet term for a prosperous peasant, but it came to apply to any independent farmer. One Russian remembered believing kulaks were "bloodsuckers, cattle, swine, loathsome, repulsive: they had no souls; they stank," and were "enemies of the state." Party workers robbed farmers of their possessions, left them to starve, or even murdered them outright. Confiscated kulak land formed the basis of the new collective farms,

Transforming the Economy and Society

totalitarianism A single-party form of government emerging after World War I in which the ruling political party seeks to control all parts of the social, cultural, economic, and political lives of the population, typically making use of mass communication and violence to instill its ideology and maintain power.

five-year plan One of the centralized programs for economic development instituted by Joseph Stalin in the USSR and copied by Adolf Hitler in Germany; these plans set production priorities and targets for individual industries and agriculture.

central economic planning A policy of government direction of the economy, established during World War I and increasingly used in peacetime.

Socialist Realist Art

The early days of the Bolshevik Revolution witnessed experimentation in social and sexual relationships and in the arts. Under Stalin the government sponsored the official artistic style called "socialist realism"; it featured smiling workers with glowing complexions who radiated a sense of supreme happiness. Often taken as hypocritical, given the actual living conditions in the Soviet Union, socialist realist art in fact looked to the future—what socialist society would be when it reached the state of perfection for which everyone should strive and sacrifice. (akg-images/Michael Teller.)

where the remaining peasants were forced to live and to share facilities and modern machinery. Traditional peasant life was brought to a violent end as the social and economic connections that bound rural residents to one another and to society at large were redrawn.

The result of the Communist experiment with collective farming was mass starvation, as Soviet grain harvests declined from 83 million tons in 1930 to 67 million in 1934. Economic failure became a political issue, and Stalin blamed the crisis not on inexperienced workers but on enemies of communism. He instituted **purges**—that is, state-approved violence that included widespread arrests, imprisonments in labor camps, and executions. Beginning in 1936, a series of "show trials" based on trumped-up charges and fabricated evidence resulted in the conviction and execution of former Bolshevik leaders and thousands of military officers for conspiring against the USSR. Simultaneously, the government expanded the system of lethal prison camps—called the *Gulag*, an acronym for the department that ran the camps—to stretch several thousand miles from Moscow to Siberia. Prisoners did every kind of work, from digging canals to building apartment complexes in Moscow. With 1 million dying annually from the harsh conditions, the casualties of the Soviet system far exceeded those in Nazi Germany in the 1930s.

Militarization in the 1930s curtailed personal freedom. As the population declined from famine, purges, and a rapid drop in the birthrate in the 1930s, the USSR ended the reproductive freedom of the early revolutionary years, restricting access to birth-control information and abortion and criminalizing homosexuality. Yet because of state programs, women across the Soviet Union made gains in literacy and received better health care. Positions in the lower ranks of the Communist Party opened to women as the purges continued, and women increasingly were accepted into the professions. Still, the burden on women was great. After working long hours in factories, they had to stand in line for scarce consumer goods and perform all household and child-care tasks.

Stalin used artists and writers—"engineers of the soul," he called them—to help mobilize the masses. In return for housing, office space, and secretarial help, the "comrade artist" adhered to the official style of "socialist realism," which depicted workers as full of rosy emotions—a rosiness reflecting less communist reality than its promises for future fulfillment. Some artists, such as the poet Anna Akhmatova (ahk-MAH-toh-vah), protested the harsh Soviet reality. "Stars of death stood above us, and Russia, / In her innocence, twisted in pain / Under blood-spattered boots," wrote Akhmatova of the 1930s, as she stood in line outside a Soviet prison, waiting for news of her son, who was being held there. Once a prosperous and celebrated writer, Akhmatova was reduced to living off the generosity of her friends as a result of her resistance.

Despite such notable exceptions, Stalin triumphantly militarized the masses in his warlike campaign to industrialize in the 1930s, becoming to them, as one worker put it, "a god on earth."[4] Admirers from around the world headed to the USSR to see the "workers' paradise" for themselves and to learn how to mobilize mass support in other countries.

purge In the USSR in the 1930s, one of a series of attacks on citizens accused of being enemies of the state.

Japanese Expansionism

The Great Depression struck Japan's economy as it was recovering from a catastrophic earthquake that had killed more than 140,000 people and laid waste to both the capital of Tokyo and the bustling port city of Yokohama. The earthquake sparked murders—led by the military—of Korean and Chinese workers in the area as somehow responsible for the devastation. In 1925, men over the age of twenty-five had received the vote and the young Hirohito (heer-oh-HEE-toh) had become emperor, but the economic downturn and social unrest made Japan unstable.

An ambitious military, impatient with Japan's weak democratic institutions, sought control of the government, as did politicians favoring improved representative government. A modernizing economy and growing world trade had unleashed social change, and reformers challenged traditional values such as women's obedience. Author Junichiro Tanizaki captured the clash of old and new worldviews in novels such as *Naomi* (1924–1925), in which an engineer is totally obsessed with an independent "new woman," and *The Makioka Sisters* (1943–1948), some of whose protagonists struggle to protect tradition amid relentless change.

The Japanese military won out over the liberal politicians. Military leaders offered their own solution to the depressed conditions of workers, peasants, and business people: conquer nearby regions to provide new farmlands and create markets. Japanese peasants, hampered in the pursuit of their livelihoods, would settle new areas such as Manchuria, while business people would benefit from a larger pool of consumers, workers, and raw materials in annexed lands. Viewing China and the Western powers as obstacles to Japan's prosperity, Japan's military leaders promoted the idea that the military was an institution unto itself, an "emperor's army" not subject to civilian control, and that it would bring about a new world order and the fulfillment of Japan's destiny. By the 1930s, Emperor Hirohito and his advisers had built public support for a militaristic imperial system. Renewed military vigor was seen as key to Japan's claims to racial superiority and its entitlement to the lands of people they considered "inferior"—such as the Chinese. Such claims linked Japan with Germany and Italy in the 1930s, setting the stage for a menacing global alliance.

The Japanese army took the lead in making these claims a reality: in September 1931 it blew up a Japanese-owned train in the Chinese province of Manchuria and made the incident look like an attack on Japan by placing corpses dressed in official Chinese uniforms alongside the tracks. The military then used the explosion as an excuse to invade the territory, set up a puppet government, and push farther into China (see Map 28.1). Journalists back in Japan rallied the public to condemn Chinese aggression and support expansion into China. China appealed to the League of Nations in protest. Although the League condemned the invasion, it imposed no penalties or economic sanctions against Japan. Meanwhile the Japanese army dealt with the democratic opposition by simply assassinating them.

The Chinese did not sit idly by in the face of Japan's invasion. In 1934 Jiang Jieshi (Chiang Kai-shek) introduced the "New Life" Movement, whose aim was "to militarize the

The Manchurian Incident

China's New Life Movement

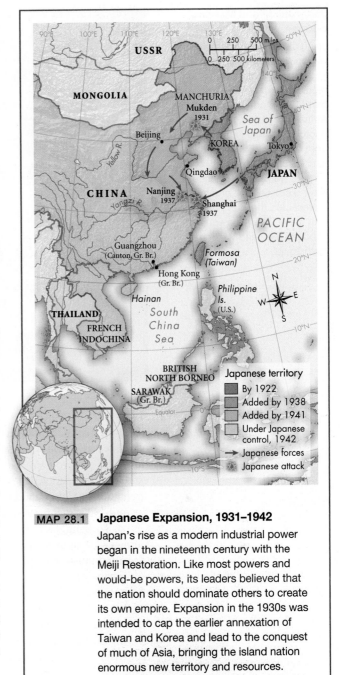

MAP 28.1   **Japanese Expansion, 1931–1942**

Japan's rise as a modern industrial power began in the nineteenth century with the Meiji Restoration. Like most powers and would-be powers, its leaders believed that the nation should dominate others to create its own empire. Expansion in the 1930s was intended to cap the earlier annexation of Taiwan and Korea and lead to the conquest of much of Asia, bringing the island nation enormous new territory and resources.

Jiang Jieshi and Mai-ling Soong

Jiang Jieshi took control of the Nationalist government in China and campaigned to promote regular exercise and hygiene as part of his modernization efforts. At the time of this 1927 photograph, Mai-ling Soong, from one of China's wealthiest families and sister-in-law of Sun Yatsen, was Jiang's fiancée. Having crossed the globe, she represented the "new woman" with her U.S. college education, unbound feet, and Western clothing. (Bettmann/Corbis.)

life of the people" and to make them "willing to sacrifice for the nation at all times."[5] The New Life Movement was inspired by European fascist militarism, with its promise of national unity, but the program also promoted discipline in everyday life through cleanliness and exercise. Some nationalist reformers saw the position of women as key to modernizing and strengthening China. Traditions such as foot-binding were attacked as old-fashioned, and by the mid-1930s there were some six thousand institutions of higher education for women in China. To Jiang, national unity demanded mobilization on the political level against the Chinese Communist Party—not the Japanese. Ultimately, however, Jiang was forced to join the Communists in fighting the Japanese instead of fighting one another.

Mobilization of the Masses in Japan

Japanese army leaders, countering increasing Chinese unity and purpose, mobilized their own people, using the mass media to create a "people's patriotism" among poor farmers and factory workers. In 1933, the film *Japan in the National Emergency* depicted the utopian mission of Japan "to create an ideal land in East Asia" where under Japanese leadership the races would harmoniously join together. Decadent Western culture—notably its racism, the film claimed—showed that Japan as a whole needed to turn away from the West and return to protecting the "sacred spirit" of the nation.[6] Propagandists encouraged Japanese citizens to renounce individual rights: "even in our private lives we always remember to unite with the emperor and serve the state."[7] Labor unions supported militarization, pressing impoverished workers to contribute funds for the military. By 1937, Japan's government was spending 47 percent of its budget on weaponry, thanks to the successful mobilization of people from all classes.

Hitler's Rise to Power

Mass politics reached terrifying proportions in Germany when Adolf Hitler finally achieved his goal of overthrowing German democracy. In his book *Mein Kampf* ("My Struggle," 1925), he laid out his vision of "scientific" anti-Semitism and the rebirth of the German "race," a vision he attempted to implement through his leadership of the Nazi

Party (National Socialist German Workers' Party). When the Great Depression struck Germany, the Nazis began to outstrip their rivals in elections, thanks in part to support from some big businessmen and the press. Hitler's election as chancellor in 1933 launched twelve years of violent Nazi rule.

Foremost among the Nazis' supporters were idealistic youth, who believed that Germany could recapture its former glory only if Hitler took control, and also white-collar workers and the lower middle class, who were still hurting from the postwar inflation that had destroyed their savings. By targeting all their parliamentary opponents as a single, monolithic group of "Bolshevik" enemies, the Nazis won wide approval for confronting those they accused of causing the depression. Many thought it was time to replace democratic government with a bold new leader who would take on these enemies militarily, without concern for constitutions, laws, or individual rights.

Appeal of Nazism

Hitler devised modern propaganda techniques to build his appeal. Thousands of recordings of Hitler's speeches and other Nazi souvenir items circulated among the public, and Nazi rallies were masterpieces of mass spectacle. Hitler, however, viewed the masses with contempt: "The receptivity of the great masses is very limited, their intelligence is small. In consequence of these facts, all effective propaganda must be limited to a very few points and must harp on those in slogans." Germany's power brokers from the military, industry, and the state bureaucracy, fearing the Communists for their opposition to private property, saw to it that Hitler legally became chancellor in 1933. Millions celebrated. "My father went down to the cellar and brought up our best bottles of wine. . . . And my mother wept for joy," one German recalled. "Now everything will be all right," she said.

Hitler took command brutally and forcibly closed down representative government. Nazis suspended civil rights, imposed censorship of the press, and prohibited meetings of the political parties. Hitler made his aims clear: "I have set myself one task, namely to sweep those parties out of Germany." Storm troopers—the private Nazi army that existed in addition to Germany's regular forces—so harassed democratic politicians that at the end of March 1933 intimidated delegates let pass the Enabling Act, which suspended the constitution for four years and allowed Nazi laws to take effect without parliamentary approval. The elite SS (*Schutzstaffel*) was yet another military organization, and along with the Gestapo, or political police, it enforced complete obedience to Nazism. These organizations had vast powers to arrest Communists, Jews, homosexuals, and activists and either executed them or imprisoned them in concentration camps, the first of which opened at Dachau near Munich in March 1933.

Repression in the Nazi State

The Nazis knew that their power depended on improving economic conditions and, in that context, the government pursued pump priming, that is, stimulating the economy by investing in public works projects such as constructing tanks, airplanes, and highways. Unemployment declined from a peak of almost 6 million in 1932 to 1.6 million by 1936. The Nazi Party closed down labor unions, and government managers classified jobs and set pay levels, rating women's jobs lower than men's regardless of the level of expertise required. The belief grew that Hitler was working an economic miracle.

The Nazi government took control of all aspects of everyday life, including gender roles. A law encouraged Aryans (those people legally defined as racially German) to have children by providing loans to Aryan newlyweds, but only if the wife left the workforce. Nazi marriage programs enforced both racial and gender ideology; women were supposed to be subordinate so men would feel tough and industrious despite military defeat and economic depression. A woman "joyfully sacrifices and fulfills her fate," one Nazi leader explained. Censorship flourished. Radio broadcasts were clogged with propaganda; book-burnings destroyed works by Jews, socialists, homosexuals, and modernist writers. Hitler claimed to be rebuilding the harmonious community destroyed by modernity even as his government used very modern tools of surveillance and big government programs to enforce the Nazi program. For millions of Germans, however, Nazi rule brought anything but harmony and well-being.

The Nazis defined Jews as an inferior "race" dangerous to the superior Aryan "race" and as responsible for both Germany's defeat in World War I and the economic crisis that

Nazi Racism

followed. National Socialism, Hitler insisted in a 1938 speech, was not based on old fashioned anti-Semitism but on "the greatest of scientific knowledge." Jews were "vermin," "parasites," and "Bolsheviks," whom the Germans had to eliminate. In 1935, the Nuremberg Laws deprived Jews of citizenship and prohibited marriage between Jews and other Germans. Whereas women defined as Aryan had increasing difficulty obtaining abortions or birth-control information, these were readily available to Jews and other outcast groups. In the name of improving the Aryan race, doctors in the late 1930s helped organize the T4 project, which used carbon monoxide poisoning and other means to kill two hundred thousand "inferior" people—especially the handicapped.

Jews were forced into slave labor, evicted from their apartments, and prevented from buying most clothing and food. In 1938, a Jewish teenager, reacting to the harassment of his parents, killed a German official. In retaliation, Nazis attacked synagogues, smashed windows of Jewish-owned stores, and threw more than twenty thousand Jews—including Eva Kantorowski's father—into prisons and work camps. The night of November 9–10 became known as *Kristallnacht* (kris-TAHL-nahkt), or the Night of Broken Glass. Faced with this relentless persecution, by 1939 more than half of Germany's five hundred thousand Jews had emigrated. Hitler mobilized the masses by targeting an enemy—the Jews—not just in wartime but in peacetime, not outside the country but within it. Persecution of the Jews brought Germans new financial resources as they simply stole Jewish property and took Jewish jobs.

Democracies Mobilize

Facing the double-barreled assault of economic depression and totalitarian aggression, democracies rallied in support of freedom, individuals' rights, and citizens' well-being, though they often limited their efforts to whites. In the eyes of many, however, representative government appeared feeble compared with totalitarian leaders' military style of mobilizing the masses. Democracy was difficult to support in tough economic times, but as the depression wore on, some governments—notably the United States and Sweden—undertook bold experiments to solve social and economic crises while still maintaining democratic politics.

The United States   In the early days of the depression, U.S. lawmakers opposed giving direct aid to the unemployed and even used military force to put down a demonstration by jobless veterans in the nation's capital. Government policy changed, however, after Franklin Delano Roosevelt was elected president in 1932. Roosevelt pushed through a torrent of legislation: relief for businesses, price supports for struggling farmers, and public works programs for the unemployed. The Social Security Act of 1935 set up a fund to which employers and employees contributed to provide retirement and other benefits for citizens. Like other successful politicians of the 1930s and thereafter, Roosevelt used the new mass media expertly, especially in his radio series of "fireside chats" to the American people. In sharp contrast to Mussolini and Hitler, Roosevelt—with the able assistance of his wife Eleanor—aimed to build faith in democracy rather than denounce it: "We Americans of today . . . are characters in the living book of democracy," he told a group of teenagers in 1939. The president's bold programs and successful use of the media kept the masses, even those facing racial discrimination, mobilized to believe in a democratic future.

Sweden   Sweden's response to the crisis of the 1930s became a model for the postwar welfare state. The Swedish government turned its economy around by instituting social welfare programs and central planning of the economy. It devalued its currency to make Swedish exports more attractive. Pump-priming projects increased Swedish productivity by 20 percent between 1929 and 1935, a period when other democracies were floundering. Government programs also addressed the population problem, but without the racism and coercion of totalitarianism. One architect of the program to boost childbirth was the activist Alva Myrdal (MEER-dahl), a young sociologist and leading member of parliament. Myrdal's mother had been so against modern education that she forbade library books in the house, claiming that they promoted diseases. Myrdal made it to university, but after her topics for a doctoral dissertation were rejected, she turned to activism, promoting causes such as "voluntary parenthood" and improved work opportunities for women—even married ones. Following Myrdal's lead, the Swedish government started a loan program for married couples in 1937 and introduced prenatal care, free childbirth in a hospital, and subsidized housing for large families. Because all families—rural and urban, poor or prosperous—received these benefits, there was widespread support for this experiment with developing a welfare state alongside democracy. Alva Myrdal went on to become ambassador to India, a tireless worker for the United Nations and world peace, and a Nobel Prize recipient.

France

Like Germany, France faced economic and political turmoil and only narrowly avoided a fascist takeover. Deputies with opposing views frequently came to blows in the Chamber of Deputies, and right-wing paramilitary groups took to the streets, attracting the unemployed, students, and veterans to demonstrations against representative government. The growing attraction of fascism shocked French liberals, socialists, and Communists into an antifascist coalition known as the Popular Front. This alliance was made possible when Stalin allowed Communist parties, whose policies he determined, to join in the protection of democracy rather than work to destroy it. For just over a year in 1936–1937 and again very briefly in 1938, the French Popular Front, headed by socialist leader Léon Blum, led the government. Like American and Swedish reformers, the Popular Front enacted welfare benefits and mandatory two-week paid vacations for workers. Bankers and industrialists greeted Blum's costly programs by sending their savings out of the country, however, leaving France financially strapped and the government mortally wounded. "Better Hitler than Blum" was the slogan of the upper classes, and the Popular Front fell. The collapse of the antifascist Popular Front showed the difficulties of democratic societies facing economic crisis and the revival of militarism.

Cultural Mobilization in the West

Democratic cultural life also fought the lure of fascism. During its brief existence, the Popular Front encouraged the masses to celebrate democratic holidays such as Bastille Day with new enthusiasm. Artists made films, wrote novels, and produced art that celebrated ordinary people and captured their everyday struggles. In Charlie Chaplin's film *Modern Times* (1936), his famous character, the Little Tramp, was a worker in a modern factory molded by his monotonous job to believe that even his co-workers' bodies needed mechanical adjustment. Viewers laughed with him instead of growing resentful. Heroines in immensely popular musical comedies behaved bravely, pulling their men out of the depths of despair and thus away from fascist temptation. In the film *Keep Smiling* (1938), for example, British comedienne Gracie Fields portrayed a spunky working-class woman who remained cheerful despite the challenges of living in hard times.

Novelists affirmed human rights and the dignity of the poor in the face of dictatorial pomp and bombast. In a series of novels based on the biblical figure Joseph, German writer and Nobel Prize winner Thomas Mann conveyed the conflict between humane values and barbarism. The fourth volume, *Joseph the Provider* (1944), praised Joseph's welfare state, in which the granaries are full and the rich pay taxes so the poor might live decent lives. Chinese author Pa Chin used his widely influential novel *Family* (1931) to criticize the dictatorial powers of traditional patriarchy, which destroyed humane values and loving relationships. In one of her last works, *Three Guineas* (1938), English writer Virginia Woolf abandoned the experimental novel in favor of a direct attack on militarism, poverty, and the oppression of women, showing that these were interconnected parts of the single, dangerous worldview of the 1930s.

Global War 1937–1945

The depression intensified competition among nations as politicians sought to expand their country's access to land, markets, and resources. Mobilizing the masses around national and military might, Hitler, Mussolini, and Japan's military leaders marched the world toward another catastrophic war.

> **FOCUS**
> How did World War II progress on the battlefront and the home front?

Democratic statesmen hoped that sanctions imposed by the League of Nations would stop new aggression, but military assaults escalated with Japan's invasion of China and the outbreak of war in 1937. An era of destruction opened that at war's end left some 100 million of the world's peoples dead and tens of millions more starving and homeless.

Europe's Road to War

The surge in global imperialism that occurred during the 1930s has shaped international politics to the present day. Hitler's harsh anti-Jewish policies drove increasing numbers of European Jews to migrate to Palestine, bringing clashes between Palestinians and Jewish newcomers. Western imperialist powers, including Britain, France, the United States, and the Netherlands, increased their exploitation of resource-rich regions outside their borders amid mounting local resentment. The most severe challenge to the global order, however, came from Germany, Italy, and Japan, whose authoritarian regimes and drive for empire became ever bolder.

Uncontested Aggression   Like Japanese leaders, Hitler and Mussolini presented their countries as "have-nots" and demanded more power, resources, and land. Hitler's agenda included gaining more *Lebensraum* (LAY-buns-rowm), or living space, in which supposedly superior "Aryans" could thrive. This space would be taken from the "inferior" Slavic peoples, who would be moved to Siberia or would serve as slaves. In 1935 Hitler loudly rejected the Treaty of Versailles's limitations on German military strength and openly began rearming. In the same year, Mussolini invaded Ethiopia, one of the few African states not overwhelmed by European imperialism. "The Roman legionnaires are again on the march," one Italian soldier exulted at this colonial adventure. Despite the resistance of the poorly equipped Ethiopians, their capital, Addis Ababa, fell in the spring of 1936. The League of Nations voted to impose sanctions against Italy, but Britain and France opposed any embargo on oil, suggesting a lack of will to fight aggression.

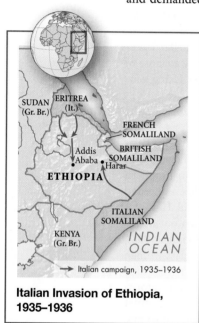

Italian Invasion of Ethiopia, 1935–1936

Nazi territorial expansion began with the annexation of Austria in 1938 (see Map 28.2). Aiming to unite all German peoples, Hitler's troops entered Austria, and the enthusiasm of Nazi sympathizers there made Germany's actions appear to support Wilsonian "self-determination." Nazis generated support in Austria by building factories to solve the unemployment problem and by reawakening Austrians' sense that they belonged once more to a mighty empire. Hitler turned next to Czechoslovakia and its rich resources. Hitler gambled correctly that the other Western powers would not interfere with any takeover if he could

The Fall of Central Europe   convince them that this was his last territorial claim. In the fall of 1938, British Prime Minister Neville Chamberlain, French Premier Édouard Daladier, and Mussolini met with Hitler in Munich, Germany, and, despite strong Czech opposition, agreed to allow Germany's claim to the Sudetenland (sue-DAY-ten-lahnd)—the German-populated border region of Czechoslovakia. Their strategy was to make concessions for grievances (in this case, injustices to Germany in the Peace of Paris), a policy called **appeasement**. As Europe outside of Czechoslovakia rejoiced, Chamberlain announced that he had secured "peace in our time" for a continent fearing another devastating war. Appeasement proved a failure: in March 1939, Hitler invaded the rest of Czechoslovakia.

The Early Years of the War 1937–1943

appeasement The strategy of preventing a war by making concessions to aggressors.

While this expansion was unfolding, the first phase of World War II had begun in East Asia. In 1937, the Japanese military, after skirmishes around Beijing, attacked Shanghai, justifying its offensive as the first step in liberating the region from Western imperialism (see again Map 28.1). Moving to capture major cities along the coast, the Japanese army

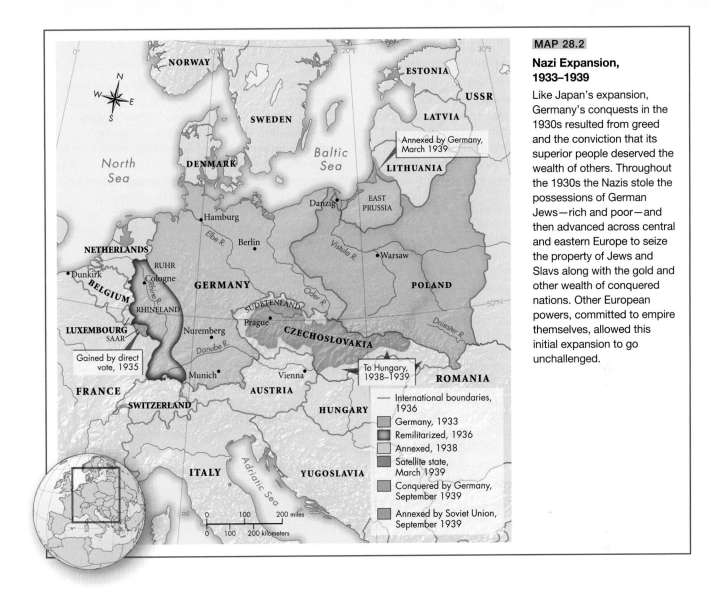

MAP 28.2

Nazi Expansion, 1933–1939

Like Japan's expansion, Germany's conquests in the 1930s resulted from greed and the conviction that its superior people deserved the wealth of others. Throughout the 1930s the Nazis stole the possessions of German Jews—rich and poor—and then advanced across central and eastern Europe to seize the property of Jews and Slavs along with the gold and other wealth of conquered nations. Other European powers, committed to empire themselves, allowed this initial expansion to go unchallenged.

took the Chinese capital of Nanjing, massacring hundreds of thousands of Chinese in the "Rape of Nanjing," an atrocity so named because of the special brutality toward girls and women before they were killed. Japan's invasion of China marked the Asian beginnings of World War II.

Despite the slaughter, many in the West continued to believe that the highly militarized and industrialized Japanese were more fit to rule China than the Chinese themselves. In 1938, the Japanese government described its expansionism as the foundation for a "New Order" in Asia, the **Greater East Asia Co-Prosperity Sphere** that Japan would use to help free Asians and indeed the world from the oppressive white race. In reality, however, the Japanese made enormous demands on Asians for resources while treating Chinese and Koreans with brutality (see Reading the Past: "Comfort Women" in World War II).

As the Japanese fought to conquer China, Hitler launched an all-out attack on Poland on September 1, 1939. The way was prepared a week earlier on August 23, 1939, when Germany and the USSR signed a nonaggression agreement—the Nazi-Soviet Pact—providing that if one country became embroiled in war, the other country would remain neutral. Feeling confident, German forces let loose an overpowering *Blitzkrieg* ("lightning war"), a stunning and concentrated onslaught of airplanes, tanks, and motorized infantry, to defeat the ill-equipped Polish defenders with overwhelming speed. Allowing the army

Greater East Asia Co-Prosperity Sphere A region of Asian states to be dominated by Japan, and in theory, to benefit from Japan's superior civilization.

"Comfort Women" in World War II

Oh Omok was sixteen when she left home in Chongup, Korea, in 1937 to take up a new livelihood: that, she was told, of a factory worker in Japan. Instead, like thousands of other young Korean women, she ended up in a military brothel. This is a small part of her story, among the mildest of those gathered in the 1990s from former "comfort women" and meticulously documented by researchers.

At first I delivered food for the soldiers and had to serve the rank and file, to have sex with them. . . . On receiving orders we were called to the appropriate unit and served five or six men a day. At times we would serve up to ten. We served the soldiers in very small rooms with floors covered with Japanese-style mats, *tatami*. . . . When the soldiers were away on an expedition it was nice and quiet, but once they returned we had to serve many of them. Then they would come to our rooms in a continuous stream. I wept a lot in the early days. Some soldiers tried to comfort me saying *"kawaisoni"* or *"naitara ikanyo,"* which meant something like "you poor thing" and "don't cry." Some of the soldiers would hit me because I didn't understand their language. If we displeased them in the slightest way they shouted at us and beat us: *"bakayaro"* or *"kisamayaro,"* "you idiot" and "you bastard." I realized that I must do whatever they wanted of me if I wished to survive.

The soldiers used condoms. We had to have a medical examination for venereal infections once a week. Those infected took medicine and were injected with "No. 606" [a medicine regularly injected into the forced sex workers, often with bad side effects]. Sometime later, I became quite close to a Lieutenant Morimoto, who arranged for Okhui [a friend of Oh Omok] and me to receive only high-ranking officers. Once we began to exclusively serve lieutenants and second lieutenants, our lives became much easier.

Source: Keith Howard, ed., *True Stories of the Korean Comfort Women: Testimonies Compiled by the Korean Council for Women Drafted for Military Sexual Slavery by Japan and the Research Association on the Women Drafted for Military Sexual Slavery by Japan,* trans. Young Joo Lee (London: Cassell, 1995), 66–67.

EXAMINING THE EVIDENCE

1. How would you describe Oh Omok's attitude toward her situation?

2. How might her experience as a "comfort woman" shape her ideas about gender and class relations?

The German Onslaught to conserve supplies, the Blitzkrieg assured Germans at home that the human costs of conquest would be low. On September 17, 1939, the Soviets invaded Poland from the east, and the victors then divided the country according to secret provisions in the Nazi-Soviet Pact (see again Map 28.2). Within Germany, Hitler called for defense of the fatherland against the "warlike menace" of world Jewry.

In April 1940, the Blitzkrieg crushed Denmark and Norway; Belgium, the Netherlands, and France fell in May and June (see Map 28.3). Stalin meanwhile annexed the Baltic states of Estonia, Latvia, and Lithuania. As Winston Churchill, an early advocate of resistance, took over as prime minister, Hitler ordered the bombardment of Britain. Churchill, another savvy orator, rallied the British people by radio to protect the ideals of liberty with their "blood, toil, tears, and sweat." In the Battle of Britain, or the Blitz as the British called it, the Luftwaffe (German air force) bombed homes, public buildings, harbors, weapons depots, and factories. Britain poured resources into anti-aircraft weapons, its highly successful code-detecting group called Ultra, and further development of radar. By year's end, the British airplane industry was outproducing the Germans by 50 percent.

By the fall of 1940, German air losses had driven Hitler to abandon his planned conquest of Britain. Forcing Hungary, Romania, and Bulgaria to become its allies, Germany gained access to more food and oil. In violation of the Nazi-Soviet Pact, Hitler launched an all-out campaign in June 1941 against what he called the "center of judeobolshevism"—the Soviet Union. Deployed along a two-thousand-mile front, 3 million German and other Axis troops quickly penetrated Soviet lines and killed, captured, or wounded more than

MAP 28.3

World War II in Europe, North Africa, and the Soviet Union, 1939–1945

War in the European theater was horrendous because increasingly powerful bombers, tanks, and artillery were unleashed on soldiers and civilians alike. After its initial success in the spring of 1940, Germany was so ideologically driven that it pursued its military ambitions even after failing in the Battle of Britain and then in the war against the Soviet Union. Meanwhile, the Allies outproduced the Axis powers by a wide margin and lavishly used their own heavy weapons to achieve a final victory in May 1945. By then, much of the European continent and parts of the Middle East and North Africa had been reduced to rubble.

half of the 4.5 million Soviet soldiers defending the borders. As the campaign continued along the far-flung battlefront, the Soviet people fought back. Because Hitler feared that equipping his army for Russian conditions would suggest to civilians that a prolonged war lay in store, the Nazi soldiers were unprepared for the onset of winter. In this way, Hitler

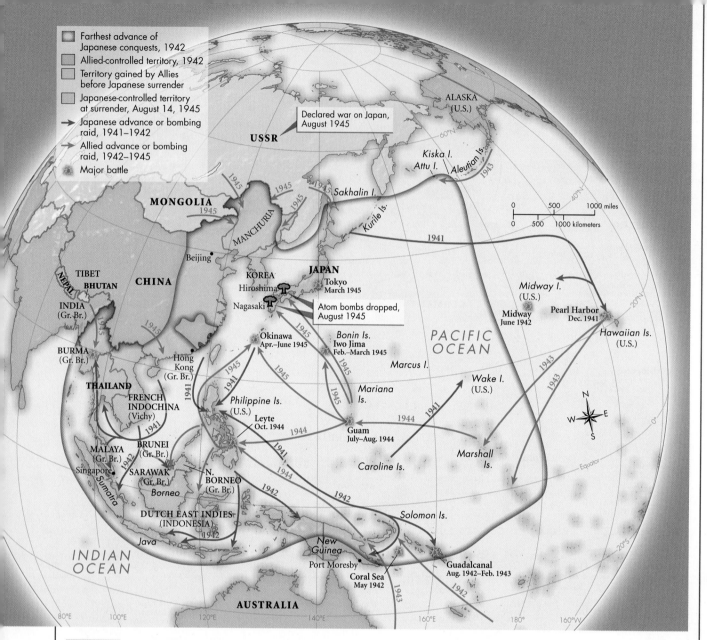

MAP 28.4

World War II in the Pacific, 1937–1945

The "Europe first" strategy of the Allies permitted Japan a comparatively free hand in the Pacific. Japan's victories were short-lived, however, despite the determined efforts of its civilians and military to sacrifice everything for victory. The many conquered peoples of the Pacific suffered mightily under Japanese rule, performing forced labor, serving as sex slaves, and bearing the brunt of the final Allied push to defeat the Axis in the Pacific.

preserved the average citizen's confidence in German might, but at the cost of undermining the actual effectiveness of his army.

As Japan swiftly captured British colonies in Asia and invaded French Indochina for its raw materials, the United States stopped supplying Japan with essential industrial goods. The Japanese government decided it should settle matters with the West, and in December 1941, its planes bombed American naval and air bases at Pearl Harbor in Hawaii and then destroyed a fleet of airplanes in the Philippines. President Roosevelt summoned the Congress to declare war on Japan. By spring 1942, the Japanese had conquered Guam, the Philippines, Malaya, Burma, Indonesia, Singapore, and much of the southwestern Pacific (see Map 28.4). As had happened with Germany's expansionist drive, the victories strengthened the appeal of the Japanese military's imperial ideology. "The era of democracy

War Intensifies in the Pacific

Allies The alliance of Great Britain, France, the Soviet Union, and the United States and their coalition partners in World War II.

Axis The alliance of Italy, Germany, and Japan and their client states in World War II.

is finished," the foreign minister announced confidently.[8] Japanese officials portrayed Emperor Hirohito as the pan-Asian monarch who would liberate Asians everywhere.

Germany and Italy quickly joined Japan and declared war on the United States—an appropriate enemy, Hitler proclaimed, as it was "half Judaized and the other half Negrified." The United States was ambivalent toward the Soviet Union despite Hitler's attack, and Stalin reciprocated the mistrust. Nonetheless, the Soviet Union joined with Great Britain, the Free French (an exile government based in London), and the United States to form the Grand Alliance. Twenty other countries joined this group of nations to form a coalition—known collectively as the **Allies**—who fought the **Axis** powers of Germany, Italy, and Japan. In the long run the Allies held distinct advantages in terms of manpower and access to resources, given the extensive terrain they controlled, but both sides faced the bloodiest fight in world history (see Lives and Livelihoods: Soldiers and Soldiering).

War and the World's Civilians

Victory in World War II depended on industrial productivity geared toward total war and mass killings. From the Rape of Nanjing to the horrors of the Holocaust, far more civilians than soldiers died in World War II. The Axis and the Allies alike bombed cities to destroy civilians' will to resist—a debatable tactic since it often inspired defiance rather than surrender. The Allied firebombing of Dresden and Tokyo alone killed tens of thousands of civilians, but Axis attacks caused far more civilian deaths. Chinese civilians, not Chinese soldiers, were the target of the Rape of Nanjing, and British people, not British soldiers, were the target of the Battle of Britain. Mass slaughter had a rationale behind it: in a total war, workers were as important as soldiers because they manufactured the tools of war. Neither Japan nor Germany took the resources and civilian morale of its enemies into full account, however.

The new "master races" believed it was their mission to rid the world of subhumans and then repopulate it themselves. As the German army swept through eastern Europe, it slaughtered Jews, Communists, Slavs, and others whom Nazi ideology deemed "racial inferiors" and enemies. The number of deliberately murdered civilian victims in China alone is estimated to be at least 2.5 million, with untold millions murdered elsewhere in the region. Some 3 million Japanese were then relocated as "civilizers" in conquered areas of East Asia, while "racially pure" Germans took over farms and homes in Poland and elsewhere. To lessen resistance, German occupiers tested the reading skills of those captured with the promise that they could avoid hard labor. Instead, those who could read were lined up and shot as potential rebel leaders.

The extermination of Jews became a special focus of the Nazis. Crowded into urban ghettos, stripped of their possessions, and living on minimal rations, countless eastern European Jews died of starvation and disease—the Nazis' initial plan for reducing the Jewish population. Soon the Nazis put into operation the "Final Solution," their bureaucratic plan for the extermination of all of Europe's Jews by rounding them up for transport to death camps. Soldiers, ordinary civilians, police, scientists, and doctors—all participated in the **Holocaust**. Extermination camps were developed specifically for the purposes of mass murder, though some, like Auschwitz-Birkenau in Poland, served as both death and labor camps. Captives, among them Hans Kantorowsky, were herded into gas chambers where they were killed by lethal gas, and then the corpses were burned in specially designed crematoria. As of 1943, Auschwitz had the capacity to burn 1.7 million bodies per year.

For all their anti-Semitic bluster, the Nazis took pains to hide the true purpose of the camps. Those not chosen for immediate murder in the camps had their heads shaved,

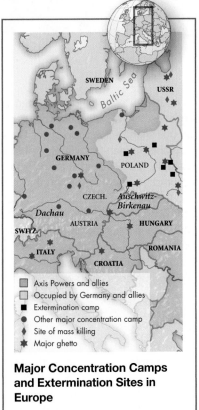

Major Concentration Camps and Extermination Sites in Europe

Holocaust The genocidal murder of some 6 million Jews by the Germans during World War II in an attempt to exterminate European Jewry.

Soldiers and Soldiering

African American Sailors in World War II

The U.S. military offered African Americans opportunity as well as danger in the struggle to defeat fascism. Even as they themselves faced discrimination in the armed forces, many saw the war as a campaign to promote universal rights and to defeat the forces of racism and ethnic supremacy. Having participated in the great moral victory of defeating violent bigotry abroad, they often joined the civil rights campaign after the war to defeat violent bigotry at home. (Bettmann/Corbis.)

Between 1930 and 1945 tens of millions of men and women worldwide became soldiers, joining both regular armies and paramilitary groups such as those run by the Chinese Communist Party and the German National Socialist (Nazi) Party. In 1927, for example, Mao Zedong, a young leader among Chinese Communists, helped decide that the groups should become a "Red Army" rather than organize into a traditional army. This paramilitary group marched northward through rural regions of China, adding recruits and ministering to the needs of peasants even as it indoctrinated them and took their resources. The German Nazi and Italian fascist paramilitary groups inflicted violence on strikers, on Communists,

and, in the case of the Nazis, on Jews. During tough economic times, when jobs in the civilian workforce were lacking, men found a livelihood in paramilitary armies.

Thus, well before World War II, there was active soldiering and warfare. Indeed, many people wondered if war ever really ended. In the deadly Chaco War (1932–1935) between Bolivia and Paraguay to increase territory, especially where oil exploration was taking place, teenage boys were drafted. One Bolivian survivor, drafted at age fifteen, recalled, "We had the luck to have bad commanders. They didn't lead us. . . . They sent all the soldiers to the front, and they stayed behind. They didn't give us a single thing to eat nor a single

The Holocaust   were disinfected, and then given prison garments—many of them so thin and tattered that they offered no protection against winter cold and rain. So began life in "a living hell," as one survivor wrote of the starvation, overwork, and disease. In the name of advancing "racial science," doctors in German concentration camps performed unbelievably cruel medical experiments and operations with no anesthesia on pregnant women, twins, and other innocent people. But prisoners developed strategies for survival, forging friendships that sustained them. Thanks to the food and favors he received from fellow prisoners, wrote Auschwitz survivor Primo Levi, "I managed not to forget that I myself was a man." In the end, 6 million Jews, the vast majority from eastern Europe, along with a mosaic of

thing to drink. . . . For this simple reason [soldiers] collapsed . . . they died."[1]

The highest ranks of the military were generally staffed by social elites and treated well. In China, Jiang Jieshi, from a relatively prosperous family, attended Baoding Military Academy. He then trained in Japan, where high levels of literacy and knowledge of the classics were central, so officers usually came from homes that were cultured. In the United States, movie stars and children from the highest ranks of society, including the sons and daughters of senators and millionaires, volunteered for World War II and were often placed in less dangerous regions. Ordinary members of the infantry, however, were on the frontlines, where the most common activity was digging, especially the foxholes in which they lived and protected themselves.

For many, political belief was a major factor in warfare. "The only thing that keeps me always on my feet and always ready: faith in God and in the Duce," one Italian soldier wrote from the front. From their training, Japanese soldiers came to believe "we are all samurai now," and an Australian soldier observed that whatever the character of the individual Japanese soldier, "good or bad, kind or sadistic, they had one supreme virtue . . . a courage that I believe to be unequalled in our time."[2]

There were failures in instilling belief, however. After their increasing exploitation during the depression, Africans often hid from recruiters and village chiefs in charge of wartime forced labor. In Southern Rhodesia, they used colonial ideology to justify their draft-dodging: "We are women. The White people are our menfolk to whom we look for guidance and protection. We have never had the courage or the ability to fight in war."[3]

War was a grim experience for most—they might face starvation in prison camps, epidemic disease, horrific wounds, wrenching physical and mental torture, suicide, cannibalism, and death. Yet soldiers' lives also had a bright side based on the loyal comradeship that developed during combat. Many professed not to fight for a cause but for the well-being of those fighting alongside them, and others found love and support on ships, in hospitals, and on the battlefield. Some believed that the military offered opportunity, among them African Americans, even though many had grown cynical when their efforts in World War I brought no relief from lynching, job discrimination, and open racism more generally. Soldiers might gain new technological skills and even find wholly new livelihoods to pursue in the future.

1. Cristobal Arancibia, quoted in "Cristobal Arancibia: The Life of a Bolivian Peasant During the Chaco War, 1932–1935," ed. W. H. Beezley and J. Ewell, *Human Tradition in Latin America: The Twentieth Century* (Wilmington, DE: Scholarly Resources, 1987), 97.
2. Quoted in John Keegan, *Soldiers: A History of Men in Battle* (New York: Viking Penguin, 1986), 51.
3. Quoted in David Johnson, *World War II and the Scramble for Labour in Colonial Zimbabwe, 1939–1948* (Harare: University of Zimbabwe Press, 2000), 18.

QUESTIONS TO CONSIDER

1. What specific advantages did soldiers from many walks of life see in joining the military?

2. How would you describe soldiers' lives from 1930 to 1945, and how did they vary?

3. What were the class dimensions of the military?

For Further Information:
Cottam, Kazimiera Janina. *Soviet Airwomen in Combat in World War II*. 1983.
Johnson, David. *World War II and the Scramble for Labour in Colonial Zimbabwe, 1939–1948*. 2000.
Keegan, John. *Soldiers: A History of Men in Battle*. 1986.
Montgomerie, Deborah. *Love in a Time of War: Letter-Writing in the Second World War*. 2005.

millions of Roma, homosexuals, Slavs, and others, were murdered in the Nazis' organized, genocidal fury.

The Axis countries remained at a disadvantage throughout the war despite their early conquests. Although the war accelerated economic production some 300 percent between 1940 and 1944 in all belligerent countries, the Allies produced more than three times as much as the Axis in 1943 alone. Even while some of its lands were occupied and many of its cities besieged, the Soviet Union increased its production of weapons. Both Japan and Germany made the most of their lower capacity, with such tactics as Japan's suicide, or *kamikaze*, attacks in the last months of the war. Hitler had to prevent wartime shortages

Societies at War

The Warsaw Ghetto, 1943

From the 1930s on, the Nazis considered Jews and others to be both dangerous enemies and inferiors unworthy of living; they drove them into ghettos, confiscated their property, took away their livelihoods, and deprived them of food and fuel. Despite being confined to these ghettos, residents learned of the ongoing Holocaust, and in 1943 the people of the Warsaw ghetto staged an uprising. Those shown here were taken prisoner, and the uprising was brutally put down. (SZ Photo/ Bridgeman Art Library.)

because he had come to power promising to end economic suffering, not increase it. Japanese propaganda, however, persuaded civilians to endure extreme scarcity for the sake of the nation. The use of millions of forced laborers and resources from occupied areas reduced Axis deprivation.

Allied governments were overwhelmingly successful in generating civilian participation, especially among women. Soviet women constituted more than half the workforce by war's end. They dug massive antitank trenches around Moscow and other threatened cities, and eight hundred thousand volunteered for the military, even serving as pilots. As the Germans invaded, Soviet citizens moved entire factories eastward. In Germany and Italy, where government policy particularly exalted motherhood and kept women from the best-paying jobs, officials began to realize that women were desperately needed in offices and factories. Japanese women rushed to help, but even changing the propaganda to stress that they should take jobs did not convince German women to join the low-paid female workforce.

Even more than in World War I, propaganda saturated society in movie theaters and on the radio. People were glued to their radios for war news, but much of it was tightly controlled. Japan, like Germany, generally withheld news of defeats and large numbers of casualties to maintain civilian support. The antireligious Soviet government found radio programming from the Russian Orthodox clergy that boosted patriotism, and Japanese propagandists taught that both the war and the emperor were sacred. Filmmakers— subject to censorship unless their films conveyed the "right" message, including racial thinking—encouraged patriotism with stories of aviation heroes and faithful wives left behind. The German government continued to advertise ugly caricatures of Jews, Slavs, and Roma; Allied propaganda depicted Germans as gorillas and "Japs" as uncivilized, insectlike fanatics.

Such characterizations eased the way for the USSR to uproot Muslims and minority ethnic groups as potential Nazi collaborators and for the U.S. government to force citizens of Japanese origin into its own concentration camps. Fred Korematsu, born in Oakland,

California in 1919, was one U.S. citizen of Japanese descent who refused to leave his home on the grounds that only a handful of Americans of Italian and German descent were similarly interned. Korematsu was arrested and ultimately sent to a camp surrounded by barbed wire, machine guns, and watchtowers. Like that of many interned Japanese Americans, his family's property was taken and sold and he was left to find odd jobs, but he continued to fight his removal to a concentration camp and became a pioneer for civil rights.

Colonized peoples were drawn into the war through conscription into the armies and forced labor. Some 2 million Indian men served the Allied cause, as did several hundred thousand Africans, even as governments stripped their families of resources. To prevent Japanese confiscation of Indian resources, the British withdrew all shipping from Bengali ports, leaving the region with no food deliveries. "When I was nine years old we had the Bengal famine," one Indian remembered. "The victims suddenly emerged in millions—it seemed from absolutely nowhere, dying in incredible numbers."[9] Some 3 to 7 million Bengali civilians died of starvation—a British-inflicted Holocaust, as many have called it. Among the peoples of the great powers, Soviet children and old people were at the greatest risk of starvation; an adolescent alive during the siege of Leningrad would probably have been among the 1 million residents of the city who starved to death. Where there were resources, bureaucrats around the war-torn world regulated the production and distribution of food, clothing, and household products, all of which were of lower quality than before the war.

Collaboration with Axis conquerors was common among colonial people who had suffered the racist oppression of the Western powers. As the Japanese swept through the Pacific and parts of East Asia, they conscripted local men into their army; many volunteered willingly. Subhas Bose, educated

Forced Labor in Vietnam

Japan promised the colonized peoples of the world—especially those in Asia—that Japanese rule would bring liberation and real benefits to those who had been dominated by the Western powers. The reality was usually quite different. Korean, Chinese, and other women were made to serve as sex slaves to members of the Japanese military, and other civilians were forced to provide manual labor, such as these Vietnamese women digging what appears to be a trench to defend the military against tanks and other enemy vehicles. (bpk, Berlin/Art Resource, NY.)

in England and accepted into the Indian Civil Service, quit his post in 1921 and became a **Collaboration** prominent member of the Indian Congress Party, spending time in British prisons for his activities. When World War II broke out and the British refused to grant India home rule, he went over to the Axis side and recruited an all-Indian army to fight the British in South Asia. "Gandhi wants to change human beings, and all I want to do is free India," Bose maintained, as he fought on Japan's side.[10] Throughout the Axis-occupied areas of Europe, collaborationist leaders such as Philippe Pétain in France and Vidkun Quisling in Norway provided workers and equipment for the Axis cause. Many an ordinary person moved up the economic ladder by spying for the Axis powers and working for the occupiers.

Resistance to the Axis also began early in the war. Escaping France in 1940, General **Resistance** Charles de Gaulle from his haven in London directed the Free French government, resisters on the continent, and Free French military—a mixed organization of troops of colonized Asians and Africans and soldiers and volunteers from France and other occupied

**Colonial Recruits
in World War II**

Colonial forces played as
significant a role in World War II
as they had in World War I.
They participated by the millions
in armies, and both the Axis and
the Allies drove colonized
people under their control into
forced labor. Often colonized
peoples used the war to work
against their imperial masters.
These North African soldiers,
who were probably under the
rule of the French before the
war, appear to have joined
forces with the Germans as they
chat with an officer. (akg-images/
ullstein bild.)

countries. Other resisters, called partisans, planned assassinations of collaborators and
enemy officers and bombed bridges and rail lines. Although the Catholic Church officially
supported Mussolini, Catholic and Protestant clergy and their parishioners were among
those who set up resistance networks, often hiding Jews and political suspects. Ordinary
people also fought back through everyday activities. Homemakers circulated newsletters
urging demonstrations at prisons where civilians were detained and in marketplaces where
food was rationed. Jews rose up against their Nazi captors in Warsaw in 1943 but were
mercilessly butchered. Resisters played on stereotypes: women often carried weapons to
assassination sites and seduced and murdered enemy officers. "Naturally the Germans
didn't think that a woman could have carried a bomb," explained one female Italian
resister, "so this became the woman's task."[11]

From Allied Victory to the Cold War 1943–1945

FOCUS

How did the Allied victory unfold, and what
were the causes of that victory?

Allied victory began to look certain by 1943, even though tough fighting
still lay ahead. The Allies crashed through German lines in the east, south,
and west of Europe, while war in the Pacific turned in the Allies' favor,
despite the Japanese policy of resistance to the death. In a series of wartime meetings, Churchill, Stalin, and Roosevelt—nicknamed the Big Three—planned the
peace that they expected to achieve, including the creation of a new organization called the
United Nations to prevent another war. On the eve of victory, however, distrust among
the Allies was about to provoke yet another struggle for supremacy—the Cold War
between the United States and the Soviet Union.

The Axis Defeated

Germany and Italy Crushed

The Battle of Stalingrad in 1942–1943 marked a turning point in the war in Europe.
In August 1942 the German army began a siege of this city, whose capture would give
Germany access to Soviet oil. The fighting dragged on much longer than the Germans

expected, and when winter arrived, the German army was ill-equipped to deal with harsh conditions. After months of ferocious fighting, in February 1943, the Soviet army captured the ninety thousand Germans who survived the freezing cold and near-constant combat. Meanwhile, the British army in North Africa faced off against German troops under General Erwin Rommel. Skilled in the new kind of mobile warfare, Rommel let his tanks move hundreds of miles from supply lines. He could not, however, overcome Allied access to secret German communication codes, and this access ultimately helped the Allies capture Morocco and Algeria in the fall of 1942. After driving Rommel out of Africa, the Allies landed in Sicily in July 1943. A slow, bitter fight for the Italian peninsula followed, lasting until April 1945, when Allied forces finally triumphed. After Italy's liberation, partisans shot Mussolini and his mistress and hung their dead bodies for public display.

The victory at Stalingrad marked the beginning of the Soviet drive westward, during which the Soviets still bore the brunt of the Nazi war machine. British and U.S. warplanes bombed German cities, and on June 6, 1944, known as D-Day, combined Allied forces attacked the heavily fortified French beaches of Normandy and then fought their way through the German-held territory of western France. Meanwhile the Soviets took Poland, Bulgaria, Romania, and finally Hungary during the winter of 1944–1945. As the military vice tightened, Hitler refused to spare the German people by surrendering. Instead, he committed suicide with his wife, Eva Braun, as the Soviet army took Berlin in April. Germany finally surrendered on May 8, 1945.

The Allies had followed a "Europe first" strategy for conducting the war, but had nonetheless steadily pursued the Japanese in the Pacific. In 1942, Allied forces destroyed some of Japan's formidable naval power in battles at Midway Island and Guadalcanal (see again Map 28.4). Japan lacked the capacity to recoup losses of ships or of manpower, while the Allies had not only their own productive power but access to materiel manufactured in Australia, India, and elsewhere around the world. The Allies stormed one Pacific island after another, gaining more bases from which to cut off Japanese supply lines and launch bombers toward Japan. In response to kamikaze attacks and the suicidal resistance of soldiers and civilians alike, the Allies stepped up their bombing of major cities, killing some 120,000 civilians in its spring 1945 firebombing of Tokyo.

Turning the Tide in the Pacific

Meanwhile a U.S.-based international team of more than one hundred thousand workers, including scientists, technicians, and other staff, had secretly developed the atomic bomb. The Japanese practice of fighting to the last man rather than surrendering persuaded Allied military leaders that the defeat of Japan might cost the lives of hundreds of thousands of Allied soldiers (and even more Japanese). On August 6, 1945, the U.S. government unleashed the new atomic weapon on Hiroshima. Three days later a second bomb was dropped on Nagasaki. The two bombings killed 140,000 people instantly; tens of thousands died later from burns, radiation poisoning, and other wounds. Hardliners in the Japanese military wanted to continue the war, but on August 15, 1945, Japan surrendered.

The Atomic Bomb

Postwar Plans and Uncertainties

Although the fighting had ended, conditions for lasting peace were poor at best. Japan, Europe, and large parts of East Asia and the Pacific lay in ruins. Governments and social order in many parts of the world were fragile if not totally broken. An estimated 100 million people had died in the war, and perhaps an equal number were homeless refugees, wandering the devastated land in search of food and shelter. Forced into armies or labor camps for war production, colonial peoples were in full rebellion or close to it. For a second time in three decades, they had seen their imperial masters killing one another, slaughtered by the very technology that was supposed to make Western civilization superior (see Seeing the Past: Technological Warfare: Civilization or Barbarism?). With their respect for empire undone, it was only a matter of time before colonized peoples would mount battles of their own for independence.

Technological Warfare: Civilization or Barbarism?

Hiroshima, September 2, 1945 (Bettmann/Corbis.)

This photograph of Hiroshima, Japan, shows the near-total destruction that resulted from the dropping of the first atomic bomb on August 6, 1945. The atomic bomb was the work of the world's top scientists during World War II, and its development resulted from the theories of brilliant people like Albert Einstein. So too, other increasingly sophisticated weaponry and methods for mass killing paralleled the great advances in a number of scientific fields. For some two centuries, the West characterized its scientific achievements as the hallmark of advanced civilization and viewed as backward those countries without them. It continued to make such claims as increasingly powerful nuclear weapons were tested in the Pacific and on the Asian continent, resulting in the annihilation of entire islands and the destruction of the environment. The visual and other evidence from Hiroshima can lead us to reflect to what degree the ability to destroy more lives than ever before and with less effort is a mark of high civilization or of barbarism.

EXAMINING THE EVIDENCE

1. How is a moral argument for the atomic bomb possible?

2. How would you situate the atomic bomb and its use during World War II in the scientific and intellectual history of the West?

The United Nations

Amid chaos, a wartime agreement led to the founding of the **United Nations** (UN). Franklin Roosevelt coined the term *United Nations* for the alliance of twenty-six countries formed on January 1, 1942, to fight the Axis. With the weakening of the League of Nations during the 1930s and its collapse after the outbreak of war, international institutions for collective security were absent, giving the formation of the United Nations a new urgency and the term a new meaning. In 1944, even as the war proceeded, delegates from the Big Three plus China met in Washington, D.C., to draw up plans for the UN. As a result of this often-ignored wartime conference, in June 1945, before the war was over, representatives from fifty countries signed the UN charter, setting the conditions for peaceful international cooperation. It remained to be seen whether this new organization would be more successful than its predecessor at maintaining world peace.

The Cold War

As the world sought to recover, a new struggle called the Cold War was taking root between the world's two military powers—the United States and the Soviet Union. At war's end, Stalin continued to see the world as hostile to his nation; the United States abruptly cut off many aid programs to the starving Soviet Union. In the face of this hostility, Stalin believed that Soviet security depended on not just a temporary military occupation of eastern Europe and Germany but a permanent "buffer zone" of European states loyal to the USSR as a safeguard against a revived Germany in particular and the anti-Soviet Western states more generally. Across the Atlantic, President Harry S. Truman, who had succeeded Roosevelt after his death in April 1945, saw the initial temporary occupation as the beginning of an era of permanent Communist expansion, especially since the Soviets were setting up friendly governments in the areas of eastern Europe they had liberated. By 1946, members of the U.S. State Department were describing Stalin as a "neurotic"

United Nations The international organization of nations established at the end of World War II to replace the League of Nations and to promote diplomacy and the peaceful settlement of disputes for countries worldwide.

Asian ruler prepared to continue the centuries-old Russian thirst for world domination. For his part, Stalin claimed that "it was the Soviet army that won" World War II and warned Anglo-American forces not to continue moving eastward. In a March 1946 speech, former British Prime Minister Churchill warned that an "iron curtain" had fallen across Europe, cutting off the East from the West and dividing the world into two hostile camps.

As the Cold War came to inflame global politics, it affected the world's peoples as World War II had done. Eva Kantorowsky was again ensnared as she and her family, like many of Shanghai's refugees, tried to emigrate to the United States. But many Americans, even though they had fought against Hitler, remained anti-Semitic, and the U.S. Congress passed legislation blocking the immigration of Jewish refugees after the war. Jews were Communists, members of Congress claimed, echoing Nazi ideology as they played the Cold War card. Eva eventually arrived in the United States despite the growing intensity of the Cold War.

COUNTERPOINT
Nonviolence and Pacifism in an Age of War

The wars of the twentieth century—hot and cold—focused the attention of peoples throughout the world on the exercise of military power. Leading nations from Germany and Japan to the Soviet Union and the United States saw military capacity as the measure of national greatness. Some activists and ordinary people, however, realized that nonviolent tactics could be powerful and effective tools to undermine colonialism and the doctrine of total war. Traditional modes of resistance shaped some efforts, while religious precepts underlay others.

> **FOCUS**
>
> In what ways did peace movements serve as a countertrend to events in the period from 1929 to 1945?

Traditional Tactics: The Example of Nigerian Women

In 1929, women in British-controlled Nigeria rebelled at the new tax the government tried to impose on them as part of its effort to resolve economic problems in England. They painted their bodies and sang and danced in the nude outside the homes of local tax collectors, who attacked and even burned some of the women's houses. Their method was called "sitting on a man," because it was generally used against rulings by men that the women considered unjust. British officials justified shooting the women, killing fifty-three of them, by calling the women's behavior irrational and dangerous. Throughout the 1930s and up into the 1980s, women in Nigeria used traditional nonviolent tactics, including removing all their clothing, to protest low prices for their palm products and the exploitative practices of oil companies in their region.

The women of Nigeria eventually became national heroes of the movement for independence, and other pacifist traditions were mobilized during the 1920s and 1930s as well. Jainism, an ancient South Asian religion, held to the belief in *ahimsa*—the idea of doing no harm—and other Asian religions adopted this belief, leading many to become pacifists.

Gandhi and Civil Disobedience

In the 1920s and 1930s, practitioners of peaceful protest adopted an approach that came to be variously called **civil disobedience** or nonviolent resistance. Mohandas Gandhi, for one, led his followers in 1930 on a twenty-three-day "Salt March" to break the law giving the British a monopoly on salt—a necessity of life that exists freely in nature. Professing to model his tactics on those of the British suffragists and the teachings of Jesus, Buddha, and other spiritual leaders, Gandhi's nonviolent protest highlighted India's difference

civil disobedience A political strategy of deliberately but peacefully breaking the law to protest oppression and obtain political change.

Mohandas Gandhi and Nonviolence

Indian leader Mohandas (Mahatma "great souled one") Gandhi led a mass movement, but his followers flocked to him because of a message entirely different from those of Mussolini and Hitler. Gandhi was neither bombastic nor wedded to material and militaristic display. Instead he denounced the violence and materialism of the West, preferring *Satyagraha*— soulforce—to physical conflict, and spinning by hand to parading tanks and rockets. (The Art Archive/Kharbine-Tapabor/ Collection NB.)

from militaristic, even genocidal Westerners, as he noted in more than one of his writings. He called his strategy *Satyagraha* (SAH-ty-ah-GRAH-hah)—truth and firmness—and rejected the view that his tactics were "passive." Rather, such acts as taking salt and then being beaten or arrested (as Gandhi was) demanded incredible discipline to remain opposed but at the same time nonviolent.

Pacifism, including the tactics of Gandhi, unfolded with real conviction both during the pre–World War I arms race and with even greater fervor in the aftermath of World War I. Feminists played key roles in the development of the Women's International League for Peace and Freedom after that war, and religious groups in many parts of the world contested what they saw as a new militarism developing in the interwar years. Many of these groups remained firmly pacifistic even with the rise of fascism, and were ridiculed either as deluded or as traitors. British novelist George Orwell called all pacifists in the 1930s "objectively fascist." After World War II, civil rights activists in the United States embraced nonviolence and civil disobedience. In the 1950s and early 1960s they "sat in" to desegregate lunch counters, buses, and public facilities that were closed to them, even as officials whipped, hosed, and murdered them. Many still see committed pacifists as deluded thinkers or as traitors to the nation-state, but none can deny that for some causes pacifists have been remarkably effective.

Conclusion

The Great Depression, which destroyed the lives and livelihoods of millions of people throughout the world, created conditions in which dictators and authoritarian rulers thrived because they promised to restore national greatness and prosperity. Mobilized by the mass media, people turned from the representative institutions that were accused of failing them and supported militaristic leaders who offered hope of a brighter future. Authoritarian leaders used aggression and violence to gain support, but others—both nonviolent resisters in the colonies and those with vivid memories of World War I—took up pacifism or a strategy of nonviolent civil disobedience to achieve their objectives, objectives that included the overthrow of authoritarian leaders.

Leaders of the Western democracies, hoping to avoid another war, permitted Hitler and Mussolini to menace Europe unimpeded throughout the 1930s. In Asia, the Japanese military convinced citizens that the nation deserved an extensive empire and that white domination must be ended. The coalition that formed to stop Germany, Italy, and Japan was an uneasy confederation among the Allied powers of France, Britain, the Soviet Union, and the United States. At the war's end, Europe's economies were shattered, its population reduced, its colonies on the verge of independence, its peoples starving and homeless. Occupied by the victorious U.S. Army, Japan was similarly devastated, as were large swaths of North Africa, Asia, and the Pacific Islands. People who had been dislocated by the war—such as Eva Kantorowsky and her family—were dislocated once again. The massive death and destruction of the war ended Europe's global dominance. Now the Soviet Union and the United States reigned as the world's superpowers, with the newly formed United Nations, a global organization, the only potential check on the two nations' unprecedented power.

In the decades following World War II, the United States and the Soviet Union competed for power and influence in every corner of the globe, seeing every local and regional development through the prism of the Cold War ideological split. Amid this growing divide, World War II brought another notable change: millions of people determined as a result of their experience of global war that colonialism, whether that of the French, British, or Japanese, would not long survive.

NOTES

1. Ana Núñez Machin, quoted in Angel Santana Suárez , "Angel Santana Suárez: Cuban Sugar Worker," in *The Human Tradition in Latin America: The Twentieth Century*, ed. William H. Beezley and Judith Ewell (Wilmington, DE: Scholarly Resources, 1987), 85, 86.
2. Quoted in Piers Brendon, *The Dark Valley: A Panorama of the 1930s* (London: Jonathan Cape, 2000), 175.
3. Quoted in Ann Farnsworth-Alvear, *Dulcinea in the Factory: Myths, Morals, Men, and Women in Colombia's Industrial Experiment, 1905–1960* (Durham, NC: Duke University Press, 2000), 124, 125.
4. Edvard Radzinsky, *Stalin: The First In-Depth Biography Based on Explosive New Documents from Russia's Secret Archives*, trans. H. T. Willetts (New York: Doubleday, 1996), 363.
5. Jiang Jieshi, quoted in Patricia Buckley Ebrey, *Cambridge Illustrated History of China* (Cambridge, U.K.: Cambridge University Press, 1996), 277.
6. Herbert Bix, *Hirohito and the Making of Modern Japan* (New York: HarperCollins, 2000), 274–276.
7. Quoted in Bix, *Hirohito*, 315.
8. Matsuoka Yosuke, quoted in Bix, *Hirohito*, 374.
9. Amartya Sen, "Interview," *Journal of Economic Perspectives* (1994).
10. Quoted in *The Washington Post*, May 23, 2005.
11. Carla Capponi, interviewed in Shelley Saywell, *Women in War: From World War II to El Salvador* (New York: Penguin, 1986), 82.

RESOURCES FOR RESEARCH

1929: The Great Depression Begins

The Great Depression was a global event, affecting peasants and farmers, factory workers and shopkeepers, and the upper classes. Balderston and Rothermund provide excellent surveys of the worldwide impact.

Balderston, Theo. *The World Economy and National Economies in the Interwar Slump*. 2003.

Brendon, Piers. *The Dark Valley: A Panorama of the 1930s*. 2000.

Feinstein, Charles H., et al. *The World Economy Between the World Wars*. 2008.

Rothermund, Dietmar. *The Global Impact of the Great Depression, 1929–1939*. 1996.

Vernon, James. *Modernity's Hunger: How Imperial Britain Created and Failed to Solve the Problem of Hunger in the Modern World*. 2006.

Militarizing the Masses in the 1930s

Many postwar politicians promised relief of economic hardship through military conquest and discipline. Regimented parades and other displays of military power attracted mass audiences. Kushner's book captures the unfolding of those promises in the case of Japan in Manchuria.

Hammer, Joshua. *Yokohama Burning: The Deadly 1923 Earthquake and Fire That Helped Forge the Path to World War II.* 2006.

Kaplan, Marion. *Between Dignity and Despair: Jewish Life in Nazi Germany.* 1998.

Kushner, Barak. *The Thought War: Japanese Imperial Propaganda.* 2006.

Naimark, Norman. *Stalin's Genocides.* 2010.

* Pa, Chin. *Family.* 1931.

Wildt, Michael. *An Uncompromising Generation: The Nazi Leadership of the Reich Security Main Office.* 2009.

Global War, 1937–1945

The scholarship on World War II is extensive. These works cover facets of global warfare.

Browning, Christopher. *Remembering Survival: Inside a Nazi Slave Labor Camp.* 2010.

Fyne, Robert. *Long Ago and Far Away: Hollywood and the Second World War.* 2008.

Johnson, David. *World War II and the Scramble for Labour in Colonial Zimbabwe, 1939–1948.* 2000.

Peattie, Mark R. *Sunburst: The Rise of Japanese Naval Air Power, 1909–1940.* 2002.

St. Andrews University in Scotland provides a number of links to sources for the diplomatic history of the origins of World War II: http://www.st-andrews.ac.uk/~pv/courses/prewar/resources.html.

Weinberg, Gerhard L. *A World at Arms: A Global History of World War II.* 2005.

From Allied Victory to the Cold War, 1943–1945

Among the many fascinating books about the war is Spector's account of the conflict's end in Asia, where Japanese soldiers and conquered peoples did not believe the war had ended and where in many cases the Allies enlisted remnants of the Japanese army to crush independence movements.

Bucur, Maria. *Heroes and Victims: Remembering War in Twentieth-Century Romania.* 2009.

Krylova, Anna. *Soviet Women in Combat: A History of Violence on the Eastern Front.* 2010.

Miner, Steven Merritt. *Stalin's Holy War: Religion, Nationalism, and Alliance Politics, 1941–1945.* 2003.

Rhodes, Richard. *Arsenals of Folly: The Making of the Nuclear Arms Race.* 2007.

Spector, Ronald H. *In the Ruins of Empire: The Japanese Surrender and the Battle for Postwar Asia.* 2007.

COUNTERPOINT: Nonviolence and Pacifism in an Age of War

Pacifism and nonviolent resistance were global phenomena. The anthology of Brock and Socknat provides a look at worldwide pacifism in the interwar years.

Allman, Jean, Susan Geiger, and Nakanyike Musisi, eds. *Women in African Colonial Histories.* 2002.

Brock, Peter, and Thomas P. Socknat, eds. *Challenge to Mars: Essays on Pacifism from 1918 to 1945.* 1999.

Matera, Marc, Misty L. Bastian, and Susan Kingsley Kent. *The Women's War of 1929: Gender and Violence in Colonial Nigeria.* 2011.

Siegel, Mona. *The Moral Disarmament of France: Education, Pacifism, and Patriotism, 1914–1940.* 2004.

Tidrick, Kathryn. *Gandhi: A Political and Spiritual Life.* 2007.

* Primary source.

▶ **For additional primary sources from this period,** see *Sources of Crossroads and Cultures.*

▶ **For Web sites, images, and documents related to topics in this chapter,** see Make History at bedfordstmartins.com/smith.

The major global development in this chapter ▶ The causes and outcomes of the Great Depression and World War II.

IMPORTANT EVENTS

1920s	Collapse of commodity prices around the world
1929	Crash of the U.S. stock market; global depression begins; Stalin's "liquidation of the kulaks"
1930	Gandhi's Salt March
1930s	Sweden begins setting up welfare state
1931	Japan invades Manchuria
1933	Hitler comes to power in Germany and ends representative government
1934	Chinese Communists begin Long March
1935	Nuremberg Laws against the Jews in Germany; Italy invades Ethiopia
1936	Purges and show trials begin in USSR
1937	Japan attacks China; World War II begins in Asia
1939	Germany invades Poland; World War II begins in Europe
1941	Germany invades USSR; Japan attacks Pearl Harbor; United States enters the war
1941–1945	Holocaust
1943	USSR defeats Germany at Stalingrad
1945	Fall of Berlin and surrender of Germany; UN charter signed; United States drops atomic bombs; Japan surrenders

KEY TERMS

Allies (p. 944)
appeasement (p. 940)
Axis (p. 944)
central economic planning (p. 933)
civil disobedience (p. 953)
five-year plan (p. 933)

Great Depression (p. 929)
Greater East Asia Co-Prosperity Sphere (p. 941)
Holocaust (p. 945)
purge (p. 934)
totalitarianism (p. 933)
United Nations (p. 952)

CHAPTER OVERVIEW QUESTIONS

1. How did ordinary people react to the Great Depression, and how did their reactions differ from country to country?

2. Why were dictators and antidemocratic leaders able to come to power in the 1930s, and how did all countries—autocratic and democratic alike—militarize the masses?

3. How are the Great Depression and World War II related historical events?

SECTION FOCUS QUESTIONS

1. What was the global impact of both the Great Depression and the attempts to overcome it?

2. How did dictatorships and democracies attempt to mobilize the masses?

3. How did World War II progress on the battlefront and the home front?

4. How did the Allied victory unfold, and what were the causes of that victory?

5. In what ways did peace movements serve as a countertrend to events in the period from 1929 to 1945?

MAKING CONNECTIONS

1. What are the main differences between World War I (see Chapter 27) and World War II?

2. In what specific ways did World Wars I and II affect the African and Asian colonies of the imperial powers?

3. How do the strengths and weaknesses of the Allies and the Axis compare?

4. How would you describe the importance of World War II not only to the unfolding of history but also to present-day concerns?

AT A CROSSROADS ▶

In 1957 Ghana became the first sub-Saharan nation to free itself from imperial rule. This woman celebrates not only Ghana's freedom but also its president, Kwame Nkrumah, who had led the campaign of civil disobedience against the British. Her clothing displays emblems of liberation, including Nkrumah's image—a preview of what would become the popular use of political heroes' faces on T-shirts and banners in the 1960s. At the time, Ghana marked a crossroads in global and African politics, as its leader and those who followed him advocated pan-Africanism and a political activism similar to that of Indian nationalist and spiritual leader Mohandas Gandhi. (Universal Images Group/SuperStock.)

The Emergence of New Nations in a Cold War World

1945–1970

During the early 1950s, on the first Thursday of the month, everyday life in Cairo and other major cities of the Arab world came to a standstill. Patrons of cafés huddled around the radio, and cabdrivers discharged their customers and dashed home to catch the broadcast. All were eager to tune in to a program featuring singer Umm Kulthum. Kulthum's repertoire included traditional desert songs, religious verses, and romantic ballads. Born at the beginning of the twentieth century, she began her career as a child disguised as a boy because girls were not supposed to perform in public. Singing verses from the Qur'an in her strong voice, she enraptured local audiences and her fame spread. By the 1950s she had become a national phenomenon, "the voice of Egypt" for the newly independent republic. In the words of one fan, her singing "shows our ordinary life." Even Egypt's leader Gamal Abdel Nasser, who in 1952 finally instituted a government totally free from British supervision, recognized the power of Umm Kulthum's popularity. He broadcast his speeches just before her program aired to link himself to her appeal. Traveling widely through the Middle East, Umm Kulthum used her vocal talent to encourage Arab-speaking people as a whole to celebrate their own culture as another way of shaking off the European powers.

The creation of a fully independent Egyptian republic was just one of the acts of liberation in the postwar world. From the Middle East through Africa and Asia, independence

BACKSTORY

As we saw in Chapter 28, imperial rivalries played a key role in the outbreak of World War II, the most destructive conflict in human history. By the time the war was over, as many as 100 million people had died, countries around the world lay in ruin, and the imperial system that had helped produce the war was in disarray. The chaos and confusion of the postwar world gave rise to a new set of global political trends. The formation of organizations such as the United Nations reflected new levels of cooperation among nations. At the same time, rising nationalism among colonized peoples sparked the process of decolonization. Finally, the Cold War between the United States and the Soviet Union shaped politics around the world and posed an unprecedented threat to world peace. These trends, along with the rising level of technological sophistication and the yearning of people around the world for peace and prosperity, would play major roles in defining the postwar world, a world that was more closely connected than ever before.

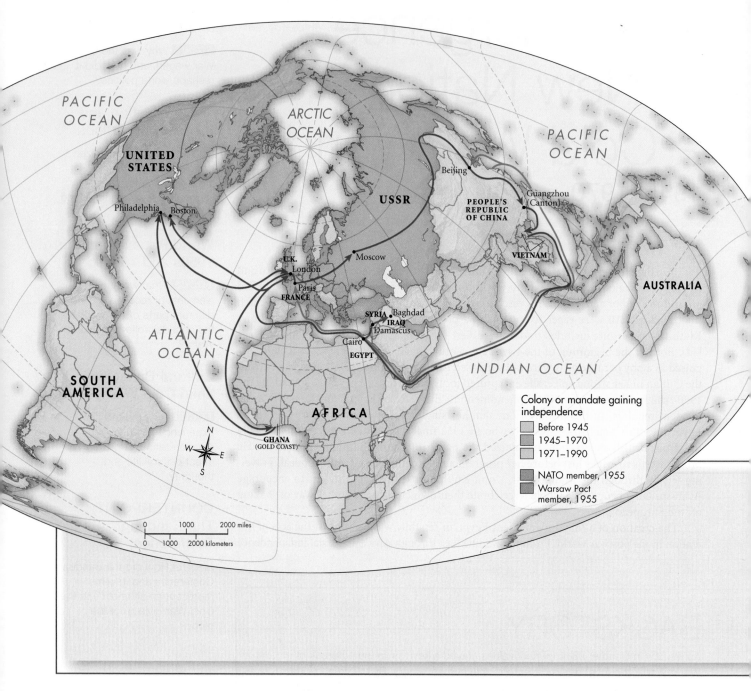

Colony or mandate gaining independence
- Before 1945
- 1945–1970
- 1971–1990

- NATO member, 1955
- Warsaw Pact member, 1955

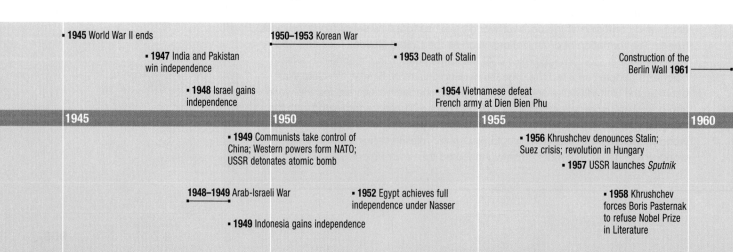

- **1945** World War II ends

- **1947** India and Pakistan win independence

- **1948** Israel gains independence

- **1950–1953** Korean War

- **1953** Death of Stalin

- **1954** Vietnamese defeat French army at Dien Bien Phu

Construction of the Berlin Wall **1961**

1945

1950

1955

1960

- **1949** Communists take control of China; Western powers form NATO; USSR detonates atomic bomb

- **1956** Khrushchev denounces Stalin; Suez crisis; revolution in Hungary

- **1957** USSR launches *Sputnik*

- **1948–1949** Arab-Israeli War

- **1952** Egypt achieves full independence under Nasser

- **1958** Khrushchev forces Boris Pasternak to refuse Nobel Prize in Literature

- **1949** Indonesia gains independence

movements toppled colonial governments that attempted to revive their control after World War II. Workers, professionals, veterans, and other activists took up arms to drive out British, French, Dutch, Belgian, and U.S. forces. **Decolonization** was followed by the difficult process of nation building. In addition to creating government structures, newly independent states had to rebuild roads destroyed in the war, erect public buildings, and create systems for educating citizens and maintaining their health. In sum, the destruction of the colonial system created the opportunity, and the necessity, for formerly colonized peoples to rebuild and redefine the connections among citizens and the relationship between newly independent nations and the rest of the world. Like Umm Kulthum, talented patriots throughout the Middle East, Asia, Africa, and Latin America devoted their livelihoods and capabilities to advancing this cause.

Postcolonial nation building took place in a vastly changed world. The old European-dominated international order was gone, replaced by the rivalry between the United States and the Soviet Union for control of a world in which many traditional political and economic systems had collapsed. The nuclear arsenals of these two "superpowers," a term coined in 1947, grew massively in the 1950s, but they were enemies who did not fight outright—at least not on their own soil. Instead, they preferred to confront each other in the developing world. The U.S.-USSR rivalry, known as the **Cold War**, set the so-called communist East against the democratic, capitalist West. When the United States discovered Soviet missile sites on the island of Cuba in 1962, the Cold War rivals took the world to the brink of nuclear disaster.

Yet there was a surge of optimistic activism after World War II. The birth of new nations and the defeat of authoritarian militarism inspired hope that life would become fairer and that people everywhere would gain the freedom to determine their own fate. Revolutionary-minded thinkers poured out new political theories, while novelists explored the often-harsh realities of independence. In rebuilding, some politicians championed the

decolonization The process of freeing regions from imperial control and creating independent nations.

Cold War The rivalry between the Soviet Union and the United States that followed World War II and shaped world politics between 1945 and 1989.

MAPPING THE WORLD
Independence Movements and New Nations

Earlier movements for freedom from colonialism were reinvigorated at the end of World War II; the Axis and Allied powers had been exhausted by this unprecedented conflict, and some were bankrupt. Independent nations emerged from the remnants of imperialism, some of them only after violent struggles with their rulers. These independent nations, however, faced a novel global situation—a bipolar world dominated by the Soviet Union and the United States and faced with a possible nuclear holocaust. This potentially disastrous confrontation was called the Cold War.

ROUTES ▼

→ Travels of Ho Chi Minh, c. 1912–1941

→ Travels of Kwame Nkrumah, c. 1930–1947

→ Travels of Umm Kulthum, c. 1932

→ Travels of Wu Guanzhong, c. 1947–1950

1962 Algeria wins independence; Cuban Missile Crisis

| 1965 | 1970 | 1975 |

c. 1966–1976 Mao Zedong's "Cultural Revolution"

well-being of their nation's citizens. Vast nation-building projects took shape; the welfare state expanded; and by the end of the 1950s economic rebirth, stimulated in part by the Cold War, had made many regions grow more rapidly than ever before. In many places, however, people caught up in events precipitated by Cold War rivalries faced a grim, and often deadly, reality. In the 1950s and 1960s, at the same time that Egyptian singer Umm Kulthum invigorated Arabs about the region's future, youthful followers of China's Mao Zedong banded together to bring about a "cultural revolution" that would transform society, killing and torturing millions of their fellow citizens in its name. The search for freedom thus differed drastically from place to place in this age of Cold War extremes.

OVERVIEW
QUESTIONS

The major global development in this chapter: The political transformations of the postwar world and their social and cultural consequences.

As you read, consider:

1. How did the Cold War affect the superpowers and the world beyond them?

2. How did the Cold War shape everyday lives and goals?

3. Why did colonial nationalism revive in the postwar world, and how did decolonization affect society and culture?

4. Why did the model of a welfare state emerge after World War II, and how did this development affect ordinary people?

World Politics and the Cold War

FOCUS

Why was the Cold War waged, and how did it reshape world politics?

In 1945, Europe's world leadership ended and the reign of the United States and the Soviet Union as the world's new superpowers began. The United States, its territory virtually untouched in the war, had become the world's economic giant, and the Soviet Union, despite suffering immense destruction, had developed enormous military might. Occupying Europe as part of the victorious alliance against Nazism and fascism, the two superpowers came to use Germany—at the heart of the continent and its politics—to divide Europe in two. By the late 1940s, the USSR had imposed communist rule throughout most of eastern Europe, while the United States poured vast amounts of money, personnel, and military equipment into western Europe and parts of Asia, Africa, and Latin America to win the allegiance of new and old nations in those areas. Both superpowers maintained dense networks of spies and conducted plots, assassinations, and other undercover operations around the world. Unwilling to confront each other head-on, they fought **proxy wars** in smaller, contained areas such as Korea, while amassing huge stockpiles of weapons—including nuclear missiles and bombs—that could annihilate the world.

The New Superpowers

The situation of the two superpowers in 1945 could not have been more different. The United States was the richest country in the world. Its industrial output had increased a

proxy war During the Cold War, a conflict in another part of the world backed by the USSR or the United States as part of their rivalry.

remarkable 15 percent annually between 1940 and 1944, a rate of growth that was reflected in workers' wages. By 1947, the United States controlled almost two-thirds of the world's gold bullion and more than half of its commercial shipping. Casting aside its post–World War I policy of nonintervention, the United States embraced its position as global leader and negotiated collective security agreements with many nations. Americans had learned about the world while tracking the progress of World War II; hundreds of thousands of American soldiers, government officials, and relief workers gained direct experience of Europe, Africa, and Asia. Although some Americans feared a postwar depression and nuclear annihilation, continued spending on industrial and military research, a baby boom, suburban housing development, and rising consumer purchases kept the economy buoyant, and most Americans were optimistic about their futures.

The Soviets emerged from the war with a well-justified sense of accomplishment. Withstanding horrendous losses, they had successfully resisted the most massive onslaught ever launched against a modern nation. Soviet citizens believed that a victory that had cost the USSR tens of millions of lives would improve everyday conditions and continue the war's relatively relaxed politics. "Life will become pleasant," one writer prophesied at war's end. "There will be much coming and going, and a lot of contacts with the West." In the 1930s, the Soviets had industrialized their nation, and in the 1940s they had defeated Nazism. With these achievements behind them, many expected an end to decades of hardship and looked forward to building a new, more open Soviet society.

Taking a very different view of the situation, Stalin moved ruthlessly to reassert control. In 1946, his new five-year plan increased production goals and mandated more stringent collectivization of agriculture. Stalin cut back the army by two-thirds to beef up the labor force, and also turned his attention to the low birthrate brought about by wartime conditions. He introduced an intense propaganda campaign emphasizing that working women should hold down jobs and also fulfill their "true nature" by producing many children.

The Cold War Unfolds 1945–1962

The Cold War, the political, economic, and ideological competition between the United States and the Soviet Union, would afflict the world for more than four decades, with lingering effects even today. Its origins remain a matter of debate. Some historians point to consistent U.S., British, and French hostility that began with the Bolshevik Revolution in 1917 and continued through World War II. Others stress Stalin's aggressive policies, notably the Nazi-Soviet alliance in 1939 and his quick claims on the Baltic states and Polish territory when World War II broke out. Even during that war, suspicions among the Allies ran deep. Stalin felt that Churchill and Roosevelt, as part of their anticommunist policy, were deliberately letting the USSR bear the brunt of Hitler's onslaught on Europe. Some Americans believed that dropping the atomic bomb on Japan would also frighten the Soviets away from seizing more land. As early as 1946, the U.S. State Department described Stalin as continuing the centuries-old Russian thirst for "world domination." In late August 1949, the USSR tested its own atom bomb, and from then on the superpowers built and stockpiled ever-more-sophisticated nuclear weapons, including hydrogen and neutron bombs. From this point on, the conflict between the superpowers carried with it the threat of global annihilation.

The United States acknowledged Soviet influence in areas the USSR occupied, but worried that the Soviets were intent on spreading communism around the world. The difficulties of postwar life in western and southern Europe made communist programs promising better conditions attractive to workers, and communist leadership in the resistance movements of World War II gave the party a powerful appeal. When in 1947 communist insurgents threatened to overrun the right-wing monarchy the British had installed in Greece, U.S. President Harry S. Truman announced what quickly became known as the Truman Doctrine, the countering of political crises that might lead to communist rule with economic and military aid. Fearing that Americans would balk at backing an antidemocratic Greece, the U.S. Congress

American Aid to Tokyo's Orphans

In addition to the homelessness, disease, and starvation caused by the war, many of Japan's citizens lost their families in the atomic- and fire-bombings. As part of the Cold War effort to win allies, the United States hurried to make things better for those most in need—including defeated enemies such as Japan and Germany—by giving them aid. These orphans in Tokyo are photographed gratefully receiving this aid. What in this image suggests both a humanitarian and a propaganda purpose to such aid programs? (Bettmann/Corbis.)

Germany Divided

containment The U.S. policy developed during the Cold War to prevent the spread of communism.

agreed to the program only if Truman would "scare the hell out of the country," as one member of Congress put it. Truman thus promoted a massive aid program as necessary to prevent global Soviet conquest, warning that "the seeds of totalitarian regimes are nurtured by misery and want."[1] As the Communists backed off in Greece, the Truman Doctrine began the U.S. Cold War policy of **containment**—the attempt to keep communism from spreading.

The Truman Doctrine was quickly followed by enactment of the European Recovery Program, popularly called the Marshall Plan, a program of massive U.S. economic aid to Europe. Announced by Secretary of State George C. Marshall in 1947, the Marshall Plan claimed to be directed not "against any country or doctrine but against hunger, poverty, desperation, and chaos." Stalin, however, saw it as a U.S. political trick that caught him without resources to offer similar economic aid to the Soviet satellite countries and thus designed to open avenues to American influence in eastern Europe. By the early 1950s, the United States had sent western Europe more than $12 billion in food, equipment, and services, and it sent the same amount to Japan alone, helping even former enemies to rebuild and thus stay in the U.S. orbit.

Taking advantage of its military occupation of the region, the Soviet Union turned its military occupation of eastern Europe into a buffer zone of satellite states directed by "people's governments." In such Soviet-allied states as Poland, Czechoslovakia, and Hungary, Stalin enforced collectivized agriculture, centralized industrialization, and the nationalization of private property. In Hungary, for example, communists seized and reapportioned all estates over twelve hundred acres. Land redistribution won the support of the poorer peasants, but enforced collectivization of farming was a brutal process for many. Others felt that ultimately their lives and their children's lives had improved. "Before we peasants were dirty and poor, we worked like dogs. . . . Was that a good life? No sir, it wasn't. . . . I was a miserable sharecropper and my son is an engineer," said one Romanian peasant.

Modernization of production in the Soviet bloc opened new technical and bureaucratic careers, but economic development in the satellite states remained slow because the USSR bought goods from these satellite states at bargain prices and sold to them at exorbitant ones. Despite this inequity, people's livelihoods changed dramatically, as they moved to cities to receive better education, health care, and jobs, albeit at the price of severe political repression. They also experienced intense immersion in Russian rather than their own national cultures.

Cold War competition led to the division of Germany. The terms of Allied agreements reached at Yalta in 1945 provided for the division of Germany and its capital city, Berlin, into four zones, each of which was occupied by one of the four principal victors in World War II—the United States, the Soviet Union, Britain, and France (see Map 29.1). The agreements provided for economic coordination among the zones, with agricultural surplus from Soviet-occupied areas feeding urban populations in the Western-controlled zones; in turn, industrial goods would be sent to the USSR. The Soviets upset this plan and instead sent equipment and dismantled industries from its zone to the Soviet Union. They transported skilled workers, engineers, and scientists to the USSR to work as virtual slave laborers. In response, France, Britain, and the United States agreed to merge their zones into a West German state that would serve as a buffer against the Soviets. The Soviets then created an East German state to act as a buffer against the West German state.

On June 24, 1948, Soviet troops blockaded Germany's capital, Berlin, located more than one hundred miles deep in the Soviet zone. The Soviets declared all of Berlin part of their zone of occupation and, expecting to starve the city into submission, refused to allow highway, railroad, and barge traffic into West Berlin. Instead of handing over Berlin, the United States flew in millions of tons of provisions to the city that just three years earlier had been the capital of the Nazi state. During the winter of 1948–1949, the Berlin airlift—"Operation Vittles," U.S. pilots called it—even funneled coal to the city to warm some 2 million isolated Berliners. The blockade was lifted in May 1949 and West Berlin remained tied to the West—a symbol of freedom to many. More than a decade later, in the summer of 1961, the East German government began construction of the Berlin Wall. The divided city had served, embarrassingly to the Soviets, as an escape route by which some 3 million people had fled to the freer, more prosperous West.

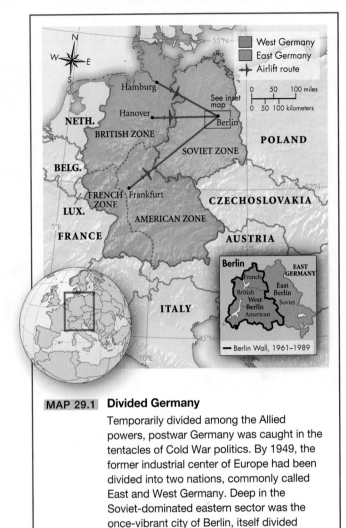

MAP 29.1   **Divided Germany**

Temporarily divided among the Allied powers, postwar Germany was caught in the tentacles of Cold War politics. By 1949, the former industrial center of Europe had been divided into two nations, commonly called East and West Germany. Deep in the Soviet-dominated eastern sector was the once-vibrant city of Berlin, itself divided east and west.

The People's Republic of China 1949

At the same time that the conflict between the superpowers in Europe was heating up, the Cold War entered a new phase with the triumph of Chinese Communist forces over the Nationalists in 1949. Before, during, and after World War II, the Nationalist government led by Jiang Jieshi (Chiang Kai-shek) and his unpopular armies had fought to eliminate rival communist forces to consolidate the Nationalist regime. With varying degrees of success, the United States and its allies did much both to prop up Jiang and to force these two Chinese enemy factions to concentrate on defeating Japan during World War II instead of annihilating one another. Once the war was over, however, the Nationalists and Communists went at each other once more.

In 1949, Mao Zedong (MOW zuh-DOONG) and his army of Communists won. From a prosperous peasant family, Mao had little in common with the farmers whom he targeted for support. He never worked as an agricultural laborer but rather spent his entire life as a politician, taking advantage of the opportunities for advancement created by the fluid conditions of modern nation building in China. At the outset he gravitated toward communism with USSR financial support. Once in power, Mao announced that Chinese communism in the new People's Republic of China would focus above all on the welfare of the peasantry rather than the industrial proletariat. Mao's government instituted social reforms such as civil equality for women and at the same time copied Soviet collectivization, rapid industrialization, and brutal repression of the privileged classes. Jiang and many of his Nationalist forces were forced to the island of Taiwan, where they refused to accept the legitimacy of Mao's communist government. With Jiang supported by the United States, Cold War fires spread to East Asia.

Mao Zedong and the Communist Victory

Proxy Wars and Cold War Alliances

The Chinese Communists' victory over the Nationalists in 1949 spurred both superpowers not only to increase their involvement in Asian politics but to form alliances with nations around the world, pulling much of the globe into the Cold War. Africa and Latin America

Cosmonauts and Astronauts

Soviet Leaders Honor Yuri Gagarin and Valentina Tereshkova
Soviet cosmonauts, like U.S. astronauts, were heroes not only in their own countries but in their Cold War blocs. The Soviets made these two cosmonauts special heroes: Gagarin (second from the left) because he was the first man in space, and Tereshkova because she was the first woman in space and represented the equality for women said to exist only in the Soviet bloc. Even today, one can find mementos of these heroes on T-shirts and caps across the former Soviet Union, reminders of the Cold War. (akg-images/RIA Nowosti.)

The space race gave rise to many new livelihoods, but none more celebrated than that of cosmonaut and astronaut, as space travelers were called in the USSR and United States, respectively. As an occupation, it attracted people of both genders and all ethnicities and classes. The parents of cosmonaut Yuri Gagarin, the first person in space, worked on a communist collective farm, and Gagarin himself labored in a foundry before the Soviet government selected him for technical education and eventual training as a pilot. His small stature, 5 feet 2 inches, helped him fit into the small cockpit of the first manned spacecraft—*Vostok I*. Television programs and films celebrate pioneers of space travel, both real and imaginary, and even today in small villages in eastern Europe one can buy T-shirts with pictures of Gagarin and other space heroes. The enduring human fascination with voyages and the longing to travel beyond the earth was on its way to being satisfied during these years.

felt the Cold War's impact as guerrilla fighters, spies, and activists for both sides blanketed their regions. The Cold War even reached into space: in 1957, the Soviets successfully launched the first artificial earth satellite, *Sputnik*, and in 1961 they put the first cosmonaut, Yuri Gagarin, in orbit around the earth. The Soviets' edge in space technology shocked the Western bloc as the superpowers continued their rivalries on the ground with more traditional weapons (see Lives and Livelihoods: Cosmonauts and Astronauts).

The Korean War

The two superpowers faced off indirectly in Korea, which after World War II had been divided into two nations, North and South Korea. After border skirmishes by both sides, in 1950 the North Koreans, supported by the Soviet Union, invaded the U.S.-backed South. The United States maneuvered the UN Security Council into approving a "police action" against the North, and UN forces quickly drove well into North Korean territory, where they were met by the Chinese army supported by Soviet planes. Fighting continued for another two and a half years, with 3 million civilian deaths, but the war remained a stalemate. The opposing sides finally agreed to a settlement in 1953 that changed nothing: Korea would remain divided as before. The United States increased its military spending from

After the successful 1957 launch of *Sputnik*, the Soviets' edge in space so shocked the Western bloc that it motivated the creation in 1958 of the U.S. National Aeronautics and Space Administration (NASA). U.S. astronauts followed Gagarin, and like him became heroes: astronaut John Glenn, for example, served as a U.S. senator. Despite the dominance of the superpowers in space, citizens of some thirty-five countries, including Afghanistan, Belgium, Brazil, China, Cuba, Malaysia, Mexico, and Saudi Arabia, contributed their citizens to the world's various space programs. In addition, individual countries such as China, Brazil, and Iran recognized that capabilities in space were needed to participate in satellite technology and to create an independent military capability. Brazil, with the most developed space program in Latin America, began its work with sounding rockets in 1964. As countries beyond the superpowers initiated their own programs and cooperated with multinational ventures, livelihoods in space multiplied, including monitoring and spying on other nations' space capabilities.

Trained space travelers are generally drawn from the ranks of jet pilots (like Gagarin) and space engineers, with mathematicians and scientists added to oversee the execution of experiments in space. Recently, teachers and space tourists have joined the ranks of those more explicitly trained for space, to give these costly and time-consuming programs more widespread appeal. Whatever their backgrounds and missions on the spacecraft, however, candidates for space travel undergo rigorous instruction in experiencing weightlessness, enduring space environments, and other space techniques. Participants in multinational space ventures also need to speak other languages well to communicate, and thus they undergo extensive language training.

Space travel is one of the more dangerous livelihoods created since the end of World War II. Not only have dozens of trained astronauts and cosmonauts died, but so have ground workers involved in space programs. In 2003, twenty-one workers and scientists died in a rocket explosion at Brazil's space site, and the next year six people in India's space program were killed when a rocket motor burst into flames. Yuri Gagarin himself died in 1968 during a jet training flight.

QUESTIONS TO CONSIDER

1. What roles did astronauts and cosmonauts play in the Cold War?

2. Why did so many countries besides the superpowers begin their own space programs?

3. What livelihoods are comparable to those of astronaut and cosmonaut?

For Further Information:

Brzezinski, Matthew. *Red Moon Rising: Sputnik and the Hidden Rivalries that Ignited the Space Age.* 2007.
De Groot, Gerard. *Dark Side of the Moon: The Magnificent Madness of the American Lunar Quest.* 2006.
Dickson, Paul. *Sputnik: The Shock of the Century.* 2001.
Wolfe, Tom. *The Right Stuff.* 1979.

$10.9 billion in 1948 to almost $60 billion in 1953 to "contain" the global threat of communist expansion. The fear that communist regimes would be established in decolonizing areas led U.S. President Dwight Eisenhower to characterize Asian countries as a row of dominoes: "You knock over the first one and what will happen is that it will go over [to communism] very quickly."[2] Thus, the Cold War mentality helped create a perception of connections between global developments, even in cases where those connections did not really exist.

Viewing the Cold War as a global conflict, the USSR and the United States formed competing military alliances that split most of the world into two opposing camps. In 1949 the United States, Canada, and their European allies formed the **North Atlantic Treaty Organization** (NATO). NATO provided a unified military force for its member countries. In 1955, after the United States forced France and Britain to invite West Germany to join NATO, the Soviet Union retaliated by establishing its own military organization, commonly called the **Warsaw Pact**, which included Albania, Bulgaria, Czechoslovakia, East Germany, Hungary, Poland, and Romania. These two massive regional alliances formed the military muscle for Cold War politics in Europe and replaced the individual might of the European powers (see Map 29.2).

North Atlantic Treaty Organization A Cold War alliance formed in 1949 among the United States, its western European allies, and Canada.

Warsaw Pact A Cold War alliance formed in 1955 among the Soviet Union and its eastern European satellite states.

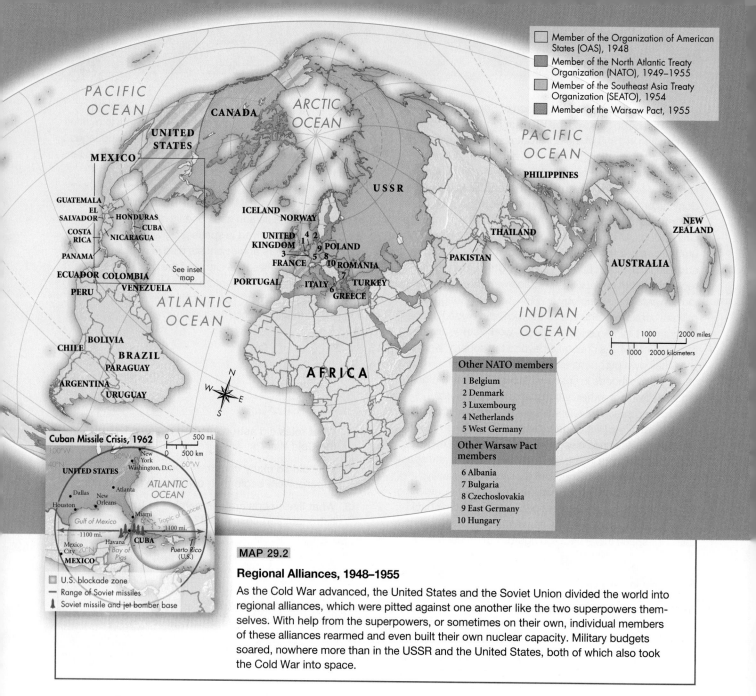

Other NATO members

1 Belgium
2 Denmark
3 Luxembourg
4 Netherlands
5 West Germany

Other Warsaw Pact members

6 Albania
7 Bulgaria
8 Czechoslovakia
9 East Germany
10 Hungary

Cuban Missile Crisis, 1962

U.S. blockade zone
Range of Soviet missiles
Soviet missile and jet bomber base

MAP 29.2

Regional Alliances, 1948–1955

As the Cold War advanced, the United States and the Soviet Union divided the world into regional alliances, which were pitted against one another like the two superpowers themselves. With help from the superpowers, or sometimes on their own, individual members of these alliances rearmed and even built their own nuclear capacity. Military budgets soared, nowhere more than in the USSR and the United States, both of which also took the Cold War into space.

Regional Alliances

Organization of American States An alliance formed in 1948 among nations in the Western Hemisphere.

Southeast Asia Treaty Organization A Cold War coalition of U.S. Asian allies formed in 1954.

Even though the most heated Cold War activity seemed to center on Europe, the largest and earliest regional alliance was far away. In 1948, some twenty-one nations from the Western Hemisphere banded together to form the **Organization of American States** (OAS). To strengthen the alliance as a Cold War vehicle, the United States gave individual Latin American countries of the OAS greater economic assistance as well as military aid and training for officers. U.S. aid guaranteed Latin American military regimes' increased prestige and power over civilians and prevented movements for democracy from succeeding. The expansion of the Cold War to Asia prompted the creation of an Asian counterpart to NATO. Established in 1954, the **Southeast Asia Treaty Organization** (SEATO) included Pakistan, Thailand, the Philippines, Britain, Australia, New Zealand, France, and the United States. Collectively, the new organizations reflected the determination of the United States to pull as much of the world as possible into its orbit.

One Latin American nation, however, refused to align with the United States. In 1959 a revolution in Cuba brought to power the young Fidel Castro. Born in 1926 to the owner of a large plantation and his housekeeper, Castro as a child played with others far less privileged than he, and he saw up close the ways of the local poor. Soon, however, the boy was separated from his poorer friends and given an elite education, leading eventually to law school. At the university, Castro was a political leader, and eventually he became a major opposition figure in Cuban politics. In 1959 Castro's forces overthrew the island's corrupt regime, which was controlled in large part by U.S. sugar interests and the mob. Peasants and well-educated guerrilla fighters like Castro banded together to end the economic plunder not only of the Cuban island but of individual workers. After being rebuffed by the United States, Castro, initially opposed to communist organizations, turned to the Soviet Union for aid to rebuild the country.

Revolution in Cuba

Cuba's connection to the Soviet Union frightened American decision makers, including John F. Kennedy. Elected U.S. president in 1960, Kennedy intensified the arms race and escalated the Cold War to a frightening pitch. In 1961 he authorized an invasion of Cuba by CIA-trained Cuban exiles at the Bay of Pigs to overthrow Castro. The CIA had backed similar coups in Iran, where it overthrew a populist nationalist regime to install the Shah, and in Guatemala, where it devised an invasion by so-called exile forces who imposed a president friendly to U.S. interests. The Bay of Pigs invasion, however, failed miserably and humiliated the United States, as Castro's tiny air force sank U.S. ships and captured more than a thousand invaders.

Cuban Missile Crisis

Another incident involving Cuba brought the world even closer to the brink of nuclear war. In October 1962, the CIA reported the installation of launching pads for Soviet medium-range nuclear missiles in Cuba (see again Map 29.2). In response, Kennedy called for a blockade of Soviet ships headed for Cuba and threatened nuclear war if the installations were not removed. For several days, superpower leaders were acutely aware that the world hovered on the brink of nuclear disaster. A high Soviet official called his wife telling her to leave Moscow immediately; men in Kennedy's cabinet reported looking at the sunset, believing it to be the last they would see. Then, between October 25 and 27, Nikita Khrushchev, Stalin's successor, and Kennedy negotiated an end to the crisis. The two leaders, who had looked deeply into the nuclear future, clearly feared what they saw.

Decolonization and the Birth of Nations

In World War II colonized peoples had been on the frontlines defending the West. They had witnessed the full barbarism of the imperial powers' warfare—and also the West's weaknesses. "We felt that the British were not supermen as we used to think," one Singapore worker put it. Another was enraged at seeing "the same old arrogance that you saw before the war."[3] Excluded from victory parades and other ceremonies so the Allies could maintain the illusion of white supremacy, veterans from the colonies were determined to be free. Workers and farmers in Asia, Africa, and the Middle East felt that they too had borne the brunt of the war effort. People from many walks of life, often led by individuals experienced in warfare and steeped in Western nationalism, fought for liberation as the postwar period opened.

> **FOCUS**
> How did colonized peoples achieve their independence from the imperialist powers after World War II?

The path to independence was paved with difficulties. In Africa, a continent whose peoples spoke several thousand languages, the European conquerors' creation of administrative units such as "Nigeria" and "Rhodesia" had obliterated divisions based on ethnic ties and local cultures. Religion also played a complicated role in independence movements. In the Middle East and North Africa, pan-Arab and pan-Islamic movements might seem to have been unifying forces. Yet many Muslims were not Arab, not all Arabs were Muslim, and Islam itself encompassed many competing beliefs and sects. In India, Hindus, Sikhs, and Muslims battled one another, though they shared the goal of eliminating British rule. Differences in religious beliefs, ethnic groups, and cultural practices—many of them invented or promoted by the colonizers to divide and rule—overlapped and undermined political unity. Despite these complications, in the three decades after World War II colonized peoples succeeded in throwing off the imperial yoke, often to become entangled in the battle between the United States and the USSR for world supremacy.

The End of Empire in Asia

At the end of World War II, Asians demonstrated against the inflation, unemployment, and other harsh conditions the war had imposed on them, while politicians continued to mobilize this mass discontent against the colonial powers. White colonizers often fought back, but able leaders and ordinary people worked together to drive out foreign rulers. Slipping as the major imperial power, Britain in 1947 finally parted with India, the "jewel in its crown." As some half a billion Asians gained their independence, Britain's sole notable remaining colony was Hong Kong.

India
During World War II, soldiers, workers, and farm tenants actively protested conditions under colonialism, sometimes using Gandhi's tactic of civil disobedience and at other times attacking the workplaces of moneylenders and landlords. Britain had promised in the 1930s to grant India its independence, but postponed the plan when war broke out. Two million Indian veterans, who had participated in the war in the Middle East and Asia, joined forces with powerful Indian Congress politicians, many of whom had helped finance the British war effort by buying out British entrepreneurs short of cash. India was now one of Britain's major creditors, and Britain had to face the inevitable by granting the colony its independence.

Independent countries emerged along the lines of religious rivalries that Britain had fomented under colonialism as a strategy to divide and conquer. In 1947, political leaders agreed to partition British India into an independent India for Hindus and the new state of Pakistan for Muslims; both were artificial divisions, because there were people from many religions living together across the subcontinent. The new state of India, in fact, had the second largest Muslim population in the world after Indonesia. Ordinary people had violent reactions as **Partition** unfolded (see Map 29.3). A powerful religious minority—the Sikhs—bitterly resented receiving nothing. Because independence as determined by the British occurred along religious rather than secular lines, tensions exploded among opposing religious groups, who used partition to struggle for resources and power. Hundreds of thousands were massacred in the great shift of populations between India and Pakistan—"appalling sights," a journalist reported, as trains reached their destination filled with nothing but corpses and hospitals treated the wounded whose hands had been cut off.[4] Indian and Pakistani soldiers began fighting for control of Kashmir along the border between the two countries. In the midst of this tragic bloodshed, in 1948 a radical Hindu assassinated Gandhi, who had loudly championed religious reconciliation and a secular Indian democracy. Delayed by bitter feelings, a Constitution emerged for India that forced wealthy, autonomous Indian states into the union.

In Indonesia in the closing days of World War II, the Japanese, eager to foil the Dutch, allowed a group of nationalist leaders, headed by the Western-educated Achmed Sukarno, to declare Indonesia an independent state. Sukarno's distinctive nationalist vision brought all the islands of the archipelago into a unified nation. His task was complicated by three factors. First, Indonesia had a tradition of local princely rule, even under Dutch control. Second, from the beginning of the twentieth century Indonesians had built an array of organizations, including a variety of Islamic ones, that pushed for freedom from Dutch exploitation. Third, Allied military forces had helped the Dutch to reclaim their empire, and after the defeat of Japan they even enlisted the occupying Japanese troops to put down all movements for independence.

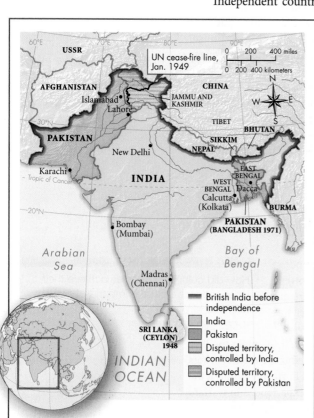

MAP 29.3 **Partition of India, 1947**

The British had whipped up religious antagonisms as part of their strategy of divide and conquer in India, and they used the same strategy in planning for decolonization. Thus, despite the commitment of Gandhi and other leaders to unity and religious toleration, Britain, along with some Indian leaders, arranged for a partition into a Muslim-dominated Pakistan and a Hindu-dominated India. Given the many religions in the region, the partition was a recipe for independence plagued by violence.

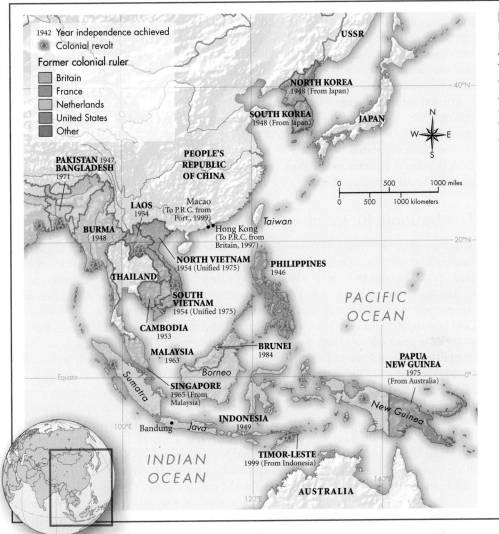

Year independence achieved 1942
Colonial revolt

Former colonial ruler
Britain
France
Netherlands
United States
Other

MAP 29.4

New States of Southeast Asia, 1945–1999

The French were determined to keep their empire in Southeast Asia, but their forces were handily defeated by the Vietnamese in 1954. Even as the Bandung Conference was held in Indonesia, the emerging nations of Southeast Asia became pivotal to the Cold War, as communist leader Ho Chi Minh stood steadfast in his vision for the region. One of the longest and most lethal proxy wars of the Cold War was fought in Vietnam, where genocide in neighboring Cambodia erupted adjacent to the war for liberation.

Indonesia

The popular forces of independence used **guerrilla warfare** that was unstoppable. In 1949 the Dutch conceded Indonesian independence, and in 1957 Sukarno, as head of the new state, legislated that all Dutch leave the country. Sukarno's policies entailed economic modernization and a cultural unity based on the belief in one God, whether Islamic, Christian, or other. Although the new Ministry of Religion fostered unity through Islamic institutions, sponsoring the building of mosques and institutions for Islamic welfare programs, ethnic, religious, and economic interests diverged and kept the archipelago involved in constant governmental struggle against dissenters. For a time, Sukarno himself was the mainstay of unity, becoming a charismatic leader by championing the power of newly independent countries (see Map 29.4).

Indochina

In Indochina nationalists struggled to prevent the postwar revival of French imperialism. From the 1930s on, their leader, Ho Chi Minh (hoe chee min), built a powerful organization, the Communist Viet Minh, to fight colonial rule. He began his career, however, by working aboard a French ocean liner, then taking jobs in London and Paris at the time of World War I, experiences that brought him in direct contact with white racism. Ho became interested in Marxism, which led him to Moscow and training as a political operative; he was first assigned to organizing strikers in China in the 1920s. Once head of the Viet Minh, he advocated the redistribution of land held by big landowners, especially in the rich agricultural area in southern Indochina where some six thousand owners held more than 60 percent of the land.

Partition The division of the Indian subcontinent into different states in 1947 and the violence accompanying it.

guerrilla warfare Unconventional combat, often undertaken by those who are not members of official armies.

During World War II, Ho worked to overthrow the Japanese, who had taken over Indochina, and at the end of the war, he declared Vietnam independent. The French, however, reasserted their control. Viet Minh peasant guerrillas ultimately forced the French to withdraw from the country after the bloody battle of Dien Bien Phu in 1954. Later that year the Geneva Conference—a meeting held in Switzerland to settle the war between the Indochinese and the French—carved out an independent Laos and divided Vietnam into North and South, each free from French control. Ho established a communist government in North Vietnam, and a noncommunist government was installed in South Vietnam (see again Map 29.4). Fearing that Ho would further the spread of communism in Asia, the United States supported the regime in South Vietnam, even its cancelling of elections in 1956 to prevent a communist victory. Ho and North Vietnam, in turn, received aid from both the Soviet Union and China.

The Struggle for Independence in the Middle East

By war's end in 1945, much of the world had become almost fully dependent on the Middle East's rich petroleum resources to fuel cars and airplanes, heat homes, and create products such as plastics. "The oil in this region is the greatest single prize in all history," as one geologist put it.[5] The Middle Eastern nations that emerged from their political domination by the European powers were thus economically and strategically important enough to maneuver between the Cold War rivals. At the same time, newly independent nations such as Syria, Lebanon, and Iraq struggled to develop a sure footing and autonomous identity. The legacy of the Holocaust complicated the political scene as the Western powers' commitment to secure a Jewish homeland in the Middle East stirred up Arab determination to hold onto their lands. From 1945 on, the Middle East was the scene of coups, power struggles, and ethnic and religious conflict, even as new nations were being born and older ones were strengthened by oil.

Israel   When World War II broke out, six hundred thousand Jewish settlers and twice as many Arabs lived, amid intermittent conflict, in British-controlled Palestine. In 1947, an exhausted Britain ceded the area to the United Nations to work out a settlement between the Jews and the Arabs. The UN voted to partition Palestine into an Arab region and a Jewish one, and in May 1948 Israelis proclaimed the new state of Israel. "The dream had come true," Golda Meir, future prime minister of Israel, remembered, but "too late to save those who had perished in the Holocaust."[6] Arguing that the UN had no right to award land to the Jewish minority in Palestine, five neighboring Arab states attacked Israel and were beaten. A UN-negotiated truce in 1949 to the Arab-Israeli War gave Israel even more territory than had been granted earlier. The result was that some two-thirds of Palestinian Arabs became stateless refugees and the war itself became but one more confrontation in a longer Arab-Israeli conflict over territory, rising Jewish immigration, and Palestinian rights to a homeland that continues to the present day.

Israel's neighbor, Egypt, had been a center of Allied efforts in North Africa and the Middle East during the war and demanded complete independence from British domination at the war's end. Britain, however, was determined to keep its control of Middle Eastern oil and Asian shipping through the Suez Canal, which was owned by a British-run company. Early in the 1950s the people of Cairo took to the streets, destroying flags of the puppet monarchy and other symbols of British rule. In 1952, army officer Gamal Abdel Nasser took part in the military ouster of the Egyptian king, a puppet of Britain's behind-the-scenes rule. The son of a postal inspector, Nasser rose quickly to become president of Egypt in 1956. As president, Nasser worked to improve the economic well-being of the peasants by redistributing land from the very wealthiest estates. Most notably, he faced down the European powers

UN partition of Palestine, 1947
- ■ Proposed Jewish state
- ■ Proposed Arab state
- — Boundary of Israel after UN truce, 1949

The Arab-Israeli War of 1948–1949

that wanted to keep control of Egyptian resources. A prime goal was reclaiming the Suez Canal, "where 120,000 of our sons had lost their lives in digging it [by force]," Nasser stated. In July 1956, after being denied a loan from the United States to build the projected Aswan Dam, he nationalized the Suez Canal so that Egypt would receive the income from tolls paid by those who used the canal. Nationalization of the Suez Canal sent Nasser's reputation soaring, making him the most popular and respected leader in the Arab world.

Egypt

Nasser's nationalization sent an angry tremor through the imperial powers, however. The Egyptians, Britain claimed, were hardly advanced enough as a people to run as complex an operation as the Suez Canal. Britain, with assistance from Israel and France, then invaded Egypt, bringing the Suez crisis to a head. American opposition made the British back down. Nasser's triumph in gaining the canal inspired confidence that the Middle East could confront the West and win.

New Nations in Africa

Displaced from their traditional agricultural livelihood during the war, many Africans flocked to cities such as Lagos and Nairobi, where they lived in shantytowns and survived by scavenging and doing menial labor for whites. After the war, struggling urban workers, including civil servants, professionals, and ordinary laborers, formed the core of the nationalist movement. High taxes imposed by white settlers gave added impetus to the decolonization movement. Another element in the drive toward independence was the transnational vision of Africans involved in trade and intellectual contact with the wider world. Leaders who had studied abroad were determined to have Western-style freedom.

In sub-Saharan Africa, these nationalists led increasingly discontented peoples to challenge the European imperialists. In the British-controlled Gold Coast of West Africa, Kwame Nkrumah (KWAH-may ehn-KROO-mah), formerly a poor school teacher, led the region's diverse inhabitants in Gandhian-style civil disobedience. A student in the United States in 1936, Nkrumah had been radicalized by Italy's invasion and defeat of Ethiopia. After the war, he joined a group of fellow West Africans in London, forging with them plans for liberation. Nkrumah returned to the Gold Coast, where he led protests that, despite determined British opposition, resulted in the formation of the independent country of Ghana in 1957 (see Seeing the Past: African Liberation on Cloth, page 975).

Sub-Saharan Africa

Nkrumah lobbied for the unity of all African states: "How except by our united efforts will the richest and still enslaved part of our continent be freed from colonial occupation . . . ?" he asked the heads of African governments in 1963 before all of Africa had been liberated.[7] But individual nation building was the order of the day. In the most populous African colony, Nigeria, workers and veterans recognized how important they were to Britain's postwar recovery and struck for higher wages, better working conditions, and greater respect. Respect did not come quickly: during a miners' strike in 1949 the British police commissioner ordered his troops to shoot because, he said, the miners were "dancing around and around" and chanting "We are all one."[8] Nonetheless, Nigeria gained its freedom in 1960 after the leaders of its many regional groups, unions, and political organizations reached agreement on a federal-style government. In these and other African states where the population was mostly black, independence came less violently than in mixed-race territory (see Map 29.5, page 974).

The numerous European settlers along Africa's eastern coast and in the southern and central areas of the continent violently resisted independence movements. In British East Africa, where white settlers ruled in splendor, the increasing mechanization of agriculture during the war drove blacks off the land. Displaced people filled cities like Nairobi or tried to eke out a living on infertile land. From the middle of World War II on, some of these displaced persons, including returning veterans, began forming secret political groups to oppose British rule. Violence erupted in the 1950s, when these rebels—including women who served as provisioners, messengers, and weapons stealers—tried to recover land from the whites. The rebels, who were mostly from the Kikuyu (kih-KOO-you) ethnic group, called themselves the Land and Freedom Army, but the whites referred to them as "Mau

MAP 29.5 New States in Africa and the Middle East, 1945–2011

To maintain their empires, the British, French, and Belgians fought lethal wars in Kenya, Algeria, and Congo, which featured brutal attacks against the local populations and killed tens of thousands. Inspired by their leaders, other African countries became independent relatively peacefully, although the costs of nation building were crushing in areas that had been so overexploited. The Middle East, in contrast, had enormous assets that drew the superpowers and other nations to compete fiercely for oil and control of the region's other assets, such as the Suez Canal.

Mau." The British responded by rounding up Kikuyus by the hundreds of thousands and placing them in secret concentration camps where conditions were so grim and mortality so high that the British deny their existence to this day. Nonetheless, despite the coordinated slaughter of an estimated 150,000 to 320,000 Kikuyus, the Land and Freedom Army finally wore the British down in costly military actions. Kenya gained formal independence in 1963.

North Africa As the tide of liberation spread, colonial leaders in Tunisia, Morocco, and French West Africa successfully convinced France to leave peaceably, in large part because European settlers were few and there was little military involvement running these areas. Having earlier been declared an integral part of France, Algeria was another story altogether. In 1954 the newly formed Front for National Liberation (FLN) rose up, attacking French government buildings, radio stations, and utility plants. A radio station in Cairo announced the FLN's goal: the "restoration of the Algerian state, sovereign, democratic, and social, within the framework of the principles of Islam." The French sent in more than four hundred thousand troops to crush the uprising, determined to keep Algeria French and to guard the well-being of over 1 million European settlers.

African Liberation on Cloth

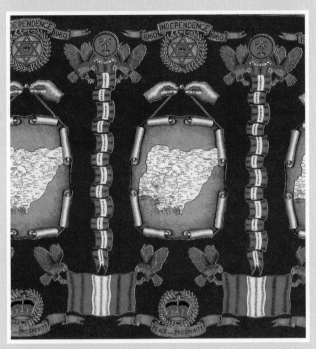

Nigerian Commemorative Textile (Textile Museum of Canada.)

Many African societies used commemorative textiles such as this vividly colored one from Nigeria to mark special occasions. Nations gaining their independence from the European powers issued such textiles in the 1960s and 1970s as they threw off imperial rule. This cloth clearly proclaims "Independence," but others presented the portraits of liberation heroes as they announced their freedom to the world. The textiles were immensely popular, hanging in homes and public buildings or serving as clothing (see At a Crossroads, page 958). Paradoxically, the independence textiles symbolized unity in the face of divisions among regions and ethnic groups within a country that had been artificially created by imperialist designs. In so doing, commemorative textiles, sometimes fashioned by women artisans, stood at the crossroads of pre-war and postwar world history.

EXAMINING THE EVIDENCE

1. What was the purpose of these commemorative textiles?

2. What accounts for their popularity, given the many divisions among the peoples of new nations?

3. Why would some commemorative textiles feature brutal dictators?

Neither side fought according to the rules of warfare: the French tortured native people, mutilating and then beheading them. The FLN fought a guerrilla war, fading into the mountains and countryside, while Algerian women, defying gender stereotypes, planted bombs in European cafés and carried weapons to assassination sites. Although France won the war with Algeria in military terms, the Algerian nationalists knew how to win the war of world opinion. Using modern public relations methods, they turned the United States and other influential nations against the French, convincing them that France stood in the way of Algerian economic development and the fight against communism. In 1962 Charles de Gaulle, leader of the Free French during World War II and new president of France, negotiated a settlement that resulted in independence for Algeria. Fearing retribution, hundreds of thousands of Europeans in Algeria as well as their Arab supporters fled to France. Having won its independence, Algeria, like the other newly independent states, now faced the challenge of establishing an effective, unified nation.

World Recovery in the 1950s and 1960s

The struggles against colonialism and the ideological clash between the United States and the Soviet Union took place alongside remarkable economic growth and social change. Some parts of the world had prospered during the war. Latin America, for example, benefited from the wartime demand for raw materials and manufactured goods. Cuba's exports of

FOCUS

What were the major elements of recovery in different parts of the world in the decades following World War II?

sugar grew almost 300 percent between 1938 and the end of the war. The population of Latin America steadily grew. Other peoples, within a few decades after suffering the deprivation and devastation of total war, came to live longer lives and to enjoy a higher standard of living than ever before in history. In Europe this newfound prosperity was celebrated as an "economic miracle." As governments took increasing responsibility for the health and well-being of citizens, the menacing Cold War was also the backdrop for rapid development of the welfare state pioneered by Sweden (see Chapter 28).

Political changes fostered some of the movement toward economic growth. New nations faced the enormous task of building effective government. India, for example, had experienced the horrors of Partition and was additionally composed of more than five hundred small and several quite large states that had enjoyed local rule under the British. "We have to make [people] feel they are parts of India, not only politically but emotionally and otherwise, and that their future is tied up with India," the first prime minister, Jawaharlal Nehru (JAH-wa-HAR-lahl NAY-roo), wrote in 1955.[9] To build loyalty to new nations and the superpowers alike, governments often turned to expensive projects such as building dams, extending railroads, and electrifying rural areas—all of which contributed to the postwar pattern of economic growth.

Expanding Economic Prosperity

In the immediate aftermath of the war, governments in new and old nations alike diverted labor and capital into rebuilding infrastructure—transportation, communications, and industrial capacity. The scarcity of consumer goods sparked unrest in many parts of the world, but the influx of U.S. funds into nations worldwide as part of its Cold War mission fueled economic recovery. Food and consumer goods became more plentiful, and demand for them increased. The growth in production alleviated unemployment among those whose livelihoods the war had destroyed. Oil-rich countries imported people from many parts of Asia and Africa to perform menial labor: women from the Philippines, Indonesia, and the Caribbean were among those who migrated as nurses, nannies, and household help. Northern Europe, short of labor, arranged for "guest" workers to arrive from Sicily, Turkey, and North and sub-Saharan Africa to help rebuild cities. The outbreak of war in Korea in 1950 encouraged economic recovery in Japan and elsewhere. Korea itself, however, was devastated. The Cold War thus spurred economic advance in some parts of the world while labor shortages led to ongoing migration and further interconnectedness of peoples and livelihoods.

During the postwar recovery, wartime technology was adapted to civilian use, and military spending continued. Civilian travel expanded globally as nations organized their own air systems based on improved airplane technology. Developed to relieve wartime shortages, synthetic goods such as nylon now became part of peacetime civilian life. Factories churned out a vast assortment of electronics, and plastic products ranging from pipes to household goods and rainwear. In the climate of Cold War, governments ordered bombs, fighter planes, tanks, and missiles, and they continued to conduct military research. Governments in decolonized countries courted the superpowers to provide up-to-date weaponry to secure their rule against internal and external foes. The number of radios in homes grew steadily around the world, and by the 1960s television had become a widely popular consumer item and the source for a host of new occupations.

The Common Market

International cooperation and economic growth led to the creation in 1957 of the **European Economic Community** (EEC), known popularly as the Common Market, the foundation of the European Union of the 1990s. In 1957, Belgium, the Netherlands, Luxembourg, France, West Germany, and Italy established the EEC, which reduced tariffs among the six partners and worked to develop common trade policies. According to its founders, the EEC aimed to "prevent the race of nationalism, which is the true curse of the modern world." Increased cooperation produced great economic rewards for the six members, and it reduced the threat of war: the Italian economy, which had lagged behind that of France and Germany, boomed, and as additional countries joined from the 1970s on, many of them flourished too.

European Economic Community A consortium of European countries established in 1957 to promote free trade and economic cooperation among its members.

The Welfare State

Even as new nations came into being, the trend in postwar and postcolonial government was to intervene in people's everyday lives to improve social conditions and to prevent the political extremism and discontent of the 1930s. This policy of intervention became known as the **welfare state**, a term suggesting that, in addition to building their military power, states would guarantee a minimum level of well-being for their citizens. Postwar governments promoted both the advance of industry and the welfare of the general population with various forms of financial assistance. Imitating the sweeping Swedish programs of the 1930s, nations expanded or created family allowances, health-care and medical benefits, and programs for pregnant women. The combination of better material conditions and state provision of health care dramatically extended life expectancy. Contributing to the overall progress, the number of medical doctors and dentists soared between 1920 and 1950, and vaccines greatly reduced the global death toll from such diseases as tuberculosis, diphtheria, measles, and polio.

State initiatives in other areas also helped raise the standard of living. Government-built atomic power plants brought electrification to many more rural areas. States legislated for better conditions and more leisure time for workers and sponsored construction to alleviate housing shortages resulting from three decades of economic depression and war. Such efforts often drained the economies of newly independent countries. Moreover, despite the new construction, housing shortages persisted, and growing cities like Rio de Janeiro were surrounded by shantytowns. Nonetheless, the modernized appearance of many of the world's largest cities suggested that the century's two cataclysmic wars had swept away much that was old and traditional.

The welfare state became the backbone of politics in many regions. Juan Perón, a colonel in the Argentine army, became president in 1946 on a platform of welfare for workers and independence from the financial domination of Britain and the United States. During the war, as manufacturing jobs multiplied and migration to cities in search of industrial jobs swelled, Perón had forced American meatpacking plants around Buenos Aires to raise wages. Hundreds of thousands of workers backed Perón's array of economic benefits for "the shirtless ones," and his dramatic use of surplus government funds to buy out British-owned telephone companies and railroad lines was said to free Argentina from Western business imperialism domination. While Perón added to workers' wallets with rising social security and wages, his wife Eva, who was from the lower class, won their hearts. During the depression,

Welfare for Workers in Argentina

welfare state The postwar system of government-sponsored programs designed to provide citizens with basic standards of health care, housing, and income.

The Great Leap Forward in China

In 1949, life in China changed for most people because of the communist revolution that brought Mao Zedong to power. Kang Zhengguo was a student in the 1950s as the full weight of change began. His grandfather owned land and was a Buddhist leader; his father was a highly trained engineer. In this early passage from Zhengguo's memoir, he describes one of Mao's earliest programs, "The Great Leap Forward," when China was supposed to industrialize rapidly as the Soviets had done. Later parts of his memoir present bloody and terrifying incidents, including those that he himself endured.

In 1958, the year of the Great Leap Forward, the nation became caught up in a frenzy of smelting "backyard steel." It was our "glorious mission" to donate scrap iron to this cause, so our school playground, like most other work units, was heaped with it, along with piles of burned charcoal. Some enthusiasts had tossed in their pots and pans or drawer handles for good measure, even if they were made of copper or tin. The student cafeteria had been temporarily converted into a foundry, equipped with a mighty blower that shook the classrooms with its roar and filled the air with a sooty purplish haze. Nobody seemed to have time for mundane pursuits like eating and sleeping. The upperclassmen manned the furnaces around the clock with holiday spirit, belting out all of their new songs and

cheering for the molten "steel" as it poured out of the furnaces. Once it congealed into hard black slag, we deemed it a success and swathed it in bright red silk. Then, banging on drums and gongs and carrying big red paper placards that read "SURPASS ENGLAND AND CATCH UP TO AMERICA," we marched it triumphantly over to the district party committee.

Classes were canceled more often than not, and even we younger students had to help out at the foundry.

Source: Kang Zhengguo, *Confessions: An Innocent Life in Communist China*, trans. Susan Wilf (New York: W. W. Norton, 2007), 14–15.

EXAMINING THE EVIDENCE

1. What impression does this passage give you of the Great Leap Forward?

2. What is the place of politics in education, as suggested by this excerpt?

3. How would you describe the industrialization taking place during the Great Leap Forward?

4. How would you describe the student life?

---

at the age of fifteen, she had migrated from the countryside to Buenos Aires, quickly leaving her poverty behind when she succeeded in radio and film. As Perón's wife, "Evita" joined him in providing the poor with housing, unemployment funds, and personal charity, which she virtually extorted from businesses. In exchange, the masses loyally supported the Peróns, even as the upper and middle classes stewed in silent protest. Eva Perón died from cancer at the age of thirty-two, leaving the Argentine masses heartbroken and the government strapped for funds to continue its welfare policies. In 1955, the military drove Perón out, reducing both the welfare state and the anti-American rhetoric.

Building and Rebuilding Communism

Two countries in particular bore the brunt of World War II in terms of population loss and outright destruction. The Soviet Union lost between 42 and 47 million people, new estimates suggest, while the Japanese invasion and more than a decade of civil war killed some 30 million people in China. Both Stalin and Mao Zedong were committed to rebuilding and modernizing their countries, and both revived the crushing methods that had served before to modernize and industrialize traditional peasant economies. An admirer of American industrial know-how, Stalin prodded all Soviet-bloc nations to match U.S. productivity. In China Mao had similar goals, and reaching them produced losses in both lives and jobs.

The Soviet Union   Stalin's death in 1953 created an opportunity to create a less repressive society in the USSR. Political prisoners in the labor camps pressed for reform, leading to the release of millions. Cold War competition and growing protests over shortages of food and other consumer items led the government to increase production of consumer goods. Nikita Khrushchev, an illiterate coal miner before the Bolshevik Revolution, outmaneuvered other rivals to become in 1955 the undisputed leader of the Soviet Union, but he did so without the usual executions. At a party congress in 1956, Khrushchev attacked the "cult of personality" Stalin had built about himself and announced that Stalinism did not equal socialism. The so-called Secret Speech—it was not published in the USSR but became widely known—sent tremors through hard-line Communist parties around the world.

In 1956, discontented Polish railroad workers successfully struck for better wages. Inspired by the Polish example, Hungarians rebelled later that year against forced collectivization and wage cutbacks, but the protest soon targeted the entire communist system. Tens of thousands of protesters filled the streets of Budapest, urged on both publicly and privately by the United States and its allies. When Hungary announced that it might leave the Warsaw Pact, Soviet troops moved in, killing tens of thousands and causing hundreds of thousands more to flee to the West. The U.S. refusal to act showed that, despite its rhetoric of "liberation," it would not risk World War III by military intervention in the Soviet sphere of influence.

In the People's Republic of China, Mao Zedong faced the problem of rebuilding a war-torn peasant society. Like Stalin, Mao saw modernization as the answer, but to keep Chinese communism and himself in power, Mao tacked back and forth, uncertain of what to do. In 1959 he initiated the **Great Leap Forward**, an economic plan intended to increase industrial production. The plan ordered country people to stop tending their farms and instead produce steel from their shovels, pots, and pans in their own small backyard furnaces (see Reading the Past: The Great Leap Forward in China). This decentralized plan of industrial production proved to be a disaster, as much of the do-it-yourself iron and steel was worthless. Meanwhile, the halting of agriculture resulted in massive famine. An estimated 30 million people died, and millions more went hungry. "Communism is not a dinner party," Mao remarked with grim irony, and his government touted the virtues of being thin. During this and other projects, livelihoods deteriorated and education was devalued in the name of participating in different communist schemes.

In the early 1960s, Mao's slipping popularity and rising threats from outside the country led to the brutal development known as the **Cultural Revolution**. To break the opposition that had emerged during the Great Leap Forward, Mao turned against his associates in the Communist Party, appealing to China's youth to reinvigorate the revolution. Brought up to revere Mao, young people responded to his call to rid society of the "four olds"—old customs, old habits, old culture, and old ideas. In Mao's name they destroyed artistic treasures and crushed individual lives, striking yet another blow at ordinary people's ability to pursue productive lives.

During the Cultural Revolution, any kind of skilled person was branded uncommunist and thus criminal, as seen in the experience of painter Wu Guanzhong. Wu went to Paris in 1947 on a government scholarship to learn the techniques of Western masters, but after three years Mao's administration summoned him back to teach in Beijing. By the mid-1950s, the Chinese leadership had come to see Wu's work, which mixed Chinese and Western

Wu Guanzhong, *Willows on a Hillside*

Wu Guanzhong's studies in Europe influenced his art after his return to China to teach in Beijing in the 1950s. Forbidden to paint during the Cultural Revolution of the 1960s, Wu returned to his hybrid style, which mixed abstract representations from the West with Chinese styles that he modernized in his work. For many critics, Wu's work reflects both his own artistry and the influence of other contemporary artists, such as Jackson Pollock (see page 983). (Christie's Images/Corbis.)

China

Great Leap Forward The Chinese communist program of the mid-1950s designed to push the country ahead of all others in industrial and other production.

Cultural Revolution The Chinese communist program of the 1960s and early 1970s carried out by Mao Zedong's youthful followers to remake Chinese thought, behavior, and everyday life.

styles, as a "poisonous weed." In their view, the only acceptable approach to art was Soviet-style socialist realism. Wu was removed from his prestigious teaching post and sent to farm in the countryside, where he was forbidden to paint or to talk to his wife, who accompanied him. In 1972 Wu was allowed to resume his artwork "for relaxation" one day a week, but he had trouble finding materials and came ultimately to describe himself as a "cow-dung painter." After Mao's death in 1976 the brutality of the Cultural Revolution eased. Wu Guanzhong's reputation as one of the world's outstanding artists was restored, and the skills of the Chinese people in artistic, agricultural, industrial, and other pursuits were once again valued.

Cultural Dynamism amid Cold War

FOCUS

How did the experience of world war, decolonization, and Cold War affect cultural life and thought?

As the Cold War unfolded, people around the world vigorously discussed the devastating World War II experience, the rationale for decolonization, and the dangers of the Cold War itself. Writers tried to understand the meaning of war and genocide. Literature exploring concepts of freedom and liberation poured out of Africa, Latin America, and Asia and reached the West, where oppressed minorities were likewise demanding better treatment. Thus, the postwar period was one of intense cultural ferment and unprecedented levels of cultural exchange within each Cold War bloc.

Confronting the Heritage of World War

In 1944, during the last months of the war, University of Tokyo professor Tanabe Hajime began a soul-searching book, turning to Buddhism for enlightenment. In *Philosophy as Matonetics* (the title refers to an act of repentant confession), Tanabe urged the Japanese to enter higher realms of wisdom as they faced defeat. His program for a return to Buddhist values allowed the Japanese to see in their defeat a lofty purpose, elevating them above the brute power politics of the Western victors. Such programs for exalting the wartime losers took place alongside intense indoctrination in democratic values and the dramatic trials of Axis leaders conducted at Nuremberg, Germany, in 1945 and in Tokyo, Japan, in 1946. Both sets of trials revealed a horrifying panorama of crimes and led to death sentences or long imprisonment for most of the defendants. These trials introduced the concept of "crimes against humanity" and an international politics based on demands for human rights.

Nonetheless, as civilians in the defeated Axis nations struggled with starvation, rape, and other postwar hardships, many Japanese and Germans came to believe that they were the main victims of the war. The Cold War helped reinforce that view. American officials themselves, eager to fight the communists, began to rely on the expertise of high-ranking Japanese militarists, fascists, and Nazis, overlooking war crimes as trivial when compared to the evil menace of the USSR. The work of Tanabe and others justified the speedy rehabilitation of the Axis powers, as the war temporarily came to be explained as one of idealism on both sides.

Memoirs of the death camps and tales of the resistance evoked a starkly different side of the events of the 1930s and 1940s. Anne Frank's *Diary of a Young Girl* (1947) was the poignant record of a German Jewish teenager hidden with her family for two years in the back of an Amsterdam warehouse before they were discovered and sent to concentration camps, where all died except Anne's father. Confronted with the small miseries of daily life and the grand evils of Nazism, Frank wrote that she never stopped believing that "people are really good at heart." Histories of the resistance addressed the public's need for inspiration after the savagery of World War II. After years of censorship and privation, Japanese publishers tapped a market thirsty for books by putting out moving collections of letters from soldiers that quickly became best sellers. Only phrase books teaching the language of the conquerors outsold the books of soldiers' letters. Filmmakers from around the world also depicted war, as memories and nightmares of World War II haunted the screen into the twenty-first century.

By the end of the 1940s, **existentialism** had become popular among the cultural elites and students in universities around the world. This philosophy explored the meaning of human

existentialism A philosophy prominent after World War II, developed primarily by French thinkers, that stresses the importance of active engagement with the world in the creation of an authentic existence.

existence in a world where evil flourished. The principal theorists of existentialism, Frenchmen Jean-Paul Sartre and Albert Camus, wrote plays and essays in which they asked what "being" meant, given what they saw as the absence of God and the breakdown of morality under Nazism. Their answer was that "being," or existing, was not the automatic process either of God's creation or of birth into the natural world. Instead, through action and choice, the individual created an "authentic" or meaningful and valuable existence. As existentialists, Sartre and Camus emphasized political activism and resistance to totalitarianism.

In 1949, Simone de Beauvoir, Sartre's lifetime companion, published *The Second Sex*, the twentieth century's most influential work on the condition of women. Examining women's status as mothers, wives, and daughters, de Beauvoir concluded that most women had failed to take the kind of action necessary to lead authentic lives. Instead of acting based on their individual reasoning, they devoted themselves to reproduction and motherhood because it was a social expectation. Failing to create an authentic self through considered action, they had become its opposite—an object, or "Other," who followed cultural norms set by men. Translated into many languages, de Beauvoir's book asked women to change by creating their own freedom.

Liberation Culture

In decolonizing areas, thinkers mapped out new visions of how to construct the future. In the 1950s and 1960s Frantz Fanon, a black psychiatrist from the French Caribbean colony of Martinique, wrote that the mind of the colonized person had been

Frantz Fanon

Frantz Fanon was one of the most influential thinkers during anti-imperial liberation struggles of the 1950s. He justified the use of violence against colonizers by arguing that brute force was all the imperialists understood, and indeed it was what colonized peoples themselves understood best because of the violence regularly inflicted on them. He also raised the question of how one "decolonized" one's mind of such propagandistic notions as the superiority of whites and the inferiority of blacks. (© Abdelhamid Kahia/Kaha Studio.)

traumatized by the brutal imposition of an alien culture. Ruled by guns, the colonized person knew only violence and would thus naturally decolonize by means of violence. Translated into many languages, Fanon's *Black Skin, White Masks* (1952) and *The Wretched of the Earth* (1961) posed the question of how to "decolonize" one's mind. South African writer Bessie Head, the daughter of a white mother and an African father, developed Fanon's themes in her novels. Her characters danced on the edge of madness because of their complicated identities springing from colonialism, clashing ethnicities, and education. A teacher in Head's novel *Maru* (1971) has an English education but is despised and disdained by other Africans because she belongs to the darkest-skinned group of Bushmen. Liberation culture characterized independence as something emotionally confusing for individuals, with the meaning of freedom remaining to be puzzled out.

Ideas about the meaning of liberation circled the world. Mao Zedong's "Little Red Book" contained brief maxims intended to guide hundreds of millions of postcolonial citizens. Fanon's ideas also circulated among Africans, North Americans, and Latin Americans. They intersected with those of Jamaica-born Marcus Garvey, who in the interwar years had promoted a "back to Africa" movement as the way for African Americans to escape racial discrimination in the United States. In the 1960s the physician and upper-class guerrilla warrior Che Guevara, though a Marxist, wrote of avoiding the centralized and dictatorial Marxism of both the USSR and China. His popular works advocated a compassionate Marxism based on an appreciation of the oppressed rather than on a determination to direct them.

The Spread of Ideas

Inspired not only by their own situation in the United States but by decolonization movements throughout the world, African Americans intensified their agitation for civil rights in the 1950s. In principle, African American troops had fought to defeat the Nazi idea of white racial supremacy; now African Americans hoped to end ideas of white racial superiority in the United States. In 1954, the U.S. Supreme Court declared segregated education unconstitutional

The U.S. Civil Rights Movement

The "New Look" for Women After World War II

Designers and marketers aimed to return women in the West to a state of hyperfemininity in the postwar world, even though women in war-torn areas often lacked the bare necessities. In some places, clothing and food were rationed into the early 1950s, making the attire shown here more a fantasy than a reality. (Bibliotheque des Arts Decoratifs, Paris/Archives Charmet/Bridgeman Art Library.)

in *Brown v. Board of Education*, a case initiated by the National Association for the Advancement of Colored People (NAACP). Over the course of the 1950s, many talented individuals emerged to lead the civil rights movement, foremost among them Martin Luther King, Jr., a minister from Georgia whose powerful oratory galvanized African Americans to peaceful resistance in the face of brutal white retaliation. By the 1960s, other activists came to follow thinkers such as Fanon, proclaiming "black power" to achieve rights through violence if necessary.

The Culture of Cold War

In the effort to win the Cold War, both sides poured vast sums of money into high and popular culture. The United States secretly channeled government money into foundations to promote favorable journalism around the world and to sponsor specific artists. In the USSR, official writers churned out spy stories, and espionage novels topped best seller lists as well in the West. *Casino Royale* (1953), by the British author Ian Fleming, introduced James Bond, British intelligence agent 007, who survived tests of wit and physical prowess at the hands of communist and other political villains. Soviet pilots would not take off for flights when the work of Yulian Simyonov, the Russian counterpart of Ian Fleming, was playing on radio or television. Daily reports of Soviets and Americans—fictional or real—facing one another down fed many of the world's fantasies and nightmares.

In postwar Europe and the United States, everyday life also revolved around the growing availability of material goods and household conveniences. A rising birthrate and a bustling youth culture encouraged spending on newly available goods. The advertising business boomed, confronting the thriftiness of the Great Depression and wartime with messages that described new products and encouraged the desire to

Consumerism in the West

buy them. These were the years when American-style consumerism came to stand for freedom and plenty versus the scarcity in the communist world. Women's magazines in the West publicized a "new look" that encouraged women to be sexy and feminine—unlike women in communist countries—and urged them to return to the "normal" life of domesticity and shopping. European communists debated the "Americanization" they saw taking place. Many wanted American products; nonetheless, Communist parties worked to get American products banned. The Communist Party in France, for example, led a successful campaign to ban Coca-Cola for a time in the 1950s, and the Soviets tried unsuccessfully to match the West's production of consumer goods.

Spreading Cold War Culture

Radio was key to spreading Cold War culture and values; both the United States and the USSR used the medium to broadcast news and propaganda. During the late 1940s and early 1950s, the Voice of America, broadcasting in thirty-eight languages from one hundred transmitters, provided an alternative source of news for people around the world. The Soviet counterpart broadcast in Russian around the clock but initially spent much of its wattage jamming U.S. programming. Russian programs stressed a uniform communist culture and values. The United States, by contrast, emphasized diverse programming and promoted debate about current affairs—even while a U.S. senator, Joseph McCarthy, began a witch hunt for communists to win an election in 1950. Radio and television helped the events and developments of the Cold War acquire a far-reaching emotional impact: both the United States and USSR whipped up fear of enemies within, persecuting millions of citizens for allegedly favoring the opposing side. People heard reports of nuclear build-ups; in school, children rehearsed what to do in case of nuclear war; and families built bomb shelters in their backyards.

Abstract Expressionism

As leadership of the art world passed from Europe to the United States, art became part of the Cold War, along with consumer goods and books. **Abstract expressionism**, developed primarily by American artists, encompassed many diverse styles but often featured large canvasses depicting nonrepresentational forms in bold colors. Abstract expressionists spoke of the importance of the artist's self-discovery, spiritual growth, and sensations in the process of painting. American artist Jackson Pollock produced abstract works by dripping, spattering, and pouring paint. Dutch-born artist Willem de Kooning commented on his relationship with his canvas, "If I stretch my arms next to the rest of myself and wonder where my fingers are, that is all the space I need as a painter." Said to exemplify Western freedom, such painters were awarded commissions at the secret direction of the U.S. Central Intelligence Agency. Pro-Soviet critics in western Europe condemned abstract art as "an infantile sickness" and favored socialist realist art with "human content," showing the condition of the workers and the oppressed races in the United States. When a show of abstract art opened in the Soviet Union, Khrushchev yelled that it was "dog shit."

Official Communist Culture

The USSR promoted an official communist culture based on the socialist realist style highlighting the heroism of the working classes. The government sponsored classical training in ballet and music and harassed innovators in the arts. Communist culture emphasized Soviet successes, celebrating Soviet wartime victories and the USSR's progress toward Stalin's goal of economic modernization. Dissenters in the USSR were both feared and bullied. For example, Khrushchev forced Boris Pasternak to refuse the 1958 Nobel Prize in Literature because Pasternak's novel *Doctor Zhivago* (1957) cast doubt on the glory of the Bolshevik Revolution and affirmed the value of the individual. Yet Khrushchev himself made several trips to the West and was a more cosmopolitan, public figure than Stalin had been. With growing confidence and affluence, the Soviets concentrated their efforts on spreading official socialist culture and influence in Asia, Africa, and Latin America.

COUNTERPOINT
The Bandung Conference 1955

In April 1955, Achmed Sukarno, who led the struggle for Indonesian independence from the Dutch, hosted a conference in Bandung, Indonesia, of emerging nations. The Bandung Conference, also known as the Asian-African Conference, was meant to ensure the independence of the emerging Asian and African nations despite the temptations of loans and military aid from the superpowers. The conference was thus a counterpoint to the seemingly global grip of the Cold War and the superpowers' hold on international politics.

FOCUS

How did the Bandung Conference and its aims represent an alternative to the Cold War division of the globe?

Cosponsored by Egypt, Indonesia, Burma, Sri Lanka, India, and Pakistan, the conference was attended by representatives from twenty-nine countries, most of them newly independent. They constituted a who's who of anticolonialism: Kwame Nkrumah of Ghana, Gamal Abdel Nasser of Egypt, Zhou Enlai of China, and Ho Chi Minh of Vietnam attended alongside Sukarno and Jawaharlal Nehru, prime minister of India. Activists throughout the world were inspired

abstract expressionism A postwar artistic style characterized by nonrepresentational forms and bold colors; often associated with the freedom of the Western world.

The Bandung Conference

In 1955, leaders from Asia and Africa met in newly independent Indonesia at the Bandung Conference, with the goal of building unity among emerging nations. Participants listened to inspiring and hard-hitting speeches as they began a policy of "nonalignment" in the Cold War. This policy was a refusal to become pawns of the superpowers, but it was hard for many to maintain because the need for support was so great in regions devastated by imperial greed and total war. (AP Photo/Asia-Africa Museum, HO.)

by the independent, even defiant stand against the superpowers taken by the leaders gathered at Bandung. African American author Richard Wright, who attended the conference, was riveted by the meaning of such an assembly: "The despised, the insulted, the hurt, the dispossessed—in short, the underdogs of the human race were meeting. Here were class and racial and religious consciousness on a global scale. Who had thought of organizing such a meeting? And what had these nations in common? Nothing, it seemed to me, but what their past relationship to the Western world had made them feel. This meeting of the rejected was in itself a kind of judgment upon the Western world!"[10] Leaders at the conference, speakers noted, represented more than half the world's population.

Shared Goals

Issues discussed at the Bandung Conference included economic development outside the structures of colonialism, and the achievement of political well-being without following the dictates of either the Soviet Union or the United States. Nehru argued strongly for nonalignment, maintaining that nations affiliating with one side or another would lose their identity. Moreover, Nehru claimed, the superpowers had come to equate a nation's worth with its military power. To his mind this was evidence that "greatness sometimes brings quite false values, false standards. When they begin to think in terms of military strength—whether it be the United Kingdom, the Soviet Union, or the U.S.A.—then they are going away from the right track and the result of that will be that the overwhelming might of one country will conquer the world."[11] In India, Nehru tried to follow a middle course between the superpowers in his own economic policies, even though he simultaneously offered support to communist China.

Nehru had high hopes for Bandung, but he also had concerns that proper conditions such as first-rate accommodations and sanitary facilities be provided for delegates of the emerging nations to the conference. They needed to be recognized as valuable through their treatment, as they were at the meetings of the United Nations in New York. Nehru admired the more lofty goals of the UN, including the charter outlining a collective global authority that would adjudicate conflicts and provide military protection to any member threatened by aggression. Meetings of both the UN and emerging nations began shifting global issues away from superpower priorities. Human rights and economic inequities among developing countries and the West nudged their way into public consciousness.

Divisive Issues

Yet for all the desire to be an influential third force between the superpowers, serious issues divided participants at the Bandung Conference. For one, the legacy of mistrust between India and Pakistan grew increasingly bitter and violent over their rival claims to the state of Kashmir. The leaders at Bandung argued both in favor of nationalism and in support of movements that transcended nationalism, such as pan-Islam and pan-Africanism. Although the Bandung Conference did not yield an enduring world power bloc, it did articulate a position that after the end of the Cold War would evolve into the idea of a North-South divide. Those living in the northern half of the globe were wealthy compared with those in the south, impoverished because imperialism's legacy had relegated them to poorly remunerated production of commodities. In the 1950s and 1960s, however, the notable achievement of the Bandung Conference was that it strengthened the commitment of new nations to remain independent in the face of the superpowers' military and economic might.

Conclusion

The Cold War began the atomic age and transformed international power politics. The two new superpowers, the Soviet Union and the United States, each built massive atomic arsenals, replacing the former European leadership and facing off in a Cold War that menaced the entire world. The Cold War saturated everyday life, producing a culture of bomb shelters, spies, and witch-hunts. Yet within this atmosphere of division and nuclear rivalry an astonishing worldwide recovery occurred. New housing, transport, and industrial rebuilding—often sponsored by a burgeoning welfare state and using wartime technology—made many people healthier and more prosperous.

World War II promoted further discontent and activism—like that of Umm Kulthum—among the colonized peoples of the world and simultaneously loosened the grip of the colonial powers. From India to Ghana and Nigeria, colonial peoples, often led by Western-educated and nationalist politicians, won their independence and turned to nation building. Many, as in the case of Algeria and Kenya, had to take up arms against the brutality of the imperialists to become free. Nation building in newly independent states, however, turned out to be slow and halting, even though many of these nations also enjoyed a burst of postwar prosperity.

As the world grew overall in prosperity, its cultural life focused on eradicating the evils inflicted by the Axis and on surviving the atomic rivalry of the superpowers. Frantz Fanon and other thinkers developed theories to explain the struggles of decolonized peoples for their full independence. In the midst of postwar intellectual introspection and heated Cold War rhetoric, many came to wonder whether Cold War was really worth the threat of nuclear annihilation and whether there might be an alternative way of living as individuals and as a world community. Leaders of newly independent nations, through such activities as the Bandung Conference, promoted the idea of nonalignment with either superpower, but they often had difficulty overcoming their own differences, rivalries, and internal corruption. These hopes matured into a burst of technological creativity and further activism to improve the world—including putting an end to the Cold War.

NOTES

1. Harry S. Truman, "Truman Doctrine Speech," March 12, 1947.
2. Dwight D. Eisenhower, press conference, April 7, 1954.
3. Quoted in Ronald J. Spector, *In the Ruins of Empire: The Japanese Surrender and the Battle for Postwar Asia* (New York: Random House, 2007), 78.
4. Quoted in Alex von Tunzelmann, *Indian Summer: The Secret History of the End of an Empire* (New York: Henry Holt, 2007), 225.

5. Everette Lee DeGoyler, quoted in Daniel Yergin, *The Prize: The Epic Quest for Oil, Money, and Power* (New York: Simon and Schuster, 1991), 393.

6. Golda Meir, *My Life* (New York: Putnam, 1975).

7. "Africa Must Unite" (1963), quoted in Michael Hunt, *The World Transformed, 1945 to the Present* (Boston: Bedford/St. Martin's, 2004), 144.

8. Superintendent of Police Philip, quoted in Carolyn A. Brown, *"We Were All Slaves": African Miners, Culture, and Resistance at the Enugu Government Colliery* (Portsmouth, NH: Heinemann, 2003), 310.

9. Quoted in Judith M. Brown, *Nehru: A Political Life* (New Haven, CT: Yale University Press, 2003), 229.

10. Richard Wright, *The Color Curtain: A Report on the Bandung Conference* (Jackson, MS: Banner, 1995).

11. *Selected Works of Jawaharlal Nehru: 1 February–31 May 1955*. vol. 28.

RESOURCES FOR RESEARCH

World Politics and the Cold War

The Cold War replaced the great-power politics of the previous hundred years, making the world increasingly dangerous. Spector's history of the immediate postwar years in Asia shows the chaos and violence that provided the setting for the Cold War division of the world and the transformation of world politics.

Cumings, Bruce. *Korea's Place in the Sun: A Modern History.* 2005.

The Korean War Educator. http://www.koreanwar-educator.org.

Meisner, Maurice. *Mao Zedong: A Political and Intellectual Portrait.* 2007.

Skierka, Volker. *Fidel Castro: A Biography.* 2007.

Spector, Ronald H. *In the Ruins of Empire: The Japanese Surrender and the Battle for Postwar Asia.* 2007.

Statler, Kathryn, and Andrew Johns, eds. *The Eisenhower Administration, the Third World, and the Globalization of the Cold War.* 2006.

Decolonization and the Birth of Nations

New nations emerged in a variety of ways, with differing levels of violence and styles of leadership. Elkins's book starkly details the British torture and slaughter of Kenyans who wanted freedom.

Connelley, Matthew. *A Diplomatic Revolution: Algeria's Fight for Independence and the Origins of the Post–Cold War Era.* 2002.

Danielson, Virginia. *Umm Kulthum, Arabic Song, and Egyptian Society in the Twentieth Century.* 1998.

Duara, Prasenjit, ed. *Decolonization: Perspectives from Then and Now.* 2004.

Elkins, Caroline. *Imperial Reckoning: The Untold Story of Britain's Gulag in Kenya.* 2005.

Guha, Ramachandra. *India After Gandhi: The History of the World's Largest Democracy.* 2008.

Hyam, Ronald. *Britain's Declining Empire: The Road to Decolonisation, 1918–1968.* 2007.

World Recovery in the 1950s and 1960s

Recovering from the devastation of World War II and the trials of nation building was no easy task. Notable leaders of new nations worked to overcome poverty, illiteracy, and lingering factionalism. Brown's biography of Nehru provides a good example.

Allen, Larry. *The Global Economic System Since 1945.* 2005.

Brown, Judith M. *Nehru: A Political Life.* 2003.

Estévez-Abe, Margarita. *Welfare and Capitalism in Postwar Japan.* 2008.

Rhodes, Richard. *Arsenals of Folly: The Nuclear Arms Race.* 2007.

Sturgeon, Janet C. *Border Landscapes: The Politics of Akha Land Use in China and Thailand.* 2005.

Tignor, Robert. *W. Arthur Lewis and the Birth of Development Economics.* 2006.

Culture Dynamism amid Cold War

An array of thinkers and artists considered the birth of new nations amid immense postwar suffering. Frantz Fanon was one of the most influential theorists of decolonization of his time, but Cold War rivalries also led to cultural competition, as seen in Von Eschen's work.

Fanon, Frantz. *The Wretched of the Earth.* 1963 [orig. pub. 1961].

Hoerder, Dirk. *Cultures in Contact: World Migrations in the Second Millennium.* 2002.

Igarashi, Yoshikuni. *Bodies of Memory: Narratives of War in Postwar Japanese Culture, 1945–1970.* 2000.

Von Eschen, Penny. *Satchmo Blows Up the World: Jazz Ambassadors Play the Cold War.* 2005.

Wright, Michelle M. *Becoming Black: Creating Identity in the African Diaspora.* 2004.

COUNTERPOINT: The Bandung Conference, 1955

Taylor's people-oriented book provides the Indonesian background to Bandung and shows the stresses and strains of nation building amid postwar turbulence.

Jankowitz, Odile, and Karl Sauvant, eds. *The Third World Without Superpowers: Collected Documents of Non-Aligned Countries.* 1973–1993.

Legge, John David. *Sukarno: A Political Biography.* 2003.

Taylor, Jean Gelman. *Indonesia: Peoples and History.* 2003.

Wright, Richard. *The Color Curtain: A Report on the Bandung Conference.* 1995.

▶ **For additional primary sources from this period,** see *Sources of Crossroads and Cultures.*

▶ **For Web sites, images, and documents related to topics in this chapter,** see Make History at bedfordstmartins.com/smith.

The major global development in this chapter ▶ The political
transformations of the postwar world and their social and cultural consequences.

IMPORTANT EVENTS

1945	World War II ends
1947	India and Pakistan win independence
1948	Israel gains independence
1948–1949	Arab-Israeli War
1949	Communists take control of China; Western powers form NATO; USSR detonates atomic bomb
1949	Indonesia gains independence
1950–1953	Korean War
1952	Egypt achieves full independence under Nasser
1953	Death of Stalin
1954	Vietnamese defeat French army at Dien Bien Phu
1956	Khrushchev denounces Stalin; Suez crisis; revolution in Hungary
1957	USSR launches *Sputnik*
1958	Khrushchev forces Boris Pasternak to refuse Nobel Prize in Literature
1961	Construction of the Berlin Wall
1962	Algeria wins independence; Cuban Missile Crisis
c. 1966–1976	Mao Zedong's "Cultural Revolution"

KEY TERMS

abstract expressionism (p. 983)
Cold War (p. 961)
containment (p. 964)
Cultural Revolution (p. 979)
decolonization (p. 961)
European Economic Community (p. 976)
existentialism (p. 980)
Great Leap Forward (p. 979)

guerrilla warfare (p. 971)
North Atlantic Treaty Organization (p. 967)
Organization of American States (p. 968)
Partition (p. 971)
proxy war (p. 962)
Southeast Asia Treaty Organization (p. 968)
Warsaw Pact (p. 967)
welfare state (p. 977)

CHAPTER OVERVIEW QUESTIONS

1. How did the Cold War affect the superpowers and the world beyond them?

2. How did the Cold War shape everyday lives and goals?

3. Why did colonial nationalism revive in the postwar world, and how did decolonization affect society and culture?

4. Why did the model of a welfare state emerge after World War II, and how did this development affect ordinary people?

SECTION FOCUS QUESTIONS

1. Why was the Cold War waged, and how did it reshape world politics?

2. How did colonized peoples achieve their independence from the imperialist powers after World War II?

3. What were the major elements of recovery in different parts of the world in the decades following World War II?

4. How did the experience of world war, decolonization, and Cold War affect cultural life and thought?

5. How did the Bandung Conference and its aims represent an alternative to the Cold War division of the globe?

MAKING CONNECTIONS

1. Recall Chapters 27 and 28. Why did economic well-being seem so much stronger a decade and longer after World War II than it had been after World War I?

2. Why did proxy wars play such a constant role in the Cold War? Some historians see these wars as part of a new imperialism. Do you agree?

3. What was the role of culture in shaping the Cold War?

4. What remnants of decolonization and the Cold War still affect life today?

30

AT A CROSSROADS ▶

This technician, working in 1962 in a telephone plant in Bangalore, India, stands at a crossroads of global technological innovation. Not only would satellites come to connect a range of communication devices such as telephones throughout the world, but telephones would evolve into such instruments as the iPhone, which would incorporate almost all other means of communication. By the twenty-first century, Bangalore itself would become a leader in global service work because of these and other innovations. (National Geographic/Getty Images.)

Technological Transformation and the End of Cold War

1960–1992

In 1973 the film *Bobby* opened to packed houses in cities across India. The film tells the story of Raj and Bobby, teenagers who fall in love after Raj returns to Bombay from boarding school. Infatuated with each other and the world, Bobby wears long chiffon scarves floating from her ponytail and Raj races around on his motorbike, both of them setting consumer trends among young Indians tired of postindependence seriousness. As Raj's wealthy industrialist father works to stop his son from marrying someone of a lower class, moviegoers cheered the young couple's determination to stay together, even as thugs kidnap them to obtain ransom money from the father. Rebellious young love, new fashions, and lots of song and dance filled *Bobby* and other hit Indian films, which helped "Bollywood," as the film industry centered in Bombay (Mumbai) came to be called, outpace Hollywood in ticket sales and popularity in the 1970s. Thanks to new video-recording technology, developed by the Japanese as a mass market item late in the 1970s, *Bobby* came to circulate worldwide, especially among South Asian fans who had migrated to Western countries.

Hundreds of Bollywood writers, composers, actors, designers, cameramen, editors, agents, and the other service workers who constituted an ever-growing segment of the global workforce contributed to the making of *Bobby*. Bollywood films represented the

BACKSTORY

As we saw in Chapter 29, by 1960 the two superpowers had pulled much of the world into the Cold War, using their considerable military and economic power to attract allies and counter each other's efforts. Their ability to extend their influence into developing countries rested on their successful adoption and application of the technological and industrial developments of the past two centuries. Since 1750 the Industrial Revolution (discussed in Chapter 24) had substituted mechanical energy for human power and then proceeded to develop electrical, chemical, and nuclear capacity. By the postwar period all of these technologies were being enhanced and democratized, widely improving civilian life. Those societies that could innovate, adapt, and then efficiently coordinate the use of these technologies moved ahead, as Japan and Western countries understood early on.

OPEC member
Other major oil-producing country
International borders, 1975
Pacific tiger, c. 1990
Sony Major multinational corporation, 1990s; listed by size

Exxon
IBM
Ford
General Electric
Mobil
Grace
McDonald's
Coca Cola

Toyota
Honda
Sony
Toshiba

Royal Dutch Shell (U.K.)
Nestlé (SWITZ.)
Philips (NETH.)
Asea Brown Boveri (SWE./SWITZ.)

Daewoo

Tata Steel

PACIFIC OCEAN

BELIZE MEXICO
ECUADOR
CUBA
JAMAICA
HAITI
VENEZUELA
DOM. REP.
SOUTH AMERICA
UNITED STATES
CANADA

JAPAN
S. KOREA
Taiwan
P.R. CHINA
Hong Kong
VIETNAM
BANG.
PAK. INDIA
MALAYSIA
SINGAPORE
INDONESIA
AUSTRALIA

NORWAY
U.K.
FRANCE
Frankfurt
Moscow
USSR

ATLANTIC OCEAN

ALGERIA
LIBYA
EGYPT
KUWAIT
IRAQ
QATAR
IRAN
SAUDI ARABIA
U.A.E.
OMAN

NIGERIA
GABON
AFRICA

INDIAN OCEAN

0   1000   2000 miles
0   1000   2000 kilometers

Arab-Israeli Six-Day War **1967**

Vietnam War ends; Vietnam reunited **1975**

1957 USSR launches *Sputnik*

"Prague Spring" in Czechoslovakia **1968**

1969 U.S. astronauts land on moon

1950   **1960**   **1970**

Betty Friedan, *The Feminine Mystique* **1963**

U.S. president Richard Nixon visits China; SALT I agreement **1972**

1973–1976 Aleksandr Solzhenitsyn, *Gulag Archipelago*

Arab-Israeli Yom Kippur War; OPEC raises oil prices and imposes embargo **1973**

fantasies of an increasingly service-oriented population and those aspiring to join it. Across the world, sophisticated technology devised by highly educated service workers transmitted productions via satellite and circulated them on DVDs. In **postindustrial**, service-driven economies, institutions of higher education sprang up at a dizzying rate, drawing more students away from traditional families than ever before—among them bright-eyed young people like Raj and Bobby. The high-tech youthfulness and rebellion represented by *Bobby* and Bollywood were one aspect of the unsettled, dynamic social and economic environment of the late twentieth century.

Although Bollywood presented social and economic change in lighthearted fantasies, people were also making serious efforts to tackle the most pressing problems of modern society. The same young people targeted by the makers of Bollywood films joined a wide variety of activists to strike out against the effects of technology, as well as against war and the Cold War, social inequality and repression, and prevailing attitudes of racism and sexism. Many of these activists participated in grassroots protests against national dictatorships—in Latin America, for example—and against the way high-tech nations in general and the superpowers in particular were directing society. Between 1945 and 1990, more than one hundred major rebellions and civil wars erupted around the world as countries in both the Soviet and U.S. blocs headed toward political revolution. Whole nations—often with the young on the frontlines—challenged the superpowers' monopoly of international power. Agonizing wars in Vietnam and Afghanistan sapped the resources of the United States and the Soviet Union, respectively. Other states emerged to exercise surprising economic and military power as they grasped the reins of technology. The oil-producing states of the Middle East combined their efforts and reduced the export of oil to the leading industrial nations in the 1970s while also raising prices.

As the USSR failed to keep pace with high-tech innovation or to heed youthful calls for change, an invisible erosion of Soviet legitimacy took place, and soon a reform-minded leader—Mikhail Gorbachev—set the country on a new course. It was too late: in 1989, the

postindustrial An economy or society in which service work rather than manufacturing or agriculture predominates.

MAPPING THE WORLD

OPEC, Pacific Tigers, and World Migration

In the decades from 1960 to 1990, the world seemed bogged down in the Cold War order, but it was actually in tremendous flux. Technological change was transforming society and would continue to do so through the twenty-first century. Economic power was beginning to shift away from the West, and this shift would accelerate over the coming decades. Finally, under the influence of technology and global economic change, livelihoods became postindustrial in some areas and more attuned to manufacturing in formerly agricultural regions.

ROUTES ▼

→ Major oil trade routes, c. 1975

→ South Asian migrations, 1970–present

→ Southeast Asian migrations, 1975–present

→ Routes of Aleksandr Solzhenitsyn, 1945–1974

1978–1979 Islamic revolution in Iran

1992 Soviet Union no longer exists

1978 World's first test-tube baby born

1985 Mikhail Gorbachev becomes Soviet leader, introduces new policies of perestroika and glasnost

1980   1990   2000

1979–1989 Soviet war in Afghanistan

1980 Solidarity labor union organizes resistance to communism in Poland; Prime Minister Margaret Thatcher introduces neoliberal program in Britain

1989 Chinese students demonstrate at Tiananmen Square; communist regimes in eastern Europe fall

Soviet bloc collapsed, and by 1992 the USSR itself had dissolved. The dissolution of the Soviet bloc occurred in part as a result of the transformations in the rest of the world. Among these transformations were the growth of rapid global communications, revolutionary developments in technology, and the raised voices of educated young people like Raj and Bobby.

OVERVIEW
QUESTIONS

The major global development in this chapter: The technological revolution of the late twentieth century and its impact on societies and political developments around the world.

As you read, consider:

1. How did the technological developments of these decades transform social and economic conditions?

2. What were the attitudes of young people toward technology and social change during these years, and how did they reflect the Cold War climate in which these changes occurred?

3. How did the technological developments influence the fall of communist regimes in Europe and the dissolution of the Soviet Union?

4. How did the scientific and technological developments of the second half of the twentieth century affect the waging—and the end—of the Cold War?

Advances in Technology and Science

FOCUS

What were the major postwar advances in technology and science, and why were they important?

Revolutionary developments in technology and science reshaped global society after World War II, if unevenly. Wartime technology adapted for civilian use—such as the massive development of nuclear power—continued to improve daily life and boost prosperity. The spread of technology allowed billions of people access to instantaneous radio and television news, to new forms of contraceptives to control reproduction, and to the advantages of computers. Satellites orbiting the earth reported weather conditions, relayed telephone signals, and collected military intelligence. While television, cassettes, and the computer changed politics, other gadgets such as Japanese-developed electric rice cookers and electronic games made life more pleasant for consumers. New forms of information technology allowed citizens to better understand conditions in other countries—knowledge that inspired people around the world to demand more from employers and politicians alike.

The Information Revolution

Information technology catalyzed social and political change in these postwar decades just as innovations in textile making and the spread of railroads had in the nineteenth century. In the first half of the twentieth century, mass journalism, film, and radio had begun to forge a more homogeneous society based on shared information and images; in the last third of the century, television, computers, and telecommunications made information even more accessible and linked once-remote towns to urban capitals on the other side of the globe. In effect, the new information technology acted as a new kind of crossroads, giving individuals access to the ideas, beliefs, and products of societies around the world.

Americans embraced television in the 1950s; following the postwar recovery television became a major entertainment and communications medium in countries around the world. In many places the audience for newspapers and theater declined. "We devote more . . . hours per year to television than [to] any other single artifact," a French sociologist commented in 1969.[1] As with radio, many governments funded television broadcasting with tax dollars and initially controlled TV programming to tap its potential for sending political messages and to avoid what they perceived as the substandard fare offered by American commercial TV. The Indian official in charge of early television programming forbade pop music, for example, and some European countries broadcast mostly classical drama and news. Thus, states assumed a new obligation to organize their citizens' leisure time, thereby gaining more influence over daily life.

Television

With the emergence of communications satellites and video recorders in the 1960s, state-sponsored television encountered competition. Satellite technology transmitted sports broadcasts and other programming to a worldwide audience. In 1969 the Sony Corporation of Japan introduced the first color videocassette recorder to the consumer market; it was widely purchased late in the 1970s. What statesmen and intellectuals considered the junk programming of the United States—soap operas, game shows, sitcoms—arrived dubbed in the native language. More interesting to Brazilians, however, were their own soap operas and those imported from Mexico. Although under the Brazilian dictatorship news was censored from the 1960s into the 1980s, soap operas seemed to show real life, and Mexican programming added to their pool of information. By the 1980s people migrating from one continent to another could keep in touch with their home culture by watching sporting events broadcast via satellite or viewing films such as *Bobby* on videocassettes.

East and west, television exercised a powerful political and cultural influence. Educational programming united the far-flung population of the USSR by broadcasting shows featuring Soviet specialties such as ballet. At the same time, with travel forbidden or too expensive for many people globally, shows about foreign lands were often the most popular. By late in the century even some of the poorest houses in remote African oases sported satellite dishes. Heads of state such as Fidel Castro in Cuba used the medium to maintain national leadership, often preempting regular programming to address fellow citizens. Because electoral success increasingly depended on a successful media image, politicians came to rely on media experts—a new service job—as much as they did policy experts.

Computers

Just as revolutionary as television, the computer reshaped work in science, defense, and industry and eventually came to affect everyday life. As large as a gymnasium in the 1940s, computing machines shrank to the size of an attaché case in the mid-1980s and became far less expensive and fantastically more powerful, thanks to the development of sophisticated digital electronic circuitry implanted on tiny silicon chips, which replaced the clumsy radio tubes used in 1940s and 1950s computers. Within a few decades, the computer could perform hundreds of millions of operations per second and the price of the integrated circuit at the heart of computer technology would fall to less than a dollar, allowing businesses and individuals access to computing power at a reasonable cost.

Computers changed the pace and patterns of work by speeding up tasks and making them easier. By performing many operations that skilled workers had once done themselves, they rendered many livelihoods obsolete. In garment making, for example, experienced workers no longer painstakingly figured out how to arrange patterns on cloth for maximum efficiency and economy. Instead, a computer gave instructions for the best positioning of pattern pieces, and workers, usually women, simply followed the machine's directions. In 1981 the French phone company launched a public Internet server, the Minitel—a forerunner of the World Wide Web—through which French users made dinner reservations, performed stock transactions, and gained information. As in earlier

Computer Programmers in the 1940s

Early computers were massive, and programming required plugging and unplugging multiple cables, as this photograph shows. Many women, such as these U.S. workers, were among the first programmers, perhaps because the process resembled large telephone operations. Technological advances brought increasing miniaturization of ever more powerful computers—a true knowledge revolution that advanced the development of postindustrial society and globalization. (Corbis.)

times, people could work in their homes, but technology now allowed them to be connected to a central mainframe.

Failure to profit from high-tech efficiencies could have dire political consequences, as we shall see. But debate raged over the social effects of computers. Whereas in the Industrial Revolution, machine capabilities had replaced human power, in the information revolution computer technology augmented brainpower. Many believed that computers would further expand mental life, providing, in the words of one scientist, "boundless opportunities . . . to resolve the puzzles of cosmology, of life, and of the society of man."[2] Others maintained that computers programmed people, reducing human capacity for inventiveness and problem solving. Widespread access to the Internet and World Wide Web in the 1990s provoked debates over privacy, property rights, and the transmission of pornography, debates that continue to the present day.

The Space Age

The Space Race

New information and computer technology both contributed to and grew out of another mid-twentieth century development—the space race. After the Soviets' launch of the satellite *Sputnik* in 1957, the space race took off. The competition produced increasingly complex space flights that tested humans' ability to survive space exploration and its effects. Astronauts walked in space, endured weeks (and later, months) in orbit, docked with other craft, fixed satellites, and carried out experiments for the military and private industry. Meanwhile, a series of unmanned rockets filled the earth's gravitational sphere with weather, television, intelligence, and other communications satellites. In July 1969, U.S. astronauts Neil Armstrong and Edwin "Buzz" Aldrin walked on the moon's surface—a climactic moment in the space race.

Global Communication

Although the space race grew out of Cold War rivalry, the space age also offered the possibility of global political cooperation and communication. The exploration of space by a single country came to involve the participation of other countries. In 1965, an international consortium headed by the United States launched the first commercial communications satellite, *Intelsat I*, and by 1969, with the launch of *Intelsat III* covering the Indian Ocean region, the entire world was linked via satellite. Although some 50 percent of satellites were for military and espionage purposes, the rest promoted international communication and were sustained by transnational collaboration: by the 1970s some 150 countries collaborated to maintain the global satellite system. Satellite transmission allowed 500 million people to watch live reporting from the moon in 1969, and in 1978 one billion fans—or one quarter of the world's population at the time—tuned in to the World Cup soccer game. Global linkages only grew in magnitude and importance over the next decades.

Lunar landings and experiments in space brought advances in pure science. For example, astronomers used mineral samples from the moon to calculate the age of the solar system with unprecedented precision. Unmanned spacecraft provided data on cosmic radiation, magnetic fields, and infrared sources. Utilizing a range of technology, including the radiotelescope, which depicted space by receiving, measuring, and calculating nonvisible rays, these findings reinforced the so-called big bang theory of the origins of the universe and brought other new information, such as data on the composition of other planets, to scientists around the world. Long before politicians resolved Cold War differences, scientists were sharing their knowledge of the universe.

Scientific Advances

A New Scientific Revolution

Sophisticated technologies extended to the life sciences, bringing dramatic health benefits and ultimately changing reproduction itself. In 1952, English molecular biologist Francis Crick and American biologist James Watson discovered the configuration of DNA, the material in a cell's chromosomes that carries hereditary information. Simultaneously, other scientists were working on "the pill"—an oral contraceptive for women that tapped more than a century of scientific work in the field of birth control. More breakthroughs lay ahead—ones that would revolutionize conception and make scientific duplication of species possible.

Crick and Watson, young men working as a team from laboratories in Cambridge, England, solved the mystery of the gene and thus of biological inheritance when they demonstrated the structure of DNA. They showed how the double helix of the DNA molecule splits in cellular reproduction to form the basis of each new cell. This genetic material, biologists concluded, provides the chemical pattern for an individual organism's life. Beginning in the 1960s, genetics and the new field of molecular biology progressed rapidly. Growing understanding of nucleic acids and proteins advanced knowledge of viruses and bacteria, leading to effective worldwide campaigns against polio, tetanus, syphilis, tuberculosis, and such dangerous childhood diseases as mumps and measles— boosting the world's population.

Understanding DNA

Understanding how DNA works allowed scientists both to alter the makeup of plants and to bypass natural animal reproduction in a process called cloning—obtaining the cells of an organism and dividing or reproducing them (in an exact copy) in a laboratory. The possibility of genetically altering species and even creating new variations (for instance, to control agricultural pests) led to concern about how such actions would affect the balance of nature. Adding to medical breakthroughs, in 1967 Dr. Christiaan Barnard of South Africa performed the first successful heart transplant, and U.S. doctors later developed an artificial heart. By the end of the twentieth century, transplant technology circled the globe. Critics questioned whether the enormous cost of new medical technology to save a few people might be better spent on improving basic medical and health care for the many.

Technology also influenced the most intimate areas of human relations—sexuality and procreation. In traditional societies, community and family norms dictated marital arrangements and sexual practices, in large part because too many or too few children threatened the crucial balance between population size and agricultural productivity. As societies industrialized and urbanized, however, not only did these considerations become less important, but the growing availability of reliable birth-control devices permitted young people to begin sexual relations earlier, with less risk of pregnancy. These trends accelerated in the 1960s when the birth-control pill, developed in a Mexican research

Transforming Reproduction

institute and later mass-produced in the United States and tested on women in Puerto Rico and other developing areas, came on the Western market. By 1970, its use was spreading around the world. Millions also sought out voluntary surgical sterilization through tubal ligations and vasectomies. New techniques brought abortion, traditionally performed by amateurs, into the hands of medical professionals, making the procedure safe, though still controversial.

Childbirth and conception itself were similarly transformed. Whereas only a small minority of Western births took place in hospitals in 1920, more than 90 percent did by 1970 and this trend spread worldwide. Obstetricians performed much of the work midwives had once done. As pregnancy and birth became a medical process, innovative procedures and equipment made it possible to monitor women and fetuses throughout pregnancy, labor, and delivery. In 1978, the first "test-tube baby," Louise Brown, was born to an English couple. She had been conceived when her mother's eggs were fertilized with her father's sperm in a laboratory dish and then implanted in her mother's uterus—a complex process called *in vitro fertilization*. If a woman could not carry a child to term, the laboratory-fertilized embryo could be implanted in the uterus of a surrogate, or substitute, mother.

The Green Revolution

Science also helped boost grain harvests around the world. In Mexico City in the 1940s, a team of scientists led by Norman Borlaug experimented with blending Japanese strains of wheat with Mexican ones, devising hardier seeds that raised yields by some 70 percent. Borlaug became part of "an army of hunger fighters," as he called those who next worked to devise rice that would thrive in India, the Philippines, and other countries.[3]

Those most able to profit from the breakthrough, however, were large landowners who could afford the irrigation, fertilizers, and the new seeds themselves. High costs led many small farmers to fail. As a result of the **Green Revolution**, however, rural poverty nonetheless declined in countries such as India, where it fell from close to 50 percent of the population in the 1960s to 30 percent in the 1990s. Although technological innovation did not affect all societies to the same degree or in the same ways, the rate of scientific discovery and its overall impact on life around the world increased steadily in the late twentieth century. Moreover, as the century came to a close, Western nations lost their monopoly on scientific and industrial power.

Changes in the World Economy

FOCUS

How did changes in the global economy affect livelihoods and family life?

Beginning in the 1960s industrial and agrarian entrepreneurship and the development of technology rose dramatically outside the West, especially in Asia and the Middle East. Profits from both manufacturing and the sale of commodities soared during these years. In contrast, reshaped by the spread of technology, the economies of Western countries took what has been labeled a postindustrial course. Instead of being centered on industry and agriculture, the postindustrial economy emphasized intellectual work and the distribution of services such as health care and education. As Asia and Latin America in particular developed their manufacturing and service sectors in the last third of the century, the share in the world economy of the traditional industrial powers declined.

The Rising Pacific Economy

Green Revolution The application of DNA and other scientific knowledge to the production of seeds and fertilizers to raise agricultural productivity in developing parts of the world.

From Japan to Singapore, explosive productivity began to spread economic power through the Pacific region. Japan's government determined to oversee the nation's economic rebirth, with the Ministry of Trade and Industry announcing in 1959 a goal of "income doubling" within ten years. In an effort to strengthen its Cold War allies, the United States pumped some $12 billion into East Asian allies such as South Korea, contributing to its

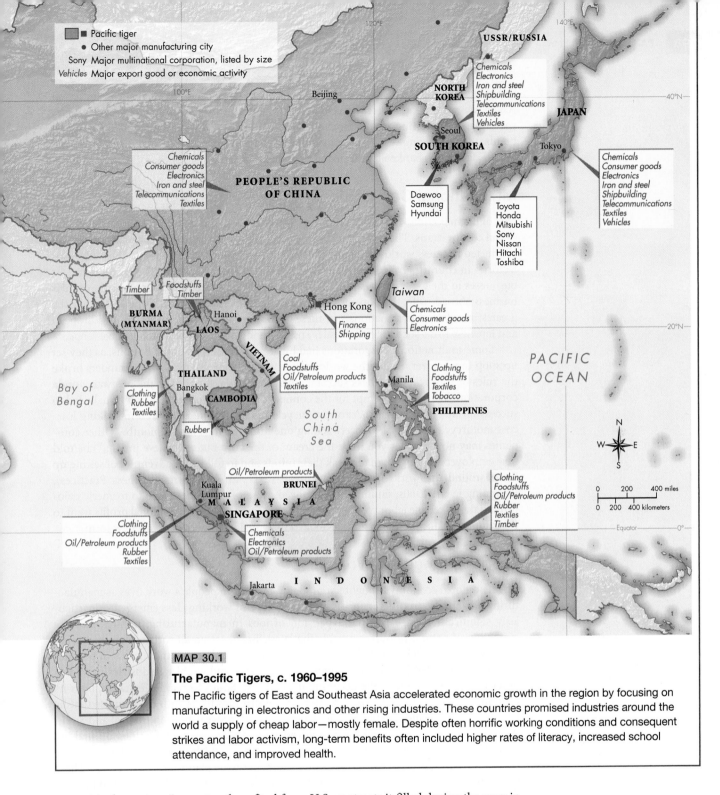

MAP 30.1

The Pacific Tigers, c. 1960–1995

The Pacific tigers of East and Southeast Asia accelerated economic growth in the region by focusing on manufacturing in electronics and other rising industries. These countries promised industries around the world a supply of cheap labor—mostly female. Despite often horrific working conditions and consequent strikes and labor activism, long-term benefits often included higher rates of literacy, increased school attendance, and improved health.

economic dynamism. Japan, too, benefited from U.S. contracts it filled during the wars in Korea and Vietnam. By 1982, Asian Pacific nations accounted for 16.4 percent of global production, a figure that had doubled since the 1960s. China abandoned Mao's disastrous economic experiments in 1978, achieving economic growth rates of 8 percent by the mid-1990s. Japan and China joined the United States and Germany as the world's top trading nations, while South Korea, Taiwan, Singapore, and Hong Kong came to be called **Pacific tigers** for the ferocity of their growth in the 1980s and 1990s (see Map 30.1).

Japan led the way in developing innovative high-tech industries. In 1982, Japan had more than four times as many industrial robots in operation as the United States. Constant government spending on technological innovation paid off as buyers around the

Pacific tiger One of the East Asian economies with ferocious rates of growth in the 1980s and 1990s.

world snapped up automobiles, videocassettes, and computers from Japanese and other Asian Pacific companies. As the United States poured vast sums into Cold War military spending, the resulting profits from the Pacific Rim went to purchase U.S. government bonds, thus financing America's national debt. Forty years after its total defeat in World War II, Japan was bankrolling its former conqueror.

Multinational Corporations

One of the major innovations of the postindustrial era was the growing number of **multinational corporations**. These companies produced goods and services for a global market and conducted business worldwide, but unlike older international firms, they established major factories in countries other than their home base. For example, of the five hundred largest businesses in the United States in 1970, more than one hundred did over a quarter of their business abroad, with IBM operating in more than one hundred countries. Although the greatest number of multinationals in these years were U.S.-based corporations, European and Japanese firms such as Shell, Nestlé, Toshiba, and Sony also had a broad global scope.

Some multinational corporations had bigger revenues than entire nations, as they set up shop in whatever part of the world offered cheap labor. Many of their founders broke the rules of traditional business success. Soichiro Honda, founder of the postwar Honda corporation, had only contempt for the connections and diplomas that traditionally led to success in Japanese business. A former bicycle repairman, he pioneered in making low-cost motorcycles that by 1961 were selling one hundred thousand a month. "Other companies may not consider you to be the cream of the crop but we believe in you,"[4] he told new employees, urging them to speak their minds and to follow his adventure of setting up firms around the world (see Reading the Past: Japan Transforms Business Practices). Beginning in the 1960s, multinationals moved more of their operations to formerly colonized states to reduce labor costs, taxes, and regulations. Most multinational profits went to enrich foreign stockholders and thus looked to some like imperialism in a new form.

Global Changes in Work

New Manufacturing Areas

The new global economy brought about major changes in people's work lives as manufacturing jobs moved to different areas and a new type of working class emerged. A particularly significant change was the expansion of jobs in manufacturing, mining, and the extraction of natural resources outside the West. Brazil set up all sorts of manufacturing enterprises in the 1960s, including what would eventually become the successful production of automobiles. Jobs in electronics and the textile and clothing industries moved to other parts of the world while declining in the West. South Korea, for instance, built its economy in the 1960s and 1970s by attracting electronics firms with the promise that its female workers would accept low wages and benefits. In sweatshops in Central and South America, young women and even children helped support their families by making sneakers and other goods. In China, rural families chose which single daughters would be sent to work in European toy factories or Taiwanese textile plants located in China. These young women performed repetitive work, yet still learned to move from plant to plant to gain small advantages either in pay or conditions in the few years during which their families allowed them to leave the village. People learned new skills: "The first time I saw those English letters I was scared to death. I couldn't recognize them, so I copied them down and recited them at night," one young Chinese worker recalled of learning English.[5] With the influx of manufacturing jobs, educational standards rose, along with access to birth control and other medical care that improved health.

Change also occurred in the West, where the number of manufacturing workers who had once labored to exhaustion declined, a trend that slowly spread to the rest of the world. Resource depletion in coal mines, the substitution of foreign oil for coal and of plastics for steel, the growth of offshore manufacturing, and automation in industrial

multinational corporation A company that produces goods and services for a global market and that operates businesses worldwide.

Japan Transforms Business Practices

Alongside technological innovation from the 1960s on came a fundamental change in the way many multinational companies were run. Japan led the way, as it did in much innovation in these years, and its businessmen introduced new responsibilities for workers—a real break from the relationships between bosses and workers in the first two hundred years of the Industrial Revolution. Akio Morita was a cofounder of Sony, the Japanese electronics pioneer that quickly became a global corporation. Its founders ushered in the cutting-edge practice of spreading responsibility for innovation and productivity across the firm instead of confining it to the managerial ranks as had been the previous practice. Morita explained the concept in his autobiography *Made in Japan* (1986).

A company will get nowhere if all of the thinking is left to management. Everybody in the company must contribute, and for the lower-level employees their contribution must be more than just manual labor. We insist that all of our employees contribute their minds. Today we get an average of eight suggestions a year from each of our employees, and most of the suggestions have to do with making their own jobs easier or their work more reliable or a process more efficient. Some people in the West scoff at the suggestion process, saying that it forces people to repeat the obvious, or that it indicates a lack of leadership by management. This attitude shows a lack of understanding. We don't force suggestions, and we take them seriously and implement the best ones. . . . After all, who could tell us better how to structure the work than the people who are doing it? . . .

I always tell employees that they should not worry too much about what their superiors tell them. I say,

"Go ahead without waiting for instructions." To the managers I say this is an important element in bringing out the ability and creativity of those below them. Young people have flexible and creative minds, so a manager should not try to cram preconceived ideas into them, because it may smother their originality before it gets a chance to bloom.

In Japan, workers who spend a lot of time together develop an atmosphere of self-motivation, and it is the young employees who give the real impetus to this. Management officers, knowing that the company's ordinary business is being done by energetic and enthusiastic younger employees, can devote their time and effort to planning the future of the company. With this in mind, we think it is unwise and unnecessary to define individual responsibility too clearly.

Source: Akio Morita with Edwin M. Reingold and Mitsuko Shimomura, *Made in Japan: Akio Morita and Sony* (New York: E. P. Dutton, 1986), 149.

EXAMINING THE EVIDENCE

1. What is Akio Morita's attitude toward employees in this statement?

2. What are the innovative aspects of his policies?

3. What role does Akio Morita see for young people in businesses?

4. How have industrial attitudes, as described in this excerpt, changed from those discussed in Chapter 24?

---

processes reduced the blue-collar workforce. Remaining blue-collar workers enjoyed improved conditions as work in manufacturing became cleaner and more mechanized than ever before. Huge new agribusinesses forced many struggling farmers to take different jobs. Governments, cooperatives, and planning agencies set production quotas and handled an array of marketing transactions for the modern farmer-entrepreneur.

Changes in the Workforce in the West

Meanwhile, the ranks of service workers swelled with researchers, health-care and medical workers, technicians, planners, and government functionaries. Jobs in banks, insurance companies, and other financial institutions also surged because of the vast sums needed to finance technology and research. Entire categories of employees such as flight attendants found that much of their work focused on the psychological well-being of customers. Already by 1969, the percentage of service-sector employees had passed that of manufacturing workers in several industrialized countries: 61.1 percent versus 33.7 percent in the United States alone (see Lives and Livelihoods: Global Tourism).

Global Tourism

International Tourism Workers in Japan
These guides at the Imperial Palace in Japan are part of the vast global pool of service workers, whose fields range from medicine and health care to teaching, law, and personal service such as beautification and domestic help. Tourism workers number in the millions and are found in thousands of capital cities, historic locations, and sites of natural beauty. (Robert Holmes/Corbis.)

Mr. Ibrahim stands outside the hotel gates near the Great Pyramids of Giza looking for customers who might want a guide around the nearby city of Cairo. Friendly, speaking several languages, he asks passersby if they need directions or a ride into town in his car. Like him, women in Guatemala wait by bus and train stations with ponchos and other craft items they have made themselves in hopes that a tourist will buy something. Native Americans ring the main square of Santa Fe, New Mexico, with lavish displays of leatherwork, jewelry, and paintings. In Bamako, capital of Mali, Muhammad waits to do such services for visitors as finding a telephone, delivering a message, or guiding

them around the museums. All of these workers make their living through the growing presence of tourists eager to visit every part of a shrinking world, and to make purchases when they get there. They are the uncounted laborers in one of the fastest-growing global livelihoods—tourism.

In 1841 Thomas Cook, a Baptist evangelist in Britain, arranged for a special train to take some six hundred people to a temperance rally. His belief was that going to a rally and then seeing the local sights was a far better way to spend time than frequenting cafés and taverns. Cook's enterprise was so financially successful that he made deals with trains and found lodging for ever-larger groups of travelers.

The Knowledge Economy

Research and education were the means by which nations now advanced their economic and military might. Common sense, hard work, and creative intuition had launched the earliest successes of the Industrial Revolution. By the late twentieth century, success in business or government demanded humanistic or technological expertise and ever-growing staffs of researchers. As one French official put it, "the accumulation of knowledge, not of wealth, . . . makes the difference" in the quest for power. Thus governments around the world expanded the welfare state's mandate for intensive development of educational and research facilities.

Research and Applied Science

Investment in research fueled economic leadership. The United States funneled more than 20 percent of its gross national product into research in the 1960s, in the process enticing many of the world's leading intellectuals and technicians to work in America—

In 1851 he provided package tours for people wanting to attend the Crystal Palace Exhibition in London—over one hundred thousand travelers from Yorkshire alone. Cook's Tours, the company he eventually founded, became so skilled in arranging long-distance travel that the government even hired it to move troops in such distant regions as Africa. With Cook's Tours, some say, tourism became an official line of work—and that was a century before the postwar boom in transportation and communication.

There have been travelers, pilgrims, and even tourists for thousands of years, using guides and drivers, porters, cooks, laundresses, and innkeepers to smooth the way. None of these could avail themselves of transport by air, of course, but in the twentieth century, flight went from being primarily a military phenomenon to one that involved tens of millions of consumers around the world after World War II. At that point the tourist industry grew to comprise employees of large multinational corporations such as airlines and banks. Transcontinental hotel chains employed so many different types of workers that postsecondary schools came to offer programs in hotel and restaurant management. These service workers made up the booming postindustrial economy of the late twentieth and early twenty-first centuries. The United Kingdom estimates tourism currently as one of its largest industries, generating approximately £74 billion annually and employing 2.1 million people in a variety of livelihoods, including those in hotels, restaurants, and tour companies. Still growing in the decolonized areas where women and children struggle to earn a living is sex tourism from wealthy societies such as western Europe and Japan.

Besides small-scale workers in tourism and large and vigorous multinational companies dealing with hundreds of thousands of people, tourism has generated livelihoods for bureaucrats, statisticians, and, increasingly, public relations experts, translators, and Web site designers. Every country and most cities had Web sites for tourists by the twenty-first century. The World Tourism Organization (WTO), which took shape in 1925 and became an agency of the UN in 1974, provided work for people who monitored, counted, and encouraged travel. Employees of the WTO, for example, have recently worked to boost tourism in eastern European countries and sub-Saharan Africa—all of these livelihoods developing the service sector still further.

QUESTIONS TO CONSIDER

1. What is the range of service occupations you can connect to tourism?

2. What skills are necessary in the tourism industry, and how do these fit the knowledge-based, technological society of the postwar world?

3. Why do you think tourism has grown so dramatically since the time of Thomas Cook?

For Further Information:

Baud, Michiel, and Annelou Ypeij, eds. *Cultural Tourism in Latin America: The Politics of Space and Imagery.* 2009.

Dallen, J. Timothy, and Gyan P. Nyaupane, eds. *Cultural Heritage and Tourism in the Developing World: A Regional Perspective.* 2009.

Segreto, Luciano, et al., eds. *Europe at the Seaside: The Economic History of Mass Tourism in the Mediterranean.* 2009.

the so-called brain drain. Soon, however, Japan was outpacing Western countries in research and new product development. Complex systems—for example, nuclear power generation with its many components, from scientific conceptualization to plant construction to the supervised disposal of radioactive waste—required intricate coordination and oversight. In the realm of space programs, weapons development, and economic policy, scientists and bureaucrats frequently made more crucial decisions than did elected politicians. Developing and developed nations alike set up special cities and research hubs where scientists lived and worked, but Soviet-bloc nations proved less successful at linking their considerable achievements in science and technology to actual applications because of bureaucratic red tape. In the 1960s, an astounding 40 percent of Soviet-bloc scientific findings became obsolete before the government approved them. Falsification of information in the Soviet system also hampered efforts to make technology work to the nation's benefit.

Growth in Higher Education

The new criteria for success fostered unprecedented global growth in education, especially in the size and number of universities and scientific institutes. The number of university students in South Korea soared from 11,358 in 1950 to 3.4 million by 2000. Countries set up networks of universities specifically to encourage the technical research that traditional elite universities often scorned and established schools to train high-level experts in administration. Meanwhile, institutions of higher learning added courses in business and management, information technology, and systems analysis. Students enrolled in schools outside their home nations as education became internationalized. In principle, education equalized avenues to success by basing them on talent instead of wealth, but in fact, broad societal leveling did not occur in many universities. So long as socioeconomic background remained a key factor in determining university attendance, universities would reinforce inequality, not reduce it.

Postindustrial Family Life

Just as education changed dramatically to meet the needs of postindustrial society, in urban areas family structure and parent-child relationships shifted significantly from what they had been a century earlier. A steady flow of migrants produced enormous variety in urban households. These varied from patriarchal households consisting of several generations to those headed by a single female parent, unmarried couples cohabiting, or traditionally married couples who had few or no children. Daily life within the urban family became increasingly mechanized. The wages that young Chinese workers earned enabled them to buy more consumer items, even in villages distant from cities, and radio and television often formed the basis of the household's common social life, yielding conversations from Australia to Chile about the plots of soap operas and the outcomes of sporting matches. By the end of the century, appliances became increasingly affordable and more households were able to own them. The increase of appliances within the home reduced the time women devoted to household work, but did not eliminate it, as the standards of cleanliness also increased. Still, the mechanization of domestic chores freed more women to work outside the home. Young women's wages went to finance the education of brothers, and working mothers supported the prolonged economic dependence of their children, who spent more years in school. Working mothers still, however, did the housework and provided child care almost entirely themselves.

Whereas early modern families organized labor, taught craft skills, and monitored reproductive behavior, the primary focus of the modern urban family was most often on psychological and financial assistance. Many children in industrialized regions did not enter the labor force until their twenties but instead attended school, thus requiring their parents' backing. Japanese parents doled out the most resources: they financed their children's after-school education beginning as early as the primary grades to give the children a competitive edge

Bobby and the Youth Revolution

In the late 1960s and 1970s, young people around the globe asserted their rights to sexual freedom and independent private lives. The 1973 hit film _Bobby_, in which the main character rebelled by choosing a partner from a different social class, featured the youth culture of these years. Made at the height of postwar prosperity, just before the first oil embargo, the film also reflected youthful consumerism, as young people bought such items as motorcycles and up-to-date fashions. (RK FILMS LTD/Ronald Grant Archive/Mary Evans/The Image Works Editorial.)

Children and Teenagers

in exams, and ambitious parents never let their children do housework or hold part-time jobs. Parents could also rely on an array of psychologists and other service workers to counsel them.

Most notably, modern society transformed teenagers' lives; they gained new roles as the most up-to-date consumers. Advertisers and industrialists saw youth as a multibillion-dollar market and wooed them with consumer items such as rock music recordings, electronic games, and eventually computers and iPods. Rock music celebrated youthful rebellion against adult culture in biting and often sexually explicit lyrics. This youth music, in the words of one 1960s Latin American commentator, was "a threat to the family."[6] Sex roles for the young did not change, however. Despite the popularity of a few individual women rockers, promoters focused on men, setting them up as idols surrounded by worshiping female groupies. Advanced technology and savvy marketing for global mass consumption contributed to a worldwide youth culture and a growing generation gap—phenomena depicted in the film *Bobby*.

A Sexual Revolution?

The global media helped spread knowledge of birth-control procedures and allowed for public discussion of sexual matters in many parts of the world. Although highly sexualized film, music, and journalism permeated the world, widespread use of birth control (by some 80 percent of the world's people at the end of the twentieth century) meant there was no corresponding rise in the birthrate—evidence of the increasing separation of sexuality from reproduction. Statistical surveys showed that regular sexual activity began at an ever-younger age, and people talked more openly about sex—another component of cultural change. Critics as early as the mid-1950s worried about the level of sexuality in media: "Reduce the sex appeal in [motion] pictures," one Indian official urged. "How can we progress in other matters if every young man is thinking of this [sex] stuff all the time?"[7] Finally, in a climate of increased publicity about sexuality, homosexual behavior became more open and accepted. Some media announced the arrival of a "sexual revolution," but many political voices denounced it as a particularly dangerous form of Westernization.

Politics and Protest in an Age of Cold War

Scientific sophistication and high-tech military elevated the United States and the Soviet Union to the peak of their power in the 1960s. Simultaneously, however, other nations' aspirations for freedom and their own growing access to technology began to limit the superpowers' ability to shape world politics. Expanding European Common Market and Pacific Rim economies were innovative and had muscle of their own. People in eastern Europe had greater contact with the West via satellite and other technology and contested Soviet leadership. Elsewhere, people refused to endure superpower-backed dictatorships. At the same time, both superpowers discovered that there were limits to their ability to dictate the outcomes of foreign struggles, notably in Vietnam and Afghanistan. Thus, popular struggles around democratization, technology, and economic well-being strained the international political order of the Cold War.

FOCUS

What developments challenged the superpowers' dominance of world politics, and how did the superpowers attempt to address those challenges?

Democracy and Dictatorship in Latin America

World War II and the early Cold War had boosted prosperity in many countries of Latin America, but a hefty percentage of profits went to multinational corporations that had taken control of resources and often shaped the economy around one or two crops such as coffee or bananas or raw materials such as copper. When prices for commodities dropped after the war, workers in undiversified economies suffered and activism grew. By providing aid to Cuba, the Soviet Union came to dominate the Cuban government, while the United States sent money and personnel to overthrow democratic leaders in Guatemala,

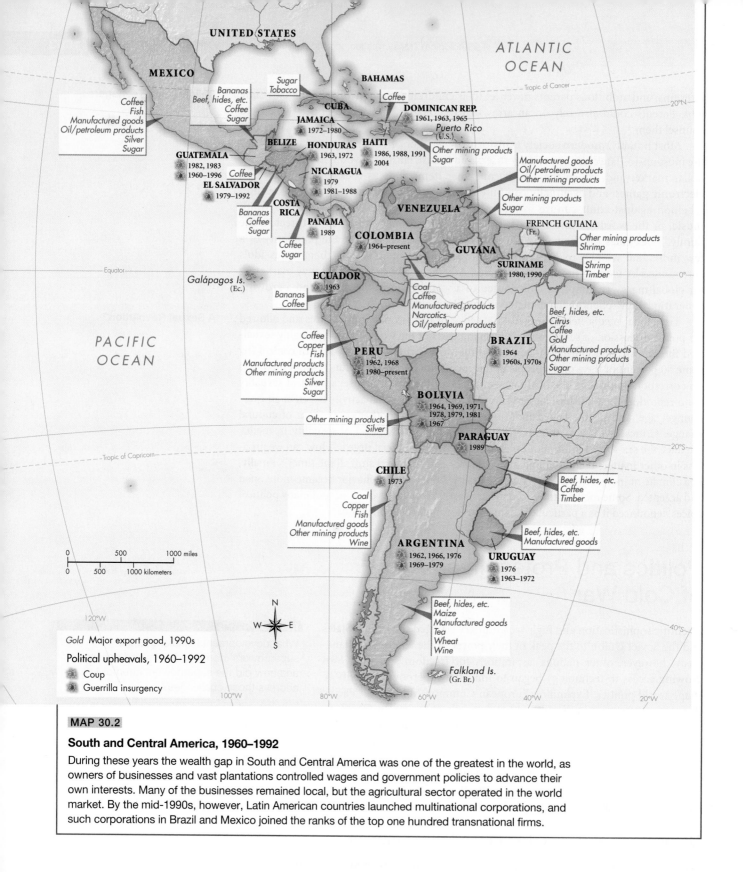

MAP 30.2

South and Central America, 1960–1992

During these years the wealth gap in South and Central America was one of the greatest in the world, as owners of businesses and vast plantations controlled wages and government policies to advance their own interests. Many of the businesses remained local, but the agricultural sector operated in the world market. By the mid-1990s, however, Latin American countries launched multinational corporations, and such corporations in Brazil and Mexico joined the ranks of the top one hundred transnational firms.

Chile, Nicaragua, and other Latin American nations with the aim of keeping communism at bay. Generous financing by the superpowers gave rise to repressive dictatorships allied to one side or the other in the Cold War. In many Latin American countries citizen activists protested against both economic difficulties in an increasingly technological world and foreign-backed political oppression (see Map 30.2).

Dictatorships grew up across Latin America to crush democratic movements for change and to provide the kind of bureaucratic planning for a technology-driven economy that was helping Common Market countries advance. Argentineans, burdened by rising prices and wage freezes along with dictatorship, took their protests to the streets in the 1960s and early 1970s. In response, the Argentinean military, having taken over from Perón in 1955, launched what came to be known as "the dirty war," silencing critics through kidnapping, torture, and murder. Mothers of the Plaza de Mayo became celebrated for opposing the "dirty war." Beginning in April 1977, a group of women, whose relatives were among the "disappeared" ones, began meeting at three-thirty in the afternoon in the plaza that fronted important government buildings. Walking in silent protest around the bustling center where Argentineans gathered to chat or conduct business, the "Mothers"—women from all livelihoods and conditions—wordlessly demanded an account of their missing brothers, husbands, and children. Hebe de Bonafini, whose two sons had "disappeared," explained the change in her everyday existence: "My life had been the life of a housewife—washing, ironing, cooking, and bringing up my children, just like you're always taught to do, believing that everything else was nothing. . . . Then I realized that that wasn't everything, that I had another world too. You realize that you're in a world where you have to do a lot of things."[8] She became an activist, helping bring the human rights abuses of the Argentinean government to the attention of a global audience (see Reading the Past: Terror and Resistance in El Salvador).

The many protests against the Argentinean government, combined with a disastrous economic situation, led to the election of civilian Raúl Alfonsin to the presidency in 1983. Alfonsin tried to deal with the nation's economic troubles brought on by a lack of investment in industry, large public expenditures, and an unequal balance of payments, but his failure to solve these problems quickly and his decision to freeze wages led to the return of a military-backed candidate in 1989. But one thing had changed: the military's policy of torture and murder was ended—a crucial victory. "There's no more official torture here; there are no more 'disappeared,'" one reporter exclaimed of the more open political climate. "Whatever else may be happening, this is terribly terribly important."[9]

Brazil also took the Argentine route of dictatorship in the name of orderly technological development, but until the mid-1970s Chile remained democratic even as it experienced the chaotic postwar rush to the cities. In country and city alike, however, poverty remained pervasive. In 1970 Chileans elected socialist candidate Salvador Allende (ah-YEHN-day), whose platform for improving the economy included taking over the country's copper resources from foreign investors, notably many Americans. The U.S. fought back against both Allende's socialism and his potential to reduce U.S. economic interests, pouring vast sums into political opposition and sending CIA operatives to murder Allende's supporters in the military. Allende hoped to improve Chile's economic position, but the measures he used failed miserably. He mandated a wage increase, but he also imposed price controls that discouraged domestic manufacturers. Inexperienced bureaucrats could not make newly nationalized industries function either well enough or fast enough. As inflation soared, opposition to Allende mounted, much of it sponsored by the CIA. In 1973 Allende was murdered in a military coup.

Chile's multiple political parties depended on the support of people from different classes. Allende's had come from the working classes, whereas professionals and small shopkeepers backed more centrist parties. General Augusto Pinochet (pin-oh-CHET), who emerged to rule after the coup, ended this tradition of political participation, closing down the elected Congress and suspending the constitution. While working to stabilize the economy, Pinochet's government kidnapped and killed dissidents. Determined opponents, braving torture and facing murder, slowly gained a foothold and finally became strong enough to defeat Pinochet. Mothers for Life, one of the opposition groups, launched a series of demonstrations, sending letters to foreign embassies and the press: "We are Chilean women from a variety of fields: workers, professionals, students, peasants, artists, and housewives, women of all ages who have survived more than a decade of a system of

Terror and Resistance in El Salvador

In a number of Latin American countries, dictators came to power in the second half of the twentieth century, using the military and private armed forces to "disappear" those who opposed them. Teenage critics, protesters, relatives of protesters, and sympathetic Catholic clergy were kidnapped, tortured, raped, and most often killed, frequently with the assistance of the superpowers. In El Salvador, the disappearance of family members beginning in 1975 sparked the development of the CoMadres ("co-mothers"), a group of mostly peasant women who—like women in other Latin American nations—gave up their normal livelihoods to protest these conditions. In the face of the increasing number of disappeared and even the torture and rape of virtually all the "mothers" themselves, the group regularly marched in protest and collected information about the capture of family members—their own and others'. Here, one of the founders explains the protest movement to an American anthropologist.

In the beginning of our struggle, it was an individual problem. But one began to discover that there were others in the same situation, and we realized we couldn't be isolated, that our struggle had to be collective. It had to be a group of people who participated in the same fight, in the same search, trying to discover the truth. . . .

We borrowed from a march of mothers dressed in black during a march in 1922 to protest a massacre of male and female teachers. They went out into the street to protest the killing of their children. We borrowed our black dress from them. . . . Black signified the condolences and affliction we carry for each person killed. And the white headscarf represents the peace we are

seeking—but it must be a peace with justice, not a peace with impunity! We also carry a red and white carnation: the red for the spilled blood, the white for the detained—disappeared and the green leaves, the hope for life. That is our complete dress. . . .

Most of us at this time were from Christian-based communities. . . . Mons[eigneur] Romero would read our public letters out loud in his Sunday homily in the Cathedral so that the CoMadres became known nationally. One month before he was assassinated, I remember that Mons[eigneur] Romero gave us his blessing by telling us, "Ah, women, you are the Marys of today. . . . All of you are suffering the same loss, the same pain."

Source: Interviews conducted by Jennifer Schirmer, "The Seeking of Truth and the Gendering of Consciousness: The CoMadres of El Salvador and the CONAVIGUA Widows of Guatemala," in *"VIVA": Women and Popular Protest in Latin America*, ed. Sarah A. Radcliffe and Sallie Westwood (London: Routledge, 1993), 32–33, 36.

EXAMINING THE EVIDENCE

1. What caused these women to leave their ordinary livelihoods to protest on a regular basis?

2. To what extent would you say that protest and the search for their children became a new livelihood for them?

3. Why did the CoMadres and similar groups of Latin American women activists become such a powerful symbol around the world?

death. . . . We accuse the military regime of throwing our nation into the greatest crisis of history. . . . It is a crisis of the future, a crisis of life."[10] The Mothers for Life were hardly alone, and by 1988 a broad coalition of the Chilean people had swept Pinochet from office, bringing in a representative government and leaving him to face international tribunals for crimes against humanity. Thus, while global developments contributed to the rise of dictatorships in Latin America, some of the same developments made it possible for ordinary individuals to forge connections with sympathetic people around the world and to serve as models for others who wanted change.

Domestic Revolution and a Changing International Order

Political change surged around the world, undermining allies of both superpowers, upsetting the Cold War order, and generally highlighting the need to advance technologically, economically, and politically. In Spain, the death of dictator Francisco Franco in 1975

The Rule of Idi Amin in Uganda

New nations emerging from colonial rule were often plagued by dictatorships headed by the military leaders who fought the imperialists. Idi Amin took power in Uganda in 1971, and during his eight-year reign his forces murdered some five hundred thousand Ugandans, forcing many thousands more to flee the country to safe havens around the world. In this image of a public execution in 1973, a supposed guerrilla fighter becomes one of Amin's victims. (Mohamed Amin/Africa Media Online/The Image Works.)

ended more than three decades of authoritarian rule. Franco's handpicked successor, King Juan Carlos, surprisingly steered his nation to Western-style constitutional monarchy that ushered in Spain's economic modernization and membership in the Common Market. In Africa, brutal killers such as Idi Amin of Uganda were overthrown, and other dictators fell, making Cold War stability uncertain.

In 1960 some thirty thousand South Korean university and high school students mounted a peaceful demonstration in Seoul to call for clean elections in their country. They stood before the presidential residence, where Syngman Rhee (SING-man REE), a U.S.-educated and U.S.-supported dictator, had ruled since before the Korean War. Playing the Cold War card, Rhee labeled any critic or democratic politician a communist and had that person arrested or assassinated. Rhee employed his usual tactics in response to the student protesters' call for honest democracy: the police fired into the crowd and killed and wounded hundreds. Citizen outrage caused the government to collapse and free elections brought to power leaders oriented toward openness and constitutional government.

In May 1961, however, Park Chung Hee, a major general in the military, overthrew the new democratic government and instituted a dictatorship, which the U.S. praised as "Korean-style democracy." Instead of democracy, however, Park opted to give Koreans economic growth, using repressive measures such as torture and imprisonment of critics as the government lured hi-tech multinationals to its shores. Student protests continued through the late 1960s and 1970s, and workers denounced the influence of General Motors and other foreign corporations even as the police beat them up. Working people fought the regime: textile worker Chon T'ae-il immolated himself in 1970, shouting as he died "Don't mistreat young girls," a reference to the fifteen-hour days with one day off per month worked by teenagers in unheated textile factories to meet the government's goals for economic development.[11] In 1979, Park ordered more severe police retaliation against demonstrators; opposing the directive, the head of the Korean CIA shot Park. A military junta took over, again with U.S. backing to keep South Korea loyal, and ruled until 1987, when a newly elected president, backed by the military, instituted reforms, including guarantees of civil rights and democratic procedures. It appeared that popular activism had finally brought greater democracy while technological advances made South Korea a looming economic power.

South Korea

Vietnam

The Cold War remained a potent force in world politics as the United States became increasingly embroiled in Vietnam. After the Geneva settlement in 1954 formally ended French domination of the region, the United States escalated its commitment to the corrupt and incompetent leadership of noncommunist South Vietnam. North Vietnam, China, and the Soviet Union backed the rebel Vietcong, or South Vietnamese communists. The strength of the Vietcong seemed to grow daily, and by 1968, the United States had more than half a million soldiers in South Vietnam. Before the war ended in 1975, the United States would in its effort to defeat communism drop more bombs on North Vietnam than the Allies had launched on Germany and Japan combined during World War II.

U.S. president Richard Nixon promised to bring peace to Southeast Asia. In 1970, however, he ordered U.S. troops also to invade Cambodia, the site of North Vietnamese bases. Americans erupted in protest, and political turmoil followed in Cambodia. The communist Khmer Rouge, led by Pol Pot, a zealot intent on returning the country to preindustrial conditions, took control in 1975 and launched genocidal murders of minority Vietnamese, Chinese, and political opponents that ultimately killed 21 percent of the population. As this brutal situation unfolded, the United States and North Vietnam agreed to peace in January 1973, but the fighting continued. In 1975, South Vietnam collapsed under a determined North Vietnamese offensive and Vietnam was forcibly reunited. The United States reeled from the defeat, having suffered the loss of some fifty-eight thousand young lives and countless billions of dollars, along with a serious blow to its international prestige. Vietnam had demonstrated that the awesome technological might of the United States did not always ensure an easy victory, or even any victory at all.

Lessons from the U.S. defeat in Vietnam did not stop the Soviet Union from becoming entangled with Islamic forces in Afghanistan when it unleashed its own high-tech military to support a communist coup against Afghanistan's government in 1979. Afghanis who saw their traditional way of life being threatened by communism's modernizing goals put up stiff resistance. By 1980, tens of thousands of Soviet troops were fighting in Afghanistan, using the USSR's most advanced missiles and artillery in an ultimately unsuccessful effort to overcome Muslim leaders. The United States, China, Saudi Arabia, and Pakistan provided aid to a group of Muslim resisters, some of whom later coalesced into the Taliban. After the Soviets pulled out of their own "Vietnam" in 1989, the fundamentalist Taliban movement took over in the 1990s, imposing strict rules said to represent true Islamic teachings and causing millions of political and religious refugees to flee the country. Involvement in the wars in Vietnam and Afghanistan undermined both superpowers, sapping them of resources despite their technological advantages over their enemies.

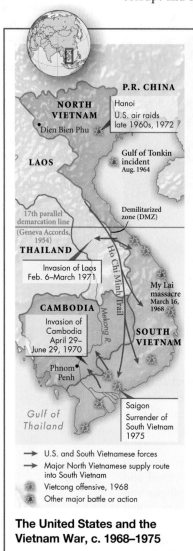

The United States and the Vietnam War, c. 1968–1975

Afghanistan

Revolution in Iran

In Iran, religiously inspired protests by students, clerics, shopkeepers, and unemployed men in 1978 and 1979 brought to power the Islamic religious leader Ayatollah Ruhollah Khomeini (a-yat-ol-LAH ROOH-ol-LAH ko-MAY-nee). The uprising was directed against Shah Mohammed Reza Pahlavi (REH-zah PAH-lah-vee), whose repressive regime the United States supported to protect its oil interests. Employing audiocassettes to spread his message, Khomeini called for a transformation of the country into a truly Islamic society, proclaiming "Neither East, nor West, only the Islamic Republic." Overturning the Westernization policy of the deposed shah, Khomeini's regime required women to cover their bodies almost totally in special clothing, restricted their access to divorce, and eliminated a range of other rights. Islamic revolutionaries believed these restrictions would restore the pride and Islamic identity that imperialism had stripped from Middle Eastern men. Khomeini won widespread support among Shi'ite Muslims, who constituted the majority but had long been subordinate to Sunni Muslims.

In the autumn of 1979, supporters of Khomeini seized hostages at the American embassy in Tehran, keeping them captive until Ronald Reagan's inauguration in January 1981. U.S. paralysis in the face of Islamic militancy, following on the heels of defeat in Vietnam, showed the possibility of superpower decline (see Seeing the Past: The Iranian Revolution as Visual News).

Activists Challenge the Superpowers

The Cold War, technological transformation, and bloody conflict gave rise to social activism that challenged the superpowers. Prosperity and the benefits of a high-tech, service-oriented economy made people eager for peace instead of the violence of war, just as those living in Latin American and South Korean dictatorships wanted to "take back the streets." Activists sought a fair chance to get education, jobs, and political influence. Students, blacks and other minorities, Soviet-bloc citizens, women, environmentalists, and homosexuals joined in what became increasingly fiery protests in the 1960s and 1970s. They protested the Cold War order that they believed denied an equal share of well-being and democracy for all.

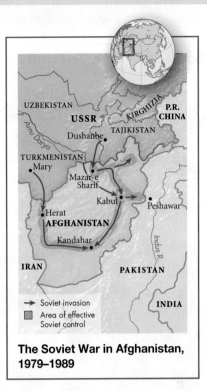

The Soviet War in Afghanistan, 1979–1989

African Americans in the United States led the way in demanding equal rights early in the 1960s, even as white segregationists murdered and maimed those attempting to integrate lunch counters, register black voters, or simply march on behalf of freedom. This violent racism was the weak link in the American claim to moral superiority in the Cold War, prompting President John F. Kennedy to introduce civil rights legislation, which, following Kennedy's assassination, was pushed through Congress in 1964 by his successor, Lyndon B. Johnson. This legislation forbade segregation in public facilities and created the Equal Employment Opportunity Commission to fight job discrimination based on "race, color, national origin, religion, and sex."

Despite the civil rights legislation, change came too slowly for some minority activists. Among those were César Chavez and Dolores Huerta, who in the 1960s led oppressed Mexican American migrant workers in the California grape agribusiness to nonviolent resistance in their struggle for their right to collective bargaining and for an end to discrimination. Chavez knew their plight firsthand—he had lived in miserable conditions as a son of migrant workers. A teacher had put a sign around his neck reading "I am a clown. I speak Spanish." Huerta, his co-organizer, had led a somewhat different life but was equally committed to the cause—"a firebrand," she was called. She had attended community college but faced racial discrimination as a Chicano despite her education.

Some African American activists, frustrated by the lack of any real change in their condition, turned militant, and urban riots erupted across the United States in 1965 and subsequent years. In 1968, civil rights leader Martin Luther King, Jr., was assassinated by a white racist. More than a hundred cities in the United States erupted in violence as African Americans vented their anguish and rage. Many felt they had more in common with decolonizing people than with Americans. They aimed for "black power," and some took up arms in the belief that, like decolonizing people elsewhere, they needed to protect themselves against the violent whites around them.

Young people, who had been critical of racism, the war in Vietnam, and the militaristic and environmentally harmful effects of technology, closed down classes in campuses around the world. In western Europe, students went on strike, invading administration offices to protest their inferior education and status. They called themselves a proletariat—an exploited working class in the new high-tech, service society—and, rejecting the Soviets, considered

Activism in the U.S. Bloc

The Iranian Revolution as Visual News

U.S. Hostages During the Iranian Revolution (Bettmann/Corbis.)

Supporters of the Ayatollah Khomeini (Abbas/Magnum Photos.)

The Iranian Revolution was a shock to the West and the world because it overthrew the ruler of a major Middle Eastern client state of the United States. Moreover, the Ayatollah Khomeini refused to ally the country with either of the superpowers because he saw them both as corrupt. In 1979, militant Iranian students stormed the U.S. Embassy in Tehran and took those in it hostage. With the development of satellite communications, images of current events circled the globe almost immediately, and newspapers and television repeatedly broadcast the two photographs shown here. The first photograph features the blindfolded hostages the day after their capture. In the second, women supporters of the hostage-taking hold their own demonstration before the U.S. Embassy to chastise the United States for backing the authoritarian rule of the Shah for so many years. The global news regularly portrayed women in Iran in this way.

EXAMINING THE EVIDENCE

1. What responses might each of these two photographs individually have provoked in viewers? What responses might they have provoked when seen together?

2. What is the historic value of these photographs? What propagandistic goal might they have served?

themselves part of a New Left. After French police beat up students, some 9 million French workers went on strike, calling not only for higher wages but also for participation in everyday decision making both in politics and in work life. With their long hair, communal living, and scorn for sexual chastity, students proclaimed their rejection of middle-class values.

Women around the world turned to feminist activism, calling for equal rights and an end to gender discrimination. Middle-class women eagerly responded to the international best seller *The Feminine Mystique* (1963) by American journalist Betty Friedan. Pointing to the stagnating talents of many housewives, Friedan helped organize the National Organization for Women in 1966 to lobby for equal pay and legal reforms. Women demonstrated on behalf of such issues as abortion rights, and they were soon joined by gays demanding the decriminalization of their sexuality. Many flouted social conventions in their attire and attitudes, speaking openly about taboo subjects such as their sexual feelings. African American women pointed to the "double jeopardy" of being "black and female." Women engaged in the civil rights and student movements soon realized that many of those protest organizations devalued women just as society at large did. As African American activist Angela Davis complained, women aiming for equality supposedly "wanted to rob [male protesters] of their manhood."[12]

Women's activism engendered some concrete changes. Just after the war, women in Chile and other Latin American countries had lobbied successfully for the vote. In Catholic Italy, feminists won the rights to divorce, to gain access to birth-control information, and to obtain legal abortions. The demand for protection from rape, incest, and battering became the focus of thousands of women's groups from the 1970s to the present, as they combated a long-held value in virtually every society—the inferiority of women.

Protests erupted in the Soviet bloc too, with students at a Czech May Day rally in 1967 publicly chanting, "The only good communist is a dead one." In 1967 the Czechoslovak Communist Party took up the cause of reform when Alexander Dubček (DOOB-chehk), head of the Slovak branch of the party, called for more social and political openness, striking a chord among frustrated party officials, technocrats, and intellectuals. Arguing that socialism should have "a human face," Dubček was made head of the entire party and quickly changed the communist style of government, ending censorship, instituting the secret ballot for party elections, and allowing competing political groups to form. The Prague Spring had begun—"an orgy of free expression," one Czech journalist called the almost nonstop political debate that followed.[15]

Dubček was unsuccessful in devising policies acceptable to both the USSR and reform-minded Czechs, and in August 1968, Soviet tanks rolled into Prague in a massive show of antirevolutionary force. Citizens turned to sabotage to defend their new rights: they painted graffiti on the tanks and removed street signs to confuse invading troops. Illegal radio stations broadcast testimonials of resistance, and merchants refused to sell food or anything else to Soviet troops. These responses could not stop the determined Soviet leadership, and the moment of reform-minded change passed even as some students, like those in Korea, immolated themselves in protest.

Mexico City Protest, 1968

Following World War II, a rising standard of living encouraged young people around the world to enter universities in greater numbers than ever before, which helped them see social and political ills more clearly. In Mexico City, which in the spring of 1968 was about to host the summer Olympics, university students protested police violence and government repression after the slaying of several high school students. They too were mowed down by the police. During the late 1960s and 1970s, reactions to student demonstrations varied worldwide. Notice in this photograph a common denominator of student protest across the world: emblems of rebellion such as the banner featuring the revolutionary Che Guevara. (Bettmann/Corbis.)

Activism in the Soviet Bloc

Activists' protests challenged superpower dominance, but little turned out the way reformers had hoped. Governments in both the Soviet and U.S. blocs turned to conservative solutions: the Soviets announced the Brezhnev Doctrine, which stated that reform movements, as a "common problem" of all socialist countries, would face swift repression and that those countries in any case had only limited independence. In 1974, Brezhnev

The Superpowers Restore Order

expelled author Aleksandr Solzhenitsyn from the USSR after the first volume of Solzhenitsyn's *Gulag Archipelago* (1973–1976) was published in the U.S.-led bloc. Solzhenitsyn's story of the Gulag (the Soviet system of internment and forced-labor camps) documented the brutal conditions Soviet prisoners endured under Stalin and his successors. More than any other single work, the *Gulag Archipelago* disillusioned loyal communists around the world. Brezhnev also expelled feminists who dared speak about communist sexism, Jews who became scapegoats for the failures of the Soviet system, and other dissenters. The brain drain from the Soviet bloc was severe, enriching the rest of the world.

In the U.S. bloc the reaction against activists was different, though order was restored there too. A current of public opinion turned against young people with the idea that somehow they—not the defeat in Vietnam or government corruption—had brought the United States down. Protesters had opened all leadership to question, helping conservatives gain power in the name of bringing back traditional values. As order returned, some young reformers turned to open terrorism in the West. In this atmosphere of reform, reaction, and radicalization, the future of prosperity became uncertain.

The End of the Cold War Order

FOCUS

Why did the Cold War order come to an end?

During the 1970s the superpowers faced internal corruption, competition from oil-producing states and rising Asian economies, and the increasing costs of attempting to control the world beyond their borders. Oil-producing nations brought a crashing halt to postindustrial prosperity in the West even as innovation continued. In response, reformers Margaret Thatcher in Great Britain and Mikhail Gorbachev in the USSR began implementing strikingly new policies in the 1980s to get their economies moving, just as Latin American countries were turning away from dictatorship. In the Soviet bloc, however, restoring prosperity was virtually impossible because a corrupt and inefficient system failed to take full advantage of technology and an unpopular war drained scarce resources. Suddenly, in 1989, the Soviet Empire collapsed and the Cold War came to an abrupt end. The USSR itself slowly dissolved, finally disappearing by January 1, 1992.

A Shifting Balance of Global Power

The United States seemed to overcome all obstacles when in 1972 it achieved a foreign policy triumph over the USSR by opening diplomatic relations with the other communist giant—China. Almost immediately a Middle Eastern oil embargo hit the United States hard, and the relationship between the United States and the Middle East began to overtake the Cold War as a major issue in global politics. In this arena, technology and Cold War muscle gave no advantage.

The United States Reaches Out to China

In the midst of turmoil at home and the draining war in Vietnam, Henry Kissinger, Nixon's national security adviser, decided to take advantage of growing tensions between China and the Soviet Union. Kissinger's efforts to forge closer ties with this other communist power led Nixon to visit China in 1972, opening up the possibility of contact and exchange between the two very different great nations. Nixon's visit served the domestic interests of both the Nixon administration and the Chinese leadership. For Nixon, the visit represented a high-profile diplomatic victory at a time when his conduct of the war in Vietnam was increasingly unpopular. Within China, the meeting helped stop the brutality of Mao's Cultural Revolution while advancing the careers of Chinese pragmatists interested in technology and economic growth.

U.S.-Soviet Rapprochement

The diplomatic success also advanced U.S.-Soviet relations. Fearful of the Chinese diplomatic advantage and similarly confronted by popular protest, the Soviets made their own overtures to the U.S.-led bloc. In 1972, the superpowers signed the first Strategic Arms Limitation Treaty (SALT I), which set a cap on the number of antimissile defenses each country could have. In 1975, in the Helsinki accords on human rights, the Western bloc officially acknowledged Soviet territorial gains in World War II in exchange for the Soviets' guarantee of basic human rights.

The Middle East's oil-producing nations dealt Western dominance and prosperity a major blow by withholding exports of oil. Tension between Israel and the Arab world provided the catalyst. On June 5, 1967, Israeli forces, responding to the buildup of Syrian, Egyptian, and other Arab armies on its border, seized Gaza and the Sinai peninsula from Egypt, the Golan Heights from Syria, and the West Bank from Jordan (see Map 30.3). Israel's stunning victory, which came to be called the Six-Day War, so humiliated the Arab states that it led them to forge common political and economic strategies. In 1973, Egypt and Syria attacked Israel on Yom Kippur, the most holy day in the Jewish calendar. Israel, with assistance from the United States, stopped the assault.

Having failed militarily, the Arab nations took economic action, striking at the West's weakest point—its enormous dependence on Middle Eastern oil. Arab member nations of **OPEC** (Organization of Petroleum Exporting Countries) quadrupled the price of its oil and imposed an embargo, cutting off all exports of oil to the United States in retaliation for U.S. support of Israel. For the first time since imperialism's heyday, the producers of raw materials—not the industrial powers—controlled the flow of commodities and set the prices. The West and many parts of the world now faced an oil crisis.

Throughout the 1970s, oil-dependent Westerners watched in astonishment as OPEC upset the balance of economic power, bringing about a recession in the West. The oil embargo and price hike caused a significant rise in unemployment in Europe and the United States,

The Politics of Oil

OPEC A consortium of oil-producing countries in the Middle East established to control the production and distribution of oil.

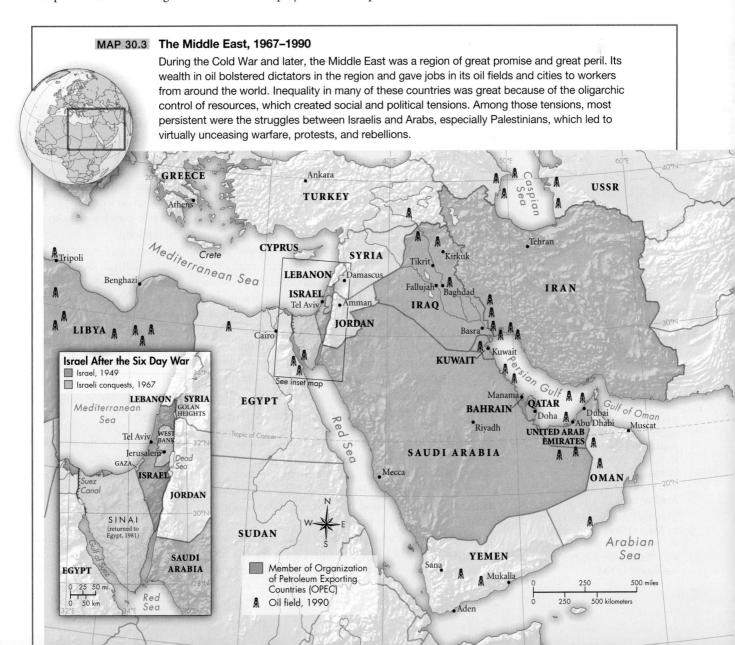

MAP 30.3   The Middle East, 1967–1990

During the Cold War and later, the Middle East was a region of great promise and great peril. Its wealth in oil bolstered dictators in the region and gave jobs in its oil fields and cities to workers from around the world. Inequality in many of these countries was great because of the oligarchic control of resources, which created social and political tensions. Among those tensions, most persistent were the struggles between Israelis and Arabs, especially Palestinians, which led to virtually unceasing warfare, protests, and rebellions.

Israel After the Six Day War
- Israel, 1949
- Israeli conquests, 1967

- Member of Organization of Petroleum Exporting Countries (OPEC)
- Oil field, 1990

and by the mid-1970s inflation soared around the world. Skyrocketing interest rates discouraged both industrial investment and consumer buying. With prices, unemployment, and interest rates surging—an unusual combination of economic conditions dubbed **stagflation**—some came to realize that both energy resources and economic growth had limits. Western Europe and Japan drastically cut back on their oil dependence by undertaking conservation measures, improving public transportation, and raising the price of gasoline to encourage the development of fuel-efficient cars. But more was clearly needed.

A Change of Course in the West

At the beginning of the 1980s, stagflation and the realignment of global economic power forced noncommunist governments in the West to put their economic houses in order. Conservative politicians, who blamed welfare state programs for the West's economic problems, were handily elected in a number of countries. Tough times also intensified feelings that the unemployed and new immigrants from around the world were responsible for the economic downturn. An emphasis on competitiveness, individualism, and privilege replaced the twentieth-century trend of promoting economic democracy—a dramatic change of political course.

Thatcherism and Reaganomics

More than anyone else, Margaret Thatcher, the outspoken leader of Britain's Conservative Party and prime minister from 1979 to 1990, reshaped the West's political and economic ideas to meet the crisis. She called herself "a nineteenth-century liberal" in reference to the economic individualism that she wanted to restore. Believing that only more private enterprise could revive the sluggish British economy, the combative prime minister rejected the politics of consensus building, targeting unions and welfare recipients as enemies of British well-being.

The policies of Thatcherism were based on monetarist, or supply-side, economic theories, which state that inflation results when government pumps money into the economy at a rate higher than a nation's economic growth rate. Supply-siders thus advocate tight control of the money supply to keep prices from rising rapidly. They maintain that the economy as a whole flourishes when businesses grow and their prosperity "trickles down" throughout the society. To implement such theories, the British government cut income taxes on the wealthy to encourage new investment and increased sales taxes on everyday purchases to compensate for the lost revenue. The result was fairly successful, but economic growth came at the price of cuts to education and health programs and an increased burden on working people, who bore the brunt of the sales tax. Thatcher's package of economic policies came to be known as **neoliberalism**, and it immediately came to shape global thinking.

In the United States, President Ronald Reagan followed Thatcher's lead in combating the economic crisis. Blaming both "welfare queens" and so-called spendthrift and immoral liberals for stagflation, he introduced "Reaganomics"—a program of income tax cuts for the wealthy combined with massive reductions in federal spending for student loans, school lunch programs, and mass transit. In foreign policy, Reagan warned of the communist threat and demanded huge military spending to fight the "evil empire." The combination of tax cuts and military expansion pushed the federal budget deficit to $200 billion by 1986. Other western European leaders limited welfare-state benefits in the face of stagflation, though without blaming poor people for their nation's economic problems.

The Collapse of Communism in the Soviet Bloc

The Soviet Union faced far more difficult challenges than the West. Since the death of Stalin in 1953, Soviet leaders had periodically taken small, halting steps toward economic and political reform. Such reforms were, however, halfhearted and often quickly abandoned. In 1985 a new Soviet leader, Mikhail Gorbachev, introduced much more thoroughgoing reforms, but instead of fortifying the economy, his programs stirred up rebellion. The corrupt system was beyond cure.

Mikhail Gorbachev, who became leader of the Soviet Union in 1985, unexpectedly opened an era of change. The son of peasants, Gorbachev had firsthand experience of the costs of economic stagnation. Years of weak and then negative growth led to a deteriorating standard of

stagflation A surge in prices and interest rates combined with high unemployment and a slowdown in economic growth.

neoliberalism A theory first promoted by British prime minister Margaret Thatcher, calling for a return to nineteenth-century liberal principles, including the reduction of welfare-state programs and tax cuts for the wealthy to promote economic growth.

perestroika A policy introduced by Mikhail Gorbachev to restructure the Soviet economy through improved productivity, increased capital investment, and the introduction of market mechanisms.

glasnost A policy introduced by Mikhail Gorbachev allowing for free speech and the circulation of accurate information in the Soviet Union.

living. After working a full day, Soviet homemakers stood in long lines to obtain basic commodities. Alcoholism reached crisis levels, diminishing productivity and straining the nation's morale. Despite its tremendous agricultural potential, the USSR imported massive amounts of grain because 20 to 30 percent of homegrown grain rotted before it could be harvested or shipped to market, so great was the mismanagement of the state-directed economy. A massive and privileged party bureaucracy stifled effective use of technology, while Soviet military spending of 15 to 20 percent of the gross national product (more than double the U.S. proportion) further lowered living standards. A new generation came of age lacking the fear instilled by World War II or Stalin's purges. "They believe in nothing," a mother said of Soviet youth in 1984.

Gorbachev Attempts Reform

Gorbachev knew from experience and travels to western Europe that the Soviet system was not keeping up, and he quickly proposed several new programs. A crucial economic reform, **perestroika** ("restructuring"), aimed to reinvigorate the Soviet economy by encouraging more up-to-date technology and introducing such market features as prices and profits. Alongside economic change was the policy of **glasnost** (translated as "openness"), which called for disseminating "wide, prompt, and frank information" and for allowing Soviet citizens freer speech.

Glasnost stirred debate across the USSR and affected superpower relations as well. Television reporting adopted the outspoken methods of American investigative journalism, and newspapers, instead of publishing made-up letters praising the Soviet state, printed real ones complaining of shortages and abuse. One outraged "mother of two" protested that the cost-cutting policy of reusing syringes in hospitals was a source of AIDS. "Why should little kids have to pay for the criminal actions of our Ministry of Health?" she asked. "We saw television programs about U.S. racism," one young man reported, "but blacks there had cars, housing, and other goods that we didn't."[14] Gorbachev cut missile production, defusing the Cold War, and in early 1989 withdrew Soviet forces from the disastrous war in Afghanistan. By the end of the year the United States started to reduce its own vast military buildup.

Solidarity Protests in Poland, 1981–1983

Even before Gorbachev's reforms of the mid-1980s unleashed free speech in the USSR, dissent had risen across the Soviet bloc. In the summer of 1980, Poles had reacted to rising food prices by going on strike and forming an independent labor movement called **Solidarity** under the leadership of electrician Lech Walesa and crane operator Anna Walentynowicz. The organization attracted much of the adult population, including a million members of the Communist Party. Waving Polish flags and parading giant portraits of the Virgin Mary and Pope John Paul II—a Polish native—Solidarity workers occupied factories in protest against inflation, the scarcity of food, and the deteriorating conditions of everyday life. The scarcity of food likewise drove tens of thousands of women, who were both workers and the caretakers of home life, into the streets crying, "We're hungry!" With Soviet support, the Communist Party imposed a military government and in the winter of 1981 outlawed Solidarity. Dissidents, using global communications, kept Solidarity alive as a force both inside and outside of Poland. Workers kept meeting and a new culture emerged, with poets reading verse to overflow crowds and university professors lecturing on such forbidden topics as Polish resistance in World War II. The stage was set for communism's downfall.

Rebellion in Poland

The disintegration of communist power in Europe was also inspired by Gorbachev's visit to China's capital, Beijing, in the spring of 1989. There, hundreds of thousands of students massed in the city's Tiananmen Square to demand democracy and greet Gorbachev as democracy's hero. They used telex machines and satellite television to rush their message of reform to the international community. China's communist leaders, while pushing economic modernization, refused to introduce democracy. Workers joined the mass of prodemocracy students: "They say and they do what I have only dared to think," one man commented after giving money to the cause.[15] As numbers swelled and the international press broadcast the events, government forces crushed the movement, killing untold numbers and later executing as many as a thousand rebels.

Revolutions of 1989

Solidarity An independent Polish trade union that confronted the communist government in the 1980s and eventually succeeded in ousting the party from the Polish government.

The televised protests in Tiananmen Square offered an inspirational model to opponents of communism in Europe. In June 1989, the Polish government, lacking Soviet support for further repression, held free parliamentary elections. Solidarity candidates overwhelmingly defeated the communists, and in early 1990, Walesa became president of Poland. In Hungary, where citizens had boycotted communist holidays and lobbied against ecologically unsound projects such as the construction of new dams, popular demand led the Parliament in the fall of 1989 to dismiss the Communist Party as the official ruling institution. Meanwhile, Gorbachev reversed the Brezhnev Doctrine, refusing to interfere in the politics of satellite nations.

East Germans had likewise long protested communism, holding peace vigils throughout the 1980s and ceaselessly attempting to cross the Berlin Wall. Satellite television brought them visions of postindustrial prosperity and of open public debate in West Germany. In the summer of 1989, crowds of East Germans flooded the borders of the crumbling Soviet bloc, and hundreds of thousands of protesters rallied against the regime throughout the fall. On November 9, East Berliners crossed the wall unopposed and protest turned to festive holiday. Soon thereafter, citizens—East and West—released years of frustration by assaulting the Berlin Wall with sledgehammers and then celebrated the reunification of the two Germanys in 1990.

The fall of communism in Czechoslovakia and Romania formed two extremes. In November 1989 Alexander Dubçek, leader of the Prague Spring of 1968, addressed the crowds in Prague's Wenceslas Square after police had beaten students who had called for the ouster of Stalinists from the government. Almost immediately, the communist leadership resigned, in a bloodless or "velvet" revolution. By contrast, Romanian president Nicolae Ceauşescu (nee-koh-LIE chow-SHES-koo), who had ruled as the harshest dictator in communist Europe since Stalin, met a far different end. Workers and much of the army rose up and crushed the forces loyal to Ceauşescu. On Christmas Day 1989, viewers watched on television as the dictator and his wife were executed. For many, the death of Ceauşescu meant that the very worst of communism was over.

The revolutions of 1989 accelerated the breakup of Yugoslavia into multiple states (see Map 30.4). Yugoslavia had the most ethnically diverse population in eastern Europe, and when Serbian president Slobodan Milosevic attempted in 1991 to seize territory and unite all Serbs (and in effect much of the former Yugoslavia) into a "greater Serbia," a tragic civil war broke out. Throughout the 1990s, the peoples of the former Yugoslavia fought one another, murdering neighbors of different ethnicities.

Meanwhile, amid deteriorating conditions and the threat of violence, the Soviet Union itself collapsed. Perestroika had failed to revitalize the Soviet economy, and by 1990 people faced unemployment and an even greater scarcity of goods than before. In 1991 a group of eight antireform top officials, including the powerful head of the Soviet secret police (the KGB), attempted a coup,

Protesters in Tiananmen Square, 1989
Student activists for democracy mounted a massive and prolonged demonstration for democracy in the spring of 1989. The protests in Tiananmen Square, where Mao Zedong had often addressed mass rallies, captured the imagination of the world and showed the protesters' own global imagination. Students displayed images of the Statue of Liberty and carried signs in English, playing to a worldwide audience. As workers joined the movement, Chinese authorities struck back, dispersing the crowds and executing many participants. (Jacques Langevin/Sygma/Corbis.)

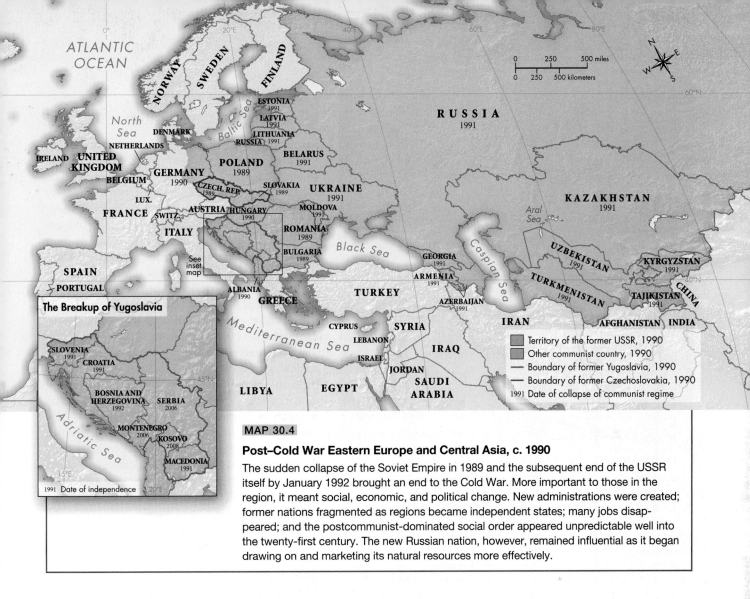

MAP 30.4

Post–Cold War Eastern Europe and Central Asia, c. 1990

The sudden collapse of the Soviet Empire in 1989 and the subsequent end of the USSR itself by January 1992 brought an end to the Cold War. More important to those in the region, it meant social, economic, and political change. New administrations were created; former nations fragmented as regions became independent states; many jobs disappeared; and the postcommunist-dominated social order appeared unpredictable well into the twenty-first century. The new Russian nation, however, remained influential as it began drawing on and marketing its natural resources more effectively.

The USSR Dissolves

holding Gorbachev under house arrest. Hundreds of thousands of residents of Moscow and Leningrad filled the streets, and units of the army defected to protect the headquarters of Boris Yeltsin, the reform-minded president of the Russian Parliament. People used fax machines and computers to coordinate internal resistance and send messages to the rest of the world. As the coup failed, the Soviet Union disintegrated and officially dissolved by January 1, 1992.

COUNTERPOINT
Agrarian Peoples in a Technological Age

As high-tech society expanded, millions of people in the world's rural areas felt themselves more hurt than helped. Even as breakthroughs in science and technology led to improved health and a higher standard of living for the majority, there were many others whom scientific advances harmed. Some farmers found that the application of scientific techniques damaged both their livelihoods and the environment. They objected especially to the genetic modification of plants and animals made possible by the discovery of DNA.

> **FOCUS**
>
> How did some agrarian peoples resist the scientific and technological developments that threatened their ways of life?

Contesting the Results of Technological Advance

As societies around the world developed technologically and economically, some of the results were shocking. Cubotão, a city in southeastern Brazil, is home to some two dozen steel, petrochemical, and other industries, which daily send about 875 tons of toxic gasses, 473 tons of carbon monoxide, and 182 tons of sulfuric oxide into the atmosphere. Residents call the area the "Valley of Death" because of the extreme air and water pollution and have lobbied successfully to curtail the most damaging dumping of toxic waste. This photograph shows a cement-producing section of the complex. (Miguel Rio Branco/Magnum Photos.)

Local Farmers Against Multinational Corporations

Farmers were especially angry about the ways in which companies took seeds from them and then patented them so that those same farmers could be sued for harvesting and using their own seeds. They also objected to the multinationals' practice of sterilizing seeds so that the resulting plants would not produce sowable seeds that farmers could harvest and plant the next year. In Africa, Asia, and Latin America, grassroots movements developed to stop the use of chemical fertilizers, the patenting of medicinal plants and seeds by multinational chemical companies, and the genetic modification of seeds, insects, fish, and other living organisms.

The immediate, practical problem of the failure of seeds to germinate and the erosion of soil caused by large-scale planting of a single crop led to the creation in the 1980s of the Institute for Production and Research in Tropical Agriculture in Venezuela. Officials from the Institute argued that the directives imposed by specialists and chemical companies from the North harmed Latin American farmers engaged in tropical agriculture. Whereas the many microclimates and diverse conditions found in Latin America should have led to the cultivation of many different crops, the Green Revolution of the 1950s and 1960s began directing farmers toward growing one crop and insisting that they use chemical pesticides. Top-down direction had depleted the soil and brought increasing poverty to many farmers. To correct this situation, the Institute collected the know-how of small and medium-sized rural producers. "We get knowledge from farmers," one worker for the Institute claimed. "We evaluate knowledge from farmers."[16]

Grassroots activists in other areas—India, for example—worked to protect local agricultural knowledge from being abused by the new postindustrial economy. Activists labeled the phenomenon of patenting plants and then suing farmers who continued to grow crops like rice in their own way as "biopiracy." "Patents are a replay of colonization as it took place five hundred years ago in a number of ways," farmers' rights activist Vandana Shiva maintained.[17] "The Basmati seed, the aromatic rice from India, which we have grown for centuries, right in my valley is being claimed as a novel invention by Rice-Tec." Biopiracy by the multinational corporations, activists charged, contributed to the impoverishment of Third World peoples: "Neem, which we have used for millennia for pest control, for medicine, . . . which my grandmother and mother have used for everyday functions in the home, for protecting grain, for protecting silks and woolens, for pest control, is treated as an invention held by Grace, the chemical company."[18] Entrepreneurs, while harming farmers, were seizing control of and profiting from their knowledge.

Government Measures to Protect Farmers

Moved by citizens' activism, governments in developing economies began taking steps to stop the piracy by multinational businesses. India, for example, began creating a database of its medicinal plants, teas, and yoga positions. The idea was to patent these as Indian property so that enterprises in other countries could not simply steal and market them as their own. The Indian government claimed to be doing just what industrialized nations had been doing for years: France, for example, sued any foreign firm that used the name *champagne* for sparkling wine. "Champagne" had been registered as a trademark branding wines from the Champagne region of France, one protected by law just as Toyota and Heinz were trademarks with full legal protection from theft by another company. These actions provided a strong counterpoint to postindustrial society's drift toward multinational markets seizing knowledge-based products and using them against the traditional livelihoods of tens of millions of agricultural workers around the world.

Conclusion

The last half of the twentieth century witnessed a surge in technological and scientific discovery with vast potential for improving people's lives and connecting them to one another. Asian Pacific nations advanced by adopting new technology and transforming their economies. Work changed, as societies across the globe expanded the service sector of their economies and entered a new, postindustrial stage. New patterns of family life, new relationships among the generations, and revised standards for sexual behavior also characterized these years. Youth culture spread globally, touching teens around the world like Raj and Bobby in India. A high-tech society demanded levels of innovation, efficiency, and coordination that spread unevenly and was especially lacking in the Soviet bloc. Despite improved postindustrial conditions, brutal coercion continued to plague workers in rapidly industrializing economies such as that of South Korea.

Inequalities in the distribution of goods and the persistent support of military dictators by the superpowers frustrated citizens worldwide, and especially pushed youths like Raj and Bobby to rebellion. From the 1960s, youth joined ethnic and racial minorities and women in condemning existing conditions, including the threat posed by the Cold War. By the early 1980s, wars in Vietnam and Afghanistan, protests against privations in the Soviet bloc, the power of oil-producing states, and the growing political force of Islam had weakened superpower pre-eminence. In the Soviet Union Mikhail Gorbachev attempted to bring about technological efficiencies and cultural reform, but he released dissent and exposed the flaws of communism. By 1992, the failure of the brutal experiment with communism had brought about both the dissolution of the Soviet Union and the end of the Cold War order. Although the former Soviet Empire faced painful adjustments, this development opened the world as a whole to the further spread of technology and the complex processes of globalization.

NOTES

1. Quoted in Ray Brown, "Children and Television," *Social Science* (1978): 7.
2. W. O. Baker, "Computers as Information-Processing Machines in Modern Science," *Daedalus* 99, no. 4 (Fall 1970).
3. Norman Borlaug, Nobel Prize Acceptance Speech, 1970, http://www.nobel.se.
4. Quoted in Sam Fiorani, "Soichiro Honda," *Automotive History Online*, http://www.autohistory.org/feature_7.html.
5. Quoted in Pun Ngai, *Made in China: Women Factory Workers in a Global Workplace* (Durham, NC: Duke University Press, 2005), 83.
6. Quoted in Peter Winn, *Americas: The Changing Face of Latin America and the Caribbean* (Berkeley: University of California Press, 2006), 447.
7. Ramachandra Guha, *India After Gandhi: The History of the World's Largest Democracy* (New York: HarperCollins, 2008), 710.
8. Quoted in Temma Kaplan, *Taking Back the Streets: Women, Youth, and Direct Democracy* (Berkeley: University of California Press, 2004), 113.
9. Quoted in Thomas E. Skidmore and Peter H. Smith, *Modern Latin America*, 3d ed. (New York: Oxford University Press, 2002), 111.
10. Quoted in Kaplan, *Taking Back the Streets*, 38.

11. Quoted in *Korea Observer* 32 (2001): 264.

12. Quoted in Paula Giddings, *Where and When I Enter: The Impact of Black Women on Race and Sex in America* (New York: William Morrow, 1984), 316.

13. Quoted in David Caute, *Sixty-Eight: Year of the Barricades* (London: Hamish Hamilton, 1988), 165.

14. Russian citizen's interview with author, July 1994.

15. Quoted in Orville Schell, "China's Spring," in *The China Reader: The Reform Era*, ed. Orville Schell and David Shambaugh (New York: Vintage, 1999), 194.

16. Quoted in *In-Motion Magazine*, http://www.inmotionmagazine.com/global/man_int.html#AnchorKnowledge-49575.

17. Quoted in *In-Motion Magazine*, 2003, http://www.inmotionmagazine.com/shiva.html.

18. Ibid.

RESOURCES FOR RESEARCH

Advances in Technology and Science

Although the powers that waged World War II led the way in converting wartime technology to peacetime uses, the impact of scientific advances was felt around the world. Marks's book on reproductive technology provides a look at science's global reach.

Borlaug, Norman. "The Green Revolution, Peace, and Humanity," Nobel Lecture, 1970. http://www.nobel.se.

Dickson, Paul. *Sputnik: The Shock of the Century*. 2001.

Marks, Lara V. *Sexual Chemistry: A History of the Contraceptive Pill*. 2004.

O'Mara, Margaret Pugh. *Cities of Knowledge: Cold War Science and the Search for the Next Silicon Valley*. 2005.

Schefter, James L. *The Race: The Uncensored Story of How America Beat Russia to the Moon*. 1999.

Changes in the World Economy

As technology swept the globe, manufacturing power began to move from the West to the rest of the world. Chu et al., Kynge, and Mazlish describe these developments.

Chu, Yun-Peng, and Hal Hill, eds. *The East Asian High-Tech Drive*. 2006.

Davis, Deborah, ed. *The Consumer Revolution in Urban China*. 2000.

Kynge, James. *China Shakes the World: A Titan's Rise and Troubled Future and the Challenge for America*. 2006.

Mazlish, Bruce. *Leviathans: Multinational Corporations and the New Global History*. 2005.

Sony history. http://www.sony.net/SonyInfo/CorporateInfo/History/SonyHistory/.

Politics and Protest in an Age of Cold War

As the Cold War advanced, citizens rose to fight off dictators and to protest superpower dominance. Suri's book shows the world-wide maneuverings that accompanied domestic instability, while Kaplan's work gives accounts of resistance to Latin American dictators.

Kaplan, Temma. *Taking Back the Streets: Women, Youth, and Direct Democracy*. 2004.

Lam, Andrew. *Perfume Dreams: Reflections on the Vietnamese Diaspora*. 2005.

Lesch, David. *1979: The Year That Shaped the Modern Middle East*. 2001.

Ngai, Pun. *Made in China: Women Factory Workers in a Global Workplace*. 2005.

Suri, Jeremy. *Power and Protest: Global Revolution and the Rise of Détente*. 2003.

The End of the Cold War Order

The year 1989 saw a series of threats to communist nations. These works describe the events in both Europe and China from a variety of perspectives.

Human Rights in China, ed. *Children of the Dragon: The Story of Tiananmen Square*. 1990.

Kenney, Padraic. *Carnival of Revolution: Central Europe, 1989*. 2002.

Kotkin, Stephen. *Escaping Armageddon: The Soviet Collapse, 1970–2000*. 2001.

Ost, David. *The Defeat of Solidarity: Anger and Politics in Postcommunist Europe*. 2005.

Thomas, Daniel C. *The Helsinki Effect: International Norms, Human Rights, and the Demise of Communism*. 2001.

Tolstoya, Tatyana. *Pushkin's Children: Writings on Russia and Russians*. 2003.

COUNTERPOINT: Agrarian Peoples in a Technological Age

The Green Revolution in agriculture provoked opposition, sometimes passionate, from many ranks of global society, as these books reveal.

Rosegrant, M., and P. Hazell. *Transforming the Rural Asian Economy: The Unfinished Revolution*. 2000.

Shiva, Vandana. *Biopiracy: The Plunder of Nature and Knowledge*. 1997.

▶ **For additional primary sources from this period**, see *Sources of Crossroads and Cultures*.

▶ **For Web sites, images, and documents related to topics in this chapter**, see Make History at bedfordstmartins.com/smith.

The major global development in this chapter ▶ The technological revolution of the late twentieth century and its impact on societies and political developments around the world.

IMPORTANT EVENTS

1957	USSR launches *Sputnik*
1963	Betty Friedan, *The Feminine Mystique*
1967	Arab-Israeli Six-Day War
1968	"Prague Spring" in Czechoslovakia
1969	U.S. astronauts land on moon
1972	U.S. president Richard Nixon visits China; SALT I agreement
1973	Arab-Israeli Yom Kippur War; OPEC raises oil prices and imposes embargo
1973–1976	Aleksandr Solzhenitsyn, *Gulag Archipelago*
1975	Vietnam War ends; Vietnam reunited
1978	World's first test-tube baby born
1978–1979	Islamic revolution in Iran
1979–1989	Soviet War in Afghanistan
1980	Solidarity labor union organizes resistance to communism in Poland; Prime Minister Margaret Thatcher introduces neoliberal program in Britain
1985	Mikhail Gorbachev becomes Soviet leader, introduces new policies of perestroika and glasnost
1989	Chinese students demonstrate at Tiananmen Square; communist regimes in eastern Europe fall
1992	Soviet Union no longer exists

KEY TERMS

glasnost (p. 1014)
Green Revolution (p. 996)
multinational corporation (p. 998)
neoliberalism (p. 1014)
OPEC (p. 1013)
Pacific tiger (p. 997)
perestroika (p. 1014)
postindustrial (p. 991)
Solidarity (p. 1015)
stagflation (p. 1014)

CHAPTER OVERVIEW QUESTIONS

1. How did the technological developments of these decades transform social and economic conditions?

2. What were the attitudes of young people toward technology and social change during these years, and how did they reflect the Cold War climate in which these changes occurred?

3. How did the technological developments influence the fall of communist regimes in Europe and the dissolution of the Soviet Union?

4. How did the scientific and technological developments of the second half of the twentieth century affect the waging—and the end—of the Cold War?

SECTION FOCUS QUESTIONS

1. What were the major postwar advances in technology and science, and why were they important?

2. How did changes in the global economy affect livelihoods and family life?

3. What developments challenged the superpowers' dominance of world politics, and how did the superpowers attempt to address those challenges?

4. Why did the Cold War order come to an end?

5. How did some agrarian peoples resist the scientific and technological developments that threatened their ways of life?

MAKING CONNECTIONS

1. Why is late-twentieth-century society in many parts of the world described as postindustrial?

2. How did technological development and the social changes it produced affect national and world politics?

3. Why did the economic, scientific, and political developments of the late twentieth century spark so many grassroots protests, and what did those protests achieve?

31

AT A CROSSROADS ▶

The Burj al Arab (Tower of the Arabs) makes a statement about its home—Dubai, the United Arab Emirates—as a global crossroads. Its name signals a regional pride, while the tower itself is a hotel that welcomes visitors from around the world. With vast international experience, Tom Wright from England and Kunan Chew from Singapore designed the exterior and the interior, respectively. Like the designers and visitors, many of the men and women who built the tower come from beyond Dubai's borders. (akg-images/Bildarchiv Monheim.)

A New Global Age

1989 to the Present

On February 11, 1990, South Africans celebrated the news that Nelson Mandela, deputy head of the African National Congress (ANC), had been freed after three decades in prison. Later that day Mandela stood before some fifty thousand cheering supporters in Cape Town, announcing his determination to end apartheid, the brutal South African system of racial discrimination. "Our path to freedom is irreversible," he stated. "Now is the time to intensify the struggle on all fronts." These were brave words in a society where the minority white population controlled the military and for decades had not hesitated to murder anyone who criticized white racist rule. But by 1990 black youth had taken up arms, protesting repression and unemployment. Their elders backed them with protests of their own, as the crowded South African ghettos became more miserable and more dangerous. Many whites hoped that Mandela's release would appease the protesters, but it became clear that white rule would not hold, and in April 1994 nearly 90 percent of South Africans went to the polls, many of them standing for hours in mile-long lines to vote in a free and fair election. One voter summed up his feelings at participating in democracy: "Now I am a human being." The ANC won 62 percent of the vote, and on May 10 that same year Nelson Mandela became president of South Africa.

Nelson Mandela's release from prison was noted not only by South Africans but by people around the world. Multinational companies had come to insist on racial equality in hiring at their South African plants, but as the apartheid government continued to torture and kill blacks, Coca-Cola, IBM, and others closed down their factories. The U.S. Congress

The Impact of Global Events on Regions and Nations

FOCUS How has globalization affected the distribution of power and wealth throughout the world in the early twenty-first century?

Global Livelihoods and Institutions

FOCUS How has globalization reshaped national economies and political institutions?

The Promises and Perils of Globalization

FOCUS What major benefits and dangers has globalization brought to the world's peoples?

Cultures Without Borders

FOCUS What trends suggest that globalization has led to a new mixing of cultures?

COUNTERPOINT: Who Am I? Local Identity in a Globalizing World

FOCUS How have peoples sought to establish and maintain distinctive local personal identities in today's global age?

BACKSTORY

As we saw in Chapter 30, a burst of technological innovation from the 1960s on changed the way many people lived and worked. In much of the West, the service sector surpassed industry and manufacturing as the most important components of the economy, with knowledge-based jobs leading the way. At the same time, industrial jobs were shipped overseas, and countries such as Korea and China joined the United States and Germany as centers of global manufacturing. As the economic balance of power began to shift, the United States and the Soviet Union found it more and more difficult to shape and control events around the world. In 1989, internal tensions led to the collapse of the Soviet Union, bringing the Cold War to a close and opening the way for still more dramatic change in the global economic and political order. With the Cold War over, technology flowed more freely across borders, and the increased pace of globalization created new connections among the peoples of the world. International tensions remained, however, and the new global landscape raised hopes around the world even as dangers persisted.

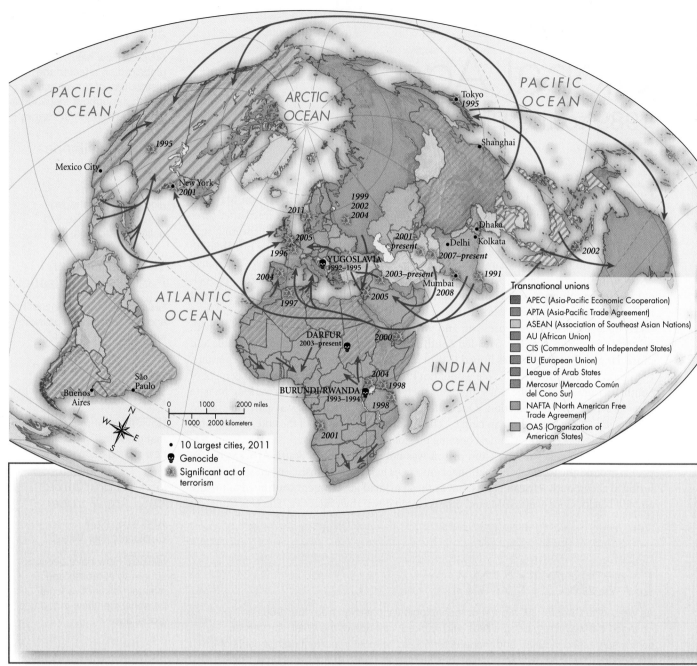

Transnational unions
- ■ APEC (Asia-Pacific Economic Cooperation)
- ■ APTA (Asia-Pacific Trade Agreement)
- ■ ASEAN (Association of Southeast Asian Nations)
- ■ AU (African Union)
- ■ CIS (Commonwealth of Independent States)
- ■ EU (European Union)
- ■ League of Arab States
- ■ Mercosur (Mercado Común del Cono Sur)
- ■ NAFTA (North American Free Trade Agreement)
- ■ OAS (Organization of American States)

- • 10 Largest cities, 2011
- ☠ Genocide
- ✺ Significant act of terrorism

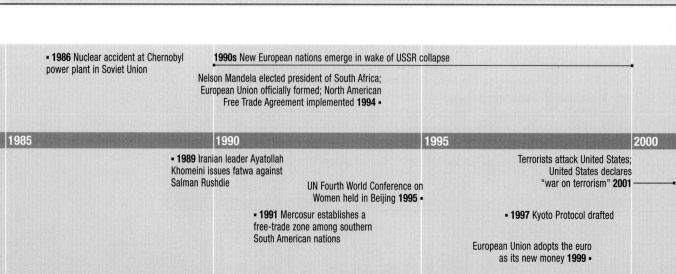

- ▪ **1986** Nuclear accident at Chernobyl power plant in Soviet Union

1990s New European nations emerge in wake of USSR collapse

Nelson Mandela elected president of South Africa; European Union officially formed; North American Free Trade Agreement implemented **1994** ▪

| 1985 | 1990 | 1995 | 2000 |

- ▪ **1989** Iranian leader Ayatollah Khomeini issues fatwa against Salman Rushdie

UN Fourth World Conference on Women held in Beijing **1995** ▪

- ▪ **1991** Mercosur establishes a free-trade zone among southern South American nations

Terrorists attack United States; United States declares "war on terrorism" **2001**

- ▪ **1997** Kyoto Protocol drafted

European Union adopts the euro as its new money **1999** ▪

banned the sale of South African gold coins, or Krugerrands, and legislated a boycott of South African products. Other countries took similar measures. The collective effect was devastating to the South African economy, whose leaders came to understand, as so many did from the 1970s on, that they were living in a world far more tightly connected than ever before. As satellite television and human rights groups brought the brutality of apartheid to the attention of the world, freedom in South Africa—like many other issues—became a concern of people everywhere. Nelson Mandela's release from prison and his election as president of South Africa symbolized a new and more intensely global stage in human history.

The end of the Cold War accelerated the continuing process of **globalization**—that is, the economic, political, social, and cultural interconnectedness of the world's regions. Now, instead of being forced to choose between two powerful and dangerous adversaries, people around the world could envision working and living together as global citizens and enjoying all aspects of one another's culture, including food, music, films, and books. Global organizations, regional trade alliances, and international businesses multiplied and drew more people into their tightening networks. Migration increased, with many migrants moving in search of opportunity. Others, however, sought to escape the dangers that cropped up after the Cold War as bitter conflicts among competing political and ethnic groups in Africa, the former Soviet Empire, India, and elsewhere brought horrific suffering. Radicals around the world publicized their aims with acts of terrorism. While improvements in medicine benefited much of the world, globalization facilitated the spread of infectious diseases, threatening people everywhere. Many soon realized that the same interconnectedness that fueled the economic boom of the late twentieth century also increased the potential for worldwide economic and environmental disasters.

Although the process of globalization drew people ever closer together, it also produced a backlash. Rejecting anything beyond the local community where they conducted their livelihoods, groups and individuals sought to retain their distinctive personal identities built on family ties and local traditions. In some cases, resistance to globalization took

globalization The economic, cultural, political, and social interactions and integration of the world's peoples.

MAPPING THE WORLD

A New Global Age

By the start of the twenty-first century, the world's peoples were bound together more significantly than ever. Migration brought unprecedented ethnic and cultural diversity to entire regions. At the same time, large regional alliances brought military, economic, and even political unity—at least superficially. No less real in their impact on everyday life were the mixing of cultures and the shared experience of terrorism and disease. Finally, the earth, humanity's common habitat, felt the effects of technological change, advancing industry, and growing population.

ROUTES ▼

→ Global migration, 1970s to present

2002 Luiz Inácio Lula da Silva elected Brazilian president

2003 United States invades Iraq

2007–2008 Global economic crisis begins to unfold

2005

2010

2015

2004 Manmohan Singh becomes prime minister of India

2005 Kyoto Protocol goes into effect

violent forms, including terrorist attacks on those seen as responsible for the erosion of traditional values and beliefs. Despite these efforts, the interdependence of the world's peoples, the connectedness of nations, and the sharing of culture that globalization had brought were nearly inescapable. In 1994 the European Economic Community (or Common Market) transformed itself from a mainly economic alliance into the European Union, which looked as if it might become a United States of Europe. When Barack Obama was elected the first African American president of the United States in 2008, it was a moment shared by the world, just as the release of Nelson Mandela had been less than two decades earlier.

As historians, the authors of this book have no firm idea how these recent events will appear a century from now, but in this chapter we follow trends that have evolved over decades and even centuries. In choosing events to recount in this analysis of the very near past we have also used generally accepted criteria for spotting historical significance. We hope—and you can be the judge several decades from now—that this account of our own global age stands the test of time and of history.

OVERVIEW
QUESTIONS

The major global development in this chapter: The causes and consequences of intensified globalization.

As you read, consider:

1. What were the elements of globalization at the beginning of the twenty-first century?

2. How did globalization affect lives and livelihoods throughout the world?

3. How did globalization affect local cultures?

4. What people do you know whose roots and livelihoods are global?

The Impact of Global Events on Regions and Nations

FOCUS

How has globalization affected the distribution of power and wealth throughout the world in the early twenty-first century?

The end of the Cold War brought many advantages in terms of free speech, human rights, and economic opportunity. Peoples around the world no longer had to toe the line set by the superpowers, and some nations began to flourish as never before, often thanks to adopting new technology. Yet the aftermath was not all positive—the weapons and other military goods given as aid by the superpowers promoted dictatorships and civil wars. Vast differences appeared between many regions emerging from colonialism and those that had long enjoyed freedom and prosperity.

North Versus South

During the 1980s and 1990s, world leaders tried to address the growing economic schism between the earth's northern and southern regions. Other than Australians and New Zealanders, southern peoples (those from Africa, South Asia, Southeast Asia, and Latin

America) generally had lower standards of living than northerners. Long ruled as colonies or exploited economically by northerners, citizens in the southern regions could not yet count on their new governments to provide welfare services or education. International organizations such as the World Bank and the International Monetary Fund provided loans for economic development, but the conditions tied to them, such as cutting government spending for social programs, led to criticism that there was no real benefit if education and health care were sacrificed in the name of balancing national budgets. Disease soared and the pace of literacy and capacity-building slowed.

Obstacles to Development

Although the Southern Hemisphere had highly productive agriculture and abundant natural resources, southern peoples often found it difficult to export their products to developed countries. Both the United States and the European Union advocated free trade but nevertheless imposed tariffs on imported agricultural products and subsidized their own farmers, raising prices for imported products and lowering them for domestic ones in the process. As Amadou Toumani Touré, president of Mali, complained in 2002, "the North cannot massively subsidize its farm exports and at the same time try and give lessons in competitiveness to the South."[1] Tariffs and financial aid to wealthy farmers in the north diverted an estimated $100 billion worth of business away from poorer nations. "We cannot compete against this monster, the United States," one Mexican farmer claimed in 2008. "It's not worth the trouble to plant. We don't have the subsidies."[2] Understanding the situation but unwilling to challenge domestic agribusinesses, leaders from wealthy nations met in 2004 to draft plans to alleviate the debt of southern countries and to sponsor health-care and education initiatives as an alternative to lifting subsidies. It remained to be seen whether these programs would materialize and whether poverty, disease and death would decline as a result.

Southern regions experienced a number of internal barriers to peaceful development. Latin American nations grappled with government corruption, multibillion-dollar debt owed to international banks, widespread crime, and grinding poverty. The situation was not, however, universally grim. Some countries—Mexico and Brazil, for example—began to strengthen their economies by marketing their oil and other natural resources effectively on the global market.

Sub-Saharan Africa suffered from drought, famine, and civil war. In the African nations of Rwanda, Burundi, and Sudan, a lethal mixture of military rule, ideological factionalism, and the ethnic antagonism that had been encouraged under imperialism resulted in conflict and genocide in the 1990s. Millions perished; others were left starving and homeless while leaders drained national resources to build up their militaries and enrich themselves. Arms dealers and aid workers poured into these regions, both groups bringing resources that governments often used against their own people. In Sudan, children were among the first victims of starvation, disease, and outright murder in the half-century-long civil war between the north and south of the country. Those in southern Sudan opposed the north's creation of an Islamic republic and its control of the country's oil and agricultural wealth. As the dispute intensified and spread to central and western Sudan (Darfur) between 1985 and 2005, an estimated 2 million people were killed and some 4 million left homeless. Common to Africa and other embattled regions was the recruitment of children into armies, a practice that contributed to the long-term militarization of affected societies. Although negotiators achieved truces, political uncertainty and the lack of stable economic institutions continued to plague many southern regions.

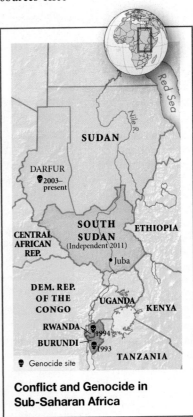

Conflict and Genocide in Sub-Saharan Africa

Advancing Nations in the Global Age

Despite the challenges, the developing world was also the site of dramatic successes. After decades of strife and economic underperformance, officials, business people, farmers, and artisans rebuilt prosperity in India, Brazil, South Africa, and China as they took advantage of global technology and markets. The same groups also helped democracy materialize in Brazil and South Africa and mature in India. Politicians worked to accommodate opposition parties instead of stifling their critics, and they pulled supporters and rivals alike into the common cause of advancing representative government.

India

By the twenty-first century, democratic India had become an economic powerhouse, possessing robust industrial and service sectors connected to markets around the world. India's path to prosperity was hardly smooth, however. Its leaders had to overcome ethnic, religious, class, and caste conflict as they tried to integrate India's diverse peoples. The Congress Party, founded in 1885 to combat British domination, remained powerful, but Nehru's daughter and grandson, who followed him as prime ministers, were assassinated by offended members of religious and ethnic minorities, leaving Gandhi's and Nehru's goals of integration unfulfilled. Nonetheless, India remained the world's largest democracy.

For a brief period the Bharatiya Janata Party (BJP), which advocated a Hindu nationalist program aimed in part at halting the technological development behind India's growing wealth and secularization, attracted voters struggling with rapid economic change. In 2004, however, Indian voters soundly defeated the BJP, rejecting Hindu nationalism in favor of the economic fairness promised by an alliance of the Congress Party and smaller parties, including the communists. New prime minister and the first Sikh to hold that position, Manmohan Singh, was an economist with international experience, having served as a director of the International Monetary Fund and other global organizations. Known as "the cleanest politician in India,"[3] Singh supported a mixed economy—that is, one with both privately and publicly owned enterprises. Even as its economy soared under Singh, however, India continued to face problems that were part of the legacy of colonialism: lack of modern infrastructure and education for all, the poverty of several hundred million citizens, and persistent ethnic and religious terrorism. Amid both turmoil and prosperity, India's cities grew and its middle class expanded, in large part thanks to the global economic activities of its innovative business people. India's internal integration and development were also importantly linked to its continued connections with peoples and markets around the world.

Globalized Agriculture in India

This up-to-date Indian farmer harvests a bumper crop of wheat using machinery from the U.S.-based John Deere corporation. Not only did this harvester have parts made in other countries, but the seeds he used were probably developed in Mexico-based scientific laboratories. These laboratories produced seeds suitable for different agricultural conditions, such as varying climate and soil composition. The result was the "Green Revolution" that began in the 1960s. (akg-images/Yvan Travert.)

Like other Latin Americans in the 1960s and 1970s, Brazilians had endured military dictatorship, soaring inflation, rising poverty, and a grossly inadequate system of education and social services. In 1985 Brazilian voters, tired of government brutality and human rights abuses, ousted the military dictatorship and installed an elected government. Civilian rule brought with it an emphasis on human rights and economic expansion, especially in the 1990s and thereafter. By the 1990s, government leaders had adopted a tight monetary policy and a commitment to pay down debts. In 2004 Brazil's economy expanded at a rate of 5.2 percent, despite the persistence of serious social problems, including crime and poverty.

There were several forces behind these developments. In the slums or *favelas* of the country's major cities, Rio de Janeiro and São Paulo, where the dictatorship provided no sanitary, educational, or other services, poverty-stricken residents organized themselves in the spirit of change, holding self-education meetings, teaching one another to read, and taking turns collecting and disposing of garbage. "I go to meetings every week now," one woman reported of her growing activism. "I think we women should participate in political parties."[4] Unions also played an important role. Luiz Inácio Lula da Silva, born in poverty in the countryside, had become a metalworker and then boosted his leftist union's membership to more than one hundred thousand. In the 1980s he brought together a broad coalition to found the Workers Party. On his fourth try for office in 2002, Lula da Silva was elected president—an incredible journey for a poor child who only learned to read when he was ten.

Global journalists described Lula da Silva as another Stalin or Mao. Yet Lula da Silva adopted an effective, pragmatic style: as president he promised that increased tax revenues on the wealthy would be used to pay off the dictatorship's foreign loans and thus free Brazil from indebtedness to the West. Alongside indebtedness, the populace was outraged at the brutal murders of reformers who wanted to stop the destruction of Brazil's rain forests by both global and local developers. The issue was one not only of murder, but of whether local peoples could keep their land in the forests or whether the government would let loggers strip the forests and murder opponents in the name of economic development. Although Lula negotiated a path between antiglobalizers and globalizers, some of the worst poverty was alleviated and the Brazilian economy surged, becoming a rising economic star in the Southern Hemisphere and indeed in the world as a whole.

As president of South Africa, Nelson Mandela faced numerous pressing issues. Foremost among them were calming interethnic tensions, ending political violence, and unifying the nation around consensus-building rather than violence. Violence against blacks and white critics had been the main political strategy of the **apartheid** government; it included taking blacks' homes and land and herding them by force into small "townships." In 1976 government troops killed and wounded some three thousand youth and children at Soweto as they protested the lack of educational opportunities. "We want equal education, not slave education," they had chanted while being mowed down. The white apartheid government also pursued a divide-and-conquer strategy, doing what it could to encourage conflict between the Zulu Inkatha Freedom Party and Mandela's African National Congress. In the 1980s, violence from many sides kept the country in turmoil. After Mandela took control, the government set up in 1995 a Truth and Reconciliation Commission to hear testimony about the violence. The Commission allowed those whom the apartheid government had persecuted to talk about their experiences in public; then it allowed those who had participated in the persecutions to confess to what they had done and request amnesty. The aim was to provide some relief to victims and to construct a new model for nation building (see Reading the Past: Testimony to South Africa's Truth and Reconciliation Commission).

While the Commission did its work, Mandela's presidency opened world markets to South African products, increased the flow of technology to the country, and created policies based on fairness to all social groups. For example, South African women had played a leadership role in opposing apartheid, and they received a quota of seats in the new government. Health care was declared a constitutional right of all citizens. The government's

apartheid The South African system of laws and behaviors that enforced segregation of the black from the white population, with the intention of creating a society dominated by whites; apartheid laws were repealed in 1991.

Testimony to South Africa's Truth and Reconciliation Commission

In 1995 the South African government established the Truth and Reconciliation Commission to hear testimony from accusers and perpetrators alike about violence and human rights abuses during the apartheid regime. Usually the commission imposed fines, but in the aftermath of the hearings victims were often angrier than before. They saw the punishment as inadequate and complained that the fines were ridiculously low or never paid. Despite the drawbacks and objections, many around the world hailed the Truth and Reconciliation model as one with great potential.

Accounts by perpetrators of the violence make for especially horrific reading. In this excerpt, researchers followed up with one member of the government security forces to hear in more depth how he pursued his grim job in the 1970s and 1980s, getting paid by the head for black resisters captured and for black resisters killed.

We would volunteer for a three-month stint on the border for the Security Branch up there. . . . It sounded like a bit of an adventure and [a] nice getting away kind of ploy, because my girlfriend and I were having hassles, probably because we were staying at my parents' place. I'd always been interested in doing something unconventional anyway, and I thought, well, this is it. This is my chance. . . .

The amount of adrenaline that we were producing on a daily level, constantly aware that we could die or be wounded at any moment. . . . Having that adrenaline pumping, we became adrenaline junkies. . . . It became like a drug to me, to go out there and follow up on those tracks. . . . [It is] almost a sexual kind of stimulation. Not physical sexual, but mental sexual. . . .

[On one particular captive] I knew that he was a veteran and that he would have been an excellent source of info. Sean, the Army medic, started patching him up while I was busy interrogating him. . . . Even at that stage he was denying everything and I just started to go into this uncontrollable [expletive deleted] rage and I remember thinking, "How dare you?" And then— this is what I was told afterwards—I started ripping. I ripped all the bandages, the drip that Sean had put into this guy . . . pulled out my 9 mm, put the barrel between his eyes and . . . I executed him.

Source: Don Foster et al., *The Theatre of Violence: Narratives of Protagonists in the South African Conflict* (Oxford, U.K.: James Currey, 2005), 130, 137, 140.

EXAMINING THE EVIDENCE

1. What values appear to have motivated this member of the security forces as he pursued his livelihood?

2. Do you detect a change over time in his conduct, and if so, how do you explain it?

3. Why do you think the Truth and Reconciliation Commission came to be viewed as a powerful model in nation building?

approach to land reform reflected its commitment to national integration and consensus-building. Instead of simply seizing land held by whites and giving it to blacks, the government set up a process by which the claims of dispossessed whites and blacks alike could be resolved. Nonetheless, South African blacks still remained an underclass, and migrants from neighboring Zimbabwe, Mozambique, and other hard-pressed African regions competed with them for jobs (see Map 31.1). Business people and farmers often fired their former employees and hired the migrants at rock-bottom wages.

At the same time, the rapid spread of HIV/AIDS (discussed later in the chapter) engulfed the nation in a horrific health crisis. South Africans themselves contracted the disease, and because of South Africa's growing prosperity, tens of thousands of other afflicted Africans came there to receive treatment. Twenty-four percent of all inhabitants of South Africa were HIV-positive in 2007. This trend, combined with ethnic tensions, economic inequalities, and the rise of new political factions, challenged the gains made after South Africa's hard-won victory over apartheid.

China Of all the developing nations, China's was the most striking success story. Deng Xiaoping came out on top in the power struggle that followed Mao's death in 1976. Under his leadership, China began its drive to become an economic titan, at once producing an array of inexpensive products for the global marketplace and providing its citizens with jobs that raised their standard of living. As people from the countryside flocked to cities to find jobs in China's global workplace, skyscrapers sprouted like mushrooms, transforming China's urban landscape. One- and two-story buildings were demolished in a flash: "Buildings are being knocked down at such a rate that one doesn't even have time to film them anymore," said one Beijing resident.[5] With rising prosperity, consumers sought out luxury goods that would have been unimaginable just two decades earlier. Even relatively poor workers could afford pirated DVDs, and thousands supported themselves by counterfeiting imported goods in much the same way that U.S. hustlers more than a century earlier had helped build American prosperity through counterfeiting products.

Economic development was not, however, accompanied by democratization. The Communist Party kept its grip on government, clamping down hard on free speech, even on the Internet, and meting out harsh punishments to political and religious dissidents. While maintaining control at home, China sought business partners around the world, making deals for raw materials and even for used factories, which it dismantled piece by piece and then reconstructed in new Chinese industrial parks. It also used its trade surpluses to buy vast quantities of debt, especially from the United States, making this communist country the bankroller of capitalist economies and thus an increasingly powerful player on the global stage. The flow of wealth and productive energy appeared to have changed direction away from the Atlantic and toward the Pacific.

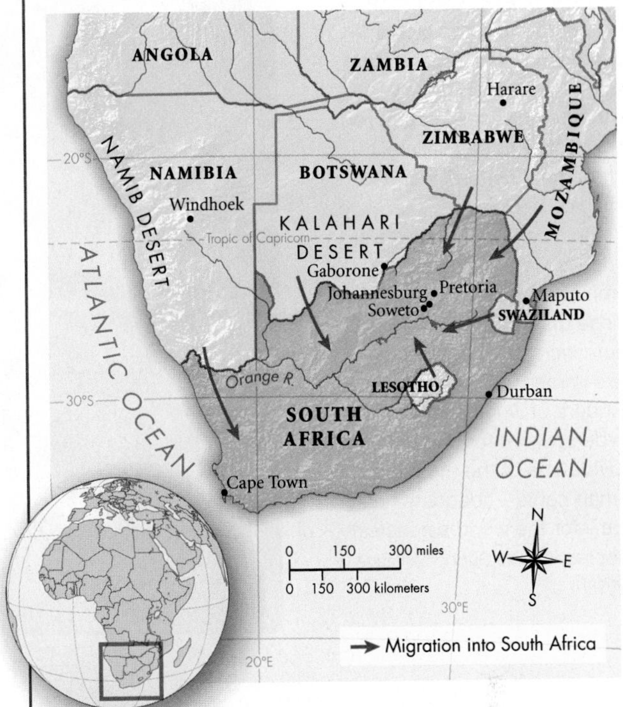

MAP 31.1   **South Africa After Apartheid**

Before the end of apartheid, legal migration into South Africa was restricted to whites and to African contract laborers who worked in the mines. After 1994, refugees seeking opportunity from the region around South Africa entered the country. The new South Africa also deported many illegal immigrants, and South Africans themselves migrated, creating a "brain drain" from the country, including people in the professions and those with technical skills.

Global Livelihoods and Institutions

The same forces that created a global market for products and services created a global market for labor. Increasingly, companies took their operations to wherever labor was cheapest. As a result, workers around the world found themselves in competition for employment. At the

FOCUS

How has globalization reshaped national economies and political institutions?

same time, workers found it easier to move to where the jobs were. Better transportation and communication led people to travel thousands of miles to work: Indonesian village women, for instance, left their families to work as domestic servants in the Middle East; nurses from the Philippines went to Japan and other countries as health-care providers in a better-paying environment. Migration, innovations in communication technology, and the globalization of business combined to create global cities. London, Tokyo, and New York became crossroads for global finance, engineering, and legal decision-making. Finally, global financial, political, and activist institutions such as the World Trade Organization, the United Nations, and Doctors Without Borders operated worldwide, transcending the borders of the nation-state and even throwing the nation-state itself into question.

Doctors Without Borders

This doctor from the global nongovernmental organization Doctors Without Borders distributes plastic sheeting to construct refugee shelters during the 1994 civil war and genocide in Rwanda. In an age of ethnic conflict and civil war, refugees were an all-too-common type of global citizen, whose displacement was traumatic and whose needs were immense. The French founders of Doctors Without Borders aimed for this NGO to provide one of the most basic human rights—adequate health care—for the world's neediest peoples. (Louise Gubb/The Image Works.)

Global Networks and Changing Jobs

The Internet and Service Work

The Internet in particular advanced the globalization that multinational corporations and satellite communications had fostered in the first decades after World War II. By the early twenty-first century, as skills spread around the world, the Internet brought service jobs to a number of previously impoverished countries. One of the first to recognize the possibilities of computing and call desk services was Ireland, which attracted global business by stressing computer literacy. From the 1990s on, the people of this traditionally poor country began to prosper as the Internet allowed them to perform service jobs for clients throughout the world. The trend reached other nations as well. Moroccans could do help-desk work for French or Spanish speakers, and Nigerians could tend to U.S. telephone and credit card bills. India and China, both of which had good if unequally distributed systems of education, and eastern Europe with its well-educated workforce profited from the Internet revolution. Three percent of Indian domestic product came from the outsourcing work it did in payroll and other services for Europe, the United States, and Austronesia, but jobs flowed in multiple directions: jobs outsourced to the United States rose from 4.9 million in 1991 to 6.4 million in 2001 and continued to grow.

Global Consumerism

Those who worked in outsourced jobs were more likely to participate in the global consumer economy. Thus, consumption soared in India, China, Brazil, and other emerging markets. Service workers in these areas received intense language training to sound like American, Spanish, or British consumers, and global advertising introduced them to products from around the world. A twenty-one-year-old Indian woman, working for a service provider in Bangalore under the English name "Sharon," was able to buy a cellphone from the Finnish company Nokia with her salary. "As a teenager I wished for so many things," she said. "Now I'm my own Santa Claus."[6] North Africans, Indians, Chinese, and eastern Europeans had access to automobiles, CD players, and personal computers that would have been far beyond their means before the 1990s. Critics called the phenomenon "Consumania."[7]

Consumerism developed unevenly, however: 30 to 40 percent of the people in eastern Europe and even larger percentages in China and Indonesia could not participate fully in the consumer economy because they lacked the means for even basic purchases. The lion's share of global consumer benefits went to urban rather than rural workers. Urban workers in the global service economy also used their rising incomes to educate their families and themselves, hoping to advance even further.

Globalization produced acute competition among lower-level workers in industrial countries for good jobs. "How can I prepare my children for a knowledge-based society when I can't even put food on the table," one French mother complained.[8] Minimum-wage workers in the urbanized countries of the north competed for jobs with people around the world. Much as rural people in the late nineteenth and early twentieth century had faced a drop in prices for their produce and a deterioration in their way of life with the development of global markets in grain and other agricultural products, now lower-level industrial and service workers faced lower wages because they competed with workers worldwide. In contrast, those with advanced managerial, technological, and other skills derived from university education fared better, showing the increasing importance of education to prosperity.

Competition for Jobs

Neoliberalism and the Global Economy

In the 1990s neoliberalism as pioneered by Margaret Thatcher and Ronald Reagan (see Chapter 30) became a central economic model for promoting growth. Reducing social programs such as health care and education for ordinary people would lower costs to employers and boost profits and investment. Neoliberal policy encouraged business mergers, the elimination of rules for the industries and banks, and the free flow of capital across national borders. German companies, like U.S. firms, increased investments abroad in the early 1990s and thereafter; Germans set up companies in the United States where benefits to the workforce were low, and U.S. firms headed to places where benefits and taxes were even lower. An important tenet of neoliberalism was that profit and investment increase through downsizing—that is, reducing the number of jobs and enhancing the productivity of any individual worker. The resulting growth would eventually produce more jobs, thus creating new opportunities for those who were put out of work.

The neoliberal model continued to challenge that of the postwar welfare state in which the government tried to create a minimum level of well-being for society as a whole. Although Europeans still believed government should provide social services and education for all, the tightening of budgetary rules in the European Union meant that these services had to constitute a smaller part of the budget. Some labor unions protested that neoliberals wanted to keep workers at bare subsistence levels. The Swedish government drastically cut pensions, leading one union member to complain: "It means that we have to work our entire life."[9] Because employers (like workers) paid taxes for social service programs, any reduction in benefits or education costs meant smaller employer contributions. Reductions in employer contributions freed up money for investment, thus advancing neoliberalism. Despite neoliberal convictions, some nations believed that certain services were too important to be left to those whose main concern was profit rather than the public good; for that reason these governments continued to run high-quality transportation systems and pave roads, for example.

Neoliberalism and the Welfare State

Beyond the Nation-State

Supranational organizations fostered globalization by creating worldwide networks to improve and regulate societies, economies, and politics. In the 1990s Europeans made immense strides in moving their governmental institutions beyond those of the traditional nation-state, while countries of the "southern cone" of South America joined the effort to speed up economic and social progress. People from around the world packed into cities such as Tokyo, New York, and London, bringing new ideas and new customs.

Supranational Organizations

The International Monetary Fund (IMF) and the World Bank had been in existence for decades, but with globalization these supranational organizations gained in power and importance. Raising money from individual governments, the IMF made loans to developing countries to support modernizing projects or to pay off debts. Such assistance, however, came on the condition that the recipient countries restructure their economies according to neoliberal principles. Other supranational organizations not connected to governments and therefore called **nongovernmental organizations** (NGOs) were charitable or policy-oriented foundations. Because they controlled so much money, these NGOs often shaped national policies. After the fall of the Soviet bloc, NGOs used their resources to bring about political reform. Some NGOs, such as the France-based Doctors Without Borders, used global contributions to provide medical aid in such places as the former Yugoslavia, where people at war lacked any medical help except what outsiders could provide.

Activists Against Globalization

Globalization entailed the rise of global activism, even against globalization itself. For example, the Association for Taxation of Financial Transactions (known as ATTAC), founded in 1998, had adherents in forty countries who opposed the control of globalization by the forces of high finance. ATTAC's major policy goal was to tax financial transactions (just as purchases of household necessities were taxed) and use the money raised to create a fund for people in underdeveloped countries. By 2011, the European Union indeed proposed such a tax, although it was to support poorer countries in the EU itself. ATTAC held a conference at Porto Alegre, Brazil, in 2002 to develop policy alternatives that would protect ordinary people from the worst effects of globalization; political leaders flocked to "alternative" Porto Alegre just as they attended the more traditionally global Davos forum held annually in Switzerland for the world's leading executives.[10]

Women Activists and Globalization

Women activists also held global meetings. Feminists gathered in Beijing, China, in 1995 to discuss common issues and agree on a common platform that could serve as the basis for political action in individual countries. The event was eye-opening for many participants, especially those from industrialized countries who had thought themselves more advanced and active than women from Africa and South America. The reverse proved to be true. Sharp differences in agendas and priorities emerged, as well as dissent in shaping the final report, especially on matters of birth control and abortion. In the end, the activists created a declaration of principles and a set of specific actions designed, in the words of the Declaration, "to advance the goals of equality, development, and peace for all women everywhere in the interest of all humanity"[11] (see Reading the Past: Assessing Livelihoods for Women in a Global Economy). In the early twenty-first century, women became heads of state in Germany, Liberia, Chile, Argentina, and Brazil, a sign of women's increasing influence in politics and business.

The European Union

In 1992, the twelve countries of the European Economic Community (or Common Market) ended national distinctions in the spheres of business activity, border controls, and transportation. Citizens of member countries carried a common burgundy-colored passport, and governments, whether municipal or national, had to treat all member nations' firms the same. In 1994 by the terms of the Maastricht Treaty, the European Economic Community became the **European Union** (EU) (see again Mapping the World, page 1025), and in 1999 a common currency, the European Currency Unit—the ECU, or euro—was established. Common policies governed everything from the number of American soap operas aired on television to pollution controls on automobiles to standardized health warnings on cigarette packages. The EU parliament convened regularly in Strasbourg, France, and with the adoption of a common currency by most members, the EU's central bank gained more control over regionwide economic policy.

Between 2004 and 2007 the EU admitted ten new members, mostly from central and eastern Europe: Estonia, Latvia, Lithuania, Poland, the Czech Republic, Slovakia, Hungary, Malta, Cyprus, Slovenia, Bulgaria, and Romania. All new members hoped to

nongovernmental organization A group devoted to activism outside the normal channels of government, such as Doctors Without Borders.

European Union An expanded version of the European Economic Community, established in 1994 to increase political and economic cooperation among European nations.

Assessing Livelihoods for Women in a Global Economy

In 1995 delegates from around the world met in Beijing, China, for the Fourth World Conference on Women sponsored by the United Nations. The delegates listened, debated, and negotiated to come up with a platform for action addressing women's health, education, role in politics, safety, and—in this excerpt—their situation in the increasingly globalized economy of the 1990s.

Although some new employment opportunities have been created for women as a result of the globalization of the economy, there are also trends that have exacerbated inequalities between women and men. . . .

These trends have been characterized by low wages, little or no labor standards protection, poor working conditions, particularly with regard to women's occupational health and safety, low skill levels, and a lack of job security and social security, in both the formal and informal sectors. Women's unemployment is a serious and increasing problem in many countries and sectors. Young workers in the informal and rural sectors and migrant female workers remain the least protected by labor and immigration laws. Women, particularly those who are heads of households with young children, are limited in their employment opportunities for reasons that include inflexible working conditions and inadequate sharing, by men and by society, of family responsibilities.

In countries that are undergoing fundamental political, economic, and social transformation, the skills of women, if better utilized, could constitute a major contribution to the economic life of their respective countries. Their input should continue to be developed and supported and their potential further realized.

For those women in paid work, many experience obstacles that prevent them from achieving their potential. While some are increasingly found in lower levels of management, attitudinal discrimination often prevents them from being promoted further. The experience of sexual harassment is an affront to a worker's dignity and prevents women from making a contribution commensurate with their abilities. The lack of a family-friendly work environment, including a lack of appropriate and affordable child care, and inflexible working hours, further prevents women from achieving their full potential.

In the private sector, including transnational and national enterprises, women are largely absent from management and policy levels, denoting discriminatory hiring and promotion policies and practices. The unfavorable work environment as well as the limited number of employment opportunities available have led many women to seek alternatives. Women have increasingly become self-employed and owners and managers of micro, small, and medium-scale enterprises.

Source: The United Nations Fourth World Conference on Women, "Action for Equality, Development and Peace," Beijing, China, September 1995, http://www.un.org/womenwatch/daw/beijing/platform/.

EXAMINING THE EVIDENCE

1. According to this statement, what are the effects of globalization on women's place in the economy?

2. What other issues besides economic ones affect women's ability to pursue productive and fulfilling livelihoods?

3. Judging from this statement, what relationship do you see between women's economic participation and the well-being of nations?

---

emulate the case of Greece, which had long been considered the poor relative of other EU countries. Greece had joined the European Common Market in 1981; in 1990 its per capita gross income was 58.5 percent of the European average. By the early twenty-first century, thanks to advice from the EU and an infusion of funds, the country reached 80 percent of the EU per capita gross domestic product. Candidates in 2010 for membership included Turkey, Croatia, and Macedonia.

The economic and political successes of the EU prompted the creation of other cooperative zones that imitated the early Common Market (see again Mapping the World,

Other Transnational Unions

Mercosur, 2011

Member states of Mercosur
■ Full member
□ Candidate
■ Associate member

page 1024). In 1967 five countries—Indonesia, Malaysia, the Philippines, Singapore, and Thailand—formed the **Association of Southeast Asian Nations** (ASEAN), later expanded to include Brunei Darussalam (1984), Vietnam (1995), Laos and Myanmar (1997), and Cambodia (1999). ASEAN members engaged in a range of cooperative ventures, but they particularly set their sights on rapid economic cooperation and expansion. The **North American Free Trade Agreement** (NAFTA), implemented in 1994, eliminated nearly all tariffs on goods traded between Canada, the United States, and Mexico. **Mercosur**, formed in 1991, established a free trade zone among South America's "southern cone" countries: Argentina, Brazil, Uruguay, and Paraguay, all of which were full members, and Chile and Bolivia as associates. These transnational organizations hardly matched the integration of the EU, and NAFTA explicitly rejected the kind of borderless opportunities for workers that the EU allowed. Workers in the United States watched in dismay as many jobs moved to Mexico, but as trade blossomed among the partners, the country's industrialists, financiers, and traders came to regard NAFTA and Mercosur as successes.

Global Cities

The changing function of cities in a global world reshaped livelihoods and identities. Cities had always served as regional crossroads, acting as centers of economic, political, and cultural activity. Now, as the twentieth century came to a close, some old urban areas, including Hong Kong, Paris, Tokyo, London, and New York, became global crossroads. Taking advantage of innovations in transportation and communication, they claimed critical roles in the global economy and became magnets for migrants from all over the world. Residents of other cities who took pride in maintaining their distinctive national culture or local way of life denounced global cities, often portraying them as corrupt and cold. Global cities, many of which were in the north, also drew criticism for their concentrated wealth, as their rise to global power and influence was seen by some to come at the expense of poorer people in rural areas or southern nations.

Life in Global Cities

A global city's institutions—its stock markets, legal firms, insurance companies, and financial service organizations—operated across national borders and were linked to similar enterprises in other global cities. Within these cities, high-level decision-makers interacted with one another to set global economic policy and to transact business worldwide. Their high pay drove up living costs and sent middle managers and engineers to live in lower-priced suburbs that nonetheless provided good schools and other amenities for these well-educated white-collar workers. Living in squalid conditions in the run-down neighborhoods of global cities were the lowest of service providers—the maintenance, domestic, and other workers who needed to be at the beck and call of global enterprise. According to one commentator, those at the top envisioned these people—many of them immigrants—as "lumpentrash." Thus, suburbanization and ghettoization alike flourished as part of globalization.

Association of Southeast Asian Nations A transnational organization formed in 1967 to facilitate economic cooperation among Southeast Asian countries.

North American Free Trade Agreement An agreement among Canada, Mexico, and the United States established in 1994 that eliminated most tariffs on goods traded among the signatories.

Mercosur The establishment in 1991 of a free trade zone among nations of South America's "southern cone."

Huge numbers of willing migrants flocked to leading global cities. In the mid-1990s, for example, an estimated ninety thousand Japanese lived in England staffing Japan's global enterprises located there. Sometimes said to be "invisible migrants," they did not aim to become citizens, nor did they make any economic or political claims on the adopted country. The presence of massive numbers of like-minded wanderers and a rich array of cultures and peoples in their communities often kept these global citizens from suffering the trauma of exile from their native country. Global cities were sometimes criticized for producing a "de-territorialization of identities"—meaning that residents of these areas lacked both a national and a local sense of themselves, so much so that they were at home anywhere in the world (see Seeing the Past: The Globalization of Urban Space).

The Globalization of Urban Space

The New Louvre, Paris, France (The Art Archive/Richard Nowitz/NGS Image Collection.)

One everyday sign of globalization is the homogenization of urban architecture. Travelers to urban capitals may see carefully preserved and distinctive buildings from centuries past that differ from one continent to another. Alongside these ancient buildings are recent ones, similar in style whether they are in Dubai, Malaysia, Japan, Brazil, or the United States. The similarity arises not only from the globalization of style but from the globalization of architects themselves, who bid on and construct buildings far beyond their home countries, often in collaboration with architects from other parts of the world.

The Louvre was once a royal palace. It evolved from a twelfth-century fortified residence of kings to a museum not only for the French but for millions of tourists from around the world. In the 1980s the French government undertook a major renovation of the central entrance to the Louvre, which was no longer adequate to deal with the throngs of visitors. The architect I. M. Pei, who designed buildings around the world, produced this entryway through a glass pyramid.

EXAMINING THE EVIDENCE

1. Why might so ancient a structure as a pyramid have been chosen to be placed in front of the Louvre?

2. Why might glass have been used instead of the stone from which the Egyptian pyramids were constructed?

3. What message does this update of the entrance to the Louvre convey?

The Promises and Perils of Globalization

Despite growing prosperity for many, the global age was filled with challenges. First, the health of the world's peoples and their environments came under a multipronged attack from industrial disasters, acid rain, epidemics, and global warming. Second, a surging population, especially

FOCUS

What major benefits and dangers has globalization brought to the world's peoples?

in southern regions, although fueling economic growth in many places, increased demands on resources and often fed strife. Migration from imperiled areas mushroomed, and transnational religious and ethnic movements also competed for power around the world, sometimes through the use of terrorism. Growing prosperity in regions outside the West boosted confidence that the time had come for the redistribution of global power, especially as the West was hit with a devastating economic crisis.

Environmental Challenges

In the late twentieth century people became concerned that technological development threatened the environment and human well-being on a disastrous scale. In 1984 poisonous gas leaking from a Union Carbide plant in Bhopal, India, killed an estimated ten to fifteen thousand people, with many tens of thousands more permanently harmed and the region completely contaminated by chemicals. This was followed by the 1986 explosion at the Chernobyl nuclear power plant in present-day Ukraine, which killed thirty people instantly and left many more dying slowly from the effects of radiation. Levels of radioactivity rose for hundreds of miles in all directions, and by the 1990s cancer rates in the region were soaring, particularly among children. Fossil-fuel pollutants such as those from natural gas, coal, and oil mixed with atmospheric moisture to produce acid rain, a poisonous brew that destroyed forests and inflicted ailments such as chronic bronchial disease on children. In less populated areas, clearing the world's rain forests depleted the global oxygen supply and threatened the biological diversity of the entire planet.

Climate Change   By the late 1980s, scientists determined that the use of chlorofluorocarbons (CFCs), chemicals found in aerosol and refrigeration products, had blown a hole in the earth's ozone layer, the part of the blanket of atmospheric gases that prevents harmful ultraviolet rays from reaching the planet. Simultaneously, automobile and industrial emissions, especially of carbon dioxide produced by the burning of fossil fuels, were adding to that thermal blanket. The buildup of CFCs, carbon dioxide, and other atmospheric pollutants produced a "greenhouse effect" that resulted in **global warming**, an increase in the temperature of the earth's lower atmosphere. Changes in temperature and dramatic weather cycles of drought or drenching rain indicated that a greenhouse effect might be permanently warming the earth and thus causing climate change. Already in the 1990s, the Arctic ice pack was breaking up, and scientists predicted dire consequences: the rate of global ice melting, which had more than doubled since 1988, would raise sea levels 27 centimeters by 2100, flooding coastal areas, disturbing fragile ecosystems, and harming the fresh water supply (see Map 31.2).

Environmental Activism   Activism against unbridled industrial growth took decades to develop as an effective political force. American biologist and author Rachel Carson wrote a powerful critique, *Silent Spring* (1962), which advocated the immediate rescue of rivers, forests, and the soil from the ravages of factories and chemical farming. In 1979, the Green Party was founded in West Germany, and across Europe Green Party candidates came to force other politicians to voice their concern for the environment.

Competing voices and the demands of nation building, however, led politicians to push massive and questionable projects such as superhighways and dams. Egypt's Aswan Dam, built in the 1960s, and China's Three Gorges Dam, on which construction began in the 1990s, destroyed miles of villages and farmland and cost thousands of lives even as they produced much-needed hydroelectric power. Chinese Nobel Laureate Gao Xingjian explored questions of ecological disaster, as he described peasant reactions to the destruction and invoked the responsibilities of the human community for the earth's well-being in his novel *Soul Mountain* (2000). Gao had been punished more than once during times of political extremism in China, the final time leading to his self-imposed exile, during which he gathered thoughts, stories, and impressions for his novel. Modernizers around the world denounced Gao's work and that of other environmental critics, and there were many attempts to silence protesting voices. In 2007, former U.S. vice president Al Gore

global warming An increase in the temperature of the earth's lower atmosphere, resulting in dramatic weather cycles and melting of glaciers.

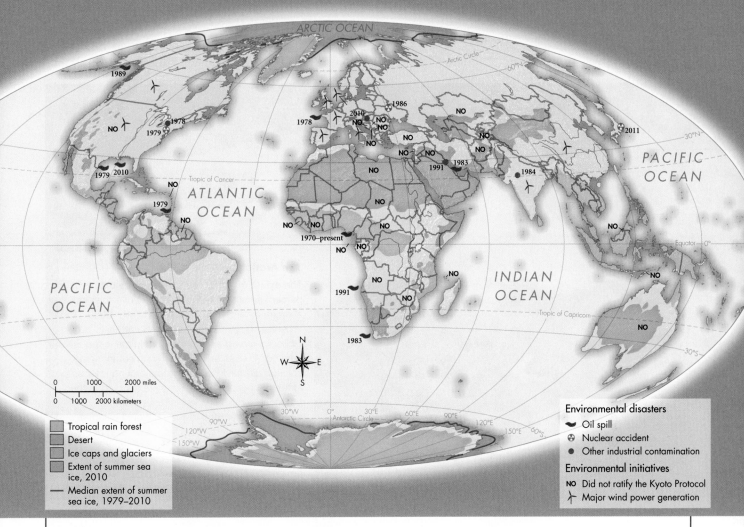

MAP 31.2

The Global Environment of the Early Twenty-First Century

As industry advanced and population grew, the earth itself came under assault. Degradation of the environment— including desertification (the transformation of formerly agrarian land into desert), depletion of rain forests, climate extremes, industrial catastrophes, and other changes caused by humans—threatened the sustainability of life.

won the Nobel Peace Prize for his fight to relieve the environmental crisis—"a moral and spiritual challenge to all of humanity," he called it.

People attacked environmental problems on both the local and global levels. Beginning in 1977, Wangari Maathai (wan-GAH-ree mah-DHEYE) enlisted women to plant trees to create green belts around Kenya's capital city of Nairobi. Born in Kenya, Maathai had studied botany in the United States and then returned to Africa to receive her doctorate in veterinary medicine. Local deforestation led her to take action and create a citizens' movement. "It's important for people to see that they are part of the environment and that they take responsibility for it," she explained. Maathai's project went against the wishes of powerful politicians and business people, who had her beaten up and run out of the country. Maathai returned, more powerful than ever, and in 2004 won the Nobel Peace Prize for her efforts to improve the environment and livelihoods of Africans.[12]

Frankfurt, Germany, and other European cities developed car-free zones. In Paris, when pollution reached dangerous levels, cars were banned. The Smart, a very small car using reduced amounts of fuel, became a popular way for Europeans to cut their use of fossil fuels. Cities also developed bicycle lanes on major city streets. Germany, Spain, the

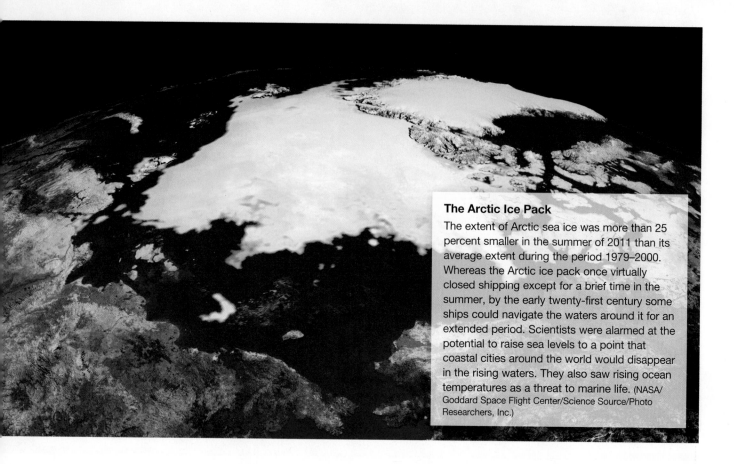

The Arctic Ice Pack

The extent of Arctic sea ice was more than 25 percent smaller in the summer of 2011 than its average extent during the period 1979–2000. Whereas the Arctic ice pack once virtually closed shipping except for a brief time in the summer, by the early twenty-first century some ships could navigate the waters around it for an extended period. Scientists were alarmed at the potential to raise sea levels to a point that coastal cities around the world would disappear in the rising waters. They also saw rising ocean temperatures as a threat to marine life. (NASA/Goddard Space Flight Center/Science Source/Photo Researchers, Inc.)

United States, Denmark, and China had some 80 percent of the world's wind installations to generate electricity in 2005, and in 2007 China and the United States led in the creation of new capacity. By 2007 some one hundred ninety countries had signed and ratified the **Kyoto Protocol**, an international treaty fashioned in 1997 to reduce the level of emissions of greenhouse gases and other pollutants around the world. Even though the United States refused to ratify the agreement, much of the rest of the world began working to preserve the environment (see again Map 31.2).

Population Pressures and Public Health

Nations with less-developed economies struggled with the pressing problem of rapidly rising population. The causes of the population surge were complex. By 1995 Europe was actually experiencing negative growth (that is, more deaths than births), but less industrially developed countries accounted for 98 percent of worldwide population growth, in part because the spread of medicine enabled people there to live much longer than before. By late 2011, the earth's population had reached 7 billion and by 2050 was projected to reach 8 to 10 billion (see Map 31.3).

Life Expectancy and Birthrates

Life expectancy globally rose by an average of sixteen years between 1950 and 1980. The world's sole remaining superpower did not fare particularly well by this measure of social health: by 2009, the United States had fallen to fiftieth place in average life expectancy, below Albania and Puerto Rico. However, life expectancy in Russia and its former satellites was catastrophic, falling from a peak of seventy years for Russian men in the mid-1970s to fifty-three in 1995 and to fifty-one at the beginning of the twenty-first century. Although birthrates in nonindustrial countries were much higher than in industrialized ones, overall birthrates were rapidly declining, leading to great uncertainty in forecasting population growth. These rates had been dropping in the West for decades, and by 1995

Kyoto Protocol An international treaty fashioned in 1997 to reduce emissions of pollutants around the world.

they had also begun to fall in the less economically developed world, where an estimated 58 percent of couples used birth control.

Population Control

Non-Western governments were alarmed at their nation's rising population and took action. In 1979 Deng introduced the idea of a one-child policy for urban Chinese families, with a considerable number of exceptions. Chinese families had their own methods of population control, mostly focused on female infanticide. Finding that its population was growing rapidly, the Iranian government under Ayatollah Khomeini at first welcomed robust growth as strengthening Islam, but by the 1990s the government was urging families to space their children: the birthrate fell from 6.5 live births per Iranian woman in the 1970s to below 2 in 2010. For a time in the 1970s, the Indian government used a policy of forced sterilization; its recent stress on voluntary family planning has kept population growth at a high level. Yet family planning appeared in unexpected places: mullahs in Afghanistan studied the problems of population. "If you have too many children and you can't control them," one reported after a class on birth control, "that's bad for Islam."[13]

Medical Treatment

Vaccines and drugs for diseases such as malaria and smallpox helped improve health in developing nations. However, half of all Africans lacked access to basic public health facilities such as safe drinking water. Drought and poverty, along with political machinations in some cases, spread famine in Sudan, Somalia, Ethiopia, and elsewhere. In the West, specialists performed heart bypass surgery, transplanted organs, and treated cancer with radiation and chemotherapy, while preventive care for the masses received less attention. Wealthy people traveled the globe to find the best medical treatment, but although the poor and unemployed suffered more chronic illnesses than those who were better off, they received less care. The distribution of health services was a hotly debated issue.

HIV/AIDS

In the early 1980s, technological expertise was challenged by the spread of a global epidemic disease: acquired immunodeficiency syndrome (AIDS), caused by human immune deficiency virus (HIV). A deadly disease that shuts down the body's entire immune system, AIDS is transmitted through contact with bodily fluid (blood or semen) of an infected person. The disease initially afflicted heterosexuals in central Africa; later it turned up in Haitian immigrants to the United States and in homosexual men worldwide. The disease spread quickly among the heterosexual populations of Africa and Asia. Action against AIDS was often sporadic, targeting the wrong audiences, and in some cases the disease was even dismissed as nonexistent. The government of Vietnam launched a dramatic campaign, with

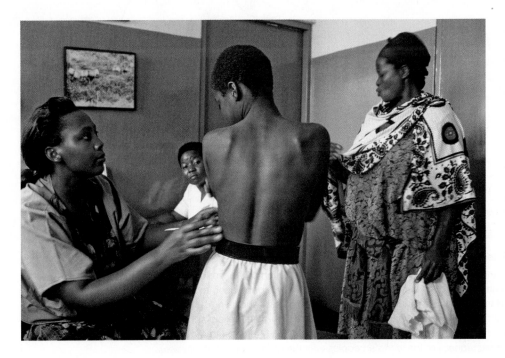

Treatment of AIDS in Uganda

Even as many Africans gained professional and technological expertise and as the continent's nations participated in the global economy, health remained a burning issue in the twenty-first century. Many diseases that had been eradicated elsewhere in the world still threatened the continent's population. Alongside the ravages of civil wars and genocide and the migration that followed, Africans also attempted to address the AIDS pandemic, often through the mobilization of local unions, doctors and nurses, and activists. (Véronique Burger/Photo Researchers, Inc.)

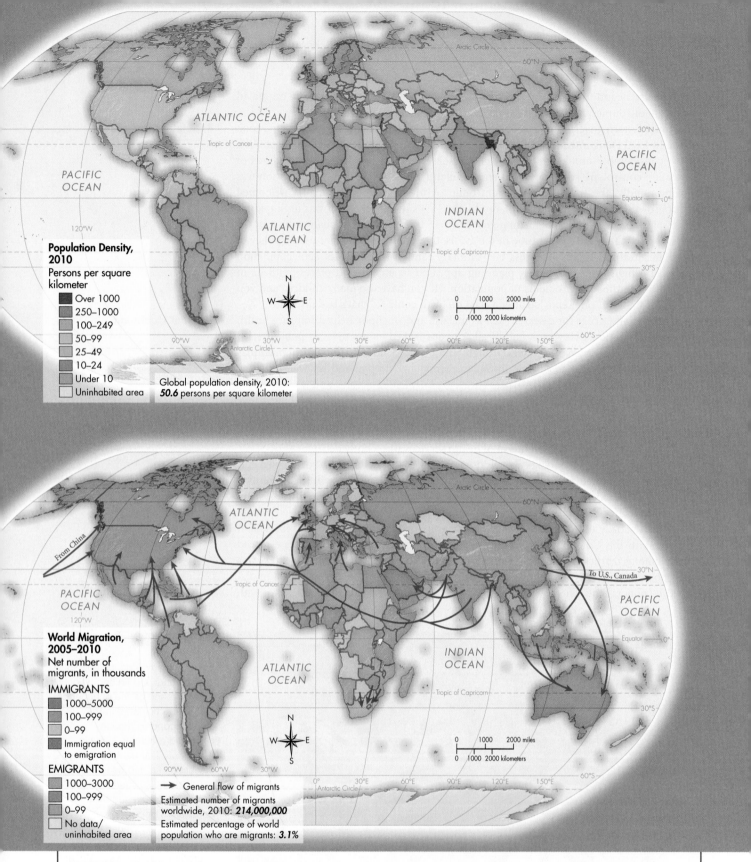

Population Density, 2010

Persons per square kilometer

- Over 1000
- 250–1000
- 100–249
- 50–99
- 25–49
- 10–24
- Under 10
- Uninhabited area

Global population density, 2010:
50.6 persons per square kilometer

World Migration, 2005–2010

Net number of migrants, in thousands

IMMIGRANTS

- 1000–5000
- 100–999
- 0–99
- Immigration equal to emigration

EMIGRANTS

- 1000–3000
- 100–999
- 0–99
- No data/ uninhabited area

→ General flow of migrants

Estimated number of migrants worldwide, 2010: **214,000,000**

Estimated percentage of world population who are migrants: **3.1%**

From China

To U.S., Canada

MAP 31.3 **The World's Peoples, c. 2010**

Migration, disease, and global religions contributed to the integration of the world's peoples in the early twenty-first century. Rising life expectancy caused the world's population to surge to 7 billion in late 2011, which led many people to migrate in search of opportunity and living space. Most of these migrants brought with them their ideas and traditions, including religious beliefs and practices, making their new homelands more culturally rich and diverse. A frightening and often tragic result of globalization and the interconnectedness of the world's peoples was the global spread of disease.

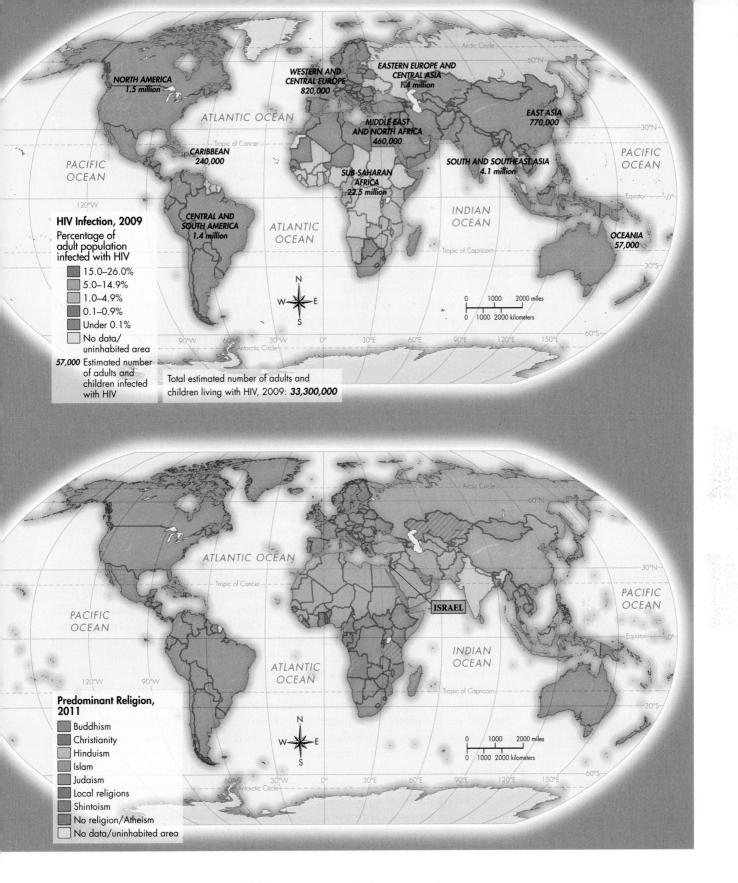

HIV Infection, 2009

Percentage of adult population infected with HIV

- 15.0–26.0%
- 5.0–14.9%
- 1.0–4.9%
- 0.1–0.9%
- Under 0.1%
- No data/ uninhabited area

57,000 Estimated number of adults and children infected with HIV

Total estimated number of adults and children living with HIV, 2009: **33,300,000**

NORTH AMERICA
1.5 million

WESTERN AND CENTRAL EUROPE
820,000

EASTERN EUROPE AND CENTRAL ASIA
1.4 million

EAST ASIA
770,000

MIDDLE EAST AND NORTH AFRICA
460,000

CARIBBEAN
240,000

SUB-SAHARAN AFRICA
22.5 million

SOUTH AND SOUTHEAST ASIA
4.1 million

CENTRAL AND SOUTH AMERICA
1.4 million

OCEANIA
57,000

Predominant Religion, 2011

- Buddhism
- Christianity
- Hinduism
- Islam
- Judaism
- Local religions
- Shintoism
- No religion/Atheism
- No data/uninhabited area

ISRAEL

posters blanketing public space that blared "Do not use or accept harmful cultural products. Do not become addicted to smoking or injecting drugs." In fact, the major culprits for the spread of AIDS in Vietnam were privileged and sexually adventurous public officials.

By 2010, no cure had yet been discovered, though strong drugs that alleviated the symptoms had been developed (see again Map 31.3). Activists in Africa and Asia raised their voices louder still, protesting that these costly drugs existed but only the lives of white victims were being saved. The mounting death toll caused some to call AIDS the twentieth-century version of the Black Death, the bubonic plague that ravaged Eurasia during the fourteenth century. In 2005 Nelson Mandela announced the death of his grown son from AIDS in hope that such publicity would help advance prevention and encourage medical attention. AIDS was not the only epidemic disease ravaging the world's population. The deadly Ebola virus, bird flu, swine flu, and dozens of other viruses harbored the potential for global pandemics. Interconnectedness via disease was all too real, showing both the promises and perils of globalization.

Worldwide Migration

Motives for Migration

The early twenty-first century witnessed migration worldwide, building on the migration that followed decolonization and adding to the diversity of many regions of the world. Often economics was the motivation for migration. An estimated 190 million rural Chinese traveled to China's industrial cities to find work in 2004, while millions more went to Malaysia, Indonesia, and other regions in Southeast Asia to get jobs. About 5 percent of the U.S. population was foreign born in the early twenty-first century, including some 11 million undocumented workers. Sometimes danger prompted migration. Africans fled civil wars in Rwanda, Congo, and Sudan, often heading for Europe, Canada, and the United States, while an easier path to safety led people in the more southerly regions of the continent to migrate to South Africa. Civil wars and ethnic oppression drove civilians from states of the former Soviet Union and its satellites to Germany, Scandinavia, Austria, France, and England. Jordan and other countries of the Middle East were home to Palestinians and Iraqis who had been driven from their homelands by violence. A particularly abhorrent form of coerced migration was the increasing trafficking in children and women for sexual and other kinds of forced labor.

Conditions of Migration

The conditions of migration varied depending on one's class, gender, and regional origin. Among the most fortunate migrants were professionals and talented innovators in science and technology. Among the less fortunate were women from the Philippines, Indonesia, and other southern regions who migrated to perform domestic service. They frequently suffered rape by their employers, oppressive working conditions including long hours and no time off, and confiscation of their wages. Women and their children who escaped on their own were often unprotected from exploitation, whereas men and women alike waited at the edges of deserts such as the Sahara or traveled packed into airless storage containers in trucks to find opportunity or to escape political turmoil. Other people migrated as part of an organized plan, such as those of Chinese or Armenian merchants around the world who planned for the migration of young relatives to participate in trade or services. Most of these migrants lived in communities of people from their own region or ethnicity.

The diverse population of the United States made it easier for migrants to meld into educational and workforce institutions, but even in the United States politics increasingly centered on the presence of migrants. In other parts of the world, prejudice against migrants was even stronger. Malaysian politicians blamed the Chinese in their midst for problems of modernization, whereas Indonesians rampaged against both Chinese and Christians. By the late twentieth century, politicians worldwide won votes simply by citing migrants as the source of their societies' problems.

The Literature of Migration

Migration stories, many of them best sellers, related dreams of magnetic other worlds, often experienced amid oppressive conditions. The appeal of Western culture, consumer goods, and democracy inspired a striking number of these. Expatriate Russian author Andrei Makine, who emigrated to France, produced lyrical accounts of Soviet people in Siberia and their powerful imaginings of a better world. *Once Upon the River Love* (1998) recounts the fantasies of a group of Siberian teens who see a French adventure film and begin to dream of Western women and life in western Europe. In this tale, the teenagers' later lives outside of the USSR are bleak and even bitterly disillusioning. *Reading Lolita in Tehran* (2003), a memoir by Iranian author Azar Nafisi, who published her book after emigrating to the United States, and *Balzac and the Little Chinese Seamstress* (2003) by Dai

Sijie, a Chinese refugee in Europe, detail the powerful influence of Western literature under conditions of oppression. Nafisi, who left her post at a Tehran university during the Iranian theocracy, writes of bringing a group of young women to her home to read forbidden literature. As they read, both teacher and students discover that forbidden works contain beauty, values, and examples of personal courage. The two young men in Sijie's novel are banished to the countryside during China's Cultural Revolution and discover there a supply of nineteenth-century Western classics.

Terrorism Confronts the World

Even as insightful literature served as a force for global understanding, the world's people also experienced their interconnectedness in terrifying ways as radicals began to use violence rather than peaceful protests or regular politics to accomplish their goals. Many such radicals came from countries with dictatorships or dysfunctional democracies, but others simply saw violent tactics as a more effective means to publicize their cause. In the 1970s, terrorist bands in Europe, such as Italy's Red Brigades, responded to the restoration of political order after 1968 with kidnappings, bank robberies, bombings, and assassinations. In 1972, Palestinian terrorists kidnapped and murdered eleven Israeli athletes at the Olympic Games in Munich. The terrorists demanded the release of Palestinian prisoners held in Israeli jails. After Bloody Sunday (January 30, 1972) in Northern Ireland, when British troops fired on unarmed civil rights demonstrators, a cycle of violence ensued that left thousands dead. Protestants, fearful of losing their dominant position, battled a reinvigorated Irish Republican Army, which carried out bombings and assassinations to end the oppression of the Catholic minority in Northern Ireland and reunite Northern Ireland with the Republic of Ireland.

Terrorists aimed at the highest levels of government and at ordinary people alike. Prime Minister Indira Gandhi was assassinated by her Sikh security guards in 1984 after the Indian government attacked a Sikh temple; Tamil separatists from Sri Lanka assassinated Indira Gandhi's son Rajiv for his lack of support for their independence in 1991; antigovernment U.S. terrorists blew up a government building in Oklahoma City in 1995; in the same year Japanese religious radicals released deadly poisonous gas in the Tokyo subway system to promote their beliefs; in 2011 a Norwegian fundamentalist Christian and anti-Muslim extremist massacred close to eighty young political activists and wounded hundreds more.

Terrorism began to play an ever-larger role in world politics. Although it appeared that growing belief in religion, nationalism, and the power of oil would naturally make the Middle East a leader in the preservation of international order, the charismatic leaders of the 1980s and 1990s—Iran's Ayatollah Ruhollah Khomeini, Libya's Muammar Qaddafi, Iraq's Saddam Hussein, and Osama bin Laden, leader of the Al Qaeda transnational terrorist organization—all used violence to gain leverage. Throughout the 1980s and 1990s, terrorists from the Middle East and North Africa planted bombs in many European cities, blew up European airplanes, and bombed the Paris subway system—among other acts. Some attacks were said to be punishment for the West's support for both Israel and repressive regimes in the Middle East.

Terrorism and the Middle East

On September 11, 2001, Middle Eastern militants hijacked four planes in the United States and flew two of them into the World Trade Center in New York and one into the Pentagon in Virginia. The fourth plane crashed in Pennsylvania. The hijackers, most of whom were from Saudi Arabia, were inspired by Osama bin Laden, who was supported by the United States during the Cold War but now wanted U.S. military forces removed from Saudi Arabia. The loss of some three thousand lives led the United States to declare a "war against terrorism."

September 11, 2001

Global cooperation followed the September 11 attacks and the continuing lethal bombings around the world. European countries rounded up terrorists and conducted the first successful trials of them in the spring of 2003. Ultimately, Western cooperation fragmented when the United States invaded Iraq in March 2003, claiming falsely that Iraq's Saddam Hussein had weapons of mass destruction and suggesting ties between Saddam Hussein and Al Qaeda, bin Laden's terrorist group (see Map 31.4). Great Britain, Spain, and Poland were among those who joined the U.S. invasion, but Germany, Russia, and

U.S. Invasion of Iraq

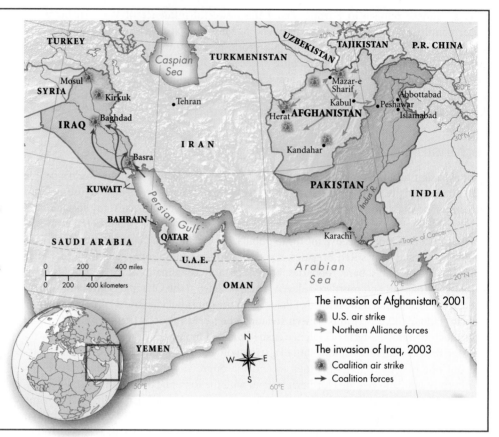

MAP 31.4

Wars in Afghanistan and Iraq, 2001–2011

In the aftermath of the terrorist attack on the United States on September 11, 2001, the U.S. government, with the help of Western allies and the Northern Alliance of Afghani groups, launched an attack on the Taliban. This group had taken control of Afghanistan in the wake of the Soviet withdrawal and supported the Al Qaeda terrorist group behind "9/11." In 2003, the United States and its allies invaded Iraq on the grounds that it had weapons of mass destruction—which was not true. Both wars caused tens of thousands of deaths and produced millions of refugees.

France refused. The public in much of the world accused the United States of becoming a world military dictatorship to preserve its only value—wasteful consumerism. Supporters of the invasion countercharged that Europeans were too selfish in their enjoyment of democracy and creature comforts to protect freedom under attack. The Spanish withdrew from the U.S. occupation of Iraq after Al Qaeda–linked terrorists bombed four commuter trains in Spain on March 11, 2004. The British reeled too, when terrorists left bombs in three subway cars and a bus in July 2005. In 2011 American forces scored a symbolic victory in the "war against terror" through the capture and execution of Osama bin Laden. Nonetheless, as the wars in Iraq and Afghanistan continued into the second decade of the twenty-first century, terrorism became an additional ingredient in the globalization of warfare.

Terrorism in the twenty-first century knew no bounds. Chechens protested the Russian destruction of their country by bombing Moscow apartment buildings, blowing up packed buses and airplanes, and taking hundreds of hostages, including schoolchildren. In Bali, terrorists blew up nightclubs and resorts, while in Jordan Al Qaeda suicide bombers slaughtered wedding guests. Alongside the many promises of globalization—including the rich mixture of peoples and cultures and the victory for democracy wrought by people like Nelson Mandela—was the incredible toll in lives taken by terrorism, civil wars and genocide, disease, and other instruments of death around the globe.

The Promise of Arab Spring

Even as terrorism continued, a new manifestation of antigovernment sentiment appeared that brought hope and promise throughout the Middle East. In late 2010, an "Arab Spring" began in a series of popular uprisings, some of which forced dictators in North Africa and the Middle East to step down in favor of democracies and representative government. Uprisings in Tunisia, Egypt, and Libya succeeded, even in the face of brutal repression. In Egypt, long-time dictator Hosni Mubarak was forced from power and put on trial for the murder of many protesters. Hard on the heels of the Egyptian success, protest mounted against dictators in Libya and Syria, with NATO planes helping the Libyan rebels defeat Muammar Qaddafi.

Arab Spring in Egypt

At the end of 2010, protests erupted in Tunisia over the corruption of longtime dictator Zine El Abidine Ben Ali and his family. The overthrow of Ben Ali inspired others across the Arab world to call for change, and although some were crushed, dictators in Egypt and Libya were driven out. The Egyptians pictured here celebrate the fall of Hosni Mubarak in February 2011, a result of protests often organized via social media. The end of Muammar Qaddafi's reign in Libya later that year was only achieved through military means and proved more costly in terms of lives and the destruction of homes and infrastructure. (Ron Haviv/VII/Corbis.)

Hopes for a speedy transition to a full-blown democracy in liberated countries were not high. Working against representative institutions and civil rights were two facts: dictators had prevented the institutions of civil society, including open debate, from developing; in their place tribal organizations often controlled decision-making. However, others who saw a more hopeful future in the near-term pointed to the sophisticated means by which protesters had mobilized: they used features of the World Wide Web such as e-mail and social networking to create meeting points and devise strategies. The protesters were relatively peaceful, unless governments fought back, forcing protesters to defend themselves. Even as the situation often appeared chaotic and uncontrolled in the face of government repression, in fact, the promise of the Arab Spring was not just in its accomplishments but in the "virtual" societies young and older citizens had constructed through technology. The Arab Spring may have looked rough and ragged, but it showed the ever-changing capacities that can be brought to bear on human problems.

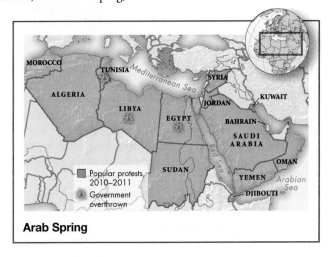

Arab Spring

Global Economic Crisis

Globalization meant tighter financial connections and a faster pace of doing business. As the twenty-first century opened, the global economy suffered a series of shocks, followed by the bursting in 2008 of a real estate bubble in the United States. Housing prices had escalated because of mortgage financing available on easy or even dishonest terms. Then, financiers distributed this often fraudulent debt around the world to those who hoped to make handsome profits because adjustable mortgage rates were set to rise dramatically. When people became unable to repay their rising debt, including credit card debt, credit became unavailable both to ordinary people and to banks and industry. A credit collapse followed, just as it had in the stock market collapse of 1929 (see Chapter 28). Banks and industries became insolvent, and governments around the world tried to prop them up with the infusion of billions of dollars. Unemployment rose as businesses and consumers alike stopped purchasing goods. Although by late 2009 Pacific economies had returned to growth, in 2011 European governments including Greece, Italy, and Spain faced possible bankruptcy. The globalization of economic crises remained yet another peril faced by the world's population.

Readers of the Qur'an

Readers of the Qur'an in Kazan, Russia

Despite the Soviet Union's official policy of atheism, Kazan has remained a center of Islamic culture and practice. It is the site of magnificent mosques and hosts expert readings of the Qur'an. In this 2008 photograph, a reader participates in a Qur'an reading contest, in which young experts from across Russia vie with one another for the best and truest performance. Although this contest is a national one, echoing secular contests in music, beauty, and even game shows, Islam remains a powerful global religion with a rising number of believers. (RIA Novosti/The Image Works.)

Among the most popular and prestigious stars in the global media are those who chant the Qur'an on cassettes, CDs, and radio. Specially trained and tested Qur'an reciters—literally thousands of them—make their recordings in dozens of cities in the Islamic world, but only after being certified to do so by official examining boards. The apprenticeship is arduous, for readers must know the Qur'an to perfection, because errors such as stopping in the middle of a word would mar recipients' understanding of the holy words of Allah as handed down through the Prophet Muhammad. Cassettes allow the Qur'an to inspire Muslims at home or work; for example, a carpenter in Cairo keeps his tape playing during the day. "I have two ears," the carpenter reports, "one for work, and one for listening to the Qur'an." Readings of the Qur'an can make up a third of sales by record companies, and cell phones now deliver Qur'an readings.

Although most reciters of the Qur'an are men, one of the best known is Maria Ulfah, a reciter from Indonesia.

Taught as a child that men and women are equal, she has traveled to many parts of the world to read. Like Ulfah, well-loved readers of the Qur'an become celebrities. In Egypt Sheik Mohammed Gebriel is the most appreciated; listeners immediately recognize his voice. He is known to bring in crowds of over half a million when reading in public. "When I hear Sheik Gebriel, I feel that the angels are reading with him," a retired army officer said.

Despite the standardization involved in procedures for certification, the reading of the Qur'an and the issuing of calls to prayer five times a day have their variations according to region and language. Muslims in Kenya, for example, prefer the sounds of the call to prayer by their country's readers to those recorded in Egypt. Saudis object to musical recitations of the Qur'an, preferring those that are direct and plain-spoken. Recordings by the thousands of reciters show, in fact, differences and nuances by region that are welcome to local worshipers, again proving that even in the face of standardization and globalization at the highest levels of religion and faith, local identities remain both powerful and important to carrying out one's daily life. "You can get bored by a song in a few days," a record store owner said in analyzing the popularity of cassettes of the Qur'an, "but no one gets bored listening to the Qur'an."

QUESTIONS TO CONSIDER

1. In the case of the Qur'an in people's lives, what has been the effect of modern communications technology?

2. How would you describe the role of the reciter of the Qur'an in modern society? Is he or she a religious leader, service worker, or media personality?

3. Over time, what has been the effect of books, television, CDs, and other media on religion generally?

For Further Information:
Douglas Jehl, "Above the City's Din, Always the Voice of Allah," *New York Times International*, March 6, 1996.
   Ali Asani lecture, November 2005.
Qur'an Explorer (recordings of recitations of the Qur'an in several languages, including Arabic, Urdu, and English). http://www.quranexplorer.com/.
Qur'an Reciters, including images of especially important reciters of the past. http://www.quranreciters.com/wp/.

Cultures Without Borders

In the global age, positive cultural values such as the quest for human rights began to mature. Communication and more extensive contact allowed widespread sharing and enjoyment of the world's cultural accomplishments in literature, art, and music. The global age, for all its deadly flaws, was rich in possibilities for improving human life and connecting people around the world.

FOCUS

What trends suggest that globalization has led to a new mixing of cultures?

The Quest for Human Rights

At the end of the twentieth century, human rights constituted a newly invigorated global value supported by people from many countries and traditions. Notions of human rights as transnational guarantees of just treatment for all people had grown up gradually over the course of the twentieth century. The idea of human rights as transcending any individual government's policies—that is, as being universal and not limited to citizens of a particular nation-state—emerged powerfully with the creation of supranational bodies such as the United Nations. In 1948 the General Assembly of the United Nations adopted a Declaration of Human Rights, which proclaimed the inalienable rights and fundamental freedoms of all people, including the rights to life, liberty, security, and equal protection of the law. In 1975 the Helsinki Accords, part of a series of agreements between the two sides in the Cold War, acknowledged Soviet gains in World War II in exchange for Soviet endorsement of human rights. This commitment to human rights, at first a pro forma statement, became central to dissidents within the Soviet bloc, and with globalization, it became a lynchpin of international activism. Some critics denounced the accords as simply another ploy for powers in the north to interfere in the political affairs of people from the south—a powerful critique once the United States began using torture during its war on terrorism.

Human Rights as a Global Value

Human rights activists found much to correct in the world around them, and after the 1970s they were better organized globally to take action. Human rights activists spoke out against the genocide in Rwanda and the former Yugoslavia in the 1990s, and the international community joined them in backing prosecution for these crimes in the International Tribunal at The Hague. Human rights activists investigated other abuses, such as violations of political freedoms, immunity from violence and torture, and the guarantee of food, clothing, and shelter. Activists protested the torture of prisoners in Turkey and the trial of Turkish novelist Orhan Pamuk for asserting Turkey's role in the Armenian genocide of 1915–1917. Latin American governments and China also wracked up long lists of abuses, which human rights activists publicized, often at their own peril. They targeted powerful leaders such as Russian president Vladimir Putin, who closed down independent television stations and imprisoned critics. Human rights activists were suppressed and sometimes murdered for speaking out. Shirin Ebadi, an Iranian lawyer who won the Nobel Peace Prize in 2005 for her human rights activism, was constantly attacked by the government; her offices were raided in December 2008 for tax fraud, even though she did not charge those she defended. Political opponents of Belarus's president Aleksandr Lukashenko, including young demonstrators on behalf of human rights, were murdered or beaten.

Targeting Human Rights Abuses

Religion Worldwide

Many religions surrendered any national identity and sought out the faithful globally. Roman Catholicism had more adherents in Latin America and Africa than in its western European heartland, where many had embraced secularism. Beginning in the 1970s, Roman Catholic popes—most notably John Paul II—traveled widely to almost every corner of the world. Although some believers found the church's message against homosexuals, birth control, and abortion distasteful, Catholic clergy, such as the nuns assassinated in Brazil or Rwanda, gained a strong record as advocates for the poor around the world. They were said to practice "liberation theology," which stressed bringing Christian compassion

Growth of World Religions

to those suffering—wherever they lived. The Buddhist sect Soka Gakkai, once identified with its Japanese origins, also had a far-flung global membership, with more than a million adherents each in Brazil and South Korea and major followings in New York, Los Angeles, Sydney, and many other parts of the world. Soka Gakkai precepts include chanting for specific goals, most important among them world peace, compassion for others, and respect for all human life. The sect sponsored cultural events, hosted conferences for women, and supported environmental protection movements, thereby, like the Catholic Church, promoting transnational values and good works.

Spread of Islam   Islam also expanded worldwide, becoming the world's second-largest faith after Christianity (see again Map 31.3). Although Muslims held Mecca and Medina in Saudi Arabia in special regard as the birthplace of their faith, the population center of Islam by the late twentieth century lay in a more easterly direction, falling on a line from eastern Pakistan through western India. As many Muslims lived east of that line, in centers such as Jakarta and Kuala Lumpur, as lived west of it in Cairo and Istanbul. While practicing the Five Pillars of their faith, including charitable giving, Muslims embraced a wide variety of interpretations of Islam. In the 1990s, young Turkish people, raised with the nation's republican and secular beliefs, began to follow "green pop" stars and to read "green romances"—green being the color of paradise in the Muslim faith. While enjoying gossip, jokes, and the company of their best friends, young women decided to wear headscarves and follow the call to prayer, maintaining "we pray like you have fun."[14] Islam spread to the New World, and places where it had mostly been rejected, such as Europe, included centers of Islamic faith. Muslims also recruited members globally, often using sophisticated techniques based on marketing and demographic knowledge (see Lives and Livelihoods: Readers of the Qur'an).

Global Literature and Music

The Boom in Latin American Literature   A crucial ingredient of globalization was the deepening relationship among cultures as books and music from many different national traditions gained a worldwide audience. Latin American authors, for example, developed a style known as magical realism, which melded everyday events with elements of Latin American history, myth, magic, and religion. The novels of Colombian-born Nobel Prize winner Gabriel García Márquez were translated into dozens of languages. His lush fantasies, including *One Hundred Years of Solitude* (1967), *Love in the Time of Cholera* (1988), and many later works, portray people of titanic ambitions and passions who endure war and all manner of personal trials. García Márquez described the tradition of dictators in Latin America, but he also emphasized the legacy of business imperialism. *One Hundred Years of Solitude*, for example, closes with the machine-gunning in 1928 of thousands of workers at the request of the U.S. United Fruit firm because they asked for a single day off per week and breaks to use the toilet. Five years of rain flood the region, erasing all trace of the slaughter, even from local memory. Wherever they lived, readers snapped up the book, which sold 30 million copies worldwide. A host of other outstanding novels in the magical realism tradition followed, including Laura Esquivel's *Like Water for Chocolate* (1989). In the 1990s the work was translated into two dozen languages and became a hit film. Set in a Mexican kitchen during the revolution of 1910, it intertwines such themes as cooking, sexuality, and brutality.

The Latin American "boom," as it was called, continued into the early twenty-first century, with innumerable authors writing in the style of Márquez and his predecessor, Jorge Luis Borges (see Chapter 29). While acknowledging these geniuses, younger novelists such as Chilean-born Roberto Bolaño questioned the right of literary-minded people to focus on aesthetics amid the brutal dictatorships, torture, and poverty that were so powerful a part of Latin American reality.

Cultural Challenges to Traditional Values   In a global age, the power of literature seemed magnified because it challenged deeply held local beliefs and widespread values. Some writers faced real danger for producing controversial works: García Márquez went into hiding from time to time and rode in a bullet- and bomb-proof car. Feminist authors were menaced and even exiled from Pakistan and other countries that felt threatened by works describing women's oppression and calling for women's equality. Egyptian feminist, medical doctor, and writer Nawal El Saadawi was criticized for producing accounts of women's plight in the region. Her opponents charged her with trying to appeal to Westerners with chilling stories of abuse and backwards customs. Indian-born Salman Rushdie, who had settled in Great Britain, produced *Midnight's Children* (1981), a novel whose fantastic characters formed part of Rushdie's fictional depiction of India's history and whose style was influenced by the magical realism of Latin American authors. Rushdie's novel *The Satanic Verses* (1988) ignited outrage among Muslims around the world because it appeared to blaspheme the Prophet Muhammad. Banned in South Africa and India, the book led to riots worldwide. In 1989 Iran's Ayatollah Khomeini issued a fatwa, or edict, promising both a monetary reward and salvation in the afterlife to anyone who would assassinate the writer. In the 1990s Rushdie went into hiding, but assassins succeeded in murdering his Japanese and Italian translators. The conflict over *The Satanic Verses* reflected a "clash of civilizations," pitting the right to free speech against the right not to have one's religion slandered.

Popular music also flourished in the global marketplace. Pop musicians mixed styles from all over the world, and people brought their music with them as they migrated. Hip-hop, rap, and salsa music, for example, combined African, Latin American, and African American traditions into new musical genres. African hip-hop artists claimed hip-hop and rap as part of an African heritage based on the poet singers, or griots, who for centuries had lyrically recited history and legends. In 1988 the South African group Black Noise produced the region's modern version of rap, and they participated in the antiapartheid movement. Other groups from East Africa rapped about the problems of HIV/AIDS and the urban crime that ruined many of their neighbors' lives. Hip-hop and rap music circled the world, soaking up influences from various cultures. Salsa music did likewise, flourishing not just in Latin America and the Caribbean, but also in the United States as more Hispanics migrated there. African influences shaped salsa too via the slave heritage of the Western Hemisphere. Countries made their own adaptations of musical styles, but the mixing of global styles remained constant, especially as promoters sought new products and novel sounds to sell globally.

Contemporary popular music was the music of diasporas as the world's peoples migrated and interacted with others. Raï, the popular music of North African cities, echoed in the Algerian suburbs of Paris, and performances by raï stars attracted tens of thousands of fans. Dangdut, a form of popular music in Indonesia, used tunes from Bollywood film while its lyrics expressed Islamic values—the combination appealing to diasporas in the world's largest Islamic state. "Chutney" generally described the fusion music of the Caribbean, but particularly the influence of the many South Asian indentured workers who settled there in the nineteenth and early twentieth centuries. As with political and economic institutions, the globalization of people's lives made literary and musical culture a dense crossroad of influences.

Global Pop Culture

Inul Daratista, a sensation in Indonesia and beyond for her singing and dancing performances, blends Indian, Middle Eastern, Malay, and Portuguese styles into unique rock routines. Inul's body moves sensuously and rapidly, and Muslim clergy object to her lack of modesty. The controversy is reminiscent of Elvis Presley's notoriety back in the 1950s in the West, but some see her moves as looking simply like sped-up aerobics, albeit with many Indian and Indonesian gestures. Although Inul Daratista's "dangdut" music originates in folk performances, she has made it not just a local but a global phenomenon. (BAZUKI MUHAMMAD/Reuters/Corbis.)

COUNTERPOINT
Who Am I? Local Identity in a Globalizing World

FOCUS

How have peoples sought to establish and maintain distinctive local personal identities in today's global age?

As globalization linked the world's people in multiple ways, individuals also claimed local, personal identities as a counterpoint to the globalizing trend. Traditionally, individuals took their identities from families, villages, and eventually nation-states. The advance of globalization produced both a sense of loss and a feeling that something other than global forces and even nation-states was needed to provide values. People sought various ways to proclaim their personal identities: through local religious customs or by emphasizing age-old local traditions of dress, food, and celebration. Personal identity also developed through showing loyalty to local sports teams, despite the fact that many such teams were allied with global business, including television networks and marketers of consumer goods.

Ethnic Strife and New Nations

One countermovement to globalization aimed at empowering smaller units of political alliance. Such groups as the Tamils in Sri Lanka and Sikhs in India struggled for autonomy for their people, threatening nation-states with fragmentation. These groups did not achieve their aims. However, by 2000 there were more nations than there were at the end of World War II in 1945. This was not only because of decolonization but because the rising tide of ethnic distinctiveness divided some countries. Since 1990, twenty-nine new nations have been born, including South Sudan in 2011. Yugoslavia splintered into several states in bloody civil wars among ethnic groups, including Serbs, Bosnians, Croatians, and Slovenians. New Asian states such as Kazakhstan and Uzbekistan came into being when they separated from Russia.

Activists also worked to assert regional autonomy, fostering movements for the independence of Quebec from Canada. Basques assassinated tourists, police, and other public servants in their quest for independence from Spain. Many a politician found campaigning for ethnic secession to be the path to public office.

Movements to Protect Tradition

The desire to maintain a local identity also encompassed the movement to preserve local customs and practices, including some of the world's thousands of languages, which were under threat of being swallowed up by Chinese, Hindi, Spanish, and English. In January 2005 Guatemalan forces killed a Maya-Kakchiquel man who sought to block a global mining firm's inroads into his community. At issue in hundreds of other similar protests across Central America was the preservation of local customs and traditional rights, including age-old rights to specific plots of land and sources of water. In late 1993 a group of activists in the Chiapas state of Mexico declared themselves a local liberation army devoted to stanching the "bleeding" of their locality by stopping the flow of oil, coffee, bananas, and other resources out of the area, leaving the local people destitute. These activists, known as the Zapatistas (recalling the name of the hero of the 1910 revolution), also decried the decline in the use of their language and the national and international ridicule heaped on their way of life. Many of these Mexicans still worshiped at ancient Maya shrines, just as locally oriented people around the world focused on their own ancient altars. In seeking to preserve their local identity, the activists were similar to the pilgrims in Vietnam, who brought fruit to special shrines around Hanoi so that it could be blessed by local gods. Native Americans in the United States worked to preserve their ancestral burial sites against industrial and agricultural development. The rap group

Local Customs in a Global Age: Mexico
This image from 2004 shows a Mexican father carrying a bouquet to the Holy Death temple in Mexico City as he presents his infant to Mictlantecuhtli and Mictecacihuatl, the "Señor and the Señora" of Mictlan—that is, the region of the dead people. In so doing, he keeps alive an Aztec custom from the fifteenth century, some six hundred years later in a much changed, cosmopolitan world. (AFP/Getty Images.)

Xplastaz in Tanzania promoted the wearing of traditional garb to fight the globalization of clothing that threatened to erase their local culture.

Although the global media have worked to make family life more standardized, individuals continued to take their identities from their families and to promote distinctiveness. They spent more effort to trace their genealogies. Despite high divorce rates, in fact there are more marriages in the twenty-first century than ever before in human history. National politicians often invoke "family values" to get people to vote for them, and in fact daily family life remains for many a shelter for individual identity, just as local activism is a bulwark against global national forces.

Conclusion

"Sometimes I tell myself, I may only be planting a tree here, but just imagine what's happening if there are billions of people out there doing something. Just imagine the power of what we can do." Wangari Maathai's motivation reflected a belief that billions of citizens, acting as individuals, can effect change on a global scale. Innovations in global communications, transportation, migration, and the development of strong transnational organizations have accelerated the pace of globalization in the past four decades. Globalization is evident everywhere: in the worldwide spread of disease and the worldwide consequences of industrialization. It is seen in the spread of campaigns like Nelson Mandela's on behalf of human rights and in dastardly acts of global terrorism.

As the world's peoples come to work on common projects and share elements of one another's cultures, their mental outlook has become more global, more cosmopolitan. The Chinese painter Wu Guanzhong, even after years of repression for his cosmopolitan style, combined elements from around the world in his work. "In my art," Wu said, "I really belonged to a hybridized breed."[15] Many rightly protest that much of value can be lost at the hands of global forces at work in the world today; others foresee some great irreconcilable clash among civilizations. The question remains whether, given the meeting of humans on the world's crossroads, we are not all hybrids—that is, mixtures of one another's thoughts, traditions, cultures, and livelihoods. Isn't this mixture of peoples and cultures what has given texture to the recent history of the world?

NOTES

1. Quoted in *Guardian Weekly*, September 19–25, 2002.
2. Quoted in James C. McKinley, Jr., "Mexican Farmers Protest End of Corn-Import Taxes," *New York Times*, February 1, 2008.
3. Soutik Biswas, "India's Architect of Reforms," *BBC News*, May 22, 2004.
4. Quoted in Yvonne Corcoran-Nantes, "Female Consciousness or Feminist Consciousness: Women's Consciousness-Raising in Community-Based Struggles in Brazil," in *Global Feminisms Since 1945*, ed. Bonnie G. Smith (London: Routledge, 2000), 89.
5. Quoted in Michael Dutton, et al., *Beijing Time* (Cambridge, MA: Harvard University Press, 2008), 10.
6. Saranya Sukumaran, quoted in Saritha Rai, "India Is Regaining Contracts with the U.S.," *New York Times*, December 25, 2002, W7.
7. Georges Quioc, "La 'consomania' de l'Europe de l'Est électrise les distributeurs de l'Ouest," *Le Figaro économie*, January 13, 2003.
8. Quoted in *Le Monde*, June 2, 2002.
9. Quoted in *Le Monde*, January 17, 2003.
10. Quoted in *Libération*, January 20 and 21, 2002.
11. Fourth World Conference on Women Beijing Declaration, 1995. http://www.un.org/womenwatch/daw/beijing/platform/declar.htm.
12. Quoted in "Nobel Peace Prize for Woman of 30m Trees," *The Guardian*, October 9, 2004.
13. Quoted in "At Birth Control Class, Mullahs Face New Reality," *International Herald Tribune*, November 12, 2009.
14. Quoted in Ayse Saktanber, "'We Pray Like You Have Fun': New Islamic Youth in Turkey Between Intellectualism and Popular Culture," in *Fragments of Culture: The Everyday of Modern Turkey* (London: I. B. Tauber, 2006), 254.
15. Wu Guanzhong, "Preface by the Artist," in Anne Farrer, *Wu Guanzhong: A Twentieth-Century Chinese Painter* (London: British Museum, 1991), 9.

RESOURCES FOR RESEARCH

The Impact of Global Events on Regions and Nations

The decades around the turn of the twenty-first century were full of events that shifted balances of economic and political power. The South African Web site provides a look at the innovative postapartheid constitution, which ensures an array of human rights.

Bayly, Susan. *Asian Voices in a Post-Colonial Age: Vietnam, India and Beyond.* 2007.

Kynge, James. *China Shakes the World: A Titan's Rise and Troubled Future and the Challenge for America.* 2006.

Prunier, Gérard. *Darfur: The Ambiguous Genocide.* 2005.

Rosefielde, Steven. *Russia in the 21st Century: The Prodigal Superpower.* 2006.

South Africa. http://www.info.gov.za/documents/constitution/1996/96cons2.htm.

Taylor, Lance, ed. *External Liberalization in Asia, Post-Socialist Europe, and Brazil.* 2006.

van Kessel, Ineke. *Beyond Our Wildest Dreams: The United Democratic Front and the Transformation of South Africa.* 2000.

Global Livelihoods and Institutions

The spread of global communication brought on by the Internet dramatically affected livelihoods and institutions. Greenspan and Rowen chart developments in information technology.

Greenspan, Anna. *India and the IT Revolution: Networks of Global Culture.* 2004.

Rowen, Henry S., Marguerite Gong Hancock, and William F. Miller. *Making IT: The Rise of Asia in High Tech.* 2007.

Sassen, Saskia. *Cities in a World Economy.* 2006

United Nations. http://www.un.org/womenwatch/. Provides ample information on women around the world and also on the UN's programs for women.

Wasserstrom, Jeffrey N. *China's Brave New World—and Other Tales for Global Times.* 2007.

The Promises and Perils of Globalization

Globalization is hotly debated, and this selection of works shows why. AIDS, terrorism, and environmental decline increased as the world's peoples became more tightly linked. Louie and Smith and Siplon, however, discuss activism and spirited movements for change.

Baldwin, Peter. *Disease and Democracy: The Industrialized World Faces AIDS.* 2005.

Hefner, Robert W. *Civil Islam: Muslims and Democratization in Indonesia.* 2000.

Khalid, Adeeb. *Islam After Communism: Religion and Politics in Central Asia.* 2007.

Louie, Miriam Ching Yoon. *Sweatshop Warriors: Immigrant Women Workers Take on the Global Factory.* 2001.

McNeill, J. R. *Something New Under the Sun: An Environmental History of the Twentieth Century.* 2000.

Smith, Raymond A., and Patricia Siplon. *Drugs into Bodies: Global AIDS Treatment Activism.* 2006.

Cultures Without Borders

As the media became a global force, culture knew even fewer boundaries than it had in the past. These works chart a variety of trends and global mixing of cultures.

Allison, Anne. *Millennial Monsters: Japanese Toys and the Global Imagination.* 2002.

Iwabuchi, Koichi. *Recentering Globalization: Popular Culture and Japanese Transnationalism.* 2002.

Kato, M. T. *From Kung Fu to Hip Hop: Globalization, Revolution, and Popular Culture.* 2007.

Lopez, A. M. *To Be Continued . . . Soap Operas Around the World.* 1995.

Osumare, Halifu. *The Africanist Aesthetic in Global Hip-Hop: Power Moves.* 2007.

Seager, Richard. *Encountering the Dharma.* 2006.

COUNTERPOINT: Who Am I? Local Identity in a Globalizing World

Whether praying or shopping, people around the world maintain local customs and practices. Even a global chain such as McDonald's needs to adjust to local preferences, as Watson's work shows.

Benjamin, Thomas. "A Time of Reconquest: History, the Maya Revival, and the Zapatista Rebellion." *The American Historical Review.* 2000.

Malarney, Shaun Kingsley. *Culture, Ritual and Revolution in Vietnam.* 2002.

Parkin, David, and Stephen C. Headley, eds. *Islam: Prayer Across the Indian Ocean and Outside the Mosque.* 2000.

Saxenian, Anna Lee. *The New Argonauts: Regional Advantage in a Global Economy.* 2006.

Watson, James L., ed. *Golden Arches East: McDonald's in East Asia,* 2d ed. 2006.

▶ **For additional primary sources from this period**, see *Sources of Crossroads and Cultures*.

▶ **For Web sites, images, and documents related to topics in this chapter**, see Make History at bedfordstmartins.com/smith.

The major global development in this chapter ▶ The causes and consequences of intensified globalization.

IMPORTANT EVENTS

1986	Nuclear accident at Chernobyl power plant in Soviet Union
1989	Iranian leader Ayatollah Khomeini issues fatwa against Salman Rushdie
1990s	New European nations emerge in wake of USSR collapse
1991	Mercosur establishes a free-trade zone among southern South American nations
1994	Nelson Mandela elected president of South Africa; European Union officially formed; North American Free Trade Agreement implemented
1995	United Nations Fourth World Conference on Women held in Beijing
1997	Kyoto Protocol drafted
1999	European Union adopts the euro as its new money
2001	Terrorists attack United States; United States declares "war on terrorism"
2002	Luiz Inácio Lula da Silva elected Brazilian president
2003	United States invades Iraq
2004	Manmohan Singh becomes prime minister of India
2005	Kyoto Protocol goes into effect
2007–2008	Global economic crisis begins to unfold

KEY TERMS

apartheid (p. 1029)
Association of Southeast Asian Nations (p. 1036)
European Union (p. 1034)
globalization (p. 1025)
global warming (p. 1038)
Kyoto Protocol (p. 1040)
Mercosur (p. 1036)
nongovernmental organization (p. 1034)
North American Free Trade Agreement (p. 1036)

CHAPTER OVERVIEW QUESTIONS

1. What were the elements of globalization at the beginning of the twenty-first century?
2. How did globalization affect lives and livelihoods throughout the world?
3. How did globalization affect local cultures?
4. What people do you know whose roots and livelihoods are global?

SECTION FOCUS QUESTIONS

1. How has globalization affected the distribution of power and wealth throughout the world in the early twenty-first century?
2. How has globalization reshaped national economies and political institutions?
3. What major benefits and dangers has globalization brought to the world's peoples?
4. What trends suggest that globalization has led to a new mixing of cultures?
5. How have peoples sought to establish and maintain distinctive local identities in today's global age?

MAKING CONNECTIONS

1. What have been the most important features of globalization—good and bad—in the past thirty years, and why are they so significant?
2. Consider Chapter 24. How have livelihoods changed since the era of industrialization, and what factors have caused these changes?
3. Do you consider local or global issues more important to people's lives? Explain your choice.
4. How do you describe your identity—as global, national, local, familial, religious—and why?

ADDITIONAL CREDITS

Text Credits

Chapter 1

Kate Wong. "Meet the Oldest Member of the Human Family," *Scientific American,* July 11, 2002. Reproduced with permission. Copyright © 2002 Scientific American, a division of Nature America, Inc. All rights reserved.

Chapter 2

H. L. J. Vanstiphout. Tale of Enmerkar from H. L. J. Vanstiphout, *Epics of Sumerian Kings: The Matter of Aratta.* Society of Biblical Literature, 2004: 85. Used by permission of the Society of Biblical Literature.

J. S. Cooper. *Sumerian and Akkadian Royal Inscriptions I,* translated by J. S. Cooper, 1986. Used by permission of the American Oriental Society, University of Michigan.

Martha T. Roth. Excerpts from the Code of Hammurabi from Martha T. Roth, *Law Collections from Mesopotamia and Asia Minor.* Society of Biblical Literature, 1997: 133–134. Used by permission of the Society of Biblical Literature.

E. Edel. Nefertari to Puduhepa from *Die agyptisch-hethitische Korrespondenz aus Boghazkoy,* by E. Edel. Nordrhein-Westfälische Akademie der Wissenschaften, 1994. Used by permission of the publisher.

Chapter 3

Burton Watson. *Records of the Grand Historian by Sima Qian: Han Dynasty II,* translated by Burton Watson. Copyright © 1993 Columbia University Press. Reprinted with permission of the publisher.

William Theodore de Bary and I. Bloom. *Sources of Chinese Tradition,* 2nd edition, edited by William Theodore de Bary and I. Bloom, translated by Burton Watson. Copyright © 1991 Columbia University Press. Reprinted by permission of the publisher.

Chapter 4

Jan Assmann. Reprinted by permission of the publisher from *Moses the Egyptian: The Memory of Egypt in Western Monotheism,* by Jan Assmann, pp. 175–177 (Cambridge, Mass.: Harvard University Press). Copyright © 1997 by the President and Fellows of Harvard College.

Chapter 5

Rex Warner. Thucydides, *History of the Peloponnesian War,* translated by Rex Warner, 1972. Reproduced by permission of Penguin Books Ltd.

S. G. Benardete. "The Persians," from *Complete Greek Tragedies: Aeschylus II,* translated by S. G. Benardete, Chicago University Press, 1991. © 1956, 1991 by The University of Chicago Press. Used by permission of Chicago University Press.

Elizabeth Wyckoff. *Antigone,* from *Sophocles I,* translated by Elizabeth Wyckoff. Copyright 1954 by The University of Chicago.

All rights reserved. Used by permission of Chicago University Press.

M. L. West. "On Women" (21 lines of poetry) from *Greek Lyric Poetry,* translated by M. L. West (1994), p. 19. Used by permission of Oxford University Press.

Chapter 6

Aimslee T. Embree. *Sources of Indian Tradition,* Vol. I, 2nd edition, edited by Aimslee T. Embree. Copyright © 1988 Columbia University Press. Reprinted with permission of the publisher.

Leonard Nathan. *The Transport of Love.* Berkeley: University of California Press, 1976. Used by permission of Julia Nathan.

A. L. Basham. Translation from E. Zurcher, "The Yueh-chih and Kaniska in the Chinese Sources," *Papers on the Date of Kaniska,* ed. A. L. Basham. Leiden: Brill, 1968: 364–365. Used by permission of Brill.

Victor H. Mair. *The Columbia Anthology of Traditional Chinese Literature,* edited by Victor H. Mair. Copyright © 1994 Columbia University Press. Reprinted by permission of the publisher.

A. K. Ramanujan. Tamil poetry from *Poems of Love and War,* translated by A. K. Ramanujan. Copyright © 1985 Columbia University Press. Reprinted by permission of the publisher and by permission of Krishna Ramanujan.

Chapter 7

Jane Rowlandson. *Women and Society in Greek and Roman Egypt,* edited by Jane Rowlandson. Cambridge University Press, 1998. Reprinted with the permission of Cambridge University Press.

Chapter 8

J. C. Beaglehole. *The Endeavour Journal of Joseph Banks 1768–1771,* edited by J. C. Beaglehole, Halstead Press, Sydney, 1962. Vol. I, p. 368, and Vol. II, p. 37. Courtesy of State Library of New South Wales.

Martin West. Sappho poetry translated by Martin West, *The Times Literary Supplement,* June 24, 2005. Reprinted with permission.

Chapter 9

N. J. Dawood. Passages from the Qur'an from *The Koran: With Parallel Arabic Text,* translated with notes by N. J. Dawood (Penguin Books, 1990). Copyright © N. J. Dawood 1956, 1959, 1966, 1968, 1990. Reproduced by permission of Penguin Books Ltd.

A. S. Tritton. *The Caliphs and Their Non-Muslim Subjects,* by A. S. Tritton (1930): "The Pact of Umar." By permission of Oxford University Press.

Chapter 11

Allen J. Christenson. Popul Vuh, *The Sacred Book of the Maya,* translated by Allen Christenson. Copyright © 2003 by O Books. University of Oklahoma Press, 2007. Used by permission of the publisher.

Choe-Wall Yangh-hi. Lady Hong, *Memoirs of a Korean Queen*, edited and translated by Choe-Wall Yangh-hi (London: KPI, 1985), pp. 1–4, 49. Used by permission of Taylor & Francis Books.

Chapter 22

Cesar E. Farah. *An Arab's Journey to Colonial Spanish America: The Travels of Elias al-Musili in the Seventeenth Century*, edited and translated by Cesar E. Farah, Syracuse University Press, 2003. Used by permission of Syracuse University Press.

Richard Price. *First-Time: The Historical Vision of an Afro-American People* (Baltimore: Johns Hopkins University Press, 1983), p. 71. Used by permission of the author.

Chapter 23

Paul Dukes. *Russia Under Catherine the Great: Select Documents on Government and Society*, edited and translated by Paul Dukes, Oriental Research Partners, 1978. Reprinted by permission of the publisher.

Chapter 24

J. N. Westwood. *A History of the Russian Railways*, George Allen and Unwin, 1964. Used by permission of the author.

Chapter 25

Alexander Nikitenko. *Up from Serfdom: My Childhood and Youth in Russia 1804–1824*, translated by Helen Saltz Jacobson. Copyright © 2001 Yale University Press. Used by permission of Yale University Press.

Anne Walthall. *The Weak Body of a Useless Woman: Matsuo Taseko and the Meiji Restoration.* © 1998 by The University of Chicago. Used by permission of the University of Chicago Press.

William R. Braisted. From *Meiroku Zasshi: Journal of the Japanese Enlightenment* by William R. Braisted, pp. 401–403, Cambridge, Mass.: Harvard University Press, Copyright © 1976 by the University of Tokyo Press.

Chapter 26

Wang Gungwu. *Community and Nation* by Wang Gungwu (2000), published by Allen & Unwin, Sydney (www.allenandunwin.com).

Chapter 27

Patricia Buckley Ebrey. Adapted with permission of Free Press, a division of Simon & Schuster, Inc., from *Chinese Civilization and Society: A Sourcebook* by Patricia Buckley Ebrey. Copyright © 1981 by The Free Press. All rights reserved.

Léopold Sédar Senghor. *The Collected Poetry*, pp. 47–48. Translated by Melvin Dixon. © 1991 by the Rector and Visitors of the University of Virginia. Reprinted by permission of the University of Virginia Press.

Chapter 28

Keith Howard. "Comfort Women" from *True Stories of the Korean Comfort Women*, edited by Keith Howard. Continuum Books, 1995. By the kind permission of Continuum International Publishing Group.

Chapter 29

Isidore Ndaywel è Nziem. *Histoire générale du Congo: De l'héritage ancien à la République Démocratique*, De Boeck & Larcier, 1998. Used by permission of Edition le Cri. [English translation by Bonnie G. Smith.]

Khang Zhengguo. From *Confessions: An Innocent Life in Communist China* by Khang Zhengguo, translated by Susan Wilf. Copyright © 2005, 2004 by Kang Zhengguo, translation copyright © 2007 by Susan Wilf. Used by permission of W. W. Norton & Company, Inc.

Chapter 30

Jennifer Schirmer. "The Seeking of Truth and the Gendering of Consciousness: The CoMadres of El Salvador and the CONAVIGUA Widows of Guatemala," in Sarah A. Radcliffe and Sallie Westwood, editors, *"VIVA": Women and Popular Protest in Latin America* (London: Routledge, 1993). Used by permission of Taylor & Francis Group.

Art Credits

Opener to Part 1

Chapter 1: Bridgeman Art Library; Chapter 2: Science Source/PhotoResearchers; Chapter 3: The State Hermitage Museum, St. Petersburg, Russia/Bridgeman Art Library; Chapter 4: Kenneth Garrett; Chapter 5: The Art Archive/Gianni Dagli Orti; Chapter 6: Fitzwilliam Museum, University of Cambridge, UK/Bridgeman Art Library; Chapter 7: Somerset County Museum, Taunton Castle, UK/Bridgeman Art Library; Chapter 8: Private Collection/Boltin Picture Library/Bridgeman Art Library

Opener to Part 2

Chapter 9: Erich Lessing/Art Resource, NY; Chapter 10: Arthur M. Sackler Museum, Harvard University Art Museums/Bequest of Grenville L. Winthrop/Bridgeman Art Library; Chapter 11: Giraudon/Bridgeman Art Library; Chapter 12: Bibliothèque Nationale, Paris, France/Bildarchiv Preussischer Kulturbesitz/Art Resource, NY; Chapter 13: ISESCO; Chapter 14: The Art Archive; Chapter 15: Candace Feit

Opener to Part 3

Chapter 16: The Art Archive/Museo del Templo Mayor Mexico/Gianni Dagli Orti; Chapter 17: The Art Archive/Science Academy Lisbon/Gianni Dagli Orti; Chapter 18: Image copyright © The Metropolitan Museum of Art/Art Resource, NY; Chapter 19: Marco Pavan/Grand Tour/Corbis; Chapter 20: Photo by Ketan Gajria; Chapter 21: Yoshio Tomii Photo Studio/Aflo FotoAgency/Photolibrary;

Chapter 22: Acervo da Fundação Biblioteca Nacional, Rio de Janeiro, Brasil

Opener to Part 4

Chapter 23: The Art Archive/Museo Historico Nacional Buenos Aires/Gianni Dagli Orti; Chapter 24: Cotehele House, Cornwall, UK/Bridgeman Art Library; Chapter 25: Tetra Images/Corbis; Chapter 26: The Art Archive/Museo Civico Revoltella Trieste/Collection Dagli Orti; Chapter 27: The Granger Collection, New York; Chapter 28: Bettmann/Corbis; Chapter 29: Universal Images Group/SuperStock; Chapter 30: Jacques Langevin/Sygma/Corbis; Chapter 31: akg-images/Bildarchiv Monheim

INDEX

North America
  agrarian societies in, 356–363
  colonial crisis and revolution in, 769(m)
  commercial colonialism in, 741–745
  cultures of, 246, 342
  Eastern Woodlands people in
    (1450–1530), 538–542
  England and France in (c. 1650–1750),
    742(m)
  European claims in, 568(m)
  farming in, 23
  gatherer-hunters of (800 B.C.E.–400 C.E.),
    255–256
  lifestyle in northern colonies, 745–748
  Mississippi Valley region of, 359–363,
    359(m)
  mound-building societies in, 358–363
  plantations in, 722
  revolution in, 767–771
  societies in, 339, 340(m)
North American Free Trade Agreement
    (NAFTA), 1036
North Atlantic Treaty Organization.
    See NATO (North Atlantic Treaty
    Organization)
Northeast, in United States, 745
Northern Europe
  Atlantic slave trade and (1600–1800),
    600–607
  commerce in, 397
  economy in, 398
Northern Ireland, 910
  Bloody Sunday in (January 30, 1972),
    1045
Northern Wei people (China), 309–310,
    309(m), 313
North German Confederation, 838
North Korea, 967
North Sea region, Vikings from, 298
North-South divide (global), Bandung
    Conference and, 985
North Vietnam, 972, 1008. See also
    Vietnam War
Northwest passage, in North America, 741
Norway
  Danes in, 300
  massacre of political activists in (2011),
    1045
  World War II in, 942
Nova Scotia, 741
  commerce in, 744–745
Novels, 893. See also Literature; specific
    works
  in 1930s, 939
Novgorod region, 288
Nubia
  culture of, 112
  Egypt and, 108–109, 109(m), 113–115,
    113(i)

gold from, 61
Greece and, 115
independence of, 112
kings of, 114(i)
Meroe and, 115–117
Napata as capital of, 113
New Kingdom of Egypt and
    (1550–660 B.C.E.), 109(m)
queens in, 115
Rome and, 115
statues of kings from, 114(i)
Nuclear war, Cuban missile crisis and, 969
Nuclear weapons, 963
Number system, in India, 183
Nuns. See also Monasteries and monasticism
  in Spanish America, 732
Nuremberg, Germany
  Nazi rally in, 924(i)
  trials in, 980
Nuremberg Laws (1935), 938
Nur Jahan (Mughal Empire), 613–615, 627
Nursing
  in Crimean War, 833
  women in, 900–902
Nut (god), 65
Nyamakala (Mande professional castes),
    400(b)
Nzinga (Ndongo queen), 599–600, 601(i)

Oaxaca, 346
Oba (king of Benin), 580(i)
Obama, Barack, 1026
Obas (Yoruba political leaders), 592
Obelisk, from Egypt, 227(i)
Obsidian, 344, 345
Obstetrics, study of, 412–413(b)
Occupation (military). See Military occu-
    pation
Occupations (labor). See also Livelihood(s)
  gender and, 383
  in India, 325
  women in, 383–384
Oceania
  Near Oceania, 363
  Remote, 363
Oceans. See also specific ocean regions
  ice ages and, 16
Octavian (Rome). See Augustus
Odoacer (German king), 228, 283
Odyssey (Homer), 148
Oedipus the King (Sophocles), 152
Offshore manufacturing, 998
Ogodei (Mongol Great Khan), 441, 443,
    458, 459(m)
Oh Omok, as comfort woman, 942(b)
Oikumene (Rome), 217(i)
Oil and oil industry
  imperialism and, 912
  in mandates, 907(m)

in Middle East, 972
trade routes in (c. 1975), 990(m)
uses of, 998
Oil embargo, 1013–1014
Okinawa, 706
Oklahoma, native Americans in, 840
Oklahoma City government building,
    destruction of (1995), 1045
Old English, 416
Old Ghana, 590
Old Javanese language, 328
Old Kingdom (Egypt), 63
Old Order, Enlightenment and, 765–767
Old Persian language, 129
Old Testament. See Hebrew Bible
Olduvai Gorge, 13
Oligarchy
  in Greece, 146
  in Sparta, 147–148
  in Venice, 483
Oliver Twist (Dickens), 817
Olmec society, 247–249, 339
  Maya and, 347
  as Mesoamerican "mother culture," 249
  sculptures of, 247–248, 248(i)
Olympic Games, 146
  in Mexico City (1968), 1011(i)
  terrorism at Munich games (1972), 1045
Oman, Mesopotamian trade with, 48
Omdurman, Battle of (Sudan), 868
Omens, in Mesopotamia, 125
On Architecture (Vitruvius), 215
Once Upon the River Love, 1044
One-child policy (China), 1041
One Hundred Years of Solitude (García
    Márquez), 1050
On Restoring Ethiopian Salvation
    (Sandoval), 596
On the Measurement of the Earth
    (Eratosthenes), 163
On the Origin of Species (Darwin), 7
On the Revolutions of the Heavenly Spheres
    (Copernicus), 671
On the Wealth of Nations (Smith), 763–764
"On Women" (Semonides of Amorgos),
    158(b)
OPEC (Organization of Petroleum
    Exporting Countries), 990(m), 1013
Opera, in Mexico, 845
"Operation Vittles," 965
Opium, 660, 807
  China and, 807
  Dutch and, 711
  India and, 809(i)
Opium War (1839–1842), 807
  taxation and, 873
Oprichnina (Russian land system), 689
Oracle bones, in China, 92, 93, 94–96,
    95(b), 95(i), 260

About the authors

BONNIE G. SMITH (Ph.D., University of Rochester) is Board of Governors Professor of History at Rutgers University. She has written numerous works in European and global history, including *Ladies of the Leisure Class*; *Changing Lives: Women in European History since 1700*; and *Imperialism*. She is editor of *Global Feminisms since 1945* and *Women's History in Global Perspective*; coeditor of the New Oxford World History series; and general editor of *The Oxford Encyclopedia of Women in World History*. Currently she is studying the globalization of European culture and society since the seventeenth century. **Bonnie treats the period 1750 to the present (Part 4) in *Crossroads and Cultures*.**

MARC VAN DE MIEROOP (Ph.D., Yale University) is Professor of History at Columbia University. His research focuses on the ancient history of the Near East from a long-term perspective and extends across traditionally established disciplinary boundaries. Among his many works are *The Ancient Mesopotamian City*; *Cuneiform Texts and the Writing of History*; *A History of the Ancient Near East*; *The Eastern Mediterranean in the Age of Ramesses II*; and *A History of Ancient Egypt*. **Marc covers the period from human origins to 500 C.E. (Part 1) in *Crossroads and Cultures*.**

RICHARD VON GLAHN (Ph.D., Yale University) is Professor of History at the University of California, Los Angeles. A specialist in Chinese economic history, Richard is the author of *The Country of Streams and Grottoes: Expansion, Settlement, and the Civilizing of the Sichuan Frontier in Song Times*; *Fountain of Fortune: Money and Monetary Policy in China, 1000–1700*; and *The Sinister Way: The Divine and the Demonic in Chinese Religious Culture*. He is also coeditor of *The Song-Yuan-Ming Transition in Chinese History* and *Global Connections and Monetary History, 1470–1800*. His current research focuses on monetary history on a global scale, from ancient times to the recent past. **Richard treats the period 500 to 1450 (Part 2) in *Crossroads and Cultures*.**

KRIS LANE (Ph.D., University of Minnesota) is the France V. Scholes Chair in Colonial Latin American History at Tulane University. Kris specializes in colonial Latin American history and the Atlantic world, and his great hope is to globalize the teaching and study of the early Americas. His publications include *Pillaging the Empire: Piracy in the Americas, 1500–1750*; *Quito 1599: City and Colony in Transition*; and *Colour of Paradise: The Emerald in the Age of Gunpowder Empires*. He also edited Bernardo de Vargas Machuca's *The Indian Militia and Description of the Indies* and *Defense and Discourse of the Western Conquest*. **Kris treats the period 1450 to 1750 (Part 3) in *Crossroads and Cultures*.**

About the cover image

Istanbul, Turkey

Istanbul, the only city in the world to connect two continents, has been a global crossroads for millennia, drawing people from across Eurasia and from around the world. Armies and navies envying its strategic location originally made Istanbul a crossroads, but it has also been traversed by religions, ethnicities, commerce in goods, and a wide range of ideas. Once the capital of three great empires — the Roman, Byzantine, and Ottoman — Istanbul (formerly named Byzantium and Constantinople) today is a leading cosmopolitan center of global civilization.

How to analyze primary sources

In their search for an improved understanding of the past, historians look for new evidence, written documents or visual artifacts. When they encounter a written or visual primary source, historians ask certain key questions. You should ask these questions, too. Sometimes historians cannot be certain about the answer, but they always ask the question.

ANALYZING A WRITTEN DOCUMENT

- Who wrote the document? Is it a specific person or someone not completely identifiable whom you can merely infer from the context of the document (for example, a parent writing to a child, a traveler writing home)?

- When and where was it written?

- Why was the document written? Is there a clear purpose, or are multiple interpretations possible?

- Who was, or who might have been, its intended audience?

- What point of view does it reflect?

- What can the document tell us about the individual who produced it and the society from which he or she came?

ANALYZING A VISUAL SOURCE

- Who made the image or artifact, and how was it made?

- When and where was the image or artifact made?

- Who paid for or commissioned it? How can you tell?

- For what audience might it have been intended? Where might it have originally been displayed or used?

- What message or messages is it trying to convey?

- How could it be interpreted differently depending on who viewed or used it?

- What can this visual source tell us about the individual who produced it and the society from which he or she came?

THE CONTEMPORARY WORLD